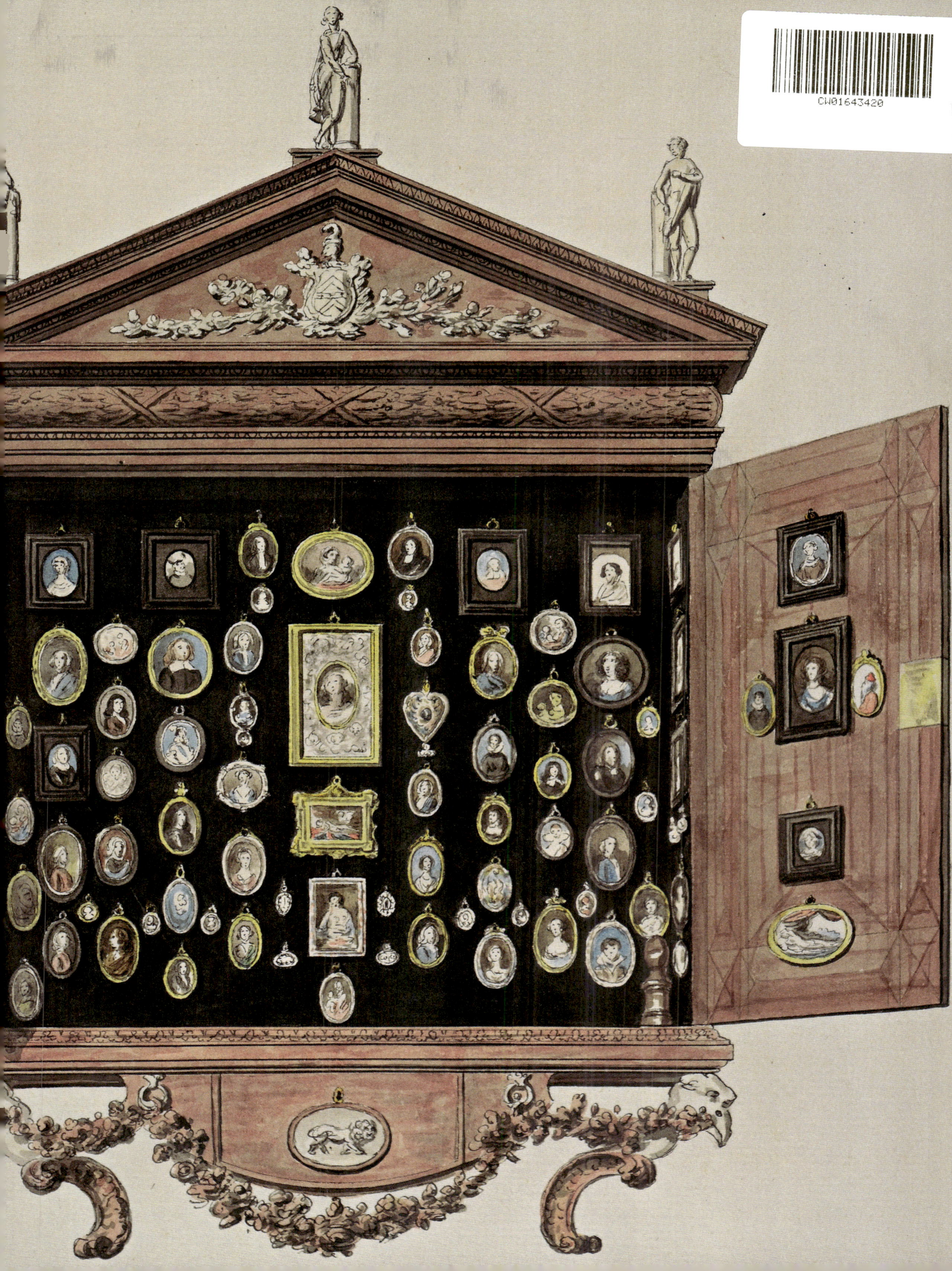

Horace Walpole's Strawberry Hill

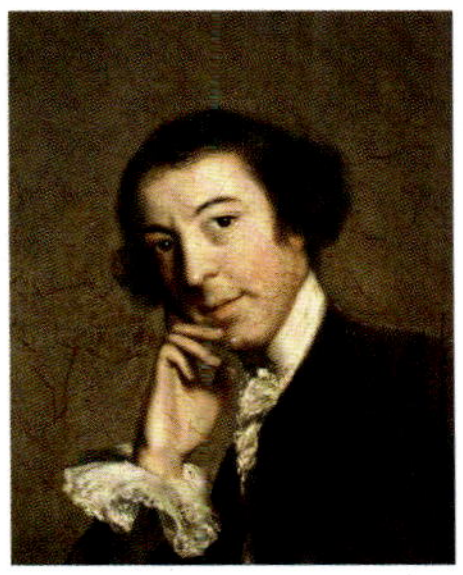

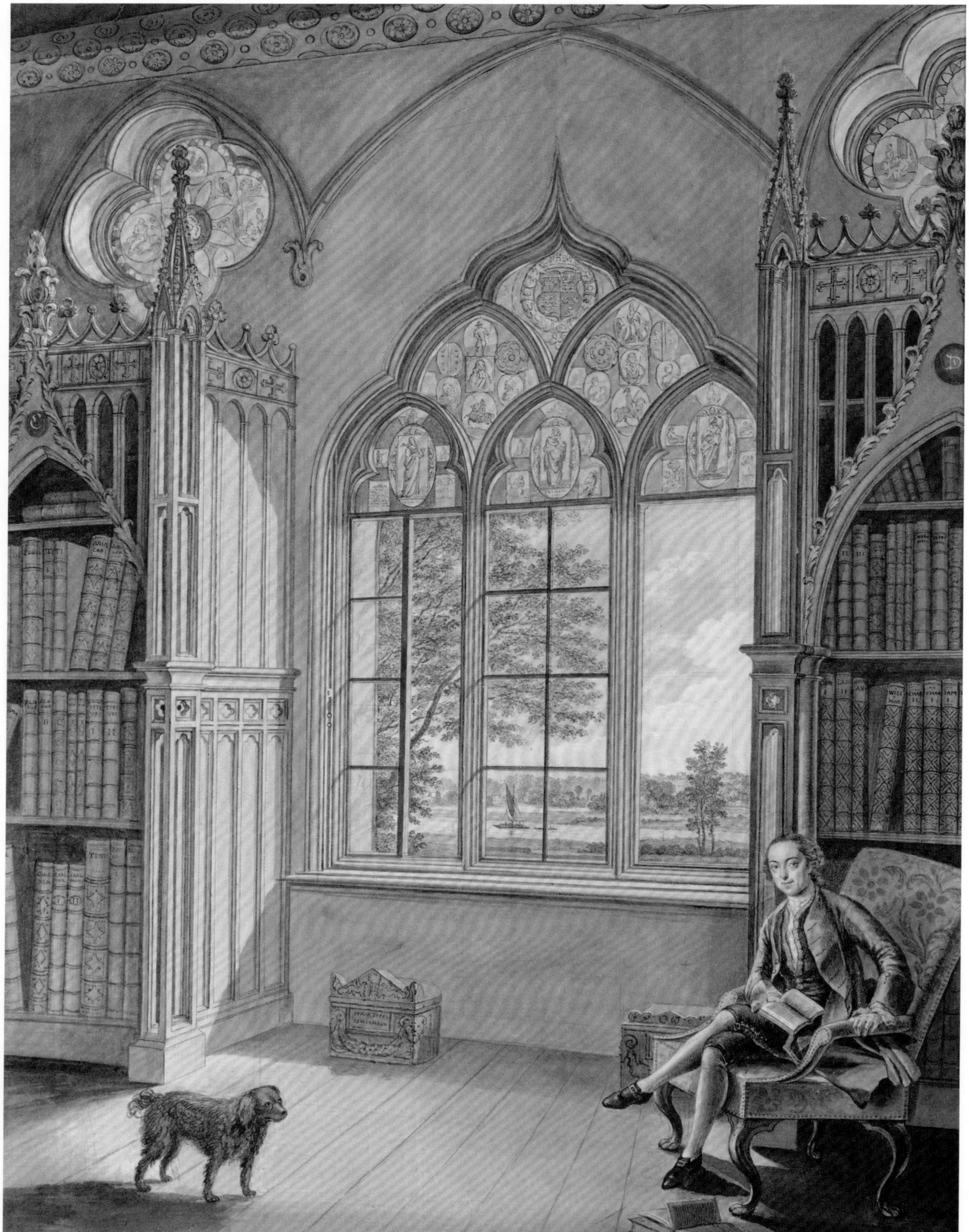

HORACE WALPOLE'S
STRAWBERRY HILL

edited by MICHAEL SNODIN
with the assistance of CYNTHIA ROMAN

THE LEWIS WALPOLE LIBRARY, YALE UNIVERSITY
YALE CENTER FOR BRITISH ART
VICTORIA AND ALBERT MUSEUM
in association with
YALE UNIVERSITY PRESS, NEW HAVEN AND LONDON

Published with assistance from the Annie Burr Lewis Fund

This publication accompanies the exhibition *Horace Walpole's Strawberry Hill* organized by the Lewis Walpole Library, the Yale Center for British Art and the Victoria and Albert Museum

On view at the Yale Center for British Art from 15 October 2009 to 3 January 2010 and at the Victoria and Albert Museum from 6 March to 4 July 2010

Set in Adobe Caslon 540
Designed by Sally Salvesen
Printed by Conti Tipolcolor SpA, Florence

Library of Congress Cataloging-in-Publication Data

Horace Walpole's Strawberry Hill / edited by Michael Snodin.
p. cm.
Publication to accompany an exhibition organized by the Yale Center for British Art in association with the Lewis Walpole Library and the Victoria and Albert Museum.
Includes bibliographical references and index.
ISBN 978-0-300-12574-0 (alk. paper)
1. Walpole, Horace, 1717-1797--Art collections.
2. Walpole, Horace, 1717-1797--Homes and haunts--England--London.
3. Art--Collectors and collecting--England--London.
4. Strawberry Hill (Twickenham, London, England)
I. Snodin, Michael. II. Yale Center for British Art.
III. Lewis Walpole Library. IV. Victoria and Albert Museum.
V. Title: Strawberry Hill.
N5247.W28H67 2009
708.0092--DC22

2009024158

ENDPAPERS: Detail from John Carter, *The Cabinet of Miniatures and Enamels*, The Lewis Walpole Library, Yale University, Fig. 128

HALF TITLE PAGE: Detail from Joshua Reynolds, *Portrait of Horace Walpole*, Marquess of Hertford, Ragley Hall, Fig. 3, Cat. 1

FRONTISPIECE: Johann Heinrich Müntz, *Portrait of Horace Walpole in his Library*, 1755–59. Private collection, Cat. 75

CONTENTS

ABBREVIATIONS

For abbreviations used only in the catalogue section see p. 277.

Accounts	Paget Toynbee, *Strawberry Hill Accounts*, Oxford: Oxford University Press, 1927
Anecdotes	Horace Walpole, *Anecdotes of Painting in England*, Strawberry Hill Press, 4 vols, 1762–71
Bib. HW	A.T. Hazen, *A Bibliography of Horace Walpole*, New Haven: Yale University Press, 1948
Bib. SH	A.T. Hazen, *A Bibliography of the Strawberry Hill Press*, New Haven: Yale University Press, 1942
Coll.	Collection
HW Corres	W. S. Lewis et al. ed., *The Yale Edition of Horace Walpole's Correspondence*, New Haven and London: Yale University Press, 48 vols, 1937–83
D 1774	Horace Walpole, *A Description of the Villa of Horace Walpole, Youngest Son of Sir Robert Walpole, Earl of Orford, at Strawberry-Hill, near Twickenham. With an inventory of the furniture, pictures, curiosities &c*, Strawberry Hill Press, 1774. References are to the expanded edition, concluding with 'more additions' (1786)
D 1784	Horace Walpole, *A Description of the Villa of Mr Horace Walpole, Youngest Son of Sir Robert Walpole, Earl of Orford, at Strawberry-Hill, near Twickenham. With an inventory of the furniture, pictures, curiosities &c*, Strawberry Hill Press, 1784. References are to the expanded edition, concluding with 'more additions' (about 1791)
HW	Horace Walpole
Library	A.T. Hazen, *A Catalogue of Horace Walpole's Library*, 3 vols, New Haven: Yale University Press, 1969
London Sale	George Robins, *The Collection of Rare Prints ad Illustrated Works, Removed for Sale in London….Collected by Horace Walpole*, 13 June 1842 and 9 following days
LWL	The Lewis Walpole Library, Yale University, Farmington, Connecticut
OHG	Orleans House Gallery, Twickenham, *Horace Walpole and Strawberry Hill*, London Borough of Richmond upon Thames, 1980.
Portraits	C.K. Adams and W.S. Lewis, 'The Portraits of Horace Walpole', *The Walpole Society*, XLII (1970), pp.1–34
1842 Sale	George Robins, *A Catalogue of the Classic Contents of Strawberry Hill Collected by Horace Walpole*, 25 April 1842 and 23 following days. The references are from the 6th (penultimate) edition; the first digit refers to the day of the sale, the second to the lot number.
SH	Strawberry Hill
V&A	Victoria and Albert Museum, London
Works	Horace Walpole, *The Works of Horatio Walpole, Earl of Orford*, 5 vols, London, 1798 (Mary Berry, ed.)

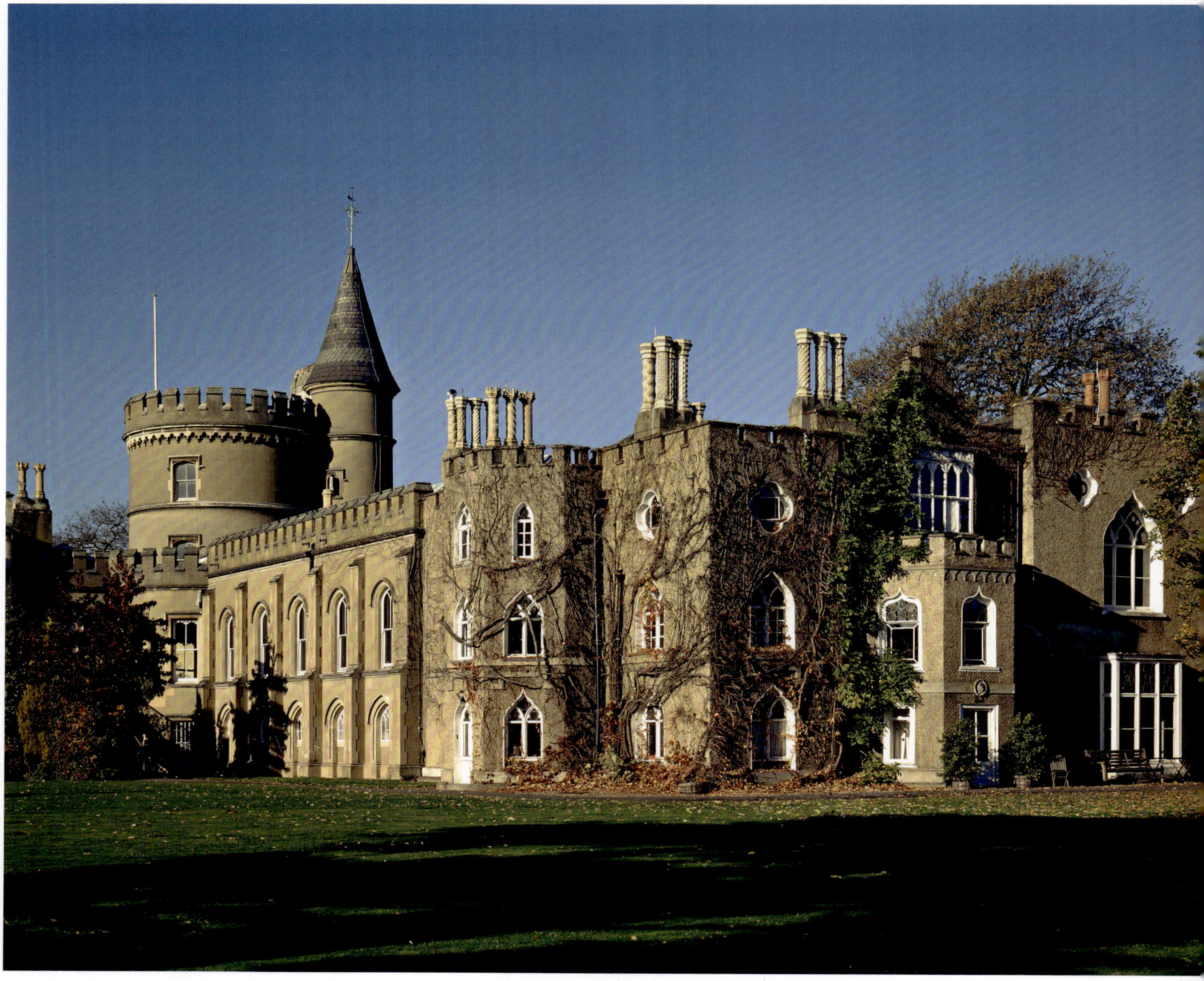

Figure 1. Strawberry Hill from the south-east, photographed in 2008

DIRECTORS' FOREWORD

THIS BOOK AND THE MAGNIFICENT EXHIBITION it accompanies remind us forcefully that for the eighteenth-century visitor, touring Horace Walpole's Strawberry Hill was an extraordinary experience. In its day, the house was a significant destination: the collection and its consciously constructed domestic setting combined to create a journey through British history and British and European art, both ancient and modern, that captivated the many who came to admire and appreciate. Bringing together many objects that have been dispersed since 1842, the exhibition inspires the same admiration and appreciation in a twenty-first-century visitor. In concert with the present volume's collection of essays, it illuminates the complex relationships Walpole established among space, history, text and objects while also adding to our understanding of the traditions of collecting and display. Such a combined exploration, effected by objects and by text, has been the happy outcome of a joint venture among institutions rich in eighteenth-century materials and connected both to Strawberry Hill and to each other. The Lewis Walpole Library, given to Yale University by Wilmarth Sheldon Lewis (Yale College Class of 1918) and his wife Annie Burr Lewis, is the most substantial repository of primary research material for any study of Walpole and Strawberry Hill; the Yale Center for British Art, the gift of Paul Mellon (Yale College Class of 1929) to his alma mater, holds the largest collection of British art outside the United Kingdom, with particular strength in the long eighteenth century; and the V&A is the single most important institution for the study of British design and material culture.

In spite of its importance, there has been no comprehensive critical study of Walpole's collection as it was formed and arranged at Strawberry Hill. All segments of the collection were part of a larger, calculated scheme. More than simply reassembling and documenting individual objects, this project addresses the totality of Walpole's collections, their installation and arrangement at Strawberry Hill, the meaning of Walpole's pursuits, and the broader cultural contexts in which he operated. In particular, the present collaboration has identified the ways in which Walpole's house and collections became a machine for manufacturing different histories: political, national, dynastic, cultural and imaginary. It is our hope that *Horace Walpole's Strawberry Hill* will be both the standard work on Walpole and his collection, and a set of debates that will enable scholarship to move forward both specifically in relation to Strawberry Hill and more broadly in the history of collecting and display.

An emerging scholarly framework contributed to our conviction that we had chosen the right moment to undertake such a re-assessment of Walpole and Strawberry Hill, and, in an instance of serendipity Walpole himself might have celebrated, the recently begun conservation of the house itself has underscored the felicity of our timing. In 2003, the house was named by the World Monuments Fund as one of the world's one hundred most endangered sites, and a conservation plan was developed for the Strawberry Hill Trust by the London firm Peter Inskip + Peter Jenkins Architects to conserve the grounds, structure and interiors so that they can be opened to the public.The process of conservation has already provided a new understanding of the architectural layout and display, and conservators and historians have made significant discoveries about the original decorative schemes.

If the three joint organizers of the project are natural partners for this topic, we have also had the great good fortune to collaborate with institutions and groups who share the same interest and commitment. The Strawberry Hill Trust, the Friends of Strawberry Hill, the World Monuments Fund, and the Samuel H. Kress Foundation, along with the architectural firm of Inskip + Jenkins, have all participated substantially in this undertaking by providing additional inspiration, expertise and support.

Michael Snodin's involvement has been essential to this most gratifying of collaborations from the very beginning. His deep understanding of Strawberry Hill and its creator Horace Walpole has informed the project all along, not only in his key roles as Guest Curator of the exhibition and Editor of this volume, but also as Chair of the Strawberry Hill Trust, and Senior Research Fellow and former Head of the Designs Collection at the V&A. Cynthia Roman's contributions to the exhibition and to the book have been immeasurable, and as the Lewis Walpole Library's Curator of Prints, Drawings, and Paintings her knowledge of the collections proved indispensable. Julia Marciari Alexander, former Associate Director for Exhibitions and Publications at the Yale Center for British Art, and now Deputy Director of the San Diego Museum of Art, initiated the logistical stewardship of the exhibition and publication with extraordinary diligence, and she has been succeeded in this complex undertaking with equal skill by Eleanor Hughes, Assistant Curator in the department. Appreciation also is due to the many staff members of the Walpole Library and the Yale Center, who helped to realize these associated projects, as well as to design consultant, Stephen Saitis, who ensured that the exhibition was mounted according to the most beautiful and effective plan. Linda Lloyd-Jones, Head of Exhibitions at the V&A, and Rebecca Lim, Head of South Kensington Exhibitions, have both made significant contributions to bringing this exhibition to fruition in London. Staff across the V&A have provided very great help and support, notably the Conservation Department, which has worked on all the UK loans. Finally Graeme Williamson of Block Architecture has produced a creative and beautiful design and worked hard to find elegant solutions to displaying the collection at the V&A.

We extend our warmest thanks to the many lenders who made possible such a remarkable reassembling of objects that had been separated for more than a century and a half. To the authors of the essays and to the many curatorial consultants who offered their expertise over the wide range objects that made up the Strawberry Hill collections, we owe great thanks, as we do to the participants in the first workshop who spent a weekend helping us consider the how best to shape the project (Brian Allen, Dana Arnold, Stephen Bann, Michael Hatt, Peter Inskip, Miles Ogborn).

The Samuel H. Kress Foundation provided funding for that first workshop and has contributed ongoing support for the development of a database to reunite the Strawberry Hill collections in a virtual environment, allowing us to share this information with the widest possible audience. We are immensely grateful for such generous and continued help. The Andrew W. Mellon Foundation generously supported another workshop, hosted by the Yale Center for British Art and the Research Department of the V&A, to bring the catalogue contributors together in the UK to see Strawberry Hill and some of the objects for the exhibition. Yale University Press allocated significant funds from the Annie Burr Lewis Fund to *Horace Walpole's Strawberry Hill*, for which we extend our greatest appreciation.

Margaret K. Powell, *W.S. Lewis Librarian and Executive Director, The Lewis Walpole Library*

Amy Meyers, *Director, Yale Center for British Art*

Mark Jones, Director, *Victoria and Albert Museum*

ACKNOWLEDGEMENTS

MAJOR INTERNATIONAL EXHIBITIONS AND THEIR PUBLICATIONS demand a huge amount of collaborative effort, both within and beyond the organising institutions. This exhibition has been no exception. We are most grateful for the institutional support of the Lewis Walpole Library, the Yale Center for British Art and the Victoria and Albert Museum.

Every member of the staff at the Lewis Walpole Library has contributed enormously to this project. The decision to create the *Horace Walpole's Strawberry Hill Collection* database and website at the Lewis Walpole Library has been central to the success of the exhibition and the breadth of its content. In particular, we would like to thank former staff members Erin Colley Monroe, Curatorial Assistant, and Hope Saska, Kress Curatorial Fellow, who contributed essentially to the development of the database and undertook considerable object research. George Ouellette, Senior Programmer Analyst, developed the database and website. Emily Lanza, Library Services Assistant, continued object research and database work, assisted with loans correspondence and was an indispensable help with compiling catalogue entries and illustrations for the publication. In addition, we want to acknowledge the good work of Brian Parker for photography of the many objects in the library collection, Ellen R. Cordes for cataloguing, Todd Falkowski for exhibition preparation, Laura O'Brien Miller for conservation of books and archival materials, and Susan Odell Walker for assistance with collection research and conservation planning of many objects. We would especially like to thank Margaret K. Powell, Librarian and Executive Director, for her generous and unwavering support for every aspect of this project, including extending an unfailing welcome to the successive waves of Walpole scholars that it generated.

The institutional resources and staff of the Yale Center for British Art contributed significantly to the practical realization of the exhibition and publication. We are deeply appreciative for the ongoing enthusiasm and support of Amy Meyers, Director of the Center. Special thanks must also go to Julia Marciari Alexander, former Associate Director for Exhibitions and Publications, and Eleanor Hughes, Assistant Curator of Exhibitions and Publications, and their staff. In particular Anna Magliaro, Publications Assistant, worked tirelessly to secure the images and permissions for this book and for related publicity. Jo Briggs, Postdoctoral Research Associate, provided vital assistance with exhibition texts. Thanks are also due to Ava Suntoke, Editorial Assistant; Diane Bowman, Senior Administrative Assistant; Andrea Wolk Rager, Postdoctoral Research Associate; and Sundari Birdsall, Intern. Center designers, Lyn Rose and Elena Grossman, produced the elegant in-house graphics for the exhibition and designed related publicity. We are also grateful for the contributions of Beth Miller, Associate Director for Advancement and External Affairs, and her colleagues; Amy McDonald, Public Relations and Marketing Manager; Ricardo Sandoval, Public Relations Coordinator; and Amelia Toensmeier, Senior Administrative Assistant. Former Head of Research Michael Hatt and Lisa Ford, Associate Head of Research, assisted by Serena Guerrette and Imogen Hart, helped to organize planning workshops and author meetings. In conservation we would like to thank Mark Aronson, Chief Conservator of Paintings, and his department colleagues,

Eric Stegmaier and Jessica David; and Theresa Fairbanks-Harris, Chief Conservator of Paper, and her staff, Mary Regan-Yttre, Dong Eun Kim, Sarah Welcome, and Sara Bisi. The contribution of the Education Department was headed by Linda Friedlaender, Curator of Education, assisted by Cyra Levenson. Jane Nowosadko, Manager of Programs, skilfully organized lectures, musical performances, and a film series to compliment this exhibition. Timothy Goodhue, Museum Registrar, has orchestrated the most complex and demanding of loan exhibitions with his usual aplomb and consummate professionalism, ably assisted by Corey Myers. Richard Johnson and his staff, Chick Cerillo, Kevin Derken, Rachel Hellereich, Rick Omonte, Greg Shea, and Dylan Vitale, skilfully managed a particularly challenging installation.

At the Victoria and Albert Museum, Stephanie Cripps, Charlotte Churchill in her role as Exhibition Co-ordinator and Hannah Hawksworth in Collections Services, were central to the practical realisation of the exhibition in London. In Conservation, the exhibition project was led by Alan Derbyshire. In the Technical Services and Collections Services Department we would like to thank Richard Ashbridge and Matthew Clarke. The gallery texts were edited by Lucy Trench and Victoria Kingston; Learning and Interpretation was in the hands of Jo Banham. In Public Affairs we would like to thank Olivia Colling, Victoria Singer and Alex Bratt and from the Web Team, Andrea Carr. Project management was in the capable hands of Sor Lan Tan and Keith Flemming; the graphics were by Lisa Pentelow in the Design Department. The film was made by Illuminations, led by John Wyver. Carolyn Sargentson and Christopher Breward, as successive heads of the Research Department, were hugely supportive, making Research the intellectual home of the project at the V&A. In addition, the project made many calls on the expertise of V&A curators. We would like especially to thank Clare Browne, Stephen Calloway, Marian Campbell, Frances Collard, Judith Crouch, Ann Eatwell, Richard Edgcumbe, Mark Evans, Norbert Jopek, Reino Liefkes, Sarah Medlam, Lesley Miller, Tessa Murdoch, Marjorie Trusted, Lucy Wood and Hilary Young.

The writing of this book represented another substantial collaborative effort and the editors would like to extend their gratitude to the authors of chapters, feature spreads and catalogue entries, both from the organising institutions and others. Timothy Wilson helped extensively with the cataloguing of the ceramics, glass and enamels, while Stephen Lloyd catalogued the miniatures and enamels, supported by a research fellowship at the Lewis Walpole Library. Ellen R. Cordes and Margaret K. Powell have catalogued the books; Susan Odell Walker, the furniture; and Stuart Pyhrr, the arms and armour. We have also called on the expertise of many other scholars, most notably Ellenor Alcorn (silver), Stephen Clarke (Walpoliana), Katherine Coombs (miniatures and enamels), Robin Emmerson (Wedgwood), Mirjam Foot and Diana Scarisbrick (bookbindings), Karen Hearn (portraits) and Rowan Watson (manuscripts). John Riely has contributed his long-standing Walpole expertise to the book as a whole. Central to the content of the exhibition and this book has been the greatly advanced understanding of Strawberry Hill that has resulted from the work of Peter Inskip, Stephen Gee and Kevin Rogers (of Peter Inskip + Peter Jenkins Architects) on the building and grounds in connection with their restoration.

An exhibition and publication of this scope and scale could not have happened without the generous contributions, practical and intellectual, of many others, including scholars, curators, conservators, and collection owners, on both sides of the Atlantic. They have included: Derek Adlam, Maryan Ainsworth, Drew Anderson, Stephen Astley, Philip Attwood, Fabienne Audebrand, Clare Baxter, Erin Blake, Rachel Bond, Catherine Bowe, Dirk Breiding, Christine Brennan, Nancy Britton, Robert Brodrick, Hugo Brown, the late Duke of Buccleuch and Queensberry KT, the

Duke of Buccleuch and Queensberry KBE, Helen Burton, Victoria Button, Jean Cadogan, Maureen Cassidy-Geiger, Anna Chalcraft, Martin Chapman, Yannick Chastang, Patricia Collins, the late Philip Conisbee, Brian Considine, Aileen Dawson, Helen Evans, Eleanor Falker, Patricia Ferguson, Hazel Forsyth, Zenon Gansziniec, Eleanor Ghey, Alden Gordon, Antony Griffiths, Judith Guston, Robert Harding, Matthew Hargraves, Kate Harris, David Haycock, Arlen Heginbotham, Peter Hill, Barbara Hinde, Bodo Hofstetter, Mindy Horn, Henry House, Mrs Sandra Howat, Amin Jaffer, Alan Jutzi, Rolf Kat, Edouard Kopp, Stephen Kornhauser, Sebastian Kuhn, Florian Knothe, Elizabeth S. Kujawski, Elizabeth Lahikainen, Alastair Laing, Janet Larkin, David Lavender, Benedict Leca, Charles Lister, Christine McCarthy Emma McCarthy, Bet McLeod, Janet McMullin, Jessie McNab, Brian Maggs, John Mallet, John Marciari, the Duke of Marlborough, Jonathan Marsden, Joseph Marshall, William Metcalf, Alain Moatti, Jeffrey Munger, Christopher Norton, David Oakey, Vlasta Odell, Magnus Olausson, Susan Palmer, Michael Peover, Julia Poole, Anne Pritchard, Vanessa Remington, Jeremy Rex-Parkes, Jane Roberts, Marcel Roethlisberger, the Countess of Rosebery, David Roth, Linda Roth, Natalie Russo, Elisa Sani, Leslie Scattone, Karen Schoenewaldt, Timothy Schroder, Günther Schuchardt, David Scrase, Catherine Sease, Jon Seydl, Katherine Sharp, Kim Sloan, Emma Slocombe, Helen Smailes, Ann Smith, Thyrza Smith, Joaneath Spicer, James Stourton, Greg Sullivan, Eleanor Summers, Mary Suzor, John Teahan, Jennifer Thompson, Katrina Thomson, Dora Thornton, Trustees of the Wedgwood Museum at Barlaston, Shelagh Vainker, Charlotte Villiers, Clare Vincent, Kirstin Waibel, the Earl Waldegrave, Robert Wenley, Wendy Walker, Mark A.F. Weiss, the Earl of Wemyss and March, Shelagh, Countess of Wemyss and March, Robert Wenley, Jon Whiteley, Audrey Wilson, John Wingfield Digby, Matthew Winterbottom, Karen Wiseman and Ghenete Zelleke. We thank them all.

Our final thanks must go to Sally Salvesen who has brought this book to glorious fruition with wonderful skill, patience and flair.

Michael Snodin, *Senior Research Fellow, Victoria and Albert Museum*

Cynthia Roman, *Curator of Prints, Drawings, and Paintings The Lewis Walpole Library, Yale University*

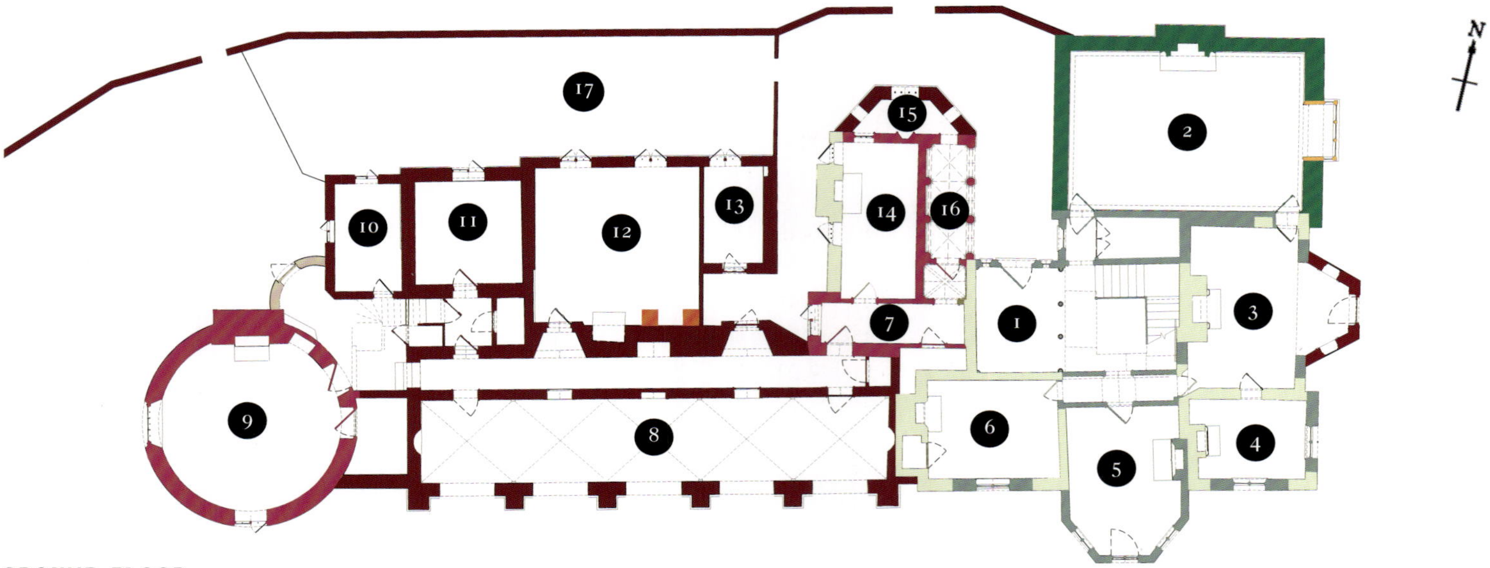

GROUND FLOOR

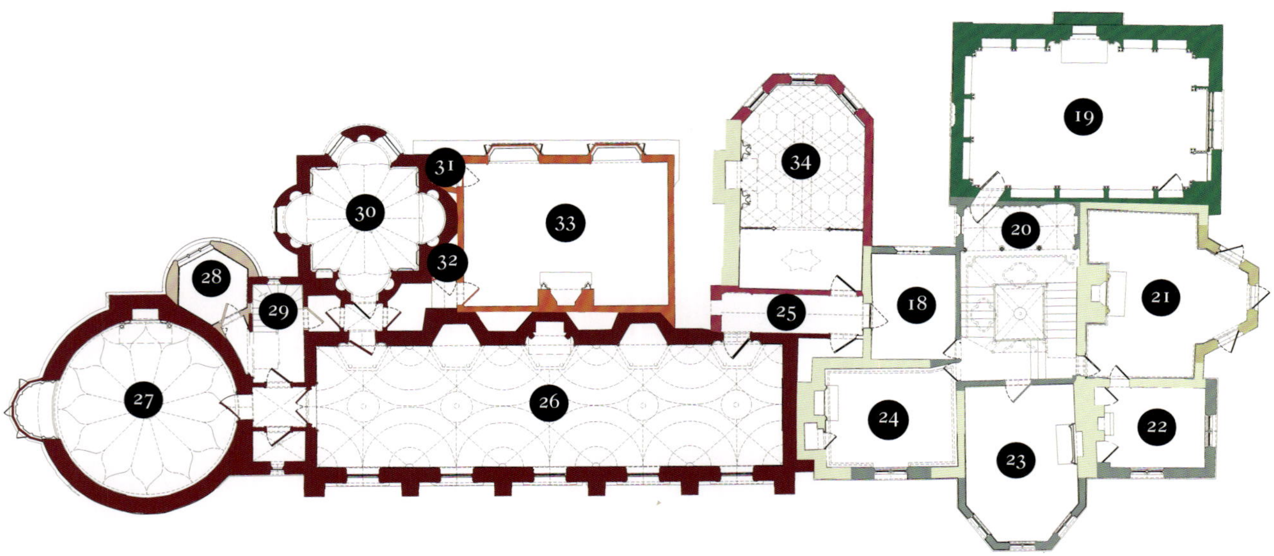

FIRST FLOOR

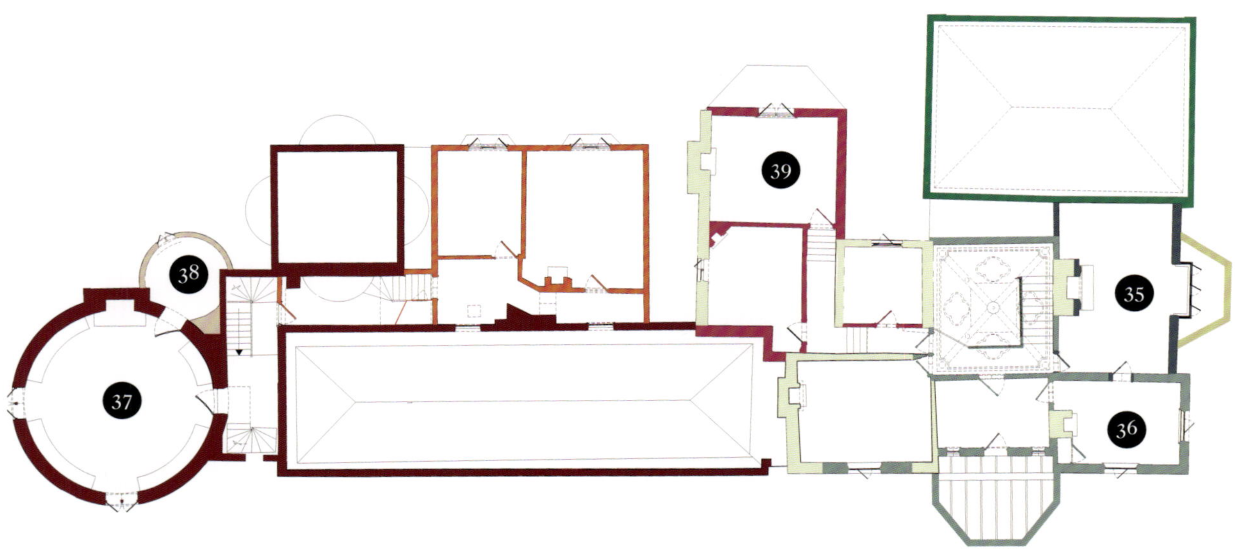

SECOND FLOOR

Figure 2. Plan of Strawberry Hill

GROUND FLOOR

1. Hall
2. Refectory or Great Parlour
3. Waiting Room
4. China Room
5. Little Parlour
6. Yellow Bedchamber or Beauty Room
7. Winding Cloister
8. Great Cloister
9. Kitchen
10. Scullery
11. Beer Cellar
12. Servants' Hall
13. Wine Cellar
14. Pantry
15. Oratory
16. Little Cloister
17. Prior's Garden

FIRST FLOOR

18. Star Chamber
19. Library
20. Armoury
21. Breakfast Room
22. Green Closet
23. Blue Bedchamber
24. Red Bedchamber
25. Trunk ceiled passage
26. The Gallery
27. Round Drawing Room
28. Beauclerk Closet
29. Back Stairs
30. Tribune
31. Glass Closet
32. Small Closet
33. Great North Bedchamber
34. Holbein Chamber

SECOND FLOOR

35. Mr Walpole's Bedchamber
36. Plaid Bedchamber
37. Round Bedchamber (later Print Room)
38. Upper Closet
39. Housekeeper's Room

1698–1747
1747/8
1752–3
1754
1756
1758–9
1760–62
1766
1771
1773–4
1776

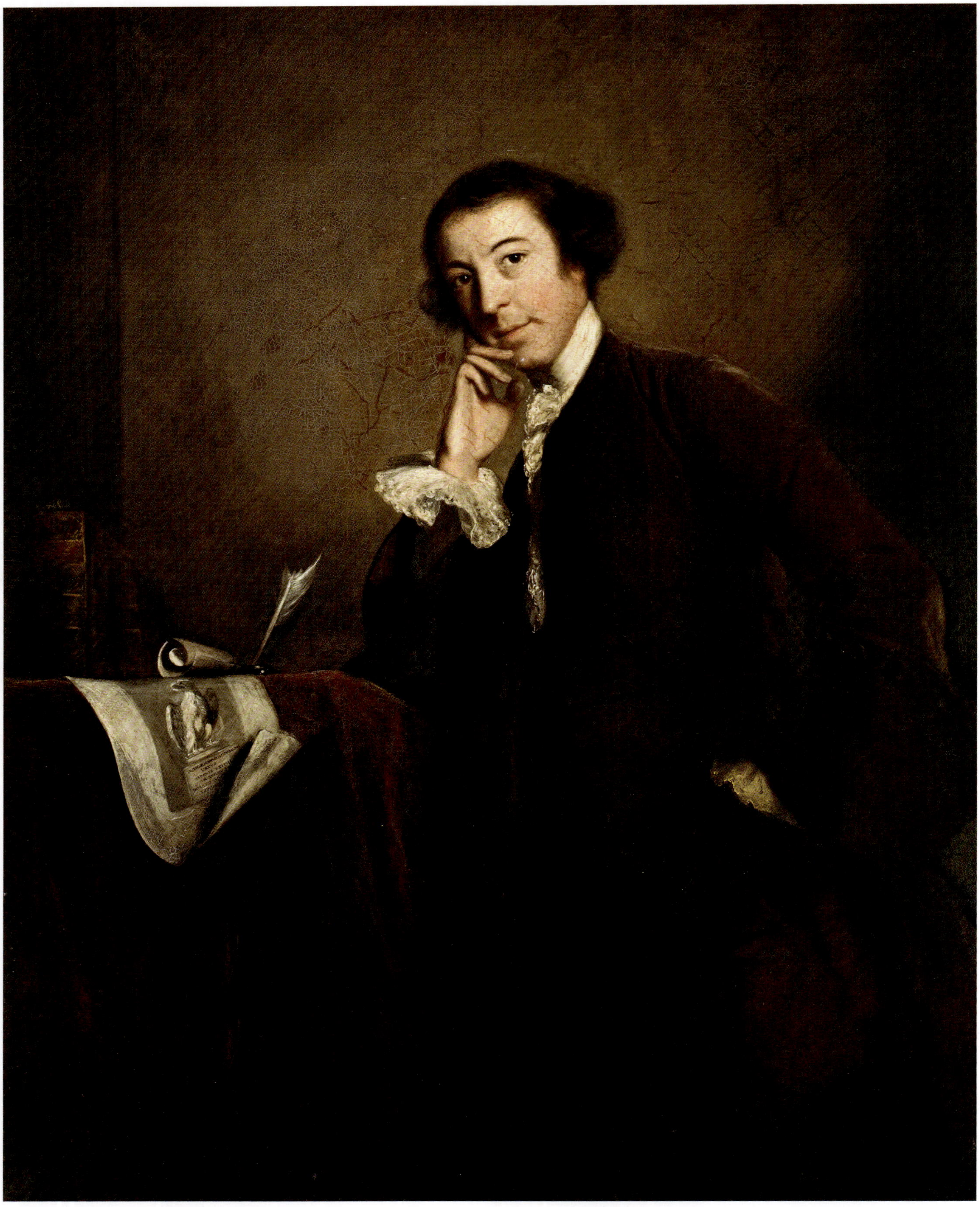

1.

HORACE WALPOLE

HIS LIFE AND CHARACTER

PETER SABOR

Horace Walpole (Fig. 3) will always be associated with Strawberry Hill, the extraordinary house that he occupied for the last fifty years of his life. He was born, however, in the heart of London, at his parents' townhouse in Arlington Street, Piccadilly. His father, Robert Walpole, who was descended from an ancient Norfolk landed family, was a powerful Whig politician who would become Prime Minister while Walpole was still a child. His mother, Catherine Shorter, was the daughter of a Baltic timber merchant. Horace, born Horatio (a name he disliked), was the youngest of six children, two of whom had died in infancy. His parents had been estranged before his birth, and the slightly built, effete son bore no resemblance to his robust, hearty father. There would later be gossip that Horace's biological father was Carr, Lord Hervey, with whom Catherine Walpole was said to have had a liaison.[1] Walpole himself, who was devoted to his mother and who in 1754 erected an elaborate cenotaph to her memory in Westminster Abbey, never alluded to this rumour, of which he seems to have been unaware and which spread only well after his death.

As a child, Walpole, eleven years younger than his next sibling, was delicate and sickly (Fig. 4). He was cherished by his mother but saw little of his father, who was often at Houghton, his Norfolk estate, in the company of his mistress, Maria Skerrett. From 1727 to 1734 Walpole attended his father's old school, Eton, then as now the most famous and prestigious in England. Here he formed friendships that would endure for most of his life. A poetically minded group known as the Quadruple Alliance, in which the other members all came from much less privileged backgrounds, was formed by Walpole, Thomas Gray, Thomas Ashton and Richard West. Other Etonian friends included his cousins Francis and Henry Seymour Conway, William Cole, George Selwyn, George Montagu, Charles Lyttelton and Lord Lincoln. In 1735, the year in which his father was knighted, Walpole entered King's College, Cambridge, following in his father's footsteps again. Gray and

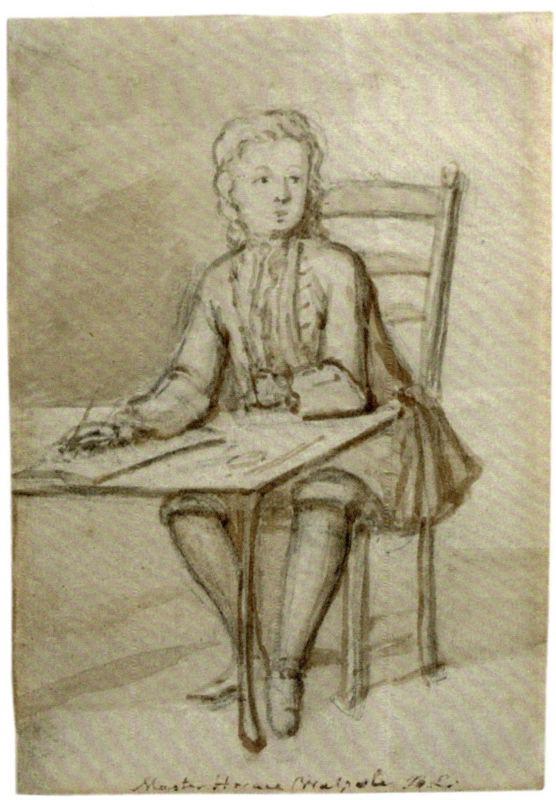

Figure 3. Joshua Reynolds, *Portrait of Horace Walpole*, *c.* 1756–7, oil on canvas, 127 × 101 cm. Marquess of Hertford, Ragley Hall, Warwickshire. Cat. 1

Figure 4. Bernard Lens III, *Portrait of Horace Walpole*, *c.* 1725–6, sepia wash, 17.5 × 11.4 cm. The Trustees of the Waldegrave Chattels Trust. Cat. 36

Ashton had also gone to Cambridge a few months earlier, while West attended Oxford. At Cambridge, where he was influenced by the deist theologian Conyers Middleton, whose collection of antiquities he was subsequently to purchase, Walpole first appeared in print: his Latin verses, signed Horatius Walpole, formed part of a volume of 1736 celebrating the marriage of the Prince of Wales.

Of greater significance than these minor verses was Walpole's personal correspondence, in which his consummate skills as a letter-writer were already being developed and refined. Walpole's letters, which occupy forty-eight volumes in Wilmarth Lewis's magisterial collected edition, are widely recognized as his greatest achievement. They are written with evident relish; the personal letter afforded Walpole full scope for his talents. Their style is often dazzling, their structure is elegant, and because they are private communications rather than formal publications, Walpole's characteristic wit, irony, use of hyperbole and rhetorical flourishes all seem entirely appropriate for the medium. Their subject matter is richly varied, and collectively they constitute an invaluable guide to eighteenth-century social, cultural and political history.

Walpole spent the summer of 1736 visiting his father, for the first time, at Houghton, his splendid, newly completed country house (Fig. 119). In August 1737 his mother died. Sir Robert married Maria Skerrett six months later, but she died in childbirth in June 1738. A few months later, Walpole attained his majority and left Cambridge without taking a degree. His father's gift of three lucrative sinecures, together worth some £2,000 annually, gave him a substantial income for the remainder of his life and ensured that he would never have to work for a living.

With Gray as his travelling companion, Walpole embarked on the Grand Tour of France and Italy in March 1739. During the next two years he became acquainted with the principal attractions of Paris, Venice, Florence, Rome and Naples. For the French part of the tour the pair were accompanied by Walpole's first cousin and lifelong

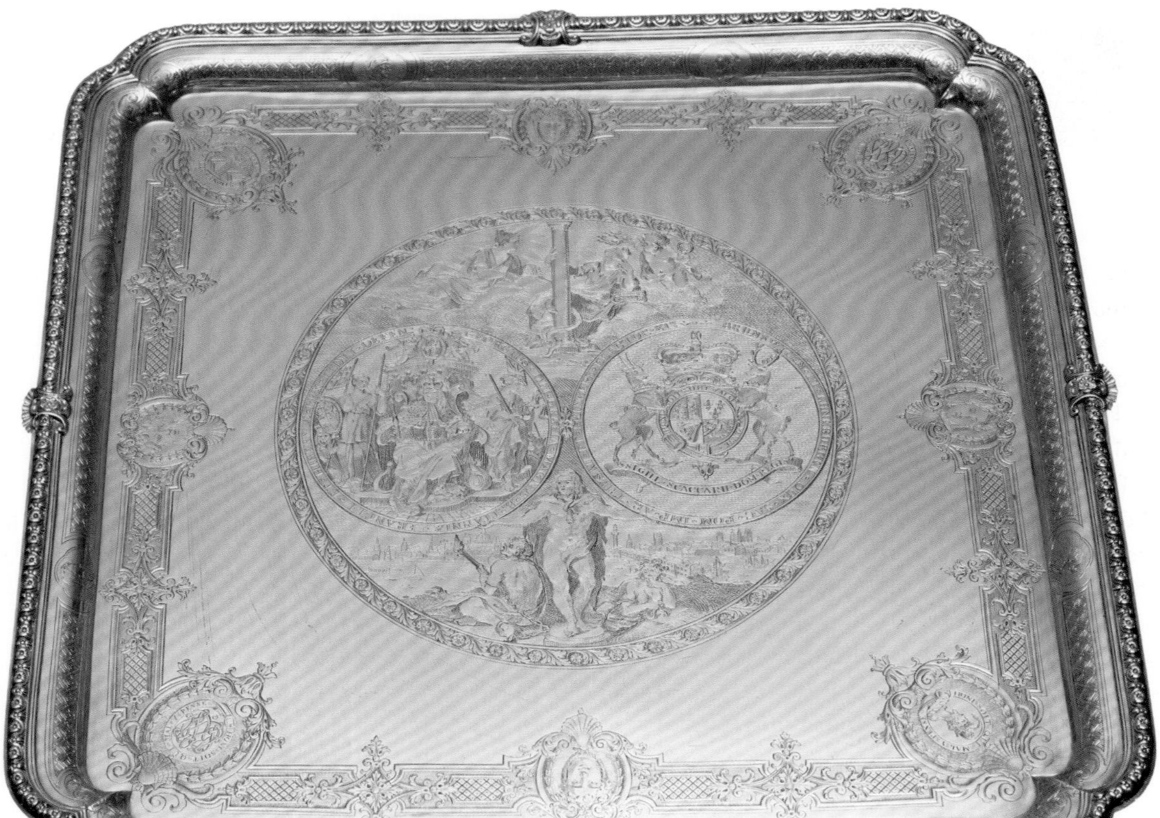

Figure 5. Paul de Lamerie, the engraving attributed to William Hogarth, *Walpole Salver*, 1728–9, Britannia Standard Silver, engraved with a composition showing the second Exchequer Seal of George I, 48 × 48.5 cm. Victoria and Albert Museum, London, purchased with the assistance of the Pilgrim Trust, the Art Fund and the Worshipful Company of Goldsmiths. M.9-1956. Cat. 35

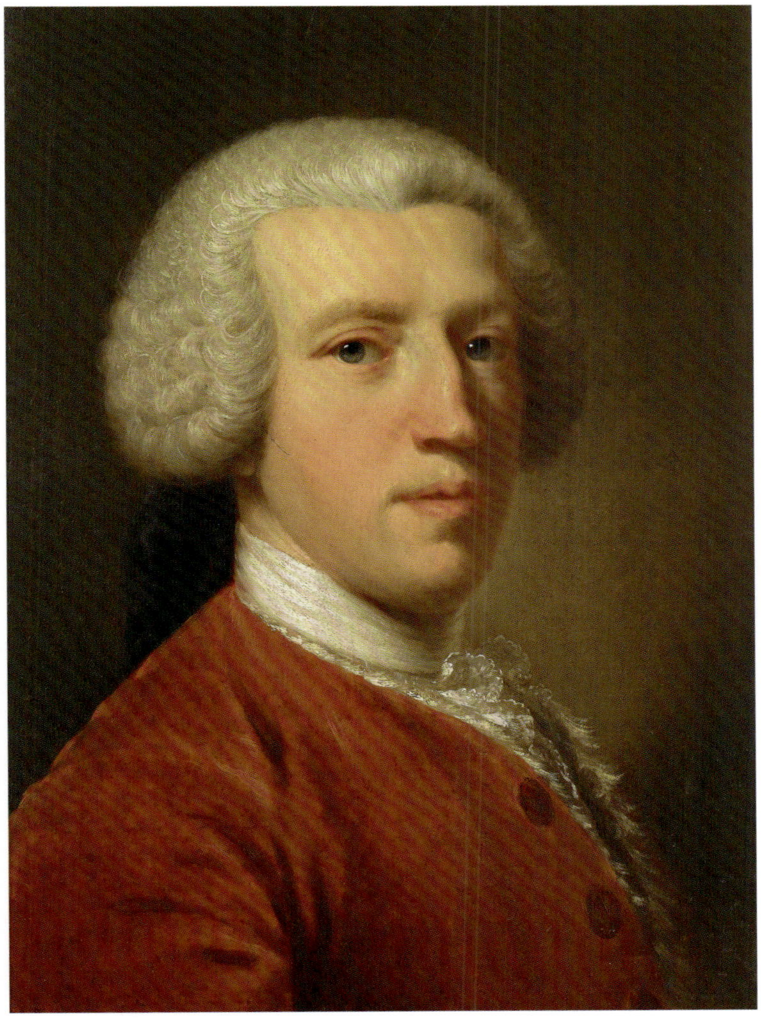

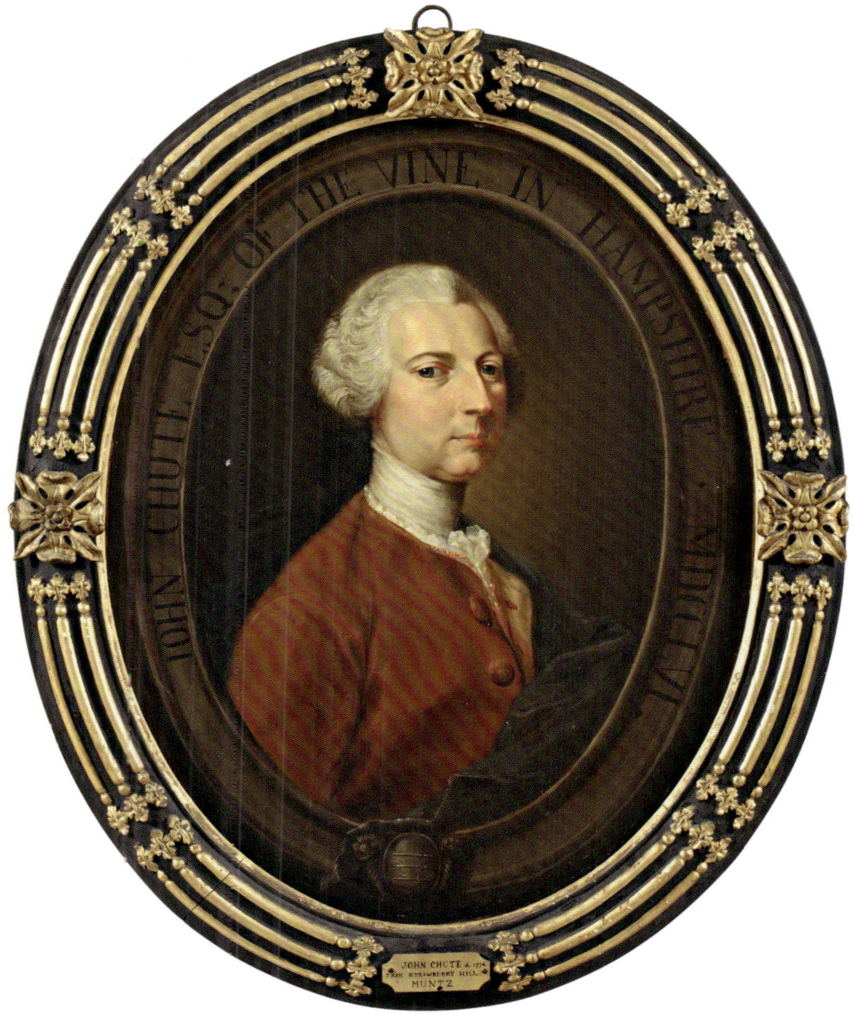

friend, the future soldier and politician Henry Seymour Conway. In Florence, where Walpole and Gray arrived in mid-December after a spectacular Alpine crossing, he formed close friendships with the British resident, Horace Mann (Fig. 6), who would become his most important correspondent for forty-six years, and with John Chute (Fig. 7), who would later contribute to the designing of Strawberry Hill. The end of the tour, however, was marred by a quarrel with Gray, of which the cause remains obscure. Sexual jealousy might have played a part; both Gray and Walpole were at least passively homosexual, and Gray might have resented the interest that Walpole took in other young men, such as Conway and another Etonian friend, the rakish Lord Lincoln. (Much later, in 1764, a scurrilous tract by William Guthrie, *Reply to the Counter-Address*, would charge Walpole with conducting a sodomitical affair, then a criminal offence, with Conway.) But the impecunious and touchy Gray, with his travelling expenses defrayed by Walpole, was in any case in a difficult position, enjoying none of the attention that his wealthy, well-born and well-connected companion commanded. In Reggio, shortly after the falling out with Gray, Walpole fell ill and might have died had not Lincoln and his tutor Joseph Spence arrived in the same city and arranged for medical care.

After his return to England in September 1741, accompanied by Lincoln and Spence, Walpole grew closer to his father, spending extended periods of time at Houghton, and despite their marked differences in taste, temperament and physical appearance, he would always be a stout defender of Sir Robert's political career. In 1742 he

Figure 6. John Astley, *Portrait of Sir Horace Mann*, 1751, oil on panel, 49.5 × 36.8 cm. The Lewis Walpole Library, Yale University. Cat. 68

Figure 7. Johann Heinrich Müntz, after Pompeo Batoni, *Portrait of John Chute*, 1756, oil on canvas, in carved gilt frame, oval: 57 × 45 cm. The Vyne, The Chute Collection (The National Trust). Cat. 45

HORACE WALPOLE'S GRAND TOUR *Eleanor Hughes*

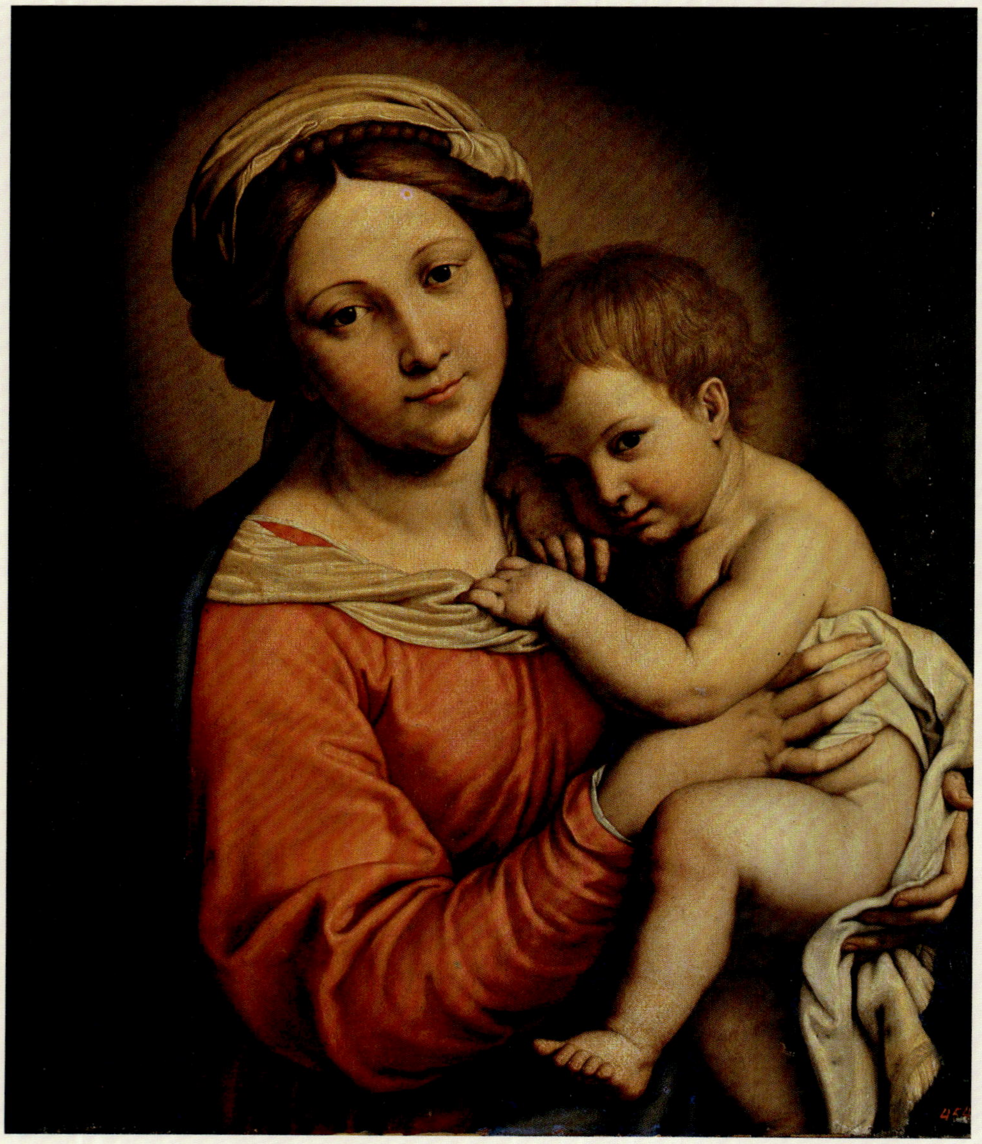

Figure 8. Giovanni Battista Salvi, *Madonna and Child*, 1774–83, oil on canvas, 96 × 73 cm. The State Hermitage Museum, St Petersburg. 1506

For Horace Walpole, as for many other elite young men of the eighteenth century, the Grand Tour offered the opportunity to continue his classical education and to acquire taste as well as to partake in the amusements of Italian high society. Walpole's Tour played a vital role in the formation of his collections, social connections and the conception of Strawberry Hill.

Unusually for a Grand Tourist, Walpole was accompanied by a friend, the poet Thomas Gray, rather than by a tutor. In March 1739 they travelled to Paris and over the Alps ('Precipices, mountains, torrents, wolves, rumblings, Salvator Rosa ... Here we are, the lonely lords of glorious desolate prospects!') to Genoa, Bologna, and Florence. Proceeding later to Rome, they made an excursion to Naples, where they saw early excavations at Herculaneum before returning to Florence in June 1740 and parting company in May 1741. Walpole travelled to Venice with Henry Clinton, Earl of Lincoln, staying for a month before returning to England via Paris in September 1741 to take up the seat in parliament to which Sir Robert Walpole had had him elected in his absence.

One of Walpole's objectives was to obtain artworks for Houghton, his father's vast country house. These included, in an episode that is both scandalous and characteristic of eighteenth-century connoisseurship, a painting of the Madonna and Child (Fig. 8) said to be by Domenico Zampieri, called Domenichino. Walpole saw the painting in Bologna and pursued it on his return to England in spite of mounting evidence that it was a copy by Giovanni Battista Salvi, called Sassoferrato, after an engraving by the French painter Pierre Mignard. Walpole participated in falsifying the painting's attribution, giving his tacit approval for the erasure of Sassoferrato's signature from the back of the canvas and excising Mignard's name from his copy of a print after the original.

Walpole also began acquiring works for his own collections: medals, prints, furniture and Venetian glass, including the set of opaque white glass (*lattimo*) plates painted with scenes of Venice (Fig. 9), of which Lincoln and John Chute, whom Walpole first met in Italy, owned identical sets. In Rome, Venice and Bologna Walpole observed the breaking up of private collections that helped to inspire the compilation and publication of the account of his father's pictures, the *Ædes Walpolianae*. At the sale of the collection of Cardinal Ottoboni, he acquired the bust of Vespasian that would eventually stand in the Gallery at Strawberry Hill (see Fig. 65).

The social connections that Walpole made on the Tour would prove to be vital. In Florence he met Horace Mann, diplomat at the court of the Grand Duke of Tuscany; their friendship and correspondence lasted over forty years. Together Chute and Mann encouraged and facilitated the acquisition of a number of works, including the 'Domenichino' and the Roman eagle and its pedestal, discovered at the baths of Caracalla in 1742 (see Fig. 84). Most significantly, of course, Chute became Walpole's 'oracle in taste … the genius that presided over poor Strawberry'.

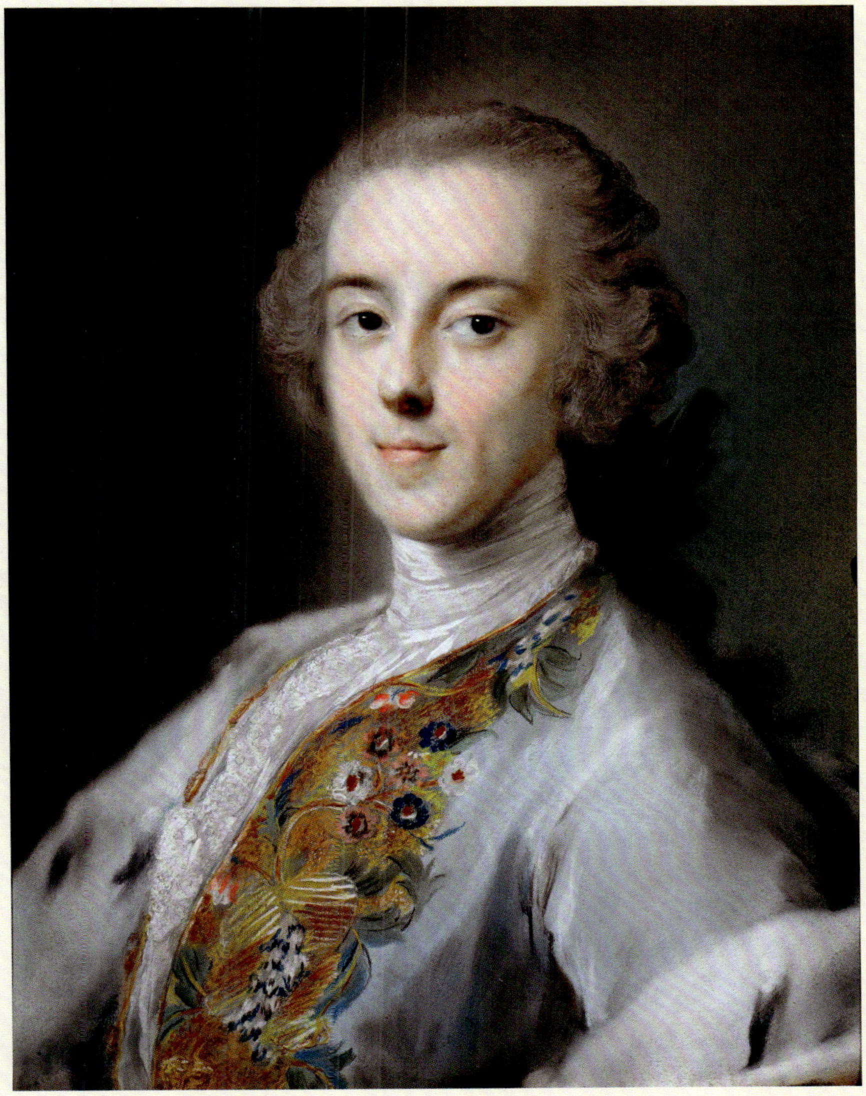

Figure 10. Rosalba Carriera, *Portrait of Horace Walpole*, *c.* 1741, pastel on paper, 61 × 46.5 cm. Houghton Hall, Norfolk. Cat. 38

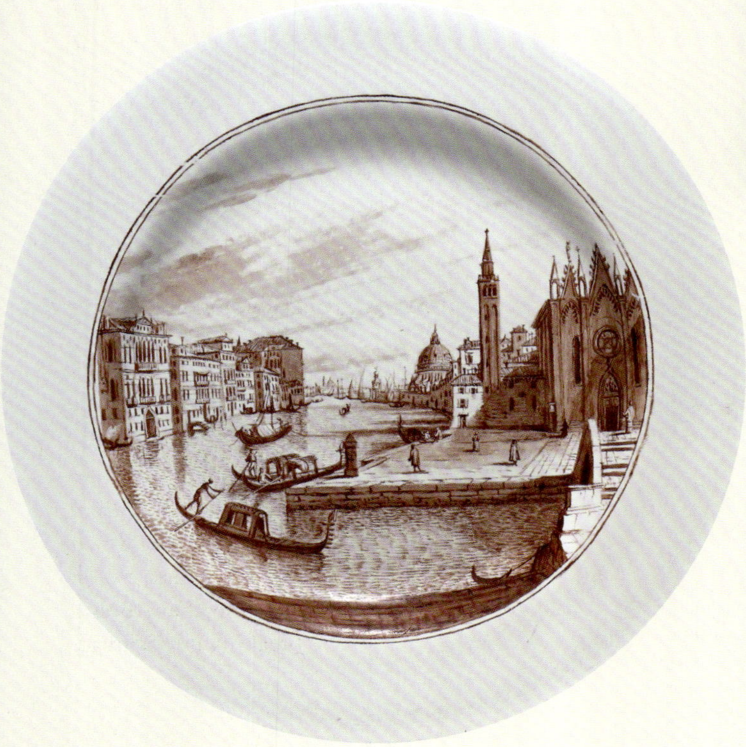

Figure 9. *Lattimo Glass Plate with View of the Church of the Carità, Venice*, probably Miotti Family glasshouse, Murano, 1741, opaque-white glass, painted in red, DIAM 22.4 cm, Murano (Venice). The Corning Museum of Glass. 66.3.38. Cat. 245

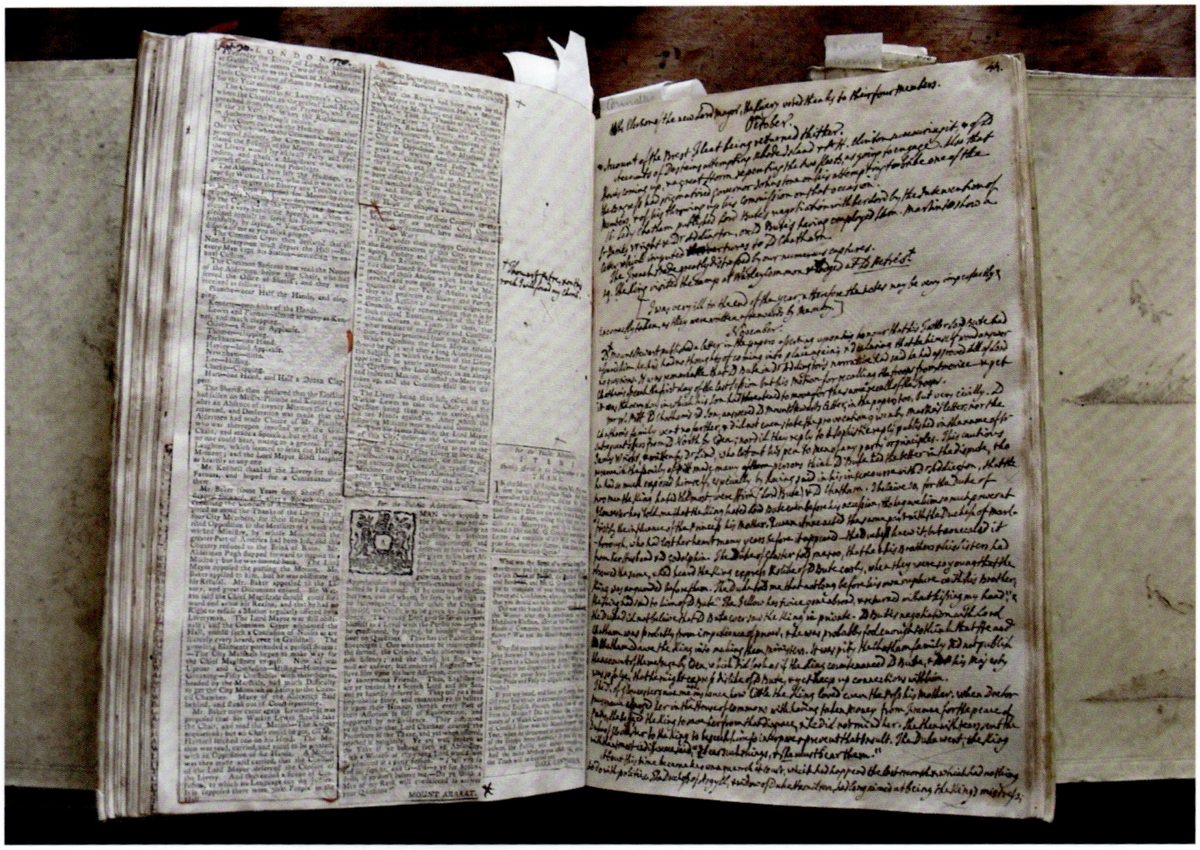

Figure 11. Horace Walpole, *Journal of the reign of George III, 1778–79*, HW's manuscript notes with pasted-in letterpress cuttings, bound in calf. The Trustees of the Waldegrave Chattels Trust. Cat. 266

wrote a witty *Sermon on Painting*, preached by his father's chaplain at Houghton, and in the following year completed his first book, *Ædes Walpolianae* ('The House of the Walpoles'), a catalogue of his father's magnificent art collection, combined with a highly idiosyncratic history of European painting; this was privately printed in 1747, two years after Sir Robert's death. He also dabbled in politics. In 1741, shortly before his return from Italy, he had been elected as a Whig to Parliament, nominally representing the Cornish borough of Callington, in which he never set foot. While he made occasional speeches in the House and published various political satires, as pamphlets or contributions to newspapers and magazines, he never wielded political power. Sir Robert's ministry was at last brought down in 1742 and the Prime Minister resigned from Parliament, retiring to Houghton after being created Earl of Orford. Horace remained an MP until 1768, later representing the Norfolk seats of Castle Rising (from 1754) and King's Lynn (from 1757). His wealth increased on his father's death in 1745; he was left the house in Arlington Street and another sinecure at the Customs, worth £1,000 annually, in addition to the three he already held. In 1746 he rented a small house in the grounds of Windsor Castle, enjoying the charms of living in the country, close to the Thames and to his old school, Eton, yet still within a few hours' carriage ride of London. In April 1747 he found a rural cottage still closer to London, near fashionable Twickenham and only 11 miles from his London house. Here, in what became his celebrated neo-Gothic miniature castle, Strawberry Hill, Walpole would write his major published works and the bulk of his massive correspondence.

In his first decade at Strawberry Hill Walpole continued to publish political pamphlets defending his father's conduct and principles and in 1751 began compiling his historical memoirs, continuing them up to 1791 (Fig. 11). This vast undertaking, totalling some three million words, remained in manuscript during his lifetime and began to appear in print only in 1822; the portion from 1783 to 1791 has still not been published. Providing a remarkably detailed and extended Whig interpretation of the politics of Hanoverian England, Walpole's memoirs are an important source for historians, but they have always been of lesser interest than his magnificently detailed and diverse correspondence. Between 1753 and 1756 Walpole also contributed some polished and entertaining essays to a fashionable periodical, *The World*, one of which describes his dangerous encounter in 1749 with the celebrated highwaymen, James Maclaine, and his confederate, William Plunkett, in Hyde Park. Walpole had no wish to be a hero, but was almost killed when a pistol was accidentally discharged. In the 'Short Notes' of his life that he compiled at various times, he wrote that the bullet 'razed the skin under my eye, left some marks of shot on my face and stunned me'.[2] In 1757 Walpole published one of his most powerful and effective tracts, *A Letter from Xo Ho, a Chinese Philosopher at London, to his Friend Lien Chi, at Peking*. The *Letter* satirizes English manners and vices, in particular the execution of Admiral Byng, whom Walpole had championed, through the mouthpiece of a Chinese commentator: a device that Oliver Goldsmith would borrow for his 'Chinese letters' collected in *The Citizen of the World* (1762). Characteristically, Walpole downplayed its merits, claiming to have written it 'in less than an hour and half'.[3] The *sprezzatura* that he displays here was a key part of his character: however difficult the task he set himself, he would always make it seem to have been undertaken with effortless nonchalance. He liked to depict himself as a gentleman amateur rather than a diligent scholar.

Among Walpole's numerous activities at Strawberry Hill was the installation in 1757 of a printing press (see pp. 242–3): the first significant private press in England. In addition to much ephemera, such as an elaborate set of regulations for visiting the house, its productions included thirty-four books, of which fourteen were by Walpole himself. Owning his own press gave Walpole the great advantage of being able to control the publication of his writings, determining precisely how many copies would be printed in each case, when and in what format they would appear, and who would or would not be given copies. Some of his works, most notably *The Castle of Otranto* (1764), were given to London publishers for commercial distribution, but most of Walpole's many publications were issued, as well as written, at Strawberry Hill.

Walpole and Gray had resumed their broken friendship in 1745, four years after their return from the Grand Tour. In 1753 Walpole had arranged for the publication of six of Gray's poems, including his great 'Elegy Written in a Country Churchyard', in an edition elaborately illustrated by Richard Bentley, a member of the committee of friends advising Walpole on the Gothicizing of Strawberry Hill. In recognition of Gray's importance as a poet, the first Strawberry Hill Press production was *Odes by Mr Gray* (1757): a slim volume containing 'The Progress of Poesy' and 'The Bard'. A year later, Walpole published two of his own works at the Press: *A Catalogue of the Royal and Noble Authors of England*, in two volumes, and *Fugitive Pieces in Verse and Prose*, a collection of his poetry and essays. Walpole always prided himself on his originality, and in *Royal and Noble Authors* he had certainly found a novel category of authorship to catalogue. After printing 300 copies of *Royal and Noble Authors* at Strawberry Hill and receiving complimentary responses from the friends to whom he had distributed it, Walpole sold the copyright to London publishers for sale in a much larger second edition of 2,000 copies. The reviews were often hostile and Walpole disliked being placed in the spotlight, as the entry in his Short Notes reveals. He complains of being 'much abused for it in the *Critical Review*, and more gently in the *Monthly Review*. By the former for disliking the Stuarts; by the latter for liking my father: opinions I am not likely to change.' He even objected to a pamphlet, probably by John Hill, written in his defence: it was, he wrote, 'full of gross flattery'.[4]

After this initial experiment in public authorship, Walpole was more cautious about exposing himself to the hazards of critical reviews. The most ambitious of his publications was his four-volume *Anecdotes of Painting in England* (1762–80), a history of British painting, engraving and architecture, largely based on some forty volumes of manuscript notes compiled by the antiquary George Vertue. Walpole deprecated its significance by using the term 'Anecdotes' in the title, as if readers would find amusing tales rather than an exhaustive survey, although he laboured long and hard on this project. He printed the work in three instalments (1762, 1764 and 1771), proceeding only after reviews proved to be positive, and then withheld issuing the final instalment until 1780, when the artists under discussion, including

THE CASTLE OF OTRANTO

Ruth Mack

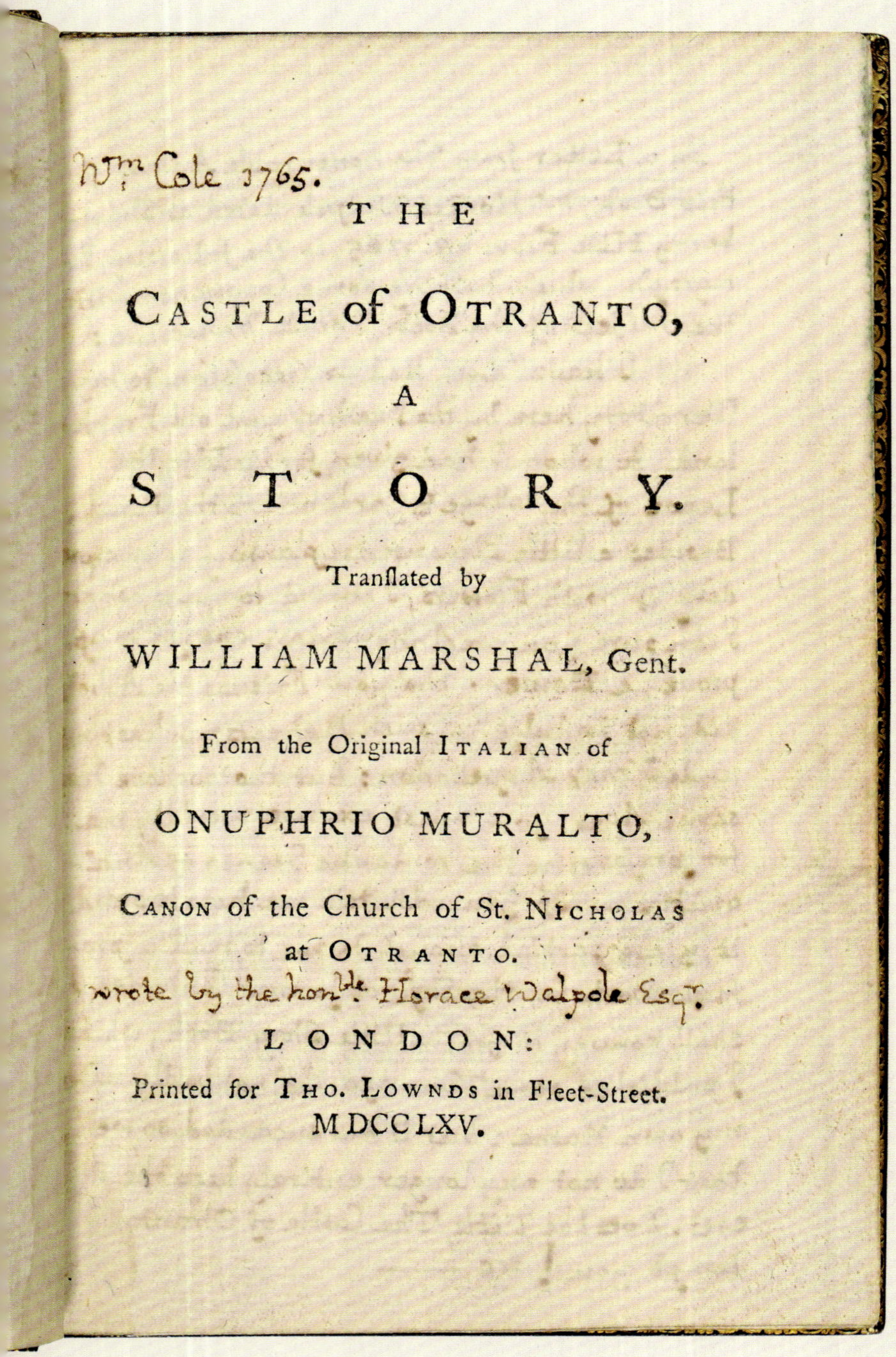

Wm. Cole 1765.

THE

CASTLE of OTRANTO,

A

STORY.

Tranflated by

WILLIAM MARSHAL, Gent.

From the Original ITALIAN of

ONUPHRIO MURALTO,

CANON of the Church of St. NICHOLAS

at OTRANTO.

wrote by the honble. Horace Walpole Esqr.

LONDON:

Printed for THO. LOWNDS in Fleet-Street.

MDCCLXV.

Figure 12. Title page, Horace Walpole, *The Castle of Otranto, a Story* (London: T. Lownds, 1765). The Lewis Walpole Library, Yale University. 24 17 765 Copy 1. Cat. 56

For over two centuries Horace Walpole's fame has mainly rested not on his creation of Strawberry Hill but on his authorship of *The Castle of Otranto*, his 'Gothic story' published in 1764. Still widely regarded as the first piece of gothic fiction, Walpole's work appeared in December 1764 as the work of Onuphrio Muralto, translated by William Marshal, Gentleman. In the preface to the first edition Walpole – writing as the supposed translator – dates the work during the time of the Crusades, analyses the political situation informing its production and comments on its 'beauties'. Only in the second edition of April 1765 does he claim the work as his own and thus as a modern text (Fig. 12).

In letters to his friends Walpole frequently links his house and book, fondly referring to Strawberry Hill as his 'castle'. He makes the most famous declaration of this connection in a letter to William Cole in 1765, when looking back on the composition of the 'story':

> I waked one morning in the beginning of last June from a dream, of which all I could recover was, that I had thought myself in an ancient castle (a very natural dream for head filled like mine with Gothic story) and that on the uppermost bannister of a great staircase I saw a gigantic hand in armour. In the evening I sat down and began to write, without knowing in the least what I intended to say or relate.

To the reader familiar with Strawberry Hill, Walpole's description recalls John Carter's drawing of the staircase (Fig. 245), with its Armoury well in view. Carter also illustrated a scene from Walpole's other castle, where the knight Frederic enters Otranto amid tall Gothic arches (Fig. 13).

In comparing these scenes, it is startling how orderly Strawberry Hill appears, how little inclined it seems towards the dark, even sublime, castle of Otranto, which would set the tone for the famous later gothic novels of Ann Radcliffe and Matthew Lewis. But if Strawberry Hill and the fictional castle at Otranto seem to embody different variants of the 'gloomth' Walpole tried to cultivate, the two importantly seem to share something else: a kind of fictionality. When he describes his dream as the

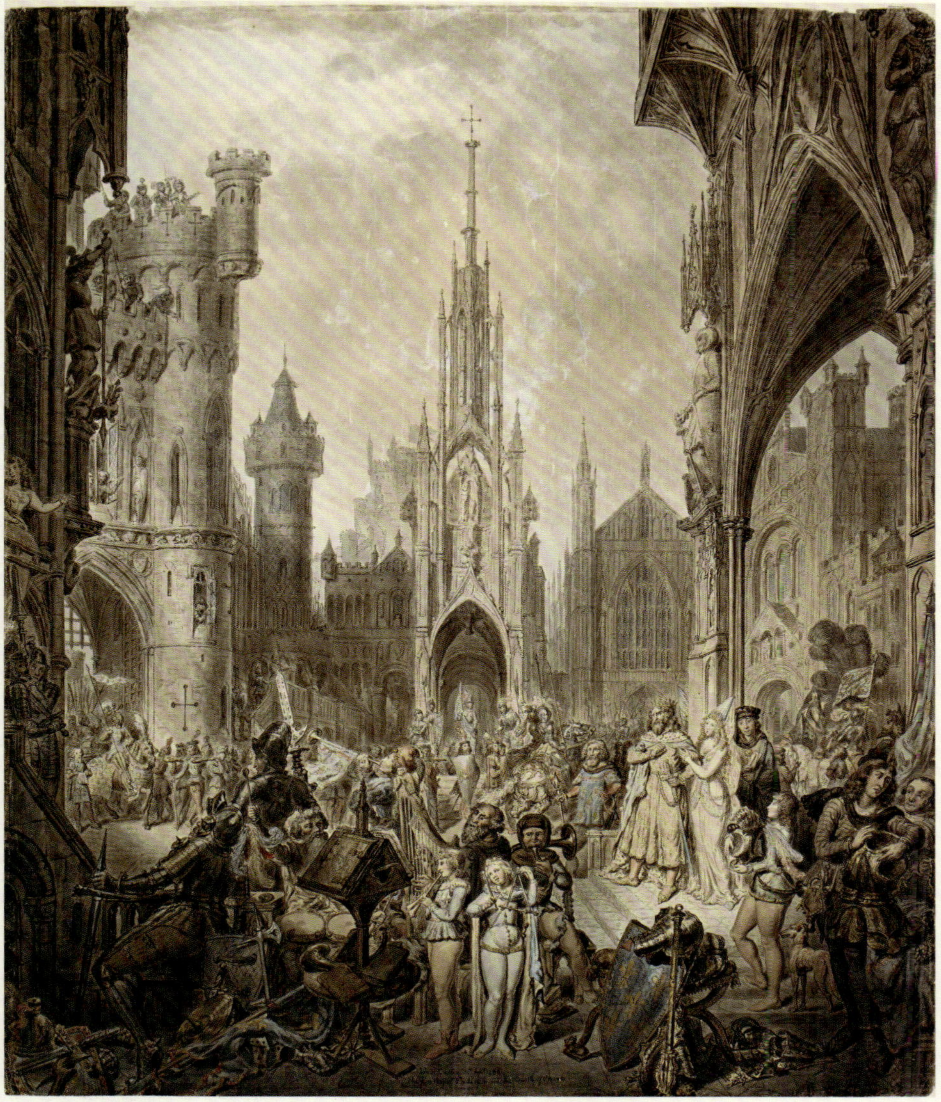

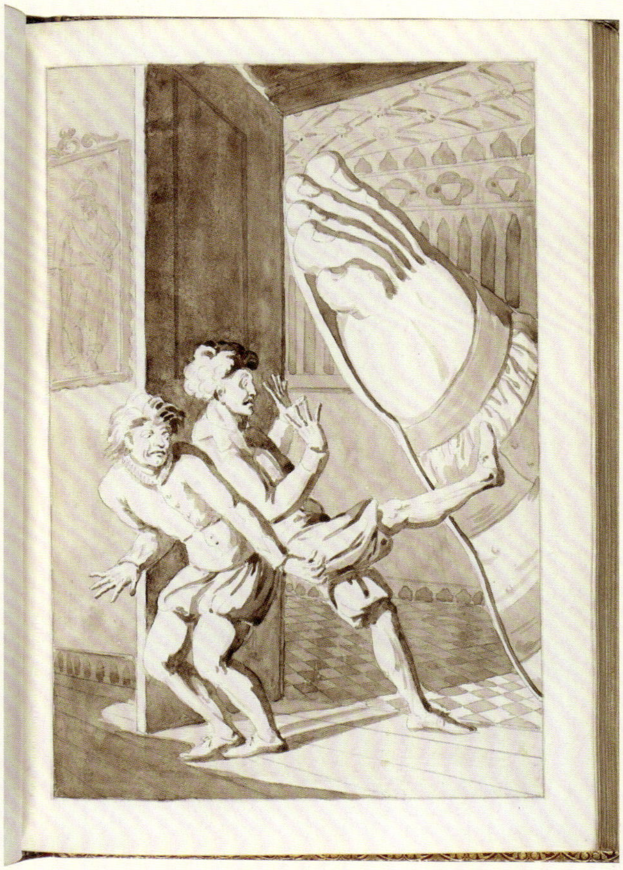

'natural' outgrowth of 'Gothic story', Walpole calls attention not only to the origin of both house and book in his fascination with medieval history but also to his creation of story through the making of Strawberry Hill. One need only recall Walpole's inventive display of his own distinguished ancestry in placing the shield of Sir Terry Robsart (a distant relation discovered by Walpole through genealogical research) alongside those of Walpole and Shorter (his parents' families), and ultimately in describing the niches on the staircase landing as containing coats of mail, shields and broadswords 'all supposed to be taken by Sir Terry Robsart in the holy wars'. Walpole's research was mistaken and Sir Terry did not fight in the Crusades; more importantly, the objects were purchased by Walpole, not inherited from this distinguished family member. But the point is that Strawberry Hill – like a fictionalized preface or the engrossing imaginary world of a novel – might encourage us to 'suppose' otherwise. If Strawberry Hill inspires *Otranto*, we might say that it does so not merely as a powerful setting but as a story whose delightful process of writing convinces its author to write again in different form.

Figure 13. John Carter, *The Entry of Frederic into the Castle of Otranto*, 1790, pen and black ink with grey and blue watercolour, 60.2 × 50.3 cm (visible). The Lewis Walpole Library, Yale University. 33 30 copy 11 Folio. Cat. 59

Figure 14. Bertie Greatheed, *Diego and Jaquez Frightened by the Giant Foot*, wash drawing inserted into the 6th edition of the *Castle of Otranto* (Parma: printed by Bodoni for J. Edwards, 1791 The Lewis Walpole Library, Yale University. 49 3729. Cat. 57

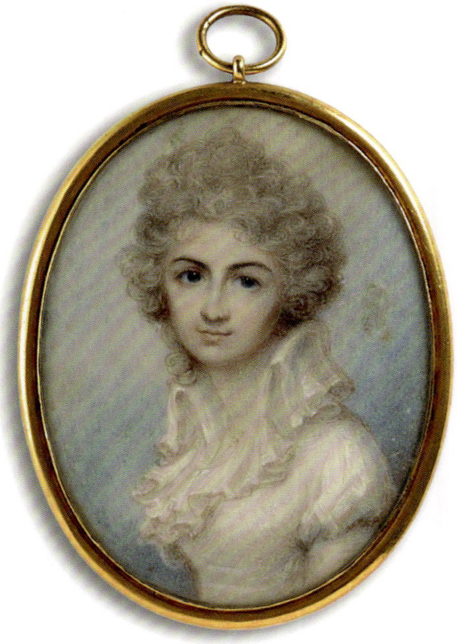

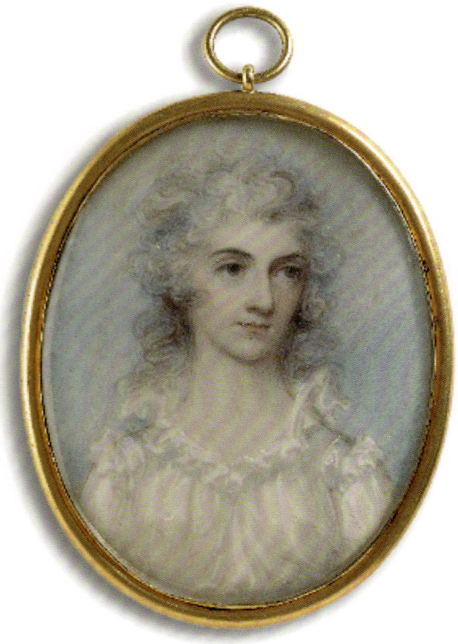

Figure 15. Anne Mee, *Portrait Miniature of Mary Berry*, 1790, watercolour on ivory set in gilt metal frame, H 7.4 cm. The Trustees of the Waldegrave Chattels Trust. Cat. 262

Figure 16. Anne Mee, *Portrait Miniature of Agnes Berry*, 1790, watercolour on ivory set in gilt metal frame, H 7.4 cm. The Trustees of the Waldegrave Chattels Trust. Cat. 263

Hogarth, were no longer alive. Volume 4 of the *Anecdotes* included Walpole's seminal 'History of the Modern Taste in Gardening', termed 'the most entertaining part of a very entertaining work'[5] by William Rose in the *Monthly Review* and a piece in which Walpole himself took particular pride. A lifelong Francophile, he was also delighted by the elegant French translation of the 'History' by the Duc de Nivernais, which he printed in a Strawberry Hill edition of 1785, with French and English texts on facing pages.

The 1760s were Walpole's most productive decade as an author. As well as publishing the *Anecdotes of Painting*, he wrote his only novel, *The Castle of Otranto*. First published on Christmas Eve 1764 in a commercial edition of five hundred copies, it appeared in the guise of a translation by William Marshal from an Italian romance by 'Onuphrio Muralto', ostensibly published in Naples in 1529, accompanied by a spurious editorial preface. Only after thus testing the waters and protecting his identity with a double pseudonym did Walpole release a second edition five months later, in which he acknowledged his authorship. It was the most popular of his works and initiated the genre of gothic fiction; the major gothic novelists of the 1790s, including Ann Radcliffe, Matthew Lewis and William Godwin, are Walpole's heirs. In 1766 Walpole published a pseudonymous 'Letter from the King of Prussia to Rousseau', which provoked a quarrel between Jean-Jacques Rousseau and David Hume, and *An Account of the Giants Lately Discovered*, a witty satire on the condition of England. Two years later, he published two more works, one commercially and the other at Strawberry Hill. The first was *Historic Doubts on the Life and Reign of King Richard III*, a revisionist defence of a widely reviled king. Sales were good but reviews were mixed, and in the 1790s, at the height of the Terror in France, Walpole himself came to doubt Richard's innocence: 'I must *now* believe that any atrocity may have been attempted or practised by an ambitious prince of the blood aiming at the crown.'[6] Shortly afterwards Walpole printed a Strawberry Hill edition of his Gothic tragedy *The Mysterious Mother*, set in medieval Narbonne and featuring incest between the Countess of Narbonne and her son (unintentional on the part of the son) and, again unintentionally, between the son and the offspring of this incestuous union, his own sister-daughter. Not surprisingly, given its scandalous subject, the play was never performed and Walpole exercised strict control over its readership. Only fifty copies were produced and Walpole retained most of them himself; it thus became an item eagerly sought by collectors.

In 1765 Walpole returned to Paris for the first time since his Grand Tour and began a close friendship with the Marquise du Deffand, the famous hostess of a literary salon, blind and twenty years his senior. They maintained an extensive correspondence in French until her death in 1780 at the age of eighty-four. Her letters to Walpole fill six volumes of the Yale Edition of Walpole's correspondence, but almost all of his letters to her were destroyed at his behest. Walpole stayed in Paris for seven months on this occasion, returning for subsequent, shorter visits in 1767, 1769, 1771 and 1775. His writings in the 1770s and 1780s included a one-act comedy, *Nature Will Prevail*, a fantasy set on a desert island, which he gave to George Colman, the manager of Covent Garden, in 1773. It had a seven-night run at the Little Theatre in the Haymarket in 1778, but remained unpublished in Walpole's lifetime. Another of his late works, *Hieroglyphic Tales*, was printed at Strawberry Hill in 1785, but in an edition of only seven copies. These six, surrealistic short stories are wilder and stranger than *The Castle of Otranto*, and Walpole seemed determined that no one should read them until after his death; every copy of the tiny Strawberry Hill edition remained in his own possession. The most important of Walpole's later publications was *A Description of the Villa of Mr. Horace Walpole*, first printed at Strawberry Hill in 1774 in an edition of 100 copies, with a second, expanded and richly illustrated edition of 200 copies following a decade later.

Walpole's printer Thomas Kirgate, who had worked for him since 1765, remained at Strawberry Hill until Walpole's death, but the Press fell silent after 1789. Visitors continued to flock to Strawberry Hill to admire the building and its contents, but its master, racked by gout, was in decline. He enjoyed the company of Mary and Agnes Berry (Figs. 15, 16), two sisters almost fifty years his junior, whom he met in 1788 and who became his closest friends; he called them his 'twin wives' and his 'StrawBerries'. They and their father became his tenants at Little Strawberry Hill in 1791, and Mary Berry collaborated with Walpole in editing his collected works, a task that she completed after his death. *The Works of Horatio Walpole, Earl of Orford* was published in five handsome quarto volumes in 1798; the last two volumes contain a selection of Walpole's hitherto unpublished correspondence (Fig. 17).

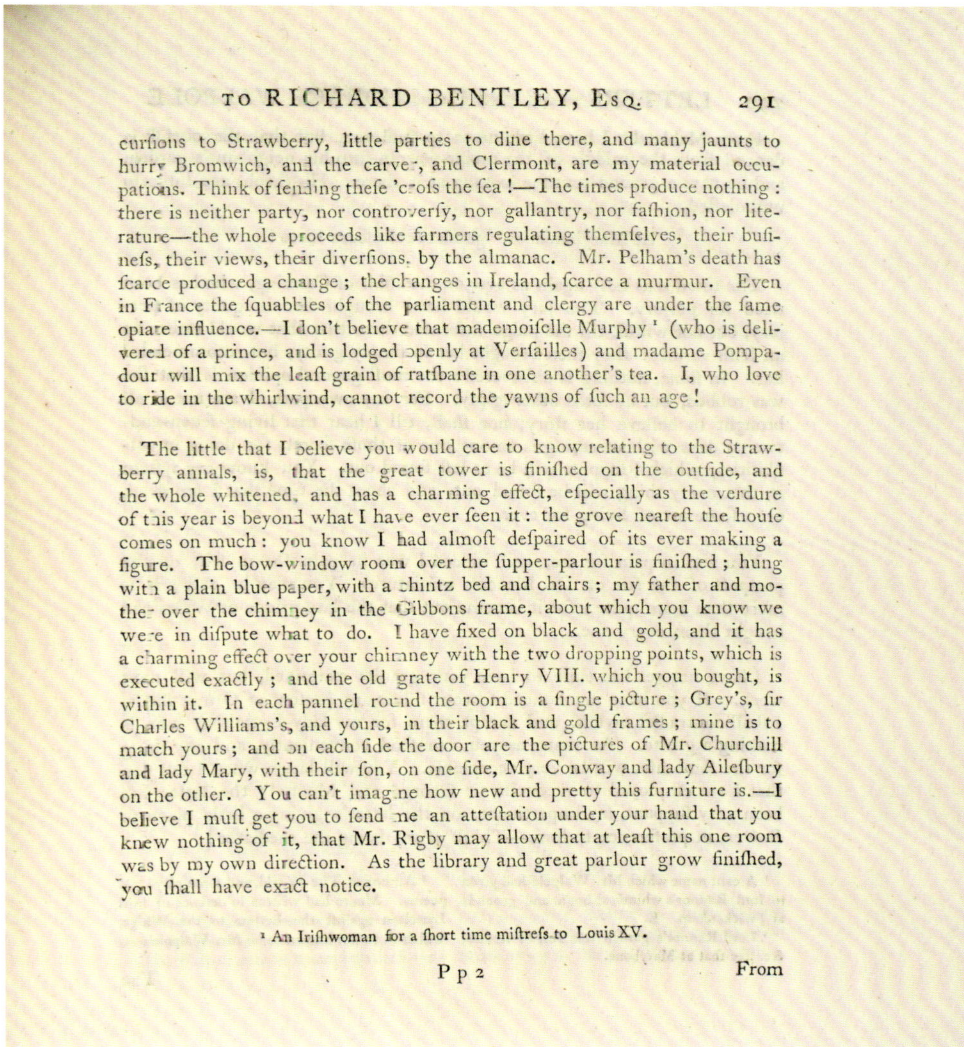
TO RICHARD BENTLEY, Esq. 291

curſions to Strawberry, little parties to dine there, and many jaunts to hurry Bromwich, and the carver, and Clermont, are my material occupations. Think of ſending theſe 'croſs the ſea !—The times produce nothing : there is neither party, nor controverſy, nor gallantry, nor faſhion, nor literature—the whole proceeds like farmers regulating themſelves, their buſineſs, their views, their diverſions, by the almanac. Mr. Pelham's death has ſcarce produced a change ; the changes in Ireland, ſcarce a murmur. Even in France the ſquabbles of the parliament and clergy are under the ſame opiate influence.—I don't believe that mademoiſelle Murphy [1] (who is delivered of a prince, and is lodged openly at Verſailles) and madame Pompadour will mix the leaſt grain of ratſbane in one another's tea. I, who love to ride in the whirlwind, cannot record the yawns of ſuch an age !

The little that I believe you would care to know relating to the Strawberry annals, is, that the great tower is finiſhed on the outſide, and the whole whitened, and has a charming effect, eſpecially as the verdure of this year is beyond what I have ever ſeen it : the grove neareſt the houſe comes on much : you know I had almoſt deſpaired of its ever making a figure. The bow-window room over the ſupper-parlour is finiſhed ; hung with a plain blue paper, with a chintz bed and chairs ; my father and mother over the chimney in the Gibbons frame, about which you know we were in diſpute what to do. I have fixed on black and gold, and it has a charming effect over your chimney with the two dropping points, which is executed exactly ; and the old grate of Henry VIII. which you bought, is within it. In each pannel round the room is a ſingle picture ; Grey's, ſir Charles Williams's, and yours, in their black and gold frames ; mine is to match yours ; and on each ſide the door are the pictures of Mr. Churchill and lady Mary, with their ſon, on one ſide, Mr. Conway and lady Aileſbury on the other. You can't imagine how new and pretty this furniture is.—I believe I muſt get you to ſend me an atteſtation under your hand that you knew nothing of it, that Mr. Rigby may allow that at leaſt this one room was by my own direction. As the library and great parlour grow finiſhed, you ſhall have exact notice.

1 An Iriſhwoman for a ſhort time miſtreſs to Louis XV.

P p 2 From

Figure 17. *The Works of Horatio Walpole, Earl of Orford*, Volume 5. The Lewis Walpole Library, Yale University. 21 798C Copy 2. Cat. 267

Walpole's nephew, the deranged George Walpole, died in 1791. Walpole took no pleasure in succeeding him as the 4th Earl of Orford and did not take his seat in the House of Lords. Nor could he salvage much of Houghton, which he inherited with his title; his nephew had encumbered it with mortgages and in 1779 had sold Sir Robert's collection of paintings to Catherine II of Russia, much to Walpole's disgust. He was appalled by the Revolution and the Reign of Terror in France and he outlived almost all of his old friends, comparing himself in his letters to the immortal but unhappy

Struldbruggs of Jonathan Swift's *Gulliver's Travels*. In November 1796 he left his beloved Strawberry Hill for the last time and was taken to his London house in Berkeley Square, where he died in March 1797 at the age of seventy-nine. He was buried with his father and brothers in the Walpole tomb at Houghton church.

A delicate child, Walpole became a frail adult, suffering much from gout in his later life. He was thin, slight and pallid, with brilliant eyes; William Cole, in 1765, refers to his 'puny Constitution' and 'meagre Frame'.[7] Laetitia-Matilda Hawkins, who became acquainted with him in the 1760s, when she was still a child, recalled the pleasantness of his voice, with its 'highly gentlemanly' tones, and the affected oddness of his gait: 'He always entered a room… knees bent, and feet on tip-toe, as if afraid of a wet floor.'[8] His portrait was painted or drawn on over twenty occasions; among those most revealing of his character are the paintings by John Giles Eccardt (1754) and Joshua Reynolds (1756) (Frontispiece and Fig. 3).

Walpole's publications, as well as his work on Strawberry Hill, were generally well received during his lifetime. After 1770, however, he was widely condemned for his dealings with Thomas Chatterton, whom he had never met but with whom he had corresponded briefly in 1769, a year before the youthful poet committed suicide. Walpole was blamed for his death, and the charge, however unjust, tainted his reputation in his later years. In the nineteenth century he was excoriated in a brilliantly written and highly influential review essay by Thomas Babington Macaulay, who termed him 'the most eccentric, the most artificial, the most fastidious, the most capricious, of men'.[9] In the twentieth century his sharpest detractor was Robert Walpole's biographer, J.H. Plumb, who found 'something incurably mannered and irrelevant about Horace Walpole. His vast correspondence touches practically no aspect of eighteenth-century life at a serious level.'[10]

Despite such negative voices, however, Walpole's reputation as one of the greatest English letter-writers, as the founder of the Gothic novel and drama, as the author of major works of art and garden history, and of course as the creator of Strawberry Hill, has endured. The breadth of his achievement is astonishing: Walpole worked in such diverse genres as prose fiction, tragic and comic drama, verse, literary criticism, historical works, political and social satire, and memoir- and journal-writing. Leslie Stephen's remark that 'the History of England, throughout a very large part of the eighteenth century, is simply a synonym for the works of Horace Walpole'[11] is certainly an exaggeration. Wilmarth Lewis, too, who devoted most of his life to collecting, editing, and writing about Walpole, was always inclined to present his subject in the most favourable possible light. But as the present volume reveals, the originality and variety of Walpole's designing, building, collecting and publishing at Strawberry Hill can hardly be overstated.

1. The standard biography of Walpole, first published almost seventy years ago but not yet superseded, remains R.W. Ketton-Cremer's *Horace Walpole: A Biography* (1940; 3rd ed. London: Methuen, 1964). It is supplemented in various ways by several subsequent biographical studies, including Hugh Honour, *Horace Walpole* (London: Longmans, 1957); Wilmarth Sheldon Lewis, *Horace Walpole* (London: Rupert Hart-Davis, 1961); Brian Fothergill, *The Strawberry Hill Set: Horace Walpole and his Circle* (London: Faber, 1983); Rex A. Barrell, *Horace Walpole (1717–1797) and France* (Lewiston, NY: Mellen, 1991); and Morris Brownell, *The Prime Minister of Taste: A Portrait of Horace Walpole* (New Haven and London: Yale University Press, 2001).
2. *HW Corres.* 13: 23.
3. *HW Corres.* 13: 27.
4. *HW Corres.* 13: 30–31.
5. *Monthly Review* 64 (March 1781): 193; see Peter Sabor, ed., *Horace Walpole: The Critical Heritage* (London: Routledge, 1987), 150.
6. Walpole, *Postscript* to *Historic Doubts*: *Works* 2: 251*. The *Postscript* was written in February 1793, shortly after the execution of Louis XVI on 21 January.
7. William Cole, *A Journal of my Journey to Paris in the Year 1765*, ed. Francis Griffin Stokes (London: Constable, 1931), 54.
8. Laetitia-Matilda Hawkins, *Anecdotes, Biographical Sketches and Memoirs* (London, 1822), I: 108; Sabor, *Critical Heritage*, 305.
9. Thomas Babington Macaulay, review essay, *Edinburgh Review* 58 (October 1833), 227; Sabor, *Critical Heritage*, 312.
10. J.H. Plumb, review of *Yale Edition of Horace Walpole's Correspondence*, *New York Review of Books* (30 September 1965), 10.
11. Leslie Stephen, 'Horace Walpole', *Cornhill Magazine* 25 (June 1872): 718.

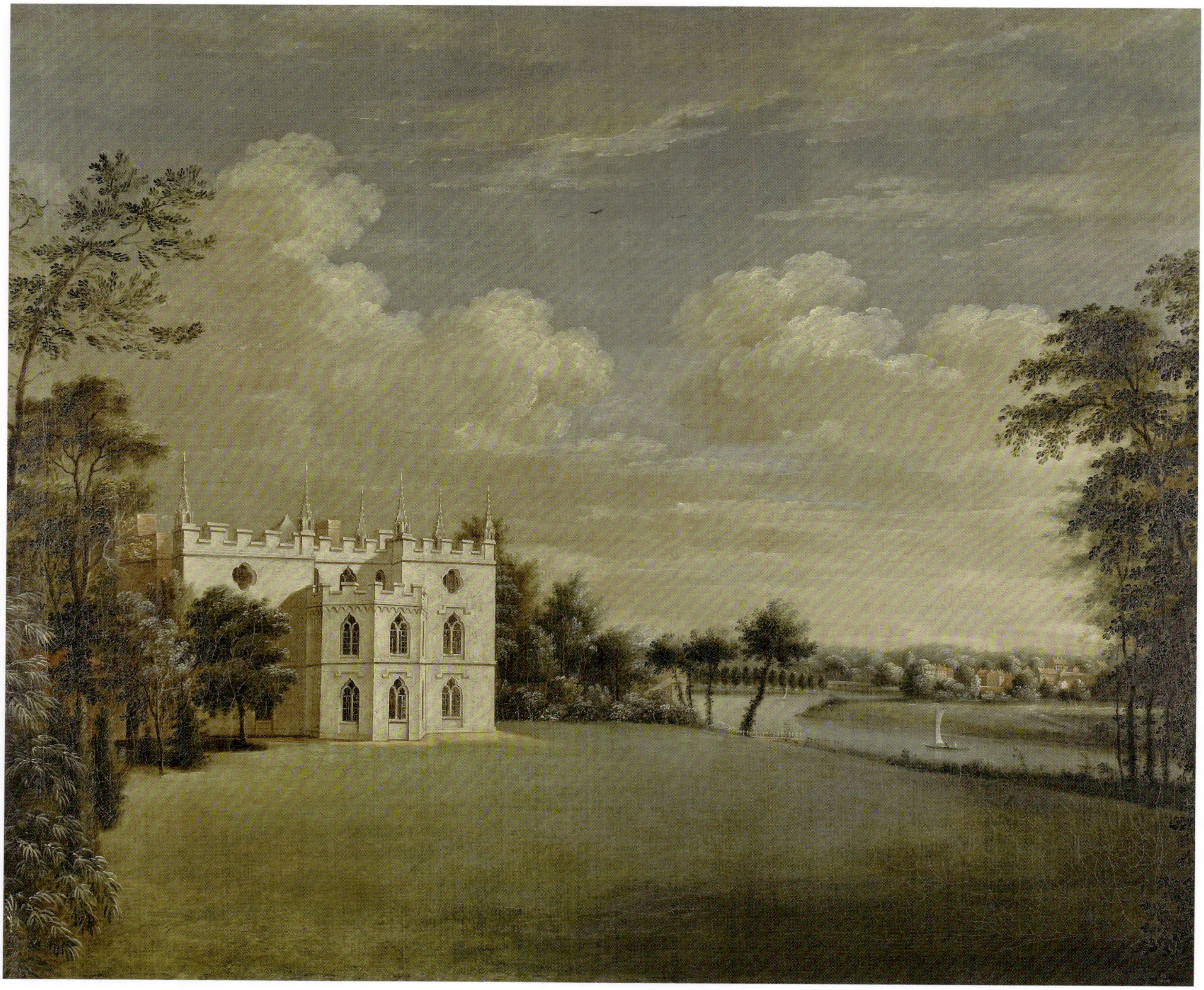

Figure 18. Johann Heinrich Müntz, *Strawberry Hill, Twickenham, from the South*, *c.* 1755–9, oil on canvas, 61.9 × 74.3 cm. The Lewis Walpole Library, Yale University. Cat. 3

2.

GOING TO STRAWBERRY HILL

MICHAEL SNODIN

> You perceive by my date that I am got into a new camp, and have left my tub at Windsor. It is a little play-thing-house that I got out of Mrs Chenevix's shop, and it is the prettiest bauble you ever saw. It is set in enamelled meadows, with filigree hedges:
>
> A small Euphrates through the piece is roll'd
> And little finches wave their wings in gold.[1]

Horace Walpole's Strawberry Hill was a place of many faces (Fig. 1). It was (and is) an actual house and garden, the Gothic summer villa of a society man who otherwise lived in a classical house in London. It was the chief setting for Walpole's collection of art, antiquities and objets d'art, and a 'fantastic fabric' and a 'new old house' that became one of the most famous buildings of the eighteenth century.[2] But it was also a place filtered through the language and imagination of its owner, and revealed through his letters and other writings. In 1747, before Walpole gave them a new Gothic skin, the conglomeration of buildings that he leased from Elizabeth Chenevix, the Charing Cross 'toywoman' (seller of trinkets), although in part a solid three storeys high, was seen in imaginative terms as a trifle from her shop, with all the studied lack of seriousness that the idea suggested.[3] With Walpole's decision two years later to adopt the Gothic style for his villa, a new imaginative model came into play. The house came to represent two highly evocative types of historical building: a monastery (or 'convent') and a 'little gothic castle', the ancient seat of the Barons of Strawberry, 'the castle (I am building) of my ancestors'.[4] Woven through with the coats of arms of the family, it was both complex and picturesquely irregular, suggesting an organic development over centuries. Like the ancient family seats studied by Walpole on his tours around England, it was filled with portraits both ancient and modern as well as historical relics and works of applied art. This approach allowed Walpole legitimately to fill the house with objects derived from several different collecting traditions. But unlike the owners of such ancient seats, Walpole was able from the start consciously to control the effects that he sought, gradually combining the house and its growing collection into a single whole that presented distinctive aspects of British and European history in a pioneering and museum-like way.

Crucial to the complex effects of Strawberry Hill was the manner in which Walpole designed the house. He worked at first with his friends John Chute and Richard Bentley as the 'Strawberry committee', more fully described on p. 349, and after 1762 with other amateurs and with professional architects. In the early stages the tension between Bentley's and Chute's very different approaches, the one imaginatively romantic and the other drier, and more correct and practical, helped to form a consistent design language. In this process Walpole was always very much the master, and Strawberry Hill his vision. Even architects as established as Robert Adam were given firm directions on historical sources, while Walpole took credit for the design of some parts himself.[5]

By the time Walpole began to Gothicize Strawberry Hill, the style had already acquired two different meanings and uses. On the one hand it

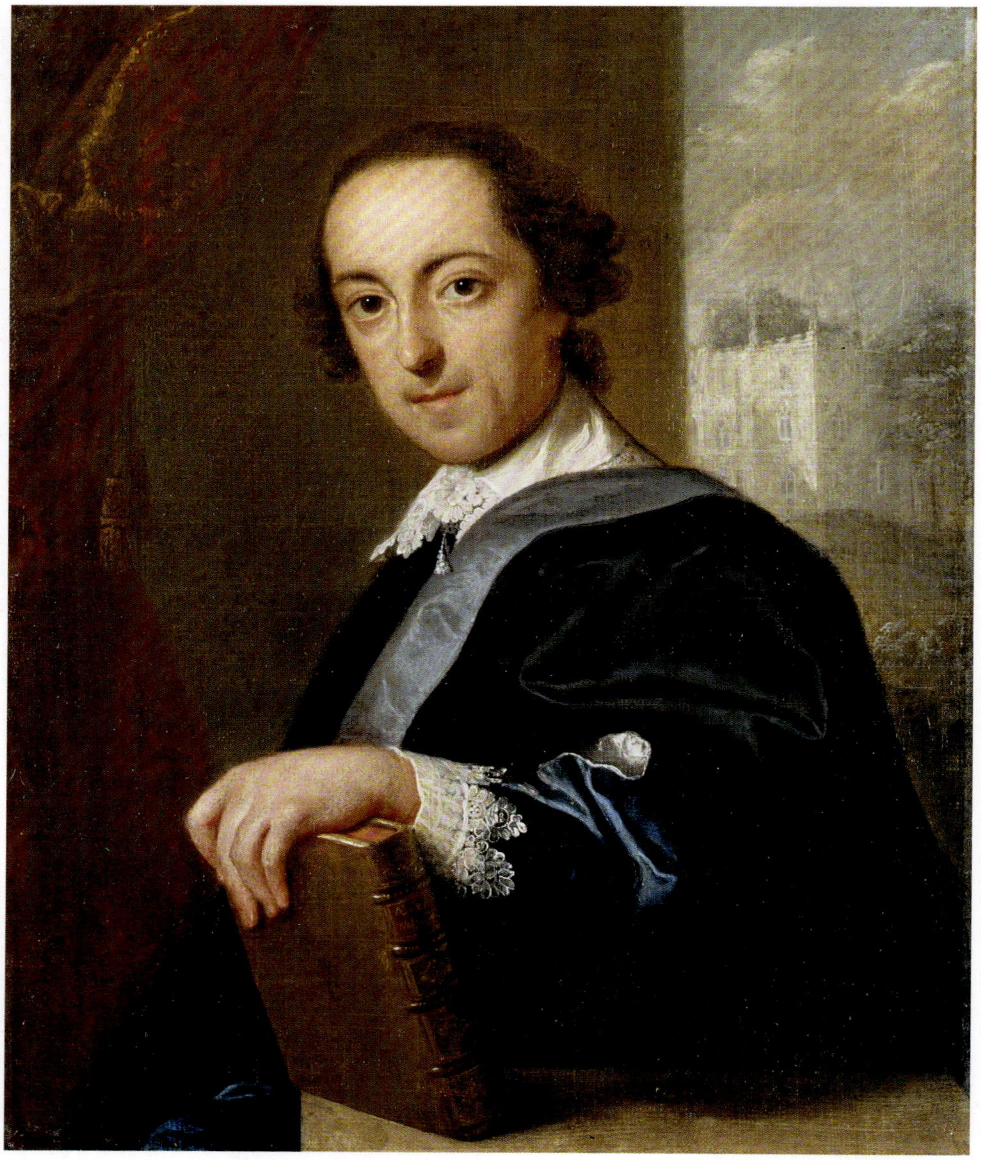

Figure 19. John Giles Eccardt, *Portrait of Horace Walpole*, 1754, oil on canvas, 39.4 × 31.8 cm. National Portrait Gallery, London. 988. Cat. 40

was a playful alternative to Chinese or Rococo while on the other, as a style for garden buildings and a handful of country houses, it had come to symbolize ancient British virtues and independence.[6] But Strawberry Hill was pioneering in three ways, firstly in the manner in which it used quotations from real ancient buildings for its architectural features, secondly in its asymmetrical picturesque planning and massing, and thirdly in its entirely consistent presentation as an ancestral building.

Walpole's word for the effects of Gothic, 'gloomth', did not mean a vision of dark and terrifying masses, but rather a world of airy and intricate effects combined with solemnity and shadow, as was suggested by a definition of Gothic in 1736: 'light, delicate, and rich to an extreme, full of whimsical and impertinent ornaments', or what Walpole called 'the irregular lightness and solemnity of Gothic'.[7] But for Walpole, Gothic had a unique ability to summon up ideas and emotions:

> I, who have great difficulty of not connecting every inanimate thing with the idea of some person, or of not affixing some idea of imaginary persons to whatever I should see, should prefer that building that furnished me most ideas, which is not judging fairly of the merit of the buildings abstractedly. And for this reason, I believe, the gloom, the ornaments, magic of the hardiness of the buildings, would please me more in the Gothic than the simplicity of the Grecian.[8]

As he put it elsewhere: 'One must have taste to be sensible of the beauties of Grecian architecture; one only wants passions to feel Gothic.'[9]

THE HOUSE AND ITS OWNER

Two portraits of Walpole throw an interesting light on the special meaning of Strawberry Hill and its links to his own self-image. The first, a portrait of 1756 by Sir Joshua Reynolds (Fig. 3), shows him as the established gentleman scholar, author and man of taste in a pose that combines that of Peter Scheemakers's statue of Shakespeare (1740; Westminster Abbey) with the aristocratic portraits by Anthony Van Dyck.[10] On the table, together with the trappings of authorship, is an example of one of the two prints he had made a year before of his most important classical antiquity, the Roman marble eagle found in the Baths of Caracalla in Rome (Fig. 184). While Walpole gave away impressions of the private mezzotint he had made from the portrait, and examples of the picture itself to his friends and relations, he owned no painted image of this statement of himself as the public man. The most significant portrait of Walpole at Strawberry Hill was painted two years earlier by John Giles Eccardt (Fig. 19). It was, by contrast, an intimate image of antiquarian make-believe and was never made into a print in his lifetime. One of a group of historicizing portraits created for the Blue Bedchamber, it shows Walpole in a costume and pose derived from a portrait by Van Dyck of the painter Simon Vouet, with Strawberry Hill in the background. While Van Dyck dress was an established form of dress at masquerades and also in portraiture, for Walpole it probably had an extra meaning, aligning him with the period that he most admired and whose collectors and collections he most wished to emulate.[11] In this portrait, too, he is shown as an author, but now the reference is specifically to the *Ædes Walpolianae*, his account (with art historical commentary) of Houghton Hall and its works of art, first published in the year after he arrived at Strawberry Hill. This is Walpole the antiquarian and art historian, who is both drawing attention to his father's great collection in its neo-Palladian setting and making a statement about his own, very different creation at Strawberry Hill.

A HOUSE FULL OF STORIES

Strawberry Hill was a house full of stories. Just as its architecture was consciously associative in its general design and borrowing of design ideas from ancient buildings, so was Walpole's approach to the display of his objects. For Walpole the past was not only just below the surface of the present, but also preferable to it:

> Visions, you know, have always been my pasture; and so far from growing old enough to quarrel with their emptiness, I almost think there is no wisdom comparable to that of exchanging what is called the realities of life for dreams. Old Castles, old pictures, old histories, and the babble of old people make one live back into centuries that cannot disappoint one. One holds fast and surely what is past. The dead have exhausted their power of deceiving – one can trust Catherine de Medicis now.[12]

For Walpole, physical objects played a key role in reaching through to history. As Alicia Weisberg-Roberts shows (Ch. 5, pp. 86–105), almost every object or group of objects told one or several stories, not usually derived from their artistic or aesthetic value but from their place in British and European history and culture. Some examples were relatively straightforward. Horace Mann's gift of a portrait of the Florentine grand duchess, Bianca Capello, in 1754 prompted the creation of a frame that incorporated her ducal coronet, her arms and those of the Medici, as well as her story, written by Thomas Gray, originally in Latin, on a label at the bottom.[13] A more complex example was the elaborate make-believe letter written by Madame du Deffand in the guise of Madame de Sévigné 'from the Elysian Fields' (Fig. 261). Perhaps even more telling was Walpole's vivid wish-fulfilment dream in which he visited Westminster Hall and Whitehall Palace in the time of Charles II (see Appendix 1, p. 341). While a visit to the hall had prompted the dream, the palace had been burnt down in 1697. The physical appearance of the historical figures was conjured out of Walpole's knowledge of historical portraiture. To visit the soon-to-be-destroyed palace, as Walpole tetchily reminded his companion George Selwyn, was a chance in a lifetime to see the much longed-for, lost masterpieces of the Stuart collections. While the Duke of York's bedchamber was well enough remembered to be shown in a sketch ground plan, it was the accurate historian in Walpole that baulked at conjuring up the Holbeins that he so wanted to see in it and of which there was no visual record. At the end of the dream a picture came to life, in the form of a portrait of Richard II. The king addressed Walpole, but Walpole could not reveal to him his impending violent fate – it was beyond even him to interfere with history.

MY HOUSE IS AS PAPER

Walpole's early presentation of Strawberry Hill as a delightful but unimportant toyshop trifle developed into the elaborate conceit that both the house and its collections were essentially ephemeral: not only was the building flimsily constructed (at least partly in papier mâché) and essentially impermanent like the medieval ruins that inspired it, but its collections would be dispersed, just like the older collections from which the objects were derived. As Ruth Mack shows (see Ch. 6, pp. 106–15), it was in another sense a true paper house, with an imaginative reality in Walpole's letters but more importantly in the *Description of... Strawberry Hill*, published in 1774 and in an illustrated edition in 1784, copies of which Walpole and others 'extra-illustrated' with prints and specially commissioned drawings of the house and contents. As a result, Strawberry Hill became one of the best-recorded houses of the eighteenth century in contemporary documents. The preface to the 1784 *Description*, which was written as if the house had disappeared and its collections dispersed, was the closest Walpole got to a public summation of the significance of the

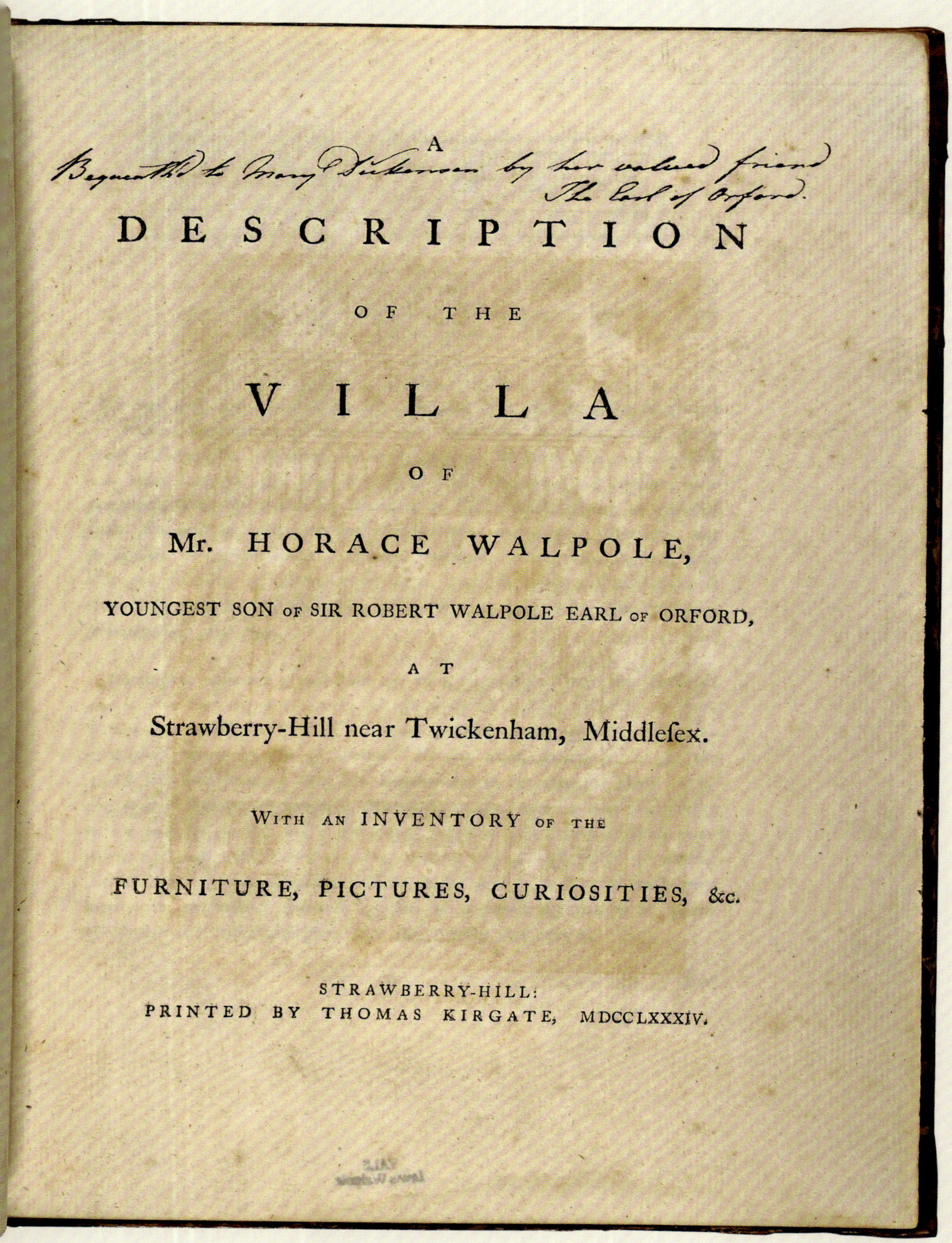

Bequeathed to Mary Dickenson by her valued friend
The Earl of Orford.

A
DESCRIPTION
OF THE
VILLA
OF
Mr. HORACE WALPOLE,
YOUNGEST SON OF SIR ROBERT WALPOLE EARL OF ORFORD,
AT
Strawberry-Hill near Twickenham, Middlesex.
WITH AN INVENTORY OF THE
FURNITURE, PICTURES, CURIOSITIES, &c.

STRAWBERRY-HILL:
PRINTED BY THOMAS KIRGATE, MDCCLXXXIV.

Figure 20. Title page, Horace Walpole, *A Description of the Villa of Mr. Horace Walpole...*, 1784, 11.75 × 9.5 cm. The Lewis Walpole Library, Yale University. Quarto 33 30 Copy 7. Cat. 21

The most important single piece of evidence of Walpole's collection, of what it contained and how it was displayed, is his *A Description of the Villa of Mr. Horace Walpole, at Strawberry Hill near Twickenham. With an Inventory of the Furniture, Portraits, Curiosities &c.* One hundred copies were printed at the Strawberry Hill Press in 1774; ten years later an expanded edition of two hundred copies was printed on larger paper, to match the size of the copper engraved plates that Walpole had commissioned (Fig. 20). These are the essential images of Strawberry: the authorized views, as Walpole wished the house to be memorialized (Figs 137, 287).

The book's title is important. It offers a description of the villa and an inventory of the collection, and its character is more inventory than country house guidebook. Despite Walpole's preface to the 1784 edition suggesting that the book was intended to assist those visiting the house, there is no evidence that it was taken round as a guide by tourists, though some form of the text, or offprints of part of it, may well have been used by Walpole's housekeeper when showing the house. Indeed, the book was not published or even circulated by Walpole in his lifetime, other than through a very few copies given to his closest friends. The preface was printed at least two years after 1784, and Walpole later drew up a list of some eighty people to whom he wished copies to be given after his death.

After a brief summary of the history of the house, and a note that you entered into a small gloomy hall and then turned left into the Refectory, the *Description* describes the rooms and lists their contents, adding comments on provenance or quality, but detailing everything: paintings, furniture, sculpture, antiquities, porcelain, the great and the small from Raphael's missal and Reynolds's celebrated painting of the Ladies Waldegrave to Admiral van Tromp's pipe case and the extended list of cups, saucers, jars and plates in the China Room. It was, as Walpole acknowledged in his preface, a catalogue and has the somewhat obsessional attention to detail that such a catalogue implies.

Walpole added to the *Description* as his collection continued to grow. His annotated copy of the 1774 edition was marked up by him, with new rooms created and new treasures secured, so that they could

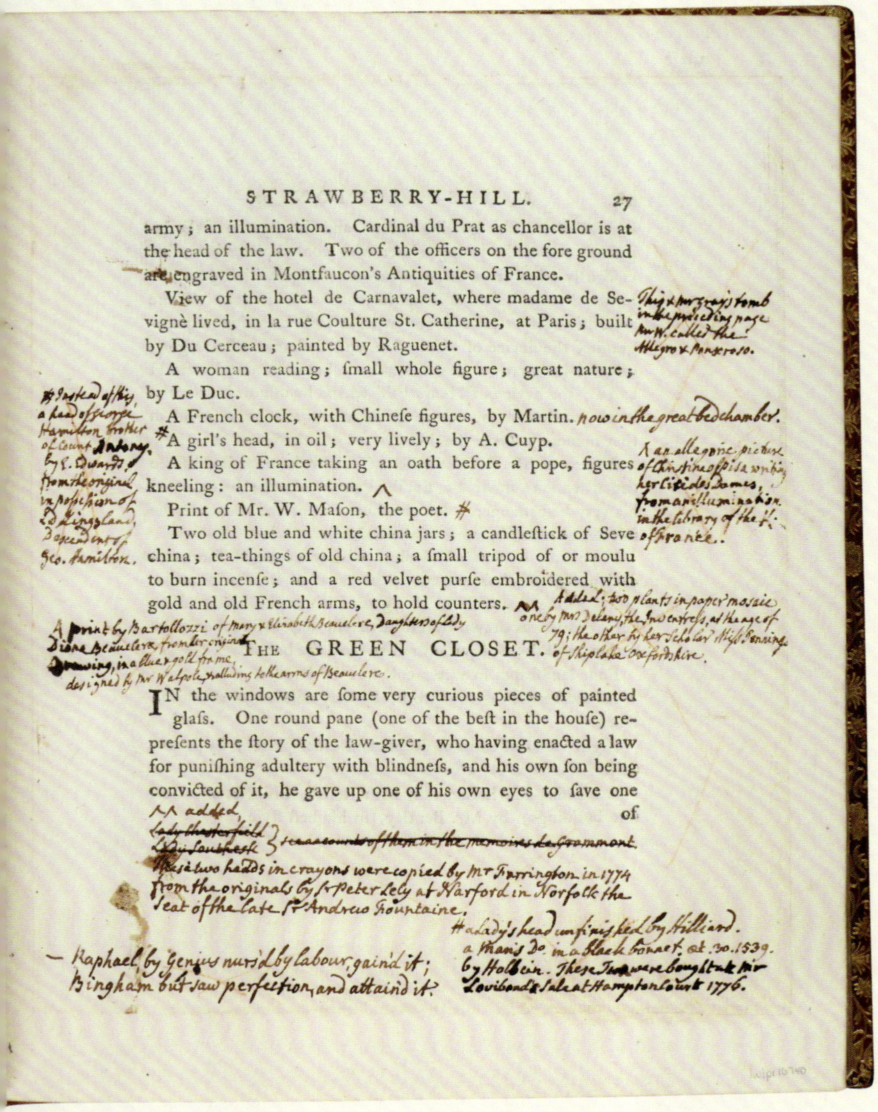

STRAWBERRY-HILL. 27

army; an illumination. Cardinal du Prat as chancellor is at the head of the law. Two of the officers on the fore ground are engraved in Montfaucon's Antiquities of France.

View of the hotel de Carnavalet, where madame de Sevignè lived, in la rue Coulture St. Catherine, at Paris; built by Du Cerceau; painted by Raguenet.

A woman reading; small whole figure; great nature; by Le Duc.

A French clock, with Chinese figures, by Martin.

A girl's head, in oil; very lively; by A. Cuyp.

A king of France taking an oath before a pope, figures kneeling: an illumination.

Print of Mr. W. Mason, the poet.

Two old blue and white china jars; a candlestick of Seve china; tea-things of old china; a small tripod of or moulu to burn incense; and a red velvet purse embroidered with gold and old French arms, to hold counters.

THE GREEN CLOSET.

IN the windows are some very curious pieces of painted glass. One round pane (one of the best in the house) represents the story of the law-giver, who having enacted a law for punishing adultery with blindness, and his own son being convicted of it, he gave up one of his own eyes to save one of

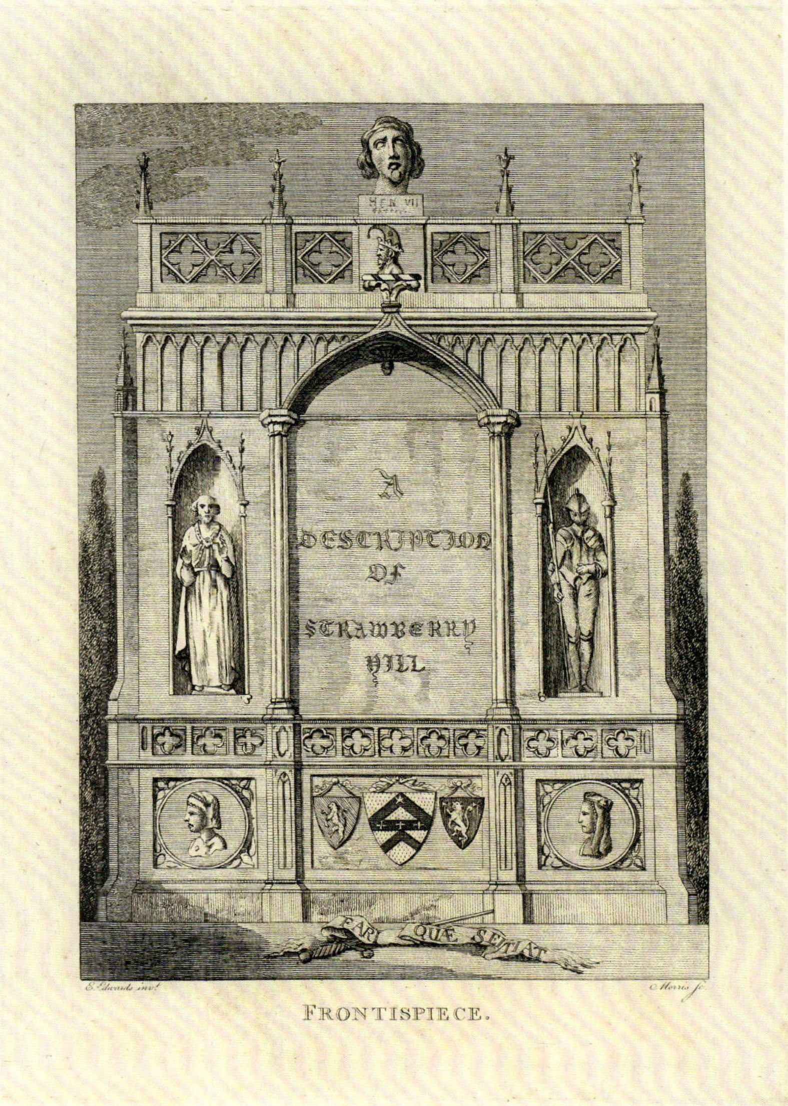

be inserted in the 1784 edition, as well as sample picture hangs for some of the main rooms (Fig. 21). Both 1774 and 1784 editions had three separate appendices noting subsequent acquisitions, and Walpole continued to make manuscript notes of further additions even in the last decade of his life.

In addition to its engravings, the *Description* inevitably attracted further illustrations, and the most famous extra-illustrated copies of it – Walpole's own and those belonging to some early collectors – became themselves collections of a collection. Posthumously presenting this extraordinary inventory to the world is Walpole's preface, opening with the words: 'It will look, I fear, a little like arrogance in a private Man to give a printed Description of his Villa and Collection, in which almost everything is diminutive.' But this typically Walpolean flourish of self-deprecation does not in any way conceal the total seriousness of his endeavour to record and illustrate, for his contemporaries and for future generations, the fragile yet curiously resilient house and collection of Strawberry Hill.

Figure 21. A page annotated by Horace Walpole from his copy of *A Description of the Villa...at Strawberry-Hill* (Strawberry Hill, 1774). The Lewis Walpole Library, Yale University. 49 2523, p. 27

Figure 22. Morris after Edward Edwards, Engraved frontispiece from Horace Walpole, *A Description of the Villa of Horace Walpole*, 1784. The Lewis Walpole Library, Yale University. Quarto 33 30 Quarto Copy 9

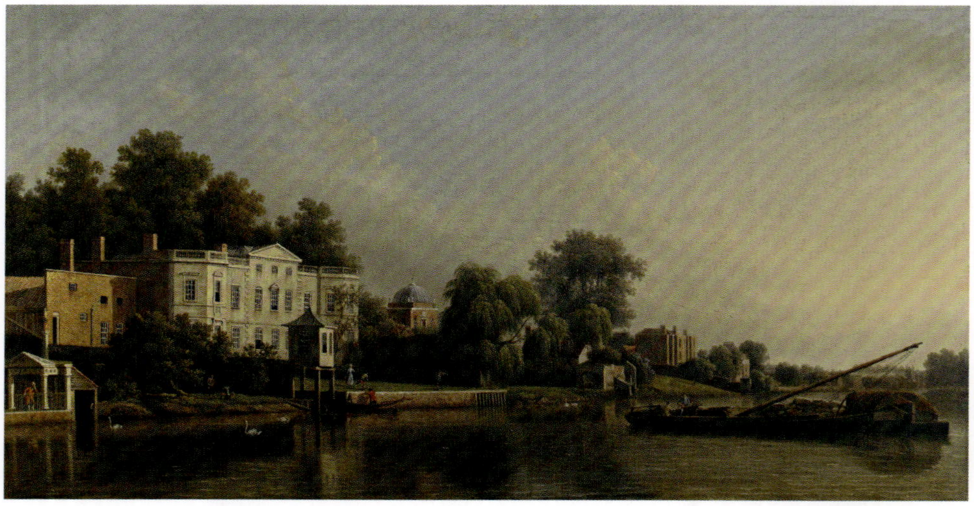

Figure 23. Samuel Scott, *A View of Alexander Pope's House at Twickenham*, *c.* 1759, oil on canvas, 47.6 × 90.8 cm. The Lewis Walpole Library, Yale University. Cat. 4

house and collections in the light of posterity, albeit characteristically described, in deference to his father's house and collection at Houghton, as a 'paper fabric and assemblage of curious trifles, made by an insignificant man'. Architecturally, he presented Strawberry Hill as a building that exhibited 'specimens of Gothic architecture' and a demonstration of how they could be applied in modern buildings, but by the end he was careful to say that it was merely a 'small capricious house ... built to please my own taste, and in some degree to realize my own visions', and he did not omit to point out that it was also 'the scene that inspired, the Castle of Otranto'.[14] The catalogue of the house's contents that formed the bulk of the book was 'given with view to their future dispersion. The several purchasers will find a history of their purchases', giving them their provenance, or 'descent': 'Such well attested descent is the genealogy of objects of virtù, not so noble as those of the peerage, but on a par with those of race horses. In all three, especially the pedigrees of peers and rarities, the line is often continued by many insignificant names.'[15] Despite the usual elegantly self-deprecating touch here, such 'pedigrees' were of course of immense importance to Walpole, who saw himself as the successor to a great English collecting tradition that had begun with the 2nd Earl of Arundel some 150 years before. Not only were previous owners carefully recorded in the *Description* but also in manuscript lists of provenances both grand and humble, on paper labels and on specially designed containers that bore the arms of the owners, mirroring the use of arms in the architecture of the house itself (Fig. 35).

In fact, Walpole had done his best to ensure that Strawberry Hill and its contents would survive, passing them at his death (with a fund for their upkeep) to his cousin's daughter, the sculptor Anne Seymour Damer (Fig. 177), who gave it up in 1811, under the will, to his great niece, Laura Waldegrave, in whose family it remained until 1883.[16] The contents, as Stephen Clarke describes in Chapter 16 (pp. 260–74), were sold in 1842, late enough to benefit from the advances in historical knowledge in the nineteenth century and to ensure, as Walpole had hoped, that his name would be added to the list of his illustrious predecessors.

A VILLA BY THE THAMES

Walpole's delight at leasing the future Strawberry Hill from Mrs Chenevix was well founded.[17] He had acquired the last piece of undeveloped Thames-side land in Twickenham, the most fashionable village in an area that for 250 years had been the site of the residences of people of wealth and fashion, attracted by the royal palaces of Richmond and Hampton Court. Already in the seventeenth century such houses were being described as villas, an idea largely based on those of the Renaissance architect Andrea Palladio, whose particular concept of the *villa suburbana* of the Veneto, especially Vicenza, became a stepping stone into Italian villa culture, both ancient and modern. The villas of Palladio, always at the centre of a working farm, were places of summer retirement not too far from the heat and tumult of the city. They were places for physical exercise where the owners' souls could be restored through study and contemplation. A highly visible architectural expression of its owner's wealth and taste, the villa could also be a cultural centre, along the lines of the academies of ancient philosophers. The Thames around Twickenham, a morning's journey from the city, was the ideal picturesque setting for the British version of the villa: designed in the latest style and highly visible, generally without a farm but often provided with a remarkable garden.[18] Free from the rules governing the design of houses in town, villas could be a field for architectural experiment on a small scale, as is suggested by Walpole's famous comparison of Strawberry Hill with the pioneering

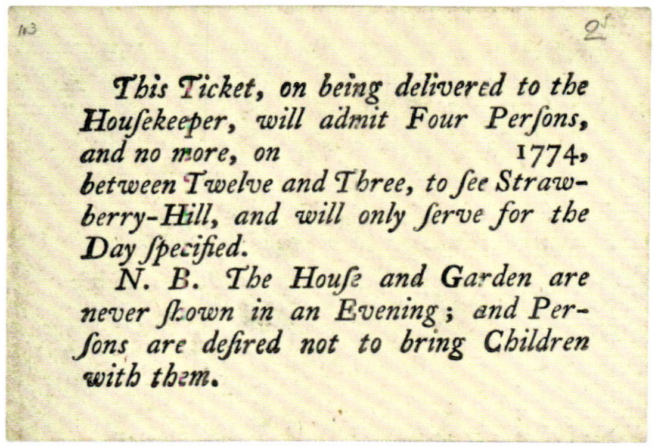

This Ticket, on being delivered to the Houſekeeper, will admit Four Perſons, and no more, on 1774, between Twelve and Three, to ſee Strawberry-Hill, and will only ſerve for the Day ſpecified.

N. B. The Houſe and Garden are never ſhown in an Evening; and Perſons are deſired not to bring Children with them.

Figure 24. Ticket to view Strawberry Hill, 6.5 × 9 cm. The Lewis Walpole Library, Yale University. Folio 336G. Cat. 22

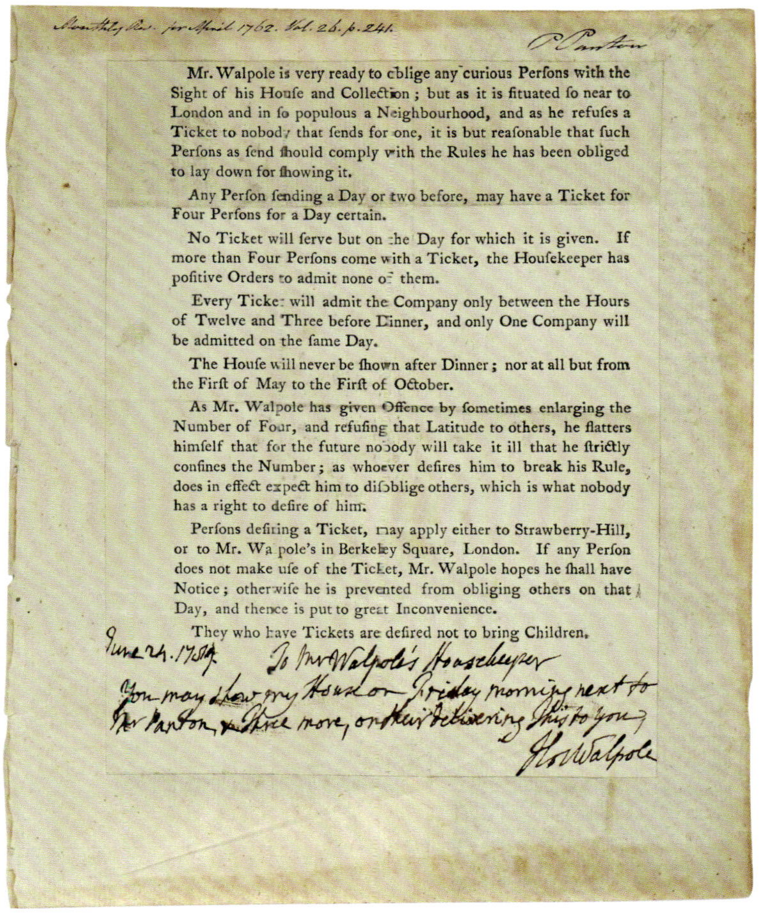

Mr. Walpole is very ready to oblige any curious Perſons with the Sight of his Houſe and Collection; but as it is ſituated ſo near to London and in ſo populous a Neighbourhood, and as he refuſes a Ticket to nobody that ſends for one, it is but reaſonable that ſuch Perſons as ſend ſhould comply with the Rules he has been obliged to lay down for ſhowing it.

Any Perſon ſending a Day or two before, may have a Ticket for Four Perſons for a Day certain.

No Ticket will ſerve but on the Day for which it is given. If more than Four Perſons come with a Ticket, the Houſekeeper has poſitive Orders to admit none of them.

Every Ticket will admit the Company only between the Hours of Twelve and Three before Dinner, and only One Company will be admitted on the ſame Day.

The Houſe will never be ſhown after Dinner; nor at all but from the Firſt of May to the Firſt of October.

As Mr. Walpole has given Offence by ſometimes enlarging the Number of Four, and refuſing that Latitude to others, he flatters himſelf that for the future nobody will take it ill that he ſtrictly confines the Number; as whoever deſires him to break his Rule, does in effect expect him to diſoblige others, which is what nobody has a right to deſire of him.

Perſons deſiring a Ticket, may apply either to Strawberry-Hill, or to Mr. Walpole's in Berkeley Square, London. If any Perſon does not make uſe of the Ticket, Mr. Walpole hopes he ſhall have Notice; otherwiſe he is prevented from obliging others on that Day, and thence is put to great Inconvenience.

They who have Tickets are deſired not to bring Children.

Figure 25. Rules for obtaining a ticket to see Strawberry Hill, 23 × 18.5 cm (Strawberry Hill, 1784). The Lewis Walpole Library, Yale University. Cat. 23

neo-Palladian Chiswick House: 'As my castle is so diminutive, I give myself a Burlington-air, and say, that as Chiswick is a model of Grecian architecture, Strawberry Hill is to be so of Gothic.'[19]

Just as at Chiswick, where Lord Burlington's private academy of the arts had included William Kent and George Frideric Handel, so Walpole strove to make Strawberry Hill a cultural centre, with attached architects, a resident artist in the person of Johann Heinrich Müntz, a poet in Thomas Gray and Britain's first private press producing a stream of antiquarian and other writing. Walpole was well aware that he was establishing himself in a place celebrated as the last home of Alexander Pope, whose villa was a stone's throw from the future Strawberry Hill (Fig. 23). When he arrived, 'Pope's ghost is just now skimming under my window by a most poetical moonlight'.[20] But Pope was neither the first nor the last, as Walpole wrote in 1755:

> Nothing is equal to the fashion of this village. Mr Muntz says we have more coaches than there are in half of France … Mrs Pritchard has bought Ragman's castle for which my lord Lichfield could not agree: we shall be as celebrated as Baiae or Tivoli, and if we have not such sonorous names as they boast we have very famous people: Clive and Pritchard actresses; Scott and Hudson painters; my Lady Suffolk, famous in her time; Mr Hickes, the impudent lawyer, mr Whitehead the poet, and Cambridge, the everything.[21]

In 1760 Joel-Henrietta Pye published a guidebook later known as *A Peep into the Principal Seats and Gardens in and about Twickenham (the Residence of the Muses)*. Walpole, whom Pye described as 'the abbot of Teddington Abbey', mocked it as a 'a silly little book … a most inaccurate, superficial, blundering account',[22] but it did suggest Twickenham's appeal:

> The genius of the inhabitants inclines not towards commerce; architecture seems their chief delight: in which, if any doubt their excelling, let him sail up river, and view the lovely villas beautifying its banks. Lovers of true society, they despise ceremony, and no place can boast more examples of domestic happiness.[23]

Strawberry Hill became a famous house to see, shown on request between May and October, with printed tickets and rules for visitors, but restricted to one party of four people a day (Figs. 24, 25). Walpole came to dread such public attention, especially after numbers grew with the opening of the State Apartment, sometimes obliging him to retreat to his new cottage in the flower garden while the house was shown by the housekeeper, and complaining in 1783 that he was 'overrun with

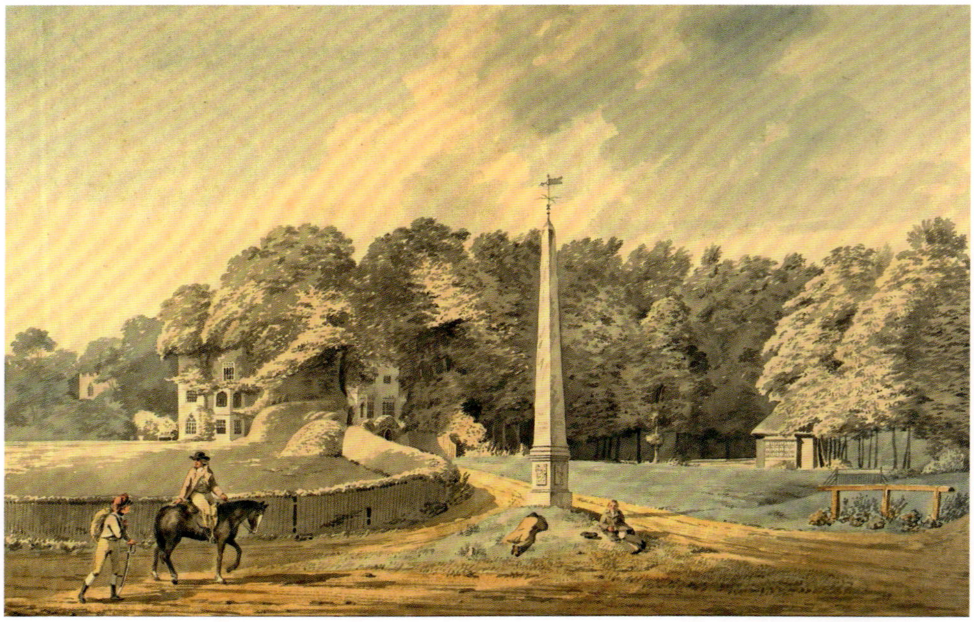

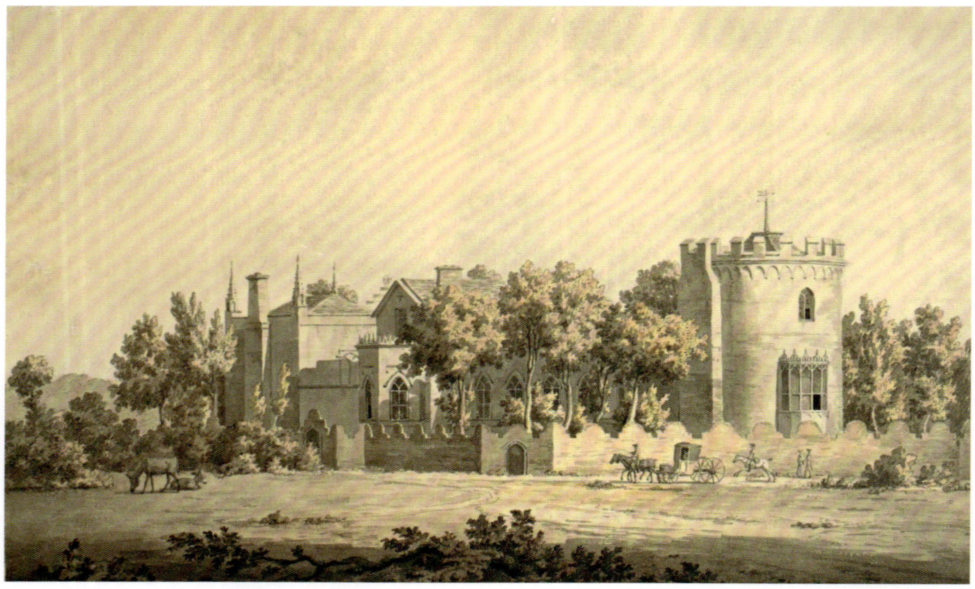

Figure 26. James Malton, *North East view of Strawberry Hill, with Obelisk*, *c.* 1791, watercolour, 29.9 × 42.4 cm. The Lewis Walpole Library, Yale University. 791.00.00.39dr. Cat. 5

Figure 27. William Marlow, *The North and West Fronts of Strawberry Hill*, 1776–80, watercolour, 32.5 × 52.3 cm. Victoria and Albert Museum, London, W.A. Sandby Bequest. D.1838-1904. Cat. 7

all the languages of Babel who come to see my house from morning to night'.[24] Important visitors, who included members of the royal family, were usually taken round by Walpole himself, as the manuscript 'Book of Visitors' from 1784 to 1796 makes clear.[25] But it was of course a house for show as well as a private retreat, a place for cards and music and the elaborately staged parties so vividly described in his letters.

Strawberry Hill's fame was enhanced by the production of drawn and printed images, largely initiated by Walpole himself. He commissioned a series of watercolours and drawings that meticulously recorded both the exteriors and the most important interiors, many of which were engraved for the *Description*. The interior views, some of which may have been produced with the aid of a camera lucida,[26] were pioneers of the genre, while the exteriors established a set of standard viewpoints for subsequent printmakers.[27] The exterior views reveal a group of carefully contrived settings of varying character showing the different fronts of the house: the more ruggedly romantic public side to the north approached via a road shaded by overhanging trees and punctuated in the foreground by an obelisk and a false bridge; and the westerly aspect of the great Round Tower from the unenclosed common field; both contrasting sharply with the private polite side on the south, best seen from the lawn (Figs. 26, 27, 102, 103). All, however, displayed the picturesque spiky silhouette, whitewashed against the green and shown to best advantage at the top of its little hill. These views of the house were of course matched by the varying and 'animated' prospects from the house, up and down the river, and across to Richmond Hill, which were the main reason for his choosing the site. They not only determined the structure and planting of the grounds but also, as we shall see, the plan of the house and the design of its interior fenestration.

Walpole conceived the garden and grounds to contrast with the house:

> You suppose my garden is to be Gothic too! That can't be; Gothic is merely architecture; and as one has a satisfaction in imprinting the gloomth of abbeys and cathedrals on one's house, so one's garden, on the contrary, is to be nothing but riant, and the gaiety of nature.[28]

The garden and grounds were an early and important example of the naturalistic style of picturesque landscape gardening promoted by Alexander Pope and William Kent, of which Walpole was the first chronicler (Fig. 29).[29] Strawberry Hill was the first such scheme to combine an ambitious naturalistic garden plan with an asymmetrical picturesque house: 'I am almost as fond of *Sharawaggi*, or Chinese want of symmetry, in buildings, as in grounds or gardens.'[30] As in other such gardens, a walk around it combined a series of associational events and picturesque planting to evoke certain moods:

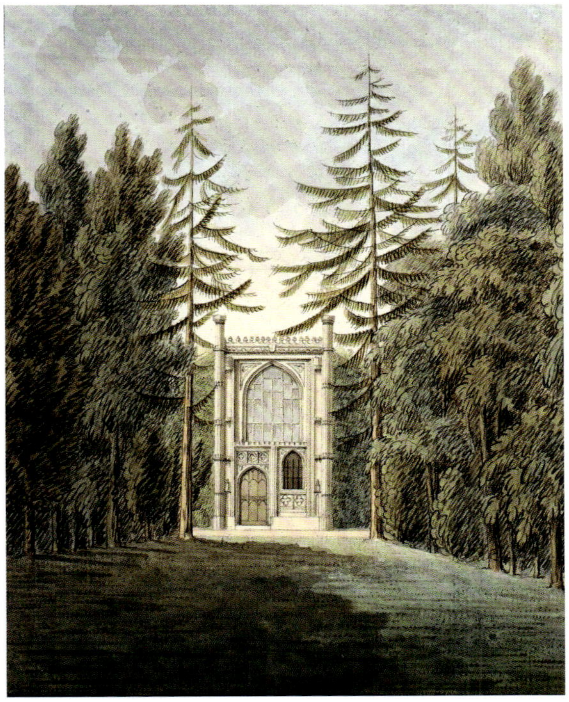

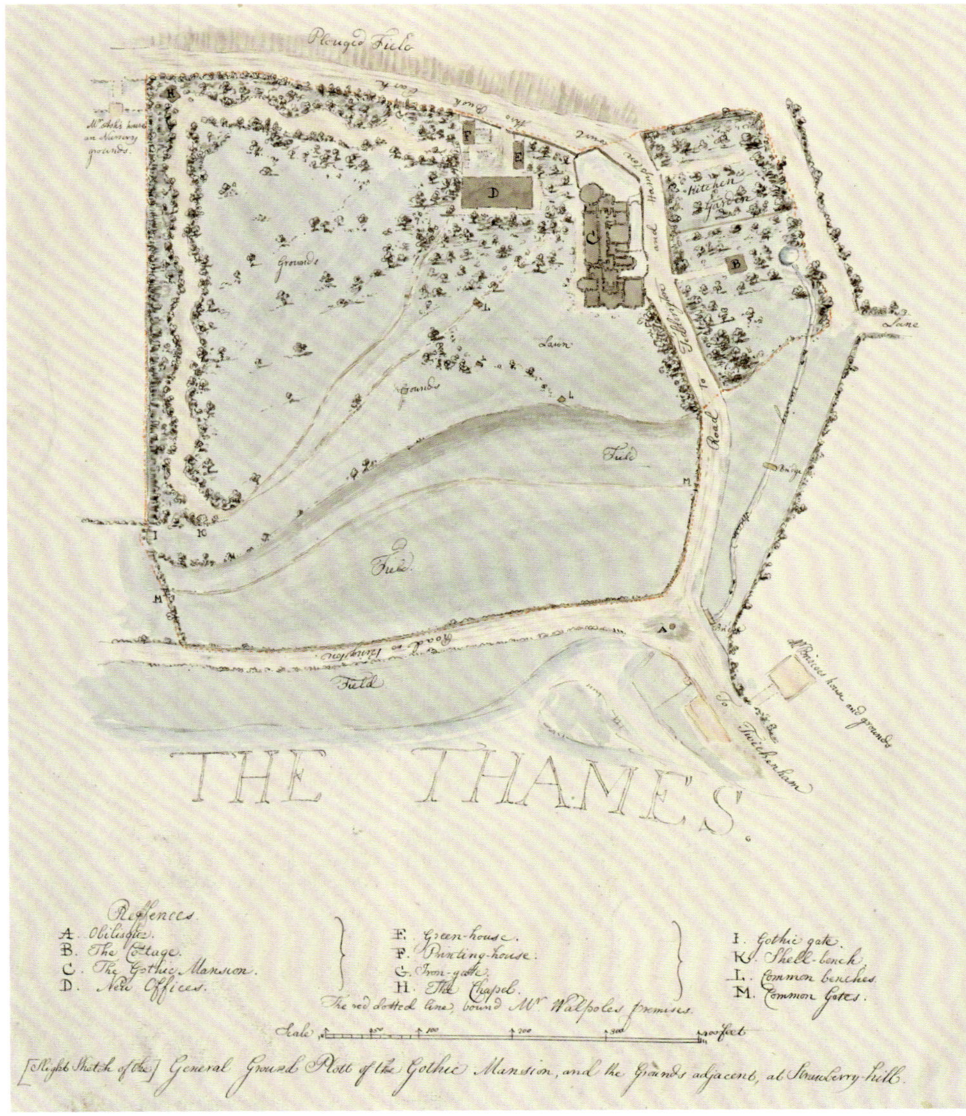

> … there is nothing so picturesque when they [i.e. cypresses] stand two or three in a clump upon a little hillock or rising above low shrubs, and particularly near buildings. There is another bit of picture of which I am fond, and that is, a larch or a spruce fir planted behind a weeping willow, and shooting upwards as the willow depends.[31]

A winding, wooded walk ran around the grounds on the west and south sides (and helped to mask a tree nursery and the common field), punctuated by built features: the Gothic Gate, the Chapel in the Wood and the Shell Seat (Figs. 28, 131, 132, 286, 287). The east side, formed by a raised terrace, was left lightly wooded to allow prospects, while on the north side the adjacent road was hidden at first by a deep 'theatrical border' of shrubs and flowers and later by trellising and trees. Facing the house on the other side of the road, a picturesque thatched cottage lay embowered in the flower garden.[32]

THE COLLECTIONS

But what drew most visitors to Strawberry Hill were the interiors and the collections that filled them. Beginning before his arrival at Strawberry Hill, Walpole was to remain a passionate collector almost to the end of his life, in spite of frequent protests to potential donors of objects that Strawberry Hill could hold no more. He collected everything except natural history and scientific objects. In 1797 Strawberry Hill contained at least 4,000 objects (excluding books, prints and drawings), acquired over some fifty-five years. They reflected three distinct collecting traditions. The first was collecting as a gentlemanly pursuit, based on connoisseurship and a set of aesthetic criteria linked to culture and learning, some aspects of which were in a tradition going back to the sixteenth-century *Kunstkammer*. It included classical antiquities, paintings, drawings and prints by the old masters, as well as the decorative arts (especially ceramics, painted enamels and glass), coins and medals, arms and armour, curiosities,

Figure 28. Artist unknown, *'Chapel in the Garden at Strawberry Hill – Twickenham, c.* 1785, pen and ink, and watercolour, 28.7 × 23.3 cm. The Lewis Walpole Library, Yale University. 49 3678.3. Cat. 15

Figure 29. John Carter, *Plan of the grounds at Strawberry Hill*, *c.* 1790–97, watercolour, wash and ink, 46 × 31 cm, from Walpole's extra-illustrated copy of the *Description*. The Lewis Walpole Library, Yale University. Folio 49 3582, fol. 2.

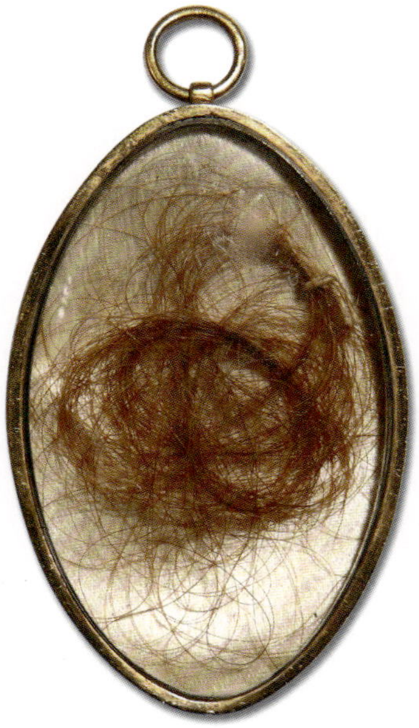

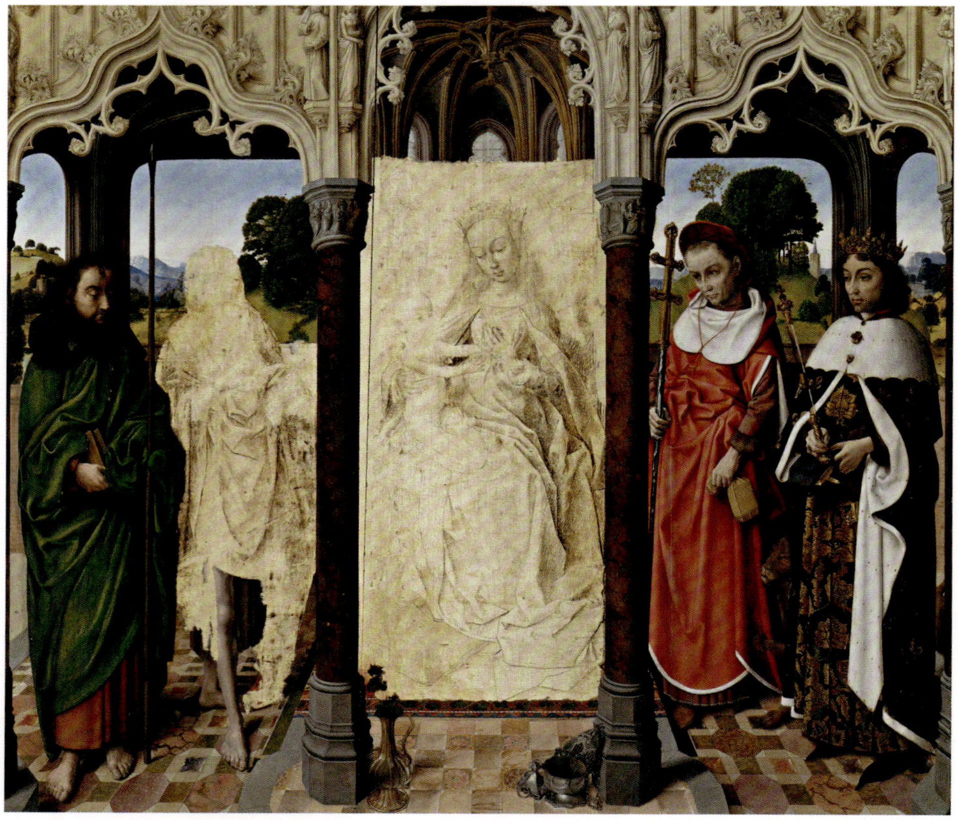

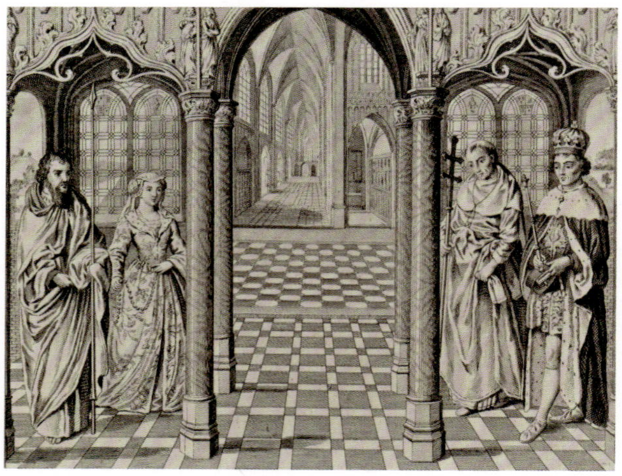

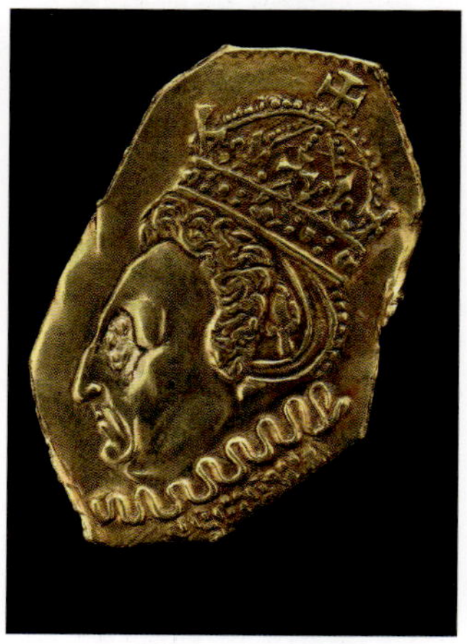

Figure 30. Hair of Mary Tudor in a Gold Locket, 1784, 5 × 3.2 cm. The Rt Hon. the Earl of Derby. Cat. 107

Figure 31. The Ghent Master, *Virgin and Child with Saints*, *c.* 1472, oil on panel, 126.1 × 111.1 cm. Private collection. The overpainting to create *The Marriage of Henry VII* has been removed, revealing the original surface and some underdrawing

Figure 32. Charles Grignion after the Ghent Master, *Virgin and Child with Saints* as altered probably in the early eighteenth century to represent *The Marriage of Henry VII*, *c.* 1762. Engraving, made for the *Anecdotes of Painting*. The original acquired by Walpole in 1753. The Lewis Walpole Library, Yale University. Folio 33 30 Copy 11, p. 137

Figure 33. Fragment of a Sovereign of Elizabeth I, 1597–1600, obverse recut by 1742 to show the queen in old age, 2.6 × 1.5 cm, gold. British Museum, Department of Coins and Medals. 1842.0523.2. Cat. 97

drawings and manuscripts. Secondly, Walpole collected historic portraits and historical objects in the British antiquarian tradition, although he was careful to distance himself from the type of dry antiquarianism that prized factual detail above aesthetic value. Historical relics, such as the hair of Mary Tudor (Fig. 30), Cardinal Wolsey's hat (Fig. 145), and Queen Bertha's comb (Fig. 146) although now often seen as characteristic of Walpole's collection, were not very numerous at Strawberry Hill. As his Whitehall Palace dream suggests, Walpole had his own 'visionary' brand of antiquarianism (to borrow Earle Havens's term[33]), in which objects (and architecture) sparked the imagination and became doorways to the past. Thirdly, he focused, particularly towards the end of his life, on collecting modern fine art, especially the work of female amateurs, and modern ceramics, notably Sèvres (see Chs. 9 and 12, pp. 154–69 and 200–219).

Some idea of Walpole's own view of his collection, and its relationship to its audience, can be gained from the preface to the 1784 edition of the *Description*: 'The most considerable part of the following catalogue consists of miniatures, enamels, and portraits of remarkable persons.'[34]

Portraits dominated the collections at Strawberry Hill in the form of paintings, prints, drawings and sculpture, and of course the collection of enamels and miniatures, which was 'the largest and finest in any country'.[35] Largely absent at Strawberry Hill was the type of old-master subject picture that he had catalogued at Houghton – and the few that he possessed were mainly from his father's collection (Fig. 75). Strawberry Hill, by contrast, was a house full of the portraits of real people. In older paintings this emphasis was to some extent the inevitable result of his concentration on the British school, but it was also a key part of his historical project. Just as he filled his Library with historical manuscripts and printed accounts, so he sought to bring that world to life by collecting the true likenesses of the principal actors. While some of these portraits were collected as the opportunity arose, others were assembled to a plan, most notably the portrait prints, which were arranged in volumes as a logically organized historical record (see pp. 150–51), and the carefully accumulated painted portraits of the English kings up to Charles II.

Such collecting, while often very successful, could have its pitfalls at a time when there was a lively antiquarian market for this type of object. Wishful thinking, coupled sometimes with personal bias, could lead to optimistic attributions, as in the case of the bust of Henry VII, 'in the agony of death' (Fig. 150), or the scene of the marriage of Henry VI, with all the characters identified (Fig. 147). On other occasions he acquired old pictures that had been cleverly altered to resemble the desired subject, as in the marriage of Henry VII (Figs. 31, 32), a process that was also applied to other types of object (Fig. 33). Portraits also dominated the modern paintings, although landscapes and subject pictures were more frequent among the small group of amateur female artists he promoted. Having emphasized the unique importance of the collection of miniatures and enamels, the preface of the *Description* went on to commend two sixteenth-century illuminated missals as the works of Raphael and Giulio Clovio (Figs. 34, 35) and, in the same sentence, wax reliefs by Lady Diana Beauclerk 'as invaluable as rare'.[36] To the 'English antiquary' he recommended the royal portraits, together with the works by and after Hans Holbein. For 'virtuosos of more classic taste', 'ancient and modern sculpture' was represented by the small busts of Jupiter Serapis and Caligula, the Cellini bell and the Boccapadugli eagle (Figs. 184, 187, 188).[37] Finally, for 'those who have more taste than consists in mere sight', he recommended Madame du Deffand's letter in the manner of Madame de Sévigné (Fig. 261).

But a rather different picture emerges from Walpole's manuscript list of the collection's 'Principal Curiosities', arranged according to room and completed in about 1789 (see Appendix 2, pp. 343–7). Comparison with comments on the same objects in the *Description* and elsewhere suggests

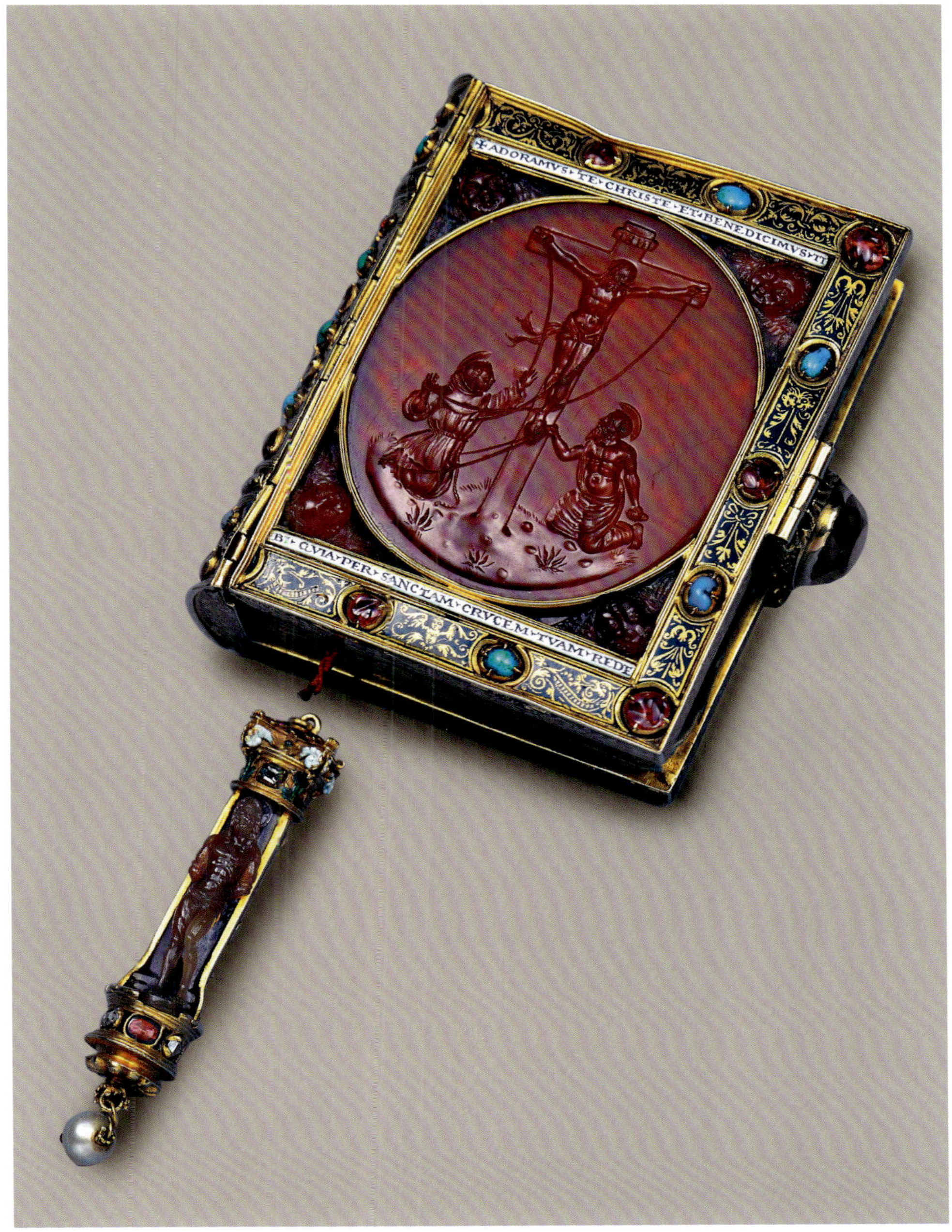

Figure 34. Unknown artist, French, *Illuminated Book of Hours*, *c.* 1532, illuminated manuscript and miniatures on vellum in a gold and jewelled French or Italian binding, 1530s; marker, French or Italian, 1560s, 8.5 × 6.5 cm; marker: 6.4 cm. S.J. Phillips Limited. Cat. 162

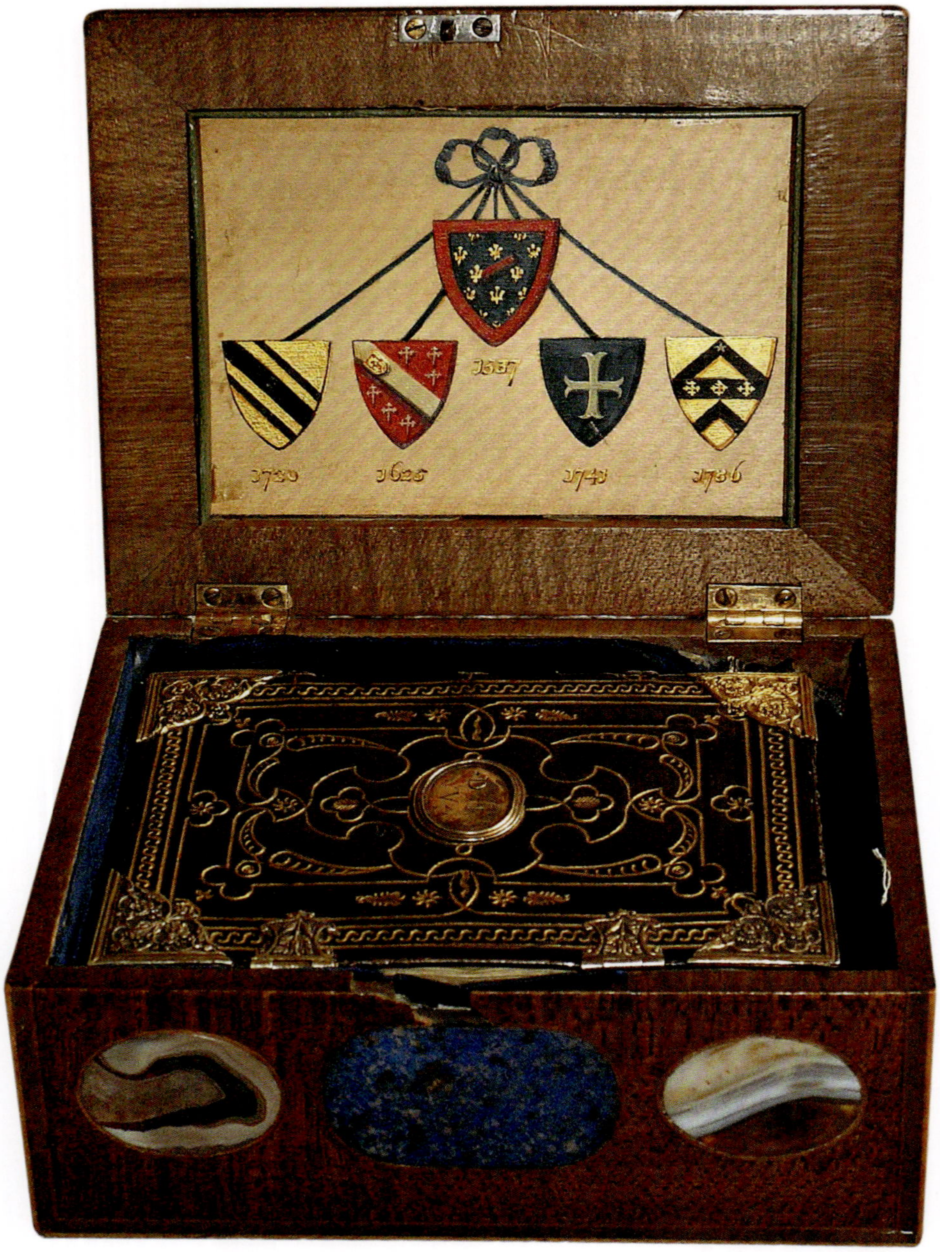

Figure 35. *Illuminated Psalter (Psalter of the Prince d'Anjou)*, 1500–25, octavo manuscript, 13.1 × 9.5 cm, bound in contemporary black Venetian goatskin and silver gilt; in an elaborate wooden box, inlaid with agate and lapis lazuli, made for Horace Walpole between 1786 and 1788. The Wormsley Library. Cat. 106

that the list is based largely on aesthetic criteria. Thus, while portraits again form the biggest single category, the early royal series emphasized in the preface is significantly omitted, while nearly all the old-master subject pictures are present. All the Isaac and Peter Olivers in the Breakfast Room are included, leaving only a Holbein, a Christian Zincke and a Carl Klingstedt to complete the miniatures group, the last perhaps selected because it was given by John Chute. Of the historical curiosities, only the Deed of King Theodore of Corsica, a relic of one of Walpole's favourite causes, had no aesthetic value. Setting aside the substantial group of works by Anne Damer and Lady Diana Beauclerk, the bulk of the list included many of the things that would now be regarded as the collection's most significant works of art. Some have become even more important: Dr Dee's magical mirror, thought by Walpole to be a British object made of cannel coal, is an Aztec artefact made of obsidian (Fig. 125). Items excluded from the list, presumably on aesthetic grounds, have also since been recognized as exceptional. 'Queen Bertha's Comb' (Fig. 146) was turned into a precious relic of early British Christianity through the addition of an inscription in the seventeenth century, awakening the interest of a train of collectors from Lord Arundel to Walpole. It is no longer thought to be Anglo-Saxon, but it is nevertheless an important Romanesque ivory.

THE COLLECTIONS IN CONTEXT

The earliest setting for Walpole's collection was not Strawberry Hill but the apartment in his father's house in Downing Street, which he occupied from 1741 to 1743,[38] and after that at his father's (and later his) house in Arlington Street. Walpole's earliest collecting was largely focused on classical antiquities, beginning during his Grand Tour (1739–41) and afterwards augmented via continuing contacts in Italy and the purchase in 1743 of the collection formed by his Cambridge mentor, the Reverend Conyers Middleton. Some sense of the character of these London rooms, which contained a life-size bust of Vespasian, bought in Rome in 1740, is conveyed in an excited letter to Horace Mann in November 1741: 'You can't think what a closet I have fitted up! Such a mixture of French gaiety and Roman virtù.'[39] A significant relic of this first phase was the boldly neo-Palladian cabinet designed by Walpole to contain his miniatures and painted enamels, made in 1743 for Arlington Street and only moved to Strawberry Hill in the 1760s (see pp. 98–99).

The 'French gaiety' at Downing Street anticipated a key characteristic of Strawberry Hill, namely the combination of objects and decorations of different periods, including the fashionably modern, in a single scheme. In the preface to the *Description* Walpole felt obliged to defend this approach:

> In a house affecting not only to obsolete architecture, but pretending to an observance of the *costume*, even in the furniture, the mixture of modern portraits, and French Porcelain, and Greek and Roman sculpture, may seem heterogenous. In truth, I did not mean to make my house so Gothic as to exclude convenience, and modern refinements in luxury. The designs of the inside and outside are strictly ancient, but the decorations are modern. Would our ancestors, before the reformation of architecture, not have deposited in their gloomy castles antique statues and fine pictures, beautiful vases and ornamental china, if they possessed them?[40]

Walpole's mixture of the old and the new (in styles both ancient and modern) was identified by Clive Wainwright as pioneering the 'romantic' or 'antiquarian' approach to interior decoration and furnishing that was to become fully established in the nineteenth century.[41] But the relative balance between old and new styles shifted as the house developed. In its first phase, culminating with the Holbein Chamber in 1758, Walpole created a series of stone-coloured Gothic interiors in which the contents were largely old (or pretended to be). In the more private rooms of this earliest phase, however, although the decorative framework was Gothic, the wall decorations, furniture and many of the contents were up to date. This latter approach was fully developed in the great rooms of the State Apartment, conceived in all their essentials in 1759, but not completed until 1776.

Getting hold of suitably ancient (or ancient-looking) furniture presented a special challenge. In 1754 the Great Parlour was supplied with a set of mirrors, chairs and table designed by Walpole and Bentley in the Gothic style (with a touch of the Baroque; Fig. 37). They strongly signalled their great age by being in what Walpole later called 'the true black blood',[42] that is, made of ebony or ebonized. Chairs with triangular seats were regarded as especially old, as indeed the form was. Seventeenth-century examples filled the Great Cloister (Fig. 36), while others were copied from chairs shown in stained glass. The problem was largely solved with the acquisition of large sets of ebony chairs and tables that Walpole believed to be sixteenth century (some having been found at Cardinal Wolsey's house at Esher) but that were

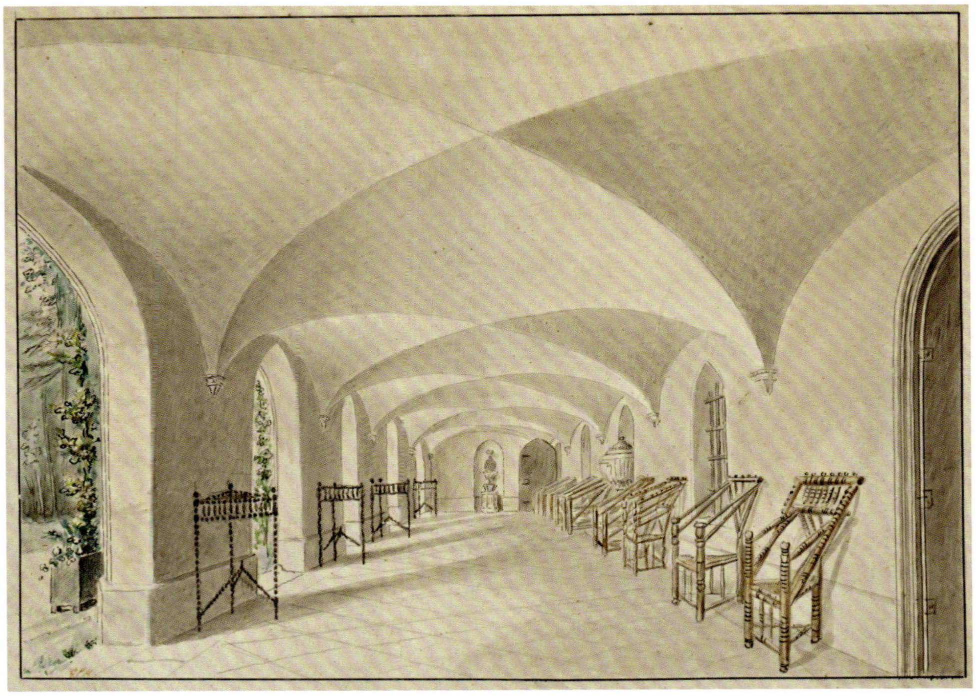

Figure 36. George Perfect Harding after John Carter, *The Great Cloister at Strawberry Hill*, c. 1800, ink, wash, watercolour, 20.5 × 27.6. The Lewis Walpole Library, Yale University.

Figure 37. George Perfect Harding, *'A Gothic Table'*, pen, ink and wash, 13.5 × 20 cm. laid in a copy of the *Description*. The Lewis Walpole Library, Yale University. Quarto 33 30 Copy 6, fol. 4b

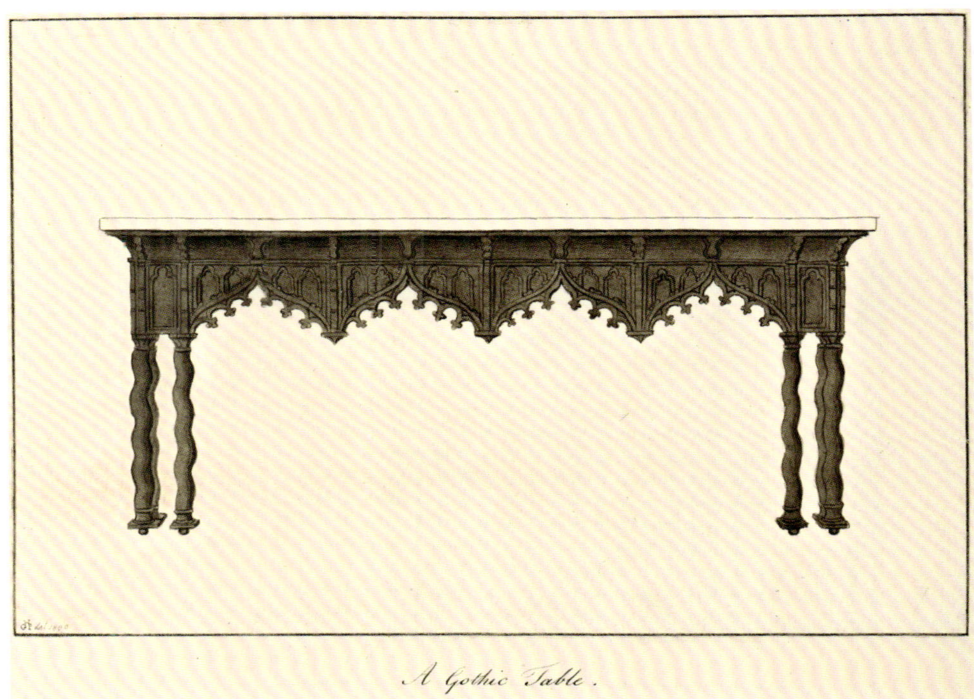

in fact made on the Coromandel Coast of India in the mid-seventeenth century (Cat. 124).[43] The whereabouts of the single piece of furniture from before 1600, the chair from the Abbey of Glastonbury, are at present unknown (Fig. 38).[44]

But for all their mixed dates and styles, the collections at Strawberry Hill were carefully assembled thematically to tell particular stories in the context of an ancient house developed over time. The themes were combined with extremely sophisticated planning, use of decoration and handling of light to manipulate atmosphere and moods. This is explained in a remarkable manuscript account (now in the Fitzwilliam Museum; see Appendix 3, p. 348) in which Walpole set out how

> great effects may be produced by the disposition of a House, & by studying lights & shades, and by attending to a harmony of colours. I have practiced all these rules in my House at Strawberry hill, & have observed the impressions made on Spectators by these arts … I do not mention my own House, which is a small one, but by comparison, & as a sample of what might be done on a magnificent scale if perspective, the effects of light & shade, Harmony in the colouring of the furniture & a picturesque taste were observed in the whole.[45]

Writing at the moment the State Apartment was completed with the Great North Bedchamber, Walpole takes the reader on a journey through the house, analysing the use of planning, changing light levels, colour harmonies and optical effects. The darkness of the 'conventual retirement of the Entrance' leads via the 'greater light' of the staircase to the cheerful, light-filled Blue Room (or Breakfast Room) and Green Closet. In these rooms and others later on, the views of the surrounding landscape form an essential part of the experience (Fig. 39). In the Great North Bedchamber 'the great size of the rest of the window, which is of plate glass, & the uncommon chearfullness of the views, make the outside as beautifull as the Inside'.[46]

When the view out is limited, as in the Gallery, which was hemmed in by trees, the interior decoration is made richer to compensate. After this lighter atmosphere the 'Star chamber and dusky passage again prepare you for solemnity: the Holbein-chamber softens that Idea, yet still maintains a grave tone'.[47] But the passage has another function, for it 'makes the richness & largeness of the gallery appear much more considerable'.[48] The most detailed analysis of visual effects is reserved for the richly colourful rooms of the State Apartment that follow, with the Great North Bedchamber getting special attention, as well as the Tribune. Again it is a journey of contrasts: 'In these large rooms a harmony is presented, tho there are differences in all according to circumstances.'[49] The picture-filled Gallery is succeeded by the calmer, grander, measures of the Round Room (or Round Drawing Room), and then by the Chapel (or Tribune). But there is a final event:

> The sobriety of the Chapel, & the idea of having seen all the House, make the opening of the great bedchamber the more surprising, from its not being expected, & from the striking contrast between the awe impressed by the Chapel, & the gush of light, gaudiness & grandeur of the bedchamber.[50]

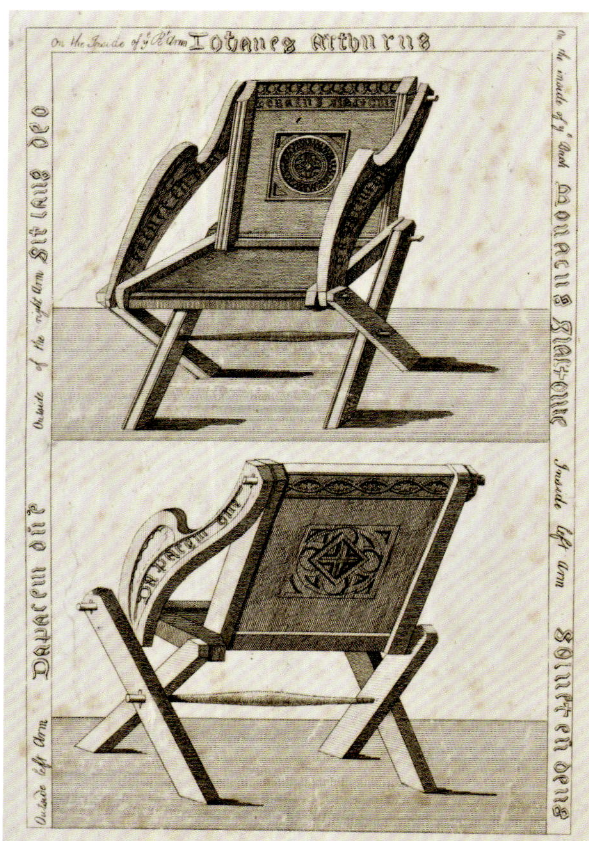

Figure 38. Unknown artist, *Two views of a Glastonbury Chair*, etching, n.d. from HW's extra-illustrated copy of the *Description*. The Lewis Walpole Library, Yale University.

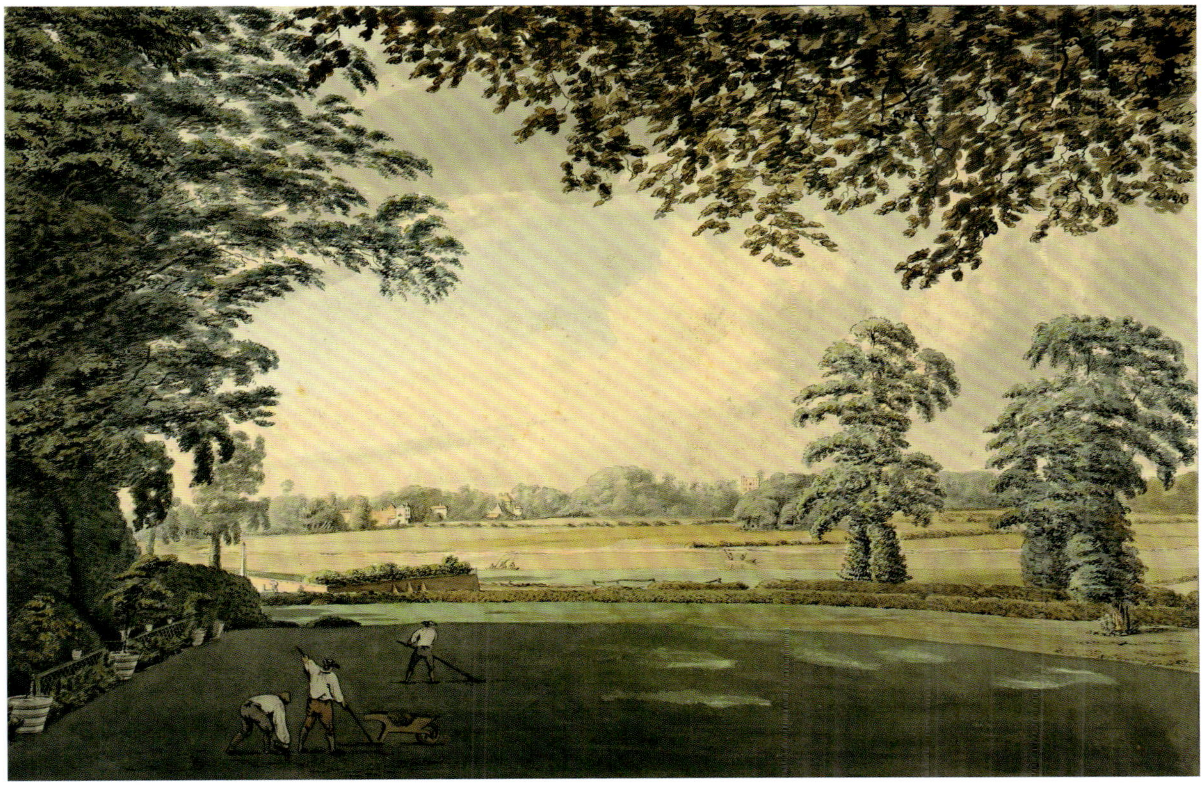

Figure 39. Joseph Charles Barrow, *View of Twickenham and part of Richmond Hill from the Blue Room at Strawberryhill*, 1789, watercolour on wove paper with wash-line mount, 33.6 × 45.4 cm, from HW's extra-illustrated copy of the *Description*. The Lewis Walpole Library, Yale University. Folio 49 3582, fol. 7. Cat. 13

It was perhaps the recent experience of furnishing this last room that led Walpole to conclude: 'I need not say how much the result of my house is improved by the humility of the Entrance, & the simplicity of the first rooms, so little promising the expence of the great Apartment.'[51] In writing in these terms in 1772 Walpole was of course post-rationalizing a scheme that had begun with the development of the pre-existing house, initially intended to go no further. But the effect worked, for once the drive westwards had begun, the 'grave' early world became a preamble to the richness of the State Apartment. The westward expansion also marked a shift in the design approach, as Walpole's conclusion makes clear. Not only were the colours brighter but also the materials were far more luxurious: worsted and silk damask (with matching suites of upholstered furniture) instead of the wallpapers and chintzes, and the chimneypieces of stone, marble and scagliola instead of painted wood. Even the 'chapel' (or Tribune), 'sober' as it was, had a touch of luxury in its carpet woven to fit the room. In the Great North Bedchamber we can almost sense that Walpole felt he had gone too far:

> In the State bedchamber, there are half the chairs of tapestry to suit the bed, with white & gold frames against the damask, while the other half are ebony with deep-rose colour'd cushions, to take off from the great gaudiness of the bed & chairs, & to bring back the room to the gothic tone of the House.[52]

VISITING STRAWBERRY HILL

By 1784, the date of the second, illustrated, edition of the *Description*, the development of Strawberry Hill, but for the building of the New Offices, was complete (Fig. 304; Cat. 17). Although objects were still being acquired, the collections had largely found their final places. It is therefore a good point at which to look in detail at the house and its interiors. The *Description* account begins with the outside, embattled wall. For the visitor it was the first of many quotations from prints of older architecture, but rather than being from a Gothic building it is in fact taken from a wall around a Jacobean prodigy house, Aston Hall in Warwickshire. Most significantly, and characteristically, the wall in the print is in the same relationship to Aston Hall as Walpole's wall is to

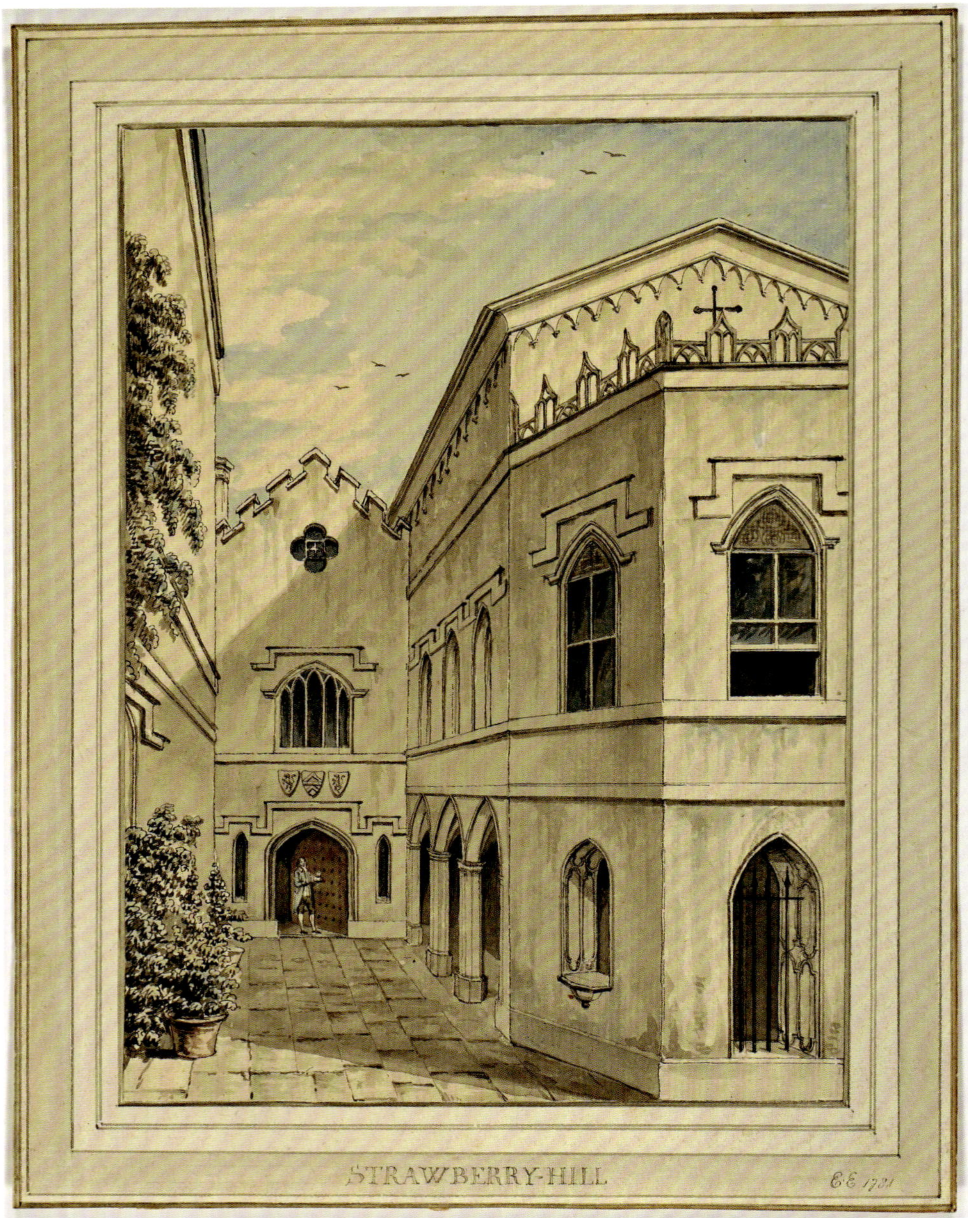

Figure 40. Edward Edwards, *'Strawberry Hill' [Entrance of Strawberry Hill]*, 1781, pen, ink and wash, watercolour, from HW's extra-illustrated copy of the *Description*. The Lewis Walpole Library, Yale University. Folio 49 3582, fol. 23. Cat. 9

Strawberry Hill. For the visitor entering via the solid wooden door of the 'great north gate' the first message was monastic (Fig. 40). He or she was immediately met by a bronze 'saint' sheltered by a small, enclosed Oratory (Figs 40, 41), complete with basins for holy water. On the right was the pierced screen of the Abbot's (or Prior's) Garden, another quotation.[53] On the left the monastic theme continued with the arcaded Little Cloister. This was the first of three connected spaces that prolonged this idea through the ground floor and into the polite grounds on the south side, all separated from the formal spaces of the house. The Winding Cloister, an L-shaped passage lit by a stained glass window, was decorated with classical reliefs, medieval alabasters and a modern brass of Ralph Walpole, Bishop of Norwich and Ely, at one point probably intended to be housed in an imitation of a medieval canopied tomb (Figs. 42, 94).[54] By 1775 the monastic character of the Great Cloister had been heightened by being filled with triangular chairs.[55] Also in the Great Cloister, from 1778, was a large classical marble vase on an altar assembled by Piranesi (Fig. 36).[56]

In the Little Cloister the visitor met with two objects linked to arresting stories with moral messages. The fish tub in which Walpole's cat Selima had drowned, an event immortalized in a poem by Thomas Gray, was playfully turned into a relic by a label quoting from the ode in which two lines are artfully changed (see pp. 32–3). Above it a relief portrait of Princess Eleanora d'Este recalled the famous romantic tale of the illicit love of the Renaissance court poet Torquato Tasso. Just as Selima lost her life through her unwise love of fish, so Tasso was imprisoned (in a monastery) for his inappropriate love of Eleanora. As always in the *Description*, provenance is carefully noted – the relief was given in 1774 by Sir William Hamilton.

The front entrance itself announced a new theme, for above the heavily studded door were the shields of the arms of Walpole, Shorter (Walpole's mother) and Robsart (the most romantic of the families to have married into the Walpoles). The visitor was moving from the monastery to the ancestral castle, although the monastic allusions were not quite over, for in 1753 the low, dark entrance hall (Fig. 45) was called 'The Paraclete',[57] after Abelard's monastery described by Alexander Pope in 'Eloisa to Abelard', published in 1717:

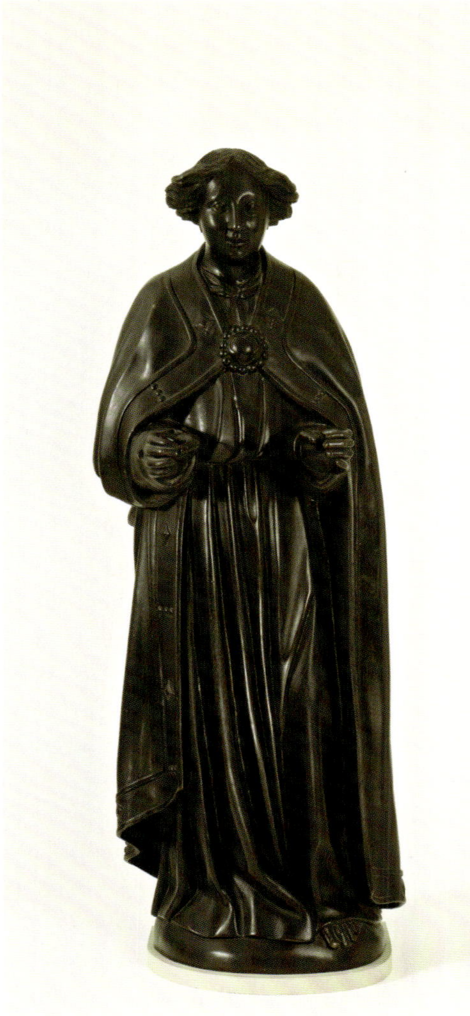

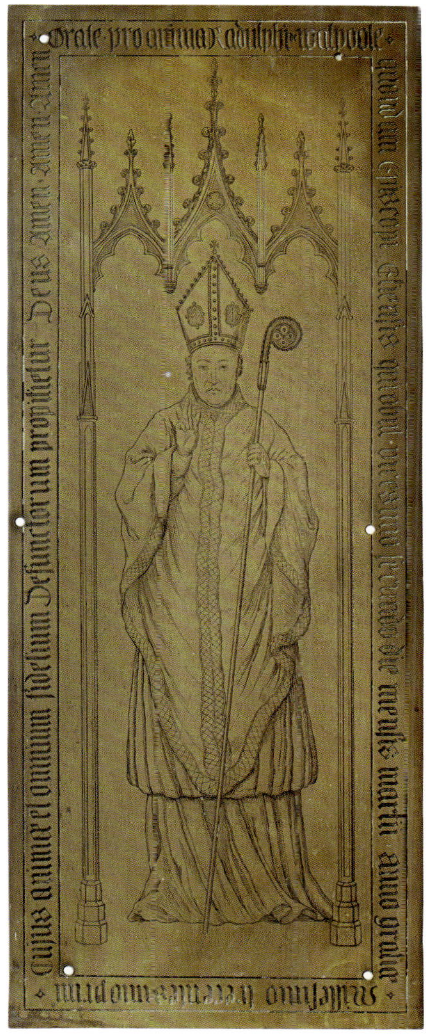

Figure 41. *Angel*, French, 1470–80, cast latten (copper alloy), 86.4 × 32 × 32 cm. Victoria and Albert Museum, London. A.3-1982. Cat. 30

Figure 42. Johann Heinrich Müntz, *Monumental Brass of Ralph Walpole, Bishop of Norwich and Ely*, *c.* 1758, engraved brass, 76.5 × 34 cm. Private collection. Cat. 34

In these deep solitudes and awful cells,
Where heav'nly-pensive contemplation dwells,
And ever-moving melancholy reigns.[58]

This was among the first of many allusive and evocative names for the spaces at Strawberry Hill, most of which, however, related not to medieval buildings but to great houses of the sixteenth and seventeenth centuries. The hall and the spectacularly dramatic staircase were part of a set of spaces completed in 1754 that included the Great and Little Parlours and the Library. A world of stone-coloured walls and woodwork, plainly planked doors, scrubbed wooden or tiled floors and brightly coloured stained glass, it sought to conjure up the atmosphere of an ancient ancestral building, albeit one that combined the Gothic with design ideas and ornament from later periods.

The skill with which the staircase was created using the floor levels of the pre-existing house is fully described by Kevin Rogers (see pp. 58–73). Its overall design, armorial supporters on the newel posts, lower columns and upper open arcade were directly inspired by the type of Jacobean staircase found at Hatfield or Knole,[59] but the painted walls quoted the screen of Prince Arthur's tomb at Worcester Cathedral and the balustrade a staircase at Rouen Cathedral, the earliest examples of this practice at Strawberry Hill.[60] Almost every wall and ceiling surface was covered with dense and startlingly illusionistic low relief ornament in paint. By day the dark entrance hall contrasted with the

WALPOLE'S CHINA FISH TUB

Bet McLeod

In common with other collectors of ceramics of his time, Walpole had a large collection of blue and white oriental porcelain. The many examples inherited from his mother, Catherine Lady Walpole, were shown in a glazed closet between the Gallery and the Round Drawing Room. Most of the remainder of the collection, some eighty-one pieces, was housed in the China Room, but a few were placed strategically throughout Strawberry Hill, often in hearths in the summer, like 'the large jar of old blue and white china' in the China Room and the blue and white vases in the Holbein Chamber, which would have matched the blue of the seat cushions. But the most famous piece of oriental porcelain was the large fish tub, immortalized in the 'Ode on the Death of a Favourite Cat, Drowned in a Tub of Gold Fishes' (Fig. 43), commemorating the unfortunate death of Walpole's cat in Walpole's house in Arlington Street. It was written by his friend Thomas Gray in 1747:

'Twas on a lofty vase's side,
Where China's gayest art had dy'd
    The azure flowers, that blow;
Demurest of the tabby kind,
The pensive Selima reclin'd,
    Gazed on the lake below.

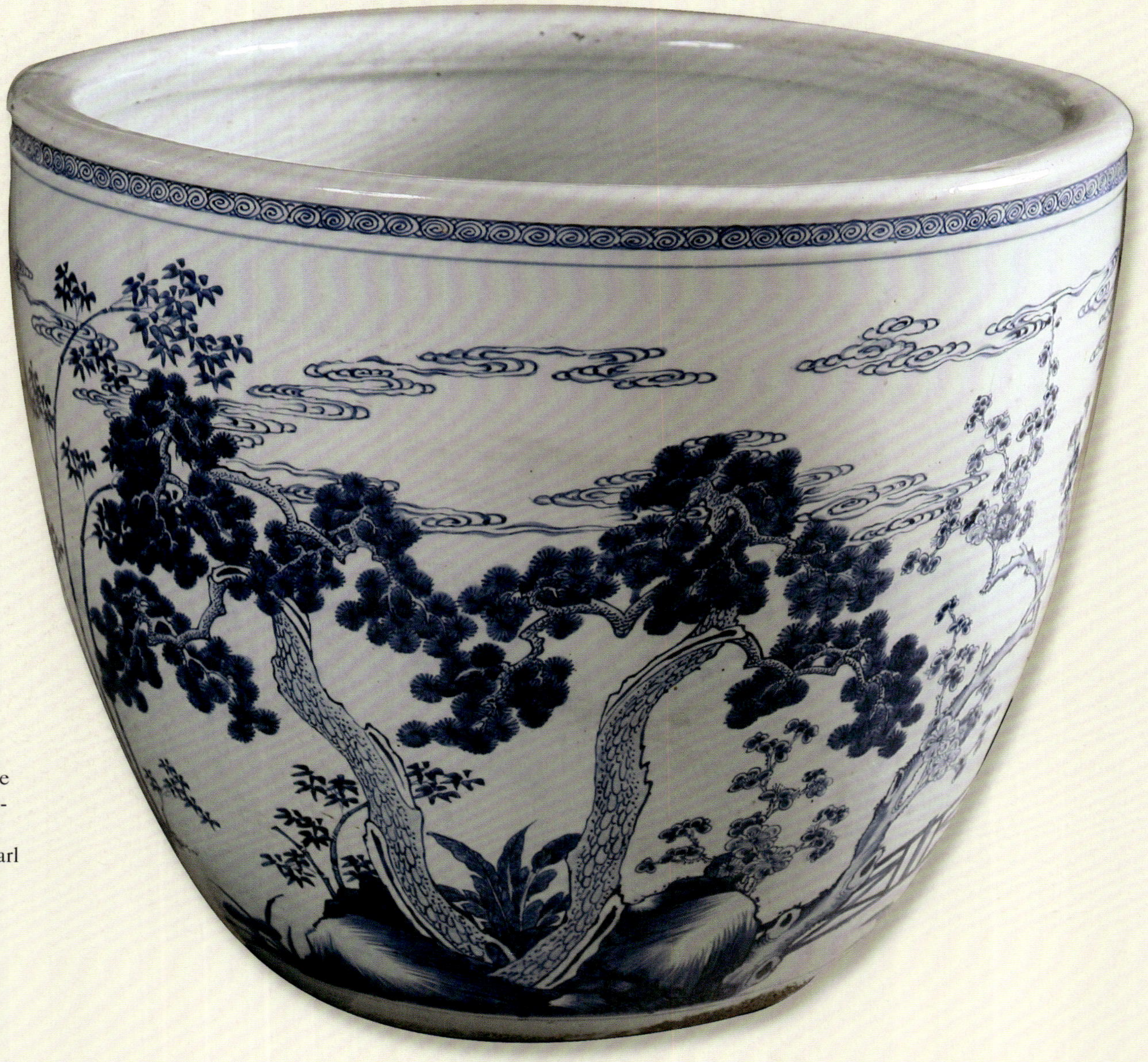

Figure 43. Goldfish Tub, Chinese, *c.* 1730, hard-paste porcelain, with cobalt decoration and lead glaze, 47 × 55 cm. The Rt Hon. the Earl of Derby. D107. Cat. 31

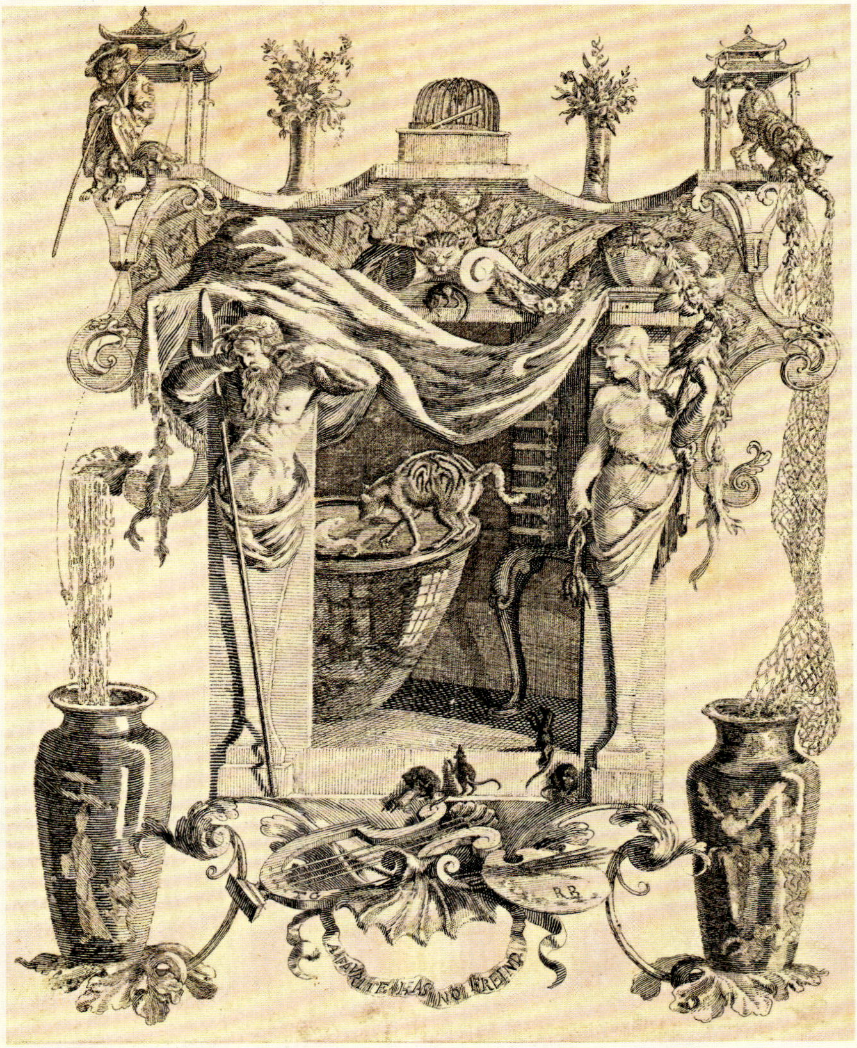

Richard Bentley, an accomplished draughtsman and a member of Walpole's 'Strawberry committee', drew the illustrations for the collection of six of Gray's poems, printed in 1753. The frontispiece to the 'Death of a Favourite Cat' shows the bowl and the inquisitive Selima perched on the rim within an interior setting, and is inscribed from the penultimate stanza of the ode: 'A favrite [*sic*] has no friend' (Fig. 44). According to the 1774 *Description*, the fish tub was the centrepiece of the Great Cloister (Fig. 45), but by the 1784 edition it had been moved to a prime position close to the entrance, in the Little Cloister, set on a splendidly ornate Gothic-style pedestal in keeping with the architecture both of the Cloisters and of the interior of Strawberry Hill (Fig. 3). On the pedestal was a label printed at the Strawberry Hill Press, repeating the ode's initial lines, but carefully altering the first two: ''Twas on this lofty vase's side' ... Where China's gayest art has dy'd.

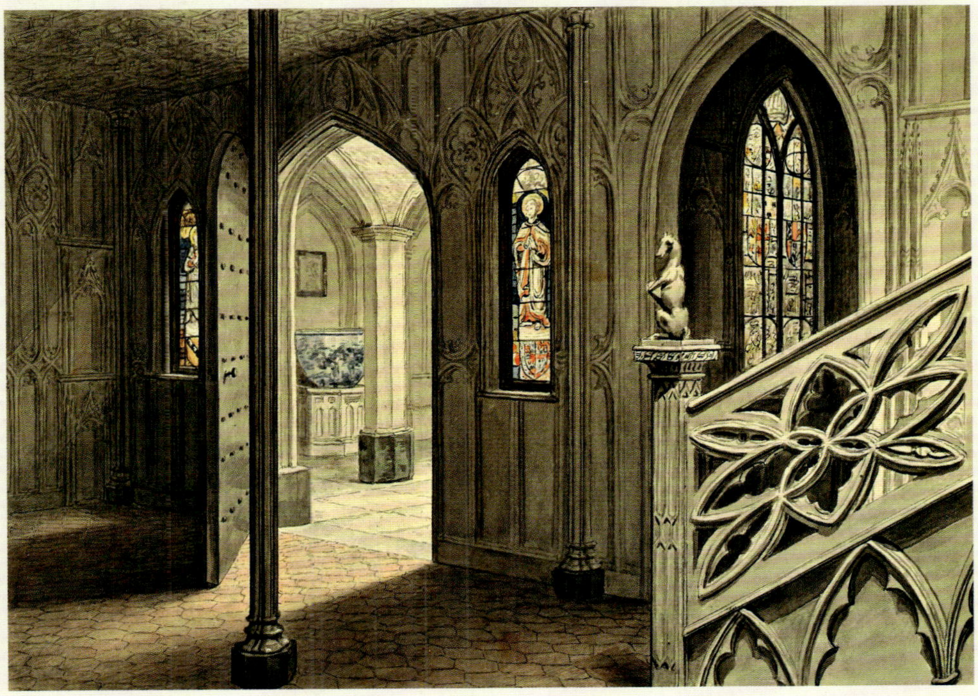

Figure 44. Richard Bentley, *Ode on the death of a favourite cat*, 1753, pen and ink, 38 × 27.5 cm, for *Designs by Mr. R. Bentley for Six Poems by Mr. T. Gray*, pen and ink. The Lewis Walpole Library, Yale University. Folio 49 3698. Opening: Ode on the death of a favorite cat. Cat. 32

Figure 45. John Carter, *View from the Hall at Strawberry Hill*, 1788, pen and ink and watercolour, 20.4 × 27.7 cm (visible), from Walpole's extra-illustrated copy of the *Description*. The Lewis Walpole Library, Yale University. Folio 49 3582 fol. 24. Cat. 47

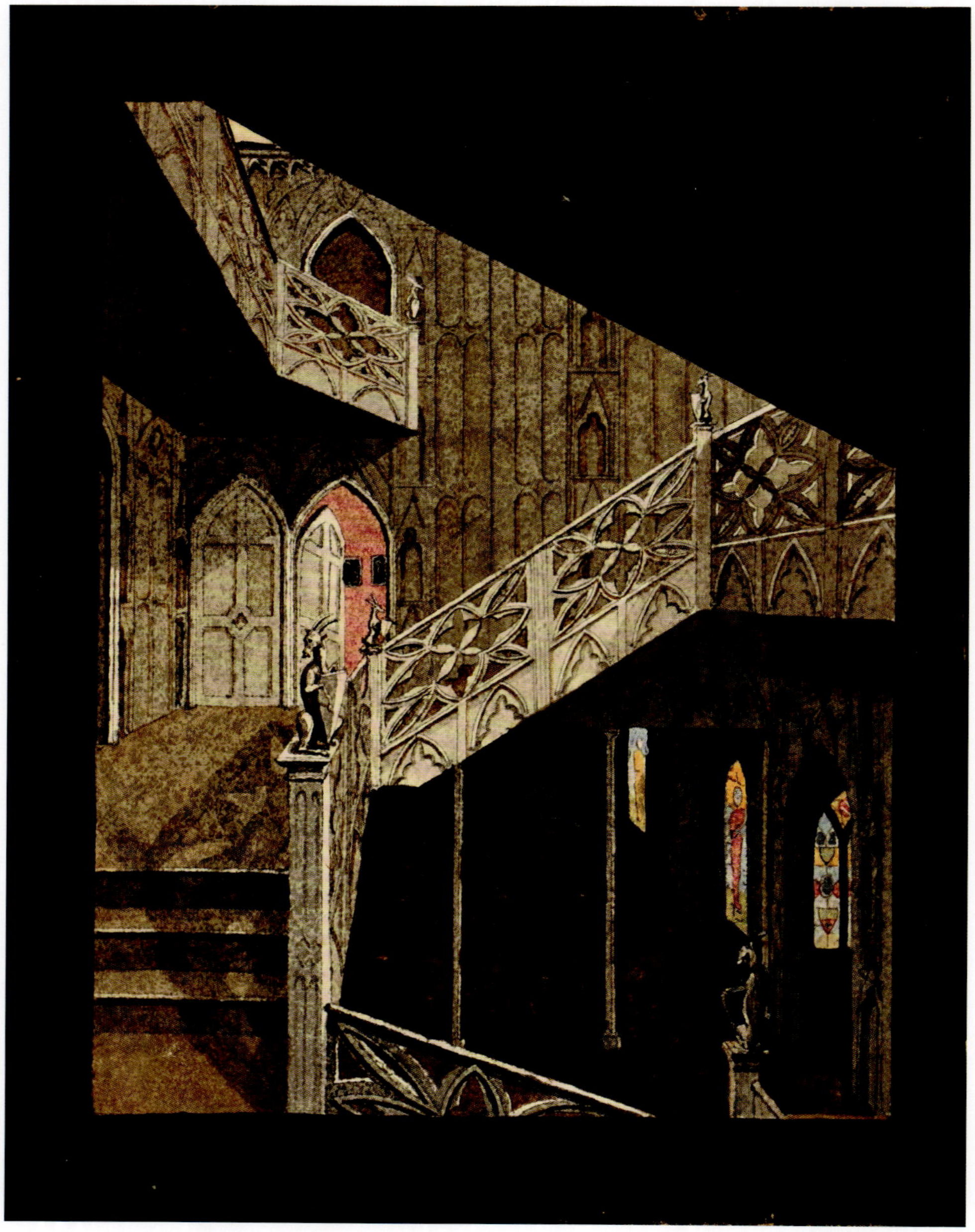

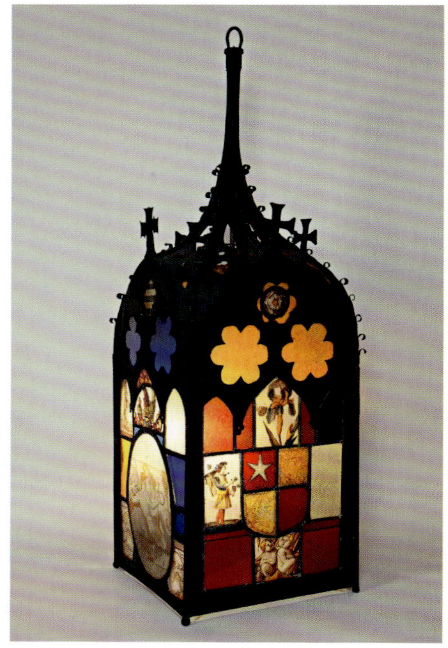

Figure 46. Richard Bentley, *Perspective of the Hall & Staircase at Strawberryhill*, *c.* 1753, pen and ink and watercolour, 22.7 × 17.7 cm, from *Drawings and Designs by Richd. Bentley* [1760, fol.30]. The Lewis Walpole Library, Yale University. Folio 49 3585 fol.30. Cat. 46

Figure 47. William Hallett, Sr, designed by Richard Bentley, Gothic Lantern, *c.* 1755. coloured, stained, and enamelled glass set in an iron, lead, and painted tin frame, 109.2 × 35.6 × 36.2 cm. The Lewis Walpole Library, Yale University. Cat. 49

staircase, strongly lit by clear-glazed quatrefoils in the roof, giving the impression of an open courtyard. By night, lit by a single candle in a stained glass lantern hung on a black and yellow rope, it was a piece of pure theatre (Figs. 46, 47) and the scene that inspired *The Castle of Otranto*.

To the south of the staircase hall, reached 'under two gloomy arches', was the Little Parlour (or Supper Parlour), created in 1754. This small room, like the hall and staircase, was a transitional space that also opened onto the garden. For forty-six years its walls were hung with trompe-l'oeil 'gothic paper of stone colour in mosaic, on which are wooden prints by Jackson of Venice'. As Walpole made clear in a letter to Horace Mann, John Baptist Jackson's 'infamous' woodcut prints after Titian were made to serve as illusionistic 'barbarous bas-reliefs': 'they succeeded to a miracle: it is impossible at first sight not to conclude that they contain the history of Attila and Tottila, done about the very era.'[61] Here, and later in the Winding Cloister, Walpole was perhaps echoing the setting of ancient reliefs into the walls of the entrance spaces in Italian palaces. The Little Parlour and the Library, also created in 1754, were the first of many rooms to have their chimneypieces derived from engravings of medieval tombs (Fig. 54). In the case of the Little Parlour the source, an engraving of the tomb

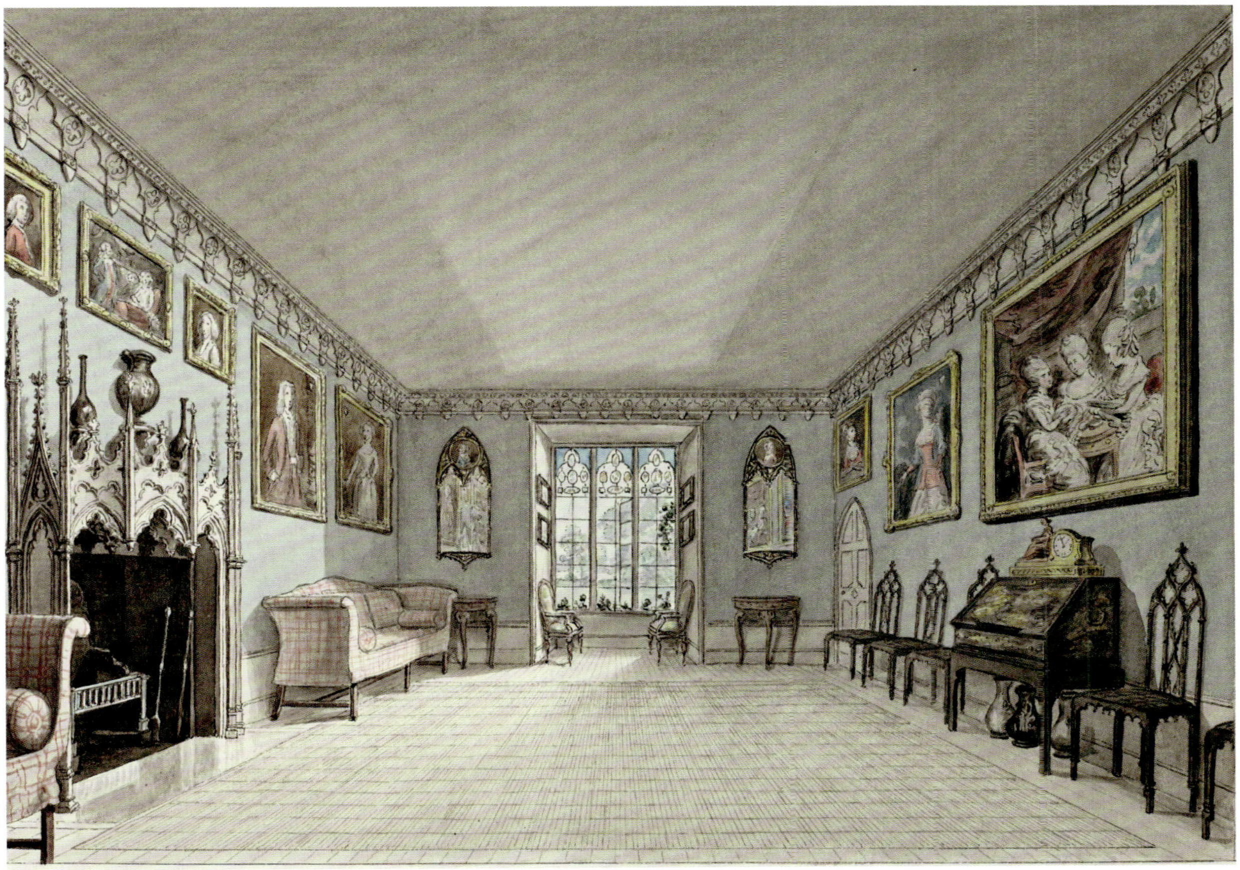

Figure 48. John Carter, *View of the Great Parlour*, *c.* 1788, watercolour and ink, 25.3 × 30.4 cm. Laid in Walpole's copy of the *Description*. The Lewis Walpole Library, Yale University. Folio 33 30, Copy 11, p. 35

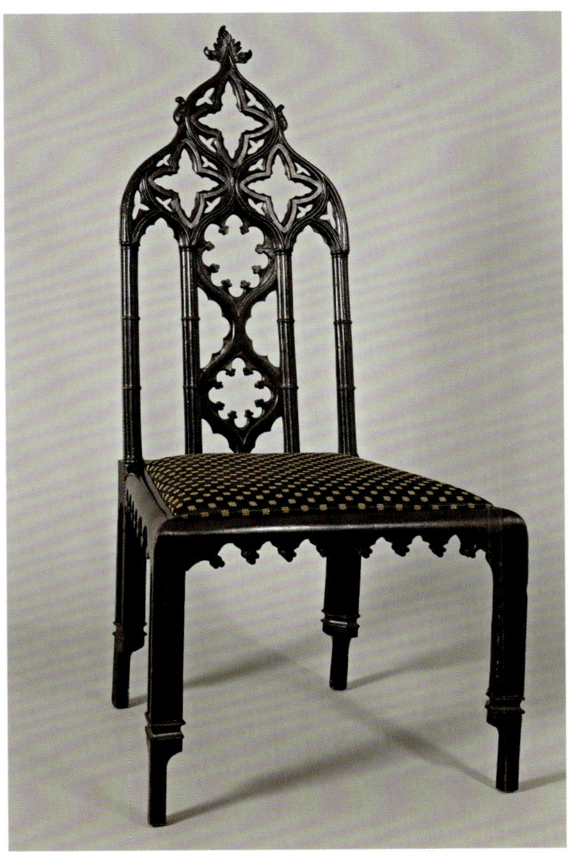

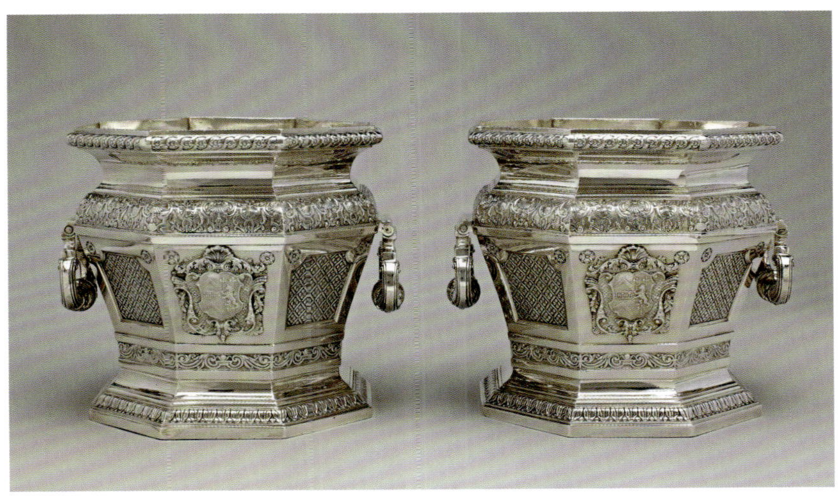

Figure 50. William Lukin, Pair of Wine Coolers, 1716–17, cast, chased and engraved silver, with large swing handles, 21 × 21.1 cm. Made for Sir Robert Walpole. The Metropolitan Museum of Art, Gift of Irwin Untermyer, 1968 (68.141.128 and 68.141.129). Cat. 66

Figure 49. William Hallett, Sr, designed by Richard Bentley and Horace Walpole, Chair, *c.* 1755. Beech, painted black to imitate ebony, 132 × 60.8 × 53 cm, the upholstery of the seat modern. The Lewis Walpole Library, Yale University. Cat. 61

Figure 51. William Hallett Sr, designed by Horace Walpole, Gothic Pier Glass with a portrait of George Walpole, 3rd Lord Orford, *c.* 1754–5, wood and glass with portrait in oil on canvas, 206 × 83.9 cm. Accepted by H.M. Government in lieu of Inheritance Tax, 2008. Cat. 63

of Thomas Ruthall, Bishop of Durham, in Westminster Abbey, was copied so literally that the illusionistic perspective of the original print was preserved. By 1784 the Little Parlour had become dedicated to showing works of 'female genius' – in 1791 it was repapered in plain brown.[62]

On the other side of the stair hall was the Refectory, also called the Great Parlour, thus combining the world of the monastery with that of the great house.[63] It was Walpole's dining room and, with the Library above, the first large room at Strawberry Hill. It was of modern shape and provided with modern equipment, but with Gothic details (Figs. 48, 50). The room must also have been rather dark, as the first window was ogee-topped, identical to that of the Library above, and set low down. The extravagantly pinnacled, stone-coloured chimneypiece was designed by Richard Bentley in his most fanciful style, with more than a hint of the Gothic of Batty Langley that Walpole came to condemn (Fig. 113). In its first form the room followed the earlier Gothic aesthetic fully, being 'hung with paper in imitation of stucco' – a type of trompe-l'oeil paper described in 1751 as 'generally a mosaic formed by a rose in a kind of a octagon'.[64] In 1773 the window was modernized into an avant-garde full-length bay. The wall decoration in plain greyish-blue painted paper seen in the first view of the room, drawn in 1788, was carried out in 1774 (Fig. 48).

The Great Parlour was the first of the rooms at Strawberry Hill to be 'pretending to an observance of the *costume*, even in the furniture', in the form of a set of eight black Gothic chairs (designed by Walpole and Bentley; Fig. 49), two Gothic mirrors (designed by Walpole; Fig. 51) and a large side table (designed by Bentley; Fig. 37).[65] The pioneering architectural forms of the chairs were intended to echo the original window. For the chairs, something of the designing process is revealed in a letter in which Walpole berated Bentley for his tardiness in producing drawings:

> In the first place my chairs! if you had taken a quarter of the time to draw what they might be, that you employed to describe what they must not be, I might possibly have had some begun by this time … My idea is to have a black back higher, but not much higher than common chairs, and extremely light, with matted bottoms. As I found yours came not, I have been trying to make out something like the windows – for example [drawing of chairs] I would have only a sort of black sticks, pierced through.[66]

The table, supporting a 6-foot (1.8 m) long piece of Sicilian jasper, combined a Gothic frieze with 'dropped points', a favourite early Gothic Revival device, reflected also in the chimneypiece, the chair frames and the mirrors. The six spiral-turned legs, however, were most probably prompted by the stands of French seventeenth-century ebony cabinets. Like a traditional great parlour, the room was a gallery for portraits of the owner's immediate family. They were positioned according to status. His father (the first Earl of Orford), mother and step-mother were above the great table, facing the window. Opposite them, the mirrors incorporated specially commissioned portraits of his legitimate nephews, one of whom was later the third Earl of Orford. On the chimney wall were his brother Robert and his wife, his brother Edward and Walpole himself (Fig. 109), while on the facing

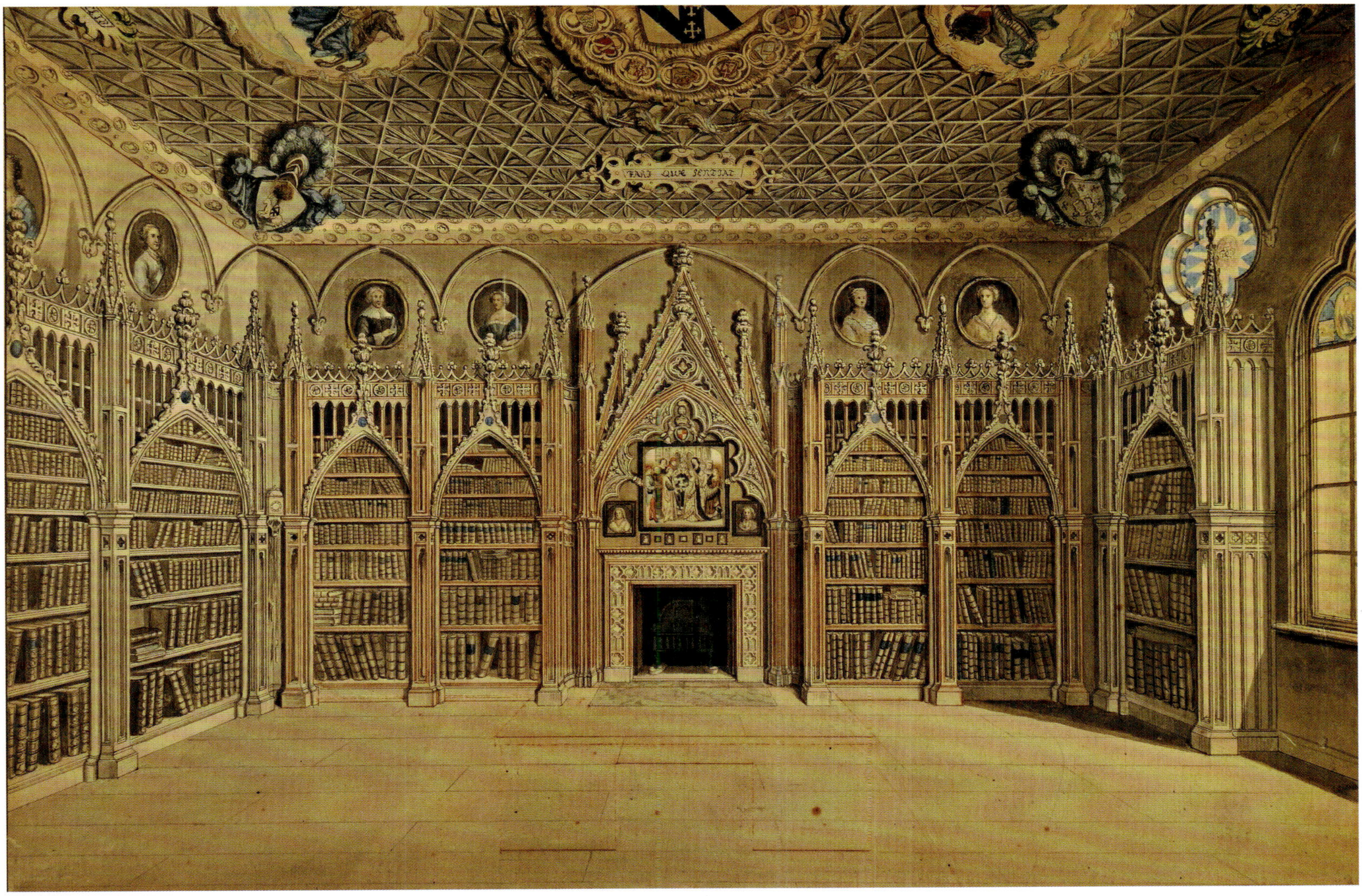

wall were his sister, half-sister and aunts. In 1781 they were joined by his brother Edward's grandchildren in the form of Reynolds's *The Ladies Waldegrave* (1780–1; Fig. 180). But into this family assemblage Walpole introduced, over the chimneypiece, pictures of some of his closest friends: Horace Mann, his brother Galfridus and the 'out of town' group of friends who visited Strawberry Hill at Christmas and Easter (Figs. 6, 144). The decorative art displayed a great range of dates, styles and origins. By 1774 a Limoges enamel horn hung over the 'ancient' table (Figs. 221, 222), two Chinese vases flanked an ancient Greek krater between the Gothic pinnacles of the chimneypiece, and opposite was a lacquer desk. It was very probably no accident that this heterogeneous collection all had blackness in common.

THE ARMOURY AND LIBRARY

When first conceived, the staircase (like its model at Rouen) was designed to culminate in the Library. In front of the Library, in a vaulted landing, was the Armoury, filled from the start with an evocative array of arms and armour and other metalware of many dates and origins, 'all *supposed* to be taken by Sir Terry Robsart in the holy wars',[67] as well as old metalwork, and later augmented by a spectacular parade armour set in a niche in the west wall (Figs. 101, 245, 255). On the wall were painted, in the medieval style, the 'quarterings of Walpole'. The ancestral and crusading references in the Armoury were a preamble to the major show of heraldry and lineage in the Library. Until the creation of the State Apartment from 1760 onwards, it was the most important room in the house. The Library

Figure 52. Edward Edwards, *The Library at Strawberry Hill*, *c.* 1781, watercolour, pencil, and pen and ink on laid paper, 31 × 45.3 cm (sheet). The Lewis Walpole Library, Yale University. 781.00.00.45dr. Cat. 74

Lisa Ford

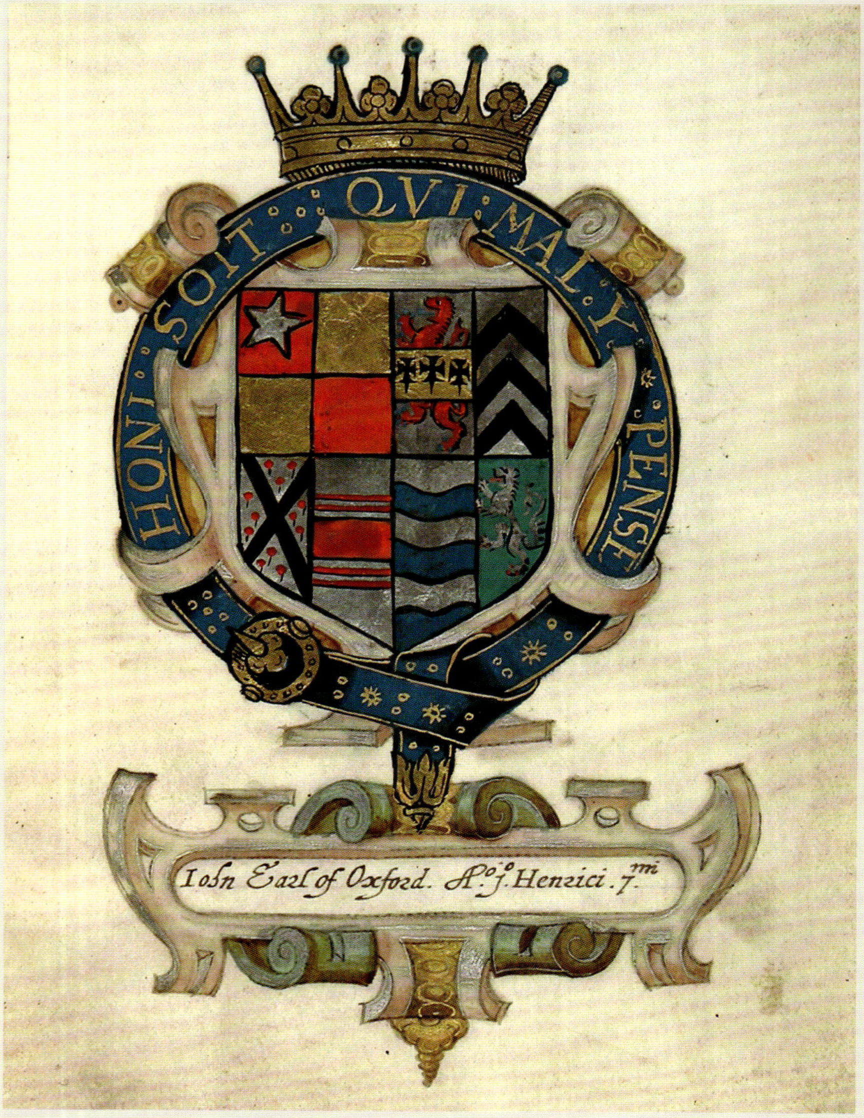

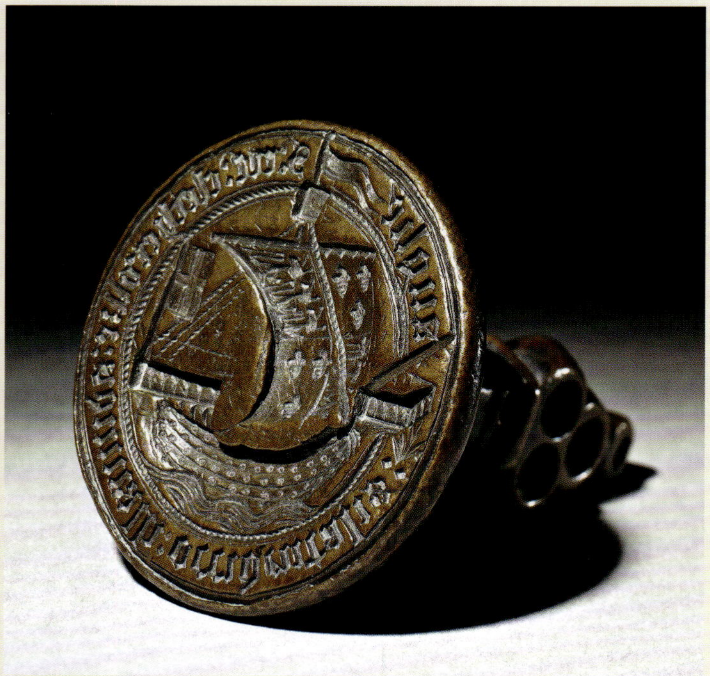

Figure 53. Sir Gilbert Dethick, 'Arms of the Earl of Oxford', from *Arms of the Knights of the Garter*, 1573, manuscript on vellum, bound in red velvet, 20 × 15 cm. The Lewis Walpole Library, Yale University. 49 2551. Cat. 83

Figure 54. Admiralty Seal Matrix for Richard Clitherowe, Admiral of the West, *c.* 1406, bronze, D 4.4 cm. British Museum, Department of Prehistory and Europe. 1858,0629.1. Cat. 165

The heraldry at Strawberry Hill, in its architecture, decoration and contents, includes numerous examples of both the Walpole genealogy and that of the Lancastrian-Tudor dynasty with which Walpole was so fascinated. The richly decorated pages of the velvet-covered arms of the Knights of the Garter (Fig. 53) installed by Richard III and Henry VII were created for Elizabeth I by her Garter King of Arms, Sir Gilbert Dethick, and they bring together in visual display the two kings whom Walpole pitted against each other in a battle of historical reputations. The intricately carved bronze seal of Richard Cletherowe, Admiral of the West (Fig. 54), shows a ship displaying the arms of Henry IV, the founder of the royal Lancastrian line. The delicately detailed clock reputed to be the wedding gift of Henry VIII to Anne Boleyn (Fig. 56) features the royal arms and Henry and Anne's mottos and initials in lovers' knots on the weights, providing an emblem of royal marriage analogous to Walpole's various portraits of Lancastrian and Tudor royal couples hung throughout the house.

The Walpole family arms were equally well presented at Strawberry Hill: William Cole commented in a manuscript describing a visit in late October 1774 that the *Description* contained 'a most fulsome enumeration, on every occasion, of the most minute titles of all the Walpole family'. As well as arms and quartering in shields over the front and other doors, in the Armoury and on the painted ceiling of the Library, the family shield of two chevrons sable on a red field with a bar across the centre featuring three crosses appeared on several windows commissioned in 1761 by Walpole for the Gallery and the Great North Bedchamber (Fig. 55). The Walpole Salver (see Fig. 5), commemorating Robert Walpole's service as Chancellor of the Exchequer, combines the artisanal skills of master goldsmith Paul de Lamerie and the artist William Hogarth, to whom the engraving is attributed, in a display of the family arms, the royal insignia and allegorical scenes. The manuscript pedigree of the Walpole family (see Cat. 33) traces his mother's family's descent, along with the kings of England, from Cadwalader of Wales, prompting Walpole's comment to Lady Ossory in a letter in December 1784: 'Thus you see, Madam, whichever way I turn myself, I have royal or Fitzroyal connections.'

Perhaps Walpole's pride in his own heredity found personal expression in the ivory figures of Rubens, François Duquesnoy and Inigo Jones atop the cabinet constructed for his miniatures and enamels (see Fig. 127). The figures perch on a pediment above a shield of the Walpole arms, to which the downturned hand of Fiammingo seems to direct the gazes of the statues of Jones and Rubens, as well as of the viewer. Certainly, Walpole's interest in pursuing a hereditary connection to the de Vere Earls of Oxford, his decoration of Strawberry Hill with Walpolean armorials, and his publication of the arms and quarterings of the Walpole Earls of Orford during both his brother George's tenure and his own suggest antiquarian interest supplemented by genealogical pride. His remark in a letter to his niece the Duchess of Gloucester in May 1778, 'I have been laughed at, perhaps deservedly, for family-pride', may be a direct comment on reactions to his Gothic villa, its contents and decoration.

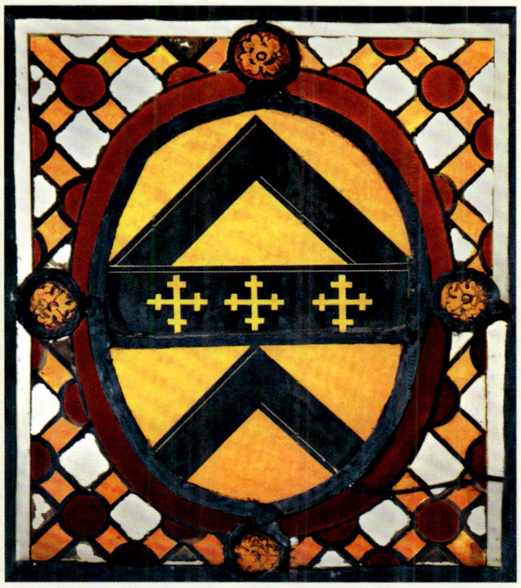

Figure 55. William Peckitt, panel with the Walpole coat of arms from the Gallery, 1762, coloured, stained and enamelled glass, 32.5 × 24.1 cm. The Lewis Walpole Library, Yale University. Cat. 132

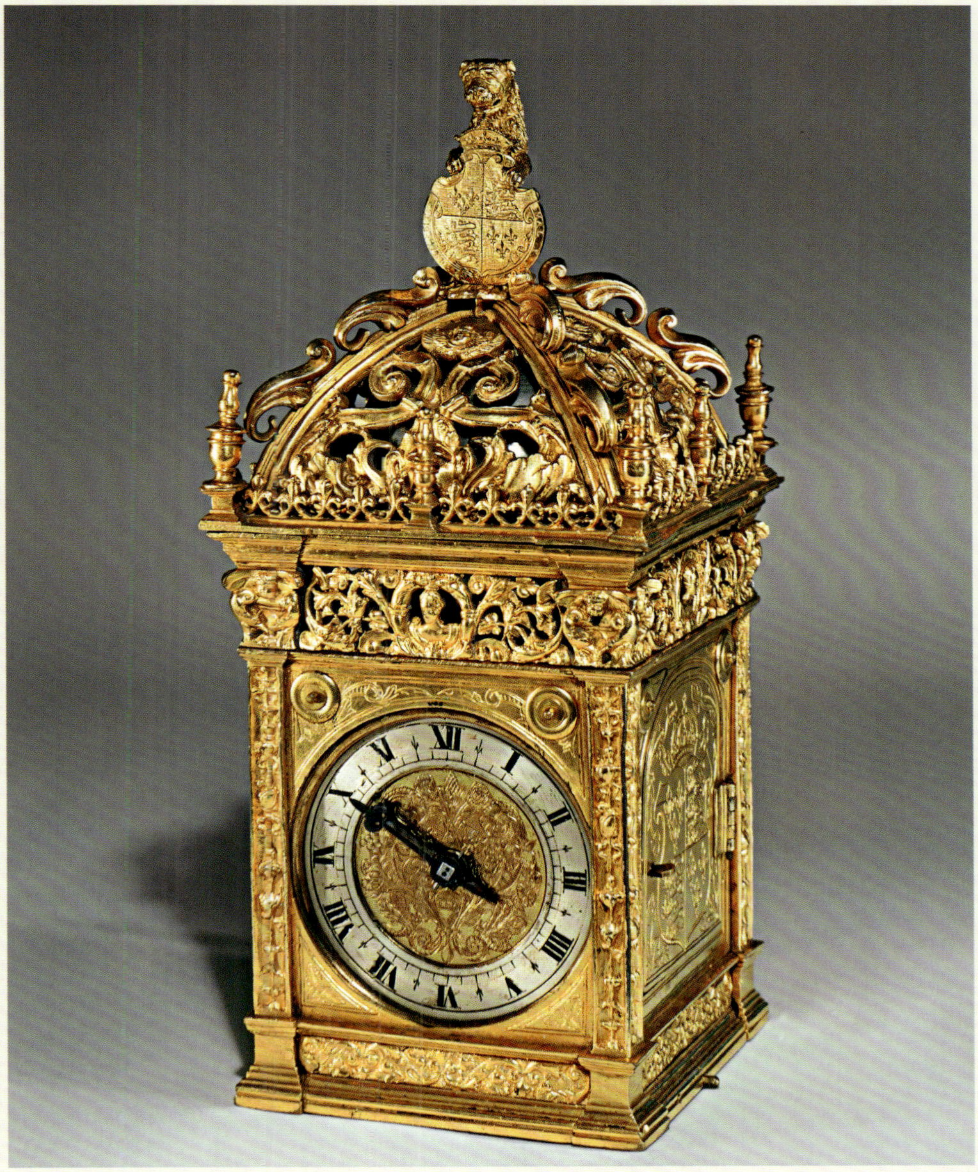

Figure 56. Maker unknown, Clock, 16th century, gilt metal, 25.5 × 10.9 × 10.7 cm. The Royal Collection

was a symbol of Walpole's antiquarian endeavour, designed to house the printed and manuscript materials of his historical projects. It was the most intensely Gothic of all the rooms at Strawberry Hill (Figs. 52, 260). Except for the functional furniture and carpets, it lacked the usual Strawberry Hill mix of ancient and modern; where the Refectory had a fire-screen worked by Lady Ailesbury and a neo-classical clock, the Library had an 'ancient curfeu' and a gilt metal clock with the arms and initials of Henry VIII and Anne Boleyn (Fig. 56). Even Anne Damer's terracotta sculpture of an osprey not only recalled the marble eagle in the Gallery ('the spoilt child of my antique one'), but was compared by Walpole with the works of Praxiteles.[68]

The walls of the Library were entirely lined with bookcases formed as a Gothic arcade, and its chimneypiece and overmantel were made up of elements from two medieval tombs.[69] Bentley's first design for the Library showed it as about the same height as the Refectory below, with a fantastic pinnacled chimneypiece and lined with arcaded Gothic bookcases, which, however, were topped with busts and vases in the manner of classical libraries of the period (Fig. 312). The entrance door – in the Jacobean style with a shell top – was to survive into the constructed scheme. His second design used the ultimate source for the arcade, a Hollar print of a doorway in old St Paul's, for the entrance door, but created for the main run an imaginative scheme with the usual 'dropping points' (Fig. 262). The final, rationalized scheme was designed by Chute, with the urns and busts replaced by real Roman funerary urns on the floor, and elements from Walpole's arms in the cresting (Fig. 264).[70] The stone-coloured woodwork translated into three dimensions the type of complex pattern-making found in the hall, with much emphasis on pierced openings and a subtle layering of elements, especially in the overmantel. The ceiling, sketched by Walpole, drawn out by Bentley and painted by Andien de Clermont, was a celebration of Walpole's medieval and (as he believed) crusader ancestry, linking his arms and initials with the Robsarts and the Fitz Osberts, who were represented as armoured knights in the form of medieval seals all around the Walpole arms in the centre (Fig. 266). Above the bookcases, under fictive painted arches, there were portraits of his Shorter ancestors and relatives. Over the chimneypiece a painting of the marriage of Henry VI, surmounted by his arms, made a direct link between the Walpoles and national history (Fig. 147). But, as in the staircase, the styles were in fact mixed: the ceiling's 'mosaic ground' and plumed and mantled helmets were of seventeenth-century inspiration, as were the strapwork cartouches and their 'Gothic' motto and date. The same was true of the painted glass, the biggest display in the house, all of it of the sixteenth or seventeenth century, although Walpole was careful to incorporate the white and red roses of the houses of York and Lancaster into the quatrefoil windows.

In addition to these Gothic spaces there were a number of much smaller rooms, chiefly for everyday living, including closets, bedrooms, a Breakfast Room, a China Room and a Waiting Room, mostly formed from pre-existing rooms in the old house between 1749 and 1756. In contrast to the stone-coloured Gothic spaces, these rooms were more colourful and comfortable and had few Gothic features except for the windows of painted glass, the chimneypieces, cornices and other details. But as in the Gothic spaces, pattern dominated, at any rate at first. All the rooms were decorated with up-to-date patterned wallpapers in a narrow range of colours: green, blue, grey and red or crimson. The most expensive paper was that in flock, including a blue and gold paper in a large damask pattern (still *in situ*), in Walpole's own bedchamber. The Waiting Room (which served as the first dining room) was papered (up to 1766) in an imitation of blue and white chinoiserie tiles (a fragment is in the Victoria and Albert Museum), perhaps to match the adjacent tile-lined China Room. The chimneypiece of the China Room was decorated with the arms 'of the principal persons who have inhabited Strawberry-hill', though in fact only from 1721 and excluding Mrs Chenevix.

The furnishings of these rooms were also up to date. In the Breakfast Room, which, like the Library, was an everyday living room, the blue and white wallpaper was echoed by 'a thousand plump chairs, couches and luxurious settees covered with linen [i.e., chintz] of the same pattern'.[71] The chimneypiece of 1748, in the style of William Kent and surmounted by Walpole's Saracen's head crest, was the earliest essay in the Gothic at Strawberry Hill, but by 1784 was condemned as 'not truly gothic'. The Green Closet next door had a small-pattern flock, the Red Bedchamber (the best bedchamber, used by John Chute) a red small-

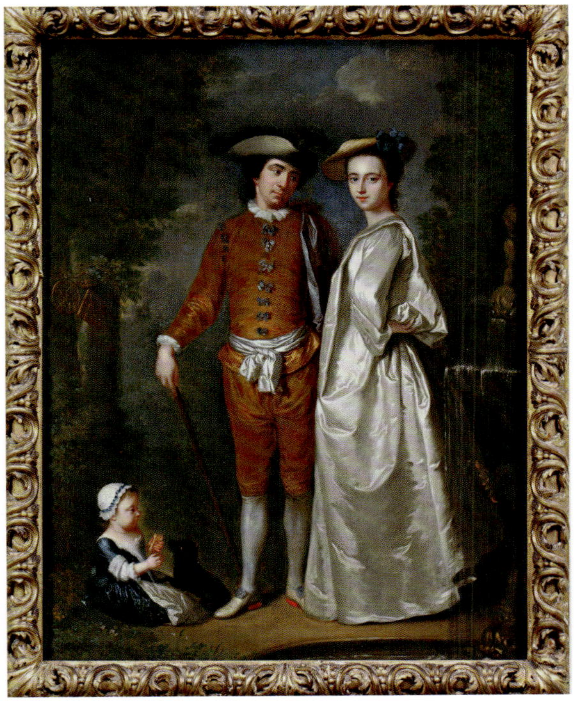

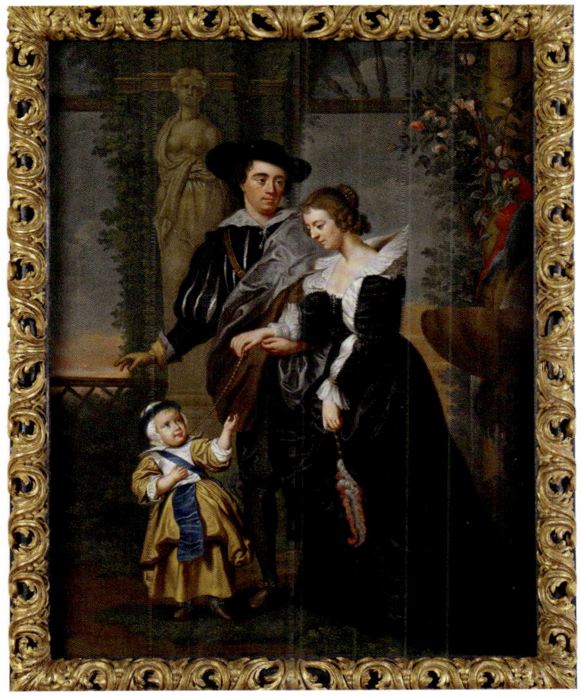

Figure 57. John Giles Eccardt, *Portrait of Henry Seymour Conway, Lady Aylesbury and Anne, their Daughter*, 1754, oil on canvas, 66 × 50.9 cm. Private collection. Cat. 43

Figure 58. John Giles Eccardt, *Colonel Charles Churchill and Lady Mary Churchill and their Eldest Son Charles*, 1750, oil on canvas, 66.7 × 50.8 cm. The Lewis Walpole Library, Yale University. Cat. 44

pattern flock, and the Blue Bedchamber was simply painted in plain blue, at any rate by 1774. The Yellow Bedchamber on the ground floor was decorated in a striking combination of yellow and black – apparently with engravings stuck to the yellow wallpaper in the new 'print room' fashion.[72] In 1776 the room was modernized with a plainer scheme, as were a number of others at about the same period, in line with the creation of the State Apartment, with its reduced emphasis on strong pattern. The wallpaper changed to 'grey spotted' for the hanging of a set of reduced copies of Sir Peter Lely's late seventeenth-century set of female portraits called the 'Windsor Beauties', and named the Beauty Room after its equivalent at Windsor Castle. By 1766 the Breakfast Room was painted plain blue.

The main showroom in this set of smaller spaces was the Blue Bedchamber, positioned on the route between the Refectory and the Library and created at the same time. It was carefully conceived as a complement to their ancestral display, containing a set of portraits by John Giles Eccardt, painted between 1747 and 1754, that placed Walpole's own portrait, discussed above, among pictures of some of those closest to him. A posthumous portrait of his parents, shown with appropriate attributes and Houghton in the background, by Eccardt and John Wootton, hung over Richard Bentley's chimneypiece (Figs. 119, 120). The families of his half-sister Lady Mary Churchill and his favourite cousin Henry Seymour Conway were on either side of the entrance door (Figs. 57, 58) and Sir Charles Hanbury Williams, Thomas Gray (Fig. 112), and Richard Bentley (Fig. 111) and Walpole himself 'in each panel round the room' (Fig. 19).[73] All the single subjects held attributes identifying them variously as poets (Gray and Hanbury Williams), an artist (Bentley) and a scholar (Walpole). While his mother was shown in simplified modern dress, and Sir Robert was wearing traditional Garter Robes, the other sitters were presented in poses and dress after pictures by Rubens, Van Dyck and Watteau. The frames reinforced the return to the *grand siècle*, Sir Robert and Lady Walpole being in an old example carved in the manner of Grinling Gibbons (and painted back and gold) and the others in new frames copied from the borders of prints after Van Dyck, the single portraits 'with emblems peculiar to each person'. But for all their historical references, these decorative treatments were seen as modern: 'You can't imagine how new and pretty this furniture is,' Walpole wrote to Bentley, 'I believe I must get you to send me an attestation under your hand that you knew nothing of it, that

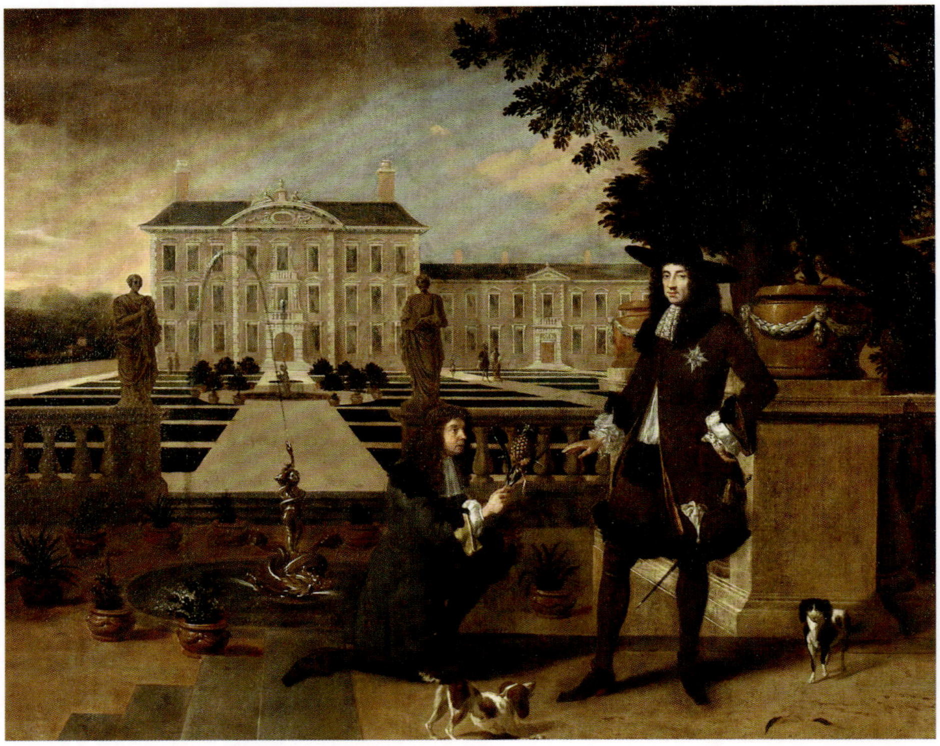

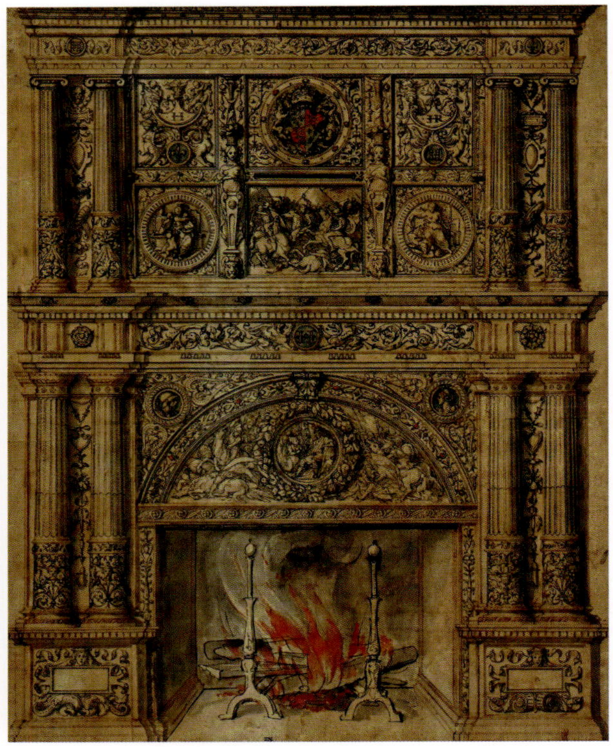

Figure 59. Hendrick Danckerts, *The Presentation of a Pineapple to Charles II* ('Rose, the Royal Gardiner, presenting the first pineapple raised in England to Charles II'), *c.* 1677, oil on canvas, 91.4 × 109.2 cm. Houghton Hall, Norfolk. Cat. 104

Figure 60. Hans Holbein the younger, *Design for a Chimney-piece*, *c.* 1537–43, black and brown ink, grey and blue wash, 53.9 × 42.7 cm. British Museum, Department of Prints and Drawings. 1854,0708.1. Cat. 125

Mr Rigby may allow that at least this one room was by my own direction'.[74]

The collections in the other, more private, small rooms were of a very different character. In the Breakfast Room, for instance, the only large paintings in 1784 were a portrait of about 1658–60 by Lely of a beautiful young shepherd, then believed to represent the poet Abraham Cowley,[75] and 'a most curious picture' of about 1677 of 'Rose the Royal Gardiner, presenting the first pineapple raised in England to Charles II' (Fig. 59). Also in the room were frames and ebony cases containing a large part of the cream of Walpole's collection of miniatures, including those of the Digby family (see pp. 188–9). Most of the other works in the room had a personal resonance, such as the drawing of Madame du Deffand by Carmontel, wax reliefs of boys by Lady Diana Beauclerk, 'set in frames with her arms, and cameos by Wedgwood and Tassie',[76] and 'a view of Stokepogeys in Buckinghamshire; the moon shining on Mr Gray's tomb in the church-yard; by Baron: a present from sir Edward Walpole'.[77] The manner in which such objects could come together in imaginative terms is shown by Walpole's acquisition of the Baron drawing: 'I have hung it here in my favourite blue room, as a companion to Madame de Sévigny's Hotel de Carnavalet, and call them my *Penseroso* and *Allegro*.'[78]

In 1753 Walpole described the 'charming' small Green Closet next door, 'where I now am writing', as 'hung with green paper and water-colour pictures'.[79] By 1784 the walls, three of which were otherwise taken up by cupboards and windows (containing some of the finest glass in the house), carried an astonishing 138 works, including 16 miniatures, oil paintings by Samuel Scott and William Hogarth (Figs. 23, 181), and landscape drawings by Andrea Locatelli. In this closet of an antiquarian there were few works with personal links of the type shown in the room next door. By 1784 the picture collections in both rooms were accompanied by Sèvres and other porcelain, and sculpture by Anne Damer, as well as modern furniture, including a table with a Sèvres top (copied for the carpet in the Round Room) and a neo-classical desk. The most personal objects were reserved for Walpole's own bedchamber, including a portrait of John Chute (Fig. 7). Its chimneypiece, designed by Chute, inspired one of the handful of value judgements on interior decoration in the *Description*: 'it has great grace'.[80]

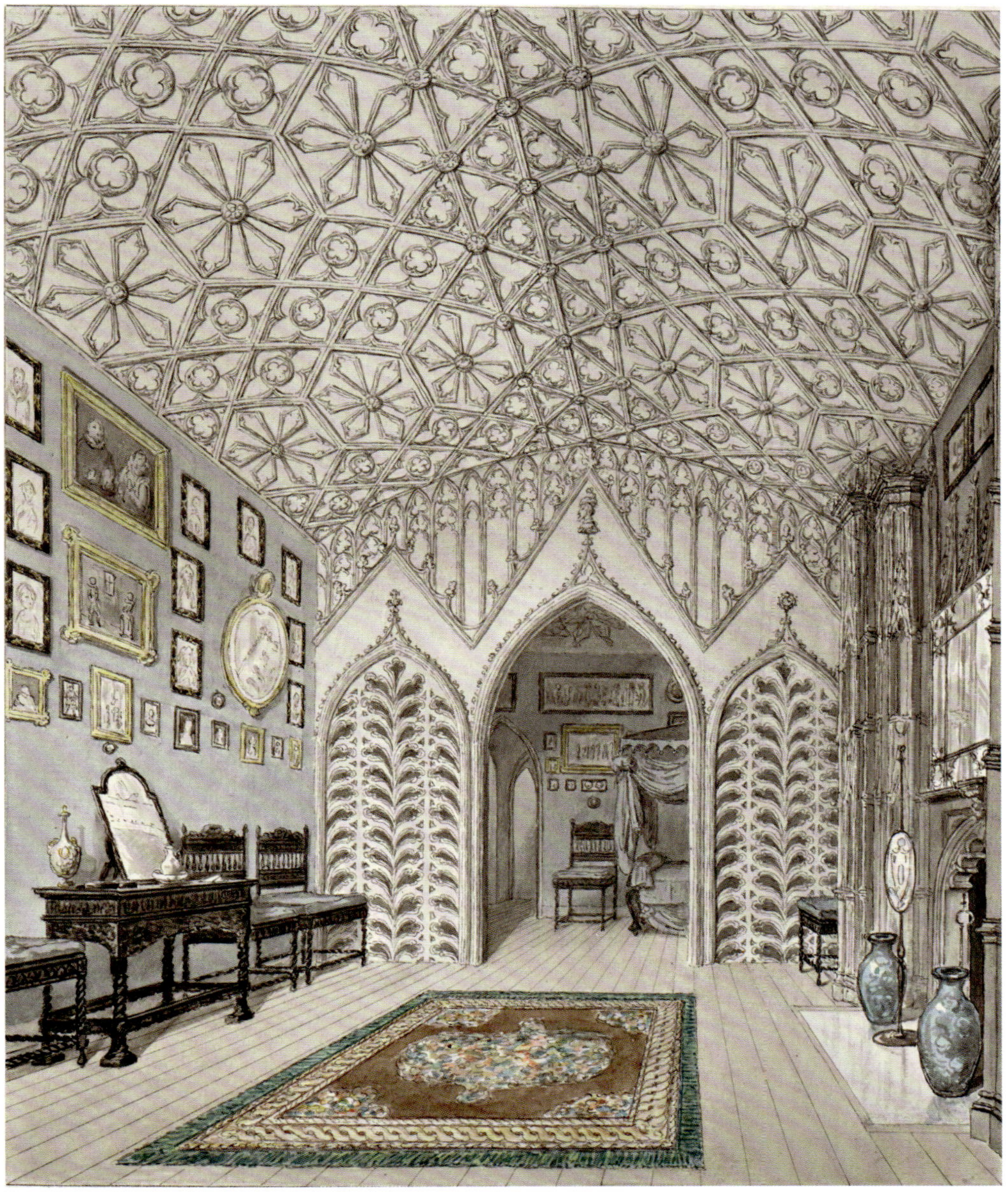

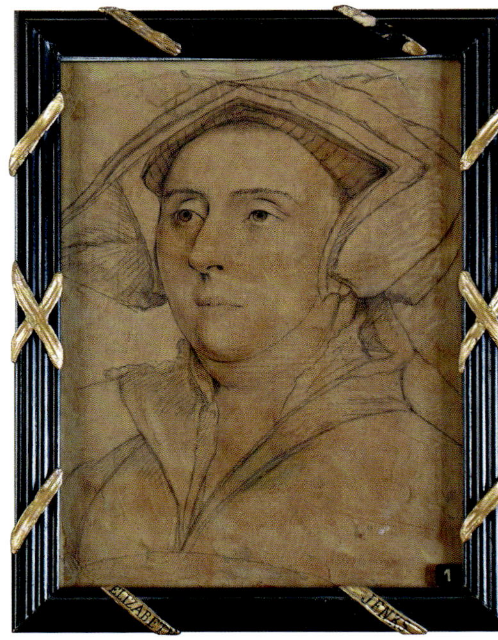

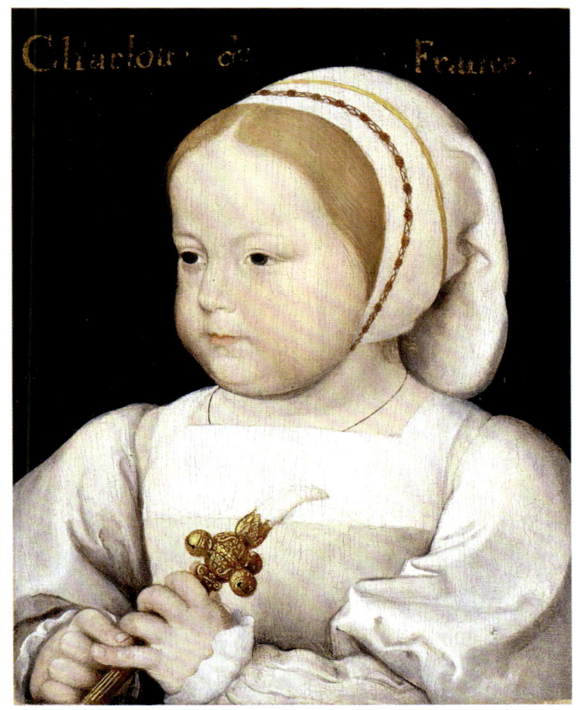

GOING WESTWARDS

In 1759 Walpole completed work on the sequence of three rooms that led to State Apartment in the western wing: the Star Chamber, the Trunk-Ceiled Passage (the 'dusky passage') and the Holbein Chamber. The first was a small, dark, transitional space, hung with green wallpaper 'with gold stars in mosaic' and lit by a window entirely filled with painted glass. Its name was also a reference to the notorious court used and abused by English monarchs from Henry VII to Charles I. The room contained more exercises in the recreation of historic furniture, in the form of a pair of chairs based on a triangular chair depicted in a piece of

Figure 61. John Carter, *'Holbien' Chamber*, *c.* 1788, watercolour, 33 × 29 cm (visible); from Richard Bull's extra-illustrated copy of the *Description*. The Lewis Walpole Library, Yale University. Folio 33 30 Copy 11, fol. 117. Cat. 114

Figure 62. George Vertue, *Elizabeth, Lady Rich*, one of a set of 33 tracings after Hans Holbein the younger, 1743–*c.* 1746, watercolour, black and red chalk, 37 × 27.5 cm. Private collection, UK. Cat. 120

Figure 63. Jean Clouet, *Portrait of Madeleine of France, 2nd Daughter of François I and Claude of France* ('Charlotte, Daughter of Francis I'), *c.* 1522, oil on panel, transferred from canvas, 16.8 × 13. 3 cm. Private collection, courtesy of the Weiss Gallery. Cat. 123

painted late-medieval glass in his bedchamber, as well as a pair of triangular 'Welch' (i.e. Welsh) chairs from the collection of his friend Richard Bateman, both blue and white with point-lace cushions. Two mahogany coin cabinets in the room were completed in a way that anticipated the State Apartment, with busts of James Gibbs (now in the Victoria and Albert Museum)[81] and a supposed Henry VII (see pp. 128–129) on top and porphyry vases below. The latter Henry VII 'in the agony of death' was placed there as a preamble to the dynastic histories in the Holbein Chamber. The dark Trunk-Ceiled Passage that led off it was a simplified imitation in applied wooden mouldings of an early sixteenth-century vaulted passage. It was terminated by a window filled with coloured glass and at night it was lit by single candle.[82] One of its functions was to make 'the richness & largeness of the gallery appear much more considerable'[83] and the other was to be an appropriate introduction to the Holbein Chamber (Fig. 326).

Nominally a bedchamber (with the bed placed in a formal arched alcove in the Baroque manner), the Holbein Chamber was the most consistently themed room in the house, most of its design and contents being focused on the momentous years of religious and political conflict of the first half of the sixteenth century (Fig. 61). Its creation was prompted by the acquisition in 1757 of thirty-three tracings by George Vertue of the Holbein portrait drawings of the court of Henry VIII, which were then, as now, in the Royal Collection (Fig. 62). The whole set was shown in a symmetrical arrangement in reeded frames bound in papier-mâché ribbons, perhaps designed by John Chute, in the key 'ancient' colours of gold and black. To these were added drawings by and after Holbein (Figs 59, 330, 332) and portraits of the English and European royal families, courtiers and others (Fig. 63). Most of the other objects in the room were also linked to the same period and personalities: Cardinal Wolsey's hat (Fig. 145), ebony furniture that Walpole believed had belonged to the cardinal, and a chair from the Abbey of Glastonbury (Fig. 38). On the table, before the dressing mirror, lay medieval and sixteenth- and seventeenth-century combs. Walpole had sought an old bed from Burghley House, but in the end had one made by William Vile in the Baroque style with plumes, tassels, and purple and white hangings (seemingly instead of a half-tester design by Bentley with heraldic antelopes at its foot).[84] The architecture and decoration of the room also referred to the sixteenth-century theme. Its shape, with a bay at one end, was dictated by the plan of the ceiling, which was copied from an example in the Queen's Dressing Room at Windsor.[85] Gently curved in section, the Strawberry Hill version was the first ceiling in the house to be decorated with mouldings in relief and the first to use papier maché. The other room details were designed by Richard Bentley: the chimneypiece 'chiefly taken' from the tomb of the catholic Archbishop of Canterbury, William Warham (who was removed from his see by Henry VIII), and the extraordinary flamboyant Gothic pierced screen derived from 'the gates of the choir at Rouen'[86] and designed to be as effective when viewed from the door as from the other side (Fig. 64). The windows were among the first examples in the house to combine old armorial glass with brilliantly coloured modern mosaic settings by William Price. The walls were painted an imperial 'purple' (in fact closer to lilac), matching the bed. In all this Walpole aimed to create 'a kind of chiaroscuro': 'Almost all the pictures are drawings faintly coloured, & the ebony

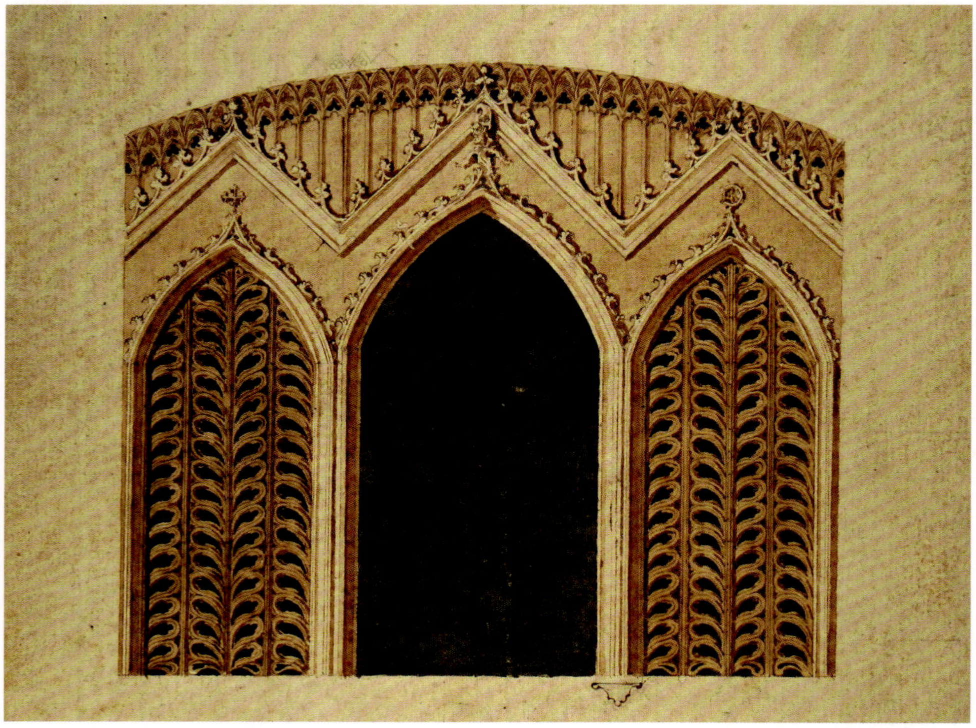

Figure 64. Richard Bentley, *Screen in the Holbein chamber at Strawberryhill*, *c.* 1750s, pen and ink with grey and brown wash on wove paper, 16.5 × 18.9 cm (visible), from *Drawings and Designs by Richd. Bentley* (*c.* 1760, fol. 55). The Lewis Walpole Library, Yale University. Folio 49 3585 fol.55. Cat. 113

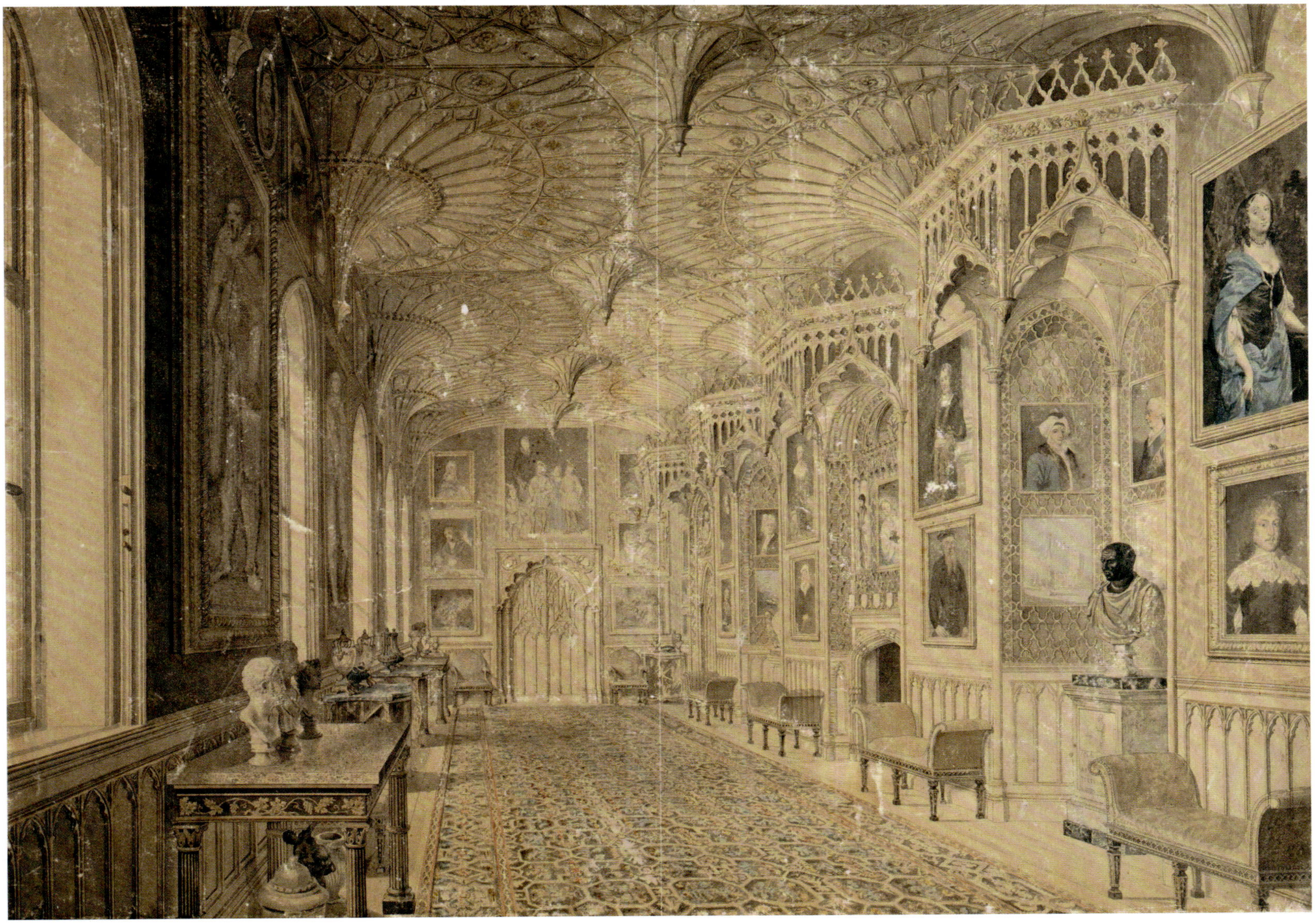

Figure 65. Thomas Sandby, Paul Sandby and Edward Edwards, *The Gallery at Strawberry Hill*, *c.* 1765(?)–1781, watercolour, 57.7 × 78.7 cm. Victoria and Albert Museum, London. Bequeathed by W.A. Sandby. D.1837-1904. Cat. 131

chairs give the darkest shade, while the white fretted cieling & a sprinkling of gold on the frames afford the lights; as the painted glass darkens part of the windows & heightens the landscapes to which they look.'[87]

THE STATE APARTMENT

Walpole announced the creation of a new State Apartment in July 1759 before the Holbein Chamber was completed, writing to Horace Mann that he was 'going to make great additions to my castle; a gallery, a round tower, and a cabinet, that is to have all the air of a Catholic chapel – bar consecration!'[88] The Apartment, consisting of the Gallery and a room in the tower (first conceived as a state bedchamber but made as a drawing room), and ultimately completed with another state bedchamber, provided the large formal rooms for entertaining that the house had lacked. It represented a marked change both in terms of scale and design approach. As before, many of the decorative elements were quotations from medieval buildings, but of an unprecedented size and seriousness, including the spectacular plaster and papier-mâché fan vaulting of the Gallery, taken from the side aisle of Henry VII's Chapel at Westminster Abbey, and the ceiling of the Round Drawing Room, adapted (by Robert Adam) from the Rose Window at Old St Paul's Cathedral.[89] But the overall approach to the decoration of the rooms, including the textile-hung walls (crimson worsted damask in the Gallery and Round

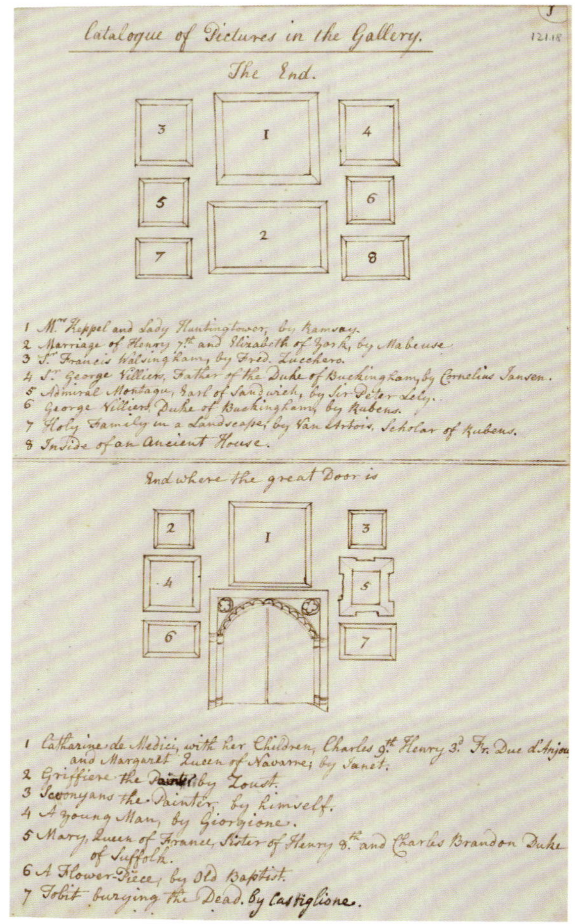

Figure 66. *Diagram of the Picture Hang in the Gallery at Strawberry Hill: 'Chimneyside'*, 1774, annotated by Walpole, pen and ink, 31 × 36 cm (approx., foldout), mounted in a copy of the *Description*, 121.19. The Lewis Walpole Library, Yale University. 49 2523. Cat. 133

Drawing Room and 'a deep rose colour' silk damask in the Bedchamber), the liberal use of gilding and the basic shapes of much of the furniture, not only marked a shift from the treatment of the earlier rooms but took its character from contemporary state rooms in the classical style.[90] The room arrangement, too, was modern, the Gallery and Round Room beyond it being the only example of axial planning in a house otherwise full of dark corners and dog-leg passages. The new state rooms crucially allowed Walpole to display, for the first time at Strawberry Hill, a substantial number of large paintings, pieces of furniture and other artefacts;[91] but, as the Fitzwilliam manuscript makes clear, even though the rooms were unified by the colours of the wall hangings, each was furnished and decorated in a slightly different way.

Thomas Gray's well-known summation of the Gallery as 'all Gothicism, gold and looking glass'[92] concealed the great showroom's complex ancestry (Fig. 65). In choosing to build a Gallery, rather than the more usual saloon or drawing room, Walpole sought not only to evoke an Elizabethan and Jacobean long gallery but also to allude to the great galleries of French and Italian Baroque palaces. Its design was directly inspired by the gallery of the Petit Château at Chantilly, which had mirrors facing the windows like its much larger counterpart, the Galerie des Glaces at Versailles, as well as by a barrel-vaulted ceiling like that in Bentley's first design, rejected because it was too low to house all the pictures (Fig. 333). In fact, the treatment of the mirror glass at Strawberry Hill, with its intricate reticulated tracery, took rather more from the German Baroque *Spiegelkabinett* than it did from the Galerie des Glaces. As in a *Spiegelkabinett*, the angled glass panels not only enhanced daylight and candlelight but also multiplied the works of art and the reflections of the viewer. The furniture in the Gallery also recalled continental European examples as well as contemporary British counterparts. Lightly Gothicized settees (Fig. 336), chairs and long stools, all covered to match the walls, were balanced by two monumental tables derived 'from a tomb at Westminster Abbey' and a pair of commodes in the Rococo style (with matching corner cabinets) made up from panels of Chinese lacquer (Fig. 67). The colours of the furniture were carefully harmonized with the walls against which they were seen: 'In the gallery, as there is a high

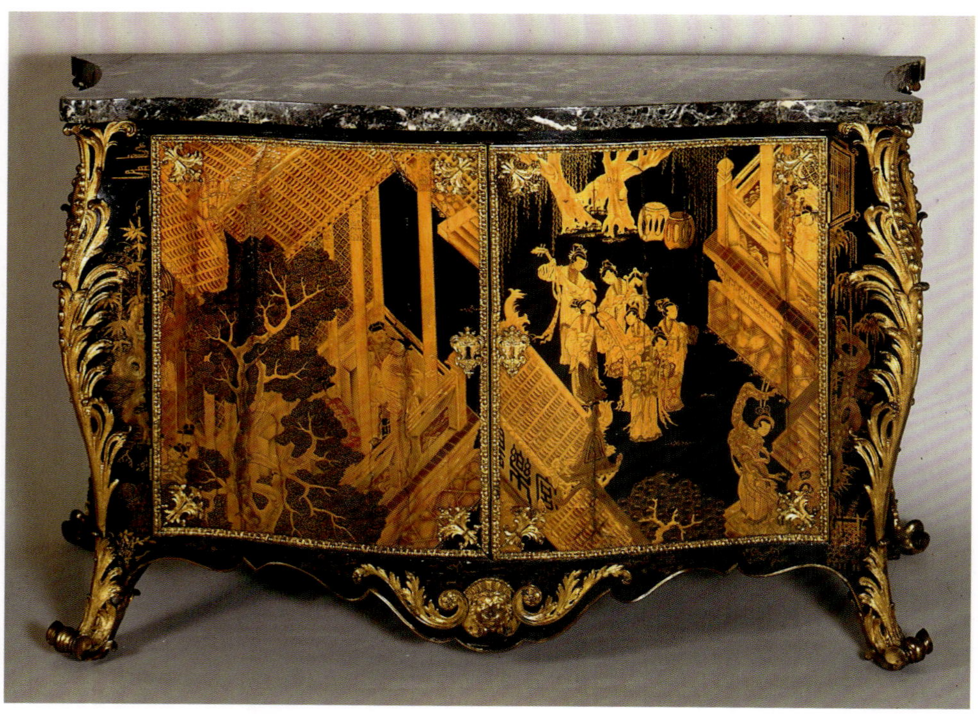

Figure 67. Pierre Eloy Langlois, *Commode*, 1763, Chinese lacquer, English japanning, softwood substrate with secondary oak, interior veneered with satinwood and Brazilian rosewood, ormolu mounts, verde antico marble veneer top, 88.6 × 148 × 59.7 cm. Fine Arts Museums of San Francisco, Gift of Mrs. William P. Roth, 1985.58a-b. Cat. 136

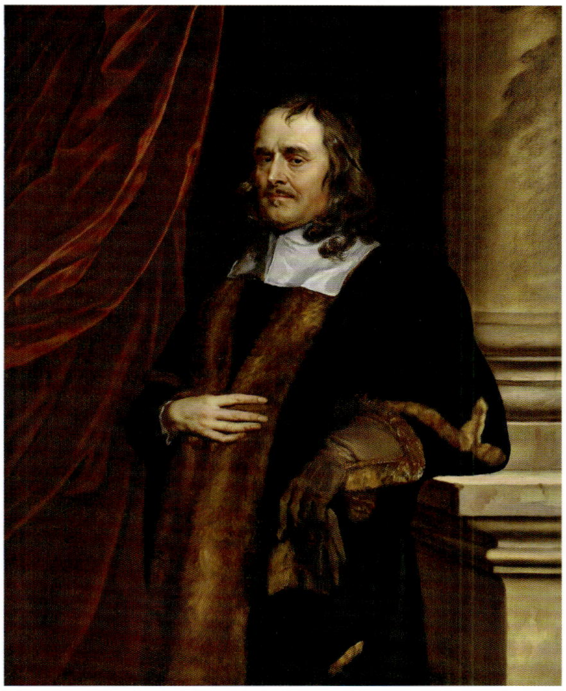

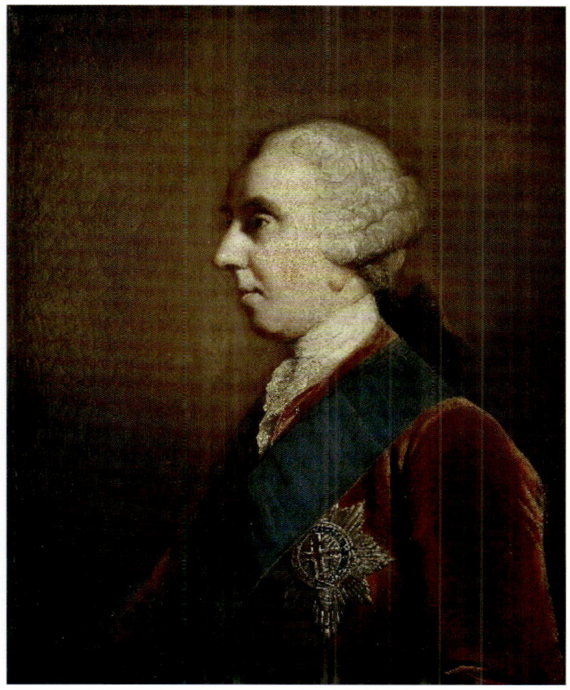

Figure 68. Sir Peter Lely, *Portrait of P. Leneve, Alderman of Norwich*, 1656–8, oil on canvas, 123.5 × 101.5 cm. The Walters Art Museum, Baltimore, Maryland. 37.231. Cat. 137

Figure 69. Sir Joshua Reynolds, *Portrait of James, 2nd Earl of Waldegrave*, 1760–61, oil on canvas, 76 × 63.5 cm. Trustees of the Waldegrave Chattels Trust. Cat. 139

Figure 70. Studio of François Clouet, *Portrait of Catherine de Medici and her Children*, 1561, oil on canvas, 198.1 × 137.2 cm. Private collection. Cat. 142

Figure 71. Allan Ramsay, *Portrait of Mrs Laura Keppel (c. 1734–1814) and her Sister Charlotte, Lady Huntingtower (1738–89)*, 1765, oil on canvas, 156.2 × 137.2 cm. Museum of Fine Arts, Boston. Bequest of Eleanor B. Winthrop in memory of Nathaniel T. Winthrop. 2009.2783. Cat. 144

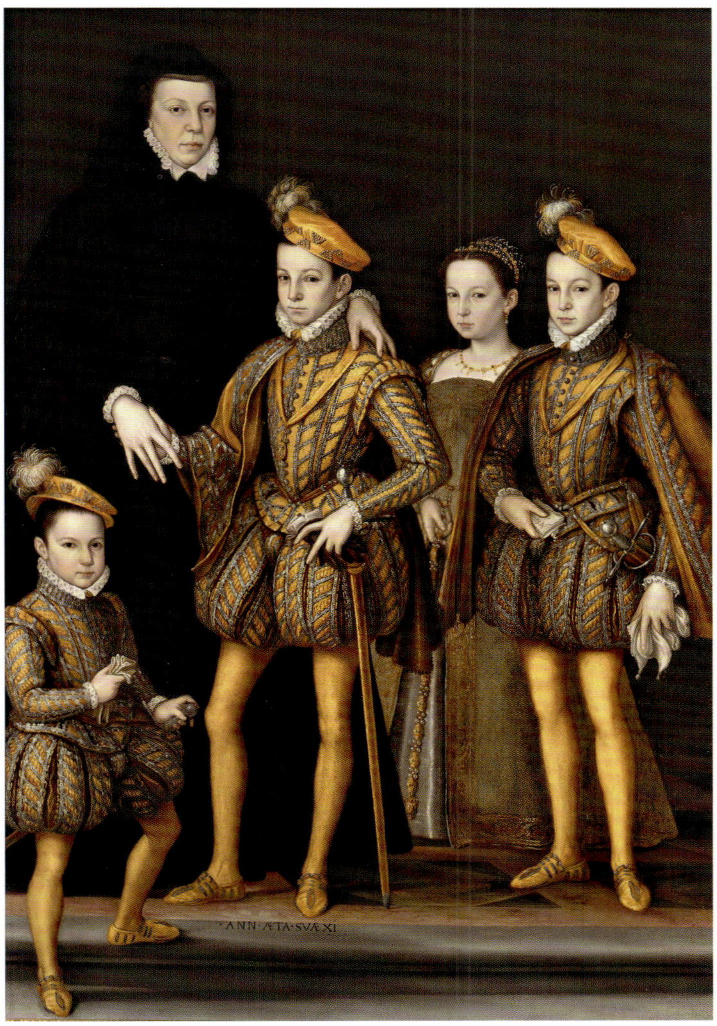

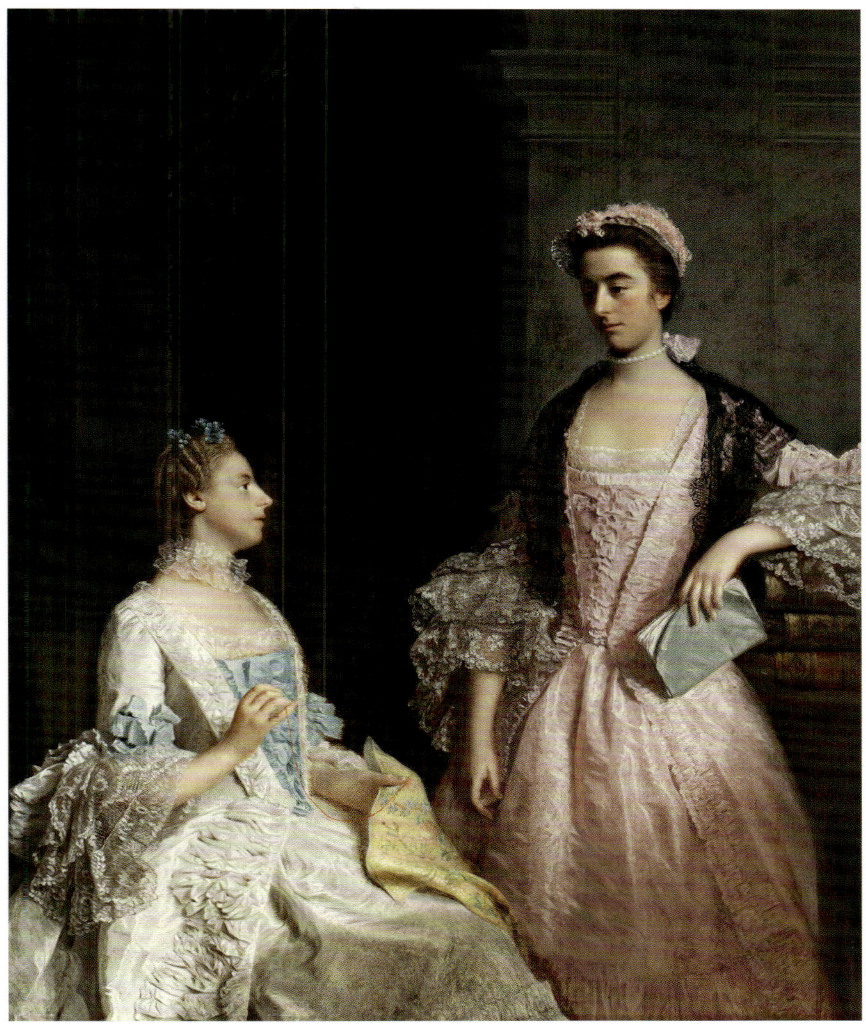

surbase of white & gold, the chairs & settees, tho crimson like the hangings, have frames of black & gold, as have the tables.'[93] Walpole brought into the Gallery his finest classical marbles, bronzes and Renaissance maiolica (Fig. 335), shown on or under the tables and on the commodes as they would have been in the gallery of an Italian palazzo. On altars in the two mirrored niches were displayed his greatest classical pieces, the eagle and the bust of Vespasian.

But the main function of the Gallery was to show pictures (Fig. 66). Although nearly all were portraits, they were arranged to fulfil a number of purposes. Unlike most of the picture displays discussed so far, the choices seem to have been dictated at least as much by artistic quality or period resonance as by subject. The darker window wall was dominated by Jacobean full-length portraits, presumably to reinforce the notion of a traditional long gallery. Above these, smaller portraits of seventeenth-century artists and poets alternated with those of Walpole's contemporaries. Most of the best pictures were on the light north wall facing the windows and were dominated by large portraits by (or believed to be by) Lely, Van Dyck and Anthonis Mor (Figs. 68, 155). The pictures in the mirrored niches, by contrast, were modern. They included pastel portraits by Rosalba Carriera and Jean-Étienne Liotard and oils by Reynolds (Fig. 69), but also a set of views and sea pieces by Samuel Scott, an artist actively promoted by Walpole. Set into the mirrored overmantel was a copy of the celebrated *Madonna and Child* that Walpole obtained for his father while on the Grand Tour, in the belief that it was by Domenichino (Fig. 8).[94] The western end wall, leading into the Round Room, continued the artists' portraits, but was dominated by a large picture of Catherine de' Medici and her children (Fig. 70). The eastern end wall had the most heterogeneous group, recalling Walpole's dictum in the Fitzwilliam manuscript: 'In hanging pictures, opposition makes harmony. Histories should be mixed with Landscapes or heads; & the two latter shd be mixed. Sizes too.'[95]Above *The marriage of Henry VII* was placed a great double portrait by Allan Ramsay (Figs. 32, 71). They were flanked by sixteenth- and seventeenth-century pictures, including an interior and a sacred landscape (Cat. 143).

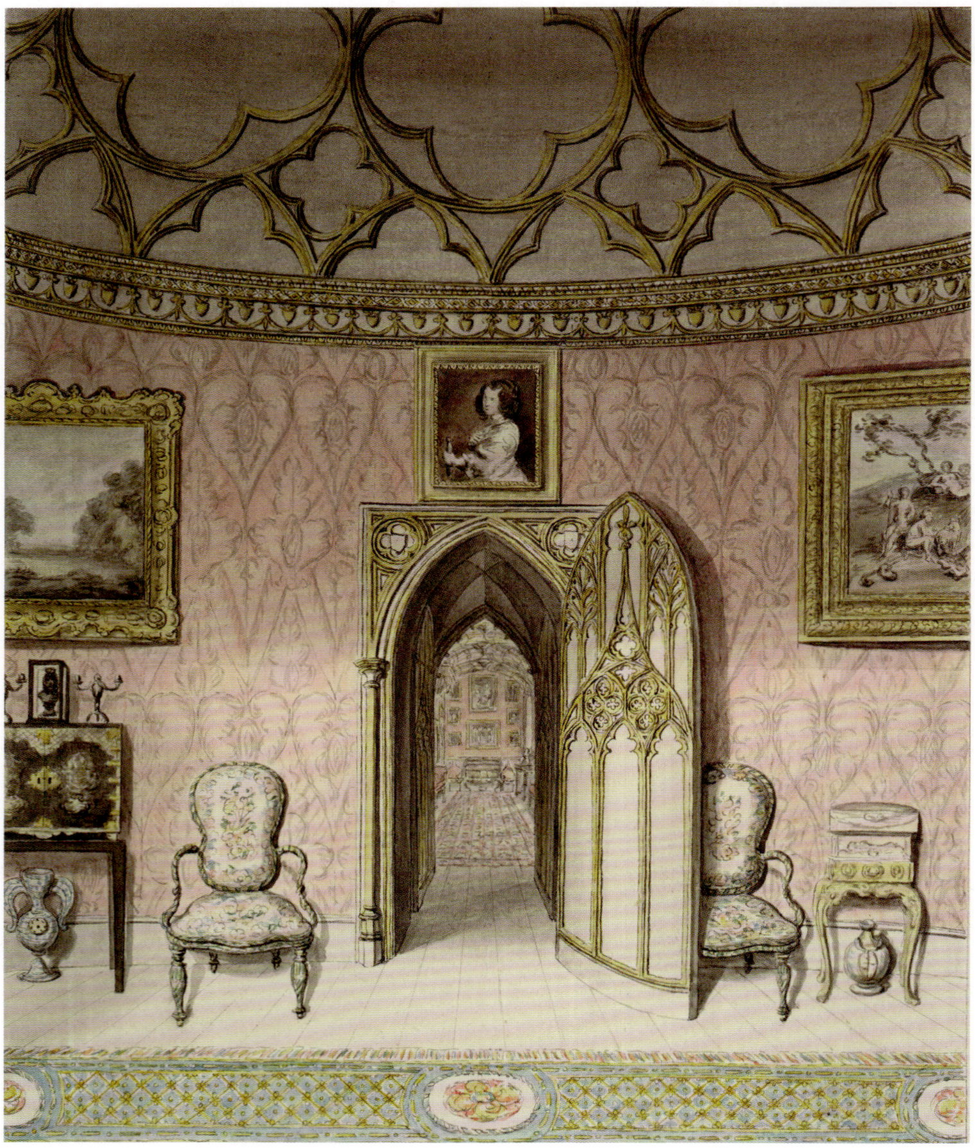

Figure 72. John Carter, *The Round Drawing Room*, n.d., watercolour, 34 × 29.5 cm, from Richard Bull's extra-illustrated copy of the *Description*. The Lewis Walpole Library, Yale University. Folio 33 30 Copy 11, fol. 153

THE ROUND DRAWING ROOM AND THE GREAT NORTH BEDCHAMBER

In its first projected form, as a state bedchamber, the Round Room was intended to contain a Gothic bed, for which designs were produced by both John Chute and probably by Robert Adam, and it was to be attached to the room's south wall in the manner of a canopied Turkish sofa.[96] When completed five years later as a drawing room, it had become subtly differentiated from the Gallery, from which it was viewed through a dark passage that would have made it appear more distant: 'The round room with its great bow-window of painted glass terminates the Gallery to great advantage by the perspective & colours, & has more effect than the same window would have if in the gallery, by

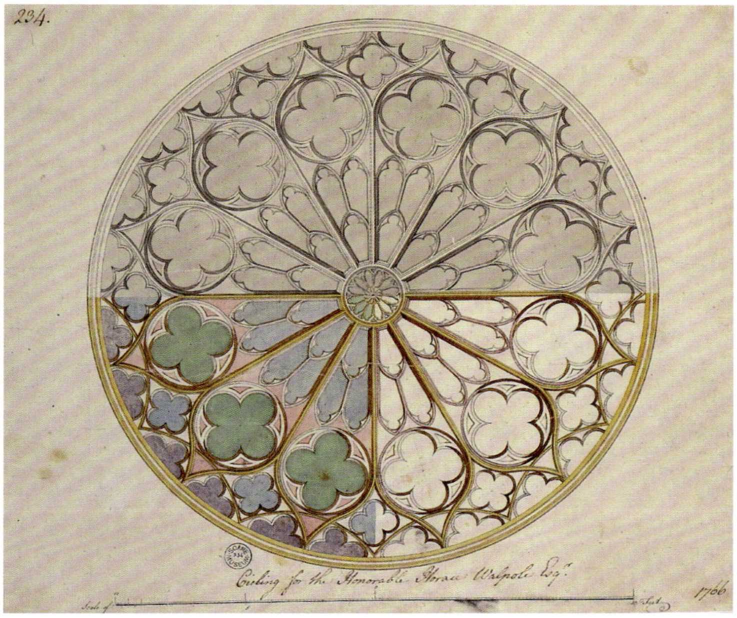

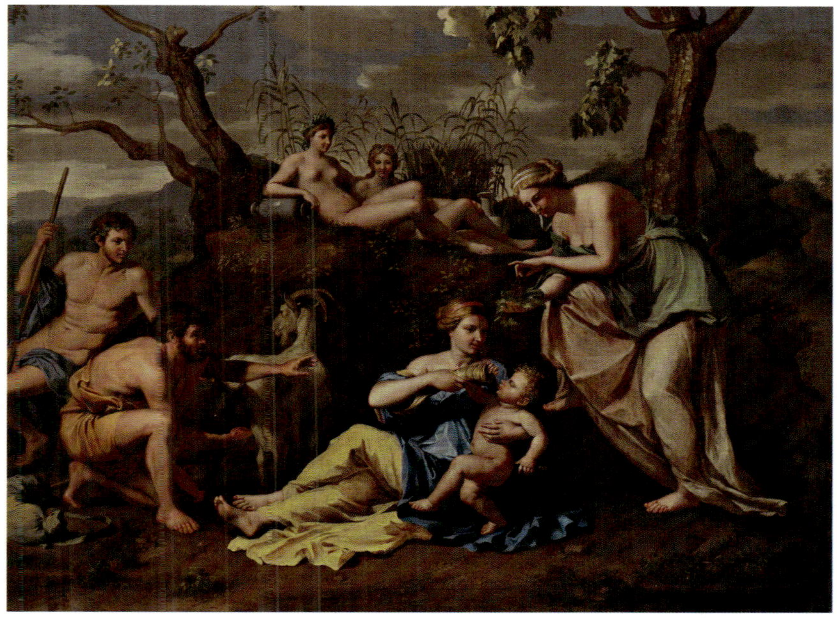

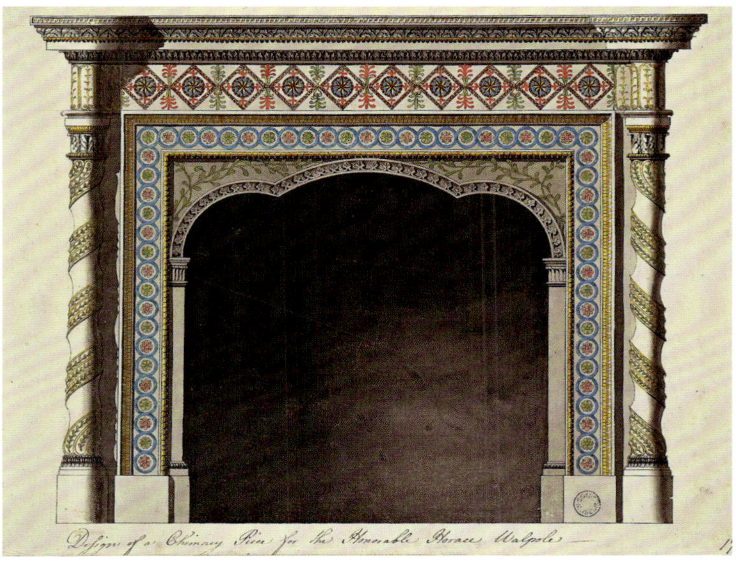

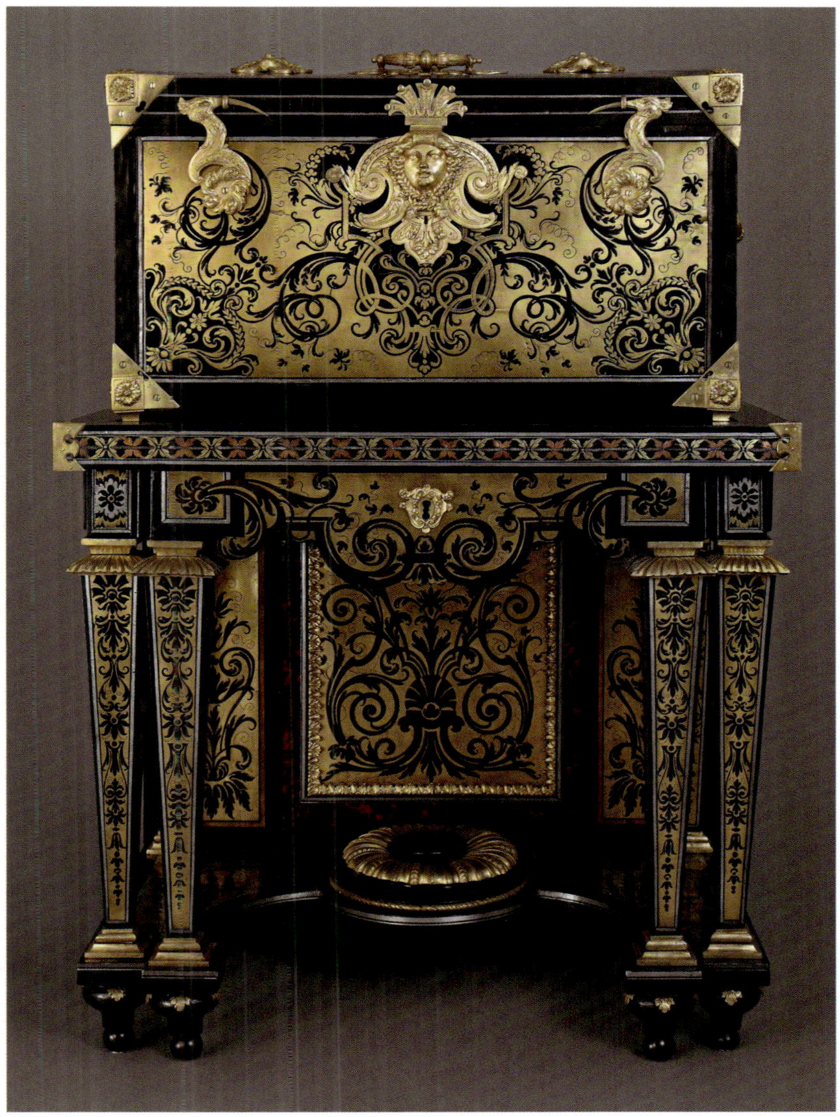

Figure 73. Robert Adam, *Design for the ceiling of the Round Drawing Room*, 1766, pencil, ink on paper, 32.6 × 37.8 cm. By courtesy of the Trustees of Sir John Soane's Museum, London, vol. 11:234. Cat. 145

Figure 74. Robert Adam, *Design for the chimneypiece in the Round Drawing Room at Horace Walpole's House*, 1767, pencil, ink and watercolour, 29.1 × 40.5 cm. By courtesy of the Trustees of Sir John Soane's Museum, London, vol. 22:229. Cat. 146

Figure 75. Follower of Nicolas Poussin, *The Feeding of the Child Jupiter*, *c.* 1640, oil on canvas, 117.4 × 155.3 cm. National Gallery of Art, Washington, D.C., Samuel H. Kress Collection. 1952.2.21. Cat. 150

Figure 76. Attributed to André-Charles Boulle, Coffer on Stand, *c.* 1710, tortoiseshell, pewter, copper, ormolu, coffer: 68.6 × 44.5 × 40.7 cm; stand: 83.8 × 71.2 cm. The Lewis Walpole Library, Yale University. 3C. Cat. 147

THIS PAGE

Figure 77. John Carter, *The Great North Bedchamber at Strawberry Hill*, *c.* 1788, watercolour, 23 × 29 cm, from Richard Bull's extra-illustrated copy of the *Description*. The Lewis Walpole Library, Yale University. Folio 33 30 Copy 11, fol. 204

FACING PAGE

Figure 79. Attributed to Nicolaes de Grebber, Nautilus Cup, 1592, silver-gilt, nautilus shell, glass and enamel, 26.5 × 19.6 × 9.9 cm. Stedelijk Museum het Prinsenhof, Delft. PDZ 3. Cat. 153

Figure 80. Roger Flynt, Spice Plate from set of 12 with Passages from the Life of the Prodigal Son, 1568–9, silver, parcel gilt and engraved, D 19.1 cm. Trustees of the Ninth Duke of Buccleuch's Chattels Fund. Cat. 156

Figure 81. John Carter, *The Tribune at Strawberry Hill*, *c.* 1789, watercolour, 59.2 × 49.5 cm. The Lewis Walpole Library, Yale University. 789.00.00.73dr++

leaving some room for expectation.'[97] But for all the impact of Robert Adam's Gothic ceiling and the window, the room's overall decoration was markedly more modern in character than that of the Gallery (Fig. 72). The crimson damask walls were set against a unified scheme of pink, green, blue, white and gold, found in the Moorfields carpet (its design adapted from a painted Sèvres table top), the upholstered chairs and sofas in a transitional neo-classical style, and the scagliola chimneypiece, which was adapted from the tomb of Edward the Confessor at Westminster Abbey, but 'improved by Mr Adam'. Adam's two designs for the chimneypiece show the emergence of a neo-classical interpretation that Walpole welcomed on grounds of cost as well as appearance (Fig. 74).[98] The approach to the contents was also different: 'The pictures in it are few & in large spaces but fine, & give an air of repose & grandeur which many pictures destroy. The Gallery is for the pictures, but the pictures in the round room serve as furniture.'[99] They included most of the best old-master subject pictures, and a fine Boulle coffer on stand (Figs. 75, 76), with a touch of ancient splendour being conveyed by the Baroque silver fire furniture, chimneypiece, wall sconces and candlesticks, all matching and enhancing a Van Dyck female double portrait over the mantelpiece.[100]

The new state bedchamber, built in an awkward position over the servants' hall, was already being created when the decoration of the Round Drawing Room was being finished in 1771. Like the other state rooms, it was a combination of the ancient and the modern. By 1774 it had been christened the Great North Bedchamber, as a conscious evocation of such rooms in ancient great houses, with their mixture of older architecture and later, often Baroque, furnishings (Fig. 77). Unlike most such rooms, its architectural details were Gothic, but like them it was filled with textiles, albeit mostly modern, floral Aubusson ones specially acquired in Paris for the purpose, as well as curtains (the only ones in the house) matching the silk walls and drawn up in the latest fashion.[101] The ceiling, however, was of early sixteenth-century type, copied from that in the North Bedchamber at the Vyne, John Chute's country house. The chimneypiece, 'designed by Mr Walpole' and perhaps the most serious piece of Gothic in the house, was copied from the tomb of William Dudley, Bishop of Durham, in Westminster Abbey (Fig. 78). It was carved out of Portland stone by Thomas Gayfere, the mason of the Abbey, and elegantly enhanced with gilding.

Other objects served to reinforce the impression of the sixteenth and seventeenth century, including Indian ebony furniture and the contents of

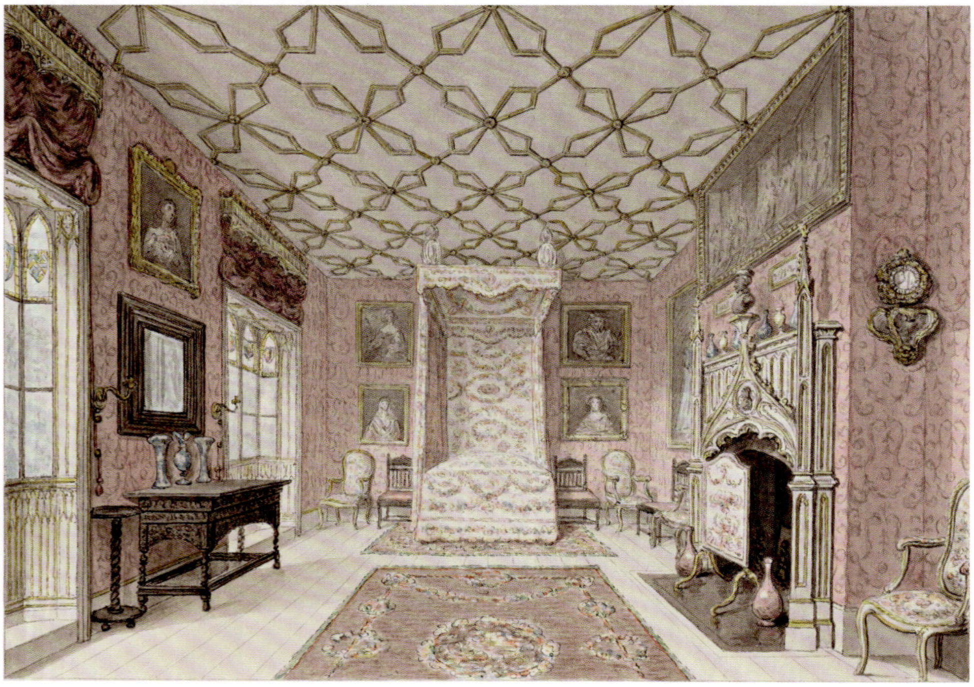

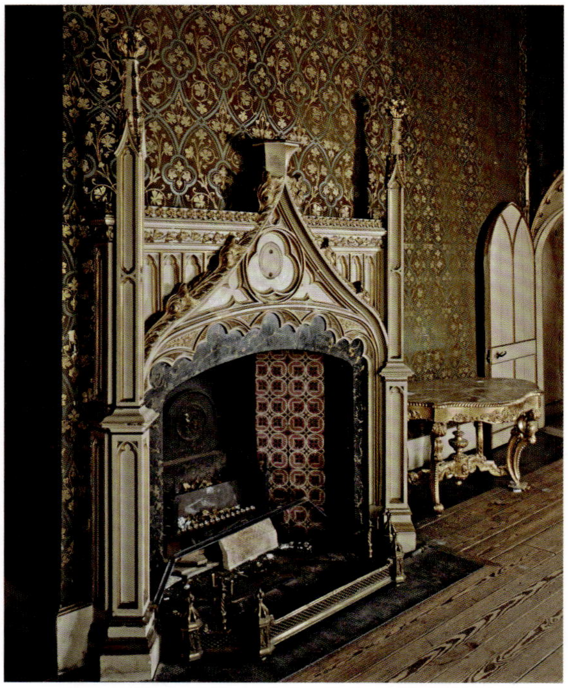

the Glass Closet in the corner, which contained, in addition to much maiolica, Dr Dee's Mirror, the gloves of James I, Admiral Tromp's pipe case, the Earl of Pembroke's billiard sticks and a spectacular set of sixteenth-century silver plates (Figs. 79, 80, 117, 125). The same was true of the paintings. Their arrangement, which had caused Walpole some difficulty, was resolved in 1785, when he wrote to Lady Ossory:

> It is really a very royal chamber now and much improved. Besides the family of Henry VIII over the chimney as before, and Queen Maintenon over one of the doors, there are Henry VII and Catherine of Braganza on one side of the bed; Henry VIII and Henriette Duchess of Orléans on the other.[102]

The picture hang was to a substantial extent a continuation of the story begun in the Holbein Chamber. Henry VIII and his children dominated the chimney wall, making a dynastic link with the bust of Francis II of France, husband of Mary Queen of Scots, on the chimneypiece below. His label, painted on the stone in Latin, matched an (English) inscription on the frame of the picture above (Fig. 149). The French royal family, including the court of Louis XIV (one of Walpole's passions), almost outnumbered the English.

THE CHAPEL, CABINET OR TRIBUNE

The names Walpole gave to his main chamber for his art treasures betrayed its multivalent nature: first a cabinet, next a chapel, then both together and finally, by 1781, the Tribune, after the Medici treasure room in the Uffizi in Florence. It was reached via a side door off the Gallery and a pierced or 'grated' inner door: 'The Chapel has the true air of a place of devotion, & that impression makes it please, tho seen after so much larger spaces. The number of curiosities in it takes up the attention, & seem to be the completion of the collection.'[103] In terms of design, it was one of the most complex and interesting rooms at Strawberry hill. The first scheme by Richard Bentley, for a different position in the house, was for a cruciform space in strongly attenuated Gothic (Fig. 115).[104] Bentley's second scheme and John Chute's many sketch designs for the room as built show them working out the complexities of the vaulting and decorative details on a ground plan of a square with semicircular additions on all four sides (Fig. 114).

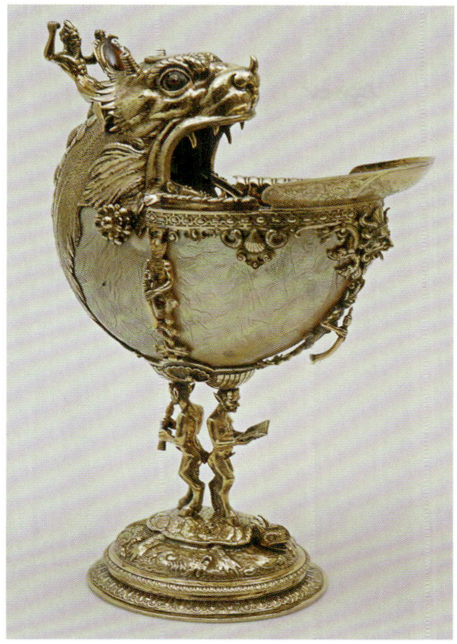

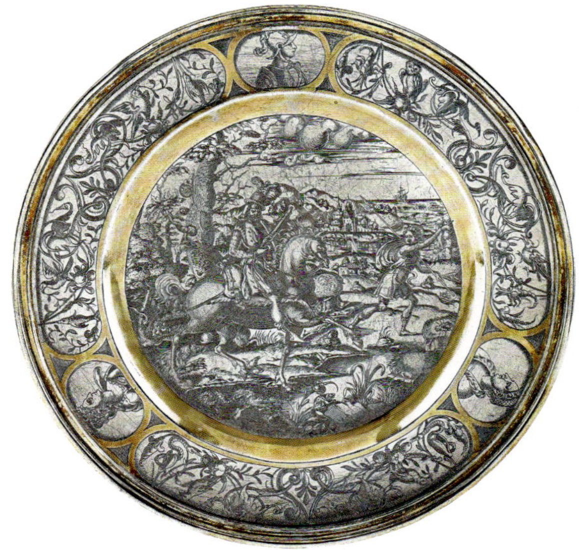

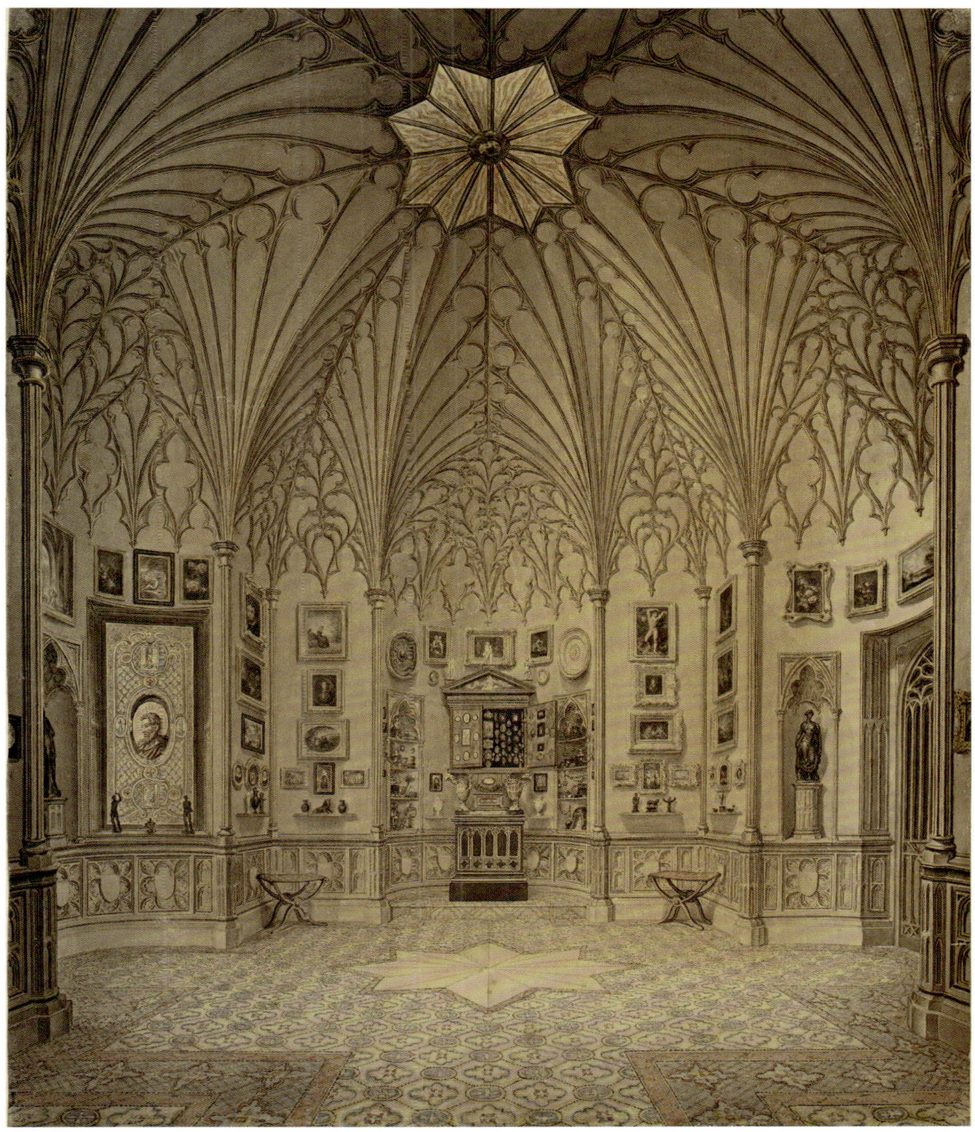

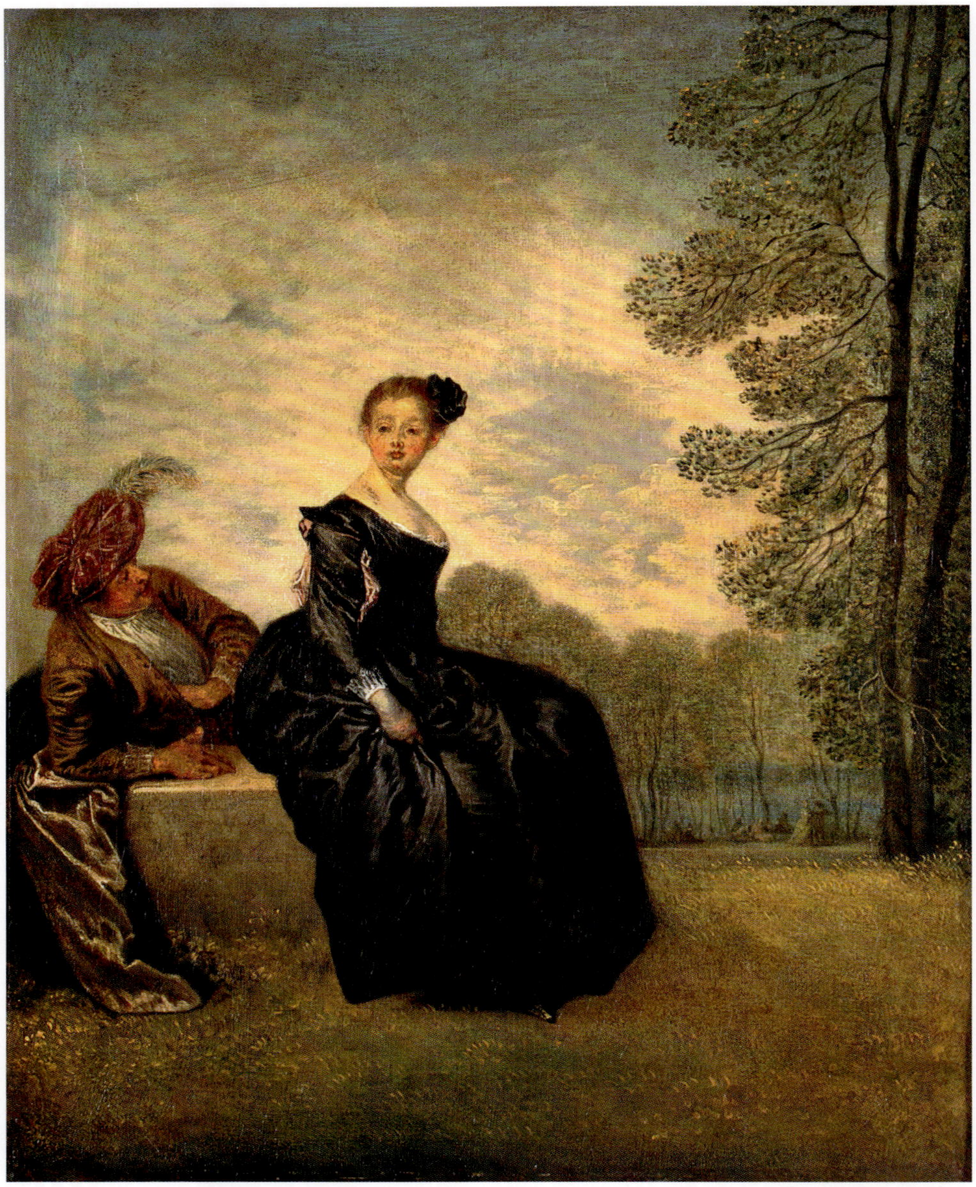

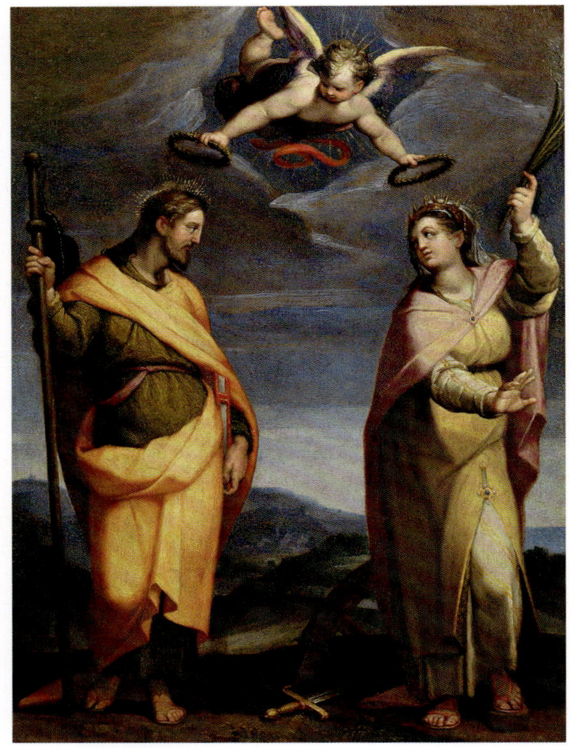

Figure 82. Jean-Antoine Watteau, *La Boudeuse (The Capricious Girl)*, *c.* 1717–18, oil on canvas, 42 × 34 cm. The State Hermitage Museum, St Petersburg. 4120. Cat. 192

Figure 83. Orazio Samacchini, *St Catherine of Alexandria and St James Major*, mid- to late 1560s, paint on white metal, 21.4 × 16 cm. Culture and Sport Glasgow (Museums). Bequeathed by Archibald McLellan, 1854. 164. Cat. 194

This was a Renaissance or Baroque form, used for domed bath houses, top-lit garden grottoes and also, interestingly, for Louis XIV's treasure cabinet at Versailles, which was separated from the State Apartment in a similar manner. But at Strawberry Hill the vault was Gothic, as were all the details except for the rectangular windows.[105]

Walpole's view of the room's intended atmosphere ('all the air of Catholic chapel – bar consecration') was borne out in practice: for all the 'gaudiness that was a little profane', it had 'all the glory of Popery' (Fig. 81).[106] This effect was mainly achieved by an almost Baroque handling of colour and light set against the stone-coloured roof and walls picked out in gold. In the centre of the vault a glass star painted with wavy rays like a medieval ceiling boss gave the room a 'golden gloom', while the windows were entirely filled with coloured glass. But the glass could also be removed, allowing the room to be lit through ordinary sashes. The 'grated door', painted brown to imitate bronze, functioned like the metal screen of a Catholic side chapel, allowing the treasures to be viewed but keeping the sacred space secure. As Walpole made clear in his final name for the room, the Tribune (like the original in the Uffizi) contained his finest things, but even then some of these were disposed to match the chapel theme. Facing the grated door was the *modello* for his beloved mother's cenotaph in Westminster Abbey. The subjects of the window glass were largely sacred, while on the east wall the pedimented cabinet of miniatures and enamels was placed like a triptych (as Rowlandson later spotted; see Fig. 279) above a black and gold 'altar' on a step. In the glazed niches (or 'glass-cases') on either side the cream of the collection, like so many sacred relics, was displayed. But in other respects the room's contents and their disposition reflected *Kuntskammern* of the type developed by the end of

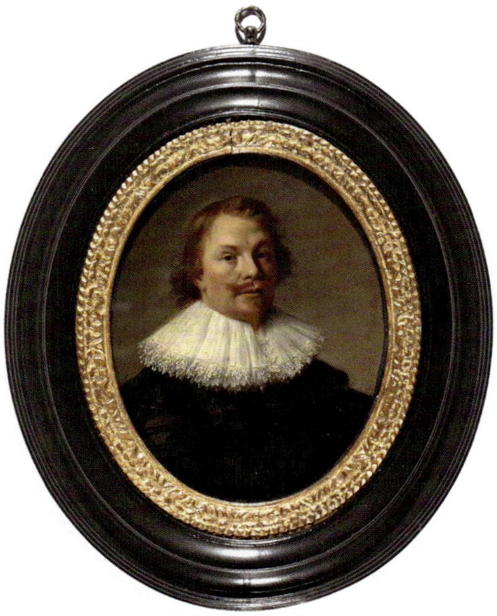

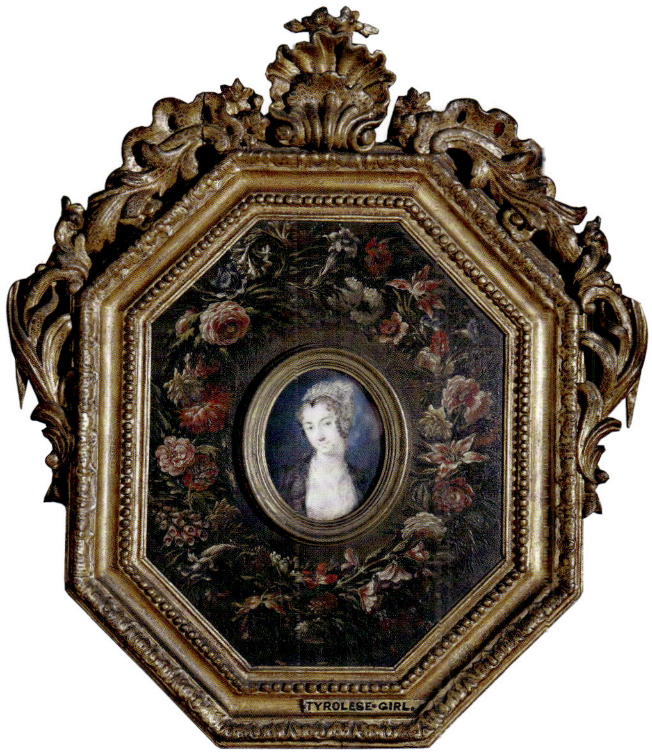

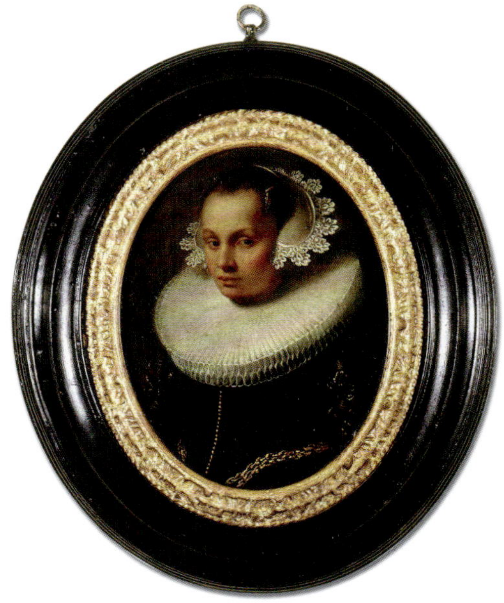

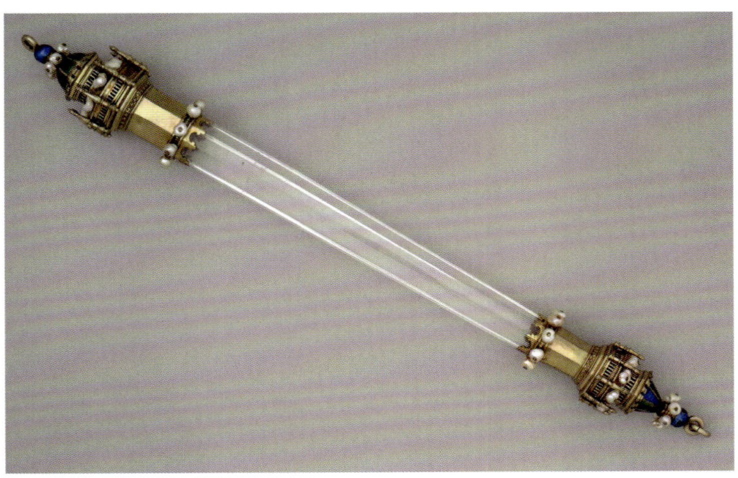

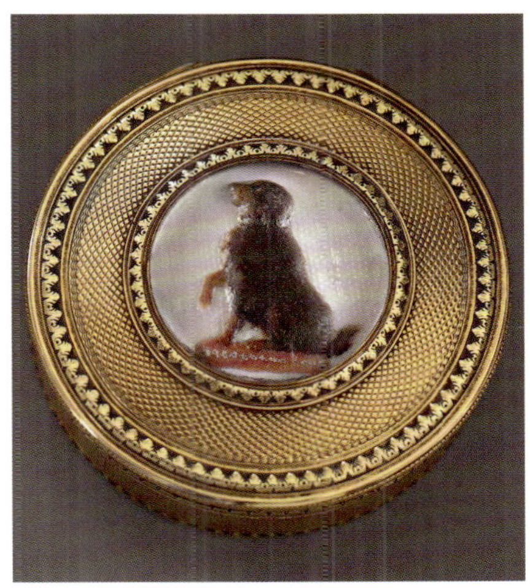

Figure 84. Artist unknown, *An Unknown Man, possibly Cornelis van Poelenburgh*, *c.* 1630, oil on copper, 22 × 18.5 cm. Victoria and Albert Museum, London. Given by Mr. W.A.J. Floersheim. P.105-1931. Cat. 195

Figure 85. Marianna Carlevarijs after Rosalba Carriera, *The Tyrolean Girl*, the surround by Philippo Laura. *c.* 1730, miniature watercolour on ivory set into oil on copper, 22.9 × 17.8 cm. The Rt Hon. the Earl of Derby, K231. Cat. 197

Figure 86. Artist unknown, *An Unknown Woman (Cornelis van Poelenburgh's Wife)*, 1631, oil on copper, 14.6 × 11.5 cm. Victoria and Albert Museum, London. Given by Mr. W.A.J. Floersheim. P.104-1931. Cat. 196

Figure 87. Baton, Italian, 1426–75, Rock crystal, mounted in silver gilt, enamelled with pearls, L 27 cm. British Museum, Department of Prehistory and Europe. 1923,1205.8. Cat. 161

Figure 88. Louis Roucel and Isaac Gosset, Snuff Box with a Portrait of Walpole's dog Tonton, *c.* 1777, silver gilt over brass with the portrait in wax, D 7 cm. The Lewis Walpole Library, Yale University. Cat. 169

seventeenth century. Small seventeenth- and eighteenth-century cabinet pictures filled the walls (Figs. 82–6), matched by ancient bronzes and modern copies of famous ancient works on narrow shelves and in the niches (as they also did in the Florentine Tribuna).[107] The objects crammed onto the shelves of each glazed niche were a startlingly heterogeneous mix, including classical rings, 'a model of the shrine of Thomas a Becket, enamelled' (Fig. 151), the missal of 'Queen Claude of France' (Fig. 34), 'Henry VIII's dagger' (Fig. 253), the 'Cellini Bell' and 'a point cravat carved by Gibbons' in limewood (Fig. 116), but also Chelsea porcelain (Fig. 334) and a toothpick case in enamelled gold given by Lady Diana Beauclerk (Fig. 152).

THE BEAUCLERK CLOSET

The Beauclerk Closet was the last room to be made at Strawberry Hill. Its decoration and contents exemplify the great steps that had been taken from the stony rooms of the early house. An elegant retreat off the great rooms of the State Apartment, the closet – by the scholarly architect James Essex, who also designed at the same time the garden gateway and the New Offices – resembled a contemporary French boudoir translated into a Gothic free from quotations.[108] The colour scheme combined blue Chinese silk walls with off-white woodwork picked out in gold and was lit by painted glass and two modern, French, lily-shaped sconces. It was shown to very few, not only because of its tiny size but also because it was mainly created to display Lady Diana's Beauclerk's seven illustrations to Walpole's verse tragedy *The Mysterious Mother*, which dealt with incest (Fig. 171). The text of the play was kept in an elegant papier-mâché table decorated by Paul Sandby. In fact, the room served as a shrine to amateur genius, one of Walpole's main causes late in life, most of the other pictures and drawings reflecting the creative efforts of Walpole's cousin Henry Seymour Conway, his daughter Anne Damer and John Chute.

CONCLUSION

Only one image survives of Walpole in Strawberry Hill (frontispiece). Drawn by Johann Heinrich Müntz at about the same time as the portraits by Reynolds and Eccardt, it shows him in the newly built Library, then the most important room of the house. It is at least as much a record of the room as of its owner. The strong sun of a summer morning slants into the Gothic space, illuminating the intricately pierced woodwork and the plain planked floor. In deep shadow are the great folios of old-master and portrait prints, and in the peaks of the bookcases, the Gothic press letters, painted by Müntz himself. But the main focus is on the window. Filled at the top with painted glass, it concentrates and frames the prospect of the river and Richmond Hill as if it was a painted landscape. This is the contrasted inside-outside world of Strawberry Hill that so delighted Walpole. But what of Walpole himself? For all the carefully recorded scholarly apparatus that surrounds him, he is shown at his gentlemanly ease and without pen in hand. Does the open book on the floor signify the dilettante or the busy checker of facts? We cannot know, but the former seems the more likely, for Walpole, like his creation Strawberry Hill, was always at pains to conceal his seriousness beneath a casual mask. But the other life of Strawberry Hill has intruded, as his dog waits to be taken out into the sunny garden.

Acknowledgements
For the discussion of the architecture and interiors of Strawberry Hill I am greatly indebted to Peter Inskip, Stephen Gee and Kevin Rogers, of Peter Inskip + Peter Jenkins Architects, whose research and investigations for the restoration of the building have hugely advanced the understanding of the physical nature and practical functioning of Strawberry Hill. I am also very grateful to Susan Walker of the Lewis Walpole Library for drawing my attention to the Fitzwilliam manuscript.

1. *HW Corres.* 37: 269 (HW to Conway, 8 June 1747).
2. *Works* 2: 398.
3. *HW Corres.* 19: 414 (HW to Mann, 5 June 1747).
4. *HW Corres.* 10: 127 (HW to Montagu, 18 June 1764); *HW Corres.* 20: 111 (HW to Mann, 10 June 1750); *HW Corres.* 9: 149 (HW to Montagu, 11 June 1753).
5. See W.S. Lewis, 'The Genesis of Strawberry Hill', *Metropolitan Museum Studies* V (1934): 57–92; PhD thesis (University of Toronto, 1986); Norbert Miller, *Strawberry Hill: Horace Walpole und die Ästhetik der schönen Unregelmässigkeit* (Munich: Hansen, 1986); Michael McCarthy, *The Origins of the Gothic Revival* (New Haven and London: Yale University Press, 1987), 63–88; Peter Guillery and Michael Snodin, 'Strawberry Hill: Building and Site', *Architectural History* 38 (1995): 102–28; John Wilton-Ely, '"Gingerbread and sippets of embroidery": Horace Walpole and Robert Adam', *Eighteenth-Century Life* 25, no. 2 (Spring 2001): 147–69; John Cornforth, *Early Georgian Interiors* (New Haven and London: Yale University Press, 2004), 232–4.
6. See [London]: Georgian Group [1983]; McCarthy, *Origins*, London: Phaidon, 1994); Leeds: Maney in association with the Society of Antiquaries of London, 1995; Chris Brooks, *The Gothic Revival* (London: Phaidon Press, 1999); Marion Tuting, *Rokoko Gothik. Ein Phänomen des englischen 'Gothic Revival' im 18. Jahrhundert* (Hildesheim: Olms, 2004); Cornforth, *Early Georgian Interiors*, 217–36.
7. Nathan Bayley, *Dictionarium Britannicum* (2nd ed., London, 1736); *HW Corres.* 21: 250 (HW to Mann, 24 Oct. 1758).
8. Frederick W. Hilles and Philip B. Daghlian, *Anecdotes of Painting in England (1760–1795) ... collected by Horace Walpole; and now digested and published from his original MSS* (New Haven: Yale University Press; London: Oxford University Press, 1937), 158–9. For Walpole's attitudes to style in architecture, see Stephen Clarke, 'Horace Walpole's architectural taste', in Peter Sabor (ed.), 'Horace Walpole: Beyond the Castle of Otranto', *1650–1850: Ideas, Aesthetics, and Inquiries in the Early Modern Era* 16 (2009): 189–362.
9. *Anecdotes* 1: 107–8.
10. Martin Postle (ed.), *Joshua Reynolds: The Creation of Celebrity* (London: Tate Publishing, 2005), 142.
11. Aileen Ribeiero, *Dress in Eighteenth-Century Europe* (New Haven and London, Yale University Press, 2002), 275–82. Karen Hearn (ed.), *Van Dyck and Britain* (London: Tate Publishing, 2009), 205–8.
12. *HW Corres.* 10: 192 (HW to Montagu, 5 Jan. 1766).
13. *HW Corres.* 20: 407 (HW to Mann, 28 Jan. 1754).
14. *Works* 2: 395, 398.
15. *Works* 2: 396.
16. It was sold to the De Stern family, and then in 1923 it was bought on behalf St Mary's College by the forerunner of the Catholic Education Service. The Walpole house and most of the formal grounds are currently leased to the Strawberry Hill Trust, which is restoring them.
17. He named it after Strawberry Hill Shot, the plot of land on which the house stood. *HW Corres.* 19: 486 (HW to Mann, 7 June 1748).
18. New Haven and London : Yale University Press, 1994) Stroud: Sutton, 1996).
19. *HW Corres.* 20: 361–2 (HW to Mann, 4 March 1753).
20. *HW Corres.* 37: 270 (HW to Conway, 8 June 1747).
21. *HW Corres.* 35: 234 (HW to Bentley, 5 July 1755).
22. *HW Corres.* 1: 367 (HW to Cole, 25 April 1775).
23. Joel-Henrietta Pye, *A Peep into the Principal Seats and Gardens in and about Twickenham (the Residence of the Muses)*
24. *HW Corres.* 35: 531 (HW to Harcourt, 5 August 1783).
25. *HW Corres.* 12: 219–74.
26. This was William Storer's 'Royal Delineator', see *HW Corres.* 28: 328–9 (HW to Mason, 21 Sept. 1777) and John H. Hammond, *The Camera Obscura: A Chronicle* (Bristol: Adam Hilger Ltd, 1981), 78–80.
27. Bamber Gascoigne and Jonathan Ditchburn, *Images of Twickenham* (Richmond-upon-Thames: Saint Helena Press, 1981), cats 252–319.
28. *HW Corres.* 20: 372 (HW to Mann, 27 April 1753).
29. 'The History of the Modern Taste in Gardening', first published in vol. IV of the *Anecdotes of Painting in England*, 1771; it is in *Works* 2: 519–45. See also Isabel Wakelin Urban Chase (ed.), *Horace Walpole: Gardenist* (Princeton: Princeton University Press, 1943); Mavis Batey, 'Horace Walpole as modern garden historian', *Garden History* 19, no. 1 (Spring 1991): 1–11; Heinz Joachim Müllenbrock, 'Horace Walpole's Place in the Historiography of the English Landscape Garden', in Sabor, 'Beyond the Castle of Otranto'.
30. *HW Corres* 20: 127 (HW to Mann, 24 Feb. 1750).
31. *HW Corres* 9: 177 (HW to Montagu, 3 Nov. 1755).
32. Mavis Batey, 'Horace Walpole as modern garden historian', *Garden History* 19, no. 1 (Spring 1991): 1–11; Mark Laird, *The Flowering of the Landscape Garden: English Pleasure Grounds 1720–1800* (Philadelphia, Pa.: University of Pennsylvania Press, 1999); Marion Harney, 'Strawberry Hill', *Architectural Review* 224, special issue, no. 1341 (Nov. 2008): 72–7.
33. Earle Havens, 'Books, Antiquity and Virtu: Horace Walpole's Antiquarian Book Collecting', in Sabor, 'Beyond the Castle of Otranto'.
34. *Works* 2: 396.
35. *Works* 2: 396.
36. *Works* 2: 396.
37. *Works* 2: 397.
38. For Downing Street see Larissa Dukelskaya and Andrew Moore, *A Capital Collection: Houghton Hall and the Hermitage* (New Haven and London: Yale University Press, 2002), 23–8.
39. *HW Corres.* 17: 213 (HW to Mann, 26 Nov. 1741).

40. *Works* 2: 397–8.
41. Clive Wainwright, *The Romantic Interior: The British Collector at Home* (New Haven and London: Yale University Press, 1989), 71–107.
42. *HW Corres.* 10: 77 (HW to Montagu, 30 May 1763).
43. Two tables and eighteen chairs were acquired at Lady Conyers' sale in 1763: see *HW Corres.* 10: 77 (HW to Montagu, 30 May 1763). See also Wainwright, *Romantic Interior*, 90–91; Clive Wainwright, 'Only the True Back Blood', *Furniture History*, XXI (1985): 250–5; Amin Jaffer, *Furniture from British India and Ceylon: A Catalogue of the Collections in the Victoria and Albert Museum and the Peabody Essex Museum* (London: V&A Publications, 2001), 130–34; Cornforth, *Early Georgian Interiors*, 234–6.
44. Wainwright, *Romantic Interior*, 97.
45. Fitzwilliam Museum, Cambridge, MS 13-1947.
46. Ibid., f. 3.
47. Ibid., f. 1.
48. Ibid., f. 1.
49. Ibid., ff. 2, 3.
50. Ibid., f. 2.
51. Ibid., ff. 3, 4.
52. Ibid., f. 3.
53. The tomb of Roger Niger, Bishop of London, in Old St Paul's Cathedral.
54. Shown in John Chute's drawings: Guillery and Snodin, 'Strawberry Hill: Building and Site', figs. 23, 24.
55. *HW Corres.* 32: 245 (HW to Lady Ossory, 3 Aug. 1775).
56. Bought from Giovanni Battista Piranesi by Charles Townley and taken to England in 1768; sold by him to Chace Price in 1773; acquired by HW at the Price sale 1778. HW seems to have been unaware of its earlier origin. Engraved as Townley's in Piranesi's *Vasi, Candelabri, Cippi, Sarcofagi, Tripodi, Lucerne ed Ornamenti Antichi* (Rome, 1778), 45. An Italian drawing of the vase and supporting altar is inscribed by Townley with its history (Victoria and Albert Museum, 9196.c).
57. *HW Corres.* 20: 372 (HW to Mann, 27 April 1753).
58. Alexander Pope, *Works* (London: W. Bowyer for Bernard Lintot, 1717).
59. Knole, in particular, includes an arcade on the first floor and shield-bearing beasts on the newels. HW and John Chute visited Knole in 1752, although HW remarked 'there is never a good staircase' (*HW Corres.* 35: 132, HW to Bentley 5 August 1752).
60. Rouen was not mentioned by HW.
61. *HW Corres.* 20: 380 (HW to Mann). See also Jacob Kainen, *John Baptist Jackson: Master of the Color Woodcut* (Washington: US Government Printing Office, 1962).
62. *HW Corres.* 11: 121 (HW to Mary Berry, 16 October 1790).
63. Cornforth, *Early Georgian Interiors*, 42.
64. Wainwright, *Romantic Interior*, 81.
65. *HW Corres.* 35: 191, 208.
66. *HW Corres.* 35: 181–2 (HW to Bentley, 27 July 1754).
67. *HW Corres.* 20: 381 (HW to Mann, 12 June 1753).
68. *HW Corres.* 33: 564 (HW to Ossory 14 June 1787).
69. Thomas, Duke of Clarence, at Canterbury Cathedral and John Eltham, Earl of Cornwall, at Westminster Abbey.
70. McCarthy, *Origins*, 81–4.
71. *HW Corres.* 20: 382 (HW to Mann, 12 June 1753).
72. For print rooms, see Cornforth, *Early Georgian Interiors*, 207. The prints could also be put onto stretchers with printed borders and hung like pictures.
73. *HW Corres.* 35: 174 (HW to Bentley 18 May 1754).
74. *HW Corres.* 35: 174 (HW to Bentley, 18 May 1754).
75. HW compares the subject with a descriptive passage from Phineas Fletcher's verse narrative, *Britain's Ida* (London, 1628): *Works* 2: 424.
76. *Works* 2: 423.
77. *Works* 2: 425.
78. *HW Corres.* 28: 196 (HW to Mason, 7 May 1775).
79. *HW Corres.* 20: 381–2 (HW to Mann, 12 June 1753).
80. *Works* 2: 452.
81. By John Michael Rysbrack (1726), now in the Victoria and Albert Museum (A.6-1988).
82. *Works* 2: 454.
83. Fitzwilliam Mueum, Cambridge, MS 13-1947, f.1.
84. See two designs by Bentley for the same bed in the Lewis Walpole Library (49.3585.b). One notes the 'alcove' as 7 ft 6 in (2.3 m) wide.
85. The Dressing Room lay between the Elizabethan long gallery and the Baroque Queen's apartment, in a relationship very similar to that of the Holbein Chamber and Gallery at Strawberry Hill. All these rooms were substantially altered when they were absorbed into the Royal Library in the nineteenth century. (Joseph Pote, *The History and Antiquities of Windsor Castle, and the Royal College, and Chapel of St George* [Eton, 1749], 49, 418–19.)
86. Wainwright, *Romantic Interior*, 301; Jean François Pommeraye, *Histoire de l'Abbaye de S. Ouen de Rouen* (Rouen, 1662), plate p.192.
87. Fitzwilliam Museum, Cambridge, MS 13-1947, f. 1.
88. *HW Corres.* 21: 306 (HW to Mann, 8 July 1759).
89. The other sources are the North Door of St Alban's Abbey (Gallery doors and canopy crestings, and Tribune niches); the tomb of Archbishop Bourchier in Canterbury Cathedral (Gallery canopies); the tomb of William Dudley, Bishop of Durham, in Westminster Abbey (Great North Bedchamber chimneypiece); the tomb of two children of Edward III, Westminster Abbey (altar in Tribune); the tomb of Queen Eleanor, Westminster Abbey (Round Drawing Room, surbase of window); and the tomb of Edward the confessor, WestminsterAbbey (Round Drawing Room chimneypiece).
90. Like Strawberry Hill, the picture gallery at Houghton was hung with crimson Norwich wool damask (Dukelskaya and Moore, *Capital Collection*, 43).
91. Presumably brought from London.
92. Letter from Gray to Wharton, 5 Aug. 1763 (Duncan C. Tovey, *Letters of Thomas Gray* [London: G. Bell & Sons, 1912], 15–16).
93. Fitzwilliam Museum, Cambridge, MS 13-1947, f. 3.
94. Dukelskaya and Moore, *Capital Collection*, 18–19.

95. Fitzwilliam Museum, Cambridge, MS 13-1947, f. 4.
96. Undated pen-and-ink sketch design by John Chute for a canopied bed placed opposite the chimneypiece, based on the tomb of Sir Simon Burleigh at Old St Paul's, and accompanied by eight stools (*D 1774*, LWL 49 2523, 121.8). On the verso is a sectional profile of the bed and an elevation of the chimneypiece, but not in its final form (suggesting a date before 1767). A design by Robert Adam in the LWL for a similar bed can presumably be linked to HW's request on about 26 September 1766 for a design for a bed for 'the enclosed little end' (*HW Corres.* 41: 39). See also Wilton-Ely, 'Gingerbread and Sippets of Embroidery', which suggests that it was designed for the Gallery. The scheme was seemingly still under consideration on 25 June 1769, when Madame du Deffand referred to the 'cabinet rond' in which 'le lit est un trone' and had 'tabourets' (*HW Corres.* 4:249).
97. Fitzwilliam Museum, Cambridge, MS 13-1947, f. 2.
98. *HW Corres.* 35: 406–7 (HW to Hamilton, 22 Sept. 1768). Adam's first idea is much closer in design to the Confessor's tomb (Soane Museum, Adam Drawings, vol. 22, no. 228).
99. Fitzwilliam Museum, Cambridge, MS 13-1947, f. 2.
100. For the painting, now at Sudeley Castle, see Appendix 2, p. 344.
101. The bed hangings are now at Sudeley Castle.
102. *HW Corres.* 33: 472 (HW to Ossory, 30 June 1785).
103. Fitzwilliam Museum, Cambridge, MS 13-1947, f. 2.
104. Bentley design for the ground plan with, on the verso, a sketch plan of the western extensions with chapel apparently attached to the earlier house (LWL 49 3698).
105. The overall design was partly inspired by the vault of the Chapter House at York Minster, with the lower relief tracery taken from that of the Minster west window.
106. *HW Corres.* 10:168 (HW to Montagu, 23 Aug. 1765).
107. For the display of bronzes see Malcolm Baker, 'Collecting and viewing small bronzes 1750–1850', in M. Baker, *The Making and Viewing of Eighteenth-Century Sculpture*. (London: V&A Publications, 2000), 144–58.
108. Cf. also the two private boudoirs or closets off the long gallery at Syon House.

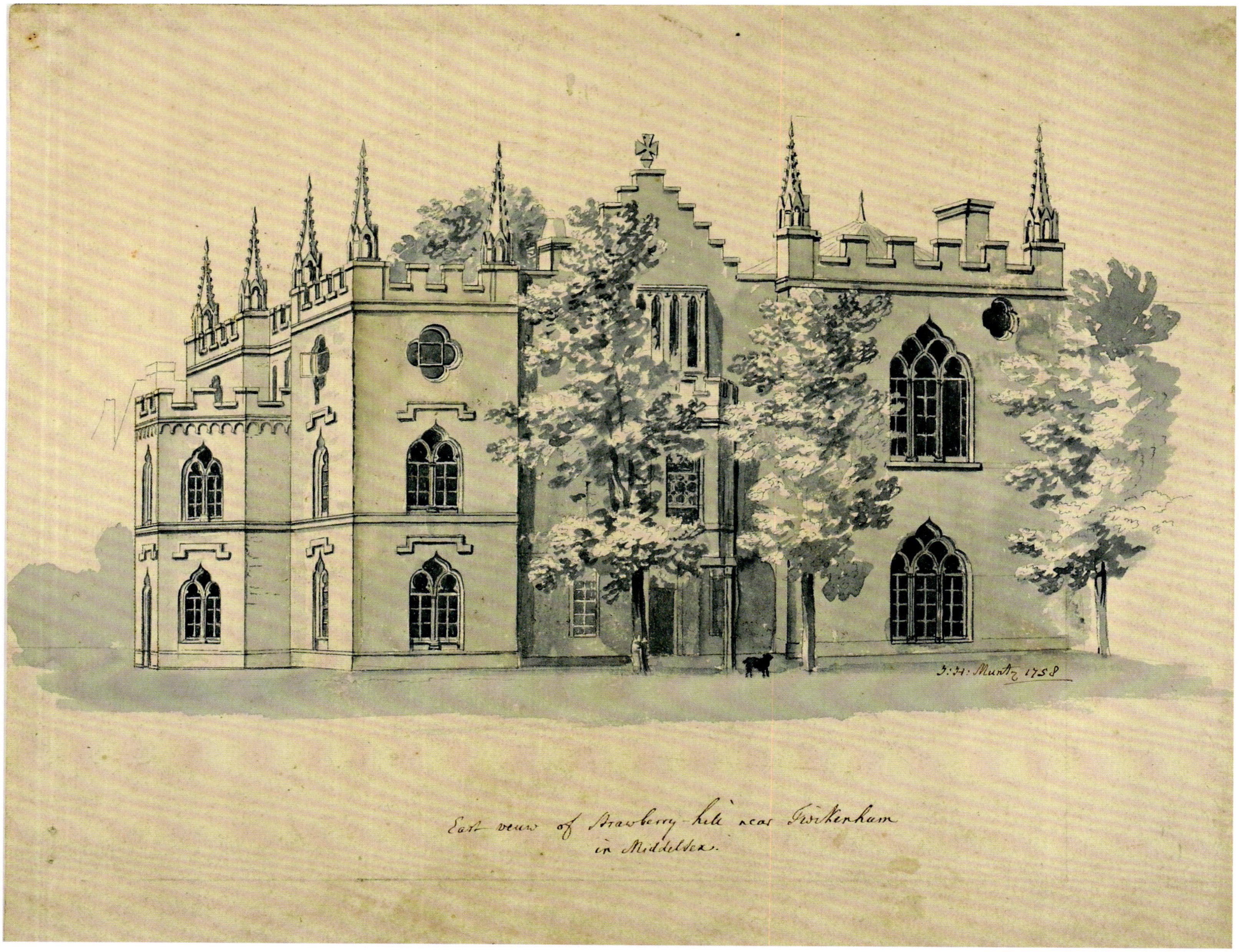

Figure 89. Johann Heinrich Müntz, *'East view of Strawberry hill near Twickenham in Middlesex'*, 1758, pen and ink, blue wash with graphite, 23.5 × 29.4 cm. The Lewis Walpole Library, Yale University. 758.00.00.40dr. Cat. 12

3.

WALPOLE'S GOTHIC

CREATING A FICTIVE HISTORY

KEVIN ROGERS

IN 1747, at the age of twenty-nine and having returned from the Grand Tour more than five years before, Horace Walpole took the lease of a modest tenement, or lodging house, from Mrs Chenevix, the London toy-woman à la mode. It was set on a five-acre plot of land with the key advantage of being on the banks of the Thames. Within the year he began the first of an elaborate sequence of alterations that was to encase the tenement, which was formed of two different structures, one modestly grand and the other more akin to a cottage, and joined together by a simple staircase (Fig. 100). The inclusion of these earlier structures contributed greatly to Walpole's villa, visually representing and giving the experiential sense of a fictive architectural history – a modern Gothic castle that suggested an accretive building with changing levels and irregular plan formed over many hundreds of years.

When Walpole arrived in Twickenham, the Gothic Revival was well established. In the same year Batty and Thomas Langley published *Gothic Architecture*, which was later to be derided by the anti-antiquarian Gothic Revivalists of the nineteenth century for its decorative handling of the Gothic. Considering Walpole's opinion of building in the Gothic style in later life, it is surprising to find him as a subscriber to the 1742 edition of this book entitled *Ancient Architecture, Restored and Improved*. While the elevations of Strawberry Hill by John Chute have no direct connection to the Langleys' plates, there is at least a superficial relationship between them and Chute's choice of details for the villa, the quatrefoil and ogee-headed windows, as well as individual elements of ornament and the profiles for the window joinery. That Chute drew on *Ancient Architecture*, albeit in a superficial way, is also suggested by his sketch for the south-east corner of Strawberry Hill in Walpole's own copy of the work (Fig. 90).

More broadly, Chute's design for the new south front, realized in 1752, can be seen in the context of Stainborough Castle, the mock-fortified modern Gothic folly of William Wentworth, 2nd Earl of Strafford, which was completed in the same year. Strawberry Hill's friendly Gothic 'rival' was created from an existing banqueting house with the addition of curtain walls punctuated by diminutive towers and pierced by lancet and quatrefoil-form windows that have a more than passing resemblance to Walpole's 'Great Tower' at the south-east corner of Strawberry Hill.[1] Even within the immediate environs of Walpole's little Gothic castle, Lord Radnor's villa had been recast by 1745 in the style of an Elizabethan prodigy house, albeit in reduced form, its river front articulated with canted bays and its windows filled with painted glass. It is thus not surprising that Horace Mann responded with disappointed surprise at Walpole's initial interest in building in the style: 'Why will you make it Gothic? I know it is the taste at present, but I really am sorry for it. *Basta*, I may be mistaken – *mi pare però un gusto gotico!*'[2]

Horace Mann's response was no doubt as much an expression of his own architectural opinion as it was a reflection of Walpole's relatively late conversion to the mode. For Walpole, adopting the

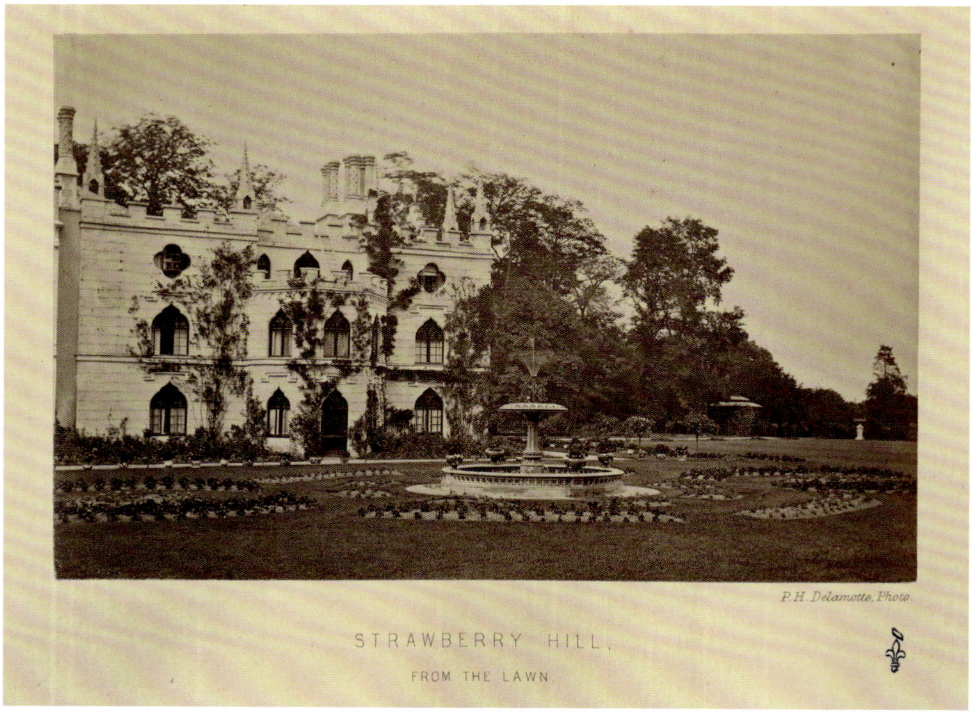

Figure 90. Philip-Henry Delamotte, *Strawberry Hill from the lawn*, 1863, calotype, 11 × 16.7 cm. Chantilly, musée Condé. PH 487

Figure 91. Chimney-piece in the Breakfast Room, designed by William Robinson, photographed 2008. The original pinnacles are not in place. The tiles are mid-nineteenth century. The wall covering has been removed to show Walpole's wooden wall lining

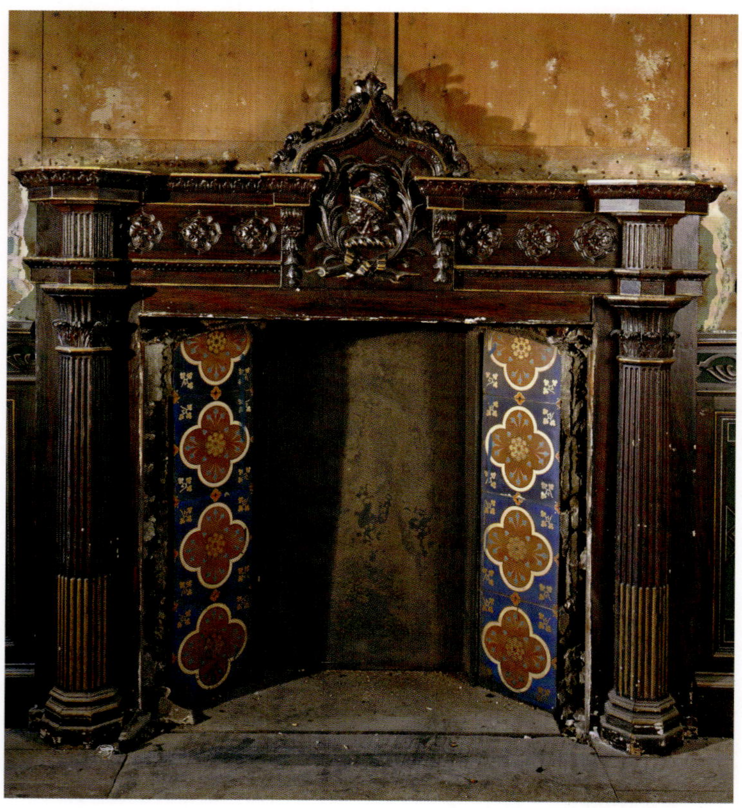

Gothic at the earliest stages of the building project (1747) was clearly not the result of a profound passion for discovering the ancient origins of English architecture, but rather the taking up of a fashionable style. His first use of the Gothic – the pretty pointed windows to the Breakfast Room and the accompanying chimneypiece – followed the established taste of decorating with Gothic ornament as used by William Kent in about 1733 in the decoration and extension of Esher Place, Surrey. The Breakfast Room chimneypiece (Fig. 91) is designed in the Corinthian order but dressed with Gothic ornament, with pinnacle finials bundled in leaves and rising from the columns below.[3] Walpole's architect, William Robinson, later became Secretary to the Board of Works, but at this stage was Clerk of Works at Greenwich Hospital. Although Walpole dropped him as a designer (and was careful to disparage his efforts), he kept him on as the surveyor dealing with the practical aspects of building the villa until 1772.

From 1750 Walpole's architectural ambitions for the villa became clearer. The existing structures with their differing floor levels were to be retained but wholly transformed, by being encased and extended to create a modest retreat. This was an opportunity for Walpole to depart from the norms of the revived Gothic and formulate his own architectural ideal. Consequently, after William Robinson's creation of the new Breakfast Room, all further architectural authorship and the design of many of the fittings for the villa were achieved by Walpole closely directing his inner social circle of highly informed gentlemen and sympathetic artists, his 'committee', whom he had organized to collaborate with him on the design.

The committee was made up of a range of talents, architectural, literary and historical. It included friends of long standing from Walpole's time at Eton: the poet Thomas Gray, who was Walpole's companion on the Grand Tour, the politician and wit George Selwyn, and the Reverend William Cole, rector successively of Milton, Waterbeach and Bletchley. Cole's contribution included his exhaustive knowledge of heraldry (matching that of John Chute), his unique role in correcting and augmenting Walpole's *Description of the Villa* and his continuing discussions of historical fact with Walpole, which also concerned questions of artistic attribution. Though not directly involved in the formulation of the design of the house, these three figures, and Thomas Gray most significantly, contributed their scholarly knowledge and a passion for historical understanding in the broadest sense, in particular the association of historical personages with ancient buildings. While Walpole's architectural expression was individual, neither following the Langley tradition nor the emerging archaeological theories, Gray probably introduced Sir Christopher Wren's 'Saracenic' or 'Southern' theory on the origin of Gothic to the group.[4] Although Wren's theory probably had little influence on the detailed design of the house, the understanding of Iberian Gothic or the Manueline style as found in the monastery of Santa Maria da Vitória at Batalha, Portugal, was of importance in the design and decoration of the Tribune, planned in 1758–9 and realized by 1760, with its unusual top lighting, and of the Gallery, planned in 1758–62 and realized in 1765, with its ostentatious bays of ornament, fretwork and inbuilt pictures. These architectural forms had probably been directly experienced by Cole, who toured the Iberian peninsula in the 1730s, and by Johann Heinrich Müntz, originally of Mülhausen in the Alsace, who had worked as a military engineer in Spain just prior to his introduction to Walpole by Richard Bentley. Müntz, however, had left the group by 1759, and although Thomas Pitt, Lord Camelford, another Iberian traveller, was introduced to Walpole's committee in 1761, his contribution to the design was limited to the overmantel of the Gallery chimneypiece and the grille-form door to the Tribune.

Most significant for his role in the shaping of all the elevations and the interiors of the new western rooms of the State Apartment was John Chute, who met Walpole on the Grand Tour and whom Walpole described on his death as 'my oracle of taste, the standard to whom I submitted my trifles, and the genius that presided over poor Strawberry'.[5] While Walpole directed every element of the design process, and the retention of the existing buildings dictated all further development of the plan, Chute's influence is most strongly seen in the creation of the house. John Chute's experience of architecture, particularly on the Continent, was far more extensive than that of any other member of the committee. We know from the post accounts kept by the solicitor Thomas Puckridge with the goldsmith-banker Samuel Camner that Chute's Grand Tour was far more ambitious than revealed by his correspondence with Walpole. Over seven years he travelled several circuits between the north and south of Europe.[6]

Chute's proto-archaeological approach was realized in every elevation, with the exception of the modest north entrance front, which, though described by Walpole as conceived by Chute, was in fact drawn by Richard Bentley (Fig. 92). The success of Chute's designs lay in his ability to visually refer to real Gothic buildings in the overall architectural composition. This is most clearly seen in the east elevation as completed by 1755 with its

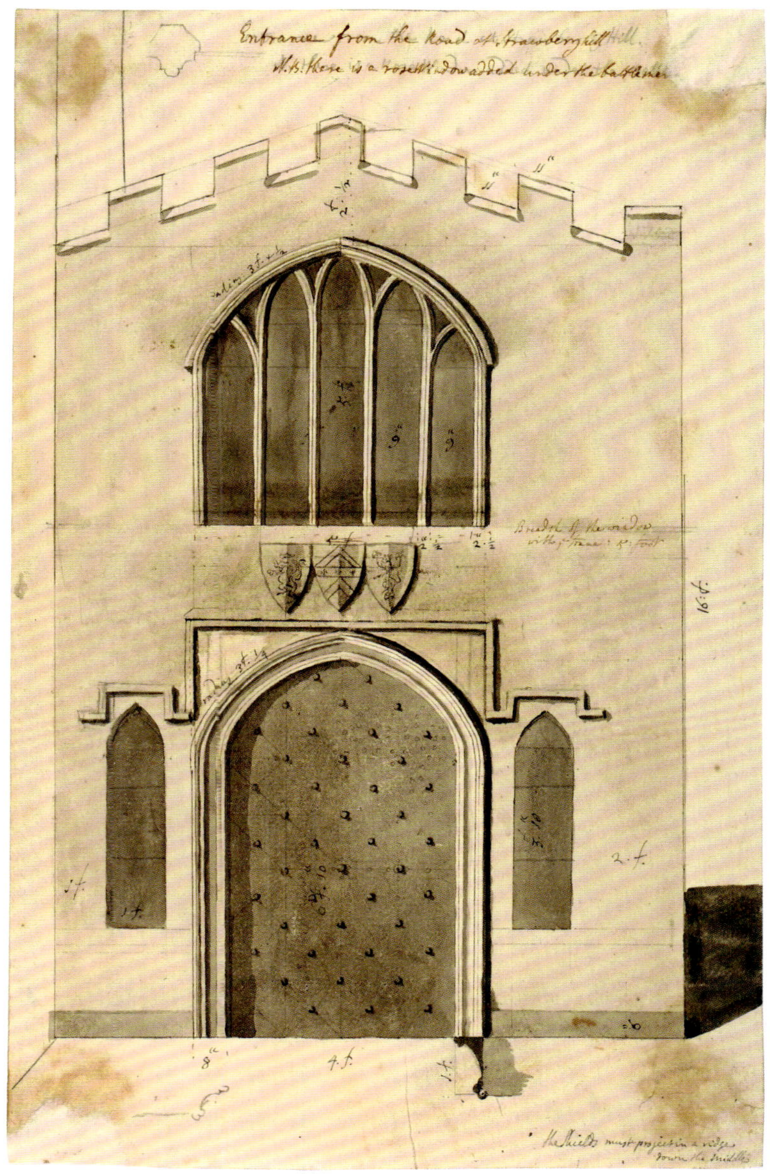

Figure 92. Richard Bentley, *'Entrance from the Road at Strawberry Hill'*, 1751–3, pencil and ink wash, 31.3 × 19.7 cm, from *Drawings and Designs by Richd. Bentley*, 1760. The Lewis Walpole Library, Yale University. Folio 49 3585 fol. 29. Cat. 18

allusion to the Venetian Palazzo Ducale. As the footprint of the villa developed, Chute successfully amalgamated his earlier work, without modification, into the new design to produce the most picturesque of architectural compositions. Even the slender Beauclerk Tower, built the year of Chute's death, was in its concept his contribution, its form appearing in his ideas for extending the house in the late 1750s (Fig. 104). In contrast is the work of Richard Bentley, who was an artist and the most creative of the group. He transformed Gothic into a playfully decorative style, abandoning the earlier approach of Kent and Langley with its deference to classical rules of hierarchy and proportion. In the interiors John Chute and Richard Bentley, working separately, even competitively, produced alternative designs for the fitting out of the Library, Gallery and Tribune. Although Chute's schemes for these principal rooms were eventually realized, Bentley's successful designs for the Great Parlour chimneypiece and for the staircase and hall, contributed to these most convincingly Gothic of all spaces in Walpole's villa as constructed by 1756, with its constantly changing plan, shifting levels and fictive architecture created in paintwork.

Walpole's unique approach was to create a house based on first-hand observations of real buildings or their representation in prints in Britain or on the Continent. The design of the elevations and many of the interiors was a pastiche of architectural quotations, utilizing details of buildings that were recognizable to the informed eighteenth-century eye. A good example is to be found in the antiquarian manual of design, William Dugdale's *History of St. Paul's Cathedral* (1658). It was used by John Chute when producing an alternative design for the fitting out of the Library (1754) in Chute's own copy. Hollar's plate depicting the choir screen was mutilated, the door case to the south of the screen being cut from the plate and the engraving used by Chute as the basis of a drawing developing the architectural form of the new book presses for the Library. The drawing is to be found in Chute's copy of *Les Cinq Ordres d'Architecture*.[7] However, not all the historical references used to evoke the ancient were Gothic; the black and gold decoration of the Gallery seat furniture and the nomenclature of the rooms were references to the comparatively recent past, or what Walpole described as 'all of the good King James I Gothic'.[8]

But the strongest influences on the overall design of the house as realized by 1756 were not in fact ancient structures but modern Gothic buildings. These included Kent's Esher Place, mentioned above, the Temple of Liberty at Stowe (1739) by James Gibbs, and Gibbs's and Sanderson Miller's modern alterations to the truly ancient Wroxton Abbey, which, notwithstanding Gibbs's rivalry with the already established Goth Miller, were given the accolade by Walpole of being 'in a pretty Gothic taste'.[9] The Temple of Liberty, which he saw in 1753, inspired Walpole to write:

> In the heretical corner of my heart I adore the Gothic building, which by some unusual inspiration Gibbs has made pure and beautiful and venerable ... The style has a propensity to the Venetian or mosque-Gothic, and the great column near it makes the whole put one in mind of the Place of St Mark.[10]

Although the three facades of the triangular temple are regular, its overall composition is unbalanced by the raised tower, while the geometric play internally creates a non-traditional conjunction of spaces in the plan and section of the building. To

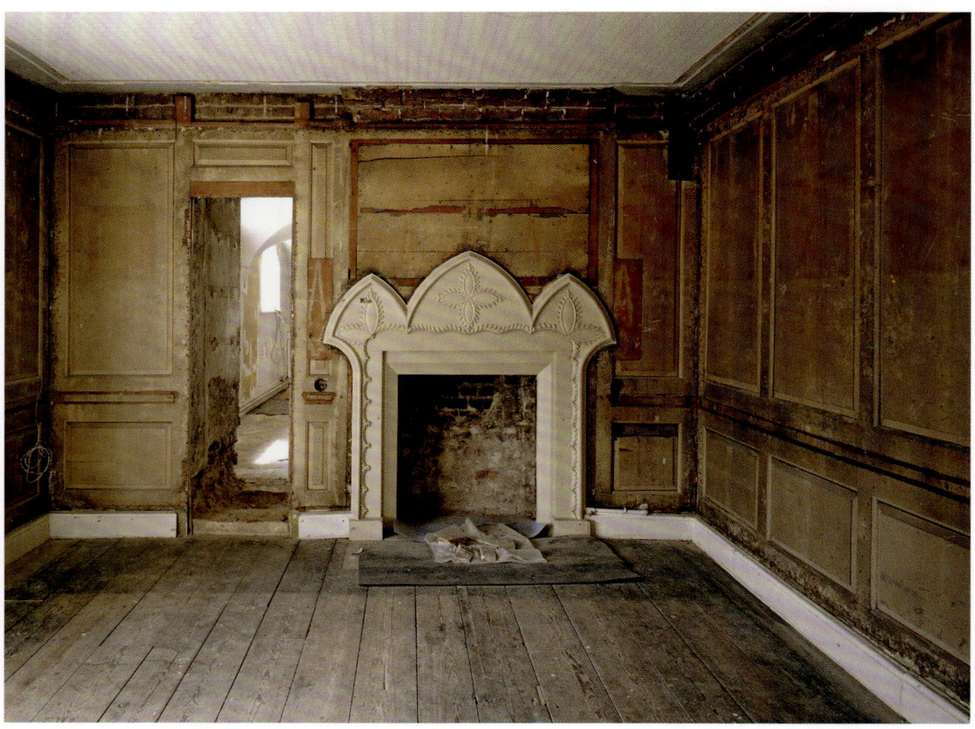

Figure 93. The Yellow Bedchamber or Beauty Room, photographed in 2008. The wall-coverings have been removed to show the early-eighteenth century panelling and Walpole's chimneypiece, designed by Richard Bentley. The opening to the Great Cloister was created in the nineteenth century

the eye of the neo-Palladian this radical reaction to the balanced formality of the accepted architectural mode must have been shocking; Gibbs's composition was one of the first formal buildings in post-medieval Europe to use asymmetrical massing.

The origin of Walpole's little Gothic castle was firmly fixed in the tenement acquired from Mrs Chenevix. The decision to integrate the Chenevix 'lodging house', with its irregular levels and plan, and its situation at the northernmost boundary of the property, at the very beginning of the alterations, determined what could be realized through each further architectural development. The physical evidence of the earlier structure to the west can be seen most clearly in the westernmost of the two pre-Walpole buildings and in the rooms that became the Beauty Room and the Red Bedchamber. It is also present in the Breakfast Room and in the reuse of salvaged materials incorporated into the wall linings of the hall. Within the Beauty Room (Fig. 93) is the early-eighteenth-century timber panelling with the imprint of a conventional box cornice (removed in the 1970s), which was extended by Walpole when an earlier pair of windows was removed to regularize the elevation in 1753. The sense of irregularity of the elevations is heightened by Walpole's development of the house over six construction phases, but it can be thought of as two principal periods of works: that up to 1756, as shown by Müntz's formally presented house portrait (see fig. 89), with the western boundary of the public rooms ending with the hall and Star Chamber above; and the post-1760 large-scale expansion to the west with its Gallery and Round Tower, as depicted by Paul Sandby (see fig. 102). While Walpole had begun the active collection of surrounding plots of land from his first occupation of the site, the lack of land prevented any major expansion of the house until after 1757.

The radical elements of Strawberry Hill lay not in its use of the revived Gothic but in its suggestion of an elaborate fictive history, not a house built over fifty years but an ancient seat, developed and extended over generations. Its asymmetrical plan, varied silhouette and circuitous internal routes all contributed to this effect. Above all, unlike a neo-Palladian house, each elevation was of equal importance, containing rooms of all types within the hierarchy of the plan. As in a real

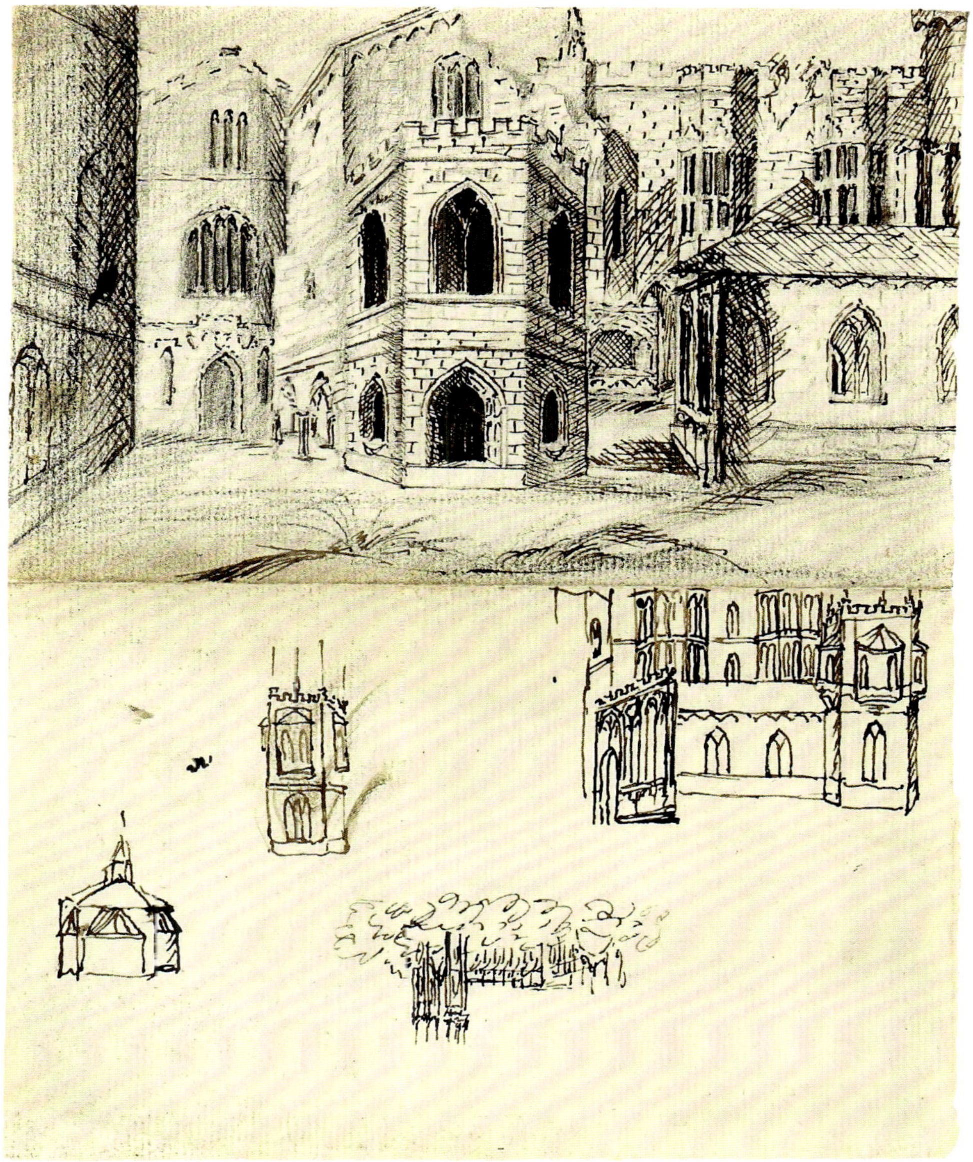

Figure 94. John Chute, *Sketch Designs for the North Front of Stawberry Hill, a sketch of Westminster Abbey and another building.* After 1757, pen and ink. Hampshire County Record Office

Gothic building, the room arrangements were directly expressed on the exterior in a variety of window types. This is most obvious on the north elevation, composed of separate blocks or wings with window types varying from the leaded diamond quarries of the lesser rooms to the large plates of French glass in the Great North Bedchamber and the elaborate coloured glass of the Beauclerk Closet (Figs. 94, 105).

Initially, Walpole toyed with integrating fragments of real Gothic buildings, but in practice this approach was limited. Horace Mann wrote: 'I am totally at a loss where to search for the

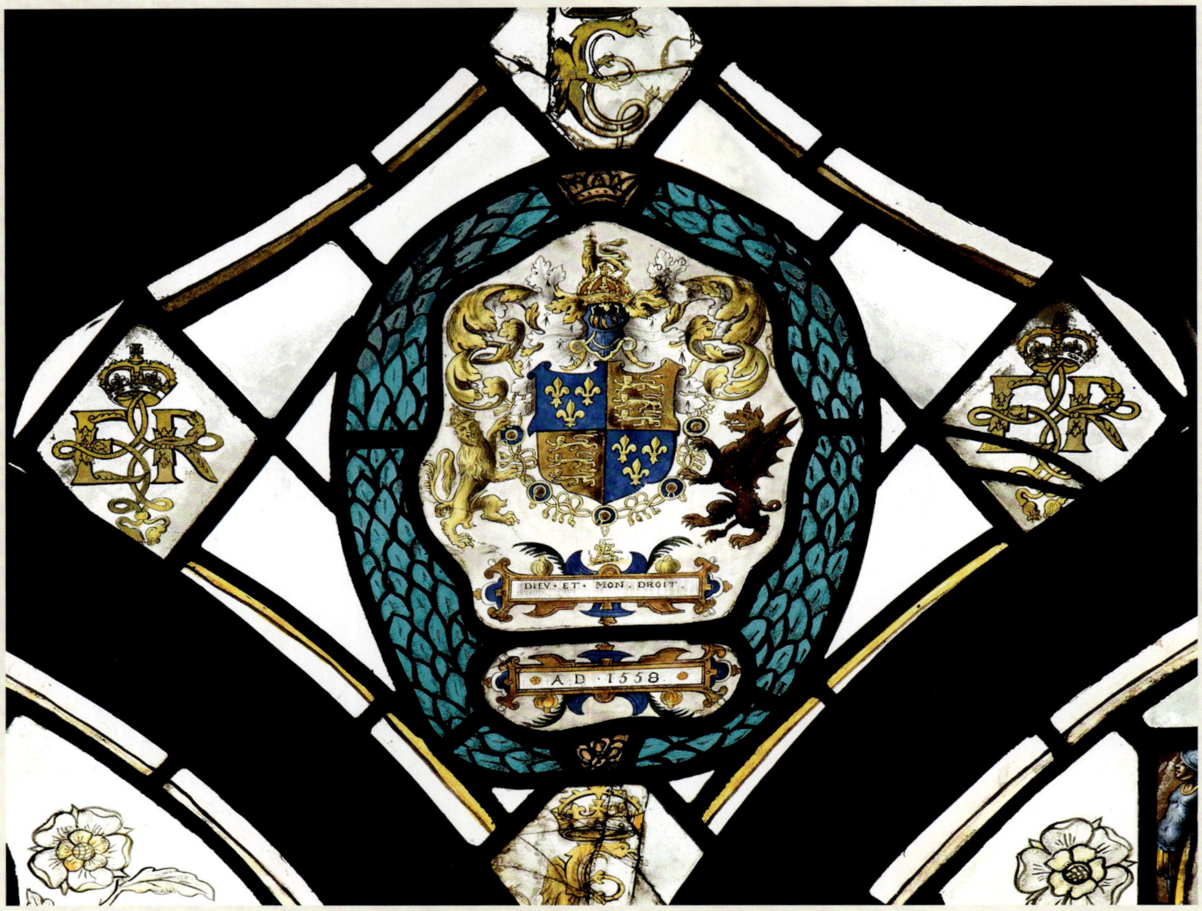

Figure 95. Royal armorial and badges of Elizabeth I, top centre window in the Library, Strawberry Hill

Strawberry Hill was remarkable for its display of stained and painted glass, which was of three periods: medieval, early Renaissance and eighteenth century. Walpole actively collected English medieval armorials, shields and badges, particularly royal Tudor badges such as the red rose of Lancaster, the hawthorn bush commemorating the Battle of Bosworth Field, and the Beaufort portcullis, all of which he would have seen in abundance in the windows of King's College Chapel, Cambridge, during his years there in college. Other badges of royalty in his windows included a rose dimidiating a split pomegranate, for Queen Catherine of Aragon; a white falcon on a tree stump holding a sceptre, for Anne Boleyn; the feathers of Edward VI; the cipher of Elizabeth I; and innumerable royal shields such as Elizabeth's of 1558 (Fig. 95). Armorials included those of Robert Dudley, Earl of Essex, and of Anne Boleyn. Numerous other pieces represented noble families, the whole providing a celebration of English Tudor history.

But the majority consisted of Netherlandish sixteenth- and seventeenth-century domestic glass showing biblical and classical subjects, armorials and small items such as birds, flowers and single figures that would have formed the original decorative surrounds of larger panels. Although Walpole was not the first collector in the eighteenth century to import stained glass, he did so on a large scale, buying 450 Netherlandish pieces in 1750. His appreciation of the

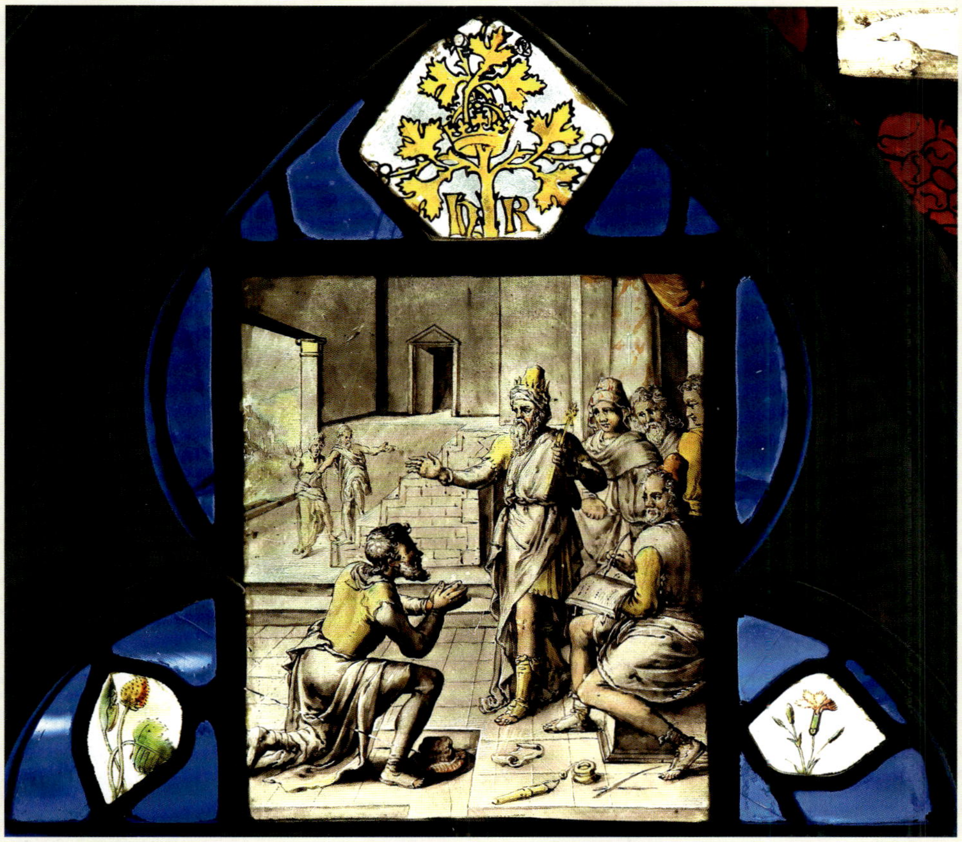

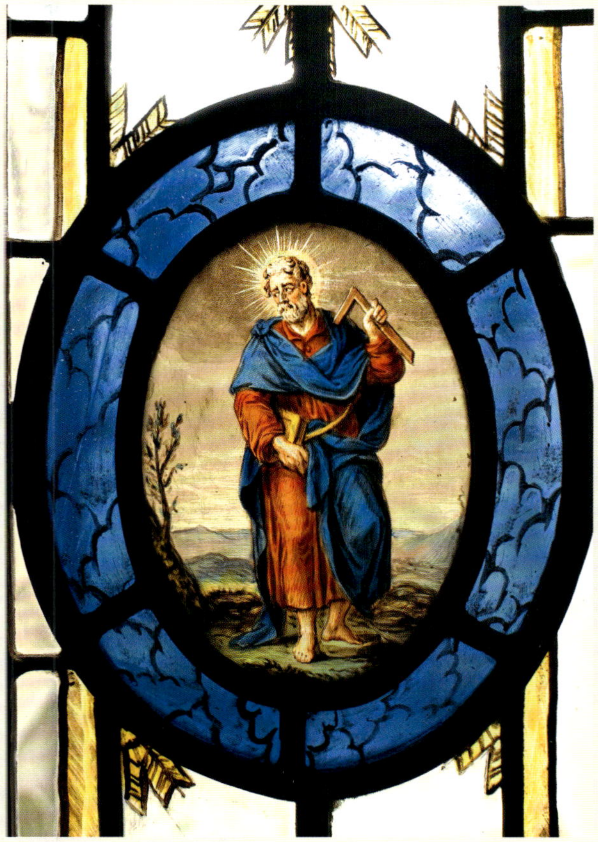

work of Netherlandish glass painters he had seen in Cambridge is shown by his treatment of them in his *Anecdotes of Painting*. The designs of the history panels were frequently copied by the glass painters from the prints of well-known contemporary artists and they complemented the Netherlandish paintings on the walls, no fewer than forty-one artists being represented.

Walpole adapted the Netherlandish panels to his Gothic windows and used the smaller pieces like medieval quarries. He supplemented the foreign glass with small pieces of coloured glass to bring additional colour to the windows in a simplified version of medieval mosaic glass, often incorporating his English medieval pieces in the same window (fig. 96). It was as much the way in which the glass was displayed as the glass itself that was innovative, creating the overall effect of colourful medieval windows with the later, Renaissance glass. His aim was to create a sense of richness throughout the house, so that by 6 June 1753, in a letter to Horace Mann, he describes the tops of his windows as being 'glutted with the richest painted glass'.

Finally, Walpole commissioned sets of family armorials from the English glass painters: William Price the younger, James Pearson and William Peckitt. Price even provided for him a set of saints in a deliberately Netherlandish style to match other glass in his Tribune windows (fig. 97). Peckitt's set of quarterings of the Walpole family graced the Long Gallery (see Fig. 55). By 1772 Walpole's taste was becoming even more medieval, and Peckitt's set of shields of family intermarriages in the Great North Bedchamber are surrounded by simple bands of colour, close to late fifteenth-century practice (Fig. 98).

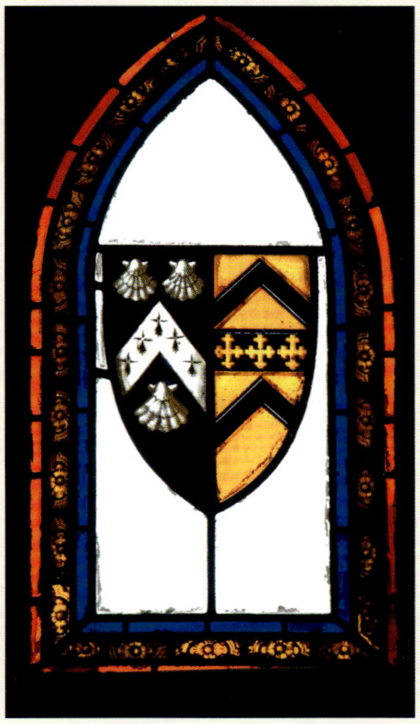

Figure 96. Netherlandish Renaissance panel and English Royal Badge in the centre window of the Blue Bedchamber, Strawberry Hill

Figure 97. William Price the younger, *Saint*, Star Chamber, Strawberry Hill

Figure 98. William Peckitt, Armorial of an intermarriage of the Walpole family, Great North Bedchamber, Strawberry Hill

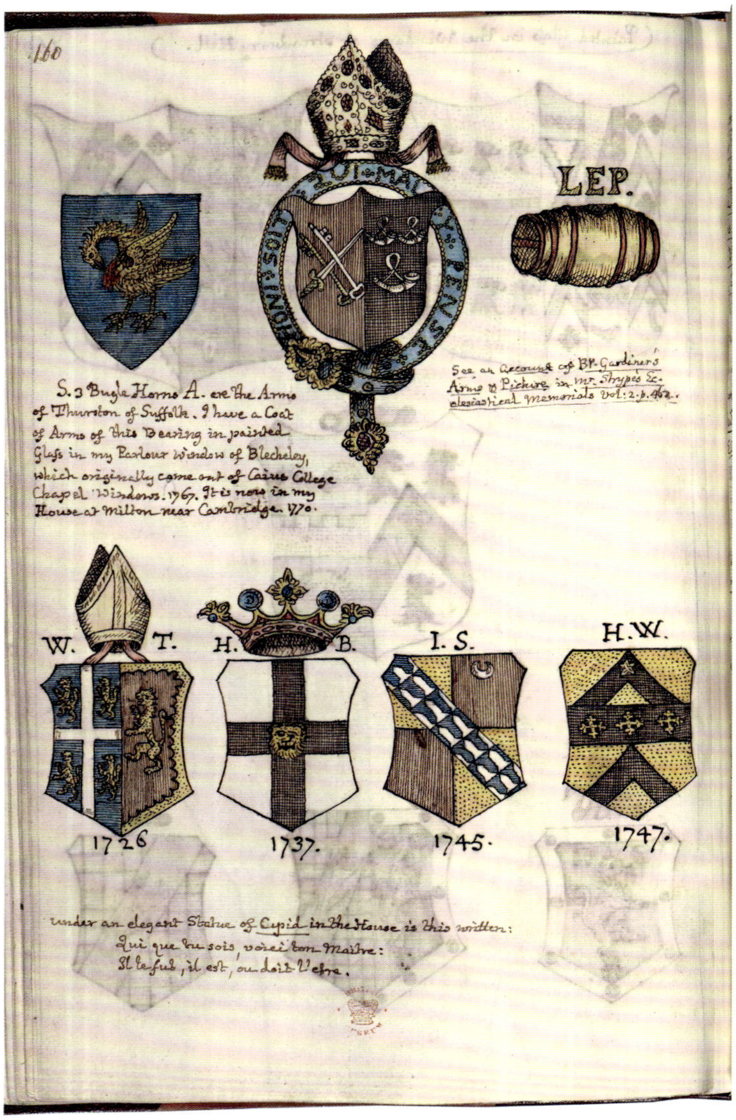

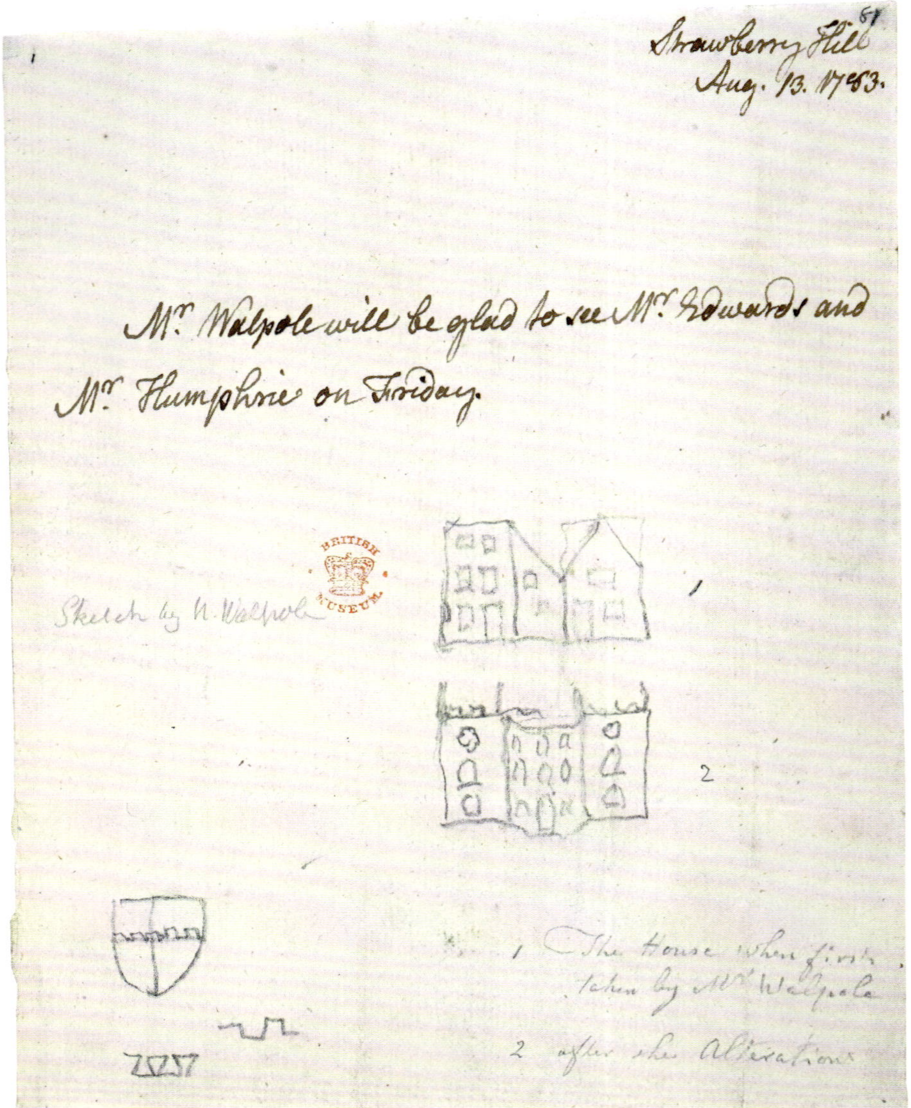

Figure 99. Rev. William Cole's description of the English Heraldry glass at Strawberry Hill; above: the glass from the Back Stairs, below: the armorials from the China Room. British Library. Add Mss 5841 f 80v

Figure 100. Letter from Horace Walpole to Edward Edwards, 13 August 1783, with a sketch by Walpole showing the house as he found it and after alteration. British Library. 29927 128

fragments you want for your little Gothic castle.'[11] The integration of real ancient material was limited to the Winding Cloister, a ground-floor room that was the culmination of the formal tour in the eighteenth century, where the *Description* draws attention to 'some ancient bas-reliefs', a pair of Norwich alabasters given to Walpole by William Cole, and four classical reliefs built into the wall that remarkably escaped the succession of sales in the house and were enhanced by a neo-Gothic 'brass plate with the effigies of Simon Walpole, bishop of Norwich and Ely, engraved by Müntz'.[12] More comprehensive was the incorporation of medieval and Renaissance glass into the fabric of the house (see pp. 64–65), together with contemporary commissions. The varying colours of the glass complemented the monochromatic decorative paint schemes of the rooms. Externally, the glass was perceived in the early nineteenth century as 'chequered like a harlequin's coat, with all the colours of the rainbow'.[13] This was both a means for Walpole to display his interest as an antiquarian collector and to contribute to the suggestion of an ancient, though wholly fictive, origin for the house.

Following the creation of the Breakfast Room on the east front, the real work on the house began with the new south front (Fig. 103), to the design of John Chute (1753), which threw together the two very different pre-existing structures to form a three-bay elevation. Unusually for Walpole, it was designed with symmetrical fenestration and a central projecting two-storey bay. However, this formal symmetry of the south front not only concealed the different widths of the bays but also the irregularity of the internal levels. At ground-floor level in the south-east corner or Great Tower the ceiling cut across the window heads, relating to the floor levels of the earlier cottage that was entombed within Walpole's new villa. The low ceiling also permitted the grander proportions of the room above, the Green Closet. The regularity of the glazing at first-floor level also concealed a shift of levels in the other direction, the Green Closet being some three steps lower than the adjacent (but unconnected) Blue Bedchamber in the south bow window. The view of the house by Johan Heinrich Müntz (1757), now in the Lewis Walpole Library, shows the formal south elevation, its three neat vertical bays all given the same glazing typology (Fig. 18). However, the symmetry of the south was only achieved by the discrete

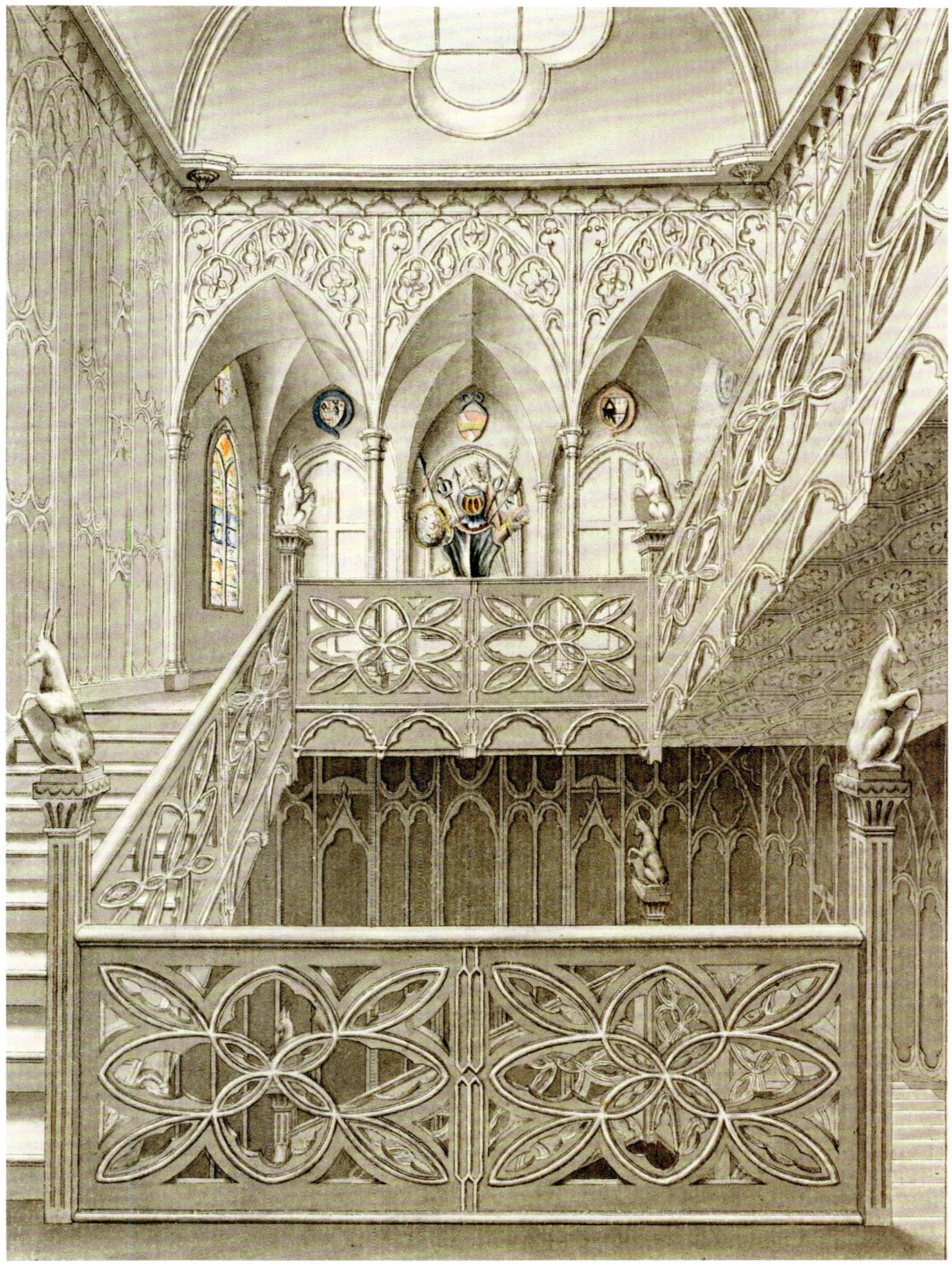

Figure 101. Anonymous artist (Edward Edwards?), *Staircase At Strawberry Hill*, ink wash with watercolour, p. 93 of HW's extra-illustrated copy of the *Description*. The Lewis Walpole Library, Yale University. 33 30 copy 11 Folio

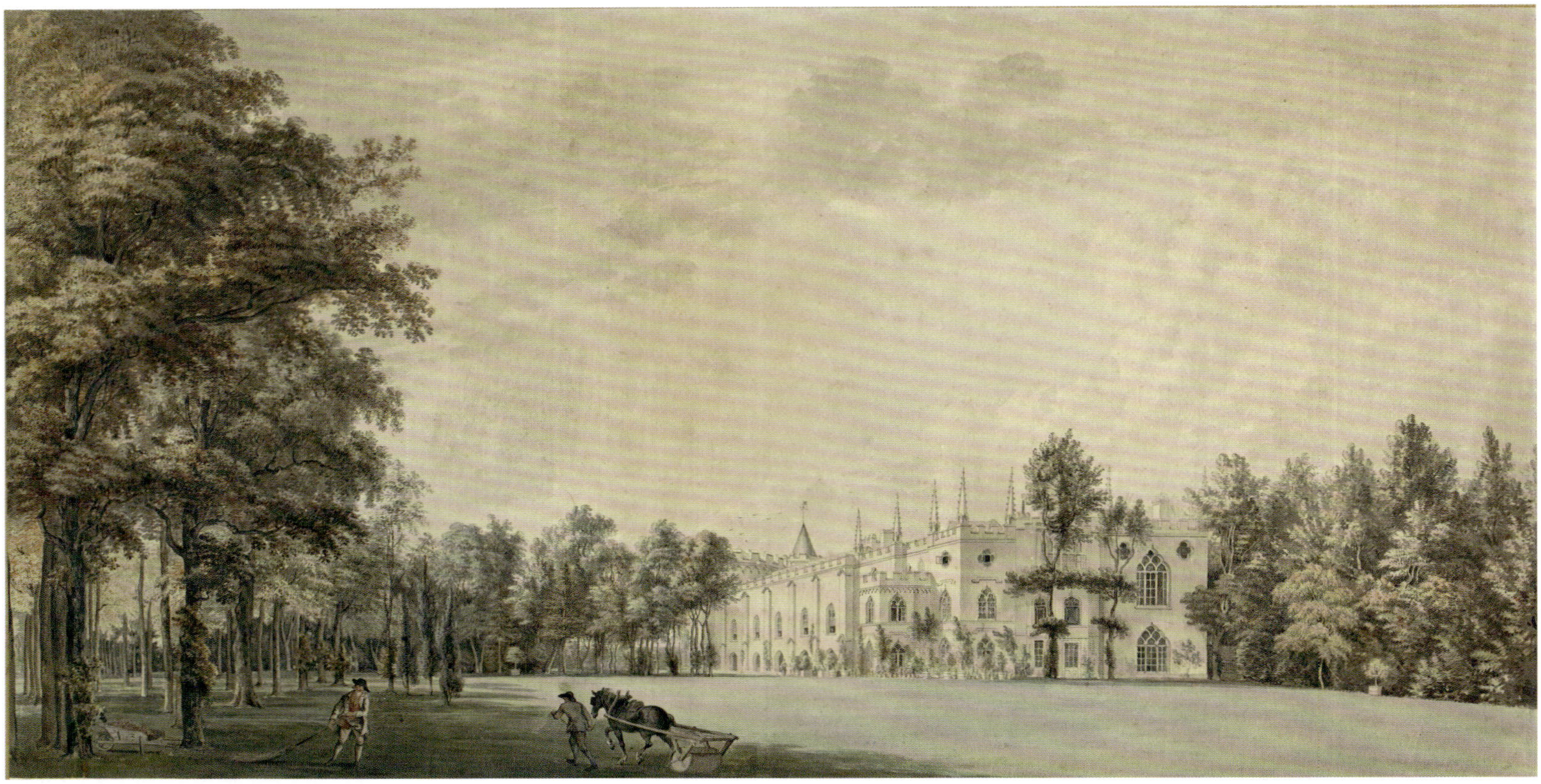

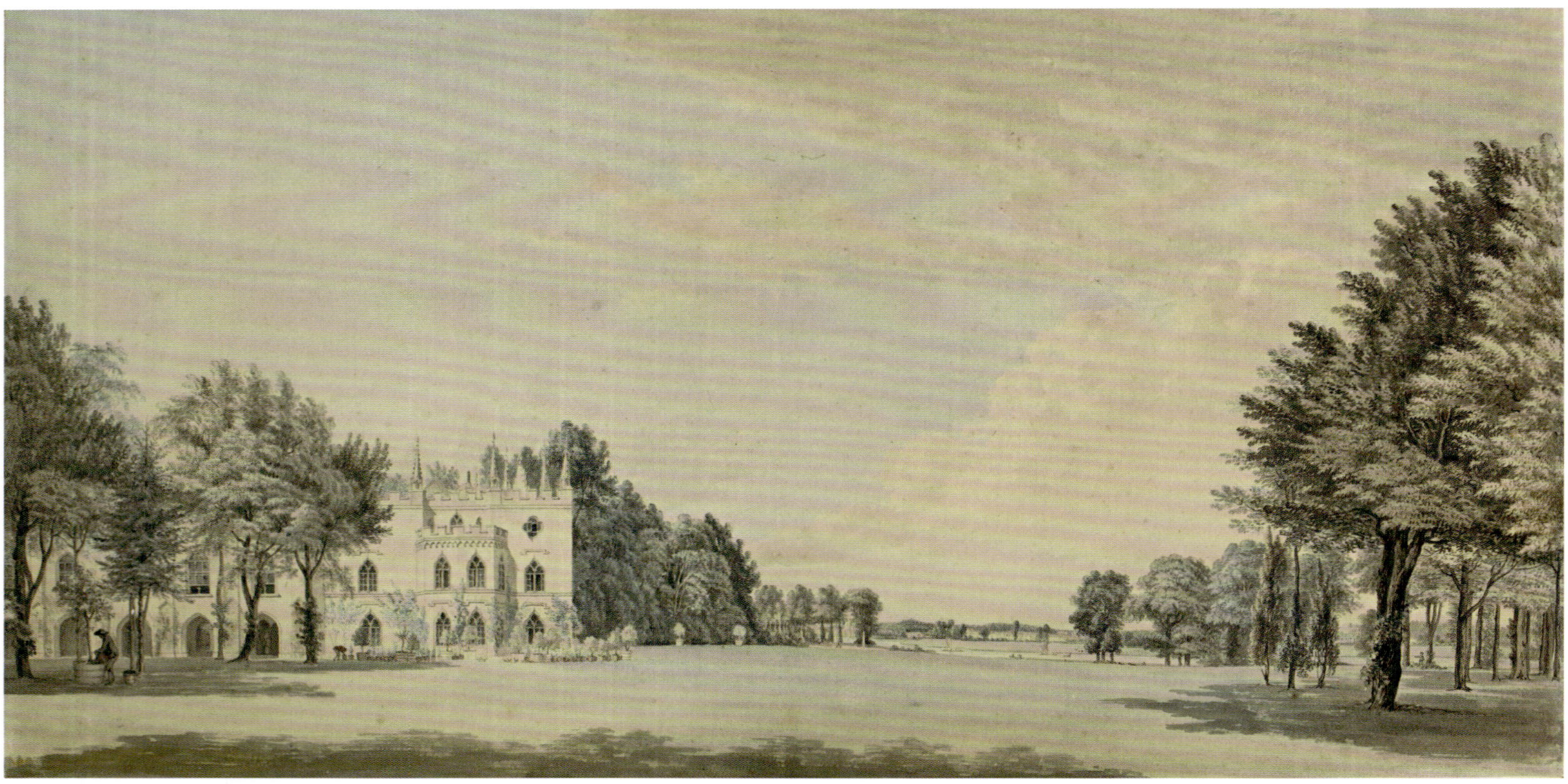

placing of trees in front of the service block (built in 1748) sitting to the west of the villa. The red-brick humbler buildings, later demolished for the building of the Gallery wing, can only just be seen as an outline in Müntz's carefully composed portrait (Fig. 89).

The early development of the villa was modest in scale, with only two new large rooms, the Great Parlour and Library, which completed the east front asymmetrically at its northern end, and a new, centrally positioned staircase; the majority of the rooms retained their original small scale. Overtly Gothicized decoration complementing the external architecture was limited to three principal spaces, namely the staircase and hall, the Great Parlour (though greatly simplified in 1774 with the plain-painted walls) and the Library. The small, south-east corner rooms were concealed from the principal circulation route and could only be accessed via other chambers, reflecting an earlier pattern of room use. Externally, the separation of the rooms was emphasized by their being disengaged from the main structure in the Great Tower.

The most successful of Walpole's spaces in suggesting an ancient history was the hall and staircase, described by him as 'the chief beauty of the castle' (Fig. 101).[14] Built in a single construction campaign (by April 1753) with a remarkable ever-changing plan at each level, it was enlivened by fictive architecture painted in trompe l'oeil to the design of Richard Bentley but based on an engraving owned by Walpole of Prince Arthur's Chantry in the sanctuary of Worcester Cathedral.[15] It was the most convincing of Walpole's new Gothic spaces. Linking the retained three-storeyed structure at the south and the two new great rooms at the north, the staircase had to accommodate the existing uneven levels. The plan was given further complexity by changing the layout and run of the stair at each level. The pierced balustrade was a subtle quotation, derived from the staircase to the canon's library at Rouen Cathedral, a model known first hand by both John Chute and Richard Bentley. At ground-floor level a complex of lobbies and a columnar screen was added, which visually suggested a screens passage. In addition to filling the lancet windows with some of the most important painted glass in the house, Walpole finished the monastic allusion by first calling the hall 'the Paraclete, in memory of Eloisa's cloister' (a reference to Alexander Pope's 'Eloisa to Abelard' – see pp. 30–31).[16]

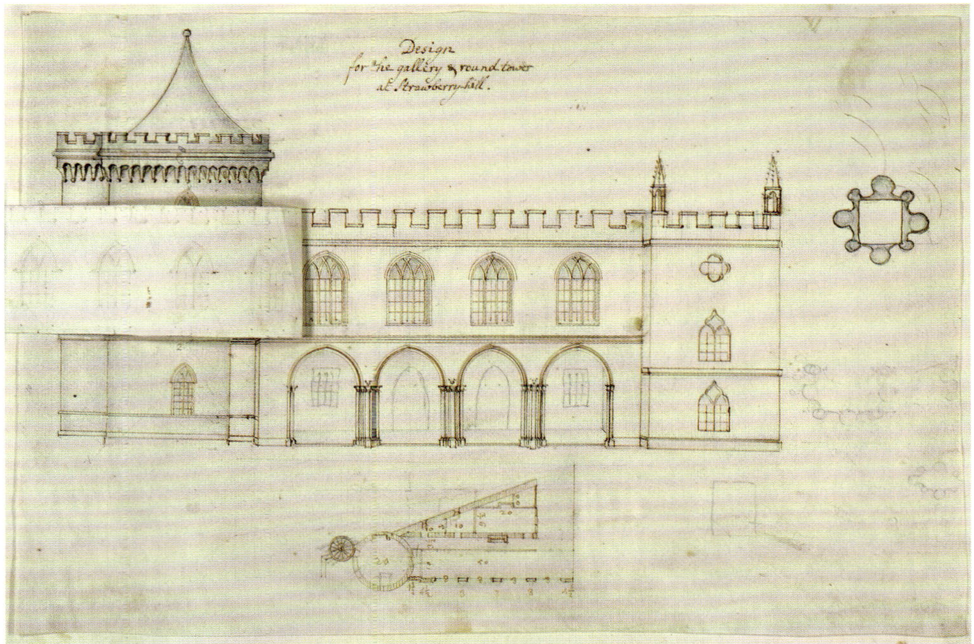

Figure 104. John Chute, *'Design for the gallery and round tower, at Strawberryhill'*, *c.* 1759, ink and pencil, 21 × 31.2 cm, mounted in the volume of John Chute's 'Original Drawings and Sketches'. The Lewis Walpole Library, Yale University. Folio 49 3490 fol. 17. Cat. 19

It is difficult to imagine the north elevation at this time, as the westernmost extent of the plan was the hall, and the Little Cloister and Holbein Chamber above (added from 1758) were not yet built. On the east front, and above Walpole's own bedchamber, the castle-like aspect of the villa was accentuated in 1755 by a crow-step gable. The irregular design of this elevation introduced an architectural idea that was truly Gothic, namely the expression of the room hierarchy through the elevation, the large-scale windows of the great rooms showing their importance in contrast to the smaller-scale openings of the bedchambers and cabinets.

The new Gallery range to the west followed almost immediately after the creation of the Holbein Chamber, its addition completely transforming the house, both in scale and decoration (Fig. 104). It was planned from 1758,[17] and work began in 1759 in the most practical way by first constructing only the base storey of the Round Tower to house the new kitchen, thus allowing the demolition of Walpole's first service buildings sited in the future eastern portion of the Cloister and Gallery wing. The building of the new Cloister and Gallery followed immediately with the structure for the upper levels of the Round Tower and Tribune completed by 1762. The

Figure 102. Paul Sandby, *'Strawberry Hill chiefly taken in the year 1769 by Mr. Sandby'*, *c.* 1769, watercolour, 39.2 × 75.7 cm (visible), The Lewis Walpole Library, Yale University. 769.00.00.77dr++. Cat. 10

Figure 103. Paul Sandby, *South Front of Strawberry Hill*, *c.* 1769, watercolour, 39 × 76.1 cm (visible). The Lewis Walpole Library, Yale University. 9.00.00.78dr++. Cat. 11

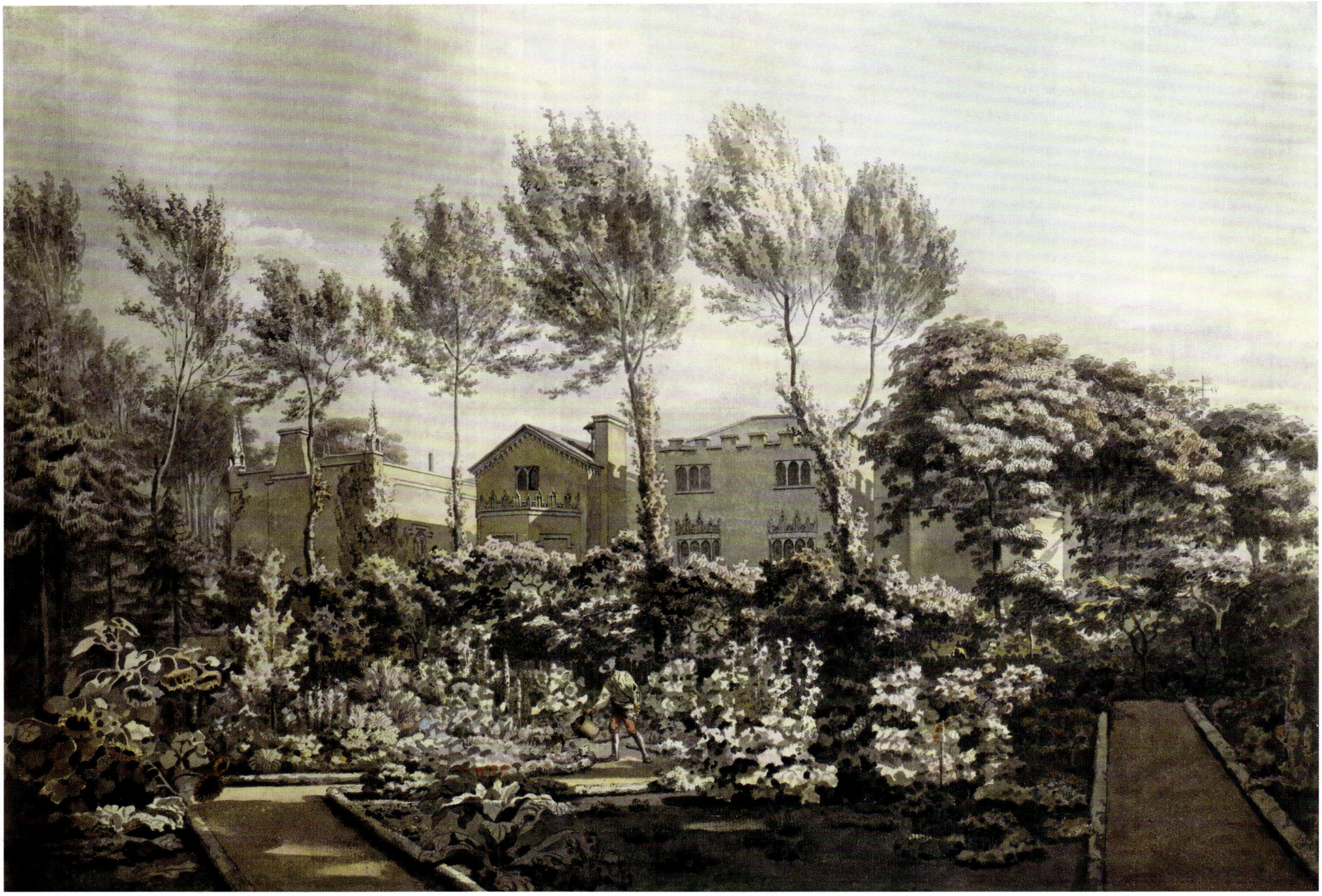

Figure 105. William Pars, *Strawberry Hill from the Garden*, *c.* 1772, watercolour, 37.5 × 53.3 cm. Victoria and Albert Museum, London. P.10–1985. Cat. 16

decoration and furnishing continued in stages over nearly the next decade, initially with the back stairs (1761) and Tribune (1763), followed by the Gallery (1765) and finally the Round Room (1770). From 1772 the State Apartment was extended with the Great North Bedchamber (Fig. 105). It was inserted against the bay of the Tribune, creating two 'closets' that were specifically designed for the display of objects and enclosed by glazed, lancet-shaped tracery doors. The Small Closet facing into the Tribune passage, with its proto-Soaneian top lighting, provided the only source of light into this otherwise interior space, while the Glass Closet was within the bedchamber itself. The culmination of the house's development in the eighteenth century was the addition of the Beauclerk Tower. Though first planned with the new State Apartment, its construction was deferred until 1776. Externally, the tower broke 'the long line of the house picturesquely, and looking very ancient'.[18] Internally, it created two new rooms: on the first floor, the Beauclerk Closet, a private retreat from the great rooms within the State Apartment; and above it on the second floor, the Upper Closet, accessible from the Round Bedchamber (Print Room from 1790).

In its planning the State Apartment discarded the concept of the enfilade in favour of allocating the new state rooms to each elevation of the house. To the south a whole new elevation was formed to the design of John Chute, extending the early villa with a double range of galleries, the lower one open to form a loggia. The architectural composition was terminated by the massive, brick-built Round Tower, but overall it focused on the bays formed by the vertical pairings of Gallery and Cloister openings. The Round Tower made its greatest impact on the approach to the house from the west. It was a striking architectural contribution, with its projecting oriel window indicating the position and importance of the Round Room. Like the north elevation, the west was immediately adjacent to the road and was only buffered by a 'piecrust'-headed wall, evoking the brick-built mansions of the English Renaissance.

The divisions retained between the earlier villa and the new western rooms were significant. At ground-floor level the hall was separated from a sequence of new austere spaces to the west, the Great and Winding Cloisters, which were intended to be seen only after the richness of the fine rooms and were the introduction to the Pleasure Ground to the south and the Abbot's or Prior's Garden, Walpole's *hortus conclusus* – an allusion, at least in spirit, to the enclosed garden of an earlier age – to the north. The main floor was linked to the original house on the first floor via an existing bedchamber rechristened the 'Star Chamber', which, with the new Trunk-Ceiled Passage, was the introduction to the State Apartment. The new western rooms worked together as a single entity on which were lavished all of the architectural conceits that coyly mimic real gothic buildings.

The ground and first floors were linked by what Walpole called the 'Back Stairs' (Fig. 106), a name that Walpole chose to consciously play down its elaborate plan, with changes at every level and windows filled with an important grouping of pre-Reformation English heraldic glass celebrating the Tudor Bishops of Winchester.[19] Although it was painted plain grey during Walpole's lifetime, it was no less sophisticated in its design than the earlier principal stairs to the east and was a consciously austere foil to the richly complex quality of the rooms that came before. However, the back stairs were not just the conclusion of the new rooms but also the link between two key spaces. Embedded within the plan and elevation of the new rooms to the west was, in effect, a double gallery. Designed by John Chute, this arrangement intentionally imitated his own house, the Vyne in Hampshire, by reproducing the idea of the double gallery that William Sandys, Lord Chamberlain to Henry VIII, had built in 1527 (Fig. 107). At Strawberry Hill the upper element, the Gallery, remains, although the

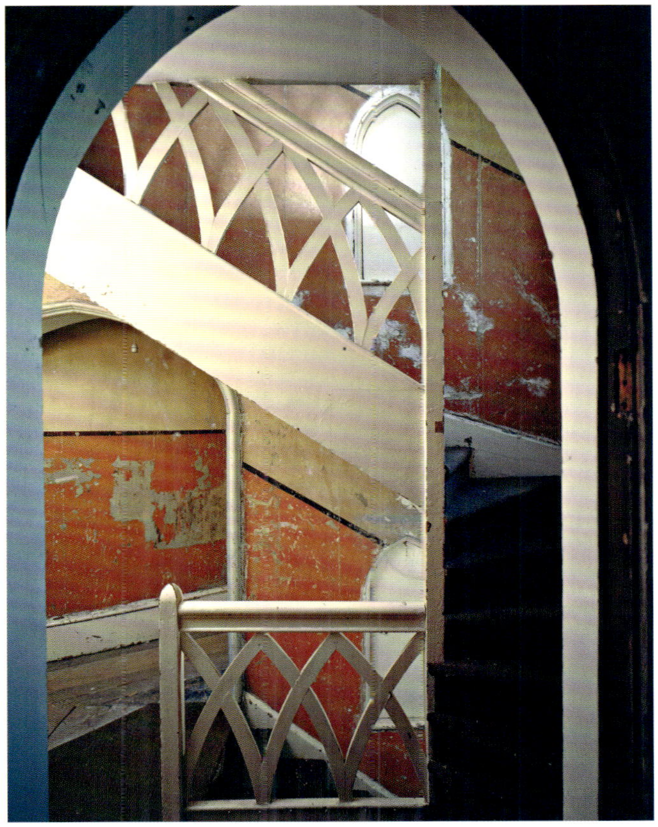

Figure 106. The back stairs at Strawberry Hill, photographed in 2008. The painting dates from after *c.* 1925

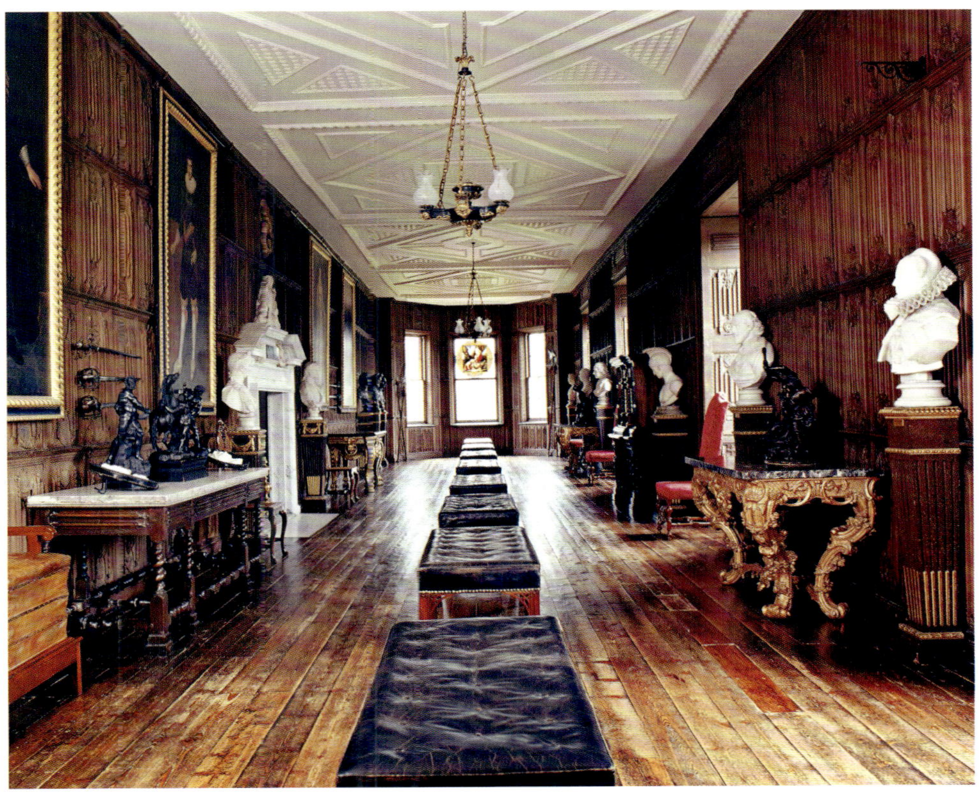

Figure 107. Modern View of Oak Gallery, The Vyne, looking south. National Trust Picture Library

lower gallery, Walpole's Great Cloister, while taking its inspiration from the middle reign of Henry VIII, was also unquestionably Italian in character, with an open loggia giving on to the Pleasure Ground and its internal wall pierced by arches with grilles that reveal a carefully articulated wall behind.

During Walpole's own lifetime the architecture of his villa was celebrated as a new approach to the revival of Gothic. By adapting the existing buildings on the site and by chance, through the accretive development of the villa over more than thirty years, Walpole achieved a building that could be experienced as a truly ancient structure, while the sequence of architectural quotations gave the design authenticity. The romance of Strawberry Hill for the informed eighteenth-century tourist was its ability to evoke the Gothic both visually and experientially, as Frances Burney described:

> All that was peculiar, especially the most valuable of his pictures, he had the politeness to point out to his guests himself; and not unfrequently, from the deep shade in which some of his antique portraits were placed, and the lone sort of look of the unusually shaped apartments in which they were hung, striking recollections were brought to their minds of his Gothic story of the Castle of Otranto.[20]

Through such architectural conceits Walpole was able to suggest an elaborate fictive history, uniquely achieved at Strawberry Hill. While Walpole's approach was new, it was to be overtaken by the development of a better understanding of Gothic architecture. Within a few decades of Walpole's death the architecture of the villa had lost its appeal, typically being dismissed by Harriet Arbuthnot as 'dull and shews a good deal of bad taste'.[22]

1. Batty and Thomas Langley, *Ancient architecture, restored, and improved, by a great variety of grand and usefull designs, entirely new in the Gothick mode* (London, 1742). Walpole's own copy is at the Lewis Walpole Library, and the endpaper contains a design for the 'Great' or 'South' Tower.
2. *HW Corres.* 20: 119.
3. The finials were disassociated from the chimneypiece at the end of the nineteenth century, when a standard Turkish-style overmantel was hung, and installed in the south-east corner room, Walpole's Plaid Bedchamber, on the second flooor.
4. Allen T. Hazen, *Catalogue of Horace Walpole's Library*, 3 vols. (New Haven and London: 1969), 1: 306. The theory first circulated as a manuscript, but was later published within Stephen Wren's *Parentalia: or, Memoirs of the Family of the Wrens* (London, 1750) and owned by Walpole from 1759. Hazen states that Walpole made notes from *Parentalia* in his Books of Materials dated by Hazen to *c.* 1759–61.
5. *HW Corres.* 24: 209.
6. 'Unpublished Collections: Norton Court Papers', Hampshire County Record Office, series 5M50, bundle 2100.
7. Vincent Scamozzi, *Les Cinq Ordres d'Architecture* (Paris: Jean Paptiste Coignard, 1705). Chute's own copy remains at the Vyne, Hampshire, part of the collection bequeathed by Sir Charles Chute to the National Trust.
8. *HW Corres.* 35: 184.
9. *HW Corres.* 35: 72.
10. *HW Corres.* 3: 77.
11. *HW Corres.* 20: 119.
12. *D 1774*, 3.
13. Louis Simond, *Journal of a tour and residence in Great Britain, during the years 1810 and 1811*, 2 vols., 2nd ed. (Edinburgh: Constable, 1817), 1: 192.
14. *HW Corres.* 20: 381.
15. *HW Corres.* 35: 234.
16. *HW Corres.* 20: 372.
17. *HW Corres.* 21: 238.
18. *HW Corres.* 2: 24.
19. 'The Rev. William Cole Papers', British Library Add Ms 548[illegible].
20. Charlotte Barrett, *Diary and Letters of Madam D'Arblay*, 7 vols. (New York: Macmillan & Co., 1904), 2: 483.
21. Francis Bamford and Duke of Wellington, eds., *The Journal of Mrs [Harriet] Arbuthnot (1820–1832)*, 2 vols. (London: Macmillan & Co., 1950): 176.

Strawberry hill
Nov. 4th 1759.

Well, how delightfull! how the deuce did you contrive to get such proportion? you will certainly have all the women with short legs come to you to design high-heeld shoes for them. The Cloyster instead of a Winecellar, has the air of a College. It has already passed the Seals. Mr Müntz has commended it in a piece of every language, & Mr Bentley is at this moment turning it outside inwards. — I assure you, Mr Chute, you shall always have my custom. You shall design every scrap of the ornaments; & if ever I build a palace or found a City, I will employ nobody but you. In short, you have found a proportion & given a simplicity & lightness to it, that I never expected. I have but one fault to find, & that is no bigger than my little finger; I think the buttresses too slight; & yet I fear, widening them would destroy the beauty of the space round the Windows. There is another thing which is more than a fear, for it seems an impossibility, that is, of getting pictures over the windows within; & if I cant, what shall I do with the spaces?

4.

STRAWBERRY HILL: FRIENDSHIP AND TASTE

GEORGE E. HAGGERTY

IN THIS CHAPTER I will discuss Horace Walpole's attitude towards Strawberry Hill as expressed in his letters. The forty-eight volumes of *The Yale Edition of Horace Walpole's Correspondence* constitute the outstanding series of letters in English,[1] and if they have been well plumbed for literary, historical, art-historical and cultural fact, they have rarely been read as the astonishing literary achievement that they are. Along with their artistic merit, they can also be seen to reveal Horace Walpole's attitudes towards Strawberry Hill, and they often articulate those features of the house that he most cherished. Much of his interest in the house depended on the shared interest of his closest friends, and I will explore some of the eighteenth century's most intriguing accounts of male friendship and taste and how the two come together in discussions of Strawberry Hill.

Strawberry Hill is a treasure trove of eighteenth-century attitudes towards architecture, fashion, wealth and the past. The house is famous as a monument to all things Gothic, and its image, still strong against the English sky, reminds us all of the almost ludicrous extent to which Gothic antiquity had captured the imagination of mid- and later eighteenth-century Englishmen, and one rather wonderful eighteenth-century Englishman in particular. But Walpole's case is illuminating in this regard. The building was a collaborative project with his dearest friends, and he never tired of advertising it as a resort for those who shared his taste. What these men had in common is difficult to describe, but we can begin to examine the mutual sensibility of the group of mostly unmarried gentlemen by remembering the term that the contemporary Swiss writer Charles Victor de Bonstetten used when talking about the poet Thomas Gray (Fig. 112):[2] *sensibilité*.[3] Walpole and his friends, Gray included, shared a *sensibilité* that set them apart, established them as a group, like-minded in aesthetic and decorative choices as they were, and gave them a common cause. For a while, for Walpole and his closest friends, Strawberry Hill was that cause.

What is at stake here is something about identity that Walpole and his friends understood but rarely expressed. They did not identify themselves and were not identified by their contemporaries as sodomites, although several of them, Thomas Gray included, were known to feel erotic desire for members of their own sex, including at times for their own friends. This quality of shared intimacy, in which Walpole participated, however intense his experience of such feelings might be, renders the aesthetic pleasure that Strawberry Hill evokes even more multi-layered than the crenellated structure itself. Walpole's own sexuality is not at issue here. It seems unlikely that, except perhaps for schoolboy high jinks, Horace Walpole had sexual relations with other men. At the same time, the intimacy that he shared with a whole range of men who were recognized as sodomitical begins to suggest a common sexual subjectivity understood and even celebrated.[4]

As the house came to fulfill so many of Walpole's dreams, it became something like an obsession. Charles Saumarez Smith puts it like this:

Figure 108. Letter from Horace Walpole to John Chute, 4 November 1759. The Lewis Walpole Library, Yale University. Cat. 265

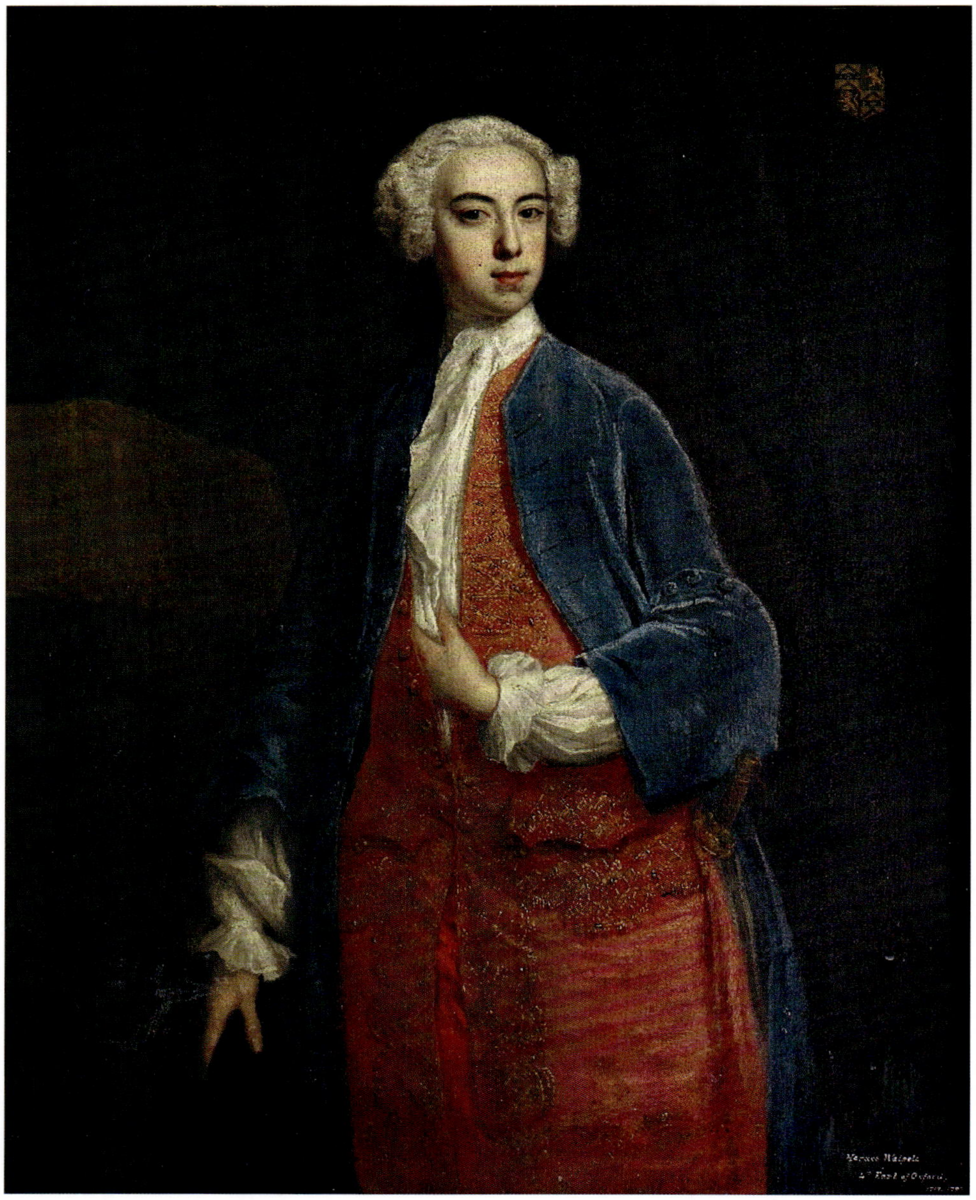

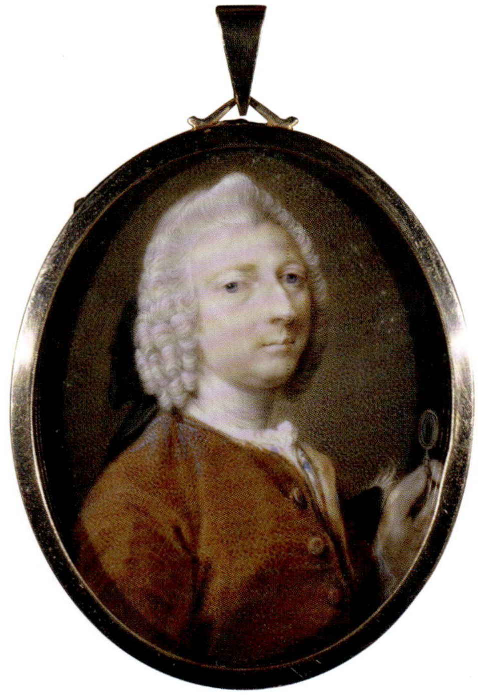

Figure 109. Jonathan Richardson, *Portrait of Horace Walpole*, 1734–5, oil on canvas, 125.7 × 86.4 cm. The Trustees of the Waldegrave Chattels Trust. Cat. 37

Figure 110. Pompeo Batoni, *Portrait Miniature of John Chute*, 1745–6, watercolour on ivory, H 5.6 cm. The Vyne, The Chute Collection (The National Trust). Cat. 191

> In building Strawberry Hill Horace Walpole became progressively more obsessional about what he was doing. What had begun as a whim, born out of a desire to irritate other people's expectations, gradually became a serious exercise in archaeology, recreating different periods of architecture from room to room. And although Walpole has suffered from his tendency to be frivolous about whatever he was doing, he did use Strawberry Hill as an experimental laboratory for different styles of building.[5]

I think the building was an 'experimental laboratory' in more ways than one. As Walpole came to inhabit Strawberry Hill, it became more than a backdrop for his artistic and creative exploits. In subtle and at times indeterminate ways it became the expression of who he was. An architectural aesthete, as well as a collector – a

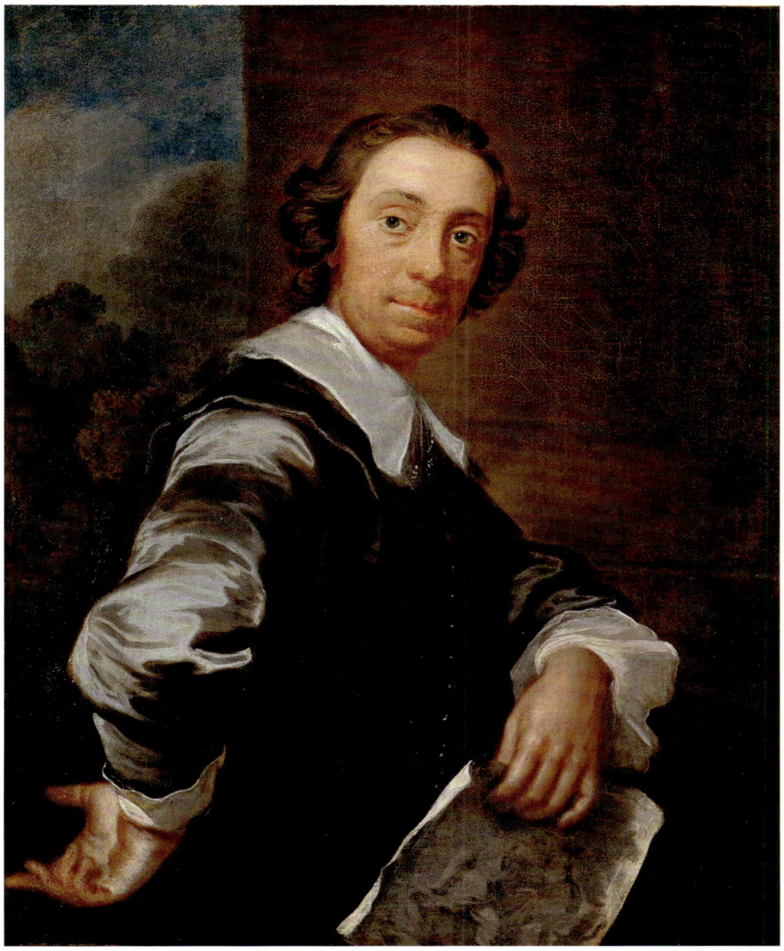

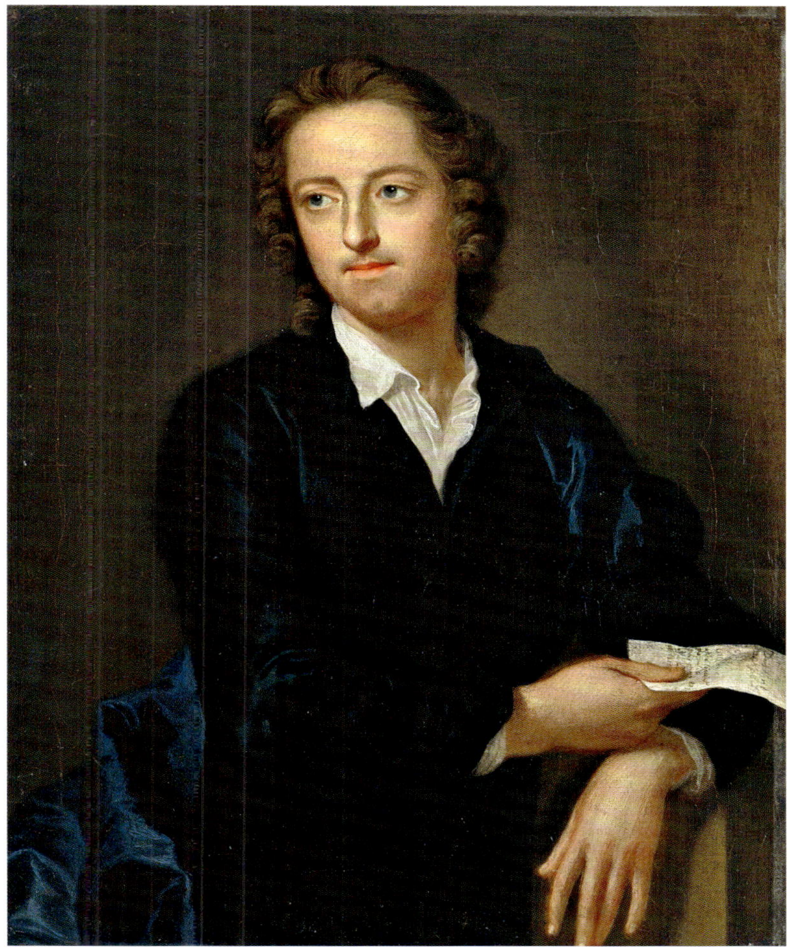

virtuoso, as Katherine Coombs's essay in this collection (pp. 183–200) explains – Walpole designed Strawberry Hill and shaped its effect. To do so he committed his little bit of plundering in the British Isles and beyond. The result is an astonishing combination of ironic aesthetics and historical pastiche. One hardly needed to look beyond the surface to realize that much of the effect was painted on, but that did not seem to bother Walpole. He was primarily concerned to achieve the effect he was looking for, and the effect of Strawberry Hill is authentic, even if nothing else about it is. That is to say, the effect *is* Strawberry Hill, and Walpole understood it precisely that way. He also understood that the effect of the house was indistinguishable, even in his own mind at times, from his own personal affect. If I have elsewhere anachronistically called this affect camp, then in the epistolary discussions of the house I can begin to show the specific contours of that proto-camp sensibility.

Into this Gothic product of his imagination, Walpole implicated his most intimate friends. The first circle of such friends included what he called the 'committee' or 'Strawberry committee' (see pp. 80–81). Walpole formed the committee with his dear friends John Chute (Fig. 110), owner of a country house called the Vyne and deeply devoted to Walpole's love of antiquities, and Richard Bentley (Fig. 111), the artist and illustrator whom Walpole sponsored and encouraged. Together these men worked to make Strawberry Hill a Gothic gem. Walpole consulted them or asked them for drawings and designs. They entered into the project enthusiastically because they saw it as an expression of their friend and benefactor.

Figure 111. John Giles Eccardt, *Portrait of Richard Bentley*, 1753, oil on canvas, 42.2 × 34.3 cm. National Portrait Gallery, London. 5885. Cat. 41

Figure 112. John Giles Eccardt, *Portrait of Thomas Gray*, 1747–8, oil on canvas, 40.3 × 32.7 cm. National Portrait Gallery, London. 989. Cat. 42

Taste became a code for a certain mode of shared sensibility that was often understood to suggest something about sexual predilection or at least qualified masculinity. John Beynon, in a chapter about William Beckford, traces taste back to its articulation in Joseph Addison's *Spectator*, No. 409 (19 June 1712), in which the periodical writer expatiates on 'that Sensitive Taste which gives us relish of every different Flavour that affects the Palate'.[6] Beynon also cites Joseph Litvak, who 'has suggested that the gustatory underpinnings of sophistication grant an erotic quality to the pursuit of good taste by claiming that the mouth and the pleasures of orality are fundamentally erotic experiences'. 'The distance between the aesthetic and culinary taste in sophistication is never as great as their distance in distinction,' Litvak claims; 'what enables their proximity ... is the psychosexual dimension of taste.'[7]

The psychosexual dimension of taste is never far from the surface when we are dealing with Walpole and his friends. Sir Horace Mann, Walpole's close friend and lifelong correspondent, and other members of his Florentine circle were labelled 'finger-twirlers', by Hester Lynch Piozzi ('"finger-twirlers" meaning a decent word for Sodomites').[8] Walpole and Mann maintained a standard of taste as a way of asserting their shared sensibility, and they understood aesthetic values and artistic judgment in similar terms. As a result, they can often take for granted a judgment or assessment that seems puzzling to us outside their circle. Walpole and his closest friends – the committee and beyond – understood taste as a definitive arbiter, something that they shared and that defined them. Like the later concept of identity, taste was a shared predilection for the artistically sophisticated, for the idiosyncratic, for the one item, or series of items, that can help to make Strawberry Hill a retreat worthy of its creator.

The house was a source of amusement to Walpole, a kind of amusement of which he never tired. Jill Campbell, in an insightful essay about incest and sexuality in Walpole, points out that Walpole 'suggests that if Strawberry Hill can exist as a flight of fancy or castle in the air, it is because it is a bachelor's rather than a family's habitation, and the collaborative project of a group of male friends'.[9] For Campbell, 'Strawberry Hill served as the extended "body" that might be playfully, innocently, shared by Walpole and his circle of male friends'.[10] Walpole and his friends used Strawberry Hill as a way of coming out of their respective privacies and sharing something that they could invest with personal meaning. The house gave them, Walpole especially, a way to express themselves in intimate, artistic and playful ways. If it all remained a facade, then that is what they preferred.

Walpole's letters to Chute show him at his most droll and self-satisfied, but also at his most posturing, all of which he uses as a gesture of closeness between friends. Here is a typical effusion that combines personal style and architectural detail, as so often in the correspondence with Chute. There is a quality to this conversation that suggests a shared attitude about all things artistic and a similar view of the social world that was their context. Walpole's voice comes through his writing as arch and a bit exaggerated, but one can almost feel the way in which the writer exaggerates for effect and rolls his eyes with pleasure as he teases his friend. Walpole is responding to Chute's design for a Gallery and cloister at Strawberry Hill (Fig. 108):

> Well, how delightful! how the deuce did you contrive to get such proportions? you will certainly have all the women with short legs come to you to design high-heeled shoes for them. The cloister, instead of a wine cellar, has the air of a college. It has already passed the Seals. Mr. Müntz has commended it in a piece of every language, and Mr. Bentley is at this moment turning it outside inwards – I assure you, Mr. Chute, you shall always have my custom. You shall design every scrap of the ornaments; and if ever I build a palace or found a city, I will employ nobody but you. In short, you have found a proportion and given a simplicity and lightness to it, that I never expected. I have but one fault to find, and this is no bigger than my little finger; I think the buttresses too slight; and yet I fear widening them would destroy the beauty of the space round the windows. There is another thing which is more than a fear, for it seems an impossibility, that is, of getting pictures over the windows within; and if I can't, what shall I do with the spaces?[11]

Walpole flatters Chute and praises his abilities before he takes issue with the design. This is typical of work-in-progress on Strawberry Hill, but it is also typical of Walpole's dealing with his friends. There is a stylistic freedom here – almost a swagger – that is meant to put Chute at his ease. This tone, as simple as it is, could misfire if these friends did not understand one another as well as they do. Instead, Walpole indulges himself in a way that moves him closer to Chute. The intimacy of friendship and shared sensibilities allows these freedoms, as does their deep and mutually instinctive understanding of the world. Campbell points to Walpole's 'profound investment of discourse itself with an erotic charge (which should remind us that sexuality is not located only in *bodily* acts) and his skeptical interrogation of the status of those bodies that perform "empirical" sexual acts'.[12] Twenty-first-century readers can sense the erotic charge in these letters, as vividly as the writers themselves do. Throughout the correspondence these men shared intimate details of their lives and bonded in as many ways as a letter can express. Chute and his companion Francis Whithead – the 'Chuteheads' Walpole called them – were devoted friends of Walpole's, and even after Whithead's early death Chute remained a fast and unfailing friend. When Chute sends suggestions for Strawberry Hill, Walpole always accepts them warmly. Even as he complains about some stylistic details, Walpole manages to flatter Chute in his typically friendly way. Walpole's aesthetic sense became in fact an end in itself. Walpole may have been up to his elbows in tradesmen and negotiations and shipments from Italy, as critics like Barrett Kalter have shown, but his purpose in creating Strawberry Hill caused all that business to fade in the shadow of the edifice itself.[13] Strawberry Hill was a kind of stage set on which Walpole performed his life, but because of that function it mattered all the more that its aesthetic effect should be precise and irresistible.

As R.W. Ketton-Cremer has said:

> The early seventeen-fifties were halcyon days at Strawberry Hill. The Committee of Taste worked together harmoniously and with enjoyment; expert visitors, like Gray and Montagu, and the inexpert throngs of the world of fashion were equally enraptured; in cathedrals and castles and ancient folios lay unexplored treasures of Gothic ready to be plundered. It was all gay and exciting; and Walpole was a happy man as he watched the rise of his battlements and the ever-increasing beauty of the trees and shrubs he planted, while the sun glittered on the Thames and splashed the colours of his painted glass about the rooms.[14]

Walpole involves other friends in the creation of this glittering abode. Writing to the Rev. William Cole, who was planning to visit in the summer of 1762, he says:

> I should name the earliest day possible; but besides having some visits to make, I think it will be more pleasant to you in a few weeks hence (I mean any time in July) when the works which I am finishing my house will be more advanced, and the noisy part, as laying floors, and fixing wainscots, at an end, and which now make me in a deplorable litter.[15]

The next year he writes to George Montagu on the continued building going on about the place:

> I am going to Strawberry for a few days *pour faire me pâques*. The gallery advances rapidly. The ceiling is Harry VII's chapel *in propriâ persona*: the canopies are all placed. I think three months will quite complete it.[16]

Later that year, he could write again to Montagu about its nearing completion:

> Gilders, carvers, upholsterers, and picture-cleaners are labouring at their several forges, and I do not love to trust a hammer or a brush without my own supervisal … Well! but I begin to be ashamed of my magnificence; Strawberry is growing sumptuous in its latter day; it will scarce be any longer like the fruit of its name, or the modesty of its ancient demeanour, both which seem to have been in Spenser's prophetic eye, when he sung of –
>
> – the blushing strawberries,
> Which lurk, close-shrouded from high-looking eyes,
> Shewing that sweetness low and hidden lies.
>
> In truth, my collection was too great already to be lodged humbly; it has extended my walls, and pomp followed. It was a neat little house, it now will be a comfortable one, and except one

George E. Haggerty

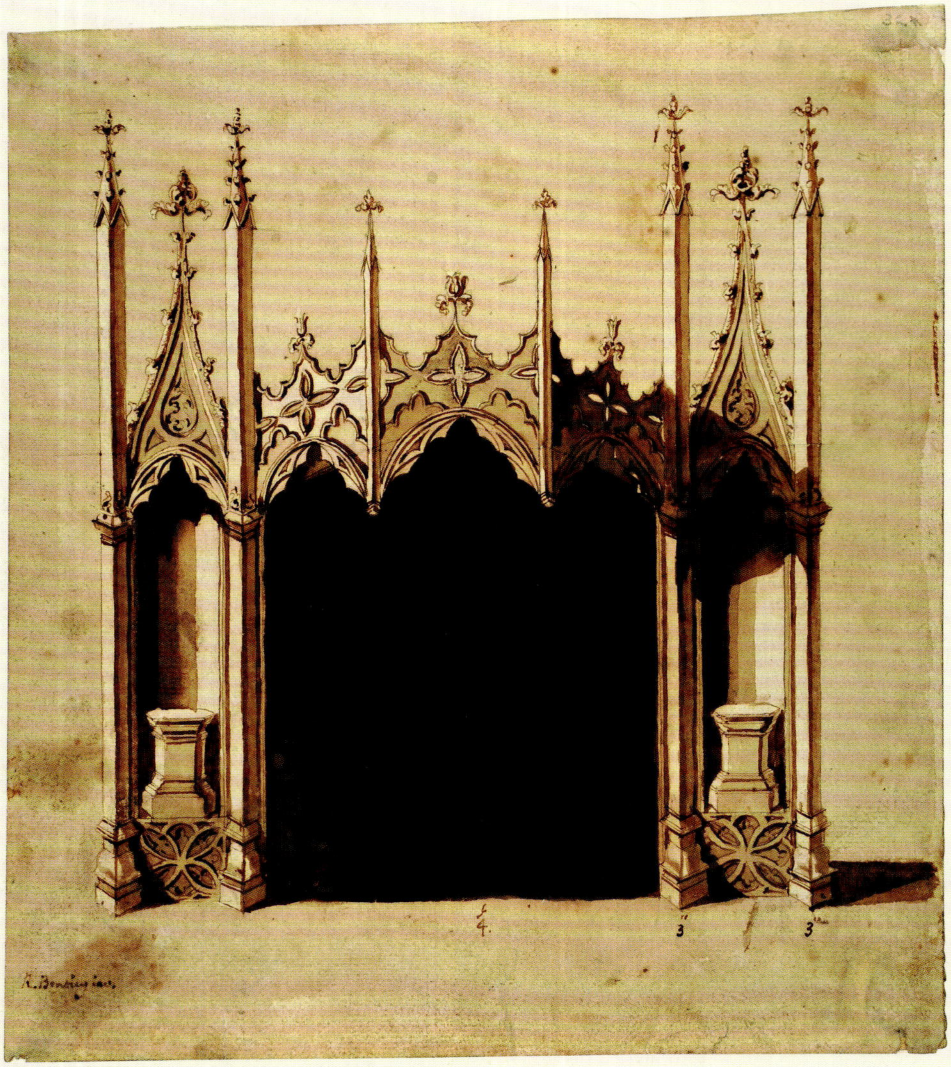

Figure 113. Richard Bentley, *Chimneypiece in the Refectory or great parlour at Strawberryhill*, 1754, ink wash and graphite on laid paper, 22.9 × 20 cm, from *Drawings and Designs by Richd. Bentley*, 1760. The Lewis Walpole Library, Yale University. Folio 49 3585 fol. 32. Cat. 60

Horace Walpole invited two friends to join him in forming the 'Strawberry Committee' (also called the 'Committee'), better known in its erroneous modern name of the 'Committee of Taste' (see Appendix 4, p. 349), to assist him with his architectural and artistic projects at Strawberry Hill. Most active throughout the 1750s, the Committee included Richard Bentley, the artist who also designed *Designs by Mr. R. Bentley for Six Poems by Mr. T. Gray*, which Walpole saw into publication in 1753 (Fig. 44), and John Chute, who lived in a country house of grand proportions at his family's estate in Hampshire, The Vyne, and used his experience there to help Walpole in many of his decisions about Strawberry Hill (Figs. 94, 104). Walpole valued the advice of both these friends and frequently consulted them as Strawberry Hill developed.

Chute and his companion Francis Whithead appear as benign and helpful friends and delightful companions throughout Walpole's correspondence. Chute was a talented architectural designer, and he threw himself into Strawberry Hill with keen enthusiasm and extraordinary care. Walpole often thanked him for his stunning designs and original conceptions. His friendship with Walpole was deep and long-standing, and when he died in May 1776, Walpole wrote to Horace Mann one of his most profound epistolary elegies.

Walpole's friendship with Bentley was slightly less stable, and Bentley's influence on the design of the house was less reliable. His designs are more extreme than Chute's, and they often add rococo excess to Chute's more controlled Gothic plans (Fig. 113). Chute's design for the Cabinet at Strawberry Hill (Fig. 114) shows this restraint, while Bentley's design for Thomas Gray's 'Elegy Written in a Country Churchyard' shows a more excessive, but wonderful, artistic sensibility (Fig. 141). Walpole found in the end that he preferred Chute's input to Bentley's, and that was perhaps best for the house itself.

The Committee helped Walpole to figure out how to create a Gothic eighteenth-century house without making it a parody of itself. In particular, decisions about architectural detail and interior decoration were all passed through the Committee, and repeatedly in the *Correspondence* Walpole can be seen to engage with his friends on topics like a staircase, the proportions of windows or a crenellated roofline. The architectural research that these three men pursued and the care with which their designs were executed established Strawberry Hill as an architectural wonder even in its own time.

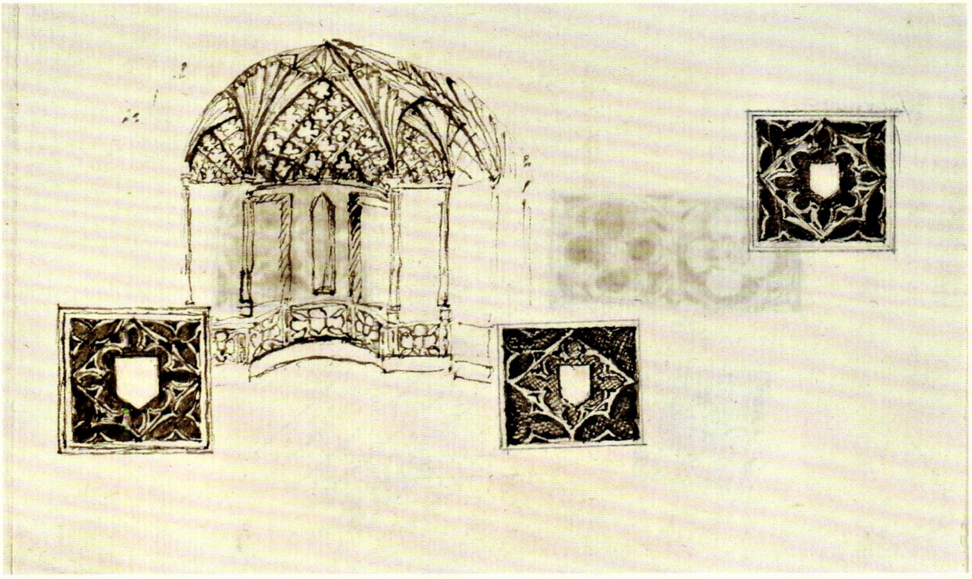

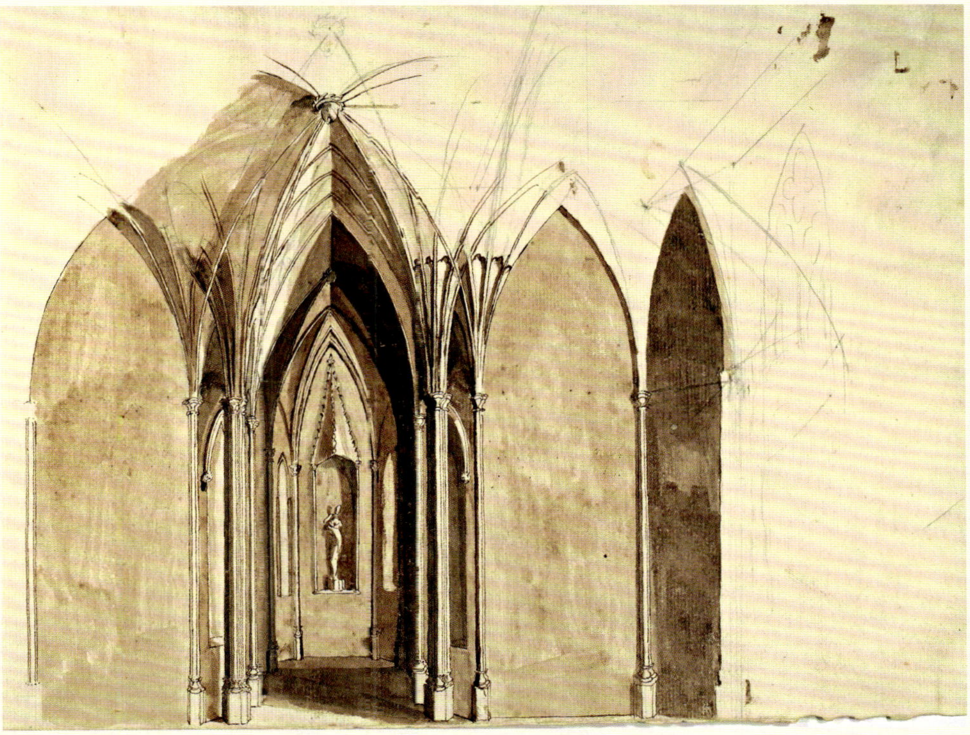

Figure 114. John Chute, *Designs for the Tribune at Strawberry Hill*, *c.* 1759, pen and ink, mounted in the volume of John Chute's 'Original Drawings and sketches'. The Lewis Walpole Library, Yale University. Folio 49 3490 fol. 16

Figure 115. Richard Bentley, *'First Idea for the Chapel Tribune at Strawberry Hill'*, *c.* 1758, pen and ink, pencil and brown wash, 23 × 37.8 cm, from *Drawings and Designs by Richd. Bentley*, 1760. The Lewis Walpole Library, Yale University. Folio 49 3585 fol. 58. Cat. 157

> fine apartment, does not deviate from its simplicity. Adieu! I know nothing about the world, care nothing about the world, and am only Strawberry's and, yours sincerely, H. Walpole.[17]

A passage like this allows us to see how the enthusiasm for works at the house turn into self-reflection; and then that reflection develops into a wonderful literary reference (not by Spenser at all); and then the literary reference develops into a kind of true confession. This is a telling example of the ways wit and taste work together in Walpole's imagination, especially when he is dealing with Strawberry Hill. The house evokes these extravagant statements because it is really more than a house. Walpole has invested Strawberry Hill with so much of himself that he is afraid to take it too seriously.

He has nicknames for the house, of course. To Montagu he calls it his 'Abbey' and signs himself 'The Abbot of Strawberry';[18] to his cousin Harry (Hon. Henry Seymour) Conway he writes more elaborately:

> I give myself airs, in my nutshell, like an old baron, and am tempted to say with an old Earl of Norfolk, who was a very free speaker, at least, if he was not an excellent poet:
>
> When I am in my Castle of Bungey
> Situate upon the river of Waveney
> I ne care for the King of Cockney.[19]

Much later in life, writing to George Nicol, who had just been to see the house in 1790 and who wrote a flattering letter in response, Walpole downplayed the house and his own devotion to it:

> Now at near seventy-four, I have neither the presumption to look forwards to duration, nor the vanity to imagine that old age, additionally enfeebled by between thirty and forty years of gout, is fit for anything but repose. My best wisdom has consisted in forming a baby-house for my second childhood, and I fear they do me more honour, especially as they amused you, than what Pope has so well called – the rattles of the Man or Boy.[20]

As the house came together, Walpole wrote about it excitedly, whether he was designing an arch or choosing a paint colour. To Mann, for instance, he expounds:

> I should like Marshal Botta's furniture that you describe if my tenure in Strawberry were as transitory as a Florentine commander's; but in a castle built for eternity and founded in the most flourishing age of the greatest republic now in the world, which has extended its empire into every quarter of the globe, can I think of a peach-coloured ground, which will fade like the bloom on Chloe's cheek? – there's a pompous paragraph! a Grecian or a Roman would have written it seriously, and with even more slender pretensions. However, though my castle is built of paper, and though our empire should vanish as rapidly as it has advanced, I still object to peach-colour – not only from its fading hue, but for wanting the solemnity becoming a Gothic edifice: I must not have a round tower dressed in a pet-en'l'air. I would as soon put rouge and patches on a stature of St. Ethelburgh.

Walpole chides himself for his own pomposity, but at the same time he asserts a preference that makes it impossible for him to consider the furniture that Mann has suggested. He desires to furnish his castle with a view to empire, and as silly as this sounds, there are times when this kind of thing is deadly serious for Walpole. This is classic Walpole: his ability to dismiss his castle as 'built of paper' in the same sentence in which he insists on Gothic solemnity. This gives a wonderful sense of the almost mock-heroic quality of the place: always a trifle, but always profoundly important at the same time.

As he proceeds in this same letter, he is more specific, and the earlier air of (false) house-humility gives way to a vivid description and almost captious assertion of Strawberry Hill grandeur:

> Three years ago I had the ceiling of my china room painted from one I had observed in the little Borghese Villa. I was hoarding ideas for a future Strawberry even in those days of giddiness, when I seemed to attend to nothing. The altar of the eagle is three feet two inches and a half high, by one foot eight inches wide. If that for the Vespasian should be a trifle larger, especially a little higher, it would carry so large a bust better; but I imagine the race of altar-tombs are pretty much of the same dimensions.[21]

In a sense, Mann is the fourth member of the Strawberry Committee. From Florence he sent materials, consulted on designs, and chided and supported Walpole as only such an old and treasured friend could. Walpole is writing in the 1760s, moreover, about something he saw in Italy almost twenty years earlier. Strawberry Hill seems to emerge from these 'days of giddiness' as a natural extension of the playful young Horace. And in a sense it does; but at the same time that giddiness gives way to the careful measure of altars and the discussion of proper dimensions for display. Giddy exterior, perhaps, but a razor-sharp mind and a vivid sense of what is correct and in the proper taste.

Walpole and Mann talked about Strawberry Hill from the time Walpole began the project, and some of his letters to Mann are the most profoundly revealing of his feelings about the place and its meaning to him:

> Your old acquaintance Lord and Lady Dacre, and your old friend Mr. Chute, dined with me today: poor Lord Dacre is carried about, though not worse than he has been these twenty years. Strawberry was in great beauty – what joy I should have in showing it to you! Is this a wish I must never indulge? – alas!

After this effusion Walpole steps back and considers what the house means to him – how his friendship with Mann and his feelings about the house are related – and this causes him to become almost philosophical:

> I have had a long chain of thoughts since I wrote the last paragraph. They ended in smiling at the word *never*. How one pronounces it to the last moment! Would not one think I counted on a long series of years to come? Yet no man has the termination of all his views before his eyes, or knows better the idleness of framing visions to one's self. One passes away so soon, and worlds succeed to worlds, in which the occupiers build the same castles in the air. What is ours but the present moment? And how many of mine are gone! And what do I want to show you? A plaything-vision, that has amused a poor transitory mortal for a few hours, and that will pass away like its master! – Well, and yet is it not as sensible to conform to common ideas, and to live while one lives? Perhaps the wisest way is to cheat one's self … Our wishes and views have given us to gild the dream of life, and if a Strawberry Hill can soften the decays of the age, it is wise to embrace it, and due gratitude to the Great Giver to be happy with it.[22]

Here the house is 'A plaything-vision, that has amused a poor transitory mortal for a few hours, and that will pass away like its master!' Its very transitory nature – and how less than transitory it has seemed – gives Walpole reason to reassert his devotion to it. If Walpole and his friends can 'gild the dream of life', then Strawberry Hill is a kind of fantasy world that these men share. And if the house can 'soften the decays of the age', as in Walpole's case it did, then what better way to expend the energy of his middle years. Walpole's happiness here suggests how dearly he held this house and how much it finally meant to him. There is no sense that this use of the house as a palliative to life was ever exhausted.

Walpole also included Cole in his plundering of the country for ideas and at times materials. In this fairly typical request Walpole asks Cole for help with Strawberry Hill:

> After gratitude, you know comes a little self-interest, for who would be at the trouble of being grateful, if he had no farther expectations? *Imprimis* then, here are the directions for Mr. Essex for the piers of my gates. Bishop Luda must not be offended at my converting his tomb into a gateway. Many a saint and confessor, I doubt, will be glad soon to be *passed through*, as it will at least secure his being *passed over* … The width of the iron gates is six feet two, and they are seven feet ten high. Each pilaster is one foot wide: the whole width with the interstices, is eight feet ten. The ornament over the gates is four feet four to the point. Perhaps you will understand me from this scrawl. The piers should certainly, I think, be a little, and not much higher than the ornament over the gates, but Mr. Essex will judge best of the proper proportion. I would not have any bas relief or figures in the bases. The tops to be in this manner – nothing over the gates themselves (I have drawn these piers too wide).[23]

The degree of detail that Walpole provides, and the care with which he makes drawings to accompany the text, all mark the seriousness of his Gothic enterprise. Walpole is precise in his desires here because he knows that Cole will be precise in his response. The detail offers a challenge to Cole, as playful a challenge as that above, and this is the kind of challenge that he is always ready to meet. More than sending a request for antiquarian aid, Walpole reaches out to Cole from a sense of what they share. At the same time he offers Cole participation in his own careless plundering of Gothic monuments for his own local effects. The Gothic spirit of this enterprise suffuses the transaction with a seriousness of purpose; and if Walpole risks offending his antiquarian friend with this crazy plan, he also knows that by pushing Cole into these almost sacrilegious plunderings, both literal and figurative, he appeals to the desire for mischievous transgression that Walpole offers. If Walpole wants to use a tomb-gate for Strawberry Hill, Cole will not be the friend to stop him.

This love of plunder animates Walpole's letters when he writes from various places around the country. To Bentley, for instance, Walpole sends a long and architecturally detailed travelogue after travelling in Worcestershire. When writing to Bentley, he uses their mutual love of Strawberry Hill as a touchstone:

> From Worcester I went to see Malvern Abbey. It is situated halfway up an immense mountain of that name: the mountain is very long, in shape like the prints of a whale's back: toward the larger end lies the town. Nothing remains but a beautiful gateway and the church, which is very large … The greatest curiosity, at least what I had never seen before, was, the whole floor and far up the sides of the church has been, if I may call it so, wainscoted with red and yellow tiles, extremely polished, and diversified with coats of arms, and inscriptions, and mosaic. I have since found the same in Glocester, and have been so fortunate as to purchase from the sexton about a dozen, which think what an acquisition for Strawberry![24]

Walpole's attachment to his home is evident here, and he does not even have to explain to his friend what he has in mind. Walpole assumes a commitment in Bentley almost equivalent to his own, and this is one of the things that makes his demands on Bentley so understandable: he would demand the same of himself. He makes the project a kind of game that engages all his friends and gives them a common cause. He writes to Mann from Strawberry Hill:

> Mr. Chute and I are come hither for a day or two to inspect the progress of a Gothic staircase, which is so pretty and small, that I am inclined to wrap it up and send it to you in my letter. As my castle is so diminutive, I give myself a Burlington-air, and say, that as Chiswick is a model of Grecian architecture, Strawberry Hill is to be so of Gothic.[25]

Chute, Bentley and Walpole conspired to make this small house something grand.

Horace Walpole felt that his own taste was impeccable, and he looked for a similar taste in others. In writing to the grandson of the architect Christopher Wren, and in an attempt to make an important distinction, Walpole says:

> That there now and then has been a genius (for a genius itself is a curiosity) without taste, and often taste without genius, is evident from example. Shakespeare undoubtedly wanted taste. In every class, which is the subject of this letter, I mean architecture, Inigo Jones seems to me to have had more taste than genius. A genius is original, invents. Taste selects, perhaps copies with judgment. If I am right, have I wronged your ancestor?[26]

When he is writing to Chute, Mann or any of his intimate friends, there is a special quality to the correspondence. These men understand the intricacies of one another's sensibilities, and they can talk about the details of wainscoting without having to stop to explain their concerns to each other. They participate, each in his own way, in the construction of Strawberry Hill because they know that it brings their friend out into the open and forces his secrets from their hiding places. Of course, the secrets turn out to be nothing more lurid than the love these men share, the project to which they are devoted, and the deep generosity of the man who has invited them to share in his vision. They do not even dream of resisting. Strawberry Hill celebrates those relations in terms that are both outrageous, as the grand gestures of the house are outrageous, and secretive, as the house harbours, like any Gothic edifice, its forbidden centre. If that centre is the erotic camaraderie of this group of aristocrats and quasi-aristocrats, then it reminds us that the history of sexuality is more complicated than we have been led to believe.

1. *The Yale Edition of Horace Walpole's Correspondence*, ed. W.S. Lewis *et al.*, 48 vols. (New Haven and London: Yale University Press, 1937–83).
2. George E. Haggerty, 'Queering Horace Walpole', *Studies in English Literature* (*SEL*) 46 (2006): 543–62.
3. George E. Haggerty, *Men in Love: Masculinity and Sexuality in the Eighteenth Century* (New York: Columbia University Press, 1999): 114. 'Gray avait la gaieté dans l'ésprit et de la mélancholie dans le caractère. Mais cette mélancholie n'est qu'un besoin non-satisfait de la sensibilité.' ('Gray had gayety in his spirit and melancholy in his character. But this melancholy was only an unsatisfied need of his sensibility.') (Bonstetten, *Souvenirs* [1831], quoted in R.W. Ketton-Cremer, *Thomas Gray: A Biography* [Cambridge: Cambridge University Press, 1955], 253); see also Jean Hagstrum, 'Gray's Sensibility', in *Fearful Joy: Papers from the Thomas Gray Bicentenary Conference at Carleton University*, ed. J. Downey and B. Jones (McGill-Queen's University, 1974), [6–19] 7–11.
4. See Haggerty, 'Queering Horace Walpole'.
5. Charles Saumarez Smith, *Eighteenth-Century Decoration: Design and the Domestic Interior in England* (New York: Harry N. Abrams, 1993), 237; see, further, 237–40.
6. John C. Beynon, 'Men of Mode: Taste, Effeminacy, and Male Sexuality in Eighteenth-Century England' (University of California, Riverside, dissertation; submitted June 2001), 145. See also '"Mr Beckford's Favourite Propensity": The Erotics of Boyhood and the Emergence of a Sexual Self in Late-Eighteenth-Century England', in *William Beckford and the New Millennium*, ed. Kenneth Graham (New York: AMS, 2004), 7–35; and Jody Greene, 'Arbitrary Tastes and Commonsense Pleasures: Accounting for Taste in Cleland, Hume, and Burke', in *Launching Fanny Hill: Essays on the Novel and Its Influences*, ed. Patsy S. Fowler and Alan Jackson (New York: AMS Press, 2003), 212–66.
7. Beynon, 'Men of Mode', 149; see also Joseph Litvak, *Strange Gourmets: Sophistication, Theory, and the Novel* (Durham: Duke University Press, 1997), 8.
8. Brian Fothergill, in his study of Walpole's circle, quotes Hester Lynch (Thrale) Piozzi, who describes Mann and his circle this way: 'I call these Fellows "Finger-twirlers," meaning a decent word for Sodomites; old Sir Horace Mann and Mr. James the Painter had such an odd way of twirling their fingers in Disccurse – I see Suetonius tells us the same thing of one of the Roman emperors' (Brian Fothergill, *The Strawberry Hill Set: Horace Walpole and his Circle* [London: Faber, 1983], 50). See also Timothy Mowl, *Horace Walpole: The Great Outsider* (London: John Murray, 1996), 58.
9. Jill Campbell, '"I Am Not a Giant": Horace Walpole, Heterosexual Incest, and Love among Men', *Eighteenth-Century: Theory and Interpretation* 39 (1998): 230–60, esp. 245.
10. Campbell, 'I Am Not a Giant', 255.
11. *HW Corres.* 35: 110–11 (4 Nov. 1759).
12. Campbell, 'I Am Not a Giant', 239.
13. Barrett Kalter, 'DIY Gothic: Thomas Gray and the Medieval Revival', *ELH/English Literary History* 70.4 (2003): 989–1019.
14. R.W. Ketton-Cremer, *Horace Walpole: A Biography* (1940, reprinted Ithaca, NY: Cornell University Press, 1964), 125.
15. *HW Corres.* 1: 11–12 (20 May 1762).
16. *HW Corres.* 10: 53 (25 March 1763).
17. *HW Corres.* 10: 84–5 (1 July 1763).
18. *HW Corres.* 10: 127 (18 June 1764).
19. *HW Corres.* 17: 406 (23 Sept. 1755).
20. *HW Corres.* 42: 285 (6 July 1790).
21. *HW Corres.* 21: 471 (27 Jan. 1761).
22. *HW Corres.* 24: 102–4 (17 May 1775).
23. *HW Corres.* 1: 178–9 (15 July 1769) nn. 6, 7. W.S. Lewis and A. Dayle Wallace remind us that Bishop Luda was William de Luda (d. 1298), Bishop of Ely 1290–98. His tomb in Ely Cathedral is the basis of Walpole's designs.
24. *HW Corres.* 35: 151 (Sept. 1753).
25. *HW Corres.* 20: 361–2 (4 March 1753).
26. *HW Corres.* 40: 352–3 (9 Aug. 1764).

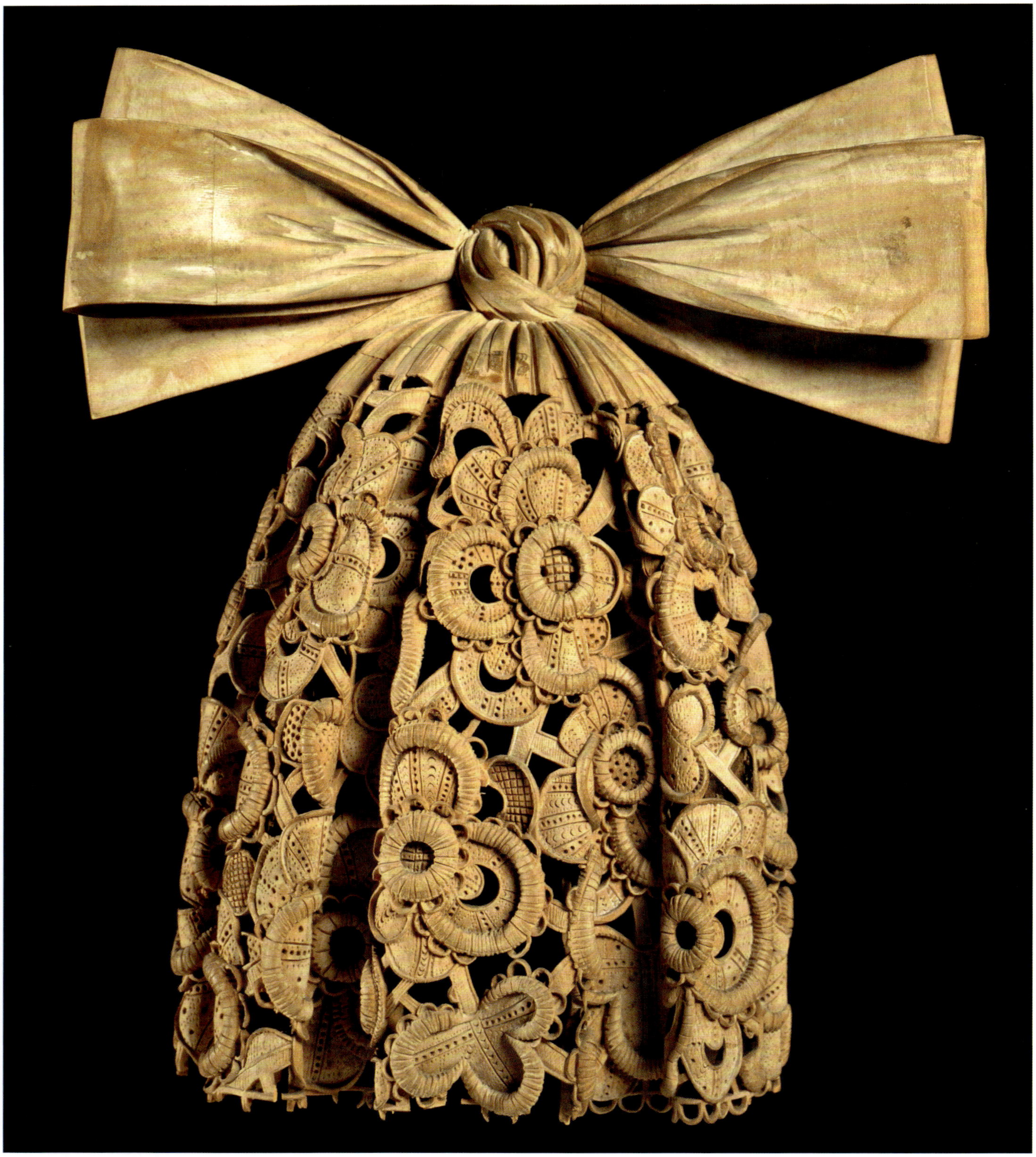

5.

SINGULAR OBJECTS AND MULTIPLE MEANINGS

ALICIA WEISBERG-ROBERTS

> The Notion I have of a *Museum*, is an Hospital for every Thing that is *singular*; whether the Thing have acquired Singularity, from having escaped the Rage of Time; from any natural Oddness in itself, or from being so insignificant, that nobody ever thought it worth their while to produce any more of the same Sort.[1]

THIS ESSAY examines the logic of display at Strawberry Hill, concentrating on objects that are not easy to classify, including some that Horace Walpole termed his 'Principal Curiosities' in the 1780s and others that he may have included in the category of 'singularities', which he advanced in a satirical letter to the editor, or 'Keeper', of *The Museum* in 1746.[2] My discussion is not intended to be an omnibus of individual object histories, although it is considerably indebted to that strain of Walpole studies.[3] Rather, I would like to explore the strategies of circulation Walpole employed throughout his collections and his various accounts of those collections.[4] A number of contemporary texts are concerned with the contents of Walpole's interiors at Strawberry Hill, many provided by Walpole himself, including the various editions of *A Description of the Villa of Mr. Horace Walpole* in its published and extra-illustrated forms, as well as bills, receipts and letters. Additionally, we have the data emerging through the restoration of Strawberry Hill, the traces of construction and revision that Walpole practised on the building fabric. However, beyond reconstruction, there is still the question of how to look at the multifarious collections at Strawberry Hill or, more precisely, what it meant to look at objects while at Strawberry Hill. This is a question as much about associative logic as physical arrangement. I have built this essay around items from Walpole's collections that, while situated in specific locations around the house, possess discursive trails that take the visitor, reader or conversationalist into more than one of Walpole's narrative contexts. To pursue these trails, I will be looking at the multiple roles that objects play in the stories Walpole constructed around their acquisition, disposition and mobilization within the interior.

Despite the susurration of dry antiquarianism that seems to issue from Walpole's general vicinity, closer inspection of specific objects and concerted assemblies of objects in the Strawberry Hill interiors indicates a much more diversified set of means and aims. Although, notionally, the collector exercises control over the items he or she possesses through strategies of classification, Walpole often seems to court the opposite impression. Maddeningly inconsistent in his attributions, just as likely to value an object for its putative associations with royalty – or better yet, royal mistresses – as any idea of quality, Walpole constantly challenges assumptions about the nature of virtuosity, connoisseurship and, indeed, basic ideas about ownership. I will be arguing that Walpole exploits the instability of possession, attribution and provenance in order to produce particular effects, rather than being subject to his collection in a passive form of self-fashioning. He inscribes a range of meanings on his possessions and then actuates them socially; Walpole is willing to hold multiple meanings in suspension and then present

Figure 116. Grinling Gibbons, Cravat, *c.* 1690, limewood, with raised and openwork carving, 24.1 × 20.9 × 5.1 cm. Victoria and Albert Museum, London, Given by the Hon. Mrs Walter Levy. W.181:1-1928. Cat. 167

them, simultaneously or in turn, to delight, bewilder and impress.

A PRIVATE SIGNAL

Walpole wrote to George Montagu on 11 May 1769:

> Strawberry has been in great glory – I have given a *festino* there that will almost mortgage it. Last Tuesday all France dined there.[5]

Walpole enumerates his twenty-four, largely foreign guests before describing the opening sally of the entertainment that he has devised:

> They arrived at two. At the gates of the castle I received them dressed in the cravat of Gibbins's carving, and a pair of gloves embroidered up to the elbows that had belonged to James I. The French servants stared and firmly believed that this was the dress of an English country gentleman.[6]

In this famous jest Walpole wore a limewood cravat, carved by Grinling Gibbons (Fig 116) in imitation of the type of point or needle lace fashionable in the last quarter of the seventeenth century, together with a pair of early seventeenth-century gloves, enhanced by their royal provenance (Fig. 117).[7] Walpole had acquired the gloves at the 1764 sale of the *Musaeum Thoresbyanum*, the erstwhile collection of the

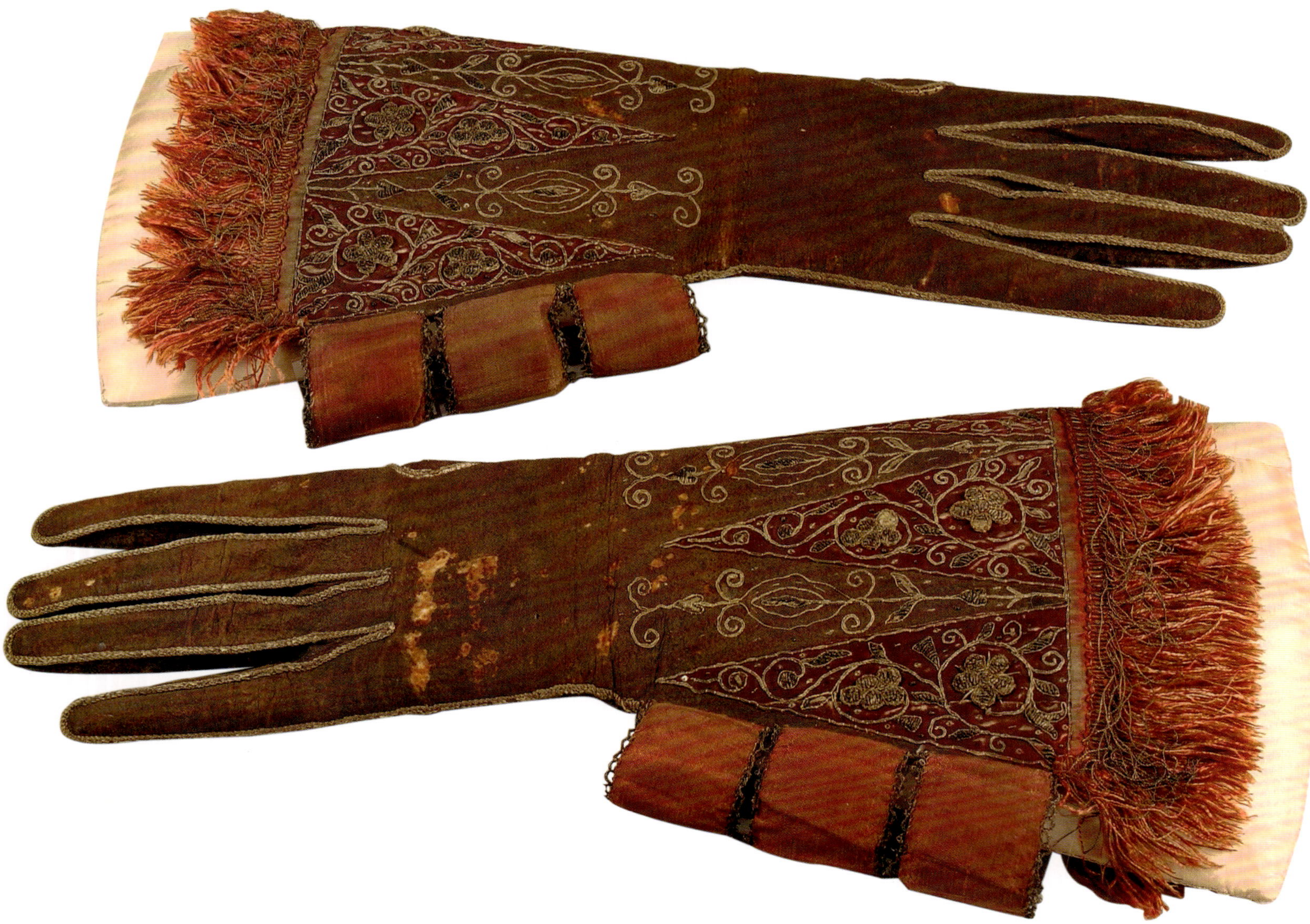

Figure 117. Pair of Gauntlet Gloves ('The Gloves of James I'), English, *c.* 1610–25, leather trimmed with silk, metal and lace, 44 × 22 cm. Gloves Collections Trust, courtesy of the Fashion Museum, Bath, and North East Somerset Council. BATMC GLO 23337. Cat. 109

celebrated Leeds antiquarian Ralph Thoresby.[8] In his published *Description* of Strawberry Hill of 1774 Walpole locates the gloves, noting their provenance specifically, in the Glass Closet of the Great North Bedchamber in the company of pieces purchased at the sale of the Comte de Caylus, an association that must have strengthened the sense of Walpole's lineage among collectors.[9] The *Description* also records the presence of the cravat, which had been a gift of his deputy at the Exchequer, Grosvenor Bedford, in one of the glass cases flanking his rosewood cabinet of enamels and miniatures in the room he referred to as both the Cabinet and the Tribune (see pp. 51–53; Fig. 81).[10] As I will discuss later in this essay, Gibbons's carving in this juxtaposition acted as an index to a range of associations linking the Tribune and Strawberry Hill to Houghton and beyond. However, on the afternoon of 11 May these objects figured in a different narrative, when their archaic qualities rather than their antiquarian associations came to the fore. As in a *fête galante*, the anachronistic use of seventeenth-century clothing signals an arcadian idyll.[11] Walpole and his guests continue their itinerary:

> After taking a survey of the apartments, we went to the printing-house, where I had prepared the enclosed verses, with translations by Monsieur de Lisle, one of the company. The moment these were printed off, I gave a private signal, and French Horns and clarinets accompanied the compliment. We then went to see Pope's grotto and garden, and returned to a magnificent dinner in the refectory. In the evening we walked, had tea, coffee and lemonade in the gallery, which was illuminated by a thousand, or thirty candles, I forget which, and played at whisk and loo till midnight. Then there was a cold supper, and at one the company returned to town, saluted by fifty nightingales, who, as tenants of the manor, came to do honour to their lord.[12]

Proceeding from the first deception, Walpole establishes an alternating rhythm of the delights of nature and artifice. The visit to Alexander Pope's grotto, with its *rocaille* surfaces and classical allusions, at the mid-point of Walpole's account serves as an emblem of this duality.[13] The tone of this narrative – playful and, above all, sociable – is as important as its content. In outline this event has all the appurtenances of a grand occasion, but it is inflected by Walpole's play with scale. This is present in Walpole's aside – 'a thousand, or thirty candles, I forget which' – and the casting, against type, of Strawberry Hill as a 'manor' owned by an 'English country gentleman', albeit a manor tenanted exclusively by printers, concealed musicians and song birds. Walpole's own persona as master of ceremonies is punctuated by self-deprecation and enveloped in an air of diminution. His willingness to incorporate precious, well-provenanced objects into this performance reveals the relation between the collector and his collection; Walpole animates his collection like a hand in a glove.

As well as extending Walpole's shifts in scale, this physical insertion of the body of the owner into his possessions is reminiscent of the central supernatural motif of Walpole's seminal Gothic fiction, *The Castle of Otranto*.[14] Here, too, the servants act as witnesses: first to the giant helmet that takes the life of Conrad, Otranto's heir, then to the colossal leg and foot in the gallery chamber and eventually to the monstrous hand on 'the uppermost banister of the great stairs'.[15] This last image had appeared to Walpole in a dream, which he identified as the 'origin of this romance'.[16] The plot of *Otranto* reveals that the giant knight who appears piecemeal at critical moments is the true owner of the castle, to whom lesser claims must yield. I would suggest that this is part of a complex act of self-representation as a collector because of, rather than despite, its appearance in the context of a fiction originally ascribed to Onuphrio Muralto (a transparent pseudonym). Walpole openly anticipated that the novel would be recognizable as a portrait of Strawberry Hill.[17] Without wishing to confine *Otranto* to the role of a *roman à clef*, I would like to place it in a series of calculated excursuses that surrounded Strawberry Hill and the objects it housed.

The objects in Walpole's collection exceed discursive boundaries by simultaneously inhabiting more than one physical or narrative context, a circumstance that allows them to jump between valencies, as with the Gibbons cravat, which is a treasure housed in the Tribune and also a joke worn on Walpole's person. Walpole's effects rely on the profusion of contextualizing strategies – from framing, casing and 'restoring', through annotation, extra-illustration and attribution, to

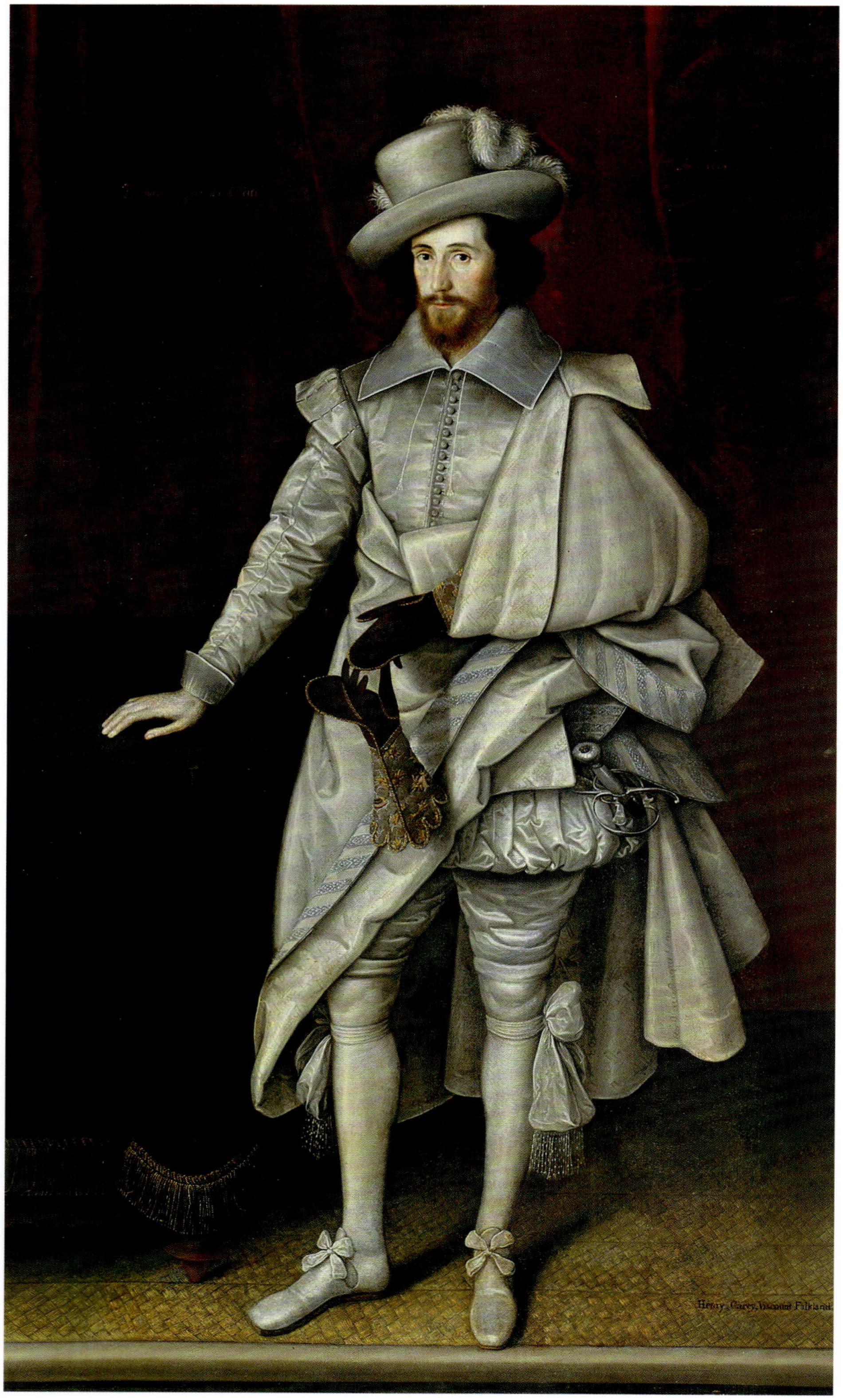

Figure 118. Marcus Geeraerts the Younger, *Portrait of Henry Carey, Lord Falkland, Deputy of Ireland*, *c.* 1603, oil on canvas, 217.2 × 127 cm. Sarah Campbell Blaffer Foundation, Houston. Cat. 58

romance, epistle and history – that he applies to his possessions. This endless re-inscription of the objects in the collection ultimately produces a vertiginous, even 'Gothick,' effect characterized by sudden reverses, striking and logically contradictory impressions, and misleading, unreliable and nested narration. The effect of these devices, and Walpole's relentless elaboration of them, is continually to surprise the reader (or viewer), and to make the beholder complicit in the game-like nature of his narratives and installations. A paradigmatic example would be the *Portrait of Henry Cary, 1st Viscount Falkland* (1603), now attributed to Marcus Geeraerts the Younger, but given to Paul Vansomer in the 1784 *Description*, with the footnote, 'The idea of the picture walking out of its frame in the Castle of Otranto, was suggested by this portrait' (Fig. 118).[18] This painting steps out of its frame in the 'real' Strawberry Hill and into the *Castle of Otranto*. The painting hung on the window side of the Gallery, an interior that operated both as a picture gallery, in the sense that Walpole hung some of his more prestigious pictures here, and as an imitation of the 'long gallery' form familiar from the Tudor period onwards. The long gallery experienced something of a revival in the mid-eighteenth century, not least at Strawberry Hill.[19] Walpole explicitly identified this room type with the display of ancestral quarterings.[20] However, Walpole's own relatives were less prominent in the hang than the group of non-family seventeenth-century portraits, including Lord Falkland, which acted as a kind of ancestral gallery manqué. This has a particular resonance with the passage in the *Castle of Otranto* to which Walpole refers:

> At that instant the portrait of his grandfather, which hung over the bench where they had been sitting, uttered a deep sigh, and heaved its breast. Isabella, whose back was turned to the picture, saw not the motion, nor knew whence the sound came, but started, and said –'Hark, my Lord! What sound was that?' and at the same time made towards the door. Manfred, distracted between the flight of Isabella, who had now reached the stairs, and yet unable to keep his eyes from the picture, which began to move, had, however, advanced some steps after her, still looking backwards on the portrait, when he saw it quit its panel, and descend on the floor with a grave and melancholy air.[21]

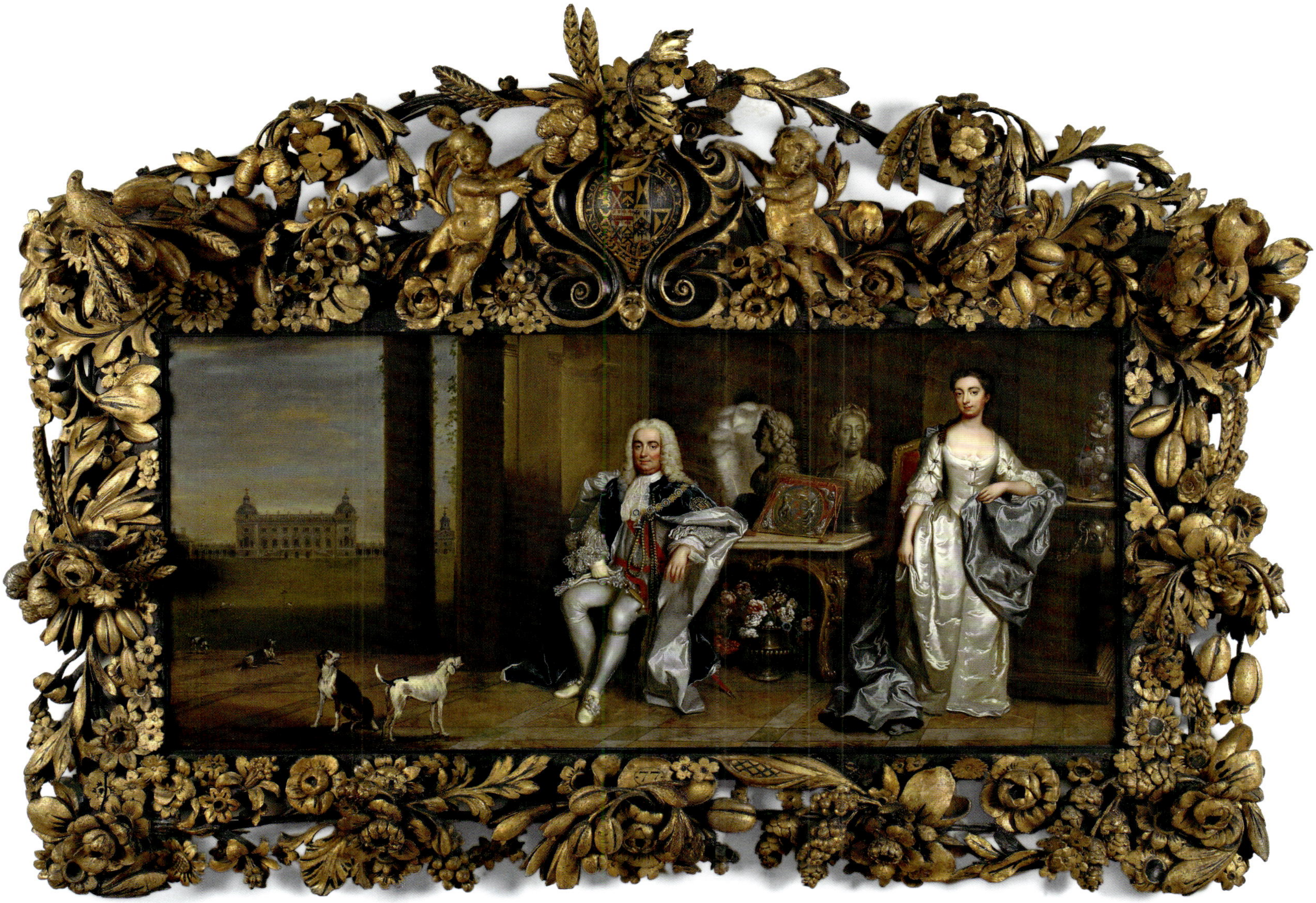

Figure 119. John Giles Eccardt and John Wootton, *Portrait of Sir Robert Walpole and Catherine Shorter, his first Wife*, *c.* 1746, oil on canvas, 50.8 × 101.6 cm; frame in the style of Grinling Gibbons, *c.* 1680. The Lewis Walpole Library, Yale University. Cat. 39

The animated portrait has proven to be an evergreen motif in gothic fiction, sometimes preserving the admonitory charge of this visitation, at other times merely as an eerie effect.[22] However, to touch on the idea of reading objects through interiors and vice versa, it is intriguing to note that the idea of the ancestor stepping from his frame arises from Walpole's gallery of ancestor surrogates and turns into the forbearer in the fiction who, it transpires, is no grandfather to Manfred. The picture has stepped out of its frame on many levels: genealogically, generically, historically. This was by no means the first or the last time that Walpole would make this kind of imaginative leap. Through text, through architecture and in literal ways Walpole framed the experience of his objects and attempted to negotiate the distinctions between miscellany, ensemble and collection.

'THE LOOSE AND AIRY LIGHTNESS OF THE FLOWERS ... CHAINED TOGETHER THE VARIOUS PRODUCTIONS'

Of course, works of art were also framed for entirely conventional reasons at Strawberry Hill: for security, for preservation and to facilitate installation. However, the practical reasons for putting paintings in frames and objects in cabinets should not obscure the fact that for Walpole, whether he was having his possessions framed or enjoying the frisson of having them transgress the boundaries of those frames, the act of encasement also provided an opportunity for identifying those possessions, ascribing histories, creating and

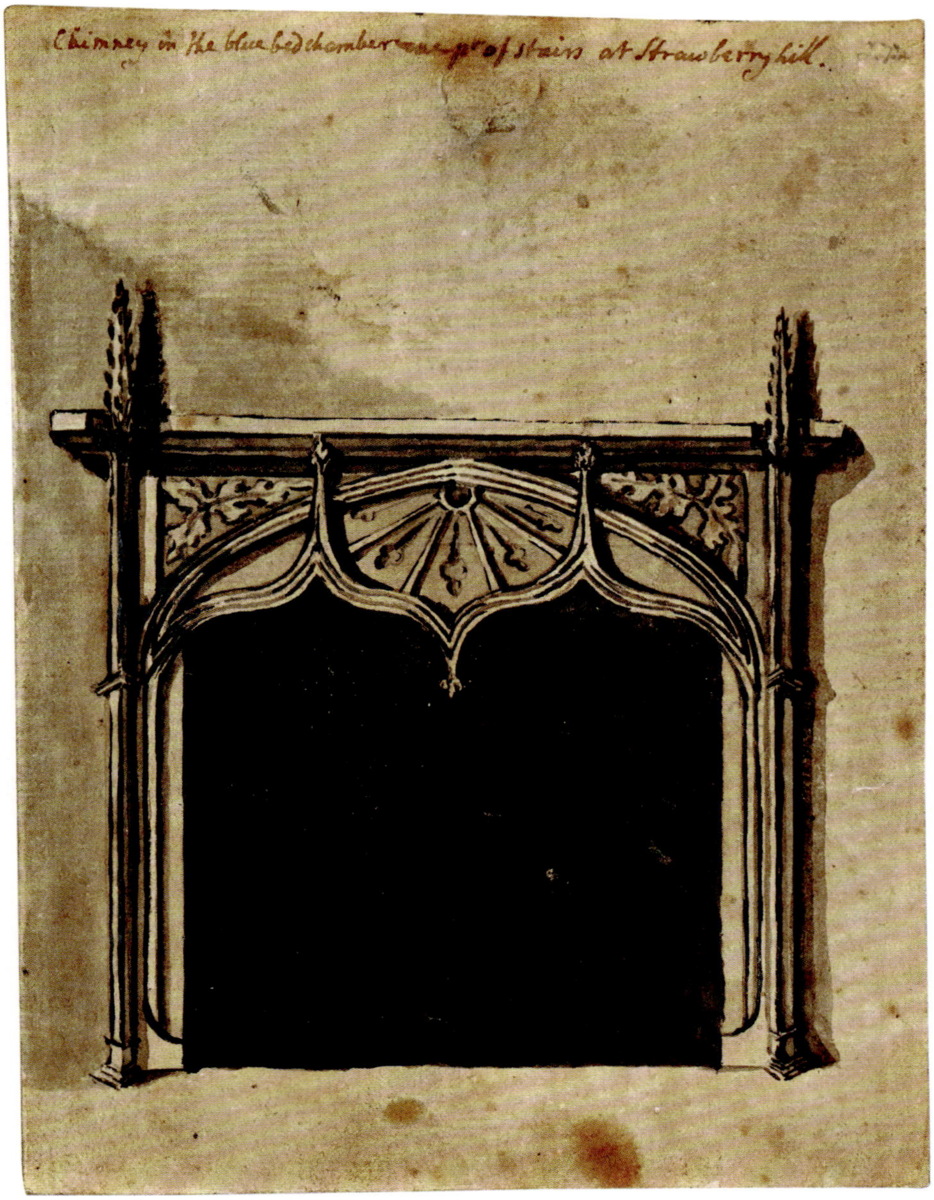

Figure 120. Richard Bentley, *Chimney in the Blue Bedchamber One Pair Of Stairs At Strawberry Hill*, ink and ink wash, 15.5 × 11.7 cm, from *Drawings and Designs by Richd. Bentley*, 1760. The Lewis Walpole Library, Yale University. Folio 49 3585, fol. 27

disrupting chains of association.[23] In the interiors of Strawberry Hill, objects were nested in frames and cabinets that were themselves the products of trails of correspondence, flights of attribution and conceptually complex, as well as physically elaborate, execution. It is not an accident that the technology of framing, of papier-mâché, of stucco and of gilding, seems to echo the project of Walpole's 'paper house' as a whole.[24] The ascendancy of ornament over structure is a key characteristic of both the decor and fabric of Strawberry Hill.

While this mode of framing and ornamentation is a general strategy, which would have been experienced repeatedly at Strawberry Hill, it was enacted through specific objects and ensembles. Accordingly, the nature of Walpole's practice, and the particular textures of allusion it conferred, becomes more evident when his possessions and their arrangement are considered in detail. The *Portrait of Sir Robert Walpole, 1st Earl of Orford, and Catherine Shorter* by John Giles Eccardt, now at the Lewis Walpole Library (Fig. 119), is still displayed in the remarkable carved frame (attributed by Walpole to Grinling Gibbons) into which Walpole inserted it. In the 1750s the painting and its frame were incorporated into the decor of the Blue Bedchamber at Strawberry Hill.[25] Walpole first wrote about the painting and its setting in a letter of 1754 and returned to it again in the published *Description* of 1774. Thanks to the richness of these accounts, it is possible to reconstruct the ways in which this inherently composite artwork, when placed in the interior, intersects with multiple histories. As Walpole sited it, the portrait evokes overlapping narrative associations: with Walpole's socially ascendant family history; with his personal formation as a collector; and with the national history and progress of the arts in England, which he was attempting to construct.

We first encounter this portrait fully embedded, even enmeshed, in the fabric of Strawberry Hill. Walpole reports on the progress of the decoration of the Blue Bedchamber to Richard Bentley, an original member of the 'Strawberry committee' and a designer of many features of the house, on 18 May 1754: 'My father and Mother over the chimney in the Gibbons frame, about which you know we were in dispute what to do. I have fixed on black and gold, and it has a charming effect *over your chimney with the two dropping points*, which is executed exactly.'[26] This vigorously Baroque frame, with its swags, armorials, putti and garlands of fruit and flowers, was originally set behind the pinnacles of Bentley's chimneypiece, which were carved out from behind in order to accommodate it (Fig. 120). Arranged in front of the frame across the chimneypiece, and again visually breaking up its lower edge, was a small collection of French porcelain: 'A boy and girl in Seve biscuit. Three small flower-pots, ditto. Two cups and saucers, ditto. Four blue and white cream-cups.' Walpole hung a number of portraits executed by John Giles Eccardt on the other walls of the Blue Bedchamber, in which close friends and relatives, including Bentley himself, appear in the clothing and compositions of Rubens, Van Dyck and Watteau.[27] These formed a relatively homogenous ensemble and were uniformly framed in 'black and gold carved, after those to Lombard's prints from Vandyck, but with emblems peculiar to each person' (Figs. 19, 57, 58, 111, 112).[28]

The painting in the 'Gibbons' frame, also executed by Eccardt, leaving to one side its role in this interior for the moment, contains in itself a variety of other works. Walpole describes it as

> Sir Robert Walpole and Catherine Shorter … after Zincke: the hounds and view of Houghton by Wootton. Sir Robert is sitting; by him, on a table, is the purse of chancellor of the exchequer, leaning against busts of George 1st and 2nd to denote his being first prime minister to those kings: by lady Walpole are flowers, shells, a pallet and pencils, to mark her love of the arts.[29]

Incorporating the possessions of the sitter into a portrait is a commonplace manoeuvre, as are the attributes of office and accomplishment that Walpole describes. However, Eccardt not only depicts Sir Robert Walpole's goods and chattels – Houghton, hunting dogs and so forth – he also portrays them in a manner that Walpole identifies with representations of those goods that Sir Robert owned (Fig. 121). The painted double portrait is only one in a series of Walpole's deployments of a pair of enamel miniatures of Sir Robert and Catherine Shorter by Christian Friedrich Zincke (Fig. 124).[30] These were housed in Walpole's rosewood miniature cabinet in the Tribune and elaborately reproduced by George Vertue in 1748. The resultant prints of the miniatures were used as frontispieces in the *Ædes Walpolianae*, Walpole's description of his father's collection at Houghton, and eventually affixed in Walpole's extra-illustrated copy of the 1784 version of his own *Description*.[31]

The frame, unlike the cravat, is no longer attributed to Gibbons, but Walpole's use of what he firmly believed to be, and repeatedly published as, Gibbons's work is significant.[32] Gibbons's name recurs frequently in the *Ædes Walpolianae*, not only for his carvings but also as the previous owner of major works in Sir Robert's collection, including Frans Snyders' *Bird's Concert* (*c.* 1630–40) and Luca Giordano's *Vulcan's Forge* (*c.* 1640).[33] Walpole reserves special praise for the portrait of Gibbons by Godfrey Kneller, which hung in the Common parlour at Houghton As in his later description of the arrangement in the Blue Bedchamber at Strawberry Hill, the surround precedes the picture and reinforces its claims: 'Over the Chimney is some fine Pear-tree Carving, by *Gibbins*, and in the middle of it hangs a Portrait of him by Sir *Godfrey Kneller*. It is a Master-piece, and an equal to any of *Vandycke's*.'[34] However, we can connect the hang of the Blue Bedchamber even more closely with that at Houghton via the first entry in Walpole's catalogue: 'On the right hand as you enter a small Breakfast Room. Over

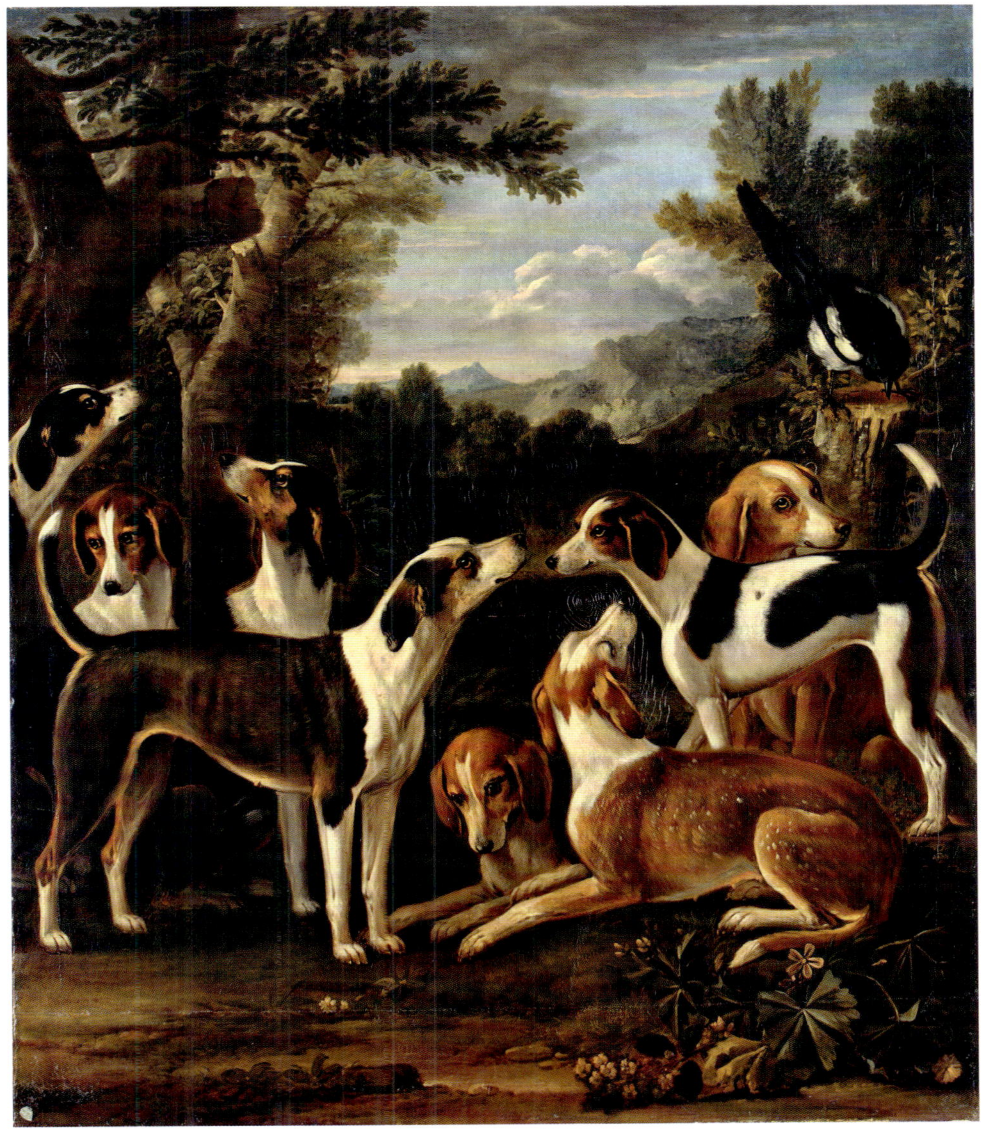

Figure 121. John Wootton, *Hounds and a Magpie*, *c.* 1740, oil on canvas. 152 × 128 cm. The State Hermitage Museum, St Petersburg. 9781

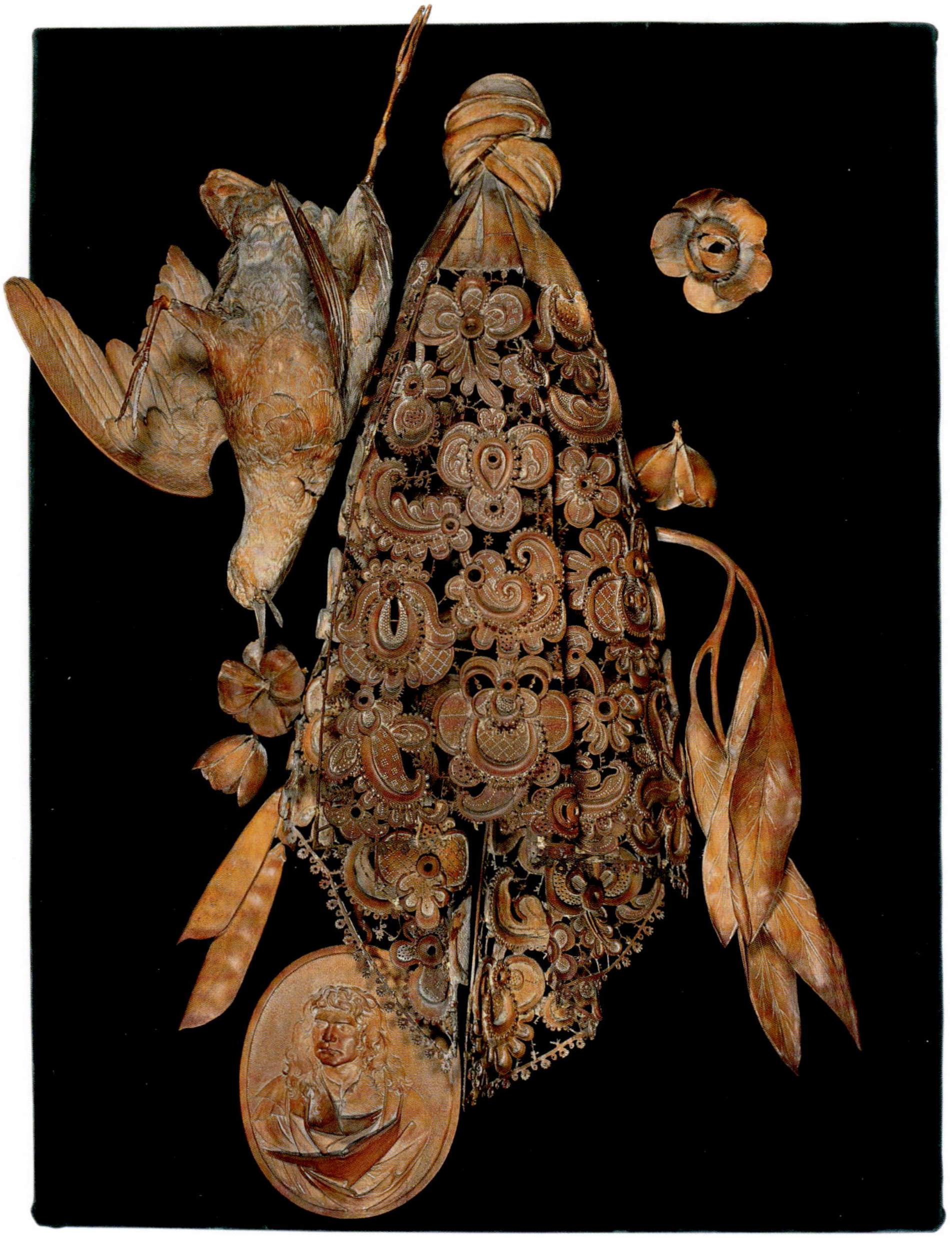

Figure 122. Samuel Watson, *Assemblage of carvings in a case*, limewood, 71 × 57 × 15 cm. Devonshire Collection, Chatsworth

the Chimney is a very good Picture of Hounds, By *Wooton*' – the picture within Eccardt's picture at Strawberry Hill. This is immediately followed by 'A Concert of Birds by Mario di Fiori; a very uncommon picture for he seldom painted anything but Flowers; it belong'd to *Gibbins* the Carver, and is four Feet seven Inches high, by seven Feet nine and a quarter wide.'[35]

Given these associations, it is perhaps unsurprising that Gibbons features prominently in Walpole's *Anecdotes of Painting in England*. Walpole saw Gibbons as crucial to the constitution of an English school, despite the fact that he was a 'carver' rather than a painter, and that his Englishness could only be established by special pleading. Gibbons was 'an original genius, a citizen of nature; consequently, it is indifferent where she produced him'.[36] Walpole describes Gibbons's craft in terms that evoke the divine powers of creation (and coincidentally elides the Netherlandish traditions in which he had trained): 'There is no instance of a man before Gibbons who gave to wood the loose and airy lightness of flowers, and chained together the various productions of the elements with a free disorder natural to each species.'[37] This praise of *artificialia* should remind us of Walpole's escapade with the cravat, which we can now see as part of a circuit that takes in Walpole's ancestral seat and his historiographical project, via the most prestigious royal and aristocratic circles. Describing the courtly transactions at Chatsworth, Walpole writes: 'When Gibbons had finished all his works in that palace, he presented the Duke with a point cravat, a woodcock and a medal with his own head, all preserved in a glass case. I have another point cravat by him, the art of which arrives even to deception.'[38] Walpole's joke, then, actuates the quality in Gibbons's work that Walpole most values.

In the same passage Walpole also attributes a 'Herodias with St. John's head, alto relieve in ivory' to Gibbons.[39] This relief, now known to be after Francis van Bossuit, can be found in the centre of the right-hand door of the same rosewood cabinet that housed the Zincke miniatures of Walpole's parents (Figs 123, 124).[40] As I have already mentioned, the Gibbons cravat was kept in a glass case alongside the rosewood cabinet, which formed the focal point of the Tribune. Virtually all of the rooms at Strawberry

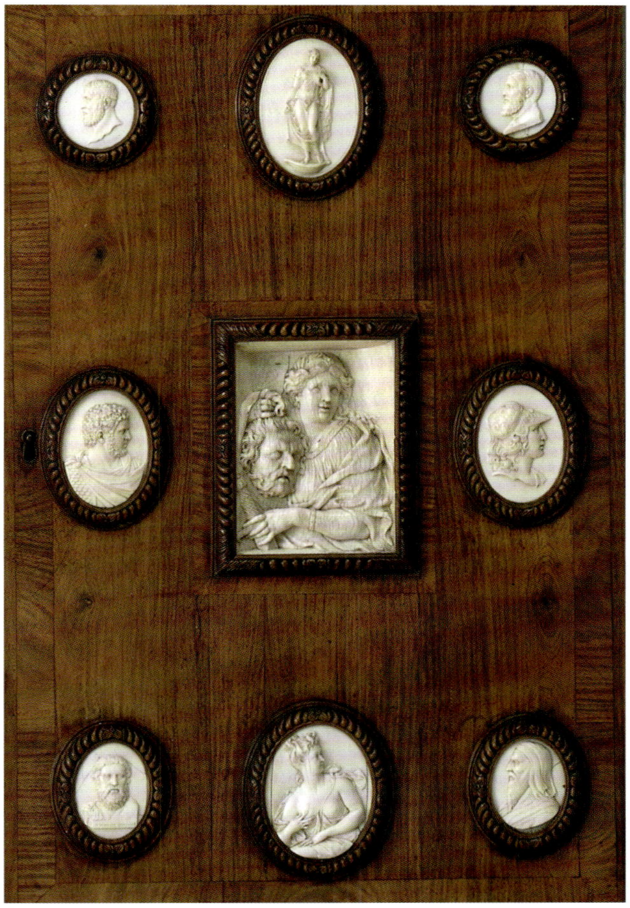

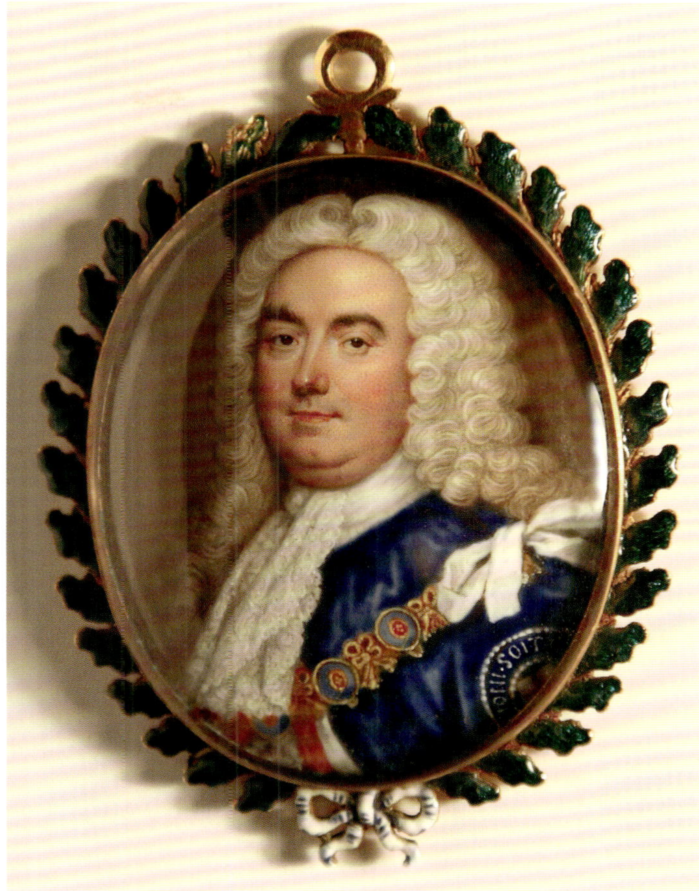

Hill expressed something of Walpole's identity as a collector, but this was the Tribune's sole function. In the section that follows we will examine the narrative that Walpole constructs around the identification and acquisition of one of his 'Principal Curiosities,' a group of objects that Walpole accorded special esteem but that in some sense formed the limits of his collection and connoisseurship.

'OH LORD! I AM THE ONLY MAN IN ENGLAND THAT CAN TELL YOU!'

On the night of Sunday, 17 March 1771, Horace Walpole's townhouse in Arlington Street was burgled. The following Friday he wrote to his friend Horace Mann, the British Resident to Florence, describing the aftermath of the crime in some detail. Walpole claimed that he had left the house 'under no guard but that of two maidens, whom lions you know will not touch, but are very ravishable by house-breakers, a much more hungry kind of wild beast'. The passage that follows this promising opening is a rare insight into the way in which Walpole displayed his collections at his London home. Despite the fact that Walpole was born in this house in Arlington Street, which he eventually inherited from his father, and that he actually spent half the year there, from at least the 1740s onwards, Walpole never lavished its rooms with the dense and novel forms of description he reserved for Strawberry Hill. The very probably unexceptionable Palladian interiors of Arlington Street served as a kind of a cradle for Walpole's changeling Gothic. Pieces like the rosewood cabinet, which was commissioned in harmony with its decor, reappeared like *spolia* in new, historiated contexts (Fig. 127). Thus this glimpse behind the sash windows afforded to us by a bit of housebreaking is of considerable interest, not least because it is narrated as an unconsummated rape: 'A glass case of china wide open, the locks not picked but forced and the doors of them broken to pieces.' Coins all out of their sorts, papers 'scattered and

Figure 123. Detail of the right-hand door of the Cabinet of Miniatures and Enamels, designed by Horace Walpole, 1743, ivory plaque depicting *Herodias with the Head of St John*, after Francis van Bossuit. Victoria and Albert Museum, London, Purchased with the assistance of the Murray Bequest. W.52:1, 2-1925. See Fig. 127, Cat. 171

Figure 124. Christian Friedrich Zincke, *Portrait Enamel of Sir Robert Walpole, 1st Earl of Orford*, 1735, enamel on copper set in enamelled gilt metal frame with green enamelled laurel surround, 5.7 × 7.7 cm. The Rt Hon. the Earl of Derby. Cat. 189

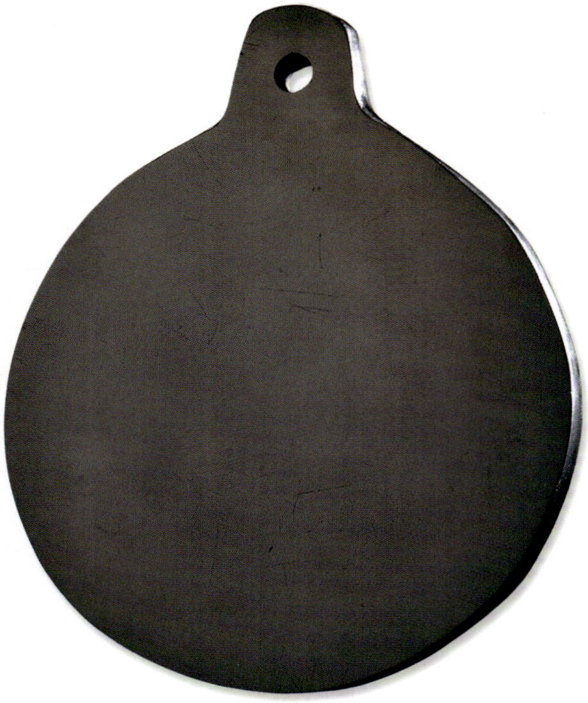

Figure 125. Dr Dee's Mirror, Aztec, 14th–16th century AD, obsidian, 22 × 18.4 × 1.3 cm. British Museum, Department of Prehistory and Europe. 1966,1001.1. Cat. 108

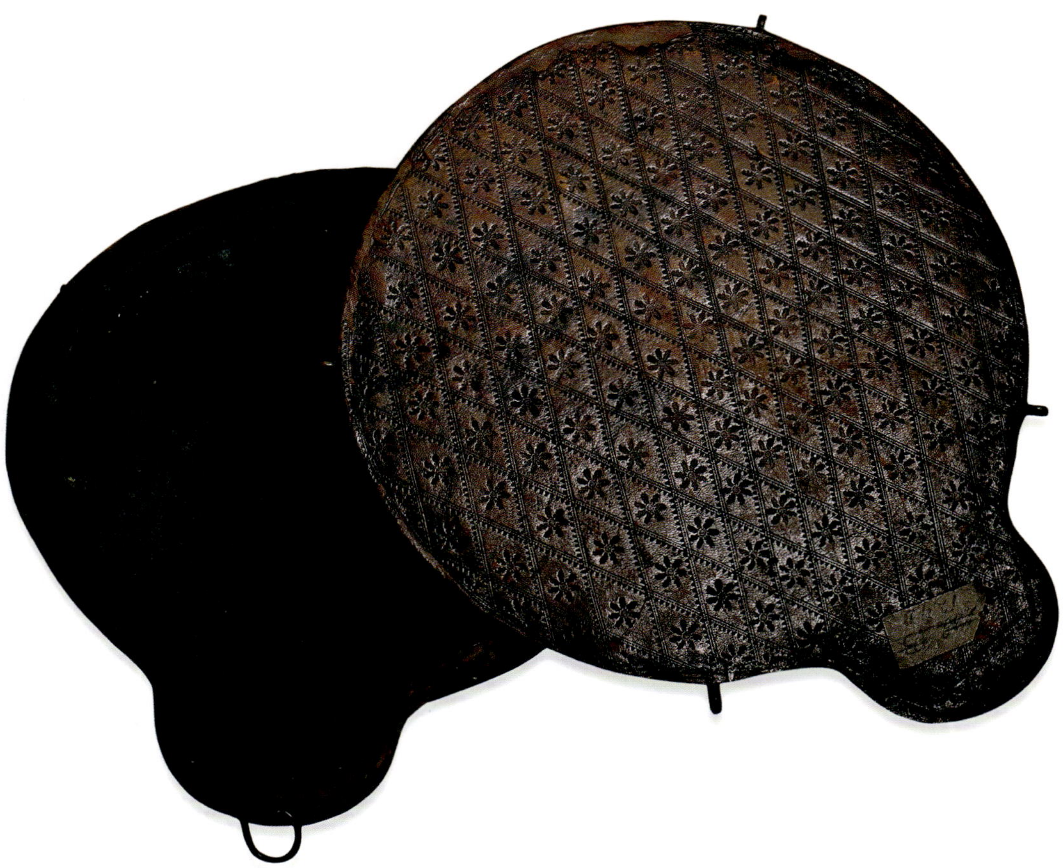

Figure 126. Case for Dr Dee's Mirror, with Walpole's inscription, 18th century, wood covered with tooled leather, 25.5 × 21 × 3 cm. British Museum, Department of Prehistory and Europe. 1966,1001.1. Cat. 108

tumbled'. His father's chest with its 'great flapper of brass' 'wrenched with such violence as to break it into seven pieces;' the contents all 'turned topsy-turvy'. 'The glass case and the cabinet of shells had been handled as roughly by these impotent gallants.'[41] The actions of the would-be thieves, which Walpole rehearses with some relish, run backwards over the acts of casing, framing, restoring and installing, set down in such detail in Walpole's letters and *Descriptions*. In the end nothing of value is stolen: the collection has been ravished, but Walpole's *virtù* is miraculously left intact. To 'all London ... reasoning on this marvelous adventure' Walpole can only offer the puzzling explanation that he possesses 'a talisman'.

The letter goes on to explain, via another tale of *virtù* lost and regained, Walpole's acquisition of the magic mirror of the Elizabethan magus and mathematician Dr Dee (Fig. 125). He writes:

> You must know that last winter being asked by Lord Vere to assist in settling Lady Betty Germaine's auction, I found in an old catalogue

> of her collection, this article, '*The black stone into which Dr Dee used to call his spirits.*' Dr Dee, you must know, was a great conjuror in the days of Queen Elizabeth, and has written a folio of the dialogues he held with his imps. I asked eagerly for this stone; Lord Vere said he knew of no such thing, but if found, it should certainly be at my service. Alas, the stone was gone![42]

Walpole quickly establishes the apparatus of the antiquarian transaction – the estate sale, the ancient catalogue, the artefact and its historical interest – and pauses for effect before plunging ahead:

> This winter I was again employed by Lord Frederic Campbell, for I am an absolute auctioneer, to do him the same service about his father's collection. Among the other odd things he produced a round piece of shining black marble in a leathern case, as big as the crown of a hat, and asked me what that could possibly be? I screamed out, 'Oh Lord! I am the only man in England that can tell you: it is Dr Dee's black stone!'[43]

This story, even to its supernatural fillip, is a perfect rendering of the triumph of the collector. The uniqueness of the object can only be matched and mastered by a connoisseur whose insight is equally unique. It concludes with Walpole's facetious assertion: 'If it was not this magical stone, which is only of high polished coal, that preserved my chattels, in truth I cannot guess what did.'[44] Today the mirror, along with the case in which Walpole kept it, is in the British Museum (see Cat. 108). It is one of a number of objects from Walpole's collection that have survived with his labels and inscriptions intact.[45] We might think of this practice of appending texts to objects as an inversion or corollary of extra-illustration; indeed the mirror appears as a gnomic image in Richard Bull's extra-illustrated *Description*.[46] Walpole writes on the sheet pasted into the case of the mirror:

> The Black Stone into which Dr Dee
> used to call his spirits. v. his book,
> This was mentioned in the Catalogue
> of the earls of Peterborough
> from whom it came to Lady Elizabeth
> Germaine.
> HW.

Dr Dee's 'book' might refer to one of several manuscripts and posthumous publications of his 'angelic conversations', but it is most likely to have been the copy of *A true & faithful relation of what passed for many yeers between Sr. John Dee … and some spirits … His private conferences with Rodolphe, emperor of Germany, Stephen k. of Poland, and divers other princes …* (1659) that Walpole himself owned.[47] The esoteric qualities of the mirror may have appealed to Walpole, but so, too, would the association of the mirror and its earliest known owner with emperors, kings and princes. As in his letter to Mann, Walpole is also careful to note the object's equally interesting immediate provenance. Lady Betty Germain was a notable collector in her own right, particularly of oriental porcelain, but she was also, through a curious set of circumstances, the heir to the collections of the Earls of Peterborough and those of Henry Howard, 7th Duke of Norfolk.[48] These connections held considerable glamour for Walpole; he eventually acquired no fewer than fifteen pieces from Lady Betty's collections, including another Principal Curiosity, the so-called dagger of Henry VIII.[49] In the introduction to the 1784 *Description* he lists Lady Betty's collection among the 'many renowned cabinets' whose 'spoils' constitute his own.[50]

At some later point Walpole penned an addendum in the corner of his label: 'Kelly was Dr Dee's Associate and is mentioned with this very stone in *Hudibras*, Part 2. Canto 3 v. 631, Kelly did all his feats upon The Devil's Looking-glass, a Stone.' The verse that Walpole quotes indeed comes from Samuel Butler's *Hudibras*, first published in 1663, and another hand has duly written on a second sheet of paper affixed to the mirror's case:

> Kelly did all his feats upon
> The Devil's Looking-Glass, a stone;
> Where playing with him at Bo-peep,
> He solv'd all problems ne'er so deep.[51]

Edward Kelly, Dee's medium and assistant, is evoked several times in Samuel Butler's mock epic as a pattern of imposture, reinforcing the charlatanry of the astrologer Sidrophel. This overtone is present in the entry in the 1774 *Description*, where Walpole records the mirror as 'a speculum of kennel-coal, in a leathern case. It is curious for having been used to deceive the mob

THE CABINET OF MINIATURES AND ENAMELS *Stephen Lloyd*

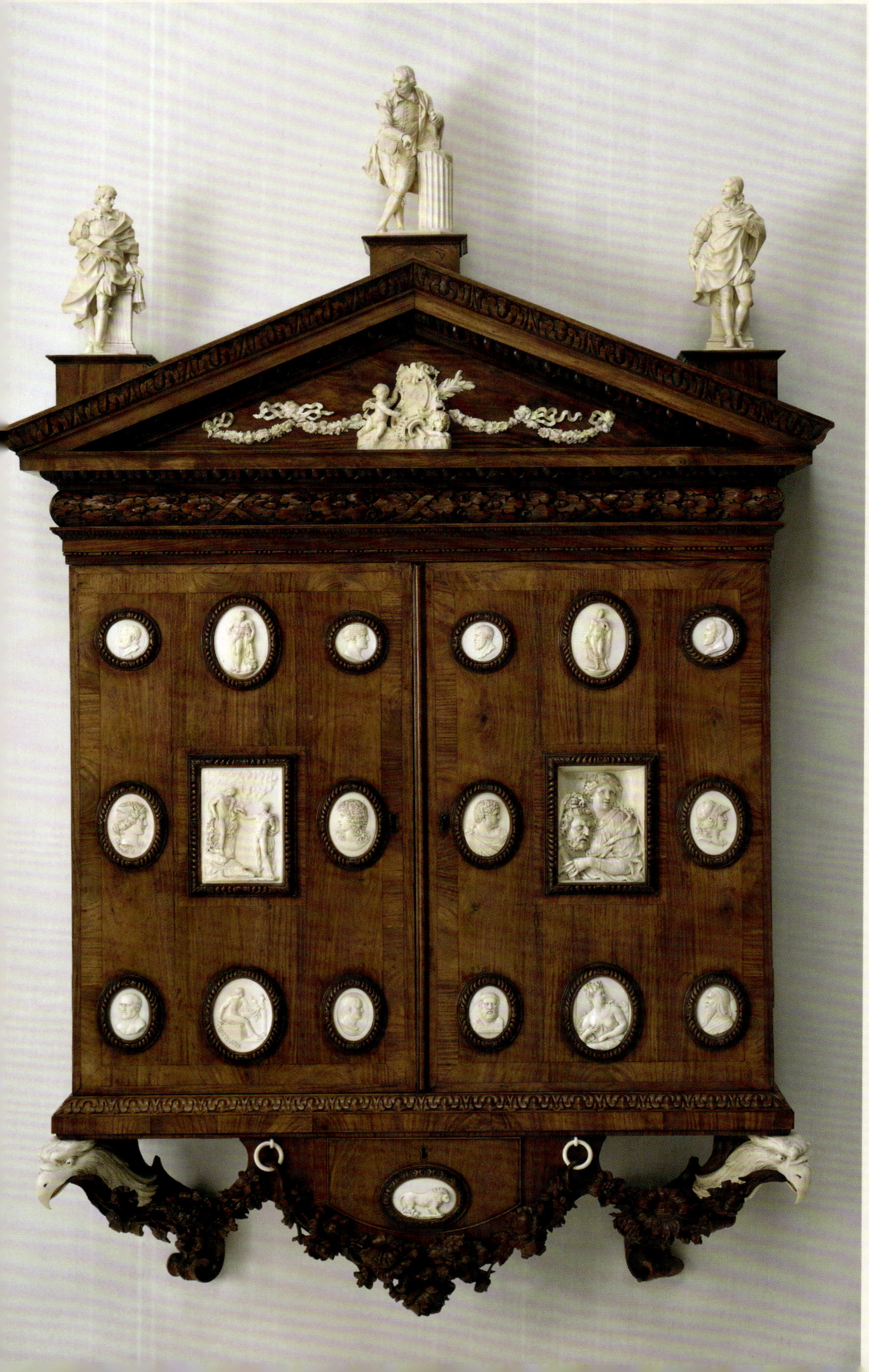

The centrepiece of the Tribune at Strawberry Hill was the hanging cabinet for the display of Walpole's portrait miniatures and enamels, which was made in 1743 and contained some of the most precious objects in his whole collection. It was introduced in the 1774 *Description* as 'A Cabinet of rose-wood, designed by Mr. Walpole; on the pediment, statues in ivory of Fiamingo, Inigo Jones and Palladio [in fact Rubens], by Verskovis, after the models by Rysbrack'. It can be seen as both a microcosm and a manifesto of Walpole's attitudes to architecture, sculpture and painting. Designed by the collector himself, the cabinet is in a Palladian style that may well have been strongly influenced by William Kent, who had worked on the interiors at Houghton for Sir Robert Walpole. It was most probably made by one of the leading London cabinet-makers, possibly William Hallett, who later provided furniture for Strawberry Hill. A similar cabinet, based on Walpole's, though decorated with ivories showing erotic scenes, was made at this date for one of the collector's friends, Thomas Brand, who was a member of the Society of Dilettanti.

Walpole's pride in the cabinet, which was made for his own rooms in his father's house in Arlington Street, was shown in a letter of 19 July 1743 to Horace Mann in Florence: 'I have a new cabinet for my enamels and miniatures just come home, which I am sure you would like: it is of rosewood; the door inlaid with carvings in ivory. I wish you could see it!' Initially, Walpole would have filled the cabinet with portraits of his family, such as his father and mother, as well as of close friends like John Chute (see Figs. 110, 124). As he developed his collection, he added outstanding pieces of jewellery such as the Darnley Jewel (Fig. 129), masterpieces of English limning such as Isaac Oliver's self-portrait (Fig. 130) and prized enamels like Jean Petitot's *Comtesse d'Olonne as Diana* (Fig. 217), set in its glamorous original frame, as well as Boit's copy after Samuel Cooper's miniature of Oliver Cromwell. Walpole's collecting interests were focused on 'portraits of remarkable persons', with, if possible, distinguished provenances, that had been painted by the best English limners and continental enamellers working over the previous two centuries in the Tudor and Stuart courts in addition to that of Louis XIV.

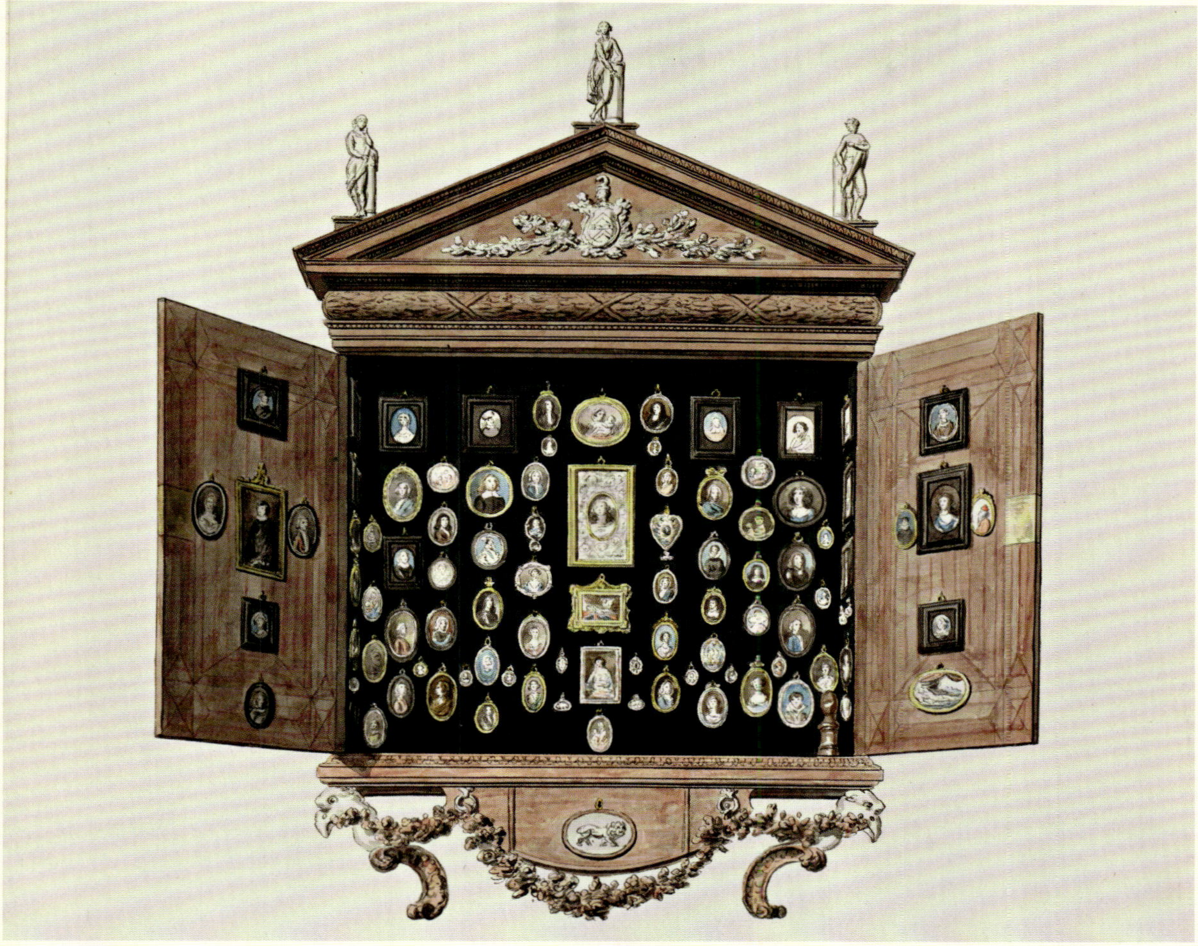

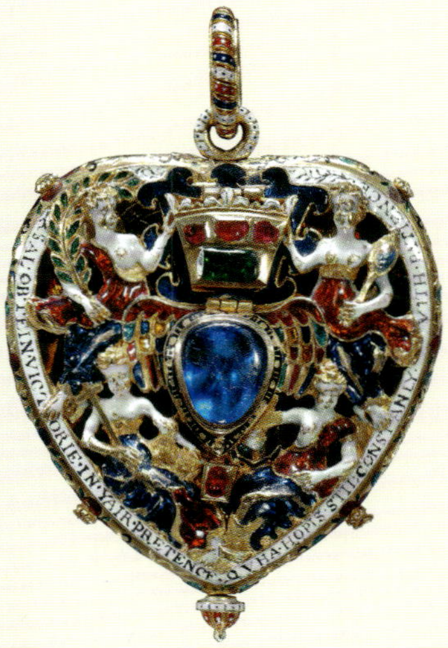

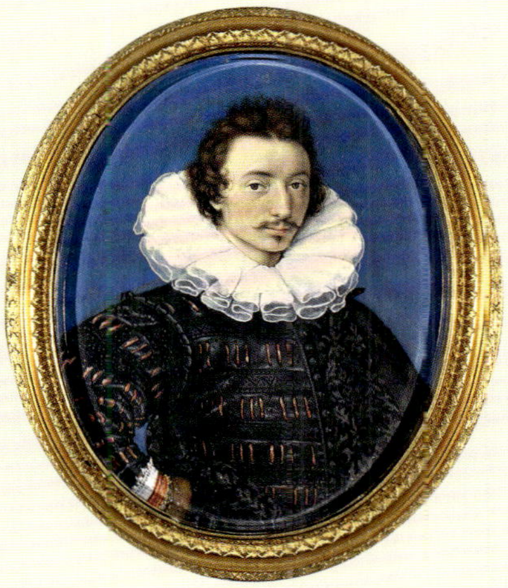

FACING PAGE

Figure 127. *Cabinet of Miniatures and Enamels*, designed by Horace Walpole, 1743, kingwood with ivory; veneered with padouk, and set with carved ivory plaques, figures and mounts, 152.4 × 91.5 × 21.6 cm. Victoria and Albert Museum, London, Purchased with the assistance of the Murray Bequest. W.52:1, 2-1925. Cat. 171

THIS PAGE

Figure 128. Detail from John Carter, *'Dispoition of the Miniatures in the Rosewood Cabinet in the Tribune'*, n.d., watercolour, 32.6 × 27.5 cm, mounted, from Walpole's copy of the *Description*, 1784. The Lewis Walpole Library, Yale University. Folio 33 30 Copy 11, p. 161

Figure 129. *The Darnley Jewel* ('Lennox Jewel'), probably Scottish, *c.* 1571–8, gold, enamel, and gemstones. The Royal Collection

Figure 130. Isaac Oliver, *Portrait Miniature of the Artist*, 1590, watercolour on vellum, stuck on card, set in chased gold frame, H 6.2 cm. National Portrait Gallery, London. Purchased with the help from H.M. Government, 1971.4852. Cat. 175

The furnishing of the cabinet had been virtually completed by 1774, when in the *Description* there were eighty-five objects listed, while ten years later in the revised edition only a few more items had been added. By the time John Carter made his revealing watercolour in around 1788 of the cabinet shown open, a further handful of additional works had been included (Fig. 128). Walpole showed only the most favoured visitors into the Tribune and personally opened the cabinet to reveal its treasures to guests (perhaps using the glass shown in the corner). In the introduction to the 1784 *Description* he proudly stated that, apart from the collections of the King and the Duke of Portland, his own 'collection of miniatures and enamels is, I believe, the largest and finest in any country'.

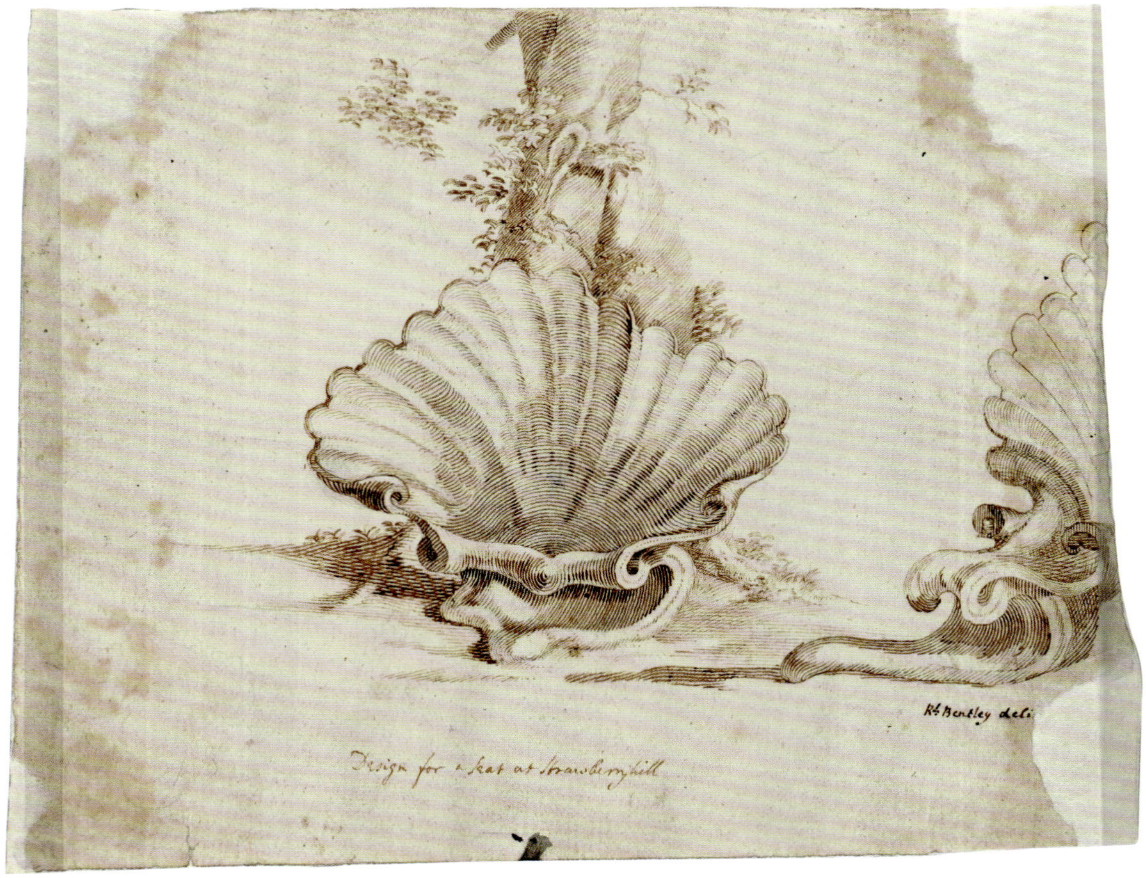

Figure 131. Richard Bentley, *Design for a seat at Strawberry Hill*, *c.* 1750, pen and ink and wash, 20 × 25.5 cm, from *Drawings and Designs by Richd. Bentley*, 1760. The Lewis Walpole Library, Yale University. Folio 49 3585 fol. 33

by Dr. Dee, the conjurer in the reign of Queen Elizabeth,' before reiterating the provenance I have already discussed.[52] Like the gloves of James I, Walpole kept the mirror in the Glass Closet in the Great North Bedchamber. It is the last object listed in the contents of the closet and is followed immediately by a description of 'the closet-window' containing 'a head of queen Elizabeth in painted glass, and another pane with men playing at cards', which would have literally shown a light on the dark surface of the mirror.[53] These installations and annotations provide us with a key to understanding the value of this delusive artefact and its true history in Walpole's collection: the mob may be fooled, but Walpole, the absolute collector, can place it precisely.

Walpole's interest in Dee's ownership of the 'Devil's Looking-Glass' and its assimilation into other illustrious collections seem to have precluded further inquiry into its ultimate origin. Walpole identified the material of the mirror as 'Kennel-coal'. Kennel or cannel coal is a relatively hard bituminous substance, which is clean to touch and can be carved and polished, like jet.[54] The only commercially exploited deposit in eighteenth-century Britain was near Wigan, Lancashire, where it had been used to make souvenirs and curiosities at least since the early seventeenth century.[55] This was plausible grounds for identifying the mirror as being of ancient English manufacture.[56] In fact, an obsidian speculum is a Mesoamerican artefact, associated with the cult of Tezcatlipoca, an Aztec god of sacrifice, conflict and divination, known as 'Lord of the Smoking Mirror'.[57] If the looking glass did indeed belong to Dr Dee, he is likely to have acquired it during his time in European courts, which were importing curiosities directly from the New World, and thus may have been aware of its origin.[58] For Walpole, however, its chief fascination resided in its connections with English history and collecting. The mirror allowed him to dramatize his pleasure and power as a connoisseur, and then to enfold that narrative within his historiographic project.

'STRAWBERRY HILL HAS GROWN A PERFECT PAPHOS'

The way that Walpole places the mirror of Dr Dee in the Glass Closet – casing, labelling and surrounding it with related objects that establish its meaning and, in a sense, create its identity – is the ancestor of the most familiar type of museological display we know. It is important, however, to understand that at Strawberry Hill this was just one form of display and part of a variety of approaches that included many other, less canonical forms of framing. Given the nature of Strawberry Hill, a modest suburban villa constantly being remade by its owner, the better to resemble an ancient and rambling keep, Walpole's collections were always juxtaposed and framed within a series of effects of contrasting scale. As we have seen, Walpole, in his guise as lord of all the nightingales in Twickenham, liked to play with miniaturization, and, as 'Onuphrio Muralto', he dreamed of the sublimity of gigantism. Moreover, the objects in Walpole's collection were not always securely fixed, physically or conceptually, within their frames and containers; they could be taken out and worn, like the gloves of James I, or they might escape their frames through representation, like the *Portrait of Lord Falkland*, or quotation, as in Eccardt's *Portrait of Sir Robert Walpole and Catherine Shorter*. This manipulation of effects of scale, and of exteriority and interiority, naturally extended into the landscape surrounding Strawberry Hill and to the framing of the human figure in its environs.

On 22 February 1754 Walpole recorded a payment for a Shell Seat, which was to be erected at the tip of the Serpentine Wood, facing the Thames.[59] Bentley contributed the initial design, rendering the bench in his peculiar, print-makerly hand as a human-sized cartouche (Fig. 131). Although the Shell Seat as executed had a more regular form, Walpole preserved the idea of it as a frame in *plein air* in his correspondence.[60] Writing to George Montagu again, less than a month after the party at which he had dressed himself in limewood and embroidery, Walpole framed three 'beauties' on the half shell: 'Strawberry Hill has grown a perfect Paphos, it is the land of Beauties. On Wednesday the Duchesses of Hamilton and Richmond, and Lady Ailesbury dined there … There never was so pretty a sight as to see them all three sitting in the shell.'[61] Paphos, where

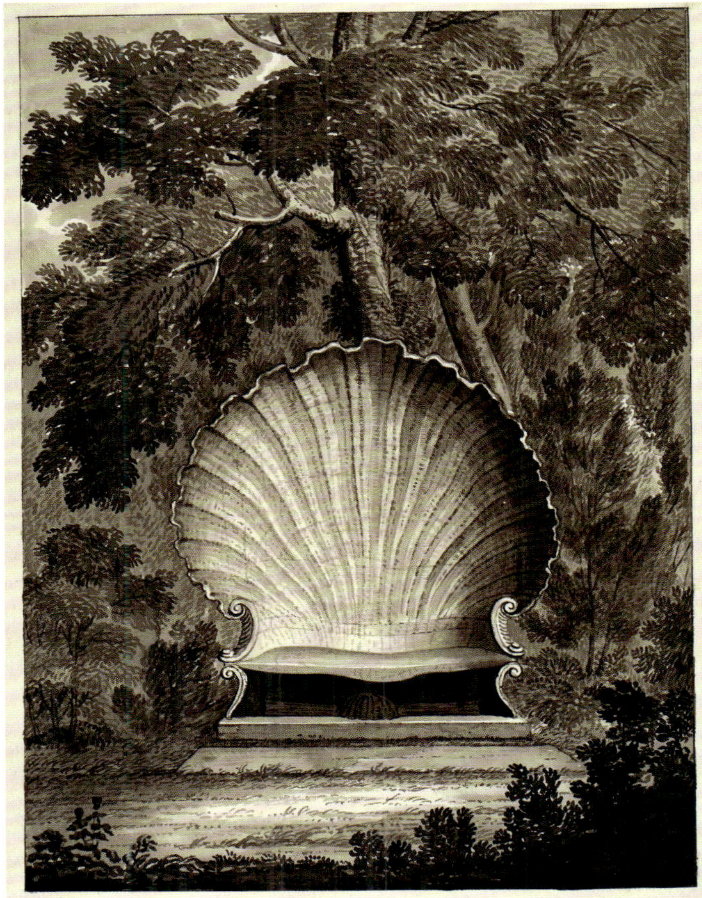

Figure 132. Artist unknown, *The shell seat at Horace Walpole's Villa at Strawberry Hill*, c. 1825, grey wash and watercolour on wove paper, 24.5 × 18.1 cm (visible). The Lewis Walpole Library, Yale University. Folio 49 3678.2. Cat. 14

Aphrodite came to shore after rising from the waters, was sacred to the goddess of love and, not coincidentally, the home of Pygmalion. Walpole's erection of an outsize ornament on the edge of his property allowed him to stage these aristocratic 'beauties' as goddesses, to frame them in a flattering allusion, that they might, in turn, transform the banks of the Thames into the shores of Cythera. What Walpole relates to Montagu is the moment – the 'sight' – when the alteration of the contents of this frame allows Strawberry Hill in its entirety to become somewhere else.

It is possible, and would undoubtedly be fruitful, to approach the objects that I have discussed in this essay as present-day antiquarians would: to date them correctly, to re-attribute them to other makers, to fix them within our own historiographies. Instead, I have attempted, through close examination of Walpole's apparatus, to tease out some of the resonances of these objects and ensembles as constituents of the collections at Strawberry Hill. Given the density of documentation surrounding Walpole, this is an operation that could be continued indefinitely, but even looking at this small sample, a number of Walpole's strategies of confabulation, destabilization and juxtaposition have emerged. Prominent among these are changes in scale and fluid exchanges between the container and the contained. In his letters and his *Descriptions* Walpole related instances where he saw his villa and its contents through fiction, poetry and dreams. Through *Anecdotes of Painting in England* and the *Ædes Walpolianae* Walpole made claims on other houses, collections and epochs. In both his fictions and his histories he populated his house with fragmentary and imaginary beings. Walpole's layers of text are complicated and complemented by his actual collections and his ludic practices of performance and display. We might think of the whole of Strawberry Hill, which eventually housed many representations of itself, as a frame whose contents were animated by the collector's presence.

ACKNOWLEDGEMENTS
Foremost, my thanks are due to Michael Snodin and the other authors for the insights they shared with me during the two workshops organized in preparation for this volume. I would like to thank Maggie Powell, Cindy Roman, Erin Monroe and the staff of the Lewis Walpole Library for their invaluable help and continuing hospitality. I am also grateful to Michael Hatt and the University of Warwick Art History Research Seminar for their valuable comments; Clare Browne for guidance on real and fake cravats; Andrew Lee, on whom many of these ideas were first tested; Adam Gardner for his assistance; and especially Opher Mansour.

1. 'Descartes [Horace Walpole], "A Scheme for Raising a Large Sum of Money for the Use of the Government, by laying a Tax on Message-Cards and Notes"', *The Museum: Or, the Literary and Historical Register* 1, no. 2 (12 March 1746): 46–53; for more on this 'fugitive piece' see *HW Corres.* 13: 15–16; *Works* 1: 132–9; and Clive Wainwright, 'Horace Walpole and his Collection', in Stephen Calloway, Michael Snodin and Clive Wainwright, *Horace Walpole and Strawberry Hill*, exh. cat., Orleans House Gallery (Richmond: London Borough of Richmond upon Thames, 1980), 14.
2. *D 1774*, 121.12.
3. See, for example, W.S. Lewis, *Horace Walpole's Letter from Madame de Sévigné* (Farmington, privately printed, 1933), and Hugh Tait, '"The Devil's Looking Glass": The Magical Speculum of Dr John Dee', in *Horace Walpole: Writer, Politician and Connoisseur: Essays on the 250th Anniversary of Walpole's Birth*, ed. Warren Hunting Smith (New Haven: Yale University Press, 1967), 95–212.
4. In its attempt to locate agency in the shifting terrain of the interior, this essay owes a debt to Katie Scott, 'Framing Ambition: The Interior Politics of Mme de Pompadour', in *Between Luxury and the Everyday: Decorative Arts in Eighteenth-Century France*, ed. Katie Scott and Deborah Cherry (London: Wiley-Blackwell, 2006), 110–52. In crossing between objects and interiors, I have also been guided by Clive Wainwright's observation that the whole character of Strawberry Hill's interiors 'was created and dictated by the objects shown within them, or in the case of the ancient tiles and stained glass, actually built into the structure ... [they] owed their whole character to the creative antiquarianism of Walpole and his friends' (Wainwright, 'Horace Walpole and his Collection', 17).
5. *HW Corres.* 10: 278 (HW to Montagu, 11 May 1769).
6. *HW Corres.* 10: 278.
7. Clare Browne, *Lace from the Victoria and Albert Museum* (London: V&A Publications, *c.* 2004), 9–11.
8. Whiston Bristow, *Musæum Thoresbyanum. A catalogue of the genuine and valuable collection of that well known antiquarian the late Ralph Thoresby* ... (London, 1764), 18, lot 55, 'A pair of King *James* I. Gloves embroidered with Gold., D.L. 481'. *D 1774*, 108: 'Curiosities in the glass closet in the great bed chamber ... A paire of gloves worn by king James the First, bought out of Thoresby's museum' (see Cat. 109).
9. *D 1774*, 107–8.
10. *D 1774*, 91.
11. Similarly, see Horace Walpole, 'History of the modern taste in gardening', in *The English Landscape Garden*, ed. John Dixon Hunt (New York: Garland, 1982), 241–2: Walpole praises the *treillages* of Paris for their 'gay and delightful effect' which suits 'the gallant and idle society who paint the walks between their parterres, and realize the fantastic scenes of Watteau and Durfé'. For another venture into the Watteauesque, see the paintings in the Blue Bedchamber, below, n. 27.
12. *D 1774*, 91.
13. See Peter Martin, *Pursuing Innocent Pleasures: The Gardening World of Alexander Pope* (Hamden: Archon Books, 1984), 45–56; Maynard Mack, *The Garden and the City. Retirement and Politics in the Later Poetry of Pope, 1731–1743* (Toronto: University of Toronto Press, 1969), 41–82; Christopher Thacker, 'Strawberry Hill and Pope's Grotto', *The Garden History Society Newsletter*, no. 15 (Nov. 1971): 10–13; and Anthony Beckles Willson, 'Alexander Pope's Grotto in Twickenham, *Garden History* 26, no. 1 (Summer 1998): 31–59.
14. Horace Walpole, *The Castle of Otranto* (1764). The identification of Strawberry Hill with the castle in the novel was suggested to me by Michael Snodin. See also W.S. Lewis, 'The Genesis of Strawberry Hill', *Metropolitan Museum Studies* 5, no. 1 (Aug. 1934): 57–92, 88–91. My use of fiction in this essay is influenced by Mimi Hellman, 'Furniture, Sociability, and the Work of Leisure in Eighteenth-Century France', *Eighteenth-Century Studies* 32, no. 4, *Sites and Margins of the Public Sphere* (Summer 1999), 415–45.
15. Walpole, *Otranto*, 4, 39, 177.
16. *HW Corres.* 1: 88 (HW to Cole, 9 March 1765). 'Shall I even confess to you what was the origin of this romance? I waked one morning in the beginning of last June from a dream, of which all I could recover was, that I had thought myself in an ancient castle (a very natural dream for a head filled like mine with Gothic story), and that on the uppermost banister of a great staircase I saw a gigantic hand in armour.'
17. *HW Corres.* 1: 88.
18. *D 1784*, 51. See also *HW Corres.* 1: 88.
19. John Cornforth, *Early Georgian Interiors* (New Haven and London: Published for the Paul Mellon Centre for Studies in British Art by Yale University Press, 2004), 67–8.
20. *D 1784*, 47: 'In the windows of the gallery, by Peckitt, are all the quarterings of the family.'
21. Walpole, *Otranto*, 19–20.
22. For a summary account see Eino Railo, *The Haunted Castle: A Study of the Elements of English Romanticism* (New York: Humanities Press, 1964), 304–6.
23. For an extended and nuanced discussion of the logic and effect of framing in the eighteenth-century interior, see Scott, 'Framing Ambition', 115–18.
24. Walpole often describes SH as being a paper castle or having a paper fabric: see *D 1774*, 13; *HW Corres.* 20: 361 (HW to Mann, 4 March 1753): 21: 471 (HW to Mann, 27 January 1761).
25. See W.S. Lewis, *Rescuing Horace Walpole* (New Haven and London: Yale University Press, 1978), 23–33.
26. *HW Corres.* 35: 173 (HW to Bentley, 18 May 1754).
27. *D 1774*, 37–8. Walpole enumerates the following, all by John Giles Eccardt: *Portrait of General Henry Seymour Conway, Caroline, Countess Dowager of Aylesbury, and their Daughter Anne*, *c.* 1744 (Cat. 43) after Antoine Watteau, *La Cascade*, *c.* 1715 (Paris, private collection) – see Michael Snodin, ed., *Rococo: Art and Design in Hogarth's England* (London: Victoria & Albert Museum, 1984), 257; *Portrait of Charles Churchill, Lady Maria Walpole and their Eldest Son Charles*, 1750 (Cat. 44) after Peter Paul Rubens

(1577–1640), *Rubens, his Wife Helena Fourment (1614–1673), and One of their Children*, mid to late 1630s, oil on wood, 203.8 × 158.1 cm (Metropolitan Museum of Art, Gift of Mr and Mrs Charles Wrightsman, in honor of Sir John Pope-Hennessy, 1981.238); *Portrait of Sir Charles Hanbury Williams*, 1746, oil on canvas (current location unknown); *Portrait of Thomas Gray*, 1750 (Cat. 42) 'taken from the portrait of a musician by Vandyck, at the duke of Grafton's' (i.e., Henricua Liberti); *Portrait of Richard Bentley*, 1753 (Cat. 41), 'from Vandyck'; *Portrait of Horace Walpole*, 1754 (Cat. 40), 'from Vandyck', i.e., after his portrait of Simon Vouet.

28. *D 1774*, 37.
29. *D 1774*, 37.
30. Christian Friedrich Zincke (1684?–1767) after Godfrey Kneller (1646–1723), *Portrait Miniature of Catherine Shorter, First Wife of Sir Robert Walpole*, 1735, enamel on gold (Ashmolean Museum, Oxford); Zincke, *Portrait Miniature of Sir Robert Walpole*, enamel on gold (The Earl of Derby, UK; see Cat. 189). See R.J.B. Walker, *Miniatures: A Selection of Miniatures in the Ashmolean Museum* (Oxford: Ashmolean Museum, 1997), 34.
31. *D 1774*, 79; Horace Walpole, *Ædes Walpolianae, or, A description of the collection of pictures at Houghton-Hall in Norfolk, the seat of the Right Honourable Sir Robert Walpole, Earl of Orford* (London, 1747), frontispiece, 115; *D 1784*, 130.
32. See H. Avray Tipping, *Grinling Gibbons and the Woodwork of his Age (1648–1720)* (London: Country Life; New York: Charles Scribner, 1914), 82–3; and David Green, *Grinling Gibbons: His Work as Carver and Statuary, 1648–1721* (London: Country Life, 1964), 208.
33. Walpole, *Ædes Walpolianae*, 38 (Snyders, *Birds' Concert*), 56 (Giordano, *Vulcan's Forge*); both works are now in the State Hermitage Museum, St Petersburg. Walpole also notes carvings by Gibbons in *Ædes Walpolianae*, 44, 51.
34. Walpole, *Ædes Walpolianae*, 44–5, referring to Godfrey Kneller, *Portrait of Grinling Gibbons*, c. 1690, oil on canvas (State Hermitage Museum, St Petersburg). Walpole repeats this praise in his *Anecdotes of Painting in England; with some account of the principal artists; and incidental notes on other arts; collected by the late Mr. George Vertue; and digested and published from his original Mss. by Mr. Horace Walpole* (Twickenham: Strawberry Hill Press, printed by Thomas Farmer, 1762–71 [i.e., 1780]), 3: 115.
35. Walpole, *Ædes Walpolianae*, 38; as mentioned, this painting is now attributed to Snyders.
36. *Anecdotes* (1765) 3: 86–7.
37. *Anecdotes* (1765) 3: 86–7.
38. *Anecdotes* (1765) 3: 89–90; for the present state of these attributions see Trevor Brighton 'Samuel Watson, Not Grinling Gibbons at Chatsworth', *Burlington Magazine* 140, no. 1149 (Dec. 1998): 811–18.
39. *Anecdotes* (1765) 3: 90.
40. Horace Walpole, designer; William Kent (bap. 1686, d. 1748), designer; William I Hallett (1707–81), furniture worker, *The Walpole Cabinet*, 1743, Rosewood Miniature Cabinet (Cat. 171).
41. *HW Corres.* 23: 284–7 (HW to Mann, 22 March 1771).
42. *HW Corres.* 23: 286.
43. *HW Corres.* 23: 286.
44. *HW Corres.* 23: 287.
45. These include 'Cup of Mr. Place's china' (Cat. 233), with a leather case and label inscribed by Horace Walpole: 'Mr Francis Places China'; a lock of Madame de Maintenon's hair (given to Horace Walpole), 1769, below label covering lock is written in Horace Walpole's hand: 'Written by Madame de Maintenon / & given to me at St. Cyr by one of the Nuns/H[or]' (The Lewis Walpole Library, Farmington); Cardinal Wolsey's hat (Cat. 129), lengthy label inscription in Horace Walpole's hand (Library of Christ Church, Oxford), a 'principal curiosity'; *Psalter of the Prince d'Anjou* (Cat. 106), Horace Walpole's descriptive notes are on flyleaves; Horace Walpole's circular bookplate (UK), a 'principal curiosity'; and most famously the Chinese fish tub (Cat. 31), which figured in Gray's 'Ode on the Death of a Favourite Cat' (1748); see *D 1784* (extra-illustrated, owned by Richard Bull), 30.
46. *D 1784* (extra-illustrated, owned by Richard Bull, LWL), 215. Another extra-illustration of the mirror, evidently derived from the image in the Bull, can be found in *D 1784* (Bawtree's extra-illustrated copy, LWL), 189.
47. See Deborah E. Harkness, 'Shows in the Showstone: A Theater of Alchemy and Apocalypse in the Angel Conversations of John Dee (1527–1608/9)', *Renaissance Quarterly* 49, no. 4 (Winter 1996), 707–8, on the publication history of Dee's conversations; John Dee, *[A true & faithful] relation of what passed for many yeers between Sr. John Dee ... and some spirits ... His private conferences with Rodolphe, emperor of Germany, Stephen k. of Poland, and divers other princes ... The particulars of his cause, as it was agitated in the Emperors court; by the Popes intervention: his banishment, and restoration in part. As also the letters of sundry great men and princes ... Out of the original copy, written with Dr. Dees own hand: Kept in the library of Sir Tho. Cotton, kt. baronet. With a preface confirming the reality (as to the point of spirits) of this Relation ... by Meric. Casaubon, D.D.* (London: Printed by D. Maxwell for T. Garthwait, 1659; LWL 49 1109).
48. Lady Betty, as the second wife of Sir John Germain (1650–1718), inherited the estates of Mary Howard, née Mordaunt, Duchess of Norfolk (1658/9–1705), the heir to Henry Mordaunt, second Earl of Peterborough (bap. 1623, d. 1697), and some of those of Mary Howard's first husband, Henry Howard (1655–1701), the seventh Duke of Norfolk. See Anne Pimlott Baker, 'Germain, Lady Elizabeth [Betty] (1680–1769)', in *Oxford Dictionary of National Biography*, ed. H.C.G. Matthew and Brian Harrison (Oxford: OUP, 2004), http://www.oxforddnb.com/view/article/10565 (accessed 5 November 2008); Stuart Handley, 'Germain, Sir John, first baronet (1650–1718)', in *Oxford Dictionary of National Biography*, ed. H.C.G. Matthew and Brian Harrison (Oxford: OUP, 2004);

online ed., ed. Lawrence Goldman, January 2008, http://www.oxforddnb.com/view/article/10567 (accessed 5 November 2008); Rachel Weil, 'Howard, Mary, duchess of Norfolk (1658/9–1705)', in *Oxford Dictionary of National Biography*, ed. H.C.G. Matthew and Brian Harrison (Oxford: OUP, 2004), http://www.oxforddnb.com/view/article/68005 (accessed 5 November 2008); Victor Stater, 'Mordaunt, Henry, second earl of Peterborough (bap. 1623, d. 1697)', in *Oxford Dictionary of National Biography*, ed. H.C.G. Matthew and Brian Harrison (Oxford: OUP, 2004), http://www.oxforddnb.com/view/article/19163 (accessed 5 November 2008); and Rachel Weil, 'Howard, Henry, seventh duke of Norfolk (1655–1701)', in *Oxford Dictionary of National Biography*, ed. H.C.G. Matthew and Brian Harrison (Oxford: OUP, 2004), http://www.oxforddnb.com/view/article/13908 (accessed 5 November 2008). See also *HW Corres.* 9: 287.

49. 'Henry VIII's dagger', Turkish, gold, diamond, ruby, 35.6 cm long (current location unknown); see *D 1774*, 89; D 1784, 13, 18, 35, 53, 61, 62, 63, 77.
50. *D 1784*, ii.
51. Samuel Butler, *Hudibras* (London, 1663), 631–4.
52. *D 1774*, 110.
53. *D 1774*, 111.
54. See Hugh Tait, 'Cannel Carvings and Robert Town of Wigan', *Connoisseur* 158 (Feb. 1965), 92–9.
55. Tait, 'Cannel Carvings', 92, 94.
56. Although the the mirror's true composition and origin were suggested in 1906, these were not actually confirmed before it entered the collections of the British Museum sixty years later. See O.M. Dalton, *Proceedings of the Society of Antiquaries* (1905–7), 2nd ser., no. xxi: 382; 'The Magical Speculum of Dr Dee (British Museum)', *Burlington Magazine* 110, no. 778 (Jan. 1968): 42–3; and Tait, 'The Devil's Looking Glass', 203.
57. See Mary Ellen Miller and Karl Taube, *The Gods and Symbols of Ancient Mexico and the Maya: An Illustrated Dictionary of Mesoamerican Religion* (London: Thames and Hudson, 1993), 125, 165–6; for an extended study of the iconography of Tezcatlipoca, see Guilhem Olivier, *Mockeries and Metamorphoses of an Aztec God: Tezcatlipoca, 'Lord of the Smoking Mirror'*, trans. Michel Besson (Boulder: University Press of Colorado, 2003); for the uses, belief systems and working methods related to obsidian, see Nicholas J. Saunders 'A Dark Light: Reflections on Obsidian in Mesoamerica', *World Archaeology* 33, no. 2, *Archaeology and Aesthetics* (Oct. 2001): 220–36.
58. Tait, 'The Devil's Looking Glass', 205. There are only a handful of Aztec mirrors in modern collections and we do not know the extent of the trade in these objects in the sixteenth, seventeenth and eighteenth centuries. However, recent work by Olivier Meslay analysing the supports of Spanish paintings in the Louvre suggests that there may be more obsidian mirrors misidentified in European collections than has previously been supposed. See Olivier Meslay, 'Murillo and "Smoking Mirrors"', *Burlington Magazine* 143, no. 1175 (Feb. 2001): 73–9.
59. Sarah R. Katz, 'Horace Walpole's Landscape at Strawberry Hill', *Studies in the History of Gardens and Designed Landscapes: An International Quarterly* 28, no. 1 (Jan.–March 2008): 9, 20, 22.
60. Ibid.: 22. See also Anon., *The Shell Seat at Horace Walpole's Villa at Strawberry Hill*, grey wash, 324.5 × 18.1 cm (sight) (LWL 49.3678.2).
61. *HW Corres.* 9: 237 (HW to Montagu, 2 June 1759).

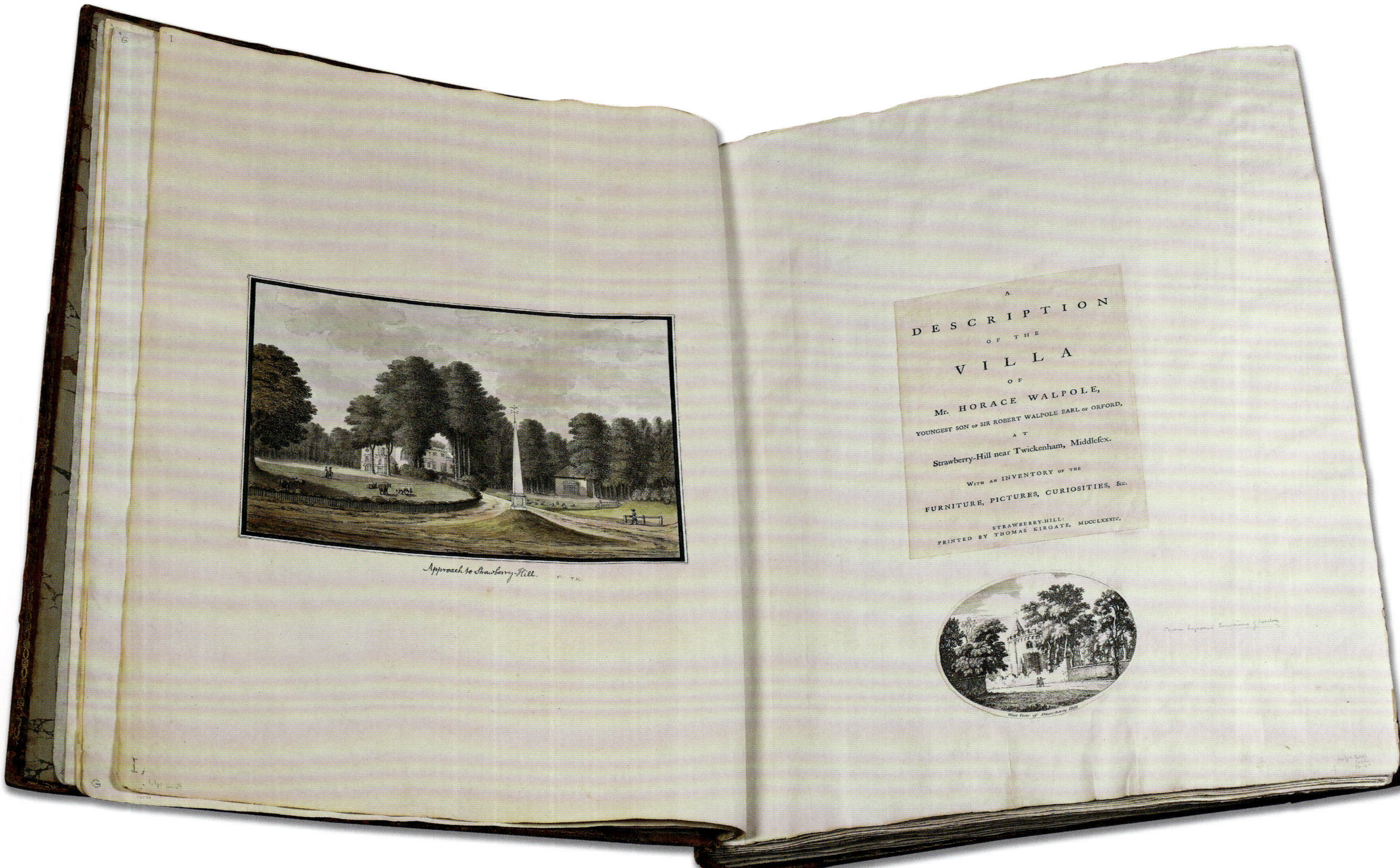

Figure 133. Horace Walpole's extra-illustrated copy of *A Description of the Villa of Horace Walpole* (Strawberry Hill Press: 1784). The Lewis Walpole Library, Yale University. 49 3582. Cat. 21

6.

PAPER CASTLE, PAPER COLLECTION

WALPOLE'S EXTRA-ILLUSTRATED COPY OF THE *DESCRIPTION OF . . . STRAWBERRY HILL*

RUTH MACK

WALPOLE WAS fond of describing on paper Strawberry Hill's existence as paper. He exclaims to Lady Ossory, '[M]y castle is of paper'; and to his cousin Henry Seymour Conway he writes, 'My buildings are paper, like my writings'. In another letter Walpole tells Horace Mann: 'For the rest of the house, I could send it you in this letter as easily as the drawing, only that I should have nowhere to live till the return of the post.'[1] Strawberry Hill is like a letter or a drawing. But as is well known, it is also, at least partly, made 'of paper' – constructed using papier mâché and made Gothic with patterned wallpaper. To say that Strawberry Hill is made of paper, then, is more than playfully to call attention to its triviality; it is also to bring up the possibility of confusing the house with representations of it (drawings) and with its materials, themselves also often representations (wallpaper).

I would like to offer this general habit of thought – this tendency to think of the house as in several senses 'of paper' – as a context for considering Walpole's extra-illustrated copy of *A Description of the Villa of Mr. Horace Walpole*. This account of the collection at Strawberry Hill – a list of objects according to the rooms in which they are displayed – is prefaced with a brief account of the house. Walpole is quite plain in indicating that he thinks of his description of the house and its contents as a kind of building, a 'paper Fabric', as he terms it in the preface. He further extends this idea of the book as a paper building when he chooses to extra-illustrate the *Description*, and it is this extra-illustrated copy of the 1784 text that will be my focus here. This volume's singularity and obvious challenges for reproduction have meant that it is largely untouched in the criticism of Walpole's work, often unmentioned even in critical writing on Strawberry Hill.[2] An extra-illustrated book is 'one into which has been bound or mounted extraneous but thematically related material both visual and verbal'.[3] In Walpole's case, this meant trimming the book's printed pages and remargining them within larger sheets of paper of uniform size, using those wide margins for images of the house and collection in a wide range of prints, watercolours, drawings and bits of written text, or simply laying these in the bound volume (Fig. 133).

It is hardly by chance that Walpole came to extra-illustrate the *Description* of 1784. The practice of extra-illustration took hold in England following the publication of *A Biographical History of England* by James Granger in 1769[4] – the origin of the term 'grangerized', a synonym for 'extra-illustrated'. It rose to great popularity by 1790, and Walpole's connections to the practice were intimate. Granger dedicates his book to Walpole and makes clear its indebtedness to Walpole's portrait collection. Walpole was also a close friend of Richard Bull, possibly the most famous extra-illustrator of the late eighteenth century and the first major extra-illustrator of Granger; Bull ultimately created of Granger's original four volumes an extra-illustrated set of thirty-six volumes. Lucy Peltz has argued that this first stage of extra-illustration, when the practice is more or less confined to an elite sphere and to the production of the book as a luxury item, begins in Walpole's circle.[5] Like Walpole, Bull extra-illustrated the *Description* of 1784, as did Walpole's printer at the Strawberry Hill Press, Thomas Kirgate, and the architect and producer of Strawberry Hill drawings, John Carter. In Walpole's context, then, this practice was both private and shared, much as were the aesthetic decisions made by the 'Strawberry committee'.

What beyond the vogue for extra-illustration would compel Walpole to extra-illustrate a catalogue of his own collection? Most obviously, this particular extra-illustrated book serves to memorialize. It is fashioned near the end of Walpole's life, after over three decades of improvements to the house and even more time spent amassing the collection; as such, it is in a position to record objects, as well as the house, in a different sort of detail than Walpole's prose, even his letters, can. The *Description* already works to such an end, printed in a small print run at the Strawberry Hill Press and made available to some of Walpole's friends only after his death. Images of the house and its objects seem to further this commemorative goal. We might note that Walpole is utterly successful in this: long after the collection is dispersed, we have not only the printed list of its contents but also images of individual objects, no insignificant thing for curators attempting to locate these objects today.

My project in this essay, however, is to look at the ways in which the extra-illustrated *Description* departs from, or at least complicates, this goal of preservation. By contextualizing Walpole's volume in terms of contemporary extra-illustration more generally, we may ask further about the 'extra' in 'extra-illustration' – that is, about those aspects of the process that are 'extraneous' to the text or even to the more ordinary practice of illustrating. And by looking more closely at Walpole's construction of individual pages than critics of extra-illustration have thus far been inclined to do, we may see something in particular about Walpole's ideas of Strawberry Hill. Nowhere in Walpole's oeuvre are the house and the collection more intimately connected than they are in this interplay of text and image, and the extra-illustrated *Description* thus serves as the perfect site for an examination of Walpole's definitions of house and collection and their relation to each other. The extra-illustrated text allows this by pointing us to concerns – visible throughout Walpole's writing – with the status of representations and with how various kinds of representations are to be read.

PAPER COLLECTION

Krysztof Pomian describes a collection as 'a set of natural or artificial objects, kept temporarily or permanently out of the economic circuit, afforded special protection in enclosed places adapted specifically for that purpose and put on display'.[6] Certainly, Walpole's collection at Strawberry Hill meets this very basic definition, and the house – as other essays in this book amply demonstrate – is designed with display in mind. Rooms within Strawberry Hill are made into particular display cabinets for the objects there, whether in the case of the Beauclerk Closet, constructed to house Diana Beauclerk's illustrations of Walpole's *Mysterious Mother* (1768), or the Holbein Chamber, created for Walpole's Holbeins as well as to showcase newly created architectural features of the house in the form of a chimneypiece based on Archbishop Warham's tomb (1507) in Canterbury Cathedral and a ceiling designed from the Queen's Dressing Room at Windsor. That Walpole so famously guided visitors through the house – despite his constant complaints about such visitors in letters to his friends – indicates the extent to which, as Pomian argues, the display of a collection is not incidental to its function but constitutive of it. That individual objects can be displayed specifies their function as objects that are seen but not otherwise used: they are outside the economic circuit and unblemished by any useful purpose.

The reason to display one's collection comes not just from pride in its objects, in other words, but from the necessity of shoring up those objects' value as beyond the economic; in this way the collector is continually fending off his or her objects' inevitable return to their status as mere commodities. Walpole gives his objects value in this way, but he also takes a rather peculiar attitude toward their eventual dispersal: he seems not just to be aware of this possibility for the objects at Strawberry Hill but in some sense to embrace it. In his preface to the *Description* he apologizes for his own audacity in cataloguing a private collection by pointing out that it is an 'illustration … allowed to many a temporary auction'.[7] Here Walpole reflects on a formal similarity like the one Cynthia Wall has noted recently in calling attention to the way that auction catalogues so closely resemble the ordinary and customary inventories of houses.[8] In such cases, 'detailed description is a sort of itemization, which actually or metaphorically breaks up a whole into distinct, perceptible, and, in some instances, purchasable bits'.[9] For Walpole, then, the formal process of memorialization in the *Description* is double-edged: even as it preserves the objects through listing them individually, it makes plain the very conditions for their eventual dispersal and redistribution.

Although we might at first assume that Walpole would find this latter aspect of the *Description* counter to his aims for the collection, the extra-illustrated version of the book suggests that this is not at all the case. In the extra-illustrated *Description* each illustration emphasizes an object's distinct and separate identity, for each may be pictured separately. But extra-illustration does more than this. In Walpole's volume this separateness is inextricable from the object's position in a larger economy of goods. Take Walpole's illustration of the antiquities in his collection: although he purchased all the antiquities from Conyers Middleton – they are at the time of the *Description* part of Walpole's own collection – Walpole chooses to illustrate them with engravings from a catalogue written by Middleton and published in 1745. (Fig. 134) In this example – typical of Walpole's practice elsewhere in the volume of choosing publicly available prints of his own objects – the larger economic world is signalled through the continued publicity, availability and circulation of the object's image, despite the object's physical presence at Strawberry Hill. In other words, these representations say something about the objects that, according to Pomian, the collector ordinarily would not want to say: the objects' circulation does not stop, despite their special removal and carefully protective environment.

The way that Walpole's images both preserve the collection and attest to the possibility that it never leaves the economic circuit also shows us an important side of the reading process entailed by extra-illustration. Critics have persistently described extra-illustration as a process of personalization. In extra-illustrating Granger's

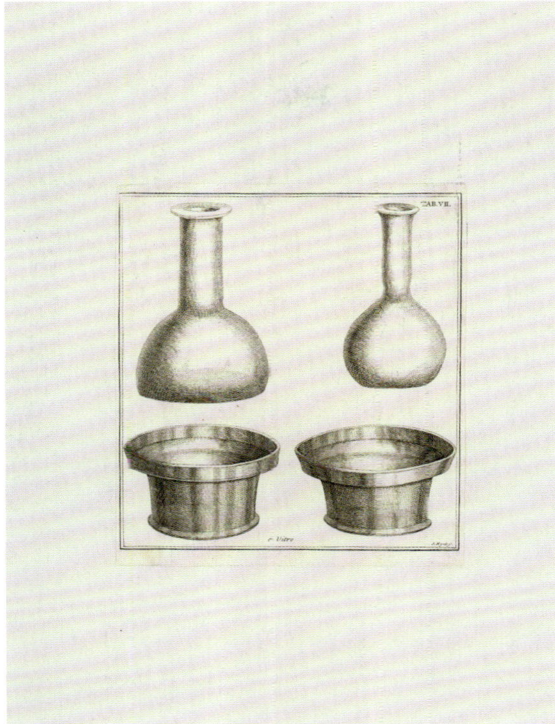

Figure 134. J. Mynde, illustrations from Middleton's *Antiquitatis*, etching, 1745, 22.6 × 20.1 cm. Page 34 of Walpole's extra-illustrated copy of the *Description*. The Lewis Walpole Library, Yale University. 49 3582

biographical history, for example, the extra-illustrator adds and arranges images in order to offer a personal view of the larger, nationalist narrative of history. But what definition of 'person' is entailed in this? Lucy Peltz argues that the process of extra-illustration constitutes what we might call a readerly trace, and she compares it to marginal notation.[10] But even if Walpole operates in the margins, what does it mean to write with images? And what does it mean to comment with images that are produced by others, or even printed and circulated in other books? At the very least we may say that the process of extra-illustration is a strangely material way of thinking about the 'personal' or about reflection. Indeed, in these terms the extra-illustrated book appears to be a stunningly literal incarnation of what Deidre Lynch has encouraged us to think about eighteenth-century texts more generally: that their very definitions of subjectivity are bound up in the materiality and the mechanisms of print culture. As Lynch observes, even Locke's memory-based subjectivity relies on the language of print-based impressions to describe how ideas make their marks.[11] Walpole's example of extra-illustration is not at all unique in this case. But as a personal reflection on what is already a very personally arranged collection, its mass-produced images

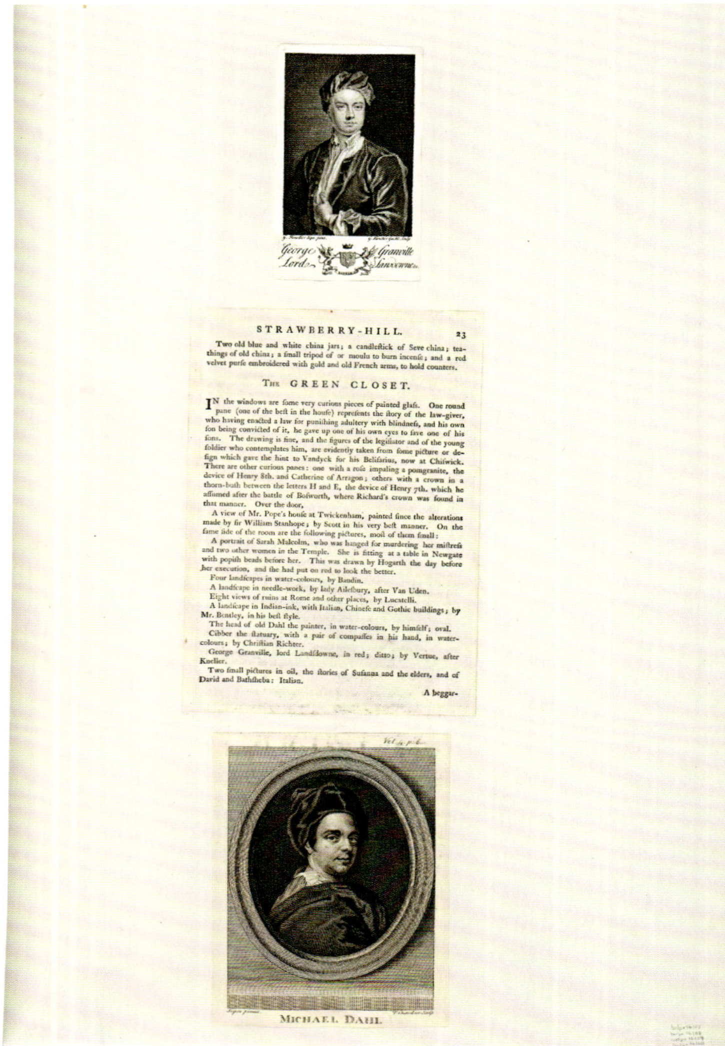

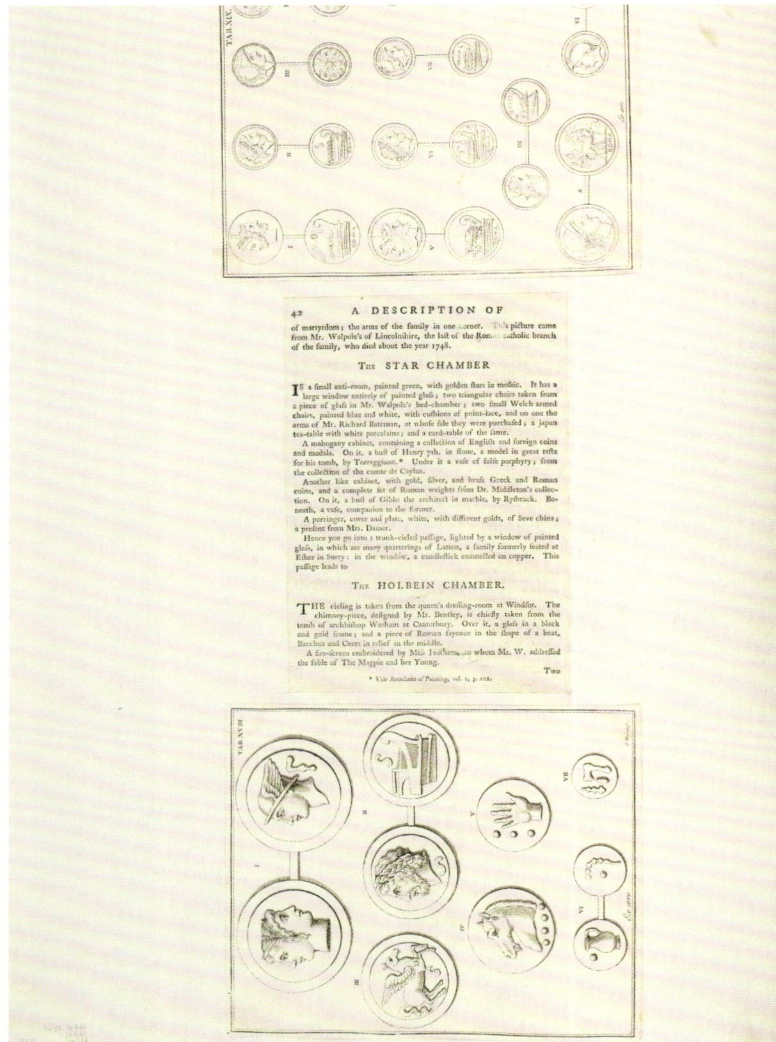

Figure 135. Page 57 of Walpole's extra-illustrated copy of the *Description*, with portraits of George Granville, and Michael Dahl. The Lewis Walpole Library, Yale University. 49 3582

Figure 136. Page 94 of Walpole's extra-illustrated copy of the *Description*, with illustrations from Middleton's *Antiquitatis*. The Lewis Walpole Library, Yale University. 49 3582

bring into exceptional focus the way that individual ideas are filtered through – even made as – printed paper objects.

If Walpole's extra-illustration thus shows us something about extra-illustrated texts more generally, it also makes clear some of the particular representational challenges involved in extra-illustrating a catalogue of a collection, as opposed to some other sort of book. To see images as a collection is part and parcel of the process of extra-illustration, and it is useful at this juncture to consider how an extra-illustrated collection might be different from the more common example of extra-illustrated history. Take Granger's *Biographical History*, which very directly involves the reader in the process of extra-illustration, describing the portraits as an aid to memory and, as Granger puts it on the title page, as a means of 'reducing our BIOGRAPHY to SYSTEM'. An extra-illustrated copy of Granger's book can indeed – page for page – look a great deal like Walpole's extra-illustrated *Description*, with portraits pasted into its pages. But there are also some critical differences between the two.

Granger describes the portraits illustrating his book as a 'collection', and he implies that portrait collection and the extra-illustrated book are analogous, calling attention to the roots of his book in the actual portrait collections of Walpole and James West.[12] Yet, as Marcia Pointon observes, extra-illustration relies on a changing role for the portrait in the eighteenth century, one in which the image does not represent the likeness of a person but instead serves as a kind of interpretation of that person.[13] For this reason, Pointon argues, extra-illustrated histories are defined by the multiplicity of images presented to illustrate a given historical person. Indeed, it is not uncommon for a page of extra-illustrated Granger to contain – as in Richard Bull's copy – so many images that they cannot fit easily on a single page; the images are then layered, producing an effect Pointon calls 'saturation'.[14] Moreover, the multiplicity of images calls attention to the different kind of system formed through extra-illustration, a system that is separate from Granger's historical narrative. In a volume of Granger, portraits order history in a way that narrative – even Granger's narrative, whose focus supposedly arose from the availability of portraits – cannot: through the extra-illustrated book 'portraiture is acknowledged as a system independent of other systems'. Pointon sees this as a marked departure from more traditional portrait collection, even collections of portrait prints, because the extra-illustrated collection aspires not to a bounded set but to a totality, to an ideal. Indeed, she speaks of the extra-illustrated book as offering a model defined by the 'elision of the portrait collection' per se, which pushes portraits toward massive Enlightenment ordering systems like those of Linnaeus and Buffon.[15]

We can see already, then, one obvious problem with thinking of Walpole's extra-illustrated collection as just another version of Granger's biographical one. Following the explosion of images in Granger, wouldn't Walpole's extra-illustrated *Description* have to be a bit circumscribed, a bit limited in how it could represent? If biographical-historical narrative allows images to provide a kind of meaning that is powerful precisely because the system they constitute need not be tied to the historical narrative through structural resemblance (thus allowing, for example, a barely mentioned historical figure to be illustrated multiple times), an extra-illustrated collection would seem unable to escape such a tie, in that its images are necessarily linked to particular objects on the collection's list. Put another way, in Granger, portraits constitute a separate system precisely because of the interpretive – as opposed to directly referential – way in which they connect to the individual depicted in the history; in Walpole's *Description*, by contrast, a portrait could not be more referential, referring to an actual portrait, rather than to a historical person (Fig. 135). Thus we might wonder whether Walpole's project, despite its apparent formal similarity to a typical extra-illustrated Granger, is doomed to merely referential – even partial – illustration.

It certainly is the case that despite the similar appearance of their pages, extra-illustrated histories and extra-illustrated collections stand to require different things of their images. Yet this does not necessarily mean that Walpole merely illustrates, for we certainly have reason to consider the images in Walpole's extra-illustrated *Description* as constituting a separate collection. Indeed, in the case of the *Description*, the extra-illustrated book cannot be an attempt to illustrate as many objects in the collection as possible, or it would have been easy enough for Walpole to commission additional sketches to fill all the margins. And although Walpole is keen to use the extra-illustrated book to display original drawings and watercolours by the likes of his talented friend Bentley and commissioned subjects by Carter, he seems just as keen on using the book to demonstrate his ability to collect from printed sources, as though he did not have exclusive ownership of the house or its objects.

What the book ultimately evidences, then, is two collections set side by side. The list of the collection, itself a system, seems to tether the organization of its images, but the image collection remains separate: collected through a different process and containing different members. Furthermore, precisely because images do not come to dominance in their own exclusive sphere, the reader of Walpole's volume is encouraged to see an equivalence – in kind – between the systems of images and of text, an equivalence Walpole offers us quite blatantly in the preface in calling the written *Description* an 'illustration'.[16] Walpole creates a related effect on the page in positioning text and images – close in size – in such a way as to offer them as two different ordering systems, as in the case of Middleton's groups of Roman coins (Fig. 136). Here it is worth stressing the extent to which the effect is importantly counter to that of an extra-illustrated Granger. Coins or medals were thought to have a historiographical function similar to portraits, allowing the viewer access to history in a different way from narrative. Not only does Walpole's collection mean that illustrations of coins refer just to coins, but if we might have been tempted to think that illustrations of objects allow us some kind of immediate access to those objects that we would not have otherwise (perhaps as portraits were thought to allow access to people), Walpole seems to emphasize through artful arrangement that this is not the case. Indeed, rather than moving toward Pointon's 'saturation', Walpole highlights the geometrical arrangement of objects on the page, calling attention to the way objects can work as a kind of ornament, by placing tiny coins above and below the printed pages or drawing our attention to the way lines of text on the coins extend lines of text on the page. In all of these cases, Walpole shows us the interaction of two kinds of ordering systems, and he suggests that both may be constituted by different kinds of textualized objects. The effect of this double collection, encouraging the reader to think of printed page and illustration as similar in kind, is to leave the real collection as a possible third – but not privileged – system.

PAPER CASTLE

Although I have been discussing Walpole's volume as an extra-illustrated collection, the *Description* is also importantly focused on the architecture of Strawberry Hill. In the preface Walpole refers to the *Description* as a 'paper Fabric' and then refers to the castle's building as a 'fantastic fabric', in both cases signalling the *OED* definition of 'fabric' as 'edifice' or 'building'.[17] If he elsewhere describes the house as paper, as I earlier mentioned, he here makes clear that the metaphor goes both ways: if buildings are like paper, then books may, too, be like buildings. The text of the extra-illustrated *Description* develops this suggestion by leading us into the collection by taking us into Strawberry Hill: the volume begins with no fewer than twenty-six images of the house and surrounding area, first offering the reader a map, directing us through a number of other representations of the house and grounds, and eventually bringing us close to the house's entrance (Fig. 137) and into the front hall.

But Walpole offers this straightforward pictorial narrative even as he complicates its terms. For, if he seems interested here in the way that a book functions like a house, he is also interested in how the house is like the collection. Indeed, in the first paragraph of the preface Walpole describes Strawberry Hill (the building) as 'exhibiting specimens of Gothic architecture, as collected from standards in cathedrals and chapel-tombs'.[18] He elaborates this statement by listing – as objects – some of the architectural features of the house and their sources. He notes, for example, of the Holbein Chamber, that 'The cieling [*sic*] is taken from the queen's dressing-room at Windsor. The chimney-piece, designed by Mr. Bentley, is chiefly taken from the tomb of archbishop Warham at Canterbury.'[19] The process of extra-illustration, however, permits Walpole to represent the idea of the house as a collection much more minutely. In one of his more freewheeling pages, the second full page of the volume, the plan for a bridge is sandwiched between two ceiling patterns for the interior of the house, below which are positioned two etchings of the exterior of the house (Fig. 138). In a manner remarkably similar to that of the 'paper' metaphors with which I began this essay, Walpole here shows us Strawberry Hill the building in the same kind of representation as the plan for the bridge and the design of parts of the building (the ceilings). In their arrangement on the page the images draw our attention to the thin, rectangular shape and geometrical design shared by bridge and pattern samples. Playing on the flatness of the bridge plan, Walpole collapses the relation between interior and exterior, and the effect is somewhat disorienting: it threatens to undo the perspective on the house so cleanly established by the two etched images. Finally, the effect of the patterned images at the top of the page is to make the two printed plates look flat, the pattern of their etched lines strikingly visible. In literally flattening the building, even as he is just beginning to depict it, Walpole offers here some very specific terms for thinking about how entering Strawberry Hill is not just entering a building: it is literally entering a collection. He shows this by leading the reader to see buildings as a collection of paper image-objects, and such an experience disrupts the narrative of readerly subjectivity that takes us through the book as though we were on a tour. Here we find Walpole experimenting with an idea of Strawberry Hill that we could never experience in an actual visit, precisely because it would be so difficult to set aside the sense that we know what a house is. Instead, our attention is drawn to what we thought was geographical space but is instead space filled with objects that seem not to know geographical rules.

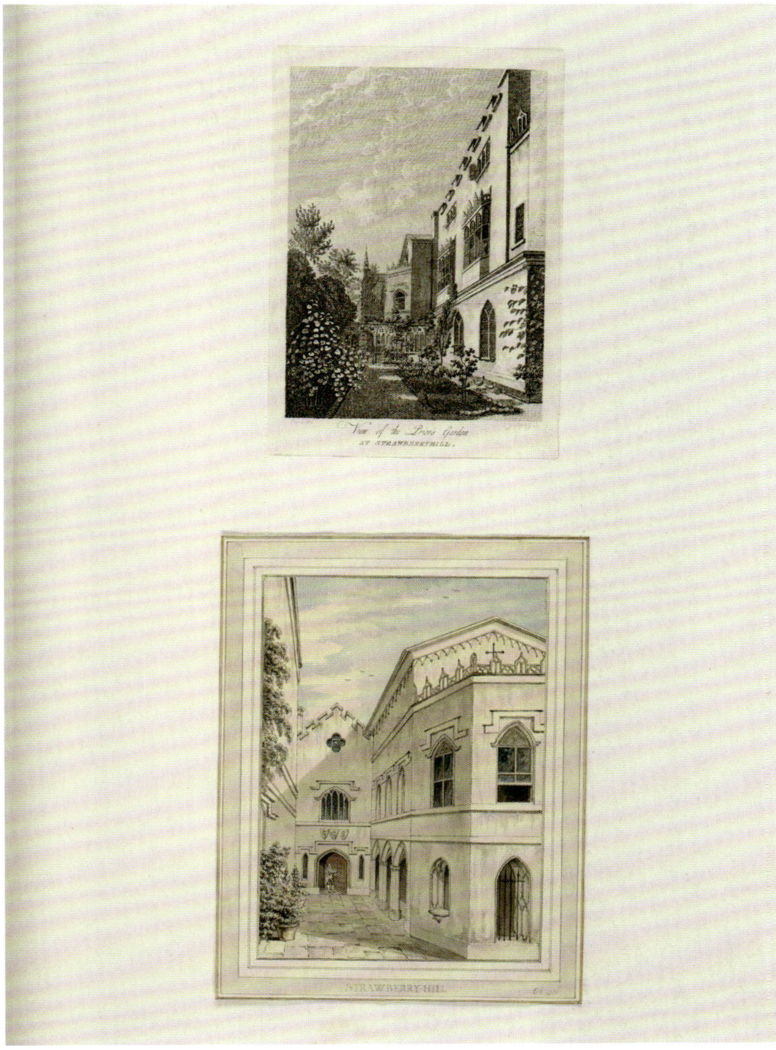

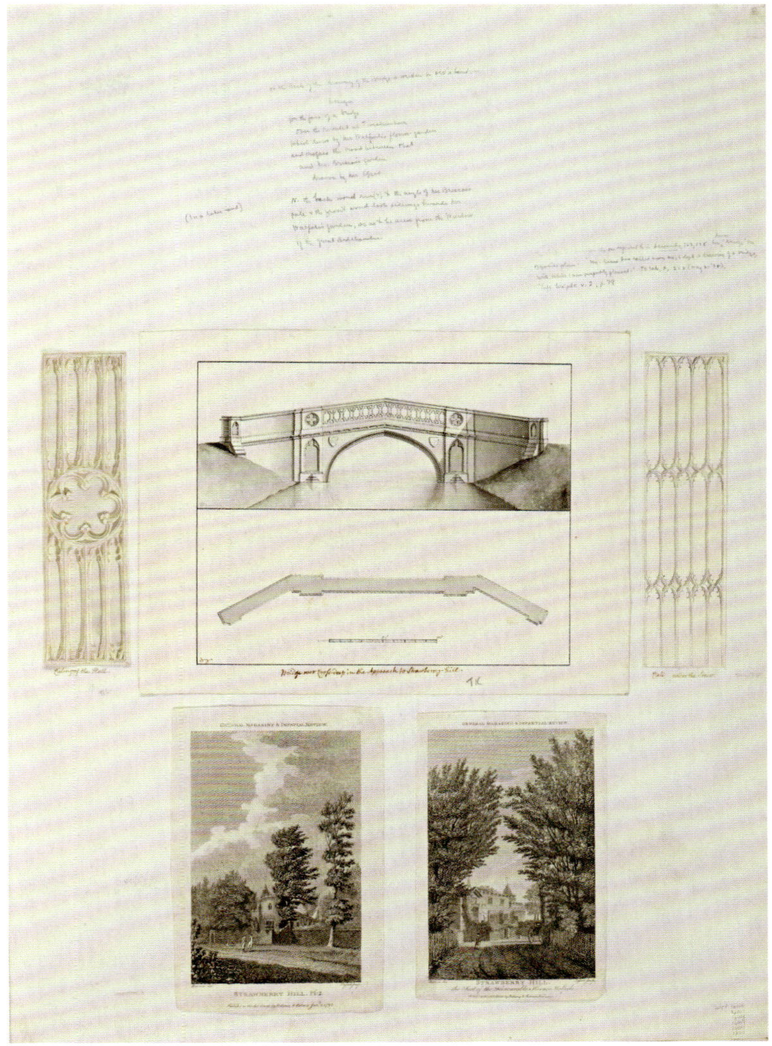

Walpole's house and collection are intimately tied, but not in the way we might at first expect when we consider the house as a display space or frame for the collection. For, if Strawberry Hill as a building seems to do this kind of work clearly enough, Walpole's project in the extra-illustrated *Description* seems to be to make clear how thoroughly such a distinction is undone when we consider the kind of thing Strawberry Hill is. The house and the collection can both be made available for the reader in the same way, through representations that attain the status of autonomous objects.[20]

Such representational equivalence emphasizes a very different aesthetic aspect of Strawberry Hill from what critics, usually contextualizing the house in terms of Gothic architecture, have described. It has long been a central issue in discussions of the house that Walpole uses both authentically historical and fabricated materials. Whether criticizing or defending this practice, critics have assumed that Walpole's aim in such fabrication is to make the actual materials employed irrelevant: to create 'gloomth' (to use Walpole's own term) through their juxtaposition, their affect.[21] Diane S. Ames argues this point, for instance, when she claims that Walpole's architectural style could be termed 'as if' and that in this he followed a long tradition of Gothic practitioners, all of whom were concerned with the production of affect over the authenticity of materials.[22]

Although certainly Walpole was well aware of this tradition, the extra-illustrated *Description* allows us to see Walpole considering Strawberry Hill through a very different understanding of

Figure 137. Page from Walpole's extra-illustrated copy of the *Description*, pasted with Edward Edwards, 'Strawberry Hill', 1781, pen and ink wash and watercolour, and a view of the Prior's Garden as engraved for the *Description*, 1784. The Lewis Walpole Library, Yale University. Folio 49 3582 fol.24

Figure 138. Page from Walpole's extra-illustrated copy of the *Description*, including the Ceiling under Hall, Bridge, Ceiling under the stairs and two views of Strawberry Hill. The Lewis Walpole Library, Yale University. Folio 49 3582 fol.3

representation: not as pointing up and towards the transcendent, but as pointing down and towards the materiality, the objectness, of the house and its contents. This understanding of representation should encourage us to revise some very widely held assumptions about Strawberry Hill's reliance on representation. As is well known, some of Walpole's central sources for the design of Strawberry Hill were not other buildings but representations of tombs in lavishly illustrated antiquarian books like William Dugdale's *Antiquities of Warwickshire* (1656) and John Dart's *Westmonasterium* (1723). From these images, Walpole had collaborators like Bentley and Chute fashion chimneypieces, screens and wallpaper. But why begin with images, especially of those things that Walpole might have travelled to see for himself? Walpole does not search out such images because they're more convenient or because he pays no regard to the distinction between original and illustration.[23] He turns to them because, in doing so, he takes the first step towards constituting his own representations as 'specimens' that can be 'collected' and that thus have an independence from their sources. Although this practice occurs long before Walpole's creation of the extra-illustrated book, that later example allows us to see the logic of Walpole's understanding of representation at Strawberry Hill all along. To understand the house as collection is to understand that it does not transcend but in fact is defined by the particularity and the materiality of its parts, however much they are representational, too.

1. *HW Corres.* 33: 43, 38: 110, 20: 382.
2. The extra-illustrated copy is in the Lewis Walpole Library, in Farmington, Connecticut. Images of Walpole's extra-illustrated *Description* are now available as part of the Lewis Walpole Library's Digital Collection (Call Number: 49 3582).
3. Marcia R. Pointon, *Hanging the Head: Portraiture and Social Formation in Eighteenth-Century England* (New Haven and London: Yale University Press, 1993), 54.
4. James Granger, *A Biographical History of England, from Egbert the Great to the Revolution: Consisting of Characters Disposed in Different Classes, and Adapted to a Methodical Catalogue of Engraved British Heads* (London, 1769).
5. Lucy Peltz, 'A Friendly Gathering: The Social Politics of Presentation Books and their Extra-Illustration in Horace Walpole's Circle', *Journal of the History of Collections* 19.1 (2007): 33.
6. Krysztof Pomian, *Collectors and Curiosities: Paris and Venice, 1500-1800*, trans. Elizabeth Wiles-Portier (Cambridge: Polity Press, 1990), 9.
7. *D 1784*, i.
8. Cynthia Sundberg Wall, *The Prose of Things: Transformations of Description in the Eighteenth Century* (Chicago: University of Chicago Press, 2006), 170.
9. Wall, *The Prose of Things*, 150.
10. Peltz, 'A Friendly Gathering', 33.
11. Deidre Shauna Lynch, *The Economy of Character: Novels, Market Culture, and the Business of Inner Meaning* (Chicago: University of Chicago Press, 1998), 33–4.
12. Granger, *A Biographical History of England*, preface.
13. Pointon *Hanging the Head*, 63.
14. Pointon. *Hanging the Head*, 59.
15. Pointon. *Hanging the Head*, 63–4.
16. *D 1784*, i.
17. *D 1784*, i , iv. *Oxford English Dictionary*, s.v. 'fabric', def. 1, http://dictionary.oed.com/cgi/entry50081398 (accessed 13 January 2009).
18. *D 1784*, i.
19. *D 1784*, 42.
20. I have considered elsewhere Walpole's related thinking about objects and representation in *The Castle of Otranto*. See Ruth Mack, *Literary Historicity: Literature and Historical Experience in Eighteenth-Century Britain* (Stanford: Stanford University Press, 2009), 109–28.
21. *HW Corres.* 20: 372.
22. Diane S. Ames, 'Strawberry Hill: Architecture of the "as if"', in *Studies in Eighteenth-Century Culture* 8, ed. Roseann Runte (Madison: University of Wisconsin Press, 1979).
23. See, for example, Michael McCarthy's account of Walpole's antiquarian patterns as problematically inaccurate and as indicating a 'naive' understanding of 'historicism in architecture' (Michael McCarthy, *The Origins of the Gothic Revival* [New Haven and London: Yale University Press, 1987], 68).

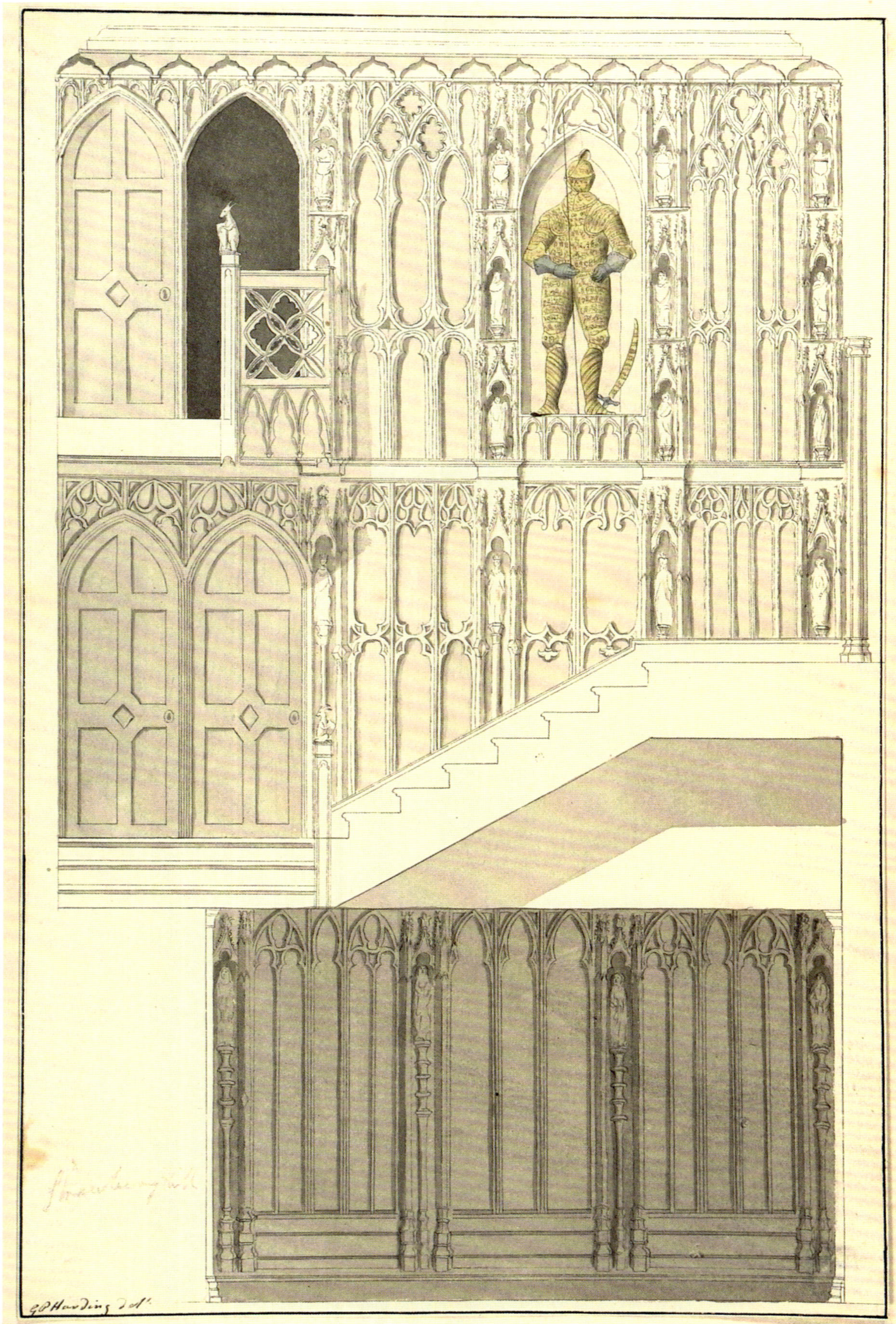
GP Harding del.

7.
HISTORICIZING HORACE

STEPHEN BANN

POPULAR WRITING ON Horace Walpole over the past half-century has reiterated the view that he stands both inside and outside his own period, while reconciling some of its major contradictions. To Matthew Hodgart, who introduced selections from the *Memoirs* in 1963, he 'exhibits the double face of his age', being at one and the same time 'a romantic medievalist, the inventor of the Gothic novel, and the inspired decorator of Strawberry Hill' and a 'rationalist, Stoic in ethics, neo-classical in many of his literary preferences, and an arch-Whig, with a strong dislike of enthusiasm in religion and politics'.[1] Hodgart here repeats the characterization of Walpole as a Janus-like figure facing towards the past and the future, which Byron popularized when terming him 'the father of the first romance and the last tragedy'.[2] A similar comment, pertaining specially to Walpole's novel *The Castle of Otranto* has been made recently in introducing a collection of 'Gothic short stories': 'The invention of literary Gothic is generally credited to Horace Walpole and dated to 1764. It was then a means of repossessing imaginative and emotional territories which had been largely surrendered in the rational, enlightened culture of the eighteenth century.'[3]

This essay will not investigate all the implications of these claims, which would lead us far away from Strawberry Hill, but it offers a broad interpretation of Walpole's many achievements in the light of their 'historical' bearing. We use the term 'history' in many different ways, and in Walpole's case this is quite significant. We might talk of him as being favoured by history, since he was the privileged son of the great Whig Prime Minister. We might talk of his historical, and historiographical, practices, since he wrote historical works of various types and, as an antiquary, occupied himself with the collecting of historical objects. We might also talk of him as leaving a legacy to history, in the form of his unpublished memoirs and his voluminous correspondence. Each of these three categories implies a different kind of historical agency, and it will be relevant to mention that Ketton-Cremer's classic biography suggests a parallel, three-fold division of Walpole's 'activities and interests': first, the 'man of position'; secondly, the '*virtuoso*', 'collector', 'antiquarian' and 'author'; and thirdly, the 'politician' and 'writer of historical memoirs'.[4] In my own account I will be attempting a three-fold analysis deriving from Friedrich Nietzsche that seeks to differentiate between Walpole's historical practices in a comparable but more systematic way. But first I need to sound a note of warning about the methodological difficulties that stand in the way of any assessment of Walpole as sitting so lightly to the conditions of his own times. Exceptional though he may have been, his very singularity has to be discussed in the light of the different models of historical agency that have been proposed in the centuries that followed his own. Needless to say, such models have been crucial in influencing the kinds of history applying to the domains of art, architecture and collecting in which he so fully engaged.

The present collection of essays focuses on Strawberry Hill, and it is with one of the major contributions to our knowledge of Walpole's 'Gothic' villa that we should begin. Clive

Figure 139. George Perfect Harding, *Elevation of the Staircase West Wall*, *c.* 1800, pen and ink, ink wash, and watercolour. 34.8 × 22.3 cm (visible). The Lewis Walpole Library, Yale University. 49.3678.5. Cat. 48

Wainwright places Strawberry Hill chronologically at the start of the series of individual case studies in his study *The Romantic Interior* which traces the development of some exceptional British home interiors between 1750 and 1850. Yet, in appropriating the term 'Romantic' for the sequence that opens with Strawberry Hill around 1750 and includes, notably, Walter Scott's furnishing of Abbotsford in the next century, Wainwright claims more than is implied in Byron's lapidary reference to the authorship of the 'first romance'. He also anticipates further debate, as he acknowledges in his conclusion:

> I have frequently stressed the importance of the motives of the collectors who were the impresarios who created these Romantic Interiors. Their individual views of the past and the character of the interiors they created to house its artefacts were very diverse. The analysis for the theoretical basis for furnishing of such interiors and the motivation of the collectors who created them have never been thoroughly investigated. Recently, however, some analysis of this type has been undertaken using the modern theoretical tools such as Michel Foucault's theories of 'epistemological totality'.[5]

Wainwright's reference is to my own study, *The Clothing of Clio*, published five years previously. He goes on to quote what I term the 'intriguing paradox' of the achievement of the creator of the Museé de Cluny, Alexandre du Sommerard, whom he acknowledges as the first practitioner of the 'Romantic Interior' in France.[6] But he does not expand on the point that, in my analysis, the discursive conditions for the emergence of Strawberry Hill in mid-eighteenth-century Britain, and for the Musée de Cluny in early nineteenth-century France, would have been significantly different. Foucault's theory of 'epistemological totality' depended precisely on underlining the concept of the 'epistemological break', and according to him, the chronological division between the 'classic' and the 'modern' *epistémès* would have intervened precisely between the historicizing practices of Walpole and du Sommerard – rendering problematic the application of the concept 'Romantic' to them both.[7]

This is not to deny the point that Walpole was conversant with the term 'romantic'.[8] Yet Foucault rightly insists (following Nietzsche) that nothing is so susceptible to historical change as the meaning of words. As Wainwright implied in 1989, this was to be a feature of the debate between the 'New Art History' and the 'antiquarian' approach with which he identified. One does not have to be a fundamentalist adherent of Foucault to see the subsequent influence of his emphasis on historical discontinuities, rather than continuities, and on 'archaeology of knowledge' as opposed to traditional history of ideas. Indeed, such an influence was especially strong in the arena of cultural activity where Horace Walpole was a prominent actor. It could be detected in the hugely influential conceptualization of the field of collecting by Krzysztof Pomian, who gave the practice of 'curiosity' a theoretical (and implicitly chronological) specificity by identifying it as 'an interim rule between those of theology and science'.[9] Admittedly, Walpole himself employed the term 'curiosity' in a self-consciously apologetic way, writing of one publication in 1758: 'This is intended as a *treatise of curiosity* … These sheets are calculated for the closets of the *idle* and *inquisitive*'.[10] Such an attitude was turned into a reproach when Thomas Babington Macaulay lacerated Walpole's reputation in his notorious essay of 1833, remarking of his 'cabinet[s] of trinkets … things, not of very great value indeed, yet things we are pleased to see': 'They are baubles; but they are made curiosities either by his grotesque workmanship or by some association belonging to them.'[11] Pomian's studies remain to advise us that, though the concept of 'curiosity' had been substantially devalued by the outset of the nineteenth century, there was an 'interim rule' in the early modern period, to which Walpole's practice remains close – though we may still decide that it should be regarded as distinct.

Walpole's 'curiosity' will indeed come into focus at a later stage in my argument. But having commenced with a reference to Wainwright's *Romantic Interior*, I first need to clarify what might be implied in ascribing, or denying, the quality of 'Romantic' to the interiors of Strawberry Hill. My own discussion of du Sommerard's Musée de Cluny relied explicitly on Foucault's distinction between the 'classic' and the 'modern' *epistémè*, as it had been described by Hayden White as a shift from 'metonymic' to 'metaphoric' and 'synecdochic' modes of discourse.[12] To put it simply, the unprecedented feature of his collection was the high degree of integration between the objects and furnishings installed in the medieval town house of the Abbots of Cluny, to the extent that visitors gained a sense of the recreated 'life' of the distant period: as one critic exclaimed, 'you walk in the midst of a vanished civilisation; you are as if enveloped by the good old chivalric times'.[13] This effect amounted to a kind of resurrection of the past. At Strawberry Hill, by contrast, this intensity of imaginative empathy was surely not achieved. Du Sommerard made his 'Room of Francis I [of France]' into a scenario of recreated history, even incorporating two suits of armour posed, as if filled with living contestants, in front of a period chess board. Walpole himself had not disdained to put medieval gaming pieces in the Great North Bedchamber (Fig. 140). He also honoured the French king, placing 'an illumination' of Francis 'receiving the homage of the clergy, law, and army' in the Breakfast Room, and installing his armour 'of steel gilt, and covered with bas reliefs in a fine taste' in a niche in the main staircase (Fig. 139).[14] Placed in such a strategic position, the regal armour seems to have taken a role in the fictive scenario of Walpole's *Castle of Otranto*. But the very multiplicity of Walpole's sitings brings out by contrast du Sommerard's more focused and thematically coherent organization of historical objects in space.

The comparison can, however, be pressed a bit further. I believe that, in early nineteenth-century France, the draw of the 'Romantic Interior' (as achieved at Cluny) relied for its power on the common memory of the French Revolution. It was the turbulence of the preceding period that caused an acute sense of being dispossessed of the past, while creating a market for the very types of historical object with which du Sommerard filled his display. His attempt to reconstitute a whole historical milieu represented a kind of imaginative rehabilitation of the past. In the case of Walpole, so different in many respects, it could be argued that the English Revolution of the seventeenth century also played a major role in structuring his attitude to the past. Michael Snodin has noted the ambiguity with which Walpole used the term Gothic, not as synonymous with 'medieval' but as delimiting precisely the period that came to an end with the English Civil War: '[A] number of features suggest that Walpole wished to recall the great Elizabethan and Jacobean ancestral houses built in what he called "good King James the First Gothic".'[15] For Walpole, then, the Tudors and Stuarts did not belong on the 'modern' side of the division between 'medieval' and 'modern'. They marked intervals in a continuous history that had been rudely interrupted in the middle of the seventeenth century.

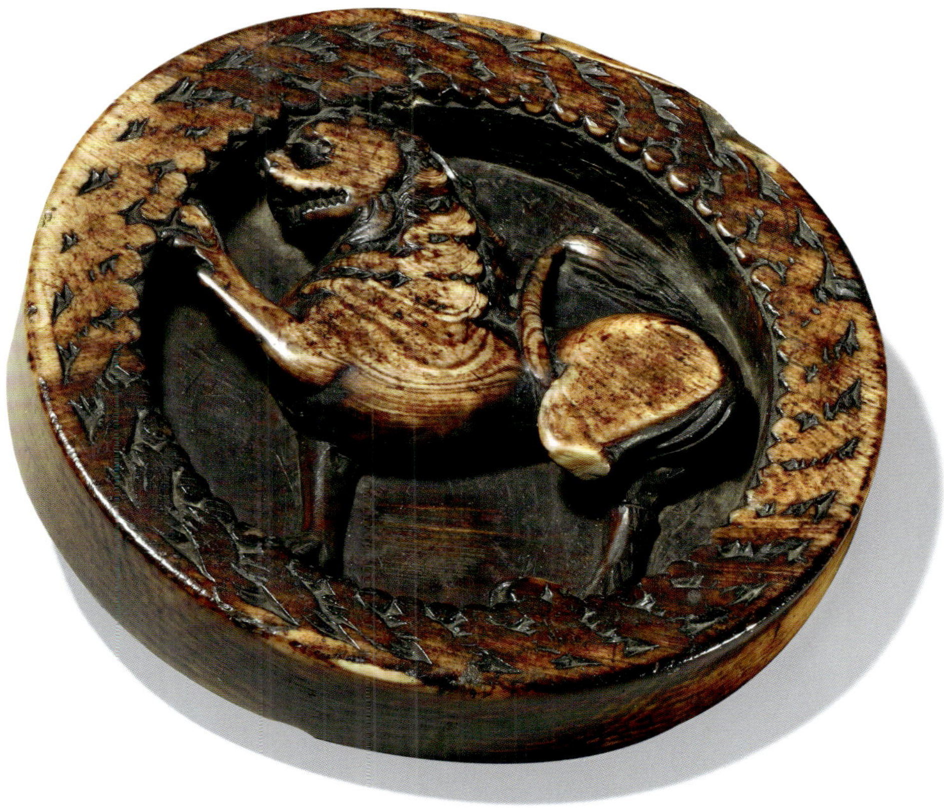

Figure 140. Tableman depicting a Lion, 12th century, carved and stained walrus ivory, 5.8 × 1 cm. British Museum, Department of Prehistory and Europe, 1892,0801.21. Cat. 155

Consequently, the relationship between the 'Romantic Interiors' of Walpole and du Sommerard could be described not in terms of historical continuity, but as a measure of the intensity with which each, in turn, evoked the existence of an *ancien régime* from which the creator was excluded – and that had acquired a mythic quality transcending historical periodization. Indeed, there is one writer who has already interpreted Walpole's activities in the light of a wholesale re-evaluation of 'aesthetic practice' in eighteenth-century Britain, while foregrounding precisely this aspect of his experience. Ronald Paulson's *Breaking and Remaking* describes as emblematic of an 'Aesthetics of Iconoclasm' the illustration by Bentley for

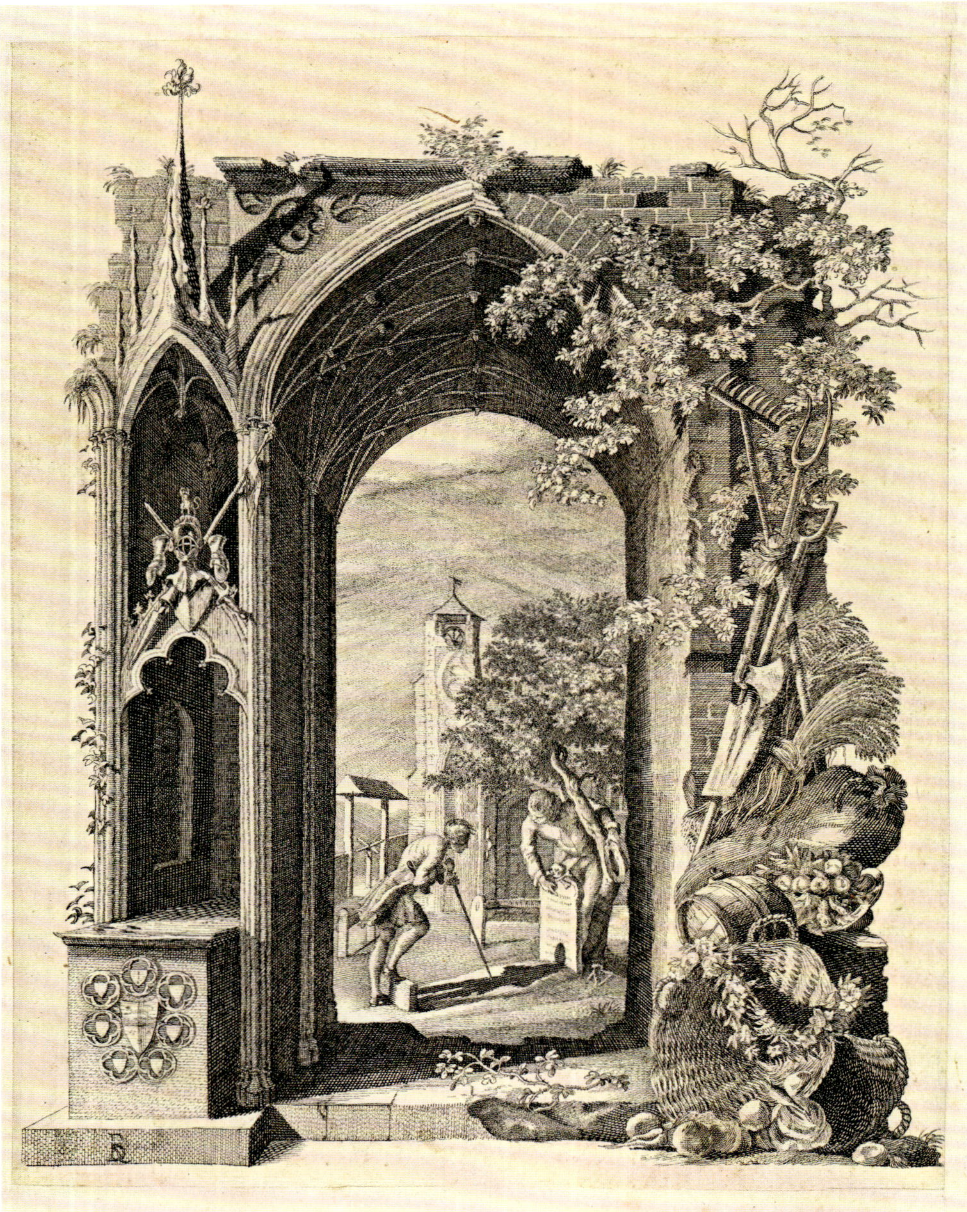

Figure 141. Richard Bentley, Drawing for the Frontispiece to *Elegy in Written in a Country Church Yard* from *Designs by Mr R. Bentley for six poems by Mr T. Gray*, 1753, pen and ink. The Lewis Walpole Library, Yale University. 49.3698 / 49 2044. Cat. 32

Gray's *Elegy* that was included in the 1753 edition of his poems (Fig. 141). Walpole himself identified this scene as 'a church-yard and a village-church built out of the remains of an abbey'. Paulson analyses it as heralding the proto-Romantic concept of the 'picturesque', but also as rehabilitating the 'broken objects' of religious iconoclasm through 'an art of the patched-together and composite'.[16] Although it comes early in the history of the development of Strawberry Hill, this image thus forms a visual prologue to the newly emerging possibilities. The future building will indeed – like Bentley's church with its ancient rose window – patch together fragments redolent of the past, and through their artful recomposition help to develop a new aesthetic.

Paulson's study also incorporates pertinent remarks on Walpole under the rubric of 'Remaking the Classical Canon'. As they imply a further clarification of the historical stance of this younger son of the great Whig Prime Minister, they are worth mentioning. The focus is on the memorial sculpture that Horace commissioned for the tomb of his mother in Westminster Abbey in 1738. The Roman sculptor, Filippo della Valle, was invited to represent Lady Walpole in the guise of the celebrated antique sculpture usually titled *Livia, Wife of Augustus*, but also known as *Pudicity* (Modesty). The ostensible reason for the choice would be that she was the wife of a great modern statesman in the Roman mould (so celebrated in the classicizing portrait bust by Rysbrack installed at his Palladian country seat). But Horace would hardly have been unaware that the alternative title 'Pudicity' implied a comment on the extra-marital activities of his father, who had married his mistress, Maria Skerrit, straight after his wife's death. Paulson sums it up: 'Horace Walpole was evoking within this sculpture both an empress and a chaste matron – the one perhaps to honour his father, the other to satisfy his own deep feelings for his betrayed mother.'[17]

This ingenious comment on Walpole's divided family loyalties brings a new dimension into my attempt to describe his historical stance. In alluding to Foucault, I referred in passing to his debt to Nietzsche. But before invoking Nietzsche's model of historical agency, I should briefly mention the nineteenth-century paradigms for the development of history that he was implicitly rejecting. For Karl Marx the individual was subject to the overriding determination of social and economic forces. As his disciple Georgi Plekhanov expressed it in the 'Role of the Individual in History', the fact that Madame de Pompadour, a French king's mistress, protected an incompetent general does not imply that she was the major causative factor in France's downfall during the Seven Years War against Britain: 'It is the relation of social forces in the last analysis, which explains the fact that Louis XV's character and the caprices of his favourite could have such a deplorable effect on the fate of France.'[18] Plekhanov was here challenging what had come to be known as the 'Cleopatra's Nose' theory of history, where momentous events were held to hang on trivial human factors. Marx himself had already taken pains to explain how individuals could only act in consonance with social forces. In analysing Louis Napoleon's coming to power in France after the Revolution of 1848, he intended to show 'how the *class struggle* in France created circumstances and relationships that made it possible for a grotesque mediocrity to play a hero's part'.[19]

Marx would surely have been no less ironic than Macaulay in questioning the historical significance of Horace Walpole. Yet, as I indicated, Nietzsche answers their anti-individualistic views of history with a theory that pluralizes historical agency, and rescues it from their iron grip. In classifying subjective attitudes to history according to a three-fold model of possible relationships to the past, he offers an adaptable tool for surveying aspects of historical culture in the broader sense of the term. The fact that my last illustration mentioned Walpole's commissioning of a monument adapts well to Nietzsche's terminology, and intimates its further potential in describing his historical role.

Nietzsche's work *The Use and Abuse of History* (1874) reacts not only against the monolithic systems of Hegel and Marx, but also against all ways in which 'excess of history' may prove deleterious to 'life'. In his view, a balance must be struck between the different subjective 'uses' of history that does not unduly privilege any one of them. 'History is necessary to the living man in three ways: in relation to his action and struggle, his conservatism and reverence, his suffering and desire for deliverance. These three relations answer to three kinds of history – so far as they can be distinguished – the *monumental*, the *antiquarian*, and the *critical*.'[20] I intend to indicate how this trio of categories encompasses the diversity of ways in which Horace Walpole established his relationship to the past – as builder, collector and historian. As Nietzsche underlines, the categories are by no means mutually exclusive. Through his different practices and the ways in which they complement one another, Walpole can be seen to create a uniquely personal blend of these 'three kinds of history'. Indeed, it is this blending of all three categories that makes his historical physiognomy so distinctive and worthy of study.

Take, first of all, the writing of *The Castle of Otranto*. Walpole published this novel in 1764, a quarter-century after commissioning his mother's memorial. Wainwright notes that he had been 'more interested in Palladianism than in any earlier style', when he set out on his Grand Tour of the continent in 1739.[21] In other words, he identified with the magnificent appearance of his father's great mansion at Houghton in Norfolk, and with the political values attaching to it by virtue of their association with the Whig magnates who took the major share of government under his father's leadership. Nietzsche's definition of 'monumental' man's approach to history involves, in particular, this adherence to heredity and tradition, which he characterizes with a distinctively classical image: 'He has no hope of reward except fame, which means the expectation of a niche in the temple of history.'[22] Walpole's schoolbooks from Eton already show a fascination with the relationships of the Roman emperors, and his interest in genealogy never waned. Yet it was with his purchase of Strawberry Hill in 1747 that Walpole began to relinquish his earlier taste for classical antiquities; pride in his own family antecedents now accompanied his cultivation of the 'Gothic' style. *The Castle of Otranto*, in this context, serves partly as an attestation of the building achieved to date at Strawberry Hill: it replicates, with a large measure of fictional aggrandizement, the 'gloomth' of the Gothic entrance hall and staircase, whose appearance in a dream Walpole asserted to be the germ of the original story.[23]

Yet the narrative succeeds precisely in defying any expectation of legitimate succession. The gigantic spectres appearing to Manfred, Prince of Otranto, wreak the revenge of an ancient line upon the present usurper. We anticipate this conclusion right from the start, when the miscreant prince's heir is crushed to death by the weight of a monstrous helmet. With the final denouement, the castle itself collapses, and there comes the moment when the legitimate Alfonso, 'dilated to an immense magnitude, appeared in the centre of the ruins'.[24] One might well imagine that, throughout this disconcerting fable, Walpole's 'antiquarian' apparatus is a vehicle for thoroughly deconstructing the 'monumental' approach He was aware of the spectres that haunted the political class since the Civil War, and his anxiety about historical succession was doubtless compounded by his own position as the son of the nation's once

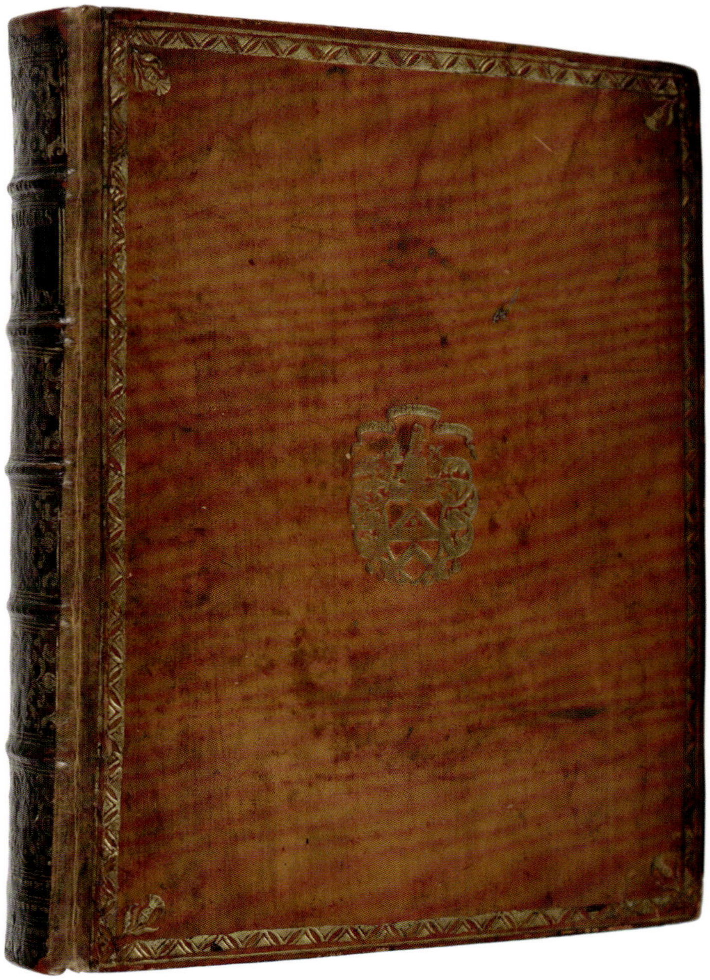

Figure 142. Count Anthony Hamilton, *Memoires du comte de Grammont,* Strawberry Hill, 1772, 23.3 × 19 cm. The Lewis Walpole Library, Yale University. 49 2511. Cat. 93

unprecedentedly powerful first minister. Yet the 'compact little Gothic villa'[25] that he had begun to fashion was a means of overcoming this anxiety, not least through its capacity to generate a compensatory fantasy.

When we pass from historicizing fantasy to the sober business of historical narration, Walpole presents a different side. He recognizes that the responsibility of the historian is to the future, rather than to his own times. Despite his personal involvement in events at the 'Cleopatra's nose' level, he is ready to stress the importance of the 'monumental' approach. While writing his copious *Memoirs*, he became especially self-conscious about his ultimate duty to posterity. Initially (he informs us), he had intended 'simply to throw together some anecdotes and characters which might cast a light on the times in which I have lived, and might lead some future and more assiduous historian to an intimate knowledge of the men whose counsels or actions he shall record'.[26] His first inclination was to reject the 'antiquarian' approach as unsuited to the sophistication of the modern age. 'A monkish writer may be qualified to record an age of barbarity and ignorance; Sallust alone was worthy to snatch the rapid episode of Catiline from oblivion; Tacitus, to paint monsters whose lives surpassed caricatura; Livy, to embrace whole ages of patriots and heroes.'[27] These noteworthy historians of Ancient Rome roll off the page because, in appropriately 'monumental' terms, the achievements of antique civilization have been rivalled, and in most respects surpassed, by the imperial reach of contemporary Britain. Walpole modestly demurs at any comparison between these Roman historians and his own efforts: 'I am no historian: I write casual memoires, I draw characters; I preserve anecdotes, which my superiors, the historians of Britain, may enchase into their weighty annals, or pass over at pleasure.'[28] Nevertheless, the care that he took to ensure that his 'memoires' should be conserved, and eventually made available to his Waldegrave heirs, in a sense disavows this self-deprecatory attitude.

Walpole's use of this term 'memoires', in the French spelling, sends an interesting signal here. It reiterates the point that the classical historians to whom he pays obeisance are not the models by whom he measures his own achievements. He was fascinated for years by the *Mémoires du Comte de Grammont*, with their lively presentation of the court of Louis XIV, and published a new edition in 1772 (Fig. 142). In view of his close personal connections with the French society of his times, it has been signalled with regret that he had no opportunity to read the more substantial memoirs of the French court by the Duc de Saint-Simon, which remained unpublished throughout his lifetime. But he certainly had access to the memoirs of major players from the troubled period of the Fronde, which preceded Louis XIV's assumption of personal power in the mid-seventeenth century. Cardinal de Retz, co-adjutor to the Archbishop of Paris and an inveterate plotter, was then on the opposing side to the Duc de La Rochefoucauld, who supported the cause of the intrepid Prince de Condé in the struggle that dominated the young king's minority.

Both left memoirs. De Retz must surely have commended himself to Walpole through the corrosive wit of his characterizations: an example is the description of Condé's younger brother, the Prince de Conti, as 'a zero, multiplied only because he was a prince of the blood'.[29] La Rochefoucauld, by contrast, was a genuinely 'monumental' historian, who even adopted the usage of Caesar's *Gallic War* in referring to his own actions in the third person. Together with the *History of the Rebellion and Civil Wars in England* (1702) by the 1st Earl of Clarendon, these Gallic precedents provided a model for the ruthless dissection of the characters of his contemporaries that we find in Walpole's own memoirs. La Rochefoucauld also offers a cartography of French society that mapped the most subtle gradations of privilege and power. For him it is not enough to be a duke; the great ambition is to acquire the privileges accorded only to the elite of French ducal families who can lay claim to former sovereign status.

Throughout Walpole's memoirs it is indeed the political role-playing of dukes, and their foibles, that provide a prime source of entertainment. Richmond and Grafton (the latter the son of Walpole's own godfather) aspire to assert the social precedence due to their status as 'Princes of the Blood'.[30] Newcastle and Bedford jockey for power and prestige at the highest level.[31] The Cavendish family, Dukes of Devonshire, consider themselves (Walpole assures us) to be 'the most distinguished in the kingdom'.[32] Walpole has no 'Fronde of the princes' to record and is soon able to dismiss the capacity of the exiled Stuarts to cause a crisis in the political order. Yet the tension persists throughout his memoirs between the purposive action of brilliant, but flawed, statesmen like Pitt the Elder and Townshend – heirs to the power of his own father – and the inertia of the vacuous princes and scheming princesses of the Hanoverian line. There is only one major exception to the habits of malevolence and negligence cultivated by the latter. William, Duke of Cumberland, the soldier son of George II who is unjustly pilloried, estranged from court and rendered powerless, acquires in Walpole's account something of the tragic dignity of La Rochefoucauld's Prince de Condé.[33]

Walpole's 'monumental' sense of history is thus permeated with a 'critical' strain. Nietzsche remarks grandiloquently: 'Man must have the strength to break up the past, and apply it, too, in order to live.'[34] Walpole is indeed aware of the greatness of the epoch in which he is living, and of his own personal stake in the genesis of that greatness. He is also painfully conscious of the negligible role that he himself has played in public affairs. His personal advocacy on behalf of the unjustly condemned Admiral Byng provides a unique occasion for him to demonstrate both his humanity and his ultimate powerlessness.[35] But the factor that supplements this 'critical' position, and arguably converts Walpole's 'breaking up' of the past into a genuine 'application', is (in Nietzsche's terms) his commitment to the 'antiquarian' mode of historical agency.

There is an amusing account by Walpole himself that can point the way in clarifying this claim. In a conversation with William Hogarth he discussed the publication of his own *Anecdotes of Painting*. 'Why, it is a critical history of painting, is it not?', asked the painter. 'No,' answered Walpole, 'it is an antiquarian history of it in England ... I believe the work will not give much offence.'[36] Here we observe straight away that Walpole had his own view of the significance of that distinction. Yet Nietzsche's broader definition brings out the more conflicting aspects of Walpole's antiquarianism. For the essence of Nietzsche's position is that the antiquarian's qualities of 'conservatism and reverence' betoken a faithful, self-denying acquiescence in the patriarchal system:

> The possession of his ancestors' furniture changes its meaning in his soul, for his soul is rather possessed by it. All that is small and limited, moldy and obsolete, gains a worth and inviolability of its own from the conservative and reverent soul of the antiquary migrating into it and building a secret nest there.[37]

The first part of this formulation is at any rate the precise opposite of all that was involved in Walpole's creation of Strawberry Hill, where the 'antiquarian' milieu was, in effect, new minted, and so in direct contrast to the Palladian splendours of Houghton – though it also sought to recover the medieval lustre of the Walpole line. It accords well with the interdependence of Nietzsche's categories to propose that, just as Walpole's historiographical ideal was monumental but also critical, so his antiquarianism was imbued with a critical element.

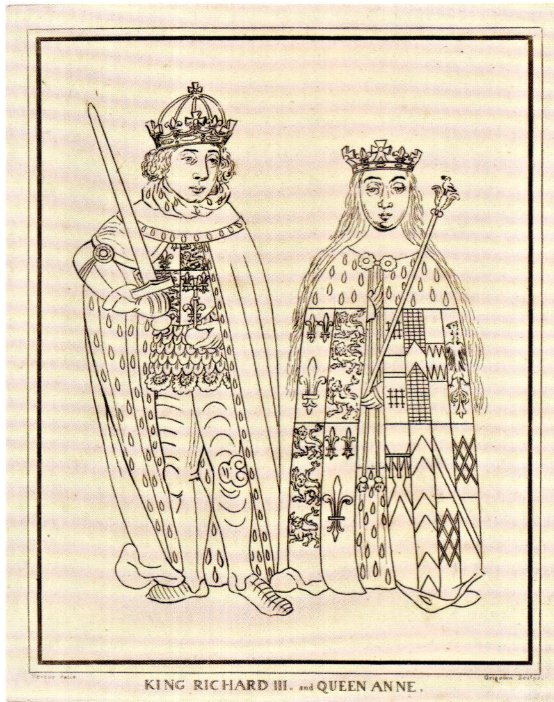

Figure 143. Charles Grignion after George Vertue, *King Richard III and Queen Anne*, *c.* 1768, etching from *Historic Doubts on the Life and Reign of King Richard the Third*, laid in Walpole's extra-illustrated copy of the *Description*, 1768. The Lewis Walpole Library, Yale University. 49 3582, p. 52

That this helps to explain Walpole's distinctiveness in his own times, as well as his legacy to the following century, can be demonstrated by two examples. First, there can be no disputing that Walpole makes a plea for a 'critical' historiography in his *Historic Doubts on the Life and Reign of King Richard the Third* (1768; Fig. 143). His epigraph, borrowed from the history of the French *Académie des Inscriptions*, recalls that histories can only be trusted if we have carefully assessed the credibility of their authors. His own intention is to question the grounds for a historical judgement that had long before achieved the status of a national myth: 'It occurred to me some years ago, that the picture of Richard the Third, as drawn by historians, was a character formed by prejudice and invention. I did not take Shakespeare's tragedy for a genuine representation.'[38] Walpole's arguments in favour of this view have never really passed muster, but it is worth noting that he supports them by questioning (with the aid of a contemporary portrait of no little ambiguity) the claim that Richard was not just a murderer by proxy but a hunchback to boot – this 'amplification of tradition' being based in his view on nothing more concrete than his possessing 'one shoulder a little higher than the other'.[39] His plea fell upon deaf ears, as far as English historical painting went, since Boydell's Shakespeare Gallery perpetuated the Bard's version of the murder of the Princes in the Tower by their uncle up to the end of the century. Yet the tradition of scepticism launched by Walpole also persisted. In 1835 the French *Magasin pittoresque* revisited the issue when it titled an article evidently in tribute to him: 'Doutes sur la mort tragique des Enfants d'Édouard'.[40]

Also resonating in the nineteenth century was another example of Walpole moderating the antiquarian with the critical sense, though in this case his role has often been deemed less creditable. This is no place to review his conduct towards the young Thomas Chatterton. Yet a judgement by the journalist Harrison Ainsworth, from 1842, is helpful in providing a perspective on the issue from an ironic, post-Romantic point of view. Ainsworth belongs to the generation that read, and no doubt endorsed, Macaulay's indictment. Yet his 'Gossip about Horace Walpole' absolves the latter from any responsibility for Chatterton's suicide on the grounds that it took place two years after they had ceased to have any contact. Ainsworth insists, nonetheless, that Walpole was persuaded of the authenticity of the purportedly medieval Rowley poems that Chatterton sent to him. 'It is clear enough', he argues, 'from this [initial correspondence] that Walpole was really taken in.'[41] This opinion explicitly runs counter to Walpole's own subsequent assertion (when he rebuked Goldsmith for his credulity) that he had always believed Chatterton's fraud to be 'palpable'.[42]

Since the issue of being 'taken in' is integral to Walpole's stance as an antiquarian, it is worth comparing this case with another 'fraud' from his lifetime that ended less catastrophically. In 1747 the antiquary William Stukeley was contacted by the young expatriate Charles Julius Bertram, then employed as an English teacher in Copenhagen.[43] Bertram claimed to have discovered 'a manuscript in a friend's hands, of *Richard of Westminster*, being a history of *Roman Britain*, which he thought a great curiosity: and an ancient map of the island annexed'.[44] Stukeley was excited by the supposed discovery and sufficiently convinced of its plausibility to do some complementary research among the rolls of Westminster Abbey. He soon claimed to have identified the author in question. With Stukeley's support, the 'history' was thus

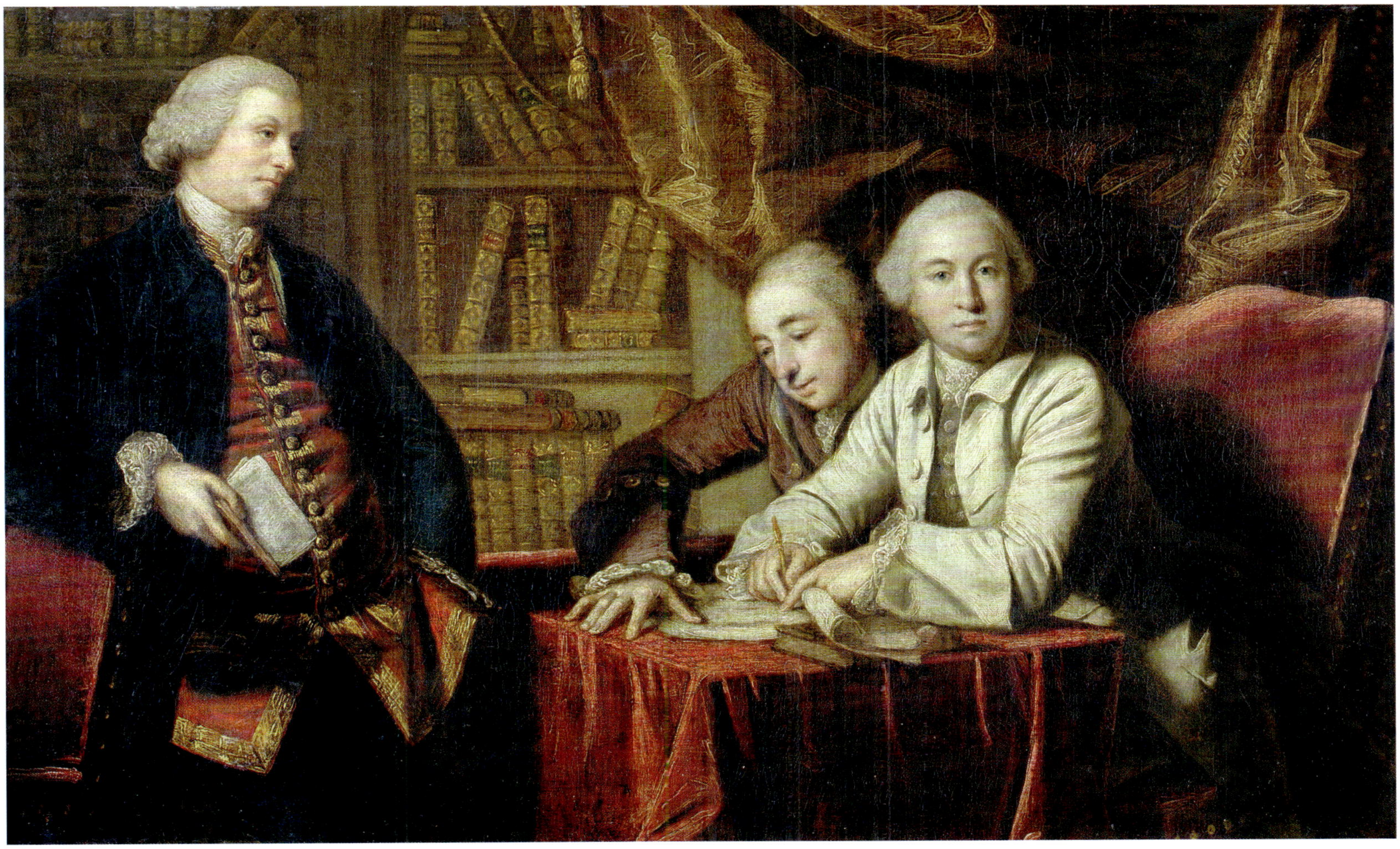

authenticated and published; together with its 'ancient map' of Britain, it acquired a spurious authority that endured until textual criticism finally demolished its claims in 1869. The comparison with Walpole's dismissal of Chatterton is a piquant one. For just when the text sponsored by Stukeley was being discredited, Chatterton was being rehabilitated by the new school of the Pre-Raphaelites who were carrying out their own idiosyncratic revision of English literary history, with Oscar Wilde claiming Chatterton as the 'founder of *our* romantic school'.[45]

There would be no point in speculating on what might have happened if Walpole also had entered with enthusiasm into the enterprises of Chatterton and provided the necessary support. Later in his life, he was ready to acknowledge the acuity of 'that strange premature Genius'.[46] Nevertheless, his reluctance to admit that he had ever been 'taken in' (in Ainsworth's words) speaks volumes about the critical limits that he placed upon his antiquarianism. A similar censoring of credulity can be observed in the episode of Walpole's two prefaces to *The Castle of Otranto*, which follows the convention of the 'found manuscript', later to be adopted by Walter Scott and other exponents of the Romantic historical novel: 'The following work was found in the library of an ancient catholic family in the north of England.'[47] The preface to the second edition abandons this subterfuge. Walpole admits to being 'the author' and 'ask[s] pardon of his readers for having offered his work to them under the borrowed personage of a translator'.[48] Despite the ostentatious humility of this second statement, it would be strange if Walpole's sense of his own elevated social position had not played a part in this reclamation of the privilege of authorship. Once again, Ainsworth

Figure 144. Sir Joshua Reynolds, *The Out of Town Party*, or *A Conversation*, 1759–61, oil on canvas, 52.5 × 81.2 cm. The picture, set in the Library, shows, from left to right, George Selwyn, George James Williams, and the Hon. Richard Edgcumbe. The group met at Strawberry Hill at Christmas and Easter. Bristol City Museum and Art Gallery. K1589

wrote shrewdly in his 'gossip' about Walpole when he intimated that the real cause of the break with Chatterton was the incommensurality of social standing between the Prime Minister's son and the pauper from Bristol. Unlike Stukeley, whose marginal gentility took second place to his passion for archaeology, Walpole allowed himself few such intemperate enthusiasms. It is characteristic to find him referring to the well-known antiquarian simply as 'one Stukeley, a parson', and no surprise to discover that he scorned the members of the 'Egyptian Society' to which Stukeley and a number of fellow clerics and academics belonged.[49] As Macaulay put it, 'the coarser morsels of antiquarian learning he abandons to others'.[50] Unlike some of his contemporaries, he had no taste for unearthing what remained underground.

Yet this image of Walpole as an aristocratic individualist must, of course, be tempered substantially to take into account the social side of his personality, as represented in particular by his hospitality at Strawberry Hill. It was there that he laid out (again in Macaulay's words) his 'entertainment worthy of a Roman epicure'.[51] From the 'Quadruple Alliance' of his Eton school-days to the 'committee' for Strawberry Hill, he willingly allied himself with like-minded friends who subscribed their talents to his projects. Sir Joshua Reynolds's group portrait of the *Out of Town Party, or A Conversation* (1759; Bristol City Art Gallery; Fig. 144), commissioned by Walpole as a painting of three friends, is a testimony to the fact that Walpole wished such cultural bonds between gentlemen to be placed on record. What may also be implicit here is a significant stage in the development of a social framework for the activities of collecting and connoisseurship that Walpole's uncharacteristic example nonetheless throws into relief. Ainsworth spoke for his own, more sceptical age when he remarked sneeringly that Walpole 'had great faith in cheap curiosities'.[52] A more considered survey of the phenomenon of 'curiosity' reveals his place in a long-term development from the early modern period onwards, as well as reminding us of the Janus-like character of his position.

Pomian's view of 'curiosity' as 'an interim rule between those of religion and science' has already been mentioned. Another approach would be to view 'curiosity' as a tendency that – though at its fullest efflorescence in the two centuries following the Renaissance – continued in existence and finally took on an institutional character in parallel with the inauguration of the modern museum.[53] If we see Walpole's collecting practice in the light of this process, some interesting features emerge. The collection of the seventeenth-century cleric John Bargrave is perhaps the most complete survival from the earlier period in Britain, and contains objects that at first sight seem not dissimilar to many that were displayed at Strawberry Hill. But as often as not their 'historical' interest is refracted through the political ideology of Bargrave, who began collecting as a self-exiled member of a Royalist family during the Civil War. When Bargrave describes a murderous Venetian stiletto with its 'oval little holes' to accommodate poison, it is evident that he recalls the attempted assassination by the Jesuits of Paolo Sarpi, the cleric and scientist who typified the independence of Venice vis-à-vis the assaults of the Counter-Reformation papacy.[54] When Bargrave reviews his 'College of Cardinals' (a set of portrait prints of the Roman curia with added commentaries), it is to underline the corruption of the ecclesiastical powers that had fomented conflict in his native land. Bargrave's notes, even to the point of commenting on the way a certain cardinal wears his cap, are directed at assuring his readers that he has been a faithful witness of this turbulent historical scene.[55] By contrast, Walpole's acquisitions invariably reflect a more disinterested and critical view of English history (Fig. 145). The red felt 'Hat, reputed to have belonged to Cardinal Wolsey' provokes no judgement on its putative owner, but is catalogued in terms of its picaresque provenance: 'found in the great Wardrobe by Bishop Burnet' and given to Walpole by the Countess of Albermarle.[56] The puzzling medieval object known as 'Queen Bertha's Comb' (Fig. 146) is validated primarily by its exalted pedigree dating back to the Earl of Arundel, who (in Walpole's words) 'was the first who began professionally to collect in this country'.[57] Bargrave, as a canon of Canterbury, was still deeply aware of the devastation caused there by Henry VIII's destruction of Thomas Becket's richly adorned shrine. Walpole acquired his Limoges reliquary (Fig. 151) in the (unsubstantiated) belief that it was a 'model of the shrine of Thomas Becket'.[58] Historical attribution had supplanted partisan outrage.

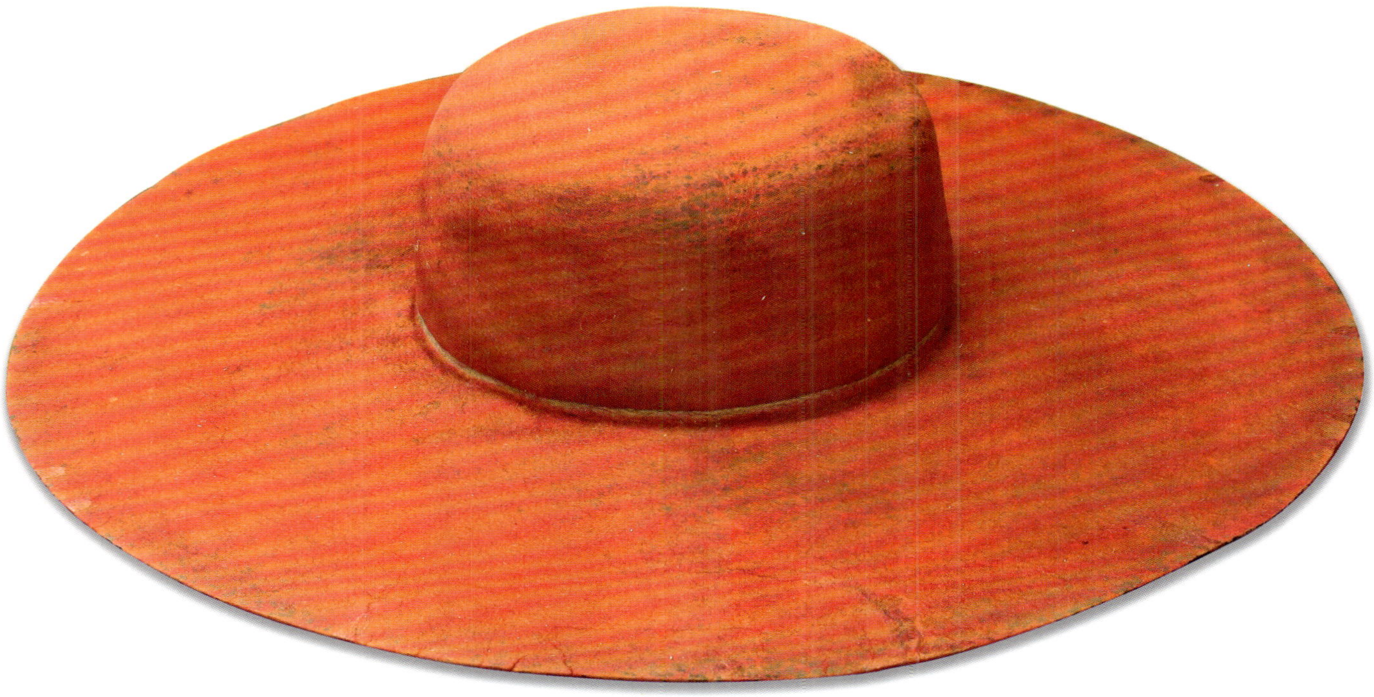

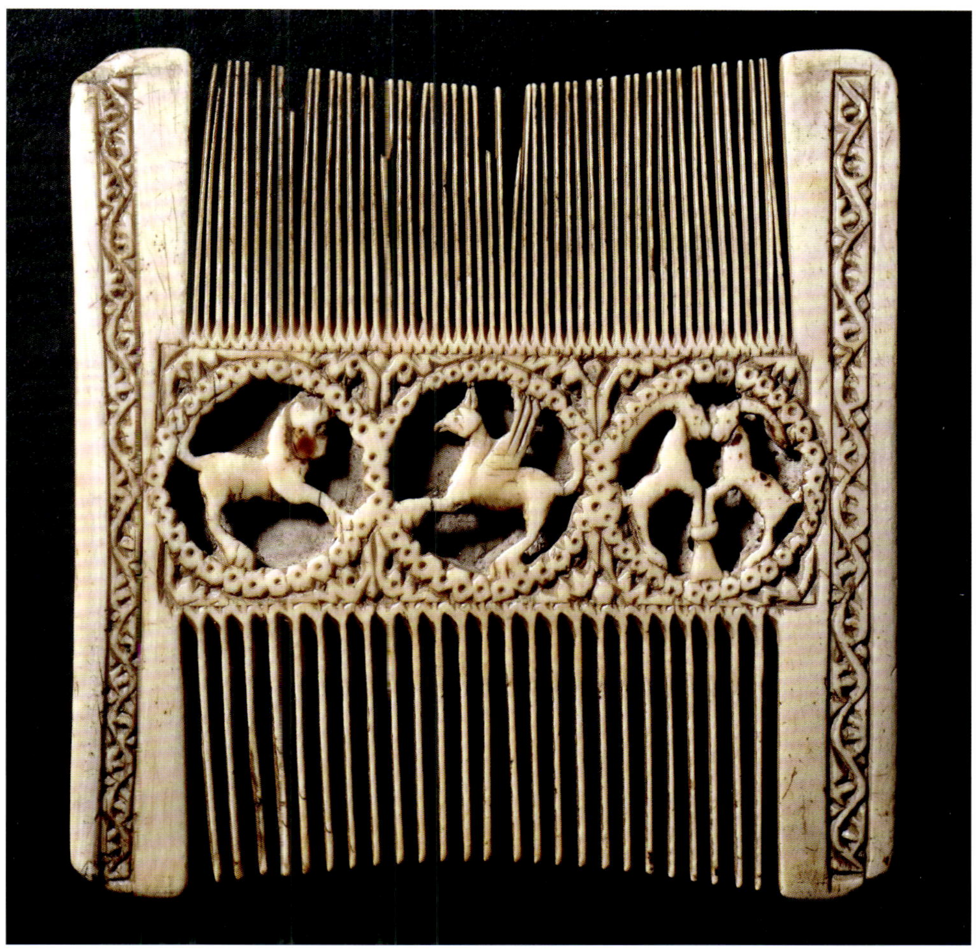

Figure 145. Hat ('The Red Hat of Cardinal Wolsey'), 16th century, felt, silk, D 47 cm. Governing Body of Christ Church, Oxford University. Cat. 129

Figure 146. Comb ('Queen Bertha's Comb'), German, late 12th century, carved ivory, 14 × 8.9 cm. British Museum, Department of Prehistory and Europe. 1916,0403.1. Cat. 105

LANCASTRIANS AND TUDORS AT STRAWBERRY HILL *Lisa Ford*

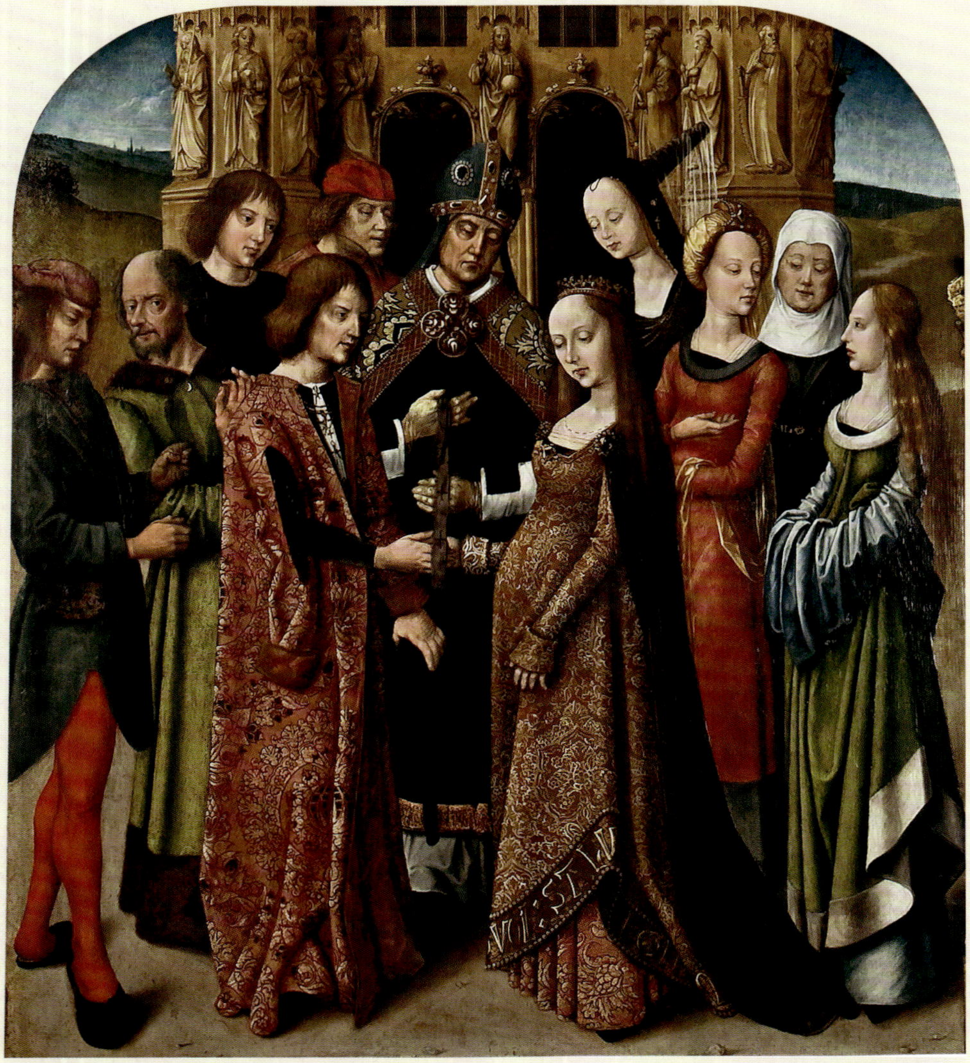

Figure 147. *Marriage of a Saint* ('The Marriage of Henry 6th'), Flemish, *c.* 1475–1500, oil on panel, 94.6 × 88.6 cm. Toledo Museum of Art, Gift of Edward Drummond Libbey. 1926.74. Cat. 99

Through his collection of images of the Lancastrian and Tudor dynasties Horace Walpole created a portrait lineage to complement his Gothic interior at Strawberry Hill. Miniatures, engravings and portraits of the royal family members and courtiers filled the walls and cabinets. In Walpole's Gallery, the ceiling of which was fashioned after that of Henry VII's Chapel at Westminster Abbey, hung the double portrait of Mary Tudor and her second husband Charles Brandon, acquired in 1763, and what he thought was the marriage portrait of Henry VII and Elizabeth of York, one of Walpole's earliest acquisitions, purchased in 1753 (Figs. 31, 32). In April 1773 Walpole wrote to his friend William Cole with great delight about the latest two additions to his set of dynastic images, a picture of Henry V and his family (later identified as the family of Henry VII) (Fig. 148) and *The Family of Henry VIII: An Allegory of the Tudor Succession* (Fig. 149): 'These two with my marriages of Henry VI and VII compose such a suite of the House of Lancaster, and enrich my Gothic house so completely, that I would not deny myself.'

Among these placid, static images of monarchs, their spouses and their progeny, the stone bust depicting a man gripped by fear or despair forms a startling contrast (Fig. 150). Walpole's identification of the bust as 'a model in stone of the head of Henry VII in the agony of death ... undoubtedly by Torreggiano' is no longer accepted for either artist or subject, and the bust differs markedly in expression from the three existing representations of Henry VII attributed to Pietro Torrigiano: Henry's funeral effigy, his tomb sculpture and a terracotta bust, all fashioned from Henry's death mask. The Strawberry Hill bust seems more representative of Walpolean romanticism than of the pattern images typical in sixteenth-century depictions of royalty and represented in Walpole's collection by the intricately detailed relief of Henry VIII after the classic Holbein pose, which has become the familiar, iconic image of the second Tudor king (Fig. 328; Cat. 122). However, considering Walpole's 'historical' assessment of the character of Henry VII, such an image may have appealed strongly to him. Through his revisionist volume, *Historic Doubts on the Life and Reign of Richard III* (1768), Walpole sought not only to cast doubt on many of the crimes ascribed to Richard by Sir Thomas More in the sixteenth century but also convince the reader that Henry VII was a far greater tyrant. Walpole did not seek to exonerate Richard, whom, in a letter to Robert Henry in 1785, he called a 'bad ambitious man', but rather to critique the chroniclers and historians of the sixteenth century who, he felt, vilified Richard unfairly in deference to Henry VII. Equally, Walpole condemned historians who, he thought, blindly followed their lead. His attempts to claim the high historical ground met with stringent criticism from the historian and philosopher David Hume and from Jeremiah Milles, President of the Society of Antiquaries. Still, he maintained his views, and perhaps this melancholy sculpture appeared to Walpole to express the anguish proper to a tyrant who, he claimed in the *Historic Doubts*, 'died mocking God', or the penitence and despair appropriate for Henry VII's supposed sins.

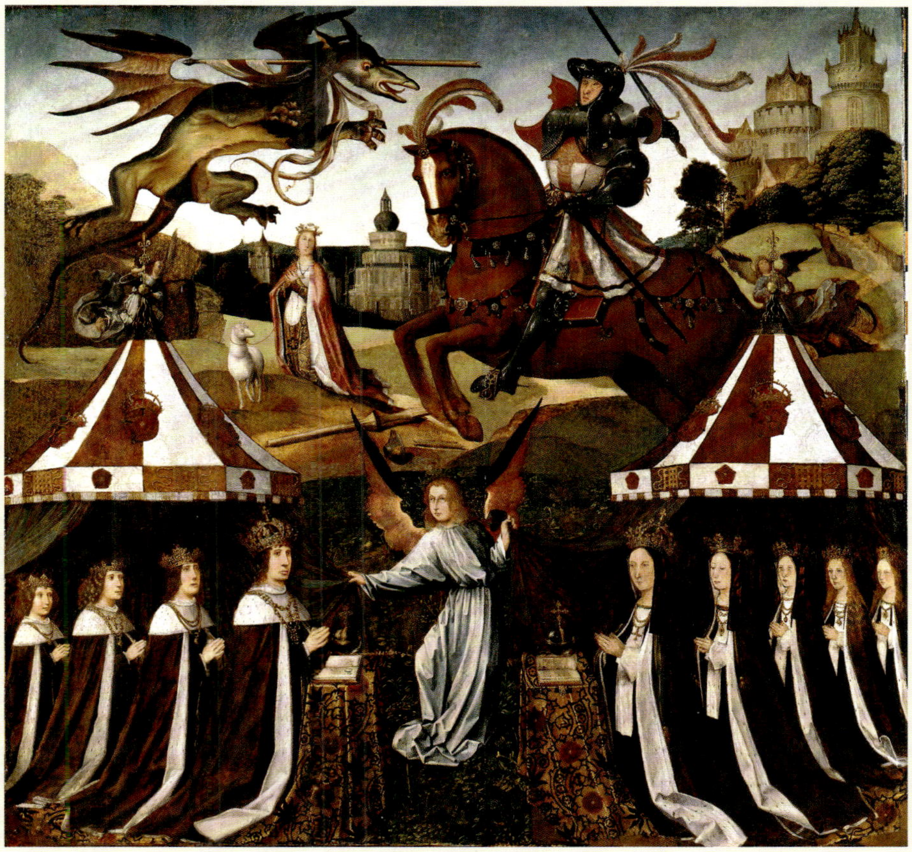

Figure 148. Flemish School, *Henry VII and his Family with St George and the Dragon* ('Henry V and his Family'), 1505–9, oil on panel, 142.2 × 146.1 cm. The Royal Collection

Figure 149. Attributed to Lucas de Heere, *The Family of Henry VIII: An Allegory of the Tudor Succession* ('Henry 8th and his children'), *c.* 1572, oil on panel, 131.2 × 184 cm. National Museum Wales, Cardiff, Wales. NMW A 564. Cat. 102

Figure 150. *Shouting Male Head* ('Bust of Henry VII in the agony of death'), probably Italian, *c.* 17th century, marble on a limestone base, H 46 cm. Collection of the Duke of Northumberland. Cat. 101

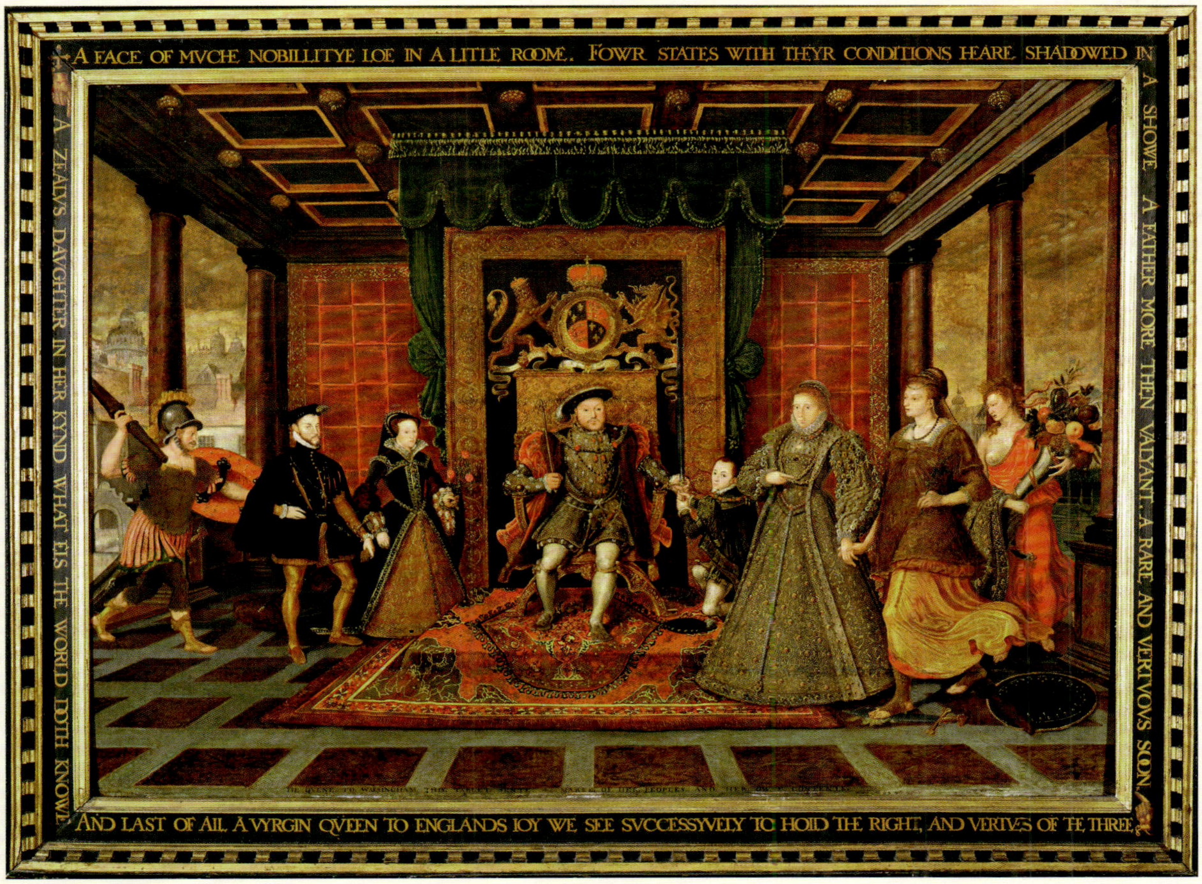

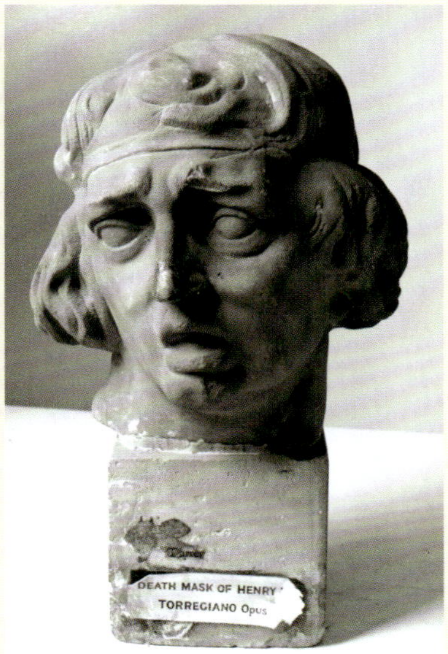

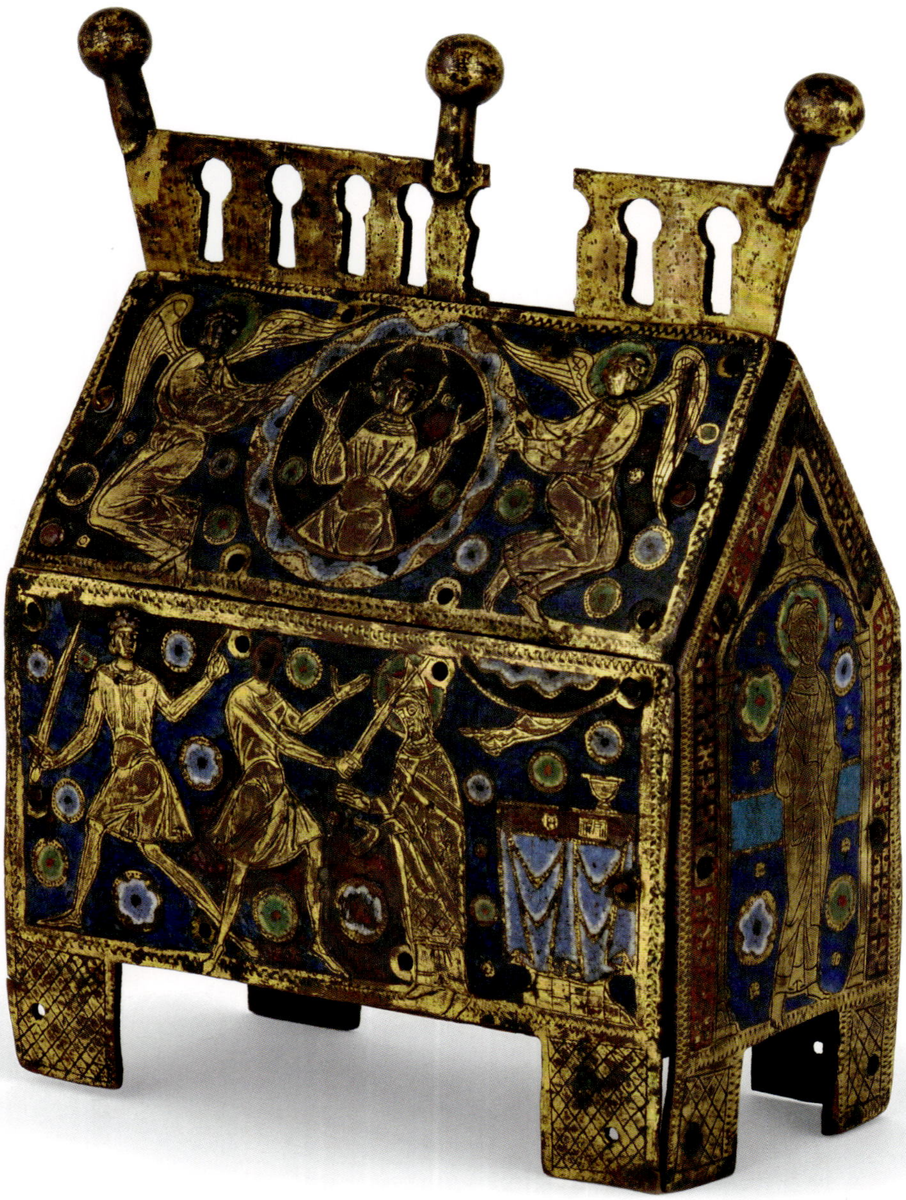

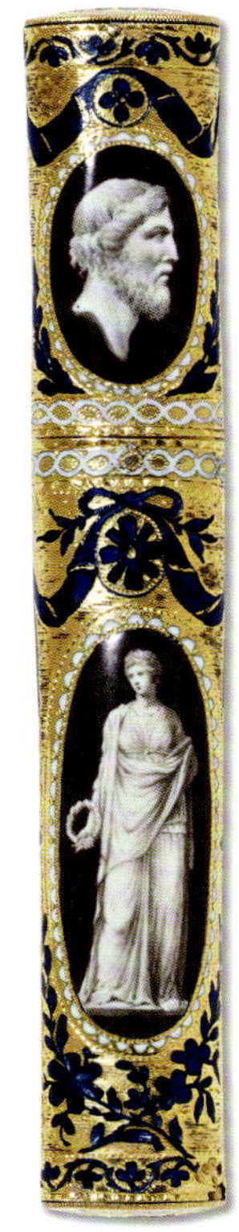

Figure 151. Chasse depicting the Murder of Thomas Becket, French, Limoges, *c.* 1200–10, copper with champlevé enamel on an oak carcase, 17.2 × 12.1 cm. Culture and Sport Glasgow (Museums). 26.6. Cat. 160

Figure 152. Toothpick case, English, *c.* 1780, enamelled gold, 9.8 × 1.5 cm. Given to Walpole by Lady Diana Beauclerk. Victoria and Albert Museum, London, acquired in memory of Professor G.M. Peterson. M7:1-1998. Cat. 170

Walpole's decision as a 'virtuoso' to extend the regime of 'curiosity' did no doubt imply a certain reserve about the practice of connoisseurship as it was developing over his own century. For the most part, it was not artistic quality that validated an object's presence at Strawberry Hill, but the richness of its associations, historical or personal . A 'Rim lock' of iron could justify its presence if it was 'from a Chest of the Period of Henry VII', and a 'Toothpick case' if it was the present of a well-connected friend (Figs. 152, 153). Yet what Macaulay dismissed as mere 'baubles' were already, in Macaulay's time, being rehabilitated and placed within the public domain. State support was becoming available to perpetuate the appeal of such objects and to display them before a mass audience newly acquainted with the rudiments of national history. Prosper de Barante, the French historian of the Middle Ages who had contributed in no small measure to this process, gave the historical curio its title of nobility when he successfully proposed the acquisition of Alexandre du Sommerard's collection by the French state:

> The sword of a great warrior, the insignia of a celebrated sovereign, the jewels of a great or an unhappy queen, the books in which a writer traced a few notes, are so many relics which people like to see and which make a different impression from the dead letter of the volume where we read their history.[59]

Following from my earlier point about the differing experiences of historical discontinuity in England and France, it comes as no surprise that France should have welcomed the first museum specifically devoted to recreating a distant historical milieu. The corollary is that Strawberry Hill was already adumbrating that aim in an embryonic form in a period when such a project was inconceivable for the French.

Here we may open up another perspective that corresponds to the originality of Horace Walpole's achievement at Strawberry Hill. One of the dramatic features of recent 'heritage tourism' has been the exponential growth of the provision of 'writers' houses'. It appears that, as recently as 1972, a survey of museums dedicated to individual persons elicited the statistic that there were 145 institutions commemorating poets and writers. In 2007 France alone laid claim to no less than 203 *maisons d'écrivains*.[60] After noting this calculation in a collection of essays devoted to 'writer's houses', Harald Hendrix speculates on what gives them their special character:

> Since by nature they cannot be straightforward demonstrations of what literature is about, they need to express [cultural status or social aspirations] in an indirect way, by using a different medium which requires a shift in expression from the immaterial to the material, from the intellectual to the tangible and visible.[61]

Strange as it may seem, Walpole's Strawberry Hill fits perfectly into this category, notable examples of which would be the medievalizing Abbotsford of Walter Scott at the beginning of the nineteenth century and the home of Pierre Loti at Rochefort-sur-mer, which cheerfully amalgamates the oriental and the Gothic half a century later.[62] Strawberry Hill's strangeness is compounded by the fact that recent research on the neoclassical culture of later eighteenth-century Britain has revealed quite a different paradigm at work. Viccy Coltman has described the country-house library of the period as 'encapsulat[ing] the neoclassical enterprise – in much the same way as the laboratory had for experimental life a century before'.[63] In Nietzsche's terms, it was a 'monumental' setting where (in Coltman's words) the 'ancient architecture, sculpture, and painting encountered on the grand tour in Italy was packaged in deluxe library volumes'.[64] As we have seen, Strawberry Hill was not devoid of such classical features, but through Horace Walpole's partial reversion to a seventeenth-century model – not of 'experiment' but of 'curiosity' – it came to enshrine a significance that was paradoxically in advance of

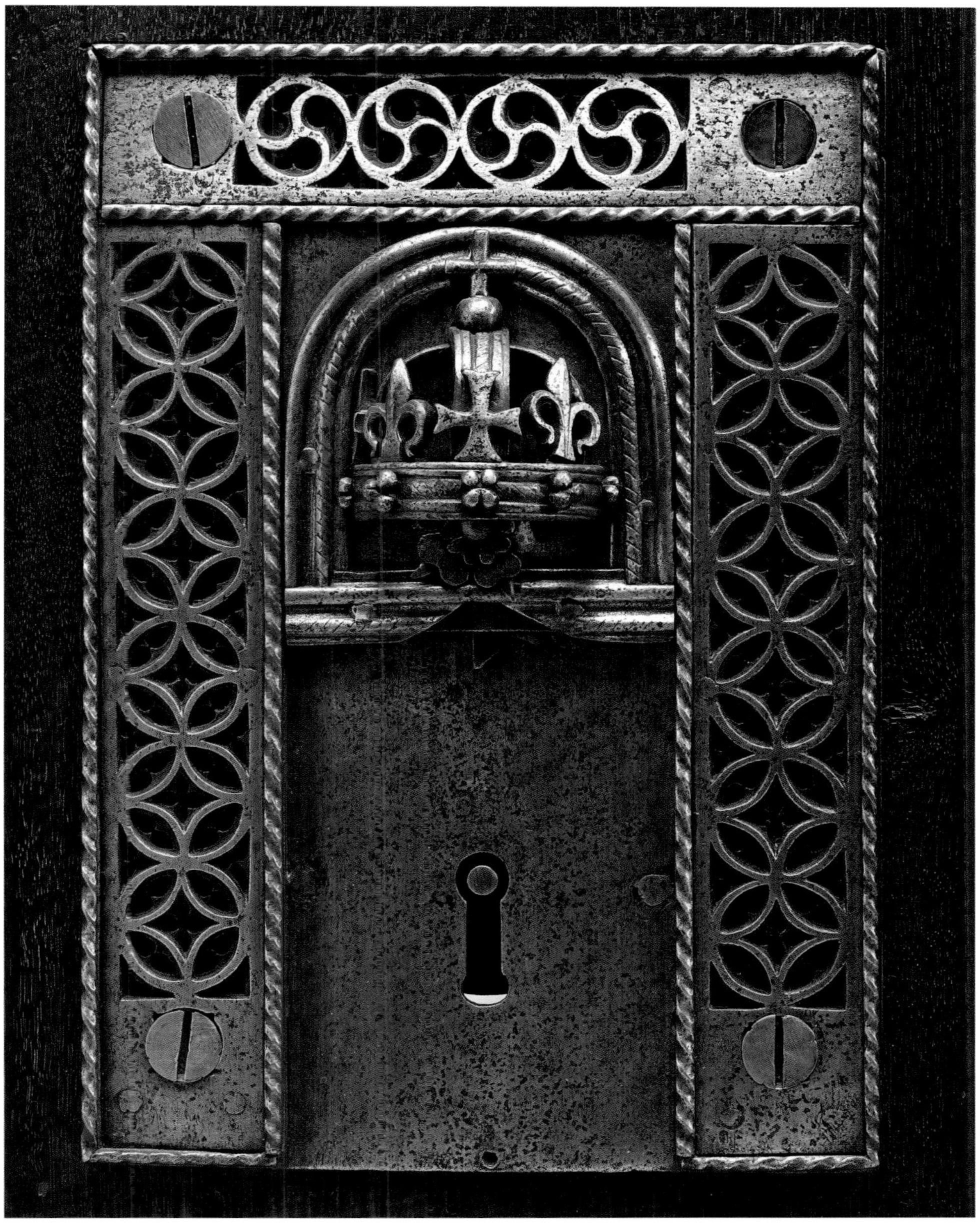

Figure 153. Door Lock, attributed to Henry Romayne, English, *c.* 1528–50, pierced iron, 25.5 × 17.7 cm. The Walters Art Museum, Baltimore. 52.91. Cat. 55

its age. There are many examples of 'writers' houses', whose fame has been established posthumously, from the sublime example of Petrarch's dwellings in France and Italy to the ridiculous case of 'Shakespeare's birthplace'.[65] But Strawberry Hill remains the first clear example (as Abbotsford is the second) of a writer's house that unites the two distinctive aspects singled out for attention throughout Hendrix's collection. It continues to work both as a theatre for 'self-fashioning' and as a repository of 'cultural memory'.[66] By turns 'monumental' and 'antiquarian' in his attitude to history, while never entirely omitting to be 'critical', Horace Walpole was eminently worthy of assimilating the two.

1. Matthew Hodgart, ed., *Horace Walpole: Memoirs and Portraits* (London: Batsford, 1963), ix.
2. Quoted Hodgart, *Walpole Memoirs*. It is in the preface to his *Marino Faliero* that Byron dubs *The Castle of Otranto* the 'first romance', while the 'last tragedy' is Walpole's play, *The Mysterious Mother*.
3. David Blair, ed., *Gothic Short Stories* (London: Wordsworth Editions, 2002), viii.
4. R.W. Ketton-Cremer, *Horace Walpole: A Biography* (London: Duckworth, 1940), 126.
5. Clive Wainwright, *The Romantic Interior: The British Collector at Home 1750–1850* (New Haven and London: Yale University Press, 1989), 296.
6. See Stephen Bann, *The Clothing of Clio: A Study of the Representation of History in Nineteenth-Century Britain and France* (Cambridge: Cambridge University Press, 1984), ch.4, 'Poetics of the Museum', 77–92.
7. See Michel Foucault, *Les mots et les choses: une archéologie des sciences humaines* (Paris: Gallimard, 1966). The preface to this work states that there have been 'two great discontinuities in the *epistémè* of western culture: that which inaugurates the classic age (around the middle of the seventeenth century) and that which, at the outset of the nineteenth, marks the threshold of our modernity' (p. 13: my translation).
8. For example, he talks of a 'wilderness' as 'much adapted to my romantic inclinations' (quoted in Ketton-Cremer, *Horace Walpole*, 45).
9. Krzysztof Pomian, *Collectors and Curiosities: Paris and Venice, 1500–1800*, trans. Elizabeth Wiles-Porter (Cambridge: Polity Press, 1990), 64.
10. Quoted in Ketton-Cremer, *Horace Walpole*, 191.
11. Lord Macaulay, *Critical and Historical Essays* (London: Longmans, 1883), 272.
12. See my formulation of a 'poetics of the museum' in Bann, *Clothing of Clio*, 77–92.
13. Bann, *Clothing of Clio*, 82.
14. *D 1774*, 48, 1.
15. Stephen Calloway, Michael Snodin and Clive Wainwright, *Horace Walpole and Strawberry Hill*, exh. cat., Orleans House Gallery (Richmond: London Borough of Richmond upon Thames, 1980), 17.
16. Ronald Paulson, *Breaking and Remaking: Aesthetic Practice in England, 1700–1820* (New Brunswick and London: Rutgers University Press, 1989), 20.
17. Paulson, *Breaking and Remaking*, 158.

18. G.V. Plekhanov, *Fundamental problems of Marxism* (London: Lawrence and Wishart, 1969), 162. The 'Cleopatra's nose' angle is here defined as 'the well-known observation that history would have taken an entirely different course had Cleopatra's nose been somewhat shorter' (p.160).
19. Karl Marx, *The Eighteenth Brumaire of Louis Bonaparte* (Moscow: Progress Publishers, 5th printing, 1967), 6.
20. Friedrich Nietzsche, *The Use and Abuse of History*, trans. Adrian Collins (Indianapolis: Bobbs Merrill, 1978), 12.
21. Wainwright, *Romantic Interior*, 73.
22. Nietzsche, *Use and Abuse*, 13.
23. See Horace Walpole, *The Castle of Otranto* (Oxford: Oxford University Press, 1996), vii, where E.J. Clery quotes the dream that Walpole alleged to be the source of the novel; it contains the detail that 'on the uppermost bannister of a great staircase I saw a gigantic hand in armour'.
24. Walpole, *Castle of Otranto*, 112.
25. Ketton-Cremer, *Horace Walpole*, 157.
26. Hodgart, *Walpole Memoirs*, 46.
27. Hodgart, *Walpole Memoirs*, 47.
28. Hodgart, *Walpole Memoirs*.
29. Quoted in La Rochefoucauld, *Mémoires* (Paris: Gallimard, 2006), 294.
30. Hodgart, *Walpole Memoirs*, 111.
31. Hodgart, *Walpole Memoirs*, 26.
32. Hodgart, *Walpole Memoirs*, 154.
33. Hodgart, *Walpole Memoirs*, 167.
34. Nietzsche, *Use and Abuse*, 21.
35. See Hodgart, *Walpole Memoirs*, 66–70. His agitation on behalf of this naval commander, who was executed on an unjust charge, allows him to align himself with the French philosopher Voltaire, who made a memorable comment on the matter.
36. *HW Corres.* 9: 366 (HW to Montagu, 5 May 1761).
37. Nietzsche, *Use and Abuse*, 18.
38. Horace Walpole, *Historic Doubts on the Life and Reign of King Richard the Third* (London: J. Dodsley, 1768), xiii.
39. Walpole, *Historic Doubts*, 103.
40. See Stephen Bann, *Paul Delaroche: History Painted* (London: Reaktion Books; and Princeton: Princeton University Press, 1997), 104–5, for discussion of this article in the light of Delaroche's *Princes in the Tower* (Louvre, 1831).
41. *Ainsworth's Magazine* I (1842): 243.
42. *Ainsworth's Magazine* I (1842): 244.
43. For this episode, see Stuart Piggott, *William Stukeley: An Eighteenth-Century Antiquary* (London: Thames & Hudson, rev. ed., 1985), 126–38. For an interpretation of Bertram's motives, see Stephen Bann, *The Inventions of History* (Manchester: Manchester University Press, 1990), 202–6.
44. Quoted Bann, *Inventions of History*, 202.
45. See Josephine M. Guy, 'Rossetti among the aesthetes', *Proceedings of the British Academy* 105 (Oxford: Oxford University Press, 2000): 174.
46. *Horace Walpole's Miscellany*, ed. Lars E. Troide (New Haven and London: Yale University Press, 1978), 23.
47. Walpole, *Castle of Otranto*, 5. John Riely points out that Walpole's witty pseudonym on the title page of the first edition – ONUPHRIO MURALTO – is an anagram of the Italian form of his own name: HORATIO MURAPALO (personal communication to the editor).
48. Walpole, *Castle of Otranto*, 9.
49. Piggott, *William Stukeley*, 142, 118.
50. Macaulay, *Essays*, 273.
51. Macaulay, *Essays*.
52. *Ainsworth's Magazine* I (1842): 244.
53. See Stephen Bann, *Ways around Modernism* (New York: Routledge, 2007), 103–72, for this alternative reading.
54. Stephen Bann, *Under the Sign: John Bargrave as Collector, Traveler and Witness* (Ann Arbor: University of Michigan Press, 1984), 112.
55. Bann, *Under the Sign*, 118–19.
56. Calloway *et al.*, *Walpole and Strawberry Hill*, 36.
57. Calloway *et al.*, *Walpole and Strawberry Hill*, 16, 41.
58. *D 1774*, 112.
59. Quoted in Bann, *Clothing of Clio*, 85–6.
60. Harald Hendrix, ed., *Writers' Houses and the Making of Memory* (New York: Routledge, 2008), 2.
61. Hendrix, *Writers' Houses*, 2–3.
62. See Stephen Bann, 'A Nomadic Investment in History', in Hendrix, *Writers' Houses*, 207–19.
63. See Viccy Coltman, *Fabricating the Antique: Neoclassicism in Britain, 1760–1800* (Chicago: University of Chicago Press, 2006), 196.
64. Coltman, *Fabricating the Antique*.
65. See Harald Hendrix, 'The Early Modern Invention of Literary Tourism', in Hendrix, *Writers' Houses*, 15–30, and Michael Rosenthal, 'Shakespeare's Birthplace at Stratford', in Hendrix, *Writers' Houses*, 31–44.
66. Hendrix, *Writers' Houses*, 5–6.

HORACE WALPOLE AND HIS BEAUTIES *Julia Marciari Alexander*

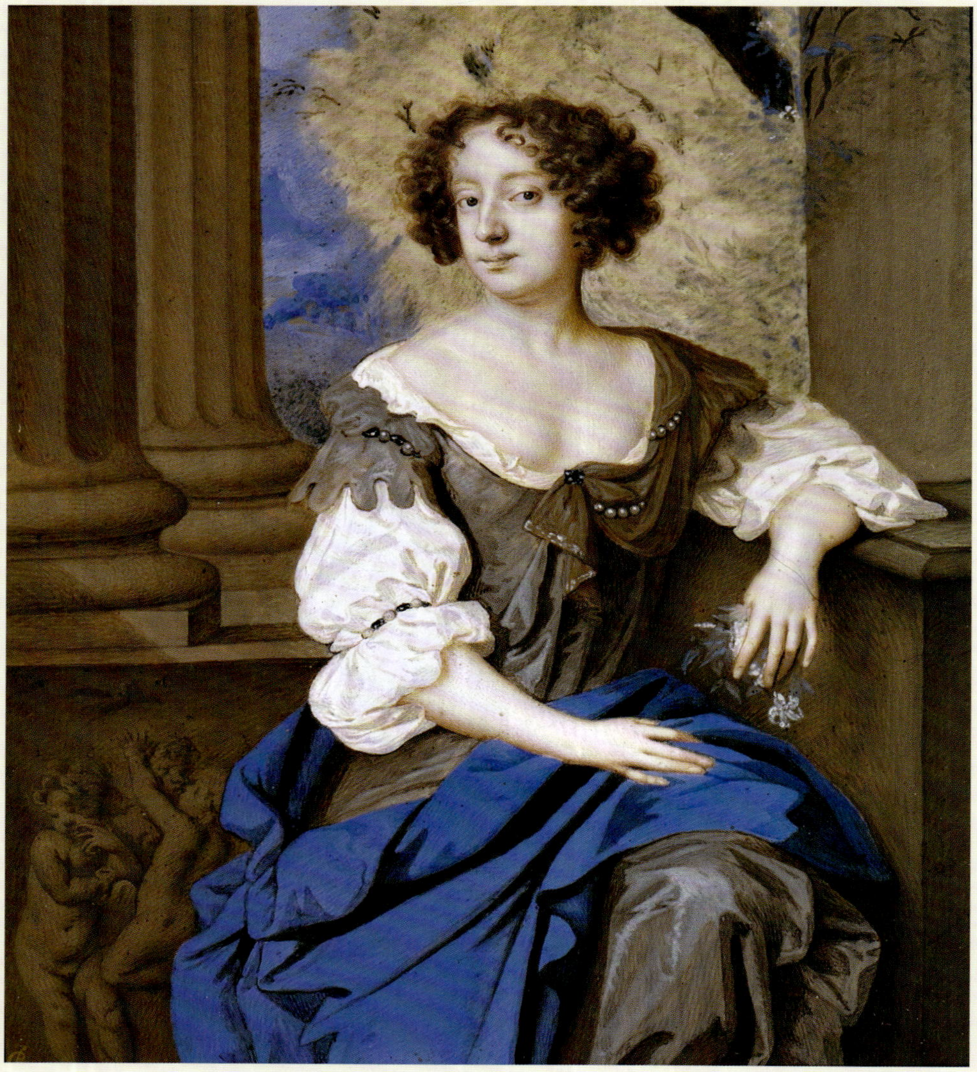

Figure 154. Charles Beale after Sir Peter Lely, *Lady Elizabeth Wriothesley, Countess of Northumberland, later Duchess of Montagu*, *c.* 1680, watercolour on vellum set in black wood frame, H 15.7 cm. Private collection c/o Robert Holden Ltd, London. Cat. 224

Walpole's relationship with Stuart England bordered on the obsessive. His project of 'history-making' employed visual and verbal tools – a careful categorization of objects, people and narratives – and the aesthetic arrangement of objects within Strawberry Hill to convey the stories he wished to tell. His narrative stemmed from the royal court culture that so repelled and fascinated him.

Although an astute collector, his connoisseurial eye has proved more hopeful than accurate. His collection of paintings of the later Stuart kings, including a portrait of Charles II by Lely and his studio and Mary Beale's small-scale portrait copy of a late Lely of James II's mistress, the Countess of Dorchester, tell us about Walpole's interpretation of the artist's style and his interest in the creation of a compelling 'history' of the Stuart court. In his *Anecdotes of Painting* Walpole's description of Lely's work exemplifies the nature of his connoisseurship of both paintings and their subjects:

> Coming to England in 1641, and seeing the works of Vandyck, [Lely] quitted his former style and former subjects, and gave himself wholly to portraits in emulation of that great man. His success was considerable, though not equal in ambition; if in nothing but simplicity, he fell short of his model … if portraits are often tame and spiritless, at least they are natural. His laboured draperies flow with ease, and not a fold, but is placed with propriety. Lely supplied the want of taste with clinquant; his nymphs trail fringes and embroidery through meadows and purling streams. Add that Vandyck's habits are those of the times; Lely's a sort of fantastic night-gown, fastened with a single pin. The latter was, in truth, a ladies' painter; and whether the age improved in beauty or in flattery, Lely's women are certainly much handsomer than those of Vandyck. (*Anecdotes* 2: 92–3.)

Walpole's praise for Sir Anthony Van Dyck is not unqualified, but he seems unwittingly drawn to the 'clinquant' (glitz) of Lely's 'nymphs' (Figs. 154, 155). Lely's ability to catch his subjects' 'reigning character' was a trait critical to Walpole's 'history-making' endeavours.

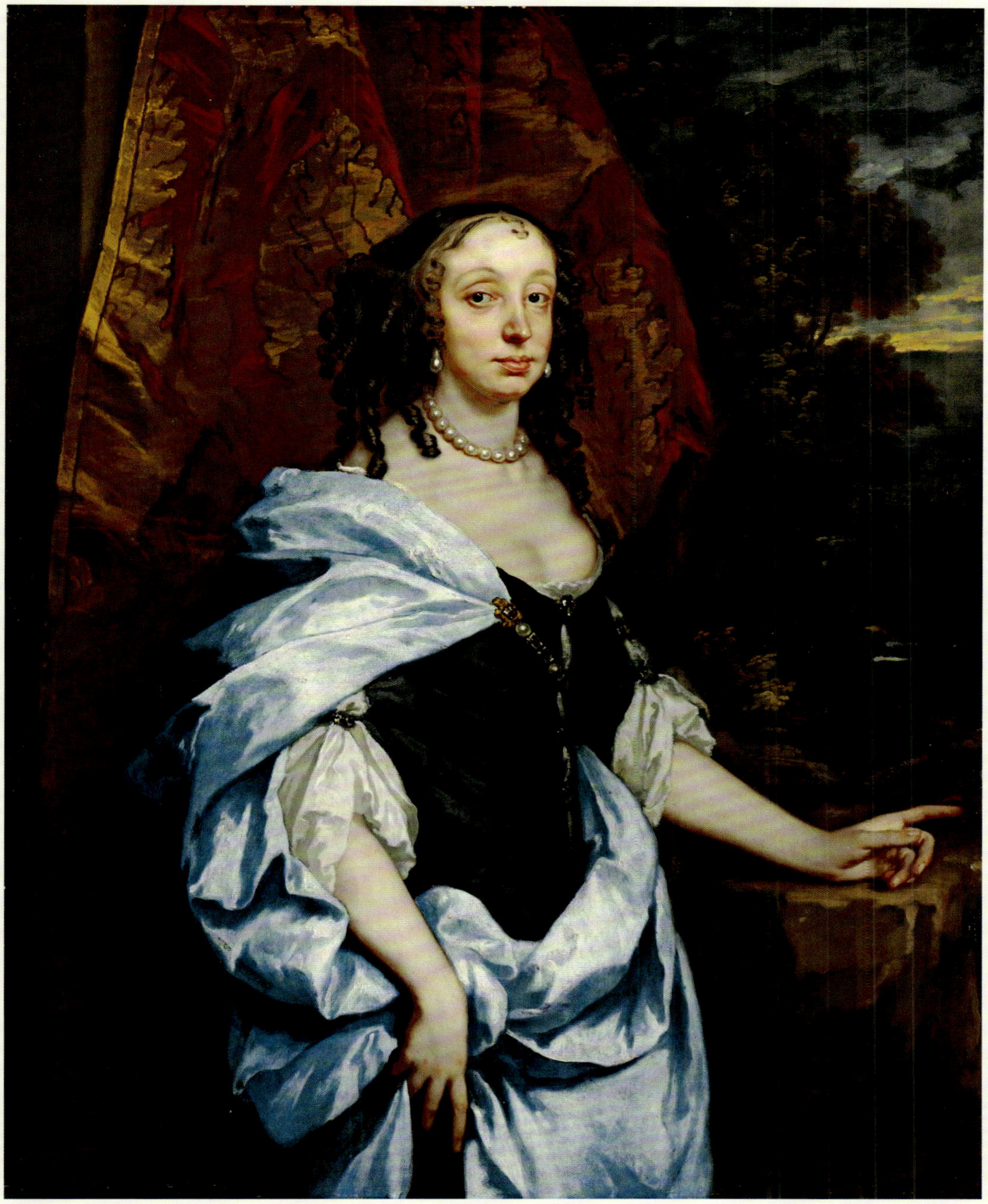

Figure 155. Sir Peter Lely, *Portrait of Mrs Leneve*, *c.* 1657, oil on canvas, 126.7 × 101.3 cm. The Cleveland Museum of Art, Gift of Mrs. Otto Miller. 1942.247. Cat. 140

At Strawberry Hill Walpole assembled his own Stuart 'Beauties', emulating the great seventeenth-century collections he saw on his travels; in 1760, for instance, he admired the 'Beauties' at Althorp (home of the Earls Spencer), which he designated 'a gallery of all one's acquaintance by Vandyke and Lely' (letter to Montagu, 1 Sept. 1760); ten years later he mentions the 'old brown gallery full of Vandycks and Lelys' at Ham House (letter to Montagu, 11 June 1770). The collections he described were relics of the fashion for portrait series between 1660 and 1715. Recording the political and affective stories created by those who assembled the portraits, they were touchstones for the portrait histories Walpole compiled at Strawberry Hill and in his engraved 'Heads' (see pp. 150–151). These pictorial compilations allowed his visitors to 'see as me' not only ancestors but recent personalities who were critical of the creation of his 'story' of Stuart Britain, one that still underpins the 'historical' account of the political and sexual (im)morality of late Stuart England.

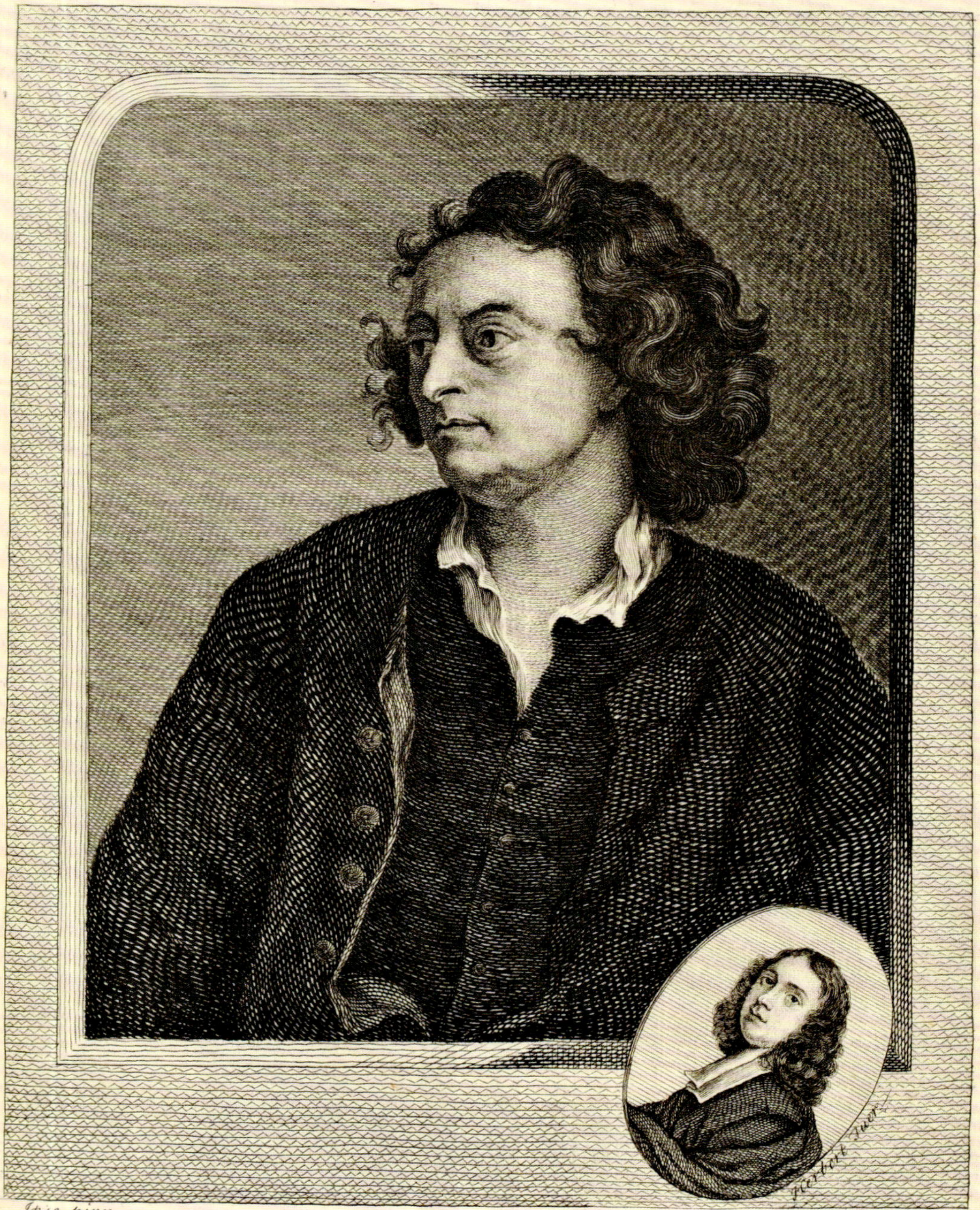

Ipse pinx. Bannerman Sculp.

SEVONYANS.

8.

THE *ANECDOTES OF PAINTING*

AND CONTINENTAL EUROPEAN ART HISTORY

NIGEL LLEWELLYN

'England's Vasari'! Such a sobriquet might seem entirely appropriate for a biographer happy to describe the seventeenth-century Scottish portrait painter, George Jamesone, as 'the Vandyck of Scotland', yet Horace Walpole's eccentric social manner and independent approach to collecting have both tended to encourage too insular a view of his work as an art historian. Like Giorgio Vasari's *Lives of the Artists* (1550), Walpole's *Anecdotes of Painting in England* (1762 et seq.) (Fig. 156) is a substantial book that collects comprehensive biographies about artists whose careers could be reconstructed from the available records.[1] It also represents an attempt to write the history of English art, since its chapters consider artists who were active in each of the reigns of the English monarchs. In terms of English historiography, Walpole's *Anecdotes* is undoubtedly innovatory yet it takes on new meanings when set in the wider continental contexts of the pan-European story of art history. The question here is: how did Walpole's stated objective to write an English history shape his response to his continental forebears? Did he simply loot their pages for content? Was he impressed by their historical strategies? The standard account of Walpole is that he was only a lukewarm co-citizen in the republic of letters and that during his youthful tour of France and Italy (1739–41) he concentrated on pleasure and social engagement, not on intellectual improvement. This essay starts with some speculations on the possible impact of Walpole's time in Florence on his intellectual formation as an art historian before concluding that the *Anecdotes* has a place in the broad sweep of European historiography as well as a place of honour in English historiography.

IN FLORENCE

Walpole's longest Italian stay during his Grand Tour was the ten months or so that he spent in Florence, being there briefly at Christmas 1739 and then for a continuous spell between July 1740 and May 1741.[2] By this date Florentine art had long been regarded as having lost the prestige it once had when the city was the cradle of the Renaissance.[3] It was seen as a somewhat parochial cultural centre, heterodox in the visual arts and with a literary scene of only modest ambitions and directed at local interests.[4] The leading Florentine scholar of his day, Anton Maria Salvini – a literary model for Thomas Gray – spent his time entertaining friends with lists of horse illustrations.[5] The sombre mood in the grand-ducal capital was somewhat lightened by the succession of Gian Gastone in 1723, and by 1744 tourism was sufficiently lively for Giuseppe Zocchi to publish the *Vedute Fiorentine*, sheets from which Horace Mann sent home to Walpole. Zocchi's views typically show elegantly dressed individuals on the city streets against a backdrop of squares or river embankments; such figures could be Walpole and his friends (Fig. 157).[6]

Had Walpole commanded the necessary conceptual vocabulary to analyse the painting styles current in Florence in the late 1730s, he would have noted a marked heterogeneity. Grand-ducal commissions tended to demand academic colouring and figure disposition, for example, in the work of Anton Domenico Gabbiani.[7] Church painters like Giovanni Domenico Ferretti – who painted an altarpiece for Walpole's friend John Chute – worked in a more traditional Tuscan style.[8] The significance of the Florentine tradition

Figure 156. Alexander Bannerman, Engraved portraits of Anton Schoonjans and Herbert Tuer, after a self-portrait, in Horace Walpole, *Anecdotes of Painting in England*... Second edition. Volume 3, [Strawberry Hill]: Printed by Thomas Kirgate at Strawberry-Hill, 1765. The Lewis Walpole Library, Yale University. 49 2520. Cat. 198

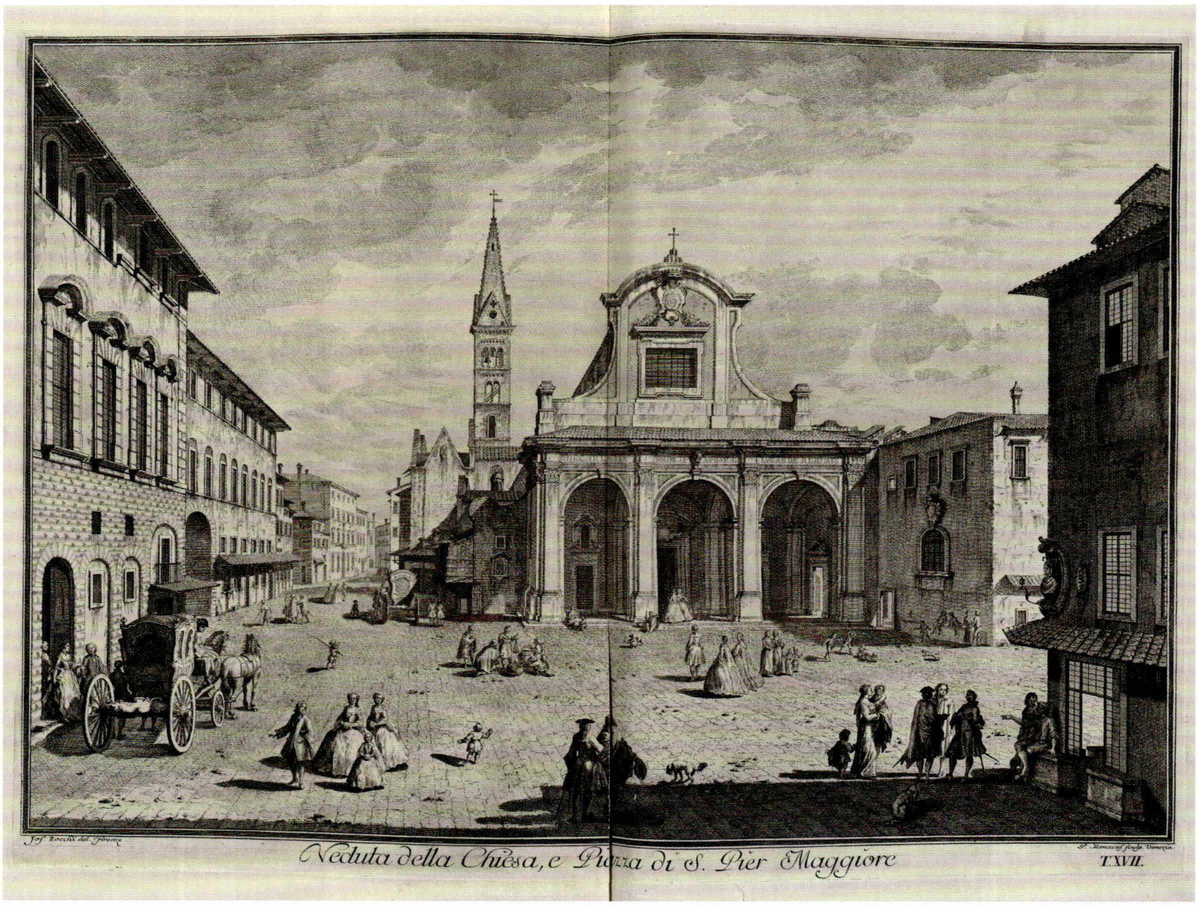

Figure 157. P. Monacus after Giuseppe Zocchi, *Veduta della chiesa, e Piazza di S. Pier Maggiore*, engraving, plate XVII from Zocchi, *Scelta di XXIV vedute delle principali contrade, piazze*… (Florence: Giuseppe Allegrini [1744?]). Beinecke Rare Book and Manuscript Library, Yale University

was important but negotiable: in 1748 Vincenzo Meucci unabashedly repainted the fire-damaged ceiling of the canonical Brancacci chapel at Santa Maria del Carmine, destroying whatever was left of Masaccio's vault, but the restoration was not criticized until much later in the century.[9] The Riccardi had replaced the Brancacci as patrons at the Carmine and restored the whole church in 1782.

Modern anglophone art history of late Baroque Florence tends to start with Rudolf Wittkower's oft-quoted argument about resistance to the Roman Baroque. To concur, Walpole would have needed to have had at his disposal agreed definitions of alternative styles and to have understood that styles could be deployed to make ideological points.[10] In fact, Pietro da Cortona, one of the exemplary figures of the Roman Baroque, was influential in Florence, and Walpole knew Poggio a Caiano, where Cortona's follower Gabbiani painted an 'Apotheosis of Cosimo the Elder' in 1698.[11] Another follower was Alessandro Gherardini, written up by the most important historiographer of art working in the peninsula at the end of the seventeenth century, the Florentine Filippo Baldinucci.[12] In fact, it was probably historiography, rather than contemporary art, that allowed Florence to project its Renaissance heritage.

At the outer limit of Florence's stylistic heterodoxy was the Grand Duke's encouragement of Alessandro Magnasco, whose inexplicably picturesque works and fixation on the superstitious placed him at the very fringes of religious orthodoxy. Magnasco made a lengthy stay at Gian Gastone's court, and had Walpole ever shown an interest in that direction, his work would surely have been cited as a source for later literary picturesque inventions such as *The Castle of Otranto* (1764).

In contrast with Magnasco's works, which tend to be constricted and dark, the great decorative pictures of Sebastiano Ricci are usually open in vision and on a lighter note. Ricci – in Florence in

1706–7 and later partially claimed by Walpole for England[13] – was by no means an academic classicist, but neither was his particular decorative style close to that of the Roman Baroque. Finally, and to complete the account of stylistic heterodoxy among the major itinerant figures, there was the Neapolitan Luca Giordano, who decorated the main gallery at the Palazzo Medici-Riccardi in 1682–3.[14] Luca represents a third distinct Baroque manner and one that Walpole seems not fully to have appreciated, since he roundly condemned him for his 'hasty and rapacious pencil'.[15]

In Walpole's day a number of major church commissions in Oltrarno Florence were still relatively fresh: for example, the decorations at San Frediano in Cestello – reconstructed in the 1680s – epitomize the stylistic diversity of the city. Gabbiani spent years frescoing the 'Glorification of the Magdalene' on the main crossing cupola (1701–18). As the son of a Whig Prime Minister, Walpole would have taken great care before entering any place of papist worship, but even a cursory glance inside this church in 1739 would have revealed a facility in the treatment of the human figure moving in space that was very rare in England in this period. If the churches were out of bounds for Anglicans, Walpole might have seen some of the same visual skills employed in secular settings, for example, at the Palazzo Capponi built by Ferdinando Ruggieri in 1705 for Scipione Capponi, where decorations by Matteo Bonechi include trompe l'oeil frescoes on the garden façade, cleverly creating the illusion that the south bay arcade continues into the garden space.

The Palazzo Capponi was near the Piazza della SS. Annunziata where the annual St Luke's Day exhibitions of the Accademia del Disegno were held. In the early eighteenth century the Florentine Academy was reforming its organization, collections and reference library. Furthermore, from 1737 it published accounts of the annual shows and also started to award prizes to the best students. Walpole seems not to have referred directly to the Academy and in later years would perhaps have disapproved of the Parisian tone of its reform programme, but he would doubtless have approved of its membership hierarchy with the *nobili* in the upper rank, then the *dilettanti* and, lastly, the practitioners or *professori*, a category that was open to foreigners.[16] It is also interesting that the Academy became sufficiently conscious of its standing for it to commission a history, by Girolamo Ticciati, whose account traces its story to 1739.[17] Such examples of Florentine veneration for its artistic past may well have impressed Walpole. In the 1730s the head of the Academy was Francesco Maria Niccolo Gabburri, whose official portrait was painted by both Bonechi and Ferretti.[18] Gabburri was a prolific if conservative biographer who adhered to the Vasarian model in writing his own set of artist's lives.[19] Among historiographers, as among painters, an awareness of the Renaissance Golden Age brought not only the advantage of pedigree but also the burden of emulation; post-Vasarian historians and painters could all find themselves unable to live up to the expectations set by past masters.

Whether or not Walpole recognized or appreciated different contemporary styles, he must have noted the central role played in Florentine art by the dynastic cultural patronage of the great patrician families. Palazzo Manetti was home to the British Resident, Horace Mann, and Walpole's base in Florence and nearby was the enormous mass of the Palazzo Corsini, where Ciro Ferri, Gherardini, Bonechi, Gabbiani and others had recently created a stupendous Baroque palace.[20] Here a grand staircase leads up to the *piano nobile* where Gabbiani's painted apotheosis of the family was displayed (1695). The Corsini, with their grand palace on the river bank, must have impressed Walpole, for their pedigree could boast not only a pope – Lorenzo (Pope Clement XII), who died during Walpole's stay in Florence – but also two saints.[21] Given his later abandonment of every known architectural rule at Strawberry Hill, Walpole's fancy might also have been caught by the grotto on the ground floor at the Corsini, an eccentric feature for a Florentine palace.

ITALIAN ART HISTORY BEFORE WALPOLE

As has been well documented, Walpole's first professional attempt at writing art history was his account of his own family's collection at Houghton.[22] However, when George Vertue's manuscripts on British art became available, Walpole acquired them to give him a starting point for the writing of an authoritative and innovative

Figure 158. Title page to vol. 1 of Raffaele Soprani, *Vite de' pittori, scultori, ed architetti genovesi*, 2nd edition (Geneva: Casamara 1768). Courtesy of Yale University Library

Figure 159. Title page to vol. 1 of Carlo Ridolfi, *La meraviglie dell'arte...* (Venice: G. B. Sgaua, 1648). Beinecke Rare Book and Manuscript Library, Yale University

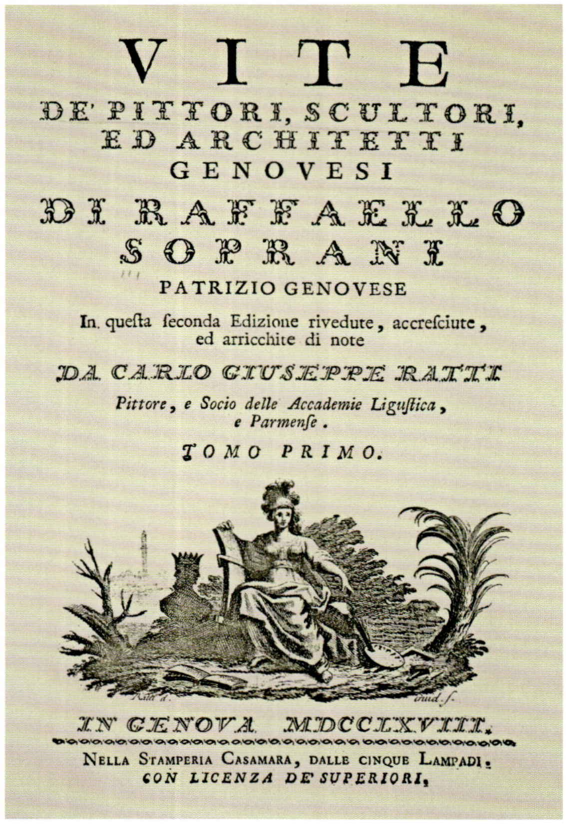

VITE
DE' PITTORI, SCULTORI, ED ARCHITETTI GENOVESI
DI RAFFAELLO SOPRANI
PATRIZIO GENOVESE
In questa seconda Edizione rivedute, accresciute, ed arricchite di note
DA CARLO GIUSEPPE RATTI
Pittore, e Socio delle Accademie Ligustica, e Parmense.
TOMO PRIMO.
IN GENOVA MDCCLXVIII.
NELLA STAMPERIA CASAMARA, DALLE CINQUE LAMPADI.
CON LICENZA DE' SUPERIORI.

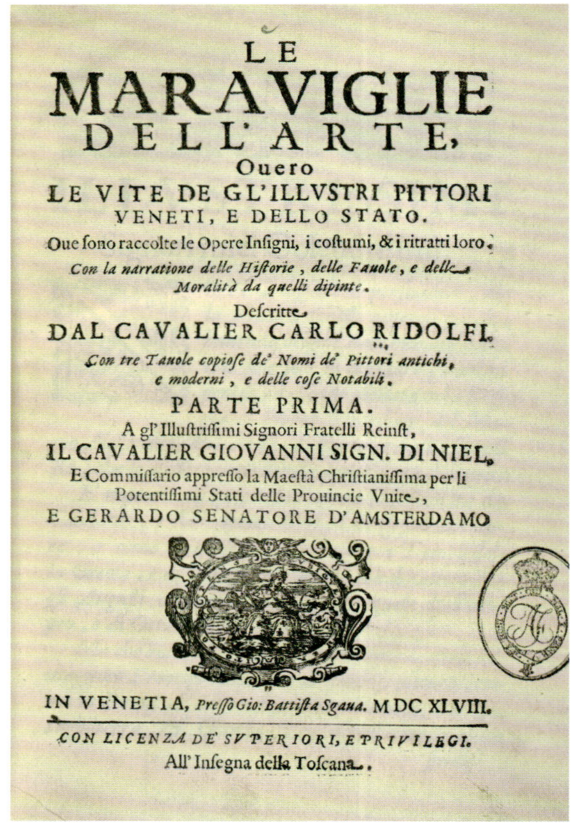

LE MARAVIGLIE DELL'ARTE,
Ouero
LE VITE DE GL'ILLVSTRI PITTORI VENETI, E DELLO STATO.
Oue sono raccolte le Opere Insigni, i costumi, & i ritratti loro.
Con la narratione delle Historie, delle Fauole, e delle Moralità da quelli dipinte.
Descritte
DAL CAVALIER CARLO RIDOLFI.
Con tre Tauole copiose de' Nomi de' Pittori antichi, e moderni, e delle cose Notabili.
PARTE PRIMA.
A gl'Illustrissimi Signori Fratelli Reinst,
IL CAVALIER GIOVANNI SIGN. DI NIEL,
E Commissario appresso la Maestà Christianissima per li Potentissimi Stati delle Prouincie Vnite,
E GERARDO SENATORE D'AMSTERDAMO
IN VENETIA, Presso Gio: Battista Sgaua. M DC XLVIII.
CON LICENZA DE' SVPERIORI, E PRIVILEGI.
All'Insegna della Toscana.

book, an art history for England; but as he himself acknowledged, there were precursors for such a project in both continental and English-language contexts. In fact, by 1700 nearly every European culture had representative publications championing the national artistic achievement through sets of artist biographies. In Italy there had been a long series of responses to the publication and influence of Vasari's *Lives*, around, against or in parallel to which local historians tended to position themselves. In Bologna, fiercely proud of its academic artistic pedigree, there was the *Felsina Pittrice* by Carlo Cesare Malvasia.[23] In the two ancient trading republics of Genoa and Venice, biographical accounts of native hero artists seem to have been published to pique international Italian competitors (Fig. 158).[24] Indeed, the first serious theorized assault on Vasari's claims about the primacy of Tuscan art had come in the form of Carlo Ridolfi's *Le meraviglione dell'arte* (1648), which argued that art had first been reborn in Venice (Fig. 159). Walpole cites Ridolfi in the *Anecdotes* as a source for the painter Girolamo da Treviso.[25] Ridolfi's arguments were consolidated in the early 1660s by compatriots like Marco Boschini.[26] Vasari famously revised his own text in 1568, after which there were some re-editions in the late seventeenth century but no new edition in the early eighteenth century.

Walpole's aim for the *Anecdotes*, comprehensively to cover every painter active in England, suggests both ambition and naivety in comparison with the works of Vasari's successors. Seventeenth-century Vasarians were increasingly selective; for example, Giovanni Baglione and Giovanni Battista Passeri, who had built on Raffaele Borghini's continuation of the Vasarian story into their century.[27] Baglione, who was mainly active as a painter, selected certain artists active in Rome from the papacy of Gregory XIII to that of Urban VIII, and Passeri wrote about Roman artists who had died between 1641 and 1673.[28] This was a kind of judicious art history that would not have suited Walpole. Any art historian seeking to build a narrative around key figures requires both a theory of taste, in order to make the selection, and sufficient data to support the argument.

The theme of national rivalry continued with Lione Pascoli, whose *Lives* were published in Rome in 1730 (second edition, 1736). That city was also the base for a key figure, Giovanni Pietro Bellori, the author of a number of learned tracts, several of them archaeological, and of a poem 'On Painting' published in 1642 to introduce Baglione's 'Lives'. Bellori's high-minded antiquarianism would probably have struck Walpole as somewhat dull. Bellori's own *Vite* ('Lives', 1672) again includes a selection of artists, on whom he had been collecting material from the 1640s. Some are Roman and others claimed for the Roman school, and the biographies are introduced by a scholarly apologia on idealization.[29] Walpole was familiar with this theory, since the *Anecdotes* had described how the sculptor John Michael Rysbrack had used ideal selection to create the form of his 'Stourhead Hercules' by assembling the best details from models like the pugilist Jack Broughton for the arms and the painter Giovanni Pietro Ellis for the legs.[30] Bellori's early intellectual training had taught him that the study of a collection could be the starting point for writing history. In his case, it was the drawings of his mentor and uncle Francesco Angeloni, which revealed to Bellori how Annibale Carracci had rescued style from mannered error. After his death Bellori's own collection of gems and medals found their way to Dresden where they helped shape J. J. Winckelmann's vision of antiquity, a highly influential account that was read right across Europe and, like Walpole's *Anecdotes*, appeared in the mid-1760s.[31] Also like Walpole, Bellori pursued a wide range of antiquarian studies: his *Nota dei Musei* (1664) catalogued private and ecclesiastical libraries and collections in Rome and included the first study of ancient painting. In the early 1660s Bellori had undertaken an extensive tour of southern Italian libraries with the personal envoy of Louis XIV. These were the kinds of projects that Walpole undertook himself in the following century. However, Bellori's 'Lives' clearly registers the increasing influence of France on late seventeenth-century Italian cultural institutions, an influence that Walpole would have deplored.

The precise impact on Walpole of these seventeenth-century Italian biographers, apart from being merely sources of information, needs a full study, but they certainly signalled the lack of an English collection of artists' 'Lives'. In the mid-1670s Malvasia had been approached for information about Bolognese painting when Baldinucci had been engaged in a comprehensive updating of Vasari, which appeared as the *Notizie de' professori del disegno da Cimabue in quà* in six volumes (1681–1728).[32] In fact, Baldinucci collected historical material over many years as he catalogued the drawings and self-portraits in the Medici grand-ducal collections. His intention was to emulate Vasari completely in producing a modern Florentine collection of artist biographies.[33] A man of great piety, modest ability and huge resolve, he attempted when young to develop his own artistic talent in print-making and sculpture but abandoned this direction as he turned to scholarship and, from the 1660s, became a grand-ducal courtier. In the early 1680s he fell in with the former Queen Christina of Sweden. She both fascinated and appalled Walpole, who censured her roundly in his account of her compatriot Michael Dahl, complaining that her pronouncements 'were rarely delicate', sometimes indeed 'gross' and that she rambled Europe in 'masculine attire' talking 'indecently with learned men'.[34] Christina prevailed on Baldinucci to add a biography of Bernini, her particular favourite, to his set of Florentine heroes.[35] Baldinucci's grand-ducal contacts were perhaps what made his work an object of particular interest for Frederick, Prince of Wales.[36]

Walpole also seems to have known or at least heard of the title of Baldinucci's great work, the title of which refers to Tuscan artists as a dynasty of professors or teachers: Walpole notes that the seventeenth-century English antiquary Sir William Dugdale had 'found some names of the professors … I call them professors, agreeably to modern estimation'.[37] In 1678 Baldinucci realized that biography needed to be supplemented by a better grasp of artistic 'terms and expressions' and in 1681 published *Il Vocabulario toscano dell'arte del disegno* (usually translated as *The Dictionary of Art Terms*) as a companion to the biographies to cover both the fine and the applied arts. This Florentine perception of the need for a more sophisticated conceptual language for the visual arts represents a key stage in the history of art history and one with many resonances in Walpole's *Anecdotes*.

By 1700 continental art historiographers were no longer simply publishing collections of biographical data. They were theorizing about taste and finding historical explanations of key epochs, particularly the antique. History was now being used to ground contemporary artistic

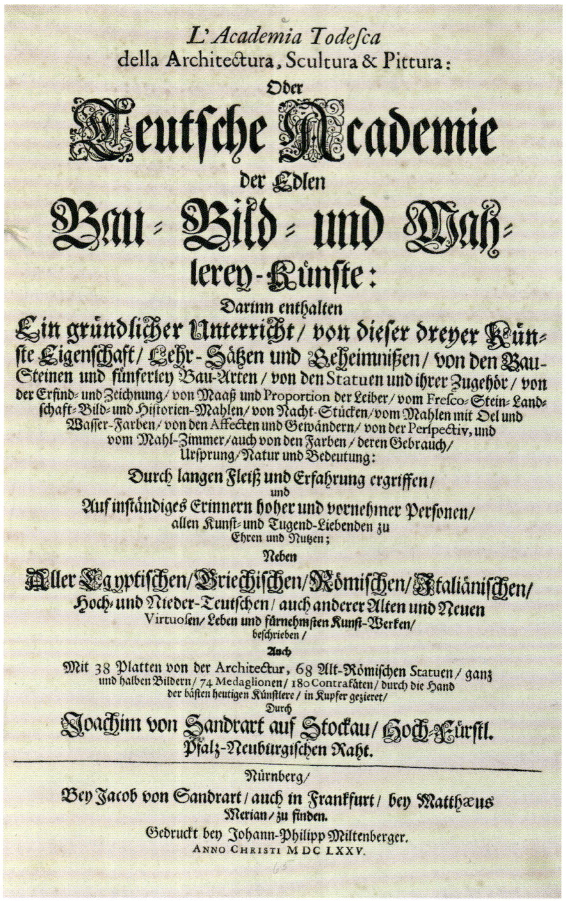

L'Academia Todeſca
della Architectura, Scultura & Pittura:
Oder
Teutſche Academie
der Edlen
Bau- Bild- und Mah-
lerey-Künſte:
Darinn enthalten
Ein gründlicher Unterricht/ von dieſer dreyer Kün-
ſte Eigenſchaft/ Lehr-Sätzen und Geheimnißen/ von den Bau-
Steinen und fünferley Bau-Arten/ von den Statuen und ihrer Zugehör/ von
der Erfind- und Zeichnung/ von Maaß und Proportion der Leiber/ vom Freſco- Stein- Land-
ſchaft- Bild- und Hiſtorien-Mahlen/ von Nacht-Stücken/vom Mahlen mit Oel und
Waſſer-Farben/ von den Affecten und Gewändern/ von der Perſpectiv, und
vom Mahl-Zimmer/auch von den Farben/ deren Gebrauch/
Urſprung/Natur und Bedeutung:
Durch langen Fleiß und Erfahrung ergriffen/
und
Auf inſtändiges Erinnern hoher und vornehmer Perſonen/
allen Kunſt- und Tugend-Liebenden zu
Ehren und Nutzen;
Neben
Aller Egyptiſchen/Griechiſchen/Römiſchen/Italiäniſchen/
Hoch- und Nieder-Teutſchen/ auch anderer Alten und Neuen
Virtuoſen/ Leben und fürnehmſten Kunſt-Werken/
beſchrieben/
Auch
Mit 38 Platten von der Architectur, 68 Alt-Römiſchen Statuen/ ganz
und halben Bildern/ 74 Medaglionen/ 180 Contrafäten/ durch die Hand
der bäſten heutigen Künſtlere/ in Kupfer gezieret/
Durch
Joachim von Sandrart auf Stockau/ Hoch-Fürſtl.
Pfalz-Neuburgiſchen Raht.
Nürnberg/
Bey Jacob von Sandrart/ auch in Frankfurt/ bey Matthæus
Merian/ zu finden.
Gedruckt bey Johann-Philipp Miltenberger.
ANNO CHRISTI MDC LXXV.

Figure 160. Title page to vol. 1 of Joachim von Sandrart, *L'Academia Todesca della Architectura, Scultura & Pittura*... (Frankfurt: Matthaeus Merian, 1675). Beinecke Rare Book and Manuscript Library, Yale University

practice. Bellori countered the Vasarian tradition that had favoured Michelangelo by championing Raphael and setting out a theory of idealism that had its origins in antique theories and presented opposing formulations of the real, either as a replication of nature or as a construction of the ideal. The history of English eighteenth-century aesthetic theory moves in the opposite direction, however, with Raphael being steadily supplanted by Michelangelo.

By Walpole's day continental art history was passing from artist-authors, seeking to improve their reputations, to scholars like Baldinucci – and Walpole himself – writing politicized art history to secure national standing. The extent of the careful crafting that was required in the writing of this kind of history can be measured by the treatment of the early phases of a nation's artistic development. Even when evidence was scarce, the antiquity of an artistic tradition, as with a family, conferred nobility and respect on a nation's art practice. If necessary, the works themselves could be largely disregarded.

BEYOND ITALY

Outside Italy, what additional art-historical precedents had been set for Walpole? The priorities of Joachim von Sandrart are signalled by the engraved portrait that opens his 'German Academy of the Fine Arts' (Fig. 160).[38] Framed within a decorated cartouche, he is portrayed in fashionable dress with one hand resting on a scholarly volume. Below this a coat of arms signals his gentle status (*von* Sandrart), and a French motto supplies a lofty moralizing note. Lines of Latin – the language of the international scholarly elite – touch on von Sandrart's social status and his mission to publicize the Apelles of his century. This kind of self-fashioned image is redolent of the gentility of painting in the late Baroque and precisely chimes with Walpole's prejudices.

In Spain, another enormous scholarly enterprise, the *Museo pictórico y escala óptica* (1715–24) by Antonio Palomino included an equally long set of artistic biographies.[39] Like Walpole, Palomino pads out his accounts with formulaic anecdotes, often derived from Pliny's *Natural History*, not a source that Walpole cites. To articulate the mass of biographical material, Palomino identifies exemplary artists. For example, El Greco – naturalized into Spain, as so many of Walpole's significant artist-subjects are naturalized into England – represents the artist who needs to distance himself from the manner of his teacher; in the case of El Greco, a (legendary) relationship with Titian. Palomino's discourse, like Walpole's, is concerned with the artist's social status: for example, his account of Velázquez's success as a courtier.

The tendency to extract moral truths from biographical histories is common across progressive late Baroque antiquarianism and has its origins in ancient historical theory, for example, Cicero. History is praised for shedding light on reality and guiding human existence. Walpole was unflattering about antiquaries who preserved the past indiscriminately and felt that progressive antiquarianism required that judgement be exercised. He used false modesty as a rhetorical figure, presenting his own historical endeavours as mere trivia, but in fact he worked into his discourse comments about the improved social standing of both painting and painters, about the relationship between higher standards in the arts, about the reputation of the nation and about the interrelations of trade, patronage and what we might now term 'the cultural sector'.

The country that in Walpole's day represented the apogee of trading success was the Dutch Republic, and Karel van Mander's *Schilder-boeck* (1603–4, usually given as *Lives of the Illustrious Netherlandish and German Painters*[40]) was a distinguished early transmontane Vasarian exercise in biography that was much cited by Walpole in the *Anecdotes*. Somewhat closer to Walpole in terms of publication date, Arnold Houbraken's *De groote Schonburgh* ... (1718–21), contains anecdotal lives of northern artists integrated like Bellori with arguments in favour of academic standards. J.B. Deschamps, in his *La vie des peintres flamandes, allemands et hollandois* ... (Paris, 1753–64), also contemporary with Walpole, does much the same (Fig. 161).[41] Finally, the *Anecdotes* has important features in common with the *Abrégé de la vie des plus fameux peintres* (1745–52) by Antoine Joseph Dézallier d'Argenville, which accepts all schools and artists and rejects the rigid dominance of the hierarchy of the genres.

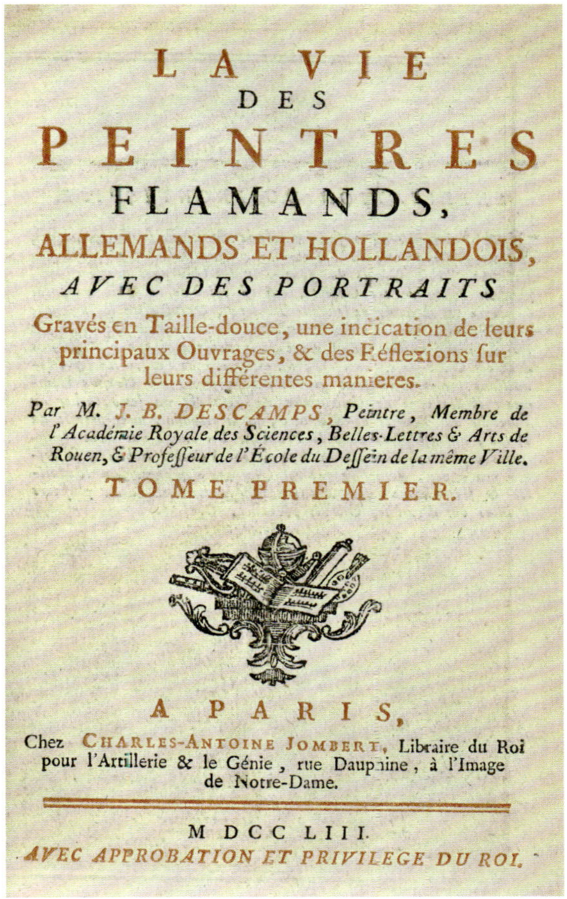
LA VIE
DES
PEINTRES
FLAMANDS,
ALLEMANDS ET HOLLANDOIS,
AVEC DES PORTRAITS
Gravés en Taille-douce, une indication de leurs principaux Ouvrages, & des Réflexions sur leurs différentes manieres.
Par M. J. B. DESCAMPS, Peintre, Membre de l'Académie Royale des Sciences, Belles-Lettres & Arts de Rouen, & Professeur de l'École du Dessein de la même Ville.
TOME PREMIER.
A PARIS,
Chez CHARLES-ANTOINE JOMBERT, Libraire du Roi pour l'Artillerie & le Génie, rue Dauphine, à l'Image de Notre-Dame.
M DCC LIII.
AVEC APPROBATION ET PRIVILEGE DU ROI.

Figure 161. Title page to vol. 1 of Jean Baptiste Descamps, *La vie des peintres flamands, allemands et hollandois*... (Paris: Charles-Antoine Jombert..., 1753). Beinecke Rare Book and Manuscript Library, Yale University

CULTURAL OLYMPICS

Biographers after Vasari were strongly motivated by national rivalry, an aspect of art writing that had an ancient lineage both in terms of geography and ethnicity.[42] Vitruvius had discussed the racial origins of the orders of architecture – the Doric, the Ionic and so on – and in the *Natural History* Pliny had used national schools of artists as one of his key organizing principles. The Renaissance tradition of art-historical writing was fundamentally grounded in nationalistic competition: artists sought fame and defeated their adversaries. In his most famous biography Vasari describes how providence plants Michelangelo in the soil of Tuscany, an appropriate seedbed for the saviour of art. Vasari argues that it is not only the endeavours of generations of predecessors that favour Tuscan artists but also the enlightened attitudes of its princes and the native qualities of its inhabitants.[43]

Elizabethan and Jacobean writers on the visual arts – Nicholas Hilliard (Fig. 218) and Richard Haydocke, for example – are equally anxious for English artists and patrons to bring honour to the nation, and Walpole himself sometimes includes insights into artists' competitive behaviour.[44] As tellingly, he claims that the main impulse behind Henry VIII's patronage was his powerful rivalry with Francis I of France.[45]

Alongside the historiographical tensions generated by art historians wrestling with the inevitability of decline post-Michelangelo, other important factors directly influenced the development of art history as a literary and historical genre. First, the geopolitical map of Italy was fragmented and made up of independent states, frequently supported by rival non-Italian powers. Second, there was the new science of the material past, antiquarianism, soon to become archaeology. Walpole uses this method, systematically drawing historical conclusions directly from surviving material evidence and works of art. Finally, there was the question of art as a sign of national status. Britain's aspiration to greatness had been key to the ideology of Walpole's father, and the lack of a national art history must have touched Horace's filial loyalty. Art history was an arena within culture and politics where he could surely make a telling contribution.

However, as we shall see, Walpole also

understands the corrupting and distorting effect of nationalistic competition. He had perhaps read Malvasia, who was a pro-Bologna counterweight to the Florentine-Roman domination of the historical debate and who promoted Annibale Carracci, born too late for inclusion in Vasari's original *Lives*. The rhetoric of Malvasia's *Felsina Pittrice* is defensive, inclined towards intemperate overstatement and inconsistent historical judgements in favour of particular political ends. A long book, it is primarily dedicated to sixteenth- and seventeenth-century Bolognese painters. Annibale Carracci is by no means simply the reviver of Raphael, who, far from being described as 'divine', is termed a mere 'mug-maker'. Another major figure from nearby Parma, Antonio Correggio, is written off by Malvasia as 'a lady'. Walpole could also be free in his criticisms, but he invariably aimed for a rather loftier tone.

THE STATUS OF PAINTING

What was the social profile of the authors with whom Walpole was aligning himself? Early art history had been written by artists, and during the Renaissance the social position of the most successful Italian artists became increasingly elevated, especially in court circles. Von Sandrart's self-presentation illustrates how early modern art historians sought to avoid illiberal social associations, and after 1600 fewer of them were also artists. The Sienese Giulio Mancini, who was physician to the Barberini pope Urban VIII and whose works circulated in manuscript form, is described as 'an early example of the lay enthusiast, the dilettante who discovers that there is more in painting than meets the average layman's eye'.[46] Walpole might well have admired Mancini's position at the papal court and sympathized with his historical methods, for they both tended to collect facts somewhat haphazardly and to rely on anecdotal evidence.

Walpole would, however, have approved of the beneficial impact that Bellorian idealist discourse had on the social status of painting itself. In Bellori's account the presiding figure of Raphael improves the arts of design (formed on the capacity to idealize) and raises their standing in the eyes of a liberal spectator:

> Painting is now greatly admired and seems as though descended from heaven, when the divine Raphael by his supreme drawing, has raised its beauty to the summit of art, restoring to it all the graces of its ancient majesty and enriching it by the attributes that had once rendered it glorious amongst the Greeks and Romans.[47]

Such an art history was more about general trends in taste than about the meaning of particular works and even less about the empirical deployment of material or historical facts. Bellori does not write about all artists, as Walpole felt obliged to do, but adopts a selective strategy. He excludes Bernini (still living in 1672) and the other major proponents of the Roman Baroque and accords his longest biography to Annibale Carracci. Furthermore, in recognizing the increasing internationalism of the late Baroque age, he gives very serious treatment to foreign artists – Rubens, Van Dyck, Duquesnoy and Poussin, whom he calls the French Apelles. It is even more telling that Bellori's *Vite* – a lavish publication, with high-quality illustrations – is dedicated to Colbert, Louis XIV's Secretary of State and the guiding hand behind the Sun King's cultural policies. Walpole would not have approved. His aim was to write a distinctively English art history within the broad European tradition of the genre.

ENGLAND AND ITALY

In its final form the *Anecdotes* comprises a short preface and more than twenty chapters, organized chronologically by reign, mostly dedicated to the history of painting but with significant coverage of the other arts of design – sculpture and architecture – and of other artistic forms like medals and, crucially in the English context, miniatures and gardens. In his preface Walpole clearly signals his awareness of the state of art historiography in continental Europe:

> In Italy, where the art of painting has been carried to an amazing degree of perfection, the lives of the painters have been written in numberless volumes, alone sufficient to compose a little library. Every picture of every considerable master is minutely described. Those biographers treat of the works of Raphael and Correggio with as much importance as commentators speak of Horace or Virgil; and indulging themselves in the inflated style of their language, they talk of pictures as works

almost of a divinity, while at the same time they lament them as perishing before their eyes.[48]

It is the very wealth of the Italian literary tradition that justifies a set of English artists' lives. Interestingly, Walpole is also implying that extant Italian discourse tends to be descriptive rather than critically analytical and to be pitched at a rhetorical level that his English readers may find off-putting. In fact, an equivocal view of the eternal and pre-eminent value of Italian art is set out in the *Anecdotes*. Walpole's recollections from Italy are few: he approves of the fountains before St Peter's, Rome, and he remembers the Piazza Navona and a work by Holbein seen at the Palazzo Delfino, Venice.[49] He shows little understanding of the powerful local identities and competitive pressures between the Italian nation-states and has even less time for Vertue's chauvinistic attempts to demonstrate that English painters were more advanced in their day than was Cimabue (a notable Tuscan hero for both Vasari and Baldinucci). In fact, Walpole's dominant thesis is that English art has improved, a trend that reflects well on the nation's growing reputation.[50] Accordingly, he opens his account by citing documentary evidence showing simply that painting existed in medieval England, without making any claims for its quality. From this point there is only one direction for English art and that is upwards.

The Italian artists whom Walpole does cite as measures of excellence are the masters of the past, not contemporaries. Somewhat unexpectedly, he notes the 'dark and unnatural' colouring of Guercino, regarded by many eighteenth-century British collectors as above reproach,[51] but he criticizes Jacopo Amigoni for abandoning the high standards of the Venetian school: '[His manner] was a still fainter imitation of that nerveless master, Sebastiano Ricci … so little attention do the modern Venetian painters pay to Titian, Tintoret, and Paul Veronese, even in Venice. Amiconi's women are mere chalk as if he had only painted ladies who paint themselves.'[52] The 'History of the Modern Taste in Gardening' published in 1780 in the final volume of the *Anecdotes* has an ambitious and authoritative historical sweep not found in the earlier chapters. In this essay Walpole regretted the passing of the 'noble simplicity' of a past (Augustan) age:

> The gigantic, the puerrile, the quaint, and at last the barbarous and the monkish, had each their successive admirers. Music has been improved till it is a science of tricks and sleight-of-hand; the sobre greatness of Titian is lost, and painting since Carlo Maratti has little more relief than Indian paper. Borromini twisted and curled architecture, as if it was subject to the change of fashions like a head of hair.[53]

To avoid such fallings-off in standards, gardening must resist the temptation to move beyond the point of perfection that has already been reached for English gardening. This is a reworking of the dilemma faced by Vasari: how to deal with the future of Italian art after perfection has been reached in the form of Michelangelo?

ENGLAND AND FRANCE

Walpole mocks other nations' attempts to rival the Italians. The historical vanity of the French has encouraged them to exaggerate the achievement of their own painters, something Walpole declines to attempt for the English. Such off-hand dismissals of French pretension colour the *Anecdotes* from start to finish: their greatest ever monarch Louis XIV was a plagiarist who copied the Whitehall masques[54] and whose 'pomp [has] infected Europe'.[55] An allegorical portrait by Philip Duval is insufficiently classical, having 'more the air of Versailles than Latium',[56] and the account of Sir John Vanbrugh gives him the opportunity to complain about the Baroque, almost certainly because of its French connotations.[57] In Walpole's own day England's architecture is thriving, in comparison with Rome where the art 'languishes' and 'wantons in tawdry imitations of the French in other parts of Europe, and struggles in vain at Paris to surmount their prepossession in favour of their own errors'.[58] Finally, he celebrates the 'private curiosity and good sense' behind enlightened publishing in England (his examples are Robert Wood's illustrated studies of the ruins of Palmyra and Baalbek, published in London in 1753 and 1757 respectively) in contrast to the potential corruption of works published at the command of 'a Louis Quatorze or at the expense of a cardinal nephew'.[59] These Francophobe comments reveal a distinct lack of gratitude for the sanctuary that Walpole found in Paris in the decade after 1765, when the political situation in England forced his retreat there.

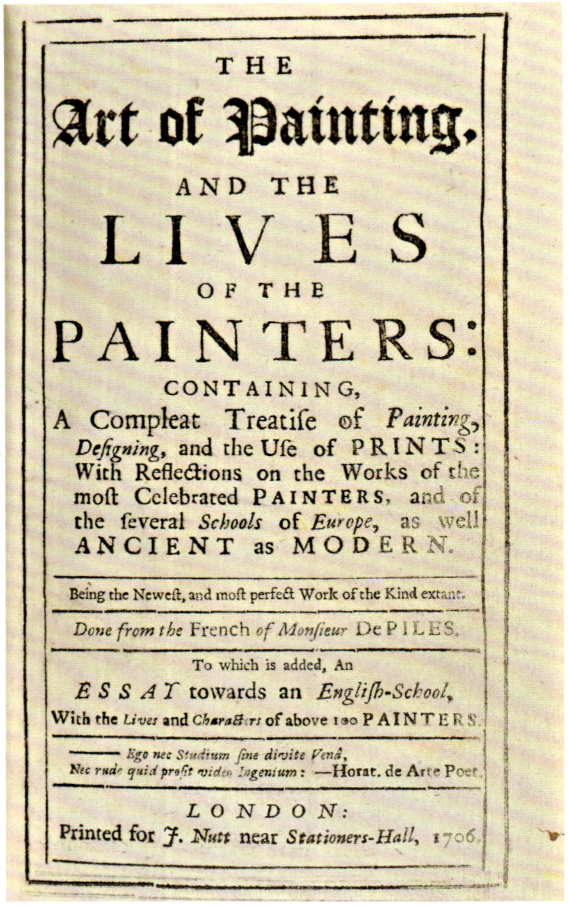

THE

Art of Painting,

AND THE

LIVES

OF THE

PAINTERS:

CONTAINING,

A Compleat Treatiſe of *Painting*, *Deſigning*, and the Uſe of PRINTS: With Reflections on the Works of the moſt Celebrated PAINTERS, and of the ſeveral *Schools* of *Europe*, as well ANCIENT as MODERN.

Being the Neweſt, and moſt perfect Work of the Kind extant.

Done from the French *of Monſieur* De PILES.

To which is added, An

ESSAY towards an *Engliſh-School*, With the *Lives* and *Characters* of above 100 PAINTERS.

——— *Ego nec Studium ſine divite Venâ,*
Nec rude quid proſit video Ingenium: —Horat. de Arte Poet.

LONDON:

Printed for *J. Nutt* near *Stationers-Hall*, 1706.

Figure 162. Title page to Roger de Piles, *The Art of Painting and the Lives of the Painters*, 1706 (London, 1705). The Lewis Walpole Library, Yale University. 72 2 06

WALPOLE'S SOURCES

Walpole makes few direct references to the continental tradition of art-history writing in his correspondence, but some of the authors we have already considered are occasionally cited in the *Anecdotes*. He picks up Vasari for his erroneous relative chronology for Pietro Cavallini and Giotto[60] and intermittently pursues the topic of the mythical Van Eyckian invention of oil painting. Finally, and somewhat embarrassedly, he cannot refrain from suggesting English origins for the method.[61] In general, he professes himself determined not to fabricate or falsely seek honour since 'our studies ... do not grow more valuable by being stuffed with guesses and invention'.[62]

Among English sources, Walpole exploits Richard Symonds's notebooks,[63] but not all his English sources are necessarily acknowledged.[64] He knows the earliest printed sources, such as Richard Haydocke's *Tracte Containing the Artes of Curious Paintinge, Carvinge & Buildinge* (translated in 1598 from Giovanni Lomazzo's *Trattato dell'arte de la pittura*, 1584),[65] Alexander Browne's *Ars Pictorica* (1675) and Sir William Sanderson's *Graphice* (1658), and relies heavily on the antiquarian literature, especially the county histories, to trace particular works in private collections. He also makes occasional use of a document or some other evidence to contest an attribution or a date. Despite citing it often, Walpole is uncomplimentary about Richard Graham's 'superficial' contributions to scholarship in *Short Account of the Most Eminent Painters* (1695).[66]

Key sources for earlier artists are Karel van Mander ('Vermander'), the first biographer of Hans Holbein, and Van Mander's copyist Deschamps.[67] Van Mander is also the probable source for a list of oil painters that starts with the name of Van Eyck. For the life of Holbein Walpole also makes extensive use of von Sandrart. Of the available French authors, Walpole takes from André Félibien an early story about a crucifix speaking to St Bridget[68] and falls back on Bernard de Montfaucon's *Collection of Regal and Ecclesiastical Antiquities of France* (1750) when he has little material to use.[69] Roger de Piles is cited throughout the *Anecdotes* (Fig. 162). Walpole relishes de Piles's high 'balance' score of 16 for Holbein, a comfortable winner against Raphael's score of 12.[70] De Piles is an interesting example of the kind of sophisticated theorizing to which English authors were aspiring, since his works combine biography with a fully developed theory of art and guidance on judgment.[71]

WALPOLE'S METHOD

Walpole is extraordinarily deferential towards his main source, George Vertue, claiming that he seeks only to polish and systematize his predecessor. Vertue's authority lies in his exploitation of personal acquaintance and his careful use of documents. Vertue's integrity is singled out, as is his disinclination to rely on conjecture, let alone fable.[72] The antiquaries who look only for information and then make 'piddling criticisms' Walpole will ignore, but he knows that his public will expect entertainment ('diversion') and instruction, and fears that his history may be too dry and too brief.[73] In another echo of the dominant continental theme, Walpole does not expect his *Anecdotes* to bring him fame and he begs indulgence for what is merely 'an essay'.

From the standpoint of the historiography of English art, nothing is more significant than Walpole's comment that there is no common language to describe and categorize works of painting in sixteenth-century England.[74] When detail is hard to come by, he adopts different strategies to pad out the narrative in the early chapters; the anecdotes are about the persons portrayed because he knows so little about the artists themselves. Another much used tactic is unabashedly or obliquely to cite works in his own collection or in that of his father. Discussing 'Pietro Cavalini', Walpole notes the shrine from Santa Maria Maggiore, Rome, that ended up partly reinstated at Strawberry Hill (Fig. 163).[75] A further tactic is to write about particular works of art because of their relation to noteworthy historical personages, rather than because of their art-historical significance. For example, there is the bizarre account of Sir Toby Matthews, who turns out not to be a painter at all;[76] the tales about the court dwarf Jeffery Hudson in lieu of information about Daniel Mytens;[77] and the history of the Mortlake tapestry factory, an excursus to the life of Solomon de Caus.[78]

Walpole is also adept at creative assemblages. The approach he takes to adapting and designing Strawberry Hill colours his work as a historian: hence the account that he elaborates of an unlucky artist called Henry Cooke whom he describes as the pupil of Salvator Rosa – widely understood among Walpole's readers to be a bandit leader as well as an artist – who lived in 'Knaves-acre' and whom he claims disappeared, having killed someone in a quarrel over a mistress. This is the neat plotting of the novelist as artist biographer at work.[79]

PATRONAGE AND THE SOCIAL STATUS OF THE ENGLISH ARTIST

Reflecting on the shortage of great historical native English painters, Walpole is puzzled since there has been no lack of patronage – 'it cannot be imputed to want of protection'. However, there have been several English rulers with no 'disposition' towards the visual arts,[80] and Walpole and his readers had been taught that great princes would be great patrons. The modern exemplar of the latter pattern was Louis XIV, generally reviled throughout the *Anecdotes*, whose patronage, Walpole has to concede, is an object of glory, indeed a reflection of his general grandeur.[81] Since it is self-evident that painting can only thrive in circumstances of economic prosperity, the increasing material prosperity of Georgian Britain gives Walpole optimism for the future: 'Genius is countenanced, and emulation will follow.'[82] We sometimes catch these glimpses of the historical model of time that underlies Walpole's overall historical schemata. In the introduction to the reign of George I, he describes art as at its lowest ebb, indeed 'dissolute': there can only be improvement, the pendulum swings forward into his own day.[83] Periods of prosperity and of high achievement in the arts will end in excess, the 'forerunner of ruin … the common course of things … tend to perfection, and then degenerate'.[84] Like so many of his continental forebears, Walpole employs biological metaphors of growth and decay in describing the improvement and decline of art. However, he also propounds mainstream Whig ideology, taking care to signal his support for free trade and for moderate centre-party Anglicanism,

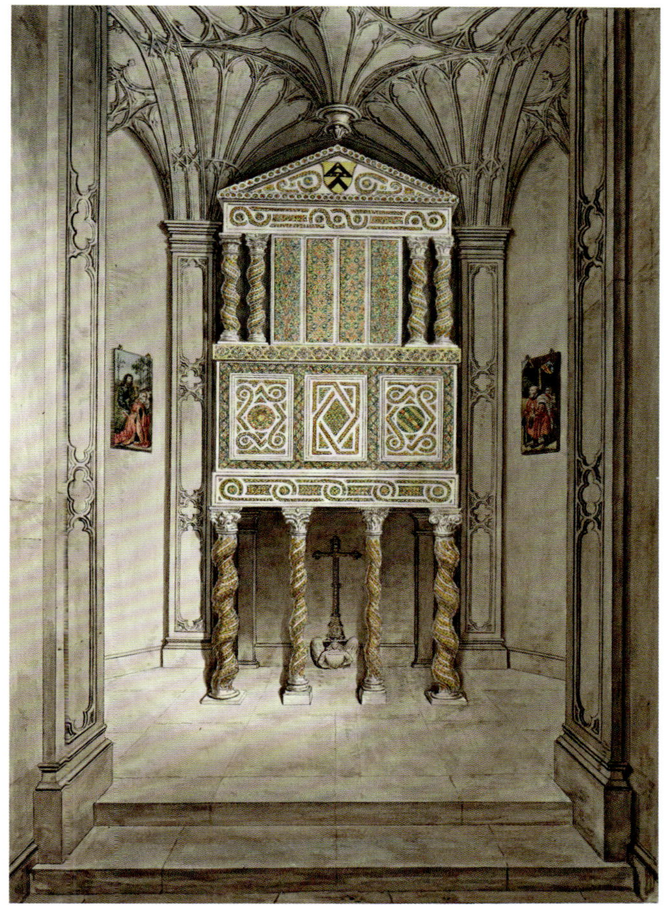

Figure 163. John Carter, *The Shrine and part of the Inside of the Chapel Taken on the Spot*, ink, wash, and watercolour, 40 × 30 cm, mounted, p. 230 of Richard Bull's extra-illustrated copy of the *Description*. The Lewis Walpole Library, Yale University. 33 30 copy 11

perhaps because his stories take him into dangerous territory. An interesting passage occurs in the strange story of Horatio Paulin, who went to the Holy Land on what Walpole calls a 'kind of promiscuous crusade ... stored with crosses, relics, etc ... and ... made many proselytes'. By way of explanation, Walpole makes it clear that he pretends 'to defend the one no more than the other ... All I meant to say was ...'[85] Although Walpole often struggles with his lack of data, there are occasional micro-histories of certain artistic genres that are remarkably authoritative, for example, his account of the English funeral monument from the Gothic to his own day, sketched in a few sentences and ending on a note of scepticism about contemporary fashions ('we seem ... to have advanced into scenery').[86] There is also the interesting suggestion that England can make a particular contribution in watercolour because its oil painters are rarely of the top rank. Walpole's most carefully observed and insightful account of any painter is perhaps his treatment of Samuel Cooper, matched only by his account of the multi-talented Inigo Jones.[87] Conscious that he was writing in an age when the status of the artist was being transformed, Walpole tackles the sensitive relationship between an artist's range of commission and his social standing: 'It may comfort the profession to know that Solimeni [i.e., Francesco Solimena], who was inferior to no painter of any age in vanity, whatever he was in merrit, painted a coach for the present King of Spain, when King of Naples, which cost £12,000.'[88]

THE STATUS OF PAINTING IN ENGLAND

But what of painting as process and practice? In the preface to the *Anecdotes* Walpole addresses his British readers directly, left raw as they have been by Reformation disputes over the legitimacy of religious imagery and the linkages made in various seventeenth-century constitutional disputes between ideology and imagery. This is the issue that lay at the heart of English post-Reformation visual culture: did scandalous images necessarily lead to the corruption of the godly? No, Walpole insists: without papist teaching, images are ineffective, pictures cannot trigger idolatry. In fact, great painting is philosophically incapable of being adapted to 'the meanest capacities': 'The people must be taught to believe in false gods and in the power of saints before they will learn to worship their images.'[89] Reflecting on the narrow sectarianism or 'party animosity' that had marred the reign of Queen Anne and had 'sharpened the genius of the age, [but] dishonoured it too', Walpole argues that iconoclasm is no longer a danger to painting.[90] But the pervasive national glory – Britain abounding in heroes, orators and patrons – has yet to be matched by the triumph of painting or of what Walpole refers to as 'the public arts' in contrast to 'private monuments' by artists from Rysbrack to Reynolds.[91]

The most sophisticated passages of style analysis in the *Anecdotes* are not directed at painting at all. The early discussion on medieval architecture stresses its associative possibilities and even suggests English primacy – 'it is difficult for the nobliest Grecian temple to convey half so many impressions to the mind as a cathedral does of the best Gothic taste'[92] – and the quality of the historical analysis of Inigo Jones is unmatched by any discussion on a painter.[93] Indeed, Jones's architecture is the first real high point: it is when English art breaks forth in 'all the lustre and purity of Rome and Athens'.[94] Otherwise, Van Dyck is the yardstick to whom the best of Cornelis Jansen and Daniel Mytens might aspire.[95]

CONCLUSION

Where does Walpole position English art within the European context? He gives primacy to William Hogarth, placing him between the epic poets and tragedians of Italy and the Dutch masters of farce and burlesque (Marten van Heemskerck's monkeys and Adrien van Ostade's drunks). In particular, Walpole admires the English middle way, leading to his condemnation of both the men of wit under Charles II and the Puritans. What the historian learns from the study of such periods ('the times of confusion and barbarism', is how to 'ascertain the ebb and flow of genius'.[96] He is especially censorious of the early Tudors – of Henry VII, who 'would have preferred a conveyancer to Praxiteles' and whose reigns had coincided with the life of Raphael, painting's 'brightest epoch' – and he voices a standard antiquarian lament for the reformations of the 'ancient monasteries and Gothic piles and painted glass'.[97] England has no ancient tradition of producing great painters, but it does have a distinguished record for patronage, especially in hosting great Netherlandish painters. This is but one of the defining qualities of a national school of painting, others relate to medium and to genre. Walpole's account of George Lambert, about whom he clearly knows very little, is prefaced by a general reflection on the surprising paucity of English landscape painters, and he makes the unexpected but apparently genuine suggestion that the Kentish hop-fields would be a challenging but appropriate choice of English subject matter.[98]

Despite some narrow but proper national concerns, the broader cultural context for Walpole's *Anecdotes* was transalpine continental Europe. As we have seen, during the seventeenth century artistic biography and other forms of art-historical writing had become a general European phenomenon. After 1700 the focus of progressive European art-historical activity had remained centred on classical and Italian material, though not exclusively so. Walpole's *Anecdotes* register a historiographic turning point, the moment when European scholars start to write more about topics of international significance and less about their own national cultures and interests. His book has been somewhat eclipsed by the near contemporary publication of Winckelmann's *History of Ancient Art* (1764) and the *Reflections on the Painting and Sculpture of the Greeks* (1765), works that are not anecdotal, narrowly nationalistic or antiquarian in character, but thoroughly theorized and overtly polemical. Winckelmann is engaged in a grand evocation of a past time as a model for future aspiration, and he understands the value and importance of historical context when citing issues such as religion, morals and the climate. He also has a theory of historical development with fixed points and artistic standards used to articulate the passage of time. He divides the broad sweep of art history into abstract but manageable divisions or cyclical epochs that are applicable to both ancients and moderns. The archaic periods lead up to Phidias and Raphael; the sublime periods of Phidias and Raphael-Michelangelo follow; then come the periods of beauty (Praxiteles, Lysippus and Apelles or Correggio to Guido Reni); finally there is the death blow struck against art by imitation, the false practice that had dominated the modern period from the Carraccis to Carlo Maratti. Furthermore, Winckelmann has a gift for ekphrastic writing that was either beyond Walpole in the 1760s or regarded as inappropriate for a scholarly work of English art history.

Perhaps the most striking point of comparison between Walpole and Winckelmann lies in their treatment of material objects. Although the German scholar was a professional curator, he relied on aesthetic idealization rather than on the minute examination of the material qualities of the objects in his care. In relation to the work of art itself, only the associated idea is of significance, not its material qualities or even the execution at the hands of the artist.[99] Since for Winckelmann beauty is immutable and was attained in the distant Greek past, all change is an inevitable decline away from that point. By contrast, Walpole was a committed collector rather than a curator and was adept both at constructive use of documentary sources and at extrapolating interpretative historical material from objects.

Walpole's *Anecdotes* need to be read in a broad European eighteenth-century context, one that accommodates models of historical evolution and concepts of the spirit of an age or of a nation, and avoids an over-reliance on a classicist and absolutist notion of beauty as an objective standard. The art history published in Walpole's day also reveals an innovative tolerance of artistic subjectivity, more tolerance than hitherto of the art of the Middle Ages and of art from outside Europe. Walpole represents the point of transition from a narrow antiquarianism to the fully documentary historical endeavours of the nineteenth century, exemplified in the work of J.A. Crowe and G.B. Cavalcaselle, whose practice derived from the methodologies of philologists as well as historians.[100] The explanation of the art object was to become something to be proved by sources cited, influences traced and documents discovered and interpreted. The model for British art history was to become continental numismatics and palaeography. This pattern was to culminate in Gaetano Milanesi's edition of Vasari's *Lives* (1878), a publication that, by harnessing the findings of connoisseurship and archival enquiry to the editing of artistic biography, heralds the birth of the authoritative artistic biography that would dominate Walpole's adopted field for the next one hundred years.

Timothy Clayton

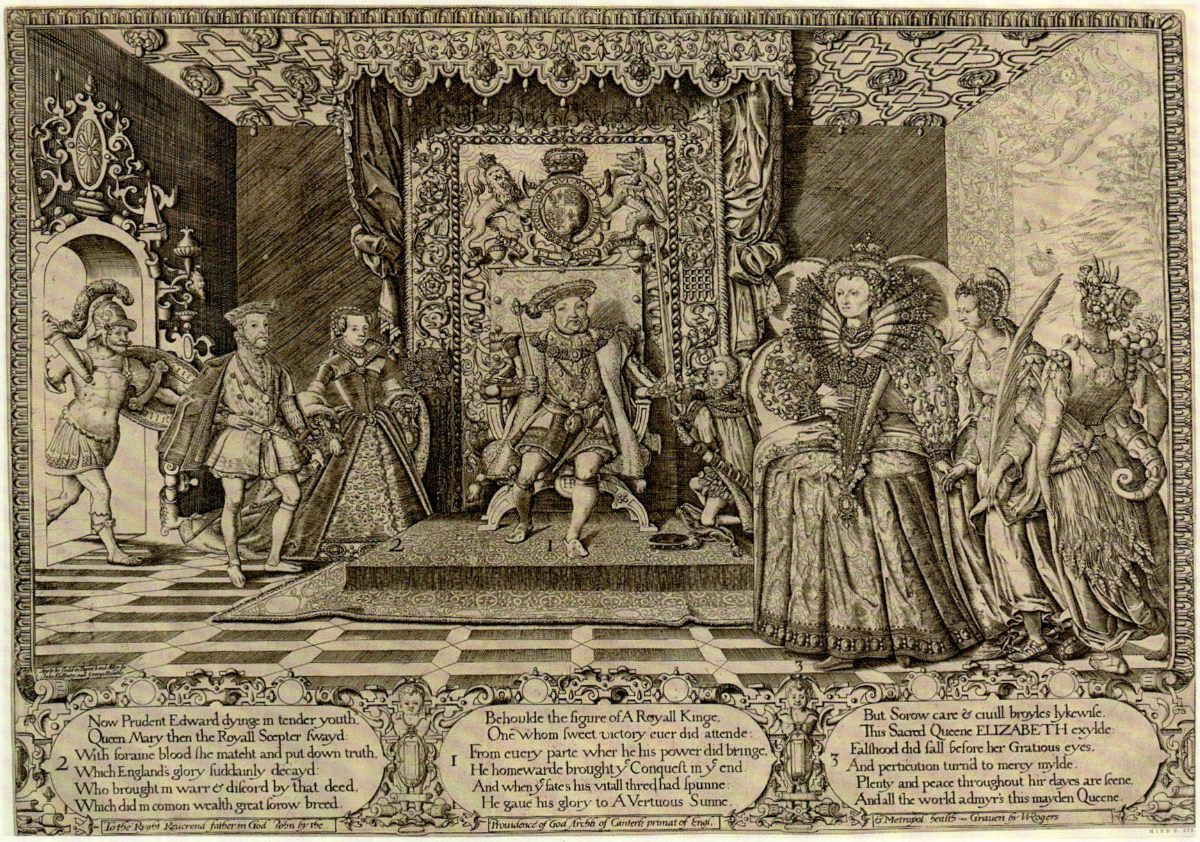

Figure 164. William Rogers after Hans Eworth, *The Family of Henry VIII*, *c.* 1572–80, engraving, 36 × 49.1 cm. British Museum, Department of Prints and Drawings. 1842,0806.373. See Cat. 102

Horace Walpole's collection of portrait heads was one of the great print collections of the day. When this 'truly valuable treasure of Chalcographic Art' was dispersed in 1842, the cataloguer, Thomas Dodd, spoke of 'innumerable gems' and 'treasures of rarity that until now have not, in many instances, come under the observation of even the most veteran collectors of the present era'.

Most libraries contained a print collection in which a selection of portrait heads was a traditional component, but French theorists of the late seventeenth century considered portraits to be central to collections formed by people whose principal interest lay in history. Portraits, they noted, were usually arranged country by country and covered sovereigns, princes and princesses; holders of high rank in the state, the church, the army and navy, the law and in various professions; and those who took some remarkable part in historical events. In England some print collectors were either exclusively or principally interested in portraits and most of them were also antiquarians.

During Walpole's youth Edward Harley, James West, John Nickolls, Joseph Ames and Andrew Coltee Ducarel, all distinguished in other walks of life, built major collections of portraits. Their efforts were supported by the engraver and historian George Vertue, who sought out rarities for them. Walpole's own generation of collectors included Sir William Musgrave, Richard Bull, Clayton Mordaunt Cracherode and James Bindley, whose collections, built with the aid of intelligent dealers like William Humphrey and John Thane, greatly expanded and codified knowledge of Britain's artistic and art-political past. Walpole's encouragement of James Granger's project to publish *A Biographical History of England … adapted to a methodical catalogue of engraved British heads* (1769) triggered an extraordinary out-

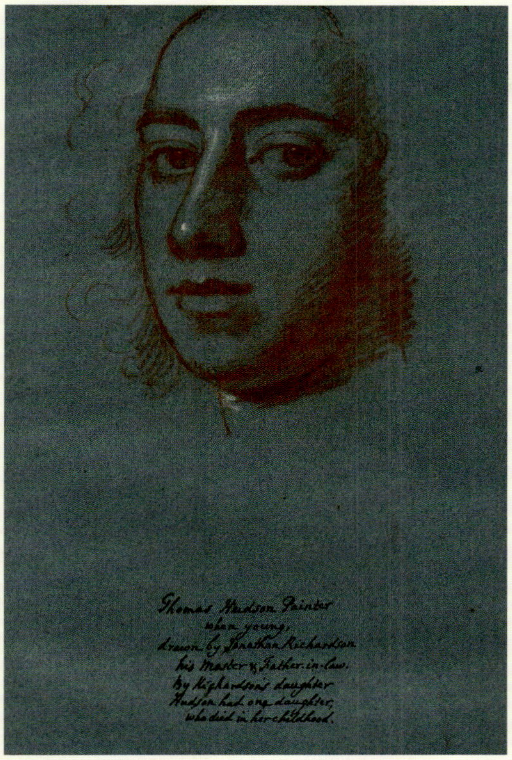

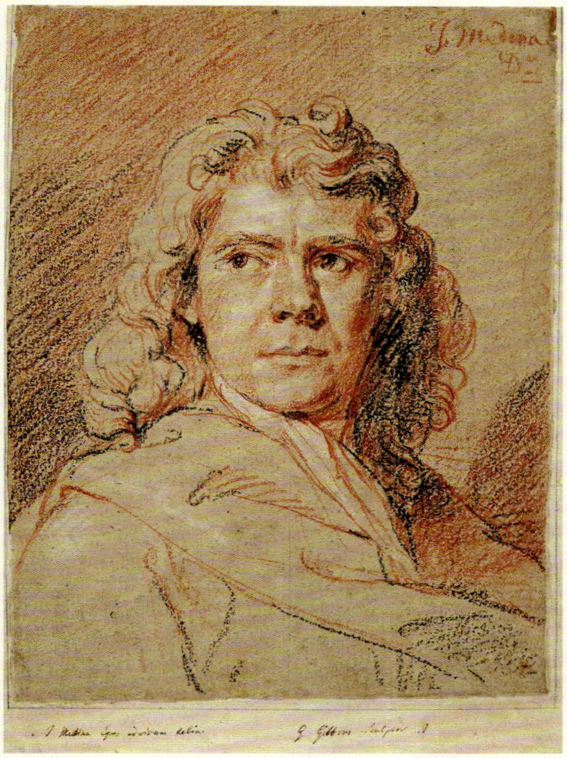

Figure 165. Jonathan Richardson, the Elder, *Portrait of Thomas Hudson*, red chalk, touched with white, on blue paper, 46.3 × 30.2 cm. British Museum, Department of Prints and Drawings. 1852,0214.370. Cat. 205

Figure 166. John Baptist de Medina, *Portrait of Grinling Gibbons*, *c.* 1686, red and black chalk, heightened with white, on buff paper, 22.7 × 17.2 cm. British Museum, Department of Prints and Drawings. 1852,0214.375. Cat. 204

Figure 167. Francis Place, *Portrait of Henry Gyles*, 1680–85, red and black chalk with watercolour on buff paper, 31.3 × 22.7 cm. British Museum, Department of Prints and Drawings. 1852,0214.372. Cat. 203

Figure 168. Horace Walpole, Detail of the title page of the album, *Portraits of English Painters Collected by Mr. Vertue and Mr. Walpole*, Strawberry Hill Press, *c.* 1771–3, 51.5 × 36.7 cm. British Museum, Department of Prints and Drawings 1852,0214.265. Cat. 200

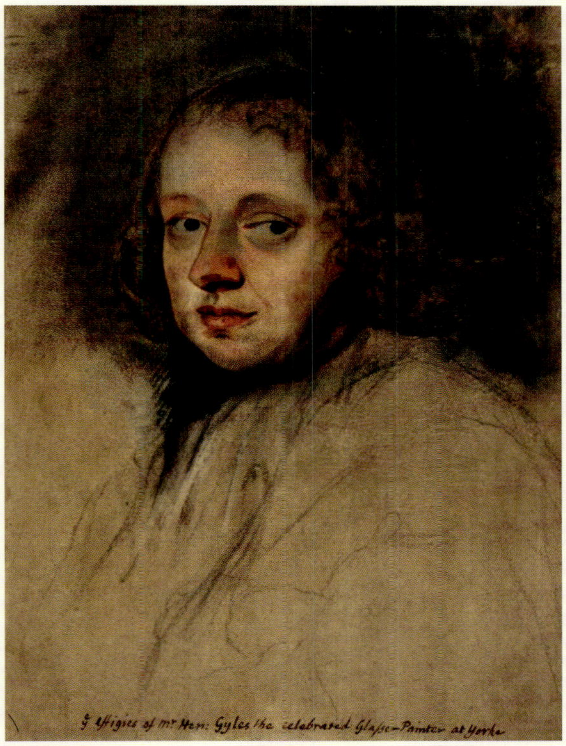

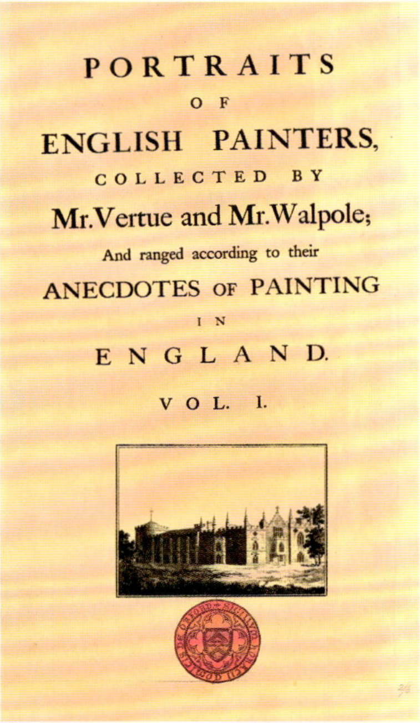

PORTRAITS
OF
ENGLISH PAINTERS,
COLLECTED BY
Mr.Vertue and Mr.Walpole;
And ranged according to their
ANECDOTES OF PAINTING
IN
ENGLAND.
VOL. I.

burst of portrait collecting in the prosperous and increasingly status-conscious Britain of that time.

The study of national history became fashionable and portrait collecting became a popular pastime. Walpole and his rivals fought over 'extra rare' prints such as that of Henry VIII and his children by William Rogers that the British Museum bought at the 1842 sale (Fig. 164). What was scarce became extremely expensive – Walpole himself bemoaned the price inflation that he had helped to cause – to the point that a writer complained in 1828 of passionate head hunters who ignored fine art but would 'contend for a base head-piece to a penny licentious ballad of the age of Charles the Second at any price'. Dealers published copies of rare prints for collectors who could not find or afford the originals.

Walpole was typically voracious. He collected drawings as well as prints, many in his very fine collection of artists' portraits from which he had copies made to illustrate his *Anecdotes of Painting in England* (Fig. 168). This was based on George Vertue's own collection, which Walpole continued chronologically and expanded in the same way that he edited and completed Vertue's notes (Figs. 165, 166). It included extremely rare portraits, such as that of the glass painter Henry Gyles (Fig. 167).

1. On Walpole's 'Vasari-hood' see especially *HW Corres.* 35: 207 and Morris Brownell, 'No Antiquary: Ghost-Writing English Art History', in Brownell, *The Prime Minister of Taste: A Portrait of Horace Walpole* (New Haven and London: Yale University Press, 2001), pp. 86–91. Vols. 1–2 of the *Anecdotes* were published in 1762, when Walpole was aged forty-five, vol. 3 in 1764 and vol. 4, which included the essay on 'Modern Gardening' in 1780. References here are to the so-called fourth edition of 1786, the final edition published in Walpole's lifetime, republished in a single volume in 1871.
2. He was about five months in Rome and there were shorter stays in Turin, Venice and Genoa.
3. For an early account see Luigi Lanzi, *Storia Pittorica della Italia*, 1792 (see M. Capucci's edition of the 1808 second edition, Florence, 1968). The final stage of Lanzi's historical scheme, as applied to Tuscany, is Epoch Five, 'I Cortoneschi', that is, the followers of Pietro da Cortona.
4. See Eric Cochrane, *Florence in the Forgotten Centuries, 1527–1800* ... (Chicago and London: University of Chicago Press, 1973), passim.
5. Cochrane, *Florence*, 319–23; *HW Corres.* 28: 109, 25: 97.
6. *HW Corres.* 17: 57–8.
7. For Gabbiani's early work at Santa Maria del Carmine, see K. Lankheit in *Mitt. Flor. Inst.* VIII, 1957–9, 48, and more recently Riccardo Spinelli, *Il Gran Principe: Ferdinando de Medici e Antonio Domenico Gabbiani: Mecenatismo e committenza artistica ad un pittore fiorentino delle fine del Seicento* (Florence: Noe Edizioni, 2003).
8. *HW Corres.* 20: 429.
9. For Meucci see Carlotta Lenzi Iacomelli, *Vincenzo Meucci 1694–1766* (Florence, 2000). Of course, Masaccio's status as one of his heroes did not stop Vasari from building an altar over the Trinity fresco at Santa Maria Novella.
10. R. Wittkower, *Art and Architecture in Italy 1600–1750*, rev. J. Connors and J. Montagu, 3 vols. (New Haven and London: Yale University Press, 1999), 3: 78 ff. In relation to the visit to England of the architect Alessandro Galilei (1714–19), see now Elisabeth Kieven, 'An Italian Architect in London: The Case of Alesandro Galilei (1691–1737)', *Architectural History* (2008), 51: 1–33, which describes Anglo-Florentine cultural relations in the generation prior to Walpole's visit. Galileo adhered to the standard Florentine view that the revival of ancient architecture had reached its apogee in Michelangelo and his contemporaries.
11. *HW Corres.* 21: 479, 481; 22: 583.
12. Filippo Baldinucci, *Notizie de' professori del disegno da Cimabue* ..., 6 vols. (Florence, 1681–1728); all the MSS and early printed editions are revised in A. Matteoli (ed.), *Vita di artisti dei secoli xvii–xviii. Prima edizione integrale del Codice Palatino 565* (Rome: [Publr?], 1975). For Baldinucci see E.L. Goldberg, *After Vasari: History, Art and Patronage in Late Medici Florence* (Princeton: Princeton University Press, 1988), and the important review by G. Perini in *Burlington Magazine* 33 (1991): 460–1.
13. *Anecdotes*, 304.
14. *HW Corres.* 22: 157.
15. *Anecdotes*, 324, a comment coming at the end of Walpole's mostly critical account of Charles Jervas.
16. Michael Wynne, 'Members from Great Britain and Ireland of the Florentine Accademia del Disegno, 1700–1855', *Burlington Magazine* (Aug. 1990), 535–8.
17. The earliest version of the MS, 'Notizie dell'Accademia del Disegno della Citta di Firenze dalla sua Fondazione fino all'anno 1739' is Bibl. Laurenziana Ashb MS 1035; see, too, P. Fanfani, *Spigolatura Michelangiolesca* (Pistoia, 1876), 193 ff.
18. In black chalk, measuring 37 x 24 cm and acquired by the Getty Trust (96.GB.324).
19. Biblio. Naz. Flor. MS Pal. E. B. 9. 5; for Walpole's visits to Gabburri's collections see *HW Corres.* 35: 47; 37: 296, 326–7, 329.
20. H. Honour, 'The Palazzo Corsini, Florence', *The Connoisseur* 138 (1956): 160; see *HW Corres.* 35: 51n. 17: 105; Mann was appointed Resident in 1740, the year of Walpole's lengthy stay, was honoured and in 1782 promoted to Envoy Extraordinary and Minister Plenipotentiary.
21. Sant'Andrea Corsini's shrine in the Carmine was by Giovanni Battista Foggini.
22. His *Ædes Walpolianae* (completed 1743, published 1748), for which see Andrew Moore, 'Aedes Walpolianae: The Collection as Edifice', in Larissa Dukelskaya and Andrew Moore (eds.), *A Capital Collection: Houghton Hall and the Hermitage* (New Haven and London: Yale University Press, 2002), 1–54.
23. First published in 2 vols. in 1678.
24. Raffaele Soprani, 1674, for Genoa.
25. *Anecdotes*, 38 n. 2.
26. The key work of Boschini (1605–81) was *La carta del navegar pittoresco* (Venice, 1660); other publications followed. For the aesthetic debates within this literature see Philip Sohm, *Pittoresco: Marco Boschini, his Critics, and their Critiques of Painterly Brushwork in Seventeenth and Eighteenth Century Italy* (Cambridge: Cambridge University Press, 1991. Extracts from some of the sources cited here are readily available in English translation in C. Harrison, J. Wood and J. Gaiger (eds.), *Art in Theory 1648–1815: An Anthology of Changing Ideas* (Oxford: Blackwell, 2000), e.g. 171–5 (Boschini).
27. Giovanni Baglione, *Le Vite de' pittori, scultori ... Dal ... 1572 ... 1642* (Rome, 1642).
28. Giovanni Passeri, *Die Kuenstlerbiographien von GB Passeri ... von Jacob Hess* (Leipzig, 1934).
29. Bellori (published in Rome by Mascardi, 1672) appropriates Poussin for Rome as Walpole appropriates Rubens for England. For extracts from Bellori see Harrison *et al.*, *Art in Theory*, 77–78, 96–101.
30. *Anecdotes*, 375.
31. J.J. Winckelmann, *Geschichte der Kunst des Altertums* (Dresden, 1764).
32. Vol. II (1686) covers the period 1300–1400; III (1728), 1400–1540/50; IV (1688), 1550–80; V (1702), 1580–1610; and VI (also 1728), 1610–1670; the posthumous volumes were supervised by Baldinucci's third son, Francesco Saverio (1663–1738).
33. Baldinucci's career has been analysed with great authority by Edward Goldberg, see note 12 above. Walpole's English predecessor, William Aglionby, had also started his collection of lives with Cimabue

(*Painting in Three Dialogues* ..., London 1685, for extracts from which see Harrison *et al.*, *Art in Theory*).

34. *Anecdotes*, 319; for the question of Christina's gender – or sex – see E. W. Nivre, 'Writing life – Writing News: Representations of Queen Christina of Sweden in Early Modern Literature', *Renaissance Studies* 33 (2; 2009): 221–39.
35. Originally intended to end with Mattia Preti.
36. *HW Corres.* 21: 481, 22: 583.
37. *Anecdotes*, 27.
38. *L'Academia todesca della architettura, scultura e pittura; Oder Teutsche Academie*, 2 vols. (Nuremberg, 1675–9).
39. In Part Three of the work; for extracts see Harrison *et al.*, *Art in Theory*, 317–26.
40. See modern facsimile editions by Hessel Miedema; a second edition with author's autobiography was published in 1616–18 and a paraphrased edition in Walpole's own day (by de Jongh, 1764).
41. On Deschamps, see now Jennifer Graham, 'The "manière Gottique": Jean-Baptiste Deschamps and the Revival of Early Netherlandish Art in Eighteenth-century France', in P. Damian-Grant (ed.), *Medievalism and manière gothique in Enlightenment France: Studies in Voltaire and the Eighteenth Century* (Oxford: Voltaire Foundation, 2006), 300–334.
42. For this strand in historiography see Thomas DaCosta Kaufmann, *Toward a Geography of Art* (Chicago and London: Chicago University Press, 2004).
43. Lanzi is still pursuing this theme in the final years of the 1700s (Lanzi, *Storia Pittorica*, 207).
44. *Anecdotes*, 242, from the life of Gerard Soest or Zoust.
45. *Anecdotes*, 37–8.
46. Mahon 329–220.
47. Erwin Panofsky, *Idea*, 175.
48. *Anecdotes*, 1.
49. *Anecdotes*, 57.
50. *Anecdotes*, 6–7.
51. *Anecdotes*, 183. For example, in 1751 Horace Mann acquired 'The Angel appears to Hagar and Ishmael' for the Marquess of Rockingham, see G. Finaldi and M. Kitson, *Discovering the Italian Baroque: The Denis Mahon Collection* (London: National Gallery, 1997), 112.
52. *Anecdotes*, 352.
53. Walpole, *Anecdotes... with additions by the Rev. James Dallaway; and Vertue's catalogue of engravers who have been or resided in England*, new edition with additional notes by Ralph N. Wornum. (London: Swan Sonnenschein, Lowrey, 1888), vol. III, 89.
54. *Anecdotes*, 210.
55. *Anecdotes*, 235, the life of Henry Gascar.
56. *Anecdotes*, 246.
57. *Anecdotes*, 310–11.
58. *Anecdotes*, 379.
59. *Anecdotes*, 6.
60. *Anecdotes*, 17.
61. *Anecdotes*, 22; and see, too, Graham, 'The "manière Gottique"'.
62. *Anecdotes*, 20–21; Vasarian claims for Van Eyck also in *HW Corres.* 29: 6. For Walpole's imitation of Vasari see, too, *HW Corres.* 35: 207, and for references to Vasari's *Vite* see *HW Corres.* 16: 96–7.
63. *Anecdotes*, 170 n. 1.
64. Dallaway spotted the use of James Burgess's *Lives of Eminent Painters* 1754 cited on Petitot (see his edition, vol. II, p. 36 note).
65. Cited in *HW Corres.* 16: 148.
66. Especially for artists in the time of Charles II Walpole appears to conflate editions of Bainbrigg Buckeridge's, *An Essay Towards an English School* ... (1706). and Richard Graham's *Short Account of the Most Eminent Painters* (1695).
67. *Anecdotes*, 42; J.C. Deschamps, *Vie des peintres flamandes*, for example, as a source for Mabuse (*Anecdotes*, 34).
68. *Anecdotes*, 18, citing Félibien I, 172.
69. *Anecdotes*, 19.
70. *Anecdotes*, 51; in a letter Walpole regrets the lack of an English de Piles, see *HW Corres.* 38: 151; T. Puttfarken, *Roger De Piles' Theory of Art* (New Haven and London: Yale University Press, 1985). For extracts, see Harrison *et al.*, *Art in Theory*, 166–20, 185–92.
71. Roger de Piles, *Dialogue sur le coloris* (1673); *Conversations sur la connaissance de la peinture* (1677); *Dissertation sur les ouvrages des plus fameux peintres* (1681 et seq.); *Abrégé de la vie des peintres* (1699); *Cours de peintures par principes* (1708).
72. *Anecdotes*, 2. See also the chapter on the *Anecdotes* in relation to Vertue's MSS in Lawrence Lipking: *The Ordering of the Arts in Eighteenth-Century England* (Princeton: Princeton University Press, 1970).
73. *Anecdotes*, 2.
74. *Anecdotes*, 40.
75. *Anecdotes*, 16 n. 2.
76. *Anecdotes*, 192–3.
77. *Anecdotes*, 115–16.
78. *Anecdotes*, 123.
79. *Anecdotes*, 290.
80. *Anecdotes*, 110.
81. *Anecdotes*, 18.
82. *Anecdotes*, 4.
83. *Anecdotes*, 316 ff.
84. *Anecdotes*, 4.
85. *Anecdotes*, 190–1.
86. *Anecdotes*, 375, discussing Roubiliac in the life of Rysbrack.
87. *Anecdotes*, 253–55, 207–14.
88. *Anecdotes*, 188, in the life of John De Critz.
89. *Anecdotes*, 4.
90. *Anecdotes*, 303.
91. *Anecdotes*, 5.
92. *Anecdotes*, 68–76 (70).
93. *Anecdotes*, 207–14.
94. *Anecdotes*, 111.
95. *Anecdotes*, 113, 114–16.
96. *Anecdotes*, 218.
97. *Anecdotes*, 33, 38; a lament at least as old as John Weever's *Ancient Funeral Monuments* (1631), a source that Walpole also cites and for which see now Phillip Lindley, *Tomb Destruction and Scholarship: Medieval Monuments in Early Modern England* (Donington: Shaun Tyas, 2007).
98. *Anecdotes*, 355.
99. A.D. Potts, 'Winckelmann's Construction of History', *Art History* V (1982).
100. For Crowe and Cavalcaselle, see Francis Haskell, *Rediscoveries in Art* (London: Phaidon Press, 1976); for connoisseurship, see this author, 'Une science du regard: les connoisseurs', in E. Pommier (ed.), *Histoire de l'Histoire de l'Art. Tome II. XVIIIe et XIXe Siècles* (Paris: Louvre, 1997), 293–325.

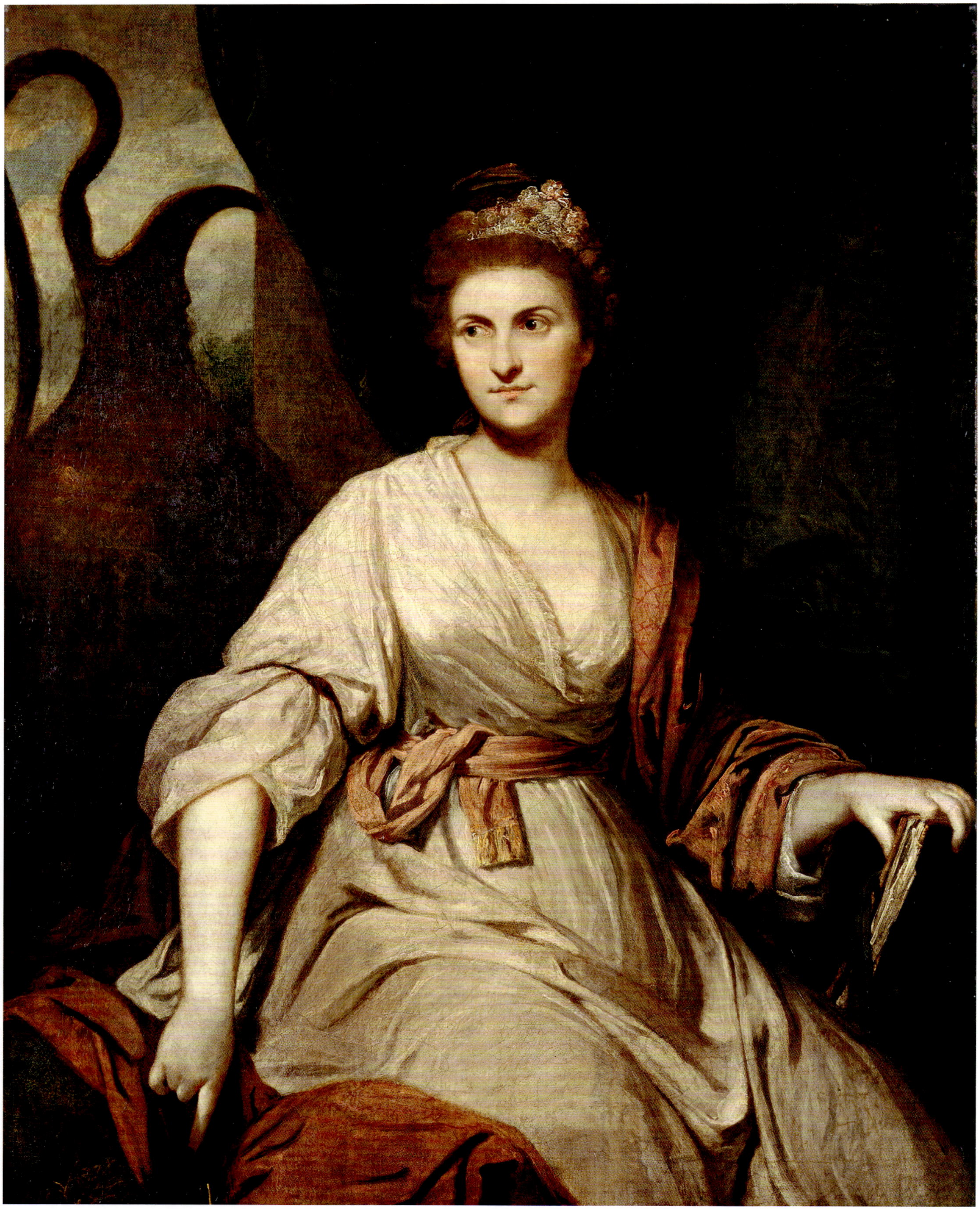

9.

THE ART OF LADY DIANA BEAUCLERK

HORACE WALPOLE AND FEMALE GENIUS

CYNTHIA ROMAN

In his later years Walpole invested considerable resources and energy in promoting the art of a number of women artists – usually amateurs – whom he identified as 'female geniuses'. He promoted their reputations in his writings and compared their achievements favourably to the works of great European masters at the apex of the canonical hierarchy. He collected their art and displayed and even enshrined it in places of honour in his house at Strawberry Hill. Walpole had long placed considerable value on the aesthetic productions of amateurs. In fact, these female geniuses were successors to an earlier group of male amateurs, including Richard Bentley, John Chute and Walpole himself, who had formed a 'committee' that designed the house itself (see pp. 80–81). The work of these female geniuses with which he adorned Strawberry Hill came to represent critical elements of his notions about modern art in England developed over a lifetime of collecting, patronage and writing.

It has been suggested that Walpole used 'genius' as a synonym for 'fine artist'.[1] None of these female artists, however, was exceptionally accomplished by most connoisseurial or aesthetic standards. Although tempered with a mocking playfulness befitting the close personal friendships he had with these women, most of whom came from his own privileged social circle, the incongruity between their real accomplishments and Walpole's exaggerated enthusiasm initially perplexes. One Walpole scholar has concluded that Walpole must have had 'tongue firmly in cheek'.[2] In any event, beneath any face value of Walpole's professed judgment of quality equal to the best masters, his evocation of female genius must signify issues beyond the artistic productions of these women. In her book, *'A Noble Art': Amateur Artists and Drawing Masters, c. 1600–1800*, Kim Sloan observed that the 'cult of sensibility' and the priority of social rather than aesthetic values cannot fully explain Walpole's admiration and lavish praise for amateur works that possess an awkwardness and lack of skill. Sloan suggested instead that Walpole's encouragement of amateur artists provided a microcosm of how a gentleman might encourage the advancement of the arts in Britain.[3] Indeed, Walpole's evaluation of these amateur works as artefacts of significant aesthetic consequence offers important insight into his thoughts on the nature and proper pursuits of both artists and patrons in England. Focusing primarily on the work of one particular favourite, Lady Diana Beauclerk (Fig. 169), this essay will suggest that Walpole's interest in amateur 'female genius' points to his alternative narrative of English art, an account that contrasts significantly with that promoted by the Royal Academy.

Walpole's exaggerated praise for the art of his favourite female geniuses can be understood as hyperbole, allowing us to assess it as a rhetorical strategy for critical dialogue with the reigning doctrine of the Royal Academy, as formulated by its first president, Sir Joshua Reynolds.[4] Reynolds's *Discourses on Art*, as characterized by his modern editor Robert Wark, were 'read by the president before his colleagues and students' and as such 'were tantamount to a statement of policy for the

Figure 169. Joshua Reynolds, *Lady Diana Beauclerk*, 1763–5, oil on canvas, 127 × 101.6 cm. English Heritage (The Iveagh Bequest, Kenwood House, London)

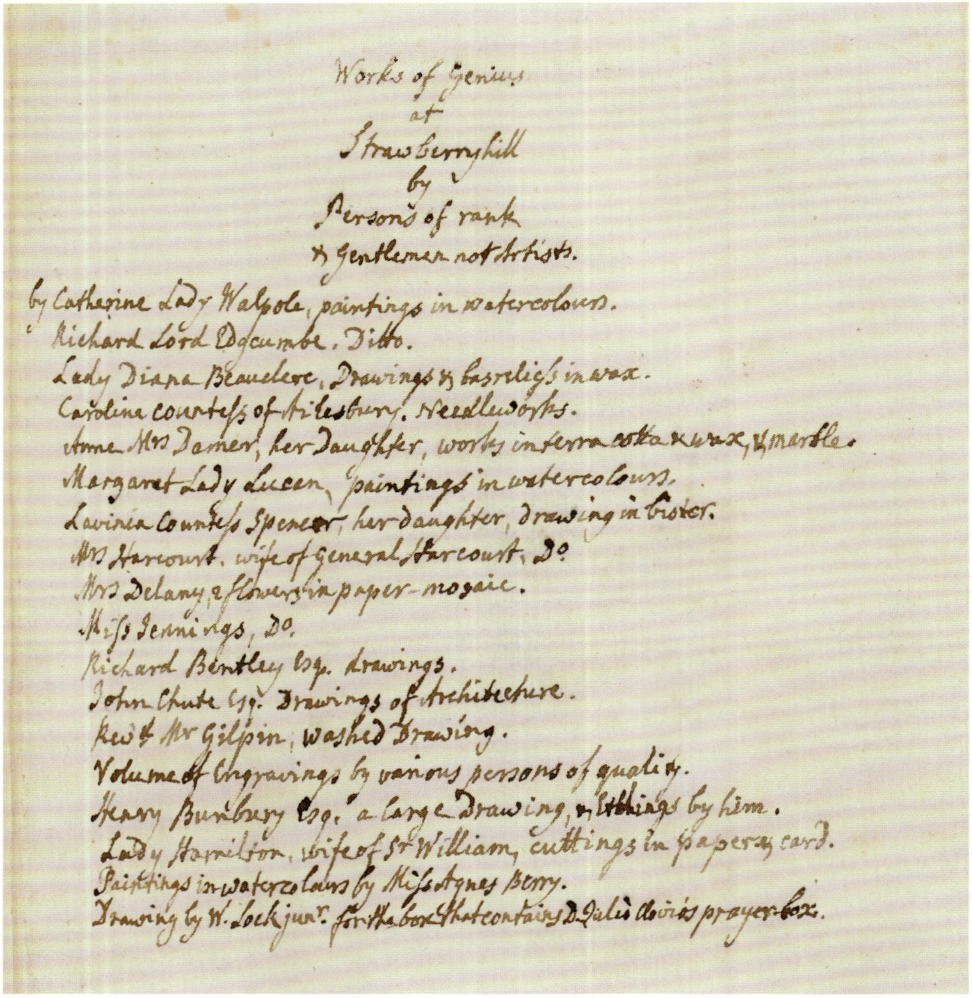

Works of Genius
at
Strawberryhill
by
Persons of rank
& Gentlemen not Artists.

by Catherine Lady Walpole, paintings in watercolours.
Richard Lord Edgcumbe. Ditto.
Lady Diana Beauclerc, Drawings & basreliefs in wax.
Caroline countess of Ailesbury. Needleworks.
Anne Mrs Damer, her Daughter, works in terra cotta & wax, & marble.
Margaret Lady Lucan, paintings in watercolours.
Lavinia Countess Spencer, her daughter, drawing in bister.
Mrs Harcourt, wife of General Harcourt, Do
Mrs Delany, & flowers in paper-mosaic.
Miss Jennings, Do.
Richard Bentley Esq. drawings.
John Chute Esqr. Drawings of Architecture.
Revd Mr Gilpin, washed Drawing.
Volume of Engravings by various persons of quality.
Henry Bunbury Esq. a large Drawing, & Ethings by him.
Lady Hamilton, wife of Sr William, cuttings in paper & card.
Paintings in watercolours by Miss Agnes Berry.
Drawing by W. Lock junr. for the box that contains D. Julio Clovio's prayer-box.

Figure 170. Horace Walpole, 'Works of Genius at Strawberry Hill by Persons of rank and Gentlemen not Artists', p.121 from *A Description of the Villa*, 1774 (Strawberry Hill Press). The Lewis Walpole Library, Yale University. 49 2523

young institution'.[5] While Walpole's critical challenge was indirect and even light-hearted, befitting a gentleman, analysis of his strategy for collecting and displaying works by female geniuses at Strawberry Hill, and of the language he used to describe these works, reveals his strong disagreement with many of the ideas set forth by Reynolds. The very idea of an artist who was both female and amateur connoted a sharp distinction from the category of professional academic artists who were normally male. The term 'amateur', borrowed from the French, had come into English usage during the eighteenth century to denote a person who understands, loves or practises the polite arts without regard to pecuniary advantage. As such, art produced by amateurs, whether for monetary gain or not, was distinguished from that produced by professional artists. Amateur artists generally belonged to noble rather than professional classes.[6]

Lady Diana Beauclerk (née Spencer) was born in 1734, the eldest daughter of Charles, 5th Earl of Sunderland and 3rd Duke of Marlborough, and his wife the Honourable Elizabeth Trevor. She grew up at Langley Park, Buckinghamshire, and was married twice, first to Frederick St John, second Viscount Bolingbroke, and then to Topham Beauclerk. From 1762 to 1768 Lady Diana was lady of the bedchamber to Queen Charlotte.[7] Her accomplishments as an artist were celebrated as early as 1765 in a portrait by the fashionable painter Sir Joshua Reynolds, who portrayed this elite young woman with a porte-crayon used to hold a pencil or chalk for drawing. Lady Diana's pursuits in the arts presumably began simply as a leisure activity common to the education of many privileged young women at the end of the eighteenth century. Making art, however, became an increasingly important aspect of her life and reputation. Her role as artist culminated with the dedicated patronage of Horace Walpole, who fashioned her as the epitome of female genius and assigned her an important place in his history of modern English art.

Debate on the nature of female genius captured considerable attention during Walpole's lifetime. He was certainly mindful of related fine art narratives, which generally excluded women from the category of artistic genius, particularly in a professional capacity. In her book, *Gender and Genius*, Christine Battersby proposed that a key obstacle to the recognition of female genius has been that the very notion of genius is a sexualized concept, rooted in ideas of male procreativity, and as such has a male gender.[8] Although feminine attributes began to be incorporated into the notion of genius during the eighteenth century, the category of artistic genius nonetheless continued to exclude women. In *Learning to Draw*, Ann Bermingham described a feminization of amateurism during the eighteenth century whereby a gender distinction came to be drawn between professional and amateur art.[9] Original works of genius (generally painting and sculpture) intended for public consumption were associated with professional male artists. Derivative works intended for domestic decoration or exchange among friends were associated with amateur female artists, who were distinguished from professional male counterparts by a lack of genius and individual style. Walpole's identification of 'female genius' with practising women artists thus embodied important elements of his views on the nature of British arts and their proper aspirations. These views diverged sharply from the institutionalized views of the Royal Academy.

Any examination of Walpole's thoughts must begin in the context of an ongoing debate about the English national school of painting, which was defined by a conflict between the practice of portraiture and the higher aspirations to paint history in the tradition of the Italian and French schools. Many connoisseurs, critics and artists advocated history painting as the highest aim of the nation's most ambitious painters, and the failure of English painters to produce a significant school of history painting was viewed by many to be a failure of national magnitude. Efforts to promote a national school of painting to rival other European schools occurred within the context of larger debates about native genius in the visual arts. Foreign writers often attributed the shortcomings of British art to some inherent mismatch of British national genius with the visual arts. English connoisseurs, art theorists and artists attributed the perceived shortcomings of British painters to other obstructions such as the lack of training and the absence of opportunity due to the misguided taste of potential patrons. To combat aspersions on native culture and talent, many in England emulated the continental model of history painting in the academic tradition; their efforts culminated in 1768 with the founding of the Royal Academy. For the first time English artists had a prestigious organization powerful enough to promote their professional status and to provide the kind of organized training that had become associated with the visual arts in every other major European country.[10]

Certainly, however, the nation's patrons and connoisseurs did not universally embrace history painting. Indeed, an alternative narrative surfaced among those who championed and patronized portraiture as the characteristic achievement of the nation's artists. Principal among these dissenting voices, Walpole celebrated portraiture, and miniature portrait painting in particular, in his *Anecdotes on Painting in England* as unique manifestations of the nation's genius.[11] Accordingly, he did not commission or acquire any history paintings by contemporary English artists. The only example of history painting in the great tradition that he displayed at Strawberry Hill, *The Education of Jupiter*, attributed then to Nichclas Poussin (Cat. 150), was inherited from his father Sir Robert Walpole and likely valued for paternal associations.

On the other hand, Walpole did assiduously collect another category of non-academic art in addition to portraiture – the work of his 'female geniuses', which he featured in his famous displays at Strawberry Hill. The works by Lady Diana Beauclerk in particular appeared alongside more conventional old-master paintings, relics and objects of virtù. The nature of Walpole's hyperbole on the accomplishments of female genius points to core issues in his dissenting views on the nature of artistic genius in the visual arts. Among the records of his collection and display at Strawberry Hill is a manuscript list of 'Works of Genius at Strawberry Hill by Persons of Rank and Gentlemen not Artists', preserved in his own extra-illustrated copy of *A Description of the Villa ... at Strawberry Hill* (Fig. 170).[12] The listed works are almost exclusively drawings or watercolours, media generally associated with amateur productions, and they include examples of needlework, sculptures in wax, and paper mosaics, media associated almost exclusively with women. The *Description* also contained a manuscript list of 'Principal Curiosities', in which Walpole itemized the objects that he prized most highly: royal relics including Henry VIII's dagger, the masterwork by Nicolas Poussin, portraits by Van Dyck and Lely, a number of fine miniature portraits, the armour of Francis I and Cardinal Wolsey's hat (see Appendix 2, pp. 343–7). While he clearly valued some of these objects more for reasons of association than for aesthetic merit, notable among these extraordinary items are no fewer than four references to Beauclerk's artwork: 'Lady Di's drawings in her closet', 'Lady's Di's flowertubs', 'Lady Di Beauclerk's Gipsies' and her 'masquerade at Vauxhall', as well as works by another favourite female genius, his cousin the sculptor Anne Seymour Damer: her terracotta dogs (Fig. 178), her eagle and her kittens.[13]

Walpole lavishly celebrated Diana Beauclerk's art with a purpose-built closet and a cabinet at Strawberry Hill. First among these commemorations of female genius was the Beauclerk Closet, built in 1776, which housed seven large 'soot-water' (i.e., bistre) drawings that Beauclerk produced to illustrate Walpole's tragic play *The*

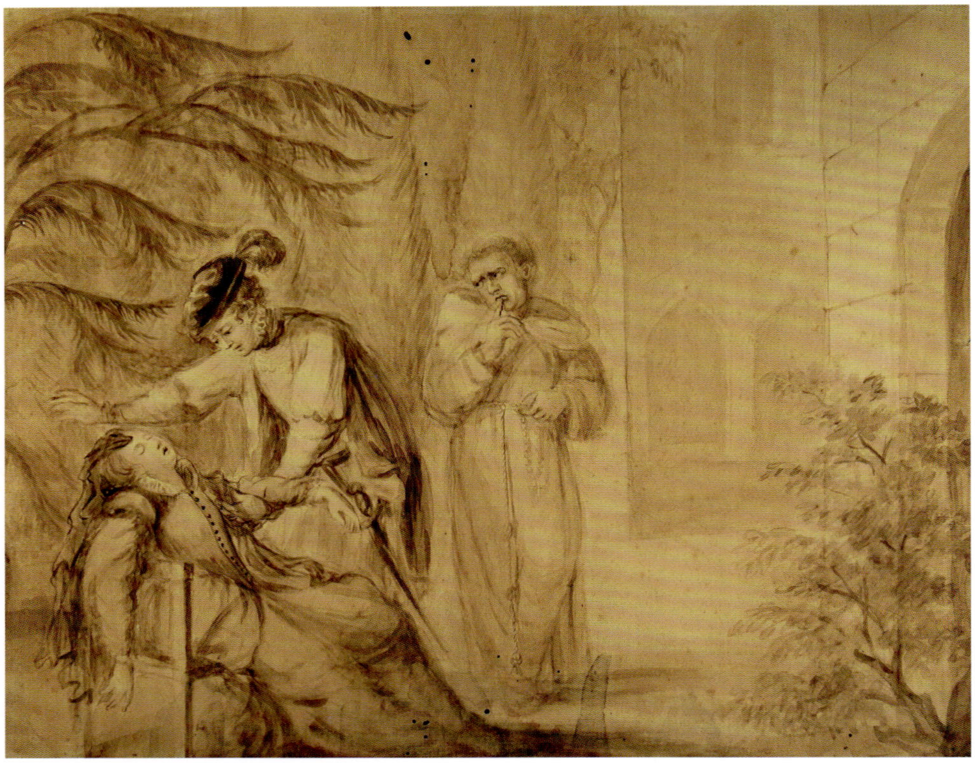

Figure 171. Lady Diana Beauclerk, *Illustration for The Mysterious Mother: The Countess of Narbonne, her Son Edmund, and Father Benedict*, 1776, wash, 32.8 × 41.6 cm. The Lewis Walpole Library, Yale University. 776.00.00.70dr. Cat. 252

Mysterious Mother (1768) – a Gothic tale of incest, dark secrets, tormenting guilt and sinister Catholic clergy (Fig. 171). The drawings, Walpole asserted, are of 'great original genius'.[14] He announced to his friend Horace Mann that his play

> has indeed received greater honour than any of its superiors, for Lady Di Beauclerc has drawn seven scenes of it, that would be fully worthy of the best Shakespeare plays – such drawings that Salvator Rosa and Guido could not surpass their expression and beauty. I have built a closet on purpose for them here at Strawberry Hill. It is called the *Beauclerc Closet*; and whoever sees the drawings, allows that no description comes up to their merit.[15]

Walpole himself, however, did describe the closet and contents at length in the *Description*: the 'Beauclerc Closet'

> is a hexagon, built in 1776, and designed by Mr. Essex, architect, of Cambridge, who drew the ceiling, door, window, and surbase. In the window is a lion and two fleur de lys, royally crowned, ancient, but repaired and ornamented by Price; and being bearings in the royal arms, serve for Beauclerc. The closet is hung with Indian blue damask, and was built on purpose to receive seven incomparable drawings of lady Diana Beauclerc for Mr. Walpole's tragedy of the Mysterious Mother. The beauty and grace of the figures and of the children are inimitable; the expression of the passions most masterly, particularly in the devotion of the countess with the porter, of Benedict in the scene with Martin, and the tenderness, despair and resolution of the countess in the last scene; in which is a new stroke of double passion in Edmund, whose right hand is clenched and ready to strike with anger, the left hand relents. In the scene of five children, some are evidently vulgar, the others children of rank; and the first child, that pretends to look down and does leer upwards, is charming. Only two scenes are represented in all the seven, and yet all are varied; and the ground in the first, by a very uncommon effect, evidently descends and rises again. These sublime drawings, the first histories she ever attempted, were all conceived and executed in a fortnight.[16]

A copy of the play, bound in blue leather and gilt, was kept in a drawer in a small table in the closet to explain the drawings. In addition, a reduced copy by John Powell of Reynolds's portrait of Lady Diana Beauclerk as an artist with porte-crayon in hand hung in the closet.[17]

Walpole later commissioned an ebony cabinet designed by Edward Edwards that was 'ordered by and Made at the Expence of Mr. Horace Walpole in 1784 to receive the Drawings which were all design'd and executed by the Right Honorable Lady Diana Beauclerc'.[18] (Figs. 173, 174) Her drawings of 'a gipsy girl and beautiful children' as well as her designs for Walpole's own Wedgwood ceramics are mounted on exterior panels, along with Wedgwood plaques. The cabinet, ornamented with ormolu and also inlaid hardstones and enamels is designed as a pastiche of seventeenth-century Dutch cabinets for the display of treasured curiosities – an association that imparted further status to Beauclerk's drawings as works of art prized and displayed in similar cabinets by earlier collectors.

Walpole's inclusion of the noble arms of Beauclerk in the closet and his own arms and crest on the cabinet, both of which he carefully points out in his *Description*, indicates the importance of the noble status of the artist as well as the patron. Beauclerk's upper-class standing imparted dignity to the merits of her accomplishments as an amateur rather than a professional artist. Similarly, Walpole carefully footnotes his comments on other 'female geniuses' with the illustrious family connections of each.[19] Distinguishing the female genius in this way as an amateur artist of notable social standing removes her art from the taint of commerce and labour associated with professional artists, which is a distinction that Beauclerk herself was keen to make. In a letter Beauclerk submitted a design for ornament.[20] Presenting her drawings, she explained first that they were 'made without measuring (or indeed light)' but 'that they may serve what I mean'. Minimizing the labour involved in producing these drawings, she requested that he 'exam this dirty paper – I wrote and sketch'd without spectacles'. The sketches, she stated, 'I only mean them to try'. In other words, she presented them not as finished professional designs but as the essays of a lady. Further denying any commercial motivation, she noted at the bottom of the drawing on the verso of the letter that if 'the drawings I make please you, I leave it to you to set the value you chuse upon them. If they do not succeed you must not think yourself obliged to take them – this is all I bargain for.'

Walpole's collection included other prized works by Beauclerk not listed in the 'Works of Genius' or the 'Principal Curiosities'. For example, a copy of the poem *Leonora* by Gottfried August Bürger, translated by W.R. Spencer and illustrated by Beauclerk (1796), earned a place of distinction in the Glass Closet in the Library where Walpole kept his most highly treasured books and portfolios of prints and drawings. Beauclerk's designs for *Leonora* were reproduced by Francesco Bartolozzi, the pre-eminent stipple engraver in England, and other fashionable printmakers (Fig. 172).

In 1781 Bartolozzi also engraved Beauclerk's double portrait in pastel of her two daughters. This print hung on the wall of Walpole's Breakfast Room in a blue and gold frame ornamented with lions and fleurs-de-lis – again an allusion to the arms of the Beauclerk family.[21] Walpole praised Lady Di's portrayal of 'the gay and sportive innocence of her younger daughter, and the demure application of the elder, as characteristically contrasted as Milton's Allegro and Penseroso'.[22] Through this comparison with poetry, like his reference to Shakespeare in his account of *The Mysterious Mother* illustrations, Walpole evoked a centuries-old tradition of academic rhetoric that raised painting to the status of a liberal art and likewise called up English national pride in the accomplishments of its literary geniuses.

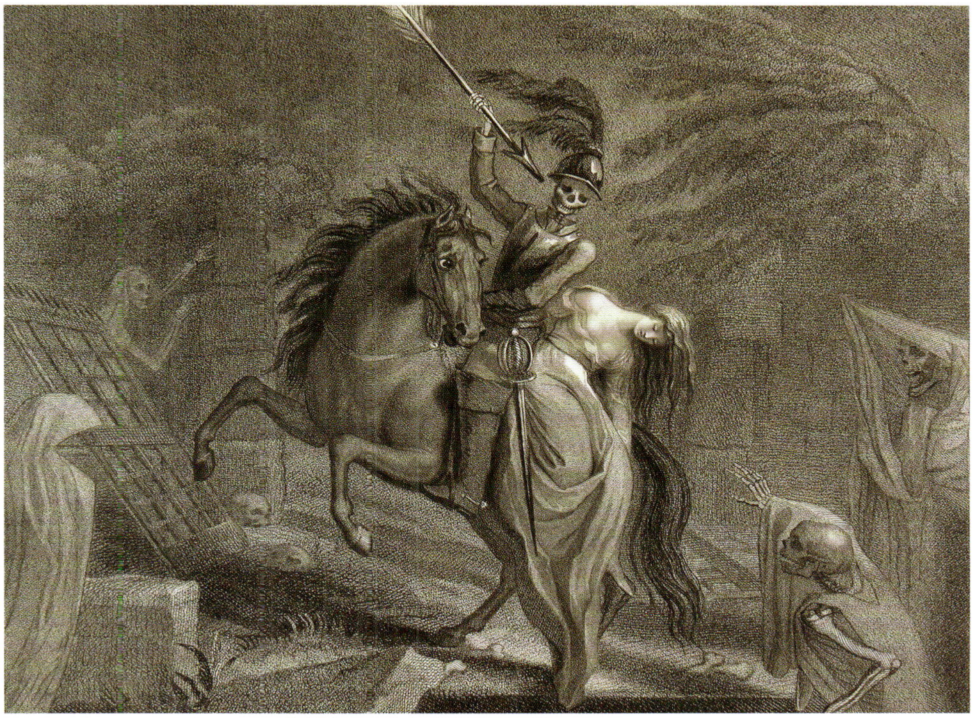

Figure 172. George Perfect Harding after Lady Diana Beauclerk, *Leonora and the Horseman* from Gottfried August Bürgher, *Leonora*, (London: 1796), stipple engraving, p. 33. The Lewis Walpole Library, Yale University. Folio 49 2349

Walpole's *Anecdotes of Painting in England* chronologically recorded the accomplishments of native British (and a few foreign-born) artists, emphasizing portrait and miniature painters while virtually ignoring painters of history. In later revisions of the text, Walpole even introduced a brief account of a number of female geniuses into his discussion of the history and merits of English painting. Most significantly, in the 'Advertisement' (written in 1780) of the fourth and final volume of the *Anecdotes*, having praised Reynolds, Gainsborough and Zoffany, but declining to deal with them later in the book as they were 'living professors', Walpole turned his attention to the accomplishments of 'female genius'.[23]

He first cited 'the wonderful progress in miniature' of Lady Lucan (Margaret Bingham, née Smith; Fig. 175), which he commended by contrasting her apparently easy genius to the lifelong labour of the artists she was copying (Isaac and Peter Oliver, John Hoskins and Samuel

'AN EBONY CABINET ORNAMENTED WITH DRAWINGS BY LADY DIANA BEAUCLERC'

Susan Odell Walker

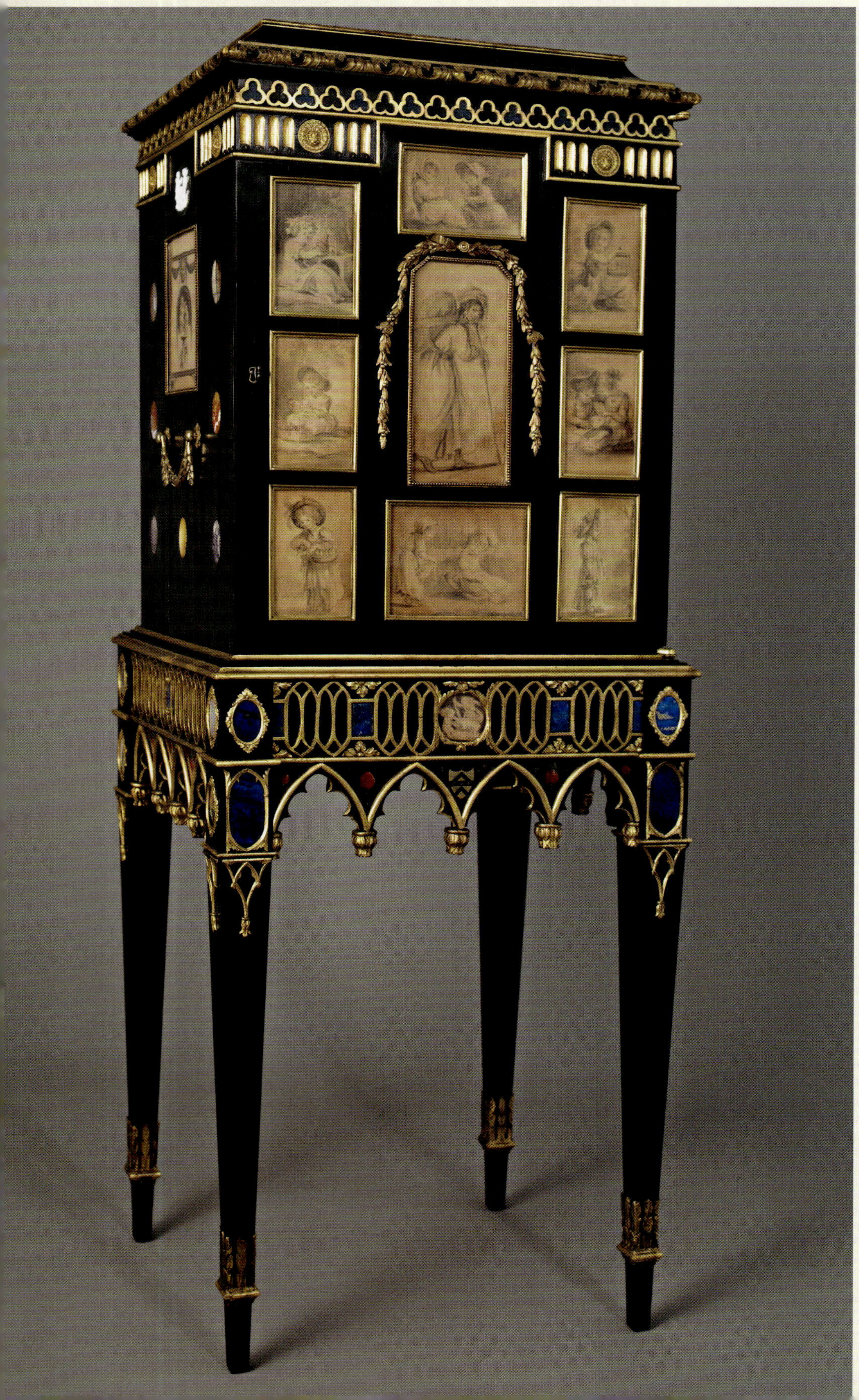

Walpole apparently commissioned the design of this cabinet from the artist Edward Edwards in 1783 and it was made by 1784, the same year that the two men are reported to have had a falling out over 'what Mr. Walpole considered an overcharge for a cabinet made by a person recommended by Edwards', according to 'An Account of the Life of Mr. Edwards' in *Anecdotes of Painters Who Have Resided or Been Born in England* (London, 1808). Edwards had come to Strawberry Hill in 1781 to draw views later engraved for the *Description*. An Associate of the Royal Academy, he had been trained early in his career in drawing patterns for furniture at the cabinetmaker William Hallett's shop and later taught drawing to young men who aimed to be 'cabinet or ornamental furniture makers'.

Although Walpole owned a number of ebony pieces and refers to his 'passion for ebony' in a 1765 letter to William Cole, this ebony cabinet held a particular place in Walpole's esteem, for it was ornamented with 'nine capital drawings' by Lady Diana Beauclerk. Walpole told Bentley in 1754 that for decorative pieces he had 'fixed on black and gold, and it has a charming effect'. The colours appear together not only in the Blue Bedchamber but also throughout the house: in the frames of the pictures and looking glasses in the Holbein Chamber and Beauclerk Closet; in the seating furniture in the Gallery; and in japanned pieces and the Boulle coffer on stand in the Round Room.

The ebony-veneered surface, adorned with pictures and hardstones, recalls seventeenth- and early eighteenth-century continental cabinets inlaid with marquetry, *pietra dura* scenes and drawings. The diminutive scale and tall form of this cabinet on its delicate, elongated legs link it to medal and jewel cabinets of the later eighteenth century. The impression given is that the top portion is separate from the base, like a casket designed to travel and able to be lifted by the handles off the stand to which, in reality, it is firmly secured.

Neoclassical decorative elements, such as the lion's head masks and Wedgwood plaques complementing Lady Diana Beauclerk's drawings, are combined with Gothic ones, like the trefoil frieze and the pointed arches, reflecting Walpole's prevailing taste throughout Strawberry Hill. Further personalizing the cabinet, which stood in the Great North Bedchamber, are the strawberries and the Walpole family coat of arms and Saracen's head crests.

The colourful hardstones inlaid into the sides of this cabinet and the fronts of the three interior drawers include marble, lapis lazuli and specimens of agates and other forms of chalcedony. These may have come from Idar-Oberstein, Germany, where agates and jasper were mined and an industry in polishing semi-precious stones flourished. The lapis lazuli probably originated in what is now Afghanistan. The two shaped pieces on the top and bottom drawers may be either agate or onyx, perhaps originally intended to be mounted for snuffboxes, and the enamel roundels are probably German, late seventeenth century, from Augsburg.

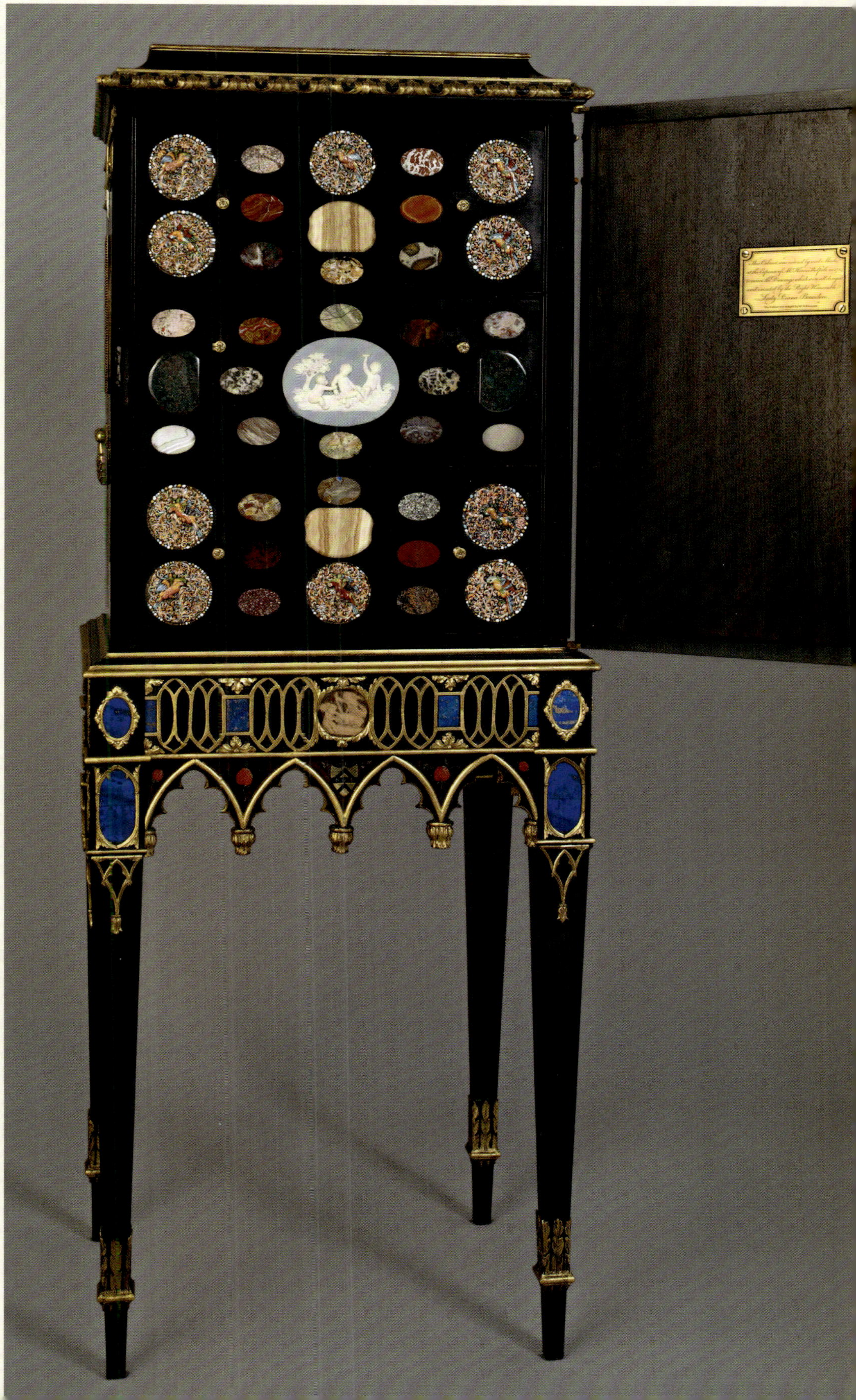

Figures 173, 174. Cabinet on stand, designed by Edward Edwards, 1783–84, ebony veneer with gilding, oak and mahogany; ormolu composition ornaments. Set with lapis lazuli and semi-precious stones, wedgwood cameos, enamels and sixteen drawings by Lady Diana Beauclerk, 127.5 × 48.5 × 40.7 cm. The Lewis Walpole Library, Yale University. Cat. 254

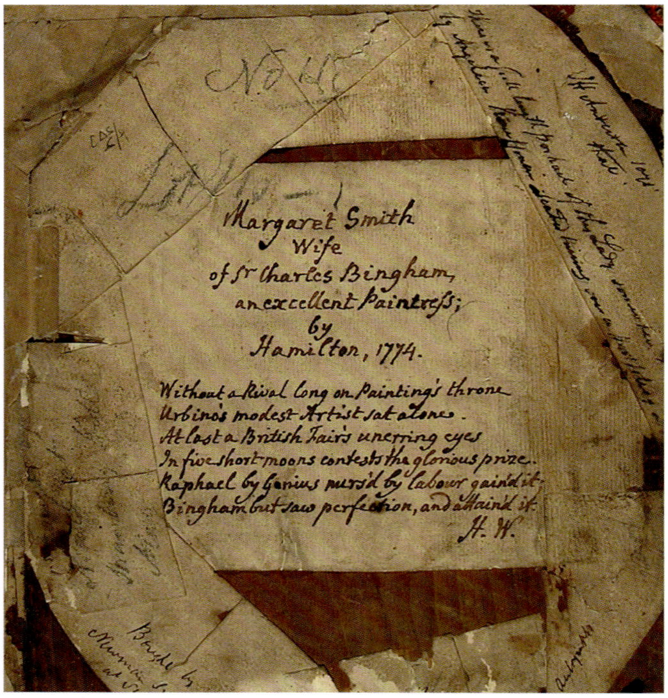

Figure 175. Poem in the hand of Horace Walpole on the back of a framed portrait of Margaret Smith, Lady Bingham (later Lady Lucan), by Hugh Douglas Hamilton. The Lewis Walpole Library, Yale University

Figure 176. Thomas Blackmore after Sir Joshua Reynolds, *Henry Bunbury, Esq.*, *c.* 1765, mezzotint, 35.6 × 25.4 cm, from *Etchings by Henry William Bunbury, Esq., and After his Designs*. The Lewis Walpole Library, Yale University, Folio 49 3562, vol. 1, fol. 1

Figure 177. Richard Cosway, *Portrait of Anne Seymour Damer*, 1790, Graphite with watercolour. The Trustees of the Waldegrave Chattels Trust. Cat. 261

Cooper), giving to her versions 'the vigour of Raphael'. Thereafter, following a laudatory account of a favourite gentleman amateur artist William Henry Bunbury ('the second Hogarth') (Fig. 176), Walpole proceeded again to uphold the example of his close friend Lady Diana Beauclerk. He boasted:

> Is there a pencil in a living hand as capable of pronouncing the passions as our unequalled poet [Shakespeare]; a pencil not only inspired by his insight into nature, but by the graces and taste of Grecian artists. But it is not fair to excite the curiosity of the public, when both the rank and bashful merit of the possessor, and a too rare exertion of superior talents, confine the proofs to a narrow circle. Whoever has seen the drawings, and bas-reliefs designed and executed by lady Diana Beauclerc is sensible that these imperfect encomiums are far short of the excellence of her works.[24]

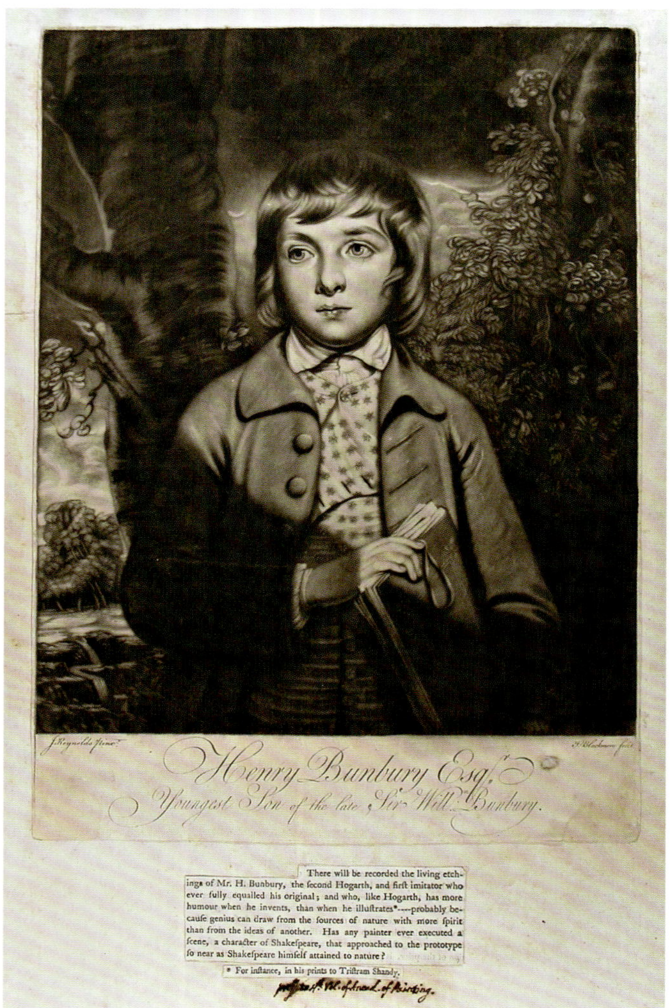

There will be recorded the living etchings of Mr. H. Bunbury, the second Hogarth, and first imitator who ever fully equalled his original; and who, like Hogarth, has more humour when he invents, than when he illustrates*----probably because genius can draw from the sources of nature with more spirit than from the ideas of another. Has any painter ever executed a scene, a character of Shakespeare, that approached to the prototype so near as Shakespeare himself attained to nature?

* For instance, in his prints to Tristram Shandy.

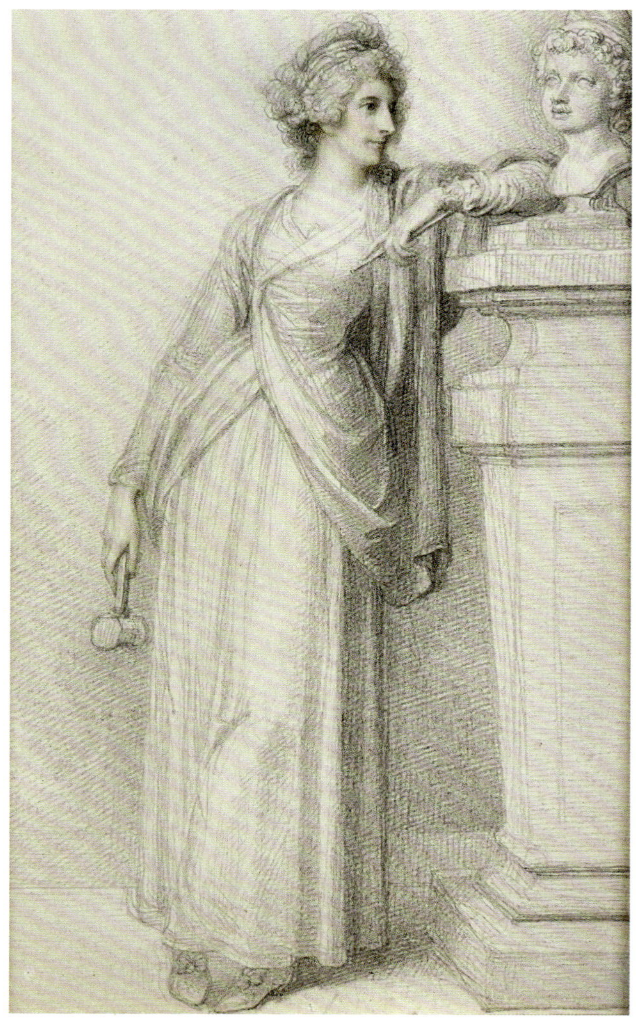

Walpole continued by comparing 'the nymph-like simplicity' of her portrait of the Duchess of Devonshire to a Greek statue of 'a dryad or a goddess of a river'. He pronounced the print by Bartolozzi after Beauclerk's drawing of her two daughters 'another singular specimen of her singular genius and taste'.

A third 'female genius', Anne Seymour Damer, is similarly identified in Walpole's *Anecdotes* as equal in merit to highly celebrated masters esteemed by the Academy (Fig. 177). Damer was another close intimate, the daughter of his favourite cousin Henry Seymour Conway, and the eventual heir to Strawberry Hill and its collections.[25] As Alison Yarrington has suggested, despite public exposure as an Honorary Exhibitor at the Royal Academy, Damer essentially held an uneasy status as an amateur rather than a professional sculptor.[26] Walpole described her extraordinary activity as a sculptor as 'a walk more difficult and far more uncommon than painting. The annals of statuary record few artists of the fair sex, and not one that I recollect of any celebrity.' His commentary continues with the evaluation of Damer's sculpture:

> [Her] busts from the life are not inferior to the antique, and theirs we are sure were not more like. Her shock dog, large as life, and only not alive, has a looseness and softness in the curls that seemed impossible to terra-cotta: it rivals the marble one of Bernini in the royal collection. As the ancients have left us but five animals of equal merit with their human figures, namely, the Barberini goat, the Tuscan boar, the Mattei-eagle, the eagle at Strawberry-hill, and Mr. Jennings's, now Mr. Duncombe's, dog, the talent of Mrs. Damer must appear in the most distinguished light.[27]

On the 'excellencies' of the Damer sculptures that he owned, and the terracotta dogs in particular, Walpole wrote to the Earl of Strafford: 'Indeed, with these dogs and the riches I possess by Lady Di, poor Strawberry may vie with much prouder collections.'[28] As in the case of Beauclerk's art, Strawberry Hill was a showcase for Damer's work. Her *Fishing Eagle* (1787) was prominently displayed on the desk in the centre of Walpole's Library (see Fig. 260). Her *Sleeping Dogs* were displayed in the Little Parlour (Fig. 178). Damer was even deemed worthy to repair the beak of the prized antique eagle from the Baths of Caracalla, eventually displayed in the Long Gallery (see Fig. 184).

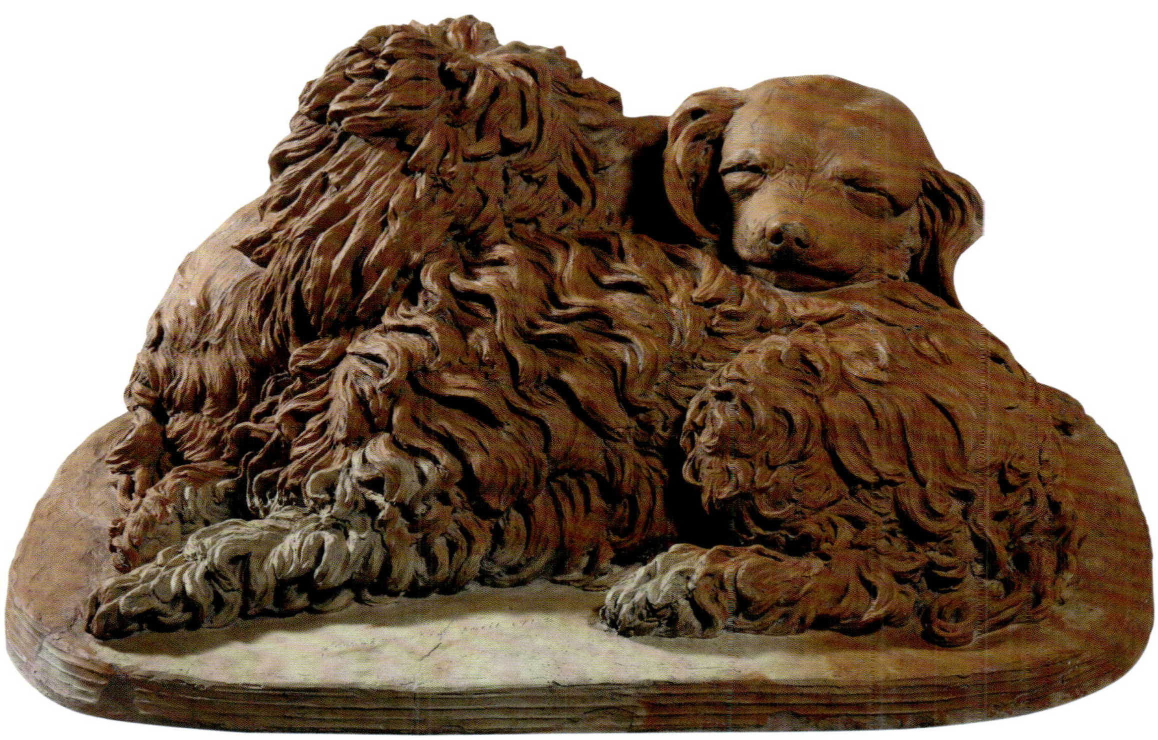

Figure 178. Anne Seymour Damer, *Two Sleeping Dogs*, 1782, terracotta, 21.5 × 42.7 × 34.4 cm. The Rt Hon. the Earl of Derby. Cat. 255

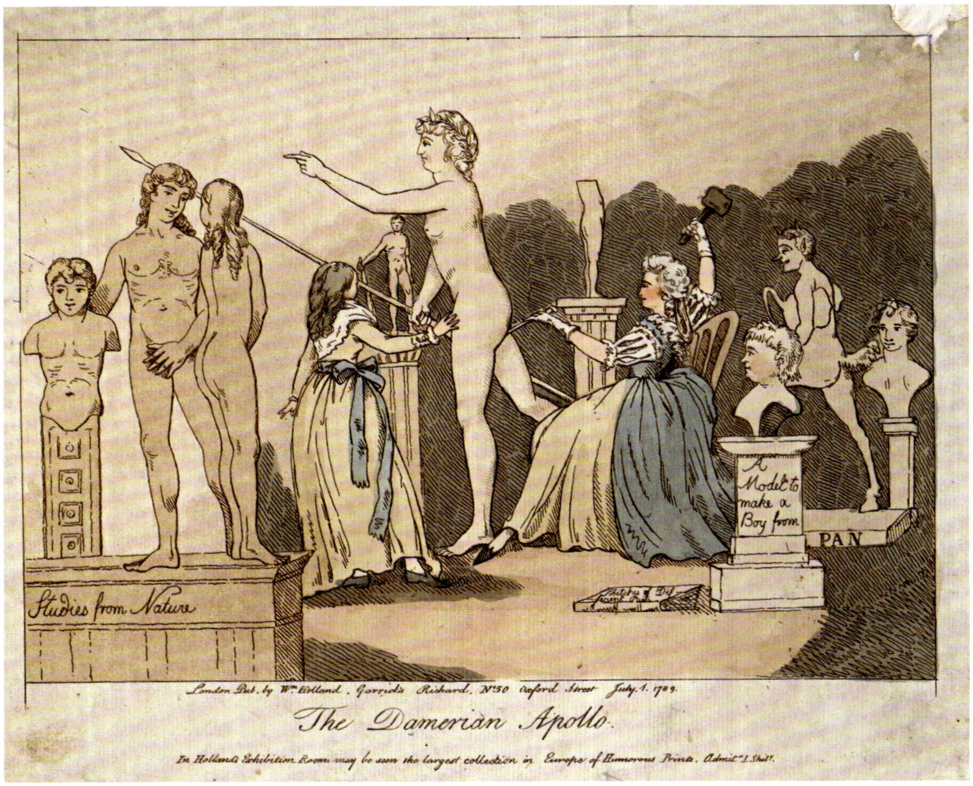

Figure 179. Anonymous, *The Damerian Apollo*, 1789, etching. The Lewis Walpole Library, Yale University. 789.7.1.2

Walpole frequently compared his female geniuses with the most celebrated members of the academic canon. Beauclerk is compared to Salvator Rosa and Guido Reni. Her mural festoon of lilacs is described as 'in as great a style as Michael Angelo would have done for a pope's villa'.[29] Lady Lucan was compared favourably to Raphael as well as to several of the English miniature painters that Walpole celebrated in his *Anecdotes*. In the *Anecdotes* Walpole listed sculpture by Damer alongside that of celebrated ancient sculpture. He expressed this comparison even more explicitly in the inscription he added to the base of her *Fishing Eagle*, which reads 'Non me Praxitiles finxit, at Anna Damer, 1787', opening a comparison between this female genius and the classical Greek sculptor Praxiteles.[30]

With such comparisons between these women artists and the male artists at the apex of the academic canon, Walpole challenged the pride of place normally given to males in the academic tradition. The Academy held all of these male artists in high esteem. Michelangelo and Raphael, in particular, representing the pinnacle of High Renaissance painting in Rome, were fixed at the top of the academic hierarchy and figured prominently in Reynolds's *Discourses* as the models to emulate in fulfilling the high ethical and public aim that Reynolds set for art.[31] In contrast, while Walpole's collections did include the standard small bronzes after Michelangelo and reproductive prints of Raphael's cartoons, Walpole, as already noted, did not collect any academic history painting by modern artists. By his choices as collector and historian of English art, Walpole defined genius in non-professional terms, and in particular identified genius in the arts with amateurs, often female.

While the Academy held painting to be the highest art form for an ambitious artist, Walpole's female geniuses executed their work almost exclusively in drawing media or even the more distaff forms of needlework or paper cut-outs; none were painters in oil. Only Anne Damer sculpted in any medium other than wax. The works by Beauclerk that Walpole admired most were in fact drawings and watercolours. Even the illustrations for *The Mysterious Mother* – the only works that can be vaguely identified as 'historical' – are drawings. Drawing had long been an accepted activity for cultured gentleman and amateurs. In the seventeenth century Henry Peacham published *The Art of Drawing with the Pen, and Limming in Water Colours*. The stated intention of this text on the title page was 'for the behoofe of all young Gentlemen, or any els that are desirous for to become practitioners in this excellent, and most ingenious Art'.[32] Identifying himself as 'Gent.', Peacham distanced himself from any rigorous professional training. In his introduction he professes that he did not benefit from any instructor save his own practice and experience. He writes:

> I have (it is true) bestowed many idle howers in it, which perhaps might have beene worse spent, yet in my judgment I was never so wedded unto it, as to hold any part of my profession, but rather allotted it the place *inter splendidas nugas*, and those things of an accomplement required in a Schollar or Gentleman, I speak not any whit to disgrace so worthy a skill, or to discommend the true & necessarie use thereof, but to give my scholler a watch word, that like a simple wooer hee should never cast off the mistres to court the maid: but estemm himselfe a great deale better graced by propounding at the table … or maintaining an argument in Philosophy or divinity, the[n] by

> intimating his skill with the pencil, or insight in the Chordes of musick.[33]

While Beauclerk kept fairly strict amateur status and never exhibited at the Royal Academy, Anne Damer did have a public presence and submitted her work to that institution, but only as an honorary exhibitor. Women were not granted membership in the Academy, with the exception of founding members Angelica Kauffmann and Mary Moser, who were both highly successful professional artists. Notably, Walpole did not collect the art of either Kauffmann or Moser and remained virtually silent on their work, commenting not at all in his voluminous correspondence, although he did make very occasional and spare notes in his Royal Academy catalogues.[34] The discomfort of many of Walpole's contemporaries with the idea of a woman artist, however, manifested itself in some negative reception of Damer's work as a sculptor.

Walpole's insistent promotion of female genius perhaps rested on the very fact of the Academy's marginalization of women, who were denied or declined participation in professional training there. In addition, Walpole's female geniuses enjoyed further social and artistic freedoms by eschewing restraints prescribed by current cultural conventions. Curiously, as the scandals surrounding their reputations attest, these women also rejected the fetters of rigid social conventions. Lady Diana Beauclerk was a notorious adulteress. She divorced her first husband, Viscount Bolingbroke, to marry her lover Topham Beauclerk. Anne Seymour Damer was separated from her husband and ridiculed as a lesbian. A satirical print entitled the *Damerian Apollo* (1784) (Fig. 179) depicts Mrs Damer in her studio and lampoons her status as an artist with an attack on her femininity. The antique sculptures cover themselves in a modesty that she by contrast clearly does not possess. She is about to chisel the buttocks of a male figure that she is sculpting in a most threatening manner. Mrs Damer was mocked in the press as a 'Sapphist', and her relationship with Mary Berry, another Walpole intimate, was the subject of attack.[35]

These transgressions of the social norms for women apparently fascinated Walpole or at least did not disturb him. Indeed, Walpole seems to have related the social freedoms of his female artists to the genesis of their artistic genius. Writing on another female genius, the author Lady Craven, Walpole confessed that she was 'infinitamente indiscreet' but concluded, 'what is that to you or me?' She 'is good-natured to the greatest degree, has not a grain of malice or mischief (almost always the associates, in women, of tender hearts) and never has been an enemy but to herself.'[36] In the first line of a poem dedicated to Lady Craven, Walpole asserted simply and directly the benefit for genius of an unfettered state. He wrote: 'Genius Howe'er sublime, pathetic, free'.[37]

Thus, notwithstanding Damer's participation in public exhibitions at the Royal Academy, Walpole's display of female genius at his own home at Strawberry Hill was primarily domestic – a context that connotes a very different meaning and invites a different social reception more fitting to a lady's accomplishments. The exclusion of women from the professional practice of public art became for Walpole, it seems, a prerequisite for their particular genius.

While the Academy marginalized women, Walpole prized the unconstrained naturalness that he associated with amateur female artists. Walpole likewise remarked that Beauclerk's mural festoon of lilacs, which he claimed rivalled works by Michelangelo, was executed 'without even making a sketch', just as he claimed, in similar denial of any excessive labour, that Beauclerk's large soot-water drawings for the *Mysterious Mother* were all conceived and executed in a fortnight. Again and again, Walpole cites ease of execution as a key characteristic in the genius of these female artists, and these accounts point to Walpole's distrust of the professional training institutionalized by the Academy. In fact, Walpole's construction of female genius so closely associated with amateurs from the leisured class suggests that labour may well conflict with this category of genius.

The Academy, by contrast, rested on the assumption that disciplined training was necessary in order to create anything of value in the arts. Reynolds considered hard work essential for any artistic achievement. As president of that institution and spokesman for its policy, he emphasized that 'refinement in the arts will not be relished without a long and industrious attention'.[38] He makes this point in the first *Discourse* and returns to it again in nearly all the later ones. In *Discourse XV* Reynolds writes:

> I have endeavoured to stimulate the ambition of Artists to tread in this great path of glory, and, as well as I can, have pointed out the track

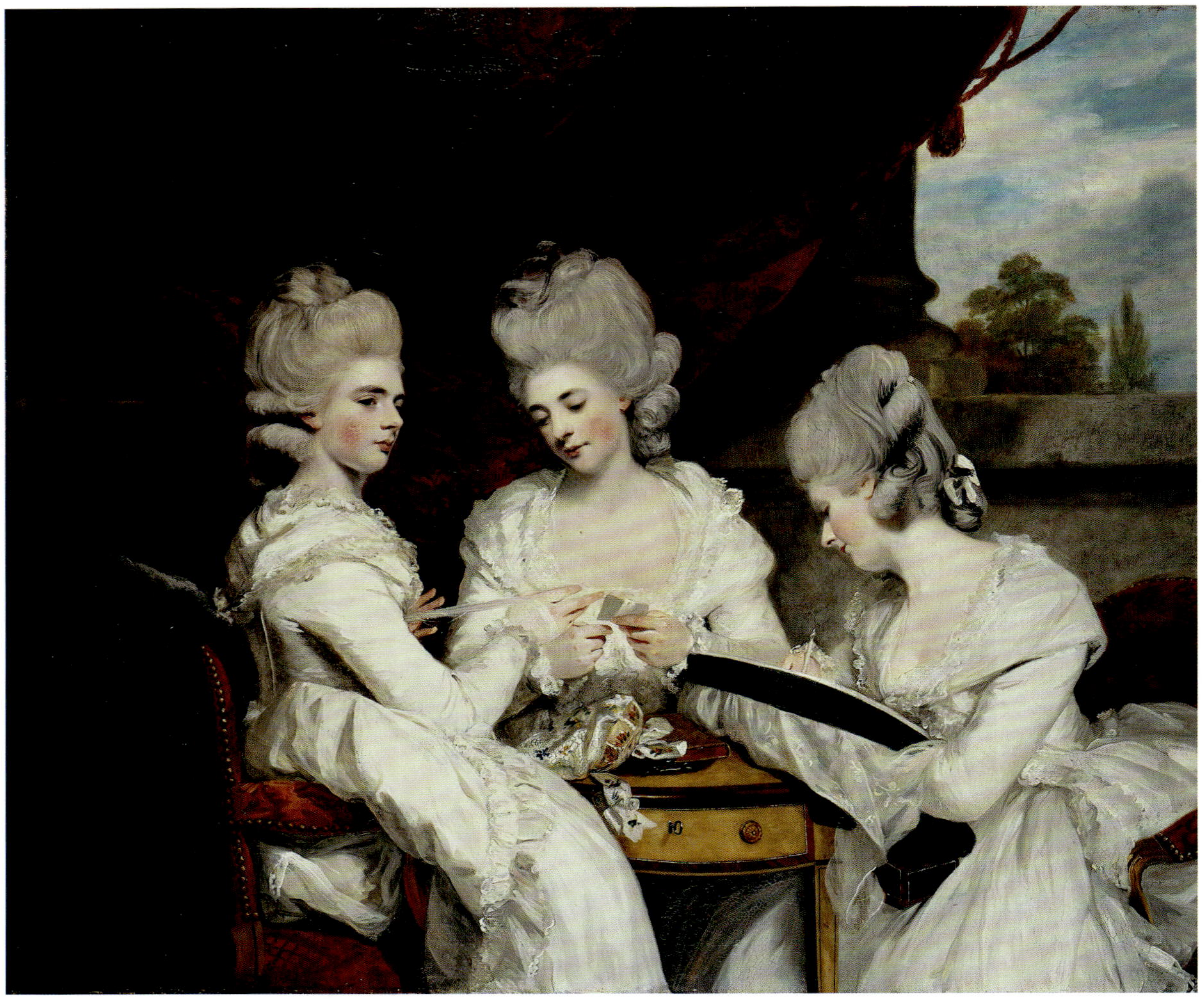

Figure 180. Sir Joshua Reynolds, *Portrait of the Ladies Waldegrave*, 1780–1, oil on canvas, 143.5 × 168 cm. National Gallery of Scotland, Edinburgh. Cat. 70

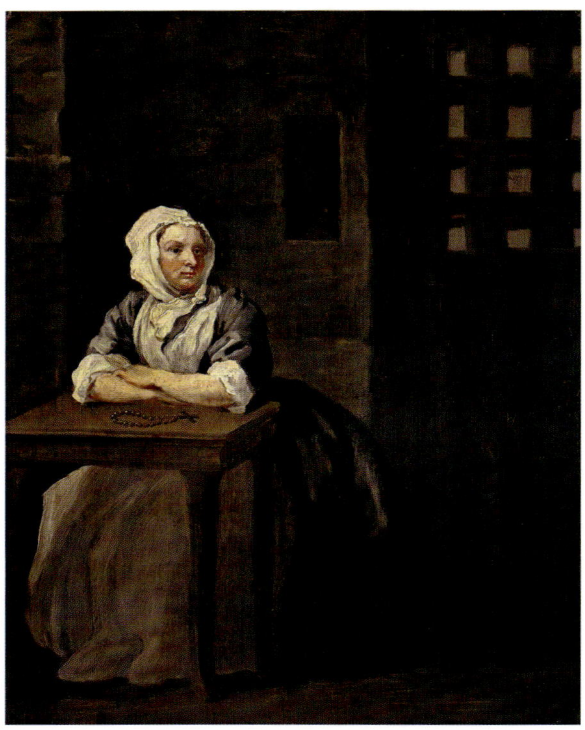

Figure 181. William Hogarth, *Portrait of Sarah Malcolm in Prison*, 1733, oil on canvas, 48.8 × 38.7 cm. National Gallery of Scotland, Edinburgh. Cat. 259

> which leads to it, and have at the same time told them the price at which it may be obtained. It is an ancient saying, that labour is the price which the Gods have set upon everything valuable.[39]

Walpole, nonetheless, objected that this Discourse 'is rather an apology for or an avowal of the object of his own style' and that 'this lesson will rather do hurt than good on his disciples'.[40] For, while Walpole credits his female geniuses Beauclerk and Damer with rivalling the art of Michelangelo and Raphael with effortless achievement, Reynolds, in his *Discourses*, presents these old masters as the exemplary models of artists who laboured intensely.

> The great Artist [Michelangelo], who has been so much the subject of the present Discourse, was distinguished even from his infancy for his indefatigable diligence ... Indeed ... he appears not to have had the least conception that his art was to be acquired by an other means than by

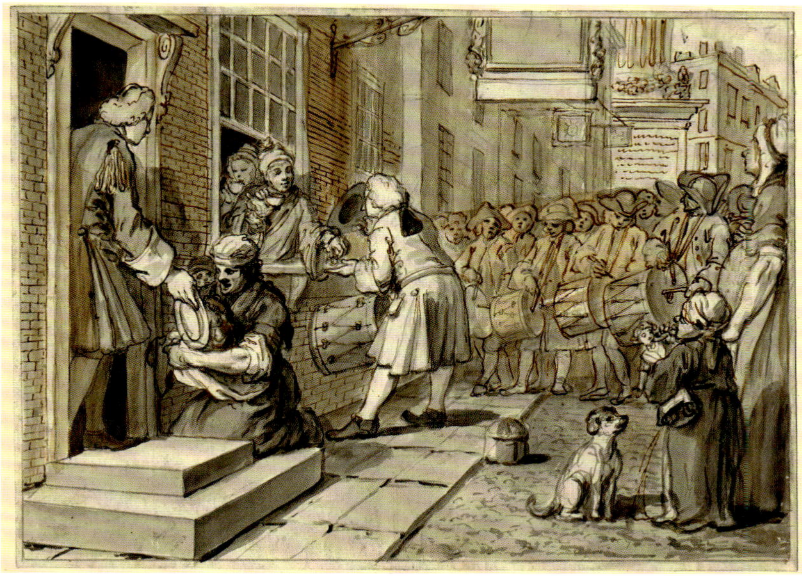

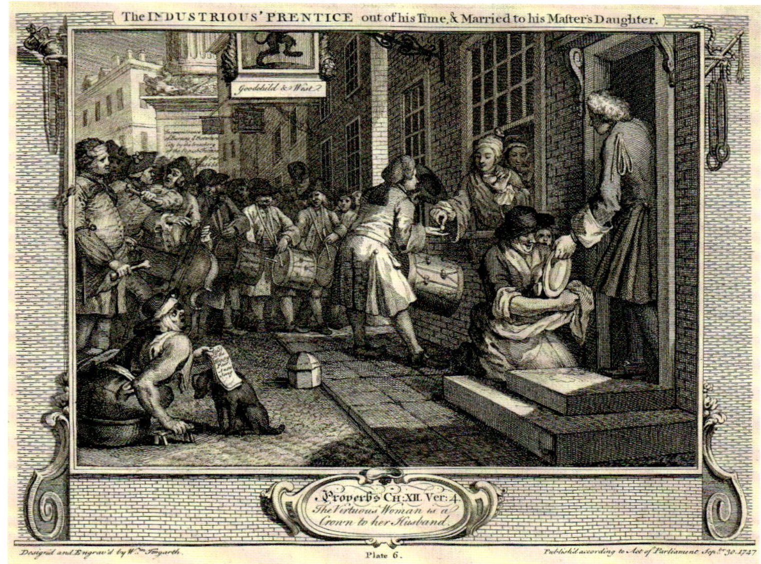

Figure 182. William Hogarth, *Drawing for Plate 6, Industry and Idleness: The Industrious 'Prentice out of his Time, & Married to his Master's Daughter*, *c.* 1746–7, pen and brown ink, and grey and brown wash, over graphite, 21.5 × 29 cm. British Museum, Department of Prints and Drawings, 1896,0710.14. Cat. 257

Figure 183. William Hogarth, *Plate 6, Industry and Idleness: The Industrious 'Prentice out of his Time, & Married to his Master's Daughter*, 1747, etching and engraving, 26.6 × 34.6 cm. British Museum, Department of Prints and Drawings, 1896,0710.15. Cat. 258

> great labour; and yet he, of all men that ever lived might make the greatest pretensions to the efficacy of native genius and inspiration. I have no doubt that he would have thought it no disgrace, that it should be said of him, as he himself said of Raffaelle, that he did not possess his art from nature, but by long study. He was conscious that the great excellence to which he arrived was gained by dint of labour, and was unwilling to have it thought that any transcendent skill, however natural its effect might seem, could be purchased at a cheaper price than he had paid for it.[41]

While Reynolds counselled young artists again and again that, whatever genius they might possess, labour was nonetheless necessary, Walpole emphasized that female geniuses laboured not at all.

Furthermore, when evaluating the work of Reynolds himself, Walpole could separate the accomplishments of labour from the charms of the effect. He commissioned Reynolds to paint several portraits of friends and family, all of which tend towards the less affected range of the artist's stylistic range. Two of these, the *Out of Town Party, or A Conversation* (Fig. 144), which depicts his close schoolboy friends Richard Edgcumbe, George Augustus Selwyn and George Williams, and *The Ladies Waldegrave* (Fig 180), which depicts his three great-nieces, Maria, Laura and Horatia, hung prominently in the Refectory at Strawberry Hill. Ironically, Walpole noted the lack of finish (i.e., meticulous labour) in some of Reynolds's portraits. Following a comment on the 'abominably bad' head and hands of a portrait of Lord Richard Cavendish (1780; Devonshire Collections, Chatsworth) that he had lately seen, Walpole wrote of *The Ladies Waldegrave*, that 'though the effect of the whole is charming, the details are slovenly, the faces only red and white'.[42]

Walpole's preference for charming effect over laboured and meticulous execution apparently extended to his patronage of professional portrait artists, as well as that of female geniuses. In both cases, Walpole clearly identified an elusive but essential capacity for expression that he deemed quite separate and distinct from the manual skill achieved through laborious practice, and he sought this expressive quality in modern English artists both professional and amateur, male and female. While the 'original genius' of Beauclerk's drawings for *The Mysterious Mother* epitomized this virtue, Walpole identified this talent in others as well. In particular, he valued highly the art of William Hogarth and described him in almost identical terms as 'a class by himself that great and original genius', despite a seemingly contradictory judgment that 'as a painter, he had but slender merit'.[43] Walpole's own collection included a number of paintings, drawings and prints by Hogarth, including the *Portrait of Sarah Malcolm* (Fig. 18[illegible]), which hung in the Green Closet at Strawberry Hill. The artist also featured prominently in *Anecdotes of Painting* with a dedicated chapter separate from the 'herd of painters in oil'. This chapter also included a catalogue of his work, the only such list of an artist's work in the publication. Notably, Hogarth, like Walpole, was a staunch advocate of English over continental art and distanced himself quite deliberately from the Royal Academy. Hogarth's best achievements, according to Walpole, were independent of adherence to prescribed models. Rather, Walpole asserted repeatedly that, with an 'intimate intuition', the artist 'drew his stores from nature and the force of his own genius, and was indebted neither to models nor books for his style', adding that Hogarth 'could not bend his talents to think after any body else'.[44] Likewise, the amateur artist William Henry Bunbury, dubbed by Walpole 'the second Hogarth', had 'more humour when he invents than when he illustrates', probably, Walpole explained, because 'genius can draw from the sources of nature with more spirit than from the ideas of another'.[45]

The debate on female genius makes women artists the natural subject of this related argument over the merit and necessity of effort. The author Laetitia Hawkins, for example, contrasted the peculiar properties of female genius found in the 'lighter regions of fancy' with the masculine tendency for exertion. She explained:

> In general, and almost universally, the feminine intellect has less strength but more acuteness; consequently, in our exercise of it, we show less perseverance and more vivacity. We are not formed for those deep investigations that tend to the bringing into light reluctant truth; but when once she has appeared, when vera incessu patuit Dea, then it is within the female province to give her spirit and decoration, which the less flexible and less volatile male mind would fail in attempting.[46]

Hawkins's identification of female genius as one achieved without the exertion or labour of male genius echoes Walpole's contrast of the ease of execution by female artists with the arduous labour advocated by Reynolds as the voice of the Academy.

Walpole's thoughts on female genius enjoyed some currency among his circle of friends, correspondents and visitors to Strawberry Hill. Sir William Hamilton agreed with Walpole on the merits of Anne Damer, describing her in a letter to his friend as 'the cleverest creature in the world next to Lady Di'.[47] A verse entitled 'Lines Sent to Mr. Walpole by an Anonymous Author, After Visiting the Curiosities at Strawberry Hill, 1790' not surprisingly shares Walpole's enthusiasm for the female geniuses.[48] The three-page pamphlet written by Lady Burrell gives considerable space and attention to the work of Anne Damer, Diana Beauclerk and Lady Lucan. They are indeed the only artists listed by name other than as comparison with these three women.

In conclusion, Walpole mobilized the irony of a clear and possibly deliberate disjunction between the non-professional accomplishments of a female genius like Diana Beauclerk and the celebrity he assigned to her. This glaring contradiction functioned effectively to support Walpole's counter-academic narrative about the history of art in England and the patronage of modern English art. By so dramatically asserting his right to 'patronize' female amateur artists, display and celebrate works of art by them that are clearly outside the purview of the Royal Academy, Walpole in effect defended himself and, by extension, the English aristocrat more generally against disparaging comments on the failure of national patronage by academic-minded artists and critics committed to the reformation of national taste and the promotion of history subjects. In his collection and display at Strawberry Hill, Walpole favoured narrative, intuitive expression and association over intrinsic aesthetic quality, and his high commitment to the art of Diana Beauclerk and her fellow female geniuses became the culmination of a masterfully orchestrated institutional critique of the Royal Academy. His concerted effort to promote this work and to display it in the domestic realm of his own home attested to his commitment to establish an alternative 'academy' of English art and validated his own choices as collector and patron.

1. Andrew Elfenbein, *Romantic Genius: The Prehistory of a Homosexual Role* (New York: Columbia University Press, 1999), 91.
2. Peter Sabor, 'A Treasure House in Farmington: The Lewis Walpole Library. Exhibition Review', *Eighteenth-Century Studies* 33.3 (2000): 454–6.
3. Kim Sloan, '*A Noble Art': Amateur Artists and Drawing Masters, c. 1600–1800* (London: British Museum Press, 2000), 216.
4. Suggested by Stephen Bann at a workshop for authors contributing to this publication, July 2007.
5. Robert Wark, 'Introduction', in Joshua Reynolds, *Discourses on Art*, ed. Robert Wark (New Haven and London: Yale University Press, 1975), xvi.
6. Sloan, '*A Noble Art*', 7; *Oxford English Dictionary*, s.v. 'Amateur', http://dictionary.oed.com/.
7. On Lady Diana Beauclerk see Carola Hicks, *Improper Pursuits: The Scandalous Life of Lady Di Beauclerk* (New York: St. Martin's Press, 2002); Beatrice Erskine, *Lady Diana Beauclerk: Her Life and Work* (London: T. F. Unwin, 1903); and Virginia Surtees, 'Beauclerk, Lady Diana', *Oxford Dictonary of National Biography* (Oxford University Press, 2004–8), http://www.oxforddnb.com/view/article/1848?docPos=4&_fromAuth=1.
8. Christine Battersby, *Gender and Genius: Toward a Feminist Aesthetic* (London: The Women's Press, 1989).
9. Ann Bermingham, *Learning to Draw: Studies in the Cultural History of a Polite and Useful Art* (New Haven and London: Yale University Press, 2000), 128.
10. William Vaughan, *British Painting: The Golden Age from Hogarth to Turner* (London: Thames and Hudson, 1999), 98.
11. See Morris R. Brownell, *The Prime Minister of Taste: A Portrait of Horace Walpole* (New Haven and London: Yale University Press, 2001), Part II: 'A Little Castle Adorned with Portraits', 93–145. On Walpole as a collector of miniature paintings see the essay in this volume by Katharine Coombs, pp. 183–200.
12. 'Works of Genius', bound in *D 1774* (extra-illustrated copy, LWL 49 3523, 121.12).
13. 'Principal Curiosities', bound in *D 1774* (extra-illustrated copy, LWL 49 3523, 121.12). See Appendix 2, pp. 343–7.
14. *HW Corres.* 28: 244.
15. *HW Corres.* 24: 524.
16. *Works* 2: 503–4.
17. *1842 Sale*, day 17, lot 30, 172.
18. From an inscription on an engraved brass plaque mounted on the interior door of the cabinet.
19. 'Advertisment', *Works* 2: 400.
20. Autograph letter, Lady Diana Beauclerk from Richmond (LWL).
21. *1842 Sale*, day 11, lot 108, 120.
22. 'Advertisment', *Works* 2: 400.
23. *Works* 2: 400.
24. *Works* 2: 400.
25. Alison Yarrington, 'The Female Pygmalion: Anne Seymour Damer, Allan Cunningham and the writing of a woman sculptor's life', *The Sculpture Journal* 1 (1997): 32–44.
26. Yarrington, 'Female Pygmalion', 32.
27. *Works* 2: 400.
28. *HW Corres.* 35: 385.
29. *HW Corres.* 28: 244.
30. *Works* 2: 445.
31. Wark, 'Introduction', xxvii.
32. Henry Peacham, *The Art of Drawing with Pen, and Liming in Watercolor* … (London, 1606).
33. Peacham, *The Art of Drawing*, 'To the Reader', n.p.
34. Horace Walpole's Royal Academy of Arts Collection of Catalogues, 1769–95, from the library of Earl of Roseberry. Photocopies: the Lewis Walpole Library, Yale University. Hazen, 3885.
35. Yarrington, 'Female Pygmalion', 33–4.
36. *HW Corres.* 25: 611.
37. Printed by Strawberry Hill Press, 1775, and reprinted in A.T. Hazen, *A Bibliography of the Strawberry Hill Press* (New Haven: Yale University Press, 1942), 216.
38. Quoted in Wark, 'Introduction', 278.
39. Quoted in Wark, 'Introduction', 280–81.
40. *HW Corres.* 29: 284.
41. Sir Joshua Reynolds, *Discourses on Art*, ed. Robert Wark (New Haven and London: Yale University Press, 1975), Discourse XV, 280–81.
42. *HW Corres.* 29: 285.
43. *Works* 2: 453 and 458.
44. *Works* 2: 455.
45. *Works* 2: 400.
46. Laetitia Matilda Hawkins, *Letters on the Female Mind, Its Powers and Pursuits* (London: Printed for Hookham and Carpenter, 1793), 6–7. My appreciation to Ruth Mack for referring me to this text by Hawkins.
47. *HW Corres.* 35: 438.
48. [Lady Burrell,] *Lines Sent to Mr. Walpole, by an Anonymous Author, After Visiting the Curiosities at Strawberry Hill, 1790* (St Albin, Newport, Isle of Wight, 1791). Twelve copies were printed at Strawberry Hill by Bull.

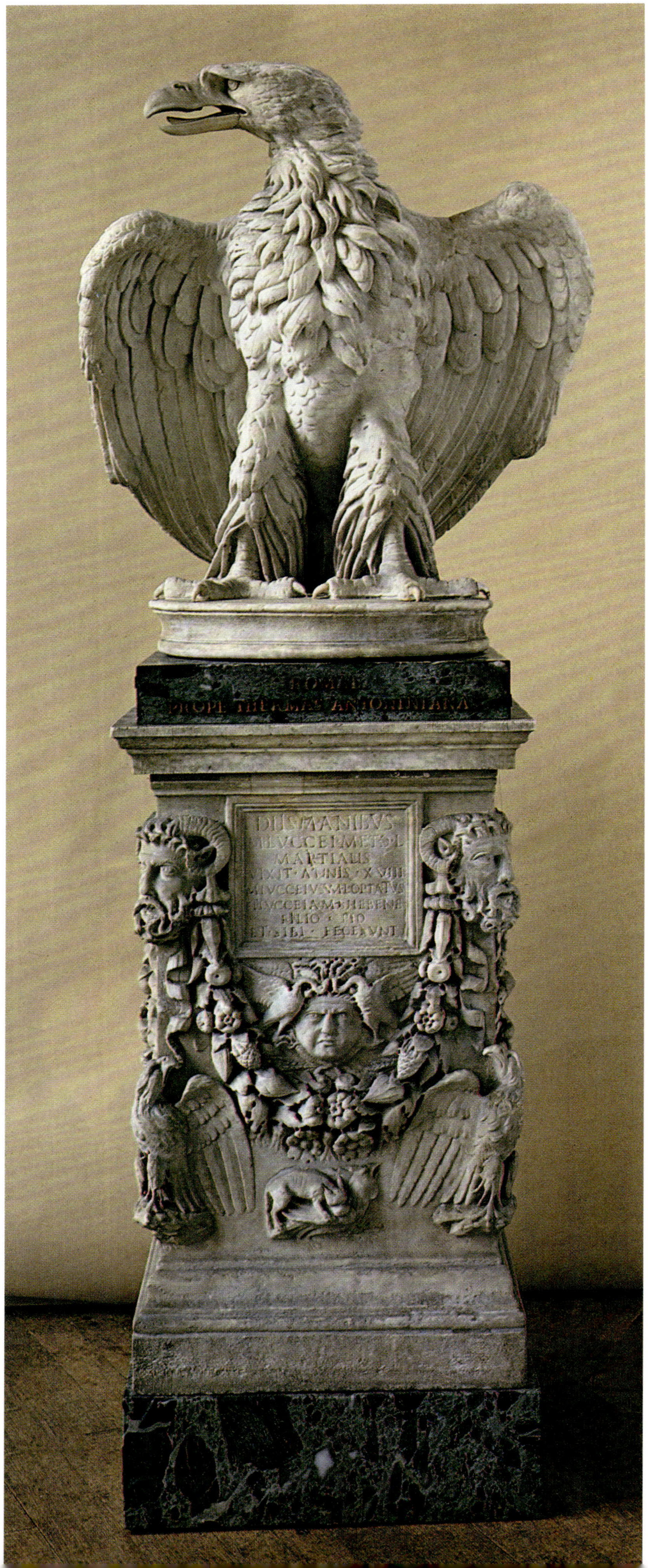

Figure 184. *Eagle*, on altar base, Roman, 1st century A.D., marble, H 77.5 cm. Earl of Wemyss and March, Gosford House, East Lothian. Cat. 138

10.

HORACE WALPOLE: ANTIQUARIAN OF HIS TIME

IRÈNE AGHION

Although Horace Walpole's collection of classical objects was never considered of pre-eminent importance, his interest in antiquity was undeniable. As a collector, Walpole conducted himself from the outset like a true connoisseur, and his aim was never merely to establish impressive displays of major works of antique art, marbles or other prestigious monuments. He belonged to a generation of antiquarians for whom collecting could no longer be considered an end in itself, who looked beyond antiquity's grand monuments of public and princely art and sought out more modest artefacts as sources for understanding the daily life of the ancients.

This new approach was exemplified by the Comte de Caylus, one of the most influential personalities in the art world of his day.[1] A frequent guest in the Paris *hôtel* of the financier Pierre Crozat, where a kind of utopian community of the arts regularly gathered, Caylus was also in contact with the artists Jean-Antoine Watteau and Rosalba Carriera, and particularly with Pierre-Jean Mariette, another collector with whom he collaborated on a number of projects. From 1731 Caylus became increasingly fascinated with antiquity and in 1742 he established a prize to be awarded by the Académie des Inscriptions et Belles-Lettres for work on the customs and traditions of the ancients that took into account both textual and material sources. Fuelled by his passion for collecting, Caylus set out his scholarly ambitions in his *Recueil d'Antiquités*,[2] in which he classified and interpreted his collection of some 2,300 antique objects, comparing them to many more. In his analyses he employed empirical, experimental and visual methods that allowed him to determine the style, age and origin of each artefact. Ancient texts thus served as complementary sources of information but were no longer accorded supremacy over monuments or artefacts. He called for the establishment of rules for geographical and chronological classification. Rather than considering the object from a purely aesthetic perspective, he championed experimental methods and, in doing so, laid down the scientific foundations of modern archaeology by comparing antiquarian practice with that of the physicist.[3]

Like so many of his contemporaries, Horace Walpole was greatly influenced by Caylus's work. Coincidence brought Walpole to Paris on the day of the scholar's death, allowing him to pay his last respects.[4] The two men never actually met, though much would have drawn them together: both were sociable, enjoying and seeking out good company, and they also shared a taste for experimentation, for the arts, and for printing and publishing techniques. Walpole bought about twenty objects at the public auction of Caylus's collection. Moreover, Walpole's Parisian friends belonged to the same circles as those of Caylus. One mutual friend was the Abbé Jean-Jacques Barthélemy; in Walpole's Library we find a carefully annotated, elegant first edition in quarto of the Abbé's famous *Voyage du jeune Anacharsis*.[5] Barthélemy was recognized by his contemporaries as one of the greatest scholars of the eighteenth century. An antiquarian, numismatist, scholar of inscriptions, writer and

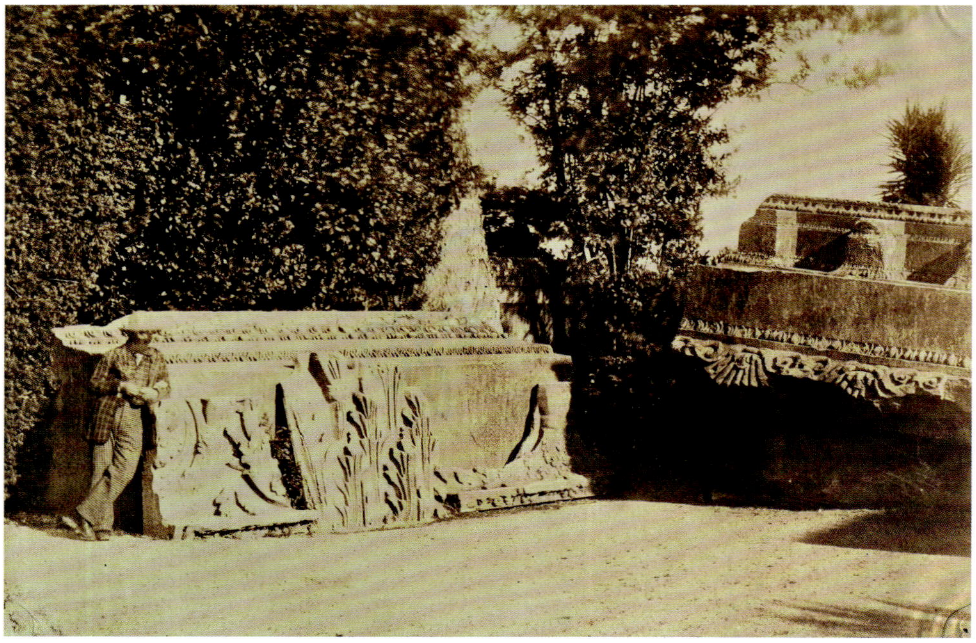

Figure 185. Giacomo Caneva, *Ruins of the Temple of the Sun (Serapis) in the Villa Colonna, Rome, c.* 1832. Fratelli Alinari Museum of the History of Photography, Florence

keeper of the King's Cabinet, he was an ardent student of modern and ancient languages. By deciphering for the first time ancient Phoenician and Palmyran texts, he paved the way for J.F. Champollion, who deciphered Egyptian hieroglyphs on the Rosetta Stone. An intimate friend of Madame Du Deffand and of Madame de Choiseul, Barthélemy introduced Walpole into Paris's most cultivated circles.[6]

Walpole was also in regular contact with Pierre-Jean Mariette,[7] whom he greatly admired. Mariette's translation of Walpole's *Anecdotes of Painting in England* straight from the press demonstrates that he was far from indifferent to Walpole's work. Similarly, Walpole was most certainly influenced by Mariette's commentary published in the *Recueil d'Estampes du Cabinet du Roi*.[8] Leaving aside the traditional focus on subject matter, he studied each painter's individual style, an altogether exceptional approach for a catalogue of the time. This method obviously inspired the *Ædes Walpolianae*, written after Walpole's return from Italy in 1741. In the complete catalogue of his father's paintings in Houghton Hall, Walpole not only commented on iconographical aspects, but also tried to identify different schools of painting.[9]

DISCOVERING ANTIQUITY

Horace Walpole and his friend, the poet Thomas Gray, set off on the Grand Tour in March 1739. They spent just over a year travelling, first through France and Switzerland, then visiting all the major towns in Italy before settling in the home of Horace Mann in Florence from July 1740 to May 1741. Walpole's letters from Italy document his growing awareness of antiquity and his interest in objects, sites and the difficulty of conserving them. He developed this passion by visiting archaeological excavations and collections and making many new friends and acquaintances who prompted him into making acquisitions of his own.

One day, while wandering through the Colonna gardens west of the Baths of Constantine in Rome, Walpole and Gray stumbled upon the ruins of a temple built by the Emperor Caracalla (r. AD 211–17) and dedicated to the Egyptian god Serapis (Fig. 185). The two explorers were stunned by the sheer size of the architectural remains: Walpole wrote to Richard West, 'Gray and I discovered a considerable curiosity lately, in an unfrequented quarter of the Colonna garden lie two immense fragments of marble, formerly part of a frieze to some building.'[10] Even today, they remain the largest architectural fragments to be seen in the city.[11] In the same letter to West, Walpole expressed his concern for Rome's ancient monuments, the destruction of which had also shocked the director of the French Academy in Rome a century earlier. Matthieu de La Teulière, writing to the Marquis de Villacerf, Surintendant des Bâtiments du Roi, on 30 June 1693, had likewise condemned the destruction of Rome's ruins, which were simply being sold as building material for new constructions.

La Teulière reported:

> It is absolutely necessary to go and study new sites as soon as they are discovered, as they may, from one day to the next, be ruthlessly destroyed for the simple profit of the price of bricks. Such is the barbarity of today's Romans; meanwhile the colours of the frescoes exposed to the open air are eaten away.[12]

Walpole concurred:

> By the remains one sees of the Roman grandeur in their structures, 'tis evident that there must have been more pains taken to destroy those piles than to raise them. They are more

> demolished than any time or chance could have effected. I am persuaded that in an hundred years Rome will not be worth seeing; 'tis less so now than one could believe.[13]

When he visited Naples and the site of Herculaneum a month later, Walpole was overwhelmed by what he saw, so much so that he left a very lively description of the history of the discoveries and the subsequent excavations made on the site. Expressing astonishment at finding whole houses preserved underground, he gave a summary of the discoveries made there and he also provided detailed descriptions of the architecture, interior decoration and planning. Walpole appreciated that the site as a whole had the potential to provide an important history lesson. He recognized the exceptional nature of the situation: the possibility of studying an entire town, undisturbed since its burial, was a unique opportunity for scholars. The excavation should be carried out by a conscientious scholar, who would keep a systematic record of everything revealed. Walpole knew that the digs organized in Herculaneum by Roque Joaquín de Alcubierre, a Spanish military engineer,[14] were being carried out in the same cavalier spirit that had already caused the plundering of so many of Rome's ruins. He was far from alone in voicing criticism; some of the leading antiquarians of the time, including Caylus and Scipione Maffei in Verona, shared his point of view. Maffei especially deplored the stupidity of the tunnel excavation system, which necessitated, for example, the cutting of mural paintings into pieces in order to extract them. This method, along with others just as damaging, could have been avoided by surface digging.[15] Additionally, objects were thoughtlessly sorted and many simply discarded. After a series of visits (in 1758, 1762, 1764 and 1767) to the Portici Museum where the discoveries from Herculaneum were displayed, the German art historian Johann Joachim Winckelmann, who was secretary to Cardinal Albani at the time, also attacked Alcubierre's methods. His writings on the subject were well known in England thanks to an anonymous translation of the *Sendschreiben von den Herculanischen Entdeckungen*,[16] taken not from the original but from Caylus's French version of the text.[17] Winckelmann vigorously questioned Alcubierre's capacity to head such a complex undertaking, illustrating his point with anecdotes of his blatant incompetence. An example was the destruction of an inscription in bronze that had been found on the wall of a public building:

> [Alcubierre] ordered these letters to be torn from the wall, without first taking a copy of them, and thrown pell-mell into a basket; and then presented them, in that condition, to the king. They were afterwards exposed for many years in the cabinet, where everyone was at liberty to put them together as he pleased. Some imagined, they made these two words, IMP.AUG.[18]

COLLECTING ANTIQUITY

Any attempt to examine Walpole's collection of antiquities in detail is destined to encounter a number of difficulties. Although quite well documented as a whole, most of the individual objects in the collection remain hard to locate. Walpole as a collector of antiquities has received little attention, and so when his objects were dispersed, their provenance was mostly lost or forgotten. His name is not mentioned in connection with objects discussed in recent publications of major English collections or more specific typological studies dealing with Roman portraits, funerary urns or other classes of objects that we know Walpole possessed.[19]

Horace Walpole began acquiring antiquities in Italy at public auctions, often with the help of Horace Mann, and he continued to do so after his return to England. While in Italy, Walpole kept abreast of current events: a letter dated 7 May 1740 shows that he had advance knowledge of the dispersal of Rome's most prestigious collections including those of Francesco Barberini and of Cardinal Pietro Ottoboni.[20]

In October of the same year, in a letter from Florence addressed to Richard West, he wrote that he had only bought a few small things.[21] However, he mentioned with some pride the acquisition of a bust of Vespasian at the Ottoboni auction: '"Tis the famous Vespasian in touchstone reckoned the best in Rome except the Caracalla of the Farnese.'[22] After the sale of Walpole's collection the bust seems to have changed hands several times and was described for the last time in Christie's catalogue of Lord Revelstoke's sale in 1893:[23] 'An

Antique bust of the Emperor Vespasian of black basalt with drapery of oriental alabaster. On socle and pedestal of variously coloured marbles.' It has yet to be located.

In her catalogue of the Ince Blundell collection of Roman portraits,[24] Jane Fejfer points out that the question of the antique or Renaissance origins of the Vitellius-Grimani bust of Vespasian in Venice[25] and the Caracalla Farnese one, which Walpole had specifically referred to as a point of comparison for the quality of his recent acquisition, is still a matter of debate. The complete catalogue of all Flavian portraits in public and private collections, drawn up by German archaeologists in 1966, does not identify the bust in question.[26] It also judiciously reminds us that the use of dark stone indicates a Renaissance origin, as in Roman times portraits of emperors were normally crafted in white material.

The marble eagle that so majestically decorated the gallery at Strawberry Hill is a happy exception in the largely fruitless quest for Horace Walpole's antiquities (Fig. 184). Supposedly found resting on an inscribed funerary altar in the Roman gardens of Boccapadugli near the Baths of Caracalla in 1742, the sculpture exudes an impression of great strength through its height of over 80 cm and the quality of its workmanship.[27] Dating from the first century AD, it may well have been conceived as an attribute of a monumental Jupiter rather than as an isolated animal figure. Having been brought to the attention of Horace Mann by John Chute, Walpole acquired both the eagle and the altar in 1745, and today they are in the collection of Earl of Wemyss at Gosford.[28]

Mann first mentioned the possibility of acquiring the piece on 13 July 1745. Cardinal Alessandro Albani was also a potential buyer. A hesitant Horace Walpole eventually consented to the transaction. Following routine procedure, Mann had a cast made to allow for a better evaluation of its quality. A few months later, the deal was settled through John Chute for the sum of 200 crowns. The latter wrote jokingly that having the eagle by his side had made him feel like John the Evangelist. When it finally reached its English home, its new owner was immediately smitten: 'It is a glorious fowl! I admire it, and everybody admires it as much as it deserves. There never was so much spirit and fire preserved, with so much labour and finishing. It stands fronting the Vespasian; there are no two such morsels in England!'[29]

Several years later, in 1756, Sir Joshua Reynolds portrayed a pensive Walpole with a book, engraving and quill pen in an altogether scholarly atmosphere. An important element is the engraving of the eagle standing on its Roman pedestal. Walpole commissioned three versions of this painting, one for his London agent, Grosvenor Bedford (1756), one for his brother-in-law Charles Churchill (1756), and a third for his cousin Francis Seymour Conway (1757).[30] Moreover, Walpole ordered prints after the painting for distribution among his friends.[31]

In the Strawberry Hill gallery Jupiter's eagle was displayed on the same wall as the portrait of Vespasian, whose rise to power in 69 BC, crushing the Emperor Vitellius, had all the ingredients of a striking and bloody tale. Roman historians described Vitellius, a fervent admirer of Nero, as vulgar and totally lacking in courage.[32] With the Roman empire in a state of chaos, he fled, dressed as a beggar, after a failed reign of only eight months. His hideout was soon discovered by Vespasian's partisans, who dragged him through the streets of Rome and forced him to witness the mutilation and destruction of his own effigies before he was tortured and thrown into the Tiber.

The troubled times that saw Vespasian's accession after the bloody assassination of Vitellius resonate with the emotional atmosphere of a 'gothic' novel, the genre created by Walpole himself. He referred to Shakespeare's *Titus Andronicus* as a source of inspiration for his own play *The Mysterious Mother* (1768). In the preface to the French edition of Walpole's play, René de Ceccatty observes that 'the political drama *Titus Andronicus* inspired by Rome's history portrays "real Goths", the ones who gave their name to the "gothic" novel, those bloody barbarians and their heads, hands and chopped-off tongues, slit throats and chunks of human flesh'.[33]

Horace Walpole displayed a series of antique and Renaissance busts of other emperors and empresses (including Tiberius, Julia Titi, Marcus Aurelius, Domitilla and Faustina) on the tables of his gallery. In aristocratic homes during the second half of the eighteenth century such 'galleries' of Roman portraits did not merely fulfill aesthetic or decorative functions. Owning and displaying a complete series of busts of Roman potentates was a means of relating to a political heritage that members of aristocratic society considered their own. However, the spirit guiding the formation of such collections changed progressively. Portraits were chosen more selectively, with greater care and attention paid to the history and quality of the pieces and in particular to the history of each figure.

But there is more to understanding Walpole's interest in collecting antiquities. After his return from Italy, in his correspondence with the English theologian and antiquarian Conyers Middleton, we find some very precise indications concerning the acquisitions that he had made during his stay. Their letters are witness to the respect and the high esteem in which Walpole held the venerable academic whose collection of antiques he was to acquire in 1744. Middleton was in the course of preparing the publication of this collection – formed during his own time in Italy between 1723 and 1729 – made up of small bronzes such as statuettes, lamps and objects used in sacrificial rituals or for cooking.

Horace Walpole volunteered whatever information he could garner from, in his words, his own modest acquisitions. In a letter dated 9 April 1743 he describes their arrival in England: 'On opening my boxes, I find what I suspected, that there is little new, or curious enough to deserve your notice.' On this occasion he gave a detailed list of all the small objects it contained: a Diana of Ephesus, an Etruscan mirror, several ex-votos, lamps, a hand of Sabazius, a Fortuna, a sistrum and so on. When Walpole acquired the Middleton collection, the illustrated publication that Middleton had been preparing was already in press and so he received the collection in 1745 with its printed catalogue (Fig. 186).

Objects similar to those mentioned in his list could be found in a number of seventeenth- and eighteenth-century collections. They would have been familiar to Walpole, thanks not only to a short manuscript illustrated with drawings, 'Scritti di varie cose antiche', by Pietro Santi Bartoli, that he later kept in the Glass Closet of his Library (Cat. 85) but also to illustrated books by Giovanni Pietro Bellori and Bartoli that he had bought in Italy (Cat. 86).[34]

Another English collection, formed more out of scientific interest than as a showpiece, was that of Dr Richard Mead, George II's surgeon. Mead had assembled it between 1695 and 1696 during his stay in Italy and visits to Florence, Rome and Naples. It mainly comprised coins and engraved gems but also included some important fragments of antique mural paintings, bronzes and an interesting series of Roman funerary urns that Walpole was to buy at the auction organized two years after the doctor's death in 1753. The quality of the collection is indicated in an entry that the Abbé Barthélemy made in his journal in 1750. He described several Greek and Roman coins in gold and silver that the doctor had given the French King's Cabinet, commenting that there 'were given [in other words, 'exchanged'] for all those precious medals several large bronze medals of very inferior worth'.[35]

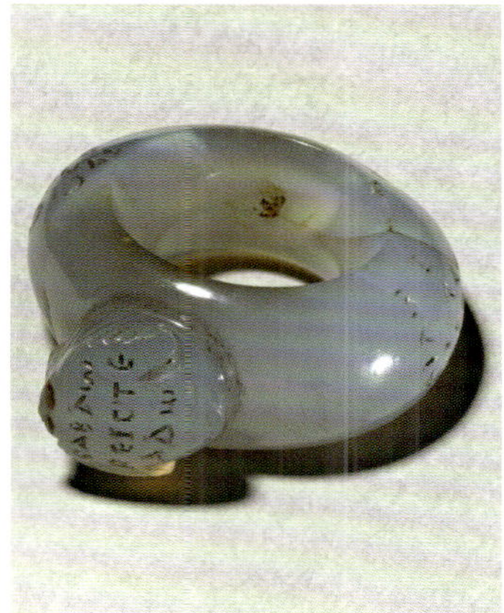

Figure 186. Finger ring (Ornament for a Horse), late Roman, chalcedony, 3.37 × 3.37 cm. British Museum, Department of Prehistory and Europe. 1917,0501.654/OA.10714. Cat. 172

Among Walpole's most cherished possessions was a small bronze head of the Roman Emperor Caligula given to him by Horace Mann. In 1767 Mann wrote to his friend that he was

> proud of having added a mite to your collection. The Caligula was indeed always admired by everybody who saw it, and the great antiquarian of whom I bought it always carried it about in his pocket, wrapped up in cotton and looked at it as often as you now do. The casts of it in gesso are sought after by strangers who have heard of it.[36]

The antiquarian mentioned in the letter was Emmanuel-Maurice of Lorraine, Prince of Elbeuf, who conducted the first excavations at Herculaneum. The prince had built his villa in the Neapolitan countryside on the exact site of the antique city. He began digging in 1714 and, using scaffolding in a nearby well, was able to retrieve marbles, statues and pieces of burnt walls from deep underground.[37] The prince continued to

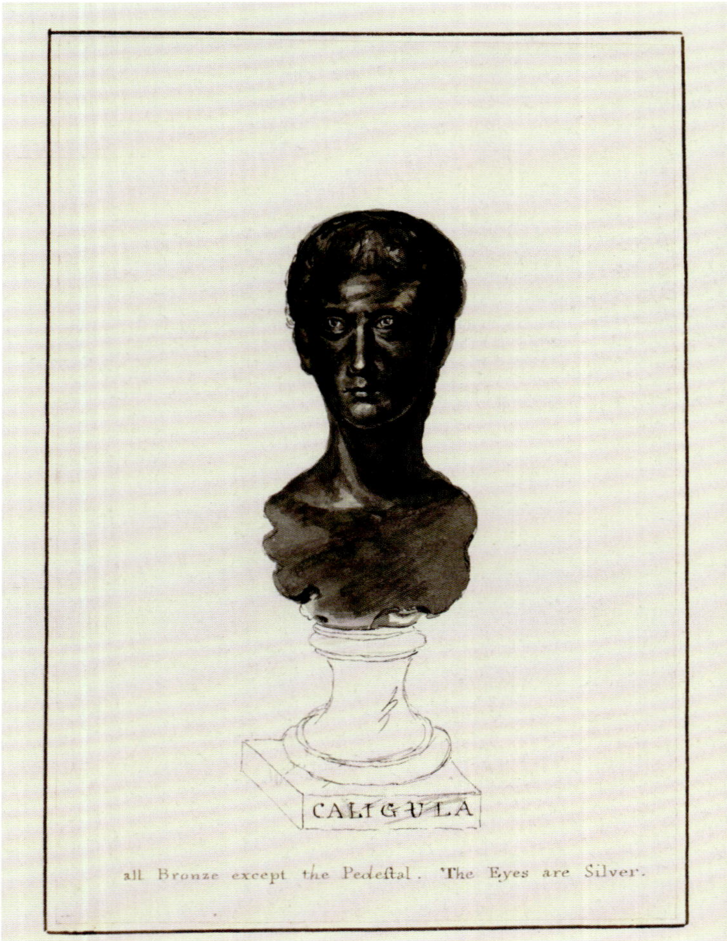

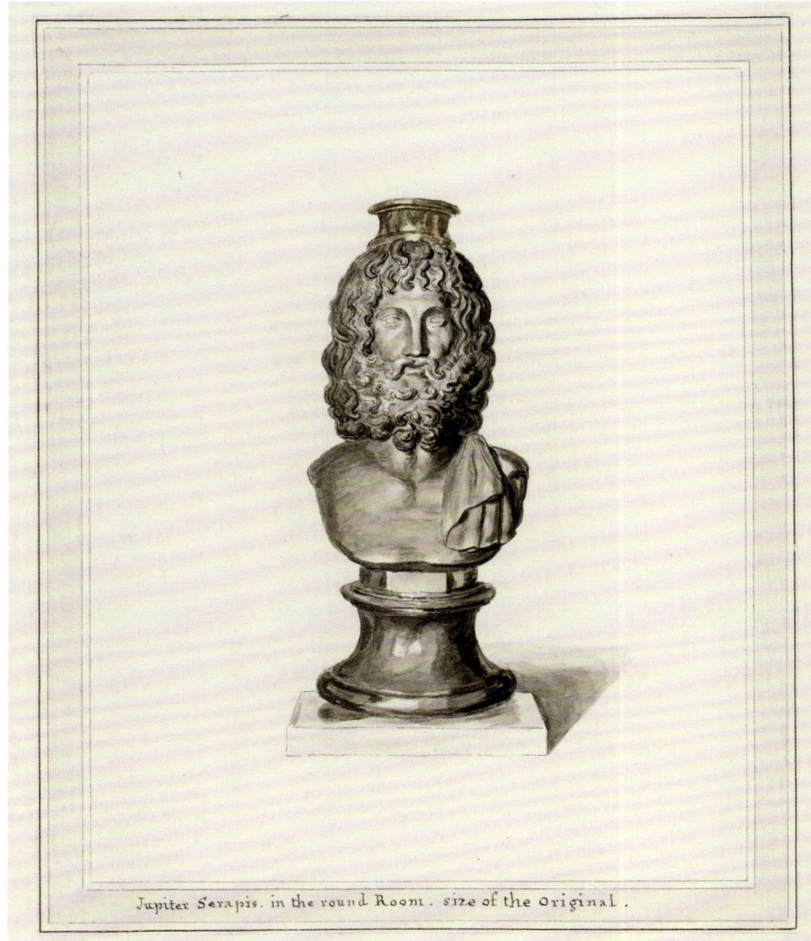

Figure 187. John Carter, *Caligula*, ink and wash, 19.8 × 13.5 cm, mounted, p. 180 of Richard Bull's extra-illustrated copy of the *Description*. The Lewis Walpole Library, Yale University. 33 30 Copy 11

Figure 188. John Carter, *Head of Jupiter Serapis*, ink, wash and watercolour, from Richard Bull's extra-illustrated copy of the *Description*. The Lewis Walpole Library, Yale University. 33 30 Copy 11.

explore the site over the next two years through a system of tunnels leading from the bottom of the well.[38] It was there that he discovered the small bust of Caligula with its exceptionally well-preserved eyes (Fig. 187). A watercolour sketch of the bust made by John Carter at Walpole's request bears an annotation by the artist stating that the eyes are in silver; strangely enough, however, the drawing itself clearly reproduces the pupil, the iris and the white of the eye, suggesting that the eyes, still in place, were made of the more usual bone. We can therefore still consider as highly probable the prestigious provenance implied by Mann's letter, since heads with their original eyes still in place are quite rare outside those uncovered at Herculanaeum and Pompei. But here again the location of the piece escapes us: none of the five small bronzes listed by Dietrich Boschung in his complete catalogue of all the identifiable busts of Caligula quite fits the description.[39] Only one is without a breastplate, or *paludamentum*. It can be traced back to the collection of the famous English chemist and archaeologist Sir Robert Ludwig Mond, from where it entered the Metropolitan Museum in New York in 1929. It does indeed bear a close resemblance to John Carter's watercolour, but differing details in the outline of the bust mean that it cannot be identified with any certainty as the one owned by Walpole.

Walpole also listed a bust of Jupiter Serapis (Fig. 188) among his 'Principal Curiosities', again known to us only thanks to one of John Carter's watercolours. This piece had been acquired by the Duchess of Portland in 1784 from Sir William Hamilton on his return from Naples at the same time as a number of other antiquities, most notably the Portland Vase, today in the British Museum. When the duchess's collection was sold a year after her death, Walpole bought the head, described as a 4-inch high Serapis in green basalt, originally from the Barberini Cabinet.

EXPERIMENTING WITH ENCAUSTIC PAINTING

Walpole, who had a great interest in drawing and painting techniques and was himself quite proficient in both, contributed enthusiastically to the rediscovery of the art of encaustic painting. The exact definition of encaustic painting has always been to some extent shrouded in mystery: not only have the ancient texts failed to provide us with anything like a recipe for the procedure, but more importantly none of the works of the ancient Greek masters like Zeuxis or Apelles mentioned in the texts have survived. For want of more precise information, it is difficult to understand why this technique was so highly valued. The word itself derives from the Greek *enkaustikos* meaning literally 'to burn from within' and was made familiar as a technique through the writings of Pliny the Elder.[40] He states that the origins of the technique are unknown, although he writes that some have credited the Greek painter Aristeides, who worked in Thebes in the fourth century BC, with its invention; Praxiteles supposedly perfected the procedure at the end of the same century. Pliny explains how the dry pigments were combined with beeswax until a paint-like mixture was obtained that could then be applied with a brush. Once painted, the picture was exposed to fire, causing the pigments to penetrate the backing in reaction to the heat and become permanently fixed.

During the eighteenth century many European artists turned to antiquity in search of new models, methods and solutions for technical problems such as the darkening of colours due to the use of fixing agents. Interest in ancient civilizations had of course been stirred by the spectacular discoveries made at Herculaneum in 1738 and Pompeii a decade later. Fascination was further fuelled by the bright and lively colours of the fragments of mural painting that travellers brought home with them from their visits to the sites. The Comte de Caylus quickly became the most famous and active protagonist in this revival of interest in encaustic painting methods.[41]

Caylus suggested the possibility of recreating the procedure by following Pliny the Elder's description in a presentation made at the Académie des Inscriptions et Belles-Lettres in 1752 under the title 'Éclaircissements sur quelques passages de Pline qui concernent les Arts' (Fig. 189). With the help of the doctor and chemist Majault and the young painter Joseph-Marie Vien, Caylus attempted to translate the classical author's rather sketchy instructions into a workable method for painting with wax. By taking on such a challenge, he wanted to prove the excellence of ancient knowledge, but he also hoped to find a new technique offering perfect preservation of colour over time that would be incomparably superior to oil painting.

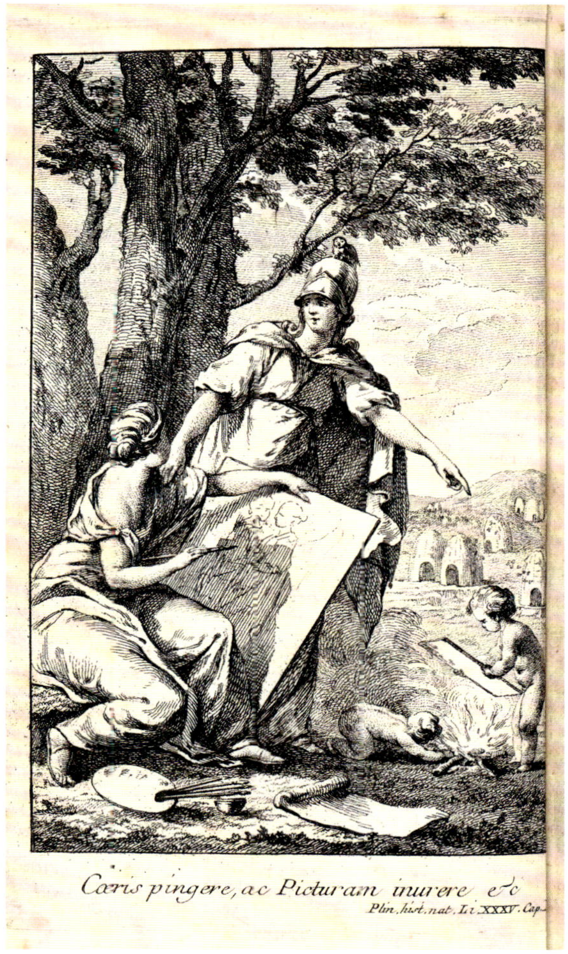

Figure 189. *Coeris pingere, ac Picturam inurere* ('Minerva shows a painter how to use bees' wax for painting'), frontispiece of Anne Claude Philippe, comte de Caylus, *Mémoire sur la peinture à l'encaustique et sur la peinture à la cire* (Geneva; Paris: Pissot, 1755). Yale University

Getting the proportions right was the main difficulty, and as wax tends to harden very quickly, it was necessary to find a means of maintaining a temperature at which the mixture of wax and pigments was fluid enough to be easily applied with a paint brush and not to hinder the artist's creativity. To achieve this, Caylus enhanced his mixture by adding turpentine, which had the advantage of being cheap and easy to find. Every colour required a specific balance of pigment and wax, which meant that a table of proportions needed to be established in order to guarantee correct mixing. The Count also developed a special stone for grinding the colours and decided that wood panels were better suited than canvas for such a technique. But wood required special preparation in order for the colours to adhere to the surface: it had to be rubbed down with white wax until the panel was fully impregnated. A specially heated palette kept the coloured wax easy to use and apply. Once the painting was finished it was placed in front of a fire, and the white background then melted into the colours. This melting process gave the colours their particular luminosity.

According to the Count, this new technique did away with problems of peeling or cracked paint, eliminating any danger of damage from sunlight or heat. Pictures would remain unalterable.[42] His experiments culminated in a small work in encaustic paint representing the head of Minerva executed by Joseph-Marie Vien.[43] It was first presented at the Academy in 1754 and then at the Paris Salon in 1755, where it was greeted with resounding enthusiasm.

In May 1756, during a meeting of the Royal Society of Arts in London, the doctor and antiquarian James Parsons read out a letter from Abbé Mazeas describing Caylus's methods and his experiments with encaustic painting. Reports of the session were made in publications such as the *Gentleman's Magazine* and *Philosophical Transactions*,[44] and several attempts to duplicate the process were made. We know of the 'IX Experiments' subsequently carried out by Josiah Colebrooke from a letter he wrote to the Earl of Macclesfield, president of the Royal Society, in 1759. Some weeks later he presented to his colleagues from the Royal Society an example of an encaustic painting executed on paper by another member of the society, the naturalist and illustrator George Edwards. It represented a bird 'on paper prepared with a ground of whitening and fish-glew, painted with water colours, and then the wax burned in', and Colebrooke claimed: 'This will roll up as easily as common paper, without cracking the varnish.' It was published again a few years later in *The Annual Register of History, Politicks and Literature*.[45]

In the meantime Walpole had employed a Swiss painter, Johann Heinrich Müntz, to carry out a series of experiments testing the new technique. On 9 September 1758 Walpole wrote to Mann:

> I have a painter in the house, who is an engraver too, a mechanic, an everything ... We are just now, practicing and have succeeded surprisingly in a new method of painting, discovered at Paris by Count Caylus, and intended to be the encaustic method of the ancients. My Swiss has painted, I am writing the account, and my press is to notify our improvements.[46]

Evidently Walpole planned to take over the more theoretical task of recording the results attained by these experiments in a memoir. But things did not go as projected and just a few months later he let Müntz go, writing in his 'Short Notes': 'I dismissed Mr Müntz for very impertinent behaviour; and upon his leaving me, laid aside the intention of publishing the account of the new encaustic.'[47] Müntz had in fact left with the accounts of the different experiments that they had made, and in 1760 he published their work in his own name under the title, 'Encaustic or Count Caylus's Method of Painting in the Manner of the Ancients'. He explained how he had imitated the procedures described by Caylus in order to ascertain which stages should be respected and how they might be perfected. Müntz had been particularly attentive to questions of colour fixation. He experimented with variations in temperature and moisture to show whether colours did indeed gain in stability compared to oils as they aged. Müntz's treatise became very popular, so much so that from 1767 onwards it could be found on sale in an unauthorized small-format version.[48]

During his stay at Strawberry Hill Müntz himself executed at least two landscapes in encaustic. One is described in the catalogue of the Strawberry Hill auction: 'The picture is painted in encaustic which this celebrated master improved from Count Caylus's rules.' Unfortunately both pictures are now lost (Fig. 190).

Walpole was so taken with the technique that he made several references to it in his letters, even after the departure of Müntz. On 14 April 1777 the Rev. William Mason wrote to tell him of a friend who had made great progress, attaining near perfect results in his experiments with encaustic painting by carefully studying fragments of text from Pliny. Though clearly somewhat disenchanted, Walpole immediately responded:

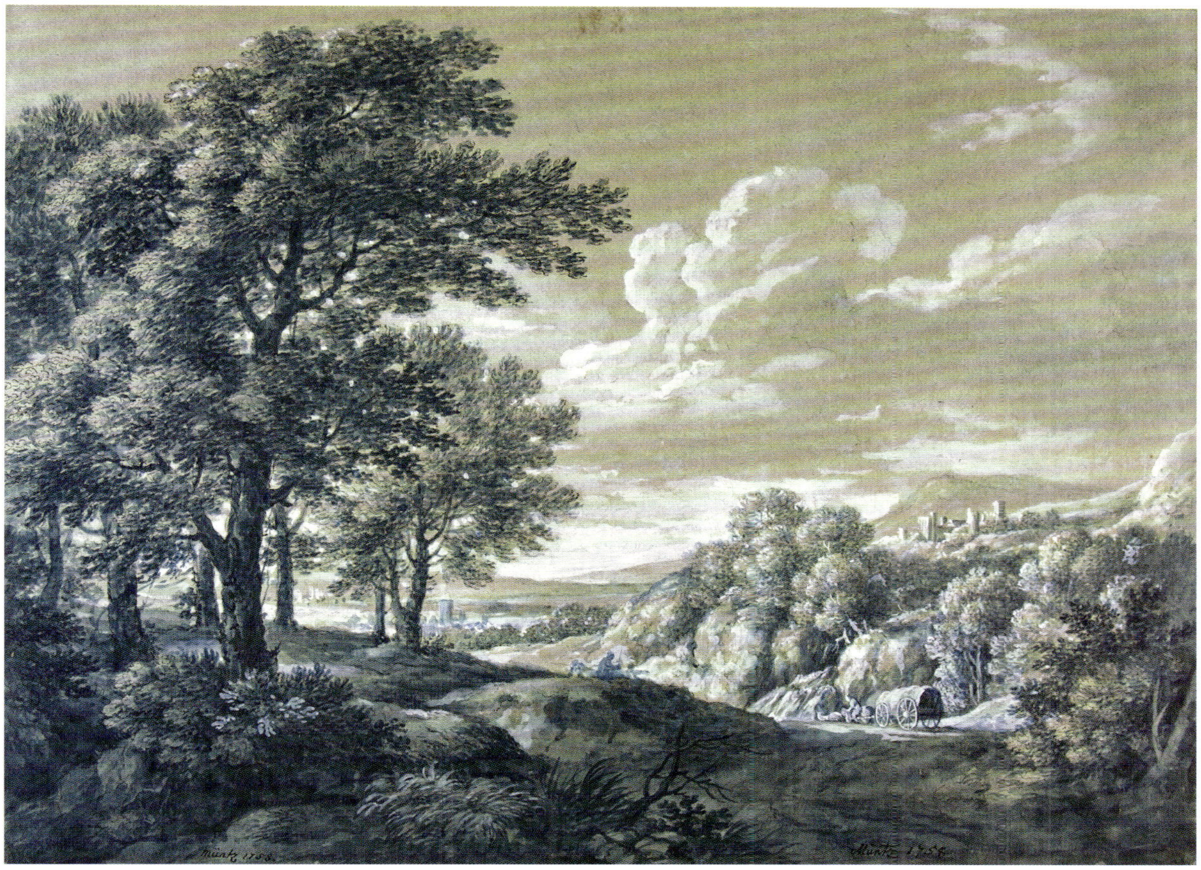

Figure 190. Johann Heinrich Müntz, *Preparatory drawing for a landscape in encaustic*, 1758, watercolour. Preparatory drawing for an encaustic landscape in the Gallery of Strawberry Hill. Eton College (Storer Collection)

> It is easy to me to believe your friend's discoveries in encaustic. Müntz went far enough to prove the facility, use and durability, but not far enough to get the method adopted; not from any defect or difficulty in the practice, but from the stupidity and obstinacy and John-trot-plodding-in-the-same-wayness of the professors. If you think, because it talks more of the arts, that the age is grown more sensible and docile, I shall not agree with you.[49]

Notwithstanding such expressions of frustration, Walpole's efforts had already contributed significantly to making this new manner of painting more widely known. The use of wax was considered an important innovation by many English artists of the time, not least Sir Joshua Reynolds and George Stubbs. Thanks to these and other experiments, artists trying to renew modern painting techniques could use the lessons of antiquity as inspiration.

Indeed, in his 'sitter-book' for 1775[50] and also in his 'Memoranda Book of Daily Practice',[51] Reynolds made notes that attest to his having bought and used wax. The most telling indication is a description of his self-portrait[52] in the 'Memoranda' as 'my own Florence upon raw cloth, cera solamente'.[53] Favourably received when shown for the first time in 1775, it continued to claim attention over the years. After seeing the self-portrait on a visit to Florence in 1826, Sir David Wilkie made note of his impressions: 'Remarked that the portrait of Sir Joshua Reynolds, by himself, has never been varnished! – is without cracks, and in surface as perfect as the day it was painted … If carnations have faded, as Irvine says they have, this is not obvious.' Wilkie's journal provides evidence for what Horace Walpole sought in copying Caylus's experiments: that encaustic painting suffered no form of alteration over time.

Chemical analyses of some of Stubbs's canvases have shown that he made use of a mixture of wax and resin in his paintings.[54] Unfortunately, for want of further documentation and due to the disappearance of such traces from repeated cleaning, little more can be said of his use of encaustic techniques.[55]

CONCLUSION: ON THE MEANING OF ANTIQUITIES

Whether as showpieces or simply as objects of quiet contemplation, the way in which his antiquities were displayed at Strawberry Hill reflects very different facets of Horace Walpole's personality. A man of the world, Walpole exhibited his most impressive pieces, including the marble eagle, in his gallery. Elsewhere, for example in the Tribune, small bronzes, vases and other objects were used as decorative elements. However, in his Library, a refuge for reading and study, Roman funerary urns were placed around the room. With their inscriptions in abridged Latin, they called for quiet scholarly attention. Walpole's books and his collection of antiques enabled him to express himself as both an aesthete and as an antiquarian.

1. Irène Aghion, ed., *Caylus mécène du roi. Collectionner les antiquités au XVIIIe siècle* (Paris: Institut national d'histoire de l'art, 2002).
2. *Recueil d'Antiquités Égyptiennes, Étrusques, Grecques, Romaines et Gauloises*, 7 vols. (Paris, 1752–67).
3. Alain Schnapp, *La conquête du passé* (Paris: Editions Carré, 1993), 241.
4. Revd William Cole, *A Journal of my Journey to Paris in the Year 1765* (London: Constable and Co. Ltd, 1931), 243–4.
5. J.-J. Barthélemy, *Le voyage du Jeune Anacharsis en Grèce*, 5 vols. (Paris, 1788).
6. Rex A. Barrell, *Horace Walpole and France*, 2 vols. (Ottawa: Borealis Press, 1979), II: 10, 83.
7. Barrell, *Horace Walpole and France*, II: 100–101, 'Mr Mariette … came to drink coffee with M. Walpole.'
8. *Recueil d'estampes d'après les plus beaux Tableaux et d'après les plus beaux dessins qui sont en France dans le Cabinet du Roy et dans celui du Duc d'Orléans, et dans d'autres Cabinets …*, 2 vols. (Paris, 1729–42).
9. L. Dukelskaya and A. Moore, *A Capital Collection: Houghton Hall and the Hermitage* (New Haven and London: Yale University Press, 2002).
10. *HW Corres.* 13–14: 213 n. 13 (HW to Richard West). This temple is sometimes mistaken for the Sun Temple built by Aurelian, which is in fact situated in a different part of the city near the Piazza S. Silvestro.
11. Filippo Coarelli, *Guida Archeologia di Roma* (Rome: A. Mondadori, 3rd ed., 1980), 220.
12. Anatole de Montaiglon, *Correspondance des directeurs de l'Académie de France à Rome avec les surintendants des bâtiments*, 18 vols. (Paris, 1887), I: 400–401.
13. *HW Corres.* 13–14: 213–14.
14. Carol C. Mattusch, *The Villa dei Papiri at Herculanum* (Los Angeles: J. Paul Getty Museum, 2005), 1–3.
15. Schnapp, *La conquête du passé*, 242–7.
16. Johann Joachim Winckelmann, *Critical account of the situation and destruction by the first eruptions of Mount Vesuvius: of Herculaneum, Pompeii, and Stabia: the late discovery of their remains: the subterraneous works carried on in them … in a letter, (originally in German) to Count Bruhl, of Saxony, from the celebrated Abbé Winckelman …, illustrated with notes, taken from the French translation* (London: printed for T. Carnan and F. Newbery, jun., 1771).
17. Mattusch, *Villa dei Papiri*, 40.
18. Quoted in Mattusch, *Villa dei Papiri*, 40.
19. e.g. Marie-Louise Vollenweider and Mathilde Avisseau-Broustet, *Camées et intailles: les portraits romains du Cabinet des médailles* (Paris: Bibliothèque nationale de France, 2003); Jane Fejfer, *The Ince Blundell Collection of Classical Sculpture: The Roman Male Portraits* (Liverpool: Liverpool University Press, 2001), vol. I, part 2; Dietrich Boschung, *Die Bildnisse des Caligula* (Berlin: G. Mann, 1989); Friederike Sinn, *Stadtrömische Marmorurnen* (Mainz am Rhein: P. von Zabern, 1987); Georg Daltrop, Ulrich Hausmann and Max Wegner, *Die Flavier* (Berlin: G. Mann, 1966).
20. *HW Corres.* 13: 214 (HW to Richard West).
21. *HW Corres.* 13: 229–34.
22. Naples, Museo Nazionale Archeologico, inv. 6033.
23. Sale catalogue: 'Objects of art … Lord Revelstoke',

London, Christie's, 28 June 1893 ff., 17, no. 138: bought by Davis for £157 10s., 'from Strawberry Hill, from the Hamilton Palace Collection'. No mention in the Davis auction: London, Christie's, 27 June 1900.

24. Fejfer, *Ince Blundell Collectio*, 10.
25. Irène Favaretto and Giovanna Luisa Ravagnan, ed., *Lo statuario pubblico della Serenissima. Due secoli di collezionismo di antichità, 1596–1797* (Cittadella: Biblos, 1997), 156, no. 18.
26. Daltrop *et al.*, *Flavier*, 74.
27. It does not appear in the recently reissued *Storia degli scavi di Roma* by Rodolfo Lanciani, a seven-volume history of the excavations carried out in Rome and its environs since 1600, based almost entirely on archive sources.
28. Gervase Jackson-Stops, ed., *The Treasure Houses of Britain* (Washington: exh. cat. National Gallery of Art, 1985), 319, no. 244; Ian Jenkins and Kim Sloan, eds., *Vases and Volcanoes: Sir William Hamilton and his Collection* (London: exh. cat. British Museum, 1996), 232, no.136.
29. *HW Corres.*19: 420.
30. Martin Postle, ed., *Joshua Reynolds: The Creation of Celebrity* (London: exh. cat. Tate Britain, 2005), 142, no. 32..
31. Postle, *Reynolds*, 142–3.
32. See, for example, Tacitus, *The Histories*, 3 vols., trans. Clifford H. Moore, Loeb Classical Library (London: William Heinemann Ltd/Cambridge, Mass.: Harvard University Press, 1962), 1: 212–13.
33. René de Ceccatty, preface to Horace Walpole, *La mère mystérieuse* (Paris: José Corti, 1991), 11: 'Titus Andronicus est un drame politique inspiré par l'histoire romaine: il y a de "vrais Goths", ces mêmes Goths desquels se réclamera le "gothique" des romans noirs, et avec leur "barbarie" sanglante, des têtes, des mains, une langue coupés, des gorges tranchées et un pâté de chair humaine.'
34. The 'Scritti di varie cose antiche' has been attributed to Bartoli by the present author and is in the process of publication.
35. MS journal of Abbé Barthélemy, Cabinet des Médailles, Rès. Ms 00001PARBN(1750)F: 'donné pour toutes ces médailles précieuses [autrement dit: en échange] plusieurs médailles de grand bronze d'un prix fort au-dessous des autres.'
36. *HW Corres.* 22: 528.
37. Comte de Caylus, *Voyage d'Italie 1714–1715*, ed. Amilda A. Pons (Paris: Fischbacher, 1914), 255.
38. Mattusch, *Villa dei Papiri*, 1. Large scale excavation only really got under way in 1738.
39. Boschung, *Bildnisse des Caligula*, 29, 50, 115 and pl. 28.
40. Pliny the Elder, *Natural History*, Book XXXV, 39; Vitruvius, *De Architectura*, VII, 9, 3.
41. Irène Aghion, 'Le Comte de Caylus, historien des techniques', in Aghion, *Caylus mécène*, 83–9.
42. Comte de Caylus, *Mémoire sur la peinture à l'encaustique et sur la peinture à la cire* (Geneva, 1755), 17.
43. Th. W. Gaehtgens and J. Lugand, *Joseph-Marie Vien, Peintre du Roi (1716–1809)* (Paris: Arthena, 1988), 152–3, no. 91.
44. *Philosophical Transactions* (London, 1757), vol.XLIX, part II, for the year 1756, 652–63.
45. *Annual Register of History, Politicks and Literature for the year 1760* (London. 1775), 135–41.
46. *HW Corres.* 21: 239.
47. *HW Corres.* 13: 34 (12 November 1759).
48. Lance Mayer and Gay Myers, 'Painting in the Age of Innovation: Stubbs's Experiments in Enamel and Wax', in Malcolm Warner and Robin Blake, *Stubbs and the Horse* (New Haven and London: Yale University Press, 2004), 131.
49. *HW Corres.* 28: 301–2 (18 April 1777).
50. 'Reproduction of Reynolds' daily journals of sitters with some sketches', Yale Center for British Art, reference library.
51. The 'Memoranda' were published as appendices to the Journal of Benjamin Haydon in Willard Bissell Pope, ed., *The Diary of Benjamin Robert Haydon* (Cambridge, Mass.: Harvard University Press, 1963), vol. 5, 1840–46, Appendix H, 572–86.
52. The portrait commissioned by the Grand Duke for his famous collection of artists' self-portraits, now in the Uffizi Gallery, Florence.
53. Pope, *Diary*, 573.
54. Raymond White, Ashok Roy, John Mills and Joyce Plesters, 'George Stubbs's Lady and Gentlemen in a Carriage: A Preliminary Note on the Technique', *National Gallery Technical Bulletin* 4 (1980), 64.
55. Mayer and Myers, 'Painting in the Age of Innovation', 130–33.

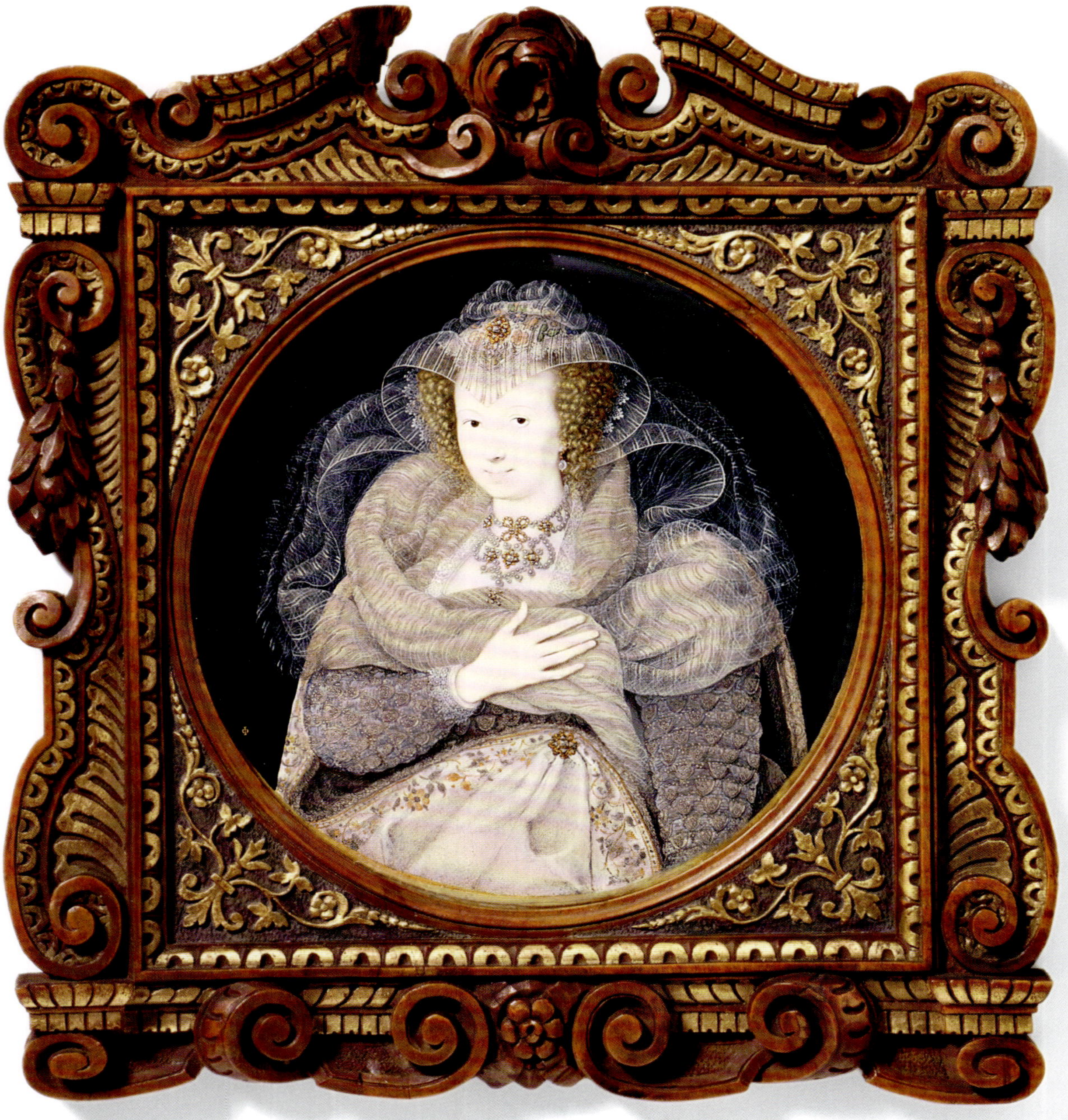

Figure 191. Isaac Oliver, *Portrait Miniature of an Unknown Lady (Frances Howard, Countess of Essex and Somerset*, *c.* 1595, watercolour on vellum, DIAM 13 cm. Victoria and Albert Museum, London, Purchased with the assistance of the Art Fund and the Pilgrim Trust. P.12–1971. Cat. 211

11.

HORACE WALPOLE AND THE COLLECTING OF MINIATURES

KATHERINE COOMBS

IN THE PREFACE to the *Description* of Strawberry Hill Horace Walpole wrote: 'The most considerable part of the following catalogue consists of miniatures, enamels, and portraits of remarkable persons. The collection of miniatures and enamels is, I believe, the largest and finest in any country'.[1] In fact, by his death in 1797 Walpole owned around 130 miniatures and nearly 40 enamels. Miniatures are paintings in watercolour on vellum and, from about 1700, on ivory. Separate, framed portrait miniatures developed in the 1520s out of the increasingly redundant art of illuminating hand-written books. Both arts were then called 'limning'; the Italian term for illumination, *miniatura*, was not introduced into England until a century later.[2] A notable early practitioner was Hans Holbein (Fig. 211), working for Henry VIII, but the art flowered in England in the hands of Nicholas Hilliard (Fig. 194) and Isaac Oliver (Figs. 191, 196), both patronized by Elizabeth I and James I. The art continued to flourish under Charles I, Cromwell and Charles II, in the hands of notable artists including Peter Oliver (Fig. 197), John Hoskins (Fig. 215) and Samuel Cooper (Fig. 195).[3] Enamel portrait painting was revolutionized in the seventeenth century by Henri Toutin (Fig. 202), and his sophisticated method was introduced at Charles I's court by Jean Petitot (Figs. 198, 212, 217), later patronized by Louis XIV of France.[4] Examples by these miniaturists and enamellists figured largely in Walpole's collection.

Morris R. Brownell in *The Prime Minister of Taste* identifies two conflicting assessments of Walpole as a collector:[5] Thomas Babington Macaulay's 1833 review characterizing Walpole as a collector 'of curiosities' and the 'Prince of Cockle Shells' (this was in fact said of Walpole by Friedrich Melchior Grimm in 1766);[6] and recent apologists representing Walpole as a 'connoisseur'. Brownell characterizes Walpole instead as a 'courtesy-book' gentleman, modelled on the kind found in Renaissance guides to gentlemanly education and manners such as the seminal *Il Cortegiano* (The Courtier) of 1528 by Baldassare Castiglione and *The Compleat Gentleman* of 1622 and 1634 by Henry Peacham. Brownell, however, considers Castiglione the more important influence and, further, compares him to Walpole's contemporary Lord Chesterfield, whose published letters to his son recommended a taste for the 'liberal arts': painting (especially Italian painting), sculpture and architecture. Inevitably, therefore, Brownell identifies a contradiction between Walpole as Chesterfield's 'Man of Taste' and Walpole as collector of what Brownell calls the 'philistine genre of portraits'.[7]

But Walpole's collection of miniatures and enamels suggests another way of understanding him as a collector, especially when considered in conjunction with the first volume of *Anecdotes of Painting in England* (1762), published by Walpole in his mid-forties. By this time Walpole had been collecting miniatures and enamels for over twenty years; in 1743 he had acquired a cabinet for 'my miniatures and enamels' (see pp. 98–9).[8] The *Anecdotes* were innovative in providing a chronology of painting in England, with volume

* Unless otherwise stated, the miniatures have been enlarged

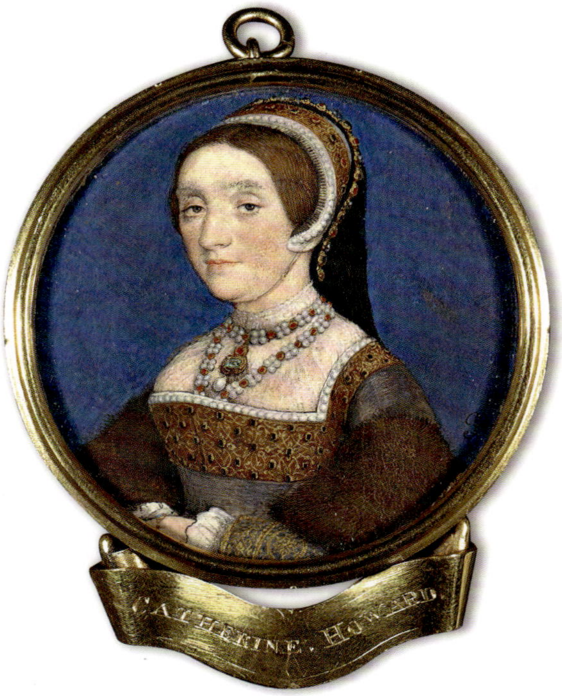
CATHERINE. HOWARD

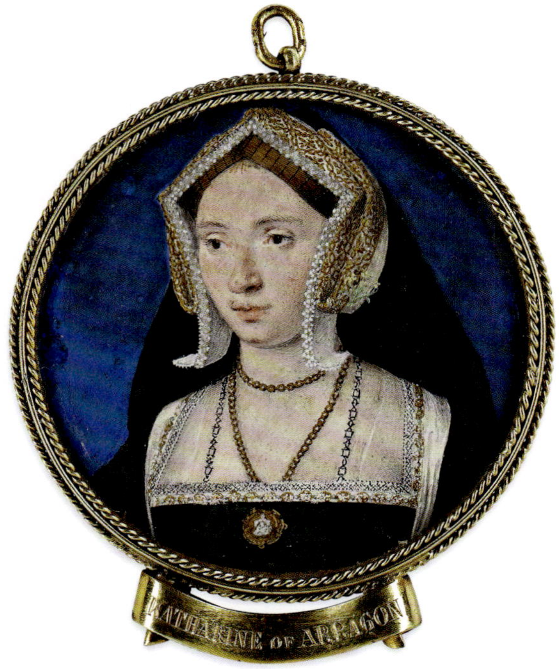

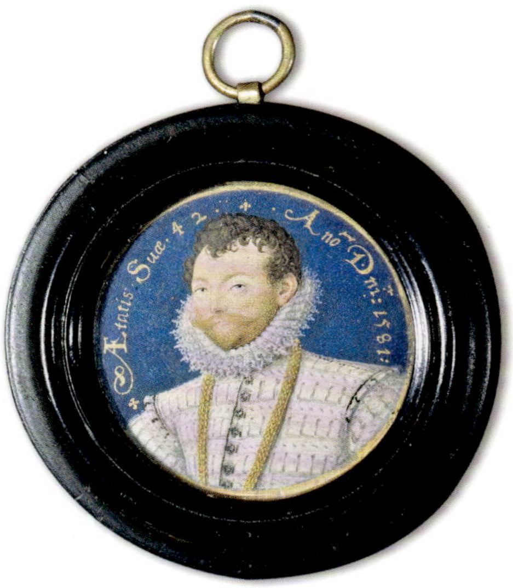
Ætatis Suæ. 42.
Ano Dni. 1581

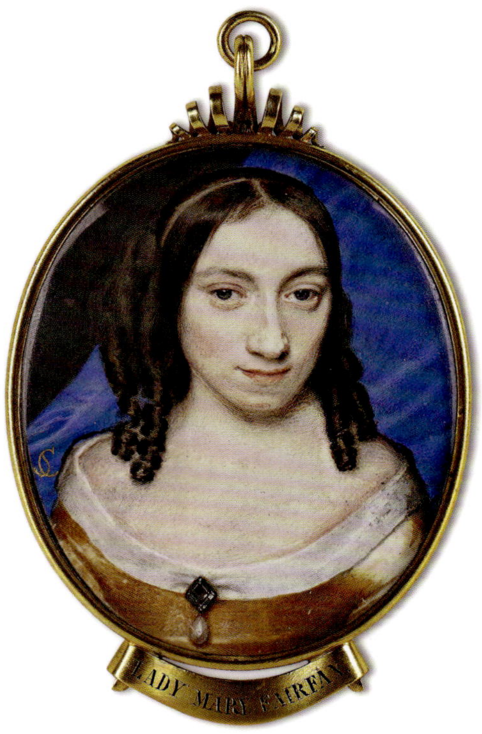
LADY MARY FAIRFAX

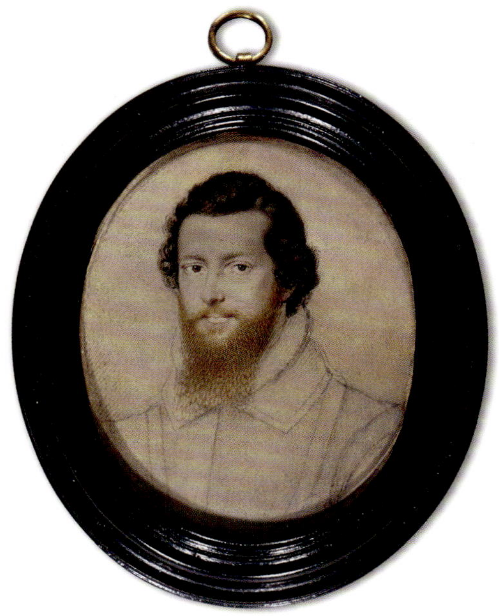

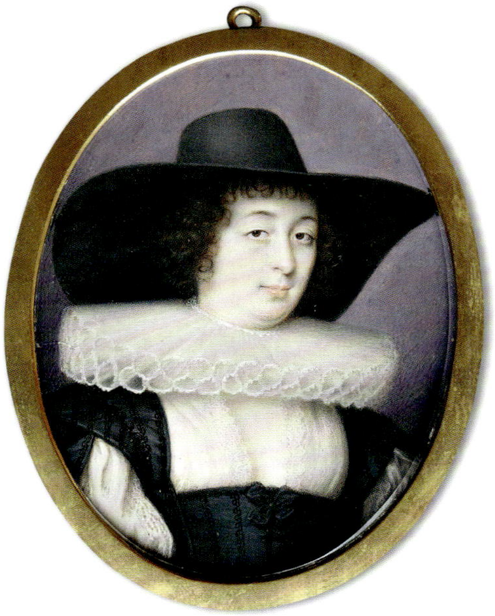

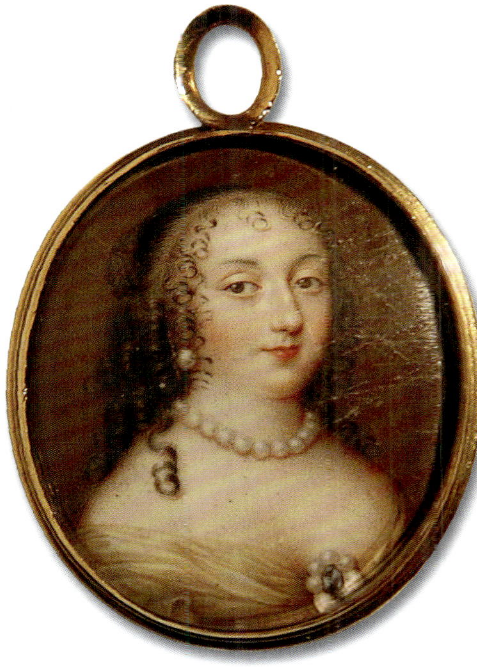

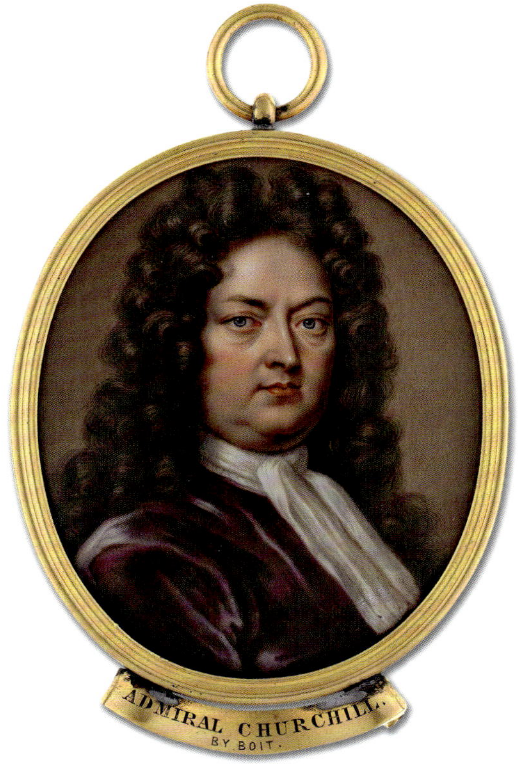

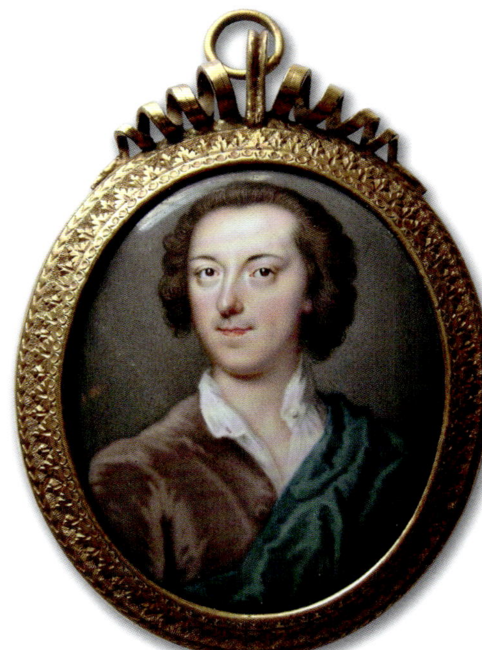

FACING PAGE

Figure 192, *top left*. Hans Holbein the younger, *Katherine Howard ('Mary Tudor, Queen of France')*, 1540–1, watercolour on vellum, set in gilt-metal frame, DIAM 5.3 cm. Trustees of the Ninth Duke of Buccleuch's Chattels Fund. Cat. 208

Figure 193, *top right*. Lucas Horenbout, *Anne Boleyn*, *c.* 1532–3, watercolour on vellum, set in gilt-metal frame, DIAM 4.2 cm. Trustees of the Ninth Duke of Buccleuch's Chattels Fund. Cat. 174

Figure 194, *bottom left*. Studio of Nicholas Hilliard, *Sir Francis Drake*, 1581, watercolour on vellum, set in pearwood frame, DIAM 2.8 cm. National Portrait Gallery, London. 4851. Cat. 210

Figure 195, *bottom centre*. Samuel Cooper, *Mary Fairfax, Duchess of Buckingham*, *c.* 1651, watercolour on vellum, set in gilt-metal frame, H 6.2 cm. Trustees of the Ninth Duke of Buccleuch's Chattels Fund. Cat. 220

Figure 196, *bottom right*. Isaac Oliver, *Robert Devereux, 2nd Earl of Essex*, *c.* 1600, watercolour on vellum, H 5.4 cm. Yale Center for British Art, Paul Mellon Collection. B1974.2.75. Cat. 178

THIS PAGE

Figure 197, *top left*. Peter Oliver, *Lady Lucy Percy*, *c.* 1620, watercolour on vellum, set in gilt-metal frame, H 7.3 cm. Wingfield Digby collection, Sherborne Castle. Cat. 213

Figure 198, *top centre*. Jean Petitot, *Maria Theresa of Austria*, *c.* 1660, enamel on copper, 2.54 × 4.2 cm. The Rt Hon. the Earl of Derby. Cat. 184

Figure 199, *top right*. Charles Boit, *Admiral George Churchill*, *c.* 1700, enamel on copper, H 6.1 cm. National Maritime Museum, Greenwich, London, MNT0129. Cat. 187

Figure 200, *right*. Christian Friedrich Zincke, *Horace Walpole*, 1745, enamel on copper, H 4.1 cm. Trustees of the Waldegrave Chattels Trust. Cat. 190

I tracing from the medieval period to Charles I. For Walpole, Charles I was a great patron and collector whose accession ushered in the 'first era of real taste in England'.[9] In this account Walpole gave miniature painters a prominent place, casting Isaac Oliver as the first national hero of painting: 'Hitherto we have been obliged to owe to other countries the best performances exhibited here in painting; but in the branch [miniature] in which Oliver excelled, we may challenge any nation to show a greater master'.[10] In 1760, as Walpole was completing volume I, George III ascended the throne, raising expectations of a renaissance of royal patronage, and the first public exhibition was held by the newly formed Society of Artists, introducing contemporary painting to a wider audience. It should be remembered, however, that the foundation of the Royal Academy of Arts was still eight years hence, as were the influential annual *Discourses* by its president, Sir Joshua Reynolds. Reynolds's discourses offered a theoretical and critical analysis of European painting, with the dual intention of extending British taste and patronage, which notoriously favoured portraiture, and encouraging a British school of art to rival France and Italy.[11] In 1719 the portrait painter Jonathan Richardson had laid the groundwork for these arguments with *The Science of the Connoisseur*, offering patrons and collectors rules for analysing European painting, and introducing the French word 'connoisseur' to British readers.[12] But although the *Connoisseur* was published around the time of Walpole's birth, the model of collecting in England in his formative years remained less narrowly focused on oil paintings. Most collectors valued a wide range of objects: antiquities such as coins and intaglios; manuscripts; prints, especially of 'illustrious' people (see pp. 150–51); sculptures; bronzes; and 'natural rarities' such as shells.[13]

Walpole knew directly or indirectly three notable collectors who fitted this model, two of whom had significant collections of miniatures and enamels: Edward Harley, 2nd Earl of Oxford, Dr Richard Mead and Sir Hans Sloane. Walpole's assessment in 1742 of Harley's posthumous sale is revealing of his own taste at this date: 'much rubbish … presents … from the Royal Society … forty volumes of prints of illustrious English personages [Walpole judged them critically as a poor selection] … few good pictures for the miniatures are not to be sold, nor the manuscripts; and the books not till next year … a few fine bronzes, and a very fine collection of English coins.'[14] Harley was the patron of George Vertue, whose copious notebooks about English art Walpole bought in 1758 and were the basis for the *Anecdotes*. Vertue, with Jacobus Houbraken, engraved portraits for *Heads of Illustrious Persons of Great Britain* published from 1734, around the time that Walpole started collecting printed 'Heads'. Remembering his first hint in 1764 of the Rev. James Granger's plan for a new edition of Joseph Ames's *A Catalogue of English Heads: Or an Account of about Two Thousand Prints* (1748), Walpole noted, 'I had [then] been thirty years collecting English heads'.[15] It is noteworthy that both Vertue and Ames sponsored Walpole in 1754 for the Society of Antiquaries. Harley also employed the miniaturist Bernard Lens in the framing and care of his miniatures. Lens had been Walpole's drawing master and undoubtedly taught him the watercolour art of miniature.[16] Like Harley, Mead and Sloane, both physicians, collected a wide variety of objects, though today Harley is known for his manuscripts and library, Mead for his oils

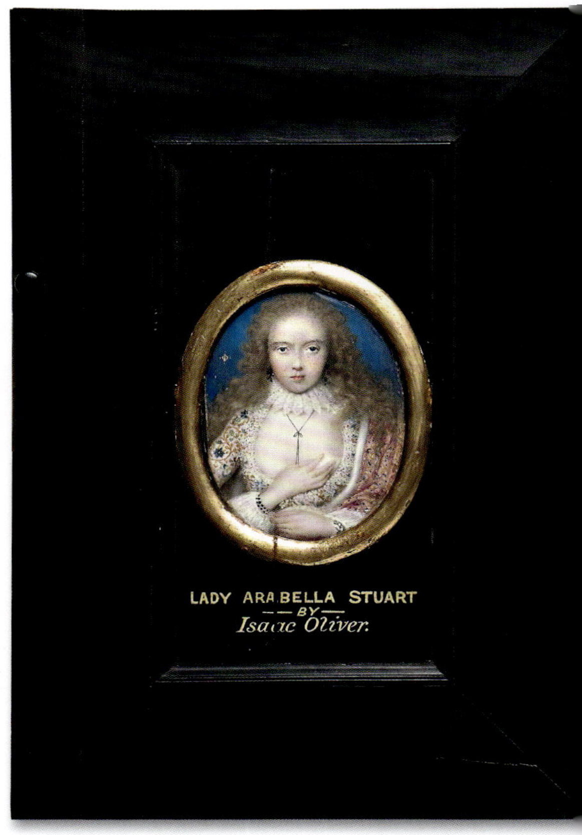

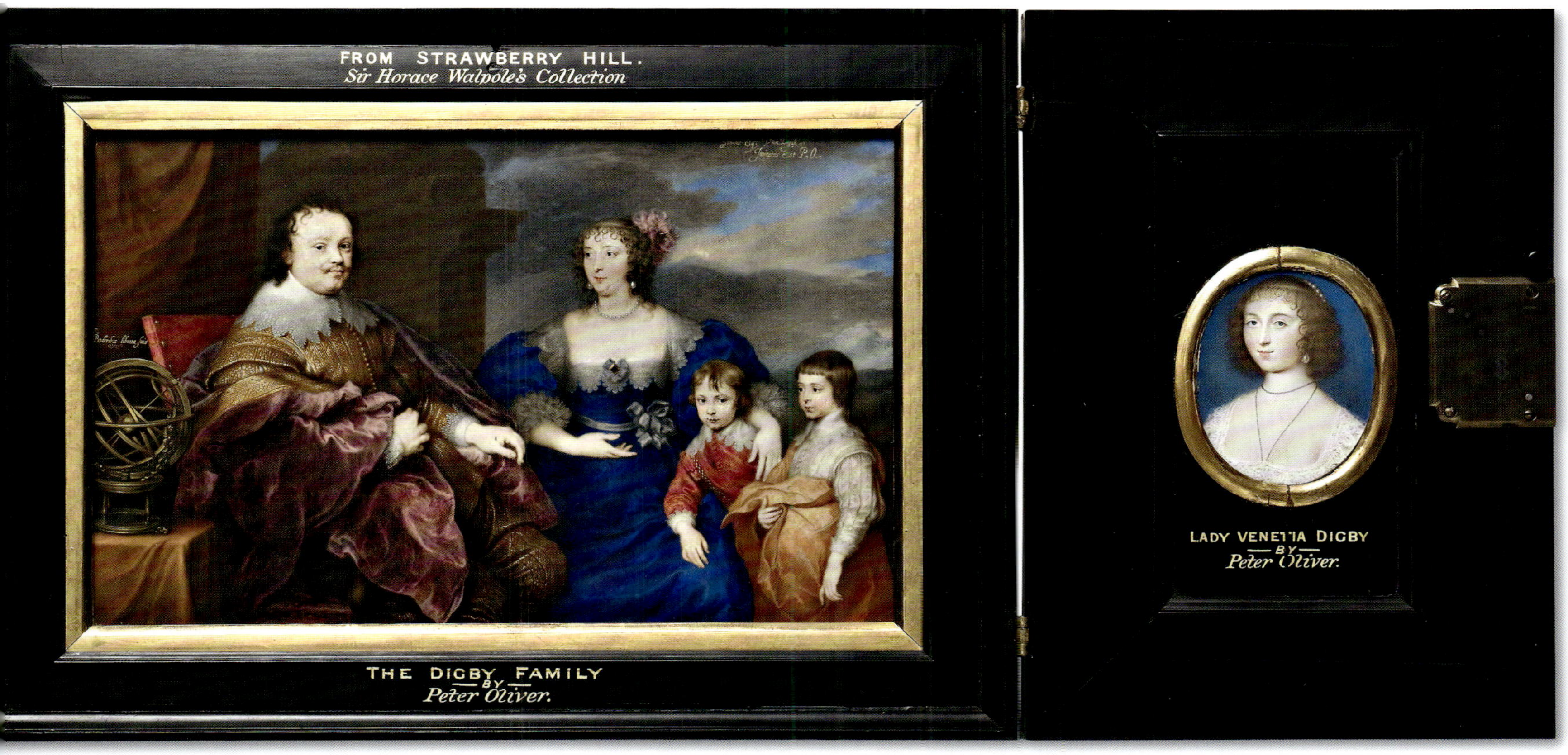

Figure 201. Peter Oliver after Sir Anthony Van Dyck, *Sir Kenelm and Lady Venetia Digby, and their sons Kenelm and John, with portraits of Lady Venetia Digby and Lady Arabella Stuart*, 1635, three miniatures in watercolour on vellum, set inside an ebony veneered wooden cabinet with inner gilt slips, two silver locks, and nineteen Wedgwood and Tassie cameos set on the outside of the doors, 15.5 × 24.6 cm. Nationalmuseum, Stockholm, Sweden. NM69. Cat. 216

and Sloane for his 'natural rarities' (scientific specimens). Mead was a friend of Walpole's father, though Walpole, while coveting his miniatures and enamels, apparently had little respect for the man. Sloane intended his collection to found a British Museum and at his death in 1753 nominated Walpole as one of his fifty trustees. Nonetheless, Walpole despised Sloane's natural rarities, commenting that while Sloane valued his collections 'at fourscore thousand … so would anybody who loves … spiders as big as geese! … It is a rent charge to keep the foetuses in spirits!'[17]

Frederick, Prince of Wales, who acquired many of Mead's miniatures and enamels, commented more positively of Sloane's collections that they 'must conduce to the benefit of Learning'.[18] The pursuit of learning was the impulse for many early collectors; Renaissance humanists, for example, collected coins and medals to illustrate ancient Roman texts such as Suetonius's *Lives of the Twelve Caesars*.[19] But in England by the end of the seventeenth century, as collectors ranged over ever wider areas of learning, satirists ridiculed these 'virtuosi', as they were known, for the purposelessness of their 'learning' and the vast sums they expended on collecting 'rarities' and 'curiosities'.[20] Originally, however, the term 'virtuosi' had had more positive connotations. It was first used in Peacham's 1634 edition of *The Compleat Gentleman*, in a chapter concerning the study and collecting of Roman antiquities such as statues and coins.[21] Peacham noted that 'possession of such rarities, by reason of their dead costliness, doth properly belong to princes, or rather to Princely minds', but a gentleman should be knowledgeable of them 'if he desire to be thought ingenious'. He added that 'such as are skilled [knowledgeable] in them are by the Italians termed Virtuosi, as if others that either neglect or despise them were idiots', and praised the collections of antiquities belonging to Thomas Howard, Earl of Arundel, and Charles I.

But, as has been noted, the concept of the knowledgeable 'virtuoso' became increasingly elastic, encompassing, for example, an interest in English 'antiquities' and the pursuit of new areas such as natural and experimental philosophy. The Royal Society, founded in 1660, provided a focus for such wide-ranging virtuoso interests; a founder member was John Evelyn, with interests ranging from numismatics and engraving to mechanics,

THE DIGBY MINIATURES

Stephen Lloyd

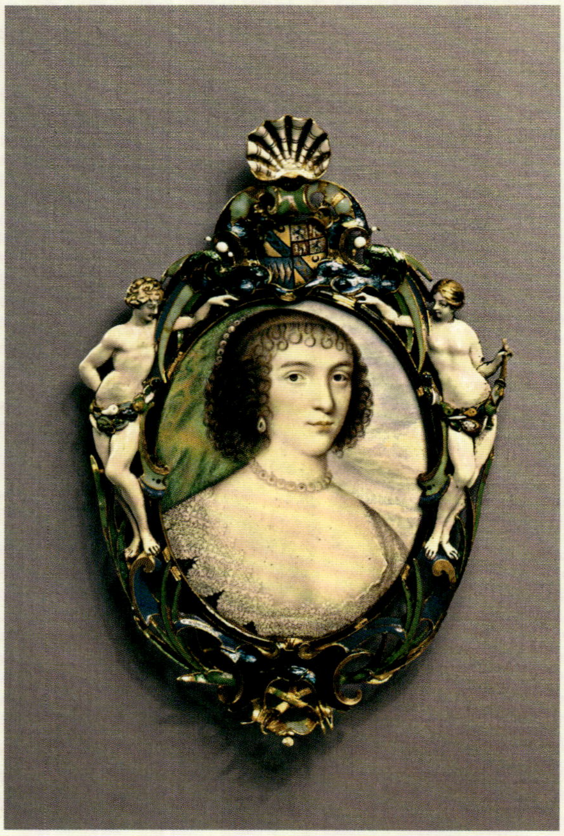

Figure 202. Henri Toutin after Peter Oliver, *Lady Venetia Digby*, 1637, enamel on gold set in gold enamelled frame by Gilles Legaré, 12.5 × 8.3 cm. The Walters Art Museum, Baltimore, Maryland. 44.177. Cat. 218

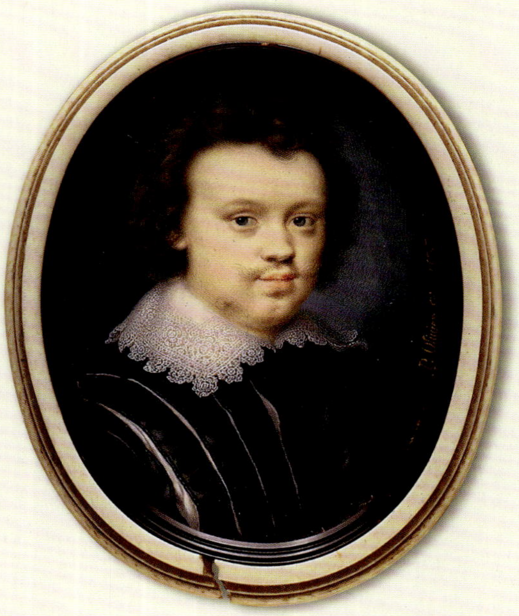

Figure 203. Peter Oliver, *Sir Kenelm Digby*, watercolour on vellum, 7 × 5.5 cm. National Portrait Gallery, London. 6274. Cat. 214

FACING PAGE

Figures 204, 205. Peter Oliver, after Sir Anthony Van Dyck, *Sir Kenelm and Lady Venetia Digby*, watercolour on vellum set in an enamelled gold diptych frame, H 8.8 cm. Wingfield Digby Collection, Sherborne Castle. Cat. 215

Figure 206. John Hoskins, after Sir Anthony Van Dyck, *Lady Frances Cranfield, Countess of Dorset* (formerly Lady Venetia Digby), watercolour on vellum set in an ebony-veneered wooden cabinet, 15.3 × 11.4 cm. The Trustees of the Ninth Duke of Buccleuch's Chattels Fund. Cat. 219

Figure 207. Peter Oliver, after Sir Anthony Van Dyck, *Lady Venetia Digby on her death bed*, after 1633, watercolour on vellum in an enamelled gold frame, 6.7 × 6.7 cm. Wingfield Digby Collection, Sherborne Castle. Cat. 217

From the *Description* of Strawberry Hill it is known that Walpole owned around 170 portrait miniatures and enamels. This highly specialized part of his collection can be seen as a microcosm of many of his collecting interests, which focused on history, the history of art and portraiture. At Strawberry Hill Walpole preserved and displayed his miniatures and enamels in various locations. Over half of the collection, including some of the most precious objects, was contained in the hanging cabinet and elsewhere in the Tribune (see pp. 98–9), while a small group of choice English miniatures was displayed over the fireplace in the Library and a miscellaneous group of about twenty works was shown in the Green Closet.

Around thirty of his finest miniature portraits were displayed in the Breakfast Room, principally in two hanging cases on either side of the fireplace. It was in this private room that the most famous group of Walpole's miniatures were preserved – those representing members of the Digby family, principally the renowned Stuart courtier and virtuoso Sir Kenelm Digby and his equally celebrated wife Lady Venetia Stanley, who died young in mysterious circumstances. Some of these outstanding miniatures were purchased by Walpole for the considerable sum of 300 guineas, as he recounted in the *Description*, having been 'found in a garret in an old house in Wales, belonging to a Mr. Watkin Williams, probably descended from Sir Kenelm'. These works, mostly by Peter Oliver – Walpole's favourite miniaturist – included a double portrait of the Digbys (Figs. 204, 205) and the deathbed portrait of Lady Venetia (Fig. 207), both after Van Dyck, as well as the miniatures of Sir Kenelm as a young man (Fig. 203) and of Lady Venetia's mother, Lady Lucy Percy (Fig. 197), which Walpole thought was by Isaac Oliver.

Also displayed in the Breakfast Room was another group of Digby family miniatures, including the very rare early enamel by Henri Toutin of Lady Venetia, set in a spectacular gold-enamelled frame by Gilles Legaré (Fig. 202) and the large cabinet miniature by Peter Oliver after Van Dyck of Sir Kenelm Digby with his wife and two sons, which Walpole had set in an ebony-veneered case decorated with

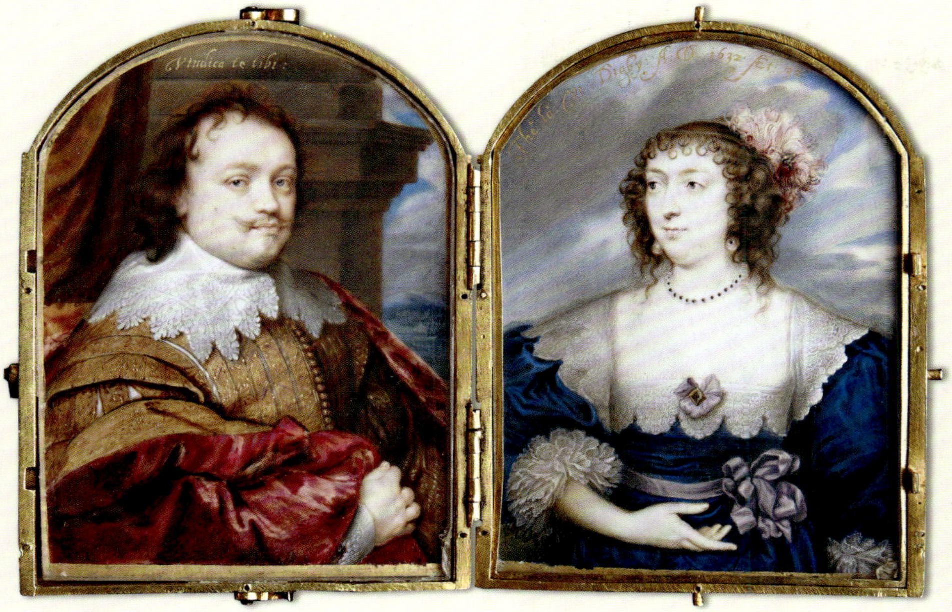

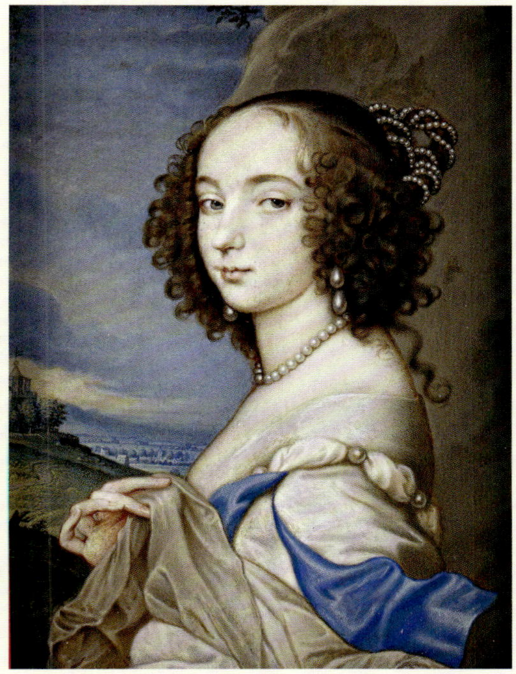

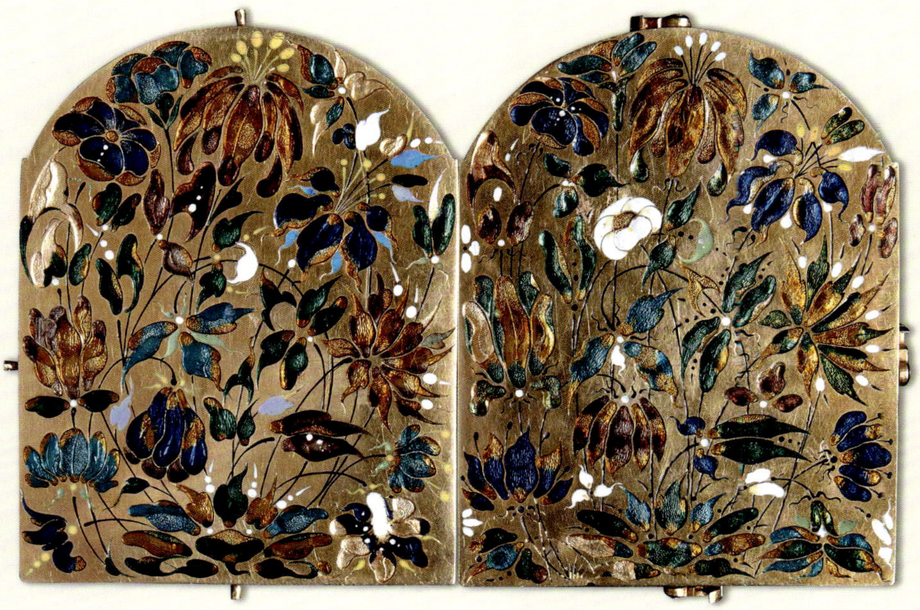

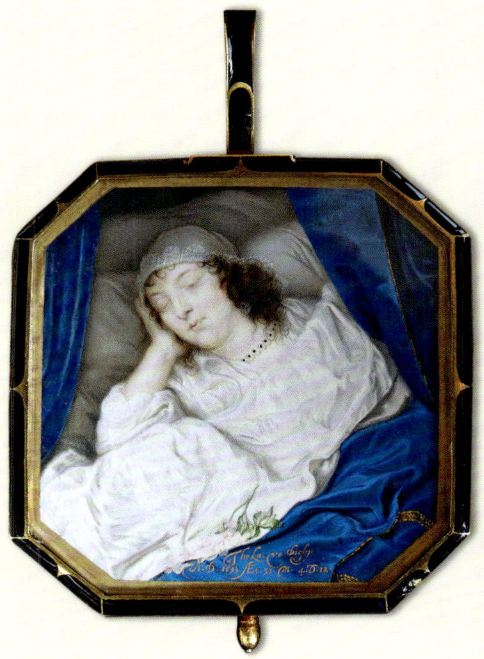

contemporary cameos, some by Wedgwood and Tassie, including a head of his father. Housed in a similarly rich manner by Walpole was the beautiful half-length miniature that he thought was Peter Oliver's copy after another supposed portrait of Lady Venetia by Van Dyck (Fig. 206). In fact this large limning is now known to have been painted by John Hoskins after Van Dyck's full-length portrait of Lady Frances Cranfield, later Countess of Dorset. Despite Walpole's failure to attribute the artist or identify the sitter correctly, perhaps due to his over-eagerness to seek out other miniatures of members of the Digby family, this work with its exceptional painting of the background landscape is a testament to Walpole's refined eye and the sensitivity of his connoisseurship and collecting.

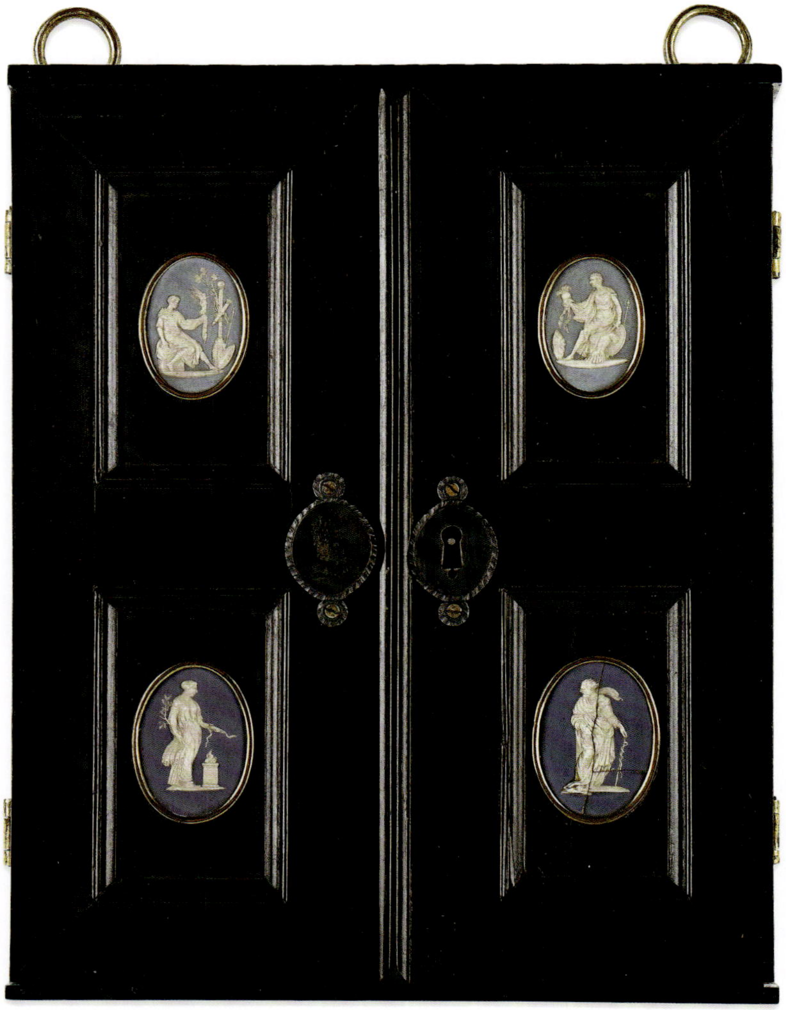

Figure 208. Ebony-veneered wooden cabinet containing the miniature of Lady Frances Cranfield, Countess of Dorset, with silver locks and ornaments and four Wedgwood cameos in gilt-metal settings mounted on exterior of two doors, closed cabinet: 22.2 × 17.7 × 3.3 cm. The Trustees of the Ninth Duke of Buccleuch's Chattels Fund. Cat. 219

and later members included Harley, Mead and Sloane. Walpole himself joined in 1747, probably sponsored by his Etonian friend Charles Lyttelton, a passionate antiquarian, who in 1754 sponsored Walpole for the Society of Antiquaries. Walpole's distaste for Sloane's natural rarities is therefore notable, especially as it chimed with comments made by early eighteenth-century commentators seeking either to rehabilitate the virtuoso or to defend a branch of learning from association with virtuosi 'curiosity'. In 1714 the Earl of Shaftesbury defended from ridicule those virtuosi who studied 'mankind and their affairs', condemning, however, 'inferior virtuosi' for privileging study of 'the Habitations and Economy of a Race of Shell-fish'.[22] Shaftesbury's target was 'philosophers' and 'virtuosi' who strayed from their proper purpose, the study of man, into 'nature's remotest operations' and he stated dismissively that 'Cockleshell abounds with each'.[23] Less robustly, Joseph Addison, defending the once respected humanist study of medals from association with virtuosi, struggled to distinguish numismatics from other subjects of curiosity such as 'spiders, lobsters and cockleshells'.[24] We can perhaps better appreciate Gilly Williams's comment that Walpole would be stung by the epithet the 'Prince of Cockle Shells'.[25] We can also recognize how Richardson's discerning 'connoisseur', while inevitably offering another type for satirists to enjoy, became established as opposite to the debased curious 'virtuoso'.

Brownell seeks to counter representations of Walpole either as a collector of 'curiosities' or a 'sober connoisseur'. Instead, despite Walpole's taste for portraiture, Brownell equates Walpole's 'attitude to the arts' with the aristocratic models of the sixteenth-century Italian 'courtesy-book' gentleman and Chesterfield's 'Man of Taste', both of whom, however, favoured Italian painting. But Walpole owned no copies of Castiglione, and Chesterfield's letters were not published until Walpole was fifty-seven. Walpole, however, possessed three copies of Peacham's *Compleat Gentleman* of 1634, one of which he kept in his Glass Closet.[26] Peacham was writing for the gentlemen of early seventeenth-century England, an era that Walpole particularly admired. Both editions paid homage to the Earl of Arundel, who was greatly respected by Walpole as a collector, and praised Sir Kenelm Digby, whose miniatures by Peter Oliver Walpole so prized as 'that noble and absolutely compleat gentleman' (see pp. 188–9; Fig. 203).[27] One cannot suggest that Walpole modelled himself on Peacham's 'compleat gentleman', especially as many of his subjects, such as fishing, would not have interested Walpole. But there is a certain congruence between Peacham's gentlemanly interests and sensibilities and those of Walpole. In these terms Peacham offers a way into understanding Walpole as a collector of the 'philistine' portrait arts of the miniature and enamel.

Much in Peacham's chapters on 'Antiquities' and on 'Historie' would have resonated with an imaginative collector like Walpole. Peacham called statues and coins 'copies and memorials of men … whose lively presence is able to persuade a man that he now seeth 2000 years ago'. They were 'highly prized, not only for the excellency of the work but also for the history ... they contain, which the learned make good use of as appeareth in their writings'. Walpole himself first studied Roman history at Eton, forming with Lyttelton and George Montagu the 'Triumvirate'; later he reminisced that 'the beginning of my Roman history was spent in the asylum, or conversing in Egeria's hallowed grove', precocious references to the history of the Seven Kings of Rome (Fig. 214).[28] He formed a taste for 'virtù' (at this date, Roman antiquities) under the tutelage of Conyers Middleton, his Cambridge tutor and collector of antiquities, and on the Grand Tour purchased 'Roman Virtù',[29] guided by the Rev. Joseph Spence, his 'master in the antique'.[30] Later Walpole invited Middleton to study his new collection, but instead Middleton offered his own collection to Walpole, a sale finally completed in 1744.[31] At this date, however, Walpole had been collecting printed 'Heads' of English sitters for ten years, and already had an established collection of portrait miniatures and enamels.

Brownell calls portraits 'philistine', a nineteenth-century term condemning Walpole's taste for portraiture as uncultured. It is notable therefore that in 1715 Richardson, author of the *Connoisseur*, echoed Peacham in arguing that portraiture 'gives strong Indications of the Mind and illustrates what the Historian says more expressly and particularly'.[32] Walpole's mercurial, even contrary, nature defies attempts to fix on him any one identity. Nonetheless, a letter written by Walpole in 1762, just following the publication of volume I of *The Anecdotes*, is revealing. Replying to William Cole, fellow Etonian and antiquarian friend, concerning Cole's offer to index Walpole's collection of portrait prints, Walpole wrote: 'I am antiquary and virtuoso enough myself not to dislike such employment, but could never think it charming enough to trouble anybody else with it.'[33] Walpole in fact often identified himself publicly as an 'antiquary', as in 'we antiquaries' in *The Anecdotes*.[34] But he skirted around the identity of 'virtuoso', never directly applying this word to himself, betraying, as has been shown, a sensitivity to its modern connotations and an awareness of the virtuoso's reputation for wasteful luxury in acquiring expensive 'rarities'; in *The Anecdotes* he said defensively of the Earl of Arundel that he was 'no selfish virtuoso'.[35] Nonetheless, in an 'advertisement' prefacing the publication of the catalogue of Charles I's collection (1757) he called Charles admiringly 'the royal virtuoso'.[36]

On balance, Walpole, like Shaftesbury, echoed Peacham in associating the virtuoso with the study of 'mankind and his affairs' and the collecting of objects redolent of civilizations such as ancient Rome and indeed England. Walpole effectively mapped many of his interests onto those of this older model of the 'virtuoso'. After his acquisition of Middleton's collection in 1744, the death of his father in 1745 and his acquisition of Strawberry Hill in 1747, his collecting of Roman antiquities dwindled. By 1752 he was writing to Montagu: 'I thank you too for the offer of your Roman Correspondences, but you know I have done with virtu, and deal only with the Goths and Vandals' (Northern tribes that had sacked Rome).[37] In his chapter on 'Historie' Peacham had advised: 'Be not a stranger in the history of your own country ... not inferior to any other in the world for matter of Antiquity and rarities of every kind worth remark and admiration.' Walpole certainly valued English 'rarities', but, unlike his friend Lyttelton, was not interested in 'barrows ... tumuli ... Roman camps, and ... bumps in the ground', preferring 'arts when perfected'.[38] He admired the 'first era of real taste in England' of Charles I and Lord Arundel.

Walpole was also drawn to the seventeenth century by the proliferation of published memoirs and letters of those intimate with the courts of Charles I, Charles II and Louis XIV. Scholars of ancient Rome had collected coins and medals, 'lively presences', to illustrate biographical accounts found in Suetonius and other writers. For Walpole. miniatures by Peter Oliver or Cooper (Figs. 209, 210) or enamels by Petitot (Fig. 212) were similar conduits to the past that so delighted him. In place of Suetonius there were the 1st Earl of Clarendon's *History of the Rebellion and Civil Wars in England* (1702); the *Mémoires du Comte de Gramont* (1713), reminiscing about life at the courts of Charles II and Louis XIV; and the letters of Madame de Sévigné, first published in French in 1725, recounting to her daughter in Provence life in the Paris of Louis XIV. For Walpole the Earl of Arundel's character was known 'by that admirable portrait drawn of him by Lord Clarendon',[39] while of Madame de Sévigné he said: 'She had the art of making you acquainted with all her acquaintance.'[40] These were accounts by those who had witnessed events and conversed with the

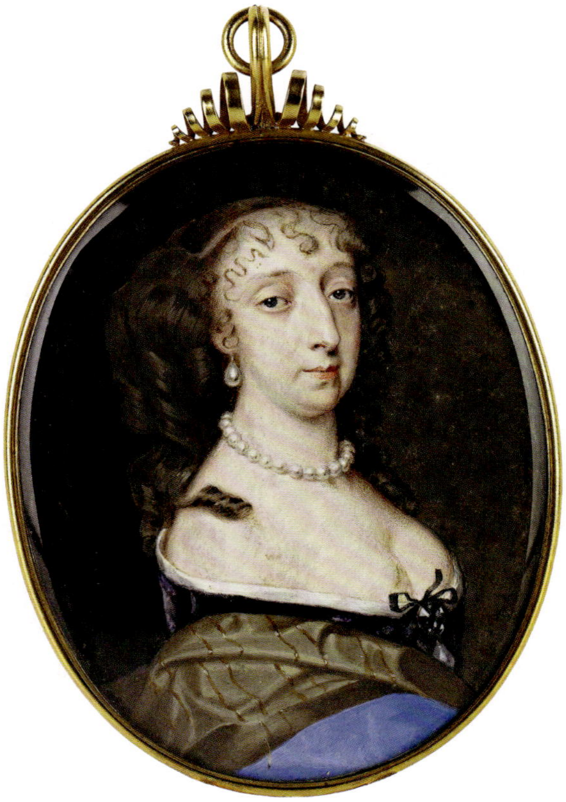

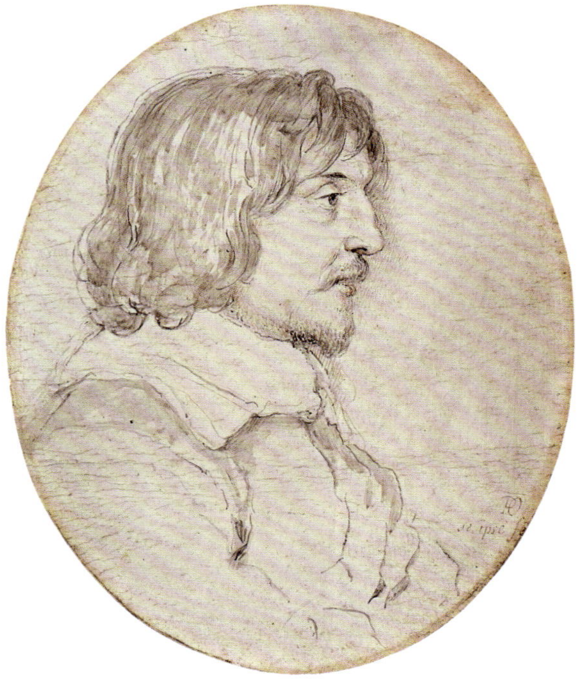

Figure 209. Samuel Cooper, *Lady Penelope Compton, wife of Sir Edward Nicholas*, watercolour on vellum, set in gilt-metal frame, H 8.9 cm. The Trustees of the Ninth Duke of Buccleuch's Chattels Fund. Cat. 221

Figure 210. Peter Oliver, *Self-portrait, with Portrait of his Wife (verso)*, graphite and watercolour on card set in pear-wood frame, 8.6 × 6.7 cm, frame. National Portrait Gallery, London. 4853. Cat. 179

protagonists. Miniatures had a similar attraction, the unique record of an encounter between artist and sitter. This of course was true of original oil paintings, but miniatures were, as Peacham said of coins when comparing them to statues, of 'small bulke' and their 'carriage lighter'.[41] Miniatures, like coins, had the prosaic advantage for collectors of portability and ease of storage. But their small size was also able to provide a powerfully evocative frisson. The sense of previous ownership is palpable with objects small enough to be held in the palm of the hand, encouraging an imaginative engagement with others who have similarly cradled the same intimate work – artist, sitter, first owner and all subsequent descendants or collectors. Walpole was acutely aware of past owners, commenting in the *Description*'s preface that 'such well-attested descent is the genealogy of the objects of virtù' and of the *Anecdotes* that they 'may be of use to collectors and virtuosi, for whose service this work is composed, to know when they meet with the ruins of that royal cabinet [Charles I's], or of the Earl of Arundel's'.[42] For Walpole, miniatures and enamels offered a particularly imaginative link to previous owners of taste. In 1760 he recorded a vivid dream in which he was wandering James II's Whitehall Palace and took the opportunity to view Charles I's collection, knowing it would soon be destroyed. He was particularly excited, thinking he had found the lost Holbein miniatures and bitterly disappointed to find he was mistaken.[43] For Walpole, miniatures by Holbein, Hilliard and Oliver had associations not only with the Tudors but with Charles I and Arundel, who, Walpole knew, had owned miniatures by these artists.[44] The miniature was a memento of the artist, sitter and collector.

It is still possible to experience the psychological power of these small objects. But it is likely that, for Walpole, his miniatures set up a further association that is harder to understand today: that between miniatures, or rather 'limning', and heraldry. Here, too, Peacham offers an insight into this most subtle of associations. In the *Compleat Gentleman* Peacham wrote at length on 'Armory or Blazon of Arms' (heraldry), a subject that fascinated Walpole (Fig. 213). Earlier, in *The Art of Drawing with the Pen and Limming* (1606), Peacham had sought to establish drawing and limning as gentlemanly activities. This was

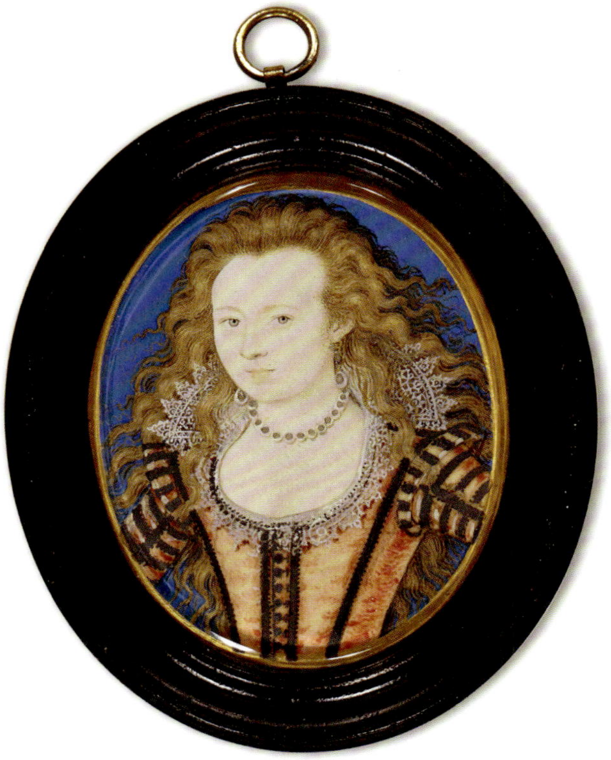

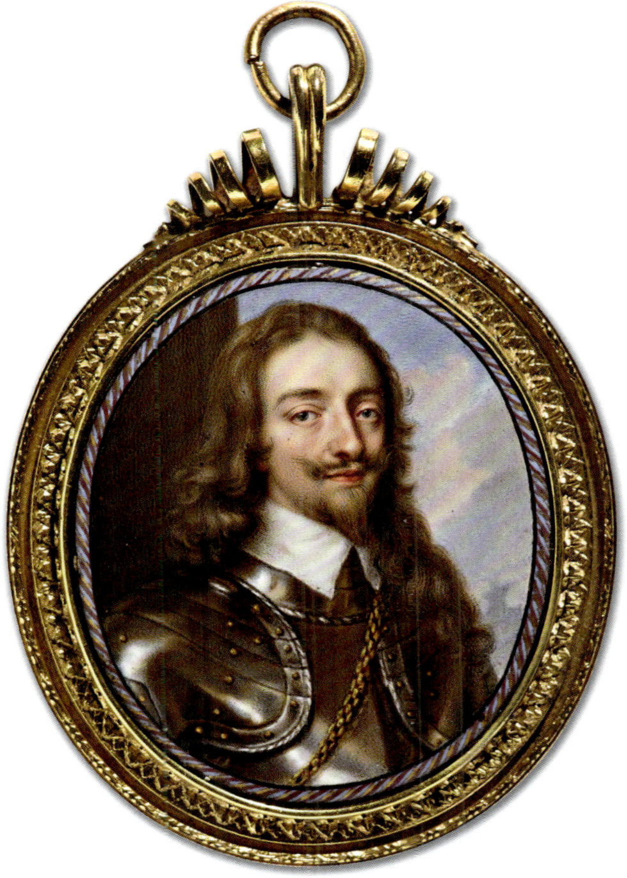

Figure 211. Nicholas Hilliard, *Portrait Miniature of an Unknown Lady* ('Queen of Bohemia'), *c.* 1605–10, watercolour on vellum, stuck on playing card with verso of four watercolour stripes alternating with black and blue, 5.1 × 4.3 cm. Yale Center for British Art, Paul Mellon Collection. B1974.2.51. Cat. 176

Figure 212. Jean Petitot I, *Portrait Enamel of Charles I*, *c.* 1638, enamel on copper, set in chased gilt-metal frame, 4 × 3.5 cm, framed 5.9 × 4.3 cm. Nationalmuseum, Stockholm. Bequest 1927 of consul Hjalmar Wicander (The Wicander Collection). NMB 989. Cat. 181

republished in 1612 as *The Gentleman's Exercise* with an added section on heraldry, setting up an association between what Peacham saw as two gentlemanly and useful arts. The term 'limning' was used for watercolour arts ranging from the decoration of manuscripts, such as grants of arms, to the small portraits by Hilliard.[45] Walpole appreciated the association between limning, in all its variety, and heraldry. In the *Anecdotes* he recorded that the guardian of Edward Norgate, 'observing his inclination to limning and heraldry, permitted him to indulge his genius'.[46] Norgate was appointed Windsor herald by the Earl of Arundel, the earl marshal, and 'illuminated' state letters for Charles I. Elsewhere in *The Anecdotes* Walpole described a 'genealogical tree' by George Jamesone, who, he said, painted 'in oil, though he sometimes practised in miniature'. It was 8 feet (2.4 m) long, 'containing in miniature' portraits of the family, and was also described by Walpole as 'beautifully illuminated'.[47] The association between heraldry, limning and miniatures was also given visible form in sets of miniatures, such as a group described in the catalogue of Charles I's collection of the Tudors as incorporating original miniatures and limned copies, presumably commissioned when no original was available.[48] Such groups, gathered in frames or cabinets, were reminiscent of limned pedigrees and similarly redolent of family. To experience the association between limning and heraldry required a particular cultural mindset; Walpole's imaginative immersion in this culture was such that he even used the language of genealogy when complaining of gout: 'If either my father or my mother had had it, I should not dislike it so much; I am herald enough to approve it if descended genealogically.'[49]

The last aspect of Walpole's taste for miniatures and enamels was, more simply, an appreciation of them as paintings. In the *Anecdotes* Walpole sometimes echoed contemporary arguments that the taste of patrons had confined English painting to portraiture; and of Peter Oliver he suggested that he was 'in some respects' a greater master even than Isaac Oliver, because he 'did not confine his talent to single heads [but] copied in watercolours several capital pictures with signal success'.[50] But essentially Walpole's imagined audience for the *Anecdotes* was not the critical

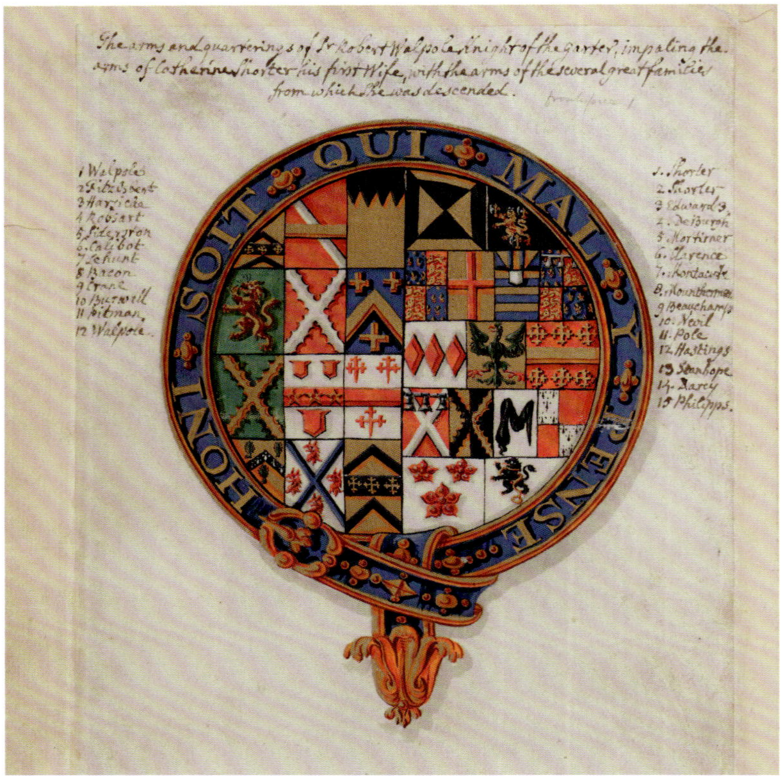

Figure 213. *The Arms and quarterings of Sir Robert Walpole Knight of the Garter, impaling the arms of Catherine Shorter, his first wife*, water and body colour. In Walpole's extra-illustrated *Description*, 1774. The Lewis Walpole Library, Yale University. 49 2523

Figure 214. Front endpapers showing a 'family Tree' of characters from Roman history in Herman Moll, *Geographia Antiqua*, 1726. The Lewis Walpole Library, Yale University. 49 2621. Cat. 88

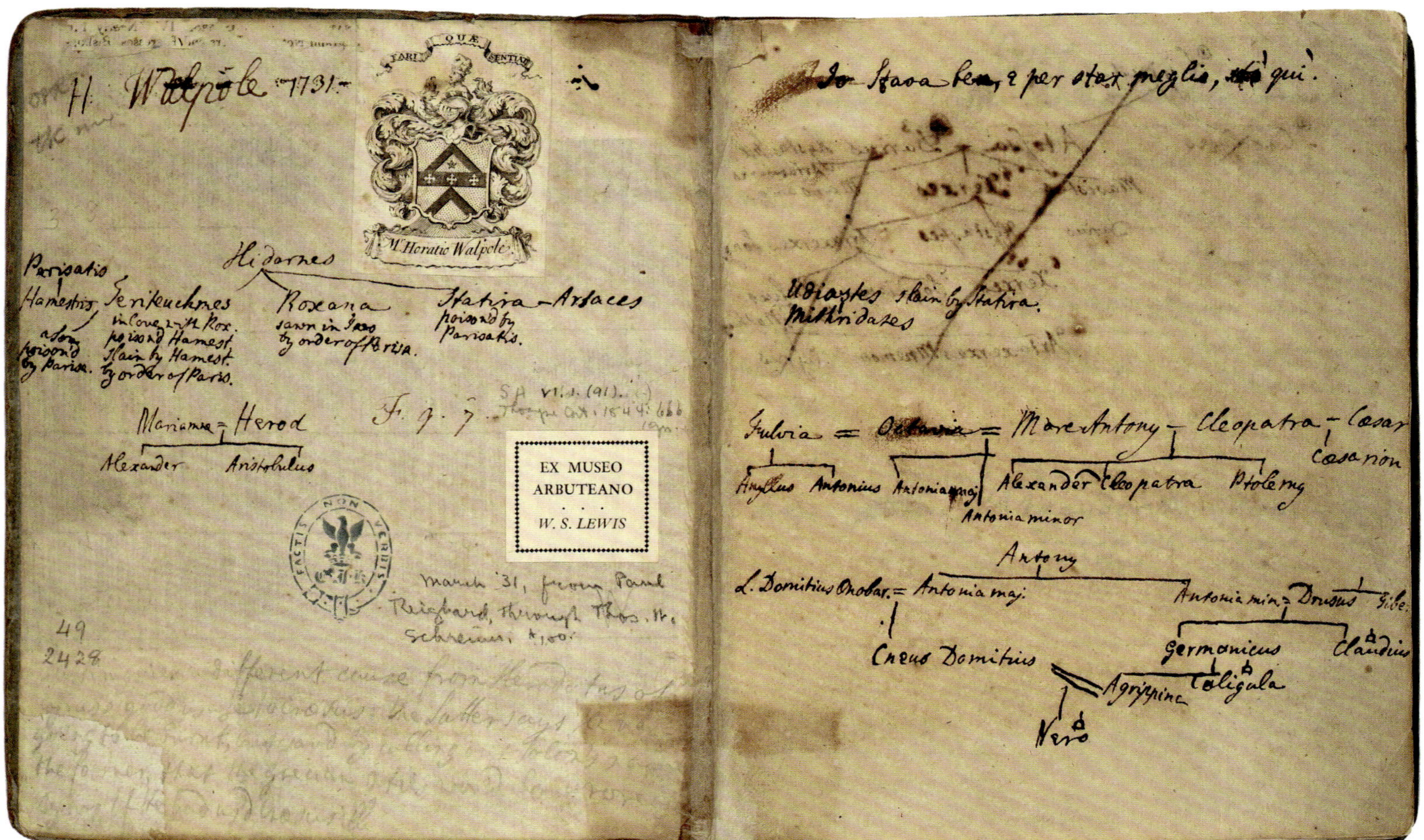

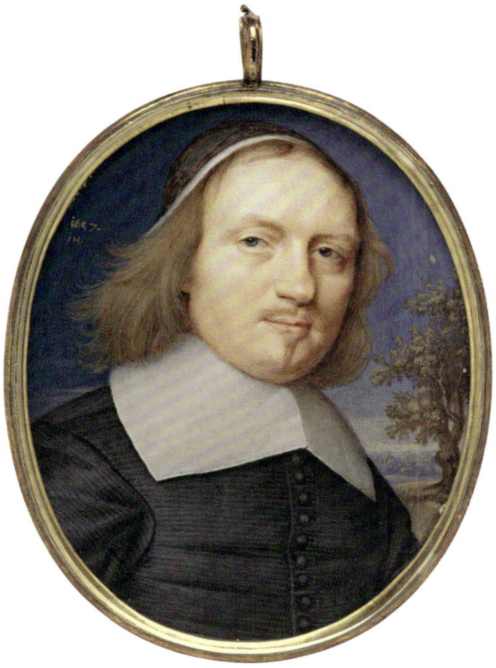

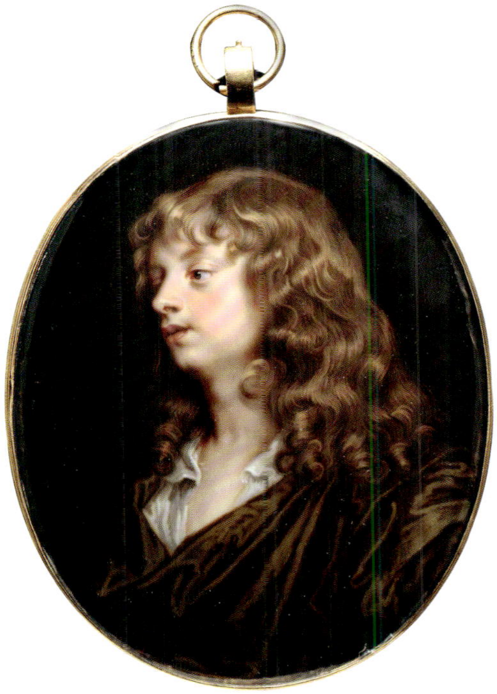

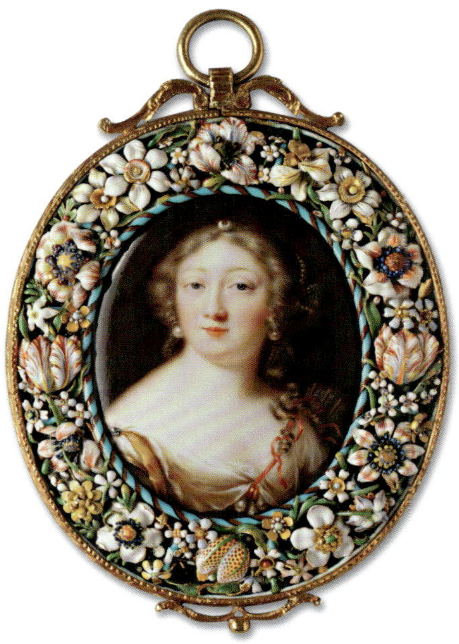

Figure 215. John Hoskins, *Dr Brian Walton* ('Sarjeant Maynard'), 1657, watercolour on vellum, laid on card, set in vermeil case, H 7.2 cm (oval). The Metropolitan Museum of Art, New York, Fletcher Fund, 1935.35.89.3. Cat. 180

Figure 216. Christian Friedrich Zincke, *Unknown youth* (formerly Abraham Cowley, 1618–97), 1716, enamel on copper, 6.8 × 5.4 cm. Fitzwilliam Museum, Cambridge. PD.7-1949. Cat. 226

Figure 217. Jean Petitot I, *Catherine Henriette d'Angennes, Comtesse d'Olonne, as Diana*, 1680, enamel on copper, 3.8 × 3.2 cm. Philadelphia Museum of Art: Gift of Mrs Lessing J. Rosenwald, 1961. 1961–37–1. Cat. 185

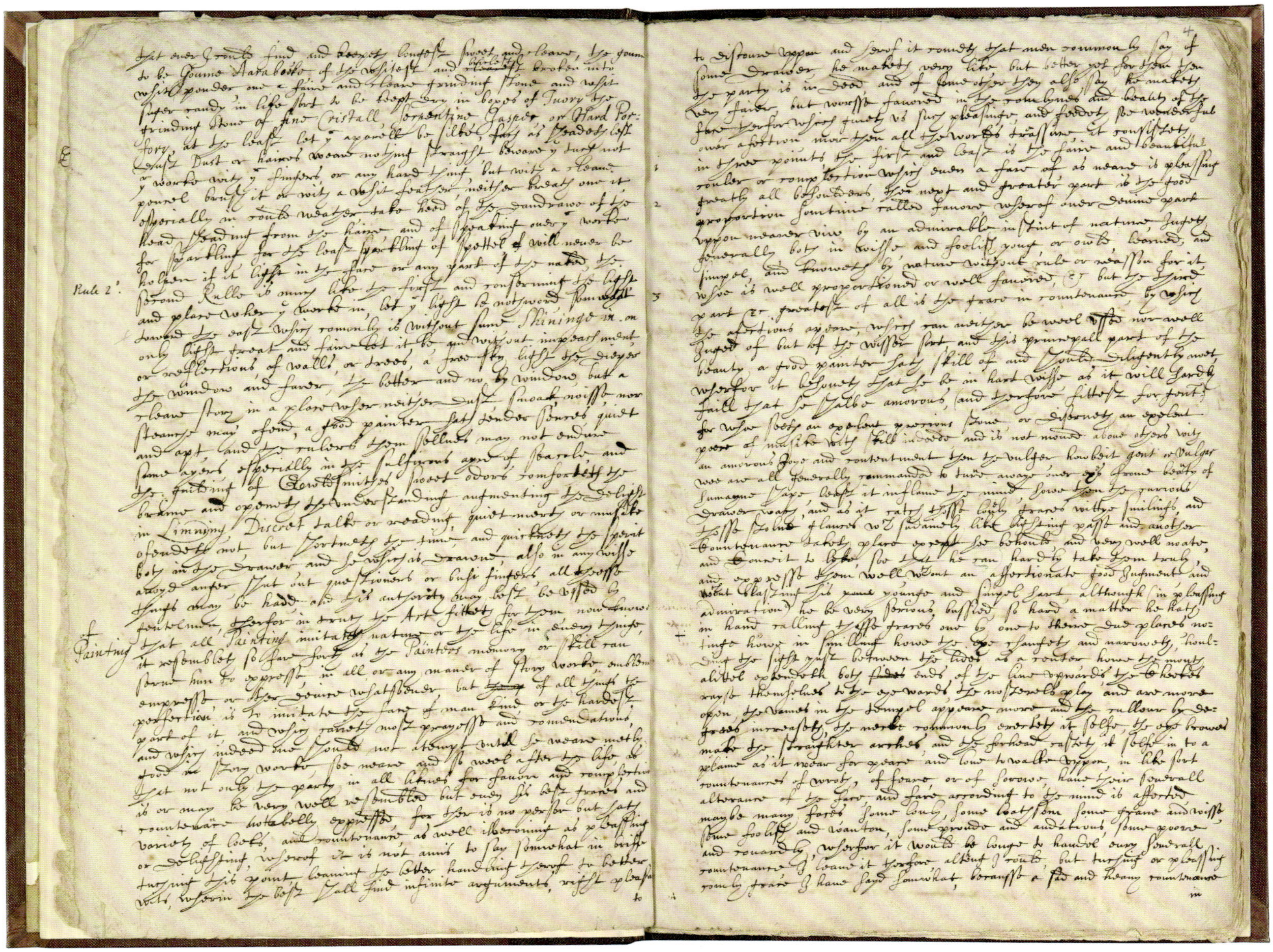

Figure 218. Unknown copyist after Nicholas Hilliard, *A Treatise Concerning the Arte of Limning*, 1624, manuscript, closed: 33 × 21.5 cm. Edinburgh University Library. Laing Mss, La.III.174. Cat. 209

'connoisseur', to whom he rarely referred, but 'collectors and virtuosi' and 'antiquaries' such as himself. For example, Holbein was 'dear to connoisseurs for the singular perfection of his colouring [but] dear to antiquaries by the distance of time in which he lived, by the present scarcity of his works, and by his connections with More and Erasmus'. The implication, however, that Walpole cared for miniatures and enamels only as 'rarities', or for evocative associations or important sitters, is contradicted by his account of John Hoskins in the *Anecdotes*. Praising 'this valuable master', Walpole noted one miniature that 'may be called perfect', adding as an afterthought 'but not known whose portrait'.[51] On another occasion he described Holbein's *Anne of Cleves*, then at Lee Priory, as 'that small most precious head … engraved, but very inadequately by Houbraken in the Illustrious [Heads]. It is by far one of the most exquisite works of Holbein and in the most perfect preservation.'[52] This is the assessment of a collector 'antiquarian and virtuoso enough', to use his own phrase, to value an important likeness, to appreciate a beautiful painting and to judge that a print has failed to do the original justice. Walpole equally valued the intrinsic beauty of enamels, calling Petitot 'a genius' and opining that '[C.F.] Zincke alone has once or twice … produced works that might stand in competition' (Fig. 216).[53]

Walpole's attributions to Nicholas Hilliard and Isaac Oliver were sometimes faulty, he occasionally muddled Isaac and Peter Oliver's work, and although warning that the number of Holbein's works was 'increased by copies, by doubtful or by pretended pieces',[54] he, too, acquired some 'doubtful' pieces. It should be noted, however, that the attribution of miniatures was then in its infancy and can still be problematic. Walpole had a real understanding and appreciation of miniatures and enamels as paintings, which he clearly studied with great attention. In *The Anecdotes* he referred to Isaac Oliver's *Self-portrait* (Fig. 130) and enthused, 'The art of the master and the imitation of nature are so great in it, that the largest magnifying glass only calls out new beauties'[55] – a self-portrait by Walpole as the knowledgeable collector poring over his small portraits.

In 1774, when Walpole was fifty-seven, Lord Chesterfield's letters to his son, from 1746 onwards, were published posthumously. One letter addressed his son's forthcoming Grand Tour:

> No days lost in poring upon almost imperceptible Intaglios and Cameos: and do not become a Virtuoso of small wares. Form a taste of Painting, Sculpture, and Architecture, if you please … those are liberal arts, and a real taste and knowledge of them become a man of fashion … But, beyond certain bounds, the man of Taste ends, and the frivolous Virtuoso begins.[56]

It is arguable that such attitudes could have written miniatures out of the history of painting in England, leaving them hidden away in cabinets of objects of virtù. But Walpole's passion for both miniatures and enamels ensured that the regard paid these arts in Vertue's notes, and reflected in collections such as that of Lord Oxford, found a voice in the *The Anecdotes*. Walpole also gave renewed voice to earlier authors who in disparate publications had registered the importance of miniatures in English painting.[57] Above all, Walpole's knowledge of the technical history of miniatures both as a collector and an 'antiquary' (he owned Vertue's copy of Nicholas Hilliard's treatise on limning; Fig. 218) ensured that the *Anecdotes* memorialized these artists' identity as painters in watercolour and did not sideline their work as mere variants of oil paintings. Similarly, in emphasizing the unique nature of enamel painting, he clearly distinguished between the two arts technically and historically. Finally, he secured a place for miniature painting in the national narrative of painting in England.

The nineteenth century saw a flowering of national institutions, such as the South Kensington Museum, now the Victoria and Albert Museum, which opened in 1857. In 1865 the museum held an exhibition of over 3000 miniatures and enamels borrowed from private families and collectors. In his 'Introductory Notice' Samuel Redgrave echoed Walpole, praising the excellence of English miniature painters compared to oil painters in the years before Van Dyck.[58] The following year Redgrave published (with his brother Richard) *A Century of Painters of the English School*, tracing the flowering of English painting from 1760. In the preface he expanded on this theme in a survey of painting prior to 1760, referring extensively to Walpole. From its inception the South Kensington Museum was 'strongly associated with British Art', with the Redgraves instrumental in encouraging John Sheepshanks to give his collection of modern British oil paintings as the foundation of a national gallery of British art.[59] In 1859 the museum published a *Catalogue of Pictures, Drawings and Etchings*, which although as yet including no miniatures, noted in the section on watercolours: 'From the earliest time there was one branch of art in which English artists had a reputation even on the continent and in which they certainly excelled the artists of other nations, namely miniature painting in water-colours.'[60] The museum adopted the role of protector of both miniature and enamel painting and is now home of the National Collection of both arts. Walpole's own collections were dispersed in 1842. But the legacy of his collection of miniatures and enamels is enshrined in the *Anecdotes*, fixing not only bare facts but a collector's enthusiasm, appreciation and knowledge.

1. *D 1774*.
2. See Katherine Coombs, 'From Limning to Miniature: The Etymology of the Portrait Miniature', in Stephen Lloyd, ed., *The Miniature Portrait c. 1500–1850: Current Research and New Approaches* (Edinburgh: National Galleries of Scotland, forthcoming 2010).
3. For a history of miniatures, see Katherine Coombs, *The Portrait Miniature in England* (London: V&A Publications, 1998).
4. For a history of enamels see Sarah Coffin and Bodo Hofstetter, *The Gilbert Collection: Portrait Miniatures in Enamel* (London: Philip Wilson, 2000), 14–44.
5. Morris R Brownell, *The Prime Minister of Taste: A Portrait of Horace Walpole* (New Haven and London: Yale University Press, 2001), 1.
6. Letter from Gilly Williams, 26 Dec. 1766, in John Heneage Jesse, *George Selwyn and his Contemporaries*, 4 vols. (John C. Nimmo, 1901), 2: 125.
7. Brownell, *The Prime Minister*, 1–7 (all references).
8. *HW Corres*. 18: 277 (HW to Mann, 19 July 1743).
9. Horace Walpole, *Anecdotes of Painting in England* (Arno Press, 1969), 1: 261.
10. *Anecdotes* 1: 176.
11. See Introduction in Robert R. Wark, ed., *Sir Joshua Reynolds: Discourses on Art* (New Haven and London: Yale University Press, 1975, 2nd printing), xv–xxxv; and Charles Harrison, Paul Wood and Jason Gaiger, *Art in Theory 1648–1815: An Anthology of Changing Ideas* (Oxford: Blackwell Publishing, 2000), 651–2.
12. Lawrence Lipking, *The Ordering of the Arts in Eighteenth-Century England* (Princeton University Press, 1970), 109–26.
13. See Barbara M. Benedict, 'The "Curious Attitude" in Eighteenth-Century Britain: Observing and Owning', in *Eighteenth-Century Life* 14 (Nov. 1990): 59–98.
14. *HW Corres*. 17: 357–8 (HW to Mann, 19 July 1743).
15. *HW Corres*. 1: 56 n. 1 (HW to Cole, 7 Feb. 1764).
16. *D 1774*, 428, 'Horace Walpole, from Murillo, watercolours on ivory'. For Lens's role in the introduction of ivory in miniature painting, see Coombs, *Portrait Miniature*, 80–83.
17. *HW Corres*. 20: 358–9 (HW to Mann, 14 Feb. 1753).
18. Frances Vivian, *A Life of Frederick Prince of Wales, 1707–1751: A Connoisseur of the Arts* (Lampeter: Edwin Mellen Press, 2006), 400.
19. See Francis Haskell, *History and its Images: Art and the Interpretation of the Past* (New Haven and London: Yale University Press, 1993), 13–79; and J.G. Pollard, 'England and the Italian Medal', in Edward Chaney and Peter Mack, eds., *England and the Continental Renaissance: Essays in Honour of J.B. Trapp* (Woodbridge: Boydell Press, 1990), 191–201.
20. The key discussion of the 'Virtuoso' remains Walter E. Houghton, Jr., 'The English Virtuoso in the Seventeenth Century, Parts I and II', *Journal of the History of Ideas*, no. 3 (1942): 51–73; and no. 4 (1942): 190–219. Since I first presented a paper on this subject in 2003 at the Paul Mellon Centre conference *Collecting and the Imagination: Horace Walpole at Strawberry Hill*, two further reassessments have been published: Brian Cowan, 'An Open Elite: The Peculiarities of Connoisseurship in Early Modern England', *Modern Intellectual History*, vol. 1, no. 2 (2004): 151–83; Harry Mount, 'The Monkey with the Magnifying Glass: Constructions of the Connoisseur in Eighteenth-Century Britain', *Oxford Art Journal*, vol. 29, no. 2 (2006): 167–83.
21. Henry Peacham, *The Compleat Gentleman* (first published 1622: 16 chapters; 2nd ed. London, 1634: 21 chapters), chapter 12.
22. Anthony Ashley Cooper, third Earl of Shaftesbury, *Characteristics of Men, Manners, Opinions, Times*, ed. Lawrence E. Klein (Cambridge University Press, 1999), 405.
23. Shaftesbury, *Characteristics*, 406.
24. *The Works of Joseph Addison* (George Bell & Sons, 1901), vol. I, 256.
25. Jesse, *Selwyn*, 2: 125.
26. Allen T. Hazen, *A Catalogue of Horace Walpole's Library* (Oxford: Oxford University Press, 1969), cat. nos. 487, 2440, 2737.
27. Quoted in *Anecdotes* 1: 90.
28. *HW Corres*. 9: 3 (HW to Montagu, 6 May 1736).
29. *HW Corres*. 17: 213 (HW to Mann, 26 Nov. 1741).
30. *HW Corres*. 40: 34 (HW to Spence, 21 Feb. 1741).
31. *HW Corres*. 15: 11–24 (HW to Middleton, 1743/4).
32. Haskell, *History and its Images*, 70.
33. *HW Corres*. 1: 29 (HW to Cole, 30 Sept. 1762).
34. *Anecdotes* 1: 28.
35. *Anecdotes* 1: 294.
36. *A Catalogue and Description of King Charles the First's Capital Collection* (London, 1757), 'advertisement', n.p.
37. *HW Corres*. 9: 144 (HW to Montagu, 14 Dec. 1752).
38. *HW Corres*. 1: 368 (HW to Cole, 25 April 1775).
39. *Anecdotes* 1: 293.
40. Brian Fothergill, *The Strawberry Hill Set: Horace Walpole and his Circle* (London: Faber, 1983), 40.
41. Peacham, *Compleat Gentleman* (1634), 125.
42. *Anecdotes* 1: 273.
43. Quoted in Brownell, *The Prime Minister*, 96.
44. *Anecdotes* 1: 179–80.
45. For an account of Peacham's publications and of limning, see Katherine Coombs, '"A kind of gentle painting": Limning in 16th century England', in Kim Sloan, ed., *European Visions: American Voices*, British Museum Research Publication no. 172 (London, 2009).
46. *Anecdotes* 1: 230.
47. *Anecdotes* 1: 348.
48. Christopher Lloyd and Vanessa Remington, *Portrait Miniatures from the Collection of Her Majesty Queen Elizabeth II* (Woodbridge: Boydell Press, 1996), 14–15, fig.3.
49. *HW Corres*. 9: 291 (HW to Montagu, 12 Aug. 1760).
50. *Anecdotes* 2: 221.
51. *Anecdotes* 2: 29–30.
52. *HW Corres*. 12: 111 n. 29.
53. *Anecdotes* 2: 31.
54. *Anecdotes* 1: 74.

55. *Anecdotes* 1: 178.
56. Quoted in Brownell, *Prime Minister*, 6.
57. Bainbrigge Buckeridge, 'An Essay Towards an English School of Painters', appended to Roger de Piles, *The Art of Painting and the Lives of the Painters* (London, 1706), 354–429.
58. *Catalogue of the Special Exhibition of Portrait Miniatures on Loan at the South Kensington Museum* (London, 1865), vii.
59. Christopher Whitehead, *The Public Art Museum in Nineteenth-Century Britain: The Development of the National Gallery* (Aldershot: Ashgate, 2005), 164.
60. Coombs, *Portrait Miniature*, 12.

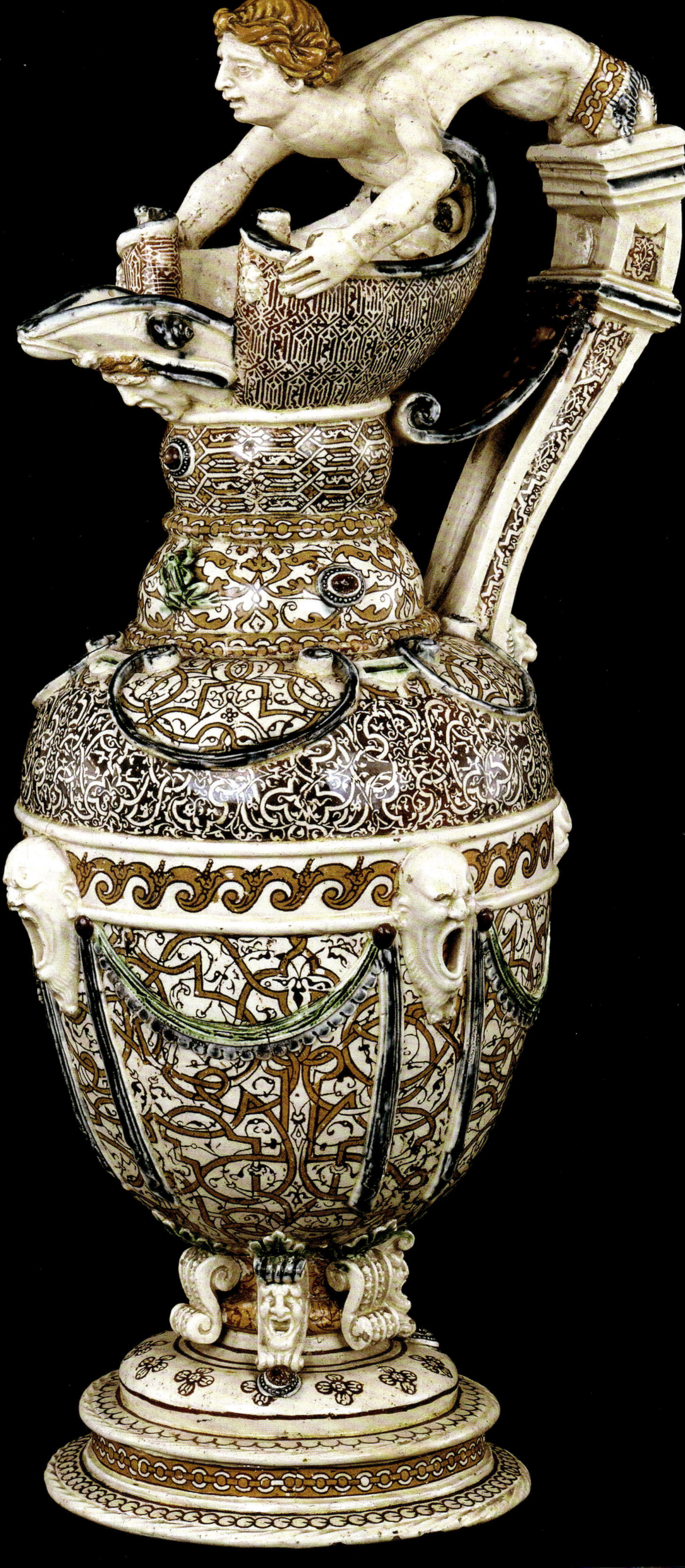

12.

'PLAYTHINGS STILL?' HORACE WALPOLE AS A COLLECTOR OF CERAMICS

TIMOTHY WILSON

In June 1785 Walpole wrote to Sir Horace Mann in Florence, requesting an example of porcelain from a grand-ducal factory he believed (wrongly) to exist:

> I should be glad if your nephew would bring me a single bit, a cup, or other trifle, as a sample. I remember that ages ago there was a manufacture at Florence belonging to Marquis Ginori, of which I wished for a piece, but could not procure one … I have a closet furnished with specimens of porcelain of various countries; besides a good deal of faience or Raphael-ware, and some pieces with the arms of Medici – but am not I an old simpleton to be wanting playthings still? – and how like is one's last cradle to one's first![1]

Among the varied accumulations at Strawberry Hill, ceramics were the most numerous category.[2] Walpole's China Room, as described in the 1784 *Description*, contained a densely packed 'collection of porcelaine, earthenware, glass, and enamel on copper, of various ages and countries', numbering some 670 items,[3] and continued to grow: one of his most celebrated possessions, the set of Delft plates painted with signs of the zodiac by Sir James Thornhill, was acquired at Mrs Hogarth's sale on 24 April 1780. Over 200 pieces were oriental (mostly Chinese, some Japanese), and about 160 were French porcelains, mostly Sèvres but also Chantilly, Saint Cloud and other factories. Alongside these were smaller groups of Chelsea[4] and other English porcelain (75 pieces) (Fig. 223); Meissen (Fig. 224) and German porcelain (33); Wedgwood and English pottery (39); maiolica (22); glasses (53) (Figs. 9, 225), including 24 marvellous plates of Venetian white glass painted with views of Venice acquired there in 1741; and smaller groups of classical pottery (Fig. 220),[5] Roman glass, medieval tiles,[6] French Renaissance pottery, German stoneware, Delft (Figs. 226, 228), sixteenth-century Limoges enamels (Fig. 229) and Islamic pottery. There were also puzzling exotic categories like 'Portuguese red earth', 'basons of most ancient Gombroon china'[7] and wares described as 'Turkish' and 'gilt within' or 'cast with leaves'. The arrangement, described in ten lovingly detailed pages of the *Description*, appears random, without any systematic attempt to group similar things together: in so dense a display the shelf heights may have been an overriding criterion. Already by 1774 ceramics had overflowed the China Room into the adjoining Waiting Room. There is nothing that sounds like a conventional

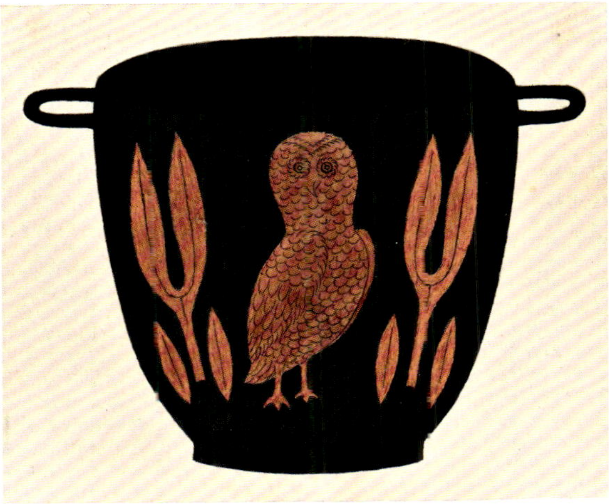

Figure 219. Ewer, 'Saint-Porchaire', *c.* 1545–60, white-bodied earthenware, inlaid and glazed, H 34.6 cm. National Museums Scotland. 1975.466. Cat. 230

Figure 220. *Ancient Greek Cup*, watercolour 10.7 × 12.8, p. 34 from Bawtree's extra-illustrated copy of the *Description*. The Lewis Walpole Library, Yale University. 33 30 copy 4

THE LIMOGES ENAMEL HORN

Timothy Wilson

In the 'Refectory or Great Parlour', as if in a medieval baron's hall, hung what the *Description* calls 'a hunting-horn, finely enameled on one side in colours, on the other in chiaro scuro, with the history of saint Hubert'. This is a unique virtuoso product of the French Renaissance, signed by its most brilliant enameller, Léonard Limousin.

Enamel painting is carried out in powdered glass on metal. Here the enamelled plaques surround a real ox horn, an unparalleled and demanding process. On one side, in coloured enamels, are scenes on a hunting theme. Nearest the opening is the story of how St Hubert (an eighth-century Bishop of Liège), while out hunting, saw a vision of Christ Crucified between a stag's horns; he became the patron saint of hunters. Three further scenes show hounds attacking a stag, a boar and a hare. On the other side, in muted *grisaille*, are roundels between scrollwork and spirited grotesques: near the opening is a Roman emperor, in front of whom a second, ghostly profile appears; next is Cleopatra applying the asp to her breast; then David playing the harp; and the last, David with the head of Goliath. Beneath the David and Goliath scene is painted (faintly) a date, apparently 1538, and the signature 'LEONARDVS.LEMOVICVS', the Latin name of Léonard Limousin.

Enamel painting on metal reached a summit of pictorial sophistication in sixteenth-century Limoges and Léonard Limousin was its greatest name. Shortly after his first-known dated work in 1533, he was introduced to the royal court in Paris, became *esmailleur pour le roi* and painted ambitious portraits

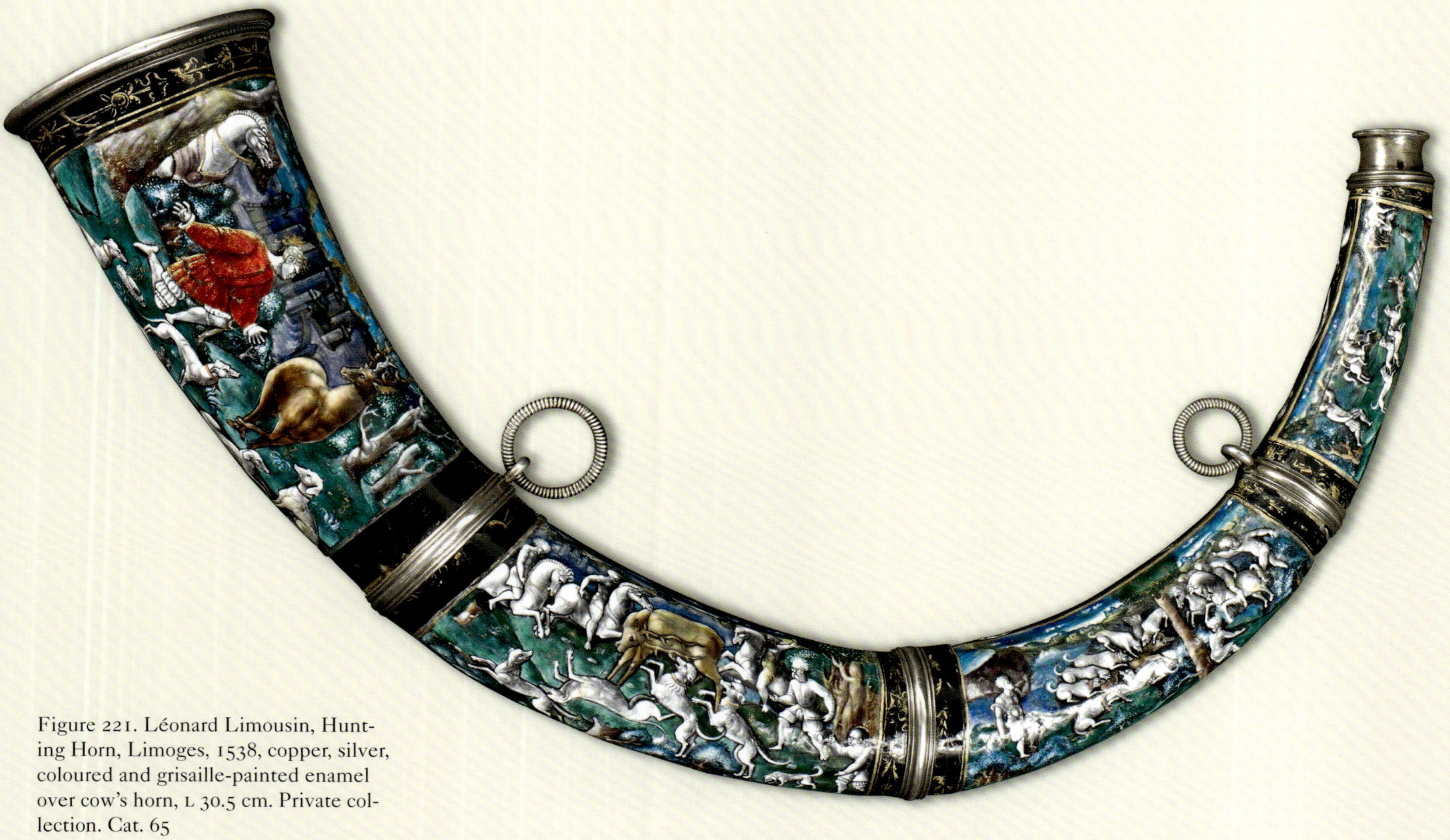

Figure 221. Léonard Limousin, Hunting Horn, Limoges, 1538, copper, silver, coloured and grisaille-painted enamel over cow's horn, L 30.5 cm. Private collection. Cat. 65

and other large-scale works. Stylistically, the horn's *grisailles* resemble another early work, a gaming board in the Louvre dated 1537. Nineteenth-century writers reported a tradition that the horn was made for Francis I. This is undocumented, but Francis had a passion for hunting with dogs and the horn is an object of high ambition, appropriate as a royal gift; the tradition might be correct.

In 1842 the auctioneer George Robins enthused: 'perfectly unique … undoubtedly one of the most remarkable gems of this rare collection, and has been highly prized by the connoisseur'. The compiler of the burlesque *Gooseberry Hall* parodied it: 'Over the chimney hangs a very large and curious cow's horn, covered with unintelligible hieroglyphics, supposed to signify that it was once the property of – the name is illegible – a celebrated Saxon swineherd.' At the sale it was bought by the dealer Webb for 135 guineas and soon passed into the collection of medieval and Renaissance works of art of the China merchant Hollingworth Magniac, who lent it to the 1850 exhibition of *Works of Antient and Mediaeval Art* at the Society of Arts in London ('this celebrated work') and to the 1862 *Special Exhibition* at South Kensington ('this exquisite work of art'). After World War II it passed into American ownership. Though it was for a time on loan at the Metropolitan Museum of Art, New York, the exhibition *Horace Walpole's Strawberry Hill* is the first public showing for many years of this long-famous object.

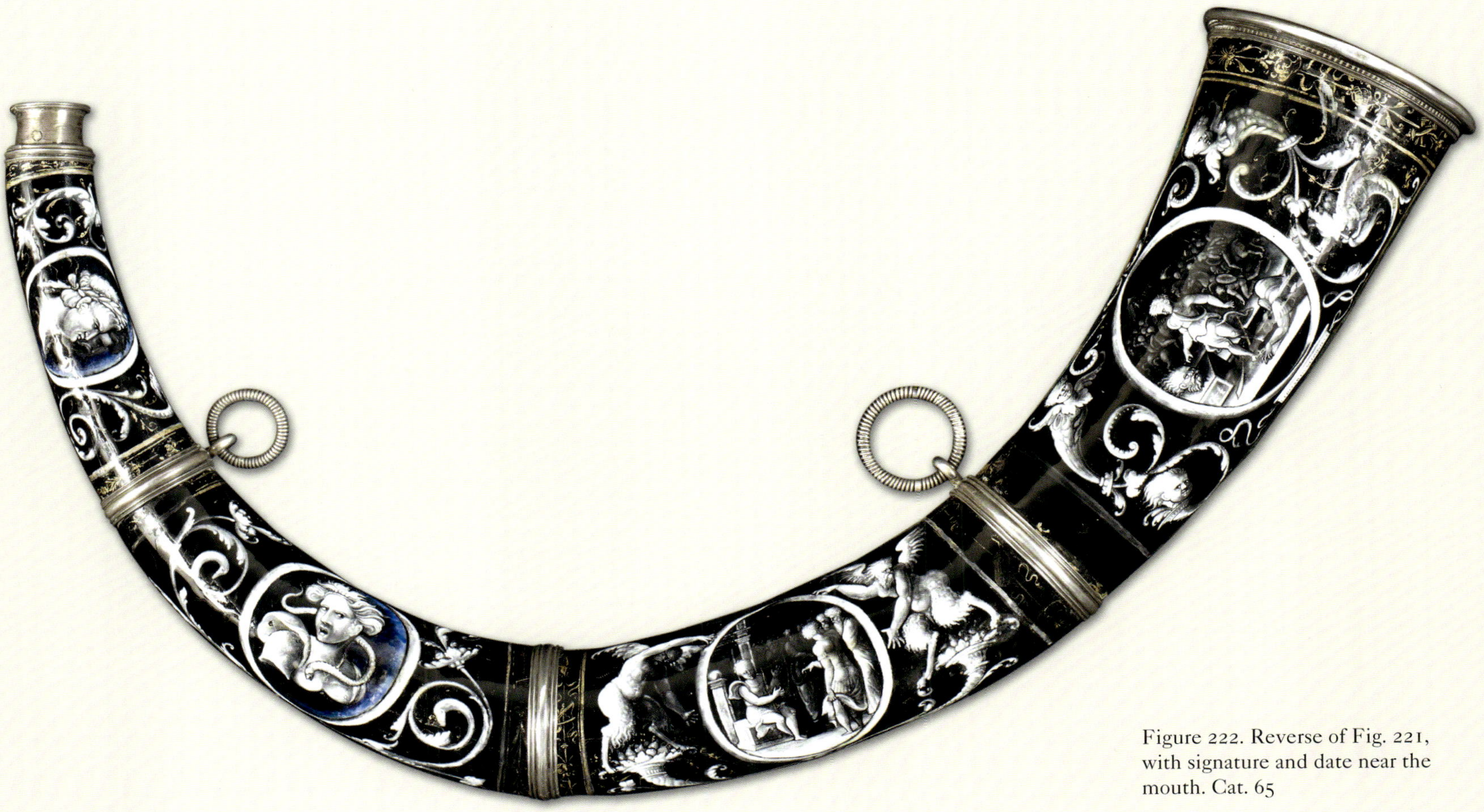

Figure 222. Reverse of Fig. 221, with signature and date near the mouth. Cat. 65

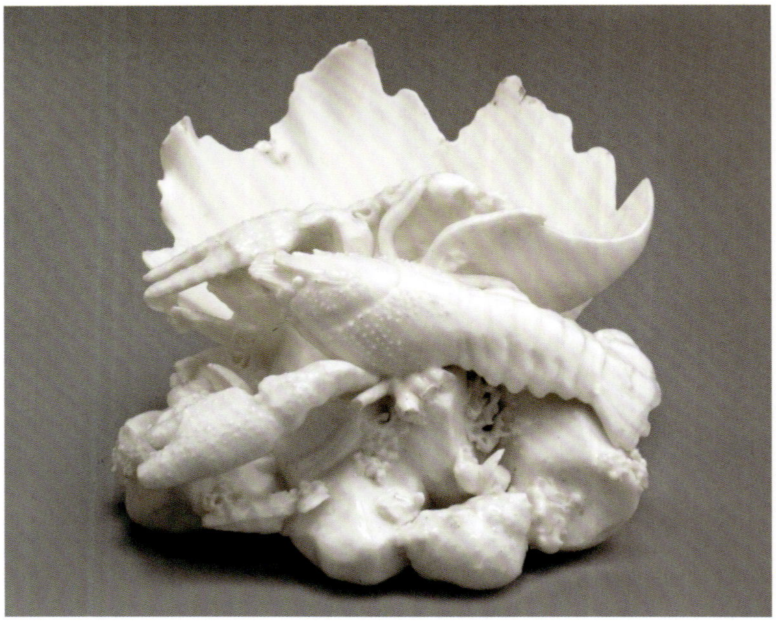

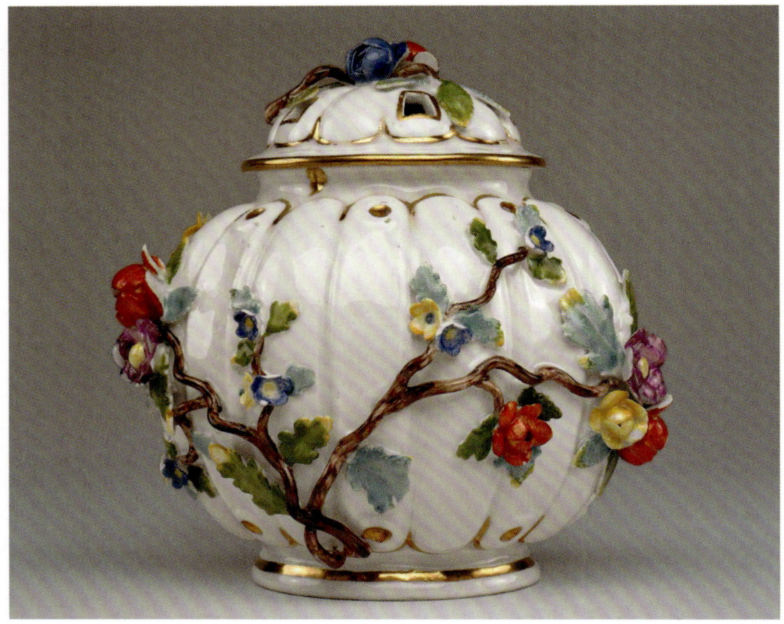

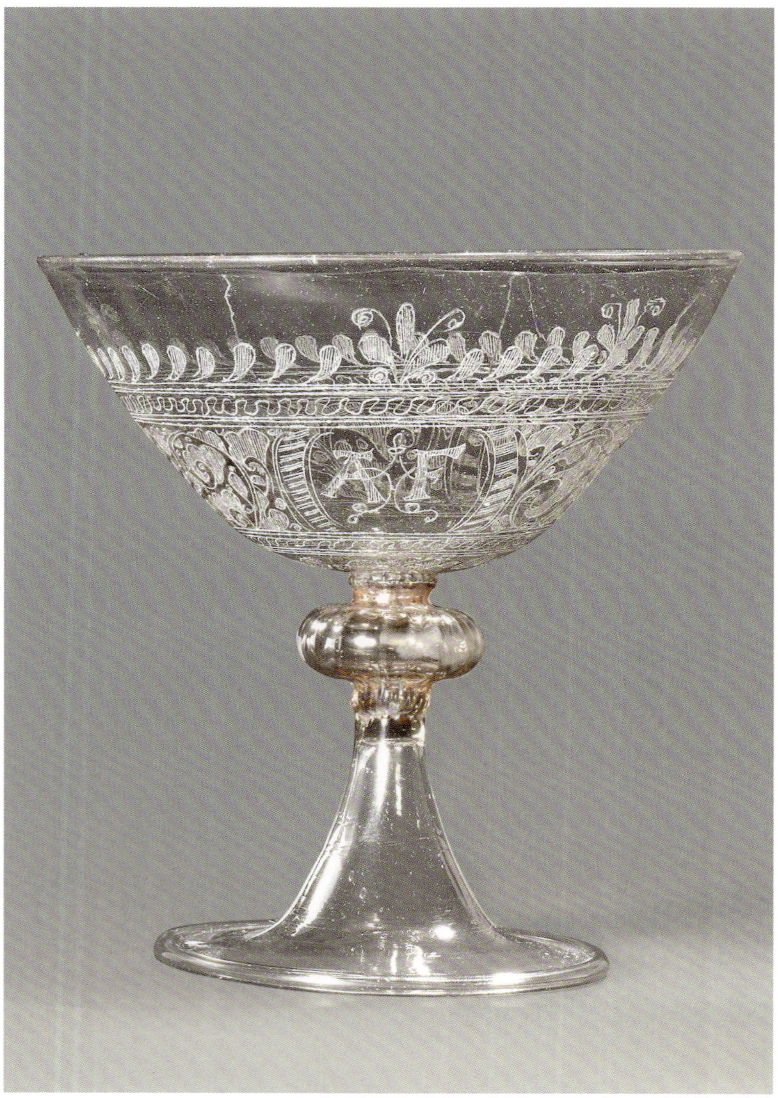

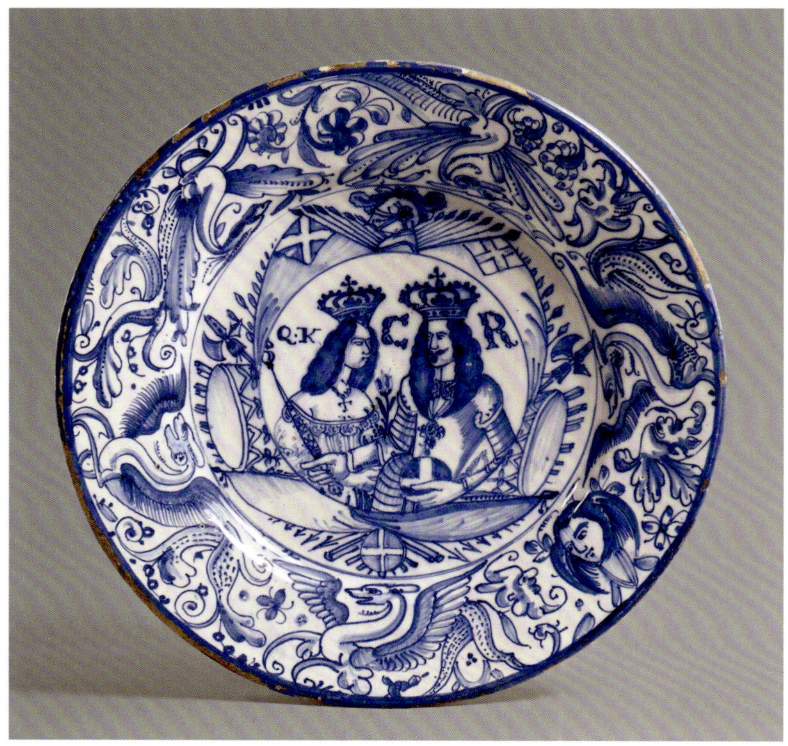

Figure 223. One of a pair of salt-cellars in the form of crayfish, Chelsea, *c.* 1745–51, soft-paste porcelain, 13.5 × 6.8 cm. British Museum, Department of Prehistory and Europe. 1887,0307,II.18. Cat. 238

Figure 224. Pot Pourri vase and cover, Meissen, *c.* 1745–50, hard-paste porcelain, painted and gilt, H 13.9 cm. British Museum, Department of Prehistory and Europe. Franks.76. Cat. 237

Figure 225. Goblet, probably by Jacopo Verzelini, glass, H 13.3 cm. Victoria and Albert Museum, London. C.1522-1936. Cat. 244

Figure 226. Dish with Portraits of Charles II and Catherine of Braganza, English or possibly Dutch, 1662–85, tin-glazed earthenware, D 33 cm. Victoria and Albert Museum, London. 3869–1901. Cat. 232

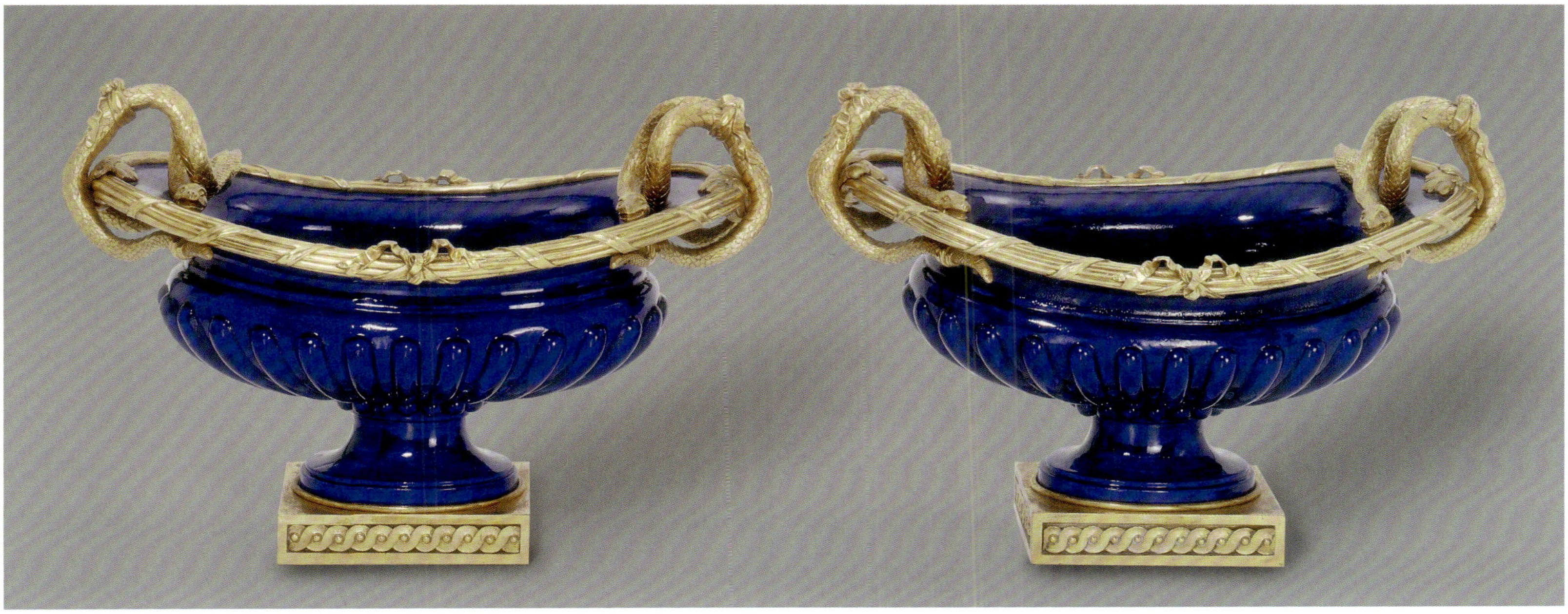

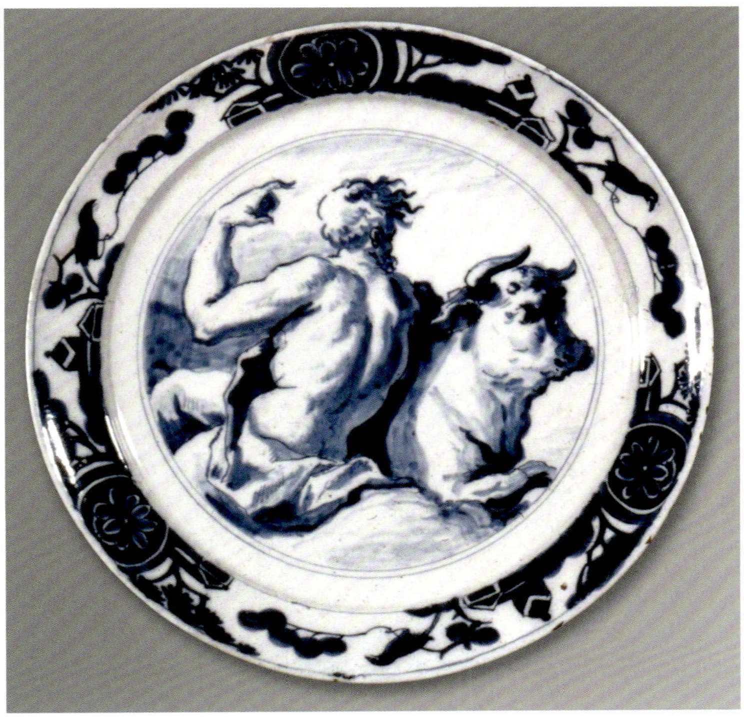

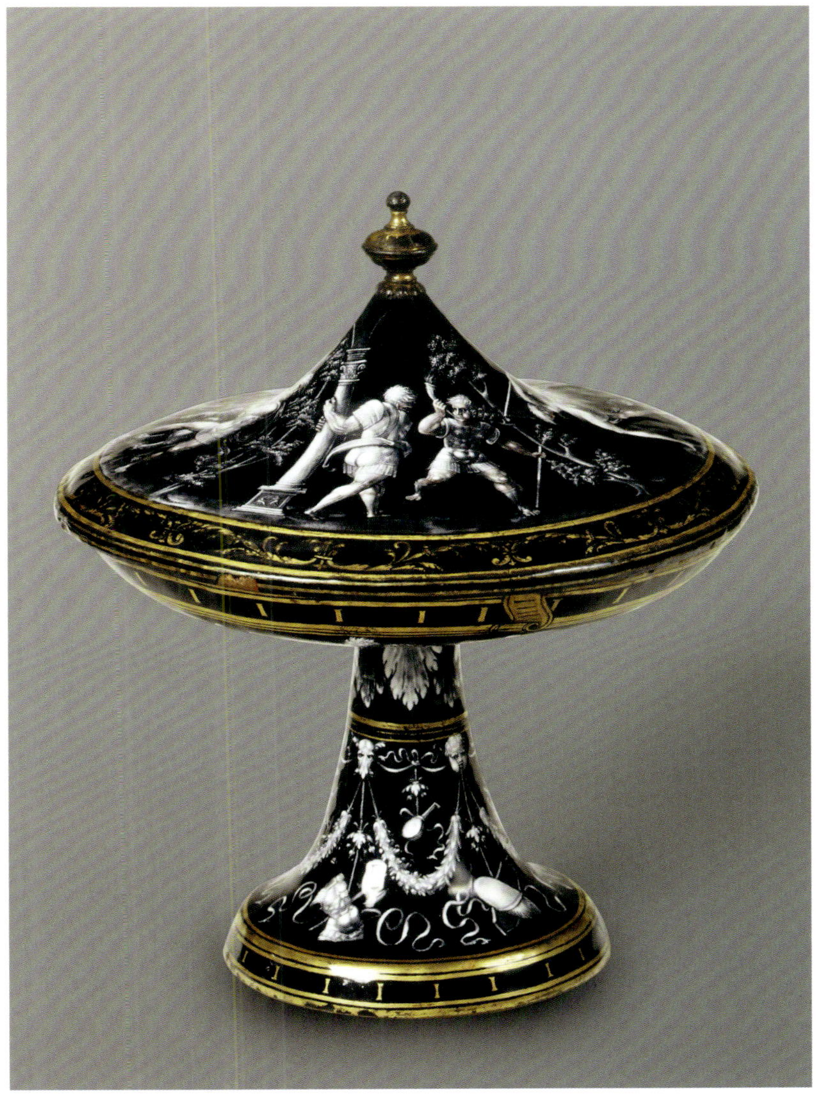

Figure 227. Pair of 'Choiseul' vases, Sèvres, 1763–9, soft-paste porcelain with gilt bronze mounts and bases, 28.8 × 43 × 25.5 cm. Victoria and Albert Museum, London, Jones Bequest. 743-1882, 743A-1882. Cat. 149

Figure 228. Sir James Thornhill, one of a set of twelve Delft plates with Signs of the Zodiac, 1711, tin-glazed earthenware, DIAM 22 cm. British Museum, Department of Prehistory and Europe. 1889.0706.67. Cat. 236

Figure 229. Jean Pénicaud II, Covered cup on a high foot with scenes from the Life of Samson, Limoges, 1539, painted enamel on copper, H 13.3 cm. Victoria and Albert Museum, London, Salting Bequest. C.2460–A-B-1910. Cat. 228

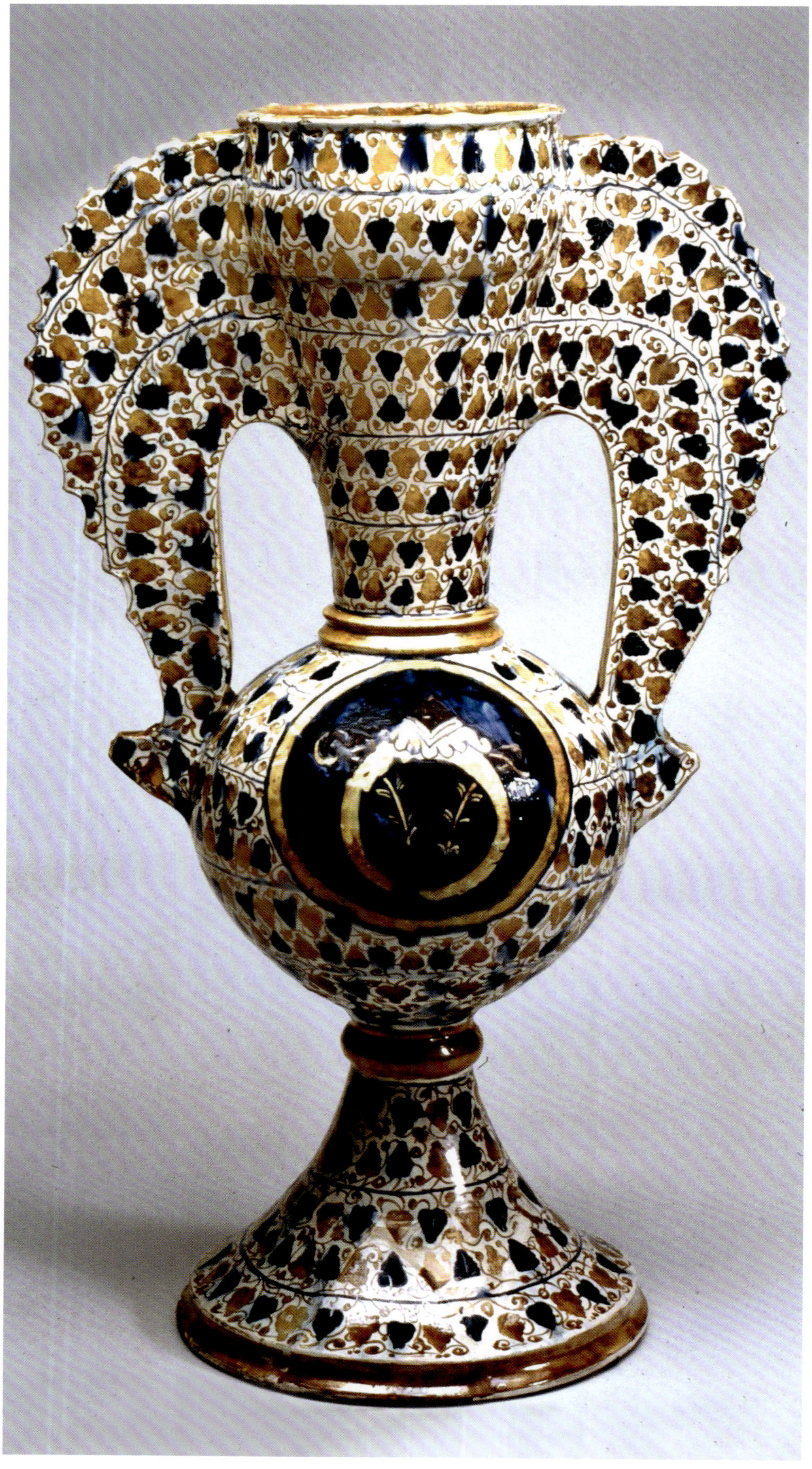

dinner service, and although Walpole's guests may sometimes have dined from special ceramics, everyday tablewares were perhaps kept elsewhere.[8] Rare ceramics were part of his lifestyle: a biographer noted that at breakfast 'the tea-kettle, stand and heater were brought in, and he drank two or three cups of that liquor out of most rare and precious ancient porcelain of Japan'.[9]

Arranged throughout the house, in cupboards, on shelves, on chimneypieces and on and under furniture, were approaching 600 other ceramics. Some were large vases or bowls (sometimes mounted) carefully positioned for display. In the Round Drawing Room, for example, in 1784 two ormolu-mounted Sèvres vases stood on a table (Fig. 227).[10] Under two Japanese lacquer cabinets were a pair of late sixteenth-century pharmacy bottles with the Medici arms, while under another cabinet was an armorial vase of Valencian lustreware, made about 1470 for Lorenzo de' Medici (Fig. 230); what connected these large items under the furniture was not style but armorials. At the end of the Gallery stood 'two commodes of old Japan with marble slabs; on one a triangular cistern of Roman fayence, finely painted with figures, probably from designs by Julio Romano; two large vases, ditto, finely painted, and inscribed *FATTE IN BOTEGA DE ORATIO FONTANA*, and mounted in or molu'; these sixteenth-century Urbino maiolica jars had been fitted in Paris around 1765 with superb ormolu mounts resembling ones applied to Sèvres.[11] On a second commode the matching Urbino 'cistern' was accompanied by 'two bottles of blue and white and gold Seve china, most beautifully designed and ornamented'.[12] The concept was not art-historical: disparate pieces were grouped for visual effect. Nearby, nearly 300 pieces[13] of oriental porcelain assembled by Walpole's mother ('a large collection of ancient porcelaine of China, which belonged to Catherine lady Walpole') were kept piously separate, crammed into a glass-fronted cupboard between the Gallery and the Round Drawing Room (Fig. 231).[14] In view of these quantities, it is not surprising that observers seeking to encapsulate what was distinctive about Walpole's near-omnivorous collecting tended to think of ceramics and especially of porcelain. William Hazlitt's pithy summary was that 'his mind as well as his house, was piled up with Dresden china, and illuminated through painted glass'.[15]

The third quarter of the eighteenth century in England was 'a heyday for upper-class interest in ceramics',[16] and particularly for female fascination with porcelain. Many great houses had 'china rooms' – sometimes hardly more than pantries containing tablewares, sometimes almost museums.[17] The most astonishing of these belonged to the Fountaine family at Narford Hall, Norfolk, where an unrivalled collection of High Renaissance maiolica, Limoges enamels and pottery by or in the manner of Bernard Palissy, formed by the 'virtuoso' Sir Andrew Fountaine, was displayed in an octagonal glazed room with a ceiling painting.[18] George Vertue, visiting in 1739, noted

> a most rare Cabinet of Earthen ware, painted, guilded and adornd, with great beauty and variety. of ancient Italian designs and painting from Raphael. Jul. Romano. del Sarto and other famous masters of that Age, being Vases of beautifull shapes and colours. cesterns. dishes. plates cupps vessels of many formes, all these are in a room ranged in the most elegant & delightfull order possible … all allow tis the most compleat collection of the kind in this part of Europe yet, he has another room adornd with great variety of china Ware for all necessary uses – and ornament. only Blew & White.[19]

Less exceptional, but still intended to impress more than to furnish a dinner table, was the china room of the Dashwoods at Kirtlington Park near Oxford. In 1778 Mrs Lybbe Powys, visiting Kirtlington, was alarmed to be challenged on her connoisseurship by the formidable châtelaine when shown

> Lady Dashwood's china-room, the most elegant I ever saw. 'Tis under the flight of stairs going into the garden; it's ornamented with the finest pieces of the oldest china, and the recesses and shelves painted pea-green and white, the edges being green in a mosaic pattern. Her ladyship said she must try my judgment in china, as she ever did all the visitors of that closet, as there was one piece there so much superior to the others. I thought myself fortunate that a prodigious fine old Japan dish almost at once struck my eye.[20]

Most china rooms were more utilitarian. The 1782 inventory of the Marquess of Rockingham's great house in Yorkshire, Wentworth Woodhouse, included coloured armorial 'China', blue and white oriental porcelain, 'Worcester China', and 'coloured Dresden'; his London house had Chelsea, Wedgwood. 'Derbyshire china', Worcester, 'Queen's Ware' and 'Swinton Ware', as well as porcelain figures.[21]

One local china room that surely impressed Horace was created at Marble Hill by his friend Henrietta Howard, Countess of Suffolk, in 1739. That year she wrote to Lord Herbert that 'my Cheney room will make you stare if not swear, tho' I must tell you 'tis the admiration of the vulgar'. It was in a separate cottage, fitted out with carved and gilded shelves and decorated probably by the French painter Andien de Clermont, whom Walpole later employed at Strawberry Hill. After Lady Suffolk's death in 1767, the China Room defeated the inventory clerks: 'Finding that it was not Possible to Take an Inventory of the China, it was agreed on to take only the amount of the pieces in japan in the Said Room.'[22]

On 31 October 1755 Walpole wrote to Richard Bentley: 'I am fitting up the old kitchen for a china-room.'[23] What was built, however, may not have been the first idea. In Walpole's copy of the 1774 *Description*, an inserted pen drawing, perhaps by John Chute (Fig. 232),[24] shows a ground plan

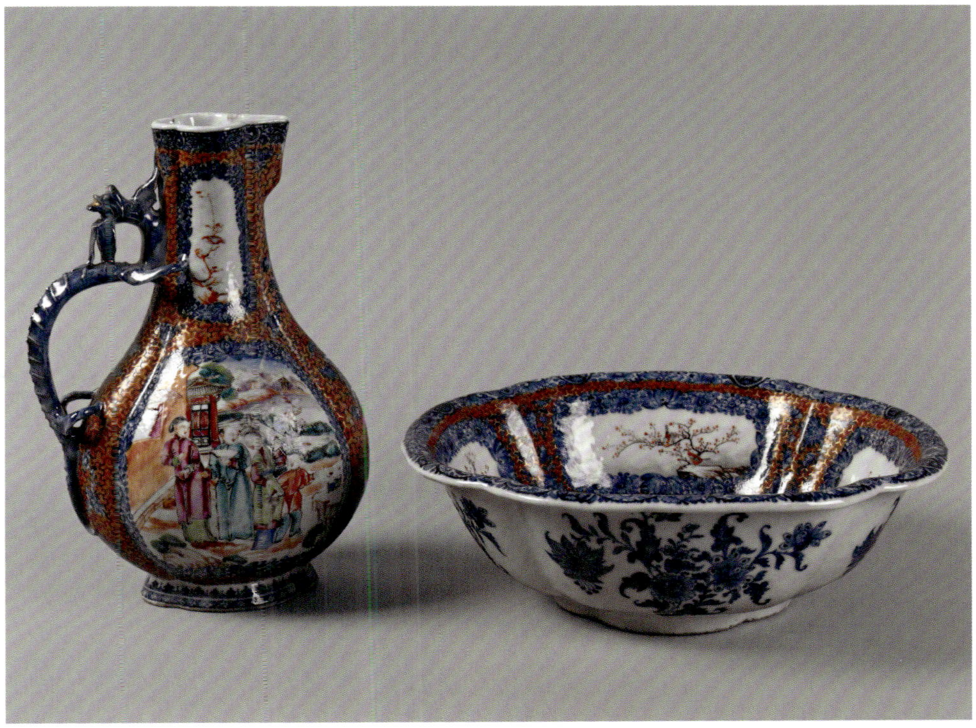

Figure 231. Ewer and Basin with Figures in a Landscape, Chinese, *c.* 1760–90, hard-paste porcelain, H 23.6 cm (ewer); H 8.9 (basin). The Lewis Walpole Library, Yale University. Cat. 242

Figure 230. Vase with Arms and Ring Device of the Medici, Spanish (Manises), *c.* 1465–80, tin-glazed earthenware, H 57 cm. British Museum, Department of Prehistory and Europe. G.619. Cat. 148

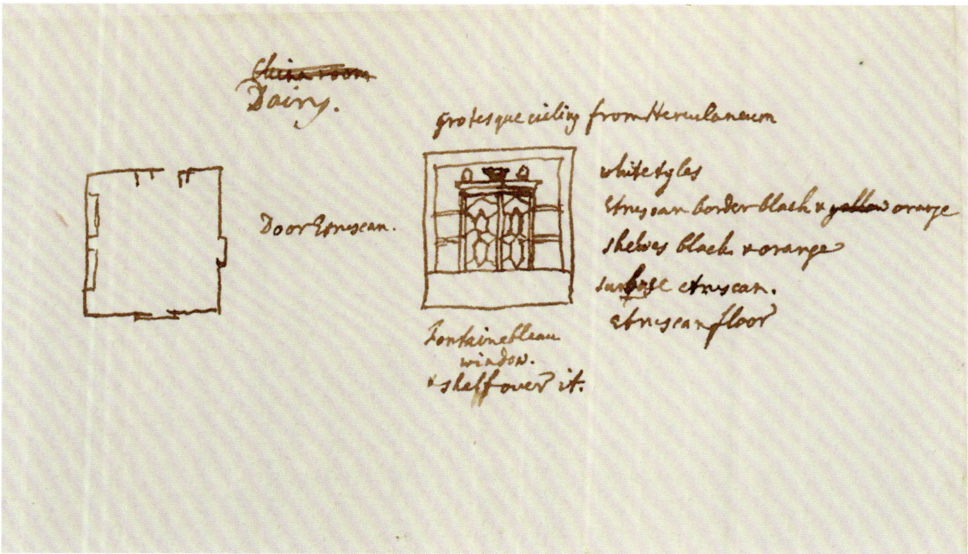

Figure 232. Perhaps by John Chute, *Sketch design for a china room or dairy*, pen and ink, from the *Description*. The Lewis Walpole Library, Yale University. 49 2523

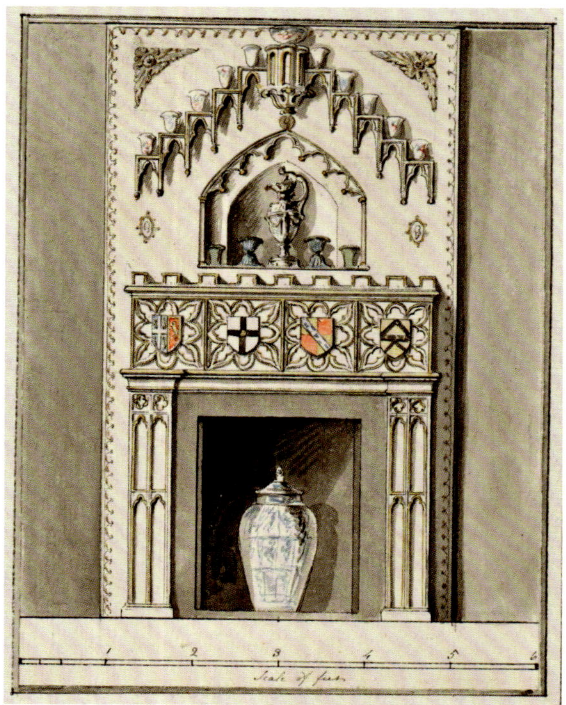

Figure 233. Edward Edwards, *Chimneypiece in China Closet*, pen and ink and watercolour, 1781. The Lewis Walpole Library, Yale University. 49 2523

and elevation of a squarish room under the heading 'China Room', which has been crossed out and 'Dairy' substituted. The annotations read: 'Door Etruscan'; 'grotesque cieling from Herculaneum'; 'white tyles'; 'Etruscan border black & ['yellow' crossed out] orange'; 'shelves black and orange'; 'surbase Etruscan'; 'etruscan floor'; 'Fontainebleau window & shelf over it'. If this was an idea for the China Room, it is an early use of 'Etruscan' ornament, but the idea was not carried foward; the final effect was more eclectic.[25]

The China Room, as it emerged, was 12 feet 4 inches by 9 feet 9 inches (3.8 × 3 m), so that, with a door, chimney breast and two windows, there was restricted shelf space. The ceiling was painted by Johann Heinrich Müntz with 'convolvuluses on poles':[26] Walpole later recorded to Mann that 'I had the ceiling of my china room painted from one I had observed in the little Borghese villa [at Frascati near Rome]. I was hoarding ideas for a future Strawberry even in those days of giddiness, when I seemed to attend to nothing.'[27] Contrasting with this sunny Italian ceiling were two windows with armorial stained glass, a wainscot of white Delft tiles with blue and white borders (possibly recalling an original Dairy concept), and an imposing wooden Gothic chimneypiece, which the *Description* meticulously noted had 'the upper part ... taken from a window of an ancient farm-house, formerly Bradfield-Hall, belonging to Lord Grimston in Essex; the lower part from a chimney at Hurst Monceaux in Sussex: it is adorned with the arms of Talbot, Bridges, Sackville, and Walpole, the principal persons who have inhabited Strawberry-Hill' (Fig. 233). Set in the floor were medieval tiles that Walpole had obtained in 1753.[28] He would have liked to have had it completely paved with them: in 1764, thanking his brother-in-law Charles Churchill for the gift of other medieval tiles, he mentioned obtaining these

> from the cathedral of Gloucester, when it was new paved; they are inlaid in the floor of my china-room. I would have got enough to pave it entirely; but the canons who were flinging them away, had so much devotion left, that they enjoined me not to pave a pagoda with them, nor put them to any profane use ... I did not know that a china-room might casuistically be interpreted a pagoda, and sued for no more.[29]

In the fireplace was a large blue and white oriental porcelain jar, while in a Gothic niche above was a ewer of the mysterious French sixteenth-century pottery known as 'Saint-Porchaire'; his description of it as 'a fine ewer of faience, designed by Julio Romano' is, in view of Giulio Romano's drawings for similar objects, quite accurate.[30] The little shelves above may have been copied from medieval originals, but their configuration seems as akin to the designs of Daniel Marot as to real Gothic;[31] they held chocolate cups, probably eighteenth-century Castelli maiolica.

The decoration of the China Room mirrored its miscellaneous contents. An eloquent idea of the impression it could still make years after Walpole's death is given in a description by the novelist Lady Morgan in 1825:

> Beakers of Indian porcelain, pails of Chelsea china, and vases of Roman *faïence* mingle their remote epochs in amicable confusion, against all rule and chronological *virtù* ... The china closet at the first glimpse looks like any body's china-closet, and, to the unlearned, is neither striking nor interesting; but to those who can trace in its little ceiling the roof of the pretty room at the Borghese villa at Frascati, or a chimney-piece copied from an old window at the ancient seat of the Grimstones (Broadfield Hall, in Essex), it is not unimportant. Regiments of Worcester china bowls, phalanxes of Sèvres mustard-pots, with cups, and dishes, and narrow-necked bottles, and wide-mouthed ewers, and mugs, and jugs, of no very striking appearance, are turned from with a sneer, by those who know not the history of this frail but venerable collection. But when cups have been painted by Pietro Cortona; and plates by Raffael; and dishes by Giulio Romano; when green-glass bottles turn out to be Roman lacrymatories, and a china figure to be Michael Angelo's Bacchus; then the China-closet becomes a precious museum; and one regrets that its dimmed stained glass windows do not throw more light upon treasures consecrated alike by the hand of time and of genius.[32]

Throughout the house provenance and association – whether historical or personal friendship, but ideally aristocratic – were evoked; armorials were sometimes no doubt Walpole's motive for a purchase. A famous 'association object' was the Chinese porcelain tub (see pp. 32–3) in which Walpole's cat had drowned, provoking Thomas Gray to write one of the most delicious poems of the century. The China Room included its share of objects with personal associations:

> An ancient tall drinking-glass, with arms and devices; a present from sir John Hawkins.[33]

> An old glass tankard ... of old Venetian glass striped with white, mounted in silver gilt: on the lid, arms of Parr enamelled[34]

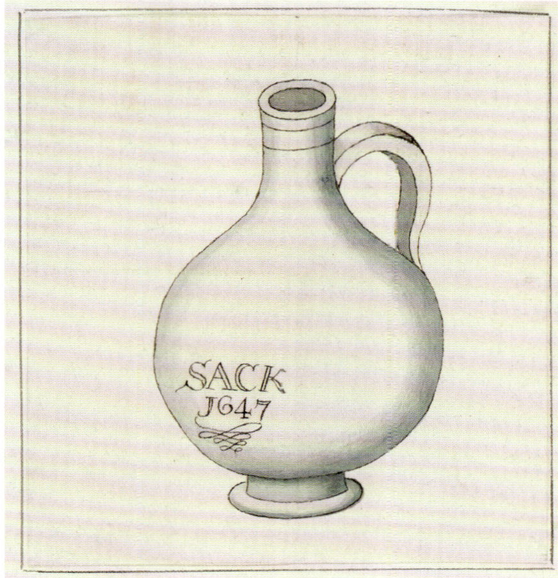

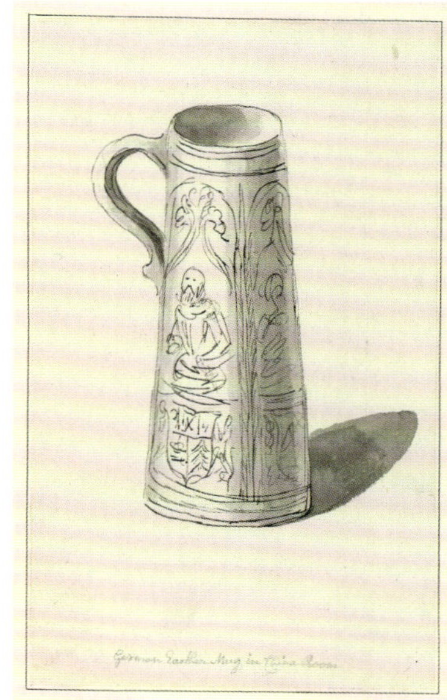

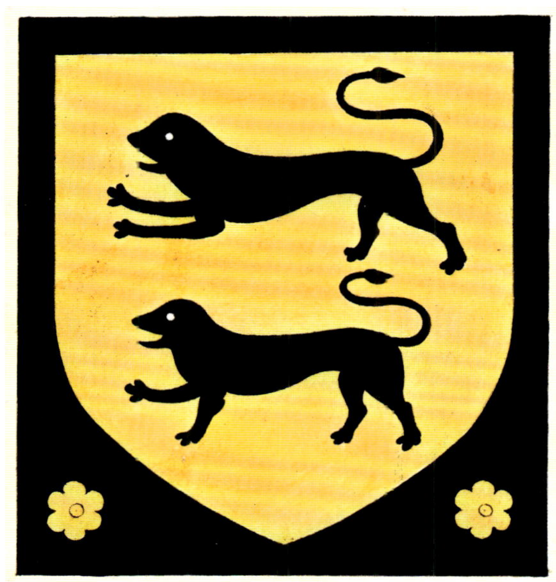

Figure 234. *Earthen bottle, painted on it 'SACK 1647'*, pen and ink, watercolour, 1674, 13 × 12.2 cm, on p.31 from Bawtree's extra-illustrated copy of the *Description*. The Lewis Walpole Library, Yale University. 33 30 copy 4

Figure 235. Perhaps by John Carter, *German Earthen Mug in China Room*, pen, ink and wash, 22.8 × 13.4 cm. The Lewis Walpole Library, Yale University. 33 30 copy 6

Figure 236. *Tile from the Kitchen of William the Conqueror*, watercolour, 14.5 × 13.5, on p. 37 of Bawtree's extra-illustrated copy of the *Description*. The Lewis Walpole Library, Yale University. 33 30 copy 4

> An earthen bottle; painted on it *Sack, 1647*: it was thus sold by apothecaries. From the collection of Mrs Kennon the virtuosa midwife (Fig. 234)[35]

> Two Saxon tankards, one with Chinese figures, the other with European. These tankards are extremely remarkable. Sir Robert Walpole drank ale; the duchess of Kendal, mistress of king George the First, gave him the former. A dozen or more years afterwards, the countess of Yarmouth, mistress of king George the Second, without having seen the other, gave him the second; and they match exactly in form and size (Fig. 235).[36]

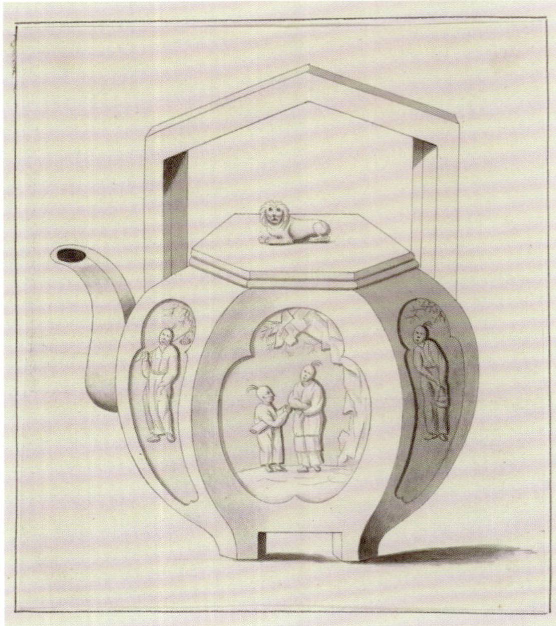

Figure 237. *The Duke of Monmouth's Tea-pot*, pen and ink and grey wash, 20.2 × 17.6, on p. 37 of Bawtree's extra-illustrated copy of the *Description*. The Lewis Walpole Library, Yale University. 33 30 copy 4

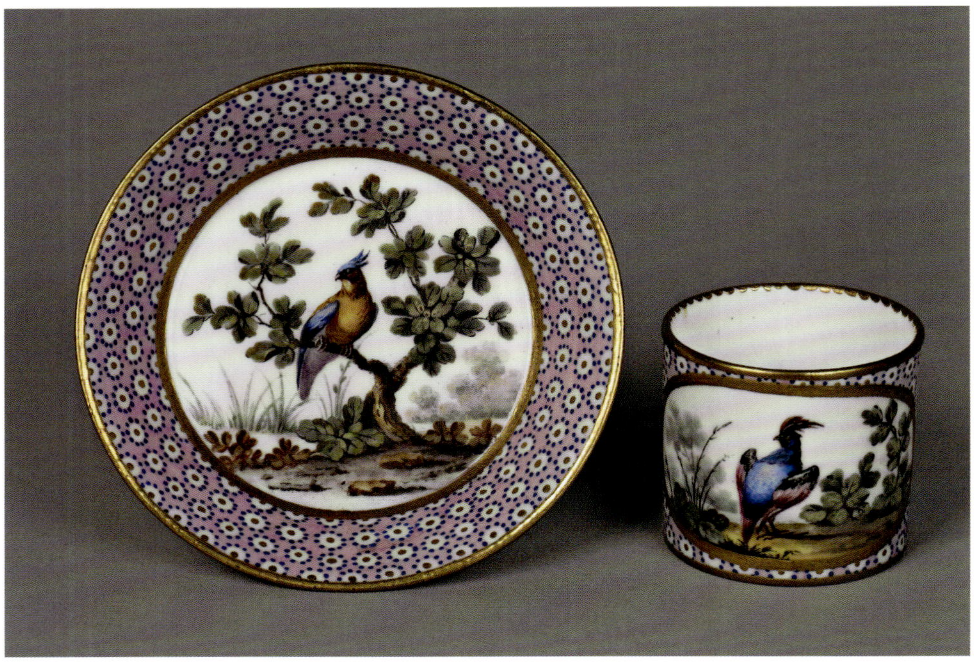

Figure 238. Cup and saucer, Sèvres, 1765, soft-paste porcelain painted in enamel with flower motifs and panels of exotic birds by François-Joseph Aloncle (active 1758–81) and gilding, D 4.7 (cup); 10.7 cm (saucer). The Lewis Walpole Library, Yale University. Cat. 240

Figure 239. Base of the cup seen in Fig. 238

> A tyle from the kitchen of William the Conqueror at Caen in Normandy (Fig. 236).[37]

> A large old white china tea-pot, that was the Duke of Monmouth's; a present from Simon second earl of Harcourt (Fig. 237).[38]

For so many objects to fit into spaces like the China Room and the closet containing Lady Walpole's porcelain, most must have been small. Walpole seems to have revelled in small, delicate objects, from miniatures to Sèvres cups and saucers (Fig. 238), and there is self-knowledge in his mock-modest disclaimer in the *Description* of 'his Villa and Collection, in which almost every thing is diminutive'.[39]

If porcelain was seen as a female taste,[40] its predominance at Strawberry Hill might be judged a 'feminine' element in Walpole's character or self-image. Many porcelain collectors had figures alongside tablewares, but Walpole, though he had a few, seems not in general to have cared for figures;[41] in 1753 he complained that

> The last branch of our fashions into which the close observation of nature has been introduced is our desserts ... Jellies, biscuits, sugar-plums and creams have long given way to harlequins, gondoliers, Turks, Chinese, and Shepherdesses of Saxon china. But these ... were soon discovered to be too insipid and unmeaning. By degrees whole meadows of cattle, of the same brittle materials, spread themselves over the whole table: cottages rose in sugar, and temples in barley-sugar; pigmy Neptunes in cars of cockle-shells triumphed over oceans of looking-glass or seas of silver tissue.[42]

Entering the China Room was not part of the general ticket-bearing visitor's tour – for security reasons, no doubt – but Walpole enjoyed showing it to kindred spirits.[43] In June 1784 Mary Hamilton recorded an invitation to Strawberry Hill:

> We did not sit long after dinner, the two gentlemen rose when we did and Mr Walpole carried us to a china closet filled with modern and old china; after we had amused ourselves there for some time, we went upstairs and spent the remainder of our time after coffee and tea in very agreeable converse.[44]

It sounds as if the men came too.

Walpole constantly insisted that he took pleasure in his objects and wanted others to, rather than regarding them as material for study. On 4 January 1762 he wrote to Mann about a discovery of 'Etrurian vases' in Tuscany: 'I shall be glad of a few, if the forms are beautiful – for what they call the *erudition* I am totally indifferent ... I hate gazing on ugliness.'[45] Furthermore, many objects in the collection were given by friends rather than systematically acquired. In 1780 Walpole wrote to a cousin about his friend Madame du Deffand:

> The last time I was at Paris she pressed me to chose and then take some of her *porcelaine.* I refused – She persisted – at last to pacify her, I took one of the cheapest cups and saucers, and pretended I preferred it because it had *strawberries on it* – and it is now in this room.[46]

Nonetheless, his pursuit of 'specimens' of Florentine porcelain and his interest in the experiments of Francis Place (the 'York virtuoso') (Fig. 240), about whom he had written in the *Anecdotes of Painting*, suggest that systematically representing factories and techniques was not entirely an alien ambition to Walpole. In Paris or at Sèvres he often bought a single cup and saucer, as a specimen or a 'bauble', whereas less meticulous, or wealthier, collectors like the Duke of Richmond ordered whole services.[47] However, his waspish note on the Duchess of Portland suggests disdain for specimen collecting regardless of quality:

> The Duchess of Portland inherited the Passion of her Family for Collecting. At first her taste was chiefly confined to Shells, Japan & old China, particularly of the blue & white with a brown Edge, of which last sort She formed a large Closet at Bulstrode; but contenting herself with one specimen of every pattern She could get, it was a collection of odd pieces.[48]

The range of Walpole's collections is unparalleled, but the quality can sometimes be hard to assess. Neither Walpole, nor Robins in cataloguing the 1842 sale, systematically applied labels, so identifying surviving ceramics can be difficult unless subsequent owners have been so proud of a Strawberry Hill provenance as to record it, as many have (Fig. 239). It is particularly hard to assess how his oriental porcelain would be judged by modern connoisseurship; few pieces can now be identified as having belonged to him. Maiolica, Sèvres and French Renaissance enamels are more frequently traceable and in each of these categories Walpole possessed masterpieces: the Valencian lustreware jar and the vases made by Orazio Fontana are now key exhibits in the British Museum; no less important are the enamelled horn in the Refectory (see pp. 202–3), the 'Saint Porchaire' ewer or the lavish Sèvres vases.

His greatest connoisseurial expertise was in French porcelain – hardly surprising for a francophile who spent months in the 1760s frequenting Paris's grandest *marchands-merciers*, Poirier or Dulac, or accompanying aristocratic friends to shop at the Manufacture at Sèvres.[49] He owned some 240 pieces of French porcelain, overwhelmingly Sèvres, far more than any other type of European ceramics. He paid such large sums in Paris for Sèvres as to shock his friend the Rev. William Cole, who wrote, awestruck, in his diary in 1765 that Sèvres

> is of a most admirable Beauty and Texture ... Indeed it ought to be superabundantly eminent & excellent, as the Price is excessive. I was with Mr Walpole one Day, at a great Shop in Paris, Mr Poirier's, where it was sold, & saw him give 10 Louis or Guineas for a single Coffee Cup, Saucer, & a little square sort of

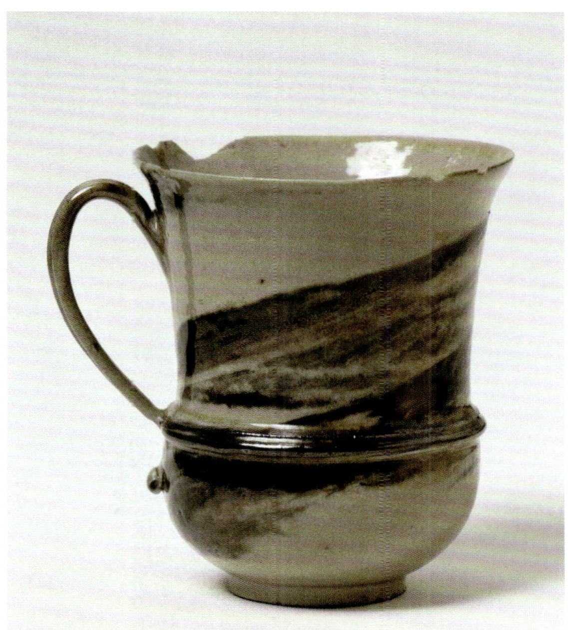

Figure 240. Francis Place, Cup, *c.* 1680–1700, stoneware, 6.4 × 5.4 cm. Victoria and Albert Museum, London. 4762&A-1901. Cat. 233

HORACE WALPOLE AND WEDGWOOD *Robin Emmerson*

Listed in the 1784 edition of Horace Walpole's *Description* are '12 plates of Wedgwood's ware, with cameos of brown and white and blue festoons, from a design of lady Diana Beauclerc' and 'two square flower-tubs of Wedgwood's ware, with antique cameos and masks in blue, from designs of lady Diana Beauclerc'. Walpole's passion for the work of the amateur artist Lady Diana Beauclerk led to the making in 1783–4 of an ebony cabinet-on-stand whose front face, sides and top are decorated with framed drawings by her (see pp. 160–61). The drawings on the ends (Fig. 241) are alternative treatments for the two flower tubs while six roundels on the sides and top, showing putti, are designs for the painted cameos on the tubs. A drawing on the top (Fig. 361) matches the description of the plates.

Figure 241. Detail of the side of the Beauclerk Cabinet, with Lady Diana Beauclerk's Design for a Flower Tub, *c.* 1777, water-colour and pencil. The Lewis Walpole Library, Yale University. Cat. 254

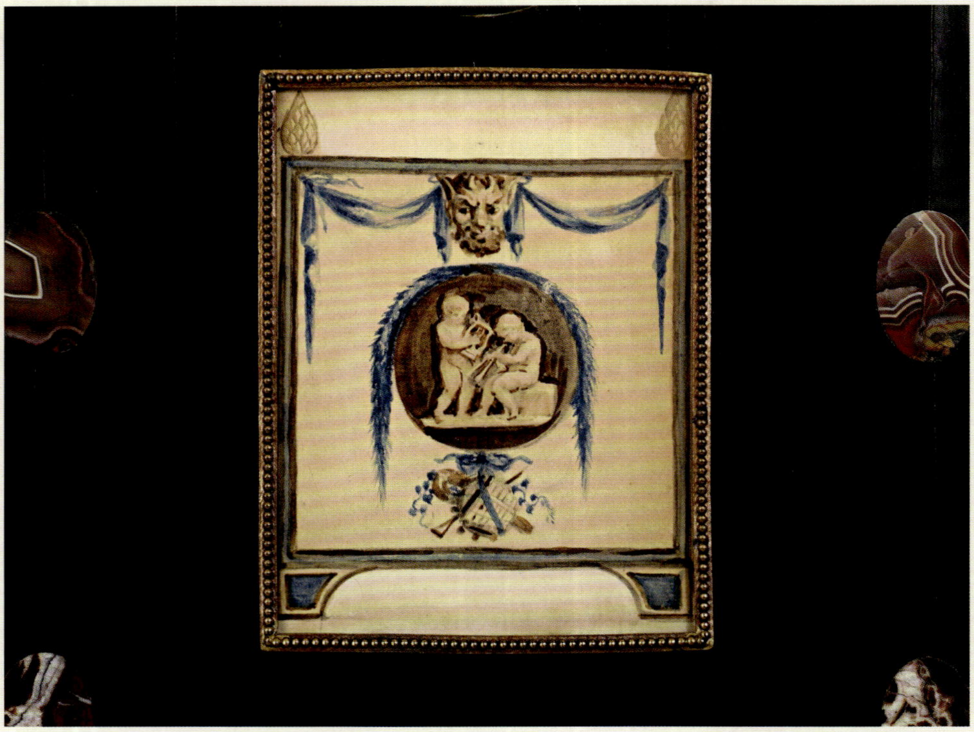

The Wedgwood flower tubs matching these drawings are here identified (Fig. 243) as Horace Walpole's for the first time since they left Strawberry Hill. Both are inscribed 'DIANA BEAUCLERC CAROLI DUCIS MARLBURIENSIS FILIA DESIGNAVIT 1777' (Diana Beauclerk, daughter of Charles Duke of Marlborough, designed [it in] 1777.) Inside the tops are pierced flower holders that are carefully fitted and lift out. This pair of flower tubs appears to be unique in Wedgwood's output and was evidently a special commission from Walpole. The tubs would have been made at Wedgwood's Etruria factory in Staffordshire, but it is most likely that they were painted at his London premises in Greek Street in Soho, and the enamel colours fixed by firing them in an enamel kiln there. None of the twelve plates has yet been found. Wedgwood probably made them at about the same time as the flower tubs, for a letter of 4 May 1777 to his partner Thomas Bentley asks, 'Pray are Mr Horace Walpoles plates done?' (Wedgwood archive MS E25/18754 – I am grateful to the Trustees of the Wedgwood Museum, Barlaston, for permission to quote this).

The cabinet is also mounted with blue and white Wedgwood cameos. In 1785 Lady Diana is known to have supplied Wedgwood with drawings, and he advertised cameos after her designs of boys as nos. 241–3 in his catalogue of 1787. Although the cameos on the cabinet are too early to be by Lady Diana, the success of Walpole's flower tubs and plates may have suggested to Wedgwood that he should ask Lady Diana for designs.

In 1774 Wedgwood made the famous 'Frog' service painted in monochrome with English views for Catherine the Great of Russia. At the same time he made a small dessert service painted with some of the same views in polychrome, without the frog badge. For some reason he also made a similarly decorated cup and saucer (Fig. 242). No other parts of a tea service have ever been recorded. Perhaps the cup and saucer were made as a sample to elicit an order that never came, or perhaps Walpole himself ordered them. Whatever the explanation, by 1784 they were at Strawberry Hill, described as 'a cup and saucer of Wedgwood's ware, finely painted with English views'. It seems entirely typical of Horace that his example of the 944-piece Frog service was a single, unique cup and saucer.

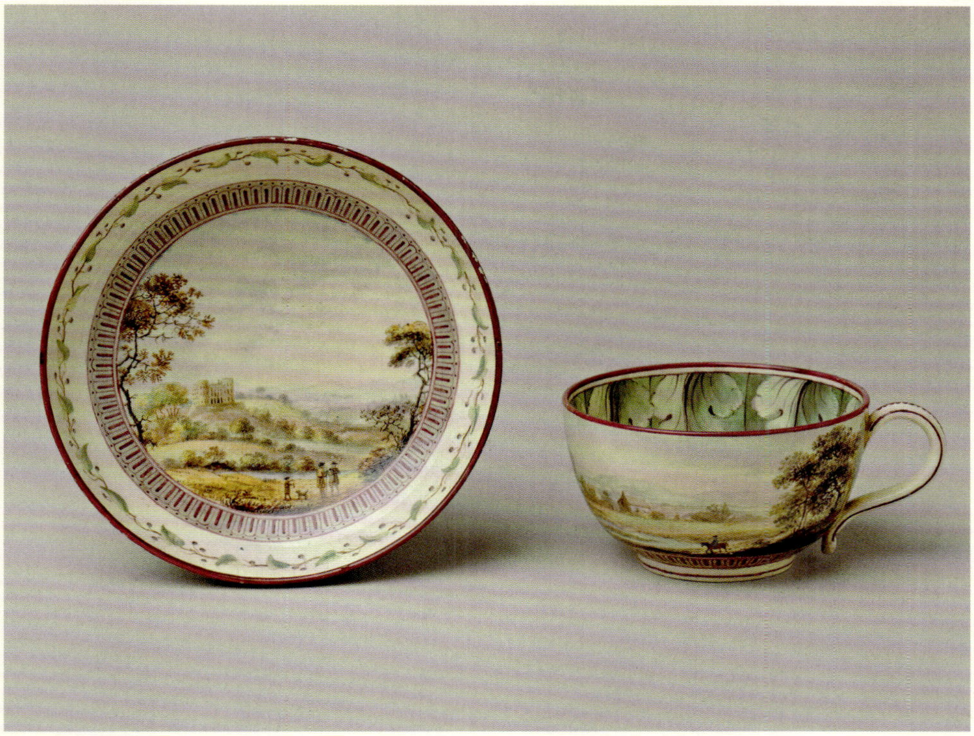

Figure 242. Cup and Saucer with English Views, Josiah Wedgwood, Stoke on Trent, 1772–80, creamware, H 5 cm (cup); 12 cm (saucer). National Museums Liverpool, Walker Art Gallery. M2768a, M2768b. Cat. 241

Figure 243. Flower Tubs, designed by Lady Diana Beauclerk, Josiah Wedgwood, Stoke on Trent, 1777, creamware, 17 × 12.4 × 12.4 cm. Private collection. Cat. 253

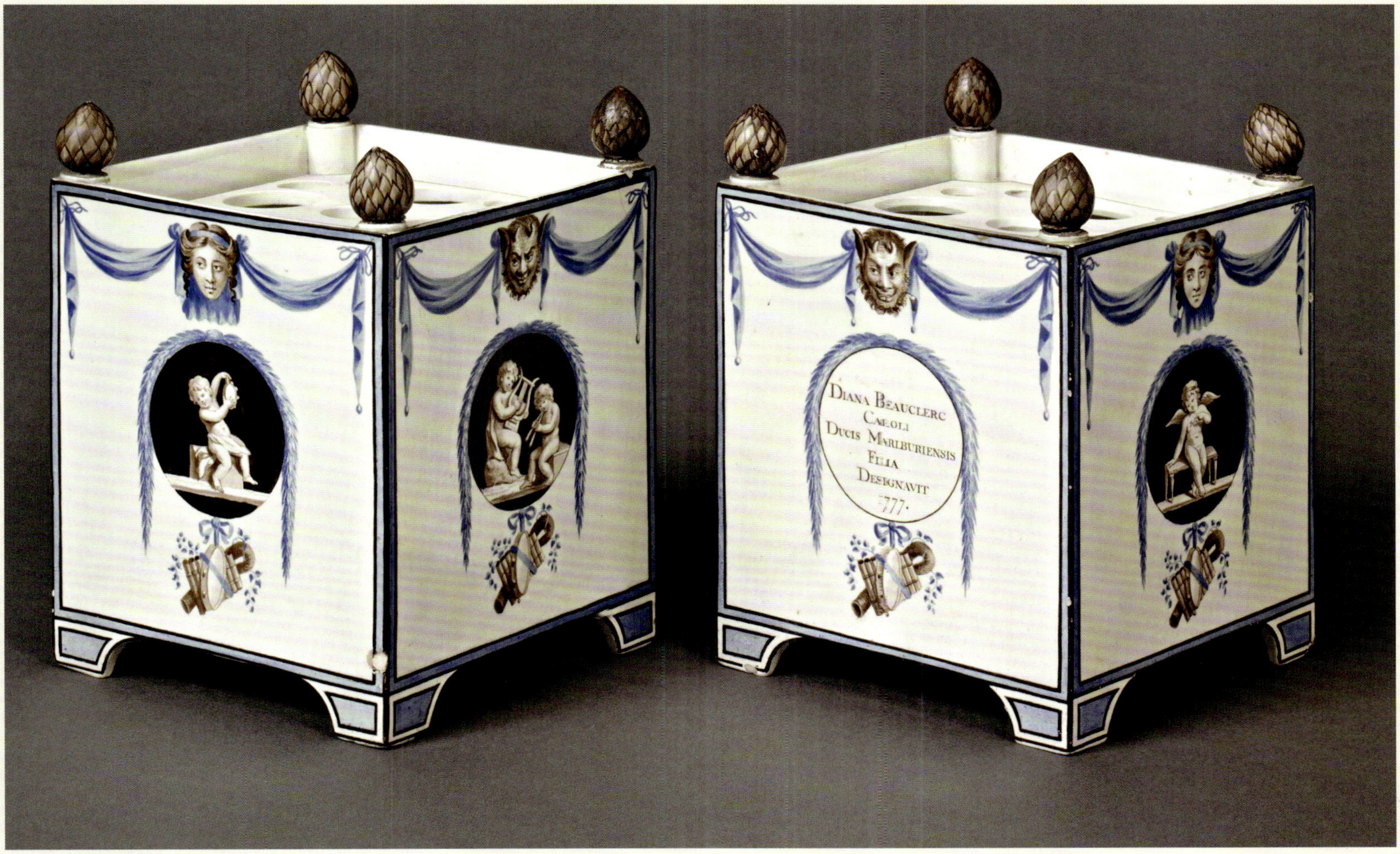

> *Soucoupe*, or under-Saucer, to set them on; they were indeed the highest finished Things of the Kind that can be conceived: perfect Jewels that deserve to be set in gold Frames to be admired and looked at, but never to be used for Fear of breaking them.[50]

Walpole himself confessed in 1766: 'I buy china faster than I can pay for it.'[51]

So enthusiastic was Walpole for Sèvres ornament that he used the design of a Sèvres table in the Green Closet as the basis for a large carpet

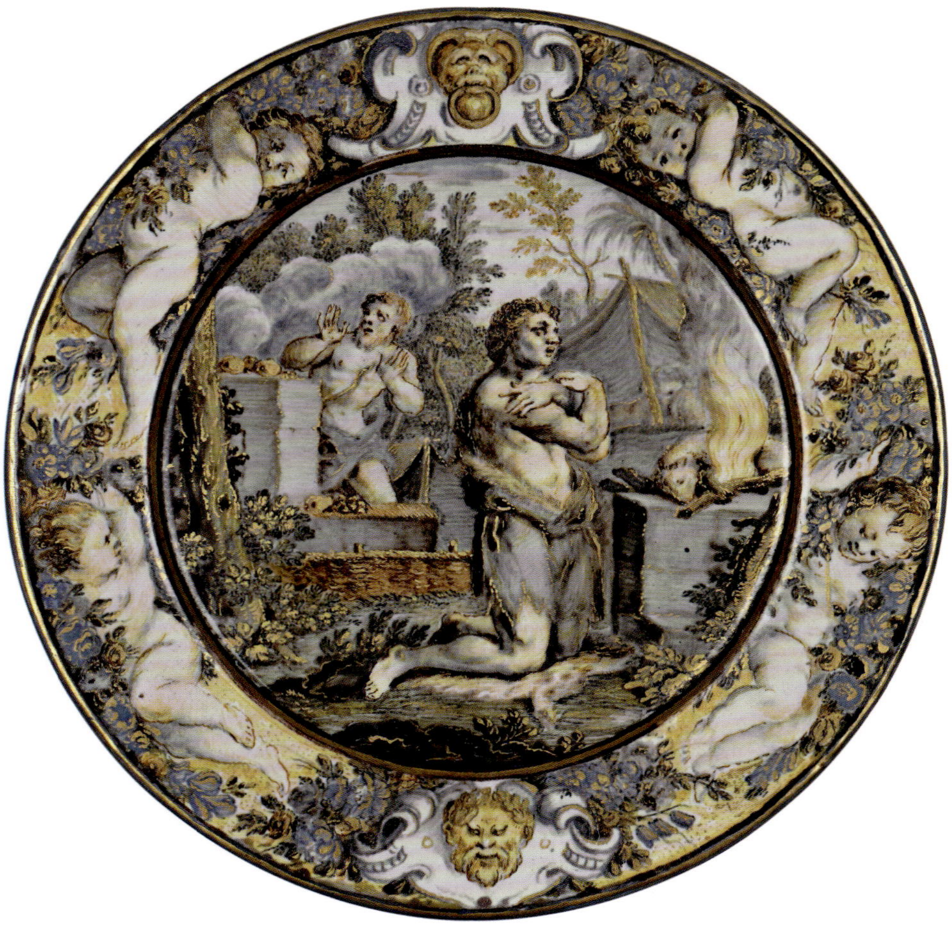

Figure 244. Italian (Castelli), workshop of Carlantonio Grue, *Cain and Abel*, *c.* 1690–1720, D 18.5 cm. The Lewis Walpole Library, Yale University. Cat. 234

in the Round Drawing Room, commissioned from the Moorfields factory; the carpet has vanished but the table has been plausibly identified.[52] In one of his 'Books of Materials' are notes on continental porcelain marks made in 1771.[53] In the China Room was 'Michelangelo's Bacchus, made in the china of the Comte de Lauragais, from the collection of the Comte de Caylus'; this sounds abstruse, but Walpole had met the Comte de Lauraguais in 1765 and seen his experimental porcelain, admiring medals of 'china, so hard that they would strike fire'.[54] The description of an early example of Sèvres hard paste as 'a white Seve saucepan that bears the fire: 1771' suggests not only that he knew the difference between soft-paste and hard-paste porcelain (introduced at Sèvres in 1769), but that he could read Sèvres date letters, a skill unlikely to have been shared by many contemporary Englishmen. Equally impressive connoisseurship, if correct, is his description of a Chinese porcelain cup with enamelled decoration as 'an old white china cup with cupids painted in Europe'.[55]

In the letter to Mann cited at the beginning of this essay, Walpole singled out his 'faience or Raphael-ware', which he also calls, in eighteenth-century terminology, 'Roman faience' or 'Roman earth'.[56] He had about fifty-five examples, including Valencian lustreware, Italian and French Renaissance maiolica, eighteenth-century Castelli (Fig. 244), 'Saint-Porchaire' and Palissy ware, and a group of *istoriato* (story-painted pieces) gathered among the 'curiosities' in a glazed cupboard in the Great North Bedchamber.[57] Walpole had no detailed knowledge of Renaissance pottery such as that possessed by specialist collectors like Andrew Fountaine or the painter Charles Jervas. Despite knowing the Fountaine collection, he seems to have failed to recognize Palissy ware or Saint Porchaire as technically different from maiolica. Describing chocolate cups and plates 'by Pietro Cortona',[58] he indulged in the old-fashioned fallacy that maiolica had been painted by (rather than copying prints by) identifiable leading artists; this was a line popular with collectors and dealers with maiolica to sell, but demolished for serious connoisseurs by Walpole's acquaintance Pierre-Jean Mariette in the 1750 Crozat sale catalogue.[59]

The name of Josiah Wedgwood, who came to dominate late-eighteenth-century European and American markets, does not appear in the 1774 *Description*, but by 1784 Walpole had acquired examples,[60] including a blue and white medallion portrait of his mother[61] and a cup and saucer 'finely painted with English views', which seems to have been a special order or one-off experiment related to Wedgwood's famous 'Frog Service' (see pp. 212–13, Cat. 241).[62] More personally important to him were pieces associated with the extravagantly admired Diana Beauclerk: 'twelve plates of Wedgwood's ware, with cameos of blue and white, and blue festoons; from a design of lady Diana Beauclerc'[63] and 'two square flower-tubs of Wedgwood's ware … from designs of lady Diana Beauclerc' (see pp. 212–13).[64] The 'Lady Di' link meant that the flower tubs, which Walpole himself had probably commissioned, were the only ceramics mentioned in his 'List of Principal Curiosities'.[65]

Like collectors before and since, Walpole liked to think of his objects as rare: the *Description* is peppered with claims like 'six fine old cups, white within; without, japanned black and mother of pearl: very rare';[66] 'a boy supporting a shell, finely modelled in red earth; the first sort of Saxon china before it was glazed and painted, and which was only given as presents by the elector: extremely rare';[67] and 'a scolloped saucer of Saxon china, the second sort, very rare'.[68] The search for unusual and innovative pieces is particularly clear with Wedgwood. Walpole's examples included a 'portrait of George Simon Earl of Harcourt, in Wedgewood's ware; the only one executed in that manner',[69] while, as described on p. 212, the flower tubs, plates, and cup and saucer were all non-standard examples.

Walpole's ceramic taste perhaps had roots in the oriental porcelain passed down to him from his mother, 'that mother on whom I doted and who doted on me'.[70] Eventually, his collection was, as he wrote, 'heterogeneous'.[71] It was larger, more varied, and – thanks to the two *Descriptions*, the watercolours in various extra-illustrated editions and the 1842 catalogue – better documented than any other English eighteenth-century collection. It was evocative and eclectic. He sometimes moved things around and there is little evidence that he bought ceramics specifically to place them in particular rooms. His collecting was not limited (as Fountaine's was) to the European Renaissance; nor was it dominated (like many ladies' china closets) by oriental porcelain. It mixed old and new and was not systematically 'Gothic', as the collections formed later by Alexandre du Sommerard[72] and Francis Douce[73] were. It had something of the (feminine) 'china closet' about it, something of the (masculine) 'cabinet of curiosities',[74] and something of Fountaine's Narford Hall type of specialist collection. Walpole showed sporadic interest in 'collecting factories', but he was the antithesis of a systematic scientist like Sir Hans Sloane.[75] One imagines the China Room, like the rest of the house, coming alive best if one was guided by its theatrical and imaginative owner, regaling his guests with anecdotes. Like its creator, Walpole's collection of ceramics is of its time yet defies comparison.

Acknowledgements

Study of Walpole's ceramics rests on foundations laid by Bet McLeod's MA thesis, 'The Ceramics at Strawberry Hill' (Parsons School of Design/Cooper-Hewitt Museum, New York, 1993), and subsequent articles, 'Horace Walpole's Ceramics at Strawberry Hill', *International Ceramics Fair and Seminar*, Handbook 1995, 28–35, and 'Horace Walpole and Sèvres porcelain', *Apollo* 147, no. 431 (Jan. 1998): 42–7. I thank her for lending me the thesis and for other help. She and John Mallet have read a draft of this essay and rescued me from some errors, as have Stephen Clarke and Michael Snodin, both generous with advice and references. I also thank Bridget Allen, Michael Archer, Hugo Brown, Julius Bryant, Maureen Cassidy-Geiger, Patricia Collins, Thierry Crépin-Leblond, Judith Crouch, Aileen Dawson, Robin Emmerson, Patricia Ferguson, Hazel Forsyth, Jonathan Horne, Sebastian Kuhn, Jessie McNab, Peter Meadows, Erin Monro, Dorothy Moore, John-Albert Moseley, Tessa Murdoch, Beverley Nenk, Christopher Norton, Brian Parker, Julia Poole, Margaret Powell, Nigel Ramsay, Dinah Reynolds, Cynthia Roman, Linda Horvitz Roth, Elisa Paola Sani, Rosalind Savill, Virginia Smithson, Denny Stone, Diana Stone, Emma Tate, Michael Vickers, Clare Vincent, Susan Odell Walker, Ian Wardropper, Jon Whiteley, Jane Wilson, and Hilary Young.

1. *HW Corres.* 25: 590–91.
2. 'Ceramics' are here understood as including vessel glass and Renaissance painted enamels, but not stained glass or enamelled miniatures.
3. This includes the Waiting Room. Counts vary depending on what is reckoned 'ceramic' and whether items like a ewer and basin are counted as one or two.
4. Walpole had reservations about Chelsea. In 1763 he wrote to Mann (*HW Corres.* 22: 121–2) about the spectacular Mecklenburg-Strelitz service: 'I cannot boast of our taste; the forms are neither new, beautiful, nor various. Yet Sprimont, the manufacturer, is a Frenchman: it seems their taste will not bear transplanting.'
5. For ancient Greek 'owl skyphoi' of the type illustrated, see Franklin P. Johnson, 'A Note on Owl Skyphoi', *American Journal of Archaeology* 59 (1955): 119–24.
6. Drawings of some tiles are reproduced in Clive Wainwright, *The Romantic Interior* (New Haven and London: Yale University Press, 1989), 106. For a type Walpole obtained from Gloucester, see Elizabeth Eames, *Catalogue of Medieval Lead-glazed Earthenware Tiles in the Department of Medieval and Later Antiquities British Museum*, 2 vols. (London: British Museum Publications, 1980), 1: 238, 298 (no. 442) design no. 1518.
7. *Oxford English Dictionary*, s.v. 'Gombroon', a 1698 citation suggesting that this term described Persian ware imitating Chinese.
8. In the Blue Breakfast Room was, by 1842, a 'Service of splendid Silver Gilt and Chased Plate'.
9. Anon., *Walpoliana*, 2 vols. (London: R. Phillips, 1799), 1: xli–xlii.
10. In 1774 these were on 'commodes of old japan' in the Gallery and by 1784 in the Round Drawing Room.
11. Dora Thornton and Timothy Wilson, *Italian Renaissance Ceramics: A Catalogue of the British Museum Collection*, 2 vols. (London: British Museum Press, 2009), vol. 1, nos 197–8; Rosalind Savill, *The Wallace Collection: Catalogue of Sèvres Porcelain*, 3 vols. (London: Wallace Collection, 1988), 1: 277.
12. *D 1784*, 52–3; *Works* 2: 468 .
13. The *Descriptions* do not enumerate them: nearly 300 were included in the sale, day 17.
14. See Oliver Impey in John Ayers, Oliver Impey and J.V.G. Mallet (eds.), *Porcelain for Palaces: The Fashion for Japan in Europe 1650–1750* (London: Oriental Ceramic Society, 1990), 56–69.
15. *Edinburgh Review* 31 (December 1818); Peter Sabor (ed.), *Horace Walpole: The Critical Heritage* (London and New York: Routledge and Kegan Paul, 1987), 187.
16. Anna Somers Cocks, 'The Nonfunctional Use of Ceramics in the English Country House During the Eighteenth Century', in Gervase Jackson-Stops *et al.*, *The Fashioning and Functioning of the English Country House* (Washington: National Gallery of Art Studies in the History of Art 25, 1989), 195–215, esp. 204.
17. Compare Roger Massey, 'Ceramics in the English Country House: Bedfordshire 1731–1817',

Transactions of the English Ceramic Circle 18, part 3 (2004): 418–46. For Lady Burlington's china room at Chiswick, see Somers Cocks, 'Nonfunctional Use', 212, fig. 25; and T.S. Rosoman, 'The Chiswick House Inventory', *Furniture History* 22 (1986): 81–106. Among other collectors was Queen Charlotte, whose porcelain and maiolica were sold anonymously at Christie's, 24–6 May 1819. At Drayton, Northamptonshire, Lady Betty Germain's porcelain led Walpole to describe the house as 'crammed with old china' (*HW Corres.* 10: 90); sale, Langford's, 7–10 March 1770 (Frits Lugt, *Répertoire des catalogues de ventes publiques*, 4 vols. [The Hague: M. Nijhoff, 1938–87], 1806); inventories of 1710 and 1724 in Tessa Murdoch (ed.), *Noble Households: Eighteenth-Century Inventories of Great English Houses. A Tribute to John Cornforth* (Cambridge: John Adamson, 2006), 119–40. For the still intact ceramic collections at Burghley, see Gordon Lang, *European Ceramics at Burghley House* (Stamford: Burghley House Preservation Trust, 1991). The china and glass then at Houghton was listed in 1792: Murdoch, *Noble Households*, 201–2.

18. Andrew Moore, 'The Fountaine Collection of maiolica', *Burlington Magazine* 130, no. 1023 (June 1988): 435–47. The contents of the 'China Room', predominantly 'China' and 'Japan', were inventoried in 1753: National Art Library, London, MS 1996.5, 34–8.
19. *The Walpole Society* 36 (1937–8), 120; see Moore, 'Fountaine Collection', 436.
20. Emily J. Climenson, *Passages from the Diaries of Mrs Philip Lybbe Powys* (London: Longman, Green, 1899), 198.
21. Sheffield Archives, WWM/A1204 (1 July 1782), 67–8, 112–14; Timothy Wilson, 'Maiolica for the Grand Tour', *Keramos* 186 (2004): 129–39.
22. Julius Bryant, *Mrs Howard: A Woman of Reason* (exh. cat., Marble Hill House, 1988), 12, 50–51, 57. For Walpole's friendship with her, see Paget Toynbee (ed.), *Reminiscences Written by Mr Horace Walpole in 1788* (Oxford: Clarendon Press, 1924), 57–68.
23. *HW Corres.* 35: 259.
24. LWL 49 2523, 121.21. Michael Snodin compares a sketch by Chute for the Round Drawing Room in the same volume (121.8). It might, however, be a design for another ceramic-heavy space, the Tea Room in the Cottage in the Flower Garden.
25. Walpole's 1740 visit to Herculaneum: *HW Corres.* 13: 222–4. For his 1778 critique of Etruscan style as executed by Robert Adam at Osterley, see *HW Corres.* 28: 414: 'The last chamber … is called the Etruscan, and is painted all over like Wedgwood's ware, with black and yellow small grotesques … I never saw such a profound tumble into the bathos. It is going out of a palace into a potter's field.'
26. Paget Toynbee, *Strawberry Hill Accounts* (Oxford: Clarendon Press, 1927), 6 (records payment to Müntz, 24 June 1756). See W.S. Lewis, 'The Genesis of Strawberry Hill', *Metropolitan Museum Studies* 5, no. 1: 57–92.
27. *HW Corres.* 21: 471; 26: 4. Toynbee, *Strawberry Hill Accounts*, 87–8.
28. *HW Corres.* 35: 151 (Walpole described visiting Malvern Abbey in 1753): 'The greatest curiosity, at least what I had never seen before, was, the whole floor and far up the sides of the church has been, if I may so call it, wainscoted with red and yellow tiles, extremely polished, and diversified with coats of arms, and inscriptions, and mosaic. I have since found the same in Glocester, and have been so fortunate as to purchase from the sexton about a dozen, which think what an acquisition for Strawberry!'
29. *HW Corres.* 36: 39.
30. In modern debates about the authenticity of 'Saint-Porchaire' the long history of Walpole's ewer was critical: Daphne Barbour and Shelley Sturman (eds.), *Saint-Porchaire Ceramics* (Washington: National Gallery of Art Studies in the History of Art 52, 1996).
31. Compare the 1703 engraving by Marot of porcelain over a chimneypiece, Somers-Cocks, 'Nonfunctional Use', 196, fig. 1.
32. Lady Morgan (Sydney Owenson), 'Strawberry Hill', *New Monthly Magazine* 1826, part 2: 261.
33. *D 1784*, 12; *Works* 2: 413; Strawberry Hill sale, day 12, lot 124.
34. *D 1784*, 9; *Works* 2: 409. For Walpole's interest in Catherine Parr, from whom he claimed descent, see Morris Brownell, *The Prime Minister of Taste* (New Haven and London: Yale University Press, 2001), 106–8; the low-key description as simply having the 'arms of Parr enamelled' reflects the fact that almost nobody in eighteenth-century England could read silver hallmarks; Walpole could not know that the mounts definitely dated from Catherine's lifetime.
35. *D 1784*, 9; *Works* 2: 408. Mrs Kennon was the midwife who assisted in delivering the future King George III. Walpole's example is untraced, but for the type see Louis L. Lipski and Michael Archer, *Dated English Delftware* (London: Sotheby's, 1984), nos. 1331–5.
36. *D 1784*, 11; *Works* 2: 411. For the type see David Gaimster, *German Stoneware 1200–1900* (London: British Museum Publications, 1997), 181–4.
37. *D 1784*, 13; *Works* 2: 414. In 1764 Walpole wrote to Charles Churchill, thanking him for tiles from the recently demolished 'Kitchen of William the Conqueror': 'I weep over the ruined kitchen, but enjoy the tiles' (*HW Corres.* 36: 39). Christopher Norton informs me that the tile is early fourteenth century and probably from Saint-Étienne, Caen, and that it was mentioned in *Gentleman's Magazine* 59 (1789): 212.
38. *D 1784*, 13; *Works* 2: 415.
39. *D 1784*, 11; *Works* 2: 395. This version of the preface cannot have been printed before June 1786, since it mentions objects acquired at the Duchess of Portland's sale.
40. Somers Cocks, 'Nonfunctional Use', 204–5, 211; compare Hilary Young, *English Porcelain 1745–95* (London: V&A Publications, 1999), 189–93.
41. The sale, day 24, lot 90, included 'A beautiful figure of St. Roche, in the fine old Faenza ware'. The only recorded such figure is a lustred one given to the British Museum by Charles Fairfax Murray in 1905

(Thornton and Wilson, *Italian Renaissance Ceramics*, no. 294). No such figure is mentioned in the *Description*, unless it was, strangely metamorphosed (with a crown added?), 'a figure of an ancient king of France, in fayence' (*D 1784*, 82; *Works* 2: 508).

42. *Works* 1: 146–50; Anna Chalcraft and Judith Viscardi, *Strawberry Hill: Horace Walpole's Gothic Castle* (London: Frances Lincoln, 2007), 28.
43. Chalcraft, *Visiting Strawberry Hill*, 7–11; Joseph Farington noted in 1793 that the 'China Closet' was 'shown but seldom' (*HW Corres.* 15: 318).
44. *HW Corres.* 31: 216.
45. The contrast is already stark in Walpole's 1743 correspondence (*HW Corres.* 15: 11–15) with the Cambridge scholar Conyers Middleton, who said his antiquities were 'not collected out of any regard for their beauty or sculpture, but as containing what the Italians call erudition in them, and illustrating some rite or custom'; this 'archaeological' perspective is the antithesis of Walpole's.
46. *HW Corres.* 36: 181–2; also stating that in 1968 the cup and saucer belonged to Miss D.W. Pears.
47. Ghenete Zelleke, *From Chantilly to Sèvres: French Porcelain and the Dukes of Richmond* (French Porcelain Society Publications 7, 1991), 9–11.
48. Wilmarth S. Lewis, *The Duchess of Portland's Museum by Horace Walpole* (New York: The Grolier Club, 1936), 5. The Duchess, alongside her enormous accumulation of natural history specimens, had much 'fine old china' (some sold at Skinner's, April–June 1786, Lugt 4028); Impey, 'Porcelain for Palaces', 68–69.
49. *HW Corres.* 7: 271, 401–14, detailing expenditure on Sèvres: F.J.B. Watson, 'Walpole and the Taste for French Porcelain in Eighteenth-Century England', in Warren Hunting Smith (ed.), *Horace Walpole, Writer, Politician, and Connoisseur* (New Haven and London: Yale University Press, 1967), 185–94, 327–36. On the *marchands-mercier*s and porcelain see John Whitehead, 'The *marchands-merciers* and Sèvres', *International Ceramics Fair and Seminar*, Handbook 1993, 36–43; Carolyn Sargentson, *Merchants and Luxury Markets: The Marchands Merciers of Eighteenth-Century Paris* (London: Victoria & Albert Museum, 1996); Bet McLeod, 'The Ceramics at Strawberry Hill', MA thesis Parsons School of Design/Cooper-Hewitt Museum, 1993, 43–6.
50. William Cole, *A Journal of my Journey to Paris in the Year 1765*, ed. Francis Griffin Stokes (London: Constable, 1931), 232–3.
51. *HW Corres.* 41: 8.
52. *D 1784*, 53; *Works* 2: 468: 'a carpet of the manufacture of Moorfields; the design taken from the Seve china-table in the green closet'. See Bet McLeod, 'Horace Walpole and Sèvres porcelain', *Apollo* 147, no. 431 (Jan. 1998): 42–7, esp. 46–7. For the Moorfields enterprise see C.E.C. Tattersall, *A History of British Carpets*, new ed. (Leigh-on-Sea: F. Lewis, 1966), 45–6; several Moorfields carpets were designed by Robert Adam.
53. LWL 49 2615, 2: 12.
54. *HW Corres.* 7: 262. For the Brancas-Lauraguais factory see Aileen Dawson, *French Porcelain: A Catalogue of the British Museum Collection* (London: British Museum Press, rev. ed., 2000), 290–93; Odile Chardon, 'Louis-Léon de Brancas, comte de Lauragais et la porcelaine dure', *Sèvres* 17 (2008), 66–79.
55. *D 1784*, 8; *Works* 2: 407.
56. A.V.B. Norman, *Wallace Collection: Catalogue of Ceramics, I: Pottery, Maiolica, Faience, Stoneware* (London: Wallace Collection, 1976), 25–7.
57. *D 1784*, 75; *Works* 2: 498–9. A few, like one with 'cupids, in relievo, ribbed border', were probably of the Palissy type. There was also some French maiolica: the seventeenth-century Nevers ewer is illustrated in Joseph Marryat, *Collections towards a History of Pottery and Porcelain* (London: John Murray, 1850), frontispiece; in *Catalogue of the … Collection of … Joseph Marryat, Esq.*, Christie's, 9 February 1867, lot 891, it is given as 19 inches high; McLeod, 'Ceramics at Strawberry', 161, suggests it is Strawberry Hill sale, day 12, no. 82 (but there described as 'small and elegant'). A French jar, now Glasgow Museums 1905.114d, was in the Refectory ('a jar of Roman fayence': *D 1784*, 4; *Works* 2: 402; *1842 Sale*, day 19, lot 42; Fountaine sale, Christie's, 16–19 June 1884, lot 233).
58. *D 1784*, 6, 12; *Works* 2: 405, 412.
59. Timothy Wilson, 'A brief history of maiolica collecting', in Timothy Wilson and Elisa Paola Sani, *Le maioliche rinascimentali nelle collezioni della Fondazione Cassa di Risparmio di Perugia*, 2 vols. (Perugia: Petruzzi, 2006–7), 2: 324.
60. Compare Julia Poole, 'Ceramics in the Household of the 4th Duke of Bedford', *Transactions of the English Ceramic Circle* 18, part 1 (2002): 132–68, concluding that, at Woburn, 'English ornamental ware was only acquired in small quantities before 1771 … [this] changed dramatically in the last third of the century.'
61. *D 1784*, 14; *Works* 2: 415; Robin Reilly and George Savage, *Wedgwood: The Portrait Medallions* (London: Barrie & Jenkins, 1973), 263–5.
62. For the relationship to the Frog Service, see Michael Raeburn, Ludmila Voronikhina and Andrew Nurnberg (eds.), *The Green Frog Service* (London: Cacklegoose Press, 1995), 401, 406; Hilary Young (ed.), *The Genius of Wedgwood* (London: exh. cat., Victoria and Albert Museum, 1995), 204–6.
63. *D 1784*, 13; *Works* 2: 415. The 1777 letter from Wedgwood to Bentley about 'Mr Horace Walpoles plates' is in the Wedgwood Archive, MS E25/18754. Thanks are due to the Trustees of the Wedgwood Museum, Barlaston, for permission to quote it here.
64. They were placed in the Great North Bedchamber: *D 1784*, 77; *Works* 2: 502. For the context rendering it likely that they were enamelled in London, see Gaye Blake-Roberts, *Wedgwood in London* (London: exh. cat., Wedgwood House, 1984), 26.
65. LWL 49.2523, 121.12. For Lady Diana supplying Wedgwood with drawings, see Robin Reilly, *Wedgwood*, 2 vols. (London and New York: Macmillan and Stockton Press, 1989), 1: 605; and for cameos made from her drawings, 2: plate C158.
66. *D 1784*, 9; *Works* 2: 409.
67. *D 1784*, 10; *Works* 2: 410; T.H. Clarke, 'Das Kind mit

der Muschel und Statuetten Augusts des Starken', *Kunst und Antiquitäten* 6 (Nov/Dec. 1980): 42–54. One in Bamberg is dated *c.* 1710–13 by Lothar Hennig, *Glanz des Barock. Sammlung Ludwig in Bamberg. Fayence und Porzellan* (Bamberg: Fränkische Tag, 1996), 98. For diplomatic gifts see Maureen Cassidy-Geiger, *Fragile Diplomacy: Meissen Porcelain for European Courts ca. 1710–63* (New Haven and London: Yale University Press/Bard Graduate Center, 2007).

68. *D 1784*, 8; *Works* 2: 408.
69. *D 1784*, 14; *Works* 2: 416.
70. *HW Corres.* 9: 348.
71. *D 1784*, iii; *Works* 2: 397.
72. Wainwright, *Romantic Interior*, 11–13.
73. Samuel Rush Meyrick, 'The Doucean Museum', *Gentleman's Magazine*, n.s. 5 (Jan.–June 1836): 245–53, 385–90; n.s. 6 (July–Dec. 1836): 158–60, 378–84, 492–4, 598–601; Bodleian Library, *The Douce Legacy* (Oxford: exh. cat., Bodleian Library, 1984).
74. Arthur MacGregor, *Curiosity and Enlightenment: Collectors and Collections from the Sixteenth to the Nineteenth Century* (New Haven and London: Yale University Press, 2007).
75. John Cherry, in Arthur MacGregor (ed.), *Sir Hans Sloane: Collector, Scientist, Antiquary* (London: British Museum Press, 1994), 216, notes Sloane's technical interest in ceramics.

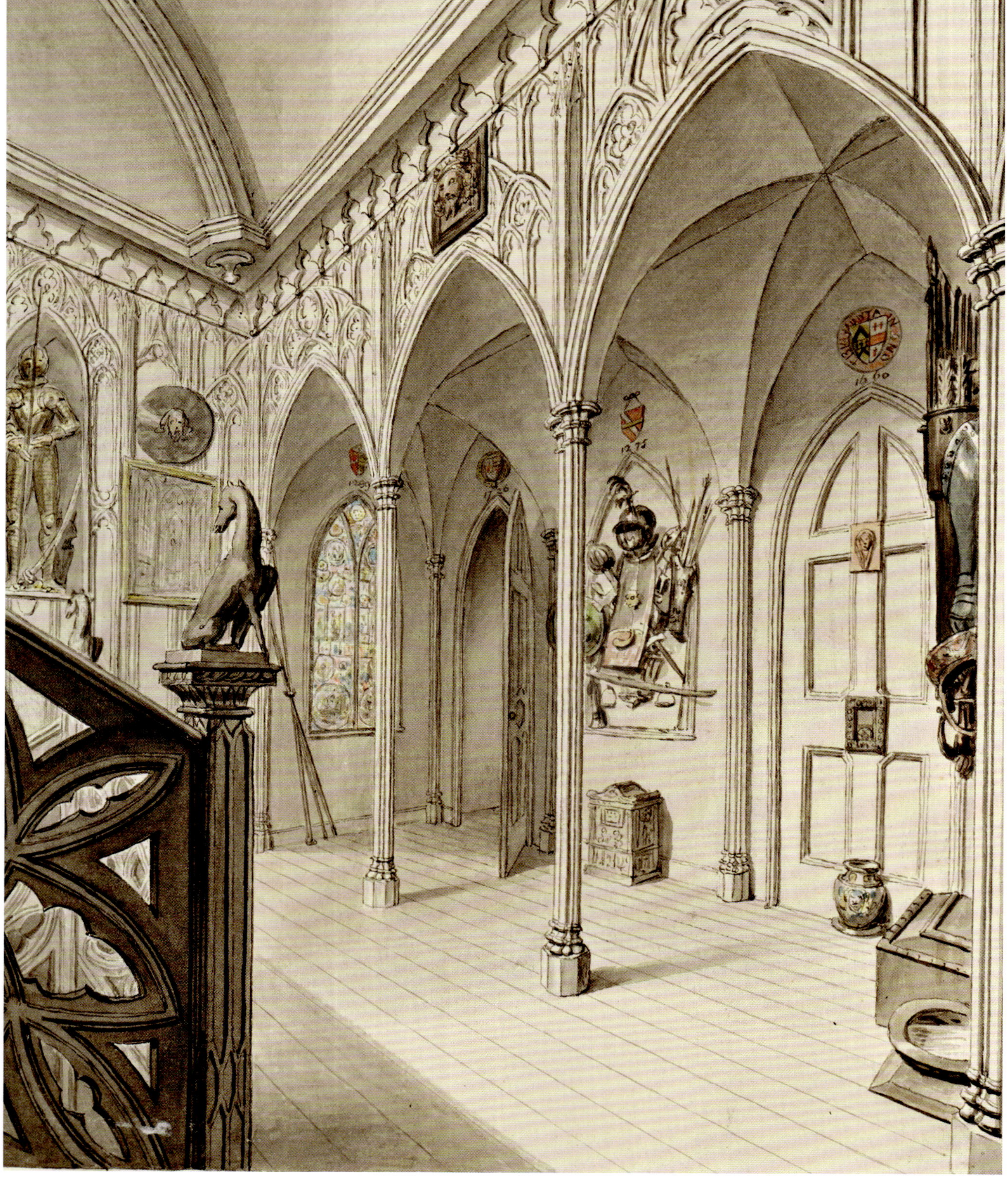

13.

THE STRAWBERRY HILL ARMOURY

STUART W. PYHRR

Horace Walpole's Armoury at Strawberry Hill occupies a special place in the history of arms and armour collecting as possibly the first, and certainly the most famous, armoury created in a Gothic-Revival setting during the eighteenth century. The Armoury's importance in the history of collecting has long been acknowledged by armour specialists,[1] while its pivotal role in the development of the Romantic interior has recently been defined by Clive Wainwright.[2] Yet the evolution of Walpole's Armoury has not been studied, and neither have its contents been examined in detail. This oversight is particularly surprising given the quality of the objects and the wealth of documentation. Walpole's guidebook, *A Description of the Villa of Mr. Horace Walpole … at Strawberry Hill* (1774), includes a survey of the Armoury, giving the provenance of some of the more important items.[3] An engraved view of the Armoury in the revised version of the *Description* (1784), and a later series of specially commissioned watercolours (Fig. 245), illustrate the Armoury's arrangement and some of the individual weapons. Walpole's correspondence offers a first-hand account of the Armoury's growth.[4] George Robins's 1842 sale catalogue of Strawberry Hill's contents contains the final and only complete inventory of the Armoury, and the list of buyers records the many directions into which the arms were dispersed.[5] This documentation, and in particular the detail and accuracy of the illustrative material, afford a unique opportunity, on the one hand, to reconstruct the arrangement of an eighteenth-century armoury and, on the other, to identify individual items with objects in public and private collections.

Since the sixteenth century, armour and weapons were commonly found in antiquarian collections in England and on the Continent. They often kept company with fossils, shells, minerals, flora and fauna, coins, medals and gems, as well as antiquities, art works, ethnological material and relics associated with historic persons or events, a heterogeneous mix of objects intended to form an encyclopedic catalogue of the natural and manmade world.[6] Arms were variously appreciated as mementoes of one's ancestors or of famous warriors, as curiosities of exotic peoples, as mechanical marvels and occasionally even as works of art. In seventeenth-century Bologna, for example, Ferdinando Cospi's cabinet included panoplies of European and non-European arms (Fig. 246) among extensive displays of *naturalia* and *artificialia*. By the mid-eighteenth century the collecting of arms and armour with a connoisseur's focus had not yet developed; no specialized market or dealers existed to supply it and there was no scholarly literature to inform and guide the collector. As a result, Walpole's collecting was unsystematic and uninformed. He had, however, a novel plan to create an armoury within a Gothic setting so as to evoke the knights and crusaders from a distant and romantically recalled medieval world, and by doing so to emphasize the antiquity and nobility of his lineage. In Walpole's words, the Armoury 'bespeaks the ancient chivalry of the lords of the castle'.[7]

The creation of an armoury was among the first renovations Walpole made to his newly acquired

Figure 245. John Carter, *The Armoury at Strawberry Hill*, *c.* 1788, pen and ink, watercolour, 33.5 × 29.5 cm (sheet), on p. 57 of Richard Bull's extra-illustrated copy of the *Description*. The Lewis Walpole Library, Yale University. 33 30 copy 11 Folio

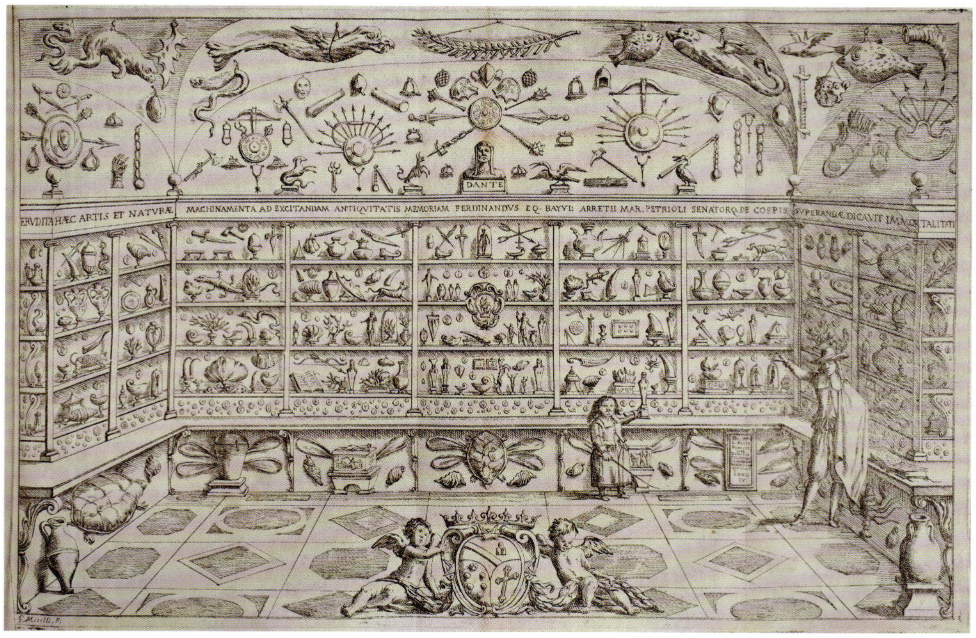

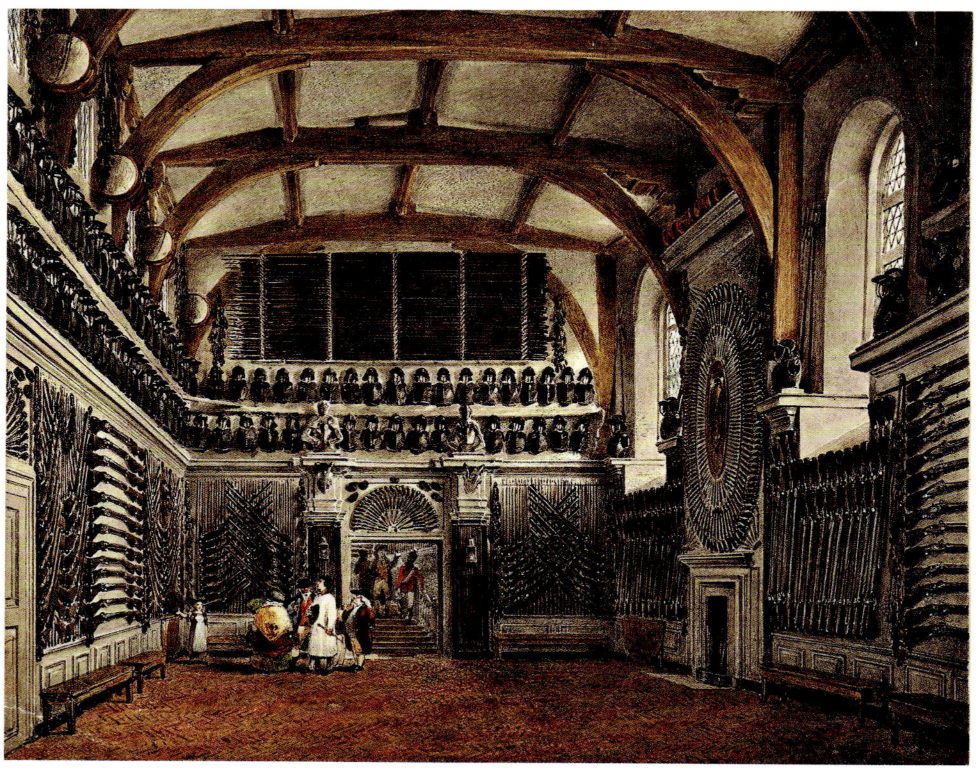

Figure 246. G. Mitelli, *Cabinet of Ferdinando Cospi in Bologna*, engraving, from Lorenzo Legati, *Mvseo Cospinao…* (Bologna: G. Monti, 1677). Courtesy of Yale University Library

Figure 247. James Stephanoff, *The Guard Chamber in the Round Tower, Windsor Castle*, 1818, watercolour. The Royal Collection

(1747) suburban villa. Already by January 1750, when he announced, 'I am going to build a little Gothic castle at Strawberry Hill', he had asked his old friend Horace Mann, British minister in Florence, to acquire old painted glass and arms for him.[8] Walpole's ideas for an armoury and its arrangement were undoubtedly influenced by his knowledge of the celebrated displays in the Tower of London, Windsor Castle (Fig. 247) and Hampton Court, as well as those in English country houses (Fig. 248).[9] From his travels abroad he would also have been familiar with some of the more famous collections of arms on the Continent, particularly those of the French royal collection (Garde Meuble) and the abbey of Sainte Geneviève (Fig. 249), both in Paris, that at the Château de Chantilly, and the Medici armoury in the Uffizi.[10]

The speed at which the Armoury took shape suggests that many of the contents were acquired in the spring of 1753. In April he announced to Mann that 'by next spring I hope to have rusty armour, and arms with quarterings';[11] by May he recorded receipt of a shield and arrows;[12] and by June the Armoury was installed. The building of the Armoury demonstrates Walpole's genius for design and his penchant for theatrical effect. Room layout, decorative displays and lighting make clear the importance he placed on the Armoury in creating an immediate medieval atmosphere appropriate to his new Gothic castle. The Armoury was sited on the narrow landing (called a vestibule) of the main staircase to the second floor. Decorative panoplies were complemented by heraldic displays, notably carved wooden antelopes, supporters of the Walpole arms, placed on the newel posts of the staircase, and shields emblazoned with Walpole's family arms set above the doors off the landing. An evocative 'gloomth' was created at night by the single lantern of coloured glass over the staircase and during the day by the stained glass window at one end of the vestibule. In his letter to Mann of 12 June Walpole described the completed ensemble:

> The hall and staircase are the chief beauty of the castle. Imagine the walls covered with (I call it paper but it is really paper painted in perspective to represent) Gothic fretwork: the lightest Gothic balustrade to the staircase, adorned with antelopes (our supporters) bearing shields; lean windows fattened with rich saints in painted glass, and a vestibule

> open with three arches on the landing place, and niches full of trophies of old coats of mail, Indian shields made of rhinoceros's hides, broadswords, quivers, long bows, arrows and spears – all supposed to be taken by Sir Terry Robsart in the holy wars.[13]

In a subsequent description Walpole noted in further detail

> a rusty helmet with rotten wadding; a coat of mail that came from Coombe, and belonged to a trooper of the Earl of Warwick ... there is a mark of its being bullet-proof ... one gauntlet; I have no more; a Persian shield enamelled, a Chinese bow, quiver, and arrows, an Indian saber and dagger, and a spear made of wood with fifty points.[14]

Much of the initial display was probably acquired in lots with the assistance of agents, family and friends. The core objects came from a single source:

> Two suits of armour, on one of which is the mark of the bullet; two helmets; a gauntlet; a round leathern quiver; and a pair of stirrups; from Coombe, near Kingston in Surrey, which seat formerly belonged to the great Richard Neville earl of Warwick. These arms therefore were probably part of those which served his troops when he marched to Westminster to awe the parliament in the reign of Henry the Sixth.[15]

Dating the Coombe pieces to the time of Richard Neville and Henry VI was naive. From Walpole's descriptions and illustrations of the Armoury it is evident that the arms date not from the War of the Roses (1455–85) but rather from the English Civil Wars (1642–51). The two armours were of 'harquebusier' type (named after the cavalry troops armed with a short-barrelled firearm called a harquebus), each comprised of an open-faced helmet (or 'pot') having a pivoted brim with triple-bar face guard, a cuirass formed of a shot-proof breastplate and a backplate, and an elbow-length gauntlet for the left hand.[16] This distinctive form of armour was worn in England throughout much of the seventeenth century and must still have been commonplace in panoplies displayed in castles and manor houses in Walpole's day. Indeed, as Walpole observed, one of his pieces bore a characteristic feature of these

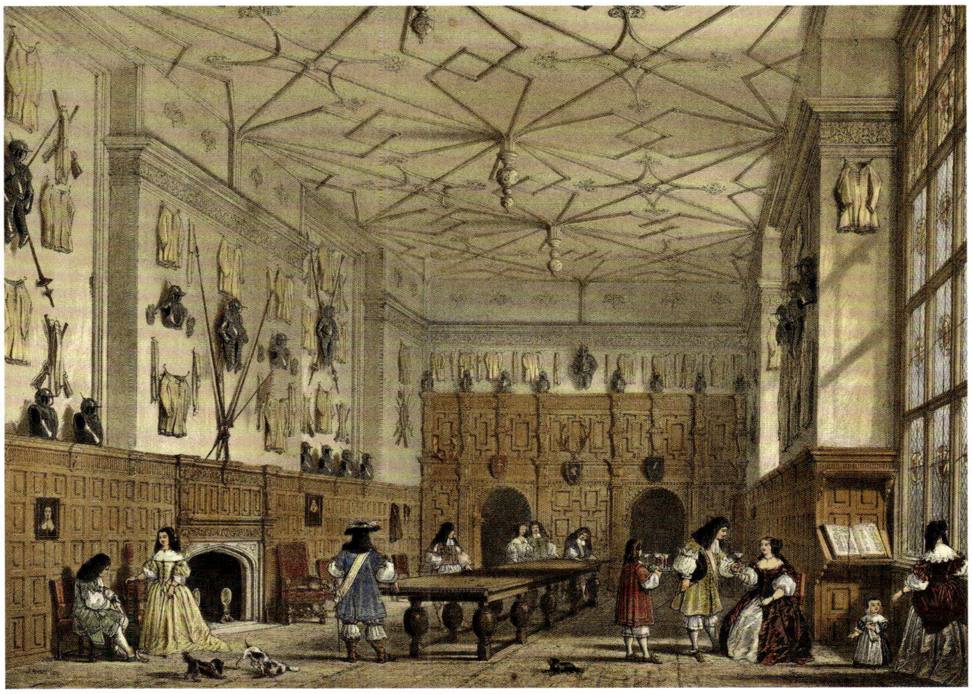

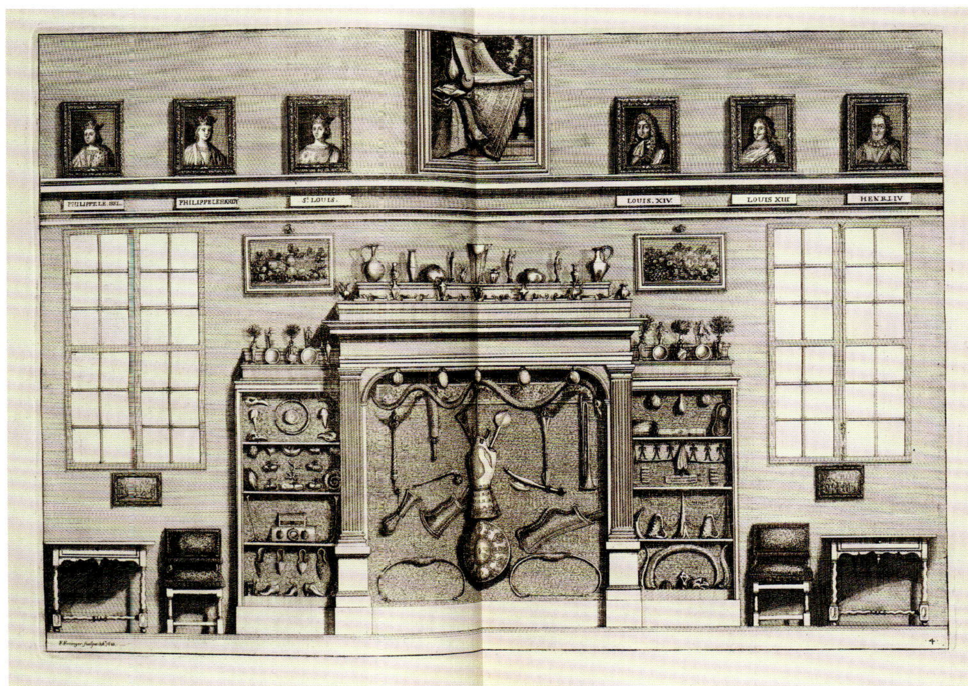

Figure 248. Joseph Nash, *Hall Littlecote Wilts*, plate 3 from *The Mansions of England in the Olden Time*. Second Series (London: Thomas M'Lean, 1839–49), vol. 2, hand-coloured lithotint. Yale Center for British Art, Paul Mellon Collection

Figure 249. F. Ertinger, *Musée Sainte Geneviève, Paris*, 1688, woodcut from C. du Molinet, *Le Cabinet de la Bibliothèk de Sainte Geneviève*, 1692. Beinecke Rare Book and Manuscript Library, Yale University

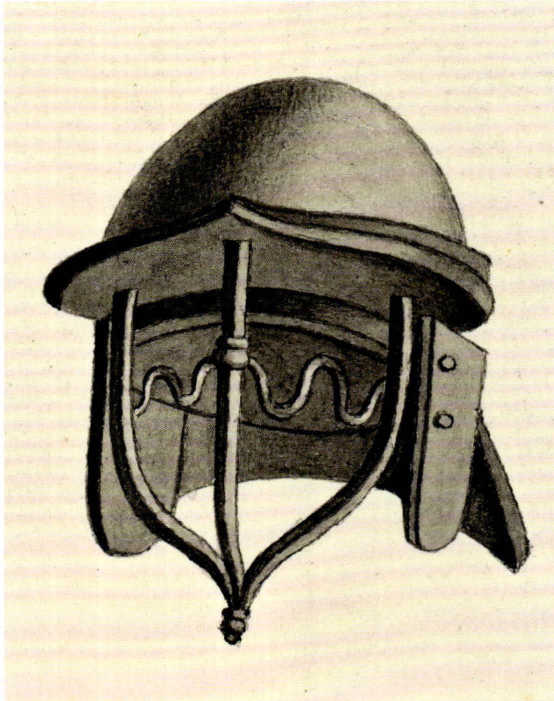

Figure 250. Harquebusier's helmet, n.d. (*c.* 1788?), pen, ink, and wash; laid in Bawtree's extra-illustrated copy of the *Description*. The Lewis Walpole Library, Yale University

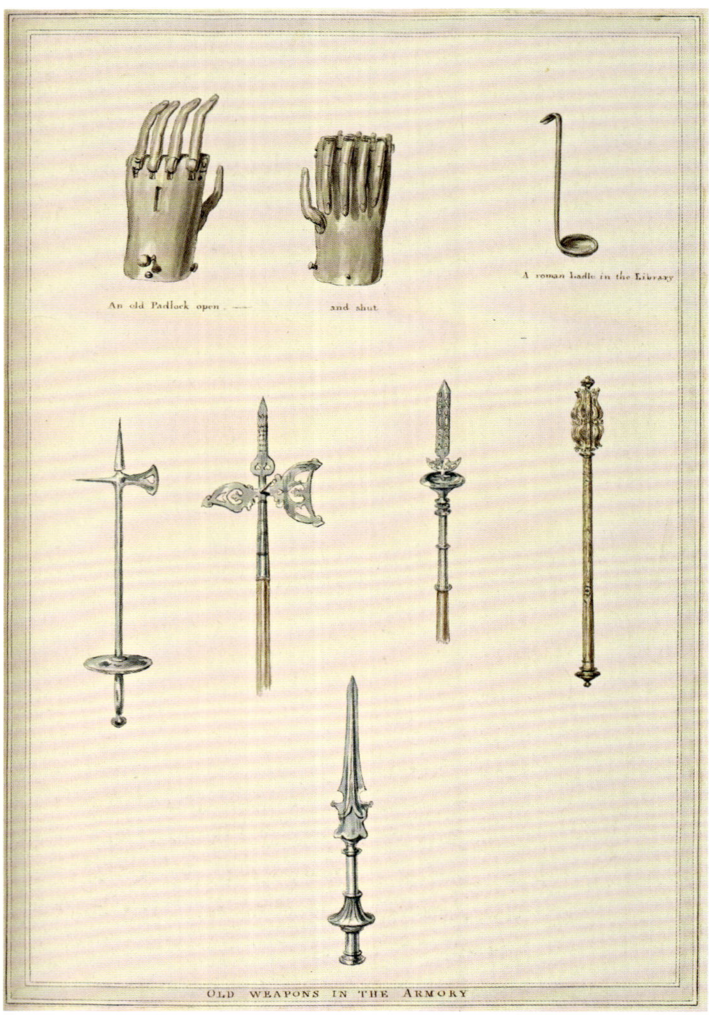

Figure 251. John Carter, *Old Weapons in the Armory*, ink and watercolour, *c.* 1788, 45.7 × 31 cm (sheet), on p. 97 of Richard Bull's extra-illustrated copy of the *Description*. The Lewis Walpole Library, Yale University. 33 30 copy 11 Folio

late armours, the deep bullet dent as evidence of having been 'proved', something never found on medieval armour.

Walpole was undoubtedly misled in his dating of the armour by the fact that Coombe was once Neville property. However, the manor house from which he acquired it dated from the late sixteenth century and the armour it contained probably belonged to one of its later owners, Charles Cockayne, Viscount Cullen of Tipperary, who was a Royalist during the Civil Wars. In 1748 the Countess of Orford, wife of Walpole's elder brother, took up residence at Coombe, and thus it was probably she who facilitated Walpole's acquisition of the manor's military relics when the house was sold in 1753.[17]

Views of the Armoury (Fig. 245) show that the main panoply opposite the stairs consisted of a console supporting a harquebusier's helmet and cuirass, framed on either side by an arrangement of weapons made up of Scottish basket-hilted broadswords, a bowcase with arrows, a gun, a curved sword and a pair of stirrups. A round Indian shield of rhinoceros hide, its convex face set with four domed bosses, was on the wall to the left. At the top of the stairs, next to the stained-glass window, rest several spears, and at the opposite end of the corridor there was apparently a second panoply, from which a round quiver and elbow gauntlet are visible, these presumably from Coombe. The helmet at the centre of the first panoply, which is a harquebusier's pot of unusual type, having a triple-bar face guard with a wavy crossbar and an acorn-shaped terminal, is the subject of a small watercolour study (Fig. 250).[18] Another sheet, entitled 'Old Weapons in the Armoury' (Fig. 251), illustrates several staff weapons, among them a horseman's axe, a halberd and several partisans (spear-like staffs); judging from their characteristic heart-shaped piercings, these were probably also seventeenth-century English.[19]

Over the next forty years Walpole made a number of important additions to the Armoury. He valued the provenance of his objects, citing in his *Description* the source of acquisitions, whether they were purchased from fellow antiquaries like Julienne, Crozat and Rawle, or were gifts from friends. Among the gifts he recorded 'an Indian scimitar, the handle and ornaments in silver, in a green case; and a dagger of the same; given by a nabob to George Morton Pitt, Governor of Fort St. George, and by his widow to Mr. Walpole'.[20] He was presented with three shields by Sir William Hamilton (discussed below), 'an ancient musket, richly carved' by his friend Moses Franks,[21] and another musket and 'pistol inlaid with ivory' by George Scott.[22] He also acquired 'an American calumet [peace pipe]; a warrior's wreath; and a neck ornament: present from Thomas Pownall', a fellow antiquary and a former governor in the American colonies.[23]

Among Walpole's purchases for the Armoury were three items from the collection of the famous French engraver and antiquary, Jean de Jullienne, which was auctioned in Paris in 1767. The arms and armour were introduced in the sale catalogue as 'piéces qui composent les trophées de la Galerie',[24] indicating that they had been used as wall decoration. This is confirmed by Walpole, who recorded after a visit to Jullienne's house in 1765 that the gallery was decorated with 'Chinese arms in festoons between the pictures'.[25] Judging from the descriptions in the sale catalogue, the majority of weapons were eastern – Turkish, Persian, Indian, Chinese or Southeast Asian – and included North and South American artefacts and 'weapons of savages'. Walpole bought 'an eastern powder-horn of steel and bronze, richly graved, and hung to a chain with a tablet of bronze, characters in the middle on a red ground; an Indian mace, inlaid with brass; [and] a hatchet, ditto'.[26] These items can be identified with the Julienne lots 1338, 1346, and 1347 respectively: 'une boite à poudre en forme de cornet de S. Hubert, revêtue d'argent travaillé & en partie doré; une très belle masse d'arme, damasquinée en or'; and 'une belle hache d'arme, dont le manche est garnie en chagrin & argent doré'.[27]

Compared to the catalogue entries, Walpole's descriptions are surprisingly careless as to the identification of materials. For example, he referred to the parcel-gilt silver powder flask as made of steel and bronze, the gold-damascened mace as brass inlaid. Several of these objects are recognizable in the watercolours and allow for more accurate dating and attribution. The powder flask on a chain, which hangs over the harquebusier's armour in the central panoply (Fig. 245) is definitely eastern, perhaps Persian or Ottoman, and probably of eighteenth-century date.[28] The mace (Fig. 251, middle row, far right)

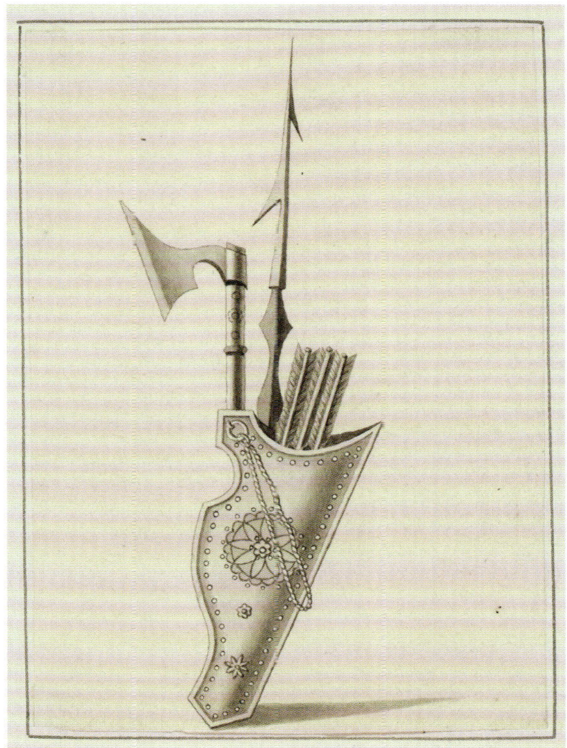

Figure 252. *Arms at Strawberry Hill*, grey wash, 14.4 × 10.3 cm, on p. 78 of Bawtree's extra-illustrated copy of the *Description*. The Lewis Walpole Library, Yale University. 33 30 copy 4

is European, probably Italian or French, from the second half of the sixteenth century.[29] The horseman's axe ('hatchet') (Fig. 252) appears to be Ottoman, perhaps Turkish or Balkan, and probably of late seventeenth-century date.[30]

The arms acquired in the 1770s were of far greater historic and artistic value than any Walpole had hitherto collected. Colourful and elaborately decorated, and appreciated as works of art in their own right, they matched in quality and importance Strawberry Hill's finest paintings, ceramics and goldsmith's work. In 1770, at Lady Elizabeth (Betty) Germain's sale, Walpole bought one of his most precious objects, 'Henry VIII^{ths} dagger, of Turkish work; the blade is of steel damasked with gold, the case and handle of chalcedonyx, set with diamonds and many rubies'.[31] The subject of several watercolours (Fig. 253), it can be identified as one of a small and distinctive group of Turkish or Persian daggers dating to the second half of the sixteenth century. The daggers are typically fitted with a hardstone grip inlaid with gold and precious stones, a guard with short curled quillons of gold set with jewels, and a straight double-edged blade damascened in gold with arabesques and inscriptions.[32] The scabbards are often of gold set with gems, whereas Walpole's was of jewelled

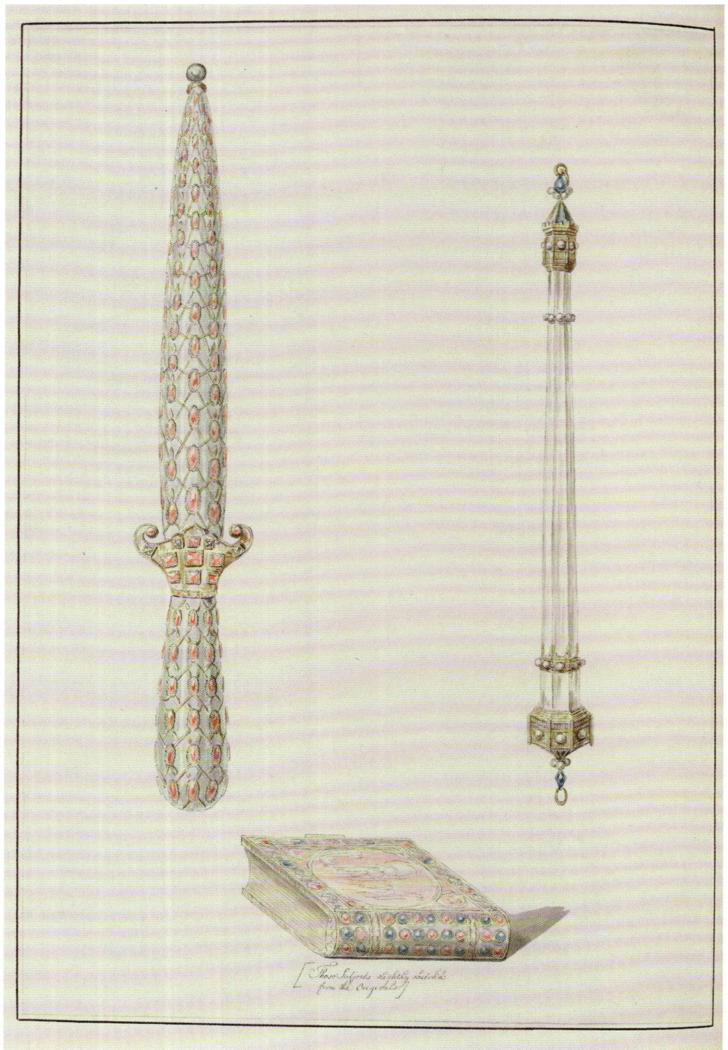

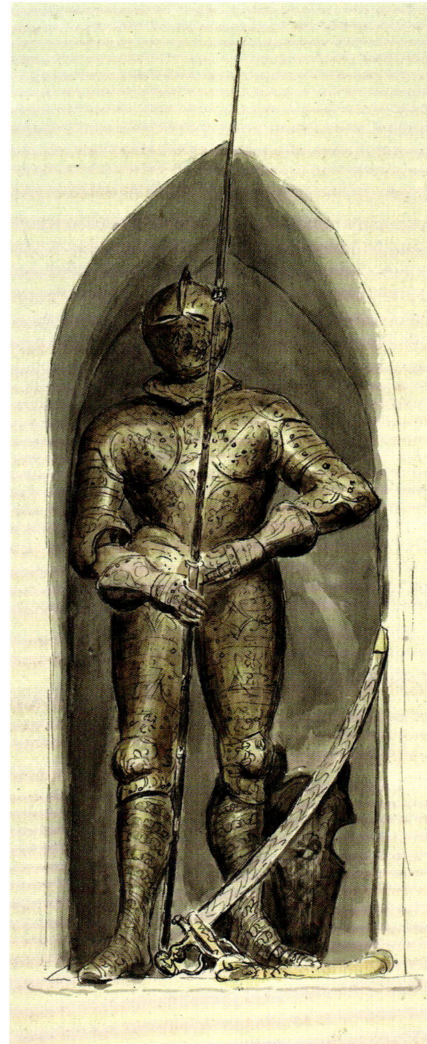

Figure 253. John Carter, *'Henry VIII's dagger, the prayer book of Queen Claude of France and a crystal sceptre'*, ink and wash and watercolour, *c.* 1788, on p.182 of Richard Bull's extra-illustrated copy of the *Description*. The Lewis Walpole Library, Yale University. 33 30 copy 11 Folio

Figure 254. John Carter, *'Suit of Armour of Francis I King of France in a nich on the Staircase at Strawberry hill'*, *c.* 1788, ink and watercolour, in an extra-illustrated copy of the *Description*. Henry E. Huntington Library, San Marino, California (vol. 1, 50v)

hardstone matching the grip. His blade, too, was unusual, having an openwork design, a virtuoso demonstration of the bladesmith's skill. Walpole's attribution of the dagger as Turkish was astute; his acceptance of its identification with Henry VIII, however, was romantic and unfounded. The association may have been based on the similarity of Lady Betty Germain's example with the jewelled dagger in the Duchess of Portland's collection, which bore an old (but equally unsupported) attribution to Henry VIII.[33] Valued as a precious Tudor relic and *objet d'art* rather than as a weapon, Walpole deposited the dagger in the Tribune, his 'treasury', rather than in the Armoury.

In 1771 Walpole bought one of the most important and famous objects in his collection, the so-called armour of Francis I of France (Fig. 254). Long missing and largely forgotten, the Francis I armour has recently been rediscovered in a German castle (Fig. 255).[34] Walpole acquired the armour from the heirs of the French collector Louis-Antoine Crozat, Baron de Thiers, whose *hôtel* he had visited on several occasions, the last time on 1 August 1771.[35] Immediately afterwards he entered into negotiations for its purchase, employing his devoted friend in Paris, Mme du Deffand, as liaison. Their correspondence chronicles the negotiations and a successful conclusion in October for the price of 50 Louis (£52 10s.).[36] The purchase included not only the armour on a wooden manikin, but also an associated sword, lance and a defence for a horse's head (shaffron).[37] The ensemble, delivered to Strawberry Hill on 19 November,

Figure 255. Detail of a Parade Armour (Armour of Francis I, King of France), French or Flemish, *c.* 1600, steel, embossed and gilt, H 140 cm. Wartburg-Stiftung Eisenach, Germany. Cat. 50

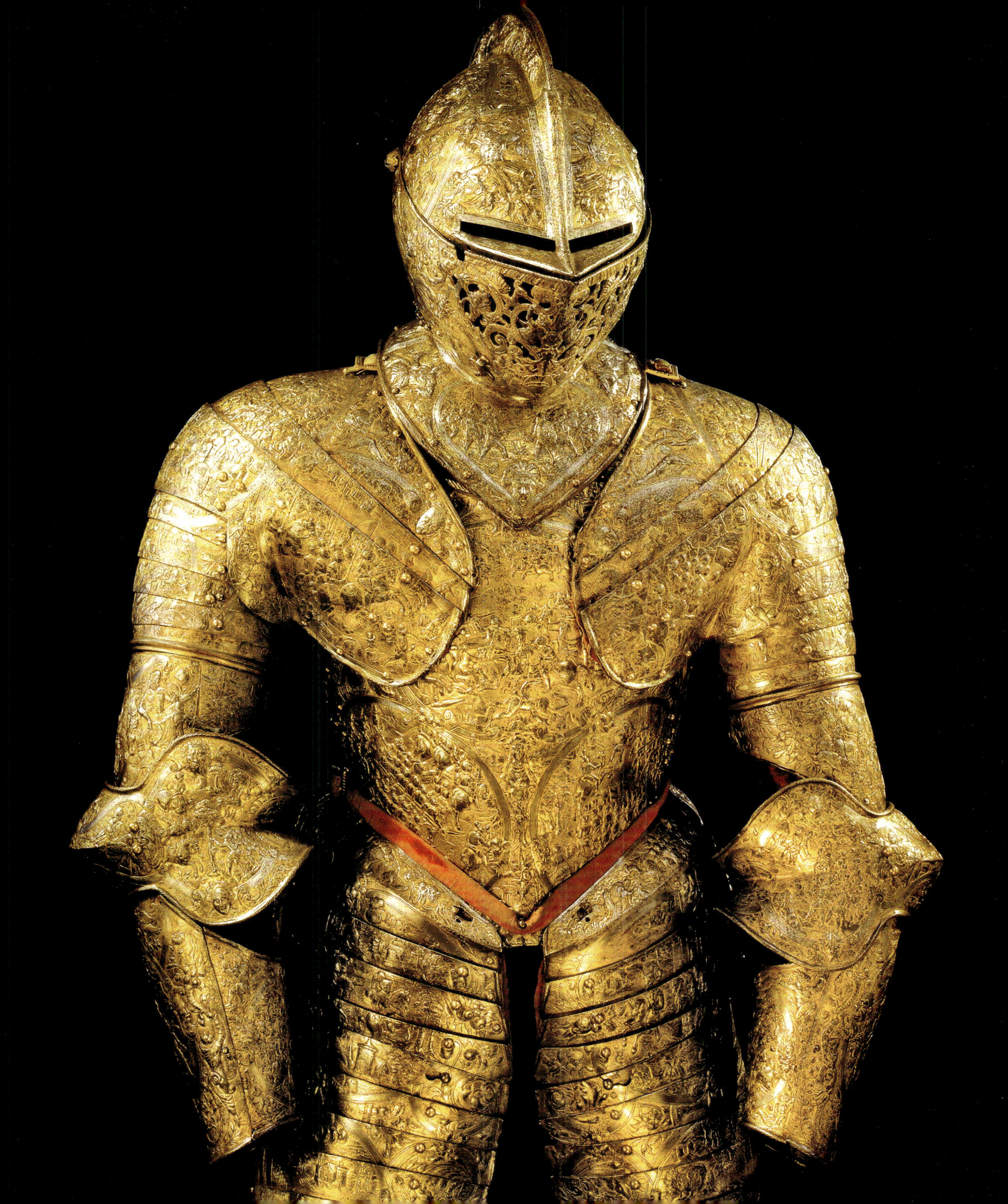

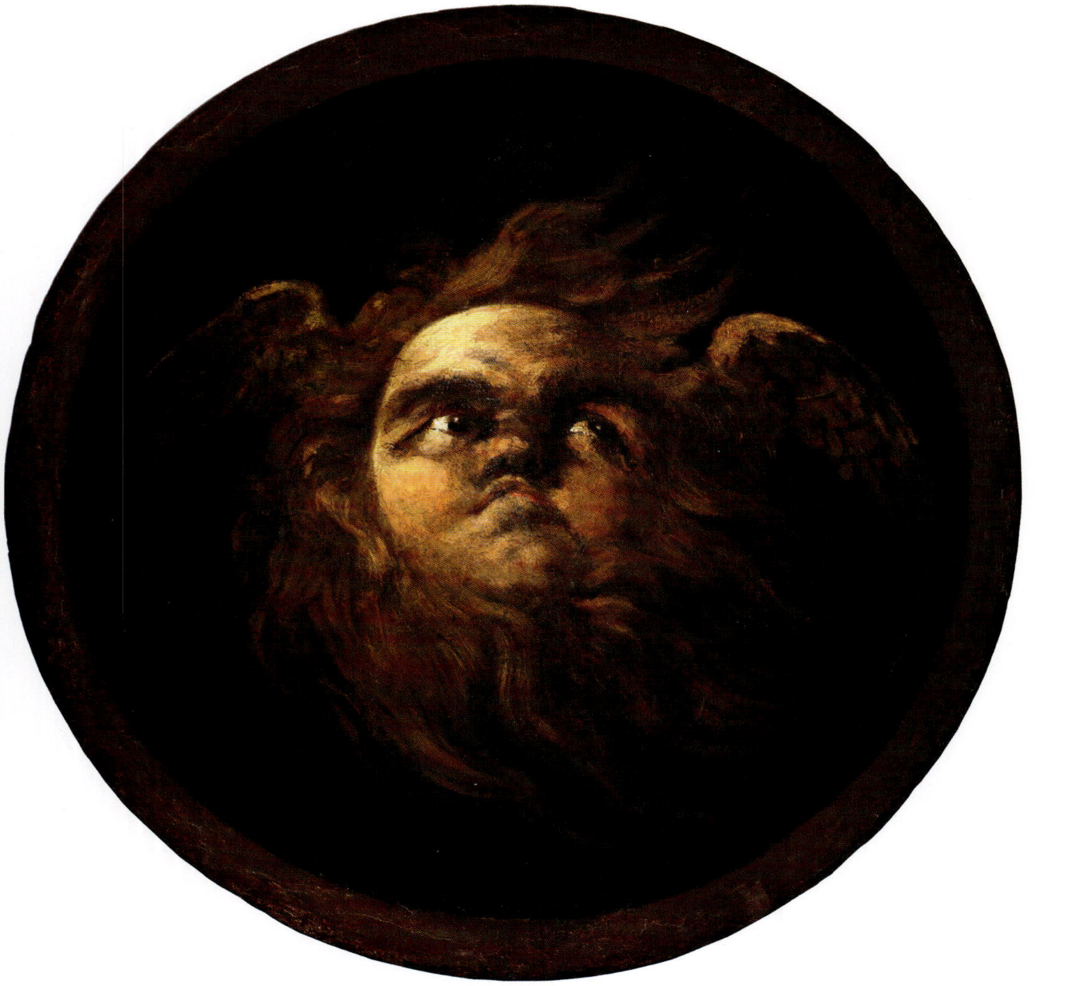

Figure 256. Shield painted with the Head of Perseus. Italian, *c.* 1525–50, painted canvas mounted on wood. Culture and Sport Glasgow (Museums). Acquired 1976 with the assistance of the National Fund for Acquisitions. Cat. 54

was immediately installed in a specially constructed niche set into the wall of the stairway leading up to the Armoury.[38] Walpole described the display:

> In a niche, the armour of Francis I. King of France, of steel gilt, and covered with bas-reliefs in a fine taste: his lance is of ebony inlaid with silver; his sword steel; beautifully inlaid with gold, probably the work of Benvenuto Cellini: there is also the armour for the horse's head. (Fig. 254)[39]

The armour became one of the highlights of the Strawberry Hill tour.

Identification of the armour with Francis I (r. 1515–47), an association that appears to have originated with Crozat, was optimistic. The form of the armour suggests instead a date during the reign of Henry IV (1590–1610).[40] It is a rare 'parade' version of cuirassier armour, a late sixteenth–century type worn by the heavy cavalry armed with pistols rather than the traditional, and by then outmoded, lance. Distinguishing features include a close-helmet, symmetrical shoulder defences (pauldrons) and long articulated thigh defences (tassets) reaching the knees, as well as the absence of armour for the lower legs and feet (greaves and sabatons). Walpole's armour is embossed in low relief with battle scenes enclosed within strapwork cartouches, as well as with allegorical figures, bound warriors, putti, trophies and foliage, the surfaces gilt overall, the strapwork blued. The Mannerist ornament, however, looks back to a mid-sixteenth-century style, evoking in particular the armour of Henry II (r. 1547–59), then in the Garde Meuble and now in the Louvre, which is embossed with scenes from the life of Julius Caesar and Pompey within strapwork cartouches.[41] In the eighteenth century the Henry II armour was mistakenly identified as Francis I's, an attribution that is likely to have been transferred to the similarly decorated Crozat armour.[42] Walpole's armour is noteworthy as probably the last embossed parade armour of this French type and for the unusual subject of its decoration, contemporary battle scenes rather than the more customary classical subject matter. The soldiers wear sixteenth-century armour and carry flags with fleurs-de-lis, suggesting that the scenes may depict recent events relating to France's Wars of Religion (1562–98).[43]

Illustrations of the armour indicate that substitutions had been made for what collectors of the day would have considered to be the missing parts necessary for a complete, 'knightly', cap-à-pie armour. The gauntlets and lower legs, the latter apparently of gilt leather, are obvious restorations and were probably made for Crozat.[44] While the armour was never intended to have lower leg defences, the original gauntlets were in fact missing; these have since been identified as a pair in the Metropolitan Museum of Art (Cat. 51, Fig. 306). The armour was displayed, as acquired from Crozat, with three arms quite unrelated to it, an association obviously intended solely for its picturesque effect. The armour holds a long spear that can be identified today as an eighteenth-century Indian example now in the Metropolitan

Museum (Cat. 53, Fig. 308). At its feet lies an eighteenth-century Indian sabre, a type with distinctive saucer-shaped pommel known as a talwar, its iron hilt and scabbard mounts damascened in gold. Behind the armour is a shaffron of French type, *c.* 1600, embossed with vertical ridges and with a small decorative disk on the forehead, identifiable now as being in a private collection (Cat. 52, Fig. 307).

Walpole's mention of Benvenuto Cellini in his description of the staircase display is noteworthy. The artist's name is also associated with two of the collector's most precious objects, the 'Cellini bell' and a small silver perfume box set with silver reliefs that came from the Medici *guardaroba*.[45] Walpole's attributions were probably prompted by his reading of the recently published English translation of Cellini's autobiography.[46] There the artist boasts of his achievements as a sculptor and goldsmith and his skills in casting and repoussé. He mentions having made a firearm entirely by himself and having learned the art of true damascening based on his study of Turkish knives. He does not, however, claim to have made or decorated plate armour. In the 1842 sale Robins catalogued the armour of Francis I as a work of Cellini, perhaps the result of having misread Walpole's description, which in fact attributed to the sculptor not the armour but the gold-damascened sword displayed at its feet.[47]

In 1774 Walpole acquired three Italian Renaissance parade shields as a gift from Sir William Hamilton, British envoy extraordinary and plenipotentiary at the court of Naples. A renowned antiquary and vulcanologist, Hamilton corresponded with Walpole, visited Strawberry Hill and on occasion contributed to Walpole's collections. In a letter to Hamilton of 22 February 1774 Walpole acknowledged that 'your Gothic shields will be extremely welcome'; on 19 June he noted their receipt two days earlier and requested more information about them, especially their provenance.[48]

Although he eagerly anticipated acquiring genuine medieval shields for his Gothic castle, Walpole was not disappointed with these Renaissance examples. Indeed, among early arms and armour collectors, little distinction appears to have been made between the Middle Ages and the Renaissance, with the result that sixteenth-century objects of the most sophisticated Mannerist taste were welcomed into Gothic settings such as Walpole's. The collector was effusive in his gratitude to Hamilton and in his praise of the shields: 'They are fine and most charming – nay, almost in too good taste, not to put my Gothic house to shame – I wish the Medusa could turn it into stone'; 'I am going to hang them by the beautiful armour of Francis I and they will certainly make me dream of another Castle of Otranto.'[49] He recorded his new acquisitions as follows, undoubtedly incorporating into his description the provenance information he received from Hamilton:

> Two shields, of leather, for tournaments, painted by Polidore. One has a head of a Medusa, the other of Perseus. On the inside are

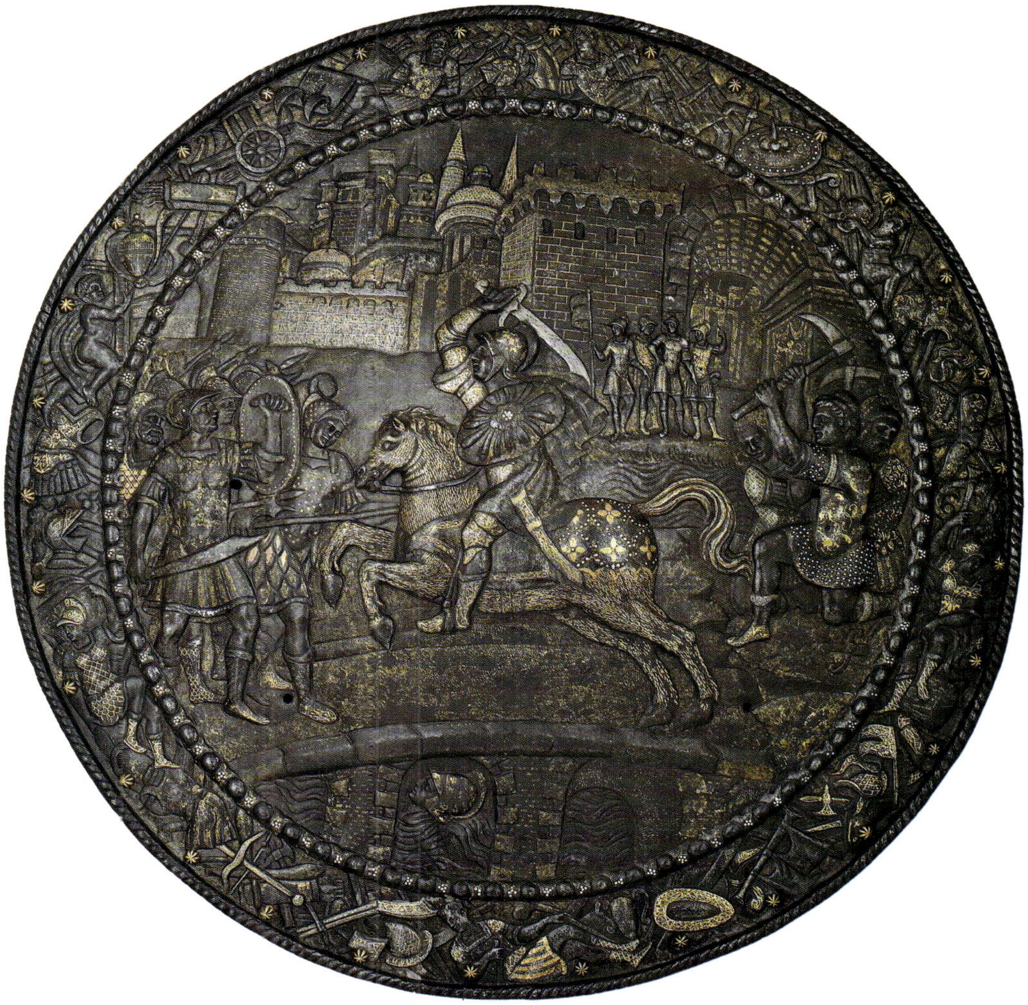

Figure 257. Parade shield depicting Horates Cocles defending the Sublican Bridge. Italian, probably Milan, *c.* 1560–70, iron, embossed and damascened in gold and silver. Wallace Collection, London

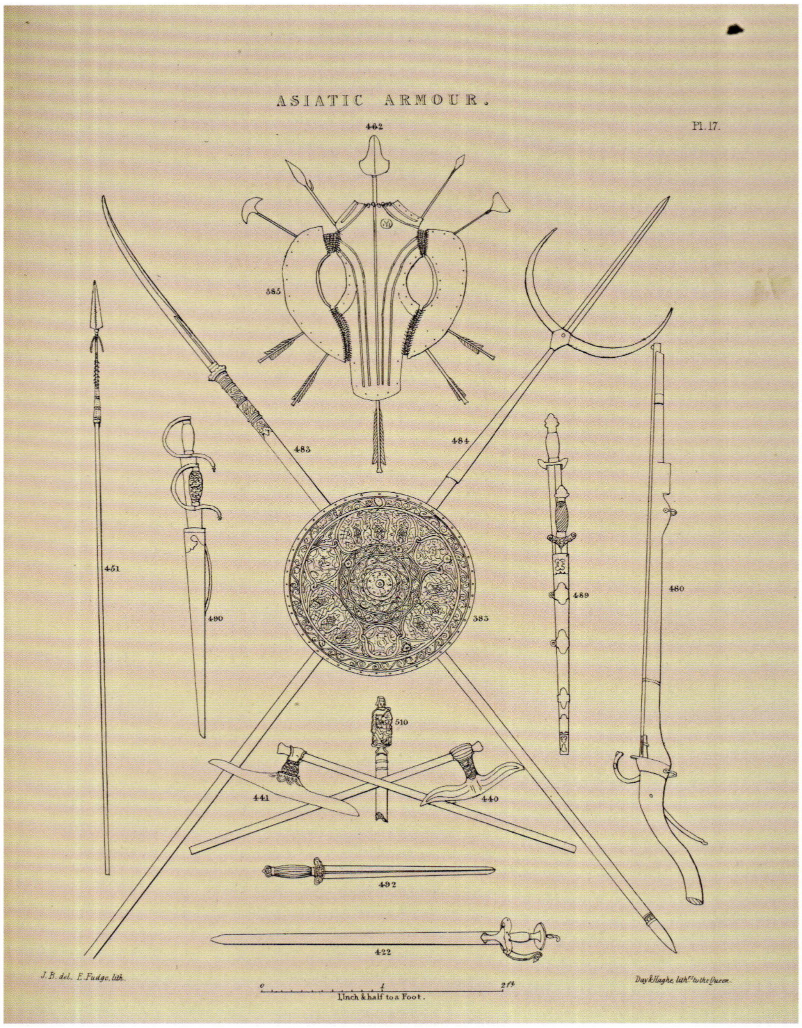

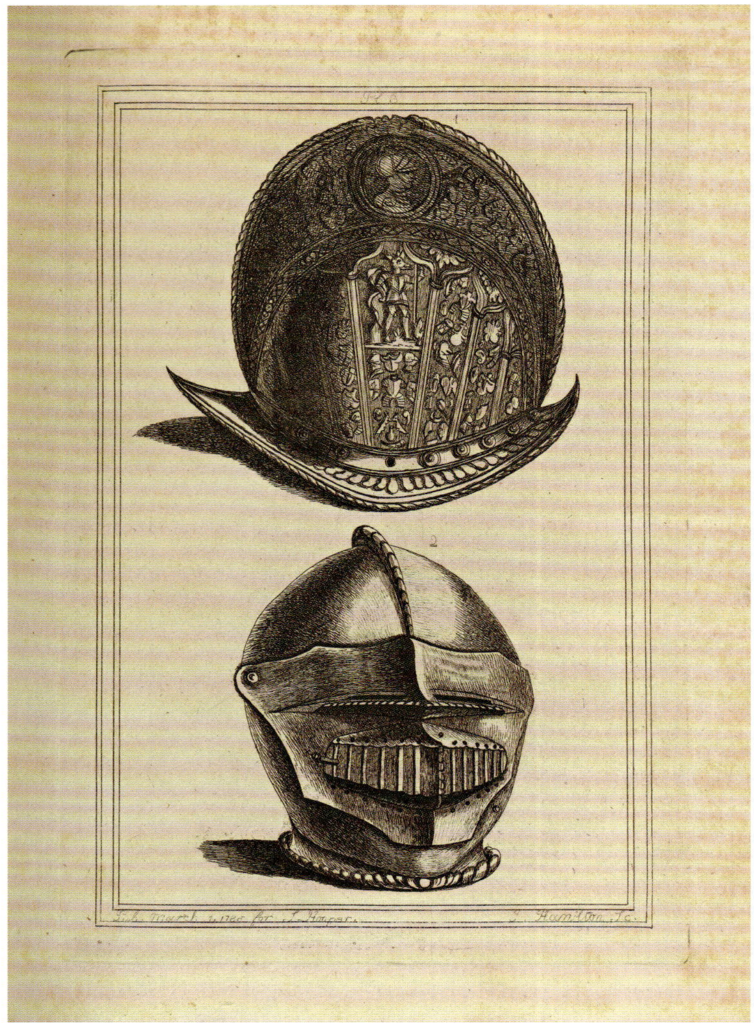

Figure 258. Plate 17 from John Beardmore, *A Catalogue with illustrations of the Collection of Ancient Arms and Armour, at Uplands, near Fareham, Hampshire*, lithograph (London: T. & W. Boone, 1845). British Library. 744.d.10. The 'Chinese, double-sword' is to the right of the shield

Figure 259. Plate 3 from Francis Grose, *A treatise on ancient armour and weapons: illustrated by plates taken from the original armour in the Tower of London*, engraving, (London: Printed for S. Hooper, 1786). Yale Center for British Art, Paul Mellon Collection. The Morion is the upper helmet

battles in gold; they came out of the collection of Commendatore Vittoria at Naples, and were sent to Mr Walpole by Sir W. Hamilton, together with a third, which hangs on the opposite side of the staircase; it is of iron and seems to have been gilt. It represents the story of Curtius; but by an embattled tower in the background ['its probably not Roman' crossed out by HW], and a cannon on the border, is certainly not antique.[50]

The two painted shields, now divided between Dublin and Glasgow (Fig. 256), are of similar size and composition and may have been pendants. The Dublin shield is painted in colours on its convex exterior with the grimacing head of the gorgon Medusa; that in Glasgow bears the winged head of a youth, perhaps Perseus. Interiors are painted in gold and grisaille with almost identical scenes from Roman history. The shields belong to a large group of Italian pageant shields with painted decoration illustrating scenes from Roman history or mythology. The majority appear to date from the second quarter of the sixteenth century and have been attributed to Giulio Romano or one of his contemporaries, notably Girolamo da Treviso the Younger or Polidoro da Caravaggio, the latter a pupil of Raphael's and a major exponent of the *all'antica* style of painting in Naples.[51] The Neapolitan provenance of Walpole's shields lends credence to the Polidoro attribution.[52]

Walpole's third shield, of embossed and gold-damascened iron, belongs to another well-documented group of Italian parade shields dating to the third quarter of the sixteenth century.[53] The subject represented on the shield was identified by Walpole (perhaps following Hamilton) as the story of Marcus Curtius, the Roman soldier who leapt with his horse into a fiery pit to save Rome.[54] A tale of virtue and self-sacrifice, it was a favourite subject for Renaissance armour decoration.[55] However, the lack of any later mention of a shield depicting Marcus Curtius suggests that Walpole's shield has been lost or, more likely, that its subject was misidentified. It seems odd that Walpole, with his knowledge of ancient history and having catalogued a painting of the same subject in his father's collection, would have misidentified the scene.[56] Still, this seems to be the case. Walpole's shield may reasonably be identified with an embossed and damascened iron example in the Wallace Collection (Fig. 257) depicting Horates Cocles defending the Sublican Bridge, another well-known subject of a hero who sacrificed his life for Rome.[57] The Wallace Collection shield displays the 'embattled tower in the background' and the 'cannon on the border' mentioned specifically in Walpole's description. Walpole's shield, which was bought at the 1842 sale by the London dealer John Swaby, is presumably the same one recorded in the posthumous sale of Swaby's collection in 1860, which included an iron shield depicting Horates Cocles said to have come from Strawberry Hill.[58]

Late in life Walpole was still making occasional additions to his Armoury. At the 1790 auction of the effects of the wealthy 'accoutrement maker' William Rawle he bought two lots, 'a singular double-handed weapon, a dagger, and other articles' and 'two ancient steel helmets'.[59] Among the first lot was a 'very rare and curious double sword', as described in the 1842 sale (lot 104); the same weapon, an eighteenth-century Chinese example consisting of two short swords fitting together within the same scabbard, is illustrated in the 1845 catalogue of John Beardmore's collection, where it is described as coming from Strawberry Hill (Fig. 258).[60] The second lot included 'a Venetian morion … engraved in Captain Grose's Armoury'.[61] Rawle's helmet of standard morion type, illustrated twice in Grose's *Treatise* (1786),[62] is of north Italian manufacture, either Milanese or Brescian, and dates to the end of the sixteenth century (Fig. 259). The etched decoration, consisting of bands of trophy ornament, is typical for Italian helmets of this type but is distinctive, nevertheless, for the inclusion of the prominent figure of Acteon on one side.

By the time of Walpole's death in 1797 Strawberry Hill was one of the most celebrated houses in Europe. The Armoury was thus well known and as a result can probably be credited with having inspired the creation of other arms and armour collections of that era. The painter Richard Cosway, for example, a friend of Walpole's and a visitor to Strawberry Hill, collected antique arms, which he displayed in his London house in a designated room, his 'armour closet'.[63] Other English artists, particularly the history painters Johann Zoffany and Philippe-Jacques de Loutherbourg, RA, were also collectors.[64] On a very different social level George Greville, Earl of Warwick, himself possessor of one of England's most important medieval castles, set about refurbishing it, including an armoury formed of indigenous Warwick pieces as well as others newly acquired on the Continent.[65] Similar stirrings of interest in armour were evident in Germany, where the Gothic Revival followed English models. By the 1780s Count Franz I zu Erbach-Erbach had assembled an important collection of armour, for which he built a neo-Gothic *Rittersaal* (Knights' Hall), complete with panoplies and stained glass, in his castle in the Odenwald, near Darmstadt;[66] by the end of the century Prince Leopold Friedrich Franz of Anhalt-Dessau had created a *Rittersaal* in his Gotisches Haus, a pleasure palace in Wörlitz;[67] and by 1805 Landgrave Wilhelm IX of Hessen-Kassel had a fully stocked armoury in his newly built Gothic 'ruin', the Löwenburg, near Kassel.[68]

When compared with some of the larger and more comprehensive armour collections formed in the following century – particularly those of the two greatest British collectors, Samuel Rush Meyrick and Sir Richard Wallace – the Strawberry Hill Armoury seems modest indeed. It occupied a narrow space and contained fewer than one hundred objects, a haphazard and heterogeneous mix of European and eastern arms without a single genuine medieval example among them. The importance of the Armoury lies rather in its unique place at the start of arms and armour collecting in eighteenth-century England, when it was the most famous, best documented and most influential collection of its kind.

Acknowledgements
In the preparation of this article I especially wish to acknowledge the valued assistance and advice of Michael Snodin, Cynthia Roman, Stephen Lloyd, Claude Blair, Thom Richardson, Donald La Rocca, Danielle Watson, Sarah Bevan Meschutt and particularly Lois Granato.

1. See, for example, Francis Henry Cripps-Day, *A Record of Armour Sales 1881–1924* (London: G. Bell and Sons, 1925), xxxiv–xxxvi; and Donald J. La Rocca, 'Carl Otto von Kienbusch and the Collecting of Arms and Armor in America', *Philadelphia Museum of Art Bulletin* 81, no. 345 (winter 1985): 4–5.
2. Clive Wainwright, *The Romantic Interior: The British Collector at Home 1750–1850* (New Haven and London: Yale University Press, 1989), esp. 101.
3. *D 1774*; *D 1784*, 31–3; the latter was reprinted in *Works* 2: 439–42. Subsequent references to the guidebook are cited as *Works*.
4. *HW Corres.*
5. *1842 Sale*; the Armoury was sold on day 19 (16 May), lots 64–105.
6. A comprehensive overview of early antiquarian collecting is provided by Arthur MacGregor, *Curiosity and Enlightenment: Collectors and Collections from the Sixteenth to the Nineteenth Century* (New Haven and London: Yale University Press, 2007).
7. *HW Corres.* 9: 150.
8. *HW Corres.* 20: 111.
9. Introduced into the royal palaces after 1660, the elaborate trophies composed of hundreds of arms arranged in decorative patterns were a tangible demonstration of the monarch's power. See Geoffrey Parnell, 'Arming the Tower: The Small Armoury at the Tower of London', *Apollo* 137 (1993): 82–5; and 'The King's Guard Chamber: A Vision of Power', *Apollo* 140 (1994): 60–64. For the more modest displays in country houses, including Strawberry Hill, see Sarah Bevan, 'Arms and the Mansion', *Country Properties: The Magazine of Fine Houses and Estates*, Strutt and Parker, 1989, 4–6.
10. For some of the highlights of these collections see, for example, Hurtaut and Magny, *Dictionnaire historique de la ville de Paris et ses environs*, 4 vols. (Paris: Chez Moutart, 1779), III: 114–15 (Garde-meuble), and II: 233–4 (Chantilly). For the history of the Medici armoury, see B. Thomas and L.G. Boccia, *Armi storiche del Museo Nazionale di Firenze, Palazzo del Bargello, restaurate dall'aiuto austriaco per Firenze* (Florence: exh. cat., Forte di San Giorgio, 1971), 13–22.
11. *HW Corres.* 20: 372.
12. *HW Corres.* 20: 375.
13. *HW Corres.* 20: 381 (and n. 11 for Terry Robsart [d. 1496], a distant relation of Walpole who never fought in the Crusades).
14. *HW Corres.* 31: 26.
15. *Works* 2: 440.
16. David Blackmore, *Arms and Armour of the English Civil Wars* (London: Trustees of the Royal Armouries, 1990), esp. 7–10, 14–17.
17. For Coombe see L.E. Gent, 'The Manor of Coombe or Coombe Neville', *Kingston on Thames Archaeological Society, Occasional Papers no. 3*, 1979, 3–6. I am grateful to Claude Blair for researching the history of Coombe on my behalf and to Jill Lamb of the Kingston Local History Room, Kingston upon Thames, for providing photocopies of Gent's paper.
18. This watercolour was a model for the engraved illustration in the 1789 *Supplement* to Francis Grose, *A Treatise on Ancient Armour and Weapons* (London: S. Hooper, 1786), pl. 62, no. 2.
19. For English staff weapons of this period, see Blackmore, *Arms and Armour*, 78–9. Two of Walpole's halberds are said to have come from his father's house at Houghton (*Works* 2: 441).
20. *Works* 2: 440; for Pitt (1693–1756), who served in India and was later a neighbour of Walpole at Twickenham, see *HW Corres.* 9: 263–4 nn. 9, 10a.
21. *Works* 2: 440; for Franks (1718–89) see *HW Corres.* 2: 373 n. 23, 10: 106n.
22. *Works* 2: 441; for Scott (1721–80) see *HW Corres.* 2: 324 n. 11.
23. *Works* 2: 441; for Pownall (1722–1805) see *HW Corres.* 1: 293 n. 4.
24. *Catalogue raisonné de tableaux, desseins & estampes, et autres effets … après le décès de M. de Jullienne ecuyer, chevalier de Saint-Michel, & Honoraire de l'Académie Royale de Peintures & de Sculpture … par Pierre Remy* (Paris, 1767), 287.
25. *HW Corres.* 7: 286.
26. *Works* 2: 441.
27. *Catalogue … Jullienne*, 288–9.
28. For comparable examples see George Cameron Stone, *A Glossary of the Construction, Decoration and Use of Arms and Armor in All Countries and in All Times* (Portland, ME: Southworth Press, 1934), Fig. 660, nos. 27, 28, 30, 32.
29. The Metropolitan Museum of Art possesses two mid-sixteenth-century damascened-iron maces of this type, acc. nos. 04.3.38 and 04.3.59, the latter signed by the itinerant Spanish damascener Diego da Çaias, and bearing the motto of Henry II of France.
30. Comparable axes, with leather-covered shafts and silver mounts, are illustrated in Bashir Mohamed, *The Arts of the Muslim Knight: The Furusiyya Art Foundation Collection* (Milan: Skira, 2008), 263–4, nos. 253–4. The watercolour (Fig. 252) served as a model for a composite illustration of non-European arms in the 1789 *Supplement* to Grose's *Treatise*, pl. 51 (mistakenly labelled as pl. 50).
31. *Works* 2: 481.
32. This group of daggers was studied by A. Ivanov, 'A Group of Iranian Daggers of the Period from the Fifteenth Century to the Beginning of the Seventeenth with Persian Inscriptions', in R. Elgood, ed., *Islamic Arms and Armour* (London: Scolar Press, 1979), 64–75.
33. The Portland dagger is discussed in Wainwright, *Romantic Interior*, 28, where Vertue's 1749 engraving of it is reproduced. Already in July of 1763, when Walpole visited Lady Elizabeth Germain's home at Drayton House, Northants, he mentioned her 'Dagger set with rubies that belonged to Henry 8th' (P. Toynbee, 'Horace Walpole's Journals of Visits to Country Seats', *Journal of the Walpole Society* 16 [1927–8]: 57). The dagger is now at Welbeck Abbey.
34. The Francis I armour will be the subject of a forthcoming article by the author.

35. Documentation for Walpole's purchase of the armour, drawn largely from his correspondence with Mme du Deffrand, is conveniently presented in Paget Toynbee, *Strawberry Hill Accounts: A Record of Expenditure in Building, Furnishing, etc. kept by Mr. Horace Walpole from 1747 to 1795* (Oxford: Clarendon Press, 1927), 138–45.
36. Toynbee, *Strawberry Hill Accounts*, 12.
37. The sword, lance and shaffron are mentioned in a report on the armour provided to Mme du Deffand by one Monsieur Bonnay (Toynbee, *Strawberry Hill Accounts*, 141).
38. Toynbee, *Strawberry Hill Accounts*, 144.
39. *Works* 2: 31.
40. For cuirassier armour see Christian Beaufort-Spontin, *Harnisch und Waffe Europas. Die militärische Ausrüstung im 17. Jahrhundert* (Munich: Klinkhardt & Biermann, 1982), 48–69.
41. Stephen V. Grancsay, 'The Armor of Henry II from the Louvre', *The Metropolitan Museum of Art Bulletin* n.s. 11 (Oct. 1952): 68–80.
42. The identification of the Louvre armour, inv. no. MR427, with Francis I is first recorded in the Garde Meuble inventory of 1673 and is repeated in subsequent inventories and Paris guidebooks throughout the eighteenth century; see Grancsay, 'Armor of Henry II', 72–3.
43. They are similar in detail and composition to the engravings published by Tortorel and Perrissin, see M. Alfred Franklin, *Les Grandes Scènes Historiques du XVI*^{e} *siècle reproduction fac-simile du recueil de J. Tortorel et J. Perrissin* (Paris: Librerie Fischbacher, 1886).
44. A watercolour by G.P. Harding (d. 1853), dating to the time of the Strawberry Hill sale, illustrates the gauntlets as of grey metal (LWL, inv. no. 49.3678), while an account of the sale in *Gentleman's Magazine* for December 1842, 602, notes that the armour 'ends at the knees, the pieces being of gilt leather'.
45. *Works* 2: 487 and 499 respectively.
46. The *Life of Benvenuto Cellini: A Florentine Artist, Written by Himself and Translated by Thomas Nugent*, 2 vols. (London: printed for T. Davies, 1771). Walpole mentioned the book in his letter to the Earl of Stafford of June 30, 1771 (*HW Corres.* 35: 342) and had a copy in his Library, for which see Allen T. Hazen, *A Catalogue of Horace Walpole's Library*, 3 vols. (New Haven and London: Yale University Press 1969), 3: no. 3181.
47. *1842 Sale*, day 19, lot 77, describing the armour as an 'undoubted work of Benvenuto Cellini'.
48. *HW Corres.* 35: 419 and 420–21 respectively.
49. *HW Corres.* 35: 420–21.
50. Walpole's MS annotation in his copy of *A Description* (1774), transcribed in *HW Corres.* 35: 419, n. 27, was printed with slight variations in the subsequent edition of 1784 (*Works* 2: 439).
51. For painted shields in general, see Stuart W. Pyhrr and Everett Fahy, 'A Renaissance Painted Shield Attributed to Girolamo da Treviso', *Studies in European Arms and Armor: The C. Otto von Kienbusch Collection in the Philadelphia Museum of Art* (Philadelphia: Philadelphia Museum of Art, 1992): 96–134.
52. The Glasgow shield (the Dublin example was then unknown) has recently been attributed to Polidoro by Pierluigi Leone de Castris, *Polidoro da Caravaggio: L'opera completa* (Naples: Electa Napoli, 2001), 201.
53. This group was most recently surveyed in José A. Godoy and Silvio Leydi, *Parures Triomphales: Le maniérisme dans l'art de l'armure italienne* (Geneva; exh. cat., Musée Rath, 2003).
54. *Works* 2: 439.
55. José Godoy (see n. 53 above) kindly informed me that he knows of no embossed shields with Marcus Curtius as the principal subject.
56. Walpole catalogued two canvases by Pier Francesco Mola (1612–66), *Marcus Curtius Leaping into the Gulf* and its pendant, *Horates Cocles Holding the Sublican Bridge*, in *Ædes Walpolianae: or a Description of the Collection of Pictures at Houghton-Hall in Norfolk, the Seat of the Right Honorable Sir Robert Walpole, Earl of Orford* (1747), reprinted in *Works* 2: 279–80
57. James G. Mann, *Wallace Collection Catalogues: European Arms and Armour*, 2 vols. (London: William Clowes and Sons Ltd., 1962), I: 203–4, no. A 328, pl. 91.
58. Strawberry Hill sale, buyers list (sold to Swaby for £42); *A Catalogue of the Rare and Beautiful Works of Art ... of the late John Swaby, Esq.* (London: Phillips, 5–13 March 1860), lot 394. Swaby also exhibited his Horates Cocles shield at the Society of Arts exhibition in 1850, but without mention of its provenance (*Catalogue of Works of Ancient and Medieval Art, Exhibited at the House of the Society of Arts* [London: exh. cat., 1850], 25, no. 181).
59. *A Catalogue of a Valuable Collection of Antiquities and Curiosities ... Late the Property of William Rawle* (London: Hutchens, 10 March 1790), lot 78 and (11 March), lot 84, respectively.
60. John Beardmore, *A Catalogue with Illustrations of the Collection of Ancient Arms and Armour at Uplands, near Fareham, Hampshire* (London: T. and W. Boone, 1845) no. 489, ill. on pl. 17.
61. *Works* 2: 511 (listed among the Additions); *1842 Sale*, day 19, lot 73.
62. Grose, *Treatise*, pls. 2, 3.
63. Cosway's collection was sold at Stanley's, London, 22–4 May 1821, the armoury on 24 May, lots 71–109, including an armour (lot 108) 'chased and engraved in a very masterly manner: of the period of Benvenuto Cellini'. For Cosway's house see Stephen Lloyd, 'The Cosway Inventory of 1820: Listing Unpaid Commissions and the Contents of 20 Stratford Place, Oxford Street, London', *The Walpole Society* 66 (2004): 80.
64. See Cripps-Day, *Record of Armour Sales*, xxvi–xxvii, for these and other eighteenth-century English collectors.
65. Examples from the Warwick Castle armoury are illustrated in Grose, *Treatise*, plates 22–8. For the Warwick Castle armoury, and the possible role that William Hamilton played in its formation, see Donald J. La Rocca, 'A Neapolitan Patron of Armor and Tapestry Identified', *Metropolitan Museum Journal* 28 (1993): 97–8, 101–2, nn. 51–62.
66. Wolfgang Glüber, 'Franz I. und der Rittersaal im Schloss zu Erbach', *Kunst in Hessen und am Mittelrhein* nF2 (2006): 35–62.
67. See Adolf Hartmann, *Der Wörlitzer Park und seine Kunstschätze* (Berlin, 1913; reprint 1991), 81–3.
68. For the formation of the Löwenburg armoury see Donald J. La Rocca, 'The Fico Armours: A Study in Connoisseurship and Secular Iconography', *The Journal of the Arms & Armour Society* 13, no. 1 (March 1989): 13–15.

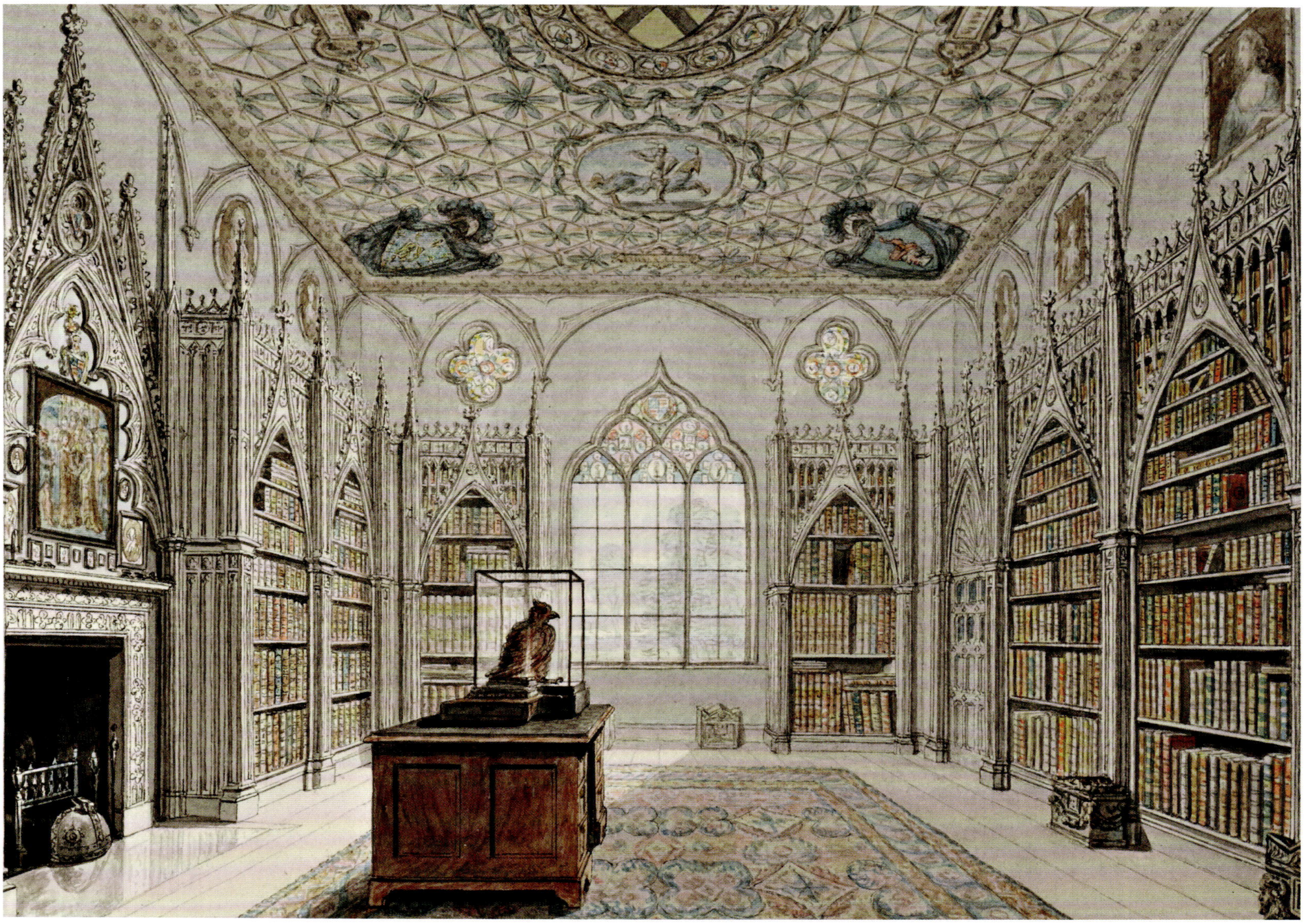

Figure 260. John Carter, *View of the Library at Strawberry Hill*, 1788, ink and wash, watercolour 24.7 × 31 cm, from Walpole's extra-illustrated copy of the *Description*. The Lewis Walpole Library, Yale University. 49.3582

14.

THE 'CURIOUS BOOKS' IN THE LIBRARY AT STRAWBERRY HILL

MARGARET K. POWELL

We know a great deal about the Library that Horace Walpole built for Strawberry Hill, his house of 'fantastic fabric' on the Thames,[1] from his own explicit statements about the room and its contents as well as from evidence gathered in decades-long research by Wilmarth Sheldon Lewis and Allen T. Hazen, two scholars who combined meticulous bibliographic detective work with a passionate dedication to Walpole.[2] We know, for instance, that the Library's design was a joint effort of the friends who formed Walpole's 'Strawberry committee' and that, unlike some of the projects undertaken by committee, the room pleased its owner greatly when it was completed by the end of 1754.[3] We know how the room was furnished and decorated, and what 'strictly ancient' sources Walpole and his friends used for the ceiling and the chimneypiece.[4] We know what books were on the shelves, how they were arranged and, in many instances, where they were moved as the Library filled up. We even know the stories of individual volumes, both before and after their years at Strawberry Hill. We have, in short, a compelling picture of the Library as a well-loved space in Walpole's 'small capricious house', filled with a very particular collection of books.[5]

It is perhaps surprising, then, how little we learn about the books themselves from reading Walpole's *Description of the Villa*, his catalogue of the 'assemblage of curious Trifles' at Strawberry Hill. 'The most considerable part of the following catalogue consists of miniatures, enamels, and portraits of remarkable persons,' he points out in his preface, apparently leaving his books out of the gathering of rarities he would introduce to the reader in the account to follow.[6] Indeed, he mentions his rich collection of books and manuscripts specifically at only one point in these introductory pages, and that comment serves merely as one more rhetorical enticement to convince an imagined reluctant connoisseur to read on: 'To those who have still more taste than consists in meer sight, the catalogue itself will convey satisfaction, by containing a copy of madame du Deffand's letter in the name of madame de Sevigné (Fig. 261).'[7]

When Walpole begins to describe the Library, he concentrates on the design and decoration of the room: the painted glass in the window; the portraits, miniatures and other pictures on the walls; the coins, medals and miscellaneous objects of virtù displayed throughout (Fig. 260). The only books that he points out to his readers are the bound collections of prints and drawings and the contents of the glazed cabinet at the south-east corner of the room, which he lists under the headings 'Rare books of prints and drawings' and 'Curious books in the glass closet'. Aside from these lists, quite spare, which fill three of the eight pages devoted to the Library, he does not categorize or describe his book collection. While it offers some hint of what its author had arranged behind the 'Gothic arches of pierced work', the *Description*'s text can only be a disappointment to anyone seeking a sense of Walpole's book collection as a whole or looking for clues to his use of that collection.[8] To discover those clues one must look elsewhere, as Lewis and Hazen demonstrated.

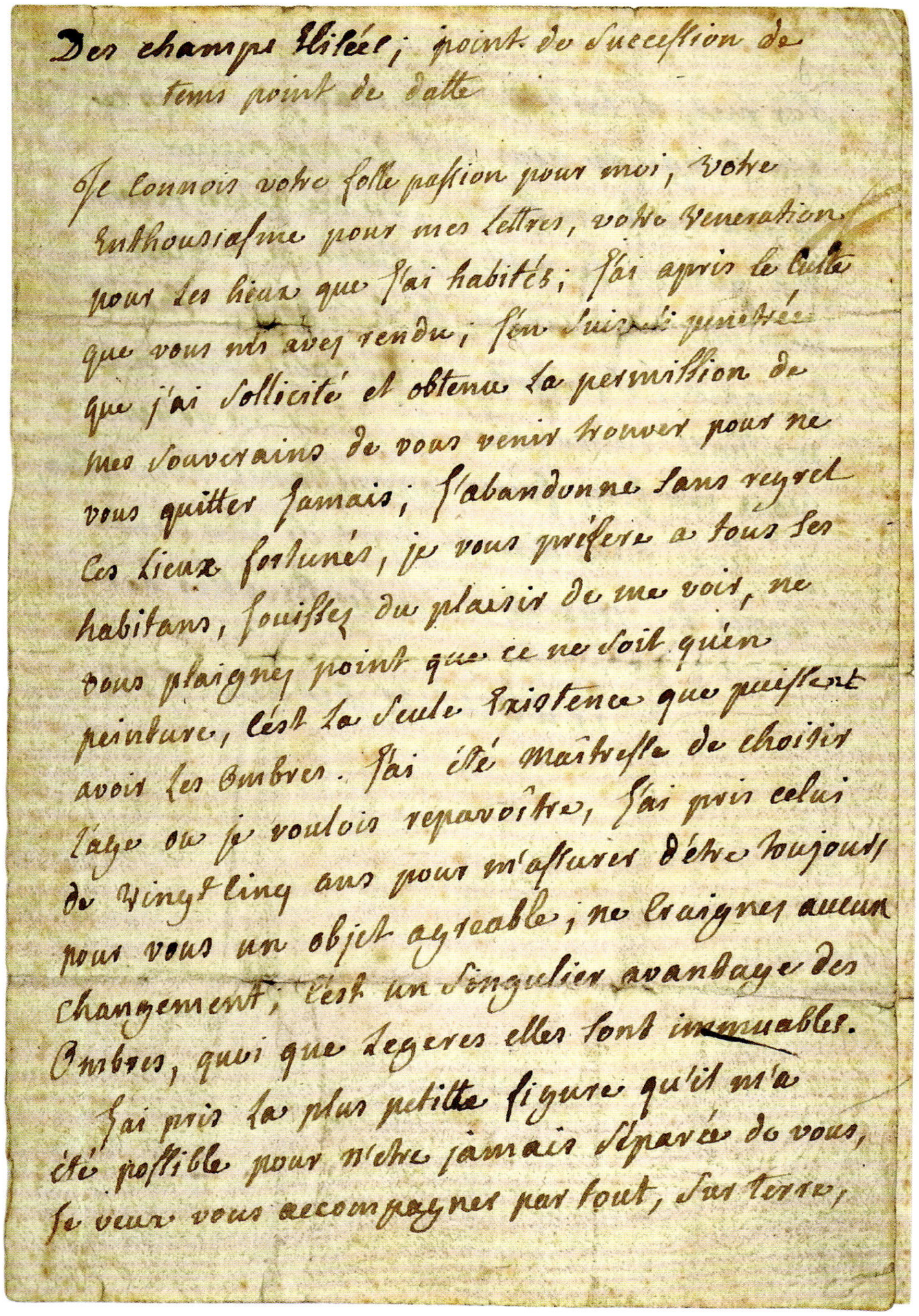

Des champs Elisées; point de succession de
tems point de datte

Je connois votre folle passion pour moi, votre
Enthousiasme pour mes lettres, votre veneration
pour les lieux que j'ai habités; j'ai appris le culte
que vous m'y avez rendu; j'en suis si penetrée
que j'ai sollicité et obtenu la permission de
mes souverains de vous venir trouver pour ne
vous quitter jamais; j'abandonne sans regret
ces lieux fortunés, je vous préfere a tous les
habitans, jouissez du plaisir de me voir, ne
vous plaignez point que ce ne soit qu'en
peinture, c'est la seule existence que puissent
avoir les ombres. J'ai été maitresse de choisir
l'age ou je voulois reparoître, j'ai pris celui
de vingt cinq ans pour m'assurer d'être toujours
pour vous un objet agreable, ne craignez aucun
changement; c'est un singulier avantage des
ombres, quoi que legeres elles sont immuables.
J'ai pris la plus petitte figure qu'il m'a
été possible pour n'être jamais separée de vous,
je veux vous accompagner par tout, sur terre,

Figure 261. Part of a letter to Horace Walpole from Madame du Deffand under the name Madame de Sévigné, May 1766. The Lewis Walpole Library, Yale University. 49 2545. Cat. 111

Between them these two twentieth-century Walpolians produced a remarkably comprehensive account of the books Walpole acquired, according to Lewis some 7,300 volumes by the time he was finished. They studied his often very detailed correspondence; the manuscript catalogue of the Library (begun at Walpole's direction in 1763, continued by him for several more years and taken up again much later by his printer, Thomas Kirgate); the catalogue of the great Strawberry Hill sale, which took place in 1842, nearly half a century after Walpole's death; book dealers' records; evidence from the books themselves; and much else besides. The painstaking work of Lewis and Hazen over many years revealed the history of individual volumes – what Walpole might well have called their pedigrees – as well as their arrangement in the main Library.[9] Walpole shelved his books by broad subject categories in the presses around the room, which were identified by letter (A through M). Each book was marked on the inside front cover with the letter of its press, the number of its shelf (from the floor up) and its position on the shelf. These pressmarks were recorded in the manuscript catalogue along with a book's size, author, title, and place and date of publication. The books in the glazed cabinet in the room's corner, the Glass Closet, had no pressmarks unless they had been moved there from another location. As Walpole acquired more and more volumes and could find no shelf space in his main Library, books were moved to other rooms in the house itself and even to outbuildings, and much of this evolution has been traced by Lewis and Hazen.

An intriguing picture of Walpole's book-collecting habits emerged from these investigations, and the development of his Library can be followed from his early years at Eton into his old age. In general, Lewis wrote, 'the library at Strawberry Hill, like the house itself, rested upon a solid eighteenth-century foundation', with particular strengths in the classical authors (mainly Latin), fine arts, belles-lettres, antiquities, history, heraldry, topography, royal and noble authors, and the French seventeenth century.[10] Walpole bought plays and poems and tracts as they were published and had them bound up in volume after volume. He appears to have acquired whatever books he wanted and to have given away very few that were not written by him or printed at his Strawberry Hill Press (see pp. 242–3). Lewis and Hazen came to believe that, despite his life-long collecting of books and his insistence on the fineness of his other collections, Walpole was not particularly interested in bibliography for its own sake. 'When he bought coins and prints,' Lewis asserted, 'he bought them as a collector mindful of states and condition; when he bought his books it was to

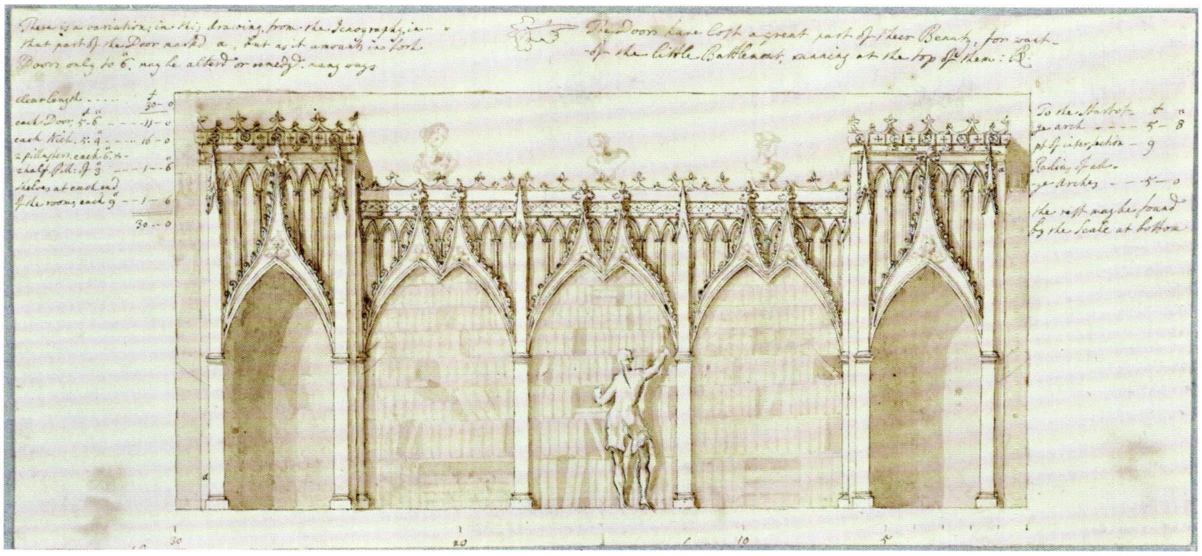

Figure 262. Richard Bentley, *Alternate Design for the Library at Strawberry Hill*, n.d., pen, ink and wash, 14.2 × 30.5 cm, from Richard Bentley, *Drawings and designs by Richd. Bentley*, 1760. The Lewis Walpole Library, Yale University. Folio 49 3585, fol. 38

build a working library.'[11] Earle Havens has recently made a persuasive case for Walpole as 'a far more active collector of early books and rarities than historians and his bibliographers have tended to admit', cautioning against dismissing 'Walpole's selective, yes, but nonetheless substantive bibliophily and rare book connoisseurship as nothing more than a utilitarian enterprise'.[12] Havens's argument is a useful reminder that there is more to be discovered and written about Walpole and his Library collecting.

If his collecting was not strictly, or merely, utilitarian, as Havens concludes, Walpole certainly did use his books repeatedly. He wrote – often copiously – in their margins. 'You know how I love writing marginal notes in my books, and there is not a word in or out of the book of which I will be ignorant,' he announced in a letter (3 April 1775) to his friend William Mason, whose *Memoirs of Gray* had just been published. Walpole asked Mason to 'fill up the asterisks' in the text of the book so that he could insert the identifications in his own copy, and he provided a list of the missing 'who is's' page by page.[13] Writing to Lady Ossory in 1787, Walpole complained:

> I have been long vexed at the ridiculous prices given for my editions. It could not be flattering to the vainest author or editor upon earth; for their dearness is solely to be attributed to their scarcity; and a collector who pays extravagantly for a rare book, will never read *in* it, or allow anybody else, for the virgin purity of the margin is as sacred with him as the text.[14]

Unlike many of his contemporaries, then, Walpole did not acquire books only for their rarity or for their potential to impress others. As Hazen has remarked,

> Perhaps the outstanding feature of Walpole's collection was its usefulness, to him ... With few exceptions the books on his shelves were there because he wanted them for use; and, again with few exceptions, he read the books as he received them, in order to mark them or take notes from them.[15]

Books were to be read actively, interrogated vigorously, amplified and corrected.

More broadly, Walpole's books often served as the sources from which his creations, both textual and physical, were made. They were the inspiration for his writing as well as for the fashioning and ornamenting of Strawberry Hill itself, the house he built 'to realize [his] own visions', visions engendered in his Library among his books.[15] Two examples may serve here. For one, Walpole appears to have compiled *A Catalogue of Royal and Noble Authors of England* (1758) using his library for reference. He included approximately 140 authors in the *Catalogue*, and more than 80 of these were well represented in his own Library.[17] Hazen and Lewis trace many of these books to Press A, perhaps the first shelves Walpole filled when, in December 1754, he wrote: 'My present occupation is putting up my books; and thanks to arches, and pinnacles, and pierced columns, I shall not appear scantily provided!'[18] Here he was addressing Richard Bentley, a

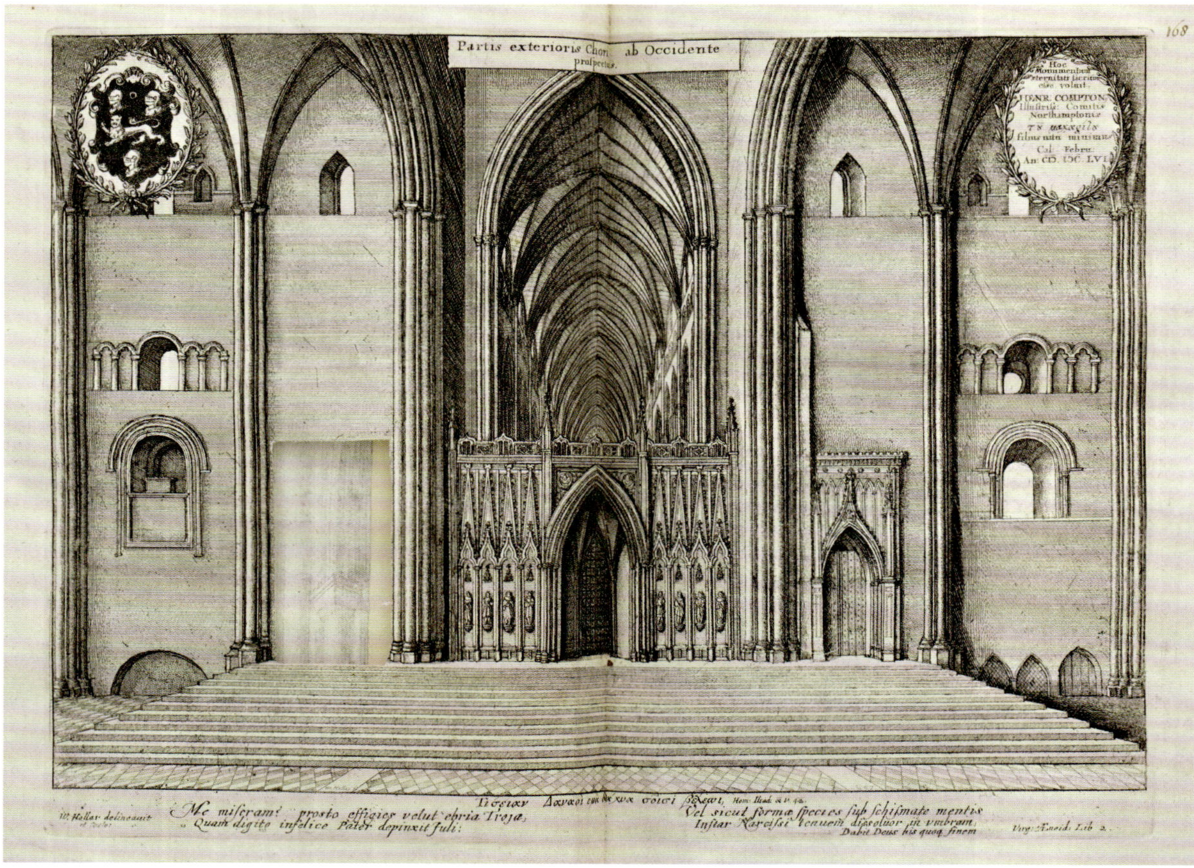

Figure 263. Wenceslas Hollar, *The Screen at Old St Paul's Cathedral*, from Sir William Dugdale, *The History of St Paul's Cathedral in London, from Its Foundation Until These Times*.... (London: Printed by Tho. Warren, 1658). 33.5 × 23 cm. The Vyne, The Chute Collection (The National Trust). Cat. 72

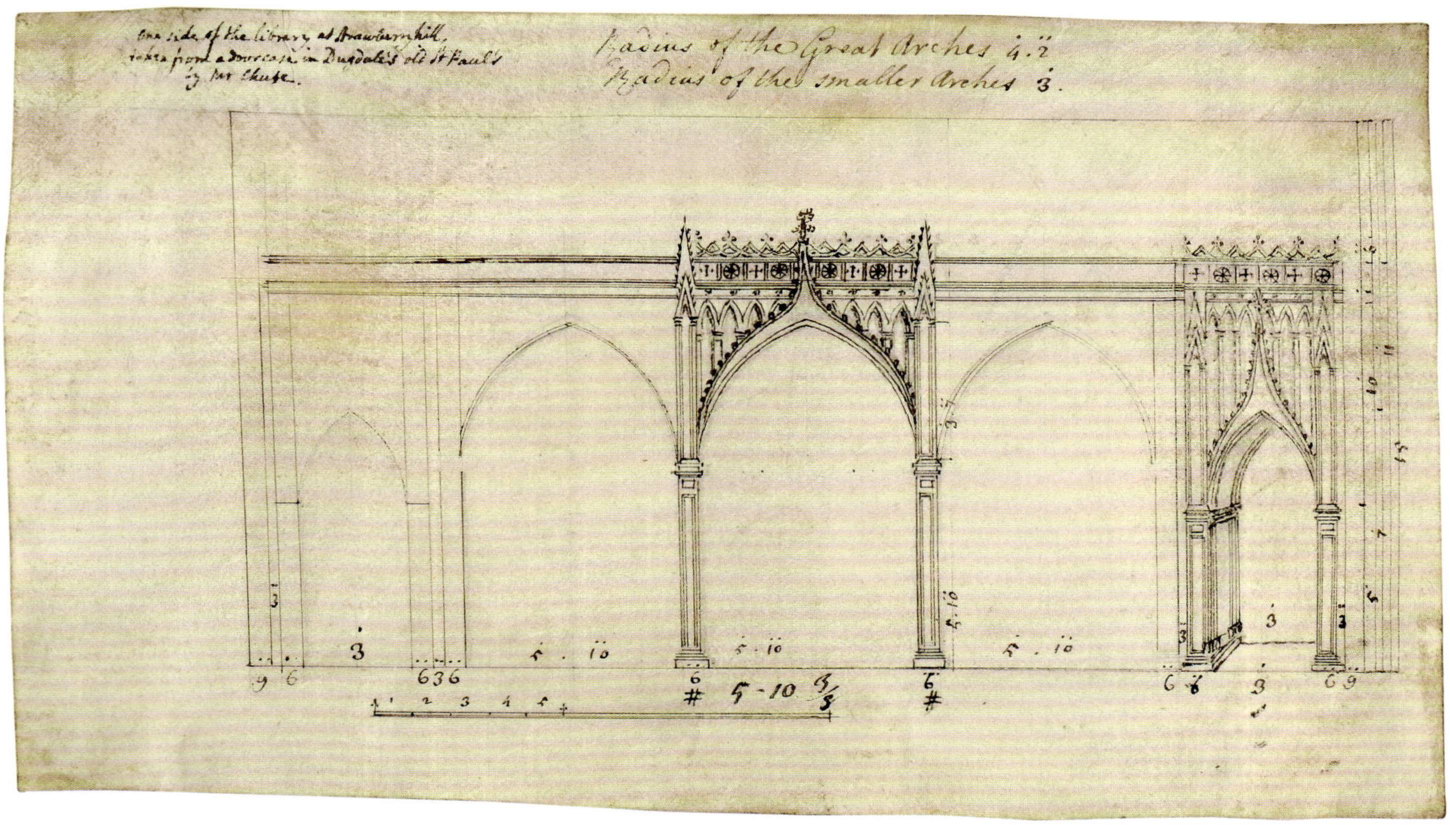

Figure 264. John Chute, *Design for the Library*, ink and pencil, in *Slight Sketches of Architecture*. The Lewis Walpole Library, Yale University. 49 3490, folio 5

member of the Strawberry committee and party to the design of those very arches and pinnacles (see Fig. 262). A second example comes from the *Description*, where the first sentence of the Library section suggests that at least one of Walpole's many illustrated volumes was a source for the room itself. Sir William Dugdale's *History of St. Paul's Cathedral in London … Beautified with sundry prospects of the church, figures of tombes, and monuments* (1658) was shelved in Press E and provided inspiration for the presses' design, as Walpole indicated in his note identifying a sketch by John Chute, the third member of the committee and Walpole's close friend and neighbour: 'One side of the library at Strawberry Hill, taken from a doorcase in Dugdale's old St Paul's by Mr Chute' (Figs. 263, 264).[19]

While Walpole mined individual books for intellectual and architectural inspiration and engaged their texts in ongoing study, he also created a spectacular space in which to house them. The Library was Strawberry Hill's first 'great room', the staircase's main destination in the early years, and its primacy strongly suggests that Walpole's books played a significant role in his self-representation. However, unlike other objects at Strawberry Hill – miniatures, coins, enamels – the Library collection would have been difficult for a visitor to appreciate individually; books must be studied, or at least read, to reveal their qualities fully. Few of Walpole's books had extraordinary bindings (Fig. 265), and in any case single volumes would not have stood out from the mass of spines on the shelves, and the arched doors to the presses would have removed them even more from a visitor's unobstructed view. Nevertheless, the impressively expensive setting, with its comprehensively intricate design of arches and pinnacles and its many references to dynastic histories on the walls and ceiling, must have functioned as an elaborate setting for a collection that was meant, at least in part, to demonstrate to viewers the range and polite learning of its owner.

If Walpole did not acquire his books primarily as objects for display, and if they were difficult for a visitor to appreciate either as words to be read or as things to be admired, why did he include his books at all in the *Description*, whose purpose was to list the rarities and curiosities displayed in Strawberry Hill? The text was, as Walpole asserts in the preface, written and printed 'to assist those who should visit the place', and, further, to exhibit 'specimens of Gothic architecture'.[20] It is possible to imagine that Walpole felt obliged to offer the reader-visitor the same variety of interesting sights in the Library as were found in other rooms in the house. And, indeed, it is easy to see those similarities in much of what he included in the text of the Library section – design, ornament, pictures, and objects precious or curious. The presence in the *Description* of his two lists of books, 'Rare books of prints and drawings' and 'Curious books in the Glass Closet', argues that Walpole did consider some of his books 'rare' or 'curious', and thus worth noting for his visitors even if they could not view them directly, as they might the decorated ceiling, the stained glass in the window, or the many portraits on the walls. Setting these two groups of books apart from the mass of volumes in the Library are two criteria: provenance and location. While Walpole may not have always cared about his books' rarity or condition, he did care passionately about their provenance, as he did about the provenance and connections of almost any object he collected. In a compelling number of instances, the volumes listed in the *Description* are described in terms of their associations with author, artist, donor or previous owner. For example, here are the first three items on his list of rare books of prints and drawings:

Figure 265. Virgil, *Publii Virgilii Maronis Bucolica, Georgica et Æneis*, white vellum binding by William Edward of Halifax, with cover painting by James Edward (Birmingham: Baskerville, 1766). The Lewis Walpole Library, Yale University. 49 2482. Cat. 91

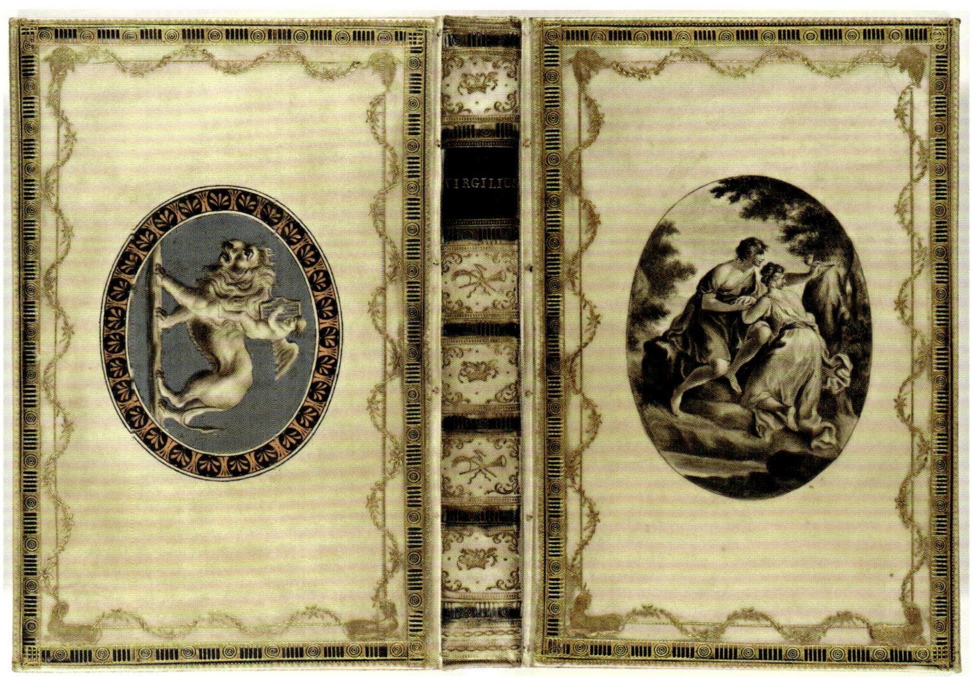

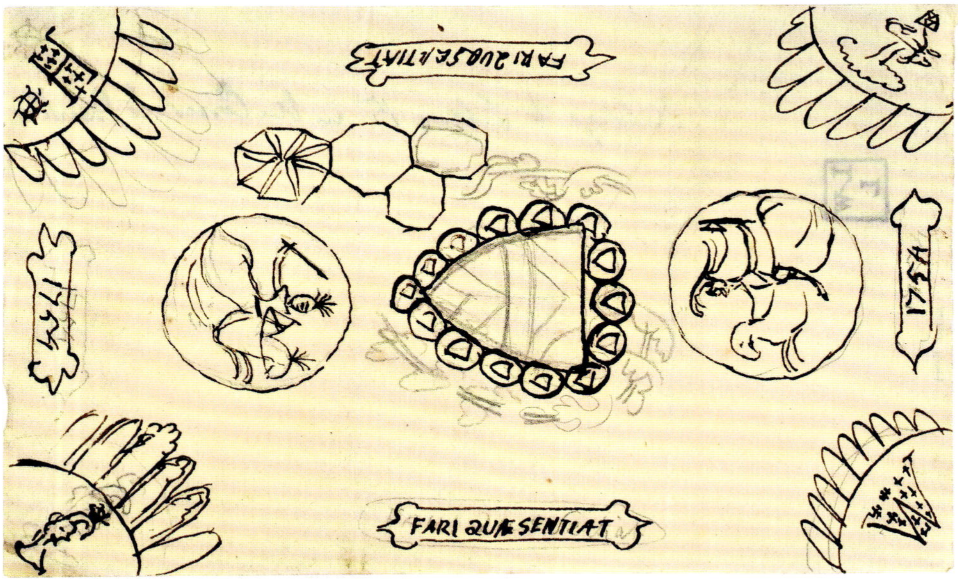

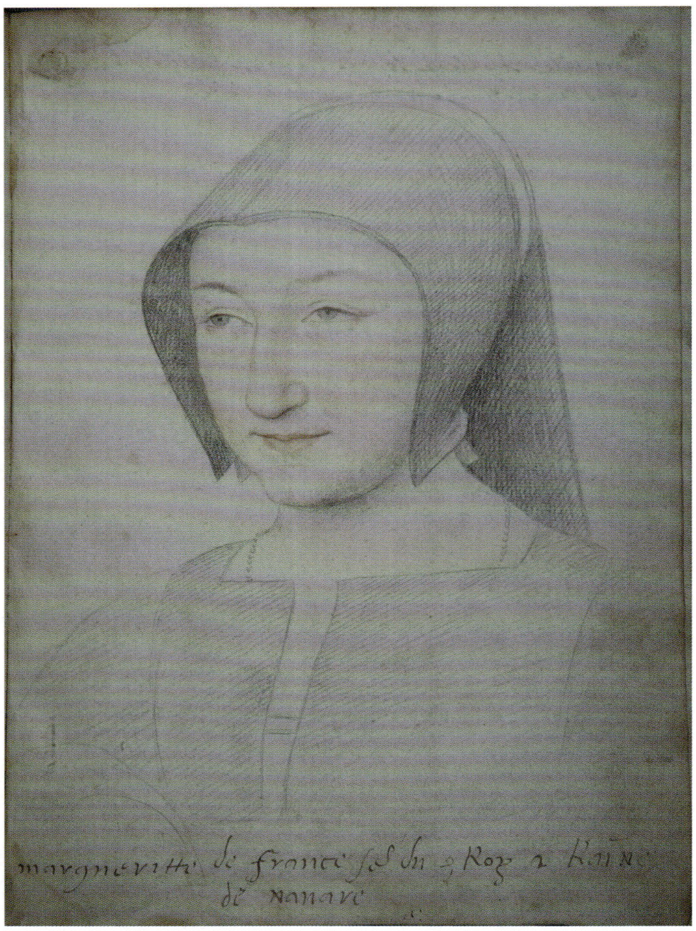

Figure 266. Horace Walpole, *Design for the Ceiling in the Library at Strawberry Hill*, 1754, pen and ink on laid paper, 18.2 × 11.2 cm (sheet). The Lewis Walpole Library, Yale University. 754.00.00.22dr. 49 3490, folio 5. Cat. 73

Figure 267. After Jean Clouet, *Margaret of France*, mid-16th century, red and black chalk, 26.8 × 18.9 cm. The Rt Hon. the Earl of Derby. W418. Cat. 81

> Thuanus, the large edition in 14 volumes, enriched with beautiful prints of the best impressions, containing portraits of the principal personages. This set was collected by sir Clement Cotterel Dormer.
>
> Ædes Walpolianae, the original drawings, with every print that has been engraved from the pictures, and with other prints and drawings of houses and buildings that belonged to sir Robert Walpole and the family of Walpole.
>
> A collection of initial letters from the beginning of printing, with some drawings of heads of the first printers; collected by Mr. Ames, author of the Typographical Antiquities.[21]

It is not the particular edition or condition of the volumes that made these objects 'rare' for Walpole but the associations attached to them and what could be found within them. The portraits of 'the principal personages' had been owned by Sir Clement Cottrell-Dormer, Master of Ceremonies at Court, whom Walpole appeared to admire for his antiquarian interests and magnificent collection of prints while also commenting acerbically on his over-fine manners and over-developed sense of protocol.[22] Joseph Ames, another antiquary from the generation just before Walpole's, was both collector and historian of early printing and portrait prints. Finally, in giving prominence to *Ædes Walpolianae* with its catalogue of his father's collections, Walpole demonstrates the insistent focus on his family's genealogy that can be seen throughout his life and that is embodied in, for instance, the design for the Library ceiling with its heraldic devices and ancestral references (Fig. 266).[23] Other books of prints he singled out for mention include

> Twelve large folios of English heads, bound in vellum, and ranged according to the reign of each king. Five larger of the reign of George III. and an additional volume of heads of different reigns collected since … A book of French portraits in the time of Francis I. It belonged to Brantome, who has inscribed the names of several of the persons. From the collection of monsieur Mariette at Paris (Fig. 267).[24]

Walpole may well have emphasized such associations and connections to make the relatively small number of books mentioned in his lists stand for a library of rare and curious objects even though

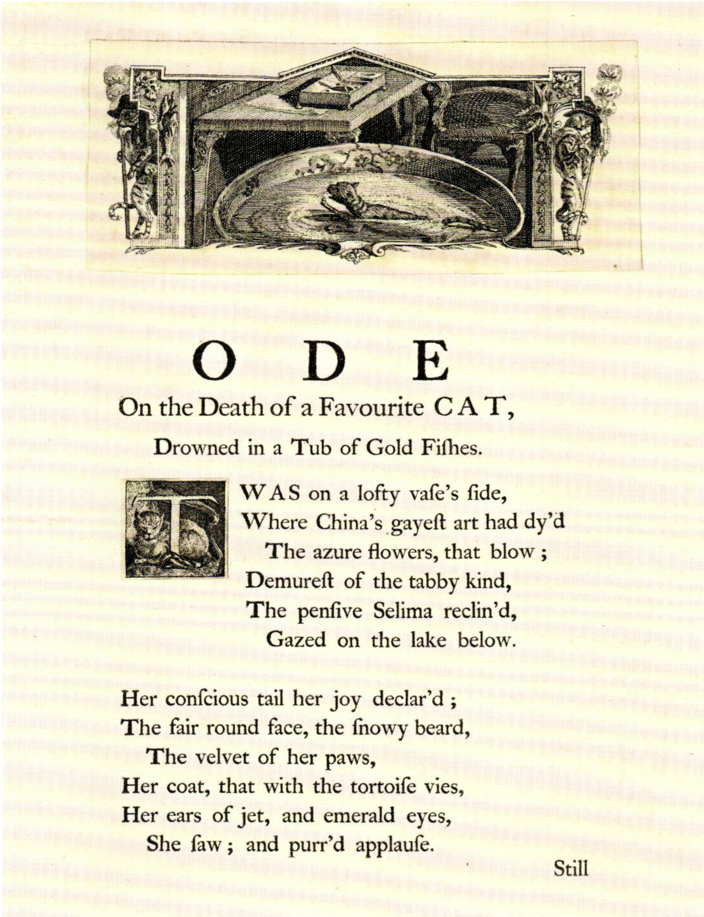

O D E

On the Death of a Favourite CAT,

Drowned in a Tub of Gold Fiſhes.

'TWAS on a lofty vaſe's ſide,
Where China's gayeſt art had dy'd
The azure flowers, that blow;
Demureſt of the tabby kind,
The penſive Selima reclin'd,
Gazed on the lake below.

Her conſcious tail her joy declar'd;
The fair round face, the ſnowy beard,
The velvet of her paws,
Her coat, that with the tortoiſe vies,
Her ears of jet, and emerald eyes,
She ſaw; and purr'd applauſe.

Still

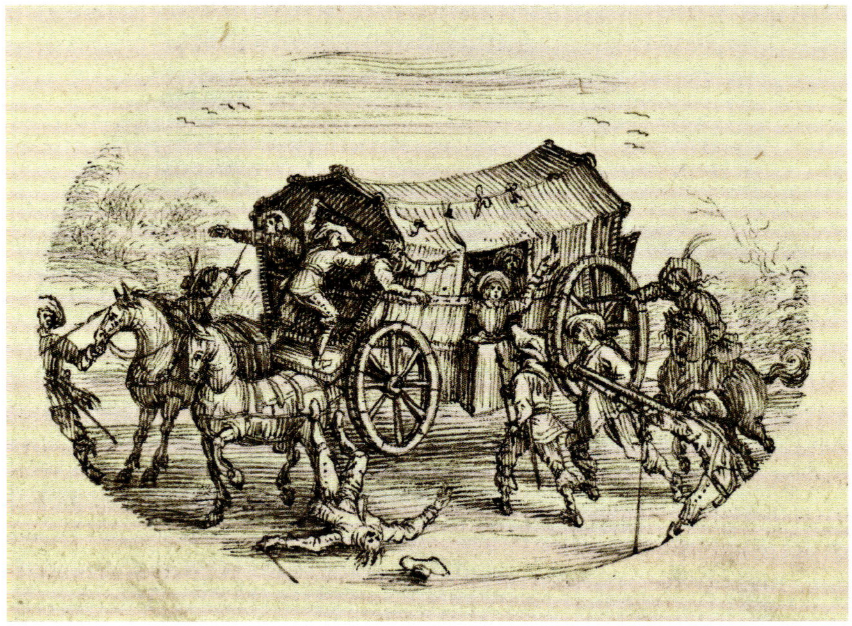

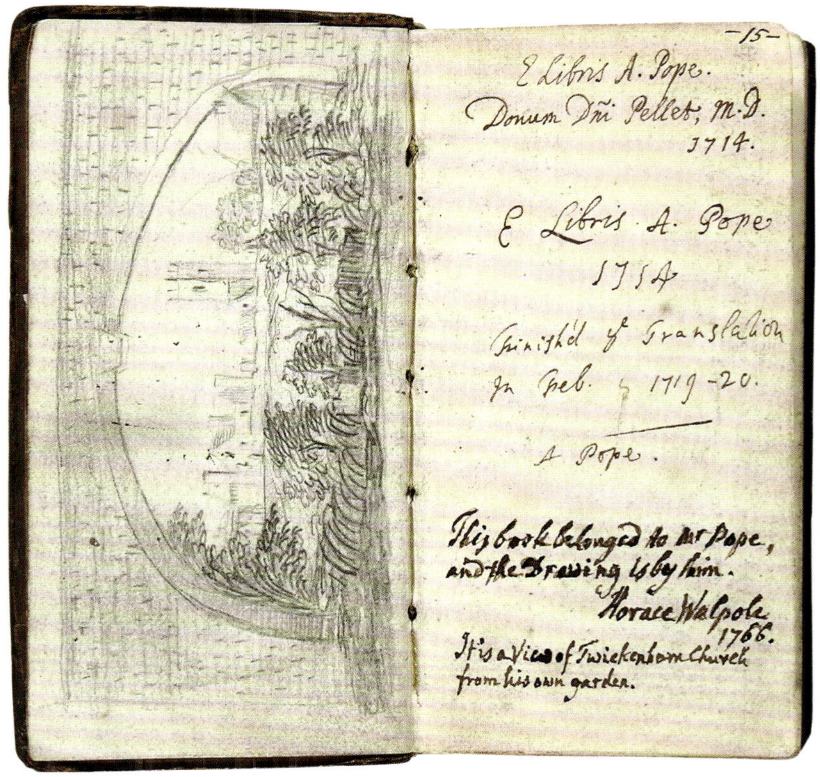

his book-collecting practices were, as we have seen, generally based on quite different principles. It is possible to understand this ambivalence, I believe, as a strategy that allowed Walpole to describe the Library and its contents in terms similar to those that he used throughout the *Description*; he was able to make his books, and the room in which they were kept, 'fit' the scheme of the house.

The books in the Glass Closet were, if anything, even more notable in their associations. A few of these were, in Walpole's words:

> Mr. Bentley's original designs for Mr. Gray's poems (Fig. 268), bound in red morocco and gilt … Callot's pocket-book (Fig. 269), with a great number of exquisite original drawings by himself: a present to Mr. Walpole from his brother Robert earl of Orford: very valuable … The arms of the knights of the garter made by Richard IIId. in their proper colours, and bound in red velvet: a present from Walter Robertson,

Figure 268. Richard Bentley, design for the headpiece to 'Ode on the Death of a Favourite Cat', pasted into Thomas Gray, *Designs by Mr. R. Bentley, for Six Poems by Mr. T. Gray* (London: R. Dodsley, 1753), pen and ink, and letterpress, 38 × 27.5 cm. The Lewis Walpole Library, Yale University. Folio 49 3698 facing p. 5. Cat. 32

Figure 269. Follower of Jacques Callot, p. 9 of *Artist's Pocket Book (Callot's Pocket Book)*, after 1633, pen and ink, 8.7 × 14 cm. National Gallery of Art, Washington, D.C., Rosenwald Collection 1943. 1943.3.2232. Cat. 84

Figure 270. Front fly with Pope's drawing and Walpole's notes, from Homer, *Homeri opera quae extant omnia* (Amsterdam: Wetsteniana, 1707). 14 × 7.5 cm. The Lewis Walpole Library, Yale University. 49 2399. Cat. 87

THE STRAWBERRY HILL PRESS

Stephen Clarke

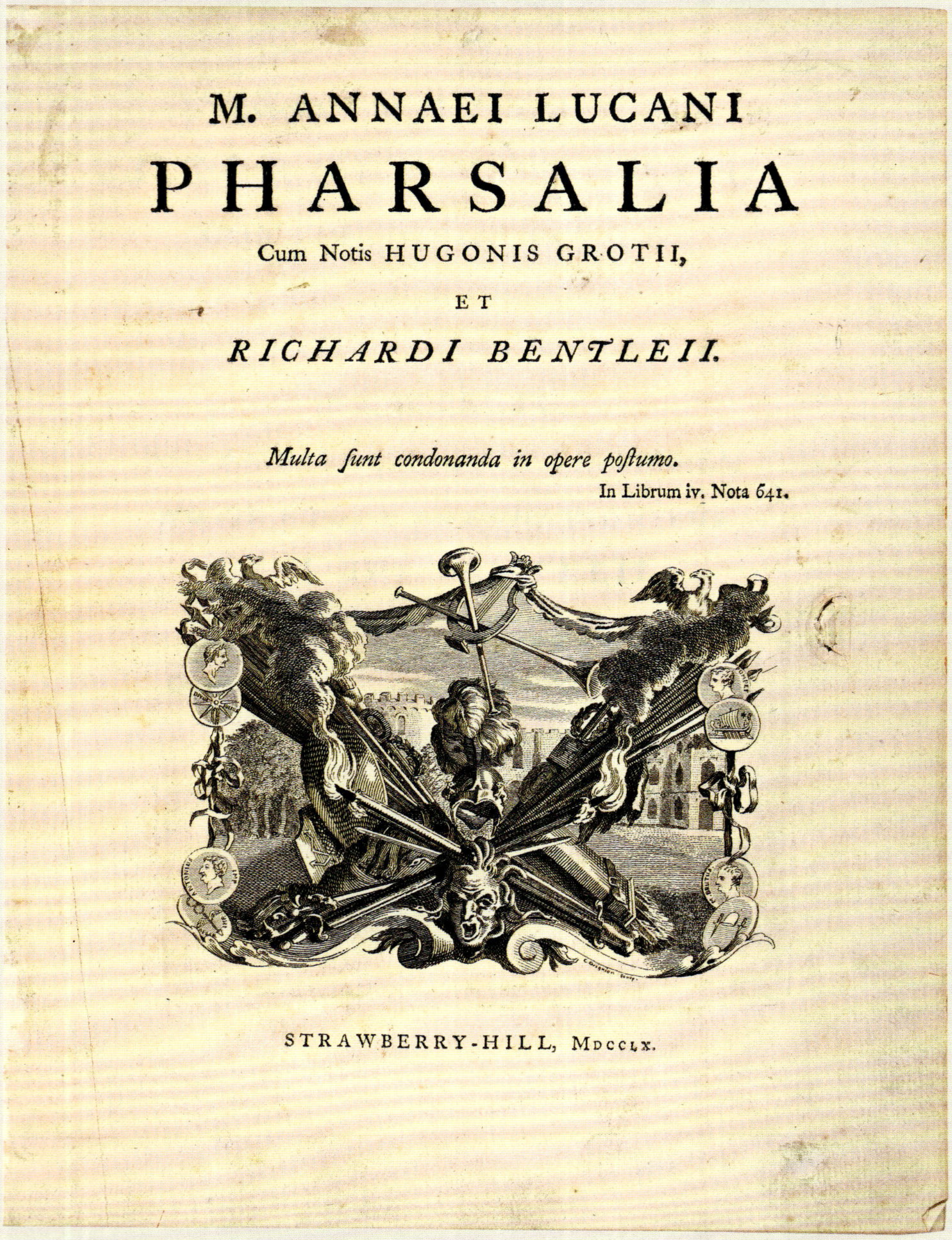

M. ANNAEI LUCANI

PHARSALIA

Cum Notis HUGONIS GROTII,

ET

RICHARDI BENTLEII.

Multa sunt condonanda in opere postumo.

In Librum iv. Nota 641.

STRAWBERRY-HILL, MDCCLX.

Figure 271. Title page of M. Annaeus Lucanus, *Pharsalia* (Strawberry Hill, 1760). The vignette engraved by Charles Grignion after Richard Bentley. The Lewis Walpole Library, Yale University. 49 3585; 33 7

The Strawberry Hill Press has long been celebrated as the first private press in England. In a letter to Horace Mann of 4 August 1757, Walpole announced its inauguration by explaining, 'I am turned printer, and have converted a little cottage here into a printing-office – My abbey is a perfect college or academy – I keep a painter in the house and a printer – not to mention Mr. Bentley who is an academy himself.' This description perfectly captures his perception of Strawberry Hill as a centre where he could dispense patronage of the arts to an appreciative, discerning audience.

The Press was used by Walpole primarily to print his own writings, antiquarian items that he had edited, and the occasional pieces of his friends. It opened with its most important literary production, two thousand copies of Gray's *Odes*. The most distinguished piece of printing to come from the Press was its edition of Lucan's *Pharsalia* (1760; Fig. 271), but the main body of work was Walpole's own, including his *Catalogue of Royal and Noble Authors* (1758; Fig. 272) and his *Anecdotes of Painting in England* (1762–71). One of its most important productions was his *Description* of Strawberry Hill (1774) and the revised *Description* of 1784, the latter illustrated by copper engravings and circulated after Walpole's death to a select list of recipients.

For Walpole, a gentleman of letters uncomfortable with the burgeoning world of late eighteenth-century commercial publishing, it was useful to be able to employ the Press to print his own work for private circulation among a circle of friends and cognoscenti. The Press also enabled Walpole to celebrate his friendships and social circle in the miscellaneous 'Detached Pieces' printed to record visits to the house by distinguished visitors, who might on entering the printing office find a sheet of suitably flattering, freshly printed verses awaiting them.

The status of the Press in the history of the private press in England has never been questioned; it was unrivalled in the range and quality of its productions and in its longevity (some forty years). It was also unrivalled in the attention it attracted from book collectors and bibliographers, its productions – some with a vignette of Strawberry Hill on the title page – being collected in Walpole's lifetime and ever since.

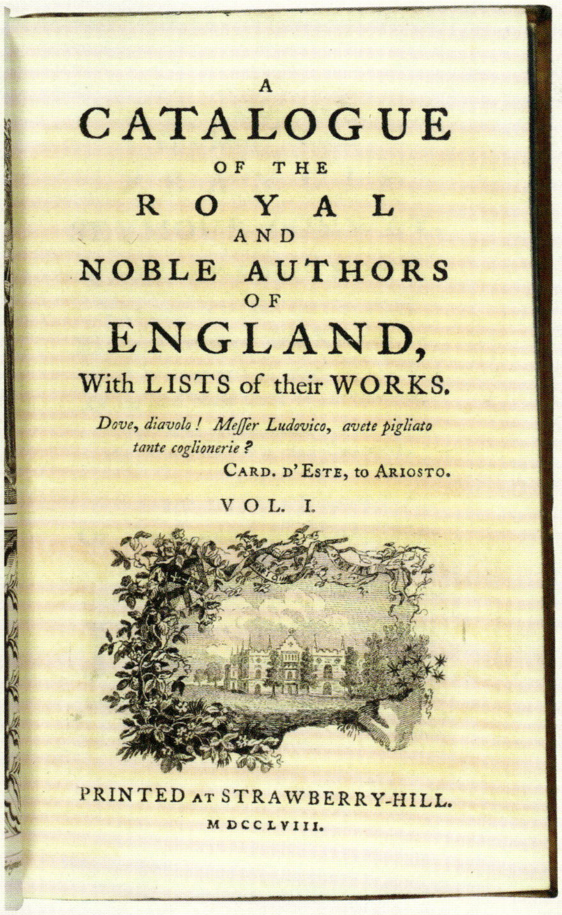

A
CATALOGUE
OF THE
ROYAL
AND
NOBLE AUTHORS
OF
ENGLAND,
With LISTS of their WORKS.

Dove, diavolo! Messer Ludovico, avete pigliato tante coglionerie?
CARD. D'ESTE, to ARIOSTO.

VOL. I.

PRINTED AT STRAWBERRY-HILL.
MDCCLVIII.

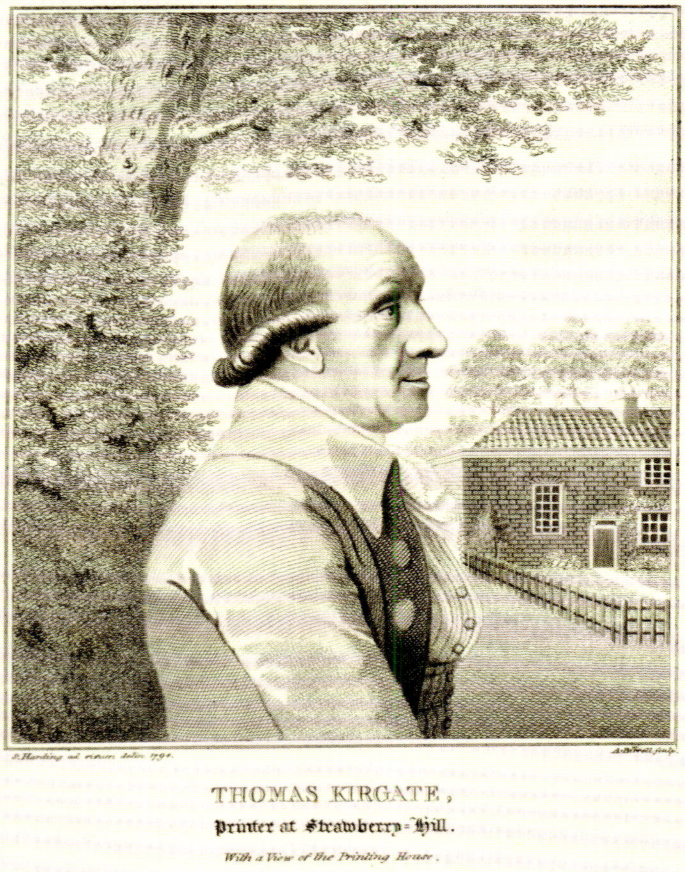

Figure 272. Title page, vol. 1, Horace Walpole, *Catalogue of Royal and Noble Authors* (Strawberry Hill, 1758). The Lewis Walpole Library, Yale University. 33 7

Figure 273. Andrew Birrell after Sylvester Harding, *Portrait of Thomas Kirgate*, 1798, engraving, on p. 187 of Richard Bull's extra-illustrated copy of the *Description*. The Lewis Walpole Library, Yale University. 33 30 Copy 11

Not only was the Press well known to contemporaries, it was also well recorded for posterity. It was originally situated on the site of the Round Tower, but in 1759–60 Walpole converted a cottage adjoining the Teddington Road into a printing house. This can be seen in the view by Edward Edwards, showing Thomas Kirgate, Walpole's printer from 1765 until Walpole's death as well as his secretary and amanuensis in later years, walking away from the simple brick building. Silvester Harding's portrait drawing of Kirgate, engraved by Birrell, shows the printer in profile and the printing house with its enclosed front garden beyond him (Fig. 273). Then there is John Carter's watercolour of the inside of the printing house, which shows Kirgate setting type in an airy, bare-boarded room with his assistant through the door on the right working the press (Fig. 274). And the records of the Press are not only visual, as Walpole's *Journal of the Printing-Office at Strawberry Hill* (first printed 1923), which lists the activities of the Press from 1757 to 1789, is an invaluable resource for its history.

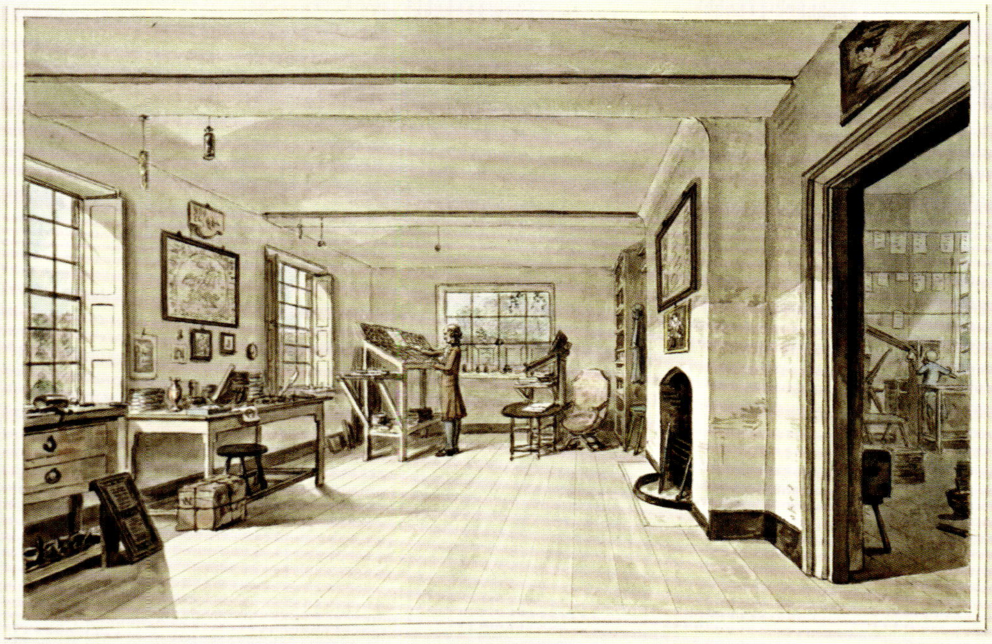

Figure 274. John Carter, *Interior of the Printing-House at Strawberry Hill*, ink, wash, and watercolour, 20.5 × 28.5 cm, mounted, p. 240 of Richard Bull's extra-illustrated copy of the *Description*. The Lewis Walpole Library, Yale University. 33 30 Copy 11

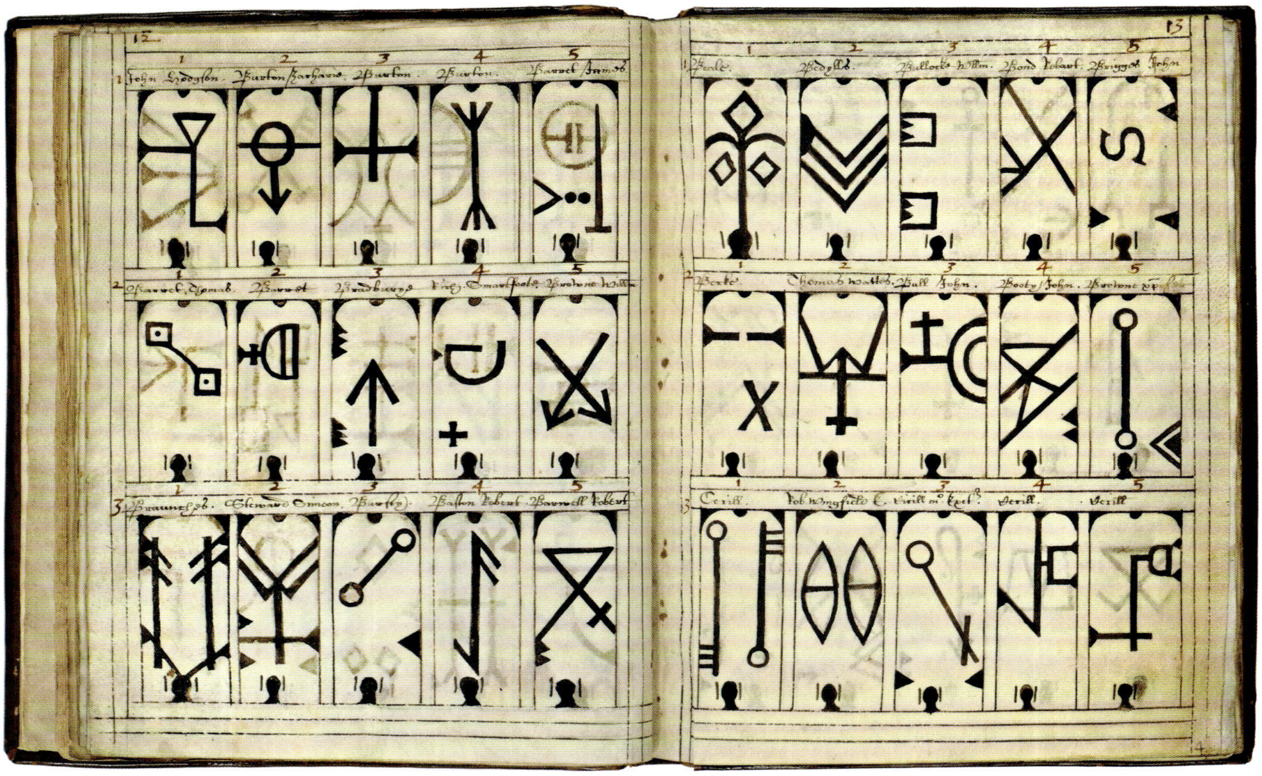

Figure 275. Book of Swan Marks, English, 16th century. Pen and ink on vellum. The Lewis Walpole Library, Yale University. 49 2601. Cat. 82

> mayor of Lynn … The Iliad and Odyssey, the very books from which Pope made his translations: in one of the volumes is a view of Twickenham, drawn by Pope (Fig. 270) … The Charter of Forests, one of the original copies finely preserved, with the great seal of Edward I. appendant; found at Hackney 1743, among writings of the ancient family of Shordich, by Robert Bygrave; presented by him to sir Edward Walpole, and by him to his brother Horace.[25]

Also included in the list of 'curious books' were illuminated missals, a set of Strawberry Hill Press publications specially bound, descriptions of some of the great country houses, books of swan marks (Fig. 275), an extra-illustrated copy of the Chevalier d'Eon's *Lettres, mémoires, et négotiations particulières* (1764), and one of Walpole's two examples of erotica, a collection of the Spintrian medals of Tiberius (bought at Sir Clement Cottrell-Dormer's sale). All of these volumes, along with others not mentioned in the *Description*'s lists but known to have been in the Glass Closet, were sequestered by Walpole behind its glazed doors, perhaps even locked up, and even further removed from 'meer sight'.

George Haggerty has suggested that the Glass Closet is the heart of Walpole's collection, if not the heart of the house itself.[26] He argues that the spaces at Strawberry Hill are intimate ones; it could be said that the Glass Closet – a cabinet within a special room within a house after 'my own taste'[27] – is one of the most intimate, and also the most secret. We might expect, then, that it would have held objects that were personal or valuable, or both. Indeed, as we have seen, there were items of great value or noted importance, but there were also homely relics of Walpole's school days, such as Herman Moll's *Geographia Antiqua Latinorum et Græcorum* (2nd ed., 1726) and a book of school exercises (Fig. 214). Here he kept his 'Books of Materials' and other commonplace books, which in some cases served as sources for his published works, and here, too, were the letters and other papers of Mme du Deffand (Fig. 276), left to Walpole at her death in 1780, as well as many historical manuscripts, including a good number on heraldry.

The Glass Closet was a place set apart and closed up, holding what were arguably the most intimate and valuable things in Walpole's Library. Yet, paradoxically, some of its contents were singled out for particular notice in the *Description* in

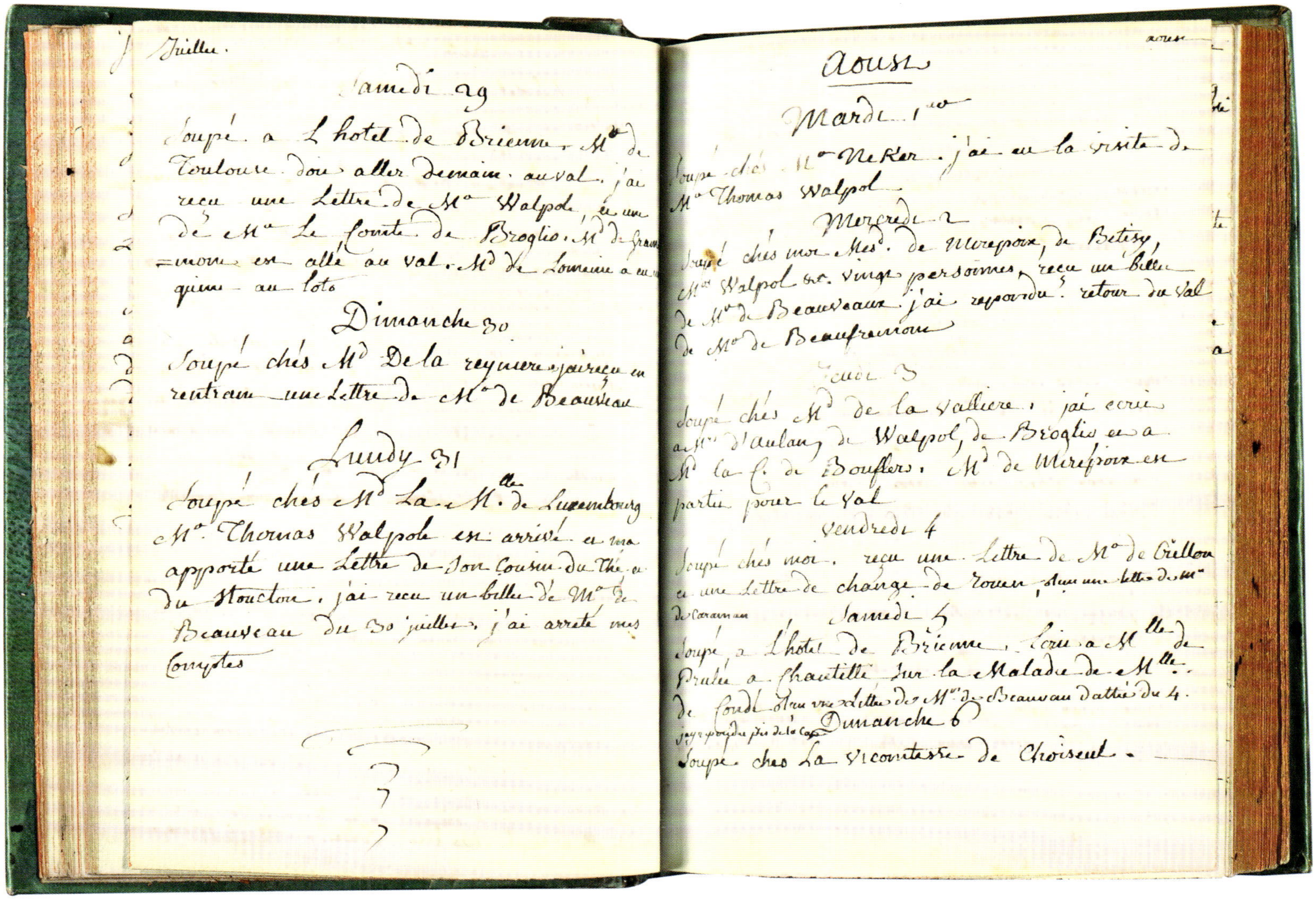

Figure 276. Madame du Deffand, *Collection of Letters and Other Manuscripts*, vol. II: Journal, 1 July 1779–10 September 1780. The Lewis Walpole Library, Yale University. 49 2545. Cat. 92

what could have been a desire to give future readers a chance to appreciate objects that would not reveal themselves immediately. The set of Strawberry Hill Press imprints shelved in the Glass Closet, with his arms stamped on their bindings, presents an interesting case. Their presence in the Glass Closet speaks of the importance Walpole placed on them, not only as evidence of his own accomplishments but perhaps also as an expression of his commitment to the making of books and of his interest in them as objects. Including his own publications in the *Description* suggests both that he believed his reader-visitors would find them just as compelling as the ancient, rare or otherwise curious books that surrounded them, and that they could hold their own with the splendid productions of the past.

It is tempting to think of the Glass Closet as, among the other possibilities suggested in this essay, a repository for Walpole's most valued associations, connections and memories, embodied in text and image within bound volumes. In a letter written to Lady Ossory late in his life Walpole offered a remarkable image. He recounted a conversation with his brother Edward, shortly before his death, in which he likened memory to a cabinet with drawers that

> can hold no more than they can. Fill them with papers; if you add more, you must shove out some of the former. Just so with the memory;

> there is scarce a day in our lives that something, serious or silly, does not place itself there, and consequently the older we grow, the more must be displaced to make room for new contents.

Edward asked:

> How do you account for most early objects remaining?

Horace's answer was that

> the drawers are lined with gummed taffeta; the first ingredients stick; those piled higgledy-piggledy upon them are tossed out with difficulty as new are stuffed in – yet I am come to think that mice and time may gnaw holes in the sides, and nibble the papers too.[28]

While it would be foolish to push the analogy very far, the Glass Closet certainly held some 'first ingredients' and continued to accept 'new contents' as Walpole added his association and other cherished volumes to its shelves. I think it is possible, however, to suggest that in the Glass Closet, in the house itself and, most tellingly, in the voluminous records he kept, Walpole found ways to defend against 'the mice and time' that may still threaten to gnaw and nibble at his extraordinary creation, Strawberry Hill.

1. *Works* 2: 398.
2. Allen T. Hazen, *A Catalogue of Horace Walpole's Library*, with Wilmarth Sheldon Lewis, *Horace Walpole's Library*, 3 vols. (New Haven and London: Yale University Press, 1969). *Horace Walpole's Library* was presented by Lewis as the 1957 Sandars Lectures, which were published in 1958 by Cambridge University Press and then later revised for inclusion in Hazen's *Catalogue*.
3. See *HW Corres.* 20: 456 (HW to Mann, 1 Dec. 1754), 35: 200 (HW to Bentley, 24 Dec. 1754).
4. *Works* 2: 397.
5. *Works* 2: 398.
6. *Works* 2: 395–6.
7. *Works* 2: 397.
8. *Works* 2: 442.
9. In his preface to the *Description* Walpole provided examples of provenance in his collection, and went on to write: 'Such well-attested descent is the genealogy of the objects of virtù – not so noble as those of the peerage, but on a par with those of race-horses. In all three, especially the pedigrees of peers and rarities, the line is often continued by many insignificant names' (*Works* 2: 396).
10. Lewis, *Horace Walpole's Library*, lii–liii.
11. Lewis, *Horace Walpole's Library*, lii.
12. Earle Havens, 'Books, Antiquity and Virtu: Horace Walpole's Antiquarian Book Collecting', in Kevin Cope and Peter Sabor, eds., *1650–1850: Ideas, Aesthetics, and Inquiries in the Early Modern Era*, vol. 16 (New York: AMS Press, 2009): 257–307.
13. *HW Corres.* 28: 187.
14. *HW Corres.* 33: 573.
15. Hazen, *Catalogue*, xiii–xiv.
16. *Works* 2: 398.
17. I am grateful to Anna Chen for these calculations.
18. *HW Corres.* 35: 200.
19. Chute's sketch is in a volume of his drawings kept by Walpole in the Glass Closet and then moved, probably in 1790, to what became a print room in the Round Tower (Hazen, *Catalogue*, no. 3490). The title, written in Walpole's hand on the flyleaf, is *Slight Sketches of Architecture by John Chute Esq. of the Vine in Hampshire*. We do not know the present location of Walpole's copy of Dugdale's *History of St. Paul's*, but we do know that there was a copy at Chute's house, The Vyne in Hampshire, with one of Walpole's bookplates inserted (Hazen, *Catalogue*, no. 591).
20. *Works* 2: 395.
21. *Works* 2: 445–6.
22. See *HW Corres.* 1: 60n, 15: 92, 31: 10, 423–4.
23. *Works* 2: 442.
24. *Works* 2: 446–7.
25. *Works* 2: 447–9.
26. George E. Haggerty, in a forthcoming book on Walpole's correspondence.
27. *Works* 2: 398.
28. *HW Corres.* 33: 576–7 (15 Sept. 1787).

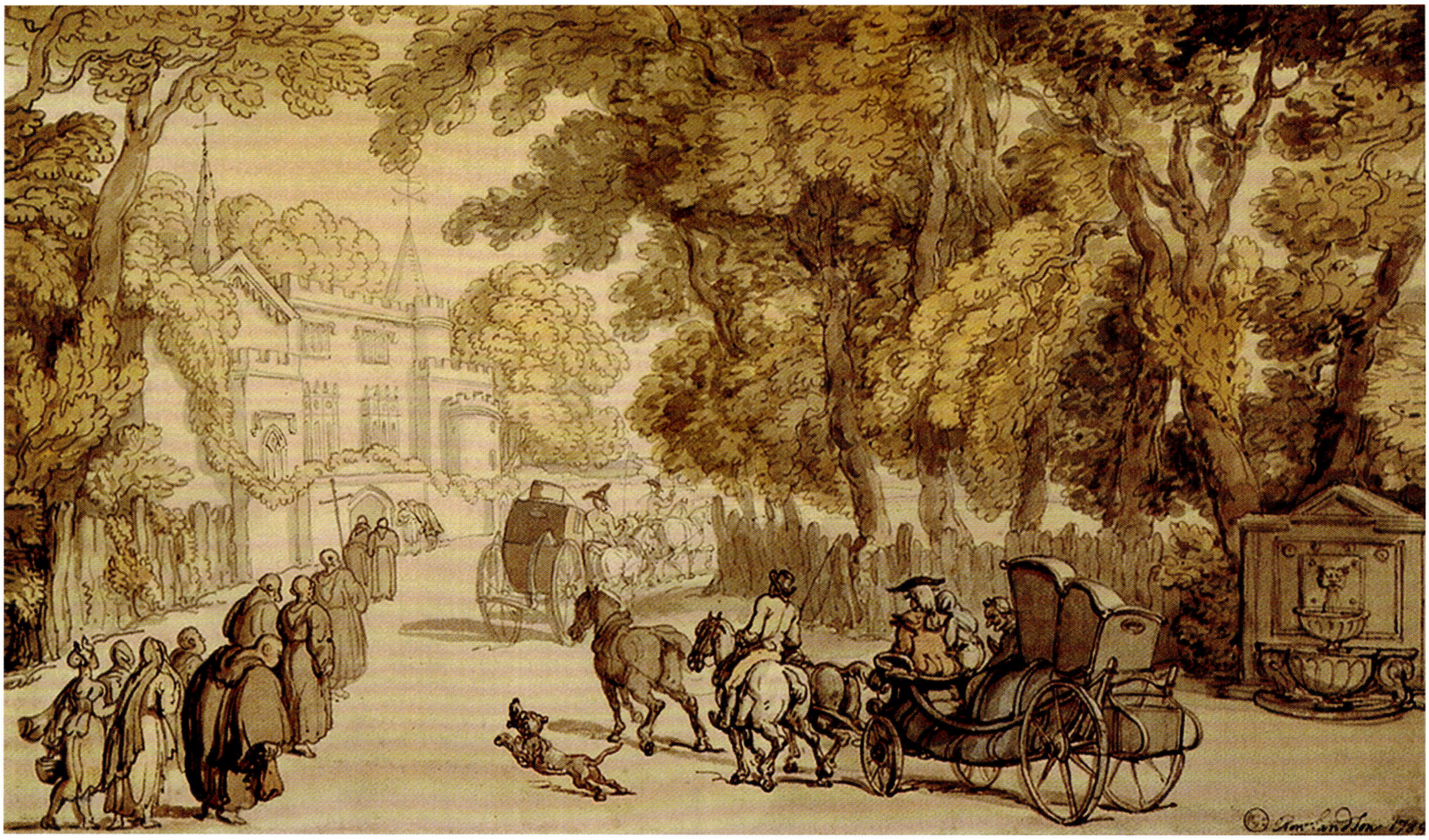

Figure 277. Thomas Rowlandson, *North Entrance of Strawberry Hill with a Procession of Monks*, probably 1805–10, watercolour, pen, and graphite, 24 × 38 cm. The Friends of Strawberry Hill for the Strawberry Hill Trust, Twickenham. Cat. 27

15.
STRAWBERRY HILL THE LAUGHING VIEW

HOPE SASKA

A GIFTED DRAUGHTSMAN who developed his talent at the Royal Academy schools, Thomas Rowlandson was renowned in the late Georgian era for compositions that lampooned the social follies of the day. Today most students of eighteenth-century British art first encounter Rowlandson through such graphic caricatures and satires. Yet Rowlandson also created elegant landscapes and detailed city views that were prized by eighteenth-century collectors. While his accomplished landscape drawings may today be less familiar, they demonstrate the range of this artist whose expressive, fluid technique has been likened to those of Thomas Gainsborough and Jean-Honoré Fragonard.[1] Rowlandson, however, seems to have been rarely able to resist a laughing view; even the loveliest of his landscapes include humorous elements, and still more of his comic drawings contain skilful landscapes. The art historian John Barrell has noted that Rowlandson enlivened his landscapes with a line that, even when delicate, 'is never far from caricature'.[2] Whether describing the rolling hills of a landscape or the generous curves of a buxom country girl, Rowlandson's playful line denotes a quick, spirited hand.

At the beginning of the nineteenth century Rowlandson produced a handful of humorous drawings that featured Strawberry Hill. This essay considers four exemplary drawings dating from about 1805–10 that depict various aspects of Walpole's retreat, including views of the facade of the house, the Chapel in the garden and, in one instance, an interior view of the Tribune. In these works Rowlandson's landscape style blends with his comic sensibility to create a small but important record of a laughing view of Walpole's famous property. In many ways, these humorous compositions speak to the cultural associations Walpole's project had for the late eighteenth-century viewer. The drawings address the contemporary fervour for the picturesque scene, mock the fashionable fascination with the Gothic and exploit antiquarian stereotypes. Rowlandson demonstrates the artifice of these categories by incorporating comedy, thereby revising the aesthetic experience. As a group, his drawings provide a counterpoint to the official topographical view of Strawberry Hill authorized, to some extent at least, by Walpole himself and substantiated by the numerous drawings of the house and grounds he commissioned and collected.

In the first drawing I discuss, known as *North Front of Strawberry Hill with Procession*, now owned by the Strawberry Hill Trust, Rowlandson imagines an encounter between a procession of monks on foot and an elderly man in a carriage (Fig. 277). Although the knowledgeable viewer easily recognizes the house as Strawberry Hill, the prominent placement of the monks generates an alternative interpretation of the building as a monastic retreat. Another exterior view, *Antiquary at Strawberry Hill*, from the Victoria and Albert Museum, juxtaposes an antiquary – a devotee of history and the historical artefact – with a strolling couple (Fig. 278). Rowlandson mocks both the rapturous antiquary, staggered by Strawberry Hill's edifice, and the couple who ignore the beauty of the building and the surrounding countryside. A drawing of the Chapel in the garden, *Solitude à*

Strawberry Hill now at the Art Institute of Chicago, assumes a view inside the walls of Walpole's estate and features the Chapel in the garden (Fig. 286). The title, inscribed on the sheet in French, indicates the level of renown enjoyed by both the artist and by Strawberry Hill. The image of country retreat features a manicured landscape that surrounds a reader who sits alone, the better to contemplate the volume open on his lap. This figure, who prefers to read his book rather than explore the garden and curious Chapel, is a model of academic absorption. The sole interior view, *Nuns at Prayer in the Tribune*, currently in a private collection, offers another type of devotion in a group of attractive young nuns who kneel in front of the altar in the Tribune (Fig. 279). The room Walpole designed to contain some of his most precious objects is here transformed into a chapel, and the cabinet built expressly for his miniatures becomes a triptych altarpiece. By placing the nuns in the Tribune, Rowlandson substitutes for the collector's reverence for objects in his collection a satire on Catholic idolatry. Even while Rowlandson pokes fun at the cultural significance of Strawberry Hill, he makes Walpole an accomplice in his comic project. Indeed, Walpole consciously and playfully constructed the Tribune in the form of a Gothic chapel, replacing religious relics and icons with miniatures, paintings and objects of virtù – objects that could be interpreted as Walpole's personal relics and that were designed to reinforce an artificial atmosphere for artefacts and create historical associations.

The drawing of the *North Front of Strawberry Hill with Procession*, falsely dated 1789, can be dated approximately to *c.* 1805–10 on stylistic grounds, placing it almost a decade or more after Walpole's death.[3] That this image circulated as a drawing, rather than a print, indicates that the subject matter appealed to a select clientele or that it was produced for a patron who suggested the theme. In either case, the *North Front*, like other drawings of the building, was intended for a viewer who was familiar with the house and could quickly grasp the humorous allusions.

In *North Front* Rowlandson uses Strawberry Hill as a backdrop against which the paths of a group of monks and an elderly gentleman in a low-slung carriage converge. Rowlandson invites the viewer to draw a comparison between the monks and the elderly man by calling attention to the similarities – a lifestyle of retreat – rather than the differences between them.[4] On the left side of the roadway, tonsured monks in long brown robes are followed by several pretty countrywomen returning from the market with full baskets. The loose garments worn by the countrywomen reveal the soft curves of their bodies underneath while the monks' bulks are enhanced by their heavy robes. The contrast between the monks and the countrywomen highlights the bodily appetites of these men of the cloth whose austere robes conceal a love of pleasure. Anchoring the procession, a monk in the middle of the group carries a crucifix at an angle so that the vertical line of the cross directs the eye to the cruciform weathervanes placed on the pinnacles of the house, a visual cue that links the monks to the building. When Rowlandson implied this connection between monks and Strawberry Hill, he could never have known that by 1923 the house would be occupied by Vincentian priests and that both the Tribune and Walpole's Chapel in the garden would be consecrated.

Other traffic on the roadway includes a stagecoach laden with passengers and parcels on the inner curve of the road. The stagecoach bypasses Strawberry Hill in favour of another destination, perhaps Hampton Court. Following apace behind the stagecoach, an elderly gentleman rides in a calèche – a low-slung carriage associated with continental modes of travel experienced by Grand Tourists. Notably, Rowlandson used a strikingly similar vignette in a drawing of Limbourg, Belgium, in which the calèche is used to signal and enhance the continental setting.[5] Just before he arrives at the gate to Strawberry Hill, the gentleman in the carriage leans forward to reveal his prominent profile and lean figure, acknowledging one of the monks with a smile and a nod. The monk, in turn, bows his head in a greeting that indicates kinship and familiarity. The white hair that frames the elderly gentleman's face and the oddness of his carriage designate him as old-fashioned and perhaps eccentric – the kind of character associated with antiquarianism and a plausible stand-in for, if not a reference to, Horace Walpole. Not only would the passenger and driver of the calèche and the processing monks be suitable in a continental setting, the Gothic style of the house and the Italianate fountain in the right foreground are architectural elements that signal European scenery. Even though Walpole based his

Figure 278. Thomas Rowlandson, *An Antiquary of Strawberry Hill*, after 1808, pen and ink, wash, 24.4 × 37.8 cm. Victoria and Albert Museum, London, Bequeathed by Rev. Alexander Dyce. Dyce 792. Cat. 26

Figure 279. Thomas Rowlandson, *Nuns at Prayer in the Tribune at Strawberry Hill*, *c.* 1805, pen and ink, and watercolour, 14 × 21.5 cm. Private collection. Cat. 159

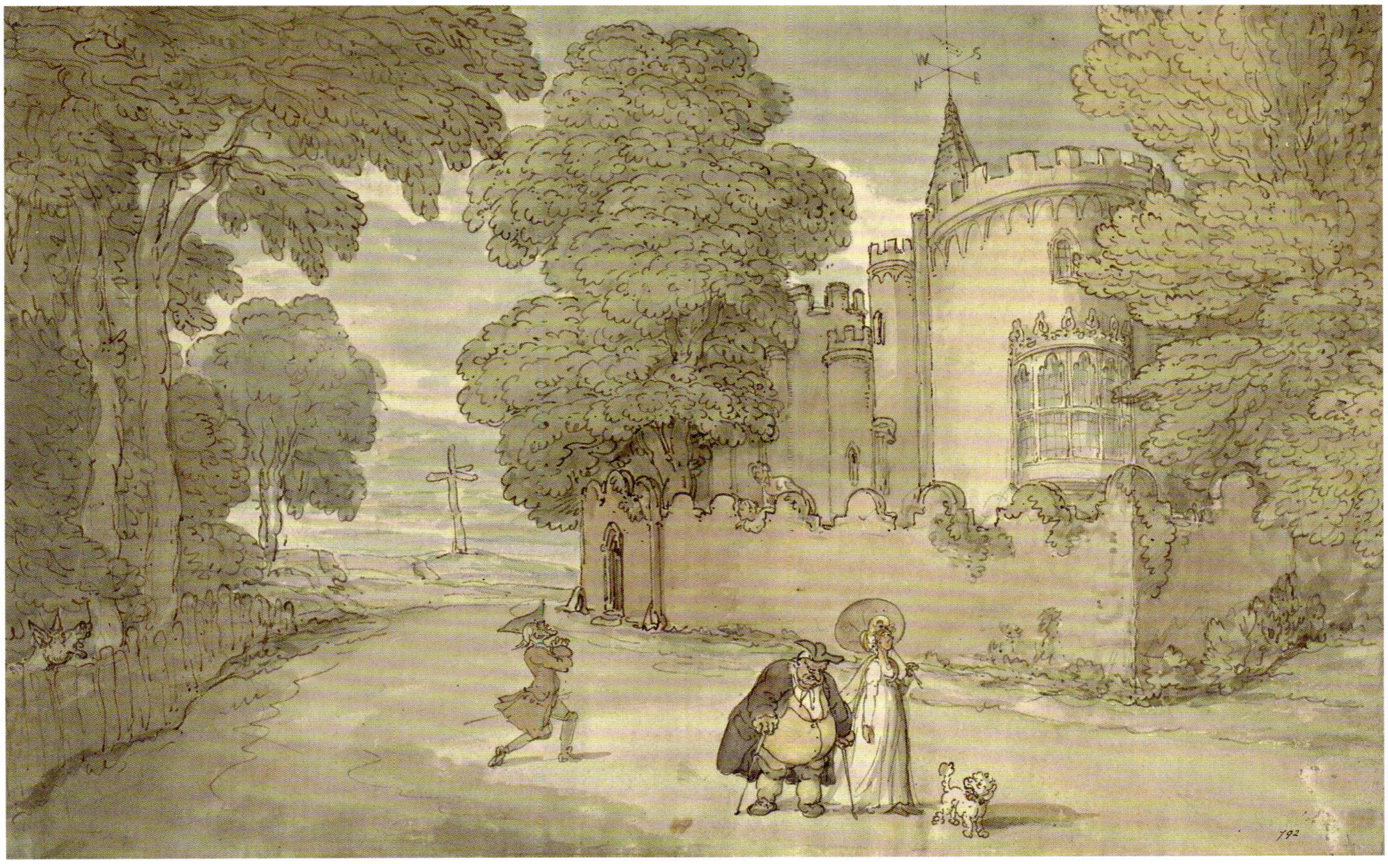

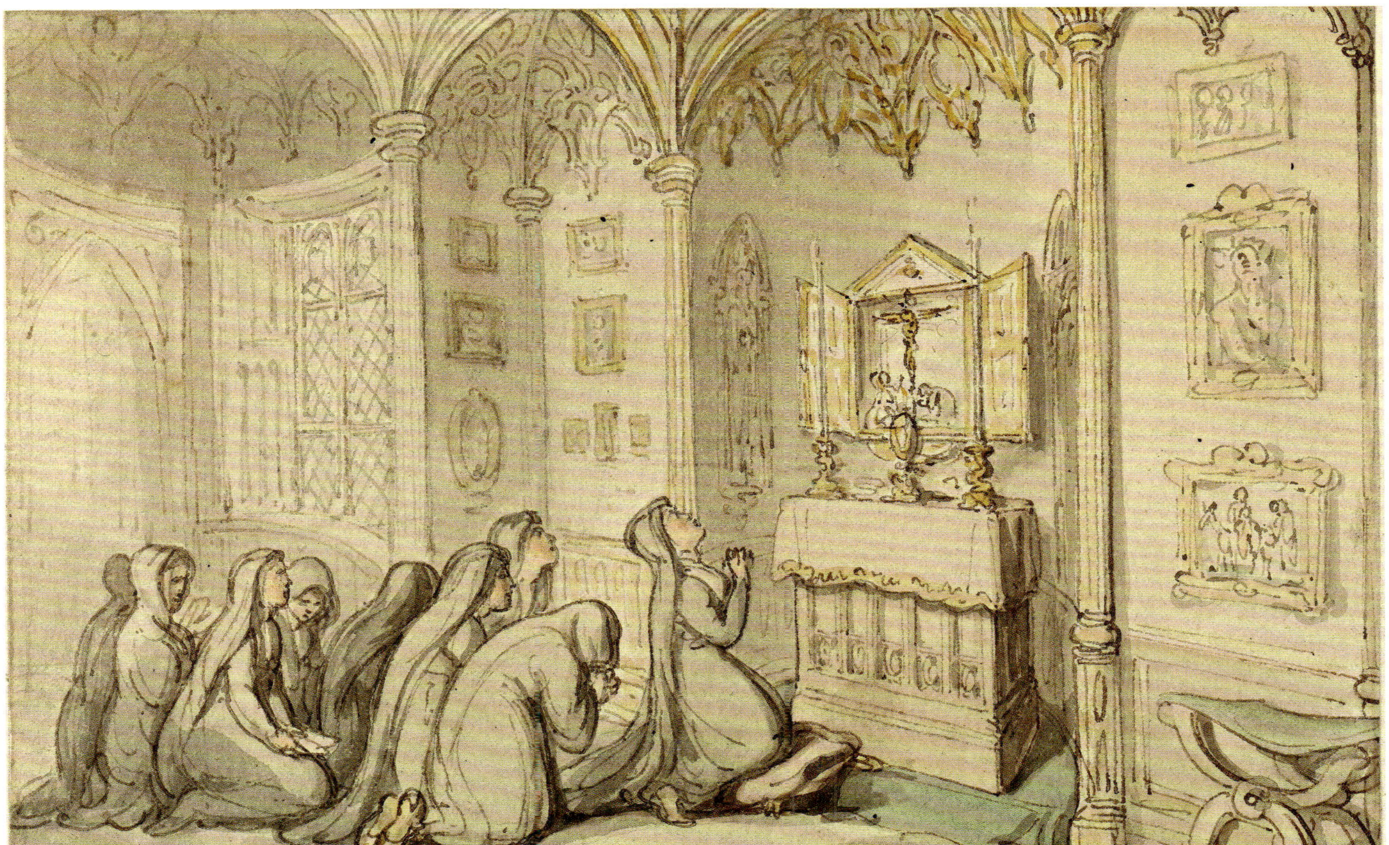

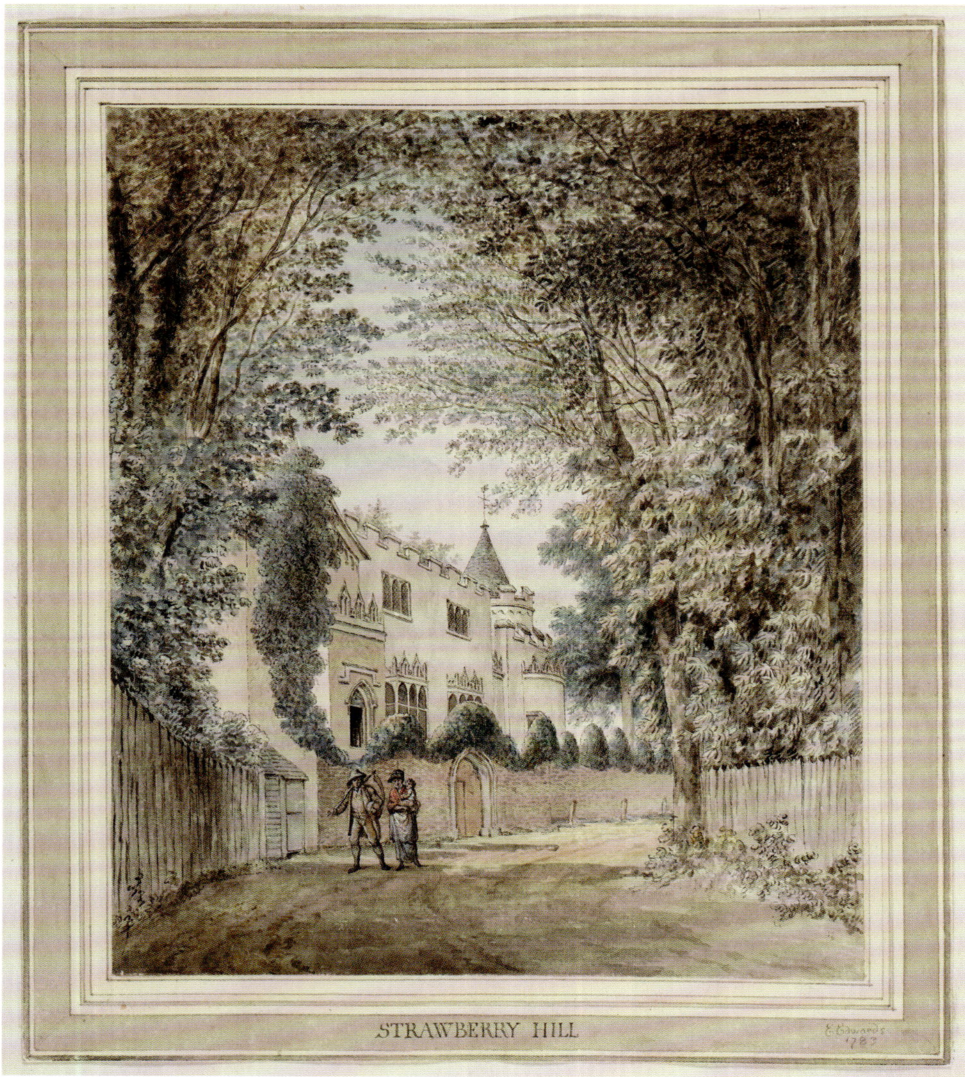

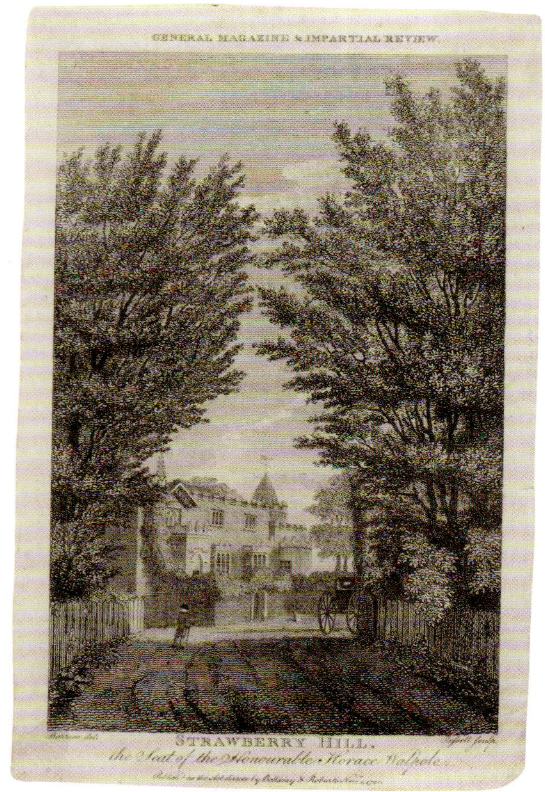

Figure 280. Edward Edwards, *Strawberry Hill*, 1783, pen, ink, watercolour, 31 × 25.9 cm, from p. 20 of HW's extra-illustrated copy of the *Description*. The Lewis Walpole Library, Yale University. 49 3582. Cat. 6

Figure 281. Russell after Joseph Charles Barrow, *Strawberry Hill: The Seat of the Honourable Horace Walpole*, etching, 1791, 17.7 × 11.3 cm p. 3 of HW's extra-illustrated copy of the *Description*. The Lewis Walpole Library, Yale University. Folio 49 3582, fol. 3

house largely on English Gothic structures and ornament, Rowlandson amplifies references to European architectural styles and the Grand Tour to play down the Englishness of Strawberry Hill and indicate that it is a fitting tourist attraction. Indeed, Walpole's admiration for Gothic architecture fills letters he penned during the Grand Tour made in his early twenties (1739–41). In one letter he reserves special praise for a Carthusian convent visited in France:

> All the conveniences, or rather (if there was such a word) all the adaptments are assembled here, that melancholy, meditation, selfish devotion, and despair would require. But yet 'tis pleasing. Soften the terms, and mellow the uncouth horror that reigns here, but a little, and 'tis a charming solitude.[6]

Perhaps Walpole had Grand Tour experiences such as this one in mind when he created his own 'charming solitude' on the banks of the Thames. Strawberry Hill thus welcomes additional interpretation as a monument to Walpole's years spent travelling in Europe in the fraternal company of his closest friends.

Rowlandson's selection of Strawberry Hill as subject matter may have been partly motivated by his familiarity with the location – he made a number of drawings of towns along the Thames, especially at Richmond and Hampton Court. The Rowlandson scholar John Riely has commented on Rowlandson's frequent use of recollection, imagination and his personal collection of prints and drawings rather than the on-site sketch to construct his compositions.[7] A sketch in a private collection that features the south-west view of Strawberry Hill demonstrates the thorny issue of the visual sources for Rowlandson's drawings of Strawberry Hill (*c.* 1805). The loose, rapidly executed lines, awkward perspective and flattened tree line indicate that this drawing was made as a preliminary study, and the inaccuracies suggest it was not made on site. Even the procession at the left is added as an afterthought to the composition. This drawing thus appears to be a precursor to two of the finished drawings shown in this exhibition: *North Front* and *Antiquary at Strawberry Hill.* It is likely that Rowlandson's drawings of Strawberry Hill were inspired by the many images of the house that circulated in book illustrations, print shops, art exhibitions and private collections during the last quarter of the eighteenth century. The deliberate arrangement of Rowlandson's comic scenes has also drawn comment from A. P. Oppé, who noted of Rowlandson's late work that: 'There is nothing ... that looks like a sketch from nature.'[8] And, as we have seen, Rowlandson recycled his own compositions with success. Of all the types of landscape views available, what were the kinds of views of Strawberry Hill that Rowlandson had to choose from? And why did these views inspire his humorous representations?

Just as Horace Walpole undertook to document the growth and arrangement of his collections at Strawberry Hill, he actively commissioned and collected topographical views of the Twickenham estate. Of the artists who produced these views, John Carter, Joseph Barrow and Edward Edwards were among the most prolific. Their designs highlight the situation of the house and grounds, record Walpole's improvements to the exterior and interior of the house and painstakingly document his collections. The extent to which Walpole participated in the design of these images is unclear but, given Walpole's involvement with the house and collection, it is probable that he at least occasionally directed the artists in their choice of composition and subject matter. That Walpole collected these drawings in various portfolios and in extra-illustrated albums indicates his appreciation and enthusiasm for representations of his estate.

Edwards's view of the entrance front of *Strawberry Hill* (Fig. 280) is an example of the type of view available to Rowlandson, who probably saw etchings made from Edward's drawings. John Barrow's nearly identical view of the house is illustrated here with an engraving published in *The General Magazine and Impartial Review* (Fig. 281). One version of Barrow's drawing is at the Lewis Walpole Library (1789), and another is in a private collection. Both Edwards's and Barrow's views describe the facade in detail and dramatize the approach to Strawberry Hill, framing the house with mature trees that screen the landscape and create an arched canopy over the rough dirt road. Dense foliage shades the foreground and accentuates the brightly rendered stucco facade of the house that presses against the masonry wall and threatens to encroach on the road. In his view Edwards elongates the facade by emphasizing the upward thrust of the windows and shortening the distance between roof line and tree line. Still other representations of Strawberry Hill focus on the open spaces around the house. Carter, for example, portrays Walpole's estate from a vantage point beyond the curve in the road in *South West View of the House from the Fields* (Fig. 282). In this view the house presides over the landscape; the trees no longer dominate the building and the windows in

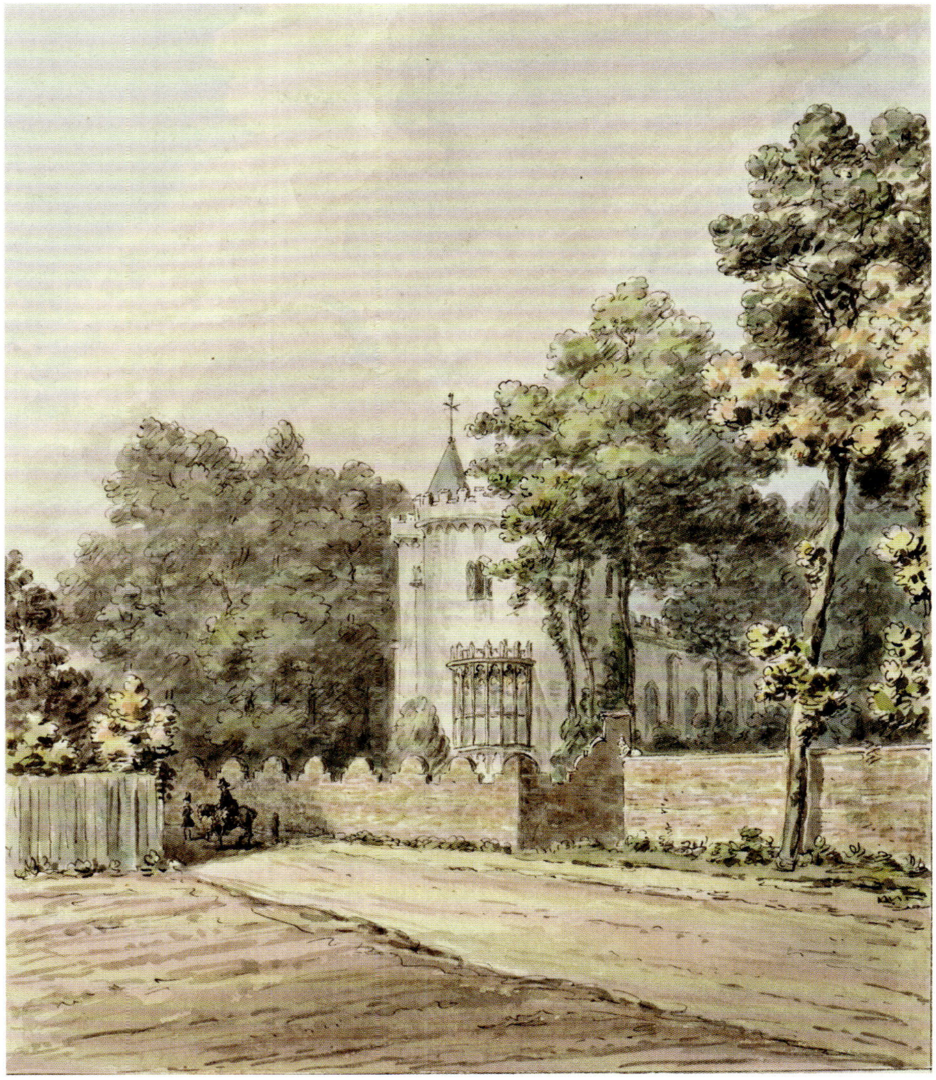

Figure 282. John Carter, *South West View of the House from the Fields*, *c.* 1790, watercolour, 23 × 20.4 cm (sheet), mounted, p. 18 of Richard Bull's extra-illustrated copy of the *Description*. The Lewis Walpole Library, Yale University. 33 30 copy 11 Folio

the Round Tower overlook a newly tilled field. Whereas many of the views Walpole collected show the house to be somewhat isolated in the countryside, Rowlandson's comedic drawings socialize the landscape in which Strawberry Hill is represented. Even though the house sits quietly behind brick walls, it witnesses an array of human activity. Here a variety of characters meet on the road – monks mingle with young women while an elderly man in a carriage and travellers in a stagecoach pass by.

While Rowlandson's drawings evoke landscapes made by Carter, Barrow and Edwards, they are rescaled and populated with animated figural groups. In Edwards's and Barrow's views figures are included as scenic elements: country folk walk on the road in front of Strawberry Hill to set off the proportion of the house, while workers tending the grounds demonstrate the extent of Walpole's property and confirm the care with which he managed his estate. The figures in Rowlandson's drawings depart from the landscape tradition practised by Carter, Barrow and Edwards and instead actively transform topographic views into comic anecdotes. The people in Rowlandson's drawings are character types drawn from eighteenth-century visual entertainments such as print caricatures and satires, stage comedies and popular novels. The monks in the *North Front*, for example, suggest the ancient traditions of the countryside and recall sensational characters found in the narratives of Gothic fiction. Here they are also shown to be lusty rustics isolated in the country, a favourite trope of Rowlandson's. Similarly, the elderly gentleman in his remarkable carriage refers to a kind of continental affect outmoded in Europe by the end of the eighteenth century and often mocked in satirical prints. By choosing a lifestyle of retirement and contemplation, both monks and aristocrat are designated outsiders from fashionable society – a status that allows them a degree of independence from the rules and strictures of that social sphere.

Strawberry Hill, replete with a catholic collection of relics, artefacts and paintings, would seem a fitting location for an encounter between a band of monks and the elderly gentleman. Walpole himself encouraged visions of his house as a monastery, decorating it with ornaments derived from ecclesiastical settings, and referred to rooms in the building as the Refectory and the Oratory, as well as a Chapel in the garden. These witty references to the traditional association of Gothic architecture with Catholicism probably appealed to Rowlandson as a ready-made satire, a folly of the true Gothic style and a fitting stage for his brand of comedy. Even for Walpole the ecclesiastical associations of the building were never fully resolved. His writings express this ambivalence, simultaneously articulating disdain and intense curiosity for the rites and rituals of Roman Catholicism. In a letter written on the Grand Tour, Walpole romantically associates himself with a variety of rustic characters who he locates in the remoter parts of Europe: 'Yesterday I was a shepherd of Dauphiné; today I am an Alpine savage; tomorrow a Carthusian monk.'[9] While the Carthusian monk was just one character he could playfully assume on a pleasure trip, Walpole also speaks of monks with reverence. For Walpole monastic retreat was also tied to an ancient tradition of western scholarship kept alive throughout the Middle Ages, when monks and the clergy 'were the only persons who had learning'.[10]

Rowlandson's drawing of monks processing in front of Strawberry Hill corresponds with the interior view, *Nuns at Prayer in the Tribune*. As discussed above, the drawing features a group of nuns in the Tribune where they kneel in front of an altar, which Walpole based on the 'tomb of the two children of Edward III in Westminster Abbey'.[11] Beautiful nuns appear regularly in Rowlandson's works, often as highly sexualized women whose vows of chastity are willingly broken. Here they are lovely objects to be admired in a room full of lovely objects, their religious devotion part of their allure. In the alcove where Walpole placed a casket, vases made of precious materials and his cabinet of miniatures, Rowlandson adds tall candlesticks and a chalice, and replaces the cabinet with a triptych including a crucifixion. Even the paintings on the walls have a religious theme, and in the niches, instead of Walpole's collection of small objects, figures hover like saints. Despite Rowlandson's modifications, the room is still recognizably Walpole's Tribune. Visions of Catholic piety, the nuns demonstrate their devotion in a substitution for the dedication of a collector. They also, of course, act as a commentary on the types of objects – rosary beads, antique artefacts and curiosities like the Becket Chasse (Fig. 151) – that Walpole displayed in the Tribune.

Rowlandson undoubtedly created this view based on Edwards's interior view of the Tribune (1781). In this watercolour, later engraved for editions of Walpole's *Description*, Edwards painstakingly documents the decorative and architectural details in the densely packed chamber, replete with paintings, sculpture, artefacts and stained-glass windows. He meticulously records the way in which the architecture frames the collection, including details like the star-shaped skylight in the ceiling and the ornamental rib vaulting above the niches. In his drawing Rowlandson edits the remarkable detail that Edwards rendered, paring it to a handful of telling characteristics and hinting at the quatrefoil shape of the room and the tracery in the arches, but omitting most of the floor and all of the vaulted ceiling. Although Rowlandson was capable of creating exact architectural views, the style of drawing he adopts here and in other drawings of Strawberry Hill is far more suited to the comic sketch. The pen strokes are loose and suggestive, and the watercolour washes light – techniques associated with the 'informal media' of these drawings.[12]

In another view of the facade of Strawberry Hill, this time from the south-western approach, Rowlandson takes on the antiquarian tourist whose pilgrimage leads him to Strawberry Hill (Fig. 278). The drawing features the Gothic window in the Round Tower and represents the rest of the facade of Strawberry Hill as a row of turrets. Rowlandson thickens the wooded area and alters the course of the road so that the crossroads are now visible; he even turns the obelisk then at the crossroads into a wooden signpost formed like a cross. Under the aegis of this cruciform signpost, the antiquary is overcome by emotion as he pays tribute to the collector and his house. With hands clasped to his chest and a gaze directed towards the crenellations and turrets of Strawberry Hill, he falls forward on bended knee in parody of an ardent lover or a religious pilgrim genuflecting in front of a relic or holy shrine. Rowlandson encourages both interpretations and includes a couple of robust girls who peer over the brick wall and laugh at the enraptured antiquary wearing old-fashioned clothing. Rowlandson raises the comedic stakes by showing that the antiquarian has not even the sense to admire female beauty and instead gazes towards the stuccoed facade. As if to comment on his asinine behaviour, a donkey brays from behind a fence at the far left side of the drawing. The antiquary's comically emotional state is underscored by the indifference of the strolling couple, who pass by the house without a second glance towards the human drama or the striking architecture behind them.

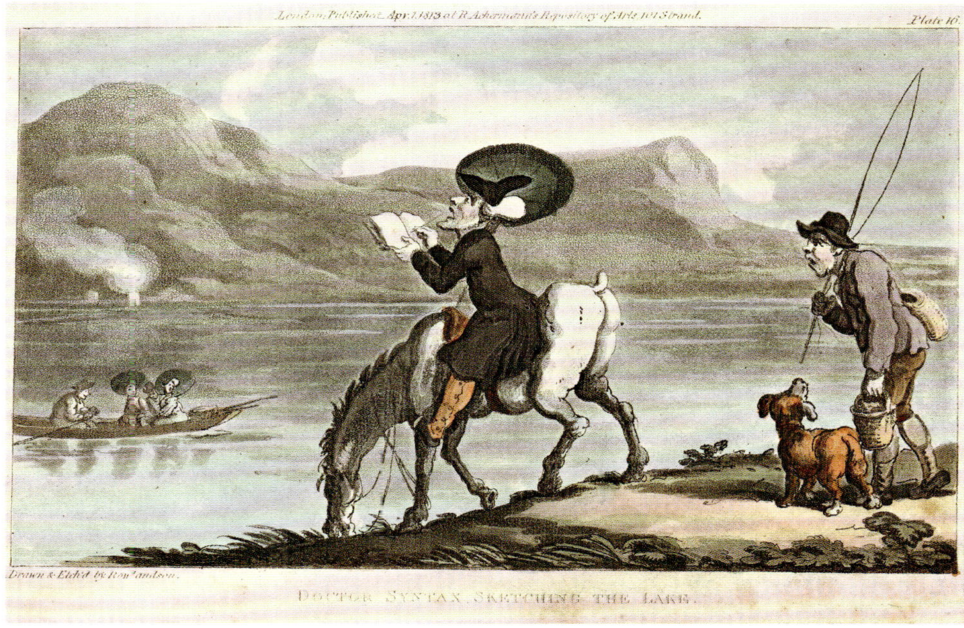

Figure 283. Thomas Rowlandson, *Dr Syntax Sketching the Lake*, 1813, etching and aquatint. The Lewis Walpole Library, Yale University. 813.4.1.3

The drawing of the antiquary formulates Rowlandson's commentary on the pursuit of picturesque tourism. Centred in the composition, immediately below the arrow-like signpost, the antiquary becomes the starting point from which the drawing is read. The laughter of the women and the braying of the mule draw attention to the antiquarian's folly; he admires the picturesque Gothic house but is blind (and deaf) to the realities of the country: the maids, the mule and the stoic couple out for a walk. In his single-mindedness the antiquarian is linked to Dr Syntax, a character Rowlandson fleshed out in a three-volume series of comic illustrations entitled *The Tours of Dr. Syntax* (1812, 1820, 1820–21) with texts by William Coombe. Modelled in part after William Gilpin, the prominent eighteenth-century theorist of the picturesque, Syntax doggedly scours the English countryside in an attempt to discover the ultimate picturesque view. His experiences are marked by his inability to moderate his emotions and by his self-absorption. Not surprisingly, numerous

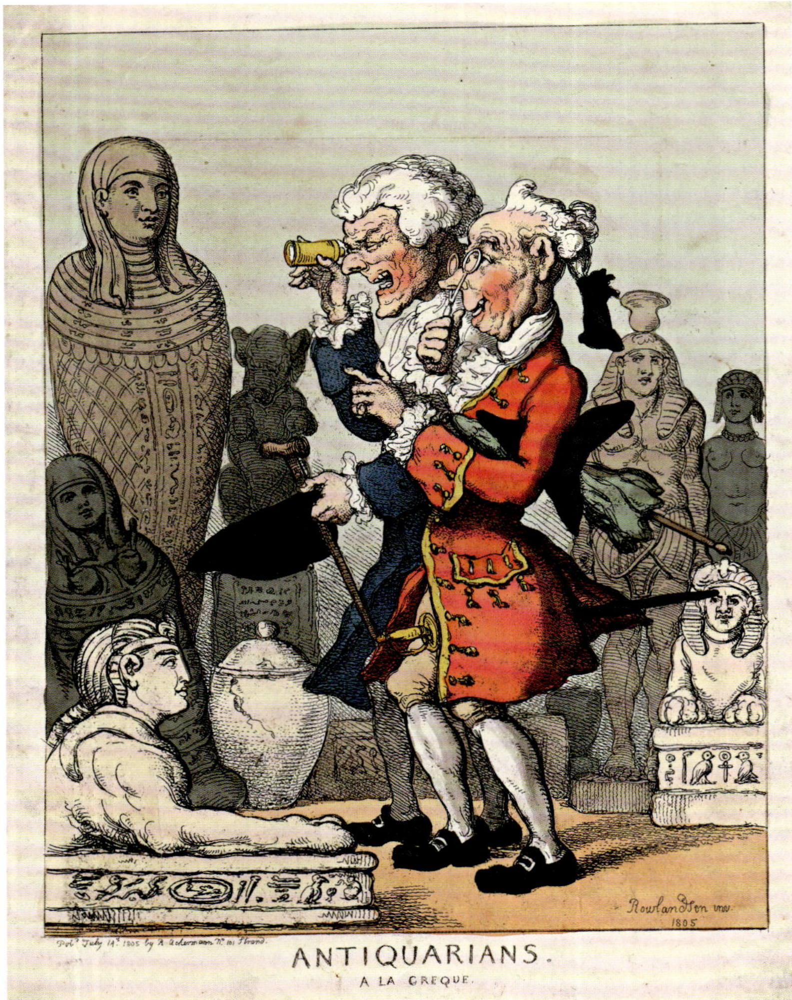

Figure 284. Thomas Rowlandson, *Antiquarians à la Greque,* 1805, hand-coloured etching. The Lewis Walpole Library, Yale University. 805.7.14.1

misfortunes assail Syntax as he encounters the inconveniences of the countryside instead of the expected idyll. Rowlandson's image *Dr Syntax Sketching the Lake* (Fig. 283) makes an excellent counterpart to the *Antiquarian at Strawberry Hill.* With his sketchbook poised above his chest and his eyes trained on the hilltop, Syntax is unaware of the boaters on the water, the boy who arrives to fish with his dog, and the fire on the opposite bank – all part and parcel of the everyday landscape. The Strawberry Hill antiquarian is likewise so enamoured with his discovery that he fails to be aware of his surroundings.

Rowlandson's representation of the antiquary at Strawberry Hill feeds into eighteenth-century stereotypes of this figure in satirical prints. A regular subject of graphic satires, antiquaries invariably appear as slender old men with irregular features and shabby or old fashioned clothing.[13] Rowlandson's graphic satire *Antiquarians à la Greque* (Fig. 284) is yet another variation on this theme. In a room packed with Egyptian sculpture and other artefacts, the antiquaries approach an upright mummy at the left of the composition. Their slight frames padded by layers of ruffles, bows and trimmings contrast with the handsome, bare physiques of the antiquities that surround them. So represented, an antiquarian is an effete modern male devoted to the study of potsherds, relics and, most damningly, the idealized male form as it was rendered in ancient sculpture. Of the collectors who were ridiculed in this vein, William Beckford, around whom rumours of pederasty swirled, and Sir William Hamilton, whose wife Emma conducted a public affair with Admiral Horatio Nelson, were among the most prominent.

While the public prints were unkind to such sensational figures as Beckford and Hamilton, Walpole remained relatively unscathed, with the exception of two satires. A small *Tête-à-Tête* portrait entitled *Mrs. Heidelburgh and Baron Otranto* (1769) romantically linked Walpole with the actress Kitty Clive, who lived at Little Strawberry Hill, then known as Cliveden, but seems not to have affected him much. Far more wounding was William Guthrie's caustically satirical response to a printed exchange that occurred between Guthrie and Walpole in 1764 over the dismissal of Walpole's cousin Henry Seymour Conway from his military command.[14] The public squabble over a political appointment turned personal in Guthrie's counter-attack when he insinuated that Walpole's defence of Conway was motivated by homoerotic affection that Walpole harboured for his close friend. With these two exceptions aside, satirists generally directed their attacks towards controversial public figures who were more easily recognized than Walpole.

Nevertheless, one gentle caricature of Walpole by John Carter depicts the bachelor aristocrat as an antiquary who is himself an antiquity in his own collection (Fig. 285). Carter's unpublished drawing, one version of which was inserted into an extra-illustrated copy of the *Description* now in the Lewis Walpole Library, tracks Walpole's movements through his house over the course of a day. (Another version is in John Carter's extra-illustrated copy of the *Description*, now in the Huntington Library.) From the left of the page to the right, Carter shows a succession of views of

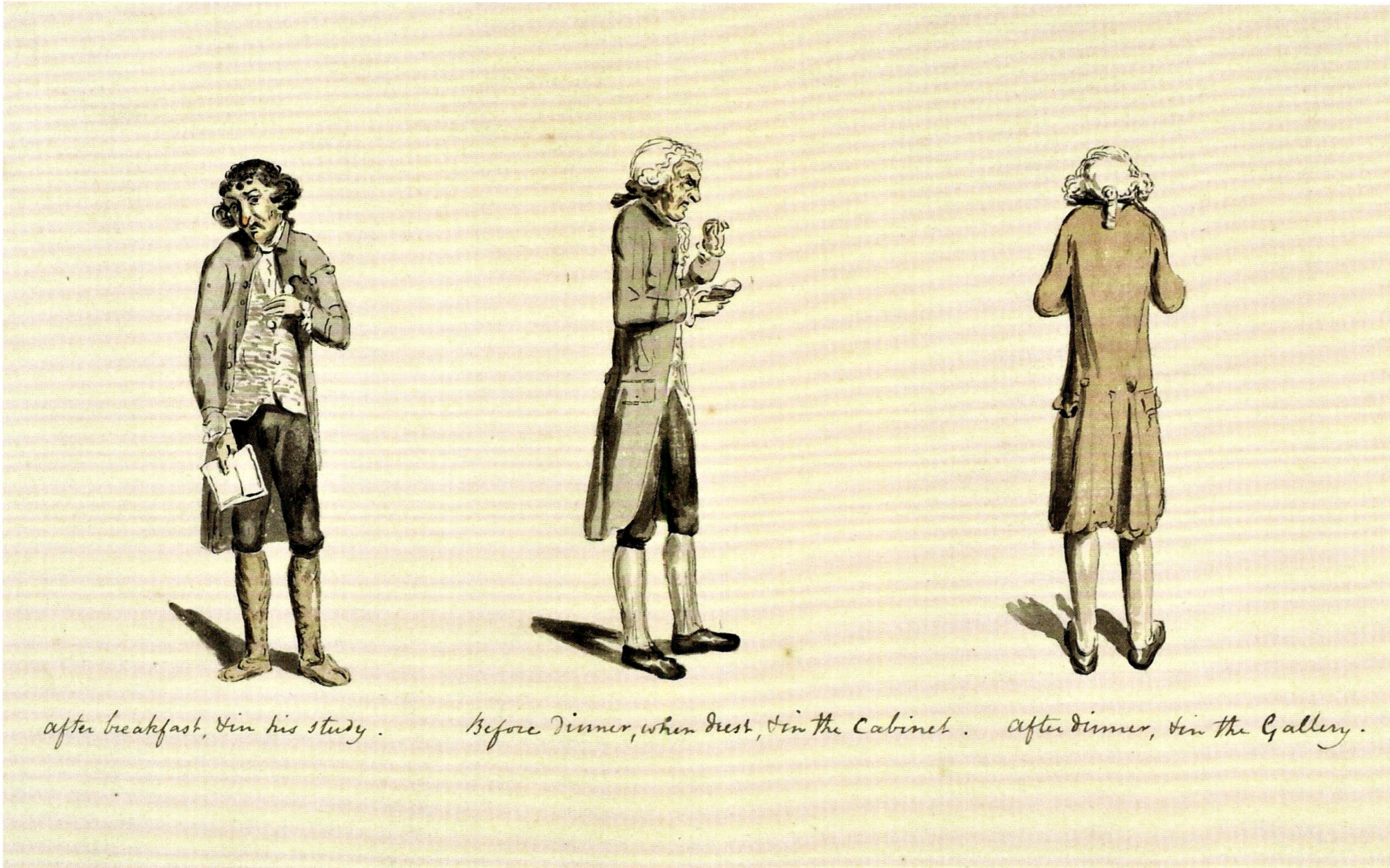

Figure 285. John Carter, *Three Sketches of Horace Walpole*, 1788, pen and ink and watercolour on laid paper, 22 × 28.3 cm (sheet), formerly in James Bindley's extra-illustrated copy of the *Description*. The Lewis Walpole Library, Yale University. 33 30 Copy 22. Cat. 25

Walpole – front, profile and back – as if he were a specimen to be examined and studied. Thus Walpole glares at the disturbance that has interrupted his reading 'after breakfast, and in his study', scowls at a pinch of snuff held between thumb and forefinger 'before dinner, when drest and in the cabinet', and concludes by turning his back on the viewer as he stalks away 'after dinner, and in the Gallery'. By locating Walpole within key rooms of his home, Carter illustrates the integral relationship between Walpole, his house and his collection. The slight exaggeration of Walpole's emaciated frame and down-turned mouth reveals Carter's intimacy with the expressions and gestures of his subject and has more in common with the type of playful caricature sketches made by Walpole and his associates than it does with the published satirical prints.

Whereas Carter's drawing can be construed as an attempt to incorporate the physical presence of Walpole into his collection, Rowlandson demonstrates no such inclination to meditate on the body of Walpole. Instead, Strawberry Hill becomes a stand-in for Walpole and the antiquarian pursuit. The character types that populate Rowlandson's drawings both enact elements of Walpole's project and embody critical reactions to it. The final Rowlandson drawing I discuss, *Solitude à Strawberry Hill* (Fig. 286), shows a figure seated in a garden setting in front of the Chapel at Strawberry Hill. The French title inscribed on this sheet is certainly a later addition, two facts that complicate the sheet's history. Moreover, another version of the drawing, known as *Garden and Entrance to a Neo-Gothic House – Strawberry Hill*, is now in the Courtauld Gallery.[15] The scene was one of twelve

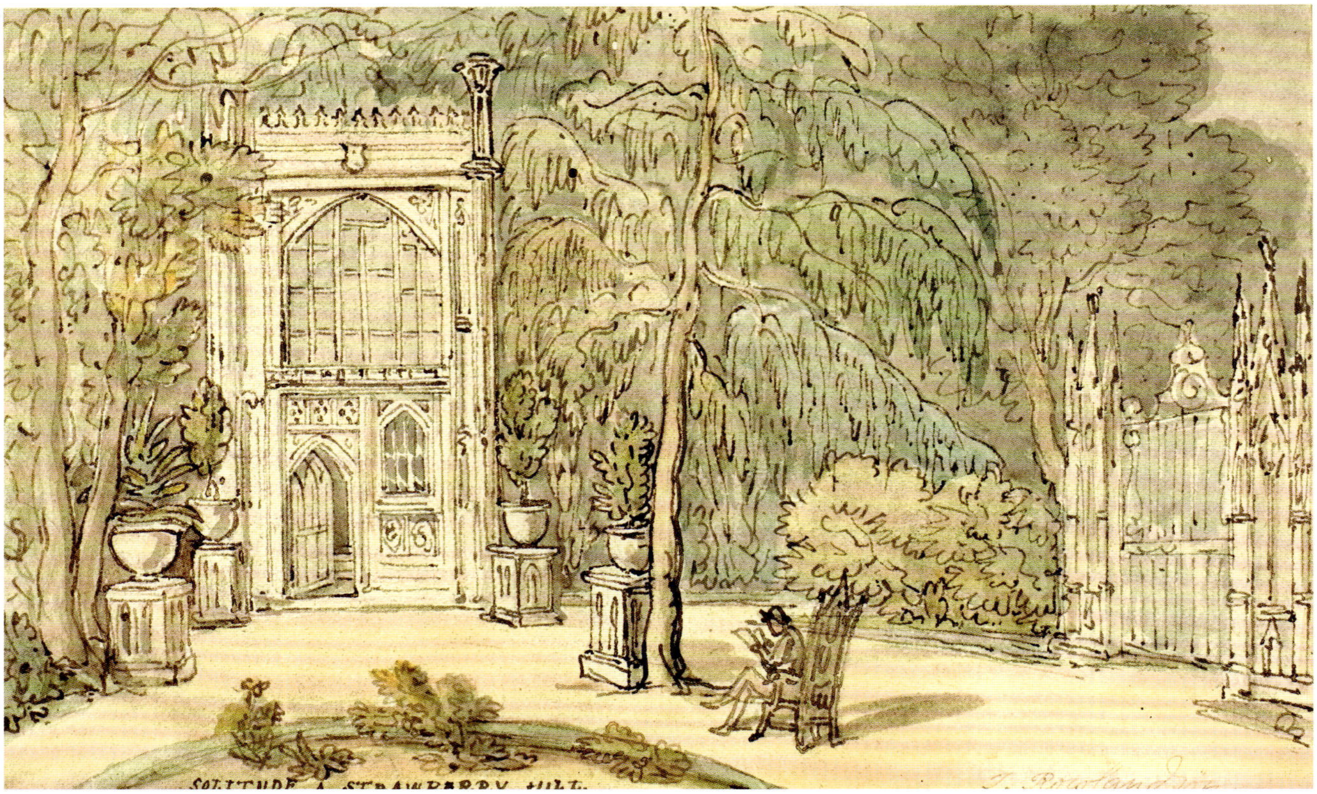

Figure 286. Thomas Rowlandson, *Solitude a Strawberry Hill*, *c.* 1809, pen and brown ink with brush and watercolour, on cream wove paper, 16.3 × 20 cm (sheet). The Art Institute of Chicago, Gift of Mrs James Ward Thorne. 1940.207.1. Cat. 28

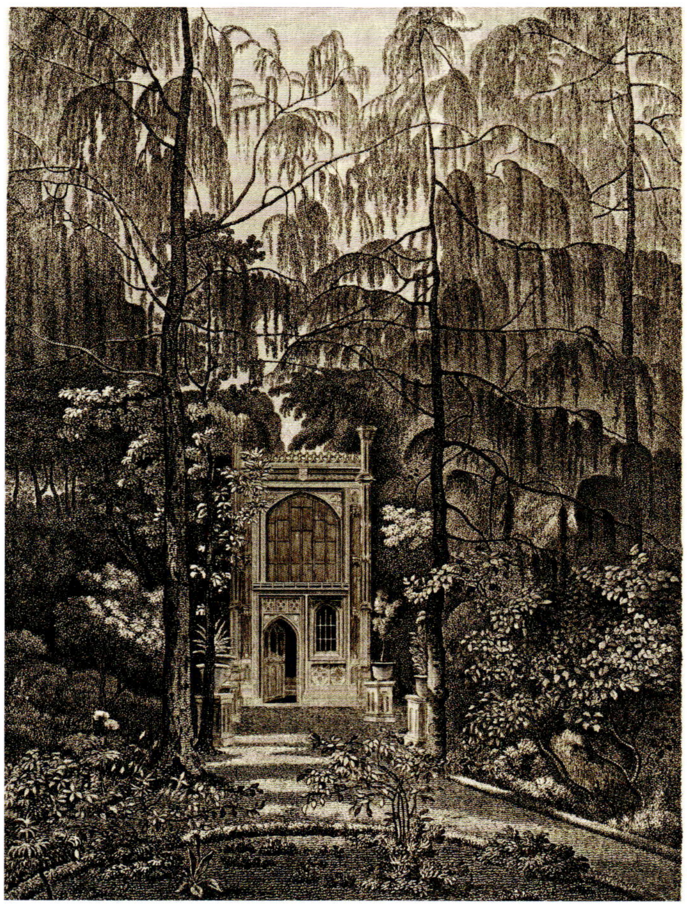

Figure 287. R.B. Godfrey, After William Pars, *View of the Chapel in the Garden at Strawberry Hill*, etching and engraving, 29.5 × 21.4 cm, made for the 1784 edition of the *Description* and mounted, p. 222 of Richard Bull's extra-illustrated copy of the *Description*. The Lewis Walpole Library, Yale University. 33 30, copy 11 Folio

subjects etched and first published by Thomas Tegg in 1809 as *Rowlandson's Sketches from Nature*, an enlarged version of which followed in 1822. Rowlandson's work incorporates a variety of architectural elements from the gardens surrounding Strawberry Hill and is clearly based on an engraving after a drawing by William Pars that had appeared in the *Description* (Fig. 287). Pars creates a brooding Gothic atmosphere by dwarfing the Chapel with weeping conifers (perhaps larches) and overgrown foliage. The Chapel windows are dark and the door opens to reveal a shadowy interior, adding to a sense of 'gloomth'. Rowlandson rejects the ominous tone of Pars's design and re-formats the scene in a horizontal frame so that it is more accommodating to the human figure. He also tames the landscape, incorporating elements of early-nineteenth-century garden design so that the setting is sunlit and open. Rowlandson includes a figure reading in a sunlit patch, seated on a straight-backed Gothic chair very like the chairs William Hallett made for Walpole. The gate nearby, which in reality was some distance from the Chapel, is likewise derived from an engraving designed by Pars in the *Description*. Although without the comic edge of drawings populated with monks, nuns and antiquaries, this drawing is not without a little joke of its own. For the scholar is so consumed by his studies that he is unaware of the picturesque scene before him, insensible to the weeping willow-like trees or the doorway to the Chapel that opens suggestively, perhaps a pathway to a Gothic adventure. Yet, the double nature of Rowlandson's works also opens the possibility that the image celebrates the experience of the solitary scholar-antiquary in his garden surrounded by all he loves – Gothic buildings, weeping willows and, most of all, his books.

Overall, Walpole's topographical views of Strawberry Hill reinforce his desire to record the property and demonstrate his taste. Rowlandson's versions, made from a perspective outside the walls, alter the landscape to represent his comic outlook. The authority of the views that Walpole collected resides in the repetition of prospect, the fairly consistent style in which they are drawn, and in the large number of images that were made. Such a project can only be effectively combatted by the comedic view, which similarly depends on repetition of imagery to revise and reassemble the official view into a laughing one. For after experiencing the pleasure and delight in Rowlandson's monks, nuns and besotted antiquary, how can any viewer put these characters out of their mind when an official view of the house is present? Thanks to Rowlandson, these are the figures that often haunt Walpole's Gothic creation.

1. Ronald Paulson, *Rowlandson: A New Interpretation* (New York: Oxford University Press, 1972), 22, 31.
2. John Barrell, 'The Private Comedy of Thomas Rowlandson', *Art History*, vol. 6, no. 4 (Dec. 1983): 423–41, esp. 425.
3. A.P. Oppé, *Thomas Rowlandson: His Drawings and Watercolors* (London: The Studio Ltd, 1923), 5, rept. There is another version of this scene of similar date in the Lewis Walpole Library, Yale University (information and dating supplied by John Riely).
4. Paulson, *Rowlandson*, 21.
5. John Baskett and Dudley Snelgrove, *The Drawings of Thomas Rowlandson in the Paul Mellon Collection* (New York: Brandywine Press, 1977), cat. no. 49.
6. *HW Corres.* 13: 168.
7. John Riely, *Rowlandson Drawings from the Paul Mellon Collection* (New Haven: Yale University Press, 1977), xxi, 11.
8. Oppé, *Thomas Rowlandson*, 25.
9. *HW Corres.* 13: 167–8.
10. *HW Corres.* 16: 352.
11. *1842 Sale*, day 13, lot 69.
12. Barell, 'Private Comedy', 432–3.
13. Bruce Redford, *Dilettanti: The Antic and the Antique in Eighteenth-Century England* (Los Angeles: J. Paul Getty Museum, 2008), 130–42.
14. Paul Langford, 'Wapole, Horatio, fourth earl of Orford (1717–1797)', *Oxford Dictionary of National Biography*, Oxford University Press, Sept. 2004; online ed., May 2008 (www.oxforddnb.com/view/article/28596, accessed 23 Dec. 2008). William Guthrie, *A Reply to the Counter-Address; Being a Vindication of a Pamphlet Entitled, An Address to the Public, on the Late Dismissal of a General Officer* (London: W. Nicoll, 1764). For William Cole's shocked comments on 29 June 1782 on Baron Otranto and Mrs Heidelburgh, see *HW Corres.* 2: 330.
15. Courtauld Gallery D.1952.RW.3600.

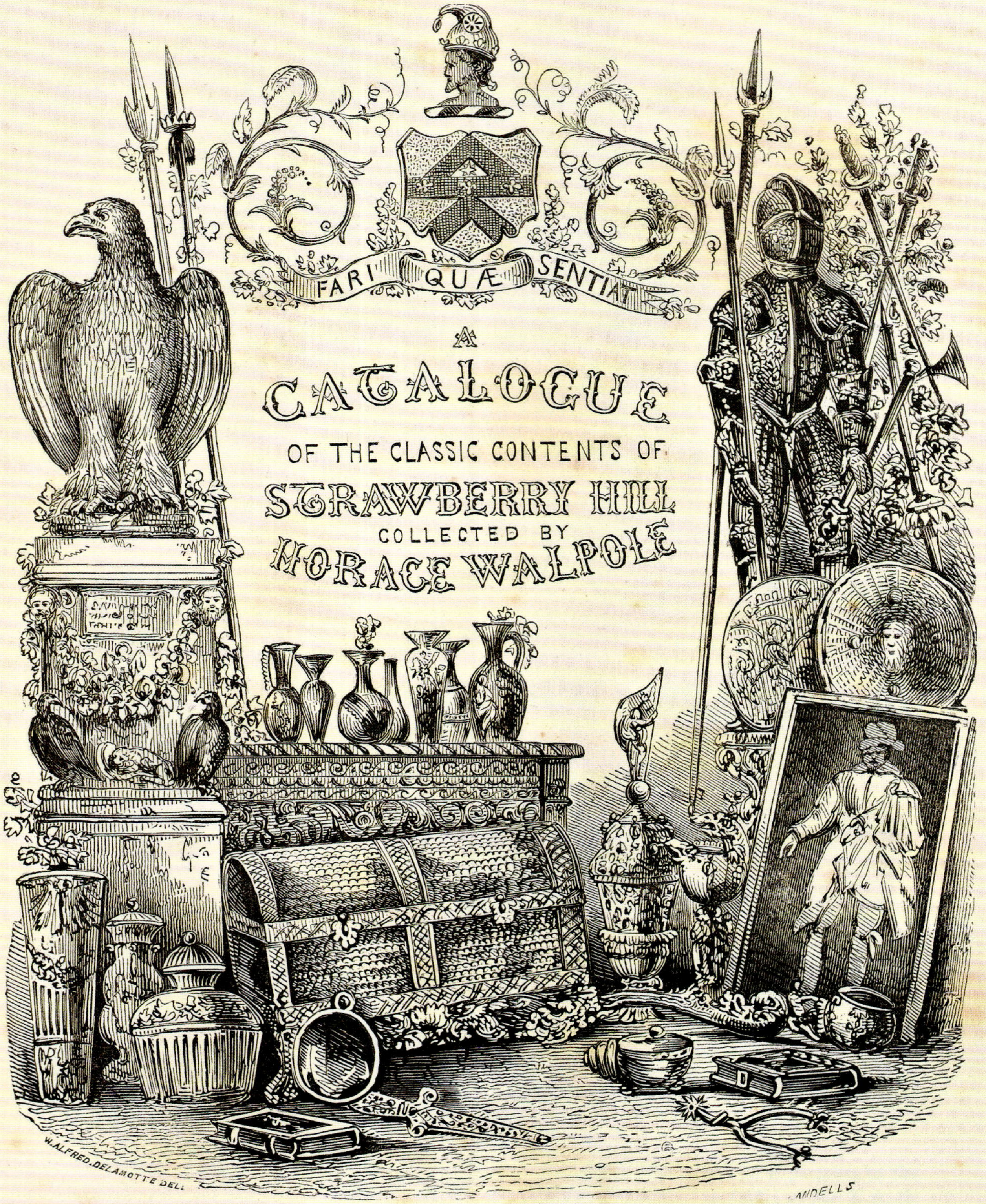

SMITH AND ROBINS, PRINTERS, KING STREET, LONG ACRE.

16.

THE STRAWBERRY HILL SALE OF 1842

'THE MOST DISTINGUISHED GEM THAT HAS EVER ADORNED THE ANNALS OF AUCTIONS'

STEPHEN CLARKE

IN THE PREFACE to his *Description* of Strawberry Hill Walpole explained that 'the following account of pictures and rarities is given with a view to their future dispersion'; but after his death at his house in Berkeley Square on the afternoon of 2 March 1797, his will revealed no such intention.[1] The Strawberry Hill estate was carefully entailed, and the will directed that the furniture, pictures, books, china, jewels, collections of curiosities and plate at Strawberry Hill should be treated as heirlooms, and kept and preserved entire.[2] And so the inherent tension between his desire to accumulate and record and his acceptance of the inevitability of dispersal was played out over a period of forty-five years after his death as the collection slumbered, out of public view, to be rudely awakened for what was to be one of the most widely publicized auction sales of the nineteenth century (Fig. 288).

Accounts of the collection in the early nineteenth century became increasingly scarce. The house was first occupied by Walpole's cousin, the sculptor Anne Seymour Damer, and from 1810 by Walpole's great niece Lady Waldegrave and her family. Its isolation increased, and in 1842 the *Athenaeum* described the house as 'almost hermetically sealed', and noted that even the German art historians Johann David Passavant and Gustav Waagen had 'found the little paper fabric impenetrable'.[3] Despite this, images of the house and its collections continued to circulate, in particular as a result of the activities of the bookseller Silvester Harding of Pall Mall, the friend and associate of Walpole's printer Thomas Kirgate, and of his son George Perfect Harding.[4]

Although Walpole's status as a gifted letter writer rose steadily as further editions of his correspondence were published, his personal reputation declined. There was a repeated suggestion that the insignificance of some of the items in his collection (Charles Burney had called the *Description of Strawberry Hill* a 'minute catalogue of cups and saucers, and saucers without cups') reflected an essential insignificance or triviality in Walpole the man.[5] William Hazlitt suggested in a review of 1818, 'His mind, as well as his house, was piled up with Dresden china, and illuminated through painted glass; and we look upon his heart to have been little better than a case full of enamels, painted eggs, ambers, lapis-lazuli, cameos, vases and rock-crystals.'[6]

This assault on Walpole's reputation was most memorably expressed in Macaulay's famous *Edinburgh Review* review of 1833, which denigrated Walpole as eccentric, artificial, fastidious and capricious, and dismissed his collection as mere trinkets and curiosities that were without intrinsic merit:

> In his villa every apartment is a museum, every piece of furniture is a curiosity; there is something strange in the form of the shovel; there is a long story belonging to the bell-rope. We wander among a profusion of rarities, of trifling intrinsic value, but so quaint in fashion, or connected with such remarkable names and events, that they may well detain our attention

Figure 288. First title page, *A Catalogue of the Classic Contents of Strawberry Hill Collected by Horace Walpole* (London: Smith and Robins, 1842), 30.5 × 25 cm. The Lewis Walpole Library, Yale University. 485 842 C76 VII Copy 2. Cat. 269

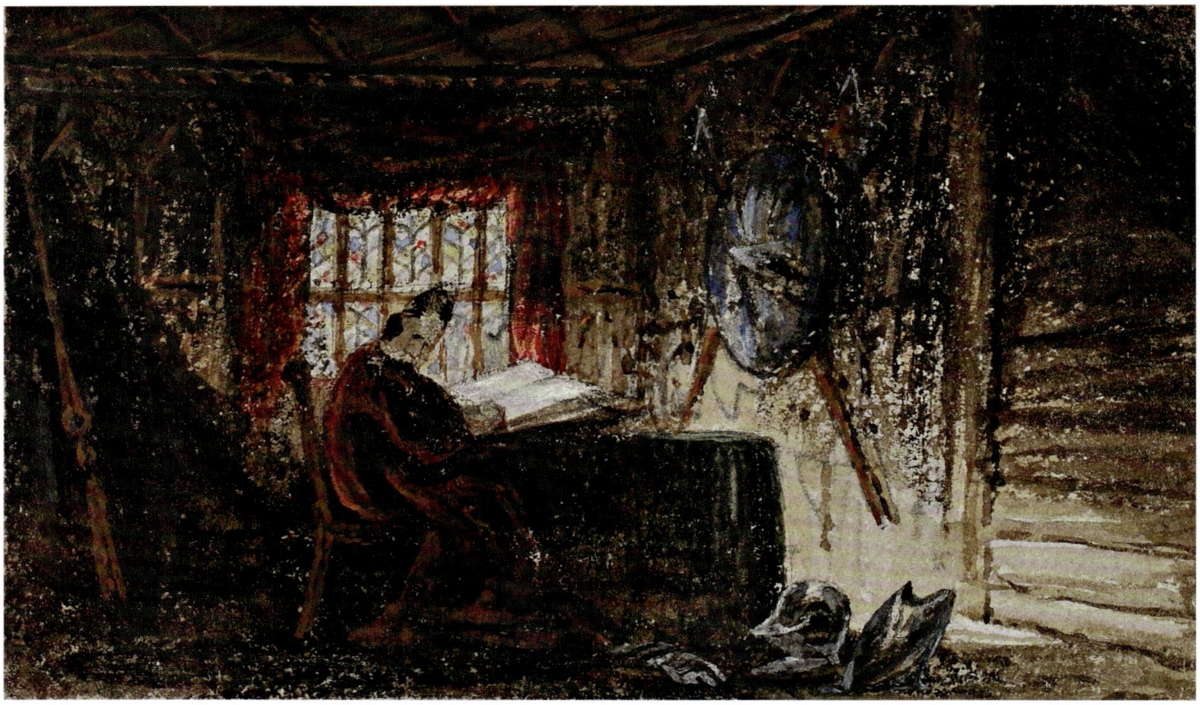

Figure 289. E. Bell and A. V., *Horace Walpole in his Study about the Year 1769*, *c.* 1842, watercolour, 5.3 × 9 cm, from Bell's copy of the *Strawberry Hill Sale Catalogue*. The Lewis Walpole Library, Yale University. 485 842 C76 V Copy 7 leaf 705

> for a moment. A moment is enough. Some new relic, some new unique, some new carved work, some new enamel, is forthcoming in an instant. One cabinet of trinkets is no sooner closed than another is opened. It is the same with Walpole's writings.[7]

But by the 1840s there were additional factors at work. The range of the collection was itself challenging and inconsistent with the more disciplined and differently structured art world that had evolved since Walpole's death. The world of Dr Sloane and the Duchess of Portland had been replaced by the world of Dr Waagen and of national art galleries. The amateur had been superseded by the scholar and the institution, and the great dispersal of paintings and other artwork triggered by the French Revolution and the Napoleonic wars had transformed what was collected and how it was acquired. The variety of Walpole's holdings – the mixture of Old Masters and modern paintings, of classical and English antiquities – did receive occasional acknowledgement, and the *Athenaeum* noted that 'no collector-like narrow-spirited mania confined his spirit to that school or t'other … his taste … ranged from Raffael and Holbein to Reynolds and Hogarth, from gothic to classic, from architecture to gardening, from books, manuscripts, coins, cameos, and armour, to household furniture and conveniences of every day life.'[8] But this response was unusually uncritical, and his collection was more commonly dismissed as a sealed cabinet of curiosities from the previous century, as can be inferred from a watercolour bound into an expanded and extra-illustrated copy of the catalogue of the 1842 sale, which purports to show Walpole in his study in the role of an antiquary (Fig. 289). It is a small, densely painted amateur vignette that bears no resemblance to Walpole or to any interior at Strawberry Hill; a far cry from the precise and controlled 1756 drawing by Johann Heinrich Müntz of Walpole in his Library, it owes rather more to images of Walter Scott at Abbotsford, with perhaps a touch of the Monk's Parlour at Sir John Soane's Museum.[9]

Meanwhile, the family circumstances of the Waldegraves that precipitated the sale were far from auspicious. By 1835 the estate was in the hands of John, the epileptic, alcoholic and illegitimate grandson of Walpole's great niece. In 1839 John married that extraordinary phenomenon, Frances Braham (who was ultimately to transform herself into the Victorian political hostess Lady Waldegrave), and they lived in a somewhat unconventional and financially rackety ménage with John's brother George, the 7th Earl Waldegrave. John died in 1840 at the age of

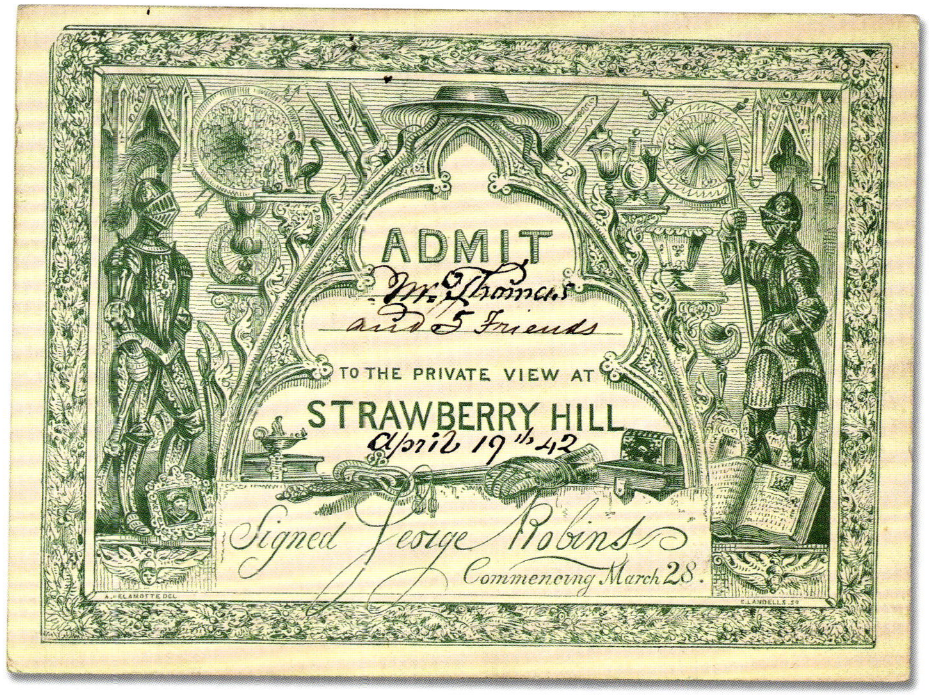

Figure 290. Admission Ticket for the Private View at Strawberry Hill, 1842, letterpress, 11.6 × 15.2 cm. The Lewis Walpole Library, Yale University. File 485 842 A19 Copy 1. Cat. 271

twenty-six, and five months later Frances married his brother George, who in turn was to die of cirrhosis within six years, at the age of thirty. In the mean time he spent six months in prison in 1841 for assaulting a police constable after a fracas at Kingston fair and, following his release that November, financially embarrassed and disenchanted with Twickenham and its bench of magistrates, he renewed a resolution he had made the previous year to sell Strawberry Hill. William Beckford's agent Robert Hume reported: '<u>He</u> and <u>She</u> rise at 5 – Breakfast at 7 – dine at 10 and are Drunk by 2 – with a regularity equal to the Steps of Time Himself.'[10] The contrast between the fastidious and self-possessed Walpole and the dissolute family wreckage of 1842 could not have been more complete.

Lord Waldegrave instructed as his auctioneer George Robins. 'The Martel of Covent Garden' had over forty years' experience on the rostrum and had acquired a reputation for showmanship and extravagant publicity, delivered with an engaging cockney vulgarity. As the *Illustrated London News* was to explain in an article following Robins's death in 1847:

> The wonderful skill and tact with which every advantage connected with the property he had to describe was seized upon and turned to profit, in his glowing descriptions and his ready wit and *repartee* in the rostrum, are well known. His announcements were unlike those of any of his contemporaries.[11]

Robins recorded in a note how he was introduced to Lord Waldegrave by a friend who

> succeeded with the noble Earl in making him believe that he would arrive at a great result by placing this important Sale to my care.

He acknowledged that

> the materials brought forward might have been very easily introduced in better taste if they had been in more able hands – If there is one thing that I may claim to commend in myself, it is this. I gave to this Sale a degree of publicity that is without any parallel case – there is nothing upon record to approach it, and I allude to this with the more satisfaction because it enabled me to atchieve [*sic*] a result as it regards the Amount of Sale that I may well be proud of.

And proud he certainly was: in a fourteen-page pamphlet produced by him after the sale, a *Condensed History* of the estates and property he had sold at auction between 1815 and 1842, he announced that he had sold over £11,470,000 of property and over 700,000 acres – both price and acreage are given in capital letters and each followed by six exclamation marks. And the penultimate item in the list of 'Splendid Miscellaneous Property over which Mr Robins has presided', and with the biggest result, was Strawberry Hill.[12]

After an initial announcement and postponement in 1841, Robins resumed placing suitably grandiose advertisements for the sale in the press in February 1842. Robins was

> honoured by having been selected by the Earl of Waldegrave to sell by public competition … the contents of Strawberry Hill; wherein will be found a repast for the lovers of literature and the fine arts, of which bygone days furnish no previous example, and it would be vain to contemplate it in times to come. This classical depository of all that is rare includes the most beautiful specimens of every known manufacture throughout the whole civilised world.[13]

Tickets were printed for a private view commencing on 28 March; the public was

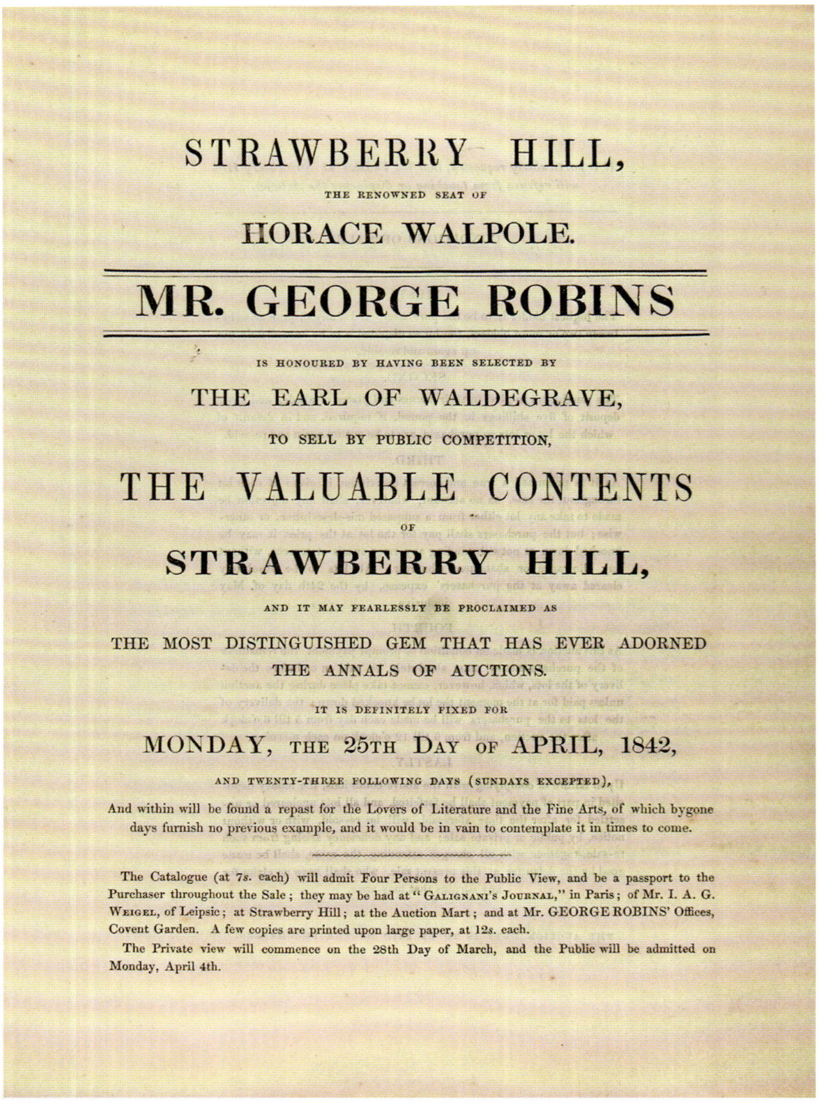

STRAWBERRY HILL,

THE RENOWNED SEAT OF

HORACE WALPOLE.

MR. GEORGE ROBINS

IS HONOURED BY HAVING BEEN SELECTED BY

THE EARL OF WALDEGRAVE,

TO SELL BY PUBLIC COMPETITION,

THE VALUABLE CONTENTS

OF

STRAWBERRY HILL,

AND IT MAY FEARLESSLY BE PROCLAIMED AS

THE MOST DISTINGUISHED GEM THAT HAS EVER ADORNED THE ANNALS OF AUCTIONS.

IT IS DEFINITELY FIXED FOR

MONDAY, THE 25TH DAY OF APRIL, 1842,

AND TWENTY-THREE FOLLOWING DAYS (SUNDAYS EXCEPTED),

And within will be found a repast for the Lovers of Literature and the Fine Arts, of which bygone days furnish no previous example, and it would be in vain to contemplate it in times to come.

The Catalogue (at 7*s.* each) will admit Four Persons to the Public View, and be a passport to the Purchaser throughout the Sale; they may be had at "GALIGNANI'S JOURNAL," in Paris; of Mr. I. A. G. WEIGEL, of Leipsic; at Strawberry Hill; at the Auction Mart; and at Mr. GEORGE ROBINS' Offices, Covent Garden. A few copies are printed upon large paper, at 12*s.* each.

The Private view will commence on the 28th Day of March, and the Public will be admitted on Monday, April 4th.

Figure 291. Second title page to Strawberry Hill sale catalogue, 1842. The Lewis Walpole Library, Yale University. 485 842 C76 IV, copy 3, vol. I

admitted on 4 April, the Sale was fixed for 25 April and the twenty-three following days, and at the very end of March Robins issued the sale catalogue (Fig. 290).

The catalogue is one of the most familiar representations of the Strawberry Hill collection, as it is of nineteenth-century auction sales generally. It used extravagant typography on its title page and also in the text (Fig. 291). This was hardly excessive by Robins's standards: his auction catalogue for Erlestoke Park ten years earlier had boasted a printed title of comfortably over 700 words, densely covering two full pages. Nonetheless, the Strawberry Hill catalogue had small and large capitals, bold and italics scattered profusely to emphasize the importance of the lots, and the descriptions were exercises in overwrought hyperbole. Robins introduced the catalogue with 'Prefatory Remarks' written in a splendidly inflated style, describing his Herculean undertaking in 'the distribution of this precious museum … far exceeding in interest and importance all that has preceded it in the chronicles of auctions'.[14] The catalogue had a frontispiece print of Walpole and, in addition to the printed title page, a wood-engraved title piled up with images of some of the more famous lots (Fig. 288). This emphasized the miscellaneous antiquarian element of the collection and, in its heaping together of particular treasures, was reminiscent of the engraved frontispiece to the sale catalogue of the Duchess of Portland's Museum of 1786, at which sale Walpole had acquired some especially prized items. Robins also incorporated into the Prefatory Remarks an article by the historical novelist Harrison Ainsworth, illustrated by wood engravings from drawings by W. Alfred Delamotte.[15] The cataloguing of lots was inadequate and inaccurate, and was much criticized. *The Times*, ever hostile to the sale, claimed that it was abounding with blunders, drawn up in a very inferior manner and 'not amongst the least of the curiosities' of the sale.[16] The blunders (and popular demand) led to the printing of seven separate editions of the catalogue, as Robins vainly tried to correct the text, though the books of prints from the Round Tower listed for the seventh and eighth days of the sale were so badly catalogued that they were withdrawn from the sale and auctioned separately in London.[17] When the elderly and experienced printseller and auctioneer Thomas Dodd re-catalogued these two days for the London sale, he expanded 305 lots to 1,331 and two days to ten. But for all its shortcomings, Robins's catalogue listed the collection as he found it, room by room, including the books in the Library shelf by shelf, and is thus of enormous importance in reconstructing how the collection was arranged.

The portentous extravagance of the catalogue invited parody and duly received it. This included a squib by Alfred Crowquill [Alfred Henry Forrestier] in *Bentley's Miscellany* and in John Mills's novel *D'Horsay, or, the Follies of the Day* (1844), in which Robins and Strawberry Hill featured as George Bobbins and Raspberry Hill.[18] But the most effective of the satires was *Gooseberry Hall* by the Irish writer Thomas Crofton Croker. This mimics the typography of Robins's Strawberry Hill sale catalogue in its title page (Fig. 292) and then mercilessly mocks Robins's Prefatory Remarks to the sale catalogue, transforming them into 'Puffatory Remarks'. The boast that the sale would be 'the most distinguished gem that has ever adorned the annals of auctions' is twisted into 'the most brilliant feather that has ever adorned the cap of an auctioneer', while the Earl of Bath's flattering Ballad of Strawberry Hill, a parody of which had already appeared in the *Illustrated London News*, was parodied again as the Earl of Noodleton's Ballad on Gooseberry Hall. The Gooseberry Hall collection is described as comprising

> Paintings by the most eminent Artists, many of whose names we are unacquainted with, – Carvings, Chasings, Crockery, and cracked China: – Roman and Greek Antiquities, designed by the revered *Old Gooseberry* himself, and executed under his direction at a most lavish expence: – a costly Library, containing books in every known language, and several in unknown languages: in various bindings, and some in no bindings at all: – legible, eligible, and illegible MSS. – Prints – Drawings - - and every object that can interest the Bibliomaniac, and all other Maniacs.

These parodies are only a small sample of the enormous volume of periodical literature occasioned by the sale. William Strange issued a cheap reprint of Walpole's *Description* to assist visitors to the sale preview, and numerous journals commented on the sale. The *Illustrated London News* and the *Magazine of Fine Arts* were complimentary; the *Morning Post* reflected on the malice and ignorance of *The Times* before 'the legacy, above all price, of this wonderfully gifted man'; the *Athenaeum* was generally approving of the wide range of the collection and appreciated how the sum of the whole was greater than the occasionally trifling items that made up the parts, and the *Gentleman's Magazine* was more detailed and detached in its six-part survey of the collection.[19] One untraced journal facetiously questioned whether the stick used by Lord Waldegrave to crack the police constable's skull might not be one of the lots.[20] But *The Times* was isolated in its unremitting hostility to the sale: Strawberry Hill was 'this dusthole of the *débris* of semi-barbarism and bad taste', which showed 'how a rich man may fool away his time in the collection of gewgaws, gimcracks, trinkets, and trumpery trifles'; even Walpole's much prized Boccapadugli eagle was 'in our judgement, a very common-place sort of bird'.[21]

Certainly the combination of items of association – such as Cardinal Wolsey's hat and John Hampden's wife's wedding gloves – and the optimistic attributions of some of Walpole's prized treasures were material issues for the journals of the day. Doubts were expressed, for example, about the Cellini bell, which was described by a visitor to the sale who annotated his copy of the catalogue, the collector J. Hughes Anderdon, as having a bluish tint and a hardness more like a cast, while the *Athenaeum* suggested that the bell and its handle might be separate items. The attribution of the illuminated psalter to Julio Clovio was

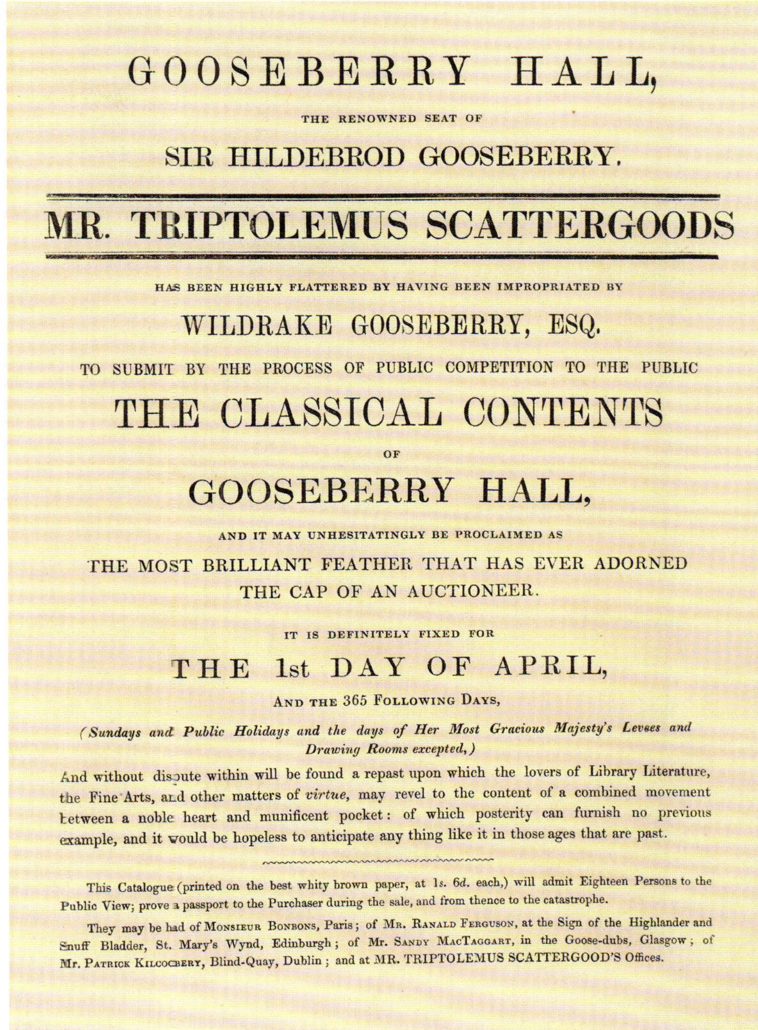

GOOSEBERRY HALL,

THE RENOWNED SEAT OF

SIR HILDEBROD GOOSEBERRY.

MR. TRIPTOLEMUS SCATTERGOODS

HAS BEEN HIGHLY FLATTERED BY HAVING BEEN IMPROPRIATED BY

WILDRAKE GOOSEBERRY, ESQ.

TO SUBMIT BY THE PROCESS OF PUBLIC COMPETITION TO THE PUBLIC

THE CLASSICAL CONTENTS

OF

GOOSEBERRY HALL,

AND IT MAY UNHESITATINGLY BE PROCLAIMED AS

THE MOST BRILLIANT FEATHER THAT HAS EVER ADORNED THE CAP OF AN AUCTIONEER.

IT IS DEFINITELY FIXED FOR

THE 1st DAY OF APRIL,

AND THE 365 FOLLOWING DAYS,

(Sundays and Public Holidays and the days of Her Most Gracious Majesty's Levees and Drawing Rooms excepted,)

And without dispute within will be found a repast upon which the lovers of Library Literature, the Fine Arts, and other matters of *virtue*, may revel to the content of a combined movement between a noble heart and munificent pocket: of which posterity can furnish no previous example, and it would be hopeless to anticipate any thing like it in those ages that are past.

This Catalogue (printed on the best whity brown paper, at 1*s.* 6*d.* each,) will admit Eighteen Persons to the Public View; prove a passport to the Purchaser during the sale, and from thence to the catastrophe.

They may be had of MONSIEUR BONBONS, Paris; of MR. RANALD FERGUSON, at the Sign of the Highlander and Snuff Bladder, St. Mary's Wynd, Edinburgh; of Mr. SANDY MACTAGGART, in the Goose-dubs, Glasgow; of Mr. PATRICK KILCOCBERY, Blind-Quay, Dublin; and at MR. TRIPTOLEMUS SCATTERGOOD'S Offices.

Figure 292. Title page to *Gooseberry Hall*. The Lewis Walpole Library, Yale University. 485 842 C76 IV, copy 3, vol. 1, fol. 113

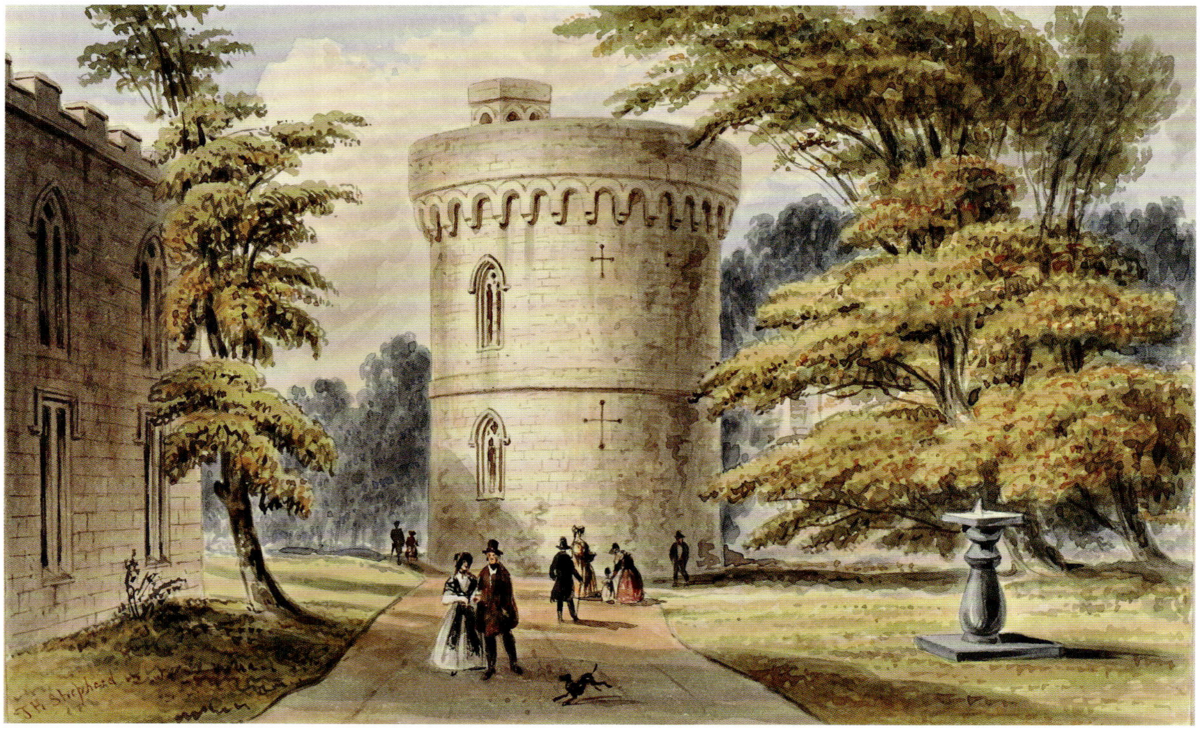

Figure 293. T. H. Shepherd, *View of the Round Tower at Strawberry Hill at the time of the Auction Sale*, 1842, watercolour, 13.8 × 21.7cm, from vol. 1 of Mackinlay's extended and extra-illustrated copy of the sale catalogue. The Lewis Walpole Library, Yale University. 485 842 C76 IV, copy 3, vol.1, fol. 124

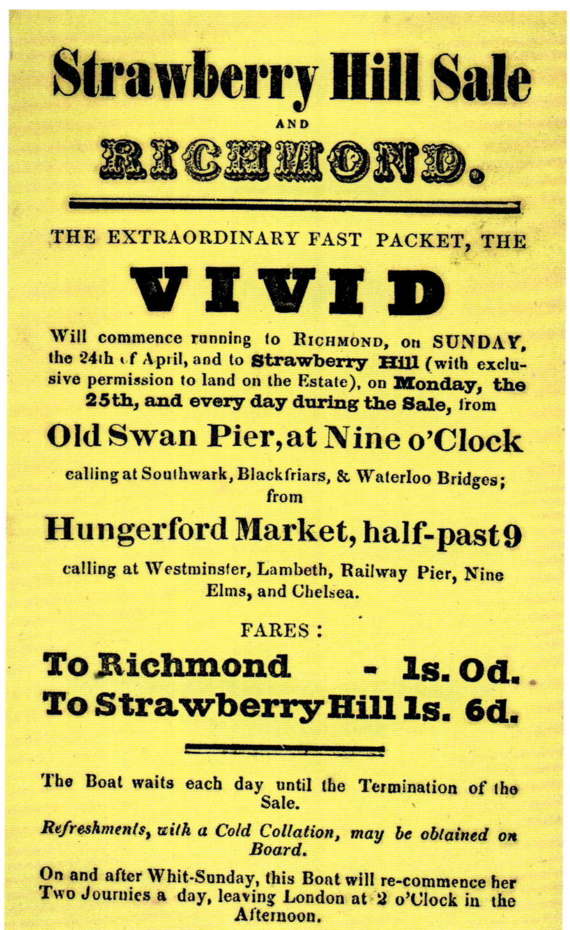

Figure 294. Handbill for 'The Extraordinary Fast Packet, the Vivid', 1842, letterpress, 19.3 × 11.5 cm. The Lewis Walpole Library, Yale University. 485 842 E96, copy 1. Cat. 272

questioned, and the sixteenth-century missal in a jewelled binding attributed to Raphael was dismissed as being 'as much by Raffael the painter as Raffael the archangel'.[22] There were also Walpole's historical English royal portraits, such as the marriages of Henry VI and of Henry VII, whose identity was widely questioned.[23]

But the fulminations of *The Times* did nothing to deter visitors to the view. A rival newspaper reported that 18,000 people attended the first fifteen days of the view and the *Morning Post* compared the level of public interest to 'the Fonthill Fever' that had raged at the time of Beckford's Fonthill Abbey sale in 1822 (Fig. 293).[24] Even *The Times* had to report that the roads from Twickenham and Teddington were almost blocked up with carriages and that on one day of the preview nearly a thousand people attended, and there were repeated complaints that the crowds in some of the rooms were so great that it was very hard to see the lots – one newspaper article deplored how 'the rooms are loaded, the walls groan under the weight' of the objects displayed.[25]

Visitors wishing to attend the sale could travel by boat: a handbill was printed for the packet *Vivid*, which took customers up the river from London

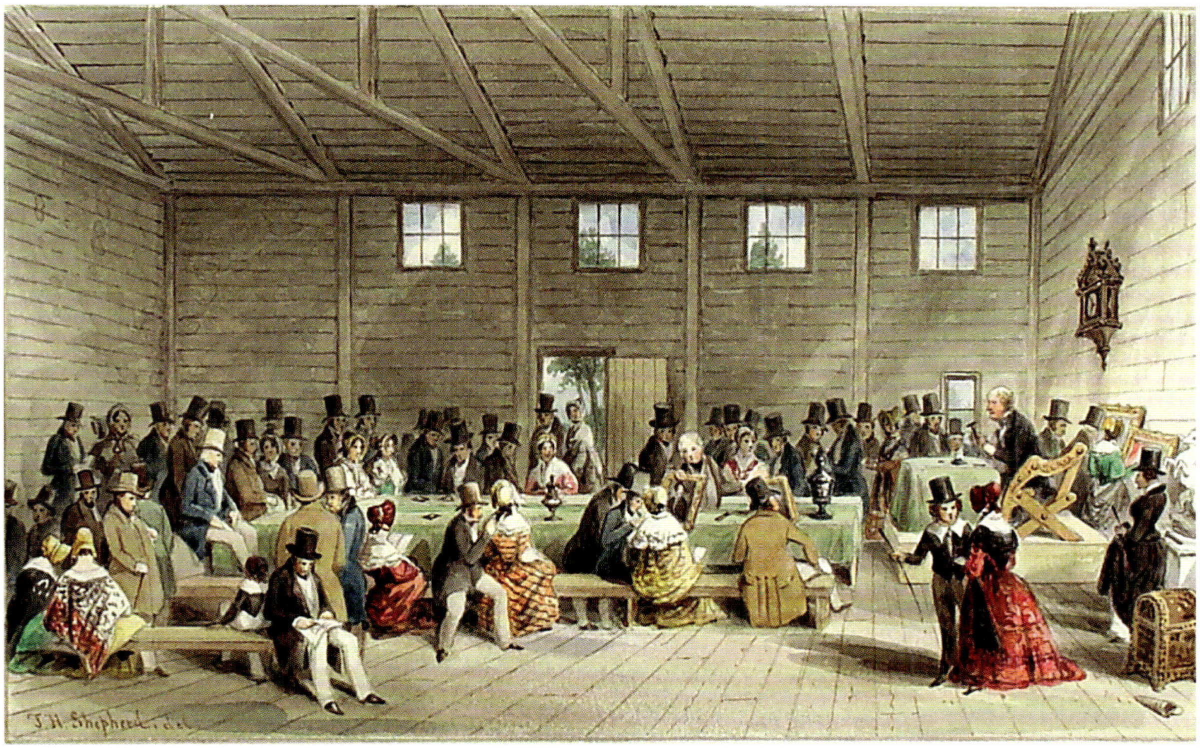

Figure 295. T. H. Shepherd, *Interior View of the Auction Room at Strawberry Hill*, 1842, watercolour, 11.2 × 17.2 cm, from vol. 1 of Mackinlay's extended and extra-illustrated copy of the sale catalogue. The Lewis Walpole Library, Yale University. 485 842 C76 IV copy 3, vol. 1, folio 127

and returned after the day's sale was over (Fig. 294). Advertisements were printed by dealers offering to bid for visitors: Mr Forster, who bid with George Robins's permission; Mr Browne of Richmond, who charged a shilling a lot; and Mr Whitaker, who offered to bid for clergymen and noblemen wishing to fit up churches, colleges or halls with stained glass, though most of the stained glass was bought in.

The Times lamented that 'the house looks wretchedly dirty, dilapidated, and deserted. It would almost appear that not a shilling had been expended upon it, or upon anything in it for half a century'.[26] Robins recognized that Strawberry Hill had no room of adequate size to house the sale, and commissioned Thomas Cubitt, the builder of much of Belgravia, to create an auction room in the grounds to the east of the house, 75 feet (22.9 m)

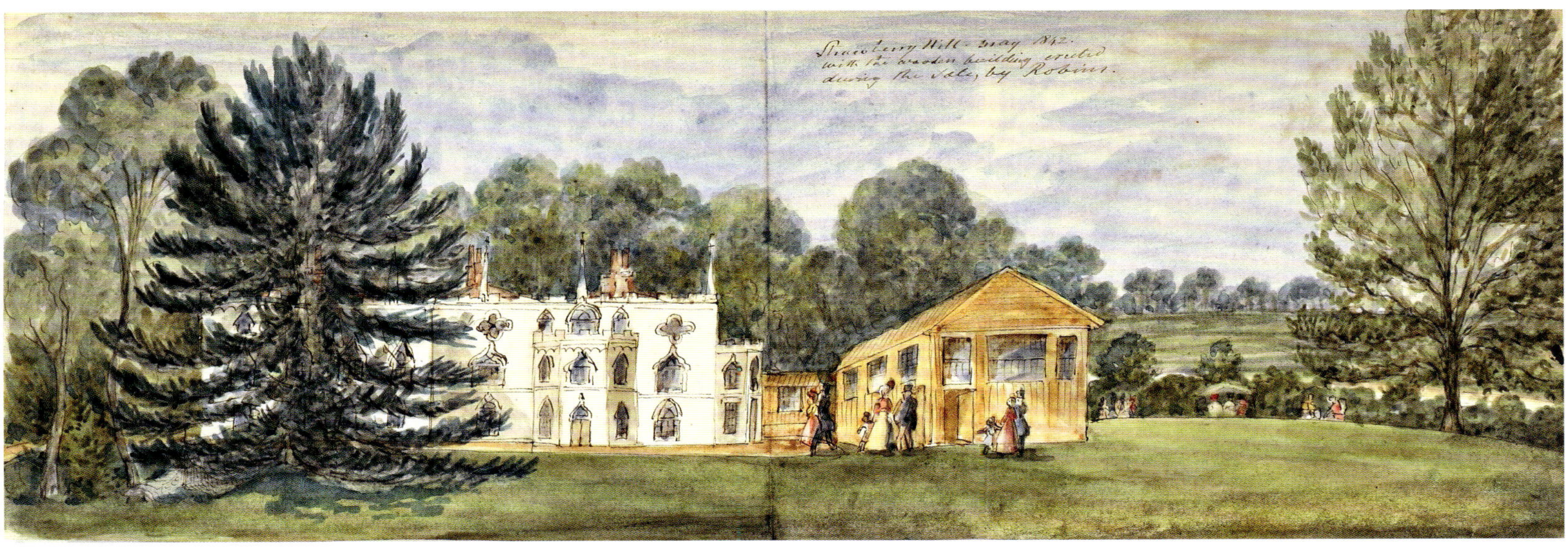

Figure 296. Artist unknown, *Strawberry Hill May 1842 with the wooden building erected during the Sale, by Robins*, 1842, watercolour with pen and ink, 12.7 × 36 cm. The Lewis Walpole Library, Yale University. 842.00.00.77dr

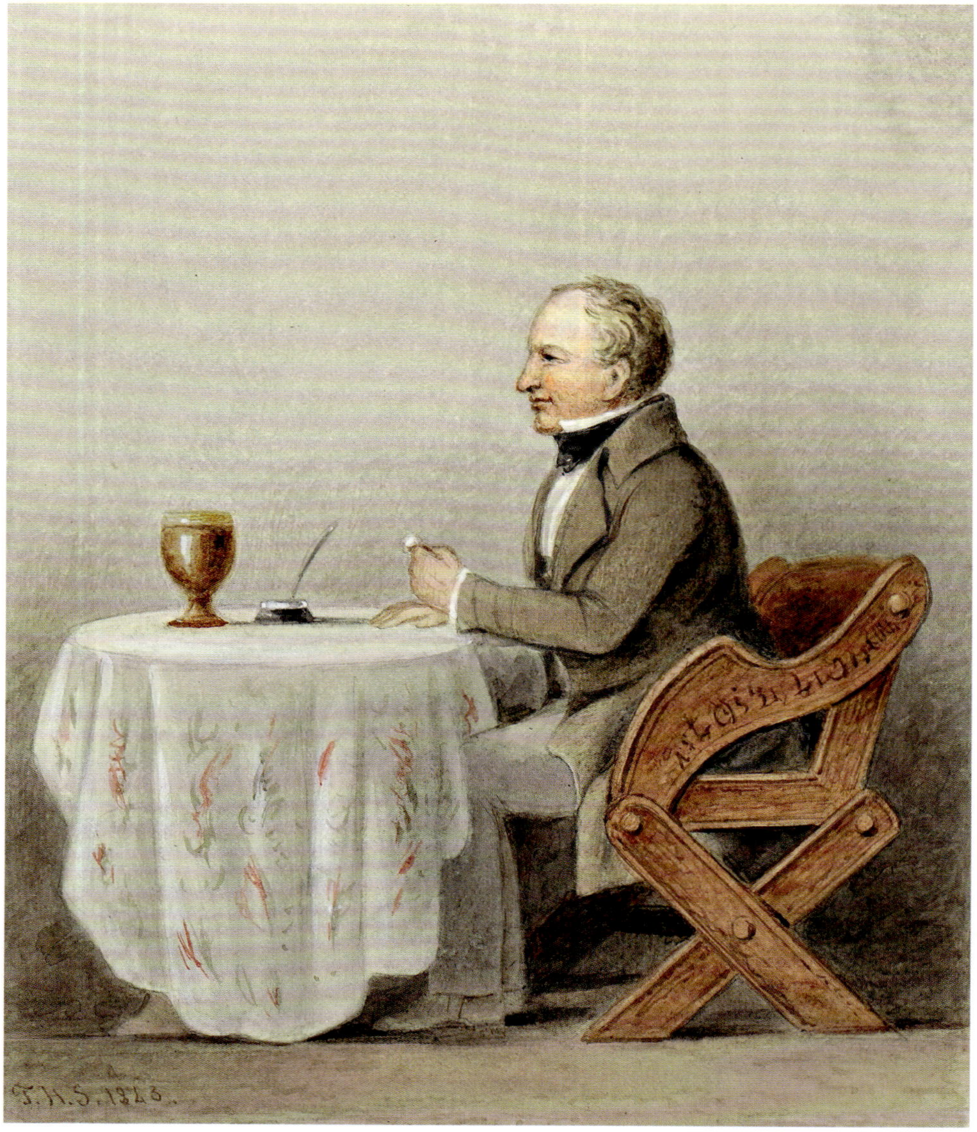

Figure 297. T. H. Shepherd, *George Robins Conducting the Sale from the Abbot of Glastonbury's Chair*, 1843, watercolour, 17.7 × 14.9 cm, from vol. 1 of Mackinlay's extended and extra-illustrated copy of the sale catalogue. The Lewis Walpole Library, Yale University. 485 842 C76 IV, copy 3, vol. 1, folio 161. Cat. 273

long and 40 feet (12.2 m) wide. It was able to hold about 700 people, though Anderdon suggested that the room was too dark and that this damaged the sale of the old portraits.[27] Contemporary watercolours survive showing both its exterior and interior with the sale in progress. Of these, the most accurate are the watercolours by T.H. Shepherd, though his external view does not show the connecting enclosed passage linking it to the house, which is visible in a charming unsigned watercolour titled *Strawberry Hill, May 1842, with the wooden building erected during the Sale, by Robins*, illustrating the auction room and house from the south with visitors to the auction strolling and possibly picnicking in the grounds.[28] (Figs. 295, 296) The contrast between Walpole's carefully controlled presentation of the house and the way in which it was now exposed 'to the vulgar stare of the multitude ... dissected, analyzed – catalogued and vulgarised as the theme of newspapers and topic of magazines' could not have been more marked.[29] Robins himself contributed to the social comedy, as recorded in a note by Anderdon. Seeing the great heiress Miss Burdett Coutts at the view, Robins followed her about:

> 'Look at this, Ma'am,' 'look at that! buy this!' and 'buy that' – 'If I was as rich as you, Ma'am, I'd buy it all' – 'what's a few thousands to you!' – The lady who is of shy & retired habits, and especially sensitive on the point so laboured by the individual who thus coarsely beset her, retired to her carriage and was unable to complete the view.[30]

Robins, 'the great Showman' (or, in the opinion of Sir Frederick Madden of the British Museum, 'impudent rascal'[31]), conducted the sale seated in the splendidly theatrical throne of the Abbot of Glastonbury's chair, from the Holbein Chamber, before a table covered with a piece of embroidered cloth of gold, on which was a handsome silver mounted cup (Fig. 297). *The Times* reported that he opened the sale with an unexpectedly brief statement that

> every lot was genuine, and precisely in the state in which it had been left by Horace Walpole; that he should have considered it sacrilege to have altered the arrangement or disposition of a single lot; and that those who did him the honour to bid should live for ever in his heart, and that he would charge them no rent for the tenancy,

and added laconically that the eloquence of this address produced good prices.[32] When the abbot's chair itself came up for sale, as lot 75 on the seventeenth day, Robins stipulated that the purchaser should consent to his continued occupation of it, until the close of the sale.[33] And it was not the only chair that participated in the auction as well as featuring as a lot. An Elizabethan armchair from the staircase hall was purchased by the Earl of Derby as the final lot on the seventeenth day of the sale for £21; a letter to the *Builder* identified the family arms with which it was decorated as belonging to Warburton of Cheshire, and noted how 'being occupied by the person who sold the Catalogue', the chair had 'escaped the observation of many of the numerous assemblage of visitors' (Fig. 298).[34]

The sale, following the catalogue, was structured almost topographically round the house. The first six days were devoted to the books – the first two days' sale were not particularly well attended, and nor was the fifth day's sale of books from the Library over the offices. After the lots of the seventh and eighth days were withdrawn for the subsequent London sale, days nine and ten were devoted to the coins and medals. The eleventh day was mostly pictures, including the Digby miniatures, and the next was china. Days thirteen and fourteen were cabinet pictures, drawings and miniatures from the Tribune, and so the auction progressed through the house. Many of the buyers were in the trade, particularly for books on the first six days and also for the china on the twelfth day, but there were also a substantial number of private buyers active throughout the sale. Among the major buyers were the Earl of Derby (numerous miniatures and other paintings, and Selima's fish tub, as immortalized in Gray's *Ode on the Death of a Favourite Cat*), John Dent (buying Tudor paintings and relics to adorn his restoration of Sudeley Castle) and Miss Burdett Coutts (who recovered from Robins's unwelcome advances to secure Digby miniatures, Petitot enamels, various intaglios and the Grinling Gibbons carved cravat). Lord Waldegrave bought in family portraits and major lots that failed to sell, such as the Raphael missal and the Cellini bell. The Revd Horace Cholmondeley, Colonel Damer and Wiggett Chute all bought items relating to their respective families. Queen Victoria, advised by Sir Robert Peel, acquired Anne Boleyn's silver-gilt clock and a portrait of Philip of Austria attributed to Holbein. Picture collectors such as Robert Holford and Lord Northwick were purchasers, and Charles Kean the actor fittingly carried away what was described as Henry VIII's dagger and also Cardinal Wolsey's hat. William Beckford was a particularly active buyer, using, as his agents, Hume for works of art, Bohn for books and Smith for prints. Beckford conducted a passionate correspondence with them, in which he confirmed his contempt for Walpole and for much of his collection, but also made transparently clear how desperately he wanted many of the lots for which he authorized bids.[35] He succeeded in carrying away the enamelled tazza after Parmigianino on day twelve, some pictures and old japan, numerous cameos and intaglios, including a cameo head of Tiberius on onyx ('the Tiberius is good – but not so decidedly fine greek as Namby-Pamby Walpole thought it' was Beckford's comment), and, to his great delight, on day fifteen the bronze bust of Caligula with silver eyes ('admirable!').[36]

In addition to the London sale of books of prints, which took place at Covent Garden on 13 June and the nine following days, Robins arranged on 12 and 13 July a third sale of essentially ordinary household furniture, but which also included 'the whole of the stone, timber and brickwork' of the Chapel in the Woods. As Robins encouragingly puffed, 'This beautiful pile is worthy the attention

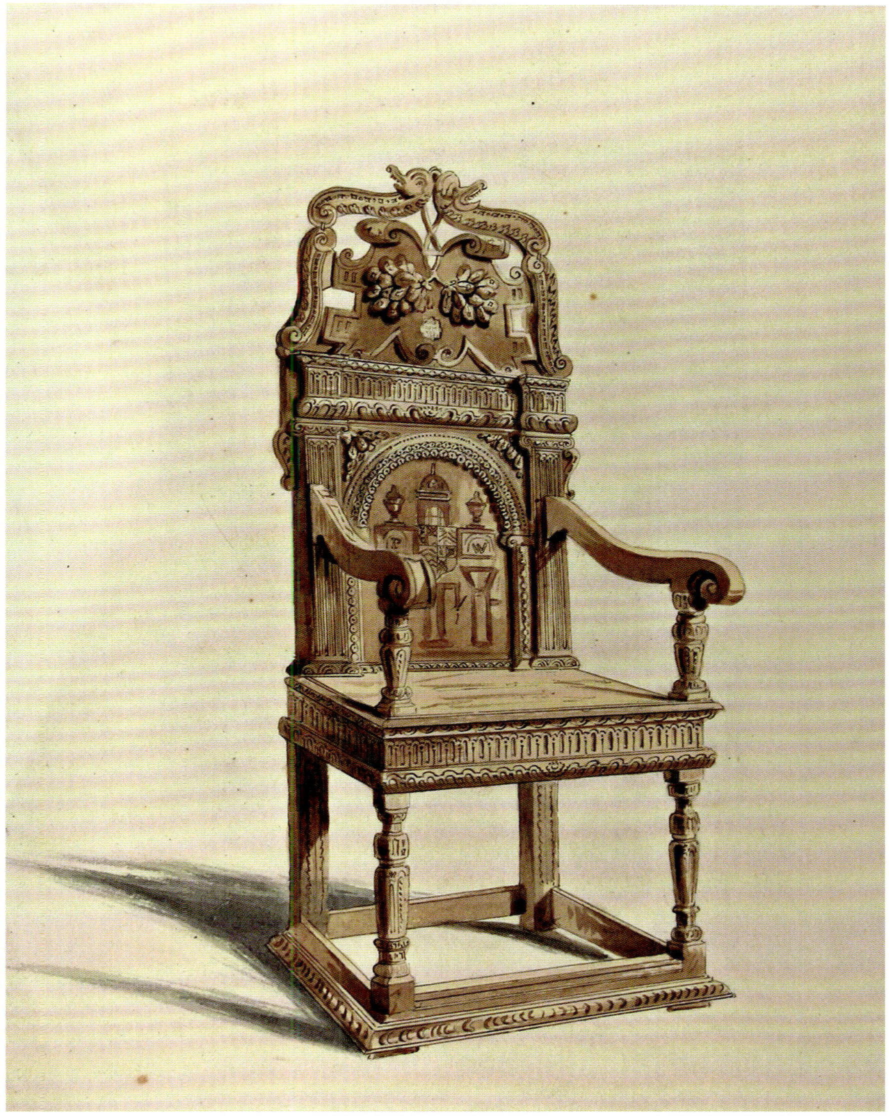

Figure 298. Artist unknown (C. J. Richardson?), *Elizabethan Armchair* (lot 117 on Day 17), cat. 1842, watercolour, 32.2 × 24 cm, from vol. 2 of Mackinlay's extended and extra-illustrated copy of the sale catalogue. The Lewis Walpole Library, Yale University. 485 842 C76 IV, copy 3, vol. 2, facing p. 178

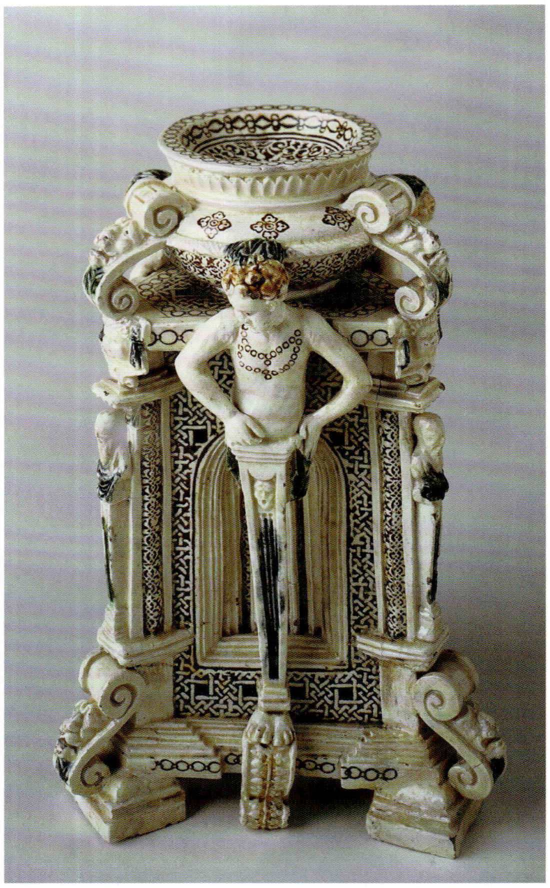

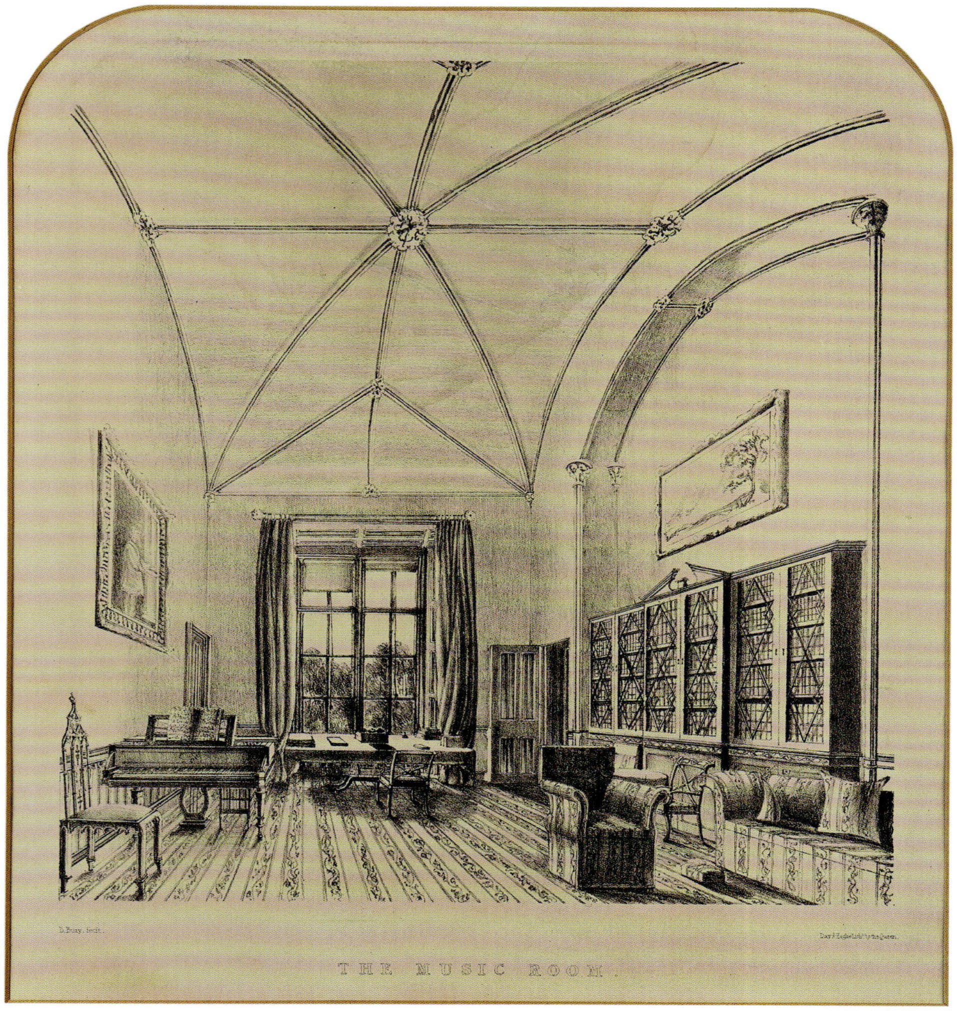

Figure 299. French (Saint-Porchaire or Paris), Salt, *c.* 1545–60, white-bodied earthenware, inlaid and glazed, H 16 cm. Taft Museum of Art, Cincinnati, Ohio. Bequest of Charles Phelps and Anna Sinton Taft. 1931.224

Figure 300. After Lady Beaujolais Bury, *The Music Room at Charleville Forest, County Offaly*, lithograph, 37.5 × 34 cm. The Knight of Glin

of all who may be desirous of possessing "An Hallowed Fane" within the precincts of their own demesne, as the removal and re-erection would be but a work of trifling consideration.' The lot was never reached, as the sale was so poorly attended that it was abandoned after a few lots were knocked down.[37]

As Robins claimed, the main sale at Strawberry Hill was generally a great success, though many complained of the high prices realized, including Beckford, who wrote of 'the egregious follies committed at this high-puff sale'.[38] The total achieved was some £33,450 11s. 9d, with a further £3,837 15s. 6d from the sale of books of prints in London. Lord Waldegrave's creditors were pacified, and Walpole's collection was scattered for ever across dealers' shops and collectors' cabinets and libraries. But despite Robins's triumph, the factors we have noted – the fulminations of *The Times*, the miscellaneous nature of Walpole's collection, the easily ridiculed items of association, the swiftly demolished attributions, and the criticisms of writers like Macaulay – cast something of a pall over the reputation of the sale, as over the reputation of Walpole himself. Allen Hazen has noted of the books at the sale how (inaccurately) 'the impression has persisted for a hundred years that prices were low', and curiously the well-informed George Redford, writing in 1888 in his survey of English art sales, expressed surprise that so little was said of the sale at the time, when in fact hardly a newspaper or journal failed to carry

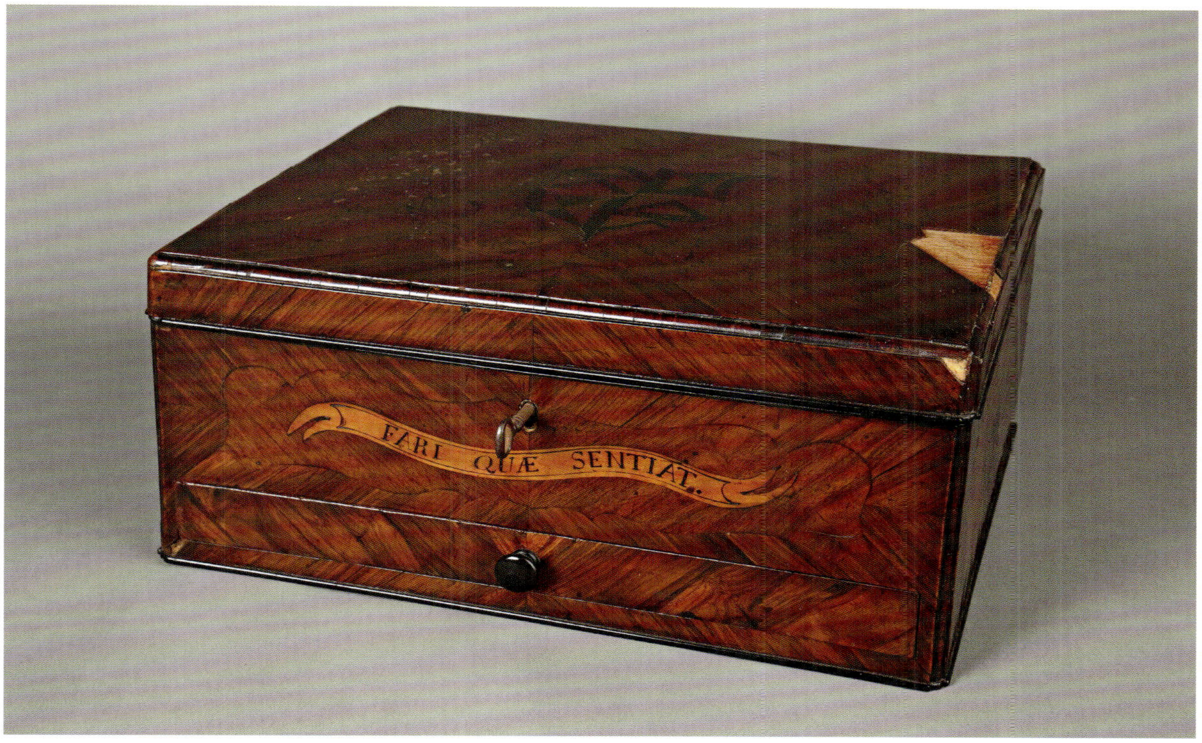

Figure 301. Pierre Eloy Langlois, Writing Box, 1760, veneer on a mahogany carcase, 13 × 29.5 × 22 cm. Josephine E. Case, James H. Case III, Samuel Case, John Case. Cat. 264

reports of it. *The Times*, despite its criticisms, reported almost daily on the lots sold and their prices, and a printed list of prices achieved was subsequently published for both the Strawberry Hill and London sales by J.H. Burn in the two issues of *Aedes Strawberrianae*.[39]

Walpole's reputation in the decades following the sale was at its lowest ebb. Macaulay's assessment of Walpole had become, as a reviewer noted in 1851, 'the general opinion', while in 1848 Abraham Hayward in the *Edinburgh Magazine* revived Hazlitt's trope of the 'quaint, curious, rich and rare repository' of Strawberry Hill as a metaphor for Walpole's mind, in which 'the rooms were deficient in size, proportion, and light; the furniture was more ornamental than useful'.[40] In 1853 John Fisher Murray reflected popular taste by noting how Walpole 'devoted the best part of his life to the collection and arrangement of whatever was curiously worthless', the collection being 'a museum of nick-nacks, rarities, and curiosities', and as for the house itself, 'a place more paltry does not exist'.[41]

There are scattered references to items from Strawberry Hill in accounts of collections and exhibition catalogues throughout the later nineteenth century, but these tend to be of the more obvious high spots. The Art Treasures exhibition held at Manchester in 1858, for example, displayed Anne Boleyn's bracket clock, the Introduction to the catalogue somewhat patronizingly describing Strawberry Hill as 'crammed full of works and curiosities of Art; apparently not devoid of interest to the public'.[42] Some of Walpole's prized objects came to rest in national museums, while nearly thirty appeared in the International Loan Exhibition at South Kensington in 1862, which included the sixteenth-century Saint-Porchaire salt from the China Room (Fig. 299). Generally, there are few nineteenth-century images of Strawberry Hill items in their new settings, though an exception is a lithograph after Lady Beaujolais Bury of the music room at Charleville Forest, County Offaly, where against the wall on the left can be glimpsed one of the Bentley chairs from the Refectory that the Earl Charleville had bought in 1842 (Fig. 300).

Some of the more modest lots from the sale have remained traceable precisely because of their identification with Walpole. One of his writing boxes, made by Peter Langlois and inlaid with the Walpole arms and motto and initials 'H.W. 1760'

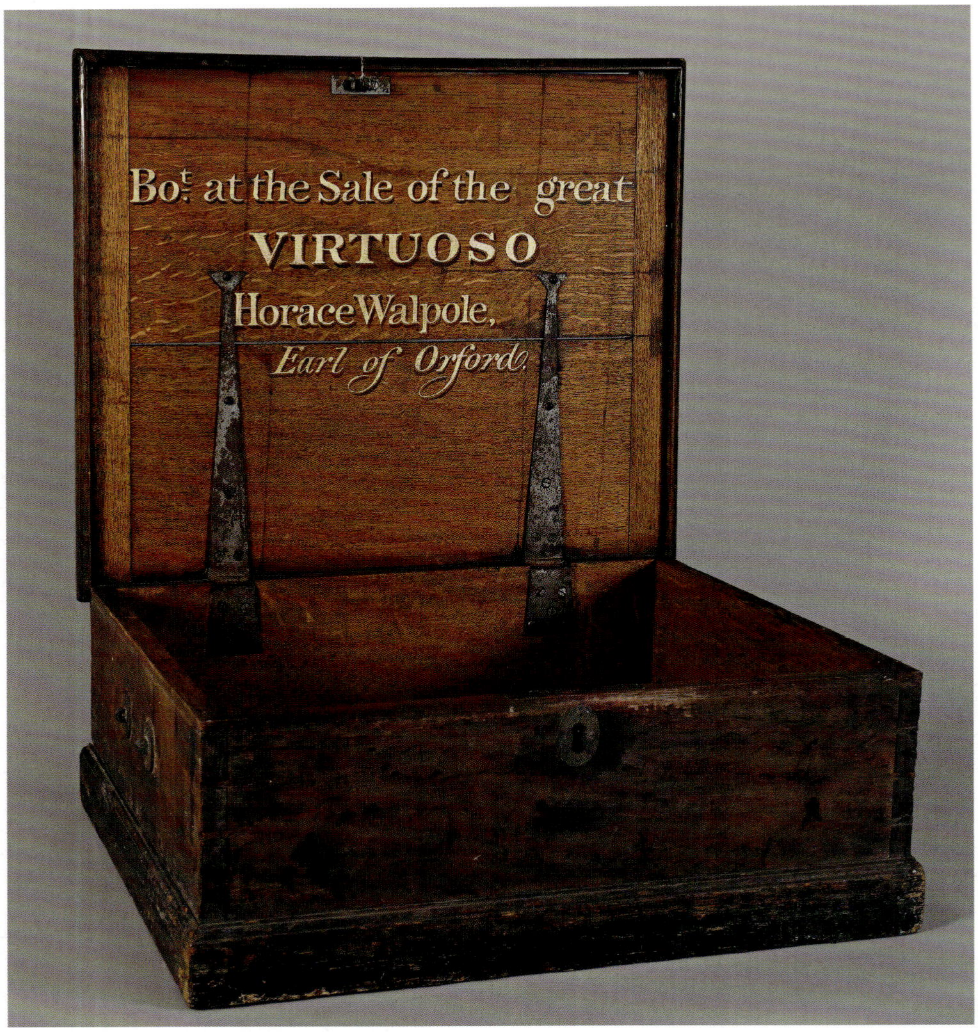

Figure 302. Oak Box, 18th century, 24.8 × 63.5 × 53.3 cm. The Lewis Walpole Library, Yale University. Cat. 275

on the back, had been kept by Walpole on the writing table in the Blue Bedchamber; when it came to be sold by the London bookseller Chas. J Sawyer in 1924, it was catalogued as 'A Fascinating Relic', implicitly pregnant with the sense of Walpole having used it to write some of his celebrated letters (Fig. 301). On a more utilitarian level, a particularly surprising survival is 'a stout wainscot box, lock and key', sold to the dealer Horatio Rodd with another box for ten shillings as lot six on day nineteen. This was then used to house the muniments of the Virtuosi Provident Fund, established in the year of the sale for the relief of picture dealers, printsellers, coin dealers, picture-restorers, and dealers in works of art, and their widows and children, when in necessitous circumstances – with Rodd as secretary. The fund's name is painted on the outside of the lid, while on its underside is painted the inscription 'B$^{ot.}$ at the Sale of the great VIRTUOSO Horace Walpole, Earl of Orford', the simple rough oak box creating an unlikely link between the exquisite, highly finished treasures of Strawberry Hill and the distressed members of the trade who participated in their dispersal (Fig. 302). The box now forms perhaps the most incongruous element in the extraordinary collection of Walpole's books, manuscripts and other treasures assembled at Farmington, Connecticut, by W.S. Lewis.

It may be fitting to conclude with one example of a particularly sympathetic reception of a Strawberry Hill item. John Dent has already been mentioned as a purchaser at the sale, his acquisitions including portraits and sculptures of Henry VIII, miniatures of some of Henry's wives, and even the Gothic lantern designed by Bentley for the hall at Strawberry Hill. In 1877 his heir's widow, Emma Dent, wrote in her *Annals of Winchcombe and Sudeley* an account of the miniature of Catherine Parr (who following the death of Henry VIII had married Lord Seymour of Sudeley Castle). She records how 'it is now preserved with the other Holbein miniatures, also from Strawberry Hill, of Sir Thomas and Jane Seymour, in the little apartment that still retains the name of "The Queen's Nursery"'.[43] The nursery at Sudeley is a heavily panelled confection of the mid-nineteenth century, a setting just as theatrical as the Tribune in which Walpole had displayed the miniature, if rather less subtle, and notwithstanding the confident assertion of Walpole and Emma Dent, doubts have recently been expressed about the attribution to Holbein. But in its appreciation of historical associations, of provenance and of setting (and despite a certain latitude in authenticity), the passage not only relates back to Walpolean ideas of presentation and the interaction of related objects but also looks forward to more modern assessments of Walpole as collector, where the range, depth and rich aesthetic and historical associations of Walpole's collecting achievement are widely celebrated, and what Macaulay recorded as failings and trivialities are seen as inherent strengths of the collection. For the Strawberry Hill sale, despite its extravagances, is itself merely one event in the provenance of the richly varied items that together formed an extraordinary collection.

1. *D 1784*, ii.
2. For a transcript of Walpole's will, see *HW Corres.* 30: 344–77, but particularly 352.
3. *Athenaeum*, 2 April 1842, 294.
4. For the activities of the Hardings see W.S. Lewis, *The Forlorn Printer* (Farmington: privately printed, 1931), 12.
5. *Monthly Review* 27 (Sept. 1798): 51–66, esp. 65.
6. *Edinburgh Review* 61 (Dec. 1818): 80–81.
7. *Edinburgh Review* 58 (Oct. 1833): 227–58, esp. 238.
8. *Athenaeum*, 9 April 1842, 317.
9. Watercolour signed 'E. B[ell]' and 'A.V.', laid onto leaf 705 of an extended and extra–illustrated copy of the sale catalogue with watercolours by E. Bell in the Lewis Walpole Library, 485 842 C76 V c7. See also Henry Stisted's painting of Scott in his armoury at Abbotsford, illustrated in Clive Wainwright, *The Romantic Interior: The British Collector at Home 1750–1850* (New Haven and London: Yale University Press, 1989), 173.
10. Letter from Robert Hume to William Beckford, 21 February 1842, Bodleian, Beckford Papers, c.22, 199.
11. *Illustrated London News*, 20 February 1847. For Robins see Robin Myers, 'George Henry Robins, Auctioneer', *The Printing Art* 1 (1973): 1–10; and 2 (1974): 8–17.
12. Note and pamphlet bound in after leaf 162 of vol. 1 of Thomas Mackinlay's extended and extra-illustrated copy of the sale catalogue at the Lewis Walpole Library, 485 842 C76 IV c3. Extending over four heavily grangerized volumes, this is the most important source of material on the sale. Mackinlay was a cousin of Robins whose help with notes of antiquarian research was acknowledged by him at the end of his Prefatory Remarks to the sale catalogue.
13. *The Times*, 31 May 1841 and 7 February 1842.
14. *1842 Sale*, v.
15. This also appeared in *Ainsworth's Magazine* 1 (1842): 100–107. There is a further article on the contents of Strawberry Hill on pp. 168–76.
16. *The Times*, 14 and 11 April 1842.
17. Percival Merritt, *An Account of Descriptive Catalogues of Strawberry Hill and of Strawberry Hill Sale Catalogues together with a Bibliography* (Boston: privately printed, 1915); see also A.T. Hazen, *A Catalogue of Horace Walpole's Library*, 3 vols. (New Haven and London: Yale University Press, 1969), 1: xxviii–xxx.
18. *Bentley's Miscellany* 7 (1842): 639–43.
19. *Illustrated London News*, 21 May 1842, 24–5; *The Magazine of Fine Arts*, 23 April 1842, 17–18; *Morning Post*, 13 April 1842; *Athenaeum*, 1842: 2 April, 293–4: 9 April, 317–19; 16 April, 340–42; 23 April, 363–4; *Gentleman's Magazine* 18 (n.s.), 1842: July, 16–24; August, 147–56; September, 257–65; October, 377–81; November, 474–80; December, 599–610. For a listing of accounts of the Strawberry Hill sale in *The Times* and in contemporary journals, see Peter Sabor, *Horace Walpole: A Reference Guide* (Boston: G.K. Hall, 1984), 41–5.
20. Newspaper cutting pasted beneath text of a copy of the *Illustrated London News* article on the sale, inserted among the preliminary cuttings in Thomas Crofton Croker's extended and extra-illustrated copy of the sale catalogue, LWL, 485 842 C76 VI c5.
21. *The Times*, 4, 11 and 7 April 1842. Robins wrote to *The Times* editor John Walter to complain of the coverage the sale had received; Walter's reply, date-stamped 14 April, refusing to interfere, is bound in as leaf 78 of vol. 1 of Mackinlay's copy of the sale catalogue. According to a note by J. Hughes Anderdon on page 121 of his copy of the sale catalogue (LWL 485 842 C76 I c4), a Dr Richardson wrote for *The Times*.
22. Note on p. 157 of Anderdon's copy of the sale catalogue; *Athenaeum*, 23 April 1842, 364; and 9 April 1842, 319.
23. *Athenaeum*, 9 April 1842, 317–19; *The Gentleman's Magazine*, 28 July 1842, 16–24; and *Notes & Queries*, 3rd series, 10 (28 July 1866): 61–2 See also Morris Brownell, *The Prime Minister of Taste: A Portrait of Horace Walpole* (New Haven and London: Yale University Press, 2001), 98–106.
24. Newspaper cutting laid in to leaf 1 of vol. 1 of Mackinlay's copy of the sale catalogue, quoted in W.S. Lewis, *Horace Walpole's Library* (Cambridge: Cambridge University Press, 1958), 48–9; *Morning Post*, 16 April 1842.
25. *The Times*, 4 and 7 April 1842; and article entitled 'An Hour at Strawberry Hill', laid into p. 11 of Bell's copy of the sale catalogue.
26. *The Times*, 29 March 1842.
27. Note on p. 132 of Anderdon's copy of the sale catalogue.
28. *Morning Chronicle*, 26 April 1842. The Shepherd images are on leaves 126 and 127 of vol. 1 of Mackinlay's copy of the sale Catalogue. There is also a watercolour of the interior of the sale room with the sale in progress and two drawings of the exterior in pen and wash by E. Bell on pages 69, 71 and 73 of Bell's copy of the sale Catalogue. A pencil sketch of the auction room in another copy of the sale catalogue also shows the connecting passage to the house (private collection).
29. *Court Journal*, 2 April 1842.
30. MS note laid in to face the title page of Anderdon's copy of the sale catalogue.
31. Diary of Sir Frederick Madden, Bodleian MS Eng. Hist. c. 155, entry for 5 May 1842.
32. *The Times*, 26 April 1842.
33. Note by Anderdon on p. 176 of his copy of the sale catalogue.
34. *Builder*, letter to the editor from C.J. Richardson, May 1844. The chair was lot 117.
35. See Stephen Clarke, '"All Ardour, all Intrepidity": William Beckford at the Strawberry Hill Sale', an analysis of the lots purchased by Beckford in *1650–1850: Ideas, Aesthetics and Inquiries in the Early Modern Era*, forthcoming.
36. Draft letter from Beckford to Robert Hume, 28 May 1842, Bodleian, Beckford Papers, c. 22, f. 220.
37. A copy of the household furniture sale catalogue is bound in at the end of vol. 4 of Mackinlay's copy of the sale catalogue. A manuscript note explaining how the sale was stopped was inserted in the copy of the sale catalogue belonging to the dealer Edward Browne of Richmond (private collection).
38. Letter, Beckford to Henry Bohn, 3 May 1842,

National Art Library, Victoria & Albert Museum, Forster Collection 48 F. 67, Bohn letter book.

39. Hazen, *Catalogue* 1: xxxiv; George Redford, *Art Sales 1628–1887*, 2 vols. (London, 1888), 1: 131; and *Aedes Strawberrianae. Names of Purchasers and the Prices to the Detailed Sale Catalogue of the Collections of Art and Vertû, at Strawberry-Hill, formed by Horace Walpole, Earl of Orford* [and] *Names of Purchasers and the Prices to the Detailed Sale Catalogue of the Collection of Early Drawings, Etchings, and Prints, Engraved Portraits of Eminent British Characters, Drawings and Rare Productions of Hogarth, Manuscripts and Works relative to the Fine Arts; withdrawn from Strawberry-Hill for Sale in London* (both London: J. H. Burn, 1842).
40. *Literary Gazette*, 17 May 1851, 339; *Edinburgh Review* 88 (Oct. 1848): 340.
41. J. Fisher Murray, *A Picturesque Tour of the River Thames in its Western Course* (London, 1853), 132–3.
42. J.B. Waring, ed., *Art Treasures of the United Kingdom from the Art Treasures Exhibition, Manchester* (London, 1858), 10.
43. Emma Dent, *Annals of Winchcombe and Sudeley* (London: John Murray, 1877), 181.

CATALOGUE

compiled by

CYNTHIA ROMAN with EMILY LANZA

CATALOGUE SECTIONS

NOTES TO THE READER

Most objects are from Horace Walpole's collection at Strawberry Hill. Exceptions from his lifetime are noted.

TITLES: those given first are current. Horace Walpole's titles, if significantly different, follow in parentheses. Titles in inverted commas are based on inscriptions on the work of art.

DIMENSIONS are given height, width, depth. Those given for paintings are for the canvas or panel exclusive of the frame unless otherwise indicated.

TRANSCRIPTIONS of Horace Walpole's text from *A Description of the Villa*... are given in full as *D 1774* and *D 1784*, with the page reference. Citations are from the last editions, with additions (see Bibliography, p. 351). The location of the item at Strawberry Hill is given in brackets whenever known. Spelling errors are maintained.

SALE TEXT is included if the object is not identified in the *Description*. This text is from the 6th edition (see Bibliography)

PRICES paid by Walpole, unless otherwise indicated, are from his own annotated copy of *D 1774* at the Lewis Walpole Library (49 2522A).

NAMES OF BUYERS and prices paid at the 1842 Strawberry Hill Sale are from the *Ædes Strawberrianae. Names of purchasers and the prices to the detailed sale catalogue of the collection ... withdrawn from Strawberry-Hill for sale in London* (London: J.H. Burn, 1842)

BIBLIOGRAPHY: these are selected references. References to HW's *Anecdotes of Painting* are to the 1st edition unless otherwise noted.

EXHIBITIONS: only 19th-century exhibitions are listed separately.

ABBREVIATIONS: in addition to those listed on p. viii, the following abbreviations are used in the catalogue:

1862 Special Exhibition: J. C. Robinson, ed., *Catalogue of the Special Exhibition of Works of Art of the Medieaeval, Renaissance, and more Recent Periods*, June 1862 (London, 1863), exh. cat., South Kensington Museum (June 1862)

Bentley illustrations: Loftus Jestin, *The Answer to the Lyre: Richard Bentley's Illustrations for Thomas Gray's Poems* (Philadelphia, 1990)

'Bentley thesis': Loftus Jestin, 'Richard Bentley the Younger, 1708–1782: A Critical Biography' (Ph. D. Thesis, Yale University, 1985)

'Genesis': W. S. Lewis, 'The Genesis of Strawberry Hill', *Metropolitan Museum Studies* 5, part 1 (1934)

Gothic Revival: Michael McCarthy, *The Origins of the Gothic Revival*, (New Haven and London, 1987), 81–4.

'Portraits': C. Kingsley Adams and W. S. Lewis, 'The Portraits of Horace Walpole', *The Walpole Society* 42 (1970)

Rescuing Horace: W. S. Lewis, *Rescuing Horace Walpole* (New Haven and London, 1978)

Romantic Interior: Clive Wainwright, *The Romantic Interior: The British Collector at Home 1750–1850* (New Haven and London, 1989)

'Strawberry Hill: Building and Site': Peter Guillery and Michael Snodin, 'Strawberry Hill: Building and Site', *Architectural History* 38 (1995)

1. INTRODUCTION

1. PORTRAIT OF HORACE WALPOLE
Joshua Reynolds (1723–1792), *c.* 1756–7

Oil on canvas, 127 × 101 cm
Marquess of Hertford, Ragley Hall, Warwickshire
Yale Center for British Art only
Fig. 3

PROV: Not Strawberry Hill Collection. Probably given by the sitter to his cousin, Francis Seymour Conway, 1st Marquess of Hertford; thence by descent.

LIT: 'Portraits': A.13.1, pl. 14. Ellis Waterhouse, *Reynolds* (London: Kegan Paul, Trench Trubner, 1941), 41, 43, 120. Nicholas Penny, *Reynolds* (New York: Abrams, 1986), no. 28. David Mannings, *Sir Joshua Reynolds: A Complete Catalogue of his Paintings*, 2 vols (New Haven and London: Yale University Press, 2000), no. 1821. John Ingamells, *National Portrait Gallery: Mid-Georgian Portraits, 1760–1790* (London: National Portrait Gallery, 2004), 369.

EXHIB: Worcester 1882, no. 62.

2. PORTRAIT OF HORACE WALPOLE
Joshua Reynolds (1723–1792), *c.* 1756–7

Oil on canvas, 127.2 × 101.8 cm
National Portrait Gallery, London. Purchased with help from the Heritage Lottery Fund, The Art Fund and the Dame Helen Gardner Bequest, 1999. 6520
Victoria and Albert Museum only

PROV: Not Strawberry Hill Collection. Apparently painted for Grosvenor Bedford (1708–71), the sitter's deputy as usher of the Exchequer; still in the Bedford family 1847, December 24, when Sir Robert Peel wrote to John Smith, dealer, declining to buy it; Lady Colum Crichton-Stuart; bt by 3rd Marquess of Lansdowne before the Grosvenor Charles Bedford sale of 1861; thence by descent until 1999 when acquired by private treaty sale from the Bowood Collection with assistance from the Heritage Lottery Fund, the NACF, and the Gallery's Helen Gardner Fund.

LIT: Ellis Waterhouse, *Reynolds* (London: Kegan Paul, Trench Trubner, 1941), 41. 'Portraits': A. 13.2, pl. 15. David Mannings, *Sir Joshua Reynolds: A Complete Catalogue of his Paintings*, 2 vols. (New Haven and London: Yale University Press, 2000), no. 1819. John Ingamells, *National Portrait Gallery: Mid-Georgian Portraits, 1760–1790* (London: National Portrait Gallery, 2004), 368–9. Martin Postle, ed., *Joshua Reynolds: The Creation of Celebrity*, exh. cat., Palazzo dei Diamanti, Ferrara and Tate Britain, London (London: Tate Publishing, 2005), no. 32.

3. STRAWBERRY HILL, TWICKENHAM, FROM THE SOUTH
Johann Heinrich Müntz (1727–1798), *c.* 1755–9

Oil on canvas, 61.9 × 74.3 cm
Inscriptions: early label on back of painting: 'Strawberry Hill Twickenham. Painted by John Henry Muntz who worked about 1755–1775. Was of Swiss origin & was brought to England from Jersey by Richard Bentley & introduced to Horace Walpole who employed him as a Painter & Engraver – He Exhibited at the Society of Arts in 1762–1763'.
The Lewis Walpole Library, Yale University
Fig. 18

PROV: Not Strawberry Hill collection. Earls Waldegrave; 1937, July, Col. M. H. Grant, Kensington, to W. S. Lewis, £200; The Lewis Walpole Library, Yale University.

LIT: *HW Corres*. 20: repro. opp. p. 380. *Collector's Progress*, repro. opp. p. 31. 'Building and Site': 102–28, fig. 14.

2. VISITING STRAWBERRY HILL

4. A View of Alexander Pope's House at Twickenham
Samuel Scott (1701/2–1772), *c.* 1759

Oil on canvas, 47.6 × 90.8 cm
The Lewis Walpole Library, Yale University
Fig. 23

D 1774, 28 [Green Closet]: Over the door, A view of Mr. Pope's house at Twickenham, painted since the alterations made by sir William Stanhope; by Scott in his very best manner.
D 1784, 23, same as *D 1774*.
PROV: Probably acquired from the artist by HW, £15.15.0 (Accounts); 1842, Strawberry Hill Sale, day 18, lot 69, bt in [Earl Waldegrave]; 1900, February 10, Christie's, Waldegrave Sale, lot 22, bt Colnaghi & Co.; property of William McKay; reappeared in London, in the possession of Mrs McKay; 1900, July 18, Robinson and Foster, lot 13, bt Colnaghi and Knoedler; 1940, December, Colnaghi bt W. S. Lewis, $1700; The Lewis Walpole Library, Yale University.
LIT: Hilda F. Finberg, 'Pope's Villa, Twickenham', *Burlington Magazine* 77, 452 (Nov. 1940): 168–70. R. Kingzett, 'A Catalogue of the Works of Samuel Scott', *Walpole Society* 48 (1980–2): 67 (d), pl. 26 (b). Greater London Council, *Alexander Pope's Villa, Views of Pope's Villa, Grotto and Garden: a Microcosm of English Landscape* (1980), no. 25.

5. North East View of Strawberry Hill, with Obelisk
James Malton (1761–1803), *c.* 1791

Watercolour on laid paper with wash-line mount, 29.9 × 42.4 cm
The Lewis Walpole Library, Yale University
791.00.00.39dr
Fig. 26

PROV: Not Strawberry Hill Collection. 1929, October, purchased from Parsons (with other drawings) by W. S. Lewis, £69; The Lewis Walpole Library, Yale University.
LIT: Mellon Lectures, no. 38.
NOTE: There is an almost identical watercolour view by Joseph Charles Barrow also at The Lewis Walpole Library, Yale University. The verso is inscribed in HW's hand: 'View of Strawberry hill from the road, by Barrow, 1789.' (49 3582, fol. 7.); and two other watercolours of the same prospect, one by an unknown artist inscribed in HW's hand on mount: 'Approach to Strawberry Hill' (49 3582, fol. 10); and the second attributed to John Carter and inscribed on the wash-line mount: 'General view coming from Twickenham, looking S.W'. (Lewis Walpole Library, Yale University. 33 30, copy 11).

6. 'Strawberry Hill'
Edward Edwards (1738–1806), 1783

Watercolour and pen and ink on laid paper with wash-line mount, 30.8 × 25.9 cm (visible); 37.2 × 32 cm (mount)
Signed and dated on the wash-line mount: 'E. Edwards. 1783'
Inscriptions: title on wash-line mount
The Lewis Walpole Library, Yale University, Folio 49 3582 fol. 20
Fig. 280

From HW's extra-illustrated copy of *D 1784*, fol. 20.
1842 Sale and *London Sale*: see cat. no. 60.
PROV: Commissioned by HW; for the volume see cat. no. 60.
LIT: *HW Corres.* 29: 150n. *Library* 3582. Bamber Gascoigne and Jonathan Ditchburn, *Images of Twickenham with Hampton and Teddington* (Richmond-upon-Thames: Saint Helena Press, 1981), no. 279 for the print.
NOTE: The drawing shows a view from the north east. It was made into an etching by Edwards in 1785.

7. The North and West Fronts of Strawberry Hill
William Marlow (1740–1813) 1776–80

Watercolour, 32.5 × 52.3 cm
Victoria and Albert Museum, London. W. A. Sandby Bequest D.1834–1904
Victoria and Albert Museum only
Fig. 27

PROV: 1900, February 10, Christie's, Ld Waldegrave Sale, bt W. A. Sandby; [1904], Bequeathed to the Victoria and Albert Museum.
LIT: *OHG* 45.

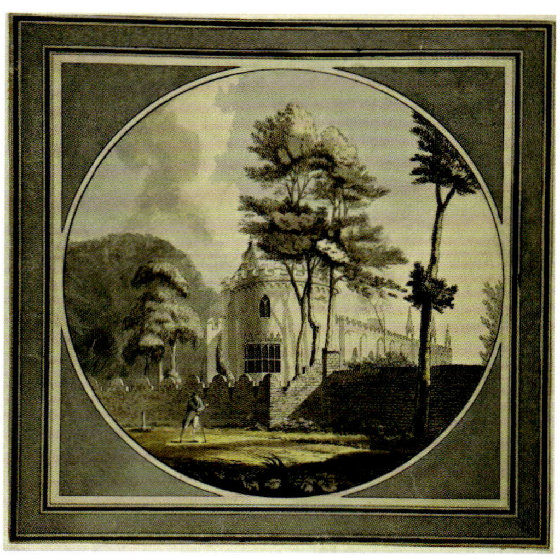

Figure 303. Catalogue 8

8. West Front of Strawberry Hill
Joseph Charles Barrow (fl. 1789–1802), 1788

Signed and dated: 'J. C. Barrow 1788'
Watercolour, D 23 cm, wash mount 34 × 34 cm
Private collection
Victoria and Albert Museum only
Fig. 304

PROV: General George Thomas Colomb (born at Strawberry Hill, son of HW's valet Philip Colomb); by descent to Rupert Colomb; by family descent; private collection.
LIT: 'Genesis': 57–92 for related image. Mellon Lectures, no. 69 for related image.
NOTE: Another version of this drawing also by Barrow is at the Lewis Walpole Library, Yale University (33 30 copy 11, fol. 15).

9. 'Strawberry Hill'
Edward Edwards (1738–1806), 1781

Pen and ink and watercolour on laid paper with wash-line mount, 19 × 13.5 cm (visible); 23.6 × 17.8 cm (mount)
Signed and dated on wash-line mount: 'E.E. 1781'
Inscriptions: title on the wash-line mount
The Lewis Walpole Library, Yale University. Folio 49 3582 fol. 23
From HW's extra-illustrated copy of *D 1784*, fol. 23.

PROV: Commissioned by HW; for the volume see Cat. 24.
LIT: 'Genesis': fig. 9 for the related etching. *HW Corres.* 29: 150n. *Library* 3582. Bamber Gascoigne and Jonathan Ditchburn, *Images of Twickenham with Hampton and Teddington* (Richmond-upon-Thames: Saint Helena Press, 1981), no. 291 for the print.
NOTE: Edwards's view was engraved by John Newton for *D 1784*, facing p. 2, as *Entrance of Strawberry Hill.*

10. 'Strawberry Hill chiefly taken in the year 1769 by Mr. Sandby'
Paul Sandby (bap. 1731, d. 1809), *c.* 1769

Watercolour on laid paper with wash-line mount, 39.2 × 75.7 cm (visible); 46.3 × 82.5 cm (mount)
Inscriptions: title in HW's hand on verso, now obscured by later mount but recorded by W. S. Lewis; on mount: 'Pa. Sandby'
The Lewis Walpole Library, Yale University. 769.00.00.77dr++
Fig. 102

PROV: Commissioned by HW; 1962, January, purchased by W. S. Lewis from Arthur U. Newton Galleries, $2000 for the pair (see cat. no. 24); The Lewis Walpole Library, Yale University.
LIT: *HW Corres.* 2: 248; 3: 575–6 (for the print). W. S. Lewis, *A Guide to the Life of Horace Walpole*

(New Haven: Yale University Press, 1973), no. 3. Bamber Gascoigne and Jonathan Ditchburn, *Images of Twickenham with Hampton and Teddington* (Richmond-upon-Thames: Saint Helena Press, 1981), no. 272 for the print.

NOTE: The watercolour was engraved for *D 1784*, probably by Richard Bernard Godfrey as East Front of Strawberry Hill. The print was produced by 1774. A reduced variant by Sandby is at the Lewis Walpole Library, Yale University (769.00.00.79dr). HW's receipt dated 1774, August 14, for payment of 25gns to Richard Godfrey for engraving two large views of Strawberry Hill for original drawings of Mr Sandby's is at the Lewis Walpole Library, Yale University.

11. SOUTH FRONT OF STRAWBERRY HILL
Paul Sandby (bap. 1731, d. 1809) *c.* 1769

Watercolour on laid paper with wash-line mount, 39 × 76.1 cm (visible); 45.7 × 82.9 cm (sheet)
The Lewis Walpole Library, Yale University. 769.00.00.78dr++
Fig. 103

PROV: Commissioned by HW; 1962, W. S. Lewis purchased from Arthur U. Newton Galleries, $2000 for the pair (see Cat. 10); The Lewis Walpole Library, Yale University.

LIT: *Rescuing Horace*, ill. p. 92. *OHG*, 41 for the print. Bamber Gascoigne and Jonathan Ditchburn, *Images of Twickenham with Hampton and Teddington* (Richmond-upon-Thames: Saint Helena Press, 1981), no. 288 for the print.

NOTE: Engraved for *D 1784*, probably by Richard Bernard Godfrey as *South Front of Strawberry Hill*. See Cat. 10 for the receipt. For a reduced variant by Sandby see *OHG* 40.

12. 'EAST VIEW OF STRAWBERRY HILL NEAR TWICKENHAM IN MIDDLESEX'
Johann Heinrich Müntz (1727–1798), 1758

Pen and ink and blue wash with pencil on laid paper, 23.5 × 29.4 cm
Signed and dated: 'J. H. Muntz 1758'
Inscriptions: on recto: by the artist, title in ink at bottom; on verso in ink: 'Strawberry hill en Middlesex maison de Campagne de Mr. Horace Walpole'; and extensive pencil notations in French
The Lewis Walpole Library, Yale University. 758.00.00.40dr
Fig. 89

London Sale: [Possibly] A ditto [folio] with leaves, containing drawings, of which eight are Costumes, and two of Scenery of Twickenham, by Samuel Scott, marine painter; the Bishop's Throne in Exeter Cathedral, by R. Leave, 1763; seven Views in the vicinity of Twickenham, by Muntz; a View of Strawberry Hill, by Edward Edwards; also sundry plans connected therewith, and two designs, by Rysbrack, for Lady Walpole's tomb in Westminster Abbey.

PROV: Commissioned by HW; 1842, Strawberry Hill London Sale, [possibly] day 10, lot 1259 (sold in a folio of drawings) bt Wm Knight, Esq., £1.14.0; 1952, July, Colnaghi to W. S. Lewis (in a collection of drawings), £95; The Lewis Walpole Library, Yale University.

LIT: *HW Corres.* 30: 370, 35: 232. 'Building and Site': 102–28, fig. 9.

NOTE: Pin pricks in drawing possibly indicate transfer.

Figure 304. Catalogue 17

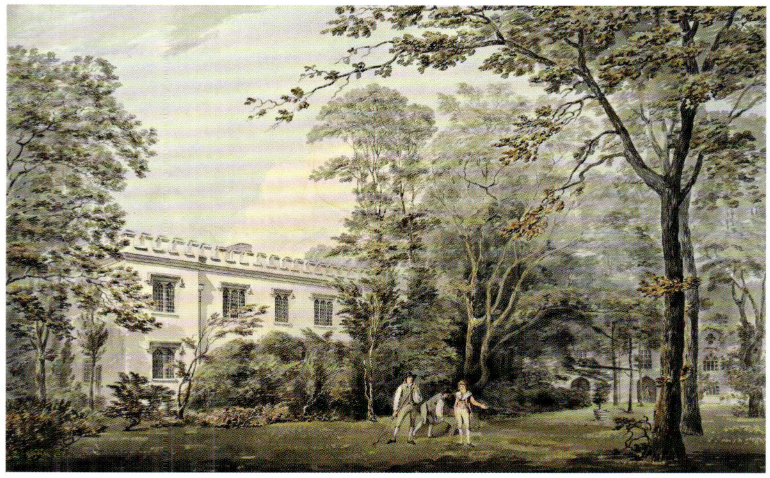

13. 'VIEW OF TWICKENHAM AND PART OF RICHMOND HILL FROM THE BLUE ROOM AT STRAWBERRYHILL'
Joseph Charles Barrow (fl. 1789–1802), 1789

Watercolour on wove paper with wash-line mount, 33.6 × 45.4 cm
Inscriptions: title in HW's hand on volume page and: 'by J. C. Barrow. 1789'; title and date on verso in pencil in a later hand
The Lewis Walpole Library, Yale University. Folio 49 3582, fol. 7
Fig. 39

From HW's extra-illustrated copy of *D 1784* (49 3582, fol. 7).

PROV: The drawing probably commissioned by HW; for the volume see Cat. 24

LIT: *HW Corres.* 11: 82n. *Library* 3582.

NOTE: A view from the Breakfast Room.

14. 'THE SHELL SEAT AT HORACE WALPOLE'S VILLA AT STRAWBERRY HILL'
Artist unknown, *c.* 1825

Grey wash and watercolour on wove paper, 24.5 × 18.1 cm (visible); 30.3 × 23.8 cm (mount)
Inscription: title in pencil in unknown hand at bottom of sheet.
The Lewis Walpole Library, Yale University. Folio 49 3678.2
Fig. 132

PROV: 1948, Lord Waldegrave to W. S. Lewis (with others); The Lewis Walpole Library, Yale University.

NOTE: From a group of Strawberry Hill views by the same hand at the Lewis Walpole Library, Yale University of which two carry watermarks dated 1821 and 1822.

15. 'CHAPEL IN THE GARDEN AT STRAWBERRY HILL – TWICKENHAM'
Artist unknown, *c.* 1785

Pen and ink and watercolour on laid paper, 25.6 × 21 cm (visible); 28.7 × 23.3 cm (mount)
Inscriptions: title at bottom perhaps in HW's hand
The Lewis Walpole Library, Yale University. Folio 49 3678.3
Fig. 28

PROV: 1948, Lord Waldegrave to W. S. Lewis (with others); The Lewis Walpole Library, Yale University.

16. STRAWBERRY HILL FROM THE GARDEN
William Edmund Pars (1742–1782), *c.* 1772

Watercolour, 37.8 × 53.3 cm
Inscriptions: inscribed in pencil '2 O Clock'
Victoria and Albert Museum, London. P.10–1985.
Fig. 105

PROV: Probably commissioned by HW; [Frances Lady Waldegrave?]; Lord O'Hagan; 1985, March 19, Christie's, bt Victoria and Albert Museum.

LIT: *HW Corres.* 24: 34–5, 35: 424.

NOTE: A view looking south from the flower garden.

17. 'VIEW OF THE OFFICES AT STRAWBERRY-HILL'
Joseph Charles Barrow (fl. 1789–1802), 1791

Pen and ink and watercolour on wove paper, 32 × 50.2 cm
Inscriptions: on verso in HW's hand: title, artist, and date; and on volume page: 'The new Offices at Strawberry Hill, designed by James Essex of Cambridge, & built in 1790 drawn by J. C. Barrow 1791.'
The Lewis Walpole Library, Yale University. Folio 49 3582 fol. 204
Fig. 304

From HW's extra-illustrated copy of *D 1784*, fol. 204.

PROV: Drawing commissioned by HW; for the volume see Cat. 24.

LIT: 'Genesis': fig. 29. Mellon Lectures, no. 46. *Library* 3582.

18. 'Entrance from the Road at Strawberry Hill'
Richard Bentley (bap. 1708, d. 1782), 1758

Pencil and ink wash on laid paper, 31.3 × 19.7 cm
Inscriptions: in HW's hand at top of drawing, with the title and: 'N.B. There is a rose window added under the battlement'; additional notes and measurements by Bentley.
The Lewis Walpole Library, Yale University. Folio 49 3585 fol. 29
Fig. 92

From the album *Drawings and Designs by Richd. Bentley* (*c.* 1760, fol. 29)
D 1774, 49 [Library]: Rare book of prints and drawings in the library…Designs by Mr. Bentley, bound in marble and gilt.
D 1784, 37, same as *D 1774*.
PROV: Design commissioned by HW; the album, 'Drawings and Designs by Rich. Bentley', assembled by HW; 1842, Strawberry Hill Sale, day 8, lot 57 [listed]; 1842, Strawberry Hill London Sale, day 10, lot 1255 [sold], bt William Knight, Esq., £4.2.0; 1926, May, Spencer through Fletcher for W. S. Lewis, £210; The Lewis Walpole Library, Yale University.
LIT: 'Genesis': fig. 8. *Library* 3585. *Collector's Progress*, 59, 102, 104–8. *Rescuing Horace*, 53–61. Bentley thesis, fig. 64. *Gothic Revival*, fig. 97.
NOTE: A design drawing of the north entrance, before it was raised by one floor.

19. 'Design for the gallery and round tower, at Strawberryhill'
John Chute (1701–1776), *c.* 1759

Ink and pencil, 21 × 31.2 cm, mounted in the volume of John Chute's 'Original Drawings and Sketches' (fol. 17)
Inscriptions: title on drawing in HW's hand
The Lewis Walpole Library, Yale University. Folio 49 3490 fol. 17
Fig. 104

D 1774, 51 [Library]: possibly: Curious books in the glass closet in the library…A book of designs of buildings, by John Chute, esq; of the Vine.
D 1784, 38, same as *D 1774*.
PROV: Design commissioned by HW; 1842, Strawberry Hill Sale, day 7, lot 25 [volume of Chute and volume of Lens drawings], bt H. G. Bohn, £4.17.6 [listed]; 1842, Strawberry Hill London Sale, lot 1256 [vol. of Chute drawings only], bt H. G. Bohn, £2.17.6 [sold]; 1847, offered in Bohn's Catalogue (Architecture), p. 223 for £5.5.0; 1948, Lord Waldegrave in a collection to W. S. Lewis; The Lewis Walpole Library, Yale University.
LIT: *Library* 3490. 'Genesis': fig. 19. *Gothic Revival*, fig. 99. 'Building and Site': 102–28, fig. 19.
NOTE: A second scheme for the windows is shown on a flap.

20. Catalogue for Shewing the House
Horace Walpole (1717–1797)

Strawberry Hill: Printed by Thomas Kirgate, 1774
Bound in blue paper, 24.1 × 19.3 × .7 cm
Inscriptions: on the cover in Thomas Kirgate's hand: 'Catalogue for Shewing the House. Little better than Waste paper'. And by HW: 'Very imperfect for many additions & alterations since this was printed'. On a label pasted to the binding: 'for Mrs Damer'
The Provost and Fellows of Eton College. ECL Cc.1.1.04A.

PROV: HW; 1810, December 4, King and Lochée, Kirgate Sale, lot 410, bt Baker, £10.0; 1825, June 8, Sotheby's, Baker Sale, lot 791, bt Cruden, £3.0; sold privately by Mr Cruden to J. W. K. Eyton; 1848, May 22, Sotheby's, Eyton Sale, lot 1464, bt Lilly, £3.0; 1904, May 7, Sotheby's, Ford Sale, lot 643, bt Sotheran, £3.5.0; Eton College Library.
LIT: Percival Merritt, *An Account of Descriptive Catalogues of Strawberry Hill and of Strawberry Hill Sale Catalogues, together with a Bibliography* (Boston: privately printed by B. Rogers, 1915), 7–12. *Bib. SH* no. 21. *OHG* 34. Anna Chalcraft and Judith Viscardi, *Visiting Strawberry Hill* (Wimbledon: Chalcraft & Viscardi, 2005).

21. A Description of the Villa of Mr. Horace Walpole: Youngest Son of Sir Robert Walpole Earl of Orford at Strawberry-Hill at Twickenham, Middlesex
Horace Walpole (1717–1797)

Strawberry Hill: Printed by Thomas Kirgate, 1784
11.75 × 9.5 cm
Inscriptions: inscribed on the title page 'Bequeathed to Mary Dickenson by her valued friend the Earl of Orford.'
The Lewis Walpole Library, Yale University. Quarto 33 30 Copy 7
Figs. 20, 133

PROV: 1784, published by HW at Strawberry Hill Press; Bequeathed to Mary Dickenson; Miss Anne Clark; Frank Woore of Derby; 1934, April, to Pickering and Chatto; 1934, April, bt W. S. Lewis; The Lewis Walpole Library, Yale University.
LIT: *Bib. SH* no. 30, copy 9.

22. Ticket to view Strawberry Hill
Strawberry Hill, 1774

Letterpress, 6.5 × 9 cm
The Lewis Walpole Library, Yale University. Folio 336G
Fig. 24

PROV: Thomas Kirgate; George Baker; William Upcott; George Smith; Lord Waldegrave; W. S. Lewis; The Lewis Walpole Library, Yale University.
LIT: *HW Corres.* 10: 98, 109, 151, 158, 215, 11: 57, 74, 12: 27, 167, 221–52, 15: 199, 267, 29: 268, 270, 31: 236, 35: 574, 635, 40: 345, 41: 441, 42: 96, 144, 384, 43: 165. *Bib. SH* 25. Mellon Lectures, xxv, ill. no. 50.
NOTE: HW issued printed tickets in 1774 only. This example has not been filled in. He otherwise wrote notes of admission to his housekeeper, after 1784 often on the printed rules for admission (see Cat. 23).

23. Rules for obtaining a ticket to see Strawberry Hill
Strawberry Hill, 1784

Letterpress, 23 × 18.5 cm
Inscriptions: HW's hand at bottom: 'June 24 1784 To Mr. Walpole's Housekeeper; You may show my House on Friday morning next to Mr. Panton and Three more, on their delivering this to you, Hor. Walpole.'
The Lewis Walpole Library, Yale University
Fig. 25

PROV: Pasted in vol. 1 of Paul Panton's copy of the first edition of *Anecdotes* (1762–3; LWL 33.10 Copy 17); 1960, February, Major Lloyd-Johnes to Maggs for W. S. Lewis. Removed from the volume of *Anecdotes* by W. S. Lewis; The Lewis Walpole Library, Yale University.
LIT: *HW Corres.* 12: 219–20, 31: 236, 33: 435–6, 35: 634–5, 43: 162–5. *Bib. SH* 33. Mellon Lectures, xxv, ill. no. 50.

24. 'View from the Holbein Chamber at Strawberry-Hill'
Joseph Charles Barrow (fl. 1789–1802), 1792

Watercolour and ink on wove paper with wash-line mount, 37 × 28.2 cm (visible); 45.7 × 36.8 cm (sheet)
Signed and dated: lower left: J. C. Barrow, Delin. 1792. Strawberry Hill Press letterpress title on a label pasted to the mount.
The Lewis Walpole Library, Yale University. Folio 49 3582 fol. 4c

From HW's extra-illustrated copy of *D 1784*, fol. 4c.
1842 Sale [Round Tower]: A Description of Strawberry Hill, illustrated with original drawings and prints of the various Pictures, Antiquities and interesting Objects; also Views of various parts of the Interior and Exterior of the Villa and the surrounding Scenery. In this vol. is that extremely rare and curious print of King Henry VIII and his Family, engraved by W. Rogers, of which only 2 other impressions are known [Fig. 164]. This Collection is perfectly unique.
London Sale: Description of Strawberry Hill and its contents, most elaborately illustrated with 32 drawings of views, exterior and interior, by J. C. Barrow, Edward Edwards, J. H. Muntz, John Carter, and about 100 engraved portraits and an infinity of engraved views, antiquities and other objects of art within the villa.
PROV: Probably commissioned by HW; 1842, Strawberry Hill Sale, day 8, lot 33 [listed]; 1842, Strawberry Hill London Sale, day 8, lot 1123 [sold] (book), bt William Knight, Esq., £22.11.6, day 1, lot 18 (print of King Henry VIII removed and sold separately), bt British Museum, £22.1.0; 1919, July 30, Sotheby's, Col. Fellows Sale, lot

159, bt Sabin; 1927, August, Sabin bt W. S. Lewis, £600; The Lewis Walpole Library, Yale University.
LIT: *Library* 3582.

25. Three Sketches of Horace Walpole
John Carter (1748–1817), *c.* 1788

Pen and ink and watercolour on laid paper, 22 × 28.3 cm (visible)
Inscriptions: by Carter below the images: 'After breakfast, & in his study, Before dinner, when drest, & in the Cabinet, After dinner, & in the Gallery.'
The Lewis Walpole Library, Yale University.
33 30 Copy 22
Fig. 285

PROV: Formerly laid in James Bindley's extra-illustrated copy of HW's *D 1784* which was bequeathed by HW to James Bindley, of the Stamp Office, London; 1949, October, Pickering & Chatto, bt W. S. Lewis, £55; The Lewis Walpole Library, Yale University.
LIT: Mellon Lectures, ill. no. 69. 'Portraits': 20, no. A.16.1. *Rescuing Horace*, 238, ill. 237. John Ingamells, *National Portrait Gallery: Mid-Georgian Portraits, 1760–1790* (London: National Portrait Gallery, 2004), 371 for another version of the drawing at The Henry E. Huntington Library, San Marino, California.

26. An Antiquary at Strawberry Hill
Thomas Rowlandson (1757–1827), after 1808 (watermark)

Pen and ink, wash, 24.4 × 37.8 cm
Victoria and Albert Museum. Dyce 792.
Bequeathed by the Rev. Alexander Dyce.
Fig. 278

PROV: Victoria and Albert Museum, London. Dyce Bequest.
LIT: *Gothick 1720–1840* (exh. cat. Brighton: Royal Pavilion, Art Gallery and Museum, 1975), cat. C.125. *OHG* 234.
NOTE: The house seen from the west, combining two viewpoints.

27. North Entrance of Strawberry Hill with a Procession of Monks
Thomas Rowlandson (1757–1827), *c.* 1805–10

Watercolour, pen, graphite, 24 × 38 cm
Signed and dated: 'T Rowlandson 1789' (probably a later addition not by the artist)
The Friends of Strawberry Hill for the Strawberry Hill Trust
Fig. 277

PROV: Earl of Warwick (Lugt 2600); 2006, June 7, Sotheby's, The Property of a Gentleman and a Lady, lot 339, bt Strawberry Hill Trust.
LIT: *OHG* 236.
NOTE: There is another version at the Lewis Walpole Library, Yale University. A sketch in reverse is in a private collection (*OHG* 236).

28. Solitude a Strawberry Hill
Thomas Rowlandson (1757–1827), *c.* 1809

Pen and brown ink with brush and watercolour, on cream wove paper, laid down on board with wash-line mount, 16.3 × 20 cm [visible]; 20.4 × 28 cm (mount)
Signed: T. Rowlandson [probably a later addition not by the artist]
Inscriptions: in French: 'Solitude A Strawberry Hill'
The Art Institute of Chicago, Gift of Mrs James Ward Thorne. 1940 207.1
Yale Center for British Art only
Fig. 286

PROV: Mrs James Ward Thorne; The Art Institute of Chicago.
LIT: See Cat. 29.
NOTE: See Cat. 29.

29. Garden and Entrance to a Neo-Gothic House: Strawberry Hill
Thomas Rowlandson (1757–1827), *c.* 1809

Pen and watercolour over pencil, scored for transfer 14.2 × 21.5 cm
Courtauld Institute of Art (Witt Collection)
Victoria and Albert Museum only

PROV: Sir Robert Clermont Witt; 1952, bequeathed to the Courtauld Institute.
LIT: J. Hayes, *Rowlandson: Watercolours and Drawings* (London: Phaidon, 1972) pl. 143. S. Jervis, *Country Life* (20 Dec. 1973) 2117. *OHG* 237.
NOTE: The same composition as Cat. 28. This drawing etched and aquatinted in reverse by J. C. Stadler as 'Temple at Strawberry Hill' in *Sketches from Nature* (1809) and again (or re-etched) in *Sketches from Nature* (1822).

30. Figure of an Angel; (Figure of a Saint)
French, 1470–80

Cast latten (copper alloy), 86.4 × 32 × 32 cm
Victoria and Albert Museum, London. A. 3–1982
Fig. 41

D 1774, 3 [Oratory]: Entering by the great north gate, the first object that presents itself is a small oratory inclosed with iron rails; in front, an altar, on which stands a saint in bronze;…
D 1784, 2, same as *D 1774*
PROV: HW; 1842, Strawberry Hill Sale, day 19, lot 28, bt Zimmerman, £3.5.0; 1977, July 14, Sotheby's, lot 188, bt Anonymous, £30,000; 1981, November 27, Sotheby Parke-Bernet, New York, lot 5, bt Daniel Katz, London; 1982, purchased by the Victoria and Albert Museum.
LIT: *Romantic Interior*, 107, pls. 88–9.

31. Goldfish Tub
Chinese, *c.* 1730

Hard-paste porcelain, with cobalt decoration and lead glaze, 47 × 55 cm
Two labels on bottom: illegible
Lent by the Rt Hon. the Earl of Derby. D107
Victoria and Albert Museum only
Fig. 43

D 1774, 112 [Great Cloister] At each end, a blue and white china flower-pot, and in the middle, the tub ditto in which Mr. Walpole's cat was drowned; on a label of the pedestal is written the first stanza of Mr. Gray's beautiful ode on that occasion,

'Twas on this lofty vase's side,
Where China's gayest art has dy'd
The azure flow'rs that blow,
Demurest of the tabby kind,
The pensive Selima reclin'd,
Gaz'd on the lake below.

D 1784, 2 [Small Cloister]: On a pedestal, stands the large blue and white china tub in which Mr. Walpole's cat was drowned; … (continues as *D 1774*)
PROV: HW, by 1747; 1842, Strawberry Hill Sale, day 19, lot 32, bt Earl of Derby, £42.
LIT: *Country Life* (5 July 1924), 25, fig. 18. 'Genesis': 57–92. *HW Corres.* 14: 23, 28: 101. *OHG* 109. Bet McLeod, 'The Ceramics at Strawberry Hill' (MA Thesis. Cooper-Hewitt/Parson's School of Design, New York, 1993), 152, no. 13, fig. 3.

32. Designs by Mr R. Bentley, for Six Poems by Mr T. Gray
Thomas Gray (1716–1771)
London: R. Dodsley, 1753

38 × 27.5 cm
HW's copy, with all the original pen and ink drawings by Richard Bentley in place of the engravings and with Gray's original sketch of Stoke House; with notes by Walpole
The Lewis Walpole Library, Yale University.
Folio 49 3698
Figs. 44, 141, 268

D 1774, 49 [Library]: Curious books in the glass closet in the library. Mr. Bentley's original designs for Mr. Gray's poems, bound in red morocco and gilt.
D 1784, 37, same as *D 1774*.
PROV: HW; 1842, Strawberry Hill Sale, day 7, lot 54 [listed]; 1842, Strawberry Hill London Sale, day 8, lot 1044 [sold], bt H. G. Bohn [for William Beckford], £8.8.0; 1882, July 3, Sotheby's, Beckford Sale, part 1, lot 802, bt Ellis & White, £20; 1882, offered by Ellis & White, cat. 50, lot 328, £65; 1933, November, bt Maggs for W. S. Lewis, £230; The Lewis Walpole Library, Yale University.
LIT: *HW Corres.* 9: 116, 134, 143, 13: 24, 14: 59–66, 172, 20: 368, 386, 35: 185, 643, 43: 191. *Bib. HW* no. 42, copy 2. *Library* 3698. *Collector's Progress*, 28, 91, 105, 107. Mellon Lectures, 56–7. *Rescuing Horace*, 62–9. *Rococo: Art and Design in Hogarth's England*, exh. cat., Victoria and Albert Museum (London: Trefoil Books, 1984), 61, cat. no. D25. Robert Halsband, 'The Rococo in England: Book Illustrators, Mainly Gravelot and Bentley', *The Burlington Magazine* (December 1985): 870–80. Bentley thesis, fig. 94. *Bentley's Illustrations*, fig. 6.

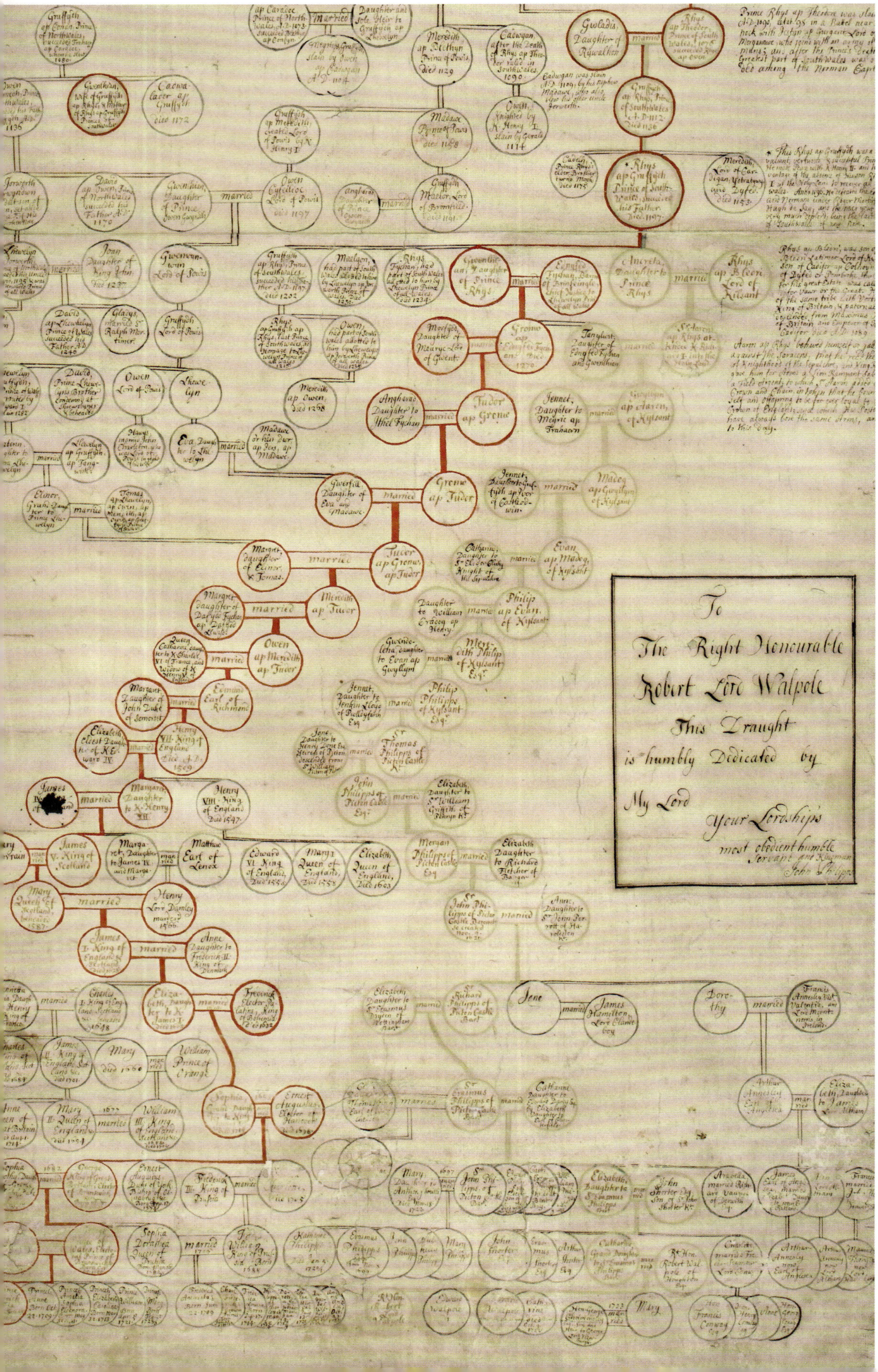

33. A GENEALOGICAL TABLE OF ALL THE KINGS AND PRINCES OF WALES FROM CADWALADER LAST KING OF BRITAIN TO LHEWELYN LAST PRINCE OF WALES OF THE BRITISH BLOOD: WITH THE DESCENT OF HIS PRESENT MAJESTY KING GEORGE AS ALSO OF THE RIGHT HONOURABLE ROBERT LORD WALPOLE FROM CADWALADER
Sir John Philipps (1700–1764), after 1723

Pen and ink on paper mounted on cloth, 132 × 47.5 cm (visible); 136.4 × 51 cm (mount)
Inscription: Inscribed with a dedication from 'his kinsman John Philipps' to the 'Right Honourable Robert Lord Walpole'.
The Lewis Walpole Library, Yale University.
49 2624
Fig. 305

1842 Sale [Library]: A curious manuscript roll on vellum, a Genealogical Tree from Noah to Lord Orford.

PROV: Given by Sir John Philipps to HW's brother Robert; HW; 1842, Strawberry Hill Sale, day 6, lot 109, bt Rodd, £4.4.0; The Lewis Walpole Library, Yale University.

LIT: *HW Corres.* 9: 69, 13: 81, 43: 114. *Library* 2624.

NOTE: HW's maternal grandmother was Elizabeth Philipps, daughter of Sir Erasmus Philipps, 3rd baronet, of Picton Castle. Sir John Philipps was the 6th baronet.

34. MONUMENTAL BRASS OF RALPH WALPOLE, BISHOP OF NORWICH AND ELY
Johann Heinrich Müntz (1727–1798), *c.* 1758

Engraved brass, 76.5 × 34 cm
Inscriptions: lettered in Latin and dated 1301
Signed: 'HM'
Private collection
Fig. 42

D 1774, 3n [Little Cloister]: In the winding cloysters on the right hand are some ancient bas-reliefs; and a brass plate with the effigies of Simon [sic] Walpole, bishop of Norwich and Ely, engraven by Muntz.

D 1784, 2n [Little Cloister]: same as *D 1774* and (A Swiss painter who lived some time with Mr. Walpole) …

PROV: Commissioned by HW; 1842, Strawberry Hill Sale, day 24, lot 95, bt Hor. Rodd, £6.6; Private collection.

LIT: *HW Corres.* 2: 105–7, 43: 67. Anthony R. Wagner, F.S.A., Richmond Herald and R. H. d'Eboux, MC, F.S.A., 'A commemorative Brass to Bishop Ralph Walpole from the cloister at

Figure 305. Catalogue 33: detail

Strawberry Hill', *Transactions of the Monumental Brass Society* (Dec. 1945): 99–102. *OHG* 111 (for an inked impression)

NOTE: Ralph de Walpole was Bishop of Norwich and Ely between 1299 and 1302. HW wrote to William Cole (*HW Corres.* 2: 106), that it was derived from a print in John Dart's *Westmonasterium* vol. 1, pl. 20, of the tomb of Robert Dalby (Walby in *Westmonasterium*), Bishop of Durham. In fact it is taken from an etching by Hollar of the brass of Robert de Braybroke, Bishop of London, in William Dugdale, *A History of St Pauls Cathedral in London*... (London: printed for T. Warren, 1658), opp. p. 84.

35. THE WALPOLE SALVER
Paul de Lamerie (1688–1751), 1728–9

Engraving attributed to William Hogarth (1697–1764)
Britannia Standard Silver, engraved, 48 × 48.5 cm
Engraved with a composition showing the Second Exchequer Seal of George I, supported by Hercules, and with a view of London
Marks: 'N' date letter for 1728–9; Britannia standard mark; Lion's head erased, town mark for London and maker's mark 'LA' below an arched crown and five pointed star above a fleur-de-lys, all in a curved shield.
Victoria and Albert Museum,London. M.9–1956
Yale Center for British Art only
Fig. 5

1842 Sale: A Magnificent 19–inch square shaped plateau, the centre exquisitely chased in medallions, representing George I, on his throne, with Figures of Britannia and Justice, and the royal arms, with a View of the City of London and Allegorical devices, richly chased border and shell edge, on scroll feet.

PROV: Sir Robert Walpole; inherited by HW; Strawberry Hill Sale, day 11, lot 120, bt Garrard, Panton Street, £101.12.06; directly to Charles Mills, Esq.; by family descent; Lord Hillingdon; 1955, December 7, Christies, Sale of the Property of Mrs Colin Davy, daughter of the late Lt-Col. Horace Walpole, lot 147; Victoria and Albert Museum, Acquired with the assistance of the Goldsmiths' Company, the Pilgrim Trust and The Art Fund.

LIT: P. A. S. Phillips, *Paul de Lamerie, His Life and Work* (London: published under the patronage of the Worshipful Company of Goldsmiths of the City of London by Batsford, 1935), 86–90, pls. LX, LXI. Charles Oman, 'English Engravers on Plate', *Apollo* 65 (July 1957): 286–9, fig. III, IV and V. J. F. Hayward, *Huguenot Silver* (London: Faber and Faber, 1959), pl. 94, 74–5. Ann Forrester, 'Hogarth as an Engraver on Silver', *Connoisseur* (1963): 112–16, fig. 6. Ronald Paulson, *Hogarth's Graphic Works* (New Haven and London: Yale University Press, 1965), no. 114, pl. 119. Ronald Paulson, *Hogarth: his Life, Art and Times* (New Haven and London: Yale University Press, 1971), vol. 1, 174–5, 235; vol. 2, 393. Carl Hernmarck, *The Art of the European Silversmith* (London: Sotheby Parke Bernet, 1977), pl. 478. Charles Oman, *English Engraved Silver* (London: Faber & Faber, 1978), pl. 109, 96–7. Philippa Glanville, *Silver in England* (Winchester, Mass. and London: Unwin Hyman, 1987), fig. 82, 216–17. Susan Hare, ed., *Paul de Lamerie: at the Sign of the Golden Ball: an Exhibition of the Work of England's Master Silversmith (1688–1751)* (London: Goldsmiths' Company, 1990), no. 50.

36. PORTRAIT OF HORACE WALPOLE
Bernard Lens III (1682–1740), *c.* 1725–6

Sepia wash, 17.5 × 11.4 cm
Inscription: probably in artist's hand: 'Master Horace Walpole B.L.'; and on verso, in pencil in HW's hand: 'Drawn from the life by Lens, / who was Master Horace Walpole's / drawing master'
The Trustees of the Waldegrave Chattels Trust
Fig. 4

PROV: HW; Earls Waldegrave.

LIT: 'Portraits': A.2, pp. 6–7, pl. 1. *OHG* 5. John Ingamells, *National Portrait Gallery: Mid-Georgian Portraits, 1760–1790* (London: National Portrait Gallery, 2004), 370.

37. PORTRAIT OF HORACE WALPOLE
Jonathan Richardson (1667–1745), 1734–5

Oil on canvas, 125.7 × 86.4 cm
The Trustees of the Waldegrave Chattels Trust
Fig. 109

D 1774, 7 [Refectory]: Horace Walpole, third son of sir Robert and Catherine Shorter; in blue velvet: by Richardson.

D 1784, 5, same as *D 1774*.

PROV: HW; 1842, Strawberry Hill Sale, day 21, lot 34, bt Earl Waldegrave, £105.0.0;

LIT: 'Portraits': A.4, pp. 7–8, pls. 2–3. *OHG* 6. John Ingamells, *National Portrait Gallery: Mid-Georgian Portraits, 1760–1790* (London: National Portrait Gallery, 2004), 371.

38. PORTRAIT OF HORACE WALPOLE
Rosalba Carriera (1675–1757), *c.* 1741

Pastel on paper, 61 × 46.5 cm
Houghton Hall, Norfolk
Victoria and Albert Museum only
Fig. 10

1842 Sale [Round Tower]: Six curious and interesting sketches, drawn at Venice, Portraits of the Earl of Lincoln, Horace Walpole, John Chute, Joseph Spence, Mr. Chaloner and Mr. Whitdsend by Rosalba.

PROV: Commissioned by HW; 1842, Strawberry Hill Sale, day 21, lot 1, bt Rev. Hor. Cholmondeley, £1.11.6; 1913, June 13, Christie's, Property of Lady Dorothy Nevill (order of the executors), lot 70, bt Asher Wertheimer, £399; 1920, June 18, Christie's, stock of Mr Asher Wertheimer (order of the executors), lot 2, bt Gooden & Fox, £120.15s; Marquess of Cholmondeley, Houghton Hall.

LIT: *HW Corres.* 18: 243n, 43: 250. Mellon Lectures, ill. no. 17. 'Portraits': A.6, pp. 9–10, pl. 5. *John Ingamells, National Portrait Gallery: Mid-Georgian Portraits, 1760–1790* (London: National Portrait Gallery, 2004), 371. Larissa Dukelskaya and Andrew Moore, eds., *A Capital Collection: Houghton Hall and the Hermitage* (New Haven and London: Yale University Press, 2007), no. 212. Bernardina Sani, *Rosalba Carriera: 1673–1757: maestra del pastello nell'Europa ancien régime* (Turin: U. Allemandi, *c.* 2007), no. 410.

39. PORTRAIT OF SIR ROBERT WALPOLE AND CATHERINE SHORTER, HIS FIRST WIFE
John Giles Eccardt (d. 1779), and John Wootton (1681/2–1764), *c.* 1754

Oil on canvas, in a carved frame of *c.* 1680, in the style of Grinling Gibbons, painted black and gilded. The painted central arms on the frame are a replacement *c.* 1754. 50.8 × 101.6 × 23 cm (visible)
The Lewis Walpole Library, Yale University
Fig. 119

D 1774, 37 [Blue Bedchamber, over the chimneypiece]: In a frame of black and gold carved by Gibbons, sir Robert Walpole and Catharine Shorter; small whole lengths; by Eckardt, after Zinck: the hounds and view of Houghton by Wootton. Sir Robert is sitting; by him, on a table, is the purse of chancellor of the exchequer, leaning against busts of George 1st. and 2d. to denote his being first minister to those kings: by lady Walpole are flowers, shells, a pallet and pencils, to mark her love of the arts.

D 1784, 28–9, same as *D 1774*.

PROV: Probably commissioned by HW; 1842, Strawberry Hill Sale, day 22, lot 84, bt Marquis of Lansdowne for £51.9.0; 1930, March 7, Christie's, (Landsdowne Sale), lot 40, bt Basil Dighton, £336; 1930, June, The Lewis Walpole Library, Yale University.

LIT: *HW Corres.* 35: 173–4. *Collector's Progress*, repro. opp. p. 23. Mellon Lectures, no. 3. John Kerslake, *Early Georgian Portraits* (London: HMSO, 1977), vol. 2, pl. 594. *Rescuing Horace*, 24. *OHG* 2. Hugh Glover, 'Two Furnishings from Strawberry Hill: Exploration and Treatment', *Postprints of the wooden artifacts group presented at the 30th annual meeting of the American Institute for Conservation, Miami, Florida, June 2002* (Washington, DC: American Institute for Conservation of Historic and Artistic Works, 2002). Larissa Dukelskaya and Andrew Moore, eds., *A Capital Collection: Houghton Hall and the Hermitage* (New Haven and London: Yale University Press, 2007), 10.

40. PORTRAIT OF HORACE WALPOLE
John Giles Eccardt (d. 1779), 1754

Oil on canvas, 39.4 × 31.8 cm
Inscriptions: on the stretcher in HW's hand: 'Horace Walpole/ youngest Son of Sr R. Walpole/ by Eckardt/ 1754'.
National Portrait Gallery, London. 988
Fig. 19

D 1774, 38 [Blue Bedchamber]: Mr. Horace Walpole; from Vandyck; leaning on the Ædes Walpolianæ: behind him, a view of Strawberry-hill. The frames are of black and gold, carved after those to Lombard's prints from Vandyck, but with emblems peculiar to each person.

D 1784, 29, same as *D 1774*.
PROV: Commissioned by HW; 1842, Strawberry Hill Sale, day 22, lot 28, bt Rev. Hor. Cholmondeley, £34.13.0; Canon Francis Vanisttart Thornton (Rev. Chomondeley's son-in-law, d. 1895); 1895, P. & D. Colnaghi, bt for National Portrait Gallery, London.
LIT: *HW Corres.* 9: 207n, 35: 174. 'Portraits': A.10, pp. 12–13, pls. 8, 10. *OHG* 10. Larissa Dukelskaya and Andrew Moore, eds., *A Capital Collection: Houghton Hall and the Hermitage* (New Haven and London: Yale University Press, 2002), repro. 18. John Ingamells, *National Portrait Gallery: Mid-Georgian Portraits, 1760–1790* (London: National Portrait Gallery, 2004), 367. Antony Griffiths, *The Print in Stuart Britain, 1603–1689* (London, British Museum Press, 1998), 182–3 (for the frame series).
EXHIB: South Kensington, 'Second special exhibitions of National Portraits', (William and Mary to MCCCC), 1867, no. 377 (lent by the Rev. F. V. Thornton).
NOTE: Adapted from a portrait by Anthony Van Dyck, engraved by Robert van Voerst, of Simon Vouet. Walpole recorded in *D 1774* that the six Eccardt portraits in the Blue Bedchamber were in frames 'of black and gold, carved after those to Lombard's prints from Vandyck, but with emblems peculiar to each person.' They were taken from the frame-like decorative borders of Pierre Lombart's series of ten female and two male portraits after Van Dyck, often known as the 'Countesses', *c.* 1661–2. This painting is no longer in its original frame

41. PORTRAIT OF RICHARD BENTLEY
John Giles Eccardt (d. 1779), 1753

Oil on canvas, 42.2 × 34.3 cm
National Portrait Gallery, London. 5885
Fig. 111

D 1774, 38 [Blue Bedchamber]: Mr Richard Bentley; from Vandyck. He holds in one hand his own design of the figure of Melancholy, drawn by him for the edition of Mr. Gray's Odes.
D 1784, 29, same as *D 1774*.
PROV: Commissioned by HW; 1842, Strawberry Hill Sale, day 22, lot 31, bt Money, £6; 1900, February 10, Christie's, 9th Earl of Waldegrave Sale, lot 35, bt Renton, £2.15; *c.* 1950, 'the Joel family'; 1986, July 9, Sotheby's, lot 42, bt Leggatt for National Portrait Gallery, £5,200.
LIT: *HW Corres.* 9: 207n, 35: 174. John Ingamells, *National Portrait Gallery: Mid-Georgian Portraits, 1760–1790* (London: National Portrait Gallery, 2004), 53.
NOTE: Adapted from a portrait by Anthony Van Dyck, engraved by Pierre de Jode, of Adam de Coster. This painting is no longer in its original frame (see Cat. 40).

42. PORTRAIT OF THOMAS GRAY
John Giles Eccardt (d. 1779), 1747–8

Oil on canvas, 40.3 × 32.7 cm
National Portrait Gallery, London. 989
Fig. 112

D 1774, 38 [Blue Bedchamber] Mr. Thomas Gray;* taken from the portrait of a musician by Vandyck, at the duke of Grafton's. *With this motto, alluding to his Ode on Eton, which, though one of his best productions was his first published, *Nec licuit populis parvum te, Nile, videre.*
D 1784, 29, same as *D 1774*.
PROV: Commissioned by HW; 1842, Strawberry Hill Sale, day 22, lot 30, bt Rev. Hor. Cholmondeley, £33.12.0; Canon Francis Vanisttart Thornton (Rev. Chomondeley's son in law, d. 1895); 1895, P. & D. Colnaghi, bt National Gallery, London.
LIT: *HW Corres.* 1: 237, 9: 207n, 14: 63n, 15: 20, 52, 56, 60, 61, 35: 174, 43: 167. John F. Kerslake, *Early Georgian Portraits* (London: HMSO, 1977), 106–7. OHG 11. Larissa Dukelskaya and Andrew Moore, eds., *A Capital Collection: Houghton Hall and the Hermitage* (New Haven and London: Yale University Press, 2002), repro. 17.
EXHIB: South Kensington, 'Second special exhibitions of National Portraits', (William and Mary to MCCCC), 1867, no. 375, (lent by the Rev. F. V. Thornton).
NOTE: Adapted from a portrait by Anthony Van Dyck, engraved by Pierre de Jode, of Henricus Liberti. This painting is no longer in its original frame (see Cat. 40)

43. PORTRAIT OF HENRY SEYMOUR CONWAY, LADY AYLESBURY AND ANNE, THEIR DAUGHTER
John Giles Eccardt (d. 1779), 1754

Oil on canvas, in carved, gilt and black frame, 66 × 50.9 cm (visible)
Dated on the tree, below the hanging shields of the arms of the sitters.
Private collection
Fig. 57

D 1774, 37 [Blue Bedchamber]: General Henry Seymour Conway, and Caroline countess dowager of Ailesbury, his wife; their daughter Anne sitting on the ground playing with a dog. The attitudes and dresses taken from Watteau. This, and all other pictures in this room, were painted by Eckardt.
D 1784, 29, same as *D 1774*.
PROV: Commissioned by HW; 1842, Strawberry Hill Sale, day 22, lot 35, bt Sir Alexander Johnston, £14.0.0; by family descent; Private collection.
LIT: *HW Corres.* 35: 174, 37: 234. *OHG* 16. *Rococo: Art and Design in Hogarth's England*, exh. cat., Victoria and Albert Museum (London: Trefoil Books, 1984), 257, cat. no. O35. John Ingamells, *National Portrait Gallery: Mid-Georgian Portraits, 1760–1790* (London: National Portrait Gallery, 2004), 113.
NOTE: The portrait is adapted from Jean Antoine Watteau, *La Cascade* (*c.* 1714). The painting is in its original black and gold frame from Strawberry Hill, derived from the border of the portrait of Elizabeth, Countess of Castlehaven or of Philip, Earl of Pembroke, engraved by Pierre Lombart (see Cat. 40)

44. PORTRAIT OF COLONEL CHARLES CHURCHILL AND LADY MARY CHURCHILL AND THEIR ELDEST SON CHARLES
John Giles Eccardt (d. 1779), *c.* 1755

Oil on canvas, 66.7 × 50.8 cm
The Lewis Walpole Library, Yale University.
Fig. 58

D 1774, 37 [Blue Bedchamber]: Charles Churchill, and lady Maria Walpole, his wife, with their eldest son Charles; taken from the picture at Blenheim, of Rubens, his wife and child.
D 1784, 29, same as *D 1774*.
PROV: Commissioned by HW; 1842, Strawberry Hill Sale, day 22, lot 36, bt Hull, Wardour Street, £16.5.0; 1961, December, P. & D. Colnaghi, bt W. S. Lewis, £400; The Lewis Walpole Library, Yale University.
LIT: *HW Corres.* 35: 174. J. Cornforth, 'The Cowles-Lewis House, Farmington, II, The Home of Mr Wilmarth S. Lewis' *Country Life* (4 May 1978): 1151, fig. 9.
NOTE: The portrait is adapted from Peter Paul Rubens's *Self Portrait with his Wife Helena Fourment, and one of their Children* (late 1630s), formerly at Blenheim and now The Metropolitan Museum of Art (1981.238). Walpole owned a watercolour of Rubens, his wife and child, by B. Lens, from the original at Blenheim. *D 1774* Appendix, 137. The painting is in its original black and gold frame from Strawberry Hill, of the same design as that on Cat. 40.

45. PORTRAIT OF JOHN CHUTE
Johann Heinrich Müntz (1727–1798), after Pompeo Girolamo Batoni (1708–1787), 1756

Oil on canvas, in carved gilt frame, oval: 57 × 45 cm
The Vyne, The Chute Collection (The National Trust)
Fig. 7

D 1774, 56 [Walpole's Bedchamber]: Over the door, Head of John Chute, esq; by Muntz, after Pompeio Battoni.
D 1784, 41, same as *D 1774*.
PROV: Commissioned by HW; 1842, Strawberry Hill Sale, day 22, lot 38, bt Wiggett Chute, Esq., MP, £1.1.0; Sir Charles Chute Collection (d. 1956); The National Trust (The Vyne, Hampshire).
LIT: Chaloner W. Chute, *A History of the Vyne in Hampshire* (Winchester and London, 1898), 143 (attributed only to Müntz). *Accounts* [6] 88, n16. James Lees-Milne, *The Vyne* (London: National Trust, 1959) [attributed to Müntz]. *The Vyne* (London: National Trust, 1969) [attributed to Müntz after Rosalba]. St John Gore, 'Supplement: Pictures in the National Trust Houses', *Burlington Magazine* 111, 793 (Apr. 1969): 258. *OHG* 13. Gervase Jackson-Stops, *The Vyne* (London: National Trust 1981) [attributed to Müntz after Batoni]. Maurice Howard, *The Vyne* (London: National Trust,1998) [attributed to Müntz after Batoni].
NOTE: The picture is taken from a miniature potrait by Batoni (see Cat. 191). The frame is probably designed by John Chute for HW: cf. a design for a frame by Chute in the Hampshire County Record Office.

4. THE ANTIQUARIAN INTERIOR: THE HALL AND ARMOURY

46. 'Perspective of the Hall & Staircase at Strawberryhill.'
Richard Bentley (bap. 1708, d. 1782), *c.* 1753

Pen and ink and watercolour on laid paper, 22.7 × 17.7 cm
Inscriptions: in HW's hand on verso: title and artist. Sketch of a reclining figure on verso.
The Lewis Walpole Library, Yale University.
Folio 49 3585 fol. 30
Fig. 46

From *Drawings and Designs by Richd. Bentley* [1760, fol. 30]
D 1774, 49 [Library]: Rare books of prints and drawings in the library…Designs by Mr. Richard Bentley, bound in marble and gilt.
D 1784, 37, same as *D 1774*.
PROV: Drawing commissioned by HW; for album see Cat. 18 [Entrance from the Road]
LIT: 'Genesis': fig. 6. *Library* 3585. *Rescuing Horace*, 53–61. Bentley thesis, fig. 47.

47. 'View from the Hall at Strawberry hill.'
John Carter (1748–1817), 1788

Pen and ink and watercolour on laid paper, 20.4 × 27.7 cm [visible]; 23.5 × 33.7 cm (visible)
Inscriptions: title, artist, and date on verso, in HW's hand.
The Lewis Walpole Library, Yale University.
Folio 49 3582 fol. 24
Fig. 45

From HW's extra-illustrated copy of *D 1784*, fol. 24.
1842 Sale [Round Tower]: A Description of Strawberry Hill, illustrated with original drawings and prints of the various Pictures, Antiquities and interesting Objects; also Views of various parts of the Interior and Exterior of the Villa and the surrounding Scenery. In this vol. is that extremely rare and curious print of King Henry VIII and his Family, engraved by W. Rogers, of which only 2 other impressions are known. This Collection is perfectly unique.
London Sale: Description of Strawberry Hill and its contents, most elaborately illustrated with 32 drawings of views, exterior and interior, by J. C. Barrow, Edward Edwards, J. H. Muntz, John Carter, and about 100 engraved portraits and an infinity of engraved views, antiquities and other objects of art within the villa.
PROV: Drawing commissioned by HW; for volume: 1842, Strawberry Hill Sale, day 8, lot 33 [listed]; 1842, Strawberry Hill London Sale, day 8, lot 1123 [sold] (book), bt William Knight, Esq., £22.11.6; day 1, lot 18 (print of King Henry VIII removed and sold separately), bt British Museum, £22.1.0; 1919, July 30, Sotheby's, Col. Fellows Sale, lot 159, bt Sabin; 1927, August, Sabin bt W. S. Lewis, £600; The Lewis Walpole Library, Yale University.
LIT: W. S. Lewis, 'f', *Metropolitan Museum Studies* 5, part 1 (1934), fig. 38. *Collector's Progress*, 74, ill. Mellon Lectures, no. 39. *Library* 3582.

NOTE: A related sketch in pen and ink, and watercolour by John Carter is in *D 1784*, extra-illustrated with prints and drawings by John Carter. The Henry E. Huntington Library, San Marino, California (vol. 1, 24v).

48. Elevation of the Hall and Staircase West Wall
George Perfect Harding (1779/80–1853), *c.* 1800

Pen and ink and watercolour on wove paper, 34.8 × 22.3 cm [visible]; 45.8 × 32 cm (mount)
Inscriptions: signed at lower left: G. P. Harding delt.
The Lewis Walpole Library, Yale University.
Folio 49 3678.5
Fig. 139

PROV: 1934, given by Geoffrey Waldegrave, Lord Chewton, to W. S. Lewis; The Lewis Walpole Library, Yale University.
LIT: *Library* 3678. Bentley thesis, fig. 49.

49. Gothic Lantern
William Hallett, Sr. (*c.* 1707–1781), designed by Richard Bentley (bap. 1708, d. 1782), *c.* 1755. The glass English 16th century and Flemish 16th and 17th century.

Coloured, stained, and enamelled glass set in an iron, lead, and painted tin frame, 109.2 × 35.6 × 36.2 cm
The Lewis Walpole Library, Yale University.
Fig. 47

D 1774, 4 [Entrance]: In the well of the staircase, by a cord of black and yellow, hangs a gothic lanthorn of tin japanned, designed by Mr. Bentley, and filled with painted glass; the door of it has an old pane with the arms of Vere, earl of Oxford.
D 1784, 3, same as *D 1774*.
PROV: 1755, made for HW by William Hallett, £2.14.0 (*Accounts*); 1842, Strawberry Hill Sale, day 17, lot 112, bt John Dent, Esq., £5.15.6; 1935, July, John Dent Brocklehurst, to W. S. Lewis, £5; The Lewis Walpole Library, Yale University.
LIT: *Accounts* [6] 83, n5. *HW Corres.* 9: 151n, 35: 644, 40: 150. *Collector's Progress*, 74, 159–69. Ralph Edwards, *The Shorter Dictionary of English Furniture* (London: Country Life, 1964), 338. John Cornforth, 'The Cowles-Lewis House, Farmington—II', *Country Life* (4 May 1978), 1233, ill. 9. *Rescuing Horace*, 57–8, 89. *Romantic Interior*, 101, fig. 81.

50. Parade Armour (Armour of Francis 1st king of France)
French or Flemish, *c.* 1600

Steel, embossed and gilt, H 140 cm
Wartburg-Stiftung Eisenach, Germany
Fig. 255

D 1774, 40–1 [Staircase]: In a niche on the staircase…The armour of Francis 1st. king of France, of steel gilt, and covered with bas-reliefs in a fine taste: his lance is of ebony inlaid with silver; his sword steel; beautifully inlaid with gold, probably the work of Benvenuto Cellini: there is also the armour for the horse's head. This very valuable suit of armour was purchased from the Crozat collection in 1772, on the death of baron de Thiers, when the czarina bought the fine collection of pictures and bronzes.
D 1784, 31 same as *D 1774*.
PROV: 1771, estate of Louis-Antoine Crozat, Baron de Thiers, bt HW, £52.10.0 (Accounts); by 1771, November 19, Horace Walpole [purchase recorded mistakenly by him as 1772]; 1842, Strawberry Hill Sale, day 19, lot 77, bt Pratt, New Bond Street, £320.5.0; Anatole Demidoff; 1863, January 16, Demidoff sale, lot 1, bt Petit-Prête, 22,500 francs; Adolphe de Rothschild; Wartburg-Stiftung, Eisenach.
LIT: *Accounts* [12] 138–45 n12 (The armour is incorrectly identified as one in the Metropolitan Museum of Art). *HW Corres.* 1: 243, 245, 5: 109–17, 115n, 119–20, 121, 123, 124, 128, 139, 141, 143, 145, 146, 147, 156, 185, 233, 260n, 7: 373, 412, 8. 185, 12: 168, 23: 350, 29: 303, 31: 234, 32: 66, 160, 33: 186, 34: 235 35: 421, 43: 56, 93.
NOTE: A Principal Curiosity.

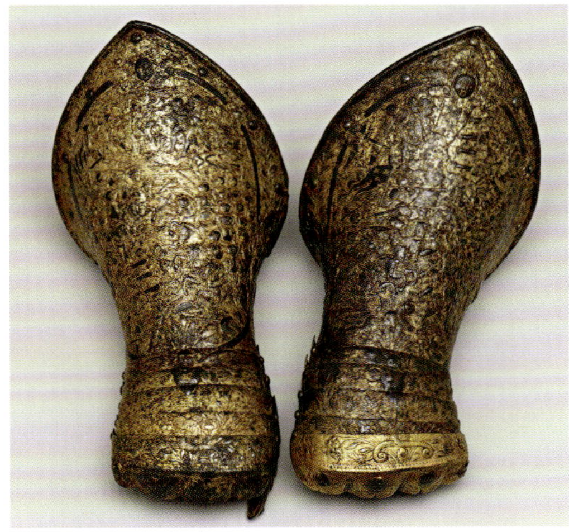

Figure 306. Catalogue 51

51. Gauntlets to a Parade Armour
French or Flemish, *c.* 1600

Steel, embossed and gilt, L 33 cm
Lent by The Metropolitan Museum of Art, Rogers Fund, 1904 (04.3.56–.57)
Fig. 306

PROV: Not Strawberry Hill Collection. Charles Stein, Paris; his sale 1886, May 10–14, lot 136, bt Fréderic Spitzer, 9,100 francs; 1895, June 10–14, Spitzer sale, lots 74 and 80, bt Maurice de Talleyrand-Périgord, Duc de Dino, Paris, 5,800

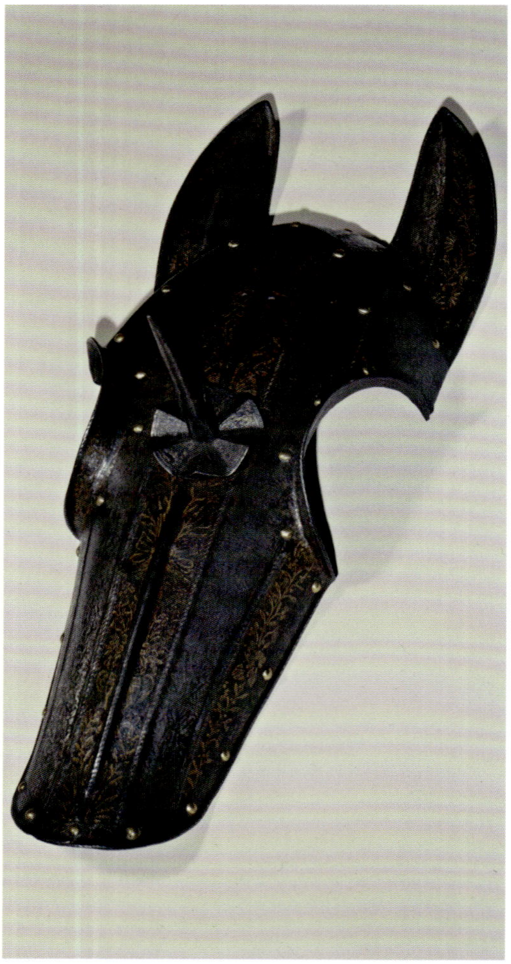

Figure 307. Catalogue 52

francs; bt 1904, Metropolitan Museum of Art.
LIT: Baron C. A. de Cosson, *Le cabinet d'armes de Maurice de Talleyrand-Périgord, Duc de Dino* (Paris, 1901), 40–1, no. C6, pl. 16. *HW Corres.* 31: 25–7.
NOTE: These gauntlets were missing from the 'armour of Francis I' when acquired by Horace Walpole in 1771.

52. SHAFFRON
French, *c.* 1600

Steel, etched and parcel gilt, brass, leather, textile, H 58.5 cm
Private collection
Fig. 307

D 1774, 40–1 See Cat. 50
PROV: 1771, estate of Louis-Antoine Crozat, Baron de Thiers, bt HW (with 'Armour of Francis I'), £52.10.0 (*Accounts*); 1842, May 16, Strawberry Hill Sale, day 19, lot 79, bt John Swaby, London, £10.10.0; 1888, July 4–11, Christie's, Earl of Londesborough sale, lot 131, £38.0.0; 1895, March 18–29, Christie's, Edwin J. Brett sale, lot 450, £52.10.0, bt Duveen; 1949, Dec. 15, Christie's, lot 40, £29.8.0; 1953, March 17, Sotheby's, William R. Hearst sale, lot 124, £24.
LIT: Guy F. Laking, *Record of European Armour and Arms* (London: G. Bell and Sons, 1920–22), vol. 3, fig. 1014 (f).
EXHIB: Alexandria Palace Exhibition of Londesborough Collection, 1875, no. 695; Tudor Exhibition, 1890, cat. no. 752.

53. SPEAR
Indian, 18th century

Iron, damascened in gold and silver, 243.2 cm
Lent by The Metropolitan Museum of Art, Bequest of George C. Stone, 1935 (36.25.1947)
Fig. 308

1842 Sale [Armoury] lot 76: A Persian lance, inlaid with gold or lot 101: An uncommonly long Indian spear, and a Persian spear with japanned handle.
PROV: Possibly 1771, estate of Louis-Antoine Crozat, Baron de Thiers, bt HW (with 'Armour of Francis I'), £52.10.0 (Accounts); 1842, Strawberry Hill Sale, day 19, lot 76, bt Pratt, New Bond Street, £5.15.6 or lot 101, bt George Corner, Esq., £0.10.6; as of 1844, Collection of John Beardmore; 1921, July 5, Christie's, Beardmore sale, lot 139, £1.11.6; W. O. Oldman, London; George C. Stone, New York; 1935 bequeathed to the Metropolitan Museum of Art.
LIT: John Beardmore, *A Catalogue with Illustrations of the Collection of Ancient Arms and Armour, at Uplands, near Fareham, Hampshire* (London: 1844), 26, no. 453, ill. pl. 16. *HW Corres.* 20: 381, 31: 25–7.

54. SHIELD PAINTED WITH THE HEAD OF PERSEUS
Italian School, 1525–50

Painted canvas, mounted on wood, D 57.8 cm
Culture and Sport Glasgow (Museums). Acquired 1976 with the assistance of the National Fund for Acquisitions. A.1976.27.f
Fig. 256

D 1784, 31–2 [Staircase]: Two shields of leather, for tournaments, painted by Polidore; one has the head of Medusa, the other of Perseus: on the insides are battles in gold. They came out of the collection of commendatore Vittoria at Naples, and were sent to Mr. W. by sir W. Hamilton …
PROV: Collection of Commendatore Vittoria, Naples; Sir William Hamilton; 1774 given to HW; 1842, Strawberry Hill Sale, day 19, lot 86, bt Pratt, New Bond Street, £10.10.0; 1842, July 21, Oxenham Sale, lot 219, £7.10 [An Italian buckler, emblazoned with Medusa head, and the inner part a Roman subject, by Julio Romano]; 1844, April 25–27, Christie's, lot 233 [A fine shield of cuir bouilli, with the head of a Fury, painted by Julio Romano, having on the inside an illustration of Roman History—from Strawberry Hill], 7gns; 1845, July 2–3, Deacon's, lot 249 [A very singular cuir bouilli shield, of the Venetian guard, with highly finished painting in Roman subjects, and finely executed illustrations of a winged fury]; by 1857, Lord Hastings; 1950, June 9, Sotheby's, Rt Hon. Lord Hastings, removed from Melton Constable, Norfolk, lot 155, bt Dr Richard Williams, £13.0.0; 1974 (donated in lieu of death duties to) Royal Armouries, H. M. Tower of London; 1976, bt Glasgow Museums, Culture and Sport.
LIT: J. R. Planché, 'The Armoury', in J. B. Waring, *A Handbook of the Museum of Ornamental Art in the Art Treasures Exhibition* (London, 1857), 76. Francis Henry Cripps-Day, *A Record of Armour Sales, 1881–1924* (London: G. Bell and Sons, 1925), xxxv. Helen Adamson, 'Armour and Weapons from the Tower of London', *Scottish Art Review*, special number vol. 15, no. 2 (1979): 23–6. *Romantic Interior*, 100, fig. 80.
EXHIB: Manchester, 'Art Treasures Exhibition', 1857.
NOTE: A second parade shield painted with the head of Medusa also from the Armoury and acquired by HW at the same time is now at the National Gallery of Ireland, Dublin.

55. DOOR LOCK
Attributed to Henry Romayne (d. 1553), English, about 1528–50

Pierced iron: 25.5 × 17.7 cm
The Walters Art Museum, Baltimore, Maryland. 52.91
Fig. 153

D 1784, 93 [Armory]: Curiosities added since this Book was completed…In the Armoury. A curious royal lock, made as early as in the reign of Henry 7th. from one of the palaces; a present from Thomas Astle, esq.
PROV: 1788, given to HW by Thomas Astle; 1842, Strawberry Hill Sale, day 19, lot 91, bt Webb, Old Bond Street, £2.12.6; Jeffrey Whitehead, London; Christie's, London, sold to Harding, London; Henry Walters; 1931, The Walters Art Gallery [now The Walters Art Museum] upon the death of Henry Walters.
LIT: *HW Corres.* 42: 223. M. C. Ross, 'A Gothic Lock from Strawberry Hill', *The American Collector* 11, no. 8 (Sept. 1942): 5. Claude Blair, 'The Most Superb of all Royal Locks', *Apollo* (Christmas 1966): 73.
NOTE: The lock was mounted on the centre of the false door in the Armoury.

56. THE CASTLE OF OTRANTO, A STORY. TRANSLATED BY WILLIAM MARSHAL, GENT. FROM THE ORIGINAL ITALIAN OF ONUPHRIO MURALTO …
Horace Walpole (1717–1797)

London: T. Lownds, 1765
18 × 11.5 cm
Inscriptions: Cole's autograph, armorial bookplate, corrections, and notes, including transcript of G. Birch's verses to Horace Walpole.
The Lewis Walpole Library, Yale University.
24 17 765 Copy 1
Yale Center for British Art only
Fig. 12

PROV: HW; gift of HW to W. Cole; 1777, gift of W. Cole to Hester Barnardiston; 1925, May, Maggs to W. S. Lewis; The Lewis Walpole Library, Yale University.
LIT: *HW Corres.* 1: 85, 86, 88, 91, 92. *Bib. HW* no. 17, copy 2. *Collector's Progress*, 89–90. Mellon Lectures, 82, 142, 157–62, 165, 166, 175, 194. *Rescuing Horace*, 181–9.

57. The Castle of Otranto. 6th Edition
Horace Walpole (1717–1797)

Parma: Bodoni, for J. Edwards, 1791
25.5 × 17 cm
Extra-illustrated with four wash drawings by Bertie Greatheed the younger (*c.* 1781–1804), 1796. With a copy of a letter to the artist's father (22 Feb. 1796) in Kirgate's hand from HW signed Orford and a letter from the publisher Edwards. Additional notes in the hand of J. W. Ford.
Rebound in red morocco.
Bookplate of HW as Lord Orford (type 1) on half-title.
The Lewis Walpole Library, Yale University.
49 3729
Fig. 14

1842 Sale [Round Tower]: The Castle of Otranto, printed by Bodoni, at Parma, 8vo, large paper with plates, with a curious manuscript letter by Lord Orford inserted …
London Sale: Il Castello di Otranto, Storia Gothica, by Onuphrio Muralto, plates coloured, Morocco, London, 1795, and a Translation of the same into English, by Wm. Marshall, Lond., 1791.
prov: HW; 1842, Strawberry Hill Sale, day 7, lot 76, [listed]; 1842, Strawberry Hill London Sale, day 8, lot 1030 [sold], bt Payne and Foss, £1.11.6; 1884, May 1, Puttick and Simpson, Gosford Sale, lot 3071, bt Harvey, £7; 1897, April 1, Christie's, Reginald Cholmondeley Sale, lot 114, bt Quaritch, £11.5.0; 1905, John W. Ford; 1909, May 21, Sotheby's, Miscellaneous Sale, lot 362, bt B. F. Stevens, £15.5.0; 1912, January 19, Hoe Sale, part 2, lot 3420, $60; 1913, December 10, Sotheby's, Hoe Books, lot 173, bt Edwards, £7; Earl of Cromer; 1937, March, Edwards to W. S. Lewis; The Lewis Walpole Library, Yale University.
lit: *HW Corres.* 11: 150, 150n, 170, 15: 212, 213, 31: 369 35: 436, 43: 145. *Bib. HW* no. 17, p. 62. *Library* 3729. Mellon Lectures, 82, 142, 157–62, 165, 166, 175, 194.

58. Portrait of Henry Carey, Lord Falkland, Deputy of Ireland
Marcus Geeraerts (1561–1635), *c.* 1603

Oil on canvas, 217 2 × 127 cm
Sarah Campbell Blaffer Foundation, Houston, Texas.
BF/1985.19
Fig. 118

D 1774, 71 [Re: Strawberry Hill version] [Gallery]: Window side…Henry Carey lord Falkland, deputy of Ireland, and father of the famous Lucius lord Falkland; in white, by Vansomer.
D 1784, 51 [same as above, with added note*] *The idea of the picture walking out of its frame in the Castle of Otranto, was suggested by this portrait.]
prov: Not Strawberry Hill Collection. Falkland Family Collection; 1985, Charles Jerdein, London, bt Sarah Campbell Blaffer Foundation.
lit: *HW Corres.* 1: 88, 42: 106. Martin Butlin, *Aspects of British Painting, 1550–1800: From the Sarah Campbell Blaffer Foundation* (Houston: the Foundation, 1988), 26–7.
note: The Strawberry Hill copy of this picture is currently untraced but is virtually identical to the version shown here. A note in HW's hand in *D 1774* (The Lewis Walpole Library, Yale University, 49.25522A) records that 'The picture walking out of its frame in the castle of Otranto was suggested by this which is all in white.'

59. 'The Entry of Frederick into the Castle of Otranto'
John Carter (1748–1817), 1790

Pen and black ink with grey and blue watercolour on laid paper, 60.2 × 50.3 cm (visible); 62.4 × 52.5 cm (mount)
Inscriptions: title and signature at lower center in artist's hand: 'John Carter int. & delt. 1790 / The Entry of Frederick into Castle of Otranto'
The Lewis Walpole Library, Yale University.
790.00.00.138dr++
Fig. 13

D 1784, 95: More Additions … Procession in the Castle of Otranto, in water-colours, by J. Carter.
1842 Sale: [In the Little Parlour]: A very fine watercolour drawing, representing the Procession in the Romance of the Castle of Otranto, an exceedingly clever composition, by J. Carter.
prov: Sold by the artist to HW, 20gns; 1842, Strawberry Hill Sale, day 22, lot 100, bt Rev Hor. Cholmondeley, £8.18.6; descended to his grandson General Sir Henry Jackson; 1962, May, Sir Henry Jackson, bt W. S. Lewis (with other prints), £575; The Lewis Walpole Library, Yale University.
lit: 'Portraits': 25 B.7, pls. 26b and 27. *Rescuing Horace*, ill. p. 185.
exhib: Royal Academy of Arts, 1790, no. 566.
note: A note by John Carter in his extra-illustrated copy of *D 1784* records that he 'was paid for it 20 guineas.' (The Lewis Walpole Library, Yale University, 33.30 copy 20).

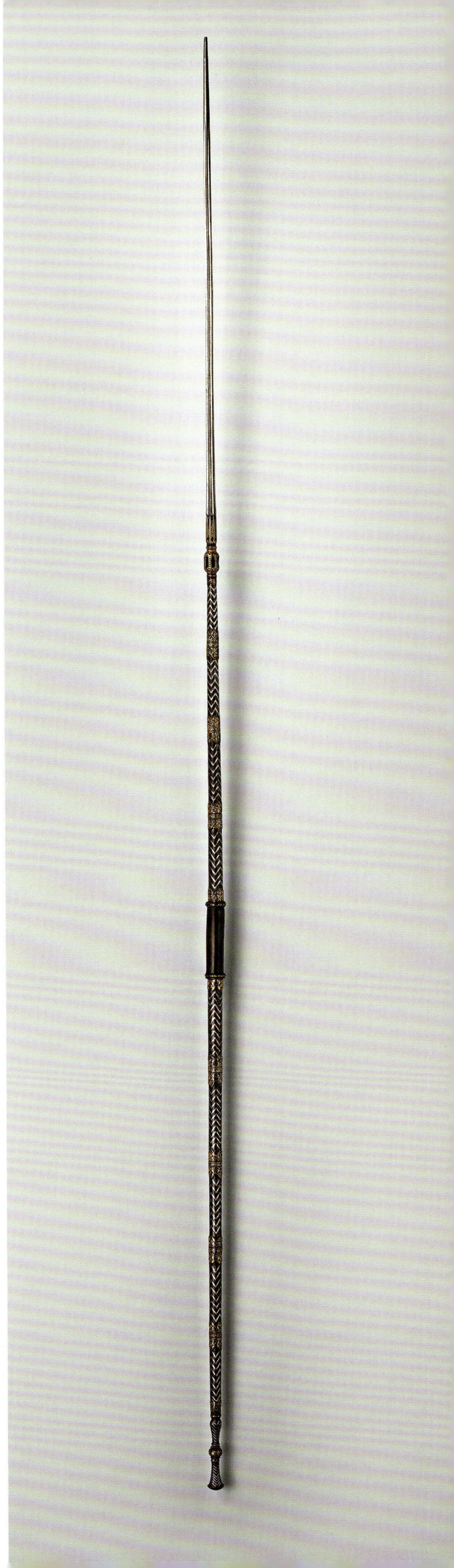

Figure 308. Catalogue 53

5. THE ANTIQUARIAN INTERIOR: THE REFECTORY OR GREAT PARLOUR

60. 'Chimneypiece in the Refectory or great parlour at Strawberryhill'
Richard Bentley (bap. 1708, d. 1782), *c.* 1754

Pen and ink, wash, and pencil on laid paper, 22.9 × 20 cm
Signed: 'R. Bentley inv.'
Inscriptions: inscribed by the artist with dimensions; inscribed with title in HW's hand on the page in his album of drawings assembled under the title *Drawings and designs by Richd. Bentley*, *c.* 1760.
The Lewis Walpole Library, Yale University.
Folio 49 3585 fol. 32
Fig. 113

From *Drawings and Designs by Richd. Bentley* (*c.* 1760, fol. 32)
D 1774, 49 [Library]: Rare books of prints and drawings in the library… Designs by Mr. Richard Bentley, bound in marble and gilt.
D 1784, 37, same as *D 1774*.
PROV: The drawing commissioned by HW; for the album see Cat. 18 [Bentley, Entry from the Road]
LIT: *Library* 3585. *Collector's Progress*, 104–8 on Bentley's drawings for Strawberry Hill. *Rescuing Horace*, 53–61. Bentley thesis, fig. 53. *Romantic Interior*, 82, fig. 59.
NOTE: Engraved by T. Morris for *D 1784*, opp. p. 3, as *Chimney in the Great Parlour*. The dimensions on the drawing suggest that it was made as a design.

61. Chair
William Hallett, Sr. (*c.* 1707–1781), designed by Richard Bentley (bap. 1708, d. 1782) and Horace Walpole (1717–1797), probably by February 1755

Beech, painted black to imitate ebony, 132 × 60.8 × 53 cm The upholstery of the seat modern.
The Lewis Walpole Library, Yale University.
Yale Center for British Art only
Fig. 49

D 1774, 5 [Refectory]: The chairs are black, of a gothic pattern, designed by Mr. Bentley and Mr. Walpole.
D 1784, 4, same as *D 1774*.
PROV: 1755, HW; 1842, Strawberry Hill Sale, day 19, lot 49, bt Piggott, Richmond, £5.15.6; or lot 52, bt Piggott, Richmond, £4.14.6.
LIT: *Accounts* [6] 83–4, note 8. *HW Corres* 14:60, 35:181–2. Ralph Edwards, *The Shorter Dictionary of English Furniture* (London: Country Life, 1964), 146, 659. John Cornforth, 'The Cowles-Lewis House, Farmington – II', *Country Life* (27 April 1978), 1153. *OHG* 84. Peter Thornton, *Authentic Décor: The Domestic Interior 1620–1920* (New York: Viking, 1984), 175. *Romantic Interior* 85–7 and 92, fig. 65. Megan Aldrich, *Gothic Revival* (London: Phaidon, 1994), 64. Chris Brooks, *The Gothic Revival* (London: Phaidon, 1999), 87, 91. Percy Macquoid and Ralph Edwards, *The Dictionary of English Furniture*, rev. ed., (Woodbridge and Wappingers' Falls, NY: Antique Collectors' Club Ltd., 2000) vol. 1, 284.
NOTE: Of the eight Gothic chairs made for the Refectory, four are at the Lewis Walpole Library and one at the Victoria and Albert Museum.

62. Chair
William Hallett, Sr. (*c.* 1707–1781), designed by Richard Bentley (bap. 1708, d. 1782) and Horace Walpole (1717–1797), probably by February 1755

Beech, painted black to imitate ebony, the upholstery of the seat modern, the finial added 2000
134.6 × 61 × 53.3 cm
Victoria and Albert Museum, London. W.29–1989
Victoria and Albert Museum only

D 1774, 5 [Refectory]: The chairs are black, of a gothic pattern, designed by Mr. Bentley and Mr. Walpole.
D 1784, 4, same as *D 1774*.
PROV: 1755, HW; 1842, Strawberry Hill Sale, day 19, lot 49, bt Piggott, Richmond, £5.15.6; or lot 52, bt Piggott, Richmond, £4.14.6; David Hicks; 1979, March 20–22, Sotheby's, Britwell House, David and Pamela Hicks, lot 11; Simon Redburn Fine Arts Ltd; 1979 Victoria and Albert Museum, purchased with the assistance of the Brigadier Clark Bequest Fund, through The Art Fund.
LIT: See Cat. 61.

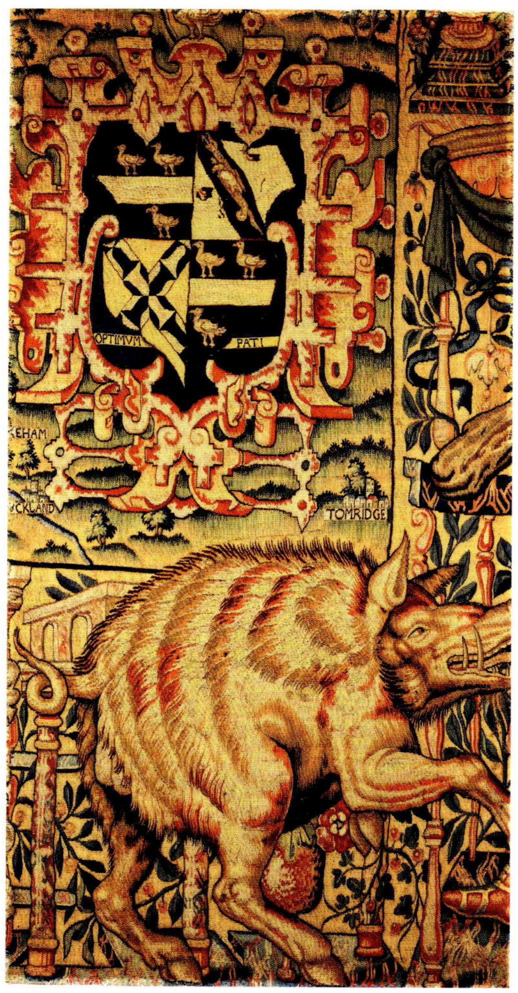

Figure 309. Catalogue 64

63. Pier Glass with a Portrait of George Walpole, 3rd Lord Orford
William Hallett senior (*c.* 1707–1781). Designed by Horace Walpole (1717–1797), *c.* 1754–5. The portrait by John Giles Eccardt (d. 1779) after Jean Etienne Liotard (1702–1789), 1755

Ebonised and gilded wood, glass. Set with a portrait in oil on canvas, 206 × 83.9 cm
Accepted by H. M. Government in lieu of Inheritance Tax, 2008.
Fig. 51

D 1774, 5–6 [Refectory]: Over each [card-tables of rose-wood], a looking-glass in a gothic frame of black and gold, designed by Mr. Walpole. Inclosed in the tops of the frames, with their arms and coronets, are the portraits of George Walpole third earl of Orford, and of George Cholmondeley viscount Malpas, eldest son of George earl of Cholmondely and of Mary second daughter of sir Robert Walpole. The former is copied by Eckardt, from a miniature by Liotard, in the cabinet above stairs: the latter is original by Eckardt.
D 1784, 4, same as *D 1774*.
PROV: 1754, HW; 1842, Strawberry Hill Sale, day 19, lot 60 (as a pair with lot 61), bt Lord Walpole, £13.2.6; Accepted by H. M. Government in lieu of Inheritance Tax, 2008.
LIT: *Accounts* [6] 84, note 9. *OHG* 85.

64. Portion of a tapestry map, showing part of Oxfordshire and Berkshire
Sheldon looms, Barcheston, Warwickshire or Bordesley, Worcesteshire, (fl. *c.* 1560–*c.* 1615), *c.* 1588

Woven in wool & silk, 126 × 65 cm
From the lower right hand corner of the map of Oxfordshire and Berkshire, showing the coat of arms of Ralph Sheldon senior (1537–1613) and the family motto OPTIMUM PATI.
Victoria and Albert Museum, London. T61–1953
Fig. 309

D 1774, 149 [Refectory]: Additions since the appendix. In the Great Parlour…A two-leafed screen, containing part of a map of Surry and Middlesex. It is a piece of the first tapestry woven in England, and came from Weston in Warwickshire, the seat of the Sheldons who introduced the manufacture. The complete suite of hangings were purchased by Mr. Walpole, and presented by him to the earl of Harcourt. This specimen had never been hung up.

D 1784, 84: Additions, same as *D 1774*.

PROV: Made for Ralph Sheldon the elder for Weston Hall, Warkwickshire. 1781, 27 Aug. and 7–12 Sept, Weston Hall Sale, Christie and Ansell, bt HW, 4 tapestries, 30gns or £; 1842, Strawberry Hill Sale, day 17, lot 59, bt Strong, Bristol, £12.12; Strong Cat, 3417, £15.15; 1920, March 26, Sotheby's, lot 133, bt Harris £1010; ?date, Property of H. Bribeck; 1936, June 18, E. of Dudley property, lot 131, bt Mallett, £1008; 1947, December, bequeathed to Mrs H. McKnight Franchot by her grandfather Charles Scott McKnight (to whom it came by will from Mrs Louisa Griswold, before 1875); 1954, presented to the Victoria and Albert Museum, London, by Mrs Franchot.

LIT: H. G. Fordham, *Studies in Carto-Bibliography* (Oxford: Clarendon Press, 1914). E. A. B. Barnard and A. J. B. Wace, 'The Sheldon Tapestry Weavers and their Work', *Archaeologia* LXXVIII (1928), 255–318; also reprinted as a monograph (Oxford, Society of Antiquaries, 1928). *HW Corres.* 16: 195n, 29: 360. G. F. Wingfield-Digby, *The Tapestry Collection, Medieval and Renaissance Tapestries* (London, 1980), no. 68. *OHG* 87. Anthony Wells-Cole, 'The Elizabethan Sheldon Tapestry Maps', *The Burlington Magazine*, 132, no. 1047 (June 1990): 392–401, fig. 4. Anthony Wells-Cole, *Art and Decoration in Elizabethan and Jacobean England* (New Haven and London, 1997), 223, pl. 379.

NOTE: The other map fragment in Walpole's screen, cut from the same map of Oxfordshire and Berkshire, also shows a part of Surrey and Middlesex very close to Strawberry Hill.

65. HUNTING HORN

French, Limoges, by Léonard Limousin (*c.* 1505–*c.* 1575), 1538

Copper, silver, coloured and grisaille-painted enamel and cow's horn, L 30.5 cm
Signed: LEONARDUS LEMOVICUS and dated 1538
Private collection
Figs. 221, 222

D 1774, 5 [Refectory]: Over the table hangs a hunting-horn, finely enamelled on one side in colours, on the other in chiaro scuro, with the history of saint Hubert.

D 1784, 4, same as *D 1774*.

PROV: Said (by 1850) to have belonged to King Francis I of France, but with no early evidence; HW paid £5.5.0; 1842, Strawberry Hill Sale, day 19, lot 48, bt Webb, Old Bond Street, £141.15.0; Hollingworth Magniac, Colworth, Bedfordshire; 1892, July 2–4, Christie's, Magniac sale, lot 403, bt Henry Pfungst, £6,615; Rothschild Family; Rosenberg & Stiebel (this dealer originally had it on consignment from the Rothschild Family; *c.* 1953), Mr and Mrs Alastair Bradley Martin, loan to the Metropolitan Museum of Art; Private collection.

LIT: *1842 Sale*, p. ix (ill.). J. C. Robinson, *Notices of the Principal Works of Art in the Collection of Hollingworth Magniac, Esq.* (London, 1861), no. 90. Yvonne Hackenbroch, 'A Limoges Enamel Hunting Horn', *Connoisseur* 133 (June 1954): 249–51. Thomas P. F. Hoving, 'Valuable and Ornamental Items: The Collection of Mr and Mrs Alastair Bradley Martin', *The Metropolitan Museum of Art Bulletin* 28 3 (Nov. 1969): 146–60. *The Guennol Collection* (New York: Metropolitan Museum of Art, 1982): 25–30.

EXHIB: [A. W. Franks], 'Catalogue of Works of Antient and Mediaeval Art exhibited at the House of the Society of Arts', London, 1850, no. 353. 1862 Special Exhibition, no. 1690. 'Special Loan Exhibition of Enamels on Metal Held at the South Kensington Museum in 1874.' London, 1875, no. 730.

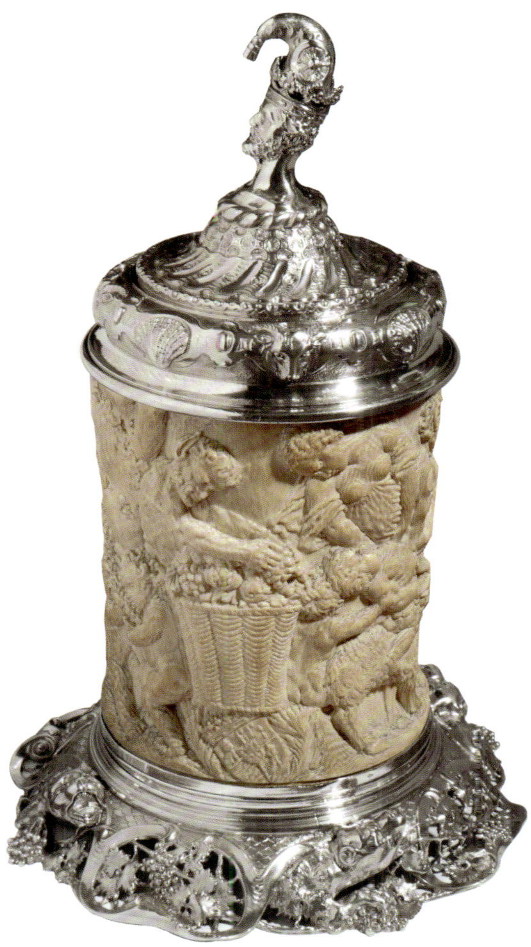

Figure 310. Catalogue 67

66. PAIR OF WINE COOLERS

William Lukin, (fl. from 1699), 1716–17

Britannia Standard Silver, cast, chased, and engraved, with swing handles, 21 × 21.1 cm
Marks: maker's mark: 'Lu', bezant below (William Lukin); Lion's head erased; Britannia standard; A in a pointed shield (London date letter for 1716–17)
Arms of Sir Robert Walpole, impaling those of his wife, Catherine Shorter
Lent by The Metropolitan Museum of Art, Gift of Irwin Untermyer, 1968 (68.141.128 and 68.141.129)
Fig. 50

1842 Sale [Blue Breakfast Room]: A pair of splendid octagon Wine Coolers, chased rose flower tablets, arabesque borders and scroll handles.

PROV: Ex-collection Sir Robert Walpole; inherited by HW; 1842, Strawberry Hill Sale, day 11, lot 127, bt Henry Hall, Esq., £208.17.9; Ashburnham Collection Sale, Christie's; 1914, March 24, lot 59; Bertram, 5th Earl of Ashburnham; Marchioness of Cholmondeley, Houghton Hall, King's Lynn; Cholmondeley Sale, Sotheby's (1950, Nov. 2) lot 150; 1968, The Metropolitan Museum of Art, New York, Gift of Irwin Untermyer.

LIT: *Highlights of the Untermeyer Collection of English and Continental Decorative Arts* (New York: Metropolitan Museum of Art, *c.* 1977), no. 80. W. W. Watts, 'Silver in the "Old London" Exhibition', *Apollo* 28 (April 1938): 189. Richard Came, *Silver* (New York: Putnam, 1961), 80, fig. 60.

67. LIDDED VASE

The ivory German, 1650–1700; the mounts in the style of Paul de Lamerie (1688–1751), *c.* 1740–5.

Ivory barrel in silver mounts and cover, cast and chased, total H 30 cm approx., D of base 20.5 cm at widest point; D of ivory section 12.4 cm
Silver cover surmounted with a finial in the form of the Walpole crest
Unmarked
Lent by the Rt Hon. the Earl of Derby, D100
Victoria and Albert Museum only
Fig. 310

1842 Sale: [Round Drawing Room]: A splendidly carved ivory cup, most elaborately and beautifully worked, representing a Bacchanalian Scene, the colour extremely pure, mounted on a finely chased silver stand, with Vine Leaves and the Hounds in full cry, the cover also beautifully chased, surmounted by the Walpole crest.

PROV: 1842, Strawberry Hill Sale, day 23, lot 40, bt. Earl of Derby, £39.18.0.

NOTE: For comparable decorative treatment cf. a cup and cover by de Lamerie of 1742–3 (Arthur Grimwade, *Rococo Silver 1727–1765* (London: Faber and Faber, 1974), fig. 7).

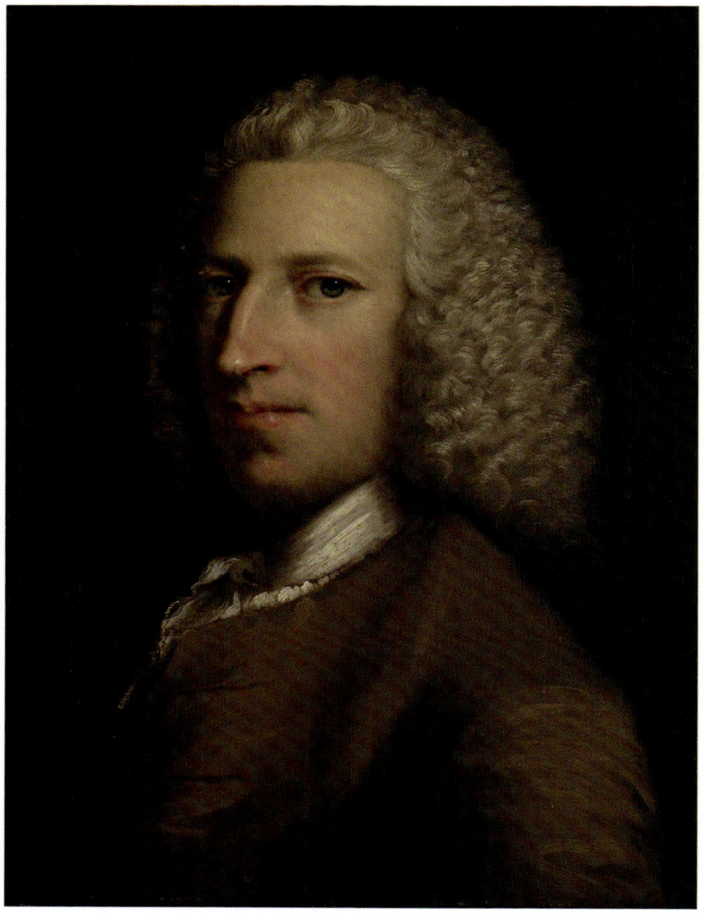

Figure 311. Catalogue 69

68. Portrait of Sir Horace Mann
John Astley (1720–1787), 1751

Oil on panel, 49.5 × 36.8 cm
Inscriptions: in ink on panel verso in HW's hand: Horace Mann, resident at Florence, by Astley, 1751
The Lewis Walpole Library, Yale University.
Fig. 6

D 1774, 5 [Refectory]: On one side of this picture [A *Conversation* by Reynolds], a head of sir Horace Mann, resident at Florence; painted there by Astley, and highly coloured: He is drest in red velvet.
D 1784, 3, same as *D 1774*.
PROV: 1752, given to HW by Horace Mann; 1842, Strawberry Hill Sale, day 21, lot 42, bt John P. Beavan, Esq., £6.6.0 [with pair Portrait of Galfridus Mann]; 1950, February 1, Sotheby's, Lord Hastings Collection, lot 71, bt Thomas Agnew & Sons for W. S. Lewis, £280; The Lewis Walpole Library, Yale University.
LIT: *HW Corres*. 20: 309–10, 313, repro. opp. p. 310. 23: 267. Mellon Lectures, pl. 18. *Rescuing Horace*, 148–9, ill. 149. J. Cornforth, 'The Cowles-Lewis House, Farmington, II, The Home of Mr Wilmarth S. Lewis', *Country Life* 4 (May 1978): 1232, ill. fig. 4.
NOTE: The portrait is in a contemporary Italian gilt wood frame.

69. Portrait of Galfridus Mann
John Astley (1720–1787), *c.* 1752

Oil on canvas, 49.5 × 49.5 cm
The Lewis Walpole Library, Yale University.
Fig. 311

D 1774, 5 [Refectory]: Opposite to it [Portrait of Sir Horace Mann], his brother Galfridus Mann, in brown; by the same [Astley].
D 1784, 3, same as *D 1774*.
PROV: 1842, Strawberry Hill Sale, day 21, lot 42, bt John P. Beavan, Esq., £6.6.0 [with pair Portrait of Horace Mann]; 1950, February 1, Sotheby's, Lord Hastings Collection, lot 71, bt Thomas Agnew & Sons for W. S. Lewis, £280; The Lewis Walpole Library, Yale University.
LIT: *HW Corres*. 21, repro. opp. p.34. *Rescuing Horace*, 148. J. Cornforth, 'The Cowles-Lewis House, Farmington, II, The Home of Mr Wilmarth S. Lewis', *Country Life* 4 (May 1978): 1230.
NOTE: The portrait is in a contemporary Italian gilt-wood frame, matching that of Cat. 68. Galfridus (1705–56) was Horace Mann's twin brother.

70. Portrait of the Ladies Waldegrave
Sir Joshua Reynolds (1723–1792), 1780–1

Oil on canvas, 143.5 × 168 cm
Marks: on the back of the painting is a label inscribed in Walpole's hand with the names of the sitters and the initials H.W.
National Gallery of Scotland, Edinburgh. Purchased with the assistance of The Art Fund 1952. NG 2171
Fig. 180

D 1784, 5 [Refectory]: Over against the chimney, a large piece of the ladies Laura, Maria, and Horatia Waldegrave, daughters of James, second earl of Waldegrave and Maria Walpole, afterwards duchess of Gloucester; by sir Joshua Reynolds, 1781.
PROV: Commissioned by HW, great-uncle of the sitters; 1842, Strawberry Hill Sale, day 21, lot 35, bt Earl Waldegrave, £577.10.0; bequeathed by Frances, widow of 7th Earl, to her 4th husband Chichester Fortescue, later Lord Carlingford; 1886, June, Lord Carlingford sold it to Agnew's via Sir Francis Bolton; Agnew's sold it to Daniel Thwaites of Blackburn, whose daughter Elma Amy married Robert Armstrong Yerburgh; 1952, November 21, Robert Daniel Thwaites Yerbury, 1st Baron Alvingham, sold it via Agnew's to National Gallery of Scotland with help from National Art Collections Fund.
LIT: *HW Corres*. 29: 45–6, 138, 285, 35: 532. Ellis Waterhouse, *Reynolds* (London: Kegan Paul, Trench Trubner, 1941), 72. Mellon Lectures, 122. Colin Thompson and Hugh Brigstocke, *National Gallery of Scotland: Shorter Catalogue* (Edinburgh, 1970), 81. Nicholas Penny, *Reynolds* (New York: Abrams, 1986), no. 122. David Mannings, *Sir Joshua Reynolds: A Complete Catalogue of his Paintings*, 2 vols. (New Haven: Yale University Press, 2000), cat no. 1810. Martin Postle, ed., *Joshua Reynolds: The Creation of Celebrity*, exh. cat., Palazzo dei Diamanti, Ferrara and Tate Britain, London (London: Tate Publishing, 2005), no. 27.
EXHIB: Royal Academy, 1781, no. 187, as 'Portraits of three ladies;' British Institution, 1823, no. 15; British Institution, 1856, no. 157; South Kensington 1867, no. 452; Grosvenor, 1883, no. 27; Guildhall, 1890, no. 104; Agnew's, 1899, no. 11.
NOTE: Shown from left to right are Lady Charlotte Maria (1761–1808), Lady Elizabeth Laura (1760–1816), and Lady Anna Horatia (1762–1801).

6. THE ANTIQUARIAN INTERIOR: THE LIBRARY

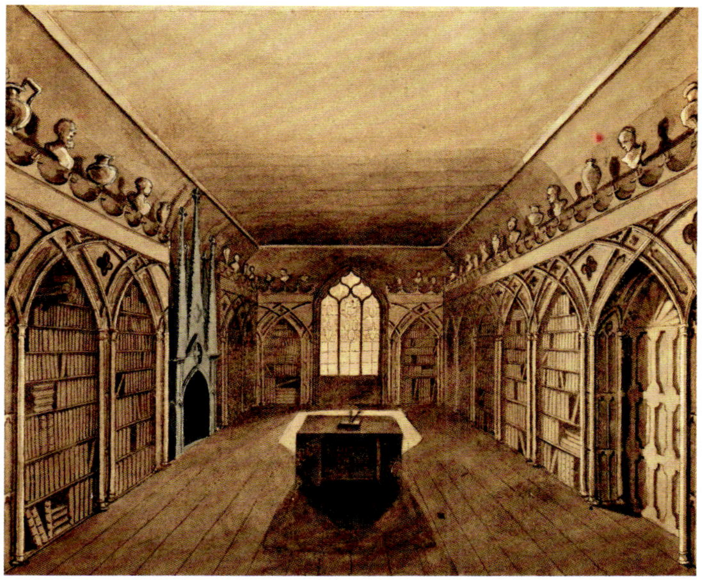

Figure 312. Catalogue 71

71. 'Design for the Library at Strawberry hill …'
Richard Bentley (bap. 1708, d. 1782), 1753

Grey and brown wash with pen and ink and pencil on laid paper, 16 × 18.3 cm (visible)
Inscriptions: title and artist on verso and on the album page in HW's hand
The Lewis Walpole Library, Yale University.
Folio 49 3585 fol. 37 from *Drawings and Designs by Richd. Bentley* (*c.* 1760, fol. 37)
Fig. 312

D 1774, 49 [Library]: Rare books of prints and drawings in the library…*Designs by Mr. Richard Bentley*, bound in marble and gilt.
D 1784, 37 same as *D 1774*.
PROV: Drawing commissioned by HW; for album see Cat. 18
LIT: *Library* 3585. *Collector's Progress*, 105. *Rescuing Horace*, 53–61. Bentley thesis, fig. 58. *Gothic Revival*, 81–4.
NOTE: This is one of two designs for the library which were mounted on a single page in the album and titled on the page in HW's hand: 'First Designs for the Library at Strawberry hill.'
NOTE: A HW bookplate has been pasted in at a later date. On a plate showing the screen one of the doorways to the side of the screen, the source of the design of the SH library bookcases, has been cut out.

72. The History of St Paul's Cathedral in London, from Its Foundation Until These Times…
Sir William Dugdale (1605–1686), 1658

London: Printed by Tho. Warren, 1658
33.5 × 23
The Vyne, The Chute Collection (The National Trust)
See Fig. 263

PROV: 1842, inventory of the library at The Vyne; The Vyne, National Trust.
LIT: 'Genesis': 57–92. *HW Corres.* 16: 143, 35: 157n, 164, 40: 221, 41: 39. *Library* 591 (HW's copy).

73. Design for the Ceiling in the Library at Strawberry Hill
Horace Walpole (1717–1797), 1754

Pen and ink on laid paper, 18.2 × 11.2 cm (sheet)
The Lewis Walpole Library, Yale University.
754.00.00.22dr
Fig. 266

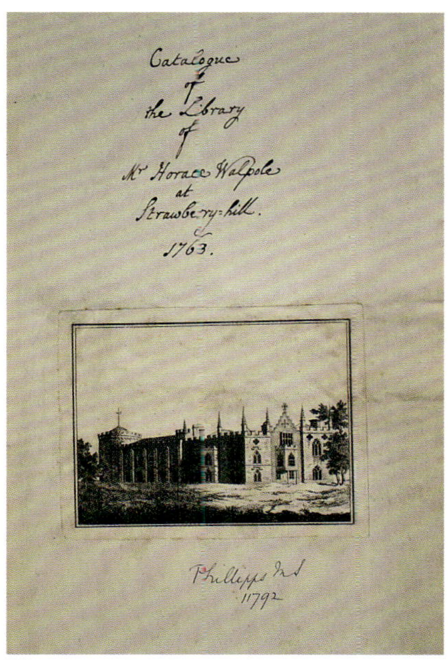

Figure 313. Catalogue 76

PROV: Probably Richard Bentley; HW?; 1947, December 15, Waller Sale, Christie's, lot 47, bt Maggs for W. S. Lewis; The Lewis Walpole Library, Yale University.
LIT: *HW Corres.* 35: 171. Bentley thesis, fig. 62.
NOTE: This is probably the drawing that was sent with HW's letter to Richard Bentley 1754, March 18. See Lit.

74. The Library at Strawberry Hill
Edward Edwards (1738–1806), *c.* 1781

Watercolour, pencil, and pen and ink on laid paper, 31 × 45.3 cm (sheet); 35.6 × 49.8 cm (mount)
The Lewis Walpole Library, Yale University.
SH Views 781.00.00.45dr
Fig. 52

PROV: Probably commissioned by HW; 1939, Gaskill Collection, bt W. S. Lewis; The Lewis Walpole Library, Yale University.
LIT: *Rescuing Horace*, 117. *Romantic Interior*, fig. 69.
NOTE: Engraved by Richard Bernard Godfrey for *D 1784*, opp. p. 33, as *Library at Strawberry Hill.*

75. Portrait of Horace Walpole in his Library
Johann Heinrich Müntz (1727–1798), 1755–59

Pen and ink and wash, 50.8 × 38.1 cm (visible); 63.5 × 48 cm (frame)
On the back of the frame is written in pencil in a 19th century hand: 'The View of the Library/at Strawberry hill / by / J. H. Muntz.'
Private collection
Frontispiece

PROV: HW?; Sir Alexander Johnston?; Lieutenant-Colonel Bruce Campbell-Johnston; Commander Colin Campbell-Johnston; Private collection.
LIT: Dorothy Margaret Stuart, *A Book of Bird and Beasts; Legendary, Literary, and Historical* (London: Methuen, 1957), 146–8 and illus. opp. p. 132. W. S. Lewis, *Horace Walpole's Library* (Cambridge: Cambridge University Press, 1958), repro. opp. p. 1. 'Portraits': A.11, 14. *Gothick 1720–1840* (exh. cat. Brighton: Royal Pavilion, Art Gallery and Museum, 1975), cat. no. D12. *OHG* 89. *Romantic Interior*, fig. 91. Chris Brooks, *The Gothic Revival* (London: Phaidon, 1999), 86 and pl. 53. John Ingamells, *National Portrait Gallery Mid-Georgian Portraits, 1760–1790* (London: National Portrait Gallery, 2004), 371.

76. Manuscript Catalogue of the Library of Horace Walpole at Strawberry Hill
Horace Walpole (1717–1797). Compiled 1763–1797

Manuscript, folio 32.6 cm × 20.3 cm × 35 cm
Bound in calf, gilt arms of Horace Walpole on covers
Inscriptions: Note by Phillips: 'From Strawberry Hill 1842. P.'
The Wormsley Library,
collection of the late Sir Paul Getty, KBE
Fig. 313

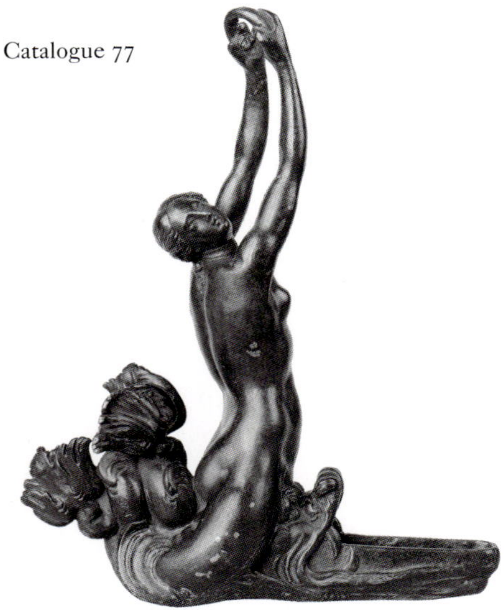

Figure 314. Catalogue 77

1842 Sale [Library]: *A Catalogue of the Books in the Library, at Strawberry Hill*, in manuscript, folio
PROV: 1842, Strawberry Hill Sale, day 4, lot 131, bt Thorpe, £4.4.0; 1899, June 10, Sir Thomas Phillipps Sale (MS 11792), Sotheby's, lot 1173, bt Eillis, £3.0.0; 1902, May 14, J. W. Ford Sale, Sotheby's, lot 5561, bt Quaritch, £24.0.0; 1902, November, offered by Quaritch in Cat. 218, lot 170, for £31.10.0, Horatio, 5th earl of Orford; by descent; 1989, Dec. 12, Christies, lot 221, bt Maggs for Wormsley.
LIT: *Library* 2164.
NOTE: This reference catalogue was kept on a table in the library. It was begun in 1763, written by a clerk, with additions added by Walpole, 1763–6, and further additions to the books in the main library by Thomas Kirgate in 1797, and a few additions by Mrs Damer in 1810.

77. OIL LAMP
Barthélemy Prieur (1536–1611)
c. 1600

Bronze, 18 × 14 cm
Paris, Musée du Louvre. OA 8982
Yale Center for British Art only
Fig. 314

D 1774, 45 [Library]: Two bronze antique lamps and chains.
D 1784, 34 same as *D 1774*.
PROV: HW; (possibly) 1842, Strawberry Hill Sale, day 17, lot 46, bt Hor. Rodd, £3.0.0; Baron Leonino; 1937, Musée du Louvre.
LIT: *1842 Sale*, ill. p. vii.

78. CLOCK AND BRACKET
Clock and weights; Maker or makers unknown, 16th century with later modifications; bracket made by B.L. Vulliamy in 1844, reproducing a bracket of *c.* 1760 perhaps designed by Richard Bentley; one silver medallion made by B.L. Vulliamy in 1844.

Surmounted by a lion finial carrying shield engraved with the royal arms, the side doors engraved with the royal arms, the weights engraved 'DIEU ET MON DROIT' the initials H and A with lover's knots and 'THE MOST HAPPYE'. The bracket set with 13 small heads in relief of Maximilian I, Francis I, Charles V and others, 12 transferred from the original.
The clock gilt metal, the two weights gilt copper over lead: the dial with a silvered chapter; bracket carved and gilt pear wood set with silver-gilt heads. Clock 25.5 × 10.9 × 10.7 cm; bracket 27.6 × 17.8 × 18.2 cm; weights: H 19.7; H 17.8.
The Royal Collection, RCIN30018.
Fig. 56

D 1774, 47 [Library]: A clock of silver gilt, richly chased, engraved, and ornamented with fleurs de lys, little heads, &c. on the top sits a lion holding the arms of England, which are also on the sides. This was a present from Henry 8th to Anne Boleyn; and since, from the lady Elizabeth Germaine to Mr. Walpole. On the weights are the initial letters of Henry and Anne, within true lovers knots; at top, Dieu et mon droit; at bottom, The most happy. One of the weights, agreeably to the indelicacy of that monarch's galantry, is in a shape very conformable to the last motto. The pedestal is adorned with small heads of bronze gilt of the age of Henry 8th but which did not belong to the clock.
D 1784, 35 same as *D 1774*.
PROV: Clock: by 1760, Lady Elizabeth Germain gave to HW; 1842, Strawberry Hill Sale, day 17, lot 48, bt [Sequier for] Her Majesty, Queen Victoria, £110.5.0; Royal Library, Windsor, Collection of H. M. The Queen. The bracket: made for HW; then as above.
LIT: *HW Corres.* 2: 334n, 9: 304, 29: 39. OHG 99 (the bracket). Cedric Jagger, *Royal Clocks: the British Monarchy and its Timekeepers, 1300–1900* (London: R. Hale, 1983), 232–9. *Romantic Interior*, 92. Delia Millar, 'Family Connections', *Country Life* 8 (March 1990), 108–11. David Starkey, *Henry VIII: A European Court in England* (New York: Cross River Press, 1991), XI.17. *A Royal Miscellany from the Royal Library, Windsor Castle* (exh. cat. London: The Queen's Gallery, 1990), no. 213.
NOTE: A Principal Curiosity. 'The Most Happy' was the motto of Anne Boleyn. A record of B.L. Vulliamy's making of the new bracket, 'carved exactly as the old one', gilding the heads and making a new one, is in the Royal Archives (LC11/12564)

79. PORTRAIT OF CHARLES II
William Faithorne (*c.* 1620–1691), published by Thomas Collins (fl. 1650–67), 1660–70

Engraving, 32.9 × 23.8 cm
British Museum, Department of Prints and Drawings. 1842,0806.376

D 1774, 48 [Library]: Rare books of prints and drawings in the library…Faithorne's works, most beautiful impressions; folio.
D 1784, 36 same as *D 1774*.
PROV: HW; 1842, Strawberry Hill Sale, day 8, lot 114 [listed]; 1842, Strawberry Hill London Sale, day 6, lot 749 [sold], bt Graves Pall Mall, £0.10.6; 1842, The British Museum.
LIT: MC D.1.28. Louis Fagan, *A Descriptive Catalogue of the Engraved Works of William Faithorne* (London: Bernard Quaritch, 1888), 8. F. O'Donoghue, *Engraved British Portraits*, vol. 1 (1908), 401, no. 113. *HW Corres.* 1: 60n. *Library* 3643. *OHG* 101.

80. CHARTA DE FORESTA (CHARTER OF THE FORESTS)
English, 1299

Manuscript, pen and ink on parchment: 32.5 × 35.9 cm; Great Seal of Edward I (damaged): 8.5 × 8.4 cm – attached to manuscript by a parchment tab, with a further tab extension. In the rolled MS a turned mahogany stick, the seal in a velvet-lined tin skippet. All contained in a shaped document case perhaps made *c.* 1743. Wood covered with stamped calf, with brass catches. The top lettered 'CHARTA DE FOREST Ao 28 EDWd I 1299'. The interior lined with waste paper, printers' scraps and decorative paper. On paper pasted into the lid an inscription, in Latin, presumably by Robert Bygrave, *c.* 1743, setting out the provenance of the document and its history, 46.7 × 14.4 × 4.1 cm, at widest point.
The Provost and Fellows of Eton College. ECL MS284

D 1774, 52 [Library]: Curious books in the glass closet in the library... The Charter of Forests, one of the original copies finely preserved, with the great seal of Edward 1st. appendant; found at Hackney 1743, among writings of the ancient family of Shordich, by Robert Bygrave; presented by him to sir Edward Walpole, and by him to his brother Horace.
D 1784, 38–39 same as *D 1774*.
PROV: The Shordich family, Hackney; Robert Bygrave to Edward Walpole; Edward Walpole gave to HW; bequeathed by him, in its 'leathern case' to Eton College Library.
LIT: 'The Great Charter of the Forest, Declaring the Liberties of it. Made at Westminster... London' (printed for John Kidgell at the Atlas in Cornhill, near the Royal Exchange, 1680). *Library* 2547.
NOTE: A Principal Curiosity. The Charter of the Forests was issued with the revised Magna Carta by Henry III in 1217. This is an example confirmed by Edward I.

81. AN ALBUM OF PORTRAIT DRAWINGS OF FRANCIS I, MEMBERS OF HIS FAMILY AND COURT, WITH ADDED FRENCH PORTRAIT DRAWINGS
Thirty drawings by an anonymous French artist after Jean Clouet, mid-16th century. Sixteen later 16th and 17th century portraits by different hands have been interpolated into the volume.

Mostly red and black chalks: some with added brown, blue and yellow, 27.2 cm
Inscriptions: by Pierre-Jean Mariette, HW (identifying the sitters on the versos), and anonymous 16th century and later hands.
Lent by the Rt Hon. the Earl of Derby. W418
Victoria and Albert Museum only
Fig. 267

D 1774, 132 [Library]: Appendix…In the Library … A book of French portraits in the time of Francis 1st. It belonged to Brantome, who has inscribed the names of several of the persons. From the collection of Mons. Mariette at Paris.
D 1784, 37 [Library]: Rare books of prints and drawings in the library…and same as *D 1774*.
PROV: 1775, November 15–1776, January 30, Pierre-Jean Mariette's Sale, lot 1414, bt HW; 1842, Strawberry Hill Sale, day 6, lot 15, bt Boone [for Lord Derby], £63.0.0.

LIT: *HW Corres.* 2: 9, 7: 307, 32: 282. Anon, 'The Treasures of Strawberry Hill III', *The Gentleman's Magazine* (1842): 258. [H. Harrison Ainsworth], 'Strawberry Hill', *Ainsworth's Magazine: a miscellany of romance, general literature and art* 1 (1842): 103. H. Harrison Ainsworth, 'Description des trésors de Strawberry-Hill', *Cabinet de l'amateur et de l'antiquaire* 1 (1842): 447–8. André Salmon, 'Nouvelles notes sur les Clouet', *Archives de l'Art Français* (1855): 297. Eugène Piot, 'Exposition des amateurs anglais au musée de Kensington', *Le cabinet de l'amateur et de l'antiquaire*, n. s., 1861–1862 (1863): 282–3. Etienne-Antoine Rouard, *François Ier chez Mme de Boisy: notice d'un recueil de crayons, ou portraits aux crayons de couleur, enrichi par le roi François Ier de vers et de devises inédites appartenant à la Bibliothèque Mejanes d'Aix* (Paris, 1863), 4. Ronald Sutherland Gower, *My Reminiscences* (London, 1885), 383. Henri Bouchot, *Quelques dames du XVIe Siècle et leurs peintres* (Paris, 1888), 11. Louis Dimier, 'French Portrait-Drawings at Knowsley', *Burlington Magazine* 18 (Dec. 1910): 162–8. Etienne Moreau-Nélaton, *Les Clouet et leurs émules* (Paris: Laurens, 1924), 2 : 111–15, figs. 386–403. Louis Dimier, *Histoire de la peinture de portrait en France au XVIe siècle* (Paris, Bruxelles: G. van Oest et cie, 1924–26), l: xi, 2: viii, 3 : 28–35. W. S. Lewis, *Horace Walpole's Library* (Cambridge: University Press, 1959), 59. *Library* 2357.

EXHIB: *1862 Special Exhibition*, no. 6925.

NOTE: A Principal Curiosity. Many of the identifications are wrong. The hands of the inscriptions do not include that of the biographer Pierre de Bourdeille, seigneur (and abbé) de Brantôme (*c.* 1540–1614). Dimier attributed some of the later drawings to Pierre Dumouter, the Master of the monogram I.D.C. and Nicolas Lagneau.

82. BOOK OF SWAN MARKS
English, 16th century

Pen and ink on vellum. Bound in calf, 25.5 × 20 cm
The Lewis Walpole Library, Yale University.
49 2601
Fig. 275

D 1774, 51 [Library]: Curious books in the glass closet in the library…Two books of swan-marks, on vellum: extremely rare.

D 1784, 38 same as *D 1774*.

PROV: By 1774, HW; 1842, Strawberry Hill Sale, day 6, lot 8, bt Boone [for Lord Derby], £8.8.0; 1953, October 19, Christie's, Knowsley Hall Sale, lots 98–99 (2 vols.), bt Maggs for W. S. Lewis; The Lewis Walpole Library, Yale University.

LIT: *Library* 2601. A. R. A. Hobson, *Book Collector* XVI (Winter 1967), 509–10 (binding only).

NOTE: All swans were Crown property by prerogative right, but licences of private ownership could be granted to individuals or institutions of appropriate status, as regulated by the Swan Act of 1482. Ownership was indicated by marks on the beak. This book refers to swans in Norfolk.

83. ARMS OF THE KNIGHTS OF THE GARTER
Sir Gilbert Dethick, 1573

Illuminated manuscript on vellum, bound in red velvet, 20 × 15 cm
HW bookplate, BP2 earlier state
The Lewis Walpole Library, Yale University.
49 2551
Fig. 53

D 1774, 51 [Library]: Curious books in the glass closet in the library…The arms of the knights of the garter made by Richard 3d. in their proper colours, and bound in red velvet: a present from Walter Robertson, mayor of Lynn.

D 1784, 38 same as *D 1774*.

PROV: 1573, prepared for Queen Elizabeth by Sir Gilbert Dethick; Garter king-of-arms; 1573, probably bound; 1639, catalogued with Lumley Mss and monogram of Charles I stamped on cover; 1740, acquired by Walter Robertson, Mayor of Lynn, 1762, given by him to HW; 1842, Strawberry Hill Sale, day 6, lot 32, bt Boone [for Lord Derby], £11 11.0; 1953, October 20, Christie's, Knowsley Hall Sale, lot 193, bt Maggs for W. S. Lewis, £135; The Lewis Walpole Library, Yale University.

LIT: *Library* 2551. Mellon Lectures, 70. *Rescuing Horace*, 123.

84. 'DIVERSES FANTAISIES DE NOBLE IAC CALLOT' (CALLOT'S POCKET BOOK)
Follower of Jacques Callot, (1592–1635), after 1633

Bound volume with 89 pen and ink drawings bound in gold-tooled calf 8.7 × 14 cm, 3 7/16 × 5 ½ in. Inscribed with title on first page. HW's bookplate (BP1) on inner cover. HW's note on fly-leaf: 'This is a very curious collection of original drawings by Callot: some he engraved exactly, others with variations; most of them were never engraved.' HW's note: 'It cost Lord Orford £10.10' in *D 1774* (The Lewis Walpole Library, 49.2522A)
National Gallery of Art, Washington, Rosenwald Collection 1943. 1943.3.2232
Yale Center for British Art only
Fig. 269

D 1774, 50 [Library]: Curious books in the glass closet in the library..Callot's pocket-book, with a great number of exquisite original drawings by himself: a present to Mr. Walpole from his brother Robert earl of Orford: very valuable.

D 1784, 37–38 same as *D 1774*.

PROV: Robert Walpole, 2nd Earl of Orford, bt for £10.10.0; Robert Walpole gave to HW; 1842, Strawberry Hill Sale, day 6, lot 46, bt Rt Hon. Tho. Grenville, £43.1.0; 1842, May 12, Grenville gave to his niece, Harriet Cholmondeley, Lady Delamere; 1926, November 17, Sotheby's (Miscellaneous Sale), lot 393, bt Maggs, £215; 1938, July 26, Sotheby's (Comte de Suzannet Sale), lot 315, bt Rosenbach, £210; Rosenbach sold to Mr Lessing J. Rosenwald; 1943, given to National Gallery of Art, Washington, DC; 1967–1993, November, loaned to The Lewis Walpole Library, Yale University; 1993, National Gallery of Art, Washington, DC.

LIT: *Library* 2351.

NOTE: The volume largely contains modifed compositions after prints by Callot, turned into an oval format. The hand is not Callot's. There are five further title pages through the book: 'Penitent et Penintentes', 'Enfant Prodigue 1631' (matching the date of the print set from which it is taken), 'Veues de France & Italie 1631', 'Les Miseres et Malheurs de la Guerre' (after prints dated 1633), and 'Varie Fantasie'. A Principal Curiosity.

85. SCRITTI DI VARIE COSE ANTICHE
Pietro Santi Bartoli, (1635–1700), probably 1690s

1 volume (149 leaves), rebound in blue morocco, 27 cm
Drawings in a variety of media (graphite, pen and ink, wash), some mounted onto the leaves, most drawn directly on the rectos.
The Lewis Walpole Library, Yale University.
49 2371

D 1774, 51 [Library]: Curious books in the glass closet in the library… A book of drawings of vases, bas-reliefs, and other antiquities.

D 1784, 38 same as *D 1774*.

PROV: By 1774, HW; 1842, Strawberry Hill Sale, day 6, lot 12, bt Boone [for Lord Derby], £8.8.0; 1953, October 19, Christie's, Knowsley Hall Sale, lot 143, bt Maggs for W. S. Lewis, £88; The Lewis Walpole Library, Yale University.

LIT: *Library* 2371.

NOTE: Information based on research by Irène Aghion.

86. LA PITTURE ANTICHE DEL SEPOLCRO DE NASONII NELLA VIA FLAMINIA DISEGNATE, ED INTAGLIATE ALLA SIMILITUDINE DEGLI ANTICHI ORIGINALI DA PIETRO SANTI BARTOLI, E DESCRITTE, ED ILLUSTRATE DA GIO. PIETRO BELLORI
Pietro Santi Bartoli (1635–1700)

Roma, Antonio de Rossi, 1702
27 cm bound to 54 cm
HW's copy; the leaves have been trimmed and mounted on larger sheets with the plates and text interspersed and pages renumbered in mss. Bound in a collection with nine other works edited by Bellori with plates by Bartoli. With Walpole's bookplate, BP1. Volumes bound in parchment with red morocco spine labels.
The Lewis Walpole Library, Yale University.
Folio 49 3598
Yale Center for British Art only

1842 Sale [Round Tower]: A collection of 620 prints, the works of Santa Bartoli, Views in Rome, Antiquities, Lamps, Vases, &c. &c, 2 vols. folio. [The above 15 Lots are bound uniform in 22 vols, in vellum].

London Sale: Two portfolios with leaves, in which are pasted upwards of 600 etchings, by P. S. Bartoli, of subjects and articles of antiquity, in painting, sculpture, bronzes, medals, vases, lamps, altars, triumphal arches and columns, with their basso relievo.

PROV: HW; 1842, Strawberry Hill Sale, day 8, lot 89 [listed]; 1842, Strawberry Hill London Sale, day 7, lot 1002 [sold], bt H. G. Bohn, £3.10.0; 1847,

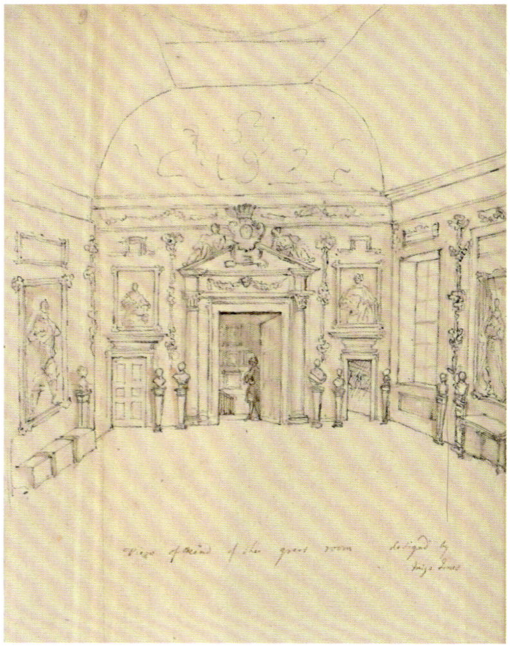

Figure 315. Catalogue 89

Bohn's Catalogue Prints, offered on p. 70 for £7.7.0; 1856, February 15, Sotheby's, Miscellaneous Sale, lot 21, bt Lilly, £2.19.0; 1931, July, Blackwell, bt W. S. Lewis, £9.0.0; The Lewis Walpole Library, Yale University.

LIT: *HW Corres.* 42: 268n. *Library* 3598.

87. HOMERI OPERA QUAE EXTANT OMNIA
Homer

Amstelaedami: Ex officina Wetsteniana, 1707
2 v., 14 × 7.5 cm
Inscriptions: in Alexander Pope's hand. In HW's hand, on the fly-leaf: 'This book belonged to Mr. Pope, and the drawing is by him. Horace Walpole, 1766. It is a view of Twickenham Church from his garden.'
The Lewis Walpole Library, Yale University.
49 2399.
Fig. 270

D 1774, 51 [Library]: Curious books in the glass closet in the library…The Iliad and Odyssey, the very books from which Pope made his translations: in one of the volumes is a view of Twickenham drawn by Pope.
D 1784, 38 same as *D 1774*.
PROV: Dr Thomas Pellett; 1714, given to Dr Pellett by Alexander Pope; by 1766, HW; 1842, Strawberry Hill Sale, day 6, lot 74, bt W. H. Miller, Esq., £11.0.6; 1971, March 29–30, Sotheby's, Christie-Miller Sale, lot 288A, bt Seven Gables, for W. S. Lewis, £1500; The Lewis Walpole Library, Yale University.
LIT: *HW Corres.* 29: 130. *Library* 2399.
NOTE: The view is taken from Pope's grotto.

88. [GEOGRAPHIA ANTIQUA] THIRTY TWO NEW AND ACCURATE MAPS OF THE GEOGRAPHY OF THE ANCIENTS, AS CONTAINED IN THE GREEK AND LATIN CLASSICKS: WHEREIN THE SEVERAL EMPIRES, KINGDOMS AND PROVINCES, THE CHIEF CITIES, TOWNS, RIVERS AND MOUNTAINS MENTION'D IN HERODOTUS, HOMER, JUSTIN, VIRGIL, OVID, FLORUS, NEPOS, CAESAR, LIVY, LUCAN, PLUTARCH, AND MANY OTHER ANCIENT AUTHORS, ARE REPRESENTED … PERFORMED ACCORDING TO THE LATEST AND MOST EXACT OBSERVATIONS … 2ND EDN
Herman Moll (d. 1732)

London: T. Bowles, 1726
19.2 cm
Horace Walpole bookplate, BP1
Inscriptions: Signed 'H. Walpole, 1731' with his notes and schoolbook memoranda on the fly-leaves and on the backs of many maps
The Lewis Walpole Library, Yale University.
49 2428
Fig. 214

1842 Sale [Library]: Cumberland's Life of Julio Bonosoni, 8vo; Moll's Maps and Geography, 4to, and Hartlib's Discoverie, 4to
PROV: 1731, HW; 1842, Strawberry Hill Sale, day 6, lot 1, bt Thorpe, £1.15.0;1842, Offered in Thorpe's Supplement, lot 13377, for £2.2.0; 1844, offered by Thorpe, lot 666, £1.1.0; 1922, December 11, Sturges Sale, lot 982, bt Anderson; 1931, March, Paul Reighard, through T. W. Schreiner, to W. S. Lewis, $100; The Lewis Walpole Library, Yale University.
LIT: *Library* 2428.

89. A DESCRIPTION OF THE EARL OF PEMBROKE'S PICTURES
Carlo Gambarini (d. 1754)

Westminster: Printed by A. Campbell, 1731
20 × 12 cm
Horace Walpole bookplate, BP1
Inscriptions: Notes by Vertue throughout, four drawings by Vertue, including interiors at Wilton, and numerous notes by HW, including lists 'Collections now in England 1757'.
The Lewis Walpole Library, Yale University.
49 2378.
Fig. 315

D 1774, 51 [Library]: Curious books in the glass closet in the library…Description of Wilton, with drawings and notes by Vertue.
D 1784, 38 same as *D 1784*
1842 Sale [In the Glass Closet in the Library]: A Description of the Earl of Pembroke's Pictures, Statues &c., at Wilton and in London, with drawings and notes, by Vertue.
PROV: George Vertue; 1757, HW; 1842, Strawberry Hill Sale, day 6, lot. 43, bt H. G. Bohn [for William Beckford], £7.17.6; 1882, December 11, Sotheby's, Beckford Sale, part 2, lot 59, bt Quaritch, £7.5.0; 1931, October, Maggs to W. S. Lewis, £14.50.0; The Lewis Walpole Library, Yale University.
LIT: *HW Corres.* 35: 296n. *Library* 2378. Ruth Guilding, *Marble Mania: Sculpture Galleries in England, 1640–1840* (London: Sir John Soane's Museum, 2001), no. 48.

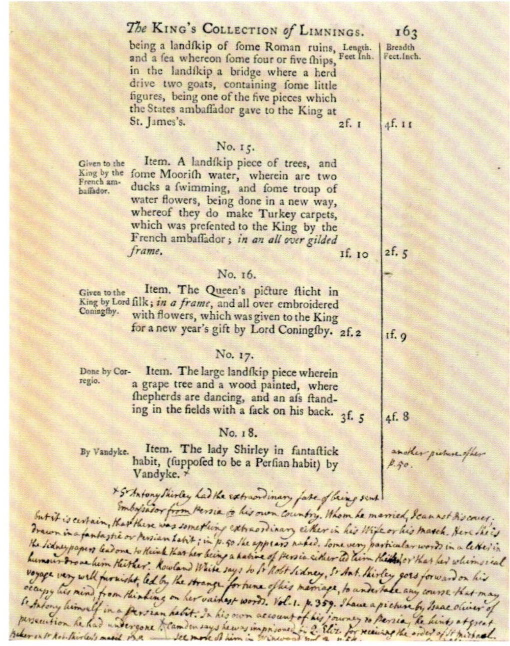

The KING'S COLLECTION *of* LIMNINGS. 163

being a landſkip of ſome Roman ruins, and a ſea whereon ſome four or five ſhips, in the landſkip a bridge where a herd drive two goats, containing ſome little figures, being one of the five pieces which the States ambaſſador gave to the King at St. James's. — Length. Feet Inh. 2f. 1 — Breadth Feet. Inch. 4f. 11

No. 15.

Given to the King by the French ambaſſador. Item. A landſkip piece of trees, and ſome Mooriſh water, wherein are two ducks a ſwimming, and ſome troup of water flowers, being done in a new way, whereof they do make Turkey carpets, which was preſented to the King by the French ambaſſador; *in an all over gilded frame.* 1f. 10 — 2f. 5

No. 16.

Given to the King by Lord Coningſby. Item. The Queen's picture ſticht in ſilk; *in a frame*, and all over embroidered with flowers, which was given to the King for a new year's gift by Lord Coningſby. 2f. 2 — 1f. 9

No. 17.

Done by Corregio. Item. The large landſkip piece wherein a grape tree and a wood painted, where ſhepherds are dancing, and an aſs ſtanding in the fields with a ſack on his back. 3f. 5 — 4f. 8

No. 18.

By Vandyke. Item. The lady Shirley in fantaſtick habit, (ſuppoſed to be a Perſian habit) by Vandyke. — another picture of her p. 50.

Figure 316. Catalogue 90

90. A CATALOGUE AND DESCRIPTION OF KING CHARLES THE FIRST'S CAPITAL COLLECTION …
Abraham Van der Doort (d. 1640), edited by George Vertue (1684–1756)

London: Bathoe, 1757
25 × 19.5 cm
Inscriptions: HW's notes including publication date on title-page; some of his notes were mutilated when the book was rebound after 1842.
The Lewis Walpole Library, Yale University.
49 2478.
Fig. 316

D 1784, 39 [Library] Curious books in the glass closet in the library… Bathoe's catalogues of the collections of Charles 1st. and James 2d. and the duke of Buckingham; with their portraits, and large additions and notes, by Mr. Walpole.
PROV: By 1784, HW; 1842, Strawberry Hill Sale, day 4, lot 170, bt Boone [for Lord Derby], £2.8.0; 1953, October 19, Christie's, Knowsley Hall Sale, lot 114, bt Maggs for W. S. Lewis, £20; The Lewis Walpole Library, Yale University.
LIT: *HW Corres.* 1: 173, 13: 27, 16: 289–90. *Library* 2478. *Bib. SH*, II, no. 43.
NOTE: Edited by Vertue from a manuscript in the Ashmolean Museum. Walpole wrote the introduction to the volume, which was in the press when Vertue died in 1756.

91. PUBLII VIRGILII MARONIS BUCOLICA, GEORGICA ET ÆNEIS
Virgil (70–19 BC)

White vellum binding by William Edwards of Halifax (1723–1808), with cover painting by James Edwards (1756–1816) and fore-edge painting, 19 cm
Birminghamiae: Baskerville, 1766, 19 cm
Inscriptions: Note in HW's hand on the fly leaf: 'This book was bound by Edwards of Halifax, and

the covers were painted by his son, 1784; on the gilt leaves, by holding them aslant, may be perceived a view of Chatsworth. The pictures will resist water'.
The Lewis Walpole Library, Yale University.
49 2482
Fig. 265

1842 Sale [Library]: Baskerville's Virgil, 8vo, curiously bound in vellum, and ornamented at the edges and on the sides with original drawings, unique.
PROV: HW; 1842, Strawberry Hill Sale, day 6, lot 39, bt Payne and Foss, £6.6.0; sold by James Toovey to J. P. Morgan; given to Junius Morgan by J. P. Morgan; bequeathed to Alexander Morgan; 1953, October, sold by him to W. S. Lewis, $1400; The Lewis Walpole Library, Yale University.
LIT: *Library* 2482.

92. COLLECTION OF LETTERS AND OTHER MANUSCRIPTS VOLUME II
Madame du Deffand (Marie Anne Vichy-Champrond, Marquise du Deffand de la Lande) (1696–1780)

Journal, 1779, July 1–1780, Sep. 10
20.2 × 14 cm
Bound in green parchment.
The Lewis Walpole Library, Yale University.
49 2545
Fig. 276

1842 Sale [Library]: The whole of the highly interesting and valuable manuscripts bequeathed to the Honble. Horace Walpole, by the justly celebrated Marie de Vichy, afterwards Madame du Deffand, who died in 1780. When we consider the rank this lady held in the *beau monde* of Paris – her splendid talents and varied accomplishments – and the terms of friendship in which she lived with most of the philosophers, poets, historians, and wits of the day, not only of her own country but with all Europe, as these papers will amply prove, what lights may be thrown on that most eventful period of French history – the commencement of the great revolution. In this collection there are upwards of 800 Letters by her to Horace Walpole, of the greatest interest. Such Letters, clothed in beautiful language, and written, as they were, by an observant and highly cultivated mind to a friend at a distance, in full confidence and without restraint, present a 'True History of the Time' and are invaluable as a literary treasure. To give anything like a complete list of these papers would far exceed the limits of a catalogue; indeed, it would require volumes to do so. The whole have been carefully preserved in the same state as they were left by Lord Orford, and are contained in a large cedarwood chest. They are divided into volumes and packets, and numbered from I. to XIII., as under. They will be offered in one or thirteen lots, as may be determined upon at the time of sale.
PROV: 1780, bequeathed to HW by Mme du Deffand; 1842, Strawberry Hill Sale, day 6, lot 107, bt [Thorpe for] Dyce Sombré, Esq., £157.10.0; bequeathed by his widow to her nephew, W. R. Parker-Jervis; 1920, Sotheby's, Parker-Jervis Sale, distributed; [Journal] bt Maggs, £25.10.0; 1923, Maggs cat. 445, lot 2971, £85; 1932, May 12, lot 427, American Art Gallery to Brick Row for W. S. Lewis; The Lewis Walpole Library, Yale University.
LIT: *HW Corres.* 36: 310, 312. *Library* 2545.

93. MEMOIRES DU COMTE DE GRAMMONT
Count Anthony Hamilton (*c.* 1646–1720)

Strawberry Hill, 1772
23.3 × 19 cm
Extra-illustrated with engraved portraits and a pen and ink drawing of Summer Hill; with Walpole's notes and corrections. Bound in calf, gilt arms of Horace Walpole on covers, uniform with other volumes in his set of Strawberry Hill Press publications.
The Lewis Walpole Library, Yale University.
49 2511
Fig. 142

D 1774, 51 [Library]: Curious book in the glass closet in the library…A complete set of the books printed at Strawberry-hill.
D 1784, 38 same as *D 1774*.
PROV: 1771, HW; 1842, Strawberry Hill Sale, day 4, lot 144, bt Strong, £16.5.6; 1847 May 3, Sotheby's, J. H. S. Pigott Sale, part 1, Sotheby's, lot 182, bt Pickering, £2.5.0; 1848, May 22, Sotheby's Eyton Sale, Sotheby's, lot 1459, bt Cunningham, £1.19.0; 1855, February 27, Sotheby's, Cunningham Sale, Sotheby's, lot 339 bt Toovey, £5.12.6; 1879, December, offered by Sotheran, lot 382 for £12.12.0; 1929, Sotheby's, Miscellaneous Sale, Sotheby's, lot 870, bt Tregaskis, £50; 1931, August, Tregaskis to W. S. Lewis; The Lewis Walpole Library, Yale University.
LIT: *HW Corres.* 1: 293, 295, 5: 268, 270, 299, 304–6, 313, 315, 436, 7: 4[illegible]6 15: 97, 28: 119n, 31: 171, 41: 470, 43: 79. *Bib. SH*:, no. 18 Copy 1. *Library* 2511. *Rescuing Horace*, 72, 80, 157.

94. COIN OF ANTONY AND OCTAVIA
Roman, 38 BC

Gold, 2 cm × 0.3 cm; 7.87g, die-axis 1
British Museum, Department of Coins and Medals.
1842,0523.1
Fig. 317

D 1774, 53 [Library]: Catalogue of the 25 most precious coins and medals in the rose-wood case…13. Gold medal of Marc Antony: reverse the head of Octavia, the only one of her known, which makes this medal of the highest value.
D 1784, 40 same as *D 1774*.
PROV: Cardinal Quirini (d. 1755); probably by 1741, HW; 1842, Strawberry Hill Sale, day 9, lot 82, bt British Museum, £66.3.0.
LIT: *HW Corres.* 15: 12, 37: 111–12. H. A. Grueber, ed., *Coins of the Roman Republic in the British Museum* 2 (London: Printed by order of the Trustees, 1910), 507, no. 144. Mellon Lectures, 122.
NOTE: A Principal Curiosity.

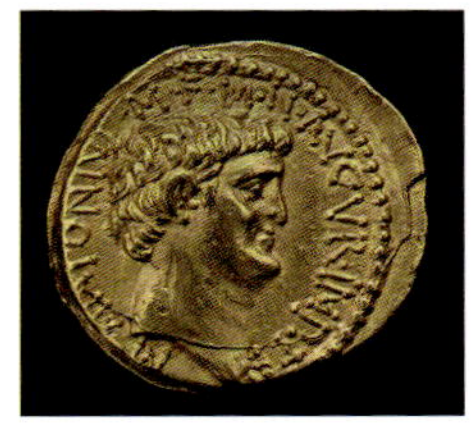

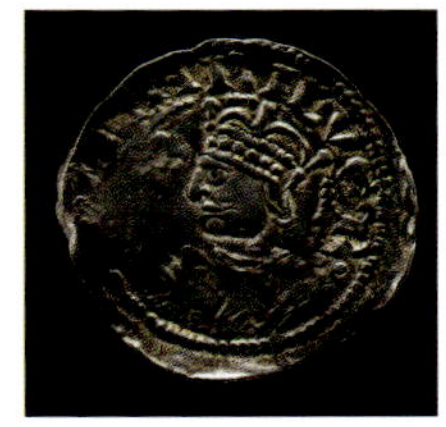

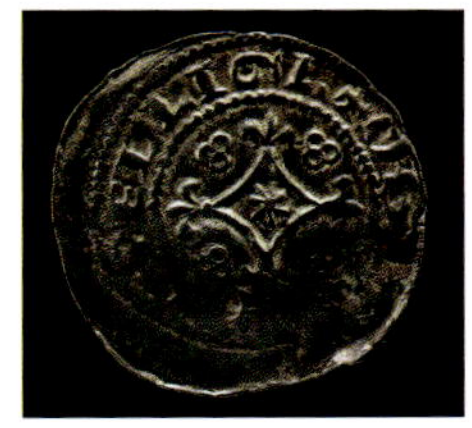

Top left
Figure 317. Catalogue 94

Top right
Figure 318. Catalogue 95

Bottom
Figure 319. Catalogue 96

95. PENNY OF HENRY I, MONEYER OSULF, MINT OF WALLINGFORD
English, *c.* 1119

Smaller Profile/Cross & Annulets type (BMC XII), Coin, D 2.1 cm, 0.1 cm (thickness); 1.37g (weight)
British Museum, Department of Coins and Medals.
1842,0523.4
Fig. 318

D 1774, 53 [Library]: Catalogue of the 25 most precious coins and medals in the rose-wood case…7. Coin of young king Henry, son of Henry 2d. From ditto [Lord Oxford's collection].
D 1784, 39 same as *D 1774*.
PROV: 1742, Earl of Oxford's Sale, bt HW; 1842, Strawberry Hill Sale, day 9, lot 108, bt British Museum, £9.0.0.
LIT: *HW Corres.* 17: 358, 374. G. C. Brooke, *A Catalogue of English Coins in the British Museum: the Norman Kings* 2 (London, 1916), 298. no. 101. Mellon Lectures, 122.
NOTE: A Principal Curiosity.

96. PATTERN (PIEDFORT) FOR SHILLING, OR PRESENTATION PIECE, OF EDWARD VI
English 1461–83

Coin, 2.8 cm × 0.4 cm; 31.18g (weight)
British Museum, Department of Coins and Medals.
1842,0523.5
Fig. 319

D 1774, 52 [Library]: Catalogue of the 25 most precious coins and medals in the rose-wood case. 1. An unique crown of king Edward 6th bought at Lord Oxford's sale in 1742.
D 1784, 39 same as *D 1774*.
PROV: 1742, Earl of Oxford's Sale, bt HW; 1842, Strawberry Hill Sale, day 10, lot 1, bt British Museum, £48.0.0.
LIT: *HW Corres.* 17: 358, 374. Mellon Lectures, 122. J. J. North, *English Hammered Coinage* 2 (London, 1991), no. 1953.
NOTE: A Principal Curiosity.

97. Fragment of Sovereign of Elizabeth I
English, 1597–1600 (in original condition). The obverse recut by 1742

Gold, 2.6 cm × 1.5 cm; 2.56g [weight]
initial mark anchor
British Museum, Department of Coins and Medals. 1842,0523.2
Fig. 33

D 1774, 53 [Library]: Catalogue of the 25 most precious coins and medals in the rose-wood case…10. Gold fragment of queen Elizabeth's last broad piece, described in the Royal and Noble Authors. Unique: from the Oxford collection.
D 1784, 39 same as *D 1774*.
PROV: 1742, Earl of Oxford's Sale, bt HW; 1842, Strawberry Hill Sale, day 10, lot 8, bt British Museum, £36.15.0.
LIT: *HW Corres.* 17: 358, 374, 42: 278. Horace Walpole, *Royal and Noble Authors*, I, 1758, 125. Mellon Lectures, 122. J. P. C. Kent, 'Five Tudor notes', British Numismatic Journal 32 (1974): 164. M. Jones, ed., *Fake: the Art of Deception* (London: British Museum Publications, 1990), 153, no. 157.
NOTE: A Principal Curiosity. Described by HW in the Royal and Noble Authors as: 'a fragment of one of her last broad pieces, representing her horridly old and deformed: An entire coin with this image is not known: it is universally supposed that the die was broken by her command, and that some workman of the mint cut up this morsal which contains barely the face….'. The head of a standard sovereign has been recut to make her appear older. The publication of this fragment prompted the production of forged complete examples.

7. ANIMATING HISTORY: ROYALS AND RELICS

98. Head of a King (Portrait of Henry III)
Maker unknown, English, *c.* 1250–60

Oak, 27.2 × 26.9 × 12.8 cm
Culture and Sport Glasgow (Museums). 50.147.
Victoria and Albert Museum only
Fig. 320

D 1774, 131 [Staircase] Appendix … Over the middle arcade is a curious ancient head of Henry 3d. carved in alto-relievo on oak, from the church of Barnwell near Oundle, which he endowed.
D 1784, 32 [Staircase] As *D 1774* and: This head is very like to the effigies on his tomb, and to that in painted glass in the chapel here at Strawberry-hill.
PROV: From the chancel of the Church of St Andrew, Barnwell St Andrew, Northamptonshire, built *c.* 1250; removed *c.* 1740 by Thomas Slater, the carpenter restoring the chancel; *c.* 1770 given by his son to a carpenter of Peterborough, who gave it to Dr John Fysche Palmer of Peterborough; 1780, Dr John F. Palmer, Peterborough, bt HW; 1842, Strawberry Hill Sale, day 19, lot 84, bt Lord Lilford, £3.5.0; 1945 or 1949, bt Albemarle Galleries; 1950, March 20, Sir William Burrell bt from Acton Surgey, Albemarle Galleries, London, £300; Gifted by Sir William and Constance, Lady Burrell to Glasgow Corporation in 1944.
LIT: *HW Corres.* 2: 275, etching dated 1782 by John Carter in John Carter, *Specimens of the ancient sculpture and painting now remaining in England, from the earliest period to the reign of Henry VIII, consisting of statues, bas-reliefs, busts, sculptures; brasses … etc.*, (London: Henry Bohn, 1838) opp. p. 108. *HW Corres.* 2: 275, 16: 192–3, 43: 73.
NOTE: A drawing by John Carter (copied in his etching) is in an extra-illustrated copy of *D 1784*, at the Lewis Walpole Library (49 3582 folio, 73). It is inscribed by the artist: 'Henry the Third. This head (carv'd in oak) is in the collection of Dr PALMER of PETERBOROUGH NORTHAMPTON shire and was brought from BRANWELL church near OUNDLE NORth

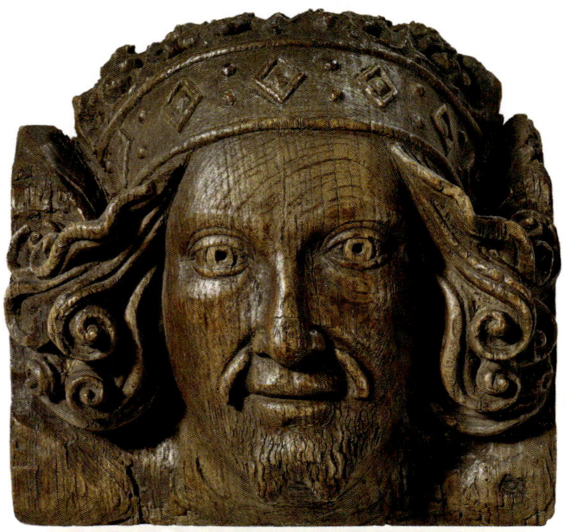

Figure 320. Catalogue 98

shire. about 40 years ago. HENRY the THIRD endow'd this church, this drawing is half the size of the original head' and in HW's hand on the drawing: 'The upper part above the crown is modern, and the date'; on wash-line mount: 'now at Mr. Walpole's at Strawberry hill'. Another drawing by Carter, mounted on the same page, shows the site in which the head was hung, and details of its later provenance. The head is now missing the framed wooden backboard on which it was mounted when HW acquired it. The board was crudely engraved with a crown and 'H R 12.III.16'. The drawing of the head was sent to HW by Lort, who wrote on the 23 December 1780: 'I send you a drawing by Carter of the Head of Henry III, which, I understand from him, Dr Palmer is willing to dispose of for four or five guineas.'

99. Marriage of a Saint (The Marriage of Henry VI)
Artist unknown, Flemish, *c.* 1475–1500

Oil on wood panel, 94.6 × 88.6 cm
Formerly inscribed with the names of the apparent subjects in upper left and right corners (now hidden by the modern frame), probably added in the 18th century, and removed by modern conservators; undecipherable inscription lower center
Toledo Museum of Art, Gift of Edward Drummond Libbey, Acc. No. 26.74
Fig. 147

D 1774, 44 [Library]: Over the chimney, an ancient and valuable piece, representing the marriage of Henry 6th of which see a description in the first volume of the Anecdotes of Painting.
D 1784, 34, same as *D 1774*.
PROV: HW, £21.0.0; 1842, Strawberry Hill Sale, day 20, lot 25, bt Duke of Sutherland, £84; 1910, February–March, loaned to the Fogg Art Museum, Harvard University, Massachusetts, by Gimpel & Wildenstein, NY, as a potential purchase (as a 'French primitive'); 1916, Edward Drummond Libbey; 1926, Toledo Museum of Art, Gift of Edward Drummond Libbey.
LIT: *Anecdotes*, vol. 1, opp. p. 33 (engraved by C. Grignion). *HW Corres.* 1: 305, 352, 2: 31, 221, 14: 68–78, 81, 16: 184, 185, 35: 158, 163, 250, 40: 316, 319, 42: 246–7, 43: 58, 183. R. H. Wilenski, *Flemish Painters, 1430–1480* (New York: Viking Press, 1960), 80, pl. 147. Mellon Lectures, 122n. Roy Strong, *Tudor & Jacobean Portraits*, 2 vols. (London: HMSO, 1969), vol. 1, no. 145. Toledo Museum of Art, *European paintings* (Toledo: the Museum, 1976), pl. 77.
EXHIB: 'Art of the Middle Ages', Royal Academy, London, 1861. 'Exhibition of National Portraits.' South Kensington Museum, London, 1866, no. 16.
NOTE: HW identifies all the participants in the *Anecdotes*. The real subject of the picture is still unclear.

100. Three Children of Christian II of Denmark; (Children of Henry VII)
Anonymous, after Jan Gossaert, called Mabuse (*c.* 1478–1532)

Oil on panel, 33 × 44.5 cm
Private collection
Fig. 321

D 1784, 96 [Holbein Chamber]: More Additions: Prince Arthur, prince Henry, and princess Margaret, children of Henry the Seventh, by Mabuse; from Cosway's collection.
PROV: Richard Cosway; 1792, Feb. 2–3, his sale, bt HW; 1842, May 17, Strawberry Hill Sale, day 20, lot 75, bt John Dent, Esq., £31.10.0; Private collection, UK.
LIT: *Anecdotes*, I, 49–50. Max J. Friedländer, *Early Netherlandish Painting* (Brussels: Editions de la Connaissance, 1967), cat. no. 79. OHG 123. George Scharf, 'Remarks on some portraits from Windsor Castlel, Hampton Court and Wilton House', *Archaeologia* XXXIX (1863), 260. Lorne Campbell, *The Pictures in the Collection of Her Majesty the Queen. The early Flemish Pictures* (London and New York: Cambridge University Press, 1985) 53–6, cat. 34, no. 6.
NOTE: The prime version, painted *c.* 1526, is in the Royal Collection. It was engraved by George Vertue in 1748 as the children of Henry VII, an identification it had assumed by 1682.

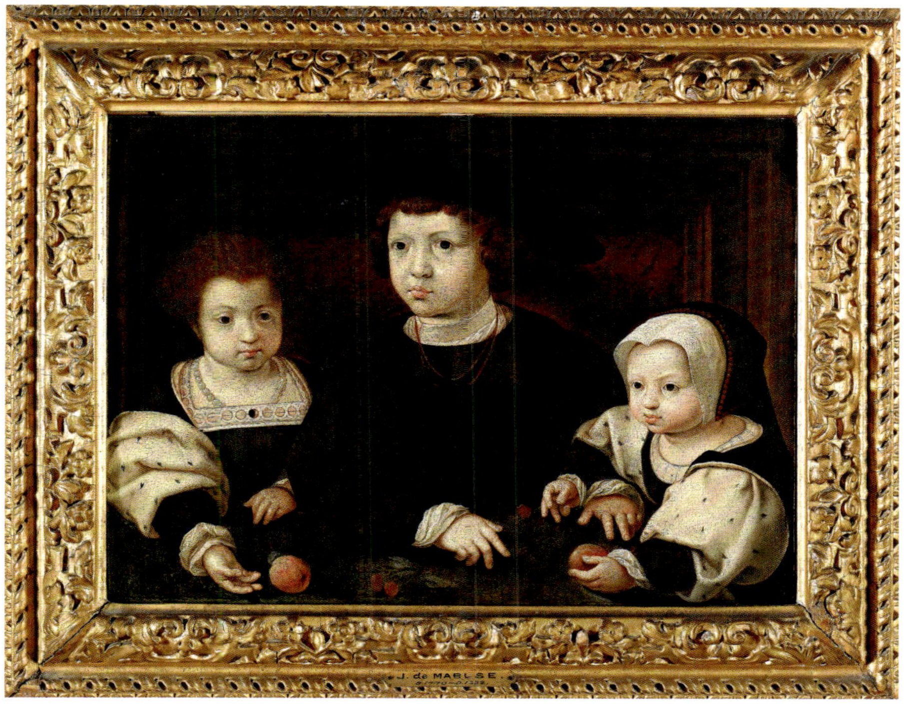

Figure 321. Catalogue 100

101. Shouting Male Head (Henry VII, 'in the agony of death')
Maker unknown, probably Italian, *c.* 1600–1650

Marble, on a limestone base, H 46 cm
Pasted onto the base the remains of a letterpress label, perhaps printed at the Strawberry Hill Press: 'H.../Torreg..', with later labels
Collection of the Duke of Northumberland
Fig. 150

D 1774, 57 [Star Chamber]: ... and a bust of Henry 7th. in stone, a model in great taste for his tomb, by Torreggiano. * * Vide Anecdotes, vol. 1, p. 102.
D 1784, 42 [Star Chamber]: A mahogany cabinet...On it, a bust of Henry 7th in stone, a model in great taste for his tomb, by Torreggiano. * *Vide Anecdotes, vol. 1, p. 102.
PROV: Bt HW, £10.10.0; 1842, Strawberry Hill Sale, day 17, lot 96, bt Algernon, Lord Prudhoe, £27.6.0; Duke of Northumberland, Syon House.
LIT: *Anecdotes, Works*, vol. 3, 87n. Etching by John Carter dated 1792 in John Carter, *Specimens of the ancient sculpture and painting now remaining in England, from the earliest period to the reign of Henry VIII, consisting of statues, bas-reliefs, busts, sculptures; brasses ... etc.*, (London: John Carter, 1780–87), pl. lxix. Preston Remington, 'A Portrait of an English Ecclesiastic of the Sixteenth Century', *The Metropolitan Museum of Art Bulletin* 31, no. 11 (Nov. 1936), 223–9. *HW Corres* 2: 174, 15: 333; 33: 403. OHG 79.
NOTE: Described by HW in the second edition of the *Anecdotes*, (*Works*, vol. 3, 87n): 'At Strawberry-hill is a model in stone of the head of Henry VIIth in the agony of death. It is in the great style of Raphael and Michael Angelo, and worthy of either, though undoubtedly by Torregiano.' A drawing of the head by John Carter (copied in his etching) is mounted in an extra-illustrated copy of *D 1784* Lewis Walpole Library (33 30 copy 11). A sketch for the drawing is in *D 1784*, extra-illustrated with prints and drawings by John Carter. The Henry E. Huntington Library, San Marino, California (vol. 2, 68r). The drawing shows the base inscribed: 'HENRICUS VII/ TORREGIANI/ OPUS/ Ao MDIX'. There is now apparently no trace of this inscription.

102. The Family of Henry VIII: An Allegory of the Tudor Succession
Attributed to Lucas de Heere (1534–1584), *c.* 1572

Oil on panel, 131.2 × 184 cm, in a 16th century black and gold frame with a painted inscription
Marks: Strawberry Hill sale mark, chalk mark, verso, center right: LOT 86.
Amgueddfa Cymru – National Museum Wales, Cardiff, Wales. NMW A 564
Victoria and Albert Museum only
Fig. 149

D 1774, 103 [Great North Bedchamber]: Over the chimney, a large picture of Henry 8th. and his children; bought out of the collection of James West, esq; in 1773. *See a description of this curious piece in the first vol. of the Anecdotes of Painting.*
D 1784, 72, same as *D 1774*.
PROV: Presented by Queen Elizabeth I to Sir Francis Walsingham, *c.* 1572; Walsingham Family, Scadbury, Kent, bt James West; 6gns (see *HW Corres.*); 1773, April 2, James West Sale, day 3, lot 66, bt Sir Joshua Reynolds; bt HW, £80.0.0 or variously £84 (*HW Corres.*); 1842, Strawberry Hill Sale, day 20, lot 86, bt John Dent, Esq. £220.10; by descent to Mark Dent-Brocklehurst, Sudeley Castle, Gloucestershire; 1991, National Museum and Gallery, Cardiff; given in lieu of tax, 1991, Amgueddfa Cymru – National Museum Wales, Cardiff.
LIT: *Anecdotes*, vol. 1, 134n. F. M. O'Donohue, *A Descriptive and Classified Catalogue of Portraits of Queen Elizabeth* (1894), ill. no. 18. 'Vertue Note Books', *The Walpole Society Journal* 24 (Oxford: University Press, 1936), 87–8. *HW Corres.* 1: 305, 42: 247n. E. Auerbach, 'Portraits of Queen Elizabeth', *Burlington Magazine* 95 (1953): 197–205. Roy Strong, *The English Icon. Elizabeth & Jacobean Portraiture* (New Haven: Yale University Press, 1969), cat no. 95. Roy Strong, *Gloriana: the Portraits of Queen Elizabeth I* (New York: Thames & Hudson, 1987), 71–7. John N. King, *Tudor Royal Iconography: Literature and Art in an Age of Religious Crisis* (Princeton, N. J.: Princeton University Press, *c.* 1989), 222–6. Christopher Lloyd and Simon Thurley, *Henry VIII: Images of a Tudor King* (Oxford: Phaidon Press, 1990), 40. Karen Hearn, *Dynasties: Painting in Tudor and Jacobean England, 1530–1630* (London: Tate Publishing, 1995), no. 35. Maurice Howard, *The Tudor Image* (London: Tate Gallery, 1995), no. 54. P. G. Matthews, 'Portraits of Philip II of Spain as King of England', *Burlington Magazine* (Jan. 2000): 13–19. Roy Strong, *The Artist & the Garden* (New Haven and London: Yale University Press, 2000), 100.
EXHIB: London, New Gallery 1890 (158).
NOTE: A Principal Curiosity.

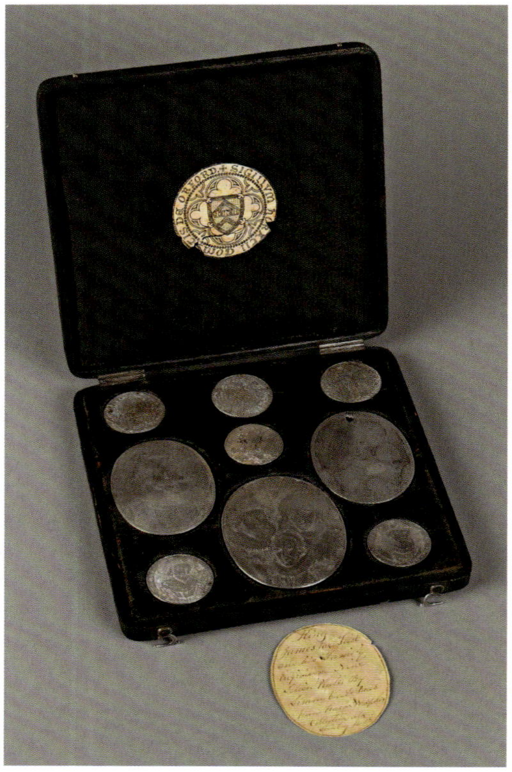

Figure 322. Catalogue 103

103. Three Portrait Medallions and Six Counters
The medallions by Simon de Passe, 1616–20; the counters by a unknown English workshop, mid-17th century, one dated 1638.

Silver, 6 round: approx. D 2.5 cm; 3 oval: approx. 5.7 × 4.4 cm, in an 18th century sharkskin-covered wood box, interior fitted and lined with velvet. Medallions of King James VI and I and Queen Anne signed: 'SP fe'. Latin inscriptions.
HW's 1792 circular book plate (Type 1) pasted to interior of box; later partial sale [?] label on exterior, loose Mss 19th century label 'King James the First and his Family Engraved on Nine Silver Plates By Simon van De Paas from Horace Walpole's Collection at Strwby Hill'
Medallions: James VI and I (reverse: royal arms); Queen Anne (reverse: royal arms of Denmark); James VI and I, Queen Anne and Prince Charles (reverse: arms of the sitters); Counters: King Frederick of Bohemia; Queen Elizabeth of Bohemia; Henry, Lord Darnley; James VI and I, (reverse: Prince Charles); Charles I (reverse: Queen Henrietta Maria); Queen Henrietta Maria (reverse; inscription dated 1638).
The Lewis Walpole Library, Yale University
Fig. 103

1842 Sale: Various Jettons and Counters of James I., his Queen; Charles I., his Queen; various on his Marriage, Birth of the Prince, and on his Death.
prov: HW; 1842, Strawberry Hill Sale, day 10, lot 54, bt Docwray, Esq., £1.10.0, or possibly day 15, lot 72, bt Miss Burdett Coutts, £4.14.6; 1938, Lord Beauchamp; as of 1940, Herbert M. Lingford; 1957, May 27, Glendining & Co., lot 211, bt Spink & Son, Ltd, for W. S. Lewis, £84; The Lewis Walpole Library, Yale University.
lit: Mark Jones, 'The Technique of Simon van de Passe Reconsidered', *The Numismatic Chronicle* 143 (1983): 227–30. Ellenor M. Alcorn, *English Silver in the Museum of Fine Arts, Boston*, vol. 1: *Silver before 1697* (Boston: Museum of Fine Arts, Boston, 1993), no. 28, for engraved version of a related jetton with portrait medallions depicting James I, Anne of Denmark and Charles, Prince of Wales. Philippa Glanville, *Silver in Tudor and Stuart England* (London: Victoria and Albert Museum, 1990) cats 116, 126, 127, 129.
note: For a discussion on the production techniques of the medallions as cast, engraved, or both, see the bibliography. These counters are stamped.

104. The Presentation of a Pineapple to Charles II (Rose, the Royal Gardener, Presenting the First Pineapple Raised in England to Charles II)
Hendrick Danckerts (*c.* 1625–1680), *c.* 1677

Oil on canvas, 91.4 × 109.2 cm
Inscriptions: in HW's hand on verso
Houghton Hall, Norfolk,
Fig. 59

D 1774, 22 [Blue Breakfast Room] [Lewis Walpole Library copy 49 2523 inscribed in HW's hand]: A very curious picture of Rose, the royal gardiner, presenting the first pineapple raised in England to Charles 2d, who is standing in the garden. The whole piece is well painted with perfect harmony, probably by Danckers. It was a present to Mr. Walpole from the Revd. Mr. Pennicott of Ditton, to whom it was bequeathed by Mr. London, grandson of London who was Partner with [Wise].
D 1784, 19 [Blue Breakfast Room]: A most curious picture of Rose the royal gardiner, presenting the first pineapple raised in England to Charles 2d. who is standing in a garden: the house seems to be Dawny-court near Windsor, the villa of the duchess of Cleveland. The whole piece is well-painted, probably by Danckers. It was a present to Mr. W. from the rev. Mr. Pennicott of Ditton, to whom it was bequeathed by Mr. London, grandson of him who was Partner with Wise.
prov: George London (*c.* 1604–1714); bequeathed by his grandson, perhaps Edward London (d. 1776) to the Rev. M. Pennicott, rector of Long Ditton; *c.* 1780, Rev. M. Pennicott gave to HW; 1842, Strawberry Hill Sale, day 11, lot 20, bt J. M. Smith, £22.1.0; E. A. V. Stanley, Esq., of Quantock Lodge, Bridgewater; 1920, July 15, Sotheby's, Taunton Heirlooms Sale, lot 133, bt Agnew Dealers for £620; Philip Sassoon; Marchioness of Cholmondeley (his sister); Private collection.
lit: *HW Corres.* 2: 200n, 12: 258n, 29: 45n. Mario Praz, *Conversation Pieces* (University Park: Pennsylvania State University Press, 1971), 137, 172, 280, fig. 319. John Harris, *The Artist and the Country House; a History of Country House and Garden View Painting in Britain, 1540–1870* (London: Sotheby's Publications, 1985), no. 36. Gervase Jackson-Stops, ed., *The Treasure Houses of Britain* (Washington DC: National Gallery of Art, 1985), 162. George Royle, 'Family links between George London and John Rose: new light on the "Pineapple Paintings"', *Garden History*, 23, No. 2, 1996, pp. 246–9.
note: A Principal Curiosity. Both the suggested location and the alleged subject are now dismissed. Pineapples were first grown in England in the 1720s. John Rose was gardener to Charles II.

105. Comb (Queen Bertha's Comb)
Maker unknown, German, late 12th century

Carved ivory, 14 × 8.9 cm
Inscriptions: carved Latin inscription probably early 17th century, in rough translation: 'This comb was sent from Pope Gregory to Queen Bertha'
British Museum, Department of Prehistory and Europe. 1916.0403.1
Fig. 146

D 1774, 156: [Small Closet]: More Additions…An ivory comb, sent by pope Gregory to queen Bertha; from the Portland collection.
D 1784, 91, same as *D 1774*.
prov: Collection of Thomas Howard, 2nd Earl of Arundel; by descent; 1720, May, sold by the 10th Earl of Stafford, bt Edward Harley, Earl of Oxford; 1741, by descent, Edward Hartley's daughter, the Duchess of Portland; 1786, April 24–June 8, her Sale, bt HW, 18s; 1842, Strawberry Hill Sale, day 23, lot 12, bt Money, £3.13.6; 1916, British Museum, donated by Sir Maurice Rosenheim.
lit: *Proceedings of the Society of Antiquaries* 28, 168–71. C. E. Wright, and R. Wright, *The Diary of Humfrey Wanley 1715–1726*, 2 vols. (London: Bibliographical Society, 1966), 46. *OHG* 154. George Zarnecki, Tristram Holland and Janet Holt, *English Romanesque Art 1066–1200* (exh. cat. London: Hayward Gallery, Arts Council of Great Britain, 1984), no. 496. *Romantic Interior*, 28, fig. 22. Mark Jones, Paul Craddock, and Nicolas Barker, *Fake? The Art of Deception* (London: British Museum Press, 1990), no. 156.

106. Illuminated Psalter; (Psalter of the Prince d'Anjou)
Italy, Venice in the workshop of Benedetto Bordon by the Second Grifo Master and another artist, 1500–25.

Octavo manuscript, brown ink on vellum, six full-page miniatures with full borders and 15 large illuminated initials with full border, bound in contemporary black Venetian goatskin, doublures with pierced gilt panel in the Veneto-Oriental style, silver-gilt cornerpieces and clasps (with Canale arms) by the Mendoza Binder; inscriptions on front and back, 13.1 × 9.5 × 43 cm

In an elaborate wooden box, fitted and hinged, made for HW between 1786 and 1788; the sides inlaid with seven panels of agate and one of lapis lazuli. Cover inset with wash drawing by William Lock the younger (1767–1847); inside lined with blue velvet and painted inside lid with the arms of Walpole, dated 1786 and four previous owners, dated 1537, 1625, 1720, 1741. A separate original gold-plated label displayed by the box at Strawberry Hill with engraved description: 'RELIGION, To whom infant Angel introduces Painting, who offers to Her the Book of Psalms illuminated by Don Julio Clovio. Designed and drawing by Willm. Lock, Junr. Esqr. 1788.'

Inscriptions: HW's descriptive notes are on flyleaves; HW's circular bookplate.
The Wormsley Library, Collection of the late Sir Paul Getty, KBE.
Figs. 35, 323

D 1784, 91 [Beauclerk Closet]: Appendix…In Lady Diana Beauclerc's Cabinet. The book of Psalms, with 21 inimitable illuminations by don Julio Clovio, scholar of Julio Romano. If any thing can excel the figures, it is the execution of the borders, which are of the purest antique taste, and unrivalled for the lustre and harmony of the colours, as well as for the preservation, which is allowed to be more perfect than any of the few works of this extraordinary master. It was painted, as is said on one of the illuminations, *Principi Andegavensi, 1537*; was afterwards in the Arundelian collection, on the dispersion of which it was purchased by the earl of Oxford in 1720, who bequeathed it to his daughter the duchess of Portland, at whose sale Mr. Walpole bought it in 1786.

PROV: Augustinian convent of Santa Maria delle Vergini, Venice; [1537, to Andrea Gritti, Doge of Venice (or the Duke of Anjou)]; 1637, given by Cassiano dal Pozzo to Thomas Howard, 2nd Earl of Arundel; William Howard, Viscount of Stafford; Henry Stafford-Howard, Earl of Stafford; 1720, May, Arundel Collection Sale; bt Robert Harley; Edward Harley, Earl of Oxford; Margaret, Duchess of Portland; 1786, April 24, Duchess of Portland's Museum Sale, lot 2951, bt Humphreys for HW, £169.1.0; 1842, Strawberry Hill Sale, day 15, lot 90, bt Earl Waldegrave, £441; 1862, repurchased by Waldegrave family, owned by Frances, Countess Waldegrave; 1886, Messrs Ellis and Scrutton, Bond Street; [1891, March] sold to Sophia Augusta Brown (or to her son John Nicholas Brown); 1901, given to the John Carter Brown Library; 1981, May 18, Sotheby Parke Bernet & Co., lot 19; Wormsley Library.

LIT: J. Holmes, 'The Strawberry Hill Julio Clovio', *Gentleman's Magazine* 17 (1842): 491–3. J. W. Bradley, *The Life and Works of Giorgio Giulio Clovio* (London: B. Quaritch, 1891), 230–35. W. S. Lewis, introduction to Horace Walpole, *The Duchess of Portland's Museum*, (New York, 1936), vi–vii. *Library* 3786.2. A. N. L. Munby, *Connoisseurs and Medieval Miniatures, 1750–1859* (Oxford: Clarendon Press, 1972), 24–5, pl. 4. *HW Corres.* 39: 442, 42: 165, 43: 357. *Western Illuminated Manuscripts. The Property of The John Carter Brown Library, Providence, Rhode Island* (auction cat. London: Sotheby Parke Bernet & Co., 1981), no. 19. George Fletcher, ed., *The Wormsley Library: A Personal Selection by Sir Paul Getty, K.B.E.*, 2nd edn, exh. cat., Pierpont Morgan Library & Museum, New York (London: Maggs Bros for the Wormsley Library, 1999), no. 22.

EXHIB: 1862 Special Exhibition, no. 6888.

NOTE: A Principal Curiosity. The attribution of the hands is per W. M. Voelkle. The drawing is included in the 'Works of Genius': drawing by W. Lock Jun. for the book that contains D. Juliò Clovio's prayer box. (HW's mss list in his copy of *D 1774* at The Lewis Walpole Library, Yale University, 49 2523). Associated with the volume is a Ms note dated 1748 by George Vertue concerning the volume, addressed to the Countess of Oxford and Mortimer.

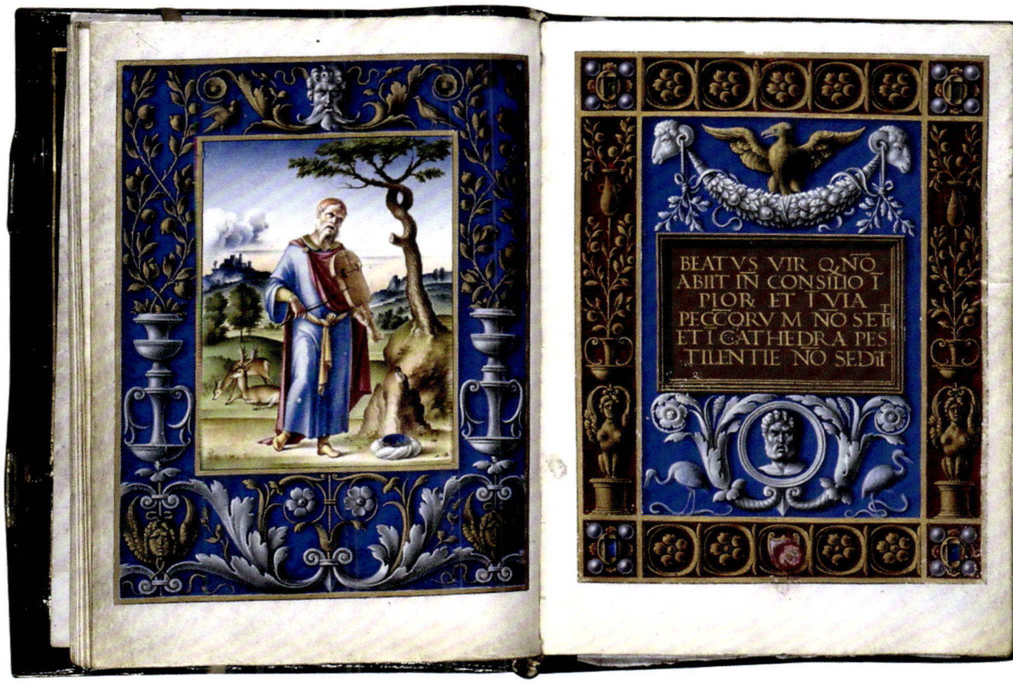

Figure 323. Catalogue 106

107. Hair of Mary Tudor in a Gold Locket

The locket: maker unknown

5.9 cm including ring (5 cm without ring), × w 3.2 cm
Engraved on the back: 'Hair of Mary Tudor Queen of France cut from her head Sep 6 1784 when her tomb at St Edmundsbury was opened H.W.'
Lent by the Rt Hon. the Earl of Derby. D240.
Victoria and Albert Museum only
Fig. 30

D 1774, 158 [Beauclerk Closet]: More Additions … A locket with hair of Mary Tudor, queen of France; whose tomb was opened in 1784; a present from miss Fauquier.

D 1784, 92 same as *D 1774*.

PROV: The tomb of Mary Tudor (1496–1533) in St Mary's church, Bury St Edmunds, Suffolk, opened 1784, September 6; before 1786, given by Jane Georgiana Fauquier (d. 1823) to HW; 1842, Strawberry Hill Sale, day 15, lot 58, bt Earl of Derby, £2.12.6; by family descent.

LIT: Samuel Tymms, *An Architectural and Historical Account of the Church of St Mary, Bury St Edmund's* (London: Simpkin and Marshall, 1854), 179, et. seq.

NOTE: Miss Fauquier married in 1786.

108. Dr Dee's Mirror

Maker unknown, Aztec, 14th–16th century AD

Obsidian, in an 18th century wooden case covered with tooled leather, H 22 × D 18.4 × W 1.3 cm (mirror); L 25.5 × D 21 × W 3 cm (case)
Inscriptions: label on case in HW's hand: 'The Black Stone into which Dr. Dee used to call his spirits…' Later HW inscription: 'Kelly was Dr. Dee's Associate and is mentioned with this very stone in Hudibras [a satirical poem by Samuel Butler, first published in 1664] Part 2. Canto 3 v. 631. Kelly did all hs feates upon The Devil's Looking-glass, a Stone.'
British Museum, Department of Prehistory and Europe. 1966,1001.1
Figs. 125, 126

D 1774, 110 [Great North Bedchamber, Glass Closet]: A speculum of kennel-coal, in a leathern-case. It is curious for having been used to deceive the mob by Dr. Dee, the conjurer, in the reign of queen Elizabeth. It was in the collection of the Mordaunts earls of Peterborough, in whose catalogue it is called, the black stone into which Dr. Dee used to call his spirits. From the Mordaunts it passed to lady Elizabeth Germayne, and from her to John last duke of Argyll, whose son lord Frederic Cambell, gave it to Mr. Walpole.

D 1784, 77, same as *D 1774*.

PROV: Dr John Dee; The Mordaunt family, earls of Peterborough; Lady Elizabeth Germain, widow of Henry Mordaunt, 2nd Earl of Peterborough; John, Duke of Argyll; 1771, given by Lord Frederic Campbell to HW, 1771; 1842, Strawberry Hill Sale, day 16, lot 84, bt Strong, Bristol, £12.12.0; 1848, October 8, (C. J. H. Smyth-Pigott, Esq., Sale), lot 238, bt Edwards; 1853, December 19,

Sotheby's, J. H. Smyth-Pigott Sale, lot 2033, bt T. Wright, £13.0.0; 1888, July 10, Christie's, Earl of Londesborough Sale, lot 694, £73.10 bt Magniac; 1892, July 15, Christie's, Collection of the late Hollingworth Magniac, lot 1534, bt R. Williams, £81.18.0; 1906, March 14, Sotheby's Sale, lot 103 (withdrawn); 1966, purchased from Rev. R. W. Stannard by The British Museum.

LIT: *HW Corres.* 12: 262, 23: 286–7, 301, 33: 323–4, 43: 355, 389. H. Tait, 'The Devil's Looking Glass', in Warren Hunting Smith, ed., *Horace Walpole, Writer, Politician, and Connoisseur* (New Haven: Yale University Press, 1967), 195–212. *OHG* 151. N. H. Clulee, *John Dee's Natural Philosophy: Between Science and Religion* (London and New York: Routledge, 1988). Kim Sloan and Andre Burnet, eds., *Enlightenment. Discovering the World in the Eighteenth Century* (Washington, DC: Smithsonian Books, 2003), 18, fig. 7.

NOTE: A Principal Curiosity.

109. PAIR OF GAUNTLET GLOVES
(THE GLOVES OF JAMES I)
Maker unknown, English, *c.* 1610–25

Leather gloves, trimmed with silk metallic fringe, silk appliqué and metal thread embroidery, metallic braid, and lace, L 44 cm (max.), W 22 cm (max.)
Gloves Collections Trust, courtesy of the Fashion Museum, Bath and North East Somerset Council. BATMC GLO 23337
Fig. 117

D 1774, 108 [Great North Bedchamber]: A pair of gloves worn by king James the 1st. bought out of Thoresby's museum.

D 1784, 75, same as *D 1774*.

PROV: Before 1713, Sir Thomas Tomlinson (as gloves of James I); Ralph Thoresby (1658–1725) (in his museum); son of Thoresby, Stoke Newington; 1764, March 5–7, Ralph Thoresby's Museum Sale, bt HW, £8.6.0; 1842, Strawberry Hill Sale, day 16, lot 54, bt W. Smith, £2.12.0; 'Mr Anthony'; [1848, July 20, Sotheby's, lot 160 for £2.10.0]; in 186, Rev. J. Fuller; 1905, July 10, Christie's sale of Different Properties, lot 131, £9.19.6; 1908, François Flameng; since 1920, collection of Mr Robert Spence (1870–1964), the Worshipful Company of Glovers, no. 23337; currently on loan to the Fashion Museum, Bath.

LIT: Eugenie Gibson, 'Some Gloves from Mr Robert Spence's Collection. Part II', *Connoisseur* 53 (Sept.–Dec. 1920): 19–23, no. 5. *HW Corres.* 10: 278, 38: 340n, 43: 136. P. Byrde and P. Brears, 'A Pair of James I Gloves', *Costume* 24 (1990): 34–42.

110. SNUFF BOX WITH PORTRAIT MINIATURE OF MADAME DE SÉVIGNÉ
Joseph Gibert, (fl. 1759–76); the portrait miniature by an anonymous artist after Jean Petitot (1607–1691). 1765

Gold, lacquered ivory, lined with turtoise shell; detachable lid with rings of marcasites and a portrait miniature, H 3.2 cm × D 7.0 cm
Cypher of Madame de Sevigné ('R' and 'S' entwined) in marcasite against blue silk at bottom of box
The Trustees of the Waldegrave Chattels Trust
Fig. 324

D 1774, 93 [Tribune]: A round white snuff-box; on the top, miniature of madame de Sevigné; at bottom, the cypher of Rabutin and Sevigné in marcasites. This box, with the letter* in it from madame de Sevigné in the Elysian fields to Mr. Walpole, was sent to him by madame du Deffand. *Letter written by madame Marie de Vichy, marquise du Deffand [the lady to whom Mr W. afterwards dedicated his edition of the Memoires de Grammont] in the name of madame de Sevigné from the Elysian fields to Mr Walpole, after his return from Paris in 1766.

D 1784, 65–66, same as *D 1774*.

PROV: 1766, sent to HW by Madame du Deffand; 1842, Strawberry Hill Sale, day 15, lot 25, bt Strong, £28.7.0; Private collection, UK.

LIT: *HW Corres.* 3: 51–2; 118–19. OHG 139. A. Kenneth Snowman, *Eighteenth Century Gold Boxes of Europe*, rev. edn (Woodbridge: Antique Collectors' Club, 1990), pls. 117 and 118.

111. LETTER TO HORACE WALPOLE FROM MADAME DU DEFFAND UNDER THE NAME MADAME DE SÉVIGNÉ
May 1766

16.2 × 11 cm
The Lewis Walpole Library, Yale University.
Figs. 261, 325

D 1774, 93 [Tribune]: See Cat. 110.

PROV: 1766, sent to HW by Madame du Deffand (the snuff box is mentioned in Walpole's correspondence in 1766); 1842, Strawberry Hill Sale, day 15, lot 25, bt Strong (the snuff box and the letter sold together?), £28.7.0; James Robins; 1933, W. S. Lewis; The Lewis Walpole Library, Yale University.

LIT: *HW Corres.* 3: 51–2. W. S. Lewis, 'Horace Walpole's letter from Madame de Sévigné', *Miscellaneous Antiquities*, vol. 8 (Farmington: privately printed, 1933).

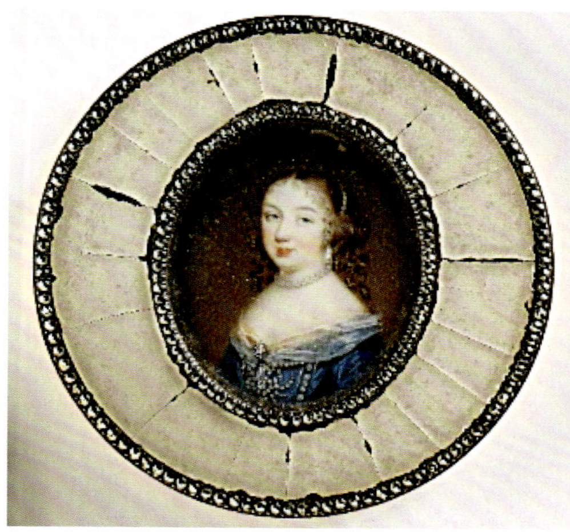

Figure 324. Catalogue 110

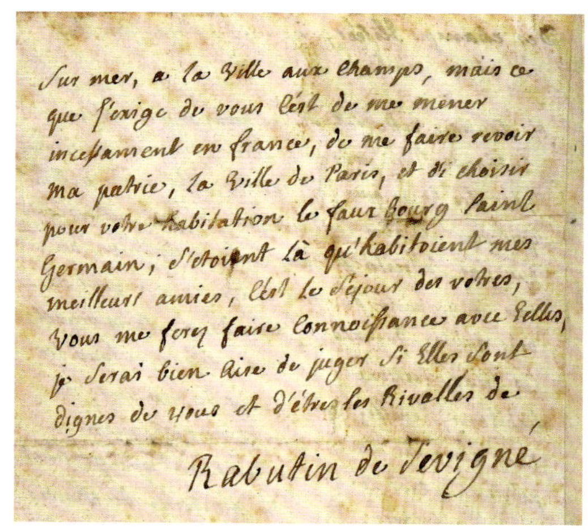

Sur mer, a la ville aux champs, mais ce
que j'exige de vous c'est de me mener
incessament en france, de me faire revoir
ma patrie, la ville de Paris, et de choisir
pour votre habitation le faux bourg saint
Germain; c'etoient là qu'habitoient mes
meilleurs amies, c'est le séjour des votres,
vous me ferez faire connoissance avec elles,
je serai bien aise de juger si elles sont
dignes de vous et d'être les rivalles de
Rabutin de Sevigné

Figure 325. Catalogue 111

8. ANIMATING HISTORY: THE HOLBEIN CHAMBER

112. 'Passage to the Gallery, and Interior of the Holbein Room at Strawberry Hill'
John Carter (1748–1817), *c.* 1790

Pen and ink and watercolour on wove paper, 27.2 × 21.8 cm (visible); 35.4 × 25.8 cm (mount)
Inscriptions: title in Thomas Kirgate's hand in pencil at bottom of sheet
The Lewis Walpole Library, Yale University.
Folio 49 3678.1
Fig. 112

PROV: 1948, Lord Waldegrave to W. S. Lewis; The Lewis Walpole Library, Yale University.
LIT: *Library* 3678. Bentley thesis, fig. 81. *Romantic Interior*, 94–5, fig. 74.
NOTE: Another version by Carter is in Cat. 114, p. 133. A sketch in pen and ink for these drawings is in a copy of *D 1784* extra-illustrated with prints and drawings by John Carter. The Henry E. Huntington Library, San Marino, California (vol. 2, p. 67).

113. 'Screen in the Holbein chamber at Strawberryhill'
Richard Bentley (bap. 1708– d. 1782), *c.* 1750s

Pen and ink with grey and brown wash on wove paper, 16.5 × 18.9 cm (visible), 31.3 × 26.5 cm (mount)
Inscriptions: title in HW's hand at bottom
The Lewis Walpole Library, Yale University.
Folio 49 3585 fol. 55
Fig. 64

From *Drawings and Designs by Richd. Bentley* (*c.* 1760, fol. 55)
D 1774, 49 [Library]: Rare books of prints and drawings in the library…Designs by Mr. Richard Bentley, bound in marble and gilt.
D 1784, 37, same as *D 1774*.
PROV: Design commissioned by HW; for the album see Cat. 18.
LIT: 'Genesis': fig. 17. *Library* 3585. *Collector's Progress*, 59, 102, 104–8. *Rescuing Horace*, 53–61. Bentley thesis, fig. 80. *Romantic Interior*, 94, fig. 73.
NOTE: One of a series of design drawings by Bentley of the screen in the Holbein Chamber. It was engraved by Morris for *D 1784*, opp. p. 43, as *Screen of the Holbein Chamber*.

114. 'Holbien Chamber'
John Carter (1748–1817), *c.* 1788

Watercolour with wash-line mount, 33 × 29 cm (visible); mounted in *D 1784*.
Inscriptions: title on wash-line mount with mispelling
The Lewis Walpole Library, Yale University.
Folio 33 30 Copy 11
Fig. 61

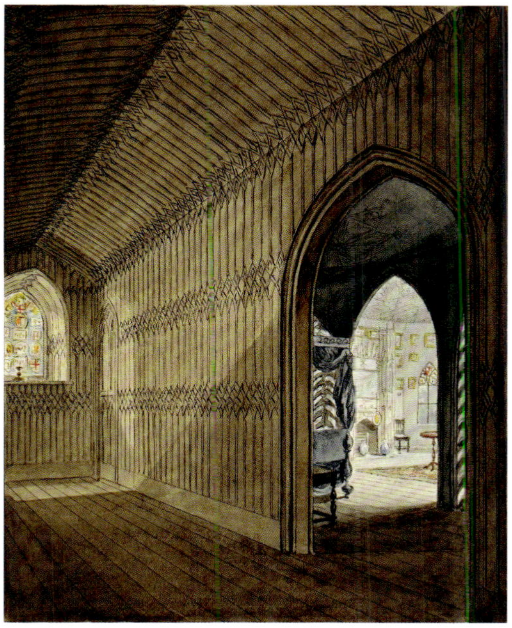

Figure 326. Catalogue 112

PROV: For the extra-illustrated album, Richard Bull (1725–1806); 1880, 29 April–1 May, Sotheby's (Bull sale), lot 886, bt Ellis, £110; 1920(?), 15 (16) June Sotheby's, lot 243, bt Lynch, £255, (for C. Constable Curtis of Langford Hall, Newark); 1937, August, Mrs. Curtis, bt W.S. Lewis £225.
LIT: *Rescuing Horace*, 93. *Romantic Interior*, 94, fig. 72.

115. Portrait of Jane Seymour
George Vertue (1684–1756) after Hans Holbein, the younger (1497/8–1543). 1743–*c.* 1746

Watercolour; black and red chalk, graphite, white watercolour highlights on oiled paper. In Strawberry Hill frame, ebonised wood bound with gilt ribbons in papier mâché, with later replacements in composition, 37 × 27.5 cm (framed)
Inscriptions: on a transferred label on the back of the frame, in HW's hand: 'Queen Jane Seymour: copied by Vertue from the original by Holbein at Kensington'. The ribbons lettered in black: 'JANE SEYMOUR'
Private collection, UK

D 1774, 62 [Holbein Chamber]: On the side opposite to the chimney … *Jane Seymour. [This and all following heads marked with an asterism, were taken off on oil-paper by Vertue from the original drawings of Holbein in queen Caroline's closet at Kensington, now removed to Buckingham house.
D 1784, 45, same as *D 1774*.
PROV: George Vertue; 1757, March 17, his sale, day 2, lot 83, bt HW, £12.12.0 for the group of heads; Strawberry Hill Sale, day 20, lot 32 (34 heads), bt Luxmoore, £36.15.0; Private collection, UK.
NOTE: A receipt for items bought at Vertue's sale of pictures, May 17, 1757 with Walpole's list including 35 drawings from Holbein. The price given is £13.2.6 (The Lewis Walpole Library). Holbein's drawing of Jane Seymour, *c.* 1536, is in the Royal Collection (RL 12267). All Vertue's Holbein tracings, initially carried out in red chalk, have been crudely strengthened with graphite at a later date.

116. Portrait of Mary, Lady Heveningham
George Vertue (1684–1756) after Hans Holbein, the younger (1497/8–1543). 1743–*c.* 1746

Watercolour; black and red chalk; graphite; white highlights on oiled paper. In Strawberry Hill frame, ebonised wood bound with gilt ribbons in papier mâché, with later replacements in composition 37 × 27.5 cm (framed)
Inscriptions: on a transferred label on the back of the frame, in HW's hand: 'Lady Henningham copied by Vertue from the original by Holbein at Kensington'. The ribbons lettered in black 'LADY HENNINGHAM'
Private collection, UK

D 1774, 60 [Holbein Chamber]: Between the bow windows … * Lady Henningham …* See Cat. 115.
D 1784, 44, same as *D 1774*.
PROV: See Cat. 115.
NOTE: Holbein's drawing, *c.* 1532–43, is in the Royal Collection (RL 12227).

117. Portrait of George Brooke, Lord Cobham
George Vertue (1684–1756) after Hans Holbein, the younger (1497/8–1543). 1743–*c.* 1746

Watercolour; black and red chalk; graphite; white highlight, on oiled paper. In Strawberry Hill frame, ebonised wood bound with gilt ribbons in papier mâché, with later replacements in composition 37 × 27.5 cm [framed]
Inscriptions: on a transferred label on the back of the frame, in HW's hand: 'George Brooke Lord Cobham an associate of Sr Thomas Wyat the younger in the rebellion against Q. Mary: copied by Vertue from the original by Holbein at Kensington'. The ribbons lettered in black 'LORD COBHAM'.
Private collection, UK

D 1774, 62 [Holbein Chamber]: On the side opposite to the chimney … *George Brook lord Cobham. …* See Cat. 115.
D 1784, 45, same as *D 1774*.
PROV: See Cat. 115.
NOTE: Holbein's drawing, *c.* 1538–40, is in the Royal Collection.

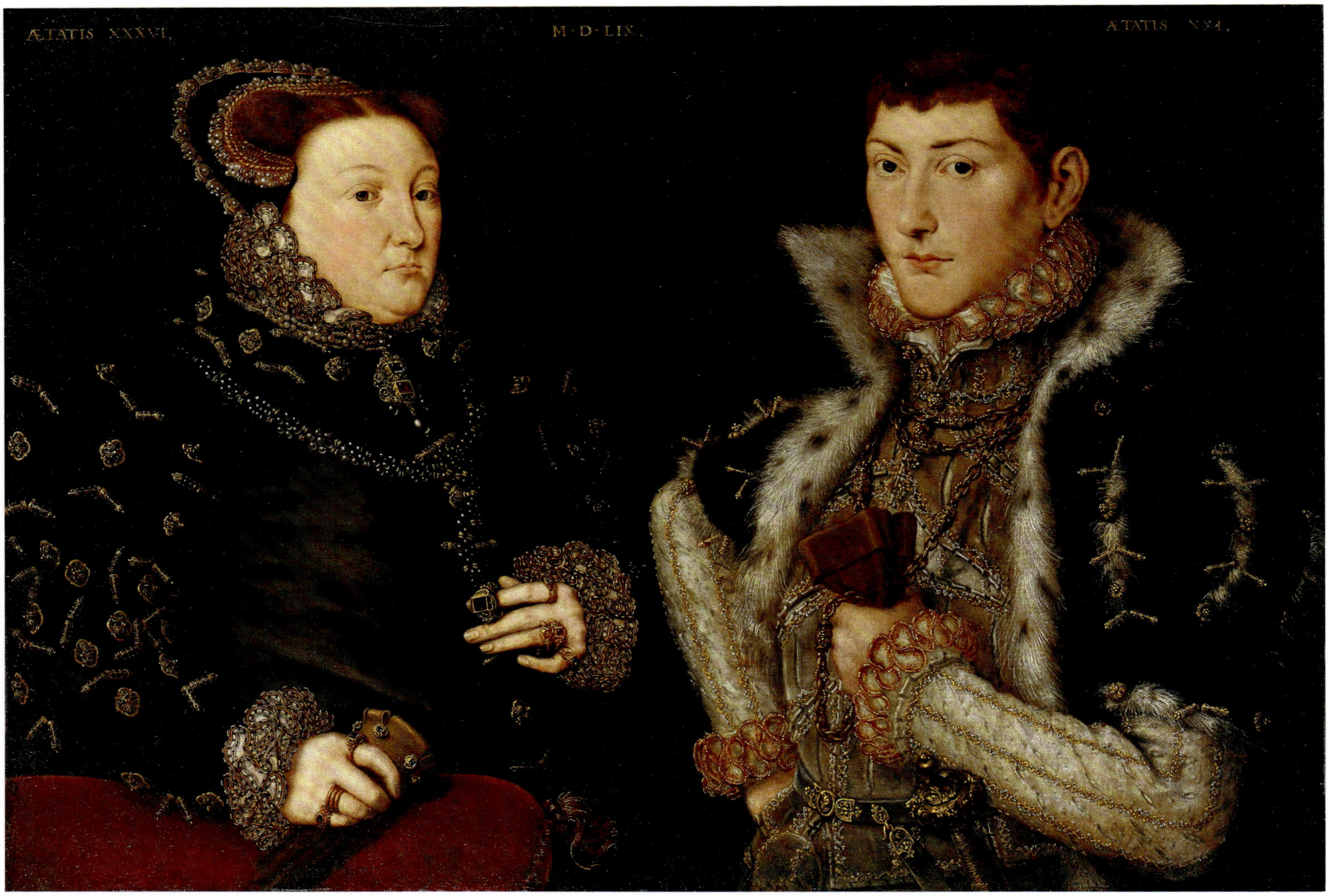

Figure 327. Catalogue 121

118. Portrait of Elizabeth Dauncey (Portrait of Lady Berkeley)
George Vertue (1684–1756) after Hans Holbein, the younger (1497/8–1543). 1743–*c.* 1746

Watercolour; black and red chalk, graphite on oiled paper. In Strawberry Hill frame, ebonised wood bound with gilt ribbons in papier mâché, with later replacements in composition 37 × 27.5 cm (framed)
Inscriptions: on a transferred label on the back of the frame, in HW's hand: 'Anne Savage second wife of Thomas Lord Berkeley copied by Vertue from the original Holbein at Kensington'. The ribbons lettered in black 'LADY BERKELEY'.
Private collection, UK

D 1774, 62 [Holbein Chamber] On the side opposite to the chimney … *Anne Savage Lady Berkeley. She held up the train of Anne Boleyn, at her coronation: Vide Stowe's Chron. p. 543. … * See Cat 115.
D 1784, 45, same as *D 1774*.
PROV: See Cat. 115.
NOTE: Holbein's drawing, *c.* 1526–7, is in the Royal Collection (RL 12228).

119. Portrait of Sir John Gage
George Vertue (1684–1756), after Hans Holbein, the younger (1497/8–1543). 1743–*c.* 1746

Watercolour; black and red chalk; graphite on oiled paper. In Strawberry Hill frame, ebonised wood bound with gilt ribbons in papier mâché, with later replacements in composition 37 × 27.5 cm (framed)
Inscriptions: on a transferred label on the back of the frame, in HW's hand: 'Sr John Gage Knight of the Garter, and Knight Banneret, Captain of the castle of Guisnes, Chancellor of the Dutchy of Lancaster, Constable of the Tower; and Lord Chamberlain to Queen Mary; copied by Vertue from the original by Holbein at Kensington.' The ribbons lettered in black: 'Sr JOHN GAGE'.
Private collection, UK

D 1774, 62 [Holbein chamber] On the side opposite to the chimney … * Sir John Gage. *See Cat. 115.
D 1784, 45, same as *D 1774*.
PROV: See Cat. 115.
NOTE: Holbein's drawing, *c.* 1535–40, is in the Royal Collection (RL 12207).

120. Portrait of Elizabeth, Lady Rich
George Vertue (1684–1756) after Hans Holbein, the younger (1497/8–1543). 1743–*c.* 1746

Watercolour; black and red chalk; graphite on oiled paper, In Strawberry Hill frame, ebonised wood bound with gilt ribbons in papier mâché, with later replacements in composition 37 × 27.5 cm (framed)
Inscriptions: on a transferred label on the back of the frame, in HW's hand: 'Elizabeth Jenks Wife of Lord Chancellor Rich. Copied by Vertue from the original Holbein at Kensington'. The ribbons lettered in black: 'ELIZABETH JENKS'.
Private collection, UK
Fig. 62

D 1774, 62 [Holbein Chamber]: On the side opposite to the chimney: *Lady Rich, his wife [Lord chancellor Rich]. *See Cat. 115
D 1784, 45, same as *D 1774*.
PROV: See Cat. 115.
LIT: See Cat. 115.
NOTE: Holbein's drawing, *c.* 1535–40, is in the Royal Collection (RL 12271).

121. PORTRAIT OF MARY NEVILL, LADY DACRE AND GREGORY FIENNES, 10TH BARON DACRE (PORTRAIT OF FRANCES, DUCHESS OF SUFFOLK AND HER HUSBAND, ADRIAN STOKES, ESQ.)
Hans Eworth (*c.* 1525–after 1578), 1559

Inscriptions: AETATIS XXXVI (t.l.); M.D.LIX (t.c.); AETATIS XXI / HE t.r.
Oil on panel, 50 × 71.4 cm
National Portrait Gallery, London, 6855. Purchased with the help from the National Heritage Memorial Fund, The Art Fund, the Portrait Fund and many other donations, 2008.
Victoria and Albert Museum Only
Fig. 121

D 1774, 61 [Holbein Room]: On the side opposite to the chimney: A fine and very valuable picture by Lucas de Heere, representing Frances duchess of Suffolk, mother of the lady Jane Grey, and Adrian Stoke, her second husband. This picture was in the collection of the earl of Oxford, and was engraved by Vertue: *Vide Walpole's Anecdotes of Painting.*
D 1784, 44–5, same as *D 1774*.
PROV: 1726–27, Collevous Sale (as Holbein, see Vertue Notebooks, II, p. 23); 1741–2, Earl of Oxford Sale, cat. 32, lot 11, bt HW; 1842, Strawberry Hill Sale, day 20, lot 37 (as de Heere), bt Hon. and Rev. Heneage Finch, £92.8.0; by descent Coll. J. C. Wynne Finch; 2008, purchased by National Portrait Gallery with the help from the National Heritage Memorial Fund, The Art Fund, the Portrait Fund and many other donations.
LIT: *Anecdotes*, vol. 1, 133. *HW Corres.* 17: 373–4. 'Vertue Note Books', *The Walpole Society Journal* 21 (Oxford: The University Press, 1938), 113 and 193. Roy Strong, 'Hans Eworth Reconsidered', *Burlington Magazine* 108 (1966): 225–33. Roy Strong, *The English Icon; Elizabethan and Jacobean Portraiture* (New Haven: Yale University Press, 1969), no. 30 (as Frances Brandon, Duchess of Suffolk and Adrian Stokes). *OHG* 116. Karen Hearn, *Dynasties: Painting in Tudor and Jacobean England, 1530–1630* (London: Tate Publishing, 1995), no. 25. Tanya Cooper, *A Guide to Tudor and Jacobean Portraits* (London: National Portrait Gallery, 2008), 37.
NOTE: Engraved by George Vertue in 1748.

122. PORTRAIT OF HENRY VIII
Unknown artist, probably German, 1537–*c.* 1600

Carved hone-stone, 15.2 × 10.2 cm
Fiorencia Foundation
Fig. 328

D 1774, 63 [Holbein Chamber]: On the side opposite to the chimney: ... Henry 8th. fine whole figure in terra cotta, by Holbein; from lady Elizabeth Germaine's Collection.
D 1784, 46, same as *D 1774*.
PROV: [Charles I of England]; Thomas Howard, 2nd Earl of Arundel; passed from Mary, Duchess of Norfolk (d. 1705), to her second husband, Sir John Germain who bequeathed it to his second wife, Lady Elizabeth Germain; 1770, March 7, Lady Elizabeth Germaine Collection Sale, by Langford (lot 48), bt HW, £16.5.6; 1842, Strawberry Hill Sale, day 20, lot 52, bt John Dent, Esq., £67.4.0; Mrs John Dent Brocklehurst, Sudeley Castle; Private collection.
LIT: *Anecdotes*, vol. 1, 92. Royal Academy of Arts, *Catalogue of the exhibition of works by Holbein & other masters of the 16th and 17th centuries*, 2nd edn (London: Royal Academy of Arts, 1950–51), no. 197. *OHG* 117 (wax cast).
EXHIB: 1862 Special Exhibition, no. 2219. Manchester, 'Tudor' 1897, no. 468; New Gallery, London, 'Tudor' 1889–90, no. 1074; London, 'Tudor Exhibition', 1889, no. 1074
NOTE: A Principal Curiosity. The relief was hung in a frame on the wall. The pose is taken from Holbein's Whitehall fresco (1537). HW's receipt dated 1770, Mar. 10, for items bought at Lady Betty Germain's sale is at the Lewis Walpole Library, Yale University.

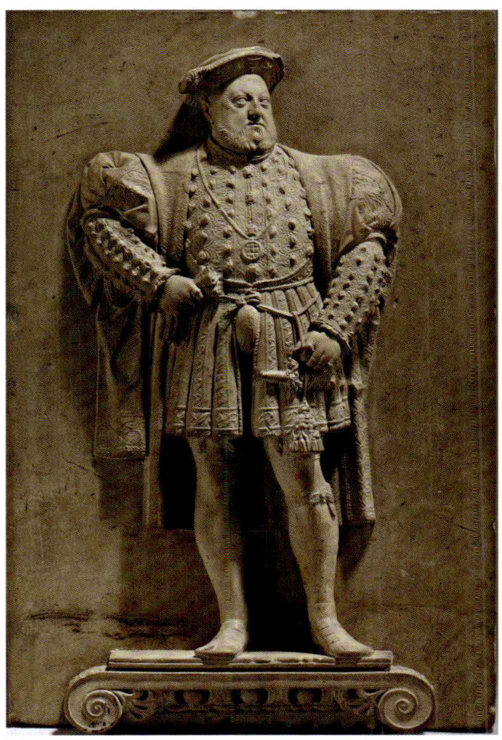

Figure 328. Catalogue 122

123. PORTRAIT OF MADELEINE OF FRANCE, 2ND DAUGHTER OF FRANÇOIS I AND CLAUDE OF FRANCE (CHARLOTTE, DAUGHTER OF FRANCIS I)
Jean Clouet (*c.* 1485–1540/1), *c.* 1522

Oil on panel, transferred from canvas, 16.8 × 13. 3 cm
Inscriptions: perhaps late 17th century, 'Charlotte de France'
Private collection, courtesy of the Weiss Gallery
Fig. 63

D 1774, 63 [Holbein Chamber]: On the side opposite to the chimney:...Charlotte, daughter of Francis 1st. died at five years of age; by Janet: fine. From sir Luke Schaub's collection.
D 1784, 45, same as *D 1774*.
PROV: François I and Queen Claude of France; Sir Luke Schaub; 1758, April 27, Sir Luke Schaub's Collection Sale, lot 20, bt Brand, £9.9.0; HW; 1842, Strawberry Hill Sale, day 20, lot 49, bt Webb, Old Bond Street, £58.16.0; Charles Baring Wall; thence to his great-nephew, Thomas George Baring, 1st Earl of Northbrook, until 1894; art market, Cologne?; Baron Alphonse de Rothschild; Baron Edouard de Rothschild (his son); 1941, Feb 8, confiscated by the Einsatzstab Reichleiter Rosenberg for Reichmarschall Hermann Goering; Dr Walter Bremen; thence to his daughter; Elisabeth Bremen; Weiss Gallery; Private collection.
LIT: Ronald S. Gower, *The Great Historic Galleries of England* (London: Sampson Low, Marston, Searle and Rivington, 1881), no. 25. Henri Bouchot, *Les Clouet et Corneille de Lyon* (Paris: Librairie de l'art, 1892). *HW Corres.* 21: 199. Peter Mellen, *Jean Clouet: Complete Edition of the Drawings, Miniatures and Paintings* (London: Phaidon, 1971), no. 137–8. *The Weiss Gallery, Historical Reflections: A Catalogue of Early Portraiture 1520–1780* (London: Weiss Gallery, 2007), no. 1.
EXHIB: British Institution, 1843, no. 90; Burlington House, 'Exhibition of Works by the Old Masters', Winter 1880, no. 209.
NOTE: A Principal Curiosity.

124. TABLE
Coromandel Coast, India, 1660–80

Ebony, carved, pierced and turned, with teak dust shelf, H 76 × W 111 × depth 75 cm
Victoria and Albert Museum, London. IS73–1981
Fig. 329

1842 Sale [Refectory]: [Possibly lot 57]: [Lot 56: A splendid solid ebony table, most elaborately and boldly carved, the top of solid ebony, with frame work, richly decorated, and lower border, on twisted legs, 3 feet 8 inches long and 2 feet 5 inches wide]. Lot 57: A ditto, perfectly similar.
PROV: Perhaps HW; 1842, Strawberry Hill Sale, day 19, possibly lot 57, bt Town and Emanuel, £50.8.0; 1980, December 12, Sotheby's, lot 141, bt Philips and Harris; 1981, purchased by Victoria and Albert Museum.
LIT: *HW Corres.* 1: 94n. Amin Jaffer, *Furniture from British India and Ceylon: a Catalogue of the Collections in the Victoria and Albert Museum and the Peabody Essex Museum* (London: V&A Publications, 2001), no. 2.

125. DESIGN FOR A CHIMNEYPIECE
Hans Holbein, the younger (1497/8–1543), *c.* 1537–43

Black and black ink with grey, blue and red wash, 53.9 × 42.7 cm
British Museum, Department of Prints and Drawings. 1854,0708.1.
Victoria and Albert Museum only
Fig. 60

D 1774, 151 [Holbein Chamber]: Additions since the Appendix…In the Holbein Chamber. A large drawing of a magnificent chimney-piece; a design by Holbein for one of the palaces of Henry 8th.
D 1784, 84 Additions: same as *D 1774*.

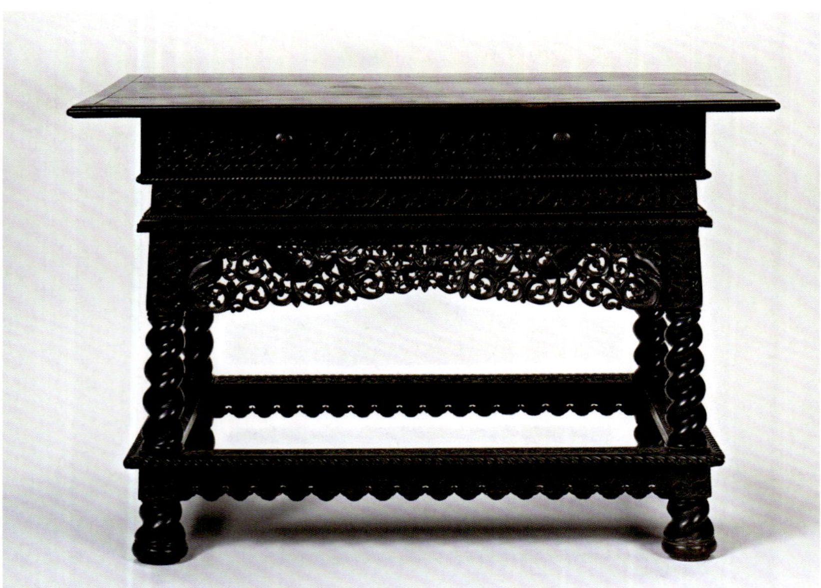

Figure 329. Catalogue 124

PROV: Thomas Howard, 2nd Earl of Arundel; Jonathan Richardson I; 1779, March 25, Thomas Hudson's Sale, lot 59, bt HW, £4.4.0; 1842, Strawberry Hill Sale, day 20, lot 64, bt Dommes, £33.12.0; 1854, Henry Graves & Co., bt British Museum.
LIT: *HW Corres.* 2: 150. Clive Wainwright, 'Some Objects from William Beckford's Collection now in the Victoria and Albert Museum', *The Burlington Magazine* (May 1971), 258, fig. 26. John Rowlands, *Drawings by German Artists: the Fifteenth & Sixteenth Centuries by Artists born before 1530*, 2 vols. (London: British Museum Press, 1993), no. 327. Susan Foister, *Holbein in England* (exh. cat. London: Tate Publishing, 2006), no. 102. Simon Thurley, *The Royal Palaces of Tudor England* (New Haven and London: Yale University Press, 1993) 40–4.

126. DESIGN FOR A CLOCK-SALT
Hans Holbein, the younger (1497/8–1543), *c.* 1543

Pen, black ink, red and grey wash, 41 × 21.3 cm
Inscriptions: in latin by Nikolaus Kratzer and in another hand, dated 1544.
British Museum, Department of Prints and Drawings. 1850,0713.14.
Victoria and Albert Museum only
Fig. 330

D 1774, 134 [Holbein Chamber]: Appendix…In the Holbein Chamber…A drawing of a clock, by Holbein; designed for sir Antony Denny as a new year's gift to Henry 8th. Bought at the sale of mons. Mariette.
D 1784, 47, same as *D 1774*.
PROV: 1775, Pierre-Jean Mariette Sale, lot 943, bt HW; 1842, Strawberry Hill Sale, day 20, lot 72, bt Graves, Pall Mall, £6.16.6; 1850, Henry Graves & Co., bt British Museum.
LIT: John Rowlands, *The Age of Dürer and Holbein: German Drawings 1400–1550* (New York: Cambridge University Press, 1988), no. 211. David Starkey, *Henry VIII: A European Court in England* (New York: Cross River Press, 1991), 135, no. IX.15. John Rowlands, *Drawings by German Artists: the Fifteenth & Sixteenth Centuries by Artists born before 1530*, 2 vols. (London: British Museum Press, 1993), no. 328. Susan Foister, *Holbein in England* (exh. cat London: Tate Publishing, 2006), no. 80.
NOTE: Kratzer, the royal astronomer records his collaboration on three occasions with Holbein. The other inscription records Denny's new-year gift to Henry VIII in 1545 (old style 1544).

127. THE TRIUMPH OF POVERTY
Lucas Vorsterman, I (*c.* 1595–1675) after Hans Holbein, the younger (1497/8–1543)

Pen and brown ink, with brown wash and black and red chalk, heightened with cream bodycolour; green wash and blue bodycolour, 43.7 × 58.5 cm
British Museum, Department of Prints and Drawings. 1894,0721.2
Fig. 332

D 1774, 63 [Holbein Chamber]: Pictures in the alcove:…The triumph of Poverty; ditto [by Frederic Zucchero, from the original of Holbein that was in the Steel-yard… *Vide a description of this and the next in the Anecdotes of Painting*, vol. I.]. These drawings, invaluable by the originals being lost, were purchased from Buckingham-house, when sir Charles Sheffield sold it to the king.
D 1784, 46, same as *D 1774*.
PROV: (?) Thomas Howard, 2nd Earl of Arundel; Sir Peter Lely; 1763, Feb. 24–25, John Sheffield, Buckingham House Sale, lot 33, bt HW with The Triumph of Riches, £10.10.0; 1842, Strawberry Hill Sale, day 20, lot 55, bt Dommes, £16.16.0 (lots 54 & 55); 1894, June 2, Christie's, collection of the late Charles Eastlake, PRA, lot 17, bt Dr Jean Paul Richter, £8.8.0; 1894, bt British Museum.
LIT: *Anedcotes*, vol 1, 83–4. A. M. Hind, *Catalogue of Dutch and Flemish Drawings preserved in the Department of Prints and Drawings in the British Museum*, vol. 2 (London: British Museum Press, 1915), 149, no. 16. Otto Kurz, 'Holbein and Others in a Seventeenth Century Collection', *Burlington Magazine*, 83, 488, Holbein Number (Nov. 1943): 279–82 on the original Holbeins. *OHG* 115. Lindsay Stainton and Christopher White, *Drawing in England from Hilliard to Hogarth* (London: British Museum Press, 1987), no. 40. John Rowlands, *Drawings by German Artists: the Fifteenth & Sixteenth Centuries by Artists born before 1530*, vol. 1 (London: British Museum Press, 1993), 178, no. 381. Susan Foister, *Holbein in England* (exh. cat London: Tate Publishing, 2006), no. 69.
NOTE: A Principal Curiosity. The corresponding 'Triumph of Riches' is in the Ashmolean Museum, Oxford. For Walpole's confused attribution of the 'Triumph of Poverty' to Federico Zuccaro (1540/2–1609) and the 'Triumph of Riches' to Vorsterman, see *Anecdotes* (*Works*, vol. 2, p. 75).

128. Young Man Holding a Missal
Circle of Rogier van der Weyden (*c.* 1399–1464)

Oil on panel, 27.9 × 21.6 cm, frame: 45.8 × 38.6 cm
Lent by the Rt Hon. the Earl of Derby, K050
Victoria and Albert Museum only
Fig. 331

D 1774, 59 [Holbein Chamber]: A man's head with a book; by Quintin Matsis: it was in sir Robert Walpole's collection.
D 1784, 43, same as *D 1774*.
PROV: 1736, Sir Robert Walpole (Downing Street, closet); HW; 1842, Strawberry Hill Sale, day 20, lot 29, bt Earl of Derby, £22.1.0.
LIT: Larissa Dukelskaya and Andrew Moore, *A Capital Collection: Houghton Hall and the Hermitage* (New Haven and London: Yale University Press, 2002), 447, No. 240. Sir George Scharf, *A Descriptive and Historical Catalogue of the Collection of Pictures at Knowsley Hall* (London: Bradbury, Agnew, & Co., 1875), no. 349. F. G. Stephens, *Notes on the Pictures at Knowsley Hall* (1881), 36.

129. Cardinal's Hat ('The Red Hat of Cardinal Wolsey')
Maker unknown, 16th century

Felt, lined with silk, D 47 cm
Inscription: on label in HW's hand: 'Cardinal Wolsey's Hat, found in the great Wardrobe by Bishop Burnet when he was Clerk of the Closet. It was left by his son Judge Burnet to his housekeeper who gave it to the Countess of Albemarle's Butler, who gave it to his lady, and her ladyship to Mr Horace Walpole in 1776'
Governing Body of Christ Church, Oxford University
Fig. 145

D 1774, 134 [Holbein Chamber]: Appendix…In the Holbein Chamber: The red hat of cardinal Wolsey, found in the great wardrobe by bishop Burnet when clerk of the closet. From his son the judge it came to the countess dowager of Albemarle, who gave it to Mr. Walpole.
D 1784, 43, same as *D 1774*.
PROV: Gilbert Burnet, Bishop of Salisbury (1643–1715); Bishop Burnet to his son, Judge Burnet (1694–1715); left by Judge Burnet to his housekeeper who gave it to the Countess of Albemarle's butler; then given to the Countess by her butler; 1776, January, Countess of Albemarle presented to HW; 1842, Strawberry Hill, day 17, lot 73, bt Charles Kean, Esq. (the actor), £21.0.0; 1898, June 24, Sotheby's, Order of Executor of Mrs Mary Logie (only child of Charles Kean), lot 531, bt Tregaskis, £27.0.0; bt for £63, by members of Christ Church, notably the Rev. A. W. Oxford, and presented to the House.
LIT: *HW Corres.* 24: 174, 28: 313, 29: 39, 41: 332–3. OHG 118. *Romantic Interior*, 95–6. Stephen J. Greenblatt, *Learning to Curse: Essays in Early Modern Culture* (New York: Routledge, 1990), 161. Anne Barton, 'The Perils of Historicism', *The New York Review of Books* (28 March 1991). John Lee, 'The Man Who Mistook His Hat: Stephen Greenblatt and the Anecdote', *Essays in Criticism* 45 (1995): 285–300.
NOTE: A Principal Curiosity. Bishop Burnet, a strong anti-Catholic, was the author of *The History of the Reformation of the Church of England, 1679–1714*. The Bishop had left the royal service by 1687.

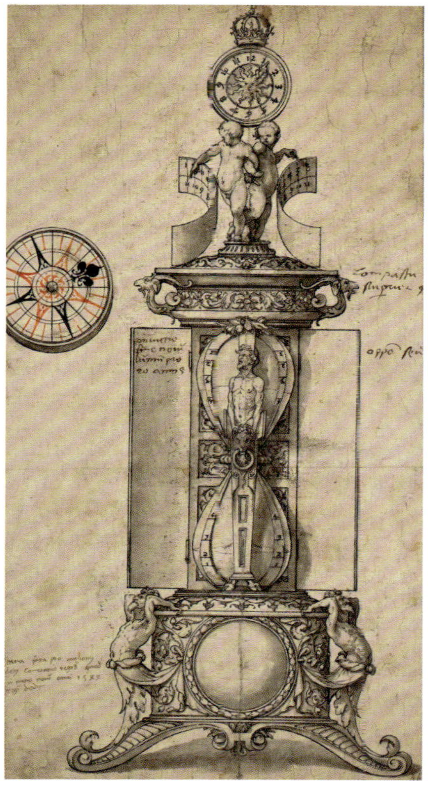

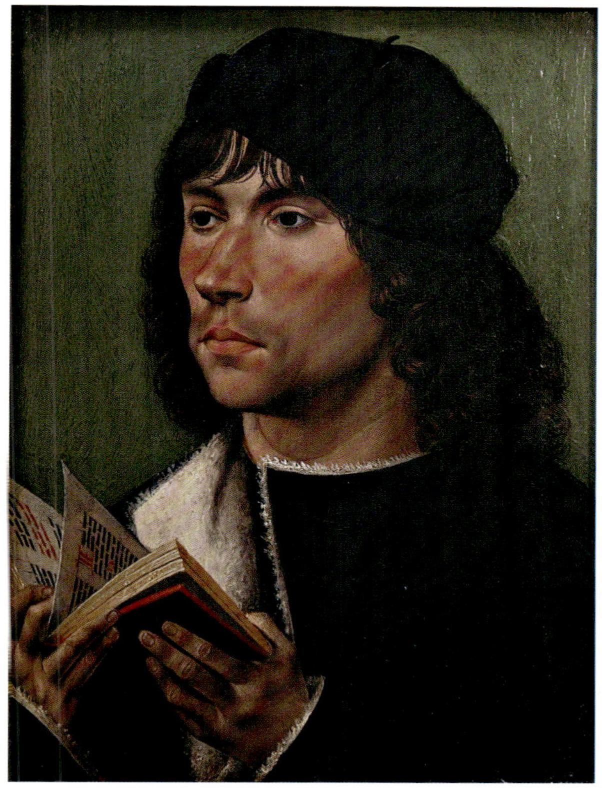

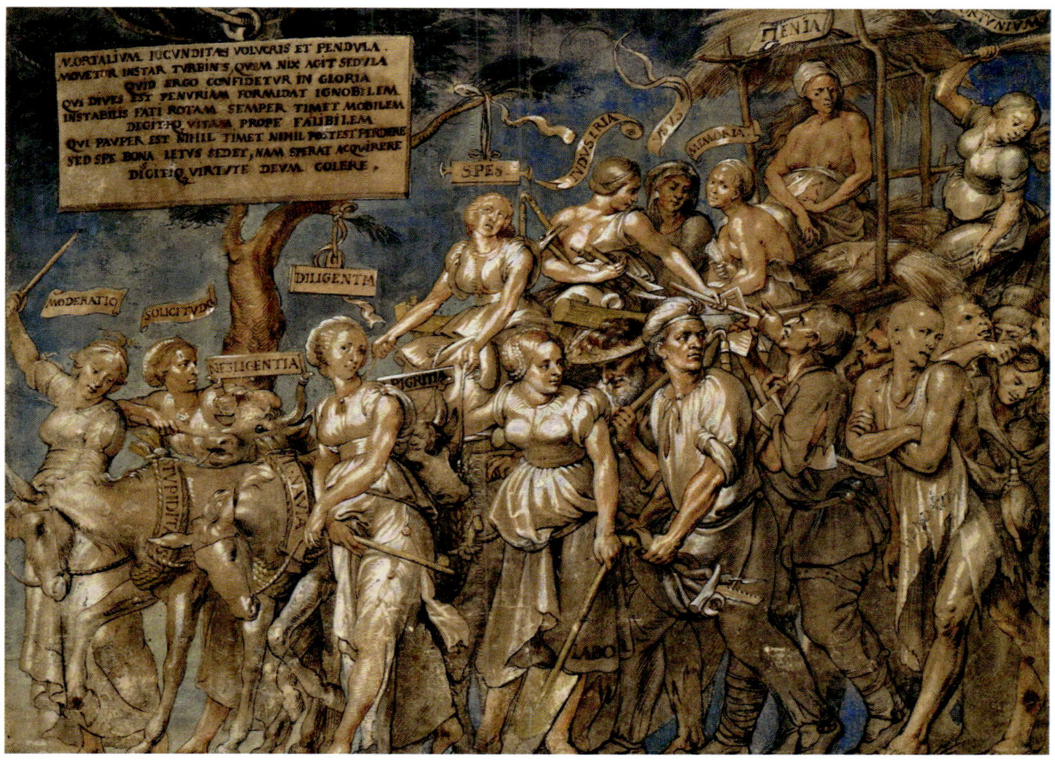

Top left, Figure 330. Catalogue 126
Top right, Figure 331. Catalogue 128
Bottom, Figure 332. Catalogue 127

9. THE STATE APARTMENT: THE GALLERY

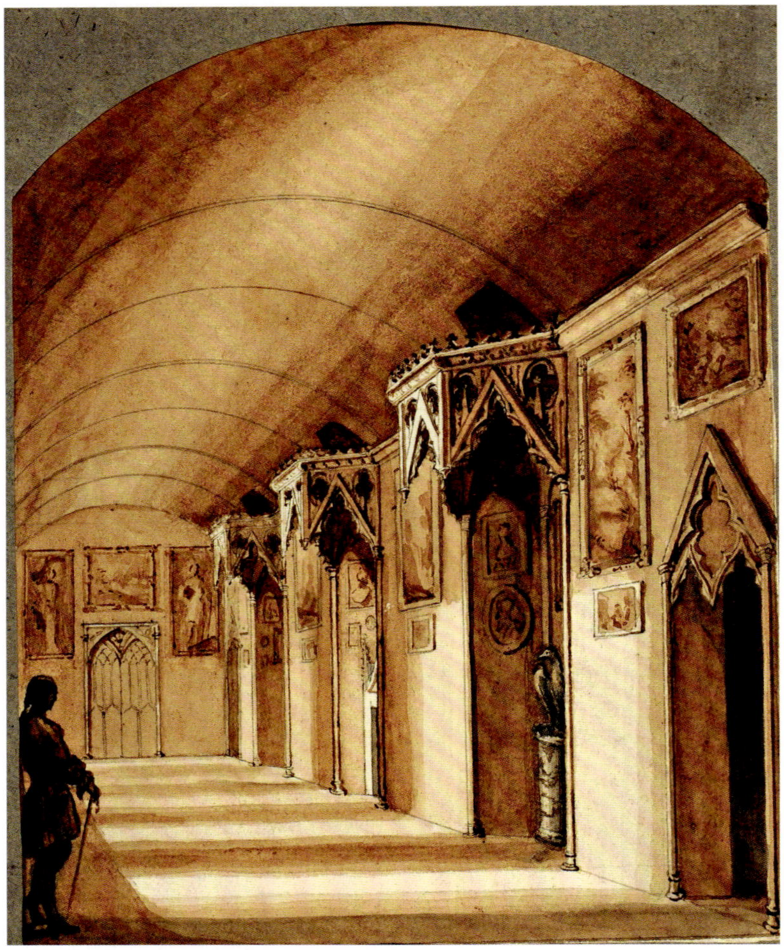

Figure 333. Catalogue 130

130. 'Sketch of the Gallery at Strawberryhill'
Richard Bentley (bap. 1708– d. 1782), *c.* 1759

Grey and brown wash on laid paper, 16.8 × 13.3 cm (visible); 23.2 × 17.4 cm (mount)
Inscriptions: title in HW's hand on the album page.
The Lewis Walpole Library, Yale University Farmington, CT. Folio 49 3585 fol. 56
Fig. 333

From *Drawings and Designs by Richd. Bentley* (*c.* 1760, fol. 56)
D 1774, 49 [Library]: Rare books of prints and drawings in the library...Designs by Mr. Richard Bentley, bound in marble and gilt.
D 1784, 37, same as *D 1774*.
PROV: Design commissioned by HW; for the album see Cat. 18.
LIT: 'Genesis': 57–92. *Library* 3585. *Collector's Progress*, 59, 102, 104–8. *Rescuing Horace*, 53–61. Bentley thesis, fig. 83.
NOTE: The earliest idea for the Gallery.

131. 'Gallery at Strawberry Hill'
Thomas Sandby (bap. 1723–d. 1798), Paul Sandby (1731–1809) and Edward Edwards (1738–1806), begun *c.* 1769? completed 1781

Watercolour, 57.7 × 78.7 cm
Inscriptions: signed on the wash-line mount with the title and: 'T.Sandby, P.Sandby & E.Edwards 1781.' Inscribed by W. A. Sandby on the back in ink on a label: 'This drawing is mentioned by Horace Walpole in a letter to the Rev. W. Cole, dated 16 June 1781. Purchased at Christies from Lord Waldegrave's sale of the Strawberry Hill collection, Feb 1900. WS.' (Walpole extract). 'A painter is to come hither on Monday to... finish T Sandby's fine view of the gallery, to which I could never get him to put the last hand.' 'Ed Edwards, ARA, a friend of TS who filled in the upper portrait on the right hand. The whole of the rest is by TS'.
Victoria and Albert Museum, London. Bequeathed by W. A. Sandby. D.1837–1904.
Fig. 65

PROV: Commissioned by HW; 1900, February 10, Christie's, Ld Waldegrave Sale, lot 20, bt W.A. Sandby; [1904], Bequeathed to the Victoria and Albert Museum.
LIT: *HW Corres.* 2: 274, 41: 189, 43: 383. Mellon Lectures, illustration no. 37. *OHG* 126. Michael Snodin, 'Representing Rooms: plans and other drawings', in Jeremy Aynsley and Charlotte Grant, eds, *Imagined Interiors: Representing the Domestic Interior since the Renaissance* (London: V&A Publications, 2006), repro. p. 129.
EXHIB: 1782, Royal Academy of Arts, no. 241, Thomas Sandby: 'View of the gothic gallery at Strawberry Hill'.
NOTE: The drawing formed the basis of smaller drawing by Edwards dated 1781 (Lewis Walpole Library 493582, p. 105) which was engraved by T. Morris for *D 1784*, opp. p. 47, as *The Gallery*.

132. Stained Glass Panel with Walpole Coat of Arms
William Peckitt (bap. 1731–d. 1795), 1762

Coloured, stained, and enamelled glass, lead, 32.5 × 24.1 cm
The Lewis Walpole Library, Yale University.
Fig. 55

D 1774, 64 [Gallery]: In the windows, painted by Peckitt, are all the quarterings of the family.
D 1784, 47, same as *D 1774*.
PROV: HW commissioned from Peckitt, £30.0.0; 1842, Strawberry Hill Sale, day 24, lot 45, bt Town and Emanuel, £30.0.0; W. J. Webb, Twickenham; 1931 November, Swift, London dealer, bt W. S Lewis, £3.10.0; The Lewis Walpole Library, Yale University.
LIT: William Cole and Edward Edwards, *British Library Manuscripts* (1762), mss 5841 ff 76–84, *Misc. Coll.* vol. XL. *HW Corres.* 1: 145, 28: 213n. *Accounts*, vol. 9, 63, note 13, and 114, note 12. Mellon Lectures, xxii. J. T. Brighton, 'William Peckitt's Commission Book', *The Walpole Society* LIV (1988): 355–6: 'No 83 March 1762 for Horace Walpole Esquire Coats of Arms and Mosaics for the tops of five windows £30.0.0'.
NOTE: The areas of glass which today appear clear had been painted in Walpole's time with blue enamel, probably once with blue florets. Remnants of the enamel can be seen in several sections, notably along the bottom edge. This piece was placed in the window opposite the chimneypiece.

133. Diagram of the Picture Hang in the Gallery at Strawberry Hill: 'Chimneyside'
annotated by Horace Walpole (1717–1797), 1774

Pen and ink, 31 × 36 cm [approx. foldout]; 27.5 × 21.5 cm [book]
mounted in *D 1774*, 121.19
Inscriptions: at top: 'Chimney Side'; and numbered with key to pictures at bottom
The Lewis Walpole Library, Yale University. 49 2523
See Fig. 66

1842 Sale for the book: [Books, printed at the Private Press of HW, at Strawberry Hill]: A ditto [A description of the Villa at Strawberry Hill, by Horace Walpole, 4to, the first edition, illustrated, 1774], bound in red Morocco.
PROV: The book: 1774, published by HW at Strawberry Hill; 1842, Strawberry Hill Sale, day 4, lot 152, bt Thorpe, £11.0.6; 1842, offered in Thorpe's Supplement, lot 13219, for £21; 1844, offered in Thorpe's Supplement; 1855, July 26, Charles Meigh Sale, Sotheby's, lot 1822, bt Toovey; 1919, November 12, Avery Sale, Anderson, lot 961, bt George D. Smith for the Spencer Collection in the New York Public Library, $375; 1950, February, New York Public Library to W. S. Lewis by exchange to Yale for the Lewis Walpole collection; The Lewis Walpole Library, Yale University.
LIT: *Library* 2523.

134. Portrait of Ludovic Stuart, Duke of Richmond and Lennox
Marcus Geeraerts, the younger (1561–1635), 1608

Oil on canvas, 213 × 130.8 cm
Lord Tollemache, Helmingham Hall
Fig. 334

D 1774, 70–1 [Gallery]: Window side:...Lodowic Stuart, duke of Richmond and Lenox; ditto [whole length, in robes of the garter]: these two last came out of Luton-house in Bedfordshire, where the latter lived.
D 1784, 51, same as *D 1774*.
PROV: Luton House, Bedfordshire, bt HW, £19.19.0 (for this and a portrait of Thomas Lord Howard of Bindon); 1842, Strawberry Hill Sale, day 21, lot 97, bt J. Tollemache, Esq. MP, £27.6.0; Private collection, UK.
LIT: *HW Corres.* 16: 191. Ellis Waterhouse, *The Collection of Pictures in Helmingham Hall* (Helmingham Hall, 1958), no. 50.

135. Wine Cooler with Bacchus and Attendants
Italian (Urbino), *c.* 1550–1570

Tin-glazed earthenware (maiolica), H 22.9 cm; W 49.8 cm (max.)
Inscriptions: Inventory number painted in red: 465
Lent by The Metropolitan Museum of Art, The Friedsam Collection, Bequest of Michael Friedsam, 1931 (32.100.368)
Fig. 335

D 1784, 52–3 [Gallery]: Window side:...Two commodes of old Japan with marble slabs; on one, a triangular cistern of Roman fayence, finely painted with figures, probably from designs of Julio Romano; ....On the other commode, another cistern* like the former... *Presents from the Earl of Exeter; and had belonged to Jervas the painter, who had a fine collection of that fayence.
PROV: Charles Jervas (1675–1739); possibly 1749, March 11, Jervas Sale, lot 469 ('a curious Antique Cistern, with the Banquet of the Gods, &c. by Raphael'); or lot 564 ('a curious Antique Cistern, with Neptune, Triton, Bacchanals, &c. by Raphael'); Earl of Exeter gave to HW; 1842, Strawberry Hill Sale, day 23, lots 81 and 82, bt Miss Burdett Coutts, £84.0.0 [each]; 1922, May 9–11, Christie's Baroness Burdett-Coutts Sale, lots 181 and 182, bt H. J. Simmonds, £241.10; 1931, bequeathed to The Metropolitan Museum of Art by Michael Friedsam (with its companion from Strawberry Hill, 32.100.367).
LIT: J. Marryat, *Collections towards a History of Pottery and Porcelain* (London, 1850), 22. 'Ceramics', *The Metropolitan Museum of Art Bulletin, Part 2: The Michael Friedsam Collection* 27, no. 11 (Nov. 1932): 60–3. *HW Corres.* 25: 591n. Bet McLeod, 'The Ceramics at Strawberry Hill' (MA Thesis, Cooper-Hewitt/Parson's School of Design, New York, 1993), 154, no. 15, fig. 12.

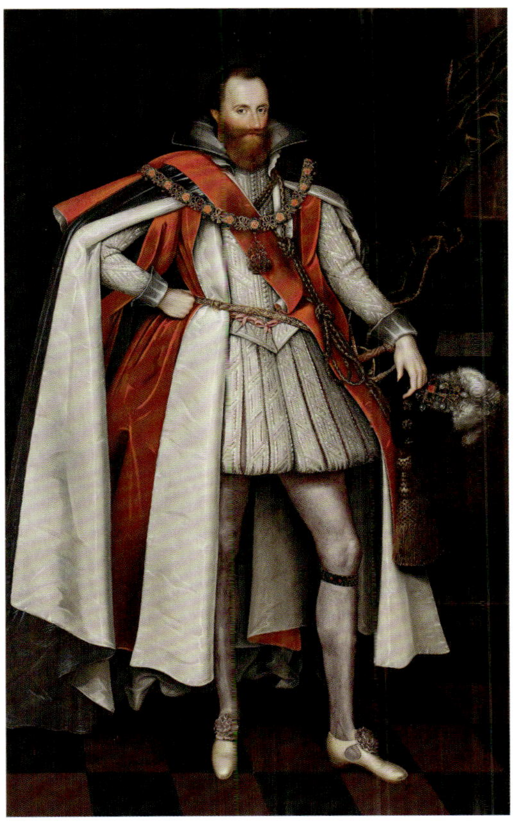

Figure 334. Catalogue 134

136. Commode
Pierre Eloy Langlois (1738–1805), 1763

Chinese lacquer, English japanning, softwood substrate with secondary oak, interior veneered with satinwood and Brazilian rosewood, ormolu mounts, verde antico marble veneer top, 88.6 × 148 × 59.7 cm
Fine Arts Museums of San Francisco, Gift of Mrs William P. Roth, 1985.58a-b
Fig. 67

D 1774, 73 [Gallery]: Window side:...Two commodes of old japan with marble slabs.
D 1784, 52, same as *D 1774*.
PROV: Made for HW (handwritten note in *D 1774* (Lewis Walpole Library 49 2422A0): 'The two commodes & 4 coins, cost, £125.0.0, without the Japan which was my own, but the bending it into the present forms by Langlois a Frenchman, was very expensive.'); 1842, Strawberry Hill Sale, day 23, lots 89 or 90, bt Redfern, Warwick £57.15.0 the pair; ?4th Earl of Shaftesbury; ?1913, April 29, Galerie Georges Petit, Eugene Kramer Collection, lot 153 (this is probably the example in the Decorative Arts Museum, Buenos Aires); 1925, February 3, Basil Dighton (Savile Row, W. London) bt W. B. Bourn Family; [Roth family purchased Bourn property called Filoli, Woodside California, that included the commode]; 1985, Fine Arts Museums of San Francisco, Legion of Honor, gift of Mrs William P. Roth.
LIT: J. de Serre, 'Porcelain and Lacquer', *Country Life*, 15 (March 1924): p. xlviii. *Accounts* [10] 120, note 4. *HW Corres.* 10: 207. Anthony Coleridge, 'Pierre Langlois and his œuvre and some recent discoveries', *Gazette des Beaux Arts* (Sept. 1967): 155–62. Peter Thornton and William Rieder, 'Pierre Langlois, Ebeniste', part 1 *Connoisseur* (Dec. 1971): 285 and part 3 *Connoisseur* (March 1972): 176–9. William Rieder, 'A Golden Age of English Furniture', *Apollo* (Feb. 1980): 113–18, 15, fig. 4. *Selected Works, Fine Arts Museums of San Francisco* (1987), 56.
NOTE: The other commode from the pair in the Gallery is in the National Museum of Decorative Arts, Buenos Aires.

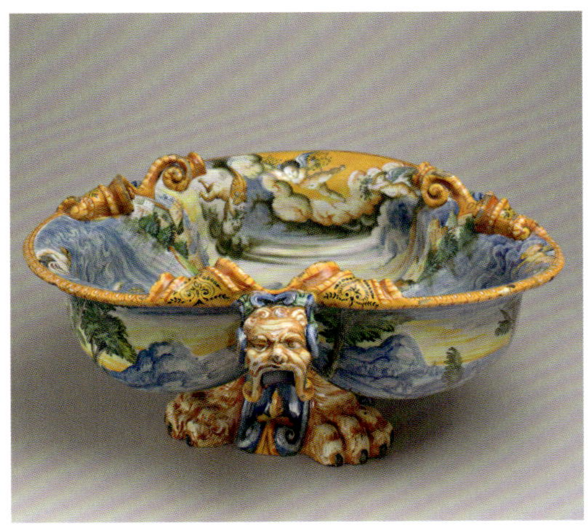

Figure 335. Catalogue 135

137. PORTRAIT OF P. LENEVE, ALDERMAN OF NORWICH
Sir Peter Lely (1618–1680), 1656–8

Oil on canvas, 123.5 × 101.5 cm, 48 ⅜ × 39 ¹⁵⁄₁₆ in.
The Walters Art Museum, Baltimore, Maryland. 37.231
Yale Center for British Art only
Fig. 68

D 1774, 68 [Gallery]: Right hand of the chimney:… —— Leneve, alderman of Norwich; son of the foregoing Leneve. The best picture sir Peter Lely ever painted, and as fine as Vandyck's countess of Exeter, before-mentioned.
D 1784, 50, same as *D 1774*.
PROV: Isabella LeNeve; 1759, September 3, bt HW, 'thirty guineas for two portraits of the LeNeve's Family'; 1842, Strawberry Hill Sale, day 21, lot 60, bt Dommes, £54.12; 1883–1894 (before), Sir Hugh Hume Campbell, Bart; 1894 June 16, Christie's, Sir Hugh Hume Campbell Sale, lot 34, bt David H. King, 25gns; 1905 March 13, American Art Association (David H. King Sale), lot 55, bt Henry Walters; 1931, The Walters Art Gallery [now The Walters Art Museum] upon the death of Henry Walters.
LIT: *Anecdotes*, vol. 2, 93. R. B. Becket, *Lely* (London, 1951), no. 196.
EXHIB: Scottish National Portrait Gallery, 1883, no. 111.
NOTE: The identity of the sitter is uncertain. HW's receipt dated 1759, Sep. 3, 'Received of the Honble Horatio Walpole, Esqr Thirty Guineas for Two portraits of the Le Neve's Family' signed by Peter LeNeve Executor of my late Aunt Isabella LeNeve' is at the Lewis Walpole Library, Yale University. HW's note in his annotated *D 1774* records variously that he paid £10.10.01 for each of the two LeNeve portraits. (*D 1774*, The Lewis Walpole Library 49 2522A.) Isabella LeNeve (*c.* 1686–1759) had a long friendship with the Walpole family and lived many years with HW and his father. (*HW Corres.* 21: 316.)

138. EAGLE ON AN ALTAR PLINTH
Roman, 1st century AD

Marble, H 77.5 cm
Earl of Wemyss and March, Gosford House, East Lothian
Not exhibited
Fig. 184

D 1774, 67 [Gallery]: Chimney-side, left hand:…The eagle, found in the gardens of Boccapadugli within the precinct of Caracalla's baths at Rome, in the year 1742. One of the finest pieces of Greek sculpture in the world, and reckoned superior to the eagle in the villa Mattei. There are extremely few fine statues of animals; the chief are these two eagles, the Tuscan boar, the Barberini goat, and the dog belonging to Mr. Jennings of Shiplake. The boldness, and yet great finishing of this statue, are incomparable; the eyes inimitable. Mr. Gray has drawn *the flagging wing*.* It stands on a handsome antique sepulchral altar, adorned with eagles too. * Ode on the Power of Poetry.
D 1784, 49, same as *D 1774*.
PROV: Eagle excavated in 1742 in the gardens of Boccapadugli within the precincts of Caracalla's bath in Rome; 1745, HW bt eagle with base for 100 zecchini (£50.0.0 and £25.0.0 for pedestal); arrived in England in 1747; 1842, Strawberry Hill Sale, day 23, lot 86, bt Earl of Leicester, £210.0.0; 1854, March 25, Christie's, property of J. D. Gardner, Esq., Bottisham Hall, lot 77, bt Hickman, £556.10; 1935, Private collection.
LIT: *HW Corres.* 10: 78, 11: 293, 303, 19: 65–6, 79, 97, 100–1, 121–2, 135, 149, 155, 161, 176–7, 197, 200, 210, 216, 220, 229, 246, 253, 256, 263–4, 268, 274, 420, 427, 20: 489, 430, 22: 522, 23: 393, 31: 377n, 33: 564, 35: 119, 217, 43: 258. Gervase Jackson-Stops, ed., *The Treasure Houses of Britain* (Washington, DC: National Gallery of Art, 1985), no. 244.
NOTE: A Principal Curiosity. The beak was repaired by Anne Damer.

139. PORTRAIT OF JAMES, 2ND EARL OF WALDEGRAVE
Joshua Reynolds (1723–1792), 1760–1
Oil on canvas, 76 × 63.5 cm
The Trustees of the Waldegrave Chattels Trust
Fig. 69

D 1774, 68 [Gallery]: Right hand of the chimney:… James earl of Waldegrave; by Reynolds.
D 1784, 50, same as *D 1774*.
PROV: HW paid £21.0.0; 1842, Strawberry Hill Sale, day 21, lot 71, bt Earl of Waldegrave, £73.10; by family descent.

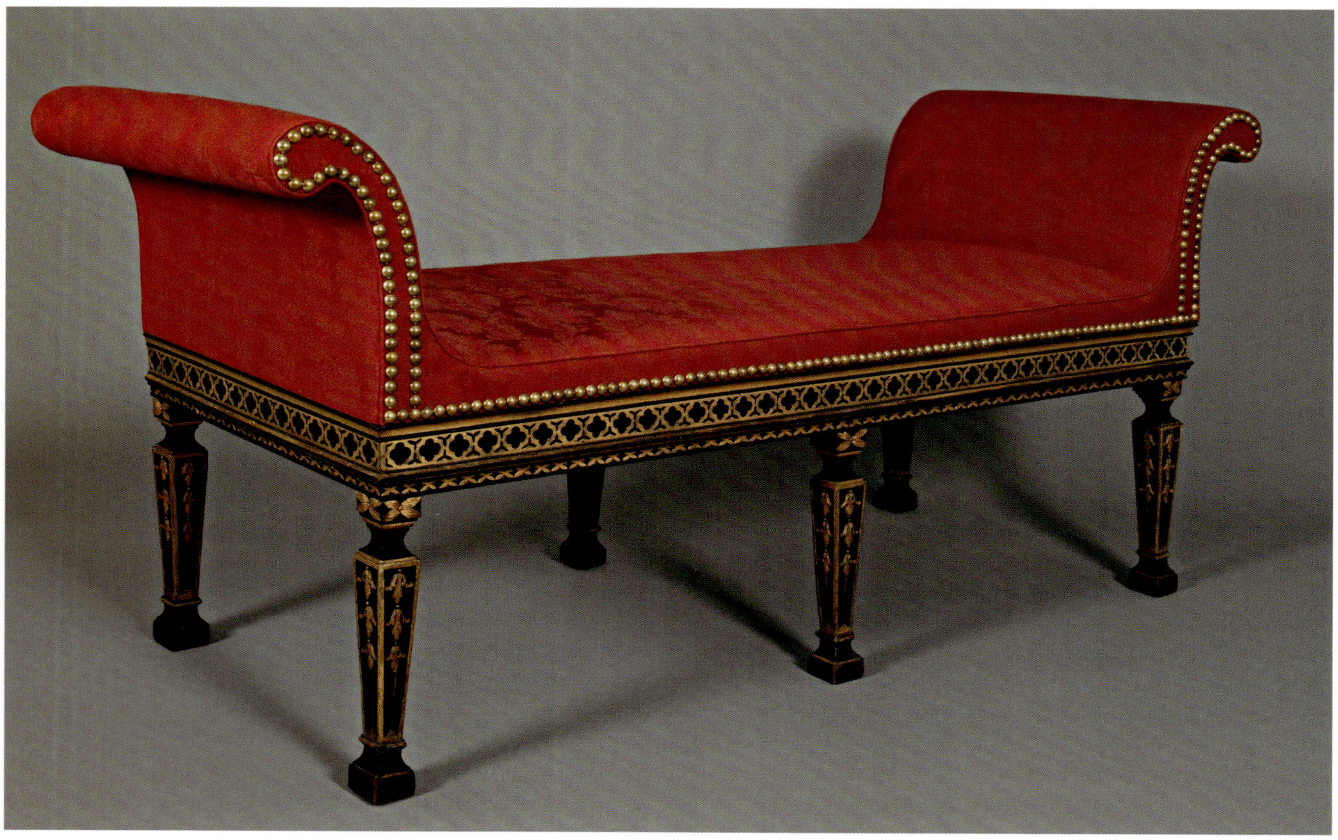

Figure 336. Catalogue 141

LIT: *Accounts* [11] 125–6 note 2. David Mannings, *Sir Joshua Reynolds. A Complete Catalogue of his Paintings* (New Haven and London: Yale University Press, 2000), no. 1808.
EXHIB: Grosvenor, 1883, no. 144.
NOTE: The painting was incorporated into one of the mirrored niches. The 2nd Earl Waldegrave was husband to HW's brother Edward's illegitimate daughter Maria Walpole. Her portrait by Reynolds was in the other mirrored niche.

140. PORTRAIT OF MRS LENEVE
Sir Peter Lely (1618–1680), *c.* 1657

Oil on canvas, 157.5 × 132.5 × 13 cm (framed), 126.7 × 101.3 cm (unframed)
The Cleveland Museum of Art. Gift of Mrs Otto Miller, 1942.247
Fig. 155

D 1774, 68 [Gallery]: Right hand of the chimney:…His [Leneve's] wife, in blue; ditto [The best picture sir Peter Lely ever painted, and as fine as Vandyck's countess of Exeter, before-mentioned.]
D 1784, 50, same as *D 1774*.
PROV: Isabella LeNeve; 1759, September 3, bt HW, 'thirty guineas for two portraits of the LeNeve's Family'; 1842, Strawberry Hill Sale, day 21, lot 61, bt Dommes, £31.10 (see also lot 60, Portrait of Mr Leneve); Mr Downe; Sir Hugh Hume Campbell; 1894, June 16, Christie's, lot 26 (Mrs Leneve) and lot 34 (Mr Leneve); [General William Earl Bulwer, Heydon Hall, Norfolk]; 1915, R. C. Vose and N. M. Vose, Boston, Massachusetts, bt Mrs Otto Miller; 1942, Cleveland Museum of Art, gift of Mrs Otto Miller.
LIT: Ronald Brymer Beckett, *Lely* (London, Routledge and Kegan Paul, 1951), no. 176. The Cleveland Museum of Art, Catalogue of Paintings, Part Three: European Paintings of the 16th, 17th and 18th Centuries (Cleveland: Cleveland Museum of Art, 1982), no. 85. Olga K. Preisner and Hedy B. Landman, The England of William Penn, 1644–1718 (exh. cat. Pennsylvania State University, Museum of Art, 1982), no. 13.
NOTE: See Cat. 137. The identity of the sitter is uncertain.

141. SETTEE
Probably made by Thomas Devenish (fl. 1756–67), working as a subcontractor to Vile & Cobb: William Vile (1714/15–1767) and John Cobb (*c.* 1715–1778), by 1762.

Beech, black and gilt, reproduction worsted damask, silk and worsted tape and yarn, 69.6 × 150.5 × 53.5 cm
Inscriptions: signed on the stretcher 'Thos. Courtney Devenish'. Incised on the frame 'IF' (probably a craftsman's mark). Inscribed in ink on the frame: 'Restuffed by H. Adams Nov. 1833'.
The Lewis Walpole Library, Yale University.
Fig. 336

D 1774, 65 [Gallery]: The room is hung with crimson Norwich damask; the chairs, the settees, and long stools are made of the same, mounted on black and gold frames.
D 1784, 47, same as *D 1774*.
PROV: Commissioned by HW from Vile and Cobb as part of a matching set of four settees, four benches, and four armchairs; 1842, Strawberry Hill Sale, day 24, part of lots 13 or 14, bt Captain Leckie, £2. 4. 0, or 14, bt Robinson, Oxford-street, £1. 3. 0; *c.* 1974, Quenby Hall, Leicester; 1975, March, Asprey & Co., bt W. S. Lewis, £4,100: The Lewis Walpole Library, Yale University.
LIT: H. A. Tipping, 'Strawberry Hill—II, Middlesex,' *Country Life* (12 July 1924): 60. *Accounts* [10] 123–4, note 16, 105, note 12. Sir Ambrose Heal, *The London Furniture Makers from the Restoration to the Victorian Era 1660–1840* (London: B. T. Batsford, 1953), xi, 189. Ralph Edwards, *The Shorter Dictonary of English Furniture* (London: Country Life, 1964), 511. John Cornforth, 'The Cowles-Lewis House, Farmington—II' *Country Life* (27 April 1978): 1153, [ill.] 7. *Rescuing Horace*, 89. Geoffrey Beard and Christopher Gilbert, eds., *Dictionary of English furniture makers, 1660–1840* (Leeds: Furniture History Society, W. S. Maney and Son Ltd, 1986), 923–8. *Romantic Interior*, 105. Percy Macquoid and Ralph Edwards, *The Dictionary of English Furniture* (Wappingers' Falls, NY: Antiques Collectors' Club Ltd, *c.* 1954; rev. edn 2000), vol. 3, 178. Christopher Gilbert and Geoffrey Beard, *A Dictionary of English Furniture Makers 1660–1840* (Leeds: Furniture History Society and W. S. Maney and Sons Ltd, 1986) 242 (For Devenish).
NOTE: In his Accounts, Walpole lists a payment [1765]: 'March 20 Pd Vile's bill for chairs, tables, stools, &c for the gallery & odd articles £146.14.0'.

142. PORTRAIT OF CATHERINE DE MEDICI AND HER CHILDREN
Studio of François Clouet (*c.* 1516–72), 1561

Oil on canvas, 198.1 × 137.2 cm
Private collection
Victoria and Albert Museum Only
Fig. 70

D 1774, 69 [Gallery]: West end: A large piece of Catharine de' Medici and her children, Charles 9th. Henry 3d. the duke d'Alençon, and Margaret queen of Navarre; whole lengths, by Janet.
D 1784, 50 [Gallery]: West end: A large piece of Catharine de' Medici and her children, Charles 9th. Henry 3d. the duke d'Alençon. and Margaret queen of Navarre; whole lengths, by Janet: bought from Mr. Byde's in Hertfordshire.
PROV: Mr Byde, Hertfordshire; bt HW, £25.0.0; 1842, Strawberry Hill Sale, day 21, lot 89, bt Hull, Wardour Street, £90.6; Scarisbrick Collection; 1892, July 2, Christie's, Hollingworth Magniac Collection, lot 94, bt L.T. Linton; 1896, June 6, Christie's, lot 80, bt Sir Tollemache Sinclair, £283.10; [1980], Private collection, UK.
EXHIB: Grafton Galleries, London, England, 'The Fair Children', 1895.
NOTE: the chief painting at the west end of the Gallery.

143. THE REST ON THE FLIGHT INTO EGYPT; (HOLY FAMILY… BY VAN ARTOIS)
Antwerp School, first half 17th century

Oil on copper, 62.2 × 85.5 cm
The Lewis Walpole Library, Yale University

D 1774, 65–6 [Gallery]: East end:…Holy family, with boy angels, in a landscape; by Van Artois, scholar of Rubens: from sir Robert Walpole's collection.
D 1784, 48 same as *D 1774*.
PROV: 1736, Collection of Sir Robert Walpole, Downing Street, closet; HW, £10.15.0; 1842, Strawberry Hill Sale, day 21, lot 57, bt G. M. Daubeney, Esq., £42; 2006 October 31, Sotheby's, Old Master Paintings, lot 47; bt Lowell Libson Ltd, London for Lewis Walpole Library, Yale University.
LIT: Larissa Dukelskaya and Andrew Moore, *A Capital Collection: Houghton Hall and the Hermitage* (New Haven and London: Yale University Press, 2002), 447.

144. PORTRAIT OF MRS LAURA KEPPEL AND HER SISTER CHARLOTTE, LADY HUNTINGTOWER
Allan Ramsay (1713–1784), 1765
Oil on canvas, 156.2 × 137.2 cm
Museum of Fine Arts, Boston, Bequest of Eleanor B. Winthrop in memory of Nathaniel T. Winthrop
Fig. 71

D 1774, 65 [Gallery]: East end: Laura and Charlotte Walpole, eldest and youngest daughters of sir Edward Walpole, and wives of Frederic Keppel bishop of Exeter, and of — Talmach earl of Dysart; Mrs Keppel in white, lady Dysart in pink: by Ramsay.
D 1784, 47 [Gallery]: East end: Laura and Charlotte Walpole, eldest and youngest daughters of sir Edward Walpole, and wives of Frederic Keppel bishop of Exeter, and of Lionel Talmach earl of Dysart; Mrs Keppel in white, lady Dysart in pink: by Ramsay.
PROV: Commissioned by HW, paid £21.0.0; 1842, Strawberry Hill Sale, day 21, lot 51, bt Earl Waldegrave, £52.10; 1900, February 10, Waldegrave Sale, Christie's, lot 48, bt Agnew's, London; Nathaniel Thayer (d. 1911); 1935, April 25, Thayer Sale, American Art Association; Private Collection; Museum of Fine Arts, Boston, Bequest of Eleanor B. Winthrop in memory of Nathaniel T. Winthrop 2009.2783.
LIT: *Accounts* [10] 124, note 18. *HW Corres.* 40: 370. Alastair Smart, *The Life and Art of Allan Ramsay* (London: Routledge & K. Paul, 1952), 84, 100. 210 (lxxxiii). Alastair Smart, *Allan Ramsay: a Complete Catalogue of his Paintings* (New Haven and London: Yale University Press, 1999), no. 295, repro. p. 57.
EXHIB: Royal Academy, 1879.
NOTE: Mrs Laura Keppel (*c.* 1734–1814) and her sister Charlotte, Lady Huntingtower (1738–89), together with their sister Maria, Lady Waldegrave (later, Duchess of Gloucester), were the illegitimate daughters of HW's brother Sir Edward Walpole. This was the chief picture at the east end of the Gallery.

10. THE STATE APARTMENT: THE ROUND DRAWING ROOM

145. Design for the Ceiling of the Round Drawing Room
Office of Robert Adam (1728–1792), 1766

Pencil, pen and ink, and watercolour on paper, 32.6 × 37.8 cm
Inscriptions: at bottom in ink: 'Ceiling for the Honorable Horace Walpole Esqr. / 1766'. Inscribed with scale.
By courtesy of the Trustees of Sir John Soane's Museum, London. Vol 11:234
Fig. 73

D 1774, 74 [Round Drawing Room]: The cieling [sic] is taken from a round window in old saint Paul's; the frieze was designed by Mr. Adam.
D 1784, 53, same as *D 1774*.
PROV: Adam family; by descent; 1833, bought by Sir John Soane from Susannah Clerk and Lord Eldin; Sir John Soane's Museum.
LIT: Eileen Harris, *The Genius of Robert Adam* (New Haven and London: Yale University Press, 2001), 92, pl. 140.

146. Design for the Chimneypiece in the Round Drawing Room
Office of Robert Adam (1728–1792), 1767

Pencil, pen and ink, and watercolour on paper, 29.1 × 40.5 cm
Inscriptions: at bottom in ink: 'Design for a Chimney Piece for the Honorable Horace Walpole / 1767'
By courtesy of the Trustees of Sir John Soane's Museum, London. Vol.22: 229
Fig. 74

D 1774, 73 [Round Drawing Room]: The design of the chimney-piece is taken from the tomb of Edward the Confessor, improved by Mr. Adam, and beautifully executed in white marble inlaid with scagliuola, by Richter.
D 1784, 53, same as *D 1774*.
PROV: Adam family; by descent; 1833, bought by Sir John Soane from Susannah Clerk and Lord Eldin; Sir John Soane's Museum.
LIT: *HW Corres.* 2: 370n, 35: 407. Eileen Harris, *The Genius of Robert Adam* (New Haven and London: Yale University Press, 2001), 8, pl. 2.

147. Coffer on Stand
Attributed to André-Charles Boulle (1642–1732), *c.* 1700–20

Oak veneered with marquetry of ebony, rosewood, brass, copper, pewter, and tortoiseshell; with gilded mounts, coffer including mounts: 42 × 72 × 49 cm; stand including mounts: 71 × 79 × 52 cm
The Lewis Walpole Library, Yale University
Figs. 76, 337

D 1774, 75 [Round Drawing Room]: A trunk of tortoishell and bronze; by Boul, on a frame of the same; a small jar of Seve china under it.
D 1784, 54, same as *D 1774*.
PROV: HW, possibly purchased in France 1765–1771; 1842, Strawberry Hill Sale, day 23, lot 25, bt Owen, New Bond Street, £44.2.0; 1922, November 9–10, Sotheby's, property of Sir Herbert Ogilvy, lot 183 (did not sell); 1935, December 6, Sotheby's, Property of Sir Herbert Ogilvy, lot 109, bt Seymour, £15; as of 1937, W. P. Wilson, Chichester, England; 1939, January 19, I. Kyrle Fletcher, London dealer, bt W. S. Lewis, £160; The Lewis Walpole Library, Yale University.
LIT: *Rescuing Horace*, 236, 238. John Cornforth, 'The Cowles-Lewis House, Farmington—II' *Country Life* (4 May 1978), 1230, [ill.] 2. Peter Hughes, *The Wallace Collection Catalogue of Furniture* (London: Trustees of the Wallace Collection, 1996), vol. 2, 674. John Hardy, 'The English Taste for Boulle', *Makers, Dealers and Collectors: Studies in Honour of Geoffrey de Bellaigue* (London: The Furniture History Society, 2007), 189.

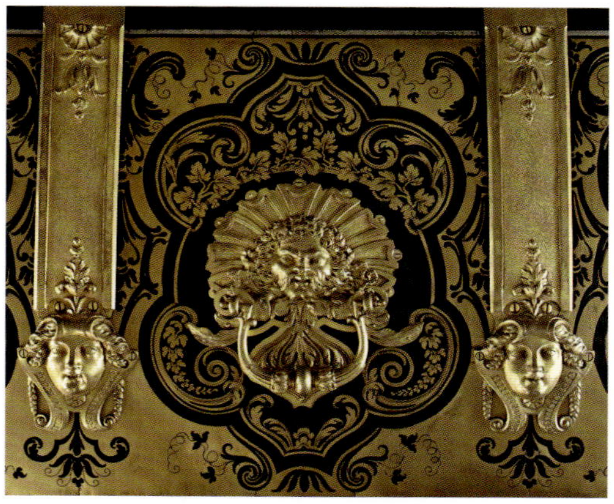

Figure 337. Catalogue 147, detail of the top of the chest

148. Vase with Arms and Ring Device of the Medici
Spanish (Manises) *c.* 1465–1480

Tin-glazed earthenware, decorated in blue and lustre; on one side the arms of the Medici of Florence; on the other the ring and feather device of Piero and Lorenzo de' Medici, H 57 cm
British Museum, Department of Prehistory and Europe. G.619
Fig. 230

D 1774, 135 [Round Drawing Room]: Appendix. In the Round Drawing-Room. A large vase of Florentine fayence, with the arms of the great duke.
D 1784, 55 [Round Drawing Room]: Under it [Japan cabinet], a large vase of Florentine fayence, with the arms of the great duke.
PROV: Before 1492, Piero or Lorenzo de' Medici; HW; 1842, Strawberry Hill Sale, day 23, lot 51, bt W. M. Smith, £22.1.0; Hollingworth Magniac (1786–1869), Colworth, Bedfordshire; 1892, July 12, Magniac Sale, lot 968, bt Durlacher, 670gns; Frederick DuCane Godman; 1983, bequeathed by Miss Edith Godman to the British Museum.
LIT: J. C. Robinson, *Notices of the Principal Works of Arts in the Collection of Hollingworth Magniac, Esq.* (London, 1861), no. 135. *The Godman Collection of Oriental and Spanish Pottery and Glass* (London, 1901), cat. 36, no. 441, p. 32, p. XI. A. Van de Put, *Hispano-Moresque Ware of the XV Century* (London, 1904), 88, pl. XXVI. A. W. Frothingham, Lusterware of Spain (New York: Hispanic Society of America, 1951), 128. Timothy Wilson, *Ceramic Art of the Italian Renaissance* (exh. cat. London: British Museum, 1987), 28–31, no. 16. P. L. Rubin and A. Wright, *Renaissance Florence* (National Gallery: London, 1999), no. 81. Luke Syson and Dora Thornton, *Objects of Virtue: Art in Renaissance Italy* (London: British Museum Press, 2001), 204, fig. 165. M. Spallanzani, *Maioliche ispano-moresche a Firenze nel Rinascimento* (Florence, 2006), 201, pl. 87a, b. Marino Marini and Giovanni Piccardi. 'Vasellame farmaceutico con emblema Medici e altre possibili dotazioni per la corte', *Centro ligure per la storia della ceramica. Atti del XLI convegno internazionale della ceramica*, Savona/Albisola Superiore 2008, p. 64.
NOTE: The vase may be one referred to as being transferred from the Medici Fonderia to the Guardaroba in 1700 (Lit: Marini and Piccardi). There is a patch of fired restoration on the foot.

149. Pair of Vases, known as 'Choiseul vases'
Sèvres Porcelain Manufactory, *c.* 1763–69

Soft-paste porcelain decorated with overglaze 'bleu nouveau' enamel, gilt bronze mounts and bases, H 28.8 cm [743–1882]; H 28.4 cm [743A-1882]
Marks: incised 'ae' on 743–1882
Victoria and Albert Museum, London. John Jones Bequest. 743–1882, 743A–1882
Fig. 227

D 1774, 73 [Gallery]: Two commodes of old japan with marble slabs; on one, a vase, boat-shaped, of deep blue Seve china, mounted in or moulu with snake handles; ...On the other commode, another blue vase like the former.
D 1784, 55 [Round Drawing Room]: On the table, two vases, boat-shaped, of deep blue Seve china, mounted in or moulu with snake handles.
PROV: HW, £19.19.0; 1842, Strawberry Hill Sale, day 23, lot 42 (erroneously described as Oriental China tazza), bt John P. Beavan, Esq., £52.10.0; 1882, Victoria and Albert Museum, John Jones Bequest.
LIT: *Handbook of the Jones Collection in the South Kensington Museum* (London, 1883), fig. 3, showing the vases displayed in the dining room of John Jones's house, 95 Piccadilly, London. Marcelle Brunet and Tamara Préaud, *Sèvres, des origins à nos jours* (Fribourg, 1978), 164, no. 120. Bet McLeod, 'The Ceramics at Strawberry Hill' (MA Thesis, Cooper-Hewitt/Parson's School of Design, New York, 1993), 134, no. 1, fig. 25. Bet McLeod, 'Horace Walpole's Ceramics at Strawberry Hill', *International Ceramics Fair and Seminar Handbook* (London, 1995): 33. Bet McLeod, 'Horace Walpole and Sèvres porcelain. The collection at Strawberry Hill', *Apollo* 147 (Jan. 1998), 43 and fig. 3. *A Grand Design. The Art of the Victoria & Albert Museum* (exh. cat. London: 1999–2000), no. 84.
NOTE: A watercolour by Thomas Sandby and Paul Sandby and Edward Edwards, completed in 1781, (see Cat. 131) shows the vases on the commodes in the Gallery.

150. Feeding of the Child Jupiter (The Education of Jupiter by Nicolo Poussin)
Follower of Nicolas Poussin (1594–1665), *c.* 1650

Oil on canvas, 117.4 × 155.3 cm, 46 ¼ × 61 1/8 in.
National Gallery of Art, Washington, DC, Samuel H. Kress Collection, 1952.2.21.
Fig. 75

D 1774, 75 [Round Drawing Room]: The education of Jupiter; by Nicolo Poussin. This picture cost sir Robert Walpole an hundred and fourteen pounds.
D 1784, 54, same as *D 1774*.
PROV: By 1736 Sir Robert Walpole, 1st Earl of Orford (1676–1745); presumably by inheritance to HW; 1842, Strawberry Hill Sale, day 21, lot 46, bt Sir J. Easthope, Bart, MP, £78.15.0; Mrs Doyle; Major Cecil Uvedale Corbett, Esq. (d. 1944); Major Uvedale Corbett, Stableford Hall, Shropshire; by descent to his son, Major Uvedale Corbett, Bridgnorth, Shropshire; 1947, sold by C. Marshall Spink to Wildenstein & Co., New York; 1947, bt Samuel H. Kress Collection; 1952, Gifted to the National Gallery of Art, Washington, D. C.
LIT: *Paintings and Sculpture from the Samuel H. Kress Collection* (Washington, DC: National Gallery of Art, 1959), 337. Anthony Blunt, 'Poussin Studies XII: The Hovingham Master', *Burlington Magazine* 103, no. 704 (Nov. 1961): 454–61. Colin Eisler, *Paintings from the Samuel H. Kress Collection: European Schools excluding Italian* (Oxford: Phaidon Press, 1977), 280–2, fig. 252, as *The Nurture of Jupiter*. John Walker, *National Gallery of Art, Washington*, rev. edn (New York: H. N. Abrams, 1984), 317, no. 416. *European Paintings: An Illustrated Catalogue* (Washington, DC: National Gallery of Art, 1985), 318. Larissa Dukelskaya and Andrew Moore, eds., *A Capital Collection: Houghton Hall and the Hermitage* (New Haven and London: Yale University Press, 2007), 447.
NOTE: A Principal Curiosity. In 1736 it was in the Dressing Room at Downing Street.

Figure 338. Catalogue 151

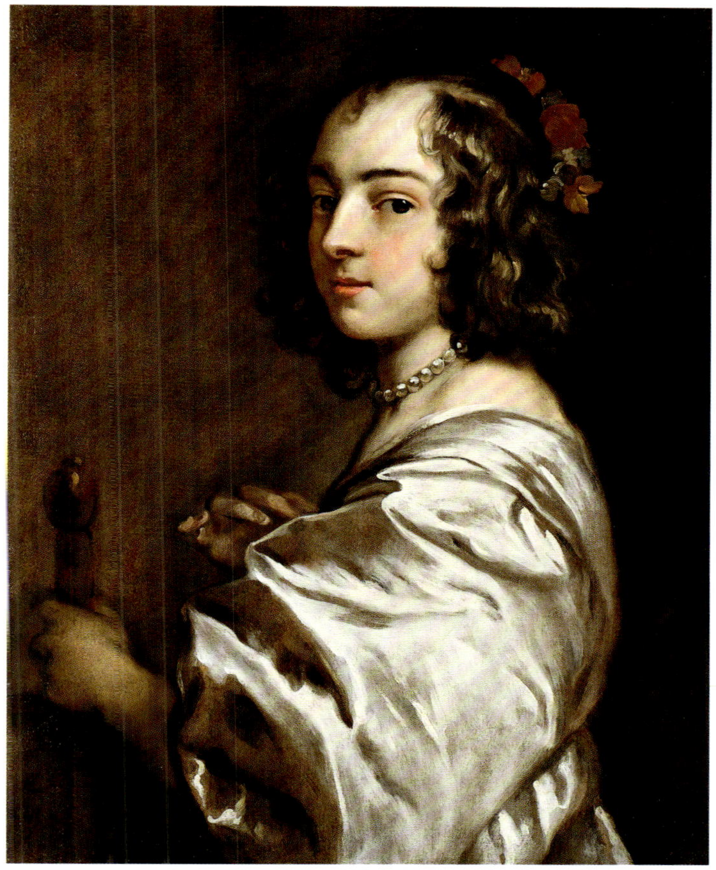

151. Portrait of Margaret Lemon
Sir Anthony Van Dyck (1599–1641), after *c.* 1641–46

Oil on canvas, [57 × 47.5 cm]
Marquess of Bath, Longleat, Wiltshire
Fig. 338

D 1774, 74 [Round Drawing Room]: Over the door, Mrs. Lemon, mistress of Vandyck, with a sword, as Judith; by Vandyck; bought out of Buckingham-house: very boldly and freely painted.
D 1784, 54, same as *D 1774*.
PROV: Probably 1763, Feb. 24–25, John Sheffield, Buckingham House; bt HW, £5.5.0; 1842, Strawberry Hill Sale, day 21, lot 45, bt B. Botfield, Esq., MP, £78.15.0; Collection of Beriah Botfield (d. 1863), Norton Hall, Northamptonshire; 1941, by inheritance to 6th Marquess of Bath, from his aunt, Lady Beatrice Thynne, Norton Hall.
LIT: Beriah Botfield, *Catalogue of Pictures at Norton Hall* (London: Chiswick Press, 1863), 42. Susan James, 'Margaret Lemon: Model, Mistress, Muse', *Jaarboek Koninklijk Museum voor Schone Kunsten Antwerpen* (Antwerp Royal Museum Annual, 1999): 90–109. Susan James, 'The Model as Catalyst: Nicholas Lanier and Margaret Lemon', *Jaarboek Koninklijk Museum voor Schone Kunsten Antwerpen* (Antwerp Royal Museum Annual, 1999), 70–89. Susan J. Barnes, Nora De Poorter, Oliver Millar, and Horst Vey, *Van Dyck: A Complete Catalogue of the Paintings* (New Haven and London: Yale University Press, 2004), no. IV, 156.

11. THE STATE APARTMENT: THE GREAT NORTH BEDCHAMBER

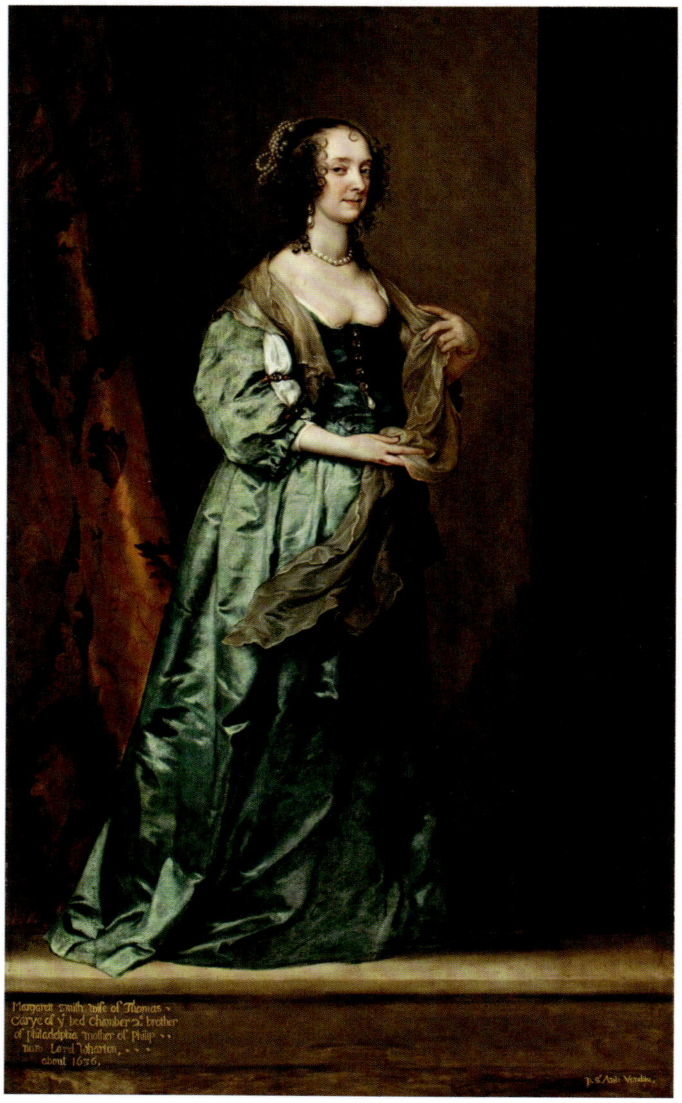

Figure 339. Catalogue 152

152. Portrait of Margaret Smith
Sir Anthony Van Dyck (1599–1641), *c.* 1638–9

Oil on canvas, 217.8 × 130.3 cm
Inscriptions: lower left and right: 'Margaret smith wife of Thomas — / Carye of ye bed Chamber 2d brother / of Philadelphia Mother or Philip - - / now Lord Wharton, - - - about 1636', and 'p. Sr. Ant: Vandike'
Private collection, England
Fig. 152

D 1774, 103 [Great North Bedchamber]: On one side of the chimney, A fine whole length, by Vandyck, of Margaret Smith, wife of Thomas Carye, groom of the bedchamber to Charles Ist. From the Wharton collection, afterwards in that of sir Robert Walpole.

D 1784, 73, same as *D 1774*.
PROV: 4th Lord Wharton (d. 1696); 1725, Duke of Wharton (his grandson), bt Sir Robert Walpole, £100; HW, £35.14.0; 1842, Strawberry Hill Sale, day 20, lot 87, bt Colonel Kemeys-Tynte, £78.15; by descent to 9th Lord Wharton (d. 1969), his great-great grandson; 1948, November 17, Sotheby's, London, Lord Wharton's Collection, lot 19, bt Leggatt of St. James's Street, £250; Private collection, England.
LIT: Susan Barnes, Nora De Poorter, Oliver Millar and Horst Vey, *Van Dyck: a Complete Catalogue of the Paintings* (New Haven and London: Yale University Press, 2004), no. IV, 133.
NOTE: A Principal Curiosity.

153. Nautilus Cup
Delft, Attributed to Nicolaes de Grebber (fl. 1574–1613), 1592

Silver-gilt, nautilus shell, glass and enamel, 26.5 × 19.6 × 9.9 cm
Marks: on underside of foot-rim: Delft, year letter B (1592) and maker's mark: a cooking-pot in a shield, attributed to Nicolaes de Grebber.
Engraved on underside of foot-rim: '13', No 7 22=11', and again '22=11.' Engraved on the book held by one of the satyrs: staves with musical notation and 'JE-PRENS/GRE-/LA-DVRE/MO[R]T.' Engraved on the upper surface of the shell is the Paston coat of arms, presumably for Sir Robert Paston, 1st Earl of Yarmouth. The two clamps securing the shell on either side are later replacements.
Stedelijk Museum het Prinsenhof, Delft. PDZ 3
Fig. 79

D 1774, 103 [Great North Bedchamber]: A nautilus mounted in silver gilt, with satyrs and the arms of Paston. ... These two pieces belonged to the last earl of Yarmouth [see Cat. 154].
D 1784, 73, same as *D 1774*.
PROV: Robert Paston, 1st Earl of Yarmouth (1631–1683); William Paston, 2nd Earl of Yarmouth (1654–1732); HW; 1842, Strawberry Hill Sale, day 16, lot 7, bt J. Morrison, Esq., MP, £37.16.0; [1887, May 5, Christie's, lot 100, bt Davis, £155]; 1942, April 22–23, Christie's, G. A. Lockett Collection Sale, (as Dordrecht); Messrs J. M. Morpurgo, Amsterdam; 1949, bt Stedelijk Museum Het Prinsenhof, Delft, with the support of the Vereniging Rembrandt.
LIT: Carl Hernmarck, *The Art of the European Silversmith*, 2 vols. (New York: Sotheby Parke Bernet, 1977), vol. 1, 113. Robert Wenley, 'Robert Paston and the Yarmouth Collection', *Norfolk Archaeology* 41, no. 2 (1991): 118, ill. pls. 1 and 4. Ger Luijten, Ariane van Suchtelen, Reinier Baarsen, Wouter Kloek, Marijn Schapelhouman, eds., *Dawn of the Golden Age, Northern Netherlandish Art, 1580–1620* (exh. cat. Rijksmuseum, Amsterdam; Zwolle: Waanders; New Haven and London: Yale University Press, 1993), no. 86. Robert Wenley, 'The Paston Treasures; Portrait of a Seventeenth Century Collection', *Silver Studies* 19 (2005): 134–5.
NOTE: The cup is included in *The Paston Treasure* (Norwich Castle Museum), a Dutch school still-life painting of the mid-1670s showing part of the enormous collection of precious objects assembled at Oxnead Hall, Norfolk, by Sir Robert Paston. The remains of his collection were dispersed at the death of his son.

154. JUG ('A CRYSTAL TANKARD AND COVER')
The crystal possibly Sassanian, late antique or early medieval; the mounts by an unidentified maker, London, 1557–8.

Rock crystal mounted in silver-gilt, H 26.4 cm
Marks: London hallmarks for 1557–8, maker's mark an anchor.
The Schroder collection
Victoria and Albert Museum only
Fig. 340

D 1774, 103 [Great North Bedchamber]: A crystal tankard and cover, mounted in silver gilt. These two pieces belonged to the last earl of Yarmouth [see Cat. 153]
D 1784, 72, same as *D 1774*.
PROV: Provenance: (probably) Robert Paston, 1st Earl of Yarmouth (1631–1683); William Paston, 2nd Earl of Yarmouth (1654–1732); (probably) HW; 1842 Strawberry Hill, Sale, day 16, lot 8, bt Baroness Anselm de Rothschild, Frankfort, £50.8.0; purchased from Crichton Brothers, 1925, March 5 (£3,500); Schroder Collection.
LIT: Timothy Schroder, *Renaisance Silver from the Schroder Collection* (London: Wallace Collection, 2007) cat. 67.
NOTE: The description of HW's 'tankard' in the 1842 sale closely matches this jug: 'A crystal tankard and cover, mounted in silver gilt, richly worked, representing Cariatic Figures supporting the mounting, the cover and foot, bordered with fruit and flowers and a serpent handle'. The hallmarks have recently been redated by Timothy Schroder from 1597–8 to 1557–8. The Paston collection inventory of 1663–73 includes a reference to a 'cristall tankard, set in a carved and silver and gilt frame, with a cover', which may be this piece.

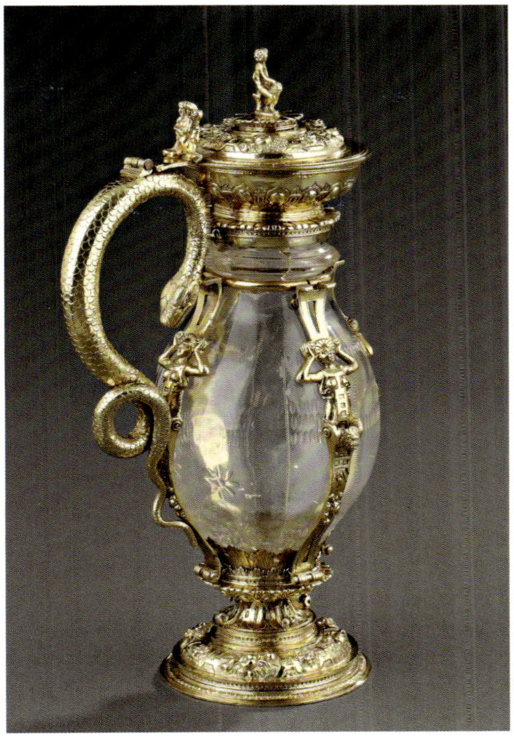

Figure 340. Catalogue 154

155. FOUR TABLEMEN, DEPICTING A LION, A BOAR, A BACTRIAN CAMEL, AND A DOG (DRAUGHTSMEN), 12th century

Carved and stained walrus ivory, D 5 8–5.9 cm × 1 cm (thickness)
British Museum, Department of Prehistory and Europe. 1892,0801.21, 1892,0801.22, 1892,0801.27, 1892,0801.39 [the last is carved only].
Fig. 140

D 1784, 76 [Great North Bedchamber: Glass Closet]: possibly: Fourteen more [draftsmen], bought at Mr. Bateman's sale.
PROV: (Possibly) 1775, March, sale of Richard Batemen, Esq., bt HW, £1.3.0; 1842, Strawberry Hill Sale, day 16, lot 72, bt W. M. Smith, £2.12.06; 1892, July 5, Christie's, Hollingworth Magniac Sale, lot 252 (29 listed), bt Sir Augustus Wollaston Franks, £89.5s (29 ivory draughtsmen); 1892, given by Sir A. Wollaston Franks to The British Museum.
LIT: O. M. Dalton, *Catalogue of Ivory Carvings ... in the British Museum* (London: Trustees of the Museum, 1909), 185, 187, 189, 191. *OHG* 153.
NOTE: Tables was a medieval board game similar to backgammon. The pieces were stained to mark the different players.

156. THREE SPICE PLATES FROM A SET OF TWELVE SHOWING THE STORY OF THE PRODIGAL SON, Roger Flynt, London, engraving attributed to the monogrammist P over M, London, 1568–9

Silver, parcel gilt and engraved with scenes: *The Prodigal Son Leaves his Father's House*; *Goes into a Far Country*; *Kisses a Woman Outside an Inn*, D 19.1 cm
London hallmark for 1568/9, one plate 1569–10;
Goldsmith's mark RF monogram for Roger Flynt;
Trustees of the Ninth Duke of Buccleuch's Chattels Fund
Fig. 80

D 1774, 140 [Great North Bedchamber, Glass Closet]: Appendix. In the Great Bedchamber: Twelve silver dessert-plates, engraved with the history of the prodigal son. They belonged to lord chancellor Clarendon, and descended to his great grand-daughter the celebrated duchess of Queensberry, and were purchased at the duke's auction.
D 1784, 78, same as *D 1774*.
PROV: Edward Hyde, 1st Earl of Clarendon (1609–1674); Catherine Hyde, Duchess of Queensberry (*c.* 1701–1777) (by descent); 1779, auction of Charles Douglas, 3rd Duke of Queensberry (1698–1778), bt HW, £31–8–0; 1842, Strawberry Hill Sale, day 16, lot 88, bt Thomas, Bond Street, £116.11; Duke of Buccleuch and Queensberry, Bowhill, Selkirk, UK.
LIT: *Accounts*, 17, 170. National Trust for Scotland, *Exhibition of Raeburns and 18th Century Silver* (exh. cat. Edinburgh: printed by G. Waterston & Sons, 1951), no. 90. Charles Oman, *English Engraved Silver 1150–1900* (London: Faber & Faber, 1978) 37, 144, figs. 36–7 and frontispiece. Philippa Glanville, *Silver in Tudor and Early Stuart England. A Social History and Catalogue of the National Collection 1480–1660* (London: Victoria and Albert Museum, 1990) fig. 116. Ellenor M. Alcorn, '"Some of the Kings of England Curiously Engraven": An Elizabethan Ewer and Basin in the Museum of Fine Arts, Boston', *Journal of the Museum of Fine Arts, Boston* (1993) 74, fig. 22.
NOTE: First displayed in the Refectory, according to a Ms note by HW in a copy of *D 1774*: 'Plate for the sideboard: ... Twelve silver water plates...' (The Lewis Walpole Library, 49 2523, p. 8).

12. THE STATE APARTMENT: THE TRIBUNE

157. 'First Idea for the Chapel Tribune at Strawberry hill'
Richard Bentley (bap. 1708– d. 1782), *c.* 1758

On the verso a sketch plan in pencil for the Gallery, Round Tower, Holbein Chamber and Tribune
Pen and ink, pencil, and brown wash on laid paper, 23 × 37.8 cm (visible)
Inscriptions: on the album page in HW's hand: 'First Idea for the Chapel Tribune at Strawberry hill, but rejected, tho beautifull, because it must have been too large or too small'.
The Lewis Walpole Library, Yale University.
Folio 49 3585 fol. 58
Fig. 115

From *Drawings and Designs by Richd. Bentley* (*c.* 1760, fol. 58).
D 1774, 49 [Library]: Rare books of prints and drawings in the library…Designs by Mr. Richard Bentley, bound in marble and gilt.
D 1784, 37, same as *D 1774*.
PROV: Designed for HW; for the album see Cat. 18.
LIT: 'Genesis': 57–92. *Library* 3585. *Collector's Progress*, 59, 102, 104–8. *Rescuing Horace*, 53–61. Bentley thesis, fig. 69.
NOTE: The sketch plan verso shows an early scheme for the western extension, in which the cross-shaped chapel is apparently attached to the southern end of the Holbein Chamber. It also shows a bed at the west end of the Round Room and the road in a different position.

158. 'The Tribune at Strawberry Hill'
John Carter (1748–1817), *c.* 1789

Watercolour on laid paper, 59.2 × 49.5 cm [visible]; 62 × 51 cm (mount)
The Lewis Walpole Library, Yale University.
789.00.00.73dr++
Fig. 81

PROV: Probably commissioned by HW; 1931, November, F. H. Swift; W. J. Webb of Twickenham, bt W. S. Lewis, £25; The Lewis Walpole Library, Yale University.
LIT: 'Genesis': fig. 25 (as by an unknown artist). Mellon Lectures, ill. no. 41. *Romantic Interior*, fig. 82 for variant composition.
EXHIB: The Royal Academy of Art, London, 1789, no. 549 as 'The Tribune at Strawberry Hill.'
NOTE: The sketch for this drawing is in *D 1784* extra-illustrated with prints and drawings by John Carter at The Henry E. Huntington Library, San Marino, California (vol. 2, p. 88 verso).

159. Nuns at Prayer in the Tribune at Strawberry Hill
Thomas Rowlandson (1757–1827), *c.* 1805

Pen and ink, and watercolour, 14 × 21.5 cm
Private collection
Fig. 279

PROV: Edward Croft-Murray, CBE FSA
LIT: *Le Gothique Retrouvé* (exh. cat. Paris, Hotel de Cluny, 1979–80), 21, no. 8. *OHG* 235.

160. Chasse depicting the Murder of Thomas Becket
French, Limoges, *c.* 1200–1210

Copper with champlevé enamel, on oak caracase, 17.2 × 12.1 cm
Culture and Sport Glasgow (Museums), 26.6
Victoria and Albert Museum only
Fig. 151

D 1774, 86 [Tribune]: In the glass-case near the window:…Model of the shrine of Thomas Becket, enamelled.
D 1784, 61, same as *D 1774*.
PROV: John Batteley (1647–1708), Archdeacon of Canterbury then to Thomas Barrett (d. 1758) of Lee Priory, near Canterbury; 1758, Feb 21, Barrett Sale, lot 80, bt HW, £1.9.0; 1842, Strawberry Hill Sale, day 13, lot 83, bt Rev. Walter Sneyd, £9.9.0; 1933 (as of), Leopold Hirsch Collection; bt John Hunt; 1934, bt William Burrell, £125; given by Sir William and Constance, Lady Burrell to Glasgow Corporation in 1944.
LIT: William Cole, *Journal*, 1761 (British Library Add.MS.5841 f77, with drawing) (*OHG* 30). Tancred Borenius, *St. Thomas Becket in Art* (Port Washington, NY: Kennikat Press, 1970), 89, no. 5. Simone Caudron, 'Les Émaux champlevés meridionaux dans les cabinets d'amateurs Britanniques des XVIIe et XVIIIe Siècles', in *Mémoire de Maîtrise d'Histoire de l'art et d'archeologie IV* (October 1975), 34–8, 65–8, 102–3, 121–2, no. 3. Jonathan Alexander and Paul Binski, eds., *Age of Chivalry, Art in Plantagenet England 1200–1400* (London: Royal Academy of Arts and Weidenfeld and Nicholson, 1987), cat. 87.

161. Baton
Italian, 1426–1475

Rock crystal, mounted in silver gilt, enamelled, with pearls, L 27 cm
British Museum, Department of Prehistory and Europe. 1923,1205.8
Fig. 87

D 1774, 88 [Tribune]: A chrystal sceptre, set in gold enamelled, with pearls ; from lady E. Germaine's collection, and given to Mr Walpole by her niece lady Temple.
D 1784, 62 same as *D 1774*.
PROV: Lady Elizabeth Germain (1680–1769); given by her niece, Anne Chambers, Lady Temple (*c.* 1709–77) to HW; 1842, Strawberry Hill Sale, day 15, lot 73, bt Webb, Old Bond Street, £14.14.0; 1892, July 12, Hollingworth Magniac Sale; 1923, British Museum, Bequeathed by Charles Borradaile.
NOTE: Drawn in pen and ink and watercolour by John Carter (*D 1784*, Lewis Walpole Library 33 30 copy 11, folio p.182). See Fig. 253.

162. Illuminated Book of Hours (the Prayer Book of Queen Claude of France)
Unknown artist, French, *c.* 1532. The binding French or Italian, 1530s. The cornelian intaglios North Italian, or from the French workshop of Matteo del Nassaro of Verona. The associated marker French or Italian 1560s.

Illuminated manuscript and miniatures, on vellum in a binding of enamelled gold, set with cornelian intaglios and cameos, rubies, and turquoises and a tourmaline. The front cover set with an intaglio of the Crucifixion, with Saints Francis of Assisi and Jerome. The back cover set with an intaglio of the Virgin and Child enthroned, with Saint Barbara and Catherine of Alexandria. The silk endleaves and pastedowns 18th century French; 8.5 × 6.5 cm. With an associated marker of enamelled gold set with an agate figure in the round of *Christ at the Column* and table-cut diamonds, rubies, or turquoises and a pearl; H 6.4 cm.
Inscriptions: the end of Matins and the end of Lauds dated 1532; the fly-leaf inscribed by HW in Latin with the history of the manuscript.
S. J. Phillips Limited
Fig. 34

D 1774, 88 [Tribune]: In the glass-case near the window:…A magnificent missal, with miniatures by Raphael and his scholars, set in gold enamelled, and adorned with rubies and turquoises; the sides are of cornelian, engraved with religious subjects; the clasp, a large garnet. This precious prayer-book belonged to Claude queen of France, wife of Francis Ist. and seems to have belonged to the father of Thuanus; *vide vol. I, p. 142, of the French edition*. It was purchased by Mr. Walpole from the collection of doctor Meade, 1755.

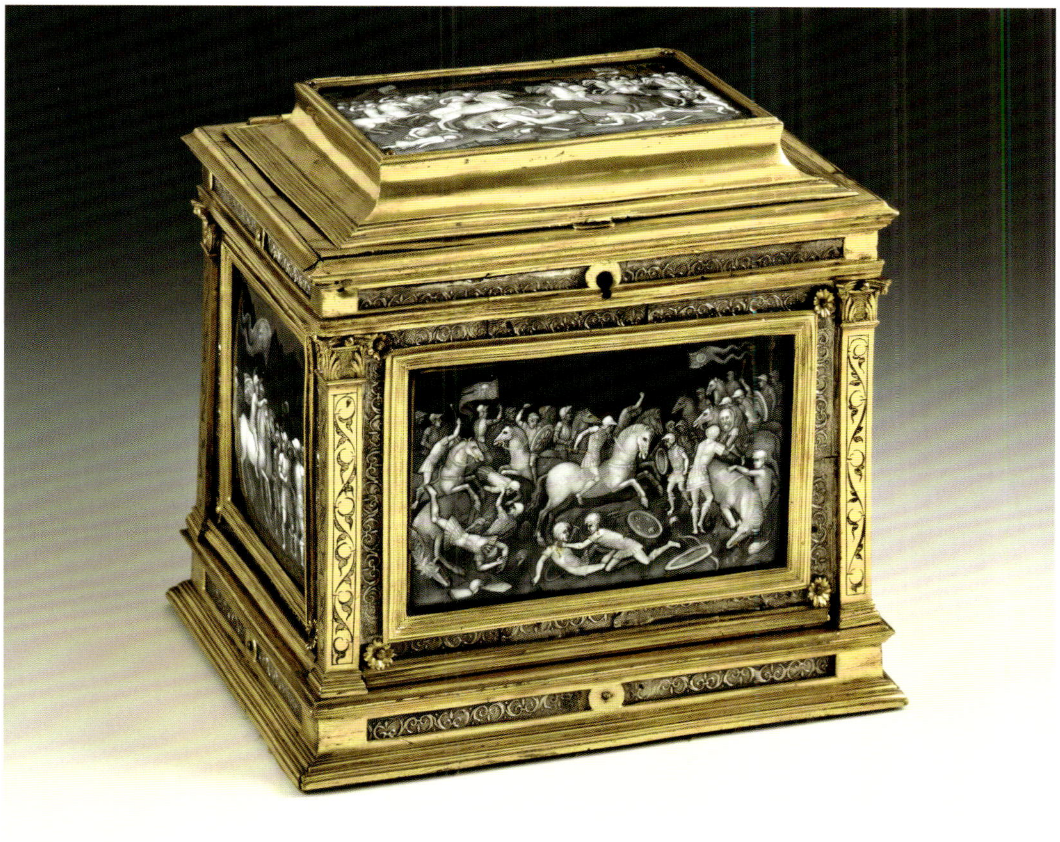

Figure 341. Catalogue 163

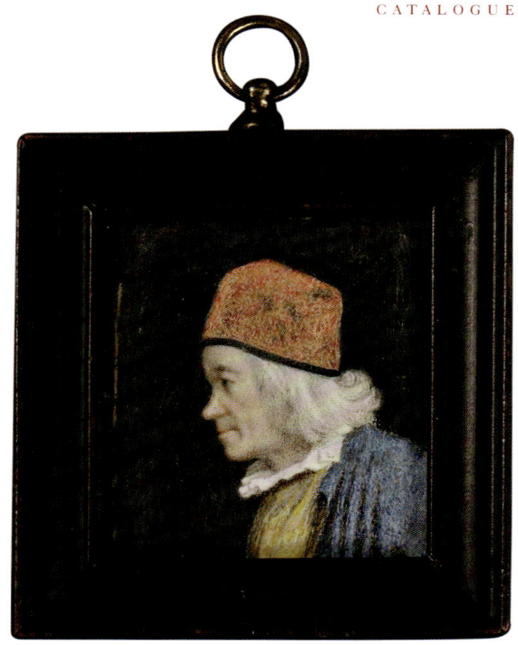

Figure 342. Catalogue 164

D 1784, 62–3, same as *D 1774*.
PROV: 1755, March 14, Dr Richard Mead Sale, Collection of Valuable Gems, bt HW, £42.0.0; 1842, Strawberry Hill Sale, day 15, lot 77, bt [Forster for] Earl Waldegrave, £115.10.0; later to Alfred de Rothschild's Collection; 1925, May 19, Christie's, Countess of Carnarvon Sale, lot 141, bt S. J. Phillips, £2100 for Lord Rothermere; 1942, March 26, Sotheby's, Property of Late Viscount Rothermere, bt Phillips, £2500; S. J. Phillips Limited.
LIT: Charles Davis, *A Description of the Works of Art Forming the Collection of Alfred de Rothschild* (London: Chiswick Press, 1884). *HW Corres.* 20: 470n. Description of An Illuminated Manuscript in a Gold and Jewelled Renaissance Binding. The Property of the late Viscount Rothermere (auction cat. London: Sotheby & Co., 26 March 1942). 'French Renaissance Manuscripts: The 1520s Hours Workshop and the Master of the Getty Epistles', *The J. Paul Getty Museum Journal* (1988), fig. 13. E. Kris, *Steinschneidekunst in der Italienischen Renaissance* (Vienna 1929), I, pp. 42, 159, 2, figs. 123, 125. *Library* 3786.1.
NOTE: A Principal Curiosity. Queen Claude, the owner of the manuscript described in Jacques-Auguste de Thou's (Thuanus) *Histoire Universelle*, died in 1524. An 18th century manuscript note accompanying the book links it to Julio Clovio and describes it as a gift of Pope Paul III to Henry VIII, who gave it to Katherine of Aragon. The manuscript was made in the Loire valley around Tours, or by someone who had worked there. It is stylistically connected to the group known as the '1520s workshop' (written communication from Rowan Watson, see also LIT). The *Virgin and Child* intaglio relates to a bronze plaquette by Maderno *c.* 1500, and a Veneto-Paduan rock crystal intaglio (see LIT). The pairing of the two men and two women Saints suggests a French origin or commission. The marker, separated from the book by 1755, was found after 1925 (written communications on the binding from Diana Scarisbrick and Mirjam Foot).

163. CASKET
Master 'KIP' (anonymous French enameller fl. in Limoges during the second third of the 16th century), *c.* 1540–45

Gilt metal set with embossed silver foil bands and five copper plaques painted in enamels *en grisaille* depicting cavalry battle scenes in part after engravings by Marcantonio Raimondi (*c.* 1470–82/1527–34), H 16.2 cm
Marks: artist's mark 'IP' painted in white enamel on top and front panels
Victoria and Albert Museum, London. C.49–1982
Fig. 341

D 1774, 87 [Tribune]: In the glass-case near the window: ...A coffer enamelled on all sides with battles, and set in silver gilt.
D 1784, 62, same as *D 1774*.
PROV: HW; 1842, Strawberry Hill Sale, day 15, lot 91, bt Town and Emanuel, £47.10; Hollingworth Magniac, Colworth, Bedfordshire; 1892, July 6, Magniac sale, Christie's, London, lot 401, bt Durlacher, £630; 1935, May 22, Edward Steinkopff Sale, Christie's, London, lot 40, bt Durlacher, £199.10s; 1977, May 31, Christie's, London, lot 43, £21,000; 1982, Victoria and Albert Museum from Sotheby's by private treaty sale.
LIT: J. C. Robinson, *Notices of the Principal Works of Art in the Collection of Hollingworth Magniac, Esq.* (London, 1861), no. 84. C. Truman, 'Acquisitions in the Department of Ceramics at the Victoria and Albert Museum 1981–82', *Burlington Magazine* 125 (May 1983): 289–90. *Romantic Interior*, 101, fig. 83.
EXHIB: 1862 Special Exhibition, no. 1687.
NOTE: The subjects of the battles are in part based on engravings by Marcantonio Raimondi. The attribution is by Fabienne Audebrand (Victoria and Albert Museum files).

164. PORTRAIT MINIATURE OF THE ARTIST
Jean-Étienne Liotard (1702–1789), *c.* 1765–7

Gouache on vellum, in a black wooden frame, 4.1 × 3.8 cm
Inscriptions: in HW's hand on paper backing of frame: 'Liotard / by / Himself. / A / legacy / to / Mr Horace Walpole / from Mrs. M. Delany / 1788'; in a later hand: ' Purchased for me by Mr. Forster at Strawberry Hill. 10th May 1842. R. R. Preston'.
The Lewis Walpole Library, Yale University.
Fig. 342

D 1784, 94 [Tribune]: Curiosities added since this Book was compleated...In the Tribune...In the glass case near the window....A small head in water-colours of Liotard, without his beard, by himself; a legacy from Mrs. Delany.
PROV: 1788, Mrs M. Delany to HW; 1842, Strawberry Hill Sale, day 14, lot 97, bt Forster, £1.1.0 for R. R. Preston; 1949, July 12, lot 9, Philips Son & Neale's, bt Sabin, £78; 1954, March, F. T. Sabin, bt

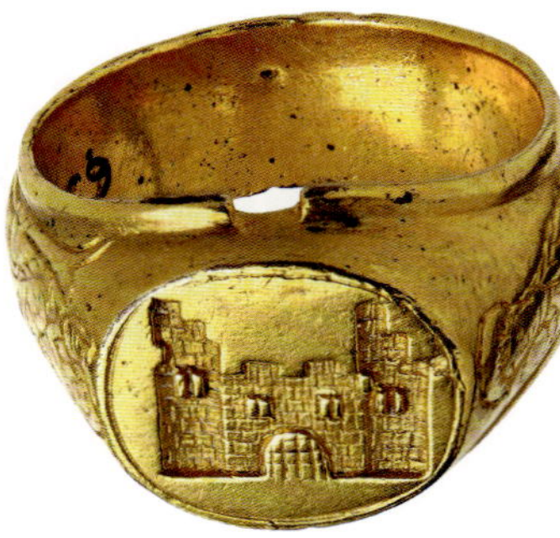

Figure 343. Catalogue 166

W. S. Lewis, £85; The Lewis Walpole Library, Yale University.
LIT: J. J. Foster, *British Miniature Painters and Their Works* (London: S. Low Marston and Co., 1898), Appendix A, p. 16. *HW Corres.* 20: 324n, 28: 197n, 43: 125. Marcel Roethlisberger and Renée Loche, *Liotard: catalogue, sources et correspondance* (Doornspijk: Davaco, 2008), 585–6, no. 445.

165. ADMIRALTY SEAL MATRIX FOR RICHARD CLITHEROWE, ADMIRAL OF THE WEST
Maker unknown, *c.* 1406

Bronze, D 4.4 cm
Inscription: 's: ric :cletherowe : admiralli: occidentalis: anglie'.
British Museum, Department of Prehistory and Europe. 1858,0629.1
Fig. 54

D 1774, 92 [Tribune]: In the other glass case:...Seal of Richard Clitherol, admiral for the west coasts in the reign of Henry 5th.
D 1784, 65, same as *D 1774*.
PROV: 1773, March 12–13?, William Bristow Collection, bt HW, £10.10.0; 1842, Strawberry Hill Sale, day 15, lot 12, bt Hor. Rodd, £4.0.0; Dr Bliss; William Chaffers; 1858, purchased by The British Museum.
LIT: A. B. Tonnochy, *Catalogue of British seal-dies in the British Museum* (London: Trustees of the British Museum, 1952), no. 21. *OHG* 140.

166. FINGER RING
English, *c.* 1450–1500, the castle on the cut-down bezel engraved on a plate added after 1720

Gold, D 2.2 cm
Shoulders engraved with the Virgin and Child and St Christopher. Engraved inside the hoop in black letter: 'en bon an'.
Victoria and Albert Museum, London. 695–1871
Fig. 343

D 1774, 92 [Tribune]: In the other glass case:...A large ancient gold ring, with a castle on it, and within, Un bon An: found in the Thames.
D 1784, 65, same as *D 1774*.
PROV: 1720, found under London Bridge; by 1761,HW; 1842, Strawberry Hill Sale, day 15, lot 11, bt John P. Beavan, Esq., £10.10.0; 1871, The Victoria and Albert Museum.
LIT: William Cole, *Journal*, 1761 (British Library Add.MS.5841). OHG 137. Shirley Bury, *Jewellery Gallery Summary Catalogue* (London: Victoria and Albert Museum, *c.* 1982), 192, Case 33 Board D, no. 14. Shirley Bury, *An Introduction to Rings* (London: HMSO, 1984), 28.

167. CARVED CRAVAT
Grinling Gibbons (1648–1721), *c.* 1690

Limewood, with raised and openwork carving, 24.1 × 20.9 × 5.1 cm
Victoria and Albert Museum. Given by The Hon. Mrs Walter Levy. W.181:1–1928.
Fig. 116

D 1774, 91 [Tribune]: In the other glass case:...A point cravat carved by Gibbons.
D 1784, 62 [Tribune]: A point cravat carved by Gibbons; a present from Mr. Grosvenor Bedford.
PROV: By 1769, given to HW by Grosvenor Bedford; 1842, Strawberry Hill Sale, day 15, lot 99, bt Miss Burdett Coutts, £9.9.0; 1922, May 11, Christie's, collection of the late Baroness Burdett-Coutts, lot 345a, bt Read, £26.5; 1928, Victoria and Albert Museum, Given by the Hon. Mrs Walter Levy.
LIT: *Anecdotes*, vol. 3, 85. *HW Corres.* 10: 278, 43: 136. David Green, *Grinling Gibbons: His Work as Carver and Statuary 1648–1721* (London: Country Life, 1964), 52, pl. 50. *OHG* 142. *Romantic Interior*, 101, fig. 83. Trevor Brighton, 'Samuel Watson, Not Grinling Gibbons at Chatsworth' *Burlington Magazine* 140, no. 1149 (Dec. 1998): 811–18.

168. PAIR OF VASES
Chelsea Porcelain Factory, *c.* 1760–65

Soft-paste porcelain, painted with Bacchanalian scenes in the style of Boucher on the front and exotic birds on the back in panels with gilding, 19.9 cm (64.101.504a) and 20.2 cm (64.101.505a)
Lent by The Metropolitan Museum of Art, Gift of Irwin Untermyer, 1964 (64.101.504a and 505a)
Fig. 344

D 1774, 91 [Tribune]: In the other glass case:...Two vases of Chelsea porcelaine, claret colour, gold and white, with cartouches of historic figures.
D 1784, 64, same as *D 1774*.
PROV: HW, £14.0.0; 1842, Strawberry Hill Sale, day 15, lot 96, bt Earl Cadogan, £16.16.0; 1903, Sir Hugh Adair; J. Pierpont Morgan; 1944, March 22, Sale of the Old English and French Furniture Objects of Art and Porcelain, from the J. P. Morgan Collection, Christie's, lot 48 [bt Major J. C. Bulteel]; 1949, November 10, Major J. C. Bulteel Collection Sale, Christie's, lot 83, bt Irwin Untermyer; 1964, given by Irwin Untermeyer to The Metropolitan Museum of Art.
LIT: Yvonne Hackenbroch, *Chelsea and other English Porcelain Pottery and Enamel in the Irwin Untermeyer Collection* (London: Thames and Hudson, 1957), 82–3, fig. 64.

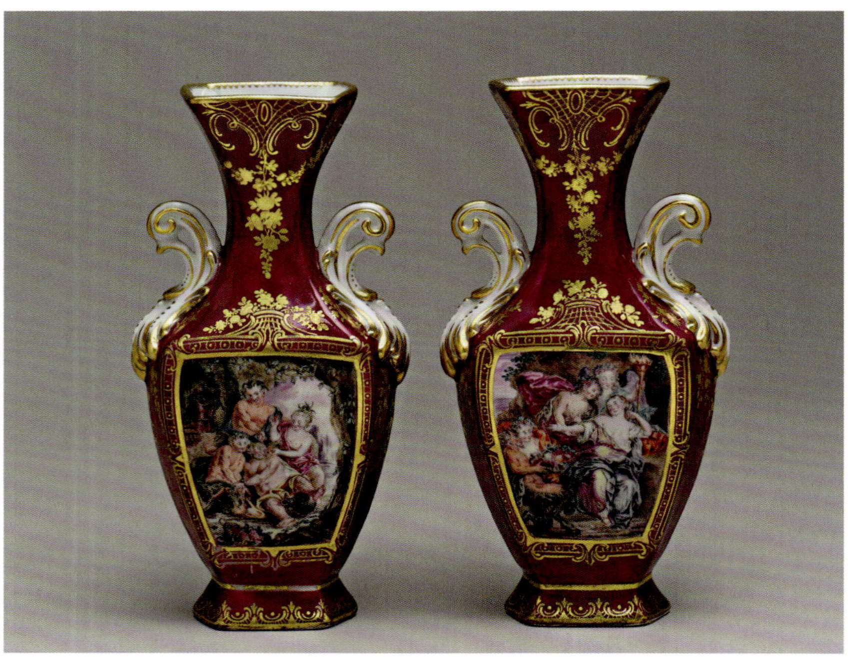

Figure 344. Catalogue 168

169. SNUFF BOX WITH A PORTRAIT OF TONTON
Louis Roucel (fl. 1763–87) and Isaac Gosset (1713–1799) (Portrait of Tonton), *c.* 1777

Silver gilt over brass with the portrait in wax, H 2.7 cm; D 7 cm
Inscriptions: engraved inside the lid: This box / with the portrait of / her Dog Tonton / was bequeathed / by / Madame la Marquise du Deffand. / to / Mr Horace Walpole, / 1780.
The Lewis Walpole Library, Yale University.
Fig. 88

D 1784, 66 [Tribune]: In the other glass case:...A gold snuff-box with the image in wax of mad. du Deffand's dog, Tonton, whom she bequeathed with this snuff-box and her MSS. to Mr. Walpole.
PROV: 1778, given by Madame de Luxembourg (1707–87) to Madame du Deffand (1696–1780); bequeathed to HW by Madame du Deffand; 1842, Strawberry Hill Sale, day 15, lot 20, bt Thomas Raikes, Esq., £14.14.0; 1899, June 11, Christie's, Different Properties, lot 106, £23.2.0; 1940, Arnold Seligmann, Rey & Co., New York, bt W. S. Lewis, $300; The Lewis Walpole Library, Yale University.
LIT: *HW Corres.* 7: 201, 33: 235. Mellon Lectures, 133. *Collector's Progress*, illus, opp. p. 151. *Rescuing Horace*, 151–60. E. J. Pyke, *Biographical Dictionary of Wax Modellers* (Supplement) (London: E. J. Pyke, 1981), 12, pl. 113A.

170. TOOTHPICK CASE
Maker unknown, English, *c.* 1780

Enamelled gold, 9.8 × 1.5 cm
Inscriptions: engraved on the inside sleeve: 'A present from Lady Diana Beauclerc to Sir Horace Walpole'
Victoria and Albert Museum, London. M7:1,2–1998
Fig. 152

D 1784, 66 [Tribune]: In the other glass case:...A tooth-pick case of gold, enamelled with cameos; a present from lady Diana Beauclerc.
PROV: Given to HW by Diana Beauclerk; 1842, Strawberry Hill Sale, day 15, lot 19, bt Farrer, Wardour Street, £11.11.0; 1963, 17 June, Sotheby's, Sir A. Chester Beatty Sale, lot 268; 1998, The Victoria and Albert Museum, Acquired in memory of Prof. G. M. Petersen.

171. THE CABINET OF MINIATURES AND ENAMELS
Designed by HW, perhaps with William Kent. Perhaps made by William Hallett Senior. Figures of Rubens, François Duquesnoy and Inigo Jones by James Francis Verskovis (Jacob Frans Vescovers) (fl. 1743) after John Michael Rysbrack (1694–1770); eagles and HW's arms in the pediment by Verskovis; reliefs by Giovnani Battista Pozzo (Pozzi) (fl. 1755–84) (perhaps as indicated in *D 1774*). Relief of Judith with the head of Holofernes by an anonymous carver after Francis van Bossuit (d. 1692). All the other ivories by anonymous carvers, the cabinet made 1743.

Veneered with padouk on a pine carcase, and set with carved ivory plaques, figures and mounts, 152.4 × 91.5 × 21.6 cm
Victoria and Albert Museum, London. Purchased with the assistance of the Murray Bequest. W.52:1, 2–1925
Fig. 127

D 1774, 77–8 [Tribune]: A cabinet of rose-wood, designed by Mr. Walpole; on the pediment, statues in ivory of Fiamingo, Inigo Jones, and Palladio [sic.], by Verskovis, after the models of Rysbrach. In the pediment, Mr. Walpole's arms, a cupid and lion, by the same: on the doors, bas-reliefs in ivory, Herodias with the head of the baptist, by Gibbons; a lady, half-length, by the same; Perseus and Andromeda; the Hercules Farnese; the Flora; Diomede with the Palladium; the Medusa of Strozzi; the Perseus of ditto; Caracalla and Alexander, by Pozzo; and eight other heads. On the drawer, the Barberini lion, by Pozzo; and heads of eagles, by Verskovis.
D 1784, 56, same as *D 1774*.
PROV: 1743, made for HW; 1842, Strawberry Hill Sale, day 15, lot 66, bt [Richards for] Mr Charles Redfern of Warwick, £126.0.0; Mr Harry Quilter; Sir George Donaldson, Private Museum in Sussex; 1925, July 9, Donaldson Sale at Hove, Sussex, lot 482, bt Sutton; 1925, The Victoria and Albert Museum, Purchased with the assistance of the Murray Bequest.
LIT: William King and M. Longhurst, 'A Relic of Horace Walpole'. *Burlington Magazine* 48, no. 275 (Feb. 1926), 98, 102–3. *HW Corres.* 9: 83, 18: 277, 34: 208n, 42: 111n, 262n. Ralph Edwards, 'Cabinets Made for Horace Walpole and Thomas Brand', *Burlington Magazine* 74, no. 432 (March 1939), 128–9, 131. H. D. Molesworth and John Kenworthy-Browne, *Three Centuries of Furniture in Color* (New York: Viking Press, 1972), pl. 189. *Romantic Interior*. 74–6, fig. 58. Christopher Wilk *Western Furniture 1300 to the Present Day* (London: Victoria and Albert Museum, 1996, 96–7. Katharine Eustace, *Michael Rysbrack Sculptor 1694–1770* (Bristol: City of Bristol Museum and Art Gallery, 1982) 142–3. M. I. Webb, *Michael Rysbrack Sculptor* (London: Country Life, 1954), 111–12. Malcolm Baker, 'Small-scale Sculpture and its Reproductions in the Eighteenth Century', in A. Hughes and E. Ranfft, eds., *Sculpture and its Reproductions* (London: Reaktion Books, 1997), 61–78.
NOTE: Rysbrack's figure of Duquesnoy was first made in 1743, with figures of Rubens and Van Dyck. On the left-hand figure of the cabinet being Rubens rather than the (usually beardless) Palladio, see Webb (LIT). The figure adds a bearded head to a body that repeats the pose and dress of Rysbrack's Palladio (at Chiswick House by *c.* 1730).

172. FINGER RING (ORNAMENT FOR A HORSE)
Maker unknown, late Roman

Chalcedony, H 3.7 cm; W 3.37 cm
British Museum, Department of Prehistory and Europe. 1917,0501.654 OA.10714
Yale Center for British Art only
Fig. 186

D 1774, 84 [Tribune]: Within the cabinet of enamels and miniatures:...A Calcedonian stone, antique, used as an ornament to a horse of a triumphal chariot. M
D 1784, 60, same as *D 1774*.
PROV: Conyers Middleton; 1744, May 14, HW bt from Conyers Middleton; 1842, Strawberry Hill Sale, day 15, lot 6, bt Roussel, Paris, £3.0.0; 1897, British Museum, London.

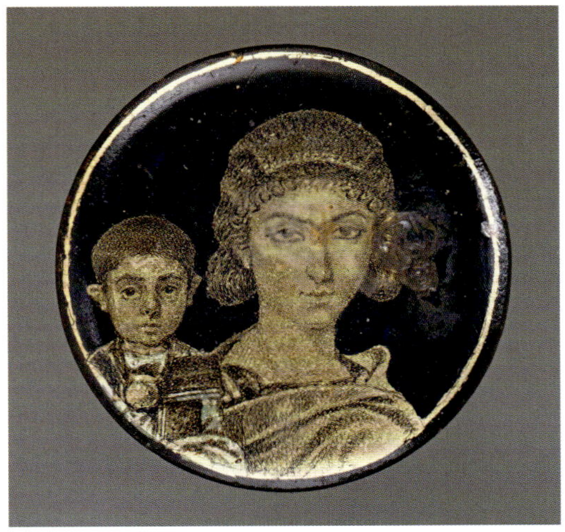

Figure 345. Catalogue 173

LIT: Conyers Middleton, *Germana quaedem antiquitatis eruditae monumenta*, 1745, p. III, no. iii. F. H. Marshall, *Catalogue of the Finger Rings, Greek, Etruscan, and Roman, in the Departments of Antiquities, British Museum* (London: Printed by the order of the Trustees, 1907), no. 654. *HW Corres.* 15: 16. *OHG* 138.
NOTE: See *D 1774*, 79: '*All the curiosities marked M. belonged to Dr. Conyers Middleton, whose whole collection Mr. Walpole bought. See an account of them in the doctor's Germana quædam Antiquitatis Monumenta. Middleton described the ring as 'A chalcedonian ring, with magical characters upon it, worn by way of amulet or charm'. HW's receipt dated 1744, May 14, for the sum of £131 for antiquities purchased from Middleton is at the Lewis Walpole Library, Yale University.

173. PORTRAIT OF A MOTHER AND CHILD; (ANTIQUE MINIATURE OF A ROMAN LADY AND HER SON)
Roman (Egypt, possibly Alexandria), 4th century AD

Verre eglomisé (in an 18th century gilt metal frame in the style of a miniature), medallion: D 4.8 cm; frame: H 6.8 cm
Inscriptions: in HW's hand on the oak slip on the back: : 'an antique miniature'; above that his cross-crosslet mark
Lent by The Metropolitan Museum of Art, Gift of J. Pierpont Morgan, 1917 (17.190.109a & b)
Fig. 345

D 1774, 82 [Tribune]: Within the cabinet of enamels and miniatures:...A curious antique miniature in gold, of a Roman lady and her son; the boy has a bulla at his neck. M.
D 1784, 58, same as *D 1774*.
PROV: [Discovered at Tivoli]; Francesco Ficorini (by 1732); Dr Conyers Middleton; 1744, May 14, bt HW from Conyers Middleton; 1842, Strawberry Hill Sale, day 14, lot 50, bt C. Wentworth Dilke, Esq., £3.3.0; 1911, June 19, Amedeo Canessa, Paris, bt J. Pierpont Morgan, no. 31; 1917, The Metropolitan Museum of Art, Gifted by J. P. Morgan.

LIT: Conyers Middleton, *Germana quaedem antiquitatis eruditae monumenta*, 1745, p. III, no. ii. (shown without a frame). *HW Corres.* 15: 16. C. Louise Avery, 'Early Christian Gold Glass', *Metropolitan Museum of Art Bulletin* 16, no. 8 (Aug. 1921): 170–5. Joseph Breck, 'The Ficoroni Medallion and Some Other Gilded Glasses in the Metropolitan Museum of Art', *Art Bulletin* 9, no. 4 (June 1927): 352–6.
EXHIB: J. L. Propert, ed., *Exhibition of Portrait Miniatures* (exh. cat. London: Burlington Fine Arts Club, 1889), no. 45 (case III).
NOTE: See *D 1774*, 79: * All those curiosities marked M belonged to Dr Conyers Middleton, whose whole collection Mr Walpole bought. See an account of them in the doctor's Germana quædam Antiquitatis Monumenta.

174. PORTRAIT MINIATURE OF ANNE BOLEYN (CATHARINE OF ARAGON)
Lucas Horenbout (*c.* 1490–1544), *c.* 1532–3

Watercolour on vellum set in gold frame, D 4.2 cm
Inscriptions: Engraved on 19th century cartouche: KATHARINE OF ARRAGON
Trustees of the Ninth Duke of Buccleuch's Chattels Fund
Fig. 193

D 1774, 84 [Tribune]: Within the cabinet of enamels and miniatures:...On the insides of the doors:...Catharine of Arragon, first wife of Henry 8th. an admirable original; by Holbein. These three were bought at the auction of lady Isabella Scott.
D 1784, 60, same as *D 1774*.
PROV: Charles II; presented to his illegitimate son the Duke of Monmouth (according to HW); his daughter, Lady Isabella Scott; at her sale purchased by HW, 1755 (as Katharine of Arragon by Holbein); 1842, Strawberry Hill Sale, day 14, lot 65, bt William Blamire, Esq., £50.8.0 (as Katherine of Aragon by Holbein); 1863, 9 November, his sale, Christie's, lot 137; purchased by Walter Francis, 5th Duke of Buccleuch and 7th Duke of Queensberry; by family descent.
LIT: J. G. Nichols, 'Remarks upon Holbein's Portraits of the Royal Family of England, and more particularly upon the several Portraits of the Queens of Henry the Eighth', *Archaeologia* 40 (1866): 71–80. A. McKay, *Catalogue of the Miniatures in Montagu House belonging to the Duke of Buccleuch*, 2nd edn, (London, 1899 [1st edn, 1896]), 21. H. A. Kennedy, *Early English Miniatures in the Collection of the Duke of Buccleuch* (London: The Studio Ltd, 1917), 3–4, 29, pl. 7. Roy Strong, *The English Renaissance Miniature* (New York: Thames and Hudson, 1983), 189, nos. 15–16. Roy Strong and V. G. Murrell, *Artists of the Tudor Court: the Portrait Miniature Rediscovered, 1520–1620* (exh. cat. London: Victoria & Albert Museum, 1983), 39–40. Stephen Lloyd, *Portrait Miniatures from the Collection of the Duke of Bucceluch* (Edinburgh: The Trustees of the National Galleries of Scotland, 1996), 32–3, cat. 5, pl. 5.
EXHIB: South Kensington Museum, 'Special Exhibitions of Portrait Miniatures', 1865, no. 1590 (as Katharine of Arragon); Royal Academy of Arts, 'Old Masters', 1879, Case F, no. 5.
NOTE: A Principal Curiosity.

175. PORTRAIT MINIATURE OF THE ARTIST
Isaac Oliver (*c.* 1565–1617), 1590

Watercolour on vellum, stuck on card, set in chased gold frame, H 6.2 cm
National Portrait Gallery, London. Purchased with help from H. M. Government, 1971. 4852
Fig. 130

D 1774, 84 [Tribune]: Within the cabinet of enamels and miniatures:...On the insides of the doors:... Isaac Oliver; by himself: perfectly fine.
D 1784, 60, same as *D 1774*.
PROV: Thomas Barrett of Lee Court, Kent to HW; 1842, Strawberry Hill Sale, day 14, lot 85, bt 13th Earl of Derby, £22.1.0. by family descent; 1971, June 8, Christie's, 18th Earl of Derby Sale, lot 79; bt Leggatt Brothers on behalf of the National Portrait Gallery, London, purchased with help from H. M. Government.
LIT: B. S. Long, *British Miniaturists 1520–1860* (London: The Holland Press, 1966), 316–20. Roy C. Strong, *The English Icon: Elizabethan & Jacobean Portraiture* (New Haven: Yale University Press, 1969), 337, fig. 61. G. Reynolds, *Nicholas Hilliard & Isaac Oliver* (London: Victoria and Albert Museum, 1971), no. 135. R. C. Strong and V. J. Murrell, *Artists of the Tudor Court: the Portrait Miniature Rediscovered, 1520–1620* (exh. cat. London: Victoria and Albert Museum, 1983), 98, no. 133. M. Rogers, *Master Drawings from the National Portrait Gallery* (London: National Portrait Gallery, 1993), 22–3, no. 3. K. Hearn, *Dynasties: Painting in Tudor and Jacobean England, 1530–1630* (London: Tate Gallery, 1995), no. 77. R. Walker, *Miniatures: 300 Years of the English Miniature illustrated from the Collections of the National Portrait Gallery* (London: National Portrait Gallery, 1998), 22–3, pl.8.
NOTE: J. Miller engraved a print of this portrait miniature in 1762 for *Anecdotes* (vol. 1, p. 152).

176. PORTRAIT MINIATURE OF AN UNKNOWN LADY; (THE QUEEN OF BOHEMIA)
Nicholas Hilliard (1547?–1619), *c.* 1605–10

Watercolour on vellum, stuck on playing card with verso of four watercolour stripes alternating with black and blue, 5.1 × 4.3 cm
Yale Center for British Art, Paul Mellon Collection. B1974.2.51
Fig. 211

D 1774, 80 [Tribune]: Within the cabinet of enamels and miniatures:...The queen of Bohemia; by Isaac Oliver: bought out of the collection of lady Isabella Scott, daughter of the duchess of Monmouth.
D 1784, 57, same as *D 1774*.
PROV: Lady Isabella Scott; 1755, Dec. 18, at whose sale purchased by HW, 7gns; 1842, Strawberry Hill Sale, day 14, lot 15, bt 13th Earl of Derby for £13.13.0; by family descent; Christie's, London, 18th Earl of Derby Sale, 1971, 8 June, lot 77; bt Fry for Yale Center for British Art, New Haven.
LIT: Sir George Scharf, *A Descriptive and Historical Catalogue of the Collection of Pictures at Knowsley Hall* (London: Bradbury, Agnew, & Co., 1875), no. 219. J. J. Foster, *British Miniature Painters and Their Works* (London: S. Low Marston and Co., 1898), 30 Appendix A, p. 9. *HW Corres.* 15, 191n. 'The Earl of Derby's Miniatures', *Connoisseur* (June 1958), 44, repro. 45. E. Auerbach, *Nicholas Hilliard* (London, 1961), 154, ill. 149. L. R. Schidlof, *The Miniature in Europe in the 16th, 17th, 18th and 19th Centuries* (Graz, 1964), 359. D. Foskett, *British Portrait Miniatures: a History* (London: Methuen and Co. Limited, 1963), 44, ill. 14. G. Reynolds, *Nicholas Hilliard & Isaac Oliver* (London: Victoria and Albert Museum, 1971), no. 97. *Yale Center for British Art, Selected Paintings, Drawings & Books* (New Haven: Yale University, 1977), repro. p. 2. Patrick J. Noon, *English Portrait Drawings and Miniatures* (New Haven: Yale Center for British Art, 1979), no. 1. *Paul Mellon's Legacy: a Passion for British Art* (New Haven and London: Yale University Press, 2007), no. 2.
EXHIB: 1862 Special Exhibition, no. 221. J. L. Propert, ed., *Exhibition of Portrait Miniatures* (London: Burlington Fine Arts Club, 1889), no. 45 (case III). S. Redgrave, ed., *Catalogue of the Special Exhibition of Portrait Miniatures ...* (London: South Kensington Museum, 1865), no. 1812.
NOTE: HW's receipt dated 1755, Dec. 18, for payment of 7gns to Rev. Dean Lyttleton and signed Js.Islene for a miniature painting of Elizabeth Queen of Bohemia by Isaac Oliver and a fine carved head of King Henry the eighth is at the Lewis Walpole Library, Yale University.

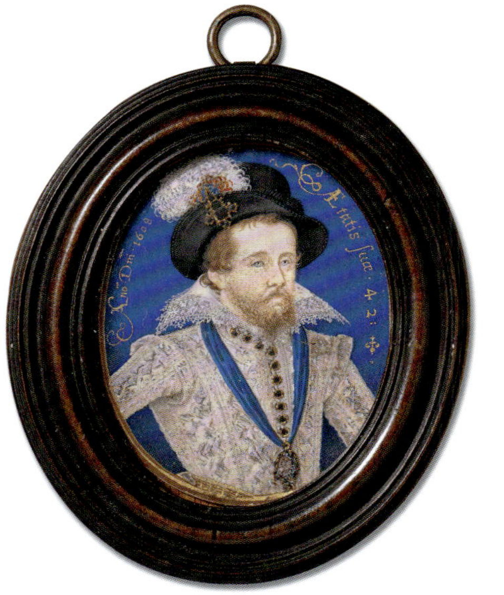

Figure 346. Catalogue 177

177. PORTRAIT MINIATURE OF JAMES VI & I
Nicholas Hilliard (1547?–1619), 1608

Watercolour, gouache, gold, and silver, on vellum set in stained fruitwood frame, 6.7 × 5.9 cm
Inscription around the portrait's edge: Ano Dni: 1608/ Aetatis Suae 42
Inscription by HW in ink on oak slip on back of frame: 'King James 1st by Isaac Oliver – HW. above that his cross-crosslet mark. In (?) another hand: 'No. 12'
Rosenbach Museum & Library, Philadelphia. 1954.1611
Yale Center for British Art only
Fig. 346

D 1774, 80 [Tribune]: Within the cabinet of enamels and miniatures:…James Ist. by Isaac Oliver.
D 1784, 57, same as *D 1774*.
PROV: HW; 1842, Strawberry Hill Sale, day 14, lot 38, bt [Colnaghi for] Robert Holford, Esq., £18.18; 1927, July 13, Christie, Manson and Woods, Holford Sale, lot 119, bt Philip Rosenbach (Reattributed to Hilliard); Rosenbach Museum & Library.
LIT: Roy Strong and V. J. Murrell, *Artists of the Tudor Court: the Portrait Miniature Rediscovered, 1520–1620* (exh. cat. London: Victoria & Albert Museum, 1983), 144–5. Roy Strong, *The English Renaissance Miniature* (London and New York: Thames and Hudson, 1983), 122–5.
EXHIB: Burlington Fine Arts Club, 'England's World of 1607', 1889.

178. PORTRAIT MINIATURE OF ROBERT DEVEREUX, 2ND EARL OF ESSEX
Isaac Oliver (*c.* 1565–1617), *c.* 1600

Bodycolour and brush and grey ink on vellum, stuck onto card, H 5.4 cm
Yale Center for British Art, Paul Mellon Collection. B1974.2.75
Fig. 196

D 1774, 81 [Tribune]: Within the cabinet of enamels and miniatures:…Robert Devereux earl of Essex; by Isaac Oliver: it belonged to Frances lady Worseley, who was descended from him. It was engraved for the *Illustrious Heads*.
D 1784, 58, same as *D 1774*.
PROV: Frances, Lady Worseley; HW; 1842, Strawberry Hill Sale, day 14, lot 45, bt 13th Earl of Derby, £7.7.0; by family descent; 1971, June 8, Christie's, 18th Earl of Derby Sale, lot 81, bt Fry; Yale Center for British Art, New Haven.
LIT: J. J. Foster, *British Miniature Painters and Their Works* (London: S. Low Marston and Co., 1898), Appendix A, p. 12, no. 45. 'The Earl of Derby's Miniatures', *Connoisseur* (June 1958), 44, repro. 45. D. Foskett, *British Portrait Miniatures: a History* (London: Methuen and Co. Limited, 1963), 55, ill. 22. D. Foskett, ed., *British Portrait Miniatures* (Edinburgh: The Arts Council Gallery, 1965), no. 27. Roy C. Strong, *Tudor & Jacobean portraits* … (London: HMSO 1969), I, 117. G. Reynolds, *Nicholas Hilliard & Isaac Oliver* (London: Victoria and Albert Museum, 1971), no. 150. Patrick J. Noon, *English Portrait Drawings and Miniatures* (New Haven: Yale Center for British Art, 1979), no. 2. *Paul Mellon's Legacy: a Passion for British Art* (New Haven and London: Yale University Press, 2007), no. 3.
EXHIB: 1862 Special Exhibition, no. 2227. S. Redgrave, ed., *Catalogue of the Special Exhibition of Portrait Miniatures…*, (London: South Kensington Museum, 1865), no. 1818. Sir George Scharf, *A Descriptive and Historical Catalogue of the Collection of Pictures at Knowsley Hall* (London: Bradbury, Agnew, & Co., 1875), no. 225. J. L. Propert, ed., *Exhibition of Portrait Miniatures* (London: Burlington Fine Arts Club, 1889), case XX, no. 7.
NOTE: This portrait miniature was made into a print by F. Bartolozzi after S. Harding, lettered i. *Earl of Essex, from an original in miniature by P. Oliver in the collection of HW at Strawberry Hill.* Published 1793, March 1, by E. Harding. The print is mounted in an extra-illustrated copy of *D 1784* at Lewis Walpole Library (33 30 copy 11 folio, p. 62).

179. PORTRAIT MINIATURE OF THE ARTIST, WITH PORTRAIT OF THE ARTIST'S WIFE, ANNE (VERSO)
Peter Oliver (1589–1647), *c.* 1625–30

Graphite and watercolour on card set in pearwood frame, 8.6 × 6.7 cm [frame]
Inscriptions: signed on recto: PO se ipse f.; inscribed on verso: P. Oliver his wife
National Portrait Gallery, London. Given by National Art Collections Fund, 1971. 4853
Fig. 210

D 1774, 84 [Tribune]: Within the cabinet of enamels and miniatures:…Peter Oliver, profile in black lead, from a leaf of his own pocket-book, and his wife, full-faced, on the other side; both fine: it belonged to Vertue the engraver.
D 1784, 59–60, same as *D 1774*.
PROV: George Vertue, his Sale, 1757, March 17, bt HW; 1842, Strawberry Hill Sale, day 14, lot 74, bt 13th Earl of Derby, £5.15.6; by family descent; 1971, June 10, Christie's, 18th Earl of Derby Sale, lot 82; 1971, bt Leggatt Brothers on behalf of the National Portrait Gallery, London, with a donation from the National Art Collections Fund.
LIT: D. Foskett, *British Portrait Miniatures: a History* (London: Methuen and Co. Ltd, 1963), 60–1, ills. 26–7. M. Rogers, *Master Drawings from the National Portrait Gallery* (London: National Portrait Gallery, 1993), 24–5, no. 5. R. Walker, *Miniatures: 300 Years of the English Miniature illustrated from the Collections of the National Portrait Gallery* (London: National Portrait Gallery, 1998), 26–7, no. 11.
EXHIB: 1862 Special Exhibition, no. 2230.

180. PORTRAIT MINIATURE OF DR BRIAN WALTON; (SERGEANT MAYNARD)
John Hoskins (*c.* 1590–1665), 1657

Watercolour on vellum, laid on card, set in gilt-metal case, H 7.2 cm (oval)
Signed and dated upper left recto in gold: 1657. / iH; on verso of case is scratched: Serjeant Maynard
Lent by The Metropolitan Museum of Art, Fletcher Fund, 1935 (35.89.3)
Fig. 215

D 1774, 80 [Tribune]: Within the cabinet of enamels and miniatures:…Serjeant Maynard; by Hoskins: given to sir R. Walpole by sir Everard Falkener.
D 1784, 57, same as *D 1774*.
PROV: 1735, Sir Everard Fawkener, Wandsworth, London, to Sir Robert Walpole; 1743, Sir Robert Walpole to HW; 1842, Strawberry Hill Sale, day 14, lot 16, bt B. Botfield, Esq. MP, £22.1.0. (as Sir John Maynard); 1863, Duke of Hamilton; 1882, July 15, Christie's, Hamilton Palace Sale, Fifth Portion, No. 1599, bt Philpot, £231, (as Maynard); 1904, May 13, Christie's, London, Collection of C. H. T. Hawkins, Esq., no. 902, bt Durlacher, £140, (as Maynard); [1906–1913], J. Pierpont Morgan, London and New York, (as Maynard); 1935, June 24, Christie's London, J. P. Morgan Sale, no. 138, bt Knoedler for Metropolitan Museum of Art, £241.10s.
LIT: *Anecdotes*, vol. 3, 254. Graham Reynolds and K. Baetjer, *European Miniatures in The Metropolitan Museum of Art* (New York: Metropolitan Museum of Art, 1996), 80–1, no. 24.
NOTE: Engraved as 'Sir John Maynard Knt.' and mounted in HW's extra-illustrated copy of *D 1784* at Lewis Walpole Library (49 3582 folio, p. 130).

181. Portrait Enamel of Charles I
Jean Petitot I (1607–1691), *c.* 1638

Enamel on copper, set in chased gilt-metal frame, 4 × 3.5 cm, framed: 5.9 × 4.3 cm
Inscriptions: on the back of the frame by HW: 'Charles I by Petitot. H.W' and with his cross-crosslet mark.
Nationalmuseum, Stockholm. NMB 989. Bequest 1927 of consul Hjalmar Wicander (The Wicander Collection)
Fig. 212

D 1774, 80 [Tribune]: Within the cabinet of enamels and miniatures:…Charles 1st. by Petitot: fine.
D 1784, 57 [Tribune]: Within the cabinet of enamels and miniatures:…same as *D 1774* and: A present from T. Walker esq; to Maria lady Walpole.
PROV: Petitot family; given by T. Walker to Maria Walpole; HW; 1842, Strawberry Hill Sale, day 14, lot 39, bt Baroness Burdett Coutts, £65.2.0; 1922, May 11, Christie's, Miss Burdett-Coutts Sale, lot 415, bt Consul Hjalmar Wicander; 1927, Wicander Collection Bequest to Nationalmuseum, Stockholm.
LIT: J. J. Foster, *British Miniature Painters and Their Works* (London: S. Low, Marston & Co., 1898.), pl. 25. Karl Asplund, *Hjalmar Wicanders Miniatursamling: Beskrivande Katalog*, vol. 2 (Stockholm: Cederquist grafiska aktiebolog, 1920–1929), 47, no. 121, pl. 45.
EXHIB: South Kensington Museum, 'Loan Exhibition', 1862. The New Gallery, London, Exhibition of the Royal House of Stuart (exh. cat. London: The New Gallery, 1889).

182. Portrait Enamel of Charles II
Jean Petitot I (1607–1691) after Philippe de Champaigne (1602–74), *c.* 1653–68

Enamel on copper set in closing gold locket with blue enamel, 3.8 × 3.1 cm
Marks: painted with crowned CR monogram on inside of lid
Nationalmuseum, Stockholm. NMB 988. Bequest 1927 of consul Hjalmar Wicander (The Wicander Collection)

D 1774, 80 [Tribune]: Within the cabinet of enamels and miniatures:…Charles 2d. ditto [by Petitot]; in a case enamelled blue; done abroad: bought of an old gentlewoman, to whom he gave it when he stood godfather to her in Holland.
D 1784, 57–58, same as *D 1774*.
PROV: HW; 1842, Strawberry Hill Sale, day 14, lot 40, bt Baroness Burdett Coutts, £78.15; 1922, May 11, Christie's, Miss Burdett-Coutts Sale, lot 416, bt Consul Hjalmar Wicander; 1927, Wicander Collection Bequest to Nationalmuseum, Stockholm.
LIT: J. J. Foster, *British Miniature Painters and Their Works* (London: S. Low, Marston & Co., 1898.), pl. 26. Karl Asplund, *Hjalmar Wicanders Miniatursamling: Beskrivande Katalog*, vol. 2 (Stockholm: Cederquist grafiska aktiebolog, 1920–1929), 48, no. 122, pl. 45. M. Olausson, ed., *Europeiskt Miniatyrmåleri i Nationalmusei samlingarna* (Stockholm: Streiffert, 1994), ill. 4b.
EXHIB: South Kensington Museum, 'Loan Exhibition', 1862, no. 2159. The New Gallery, London, *Exhibition of the Royal House of Stuart* (exh. cat. London: The New Gallery, 1889), no. 272*

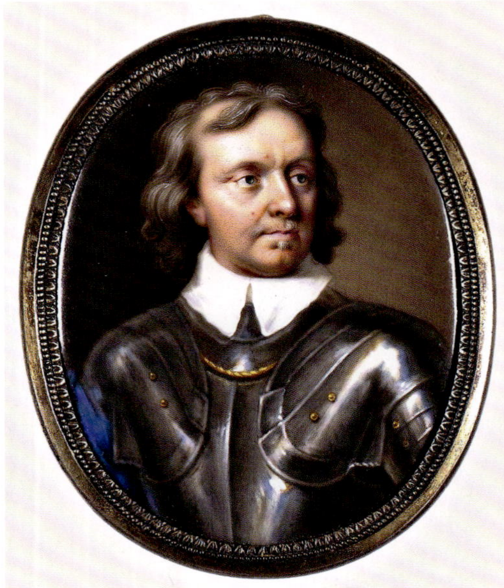

Figure 347. Catalogue 186

183. Portrait Enamel of Louis XIV
Jean Petitot I (1607–1691), *c.* 1660

Enamel on copper set in gold frame, 2.8 × 2.4 cm
Inscriptions: engraved on verso: Petitot bought at Strawberry Hill 10th May 1842
Nationalmuseum, Stockholm. NMB 2564. Purchase 2007 with the Hjalmar and Anna Wicander's Foundation.

D 1774, 82 [Tribune]: Within the cabinet of enamels and miniatures:…Louis 14th: Mary of Austria, his queen: Anne of Austria, his mother, very delicate: madame de Montespan, his mistress, beautiful. These four are small heads in enamel, by Petitot.
D 1784, 59, same as *D 1774*.
PROV: HW; 1842, Strawberry Hill Sale, day 14, lot 54, bt Mrs N. M. Rothschild, £14.14.0; 2007, May 23, Bonhams, London, lot 16, bt Nationalmuseum, Stockholm with the Hjalmar and Anna Wicander's Foundation.
LIT: J. J. Foster, *British Miniature Painters and Their Works* (London: S. Low, Marston & Co., 1898), Appendix A, p. 13.

184. Portrait Enamel of Maria Theresa of Austria
Jean Petitot I (1607–1691), *c.* 1660

Enamel on copper, H 2.54 cm; H 4.2 cm [frame]
Lent by the Rt Hon. the Earl of Derby, K513
Victoria and Albert Museum only
Fig. 198

D 1774, 82 [Tribune]: Within the cabinet of enamels and miniatures:…Louis 14th: Mary of Austria, his queen: Anne of Austria, his mother, very delicate: madame de Montespan, his mistress, beautiful. These four are small heads in enamel, by Petitot.
D 1784, 59, same as *D 1774*.
PROV: HW; 1842, Strawberry Hill Sale, day 14, lot 56, bt the 13th Earl of Derby, £21.0.0; by family descent
LIT: Sir George Scharf, *A Descriptive and Historical Catalogue of the Collection of Pictures at Knowsley Hall* (London: Bradbury, Agnew, & Co., 1875), no. 222. F. G. Stephens, *Notes on the Pictures at Knowsley Hall*, 1881, p. 42.
EXHIB: South Kensington Museum, 'Loan Exhibition', 1862, no. 2224; South Kensington Museum, 'Collection of Miniatures', 1865, no. 1815.

185. Portrait Enamel of Catherine Henriette d'Angennes, Comtesse d'Olonne, as Diana
Jean Petitot I (1607–1691), 1680

Enamel on copper in a enamelled gold frame by Gilles Légaré, 3.8 × 3.2 cm; 6.3 × 4.8 cm (framed)
Inscriptions: label on inside cover of box 'Mortimer and Hunt, Jewellers and Goldsmiths to the Queen, 136 New Bond Street, London' perhaps for a repair.
Philadelphia Museum of Art, Gift of Mrs Lessing J. Rosenwald, 1961. 1961–37–1
Fig. 217

D 1784, 59 [Tribune]: Within the cabinet of enamels and miniatures:…A beautiful enamel by Petitot, of Catherine Henriette d'Angennes comtesse d'Olonne, as a Diana, a character very different from that given of her in Bussy's Histoire amoureuse de Gaules. It is set in a frame of flowers enamelled in relief by Giles Legaré de Chaumont en Bassigni, who was famous for that sort of works: from the collection of monsieur Mariette.
PROV: 1775, Nov/Dec, lot 8, Pierre-Jean Mariette Collection Sale, bt Pierre-Francois Basan for HW, 3200 livres; 1842, Strawberry Hill Sale, day 14, lot 53, bt P. & D. Colnaghi for Robert Holford, Esq., £141.15; 1927, July 13–14, Christie's, Sale of the Property of Sir George Lindsey Holford, lot 129, bt [Amor London dealer, £588]; Lessing J. Rosenwald; 1961, Philadelphia Museum of Art, Gift of Mrs Lessing J. Rosenwald.
LIT: J. J. Foster, *British Miniature Painters and Their Works* (London: S. Low, Marston & Co., 1898), Appendix A, p. 12. *HW Corres.* 6: 95, 96–8, 102, et. al.; 7: 269; 14: 146; 32: 282; 39: 198, 208, 215. Priscilla Grace, 'A Celebrated Miniature of the Comtesse d'Olonne', *Bulletin, Philadelphia Museum of Art*, 83, no. 353 (Fall 1986): 2–21, ill. p.2.
NOTE: A Principal Curiosity.

186. Portrait Enamel of Oliver Cromwell
Charles Boit (1662–1727), after Samuel Cooper (1607/8–1672), *c.* 1700 (after original painted *c.* 1650–53)

Enamel on copper set in silver-gilt frame, H 7.7 cm
Inscriptions: in 19th century hand on paper behind glass on verso: 'Lot 71. Strawberry Hill. A fine miniature of Oliver Cromwell, enamelled by Boit or Cooper. A beautiful specimen of that Master. Given to Mr Walpole by his Brother Lord Oxford [sic]. Bt by Baldock 26 Guineas. W. Forster.'
The House of Orange-Nassau Historic Collections Trust, M338
Fig. 347

D 1774, 83 [Tribune]: Oliver Cromwell; by Boit, after Cooper: given to Mr. Walpole by his brother lord Orford.
D 1784, 59, same as *D 1774*.
PROV: Given by Robert Walpole, 2nd Earl of Orford, to HW; 1842, Strawberry Hill Sale, day 14, lot 71, bt Baldock, Hanway Street, £27.6.0; House of Orange-Nassau Historic Collections Trust (on loan to Paleis Het Loo, Apeldoorn)
LIT: *Catalogue de la Collection de Minatures appartenant à S. A. R. Mgr. Le Prince Alexandre de Pays-Bas, Prince d'Orange* (Brussels, 1882), 338. *Exposition de la Miniature à Bruxelles en 1912* (Brussels: Librarie Nationale d'Art et d'Historie, 1912), 654. F. Lugt, *Le Portrait-Miniature illustré par la collection de S. M. la Reine de Pays-Bas* (Amsterdam, 1917), 21, ill. 11. *HW Corres.* 41: 263n, 42: 125. K. Schaffers-Bodenhausen and M. Tiethoff-Spliethoff, *The Portrait Miniatures in the Collections of the House of Orange-Nassau* (Zwolle: Waanders Publishers).

187. Portrait Enamel of Admiral George Churchill
Charles Boit (1662–1727), *c.* 1700

Enamel on copper set in gold frame, H 6.1 cm
Inscriptions: Signed on counter-enamel: C. Boit pinxt.; cartouche engraved: ADMIRAL CHURCHILL. BY BOIT
National Maritime Museum, Greenwich, London MNT0129
Fig. 199

D 1774, 82 [Tribune]: Within the cabinet of enamels and miniatures:...Admiral Churchill, brother of John duke of Marlborough; very finely enamelled by Boit: it belonged to his neice, Mrs. Dunch.
D 1784, 58, same as *D 1774*.
PROV: 1761, 10–11 Dec., Sale of the Property of Elizabeth Godfrey, Mrs Edmund Dunch (niece of the sitter), bt HW, £7.8.0; 1842, Strawberry Hill Sale, day 14, lot 49, bt Hor. Rodd, £13.13; Lord Northwick, Thirlestane Collection; 1859, August 5, Colnaghi & Co., Mansion Sale, lot 785, bt Mr Philips, £22.1.0; Walter Francis, 5th Duke of Buccleuch and 7th Duke of Queensberry, frame O22; by family descent; purchased through Spink, London, by Sir James Caird in 1941 and presented by him that year to the National Maritime Museum, Greenwich.
LIT: *HW Corres.* 9: 412. A. McKay, *Catalogue of the Miniatures in Montagu House belonging to the Duke of Buccleuch* (London, 1899), 95. H. A. Kennedy, *Portrait Miniatures in the Collection of the Duke of Buccleuch* (London: The Studio Ltd, 1917), 42, pl. 66.

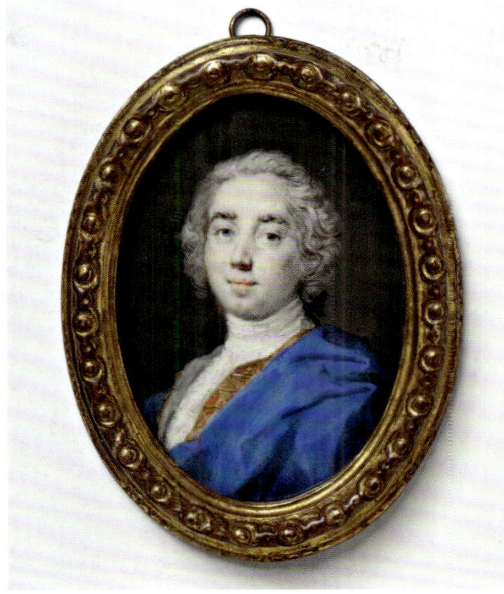

Figure 348. Catalogue 188

188. Portrait Miniature of Robert Walpole, 2nd Earl of Orford
Rosalba Carriera (1675–1757), *c.* 1720

Watercolour on ivory, H 8.4 cm
Inscriptions: in HW's hand on thin wooden backboard: 'Robert, Lord Walpole, eldest Son to Sr Robert Walpole. Earl of Orford. Drawn by Rosalba at Venice. H.W.' and with his cross-crosslet mark.
Victoria and Albert Museum, London. Salting Bequest. P.160–1910
Fig. 348

D 1774, 81 [Tribune]: Within the cabinet of enamels and miniatures:...Robert Walpole, second earl of Orford; painted in water-colours by Rosalba with all the force of oil.
D 1784, 58, same as *D 1774*.
PROV: HW; 1842, Strawberry Hill Sale, day 14, lot 47, bt Morgan, £3.5.0; 1900, purchased by Salting, £30; 1910, given to the Victoria and Albert Museum as part of the Salting Bequest.
LIT: Katherine Coombs, *The Portrait Miniature in England* (London: Victoria and Albert Museum, 1998), 77, pl. 50.

189. Portrait Enamel of Sir Robert Walpole, 1st Earl of Orford
Christian Friedrich Zincke (1684?–1767), 1744

Enamel on copper set in enamelled gilt metal frame with green enamelled laurel surround, H 5.7 cm , H 7.7 cm [frame], W 4.3 cm
Lent by the Rt Hon. the Earl of Derby, K514
Victoria and Albert Museum only
Fig. 124

D 1774, 79 [Tribune]: Within the cabinet of enamels and miniatures:...Sir Robert Walpole, earl of Orford; very like; painted in enamel by Zincke, two years before sir Robert's death: set in a frame of enamelled oak-leaves.
D 1784, 57, same as *D 1774*.
PROV: HW; 1842, Strawberry Hill Sale, day 14, lot 32, bt J. Smith of Bond Street for the 13th Earl of Derby, £27.6.0; by family descent.
LIT: *HW Corres.* 49: 249. Sir George Scharf, *A Descriptive and Historical Catalogue of the Collection of Pictures at Knowsley Hall* (London: Bradbury, Agnew, & Co., 1875), no. 227.
EXHIB: 1862 Special Exhibition, no. 2229. S. Redgrave, ed., *Catalogue of the Special Exhibition of Portrait Miniatures ...* (exh. cat. London: South Kensington Museum, 1865), no. 1820.
NOTE: This miniature by Zincke is reproduced in the frontispiece to *Ædes Walpolianae*, engraved by George Vertue, dated 1748.

190. Portrait Enamel of Horace Walpole, 4th Earl of Orford
Christian Friedrich Zincke (1684?–1767), 1745

Enamel on copper, set in gold frame with spiral cresting, H 4.4 cm
Inscriptions: in HW's hand on verso: 'HoraceWalpole 3rd son of Robert Walpole Earl of Orford by Zinck. 1745'.
The Trustees of the Waldegrave Chattels Trust
Fig. 200

D 1774, 80 [Tribune]: Within the cabinet of enamels and miniatures:...Horace Walpole, [who made the collection] youngest son of sir R. Walpole and Catherine Shorter; ditto [by Zincke].
D 1784, 57, same as *D 1774*.
PROV: HW; 1842, Strawberry Hill Sale, day 14, lot 36, bt Earl Waldegrave, £58.16.0.
LIT: J. J. Foster, *British Miniature Painters and Their Works* (London, S. Low, Marston & Co., 1898), Appendix A, p 11. 'Portraits': A.7. John Ingamells, *National Portrait Gallery Mid-Georgian Portraits, 1760–1790* (London: National Portrait Gallery, 2004), 371.
NOTE: Zincke's receipt for this miniature and three others, dated 1746, December 1, £31–10s (British Library Add MS 35,335 f.61).

191. Portrait Miniature of John Chute
Pompeo Girolamo Batoni (1708–1787), 1745–6

Watercolour on ivory, H 5.6 cm
The Vyne, The Chute Collection (The National Trust)
Fig. 110

D 1774, 82 [Tribune]: Within the cabinet of enamels and miniatures:...John Chute, esq; of the Vine in

Hampshire; finely painted in water-colours, by Pompeio Battoni, at Rome.
D 1784, 58, same as *D 1774*.
PROV: *c.* 1745–46, presumably presented by the sitter or commissioned by HW; 1842, Strawberry Hill Sale, day 14, lot 13, bt Wiggett Chute, Esq., MP, £3.0.0; The Vyne, The Chute Collection, The National Trust.
LIT: *Country Life* (23 Feb. 1984): 476. Anthony M. Clark and Edgar Peters Bowron, eds., *Pompeo Batoni: a Complete Catalogue of his Works* (Oxford: Phaidon, 1985), no. 98, pl. 92.
NOTE: A line engraving by James Heath of this portrait is mounted in an extra-illustrated copy of *D 1784* at the Lewis Walpole Library (33 30 copy 4, page 103).

192. La Boudeuse (A Man and Woman Sitting)
Jean-Antoine Watteau (1684–1721), *c.* 1717–18

Oil on canvas, 42 × 34 cm
The State Hermitage Museum, St Petersburg. 4120
Fig. 82

D 1774, 98 [Tribune]: Side opposite to the door:...A man and a woman sitting; by Watteau: from sir Robert Walpole's collection.* *All the pictures that were not at Houghton were sold after his death.
D 1784, 69 [Tribune]: Pictures and bronzes on the side where the altar is: A man and a woman sitting; by Watteau: from sir Robert Walpole's collection.* ...*All the pictures that were not at Houghton were sold after his death.
PROV: Sir Robert Walpole (after 1726?); 1748, London Sale of Sir R. Walpole's collection, day 2, lot 52, bt HW, £3.3; 1842, Strawberry Hill Sale, day 13, lot 36, bt Emery, Bury Street, £40.19; 1852, May 24, Duc de Morny in Paris, bt Henri Didiér, £1,700 FF; 1856, January 22, de Férrol Collection, no. 28. Purchased then or shortly thereafter by Count Paul S. Stroganoff of St. Petersburg. (later in the Stroganoff Gallery); 1922, transferred to the State Hermitage Museum.
LIT: Martin Eidelberg, 'Watteau's "La Boudeuse",' *Burlington Magazine* 111, no. 794 (May 1969): 273–8. Margaret Morgan Grasselli and P. Rosenberg, *Watteau, 1684–1721* (Washington: National Gallery of Art, 1984), no. 7. Larissa Dukelskaya and Andrew Moore, eds., *A Capital Collection: Houghton Hall and the Hermitage* (New Haven and London: Yale University Press, 2002), p. 456.

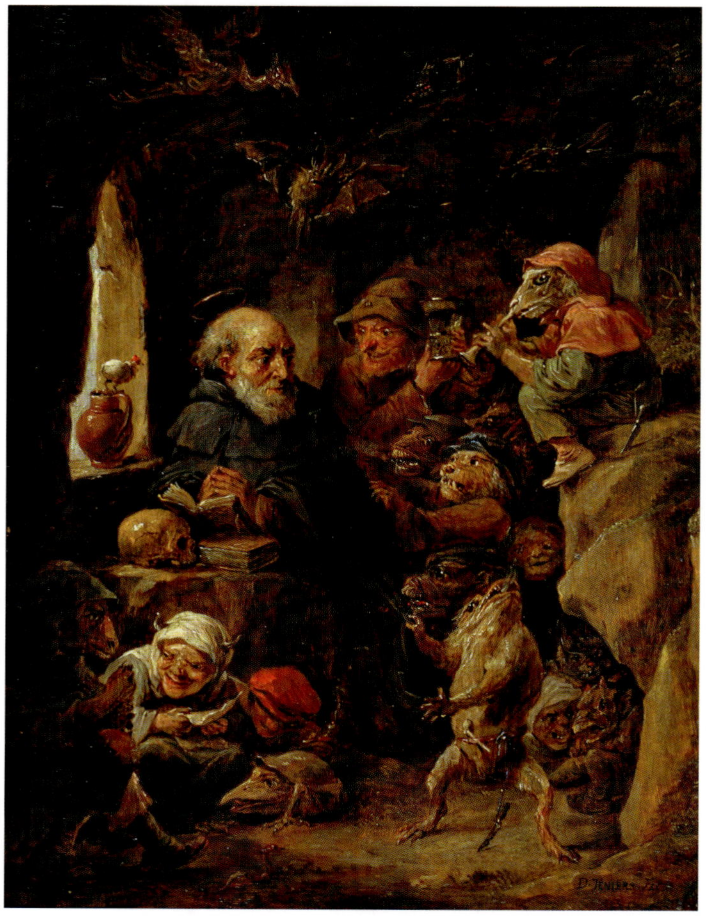

Figure 349. Catalogue 193

193. The Temptation of Saint Anthony
David Teniers II (1610–1690), *c.* 1630

Oil on panel, 24.8 × 18.6 cm
The National Trust for Scotland, Brodick Castle
Fig. 349

D 1774, 98 [Tribune]: Side opposite to the door:...Temptation of saint Antony; by Teniers.
D 1784, 68, same as *D 1774*.
PROV: HW; 1842, Strawberry Hill Sale, day 13, lot 44, bt Hume, Berners-street [for Wm. Beckford, Esq.], £45.3.0; his daughter Susan Euphemia Beckford, Duchess of Hamilton (d. 1859), wife of Alexander, 10th Duke of Hamilton (d. 1852); by descent to her grandson, William, 12th Duke of Hamilton (d. 1895); under the terms of a Trust Disposition and Settlement of 1893, to his only child Mary Louise Hamilton, later Duchess of Montrose. Accepted by Her Majesty's Treasury on death of Mary Louise Hamilton, Duchess of Montrose, in 1957, in lieu of inheritance tax and allocated by her express wish to The National Trust for Scotland, as part of the Brodick Castle estate.
LIT: Margret Klinge, *David Teniers the Younger: Paintings, Drawings*, exh. cat., Antwerp, Koninklijk Museum voor schone Kunsten (Ghent: Snoeck-Ducaju & Zoon, 1991), nos 9, 41, 90.

194. St Catherine of Alexandria and St James Major (Christ as a Pilgrim, and Saint Catherine)
Orazio Samacchini (1532–1577), mid-to late 1560s

Paint on white metal, 21.4 × 16 cm in an 18th century gilt-wood frame.
Culture and Sport Glasgow (Museums)
Reg. No. 164
Fig. 83

D 1774, 99 [Tribune]: Pictures and bronzes on the side where the altar is:...Christ as a pilgrim, and saint Catherine, crowned by an angel; by Taddeo Zucchero.
D 1784, 69, same as *D 1774*.
PROV: HW; 1842, Strawberry Hill Sale, day 13, lot 19, bt, J. M. Smith, £4.14.6, as Zucchero; 1843, June, John Smith, bt Archibald McLellan (1797–1854), £12, as Zucchero; 1854, Bequeathed to Glasgow Corporation by Archibald McLellan, principal founder of Glasgow Museums collection.
LIT: Glasgow Corporation/City Council *Paintings Catalogues* of 1855, 1882, 1935, 1970.
NOTE: The frame is from Strawberry Hill. The picture, identified as from Stawberry Hill, occurs in the accounts of John Smith, for Archibald McLellan, in June 1843 (Victoria and Albert Museum, MSL//1936/2572 [86.cc.3], f.4457. Information from Robert Wenley).

195. AN UNKNOWN MAN, POSSIBLY CORNELIS VAN POELENBURGH (CORNELIUS POLEMBERG, BY HIMSELF)
Artist unknown, *c.* 1630

Oil on copper, 22 × 18.5 cm
Inscriptions: On the back board (possibly by HW): 'Corn. Polemberg by himself'. .
Victoria and Albert Museum. P.105–1931, Given by Mr W. A. J. Floersheim
Fig. 84

D 1774, 99 [Tribune]: Pictures and bronzes on the side where the altar is:…Cornelius Polemberg, by himself, oval on copper; exquisitely finished like enamel, yet with great freedom. His wife, by ditto; inferior in freedom and labour. These two from sir Robert Walpole's collection.
D 1784, 69, same as *D 1774*.
PROV: Sir Robert Walpole, in 1736 in his Closet at Downing St; his sale bt HW £8.4.0 [pair with the artist's wife]; 1842, Strawberry Hill Sale, day 13, lot 57 [pair with portrait of the artist's wife], bt [Forster for] Newman Smith, Esq., £22.1.0; 1931, given by Mr W. A. J. Floersheim to Victoria and Albert Museum.
LIT: *Anecdotes*, vol 2, 105. J. J. Forster, *British Miniature Painters and Their Work* (London: S. Low, Marston & Co., 1898), Appendix A, p. 9. Larissa Dukelskaya and Andrew Moore, eds., *A Capital Collection: Houghton Hall and the Hermitage* (New Haven and London: Yale University Press, 2002), 447.
NOTE: A Principal Curiosity. Engraved by Thomas Chambars, for *Anecdotes* (vol. 2, 105). 'Thewife is stiff and Dutch; hs own is inimitable; though worked up to the tender smoothness of enamel, it has the greatest freedom of pencil, the happiest delivery of nature' (*Anecdotes*, vol. 2, 105).

196. AN UNKNOWN WOMAN (POLEMBERG'S WIFE)
Artist unknown, 1631

Oil on copper, 14.6 × 11.5 cm
Inscriptions: on the background on the left, apparently 'AEta s 23/1631'. On the back of the copper, apparently: 'The wife of / Poelenberg /by/ Poelenberg' .On the back of the wooden slip, in ink, probably by HW, 'Polenberg's wife by him'. In another hand, apparently: 'Bought at Strawberry Hill'.
Victoria and Albert Museum. Given by Mr W. A. J. Floersheim. P.104–1931.
Fig. 86

D 1774, 99 [Tribune]: Pictures and bronzes on the side where the altar is:…Cornelius Polemberg, by himself, oval on copper; exquisitely finished like enamel, yet with great freedom. His wife, by ditto; inferior in freedom and labour. These two from sir Robert Walpole's collection.
D 1784, 69, same as *D 1774*.
PROV: Sir Robert Walpole, in 1736 in his Closet at Downing St; his sale bt HW, £8.4.0 [pair with the artist's self-portrait]; 1842, Strawberry Hill Sale, day 13, lot 57, bt [Forster for] Newman Smith, Esq., £22.1.0; 1931, Given by Mr W. A. J. Florsheim to the Victoria and Albert Museum.
LIT: Larissa Dukelskaya and Andrew Moore, eds., A Capital Collection: *Houghton Hall and the Hermitage* (New Haven and London: Yale University Press, 2002), 447.

197. THE TYROLEAN GIRL
The portrait by Marianna Carlevarijs (1703–*c.* 1750) after Rosalba Carriera (1675–1757); the surround by Filippo Laura. portrait *c.* 1730

Miniature watercolour on ivory set into oil on copper, 22.9 × 17.8 cm, framed: 38.5 × 31.6 cm
Lent by the Rt Hon. the Earl of Derby, K231
Victoria and Albert Museum only
Fig. 85

D 1774, 99 [Tribune]: Pictures and bronzes on the side where the altar is:…A wreath of flowers; octagon; by Phil. Laura: in the middle, head of Rosalba's Tirolese girl, by Carlevares, a female scholar of Rosalba.
D 1784, 69 [Tribune]: Side opposite to the door:…A wreath of flowers; octagon; by Phil. Laura: in the middle, head of Rosalba's Tirolese girl, by Carlevares, a female scholar of Rosalba.
PROV: HW; 1842, Strawberry Hill Sale, day 13, lot 56, bt Earl of Derby, £10.10.0.
LIT: Sir George Scharf, *A Descriptive and Historical Catalogue of the Collection of Pictures at Knowsley Hall* (London: Bradbury, Agnew, & Co., 1875), no. 210.
NOTE: In the frame from Strawberry Hill. Rosalba's original was painted *c.* 1728.

13. ENGLAND'S VASARI

198. ANECDOTES OF PAINTING IN ENGLAND…SECOND EDITION. VOLUME 3
Horace Walpole (1717–1797)

[Strawberry Hill]: Printed by Thomas Kirgate at Strawberry-Hill, 1765
24 × 19 cm
Inscriptions: numerous manuscript notes by Horace Walpole.
The Lewis Walpole Library, Yale University. 49 2520
Fig. 156

D 1774, 51 [Library]: Curious books in the glass closet in the library… A complete set of the books printed at Strawberry-hill.
D 1784, 38, same as *D 1774*.
PROV: 1765, published by Horace Walpole at Strawberry Hill Press; 1842, Strawberry Hill Sale, day 4, lot 139, bt Boone [for Lord Derby] £33.12.0; 1953, October 20, Christie's, Knowsley Hall Sale, lot 314, bt Maggs for W. S. Lewis. £1000; The Lewis Walpole Library, Yale University.
LIT: *HW Corres.* 1: 53, 57–8, 61, 65, 14: 130, 132, 133, 15: 94, 198, 43: 47 132. *Bib. SH* no. 10. Library 2520. Mellon Lectures, xxvi, 44, 107, 142, 147, 153–4, 155, 167, 181. *Rescuing Horace*, 97–106.

199. 'PRINTING HOUSE AT STRAWBERRY HILL'
Edward Edwards (1738–1806), 1783

Etching, with hand colouring on laid paper with wash-line mount, 18.2 × 23.3 cm [visible]; 36.4 × 41.4 cm (mount)
Signed: 'E.E. 1783'. Lettered with title
Inscriptions: on verso: 'The seat of the Honle. H. Walpole, in the Parish of Twickenham, with the printer Thomas Kirgate standing in the right foreground.'
The Lewis Walpole Library, Yale University. 783.00.00.34
Fig. 359

PROV: 1939, August 2, Sotheby's, Property of a Gentleman, lot 163, bt Maggs for W. S. Lewis; The Lewis Walpole Library, Yale University.

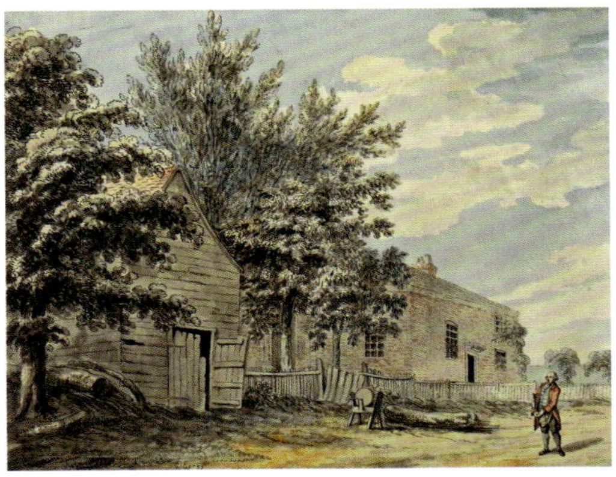

Figure 350. Catalogue 199

LIT: Bamber Gascoigne and Jonathan Ditchburn, *Images of Twickenham* (Richmond-upon-Thames: Saint Helena Press, 1981), 317.
NOTE: Thomas Kirgate (1734–1810) was HW's printer and secretary. A watercolour of the same view by an unidentified artist is at the Lewis Walpole Library. The etching reissued in 1784 with aquatint by F. Jukes as: *Farm Yard and Printing House at Strawberry Hill.*

200. DETACHED TITLE PAGE OF THE ALBUM: 'PORTRAITS OF ENGLISH PAINTERS COLLECTED BY MR. VERTUE AND MR. WALPOLE; AND RANGED ACCORDING TO THEIR ANECDOTES OF PAINTING IN ENGALND. VOL I'

Strawberry Hill Press, *c.* 1771–3
51.5 × 36.7 cm
Pasted with HW's circular bookplate as Lord Orford, printed on pink paper.
British Museum, Department of Prints and Drawings. 1852,0214.265
Fig. 168

PROV: 1771–73, printed by Horace Walpole at Strawberry Hill; 1842, Strawberry Hill Sale, day 8, lot 112 [listed]; 1842, Strawberry Hill London Sale, [part of 'Portraits of English painters collected by Mr Vertue and Mr Walpole'] day 10, lot 1270 [sold], bt Evans, £61.19.0; A. E. Evans & Sons; 1852, purchased (with others) by British Museum, London.
LIT: *Bib. SH* no. 54. Antony Griffiths, 'Walpole's Collection of Portraits', *Print Quarterly* 17, no. 3 (Sept. 2000), 290–2.

201. PORTRAIT OF AN UNKNOWN MAN (SELF-PORTRAIT BY SAMUEL COOPER)
Artist unknown, mid-17th century

Pastel, 31.5 × 26.5 × 2.5 cm [framed]
Inscriptions: on a label on the back of the frame, in HW's hand 'Samuel Cooper the famous Painter in Miniature; the only known Portrait of him, from the royal collection at Kensington palace and given to Mr Dalton (at whose auction it was bought in 1791) by King George 3. Hor. Walpole'. Another label in the hand Alexander Dyce, 'This is the portrait, which Walpole, in his description of Cooper, mentions as being in Queen Caroline's closet at Kensington and said to be by Cooper himself; but which Walpole supposes to be by Jackson, a relative of Cooper. See Anecd. of Painting in England, vol. iii. 115, ed. 1782. A. Dyce'.
Victoria and Albert Museum, London. Bequeathed by Rev. Alexander Dyce. Dyce 91
Fig. 351

D 1784, 96: More Additions… The original portrait of Samuel Cooper, the miniature painter, from the royal collection; bought at Mr. Dalton's sale.
PROV: Queen Caroline; George III; given by him to Richard Dalton, his Librarian; 1791, April, Richard Dalton Sale, bt HW, possibly lot 69 or 88; 1842, Strawberry Hill Sale, day 18, lot 166, bt Strong, Bristol, £0.19.0; [1921], Victoria and Albert Museum, London, Dyce Bequest.
LIT: *Anecdotes*, vol. 3, 115.

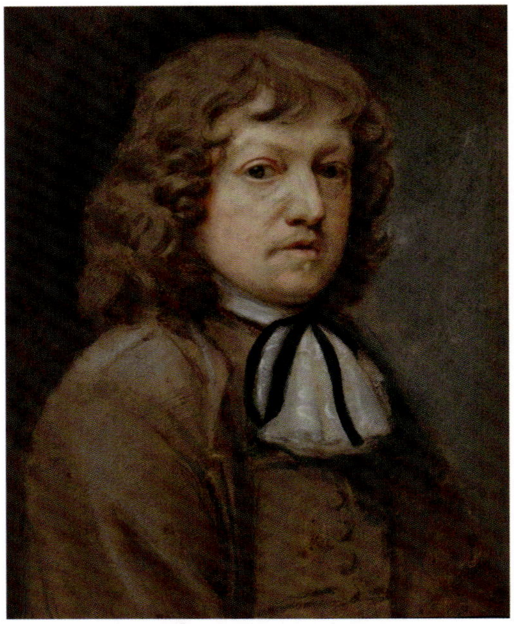

Figure 351. Catalogue 201

NOTE: The painting was engraved by Thomas Chambers for *Anecdotes*, see *Works*, vol. 3, 325. HW, writing in *Anecdotes* (*Works*, vol. 3, 327), that is before he acquired the portrait, suggests that it could be by 'one Jackson, a relation of Cooper' who had made another 'in crayons'. The engraving, however, states that it is a self-portrait.

202. PORTRAIT OF ANTON SCHOONJANS
George Vertue (1684–1756) after a self-portrait by Anton Schoonjans (1655–1726), (*c.* 1720–56?)

Red crayon with white highlights on blue paper, 14.2 cm (sheet)
Inscriptions: in George Vertue's hand at top: 'se ipse pinx'; at lower left of early mount: 'G.V.' monogram; in HW's hand: at top: 'Sevonyanse Portrait painter'; at lower left of early mount: 'now at Strawberry Hil'l; in contemporary hand in lower center of early mount: 'in poss. Mr. Judice Margate'.
The Lewis Walpole Library, Yale University.
Folio 49 3664.30
See Fig. 156

D 1774, 48 [Library]: Rare books of prints and drawings in the library…Vertue's ditto [most complete set of his works that is known, with some of his original drawings], in 2 large folios.
D 1784, 36, same as *D 1774*.
PROV: George Vertue; 1758, probably acquired by HW from the artist's widow as part of a portfolio of drawings; 1842, Strawberry Hill Sale, day 8, lot 112 [listed]; 1842, Strawberry Hill London Sale [sold], [drawing originally part of 'Portraits of English painters collected by Mr Vertue and Mr Walpole'] day 10, lot 1270, bt Evans, £61.19.0; 1949, December, James F. Drake, bt W. S. Lewis (34 drawings by Vertue), $1000; The Lewis Walpole Library, Yale University.
LIT: *Anecdotes*, vol. 3, 126. *Library* 3664.

203. PORTRAIT OF HENRY GYLES
Francis Place (1647–1728)

Red and black chalk, with watercolour, on buff paper, 31.3 × 22.7 cm
British Museum, Department of Prints and Drawings. 1852,0214.372
Inscriptions: in Thoresby's hand: 'ye efficies of Mr. Hen: Gyles the celebrated Glass-Painter at Yorke'
Fig. 167

D 1774, 48 [Library]: Rare books of prints and drawings in the library…Vertue's ditto [most complete set of his works that is known, with some of his original drawings], in 2 large folios.
D 1784, 36, same as *D 1774*.
PROV: Ralph Thoresby; George Vertue (not identified in his sales); 1758, probably acquired by Horace Walpole from his widow as part of a portfolio of drawings; 1842, Strawberry Hill Sale, day 8, lot 112 [listed]; 1842, Strawberry Hill London Sale, [drawing originally part of 'Portraits of English painters collected by Mr Vertue and Mr Walpole'] day 10, lot 1270 [sold], bt Evans, £61.19.0; A. E. Evans & Sons; 1852, purchased by The British Museum, London.
LIT: E. Croft-Murray and P. Hulton, *Catalogue of British Drawings*, vol. 1 (London, Trustees of the British Museum: 1960), 341, no. 1, pl. 138. Lindsay Stainton and Christopher White, *Drawing in England from Hilliard to Hogarth* (Cambridge, New York: Cambridge University Press, 1987), no. 137. Kim Sloan, 'A Noble Art'. *Amateur Artists and Drawing Masters c. 1600–1800* (London: British Museum Press, 2000), 36, cat. and fig. 20.

204. PORTRAIT OF GRINLING GIBBONS
John Baptist de Medina (1659–1710), *c.* 1686

Red and black chalk, heightened with white, on buff paper, 22.7 × 17.2 cm
Verso: study of a pair of legs
Signed upper right in red chalk: 'J. Medina De' and inscribed on the old mount, by George Vertue, 'J Medina Eques ad vivum delin.' and 'G Gibbons Sculptor &' [not completed]
British Museum, Department of Prints and Drawings. 1852,0214.375
Fig. 166

D 1774, 48 [Library]: Rare books of prints and drawings in the library…Vertue's ditto [most complete set of his works that is known, with some of his original drawings], in 2 large folios.
D 1784, 36, same as *D 1774*.
PROV: George Vertue (not identified in his sales); 1758, probably acquired by HW from his widow as part of a portfolio of drawings; 1842, Strawberry Hill Sale, day 8, lot 112 [listed]; 1842, Strawberry Hill London Sale, [drawing originally part of 'Portraits of English painters collected by Mr Vertue and Mr Walpole'] day 10, lot 1270 [sold], bt Evans, £61.19.0; A. E. Evans & Sons; 1852, purchased from A. E. Evans & Sons.
LIT: E. Croft-Murray and P. Hulton, *Catalogue of British Drawings*, vol. 1 (London: Trustees of the British Museum, 1960), 447, no. 1, pl. 238. *OHG* 197. Lindsay Stainton and Christopher White, *Drawing in England from Hilliard to Hogarth* (Cambridge, New York: Cambridge University Press, 1987), no. 166.

205. PORTRAIT OF THOMAS HUDSON
Jonathan Richardson, the Elder (1667–1745)

Red chalk, touched with white, on blue paper, 46.3 × 30.2 cm
Inscriptions: at bottom by HW: 'Thomas Hudson Painter/when young/drawn by Jonathan Richardson/his Master & Father in law/by Richardson's daughter/Hudson had one daughter,/who died in her childhood': on the verso by the artist: 'Mr. Tho. Hudson the Painter'.
British Museum, Department of Prints and Drawings. 1852,0214.370
Fig. 165

PROV: Jonathan Richardson Senior; Jonathan Richardson Junior; 1772, Feb. 6, Langford's, probably lot 25, bt HW; 1842, Strawberry Hill Sale, day 8, lot 112 [listed]; 1842, Strawberry Hill London Sale, [drawing originally part of 'Portraits of English painters collected by Mr Vertue and Mr Walpole'] day 10, lot 1270 [sold], bt Evans, £61.19.0; A. E. Evans & Sons; 1852, purchased by The British Museum, London.
LIT: *Thomas Hudson 1701–1779. Portrait Painter and Collector* (Kenwood: The Iveagh Bequest, 1979), cat. no. 1. Carol Gibson-Wood, *Jonathan Richardson, Art Theorist of the English Enlightenment* (New Haven and London: Yale University Press, 2000), fig. 13.

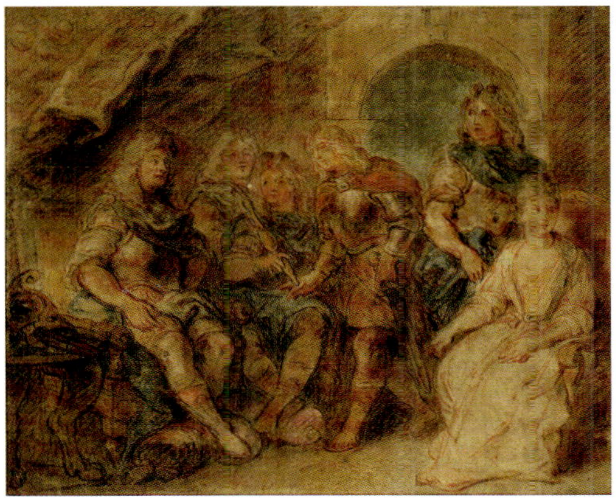

Figure 352. Catalogue 206

206. AN ALLEGORY OF LOUIS XIV (DESIGN FOR A TAPESTRY OF QUEEN ANNE'S VICTORIES)
Charles de la Fosse (1636–1716)

Coloured chalks; squared for transfer, 26.5 × 31.5 cm
Inscriptions: HW's note, on the mount, at the bottom: 'This is a curious Drawing, being a Design for a Set of Tapestry of Queen Anne's Victories, by Laguerre, in which were to have been represented the Queen, Prince Eugene, the Duke of Marlborough, and her principal Generals & Ministers. Probably the Figure on the right by the Queen was designed for Prince George, & the First on the left for the D. of Marlbourgh. See life of Louis Laguerre in 4th vol. of the Anecdotes of Painting.'
British Museum, Department of Prints and Drawings. 1962,0714.41
Fig. 352

London Sale: A folio volume of miscellaneous drawings, by various masters, ancient and modern, collected and arranged by Lord Orford, as follows: — ... Page 32 Queen Anne, and five other persons, forming a group, being a design in coloured chalks, for a series of tapestry, recording Queen Anne's victories, vide Lord Orford's note underneath. Laguerre.
PROV: HW; 1842, Strawberry Hill Sale, day 8, lot 112 [listed]; 1842, Strawberry Hill London Sale, day 10, lot 1266.32 [sold], bt Graves, Pall Mall, £53.11.0; 1962, Bequeathed by Iolo Williams to The British Museum, London.
LIT: *Anecdotes* in *Works*, vol. 3, 405.
NOTE: The drawing was formerly attributed to Louis Laguerre. HW recorded in his *Anecdotes*: 'On the union of England and Scotland he [Laguerre] was ordered by Queen Anne to make designs for a set of tapestry on that occasion, in which were to be introduced the portraits of her majesty and the principal ministers; but though he gave the drawings, the work went no further'.

14. PORTRAIT MINIATURES AND ENAMELS

207. PORTRAIT MINIATURE OF LOUIS XII
Attributed to Jean Clouet I (?1485–1540/41), after Jean Perréal, *c.* 1525–30

Watercolour on vellum, stuck on playing card, set in gilt case, D 4.1 cm
Inscriptions: engraved on verso of case: Louis XII. Holbein.
Private collection
Fig. 353

D 1774, 86 [Tribune]: Other pictures and curiosities in the same room:...Louis 12th. of France, and sir John Gage; by Holbein: in another frame. ... from the collection of lady Elizabeth Germaine.
D 1784, 61, same as *D 1774*.
PROV: 1770, Lady Elizabeth Germain Sale, by Langford, bt HW, £4.5.0; 1842, Strawberry Hill Sale, day 14, lot 94, bt Hor. Rodd, £20.0.0; 1859, Lord Northwick Sale, lot 789, bt for 5th Duke of Portland; by family descent.
LIT: Robert Goulding, 'Welbeck Abbey Miniatures', *Walpole Society* 4 (1916), no. 2.
NOTE: HW's receipt dated 1770, Mar. 10, for items bought at Lady Betty Germain's sale is at the Lewis Walpole Library, Yale University.

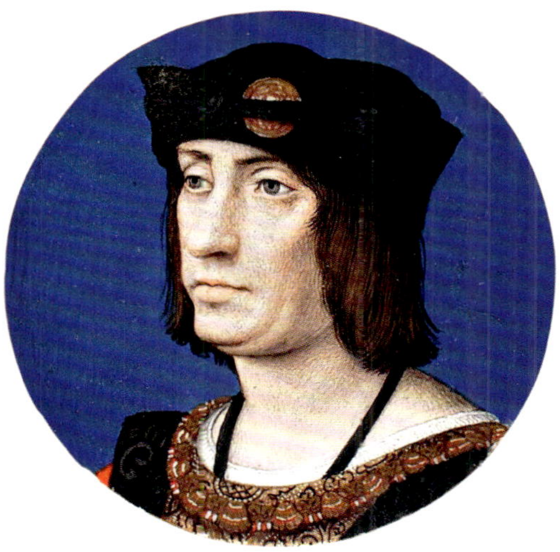

Figure 353. Catalogue 207

208. PORTRAIT MINIATURE OF KATHERINE HOWARD; (MARY TUDOR, QUEEN OF FRANCE)
Hans Holbein, the younger (1497/8–1543), 1540–1

Watercolour on vellum set in gilt metal frame, D 5.3 cm
Inscriptions: on recto: R; cartouche engraved: CATHERINE HOWARD
Trustees of the Ninth Duke of Buccleuch's Chattels Fund
Fig. 192

D 1774, 84 [Tribune]: Within the cabinet of enamels and miniatures... On the insides of the doors:...A lady, painted by Holbein; engraved by Hollar when in the Arundelian collection, and probably Mary Tudor queen of France, sister of Henry 8th. but amongst the Illustrious Heads called Catharine Howard. This was also Richardson's.
D 1784, 60, same as *D 1774*.
PROV: Thomas Howard, 2nd Earl of Arundel Collection; Jonathan Richardson, the younger; HW; 1842, Strawberry Hill Sale, day 14, lot 68, bt Conningham, Esq., £26.5.0; Walter Francis, 5th Duke of Buccleuch and 7th Duke of Queensberry (frame c4, later 1/4); by family descent.
LIT: Lionel Cust, 'A Portrait of Queen Catherine Howard, by Hans Holbein the Younger', *The Burlington Magazine* 17, no. 8 (July 1910), 1. H. A. Kennedy, *Early English Miniatures in the Collection*

of the Duke of Buccleuch (London: The Studio Ltd, 1917), 3, pl. 2a. *HW Corres.* 40: 365–6. Roy Strong, *The English Renaissance Miniature* (London and New York: Thames and Hudson, 1983), 47, 49, fig. 49. John Rowlands, *The Paintings of Hans Holbein the younger: Complete Edition* (Oxford: Phaidon, 1985), no. M7, 151 and 132. Stephen Lloyd, *Portrait Miniatures from the Collection of the Duke of Buccleuch* (Edinburgh: The Trustees of the National Galleries of Scotland, 1996), 38–9, cat. 9, pl. 8. S. Doran, ed., *Henry VIII: Man and Monarch* (London: British Library, 2009), 228, no. 224.

EXHIB: South Kensington Museum, 'Loan Exhibition', 1862, nos. 2029–30; Royal Academy of Arts, 'Old Masters', 1879, case 1, no. 3.

209. A Treatise Concerning the Arte of Limning
After Nicholas Hilliard (1547?-1619), copy made in 1624 (after lost original of *c.* 1600)

Manuscript, pen and ink on paper, H 33 cm
With HW's bookplate
Inscriptions: in HW's hand in pen and ink on inside cover: B.9 / of Limning / writ by NHilliard; / bought of the Widow /of / Mr George Vertue / Engraver; / Aug. 22d.1758.
Edinburgh University Library. Laing MSS, La.III.174.
Fig. 218

1842 Sale [Library]: A small folio manuscript, bound, a Treatise concerning the Art of Limning Writ, by Hilliard (the celebrated miniature painter), at the request of R. Haydocke, very interesting and curious to the lovers of the arts of England.

PROV: George Vertue; his widow, before 1757; 1757, purchased from her by HW; 1842, Strawberry Hill Sale, day 6, lot 122, bt Thorpe, £1.10.0; 1842, owned by Patrick Fraser Tytler; 1878, David Laing bequest to Edinburgh University Library.

LIT: *Anecdotes*, vol. 1, 150. P. Norman, ed., 'Nicholas Hilliard's Treatise concerning 'The Arte of Limning', with Introduction and Notes by Philip Norman, LL.D.', *The Walpole Society* 1 (1911–12). Library 2560. R. C. Strong and V. J. Murrell, *Artists of the Tudor Court: the Portrait Miniature Rediscovered 1520–1620* (exh. cat. London: Victoria and Albert Museum, 1983), 31–2, no. IX. *Nicholas Hilliard, A Treatise Concerning the Arte of Limning by Nicholas Hilliard*, ed., R. K. R. Thornton and T. G. S. Cain (Ashington: Carcanet Press, 1992).

210. Portrait Miniature of Sir Francis Drake
Studio of Nicholas Hilliard (1547?–1619), 1581

Watercolour on vellum set in circular pearwood frame, D 2.8 cm
Inscriptions: on recto: 'AEtatis Suae 42. Ano Dni: 1581'; in pen and ink on verso: 'Franciscus Drake Miles'
National Portrait Gallery, London. Purchased with help from the Wolfson Foundation and H. M. Government, 1971. 4851
Fig. 194

D 1774, 45 [Library]: Sir Francis Drake: ditto [a miniature], by Hilliard.

D 1784, 34, same as *D 1774*.

PROV: HW; 1842, Strawberry Hill Sale, day 20, lot 5, bt 13th Earl of Derby, £21.0.0; by family descent; 1971, June 8, Christie's, 18th Earl of Derby Sale, bt National Portrait Gallery, purchased with the help from the Wolfson Foundation and H. M. Government.

LIT: Erna Auerbach, *Nicholas Hilliard* (London: Routledge & Paul, 1961), 84, pl. 48. David Piper, *The English Face* (London: National Portrait Gallery, 1992), 57. Richard Walker, *Miniatures: 300 years of the English Miniature Illustrated from the Collections of the National Portrait Gallery* (London: National Portrait Gallery, 1998), 20. Charles Nicholl, *Shakespeare and His Contemporaries* (London: National Portrait Gallery, 2005), 27.

EXHIB: South Kensington Museum, 'Loan Exhibition', 1862, no. 2226; S. Redgrave, ed., *Catalogue of the Special Exhibition of Portrait Miniatures* (exh. cat. London: South Kensington Museum, 1865), no. 1817. Burlington Fine Arts Club, London, England, 'Exhibition of Portrait Miniatures', 1889, case XX, no. 6.

211. Portrait Miniature of Unknown Lady (Frances Howard, Countess of Essex and Somerset)
Isaac Oliver (*c.* 1565–1617), *c.* 1595

Watercolour on vellum, stuck on plain card, D 13 cm
Inscriptions: signed on recto with monogram: 'IO'; in HW's hand on verso label: 'The Lady Frances Howard Countess of Essex and Somerset, by Isaac Oliver; from the collection of James West, president of the Royal Society. H. W. 1773'.
Victoria and Albert Museum, London. Purchased with the assistance of The Art Fund and the Pilgrim Trust. P.12–1971
Fig. 191

D 1774, 98 [Tribune]: Side opposite to the door:... Frances Howard, the famous countess of Essex and Somerset ; by Isaac Oliver: from Mr. West's collection.

D 1784, 68, same as *D 1774*.

PROV: 1773, February 27, Langford's, Sale of the Collection of James West, lot 74; bt Morgan, £3.17.6; bt HW; 1842, Strawberry Hill Sale, day 13, lot 52, bt 13th Earl of Derby, £18.18.0; by family descent; 1971, June 8, Christie's, 18th Earl of Derby Sale, lot 80; Victoria and Albert Museum, Purchased with the assistance of The Art Fund and the Pilgrim Trust.

LIT: D. Foskett, *British Portrait Miniatures: a History* (London, Methuen & Co. Ltd, 1963), 52, no. 18. D. Foskett, *British Portrait Miniatures* (Edinburgh: The Scottish Arts Council Gallery, 1965), no. 30. R. C. Strong, *Tudor & Jacobean portraits...* (London, HMSO, 1969), 298. G. Reynolds, *Nicholas Hilliard and Isaac Oliver* (London: Victoria and Albert Museum, 1971), no. 146. R. C. Strong and V. J. Murrell, *Artists of the Tudor Court: the Portrait Miniature Rediscovered 1520–1620* (exh. cat. London: Victoria and Albert Museum, 1983), 163, no. 27.

EXHIB: South Kensington Museum, 'Loan Exhibition', 1862, no. 2231. S. Redgrave, ed., *Catalogue of the Special Exhibition of Portrait Miniatures...* (exh. cat. London: South Kensington Museum, 1865), no. 1811. G. Scharf, *A Catalogue of the Collection of Pictures at Knowsley Hall* (London, 1875), no. 234. J. L. Propert, *Exhibition of Portrait Miniatures* (exh. cat. London: Burlington Fine Arts Club, 1889), 11, case no. III, no. 46, pl. V. New Gallery, 1890, no. 1141.

NOTE: Stipple engraving by G. P. Harding, 'Frances Howard, Countess of Essex & Somerset. From a Picture the same Size, by Isaac Oliver at Strawberry Hill', n.d. mounted in *D 1784*.

212. Portrait Miniature of Queen Henrietta Maria
David des Granges (bap. 1611, d. in or before 1672?), after *c.* 1636

Watercolour on vellum stuck onto gesso-backed card, 8.1 × 6.9 cm
Inscriptions: engraved on reverse: Henrietta Maria/ Queen of Charles 1st/ John Hoskins?.
Inscribed on a label: No. 1 case/2nd Right hand; 84; 131m/7139
Yale Center for British Art, Paul Mellon Collection. B1974.2.62
Fig. 354

D 1774, 29 [Green Closet]: Queen Henrietta Maria; by Dixon.
D 1784, 24, same as *D 1774*.
PROV: HW, £1.11.6; 1842, Strawberry Hill Sale, day 18, lot 122, bt 13th Earl of Derby, £6.6.0; by family descent; 1971, June 8, Christie's, 18th Earl of Derby Sale, lot 84, bt Fry, for Yale Center for British Art.
LIT: Patrick J. Noon, *English Portrait Drawings and Miniatures* (New Haven: Yale Center for British Art, 1979), no. 6.
EXHIB: South Kensington Museum, 'Loan Exhibition', 1862, no. 2225. S. Redgrave, ed., *Catalogue of the Special Exhibition of Portrait Miniatures*… (exh. cat. London: South Kensington Museum, 1865), no. 1816. J. L. Propert, ed., *Exhibition of Portrait Miniatures* (exh. cat. London: Burlington Fine Arts Club, 1889), case XX, no. 5.
NOTE: Formerly attributed to John Hoskins (*c.* 1590–1665), follower of Sir Anthony Van Dyck (1599–1641),

213. Portrait Miniature of Lady Lucy Percy
Peter Oliver (1589–1647), *c.* 1620

Watercolour on vellum set in gilt-metal frame, H 7.3 cm
Wingfield Digby collection, Sherborne Castle
Fig. 197

D 1774, 23–4 [Blue Breakfast Room]: Lady Lucy Percy, daughter and coheiress of Thomas earl of Northumberland who was beheaded, wife of sir Edward Stanley, younger son of the earl of Derby, mother of Venetia lady Digby; by Isaac Oliver. She is still more beautiful than her daughter, though drest very unbecomingly in a great black hat and large ruff; only set off by a lilac ground. This is perhaps the finest and most perfect miniature in the world. All the seven last are wonderfully preserved, though found in a garret in an old house in Wales, belonging to a Mr. Watkin Williams, probably descended from Sir Kenelm, one of whose sons left only two daughters that were married into Welch families. This set of pictures cost Mr. Walpole 300 guineas.
D 1784, 18, same as *D 1774*.
PROV: Watkin Williams; bt HW, 1771 (nine framed Digby miniatures, £300) or 1775; 1842, Strawberry Hill Sale, day 11, lot 31, bt Rodd for Robert Holford, Esq., £105.0.0; the Digby family; by family descent.
LIT: *Anecdotes*, *Works*, vol. 3, 131. Basil S. Long, *British Miniaturists* (London: Holland Press, 1966), 320–3.

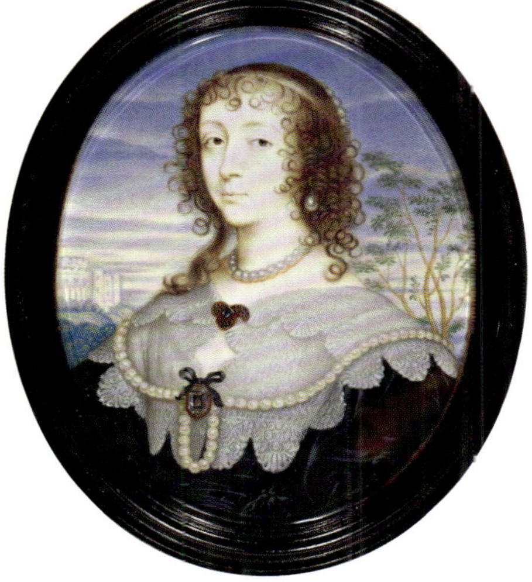

Figure 354. Catalogue 212

EXHIB: S. Redgrave, ed., *Catalogue of the Special Exhibition of Portrait Miniatures* (exh. cat. London: South Kensington Museum, 1865), no. 2174 J. L. Propert, *Exhibition of Portrait Miniatures* (exh. cat. London: Burlington Fine Arts Club, 1889), 27, no. 3, pl. VIIc.
NOTE: A Principal Curiosity. Concerning the Digby miniatures, HW noted in the *Anecdotes* (Works, vol. 3, p. 156) 'The latest are dated 1633, but being enclosed in ivory and ebony cases, and the whole collection locked up in a wainscot box, they are as perfectly preserved as if newly painted. They all represent Sir Kenelm and persons related to or connected with him. There are three portraits of himself, six of his beloved wife at different ages, and three triplicates of his mistress, all three by Isaac Oliver, as is Lady Digby's mother…. But the capital work is a large miniature copied from Vandyke, of sir Kenelm, his wife and two sons, the most beautiful piece of this size that I believe exists….' The 14 or 15 miniatures were bought in two groups from two owners, nine in 1771 for £300, and the remainder in 1775, for an unknown price. The last purchase included cat. 216. (*HW Corres.* 28: 180.)

214. Portrait Miniature of Sir Kenelm Digby
Peter Oliver (1589–1647), 1627

Watercolour on vellum, set in an early 20th century pearwood frame, H 7 cm
Signed in gold on recto: P. Oliver F 1627
National Portrait Gallery, London. Transferred from National Gallery (Alan Evans Bequest), 1994. 6274
Fig. 203

D 1774, 23 [Blue Breakfast Room] See Cat. 213 [Lady Lucy Percy] and: Sir Kenelm Digby, when young; by Peter Oliver: very fine.
D 1784, 18, same as *D 1774*.
PROV: See Cat. 213; and 1842, Strawberry Hill Sale, day 11, lot 29, bt Miss Burdett-Coutts, £25.4.0; Baroness Burdett-Coutts; 1974, Alan Evans Bequest, to National Gallery; 1994, Transferred to National Portrait Gallery, London.
LIT: *HW Corres.* 1: 358n 2: 43n, 28: 180, 32: 165. A. Sumner, ed., *Death, Passion and Politics: Van Dyck's Portraits of Venetia Stanley and George Digby* (London: Dulwich Picture Gallery, 1995), 100, no. 26, fig. 1.
NOTE: A Principal Curiosity.

215. Portrait Miniatures of Sir Kenelm and Lady Venetia Digby
Peter Oliver (1589–1647), after Sir Anthony Van Dyck (1599–1641), 1632

Watercolour on vellum set in an enamelled gold diptych frame, H 8.8 cm (each miniature); 9.6 × 14.7 cm (frame)
Inscriptions: on recto of Sir Kenelm Digby: Vindica te tibi; on recto of Lady Venetia Digby: The La: Ve Digby A:D 1632. AET: 32
Wingfield Digby collection, Sherborne Castle
Figs. 204, 205

D 1774, 23 [Blue Breakfast Room] See preceding entry [Lady Lucy Percy] and: Sir Kenelm Digby and lady Digby, after Vandyck; by ditto [Peter Oliver]: set in the form of a book with covers of gold enamelled.
D 1784, 18, same as *D 1774*.
PROV: See Cat. 213; and 1842, Strawberry Hill Sale, day 11, lot 24, bt Robert Holford, Esq., £178.10.0; the Digby family, Sherborne Castle; by family descent.
LIT: *HW Corres.* 1. 358n 2: 43n, 23: 267, 28: 180, 42: 252–3. O. Millar, ed., *The Age of Charles I: Painting in England 1620–1649* (London: Tate Gallery, 1972), no. 188. G. Reynolds, *English Portrait Miniatures* (Cambridge: Cambridge University Press, 1988), 33. A. Sumner, ed., *Death, Passion and Politics: Van Dyck's Portraits of Venetia Stanley and George Digby* (London: Dulwich Picture Gallery, 1995), 104, no. 33, pl. XII.
EXHIB: S. Redgrave, ed., *Catalogue of the Special Exhibition of Portrait Miniatures* (exh. cat. London: South Kensington Museum, 1865), no. 2172–3; J. L. Propert, ed., *Exhibition of Portrait Miniatures* (exh. cat. London: Burlington Fine Arts Club, 1889), 'Exhibition of Portrait Miniatures', 1889, Case V, ill. pl. VII.
NOTE: A Principal Curiosity.

216. Portrait Miniatures of Sir Kenelm and Lady Venetia Digby, and Their Sons Kenelm and John, with Two Portraits of Lady Venetia Digby and 'Lady Arabella Stuart'
The main portrait by Peter Oliver (1589–1647), after Sir Anthony Van Dyck (1599–1641), 1635. The other portraits by Peter Oliver.

Three miniatures in watercolour on vellum, set inside an ebony veneered 17th or early 18th century case with inner gilt slips (18th and 19th century) and silver keyhole plates with HW's crest. The outsides of the closing doors set by HW with one antique cameo and 18 other cameos, by James

Tassie and Wedgwood of classical subjects and one showing Sir Robert Walpole. 15.5 × 24.6 cm
Inscriptions: in gold lettering above central miniature: 'FROM STRAWBERRY HILL. / Sir Horace Walpole's Collection; in gold lettering below main image: THE DIGBY FAMILY / - BY - / Peter Oliver.'; in gold lettering below left-hand oval miniature: 'LADY ARABELLA STUART / -BY - / Isaac Oliver.'; in gold lettering below right-hand oval miniature: 'LADY VENETIA DIGBY / - by – / LADY VENETIA DIGBY / - BY - / Peter Oliver'. On the back of the case a label inscribed by HW: 'Sir Kenelm Digby, Lady Venetia [?], his wife and their two sons, after Vandyck HW'.
Nationalmuseum, Stockholm. NMB 969. Bequest 1927 of consul Hjalmar Wicander (The Wicander Collection)
Fig. 201

D 1774, 126 [Blue Breakfast Room]: Appendix…In the Breakfast-Room…Sir Kenelm Digby, his wife and two sons, by Peter Oliver, after Vandyck; a large miniature in the highest preservation; in an ebony case set with Wedgwood's cameos. On the insides of the doors, two other ladies of the same set.
D 1784, 22, same as *D 1774*.
PROV: See Cat. 213 ; 1775, bt HW; 1842, Strawberry Hill Sale, day 11, lot 56, bt Miss Burdett Coutts, £241.10; 1922, May 9–11, Christie's, Baroness Burdett-Coutts Sale, lot 361, bt Hjalmar Wicander, 1000gns; 1927, Wicander Collection Bequest to Nationalmuseum, Stockholm.
LIT: J. J. Foster, *Miniature painters, British and foreign, with some account of those who practised in America in the eighteenth century* (New York: E. P. Dutton & Co., 1903), vol. 1, 39. Karl Asplund, Hjalmar Wicanders Miniatursamling: Beskrifavande Katalog (Stockholm: Cederquist grafiska aktiebolag, 1920–1929), vol. 2, 65–7, no. 167, pl. 65. O. Millar, ed., *The Age of Charles I: Painting in England 1620–1649* (London: Tate Gallery, 1972), no. 187. *HW Corres.* 1: 358, 360, 23: 267, 28: 180, 41: 252–3. M. Olausson, *Europeiskt Miniatyrmåleri I Nationalmusei samlingar* (Stockholm: Streiffert, 1994), 40, fig. 15, pl. 3.
NOTE: A Principal Curiosity. For the portraits traditionally called Lady Arabella Stuart see A. Sumner, *op. cit* (LIT Cat. 214).

217. PORTRAIT MINIATURE OF VENETIA, LADY DIGBY ON HER DEATH BED
Peter Oliver (1589–1647), after Sir Anthony Van Dyck (1599–1641), after 1633

Watercolour on vellum, in an enamelled gold frame, 6.7 × 6.7 cm
Inscriptions: on recto: The La: Ve: Digby: AD 1633 AEt 32. M.4.D.12
Wingfield Digby collection, Sherborne Castle
Fig. 207

D 1774, 23 [Blue Breakfast Room] See Cat. 213 and: The same lady Digby, as she was found dead in her bed; by ditto [Peter Oliver], after ditto [Vandyck]; set in gold enamelled black; on which behind is a sphere: it seems to mean, that the world was in mourning for her. Sir Kenelm was passionately fond of this lady, who, lord Clarendon says, was of extraordinary beauty and as extraordinary fame. At Windsor is a whole length of her, by Vandyck, treading on serpents, to imply that the stories told of her were the produce of malice. At Goathurst, where they lived, are two busts of her in bronze; on the pedestal of one are inscribed these tender words, *Uxorem vivam amare voluptas defunctam religio.*
D 1784, 18, same as *D 1774*.
PROV: See Cat. 213 and; 1842, Strawberry Hill Sale, day 11, lot 28, bt Robert Holford, Esq., £52.10.0; the Digby family, Sherborne Castle; by family descent.
LIT: *HW Corres.* 1: 358n, 23: 267, 41: 252–3. O. Millar, ed., *The Age of Charles I: Painting in England 1620–1649* (London: Tate Gallery, 1972), no. 189. A. Sumner, ed., *Death, Passion and Politics: Van Dyck's Portraits of Venetia Stanley and George Digby* (London: Dulwich Picture Gallery, 1995), 104, no. 32, pl. XIII.
EXHIB: S. Redgrave, ed., *Catalogue of the Special Exhibition of Portrait Miniatures* (exh. cat. London: South Kensington Museum, 1865), no. 2166. J. L. Propert, ed., *Exhibition of Portrait Miniatures* (exh. cat. London: Burlington Fine Arts Club, 1889), 'Exhibition of Portrait Miniatures', 1889, case XIII, no. 8, ill. pl. VII.
NOTE: A Principal Curiosity.

218. PORTRAIT ENAMEL OF LADY VENETIA DIGBY
Henri Toutin (1614–aft.1683) after Peter Oliver (1589–1647), 1637

Enamel on gold set in gold and enamelled frame by Gilles Légaré, 12.5 × 8.3 cm (frame)
Inscription: around edge of frame: *Sic auferre rogis umbram centaur et ingens certamen et morte gerit curasque fatigat artificum, inque omni te quaerit amare metallo.*
The Walters Art Museum, Baltimore, Maryland. 44.177
Fig. 202

D 1774, 127 [Blue Breakfast Room] Appendix: See Cat. 216 and Appendix. In the other case, lady Digby enamelled, in a frame of the same [ebony], with her arms, and Latin mottoes, supported by two goddesses; by G. Toulin, 1637.
D 1784, 22, same as *D 1774*.
PROV: See Cat. 213 and; 1842, Strawberry Hill Sale, day 11, lot 55, bt Baroness Anselm de Rothschild, Frankfort, £37.16.0; Lady Battersea; Sir George Lindsay Holford; 1927, July 13–14, Holford Auction, Christie's, London, lot 129; Henry Walters; 1931, The Walters Art Gallery [now The Walters Art Museum] upon the death of Henry Walters.
LIT: P. Verdier, 'An Unknown Masterpiece by Henri Toutin', *Connoisseur* 162 (May 1966): no. 651, 2–7. Walters Art Gallery: *A Selection of Portrait Miniatures* (Baltimore: Walters Art Gallery, 1966), no. 26 and colour plate on front cover.
NOTE: A Principal Curiosity.

219. PORTRAIT MINIATURE OF LADY FRANCES CRANFIELD, COUNTESS OF DORSET; (A LADY OF THE FAMILY OF DIGBY)
John Hoskins, the Elder (*c.* 1590–1665), after Sir Anthony Van Dyck (1599–1641), *c.* 1637

Watercolour on vellum set in ebony-veneered wooden cabinet with silver keyhole plates with HW's crest and four Wedgwood cameos in gilt-metal settings mounted on exterior of two closing doors, 15.3 × 11.4 cm; closed cabinet: 22.2 × 17.7 × 3.3 cm; opened cabinet: 22.2 × 35.5 × 3.3 cm
Inscriptions: Gilt-metal cartouche on recto lettered in blue enamel: 'Lady Venetia Digby'; two printed labels stuck on verso of wooden backboard: 'D. of Hamilton / Hamilton Palace; envelope inside: with printed lettering: 'Montagu / House / Whitehall / S.W.'; envelope inscribed in pen and ink: 'Wedgwood / Plaque / Fell out / 15 June 90 / HS'
Trustees of the Ninth Duke of Buccleuch's Chattels Fund
Figs. 206, 208

D 1774, 126 [Blue Breakfast Room] Appendix: See Cat. 216 and Appendix: Two other ebony cases, ditto [set with Wedgwood's cameos]. In one, a lady of the Digby family, half-length, after Vandyck, with a beautiful landscape, by Peter Oliver.
D 1784, 22, same as *D 1774*.
PROV: See Cat. 213; 1842, Strawberry Hill Sale, day 11, lot 54 (as by Peter Oliver after Van Dyck, 'a lady of the Digby family'), bt Lord Northwick, £22.1.0; 1859, August 3, Christie's, Thirlestaine House, Cheltenham Lord Northwick Sale, lot 805, bt for the Duke of Hamilton; 1882, July 15, Hamilton Palace Sale, day 13, lot 1608, bt P. & D. Colnaghi and Co., £294; sold to Walter Francis, 5th Duke of Buccleuch and 7th Duke of Queensberry; by family descent
LIT: A. McKay, *Catalogue of the Miniatures in Montagu House belonging to the Duke of Buccleuch* (London, 1899), 176 ('in the cabinet at the East End of the West Drawing Room'). *One Hundred Miniatures from the Collection lent by the Duke of Buccleuch, with a Brief Guide to the Collection* (London: Victoria and Albert Museum, 1918), 3rd edn, case 15A. *HW Corres.* 1: 358n, 23: 267, 41: 252–3. John Murdoch, Jim Murrell, Patrick J. Noon and Roy Strong, *The English Miniature* (New Haven and London: Yale University Press, 1981), 101, pl. 114. Stephen Lloyd, *Portrait Miniatures from the Collection of the Duke of Buccleuch* (Edinburgh: The Trustees of the National Galleries of Scotland, 1996), cat. 33.

220. PORTRAIT MINIATURE OF MARY FAIRFAX, DUCHESS OF BUCKINGHAM
Samuel Cooper (1607/8–1672), *c.* 1657

Watercolour on vellum, set in gilt-metal frame, H 6.2 cm
Inscriptions: Signed with monogram on recto: SC; engraved on gilt-metal cartouche: LADY MARY FAIRFAX; scratched into metal on verso: Mary Fairfax / Duchess of Buckingham / by S Cooper / from Strawberry Hill
The Trustees of the Ninth Duke of Buccleuch's Chattels Fund.
Fig. 195

D 1774, 45 [Library]: Mary, sole daughter and heiress of Thomas lord Fairfax, wife of George Villiers second duke of Buckingham: ditto [a miniature], by Cooper.
D 1784, 34, same as *D 1774*.
PROV: HW; 1842, Strawberry Hill Sale, day 20, lot 8, bt Hor. Rodd, £5.5.0; Lord Northwick; 1859, August 3, Christie's, Thirlestaine House, Cheltenham Lord Northwick Sale, lot 732; Walter Francis, 5th Duke of Buccleuch and 7th Duke of Queensberry; by family descent.
LIT: A. McKay, *Catalogue of the Miniatures in Montagu House belonging to the Duke of Buccleuch* (London, 1899), 88, frame N18. Diane Foskett, *Samuel Cooper, 1609–1672* (London: Faber and Faber, 1974), 121. Stephen Lloyd, *Portrait Miniatures from the Collection of the Duke of Buccleuch* (Edinburgh: The Trustees of the National Galleries of Scotland, 1996), 85, cat. 45.
EXHIB: *1862 Special Exhibition*, no. 2050.
NOTE: Stipple engraving by S. Harding (del.) and I. Claessens (sculp.) published by E. & S. Harding, Pall Mall, London, 1793, Jan. 7, 'Dutchess of Buckingham. From an Original Picture by Cooper in the Collection of the Right Honourable the Earl of Orford Strawberry Hill', mounted in an extra-illustrated *D 1784*, fol. 85r, Lewis Walpole Library 33 30 copy 4.

221. PORTRAIT MINIATURE OF LADY PENELOPE COMPTON, WIFE OF SIR EDWARD NICHOLAS
Samuel Cooper (1607/8–1672)

Watercolour on vellum set in gilt-metal frame, H 8.9 cm
Inscriptions: Scratched on metal verso: Lady Penelope Compton / by S Cooper / from Strawberry Hill
The Trustees of the Ninth Duke of Buccleuch's Chattels Fund
Fig. 209

D 1774, 45 [Library]: Lady Penelope Compton, daughter of Spencer earl of Northampton, and wife of sir Edward Nicholas, secretary of state; by Cooper.
D 1784, 34, same as *D 1774*.
PROV: HW; 1842, Strawberry Hill Sale, day 14, lot 9, bt Hor. Rodd, £3.0.0; Walter Francis, 5th Duke of Buccleuch and 7th Duke of Queensberry; by family descent
LIT: A. McKay, *Catalogue of the Miniatures in Montagu House belonging to the Duke of Buccleuch* (London, 1899), 86, frame N9. H. A. Kennedy, *Early English Portrait Miniatures in the Collection of the Duke of Buccleuch* (London: The Studio Ltd, 1917), pl. 37.

222. PORTRAIT ENAMEL OF ANNE OF AUSTRIA, QUEEN OF LOUIS XIII
Jean Petitot I (1607–1691), *c.* 1660
Enamel on gold (unframed), 2.5 × 2.1 cm
Nationalmuseum, Stockholm. NMB 994. Bequest 1927 of consul Hjalmar Wicander (The Wicander Collection).

D 1774, 82 [Tribune]: Within the cabinet of enamels and miniatures:...Louis 14th: Mary of Austria, his queen: Anne of Austria, his mother, very delicate: madame de Montespan, his mistress, beautiful. These four are small heads in enamel, by Petitot.
D 1784, 59, same as *D 1774*.
PROV: HW; 1842, Strawberry Hill Sale, day 14, lot 55, bt J. M. Smith, £44.2.0; English collector; Bukowskis, Stockholm; bt Consul Hjalmar Wicander; 1927, Wicander's Collection Bequest to Nationalmuseum, Stockholm.
LIT: Karl Asplund, *Hjalmar Wicanders Miniatursamling: Beskrivande Katalog* (Stockholm: Cederquist grafiska aktiebolag, 1920–9), vol 2, 48 no. 123, pl. 46.

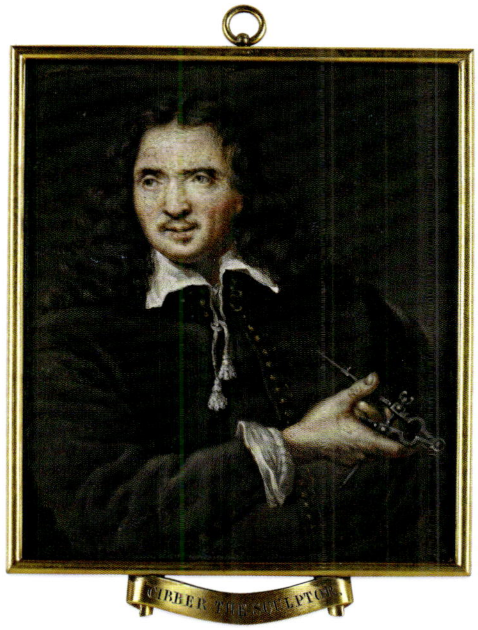

Figure 355. Catalogue 225

223. PORTRAIT ENAMEL OF THE MARQUISE DE MONTESPAN
Jean Petitot I (1607–1691)

Enamel on gold (unframed), 2.6 × 2.2 cm
Nationalmuseum, Stockholm, NMB 993. Bequest 1927 of consul Hjalmar Wicander (The Wicander Collection)

D 1774, 82 [Tribune]: Within the cabinet of enamels and miniatures:...Louis 14th: Mary of Austria, his queen: Anne of Austria, his mother, very delicate: madame de Montespan, his mistress, beautiful. These four are small heads in enamel, by Petitot.
D 1784, 59, same as *D 1774*.
PROV: 1745, Aug. 1, bt HW, £7.7; 1842, Strawberry Hill Sale, day 14, lot 57, bt J. M. Smith, £16.16.0; 1921, Bukowskis, Stockholm; bt Consul Hjalmar Wicander; 1927, Wicander Collection Bequest to Nationalmuseum, Stockholm.
LIT: Karl Asplund, *Hjalmar Wicanders Miniatursamling: Beskrivande Katalog* (Stockholm: Cederquist grafiska aktiebolag, 1920–1929), vol. 2, 48, no. 124, pl. 46.
NOTE: HW receipt dated 1745, Aug. 1, for payment of £7.7 for Petitot's miniature of Madame Montespan is at the Lewis Walpole Library, Yale University.

224. PORTRAIT MINIATURE OF LADY ELIZABETH WRIOTHESLEY, COUNTESS OF NORTHUMBERLAND, LATER DUCHESS OF MONTAGU; (ELIZABETH WRIOTHESLEY, COUNTESS OF SOUTHAMPTON)
Charles Beale (1660–d. 1726?) after Sir Peter Lely (1618–1680), *c.* 1680

Watercolour on vellum, rectangular, set in black wood frame with gilt slip, H 15.7 cm
Inscriptions: Signed on recto with monogram: 'CB'; inscribed on verso: 'Lady Elizabeth Wrotetsley / Daughter of Thomas Earl of Southampton, / first wife of ... last Earl of Northumberland / and second Wife of Ralph Duke of Montagu'.
Private collection, courtesy of Robert Holden Ltd, London
Fig. 154

D 1774, 124 [Beauty Room/Yellow Bedchamber]: Appendix...In the Yellow Bedchamber, or Beauty-Room...Elizabeth Wriothesly countess of Southampton, and afterwards first wife of Ralph the first duke of Montagu, by ditto [Charles Beale], after ditto [Peter Lely]. These three are in water- colours.
D 1784, 16, same as *D 1774*.
PROV: HW; 1842, Strawberry Hill Sale, day 22, lot 59, bt Viscount Holmesdale, £7.0.0; The David Craig Collection, London; The L. H. Gilbert Collection, Lisbon; 1963, December 3, Christie's, lot 1; The Léo R. Shidlof Collection, Vienna; 1996, June, offered to the Lewis Walpole Library by Gertrud Rudigier, Kunsthandel, Munich; 1999, April 28, Knightsbridge, Bonhams, lot 195; Private collection.
LIT: L. R. Schidlof, *The Miniature in Europe in the 16th, 17th, 18th and 19th Centuries* (Graz: Akademische Druck – u. Verlagsanstalt, 1964), III, pl. 41, fig.71.

225. PORTRAIT MINIATURE OF CAIUS GABRIEL CIBBER
Christian Richter (1678–1732), *c.* 1700

Watercolour on vellum, 9.1 × 7.8 cm (visible), 10.5 × 8 cm (frame)
Inscriptions: in HW's hand in pen and ink on verso: Cibber the Statuary father of the Player
Trustees of the Ninth Duke of Buccleuch's Chattels Fund.
Fig. 225

D 1774, 29 [Green Closet]: Cibber the statuary, with a pair of compasses in his hand, in water-colours; by Christian Richter.
D 1784, 23, same as *D 1774*.
PROV: HW; 1842, Strawberry Hill Sale, day 18, lot 129, bt Rev. John Mitford, £1.10.0; Walter Francis, 5th Duke of Buccleuch and 7th Duke of Queensberry; by family descent.
LIT: A. McKay, *Catalogue of the Miniatures in Montagu House belonging to the Duke of Buccleuch* (London, 1899), 93–4, frame O17. H. A. Kennedy, *Early English Miniatures in the Collection of the Duke of Buccleuch* (London: The Studio Ltd, 1917), fig. 52c ('perhaps by Charles Beale').
NOTE: Alexander Bannerman made an engraving, in reverse, after this miniature for *Anecdotes* (vol. 3, 80).

226. Portrait Enamel of an Unknown Youth; (Abraham Cowley)
Christian Friedrich Zincke (1684?–1767) after Sir Peter Lely (1618–1680), 1716

Enamel on copper, 6.8 × 5.4 cm
Inscriptions: signed and dated on verso: CF Zincke, Fecit 1716
Lent by the Syndics of the Fitzwilliam Museum, Cambridge.
Fig. 216

D 1774, 82 [Tribune]: Within the cabinet of enamels and miniatures:…Cowley, the poet, after sir Peter Lely; by Zincke; his master-piece, and perhaps the finest piece of enamel in the world. It was engraved for Mr. Hurd's edition of Cowley.
D 1784, 59, same as *D 1774*.
prov: 1772, Edward Lovibond Sale, bt HW, 1842, Strawberry Hill Sale, day 14, lot 51 (as a miniature of Cowley), bt Robert Holford, Esq., £63.0.0; Sir George Lindsay Holford; 1927, July 14, Christie's, Sir George Lindsay Holford Sale, lot 128; 1949, February 16, Christie's, Harry Seal Sale, lot 130, bt Friends of the Fitzwilliam Museum; Fitzwilliam Museum.
lit: *HW Corres.* 18: 347n, 22: 523, 32: 294, 33: 110. *Treasures of Cambridge* (exh. cat. London: Worshipful Company of Goldsmiths, 1959), no. 347. *OHG* 133. Bayne-Powell, *Catalogue of Portrait Miniatures in the Fitzwilliam Museum* (Cambridge: Cambridge University Press, 1985), 212–13.
exhib: *1862 Special Exhibition*, no. 2468; J. L. Propert, ed., *Exhibition of Portrait Miniatures* (exh. cat. London: Burlington Fine Arts Club, 1889), 'Portrait Miniatures', Burlington Fine Arts Club, 1889, Case XXV, no. 9.
note: A Principal Curiosity. The Lely original also owned by HW and now at Dulwhich Picture Gallery, was also a Principle Curiosity. The miniature was engraved as Portrait of Abraham Cowley, with an inscription in the plate: 'Drawn & engraved by John Hall from an Original Picture painted by Zinck in Enamel, in the Collection of the Honble Horace Walpole'. The print was published as the frontispiece in *Select Works of Mr A. Cowley* second edition (London: R. Cadell, 1772.

227. Portrait Miniature of Alexander Pope
Andrew Benjamin Lens (*c.* 1713–*c.* 1779), *c.* 1744

Watercolour on ivory, set in gilt-metal frame, d 6.1 cm
Inscriptions: signed on recto in monogram: ABL; engraved on cartouche: ALEXANDER POPE
Trustees of the Ninth Duke of Buccleuch's Chattels Fund

D 1774, 32 [Green Closet]: At the end fronting the window:…Mr. Pope, by young Lens, in water-colours; round.
D 1784, 25, same as *D 1774*.
prov: HW; 1842, Strawberry Hill Sale, day 11, lot 49, bt P. and Dom. Colnaghi, £4.4.0; Walter Francis, 5th Duke of Buccleuch and 7th Duke of Queensberry; by family descent.
lit: A. McKay, *Catalogue of the Miniatures in Montagu House belonging to the Duke of Buccleuch* (London, 1899), 113–14, frame Q27. H. A. Kennedy, *Early English Miniatures in the Collection of the Duke of Buccleuch* (London: The Studio Ltd, 1917), 26, fig. 51a.

15. CERAMICS, GLASS AND ENAMELS

228. Covered Cup on a high foot with Scenes from the Life of Samson
French, Limoges, by Jean Pénicaud II (fl. *c.* 1534–49), 1539

Painted enamel on copper, *en grisaille* with flesh tones and under the cover in gold *en camaïeu*, with gilding, h 13.3 cm
Signed in gold beneath the foot: 'Johannes Penicaudi Junior 1539'
Victoria and Albert Museum, London, Salting Bequest. C.2460–a-b-1910
Fig. 229

D 1774, 15 [China Room]: A very fine standing cup and cover, enamelled on copper with the story of Sampson, from the designs of Parmegiano.
D 1784, 10, same as *D 1774*.
prov: HW, paid £10.10.0; 1842, Strawberry Hill Sale, day 12, lot 59, bt Hume, Berners Street, £44.2.0; William Beckford (1760–1844), Bath; by descent to Duke of Hamilton, Hamilton Palace, Scotland; 1882, July 4, Christie's, Hamilton Palace Collection Sale, lot 966, bt T. M. Whitehead, £2100; 1898, May 10, Christie's, Collection of T. M. Whitehead, Esq., lot 83, bt Durlacher, £1600; 1910, bequeathed to the Victoria and Albert Museum by George Salting.
lit: Philip Hewat-Jaboor, et al. ed. Derek E. Ostergard, *William Beckford, 1760–1844: An Eye for the Magnificent* (New Haven and London: Yale University Press, 2001), no. 99 (cat. entry by Fabienne Audebrand). H. P. Mitchell, 'The Limoges Enamels in the Salting Collection', *Burlington Magazine* 20, no. 104 (Nov. 1911), 77–9, 82–5, 89. Bet McLeod, 'Some Further Objects from William Beckford's Collection at the Victoria and Albert Museum', *Burlington Magazine* 143 (June 2001), 367–70.
exhib: *1862 Special Exhibition*, no. 1676.
note: Fabienne Audebrand notes that there is restoration, but the signature was already present at the time of the 1842 sale and is likely to be original.

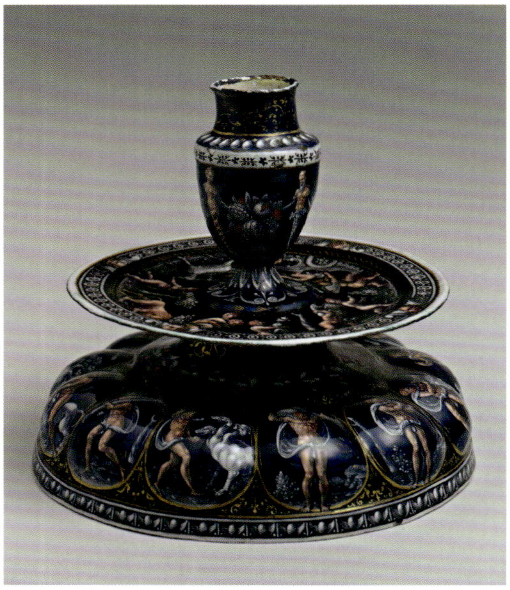

Figure 356. Catalogue 229

229. Candlestick with Medallions Depicting the Labors of Hercules
French, Limoges, *c.* 1560–80

Painted enamel on copper, h 16.4 cm
Signed 'IC' (possibly Jean Court)
Lent by The Metropolitan Museum of Art, Gift of Ann Payne Blumenthal, 1939 (39.66.1)
Fig. 356

1842 Sale [China Room]: A fine old candlestick, with beautiful medallions representing the Labour of Hercules and groups of Bacchanalians, in the finest taste.
prov: HW; 1842, Strawberry Hill Sale, day 12, lot 60, bt Webb, Old Bond Street, £26.5.0; Hollingworth Magniac, Colworth, Bedfordshire, who united it with a very similar one, now also Metropolitan Museum of Art, 39.66.2; Magniac Sale, Christie's (1892, 2–14 July), lot 245, bt Durlacher, 1250gns for the pair); Edward Steinkopff, London; 1935, May 22, Steinkopff Sale, Christie's, London lot 38; 1939, Metropolitan Museum of Art, Gift of Ann Payne Blumenthal.
lit: J. C. Robinson, *Notices of the Principal Works of Art in the Collection of Hollingworth Magniac, Esq.* (London 1861), no. 118/119. J. G. Phillips, 'Two Limoges Candlesticks', *The Metropolitan Museum of Art Bulletin* 34 (6 June 1939): 138–40. I. Wardropper, 'The Flourishing of the French Renaissance,' *Metropolitan Museum of Art Bulletin* (Summer 2004): 16.
exhib: *1862 Special Exhibition*, no. 1844 or 1845.

230. EWER
French, Saint-Porchaire or Paris, *c.* 1545–60

White-bodied earthenware, inlaid and glazed, ornamented with swags and masks, the handle formed as a human figure, H 34.6 cm
National Museums Scotland, Edinburgh. 1975.466
Victoria and Albert Museum only
Fig. 219

D 1774, 9 [China Room]: In a niche, supported by two columns of oriental alabaster, over the chimney, is a fine ewer of fayence, designed by Julio Romano
D 1784, 6, same as *D 1774*.
PROV: HW; 1842, Strawberry Hill Sale, day 12, lot 37, bt Baron Ant. de Rothschild, £19.19.0; 1948, bt Captain Norman Colville; 1975, June 17, Sotheby's, London, lot 46, bt Rainer Zietz and Cyril Humphris, £44,000; 1975, Royal Museum of Scotland.
LIT: J. Marryat, *Collections towards a History of Pottery and Porcelain* (London, 1850), 55. H. and C. Delange, *Recueil de toutes les Pièces connues jusqu'à ce jour de la Faïence Française dite de Henri Deux et Diane de Poitiers* (Paris, 1861), 33. A. C. King, *Henri Deux Ware. Photographs of Twenty Examples of This Ware Chiefly in English Collections* (London, The Arundel Society, 1868), no. 4. Bet McLeod, 'The Ceramics at Strawberry Hill' (MA Thesis, Cooper-Hewitt/Parson's School of Design, New York, 1993), 145, no. 8, fig. 18. Bet McLeod, 'Horace Walpole's Ceramics at Strawberry Hill', *International Ceramics Fair and Seminar Handbook* (London, 1995), 31. Howard Coutts, 'The "Saint-Porchaire" Ewer in the Royal Museum of Scotland', in Daphne Barbour and Shelley Sturman, eds., *Saint-Porchaire Ceramics, National Gallery of Art. Studies in the History of Art*, 52, Monograph Series II, 53–65. Daphne Barbour and Shelley Sturman, 'Index of "Saint-Porchaire" Ceramics in Public Collections', in Daphne Barbour and Shelley Sturman, *eds., Saint-Porchaire Ceramics, National Gallery of Art. Studies in the History of Art*, 52, Monograph Series II, 143, no. 35.
EXHIB: South Kensington Museum, 'Loan Exhibition', 1862, no. 1201.

231. SALT
French (Saint-Porchaire or Paris), *c.* 1545–60

White-bodied earthenware, inlaid and glazed, H 16 cm
Taft Museum of Art, Cincinnati, Ohio. Bequest of Charles Phelps and Anna Sinton Taft. 1931.224
Yale Center for British Art only
Fig. 299

D 1774, 17 [China Room]: A triangular saltcellar of fayence with fine figures on terms.
D 1784, 11, same as *D 1774*.
PROV: HW; 1842, Strawberry Hill Sale, day 12, lot 80, bt Baron L. de Rothschild, £21.0.0; Alfred de Rothschild (d. 1918); Almina, Countess of Carnarvon; [Duveen, New York] 1923, Nov. 1, Taft Collection, $22,000.00; 1931, Taft Museum of Art, Cincinnati, Ohio.
LIT: Joseph Marryat, *Collections towards a History of Pottery and Porcelain* (London, 1850), 55. H. and C. Delange, *Recueil de toutes les Pièces connues jusqu'à ce jour de la Faïence Française dite de Henri Deux et Diane de Poitiers* (Paris, 1861), 33. *Catalogue of the Taft Museum* (Cincinnati, 1939), no. 256. Jessie McNab, 'A St. Porchaire Salt in the Taft Collection', *Apollo* 128, no. 322 (Dec. 1988): 402–5 (attributing the design to Philibert de l'Orme). Bet McLeod, 'The Ceramics at Strawberry Hill' (MA Thesis, Cooper-Hewitt/Parson's School of Design, New York, 1993), 153, no. 14. Bet McLeod, 'Horace Walpole's Ceramics at Strawberry Hill', *International Ceramics Fair and Seminar Handbook* (London, 1995), p. 32. Jessie McNab, 'Saint-Porchaire Saltcellar', *The Taft Museum: its History and Collections* (New York, 1998), II, 514–17.
EXHIB: 'Exhibition of Antient and Mediaeval Art' (Society of Arts, London, 1850) no. 601; South Kensington Museum, 'Loan Exhibition', 1862, no. 120.

232. DISH WITH PORTRAITS OF CHARLES II AND CATHERINE OF BRAGANZA
English (London, Brislington, or Bristol) or possibly Dutch, 1662–1685

Tin-glazed earthenware (delftware), painted, D 33 cm
Victoria and Albert Museum, London. 3869–1901
Fig. 226

D 1774, 10 [China Room]: An earthen-ware dish, with the heads of Charles 2d. and queen Catherine in blue and white; a present from Mr. Ibbot.
D 1784, 7, same as *D 1774*
PROV: Given by Benjamin Ibbot (1709–87) to HW; 1842, Strawberry Hill Sale, day 12, lot 33, bt W. M. Smith, £2.2.0; before 1871 Museum of Practical Geology, Jermyn Street, London; 1901 transferred to Victoria and Albert Museum.
LIT: Henry de la Beche and Trenham Reeks, *Catalogue of Specimens in the Museum of Practical Geology Illustrative of the Composition and Manufacture of British Pottery and Porcelain*, 2nd edn (London: Eyre and Spottiswoode, 1871) 210, no. Y35. M. Archer, *Delftware. The Tin-glazed Earthenware of the British Isles. A Catalogue of the Collection in the Victoria and Albert Museum* (London, 1997), no. B1.

233. CUP (A CUP OF MR PLACE'S CHINA)
York or Dinsdale (County Durham), by Francis Place (1647–1728), *c.* 1680–1700

Stoneware, D 6.4 × 5.4 cm
With a tooled leather case and a label inscribed by HW: 'Mr Francis Places China'.
Victoria and Albert Museum, London. 4762&A-1901
Fig. 240

D 1774, 12 [China Room]: A cup of Mr. Place's china. *Vide* Walpole's *Catalogue of English Engravers*.
D 1784, 8, same as *D 1774*.
PROV: Ralph Thoresby, Leeds; HW; 1842, Strawberry Hill Sale, day 18, lot 21, bt Burn, £0.12.0; 1869, given to the Museum of Practical Geology, Jermyn Street, London, by Sir A. W. Franks; 1901, transferred to the Victoria and Albert Museum.
LIT: *Anecdotes*, vol. 5, 55. Henry De la Beche and Trenham Reeks, *Catalogue of Specimens in the Museum of Practical Geology Illustrative of the Composition and Manufacture of British Pottery and Porcelain*, 2nd edn (London: Eyre and Spottiswoode, 1871), 193, no. R47. A. J. Toppin, 'A Ceramic Miscellany: 1: Francis Place', *English Ceramic Circle Transactions* I (1951): 65–8. R. Tyler, *Francis Place, 1647–1728* (exh. cat. York City Art Gallery and Kenwood, 1971), 42, no. 2a. R. Tyler, 'Francis Place's Pottery', *English Ceramic Circle Transactions* 8, part 2 (1972): 203–12, no. 1, pls. 156a, 156e. OHG 106. R. J. C. Hildyard, *Browne Muggs. English Brown Stoneware* (exh. cat. London: Victoria and Albert Museum, London, 1985), no. 348. Bet McLeod, 'The Ceramics at Strawberry Hill' (MA Thesis, Cooper-Hewitt/Parson's School of Design, New York, 1993), 148, no. 19, fig. 10. Bet McLeod, 'Horace Walpole's Ceramics at Strawberry Hill', *International Ceramics Fair and Seminar Handbook* (London, 1995): 30.
NOTE: 'I have a coffee cup of his ware; it is of grey earth with streaks of black, and not superior to common earthenware' (*Anecdotes*, vol. 5, 55).

234. PLATE PAINTED WITH A SCENE OF ABRAHAM AND ISAAC
Italian (Castelli), workshop of Carlantonio Grue (1655–1723) *c.* 1690–1720

Tin-glazed earthenware (maiolica), painted and gilt, D 19 cm
Labels on verso: 'Walpole Collection Strawberry Hill Sale'; later dealer label '2575 Pair 2 gui'
The Lewis Walpole Library, Yale University.
Fig. 244

D 1774, 17 (Possibly) [China Room] Four dessert plates of fayence, with figures and boys round the borders; by Pietro da Cortona: very fine. A fifth ditto with goats, a present from Lady Diana Beauclerc.
PROV: Perhaps 1842, Strawberry Hill Sale, day 12, lot 73, (one of five) bt Pratt, New Bond Street, £5.15.6; 1949, July, given by Sir Osbert Sitwell to W. S. Lewis; The Lewis Walpole Library, Yale University.
LIT: Luciana Arbace, *Nella bottega dei Gentili. Spolveri e disegni per le maioliche di Castelli* (exh. cat. Sant'Atto [Teramo], 1998), 48–50.
NOTE: Apparently acquired by Sitwell in Chelsea in the 1930s. Nine similar plates, which look as they may all have belonged to a single set, are at The Vyne, the house of Walpole's friend John Chute. These, however, have not been found in any 18th-century inventory of The Vyne and it is not certain they belonged to Chute.

235. Plate painted with the Sacrifices of Cain and Abel
Italian (Castelli), workshop of Carlantonio Grue (1655–1723), *c.* 1690–1720

Tin-glazed earthenware (maiolica), painted and gilt, D 18.5 cm
Label on verso: Strawberry Hill; later dealer label '2575 Pair 2 gui'
The Lewis Walpole Library, Yale University.

D 1774, 17 (Possibly) [China Room] Four dessert plates of fayence, with figures and boys round the borders; by Pietro da Cortona: very fine. A fifth ditto with goats, a present from Lady Diana Beauclerc
PROV: Possibly 1842, Strawberry Hill Sale, day 12, lot 73, by Pratt, New Bond Street, £5.15.6; 1949, July, Given by Sir Osbert Sitwell to W. S. Lewis; The Lewis Walpole Library, Yale University.
LIT: Luciana Arbace, *Nella bottega dei Gentili. Spolveri e disegni per le maioliche di Castelli* (exh. cat. Sant'Atto [Teramo], 1998), 48–50.
NOTE: The scene perhaps in reverse after an engraving by Gerard de Lairesse.

236. Three Delftware Plates from a set of twelve, with Signs of the Zodiac (Pisces, Taurus, Gemini)
Made and painted at one of the Delft potteries, the central scenes probably painted by Sir James Thornhill (1675/6–1734), the borders probably by factory painters, 1711.

Tin-glazed earthenware, D 22 cm
Inscriptions: on back of Pisces Plate: 'J Thornhill f Ag Delph 1711' [with zodiac symbol]; on back of Taurus Plate: 'J Thornhill f Delph Aug 1711' [with zodiac symbol]; on back of Gemini plate: 'J Thornhill f Delph 1711' [with zodiac symbol].
The British Museum, Department of Prehistory and Europe. Gift of A. W. Franks. 1889,0706.65, 1889,0706.67, 1889,0706.68
Fig. 228

D 1784, 95 [China Room]: More Additions…Twelve earthen plates, painted at Delft, with the signs of the zodiac, by sir James Thornhill; bought at Mrs. Hogarth's sale.
PROV: 1711, James Thornhill; his son-in-law William Hogarth; 1790, April 24, Mrs Hogarth's sale, Greenwood's, at her house in Leicester Square (Lugt 4575), lot 66, bt HW, £3.10.0; 1842, Strawberry Hill Sale, day 18, lot 26, bt Lovegrove, £6.16.6; 1889, Given by A. W. Franks to the British Museum.
LIT: Katharine Fremantle, *Sir James Thornhill's Sketch-book Travel Journal of 1711* (Utrecht: Haentjens Dekker & Gumbert, 1975) II, x. Henry-Pierre Fourest, *Delftware: Faience Production at Delft* (London: Thames and Hudson: 1980), 124–5 (arguing the zodiac figures are by Delft painters after designs by Thornhill). Bet McLeod, 'The Ceramics at Strawberry Hill' (MA Thesis, Cooper-Hewitt/Parson's School of Design, New York, 1993), 151, no. 12, fig. 1. Bet McLeod, 'Horace Walpole's Ceramics at Strawberry Hill', *International Ceramics Fair and Seminar Handbook* (London, 1995), p.28.

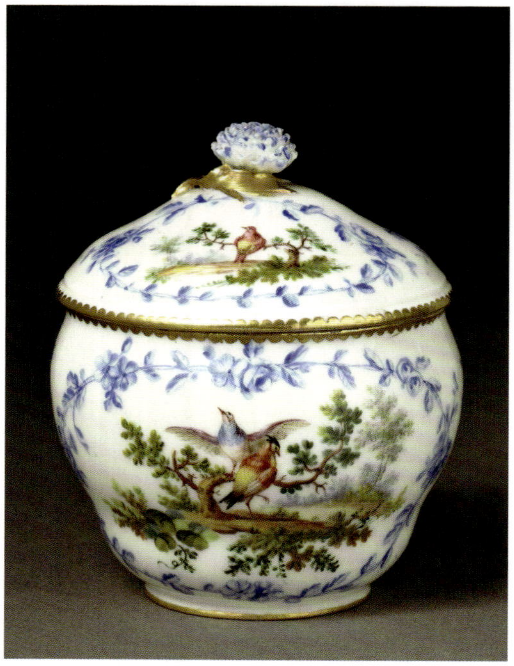

Figure 357. Catalogue 239

237. Pot Pourri Vase and Cover
Meissen Porcelain Manufactory, *c.* 1745–1750

Hard-paste porcelain, painted and gilt, H 13.9 cm
Marks: crossed swords painted in blue on base; impressed form-maker's mark 46.
British Museum, Department of Prehistory and Europe. Franks 76
Fig. 224

D 1774, 11 [China Room]: A pot pourri of Saxon china, with coloured flowers embossed.
D 1784, 8, same as *D 1774*.
PROV: HW; 1842, Strawberry Hill Sale, day 18, lot 55, bt Cooke, £3.7.6.; A. W. Franks; 1897, Bequeathed by Sir Augustus Wollaston Franks to the British Museum, London.
LIT: Bethnal Green Museum, London, Catalogue of a Collection of Continental Porcelain Lent and Described by Sir A. Wollaston Franks (1896), 10, no. 76.

238. Pair of Salt-Cellars in the Form of Crayfish and Shells
Chelsea Porcelain Factory, *c.* 1745–9

Soft-paste porcelain, (a) L 13.5 cm; H 6.8 cm; (b) L 13 cm; H 6.5 cm
Marks: both with an incised triangle; one with incised '3'
British Museum, Department of Prehistory and Europe. 1887,0307,II.18
Fig. 223

D 1774, 14 [China Room]: Two saltsellers with crawfish in relief, of Chelsea china.
D 1784, 10, same as *D 1774*.
PROV: HW; 1842, Strawberry Hill Sale, day 12, lot 115, Pratt, New Bond Street, £3.10.0; 1887, given by A. W. Franks to the British Museum.
LIT: J. Marryat, *A History of Pottery and Porcelain Mediaeval and Modern* (London, 1857), 281. R. L. Hobson, *Catalogue of the Collection of English Porcelain in the Department of British and Mediaeval Antiquities and Ethnography of the British Museum* (London, 1905), 31, no. I, 8. *Rococo: Art and Design in Hogarth's England* (exh. cat. London: Trefoil Books, 1984), Victoria and Albert Museum, 1984, 245, cat. no. O7. Bet McLeod, 'Horace Walpole's Ceramics at Strawberry Hill', *International Ceramics Fair and Seminar Handbook* (London, 1995), 30. Elizabeth Adams, *Chelsea Porcelain*, 2nd edn (London, British Museum Press, 2000), 26.

239. Cream Jug and Covered Sugar Basin
Sèvres Porcelain Manufactory, 1758

Soft-paste porcelain, painted with birds and flowers, and gilt, sugar basin: 8.9 × 7.4 cm; cream jug: H 11 cm
Marks: both have interlaced L's, and the date letter f (January 1758) and dagger mark for painter Etienne Evans
Victoria and Albert Museum, London. 276–1876 & 277–1876
Fig. 357 (sugar basin only)

D 1774, 105 [Great North Bedchamber]: On the side opposite to the bed:…a dejuné of Seve china, blue and white with coloured birds
D 1784, 74, same as *D 1774*.
PROV: 1765–66, bt HW in Paris; 1842, Strawberry Hill Sale, day 11, lot 102, bt Owen, New Bond Street, £24.3.6; 1876, May 24, Christie's, The Right Hon. Viscount Exmouth Sale, lot 72, bt Whitehead, £19.19.0; 1876, bt by Victoria and Albert Museum.

240. Cup and saucer
Sèvres Porcelain Manufactory, 1765

Soft-paste porcelain painted in enamel with flower motifs and panels of exotic birds by François-Joseph Aloncle (fl. 1758–81) and gilding, cup: D 4.7 cm, saucer: D 10.7 cm
Marks: on the saucer interlaced Ls in blue and date letter M (1765); 'N' in script underneath for Aloncle; incised numeral 3; cup incised with reversed 's'
The Lewis Walpole Library, Yale University.
Figs 238, 239

1842 Sale possibly [Blue Breakfast Room]: A beautiful lilac ground variegated pattern old Sevres China cabinet cup and saucer, the paintings enriched by Birds, of brilliant plumage.
PROV: Probably HW; probably 1842, Strawberry Hill Sale, day 11, lot 84, bt John P. Beavan, Esq., £2.12.6; possibly Alice Hay-Appleton and bequeathed by her to W. S. Lewis; The Lewis Walpole Library, Yale University.
NOTE: A later owner has proudly written STRAWBERRY HILL on a gold band on the base. This is the kind of object Walpole was buying in Paris in 1765, though it has not been specifically identified in his account books.

241. Cup and Saucer with English Views
Factory of Josiah Wedgwood, Stoke-on-Trent, 1772–80

Creamware, cup: H 5 cm; saucer: D 12 cm
Marks: incised 'C' on the cup; impressed 'O' on the saucer
National Museums Liverpool, Walker Art Gallery. M2768a and M2768b
Fig. 242

D 1784, 14 [China Room]: A cup and saucer of Wedgwood's ware, finely painted with English views.

PROV: HW; 1842, Strawberry Hill Sale, day 18, lot 49, bt Emery, Bury Street, £1.11.6; [Joseph Mayer, Liverpool]; 1867, Joseph Mayer presented to National Museums Liverpool.

LIT: Lionel Burman, 'Joseph Mayer's Wedgwood Collection', in Margaret Gibson and Susan M. Wright, eds., *Joseph Mayer of Liverpool 1803–1886* Society of Antiquaries Occasional Papers, new series XI (London, 1988), 204, pl. LIXa. Robin Reilly, *Wedgwood* (London and New York: Macmillan and Stockton Press, 1989), vol. 1, 278, fig. 336. Michael Raeburn, Ludmila Voronikhina and Andrew Nurnberg, eds., *The Green Frog Service* (London: Cacklegoose Press, 1995), 401 and 406, figs B19–B21. Hilary Young, ed., *The Genius of Wedgwood* (London: Victoria and Albert Museum, 1995), 206, no. 330.

NOTE: The coloured views were probably painted at Wedgwood's decorating studio in Chelsea, London. Around the cup is a view near Richmond Castle, Yorkshire; inside it is the Mausoleum at Castle Howard, Yorkshire. In the saucer is a view of Stoke Gifford, Gloucestershire. These views are in the style of the monochrome views on Wedgwood's 'Green Frog Service' made for Catherine the Great.

242. Ewer and Basin with Figures in a Landscape
Chinese, *c.* 1760–90

Hard-paste porcelain, ewer: H 23.6 cm; basin: D 25.4 cm
Inscriptions: handwritten label on bottom of basin: 'This Ewer & Basin belonged to Horace Walpole & bought at his Sale at Strawberry Hill – Twickenham.'; typescript label: 'Johnston'
The Lewis Walpole Library, Yale University.
Fig. 231

PROV: Possibly HW; possibly Strawberry Hill Sale; 1955, June, Cogar, Lewis & Geiger, Williamsburg, VA, bt W. S. Lewis, $275; The Lewis Walpole Library, Yale University.

NOTE: This type is one made specifically for the European market.

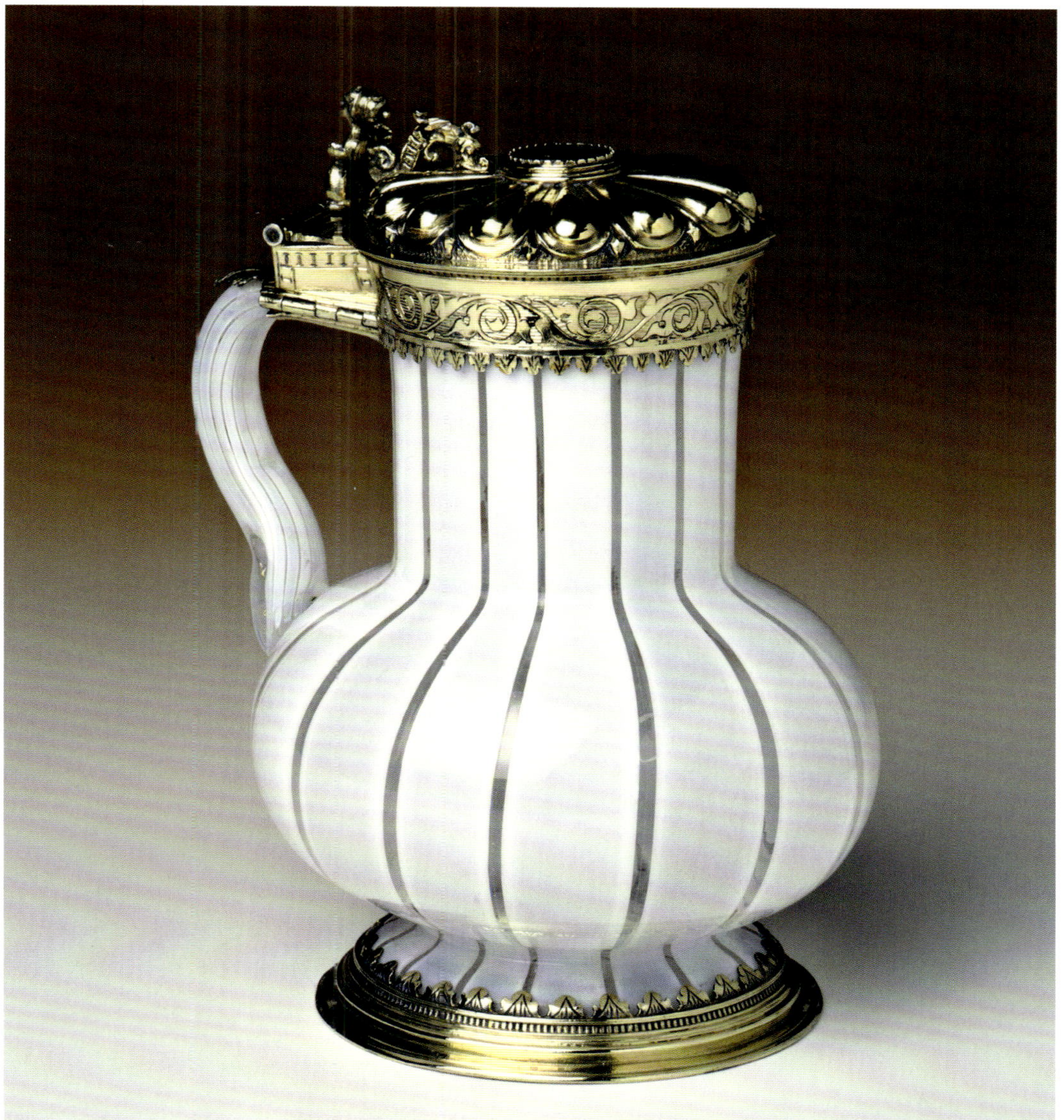

Figure 358. Catalogue 243

243. Tankard called the Parr Pot
The mounts English (London), 1546–7. The glass 18th or 19th century

Glass with silver-gilt mounts, the lid enamelled with the arms of Sir William Parr (uncle of Queen Catherine Parr), H 14 cm
Marks: mounts, London hallmarks for 1546–7, mark: a fleur-de-lis
Museum of London Collections. Purchased with the assistance of a Special Government Grant, The Art Fund, The Pilgrim Trust, The Goldsmiths' Company. 67.10
Victoria and Albert Museum only
Fig. 358

D 1774, 14 [China Room]: Ditto [An old glass tankard] of old Venetian glass striped with white, mounted in silver gilt; on the lid, arms of Parr enamelled.
D 1784, 9, same as *D 1774*.

PROV: 1758, February 21–23, Sale of Thomas Barrett of the Lee, Kent, bt HW, £2.19.0; 1842, Strawberry Hill Sale, day12, lot 120, bt John Dent, Esq., £3.13.6; by family descent, Dent-Brocklehurst family, Sudeley Castle, Gloucestershire; 1966, sold to a London dealer; 1967, purchased by the Museum of London, £18,214.

LIT: Philippa Fox-Robinson, 'Parr Pot (London Museum)', *Burlington Magazine* 110, no. 778 (Jan. 1968): 44–5, fig. 59. Philippa Glanville, 'The Parr Port', *Archaeological Journal* 127 (1970): 147–55. David Starkey, ed., *Henry VIII: A European Court in England*, exh. cat., National Maritime Museum, Greenwich (New York: Abbeville Press, 1991), 171.

NOTE: The glass imitates and replaces an original glass perhaps made by Venetian glassmakers working in London, *c.* 1546.

244. Goblet
Probably made in Jacopo Verzelini's Glasshouse, London, and engraved by Anthony de Lysle (fl. 1577–90), 1580

Glass, H 13.3 cm
Engraved 'AF' (twice) and '1580'.
Victoria and Albert Museum, London, C.1522–1936
Fig. 225

D 1784 [China Room, 89] Appendix …A large flattish drinking glass, one of the first manufacture at Venice, with the initials of an English lady's name for whom it was made, and the date 1580; a present from lady Giorgiana Smythe.
PROV: Given to HW by Lady Georgiana Smyth; 1842, Strawberry Hill Sale, day 12, lot 123, bt Forrest, Strand £0.10.0; Edward Hailstone (1818–90); 1891, Feb. 12–20, Hailstone sale, Christie's, lot 469, bt Fraser; Wilfred Buckley; 1936, Buckley Gift to Victoria and Albert Museum.
LIT: R. Charleston, *English Glass and the Glass Used in England, circa 400–1840* (London, 1984), 56, pl. 12. D. Hugh Willmott in Jutta-Annette Page, *Beyond Venice. Glass in Venetian Style, 1500–1750* (Corning, 2004), 282, fig. 12.

245. Lattimo Glass Plate with View of the Church of the Carità, Venice
Probably Miotti family glasshouse, Murano (Venice), 1741

Opaque-white glass, painted in red, D 22.4 cm
Lent by the Corning Museum of Glass, 66.3.38
Yale Center for British Art only
Fig. 9

D 1774, 9 [China Room]: Two dozen plates of Venetian glass; each plate has a different view of Venice, drawn in red.
D 1784, 7 same as *D 1774*.
PROV: 1741, Horace Walpole acquired (possibly commissioned) a set of 24 plates from a Venice glass house, £37.6.0; 1842, Strawberry Hill Sale, day 12, part of lots 41–4 (lot 41, six plates, bt W. M. Smith, £3.10.0; lot 42, six plates, bt W. M. Smith, £3.10.0; lot 43, six plates, bt Zimmerman, £3.15.0, lot 44, six plates, bt Zimmerman, £3.5.0); after 1842 sale, plates were dispersed; this plate, by 1963, Mrs Bodenheim; 1966, purchased by the Corning Museum of Glass from an art dealer in the Hague, The Netherlands.
LIT: Robert J. Charleston, 'Souvenirs of the Grand Tour', *Journal of Glass Studies* 1 (1959): 62–82. Robert J. Charleston, 'Glass Souvenirs of the Grand Tour', *Antiques* 83, no. 6 (June 1963): 665–9, fig. 9. Corning Museum of Glass, *Recent Important Acquisitions* 9 (1967): 141, no. 45. [Anon.], 'Acquisition of Glass by the Corning Museum of Glass' *Burlington Magazine* 109 (Oct. 1967): 588–9.
NOTE: The scene is after an engraving by Antonio Visentini after Canaletto. Walpole, John Chute, and the Earl of Lincoln each acquired sets of these plates when they were together in Venice. Chute's set survives at his house, The Vyne.

246. Lattimo Glass Plate with View of the Arsenale, Venice
Probably Miotti family glasshouse, Murano (Venice), 1741

Opaque-white glass, painted in red, D 22.7 cm
British Museum. Department of Preshistory and Europe S.388
Victoria and Albert Museum only

D 1774, 9 [China Room]: [see preceding entry]
D 1784, 7 same as *D 1774*.
PROV: See Cat. 245 ; Ralph Bernal (d. 1854); 1855, 19 April, Christie's Bernal Sale (1855, March 5–April 30), lot 3212, bt Felix Slade, £20; 1868, bequeathed by Felix Slade to The British Museum.
LIT: Robert J. Charleston, 'Souvenirs of the Grand Tour', *Journal of Glass Studies* 1 (1959): 62–82. Robert J. Charleston, 'Glass Souvenirs of the Grand Tour', *Antiques* 83, no. 6 (June 1963): 666, fig. 1. Hugh Tait, *The Golden Age of Venetian Glass* (exh. cat. London: British Museum Publications, 1979), no. 210. Andrew W. Moore, *Norfolk and the Grand Tour* (exh. cat. Norfolk Museums Service, 1984), no. 84.
NOTE: The scene is after an etching by Luca Carlevaris.

247. Lattimo Glass Plate with View of San Simeon Piccolo
Probably Miotti family glasshouse, Murano (Venice), 1741

Opaque-white glass, painted in red, D 22.5 cm
Victoria and Albert Museum, London. 5272–1901

D 1774, 9 [China Room]: See Cat. 245
D 1784, 7 same as *D 1774*.
PROV: See Cat. 245; Museum of Practical Geology, Jermyn Street, London; 1901, transferred to Victoria and Albert Museum.
LIT: Robert J.Charleston, 'Souvenirs of the Grand Tour', *Journal of Glass Studies* 1 (1959): 62–82. *OHG* 8. Andrew W. Moore, *Norfolk and the Grand Tour* (exh. cat. Norfolk Museum Service, 1984), no. 86.
NOTE: The scene is after an engraving by Antonio Visentini after Canaletto.

248. Lattimo Glass Plate with View of the Rialto Bridge
Probably Miotti family glasshouse, Murano (Venice), 1741

Opaque-white glass, painted in red, D 22.5 cm
Victoria and Albert Museum, London. C.185–1936

D 1774, 9 [China Room]: see Cat. 245
D 1784, 7 same as *D 1774*.
PROV: See Cat. 245; Wilfred Buckley; 1936, Buckley gift to Victoria and Albert Museum.
LIT: Robert J.Charleston, 'Souvenirs of the Grand Tour', *Journal of Glass Studies* 1 (1959): 62–82. *OHG* 8. Andrew W. Moore, *Norfolk and the Grand Tour* (exh. cat. Norfolk Museums Service, 1984), no. 85. R. Liefkes, *Glass* (London, Victoria and Albert Museum, 1997), 59, fig. 68.
NOTE: The scene is after an engraving by Antonio Visentini after Canaletto.

16. MODERN ART

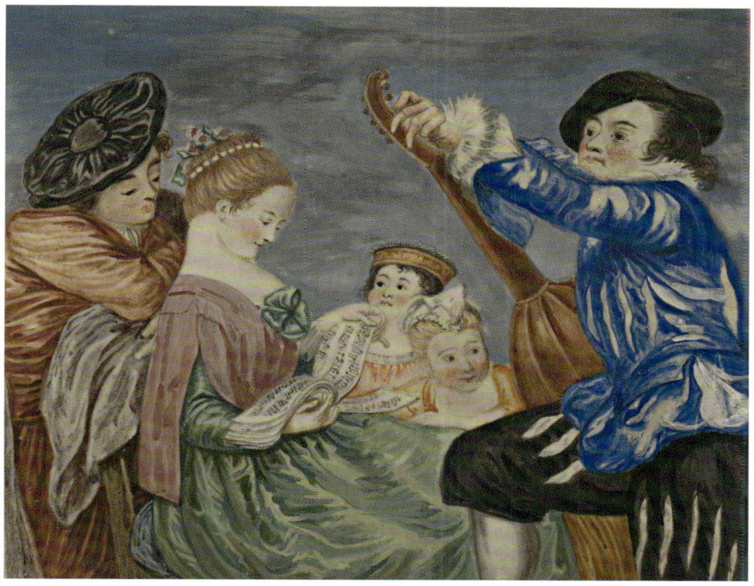

Figure 359. Catalogue 249

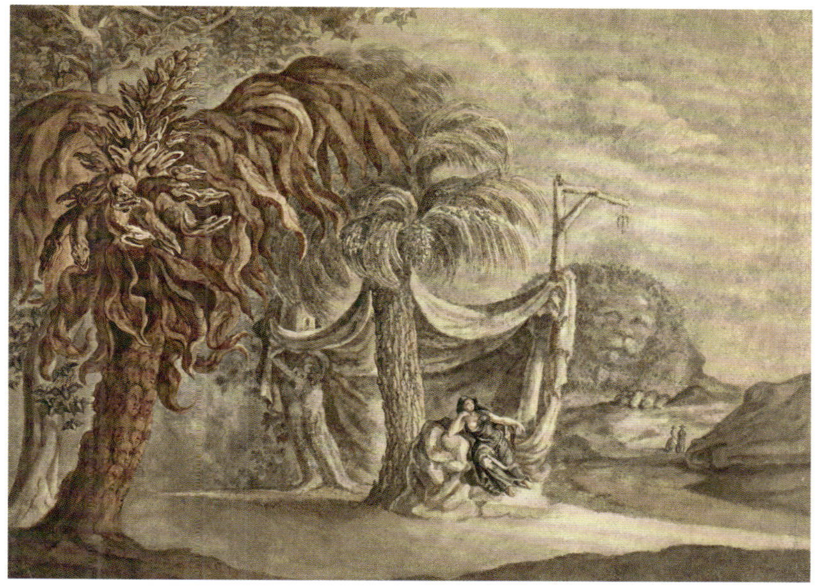

Figure 360. Catalogue 250

249. A Music Lesson ('A man and woman..after Watteau')
Horace Walpole (1717–1797), after Jean-Antoine Watteau (1684–1721), 1736

Gouache/watercolour with white highlights on paper, in original black and gilt frame, 19 × 23.4 cm (visible)
Signed and dated on side of chair: 'Hor. Walpole 1736'.
Inscriptions: on back of frame: in HW's hand: 'by Horace Walpole.'
The Lewis Walpole Library, Yale University. 736.00.00.06dr
Fig. 359

D 1774, 56 possibly [Mr. Walpole's Bedchamber]: A man and woman in water-colours, after Watteau; by Mr. Walpole. *D 1784*, 41, same as *D 1774*.

PROV: 1736, HW; 1920, May 14, Christie's, Earl Waldegrave Sale, lot 101; 1931, July 3, Parsons, lot 69, bt W. S. Lewis, £31.10 with another Walpole watercolour also after Watteau; The Lewis Walpole Library, Yale University.

LIT: Emile Dacier and Albert Vuaflart, *Jean de Jullienne et les graveurs de Watteau au XVIIIe siècle* (Paris, 1922), no. 96 for the print after Watteau. Mellon Lectures, ill. no. 5. Donald Posner, *Antoine Watteau* (Ithaca, NY: Cornell University Press, 1984), 160, ill. p. 159, fig. 118 for Watteau's painting. Margaret Morgan Grasselli and Pierre Rosenberg, *Watteau 1684–1721* (Washington: National Gallery of Art, 1984), 165 for the print after Watteau.

NOTE: The original painting by Antoine Watteau was engraved by L. Surugue in 1719. The painting is now in the Wallace Collection, London.

250. 'A Prospect of Vapourland'
Richard Bentley (bap. 1708– d. 1782), 1759

Brush and brown and grey ink over pencil on laid paper, 47 × 63.2 cm
Inscriptions: on verso possibly in HW's hand: 'By Mr. Bentley 1759'.
Label on verso in brown ink indicated by later pencil notation as Bentley's hand: 'A Prospect of Vapourland/ The Batavia Plane Tree / The Dragon Tree, / The Ficus Peoeides maximus, caule Hibernia/ foliis hirsutis./ The Rattan Palm Tree./ Lapis andromorphites./ The Gibbet Tree./ Mount Lion./ Phisic Road./ Calves-head hillock./ The sky after Polonius.'; in pencil on verso in same hand as pencil inscription above: 'from Strawberry Hill/ given to Eton (?) by Mr. Smith of L. (?)/ 1849.'
Yale Center for British Art, Paul Mellon Collection. B1975.3.188
Fig. 360

1842 Sale: The Death of Hector, a grand composition by Maria Cosway; a very singular design of a prospect of Vapour-land, by Richard Bentley, 1759, and 3 other Palaces, by Italian artists.

PROV: possibly commissioned by HW; 1842, Strawberry Hill London Sale, day 10, lot 1253, bt Smith (with 4 other items), £.0 11.0; Eton College(?): 1969, July, purchased from Christopher Mendez by Yale Center for British Art.

LIT: Diana L. Johnson, *Fantastic Illustration and Design in Britain 1850–1930* (Providence: Rhode Island School of Design, 1979), no. 18.

251. A Collection of Prints, Engraved by Various Persons of Quality. Volume I
Album containing 142 prints and drawings by various hands. Bound in red morocco, gilt, with HW's arms on the sides. 1775

Inscriptions: with notes by HW and others
60 × 49 cm
The Lewis Walpole Library, Yale University. Folio 49 3588

D 1774, 132 [Library]: Appendix...In the Library...A large volume bound in red morocco and gold, containing etchings of various persons of quality.

D 1784, 37, same as *D 1774*.

PROV: HW; 1842, Strawberry Hill Sale, day 8, lot 56 [listed]; 1842, Strawberry Hill London Sale, day 8, lot 1126 [sold], bt Pickering, £16.10.0; 1843, offered in Strong's Catalogue, lot 1867; 1851, Sotheby's Sale; 1942, October 28, Sotheby's, Miscellaneous Sale, lot 1126, bt Maggs for W. S. Lewis, £92; The Lewis Walpole Library, Yale University.

LIT: *HW Corres.* 28: 195. *Library* 3588.

252. ILLUSTRATION FOR THE THE MYSTERIOUS MOTHER: THE COUNTESS OF NARBONNE, HER SON EDMUND, AND FATHER BENEDICT
Lady Diana Beauclerk (1734–1808), 1776

Wash on laid paper, mounted on another sheet, 32.8 × 41.6 cm (visible)
Inscriptions: in HW's hand on verso: 'The Mysterious Mother. Act 3d. Scene 3d. by Lady Diana Beauclerc 1776'.
The Lewis Walpole Library, Yale University. 776.00.00.70dr
Fig. 171

D 1774, 140–1 [Beauclerk Closet]: Appendix: ... The closet...was built on purpose to receive seven incomparable drawings of lady Diana Beauclerc for Mr. Walpole's tragedy of the Mysterious Mother. The beauty and grace of the figures and of the children are inimitable; the expression of the passions most masterly, particularly in the devotion of the countess with the porter, of Benedict in the scene with Martin, and the tenderness, despair, and resolution of the countess in the last scene; in which is a new stroke of double passion in Edmund, whose right hand is clenched and ready to strike with anger, the left hand relents. In the scene of the children, some are evidently vulgar, the others children of rank; and the first child, that pretends to look down and does leer upwards, is charming. Only two scenes are represented in all the seven, and yet all are varied; and the ground in the first, by a very uncommon effect, evidently descends and rises again. These sublime drawings, the first histories she ever attempted, were all conceived and executed in a fortnight.
D 1784, 78–9, same as *D 1774*.
PROV: 1776, commissioned by HW; 1842, Strawberry Hill Sale, day 17, lot 32, bt Hon. Col. D. Damer, MP, £13.13.0; 1885, August 1, Christie's, lot 74, seven illustrations and HW's own copy of the book, bt Col. Aldridge, £37.16; 1962, May, Pickering & Chatto, bt W. S. Lewis (six drawings), £500; The Lewis Walpole Library, Yale University.
LIT: Mrs Steuart Erskine, *Lady Diana Beauclerk, Her Life and Work* (London: T. F. Unwin, 1903), 241–3. *HW Corres.* 3: 392n, 15: 318, 24: 524, 31: 206, 216, 297, 32: 289, 35: 385, 41: 322, 43: 147. Mellon Lectures, 123. *Rescuing Horace*, 107–15.
NOTE: A Principal Curiosity.

253. PAIR OF FLOWER TUBS
Factory of Josiah Wedgwood, Stoke on Trent; designed by Lady Diana Beauclerk (1734–1808), 1777

Creamware, 17 × 12.4 × 12.4 cm
Unmarked
Inscriptions: within circular medallions: 'Diana Beauclerc / Caroli / Ducis Marlburiensis / Filia / Designavit / 1777'
Private collection
Fig. 243

D 1774, 139 [Great North Bedchamber]: Appendix...In the Great Bedchamber...Two square flower-tubs of Wedgwood's ware, painted with antique cameos and masks in blue, from designs of lady Diana Beauclerc.
D 1784, 77, same as *D 1774*.
PROV: 1777, commissioned by HW; 1941, August 21, Sotheby's, lot 20, bt Dr John Blake; Private collection.
LIT: Mrs Steuart Erskine, *Lady Diana Beauclerk, Her Life and Work* (London: T. F. Unwin, 1903), 226–7 and 255–7 and 259 on work for Wedgwood. Robin Reilly, *Wedgwood*, 2 vols. (London and New York: Macmillan and Stockton Press, 1989), 1: 607.
NOTE: A Principal Curiosity. For the design drawings for tubs, see Cat. 254.

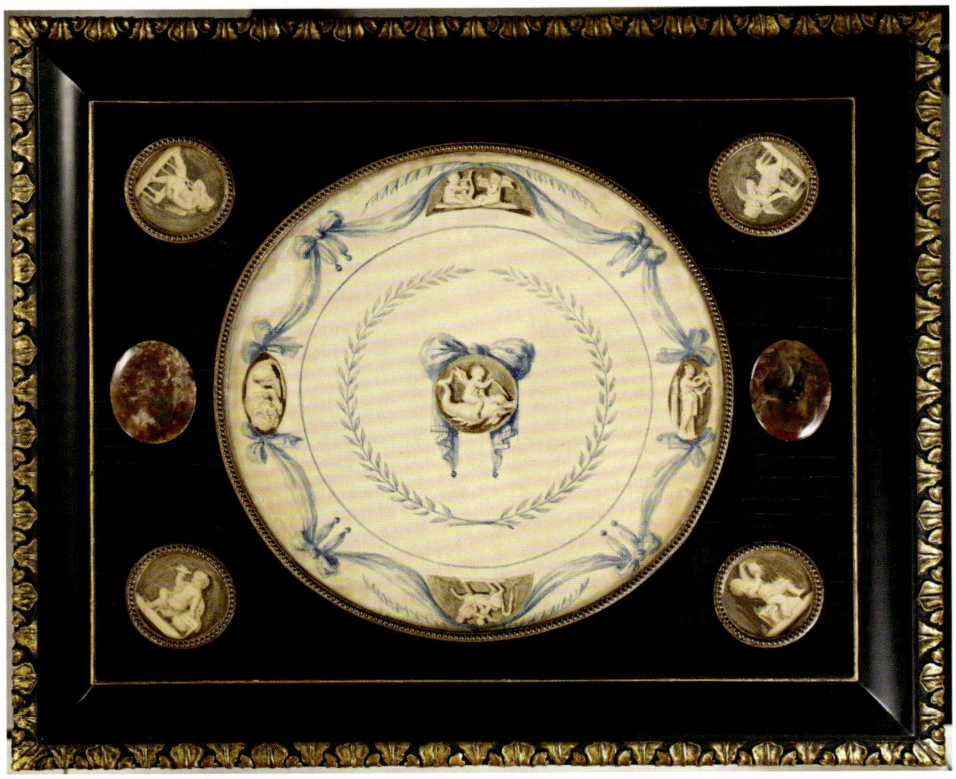

Figure 361. Catalogue 254

254. CABINET ON STAND
Designed by Edward Edwards (1738–1806). Set with drawings by Lady Diana Beauclerk (1734–1808), *c.* 1777 and later, and enamels made in Augsburg, *c.* 1680. 1784

Ebony veneer with gilding, oak and mahogany; composition ornaments; gilt metal mounts and handles; mounted on the top, sides and door fronts with drawings in watercolour and pencil on paper, set in glazed gilt-metal frames, showing children and other figures and designs for a Wedgwood plate and alternative designs for Wedgwood flower tubs, *c.* 1777. The sides with black and white jasperware plaques [one impressed 'WEDGWOOD'] and semi-precious stones. The stand set with lapis lazuli and reverse painting on glass showing strawberries and the Walpole shield and crest. The drawer fronts set with pierced enamel roundels, a blue and white Wedgwood jasperware plaque and semi-precious and other stones including agate, breccia, bloodstone, chalcedony and jasper. 127.5 × 48.5 × 40.7 cm
Brass plate inside the door engraved: 'This cabinet was ordered by and Made at the Expense of Mr. Horace Walpole in 1784 to receive the Drawings which were all design'd and executed by the Right Honorable Lady Diana Beauclerc. The cabinet was design'd by Mr. E. Edwards.'
The Lewis Walpole Library, Yale University
Figs. 173, 174, 361

D 1774, n.p. (annotated copy at The Lewis Walpole Library (49 2523) Additions since the Appendix: in HW's hand: An Ebony Cabinet ornamented with Drawings by Lady Diana Beauclerc with lapis lazuli, agates, enamels, Wedgwood bas reliefs bronze & other Decorations. The Form was designed by E. Edwards & it was executed in 1784.
D 1784, 84 [Great North Bedchamber]: Additions...In the Great Bedchamber. An ebony cabinet, ornamented with or moulu, lapis-lazuli, agates, pieces of ancient enamel, bas-reliefs of Wedgwood, and nine capital drawings of a gipsy girl and beautiful children by lady Diana Beauclerc, with other drawings by her; and with strawberries and Mr. Walpole's arms and crest. The design of the cabinet by Mr. E. Edwards, in 1783.
PROV: Made for HW; 1842, Strawberry Hill Sale, day 16, lot 26, bt John P. Beavan, Esq., £53.11.0; Collection of Sir Robert Peel; possibly bt from Peel by Edward Cazalet; by descent; 1939, Mrs Cazalet, Sussex, bt W. S. Lewis, £300; The Lewis Walpole Library, Yale University.
LIT: Mrs Steuart Erskine, *Lady Diana Beauclerk, Her Life and Work* (London: T. F. Unwin, 1903), 252. H. A. Tipping, 'Strawberry Hill—II, Middlesex',

Country Life (12 July 1924): 62, fig. 13. *HW Corres.* 43: 378. *Collector's Progress*, 136–7, ill. 13. Ralph Edwards, *The Shorter Dictionary of English Furniture* (London: Country Life, 1964), 108, fig. 48. *Rescuing Horace*, 110–12, [ills.]. John Cornforth, 'The Cowles-Lewis House, Farmington—II', *Country Life* (4 May 1978), 1230: ill. 2. Percy Macquoid and Ralph Edwards, *The Dictionary of English Furniture*, rev. edn (Wappingers' Falls, NY: Antique Collectors' Club Ltd, 2000, *c.* 1954), vol. 1, 192, fig. 65. Hugh Glover, 'Two Furnishings from Strawberry Hill: Exploration and Treatment', *Postprints of the Wooden Artifacts Group presented at the 30th annual meeting of the American Institute for Conservation, Miami, Florida, June 2002* (Washington, DC: American Institute for Conservation of Historic and Artistic Works, 2002): illustrated.

NOTE: A Principal Curiosity. For the flower tubs see Cat. 253.

255. TWO SLEEPING DOGS
Anne Seymour Damer (1749–1828), 1782

Terracotta on a marble base 21.5 × 42.7 × 34.4 cm
Inscriptions; signed in the clay 'anna damer Londiniensis fecit 1782'
Lent by the Rt Hon. the Earl of Derby, s029
Victoria and Albert Museum only
Fig. 178

D 1774, 149 [Little Parlour]: Additions since the Appendix…In the Little Parlour. Two sleeping dogs, the original model in terra-cotta, by the honorable Mrs. Damer, which she afterwards executed in marble for the duke of Richmond.

D 1784, 84, same as *D 1774*.

PROV: By 1784, HW; 1842, Strawberry Hill Sale, day 16, lot 116, bt Earl of Derby, £32.0.6 ('under a glass case').

LIT: Percy Noble, *Anne Seymour Damer, a Woman of Art and Fashion, 1748–1828* (London: K. Paul, Trench, Trubner & Co., Ltd, 1908), 78–9 and 81. Susan Benforado, 'Ann Seymour Damer (1748–1828)' Ph.D. dissertation. (The University of New Mexico, Albuquerque, New Mexico, 1986), no. 32.

NOTE: A Principal Curiosity. A marble version is at Goodwood House.

256. PORTRAIT BUST OF COLLEY CIBBER
Perhaps workshop of Sir Henry Cheere (1702–1781), *c.* 1740

Painted plaster, H 67.3 cm
National Portrait Gallery, London. 1045
Victoria and Albert Museum only
Fig. 362

D 1774, 153 [Waiting Room]: More Additions: In the Waiting-Room. Bust of Colley Cibber, poet-laureat, in a cap, when old, coloured from the life, and extremely like. He gave it to Mrs. Clive, the celebrated actress, and her brother Mr. Raftor gave it, after her death, to Mr. Walpole.

D 1784, 89, same as *D 1774*.

PROV: Colley Cibber to Mrs Catherine Clive (1711–1785); 1786, James Raftor (her brother) gave to HW; 1842, Strawberry Hill Sale, day 17, lot 106, bt

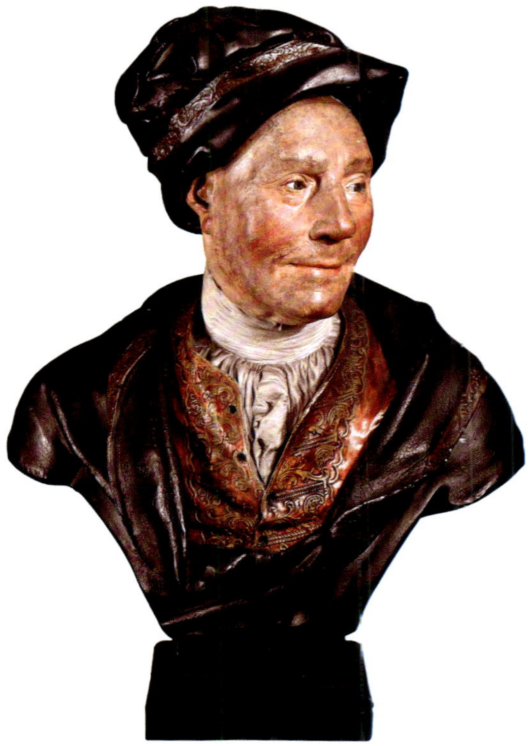

Figure 362. Catalogue 256

Buckley Bolton, Esq., £2.5.0; 1896, purchased by National Portrait Gallery, London

LIT: *HW Corres.* 42: 158. John Kerslake, *Early Georgian Portraits* (London: HMSO, 1977) 54.

NOTE: According to HW in *D 1784*, Colley Cibber (1671–1757) once rented Strawberry Hill, where he wrote *The Refusal, or the Lady's Philosophy* (1721).

257. DRAWING FOR PLATE 6, INDUSTRY AND IDLENESS: THE INDUSTRIOUS 'PRENTICE OUT OF HIS TIME, & MARRIED TO HIS MASTER'S DAUGHTER
William Hogarth (1697–1764), *c.* 1746–7

Pen and brown ink and grey and brown wash, over graphite, indented for transfer, 21.5 × 29 cm
British Museum, Department of Prints and Drawings. 1896,0710.14
Fig. 182

D 1774, 48 [Library]: Rare books of prints and drawings in the library… Hogarth's ditto [… most beautiful impressions; folio]; the most complete set of his works that is known, with some of his original drawings.

D 1784, 36, same as *D 1774*.

PROV: HW; 1842, Strawberry Hill London Sale, day 10, lot 1311, bt H. F. Standly, Esq., £111.6.0; 1896, The British Museum, London.

LIT: A. P. Oppé, *The Drawings of William Hogarth* (London, Phaidon Press, 1948), 50.

258. PLATE 6 INDUSTRY AND IDLENESS: THE INDUSTRIOUS 'PRENTICE OUT OF HIS TIME, & MARRIED TO HIS MASTER'S DAUGHTER
William Hogarth (1697–1764), 1747

Etching and engraving, 26.6 × 34.6 cm
British Museum, Department of Prints and Drawings. 1896,0710.15
Fig. 183

D 1774, 48 [Library]: Rare books of prints and drawings in the library…Hogarth's ditto [… works, most beautiful impressions; folio]; the most complete set of his works that is known, with some of his original drawings.

D 1784, 36, same as *D 1774*.

PROV: HW; 1842, Strawberry Hill London Sale, day 10, lot 1311, bt H. P. Standly, Esq., £111.6.0; 1896, The British Museum, London.

LIT: Frederic George Stephens and Mary Dorothy George, *Catalogue of Political and Personal Satires in the Department of Prints and Drawings in the British Museum* (London: by order of the Trustees, 1870–1954), no. 2945. Ronald Paulson, *Hogarth's Graphic Works*, 3rd edn (London: Print Room, 1989), 173.II.

259. PORTRAIT OF SARAH MALCOLM IN PRISON
William Hogarth (1697–1764), 1733

Oil on canvas, 48.8 × 38.7 cm
National Gallery of Scotland, Edinburgh, Bequest of Lady Dundas 1897. NG 838
Fig. 181

D 1774, 28 [Green Closet]: A portrait of Sarah Malcolm, who was hanged for murdering her mistress and two other women in the Temple. She is sitting at a table in Newgate, with popish beads before her. This was drawn by Hogarth the day before her execution, and she had put on red to look the better.

D 1784, 23, same as *D 1774*.

PROV: By 1771, HW; 1842, Strawberry Hill Sale, day 18, lot 72, bt C. K. Sharpe, Esq., £24.3.0; Bequeathed by him to Lady Jane Charteris (1811–97), daughter of the Earl of Weymss; from 1858 Lady Jane Dundas; 1897, Bequest of Lady Jane Dundas to National Gallery of Scotland.

LIT: *Anecdotes*, vol. 4, 83. *HW Corres.* 19: 460n. Mellon Lectures, 122. M. A. Doody, 'The law, the page, and the body of woman: murder and murderesses in the age of Johnson', *Age of Johnson* (New York: AMS Press, 1987), 130–1. Mark Hallet and Christina Riding, *Hogarth* (London: Tate Publishing, 2006), no. 95 for the related etching.

EXHIB: British Institution, 1863, no. 168; South Kensington, 'National Portrait Exhibition', 1868, no. 802; Edinburgh, 'International Exhibition of Industry, Science & Art', 1886, no. 1406.

NOTE: HW records his ownership in *Anecdotes*, vol. 4, published in 1771. According to J. H. Anderdon, in his copy of the 1842 sale catalogue, there is an inscription in HW's hand on back of canvas: 'Portrait of Sarah Malcolm drawn in Newgate the day before her execution' (Lewis Walpole Library information files).

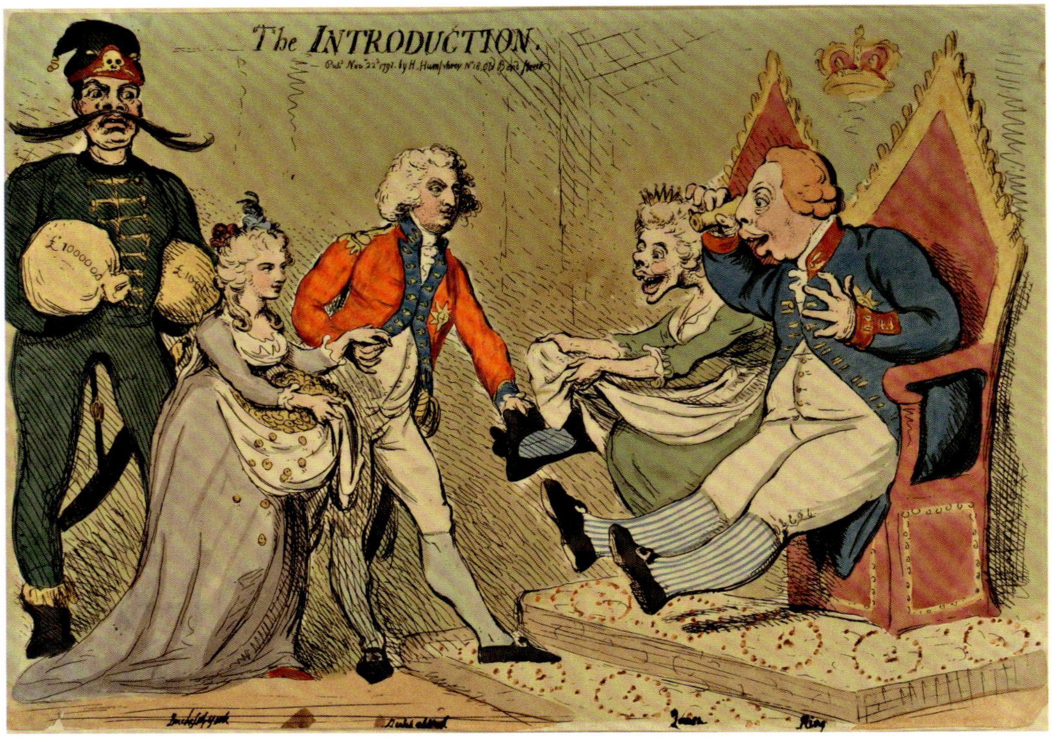

Figure 363. Catalogue 260

260. The Introduction
James Gillray (1756–1815), 1791

Etching with hand colouring on wove paper, 25 × 35.2 cm (trimmed to plate); 28 × 38 cm (mount)
Inscriptions: notations in ink at bottom in HW's hand: 'Duchess of York / Duke of York / Queen / King.'
The Lewis Walpole Library, Yale University. 791.11.22.02, Impression 1
Fig. 363

PROV: Possibly from a large portfolio, 'with numerous extra leaves containing upward of 120 political and other caricatures, of which a considerable number are by Gillray, in colours', assembled by HW and later dispersed; 1842, Strawberry Hill London Sale, day 5, lot 730, bt Strong, £4.8.0; 1843, Strong's Catalogue, lot 3364 (as 230 prints), £4.14.6; 1867, July 13, Sotheby's (George Smith Sale), lot 1641 (as 215 prints), bt Harvey, £6; Alfred Bowditch Collection; 1966, December 5, Gifted by Augustus Peabody Loring (Mr Bowditch's grandson), to W. S. Lewis as part of a collection of 1466 prints; The Lewis Walpole Library, Yale University.

LIT: Library 3563(2). Mary Dorothy George, *Catalogue of Political and Personal Satires Preserved in the Department of Prints and Drawings in the British Museum* (London: Trustees of the British Museum, 1938/1976), vol. 6, no. 7917. Richard Godfrey, *James Gillray. The Art of Caricature* (exh. cat. London: Tate Publishing, 2001), 172, no. 146 for another impression.

17. HORACE WALPOLE'S LEGACY

261. Portrait of Anne Seymour Damer
Richard Cosway (bap. 1742– d. 1821), 1790

Graphite with watercolour set in a gilt-wood frame, 22.8 × 14.0 (visible); 35.8 × 26.4 cm (frame)
Signed and dated on verso (transferred from recto): 'Rdus. Cosway R.A. Primarius Pictor Serenissimi Walliae Principis Fecit 1790'. In letterpress in the mount: 'The Honble Anne Damer'. In HW's hand on verso: 'Mrs Damer in the attitude of having just finished her bust of the young Paris. Drawn by Richd. Cosway 1790. H.W'.
The Trustees of the Waldegrave Chattels Trust
Fig. 177

D 1784, 95 More Additions…A drawing, whole length, of Mrs. Damer, in the attitude of having just carved her young Paris; by Richard Cosway.

1842 Sale: [In the Green Closet]: A Portrait of Mrs. Damer, whole length by Cosway, an original drawing …

PROV: 1790, commissioned by HW; 1842, Strawberry Hill Sale, day 18, lot 114, unsold; Earl of Waldegrave; by family descent.

LIT: *HW Corres.* 12: 273n. *OHG* 233. S. Lloyd, ed., *Richard and Maria Cosway: Regency Artists of Taste and Fashion* (Edinburgh: Scottish National Portrait Gallery, 1995), 122, no. 95.

262. Portrait Miniature of Mary Berry
Anne Mee (née Foldsone), 1790

Watercolour on ivory set in gilt metal frame, H 7.4 cm
Inscriptions: in HW's hand on verso: 'Miss Mary Berry / drawn by / Miss Foldson, / 1790. / H.W.'
The Trustees of the Waldegrave Chattels Trust
Fig. 15

1842 Sale [The Red Bedchamber?]: A pair of miniature Portraits of the Misses Agnes and Mary Berry, 1790, signed H.W. by Miss Foltson.

PROV: 1790, commissioned by HW; 1842, Strawberry Hill Sale, day 22, lot 60, bt Earl Waldegrave, £4.14.6; by family descent.

LIT: *HW Corres.* 11: 77, 133–4, 145, 193, 219, 350, 42: 292.

NOTE: The pair of miniatures of Mary and Agnes Berry is recorded in HW's hand on the free end paper in an extra-illustrated and heavily annotated copy of *D 1774*: 'Miss Mary & Miss Agnes Berry, Drs. of John Berry Esq. by Miss Foldson, 1790'. (The Lewis Walpole Library, 49 2522).

263. Portrait Miniature of Agnes Berry
Anne Mee (née Foldsone), 1790

Watercolour on ivory set in gilt metal frame, H 7.4 cm
Inscriptions: in HW's hand on verso: 'Miss Agnes Berry / drawn by / Miss Foldson, / 1790. / H.W.'
The Trustees of the Waldegrave Chattels Trust
Fig. 16

PROV: See Cat. 262.

LIT: See Cat. 262.

264. Writing Box
Pierre Eloy Langlois (1738–1805), 1760

Veneers on a mahogany carcase. H 13 × W 29.5 × depth 22 cm
Inlaid with the Walpole crest and motto, another crest of a winged wyvern and on the front, on a ribbon: 'H. 1760 W.' HW's circular bookplate as the Earl of Orford, on vellum, pasted inside the lid.
Josephine E. Case, James H. Case III, Samuel Case, John Case
Fig. 301

D 1774, 22 [Breakfast Room]: On the writing-table, an inlaid writing-box made by Langlois.

D 1784, 17, same as *D 1774*.
PROV: Made for HW; 1842, Strawberry Hill Sale; 1919, May 28, Sotheby's, Other Properties, lot 803; 1924, December 19, Charles J. Sawyer, Ltd, London, lot 345, bt Mr Owen D. Young, Esq., £22.0.0; Private collection, USA.
LIT: *HW Corres*. 30: 253, 31: 326.
NOTE: The upper, lockable part of the box, has a lift-out tray, and a place below for papers, At the bottom of the box is a shallow drawer. Walpole records travelling with his writing box.

265. LETTER FROM HORACE WALPOLE TO JOHN CHUTE
1759, November 4

23 × 18.5 cm
The Lewis Walpole Library, Yale University
Fig. 108

PROV: John Chute; *c*. 1843 sold by the 5th Duke of Grafton, as executor of the 6th Earl Waldegrave's estate, to Richard Bentley, the publisher; 1937, bt W. S. Lewis, from Mrs Bentley [estate of Richard Bentley the younger]; The Lewis Walpole Library, Yale University.
LIT: *HW Corres*. 35: 110–11.

266. JOURNAL OF THE REIGN OF GEORGE III, 1778–9
Horace Walpole (1717–1797)

68 leaves, HW's manuscript notes with pasted-in letterpress cuttings, bound in calf
The Trustees of the Waldegrave Chattels Trust
Fig. 11

PROV: HW; Earl Waldegrave; by descent.
LIT: *Bib. HW*, 93–5. Francis Steuart, ed., *The Last Journals of Horace Walpole during the Reign of George III from 1771 to 1783* (New York and London: John Lane the Bodley Head, 1910), vol. 2, p. 89 et. seq.

267. THE WORKS OF HORATIO WALPOLE, EARL OF ORFORD. VOLUME 5
Horace Walpole (1717–1797), edited by Mary Berry (1763–1853).

London: Printed for G. G. and J. Robinson and J. Edwards, 1798
30 × 24.5 cm
The Lewis Walpole Library, Yale University.
21 798C Copy 2
Fig. 17

PROV: 2007, May, Quaritch: The Lewis Walpole Library, Yale University.
LIT: *Bib. HW*. 75–85. Mellon Lectures 66, 73, 141, 166.

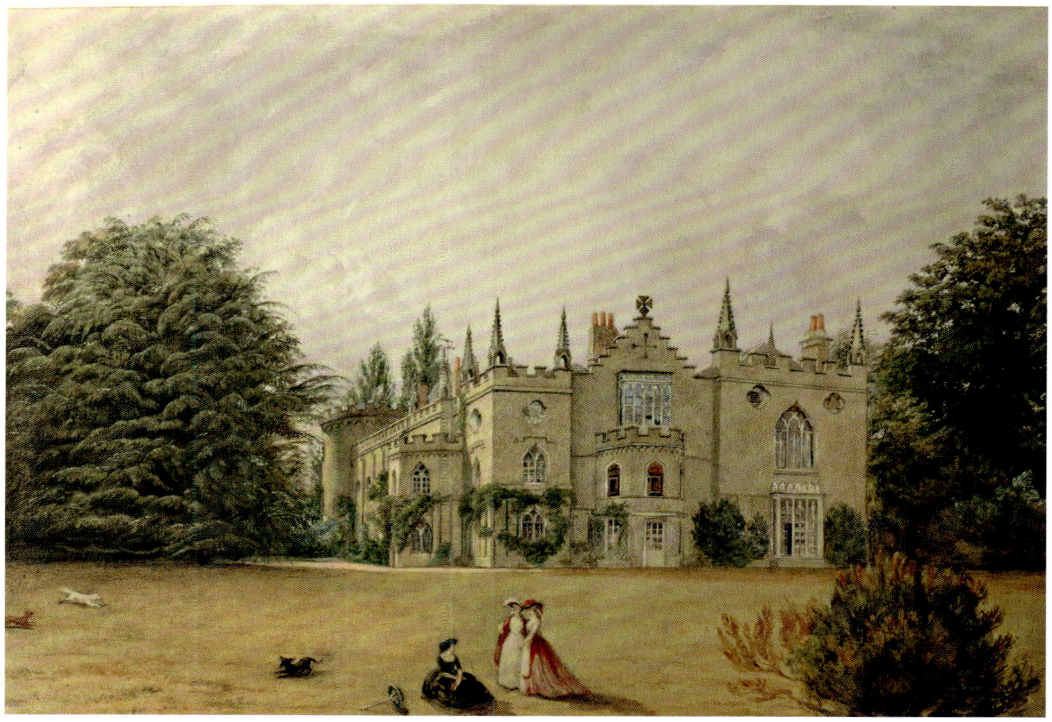

Figure 364. Catalogue 268

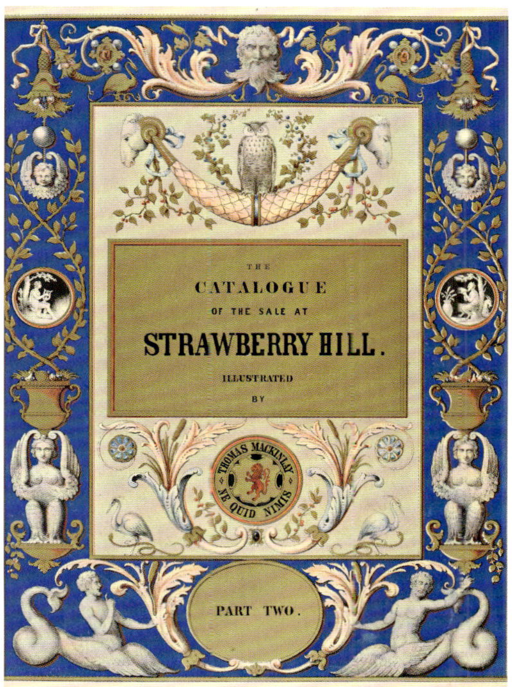

Figure 365. Catalogue 270

268. VIEW OF STRAWBERRY HILL
Gustavus Ellinthorpe Sintzenich, (exhibited 1844–56, London), *c*. 1840

Watercolour over pencil, heightened with body colour and scratching out
27.3 × 39.4 cm
Private collection
Fig. 364

269. A CATALOGUE OF THE CLASSIC CONTENTS OF STRAWBERRY HILL COLLECTED BY HORACE WALPOLE.
[London]: Smith and Robins, printers, [1842]

30.5 × 25 cm
The Lewis Walpole Library, Yale University.
485 842 C76 VII Copy 2
Fig. 288

PROV: Twisleton Fiennes; 1949, December 17, James F. Drake, Inc., to W. S. Lewis, $30. The Lewis Walpole Library, Yale University.
LIT: *Library* vol. 1, xxvii-xxv and lxxvii-xc. Percival Merritt, *An Account of the descriptive catalogues of Strawberry Hill and of Strawberry Hill sale catalogues, together with a bibliography* (Boston: privately printed by B. Rogers, 1915), 25–9 and 66–70.

270. A CATALOGUE OF THE CLASSIC CONTENTS OF STRAWBERRY HILL COLLECTED BY HORACE WALPOLE. VOLUME 2 [LONDON]: SMITH AND ROBINS, [1842]
30.5 × 25.5 cm
The Lewis Walpole Library, Yale University.
485 842 C76 IV Copy 3
Yale Center for British Art only
Fig. 365

PROV: See Cat. 273.
LIT: *Library* vol. 1, xxvii-xxv and lxxvii-xc. Percival Merritt, *An Account of the Descriptive Catalogues of Strawberry Hill and of Strawberry Hill Sale Catalogues, Together with a Bibliography* (Boston: privately printed by B. Rogers, 1915), 25–9 and 66–70.

271. ADMISSION TICKET TO THE PRIVATE VIEW AT STRAWBERRY HILL
[England: n.p.], 1842

Letterpress, 11.6 × 15.2 cm
Inscriptions: Inscribed with names and date on recto and verso.
The Lewis Walpole Library, Yale University.
File 485 842 A19 Copy 1
Fig. 290

PROV: Loose in the Strawberry Hill Sale Catalogue from Heffer, 1933, January; W. S. Lewis; The Lewis Walpole Library, Yale University.

272. HANDBILL FOR 'THE EXTRAORDINARY FAST PACKET, THE VIVID'
[England: n.p.], 1842

Letterpress, 19.3 × 11.5 cm
The Lewis Walpole Library, Yale University.
File 485 842 E96 Copy 1
Fig. 294

PROV: Handbill from the T. Crofton Croker Strawberry Hill Sale Catalogue. Gaskill Collection, 1938; W. S. Lewis; The Lewis Walpole Library, Yale University.
LIT: W. S. Lewis, *Horace Walpole's Library* (Cambridge: Cambridge University Press, 1958), 48.

273. PORTRAIT OF GEORGE ROBINS
Thomas Hosmer Shepherd (1793–1864), *c.* 1842

Watercolour on paper, 30.5 × 25.5 cm
Mounted in *Catalogue of the classic contents of Strawberry Hill Collected by Horace Walpole*. Volume I ([London] Smith and Robins [1842], 161)
The Lewis Walpole Library, Yale University.
485 842 C76 IV Copy 3 Vol. 1
Fig. 297

PROV: For the volume, Thomas MacKinlay; Sir Thomas William Boord; 1935, June 3, Mrs E. M. Copeman, Sotheby's, lot 110, bt Maggs for W. S. Lewis, £54; The Lewis Walpole Library, Yale University.

274. 'STRAWBERRY HILL MAY 1842 WITH THE WOODEN BUILDING ERECTED DURING THE SALE, BY ROBINS'
Artist unknown, 1842

Watercolour with pen and ink, 12.7 × 36 cm
Inscriptions: title at top center in contemporary hand; upper right 'se ipse pinxit'
The Lewis Walpole Library, Yale University.
842.00.00.77dr

PROV: 1959, August, Purchased from A. N. L. Munby W. S. Lewis; The Lewis Walpole Library, Yale University.

275. BOX WITH LID
Maker unknown, 18th century

Oak, with iron hinges and handles, H 24.8 × W 63.5 × depth 53.3 cm
Inscriptions: painted in shadowed letters on top: 'VIRTUOSI./PROVIDENT [the rest lost];' and on inside of lid: 'Bot. at the Sale of the great/VIRTUOSO/Horace Walpole, Earl of Orford'.
The Lewis Walpole Library, Yale University.
Fig. 302

1842 Sale [Closet Adjoining the Round Tower]: A stout wainscot box, lock and key, and a deal ditto [The deal bookcase ...]
PROV: HW; probably 1842, Strawberry Hill Sale, day 19, lot 6, bt Hor. Rodd, £0.10.0; 1964, February, H. M. Fletcher, bt W. S. Lewis $100; The Lewis Walpole Library, Yale University.
NOTE: The Virtuosi Provident Fund was a charitable fund founded in 1842 for the relief of distressed picture dealers and restorers and those working in related trades, and their families. Horatio Rodd, the dealer who purchased lot 6, on day 13 of the sale, was their original secretary, and the box would presumably have been used to keep the Fund's papers.

276. PORTRAIT OF SIR JOHN PERROT
Thomas Chambars (*c.* 1724–89), *c.* 1762

Chalk, charcoal, and graphite on brownish paper, 41.9 × 29.7 cm (visible)
Inscriptions: in HW's hand on back of frame at top: 'Sr. John Perrot, Lord Deputy of Ireland'; in Thomas Kirgate's hand: 'From the original at Sir Herbert Perrot's Packingtons at Westwood, Worchestershire.'. On paper label on back of frame: possibly in the artist's hand: 'Colours of the original now at Sir John Packingtons in Worcestershire. Hair & beard – dark brown. Eyes – dark blue. Complexions – clear & florid. Cap black velvet. Feather – white. Cloak – dark, probably black. Doublet – light greyish drab trimmed with gold. Sleeves & breeches – white satin with small black spots. Belt – gold with black pattern on it. Ribbon or scarf with jewel – red as for the Order of the Bath'.
In ink on back of wood backing: 'Bought at the Sale of Horace Walpole's House'; In chalk: '20 Lot 112 [?]'; on the wooden backing in W. S. Lewis's hand: identification of HW's hand and Kirgate's hand for inscriptions at top and 'sold S.H. xx.112 to H. Rodd £5.5.0 / Sotheby's 25 Oct. 53, lot 123, to Maggs for WSL, £4. / See Vertue's Ms Ad.d [?] 23023 (BM P.24803 [?] with HW's note that the drawing was by Chambars' On paper label at bottom of frame in W. S. Lewis's hand: '20 / Sold Sotheby's Oct. 53 (Different Properties_ lot 183 to Maggs for WSL £Sold SH xx.112 / See HW to Chas Lyttleton 16 Oct. 62'.
The Lewis Walpole Library, Yale University
762.00.00.41dr

D 1774, 106 [Great North Bedchamber]: On the window side:...Sir John Perrot, lord deputy of Ireland in the time of queen Elizabeth; in black and white chalk, by Chambars, from the original at sir Herbert Perrot Packington's.
D 1784, 74, same as *D 1774*.
PROV: Possibly commissioned by HW; 1842, Strawberry Hill Sale, day 20, lot 113, bt Strong, £4.4.0; 1953, October 26, Sotheby's (different properties), lot 183, bt Maggs for W. S. Lewis, £4; The Lewis Walpole Library, Yale University.
LIT: *HW Corres.* 40: 272n, 43: 384n. 'Vertue Note Books', *The Walpole Society Journal* 26 (Oxford: University Press, 1938), 62n.
NOTE: This picture is in its original black and gilt frame from Strawberry Hill.

APPENDICES

1. WALPOLE'S DREAM

Horace Walpole's Ms 'Book of Materials', The Lewis Walpole Library, Yale University, 49.2615, 63–4

In the night between the first & 2d of May 1760, which was soon after the Trial of Earl Ferrers in Westm. hall, I had the following entertaining Deam. I thought somebody shewed me a print of the trial of some ld Chanc. of Scotland before Charles 2d in Westm. hall. The court seem'd much smaller than what is now used on those occasions. I soon thought myself there, and that some English Earl, I can't recollect who, was tried after the Scottish Chancellor, but it did not last a minute. The King, with his crown, black wig and purple robe ermined, passed out of the court at a little door on the right hand of the great gate. A man in a light brown coat with plain gold lace, tied wig & garter, stood at the door very near me; I wondered he did not follow in the procession, for I fancied it was the Duke of York. I was very near him & examined him narrowly, and sd to myself, 'is it the duke of york? Is he like the wax head which George Selwyn has of him, that was taken off after he was dead; from the mould at Paris?' I thought he was, but much younger, as being then only Duke. Still uncertain, I said aloud, 'Is it the Duke of York? is it the Duke of York?' I thought the king heard me, & sent the present Ld Gower (master of the horse) to call me – I was surprized, but said to myself, 'it is not like me to be afraid of Kings & Princes; I will show them I am not. I went into a small low room, where the king was standing in the middle with his back to the Chimney, & six or seven persons about him. Ld Gower took a chair and turned the back towards me & bid me lean upon it, saying, 'that is the way of talking to the king'. The king asked me three or four questions, & I answered with great ease & familiarity; he then left me & went out of the room, seeming neither pleased nor displeased with me, but I was discontent, & thought he did not like me enough. I turned about , & observed that the room which was old wainscott unpainted was covered with pictures – Oh! thought I, in a rapture, this is the collection of Charles Ist. I will examine them carefully, for they will be burnt in Whitehall (where I thought I now was) I can never see them again; & then I will go home & look in the catalogue of K Charles's pictures, to see which I can find of them there. By the door where the king went out hung upright picture in an old lacquer'd frame, as most of them had, and some were inlaid with tortoiseshell. It was Adam & Eve with several beasts round them by Old Franks. The next was of the same subject but represented differently. I wondered the king had bought so many of the same kind. This room & the next had quantities of bad lacquered cabinets, trunks & boxes under the pictures; I said to myself, these are very bad, but to be sure they were the first that came over, before they knew what good Japan was. The D. of York staid in the room, but I did not mind him, nor did he seem to take it ill. Still I was determined to see all I coud, as I could never have another opportunity. I went into the next room which was the D. of York's bedchamber. Thought I, they will think me very impertinent, but I am resolved to gratify my curiosity. It was a very low old fashioned chamber & was lighted with small brass sconces, with tallow candles, the bed very old. I took down a candle and examined the pictures – & then turned peevishly to Geo. Selwyn and said, 'You pretend to love King Charles Ist. here is his collection, why don't you look at it, you never can have another opportunity, for it will be burnt.' The chimney projected much & the bed came out before it thus [Fig. 365].

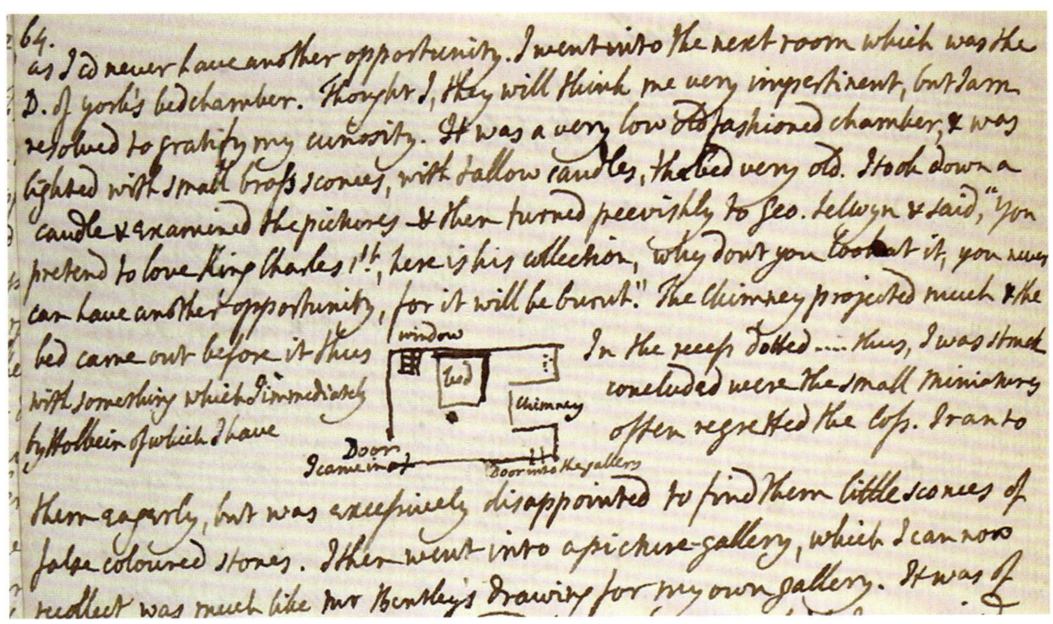

Figure 366. *The Duke of York's Bedchamber,* sketch from the 'Book of Materials', The Lewis Walpole Library, Yale University, 49.2615, 64

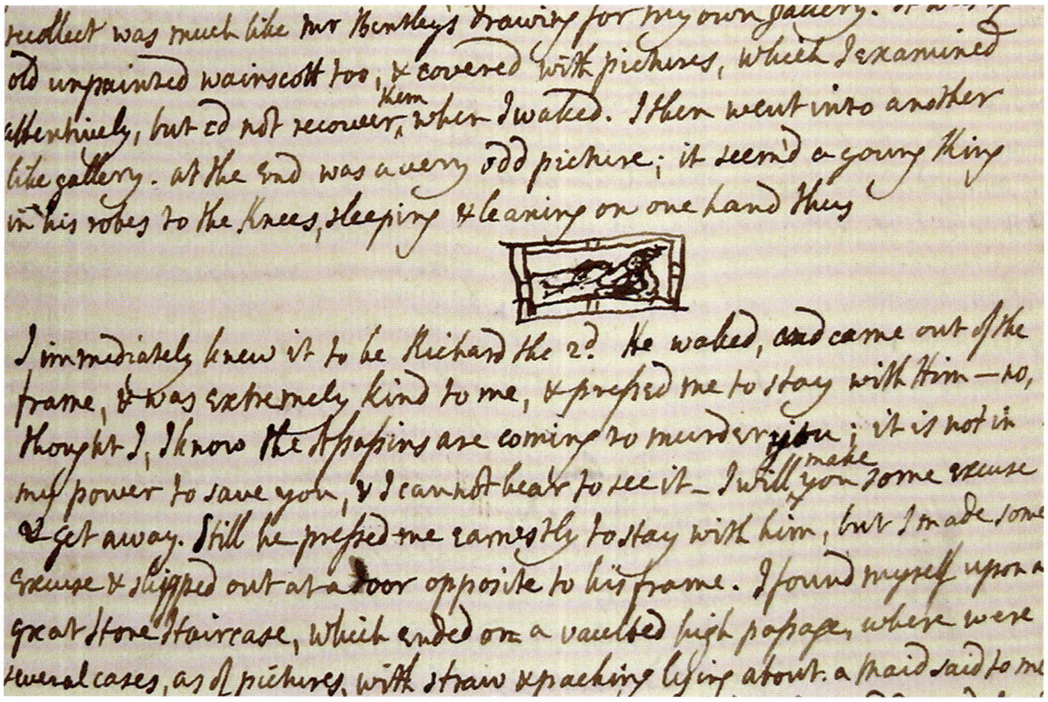
recollect was much like Mr Bentley's drawing for my own gallery.
old unpainted wainscott too, & covered with pictures, which I examined
attentively, but cd not recover them when I waked. I then went into another
like gallery. at the end was a very odd picture; it seem'd a young King
in his robes to the Knees, sleeping & leaning on one hand thus

I immediately knew it to be Richard the 2d. He waked, and came out of the
frame, & was extremely kind to me, & pressed me to stay with Him – no,
thought I, I know the Assassins are coming to murder you; it is not in
my power to save you, & I cannot bear to see it – I will make you some excuse
& get away. Still he pressed me earnestly to stay with him, but I made some
excuse & slipped out at a door opposite to his frame. I found myself upon a
great stone staircase, which ended on a vaulted high passage, where were
several cases, as of pictures, with straw & packing lying about. a maid said to me

Figure 366. *Richard II*, sketch from the 'Book of Materials', The Lewis Walpole Library, Yale University, 49.2615, 64

In the recess dotted…thus I was struck with something which I immediately concluded were the small miniatures by Holbein of which I have often regretted the loss. I ran to them eagerly, but was excessively disappointed to find them little sconces of false coloured stones. I then went into a picture-gallery, which I can now recollect was much like Mr Bentley's drawing for my own gallery. It was of old unpainted wainscott too, & covered with pictures, which I examined attentively, but cd not recover them when I waked. I then went into another like gallery. at the end was a very odd picture; it seemed a young king in his robes to the knees, sleeping and leaning on one hand thus [Fig. 366].

I immediately knew it to be Richard 2d. He waked, and came out of the frame, & was extremely kind to me, & pressed me to stay with him – no, thought I, I know the assassins are coming to murder you; it is not in my power to save you, & I cannot bear to see it – I will make you some excuse & get away. Still he pressed me earnestly to stay with him, but I made some excuse & slipped out at a door opposite to his frame. I found myself upon a great stone staircase, which ended on a vaulted high passage, where were several cases, as of pictures, with straw and packing lying about. a maid said to me, you are right, that is yr way – I wondered the palace seem'd so deserted. I turned to the right, & found myself in another vaulted passage but less, and parallel with the stairs, there was a Porter's lodge, somebody spoke to me, I went out the gate & waked.

2. WALPOLE'S LIST OF PRINCIPAL CURIOSITIES

This list, in Horace Walpole's hand, is pasted into a copy of the 1774 *Description* owned by Horace Walpole, which he annotated for the preparation of the 1784 edition (Lewis Walpole Library, Yale University, 49 2523 121 12). The contents and a change in the handwriting suggest that it was compiled in two parts. The first part up to no. 55 was written about 1783, largely following the layout of the house. From no. 56 the list contains objects in a mix of locations, acquired between 1781 and 1789.

The text of the manuscript is shown in bold. Additional references to the objects in other works such as *D 1774* and *1842 Sale* (see Abbreviations, p. 000) are also as cited in the original texts. Latest published whereabouts of the objects are given where known.

Tribune

1. Cowley enamel
See Cat. 226, Fig. 216

2. Mad d'Olonne
See Cat. 185, Fig. 217

3. Clinksted's Hermaphrodite
D 1774, 85 (Tribune): Salmacis and Hermaphroditus, a most beautiful miniature by Clinksted [Karl Gustav Klingstedt, 1657–1743]; given to Mr. Walpole by Mr. Chute: set in a gold frame enamelled blue.
1842 Sale: day 14, lot 89, bt Zimmerman, £12.1.0.

4. Catherine of Arragon by Holbein, min
See Cat. 174, Fig. 193

5. Isaac Oliver, by himself
See Cat. 175, Fig. 130

6. Ld Burleigh & Q Eliz Cameos
D 1774, 79 [Tribune]: Within the cabinet of enamels and miniatures…A valuable jewel of lord Burleigh's head on onyx, by Valerio Vicentino, cut on the reverse of an antique of Caracalla; appendent is the head of queen Elizabeth, cut likewise on sardonyx, by the same Vicentino; the whole set with 53 brilliants: given to Mr. Walpole by his father, who bought it of sir Andrew Fountaine, who had it set on purpose, with allusion to queen Caroline and sir Robert Walpole.
1842 Sale: Day 15, Lot 61 to Hertz, Marlboro Street, £84.0.0.

7. Deed of K Theodore, & his Seal
D 1774, 86 [Tribune]: Great seal of Theodore king of Corsica [Stefan von Neuhoff, Baron von Neuhoff (1694–1756)]…That very curious piece by which he took the benefit of the act of insolvency: he is only stiled, Theodore Stephen baron de Newhoff.
1842 Sale: Day 15.Lot 84, bt Charles J. Pagliano, £6.6.

8. Caligula, small bronze bust
D 1774, 87 [Tribune]: A small bust in bronze of Caligula, with silver eyes. This exquisite piece is one of the finest things in the collection, and shews the great art of the ancients. It is evidently a portrait, carefully done, and seems to represent that emperor at the beginning of his madness. It was found with some other small busts at the very first discovery of Herculaneum, which happened by digging a well for the prince d'Elbœf, who resided many years afterwards at Florence, where it was sold on his return to France, and being purchased by sir Horace Mann, was by him sent to Mr. Walpole.
1842 Sale: day 15, lot 68, bt Hume, Berners-street for Wm Beckford, £48.6.c.
Note: see p. 176, Fig. 187

9. Missal of Queen Claude
See Cat. 162, Fig. 34

10. Hen 8ths Dagger
D 1774, 89 [Tribune]: Henry VIIIth's dagger, of Turkish work; the blade is of steel damasked with gold, the case and handle of chalcedonyx, set with diamonds and many rubies. From the collection of lady Elizabeth Germaine. The duchess of Portland has such another set with jacinths.
1842 Sale: day 15, lot 79, bt Charles Kean, Esq., £54.12.0; 1898, July 11, Christie's, Mrs Mary Logie, Lot 98 bt Haigham, £215.
Note: see pp. 223–6, Fig. 253

11. Polemburg by himself
See Cat. 195, Fig. 84

12. Fiamingo's Vase
D 1774, 98 [Tribune]: A beautiful bronze vase taken from the antique by Fiamingo, who has added fine bas-reliefs of boys: from the Harleian collection.
1842 Sale: day 13, lot 74, bt Lord Charles Townsend, £21.0.0
Note: There are two drawings of this vase at the Lewis Walpole Library: one, 1759 by J.H. Müntz, laid in Horace Walpole's extra-illustrated copy of the *Description* (49 3582); and the other, n.d., attributed to John Carter and laid in Richard Bull's extra-illustrated copy of the *Description* (33 30, copy 11).

13. Bell by Benvenuto Cellini
D 1774, 96 [Tribune]: A most beautiful silver bell, made for a pope by Benvenuto Cellini. It is covered all over in the highest rilievo with antique masks, flies, grass hoppers, and other insects; the virgin and boy-angels on top, a wreath of leaves a bottom. Nothing can exceed the taste of the whole design, or the delicate and natural representation of the insects: the wonderful execution makes almost everything credible that he says of himself in his Life. It came out of the collection of the marquis of Leonati at Parma, and was bought by the marquis of Rockingham, who exchanged it with Mr Walpole for some very scarce Roman medals of great bronze, amongst which was an antique medaliuncino of Alexander Severus with the amphitheatre, in the highest preservation.
1842 Sale: day 15, lot 83, sold to Lord Waldegrave. British Museum, Waddesdon Bequest, WB.95.
Note: now attributed to Wenzel Jamnitzer, Nuremberg, mid-sixteenth century. Tait 1988.

14. Tiberius, Cameo
D 1774, 94 [Tribune]: In the box of antique rings … Tiberius, cameo on onyx, of the first Greek workmanship.
1842 Sale: day 15, lot 26, bt Hume, Berners-street [for William Beckford], £10.10.0.

15. Cigala, intaglia
D 1774, 95 [Tribune]: In the box of antique rings … A Cicada; a fine intaglio on cornelian.
1842 Sale: day 15, lot 41, Hertz, Marlboro'-street, £ 2.2.0.

16. Cupids lamp in bronze
D 1774, 101 [Tribune]: A beautiful lamp, in the shape of a foot, Cupid fallen asleep over the flame; antique bronze with silver ornaments: it was found in the temple of Cupid, is published by Montfaucon, and was bought at the sale of the Harleian collection.
1842 Sale: day 13, lot 86 bt Hertz, Marlboro'-street, 16.16.0.

17. Callots Battle
D 1784, 71 [Tribune]: A battle, in black and gold, exquisitely touched by Callot; bought at Mrs. Stanley's sale.
1842 Sale: day 13, lot 48 bt Wilkinson, £13.2.6. [Beauclerk Closet]

19. Lady Di's drawings in her closet
See Cat. 254, Fig. 361

Breakfast Room and Great North Bedchamber

20. her 4 wax pictures
D 1774, 128 [Breakfast Room]: Appendix … Two beautiful bas-reliefs of boys in wax, by lady Diana Beauclerc; set in frames with her arms, and cameos by Wedgwood and Tassie.
1842 Sale: day 22, lot 51, bt Town and Emanuel, £11.0.6 the pair.
Note: There is a related watercolour at the Lewis Walpole Library, *Sketch for the frames of her bas-reliefs* by Diana Beauclerk, 1776, laid in Horace Walpole's extra-illustrated copy of the *Description* (49 3582).
D 1774, 138 [Great Bedchamber]: Appendix … Two bas-reliefs of boys in wax on glass, designed and modelled by lady Diana Beauclerc sister of George duke of Marlborough. On the back are written these lines: [8 lines by Horace Walpole].
1842 Sale: day 18, lot 116, bt Thorne, Richmond, 2.0.0.

Round Room

21. Lady Carlisle & Leceister, Vandyck
D 1774, 74 [Round Room]: Over the chimney, lady Dorothy Percy countess of Leicester, in red, and her sister lady Lucy, the famous countess of Carlisle; a very capital picture of Vandyck, sold out of Penshurst by lady Yonge, when she inherited half of that ancient seat by the will of lady Brownlow. Mr Hoare of Stourhead offered the last earl of Leicester of the Sidney family an hundred pounds for this picture.
1842 Sale: day 21, lot 49, bt Norton, Soho-square, £231.0.0.
Private collection

22. Nicolo Poussin, birth of Jupiter
See Cat. 150, Fig. 75

23. Salvator Rosa, Isaac journeying
D 1774, 75 [Round Room]: Jacob travelling from Laban; very fine; by Salvator Rosa: a present from the same [Horace Mann].
1842 Sale: day 21, lot 47, bt Russell, King-street, £42.0.0.

24. Paul Brill, Landscape
D 1774, 75 [Round Room]: A most beautiful landscape by Paul Brill.
1842 Sale: day 21, lot 50, bt Thane, £34.13.0. [Great North Bedchamber]

25. Mrs Smith, Vandyck
See Cat. 152, Fig. 339

26. Dr Dee's black stone
See Cat. 108, Fig. 125

27. Poussin's wife's bust
D 1784, 77 [Great North Bedchamber]: A small bust in terra-cotta of Nicolo Poussin's wife, beautifully simple and natural, by Fiamingo, in terra cotta, amicitiae causa; from mons. Mariette's collection.
1842 Sale: day 14, lot 85 bt Earl of Derby, £21.0.0
Note: see Irving Lavin and Marilyn Aronberg Lavin, 'Duquesnoy's "Nano di Créqui" and Two Busts by Francesco Mochi', *The Art Bulletin* 52, 2 (Jun. 1970): 132–49.

28. Seb Ricci's concert of singers
D 1774, 106–7 [Great North Bedchamber]: Rehearsal of an opera, with caricatures of the principal performers: Nicolini stands in front, Mrs. Toft is at the harpsichord, Margarita is entering in black* [*The gentleman in blue, with the patch on one eye, sitting by the Margarita, is sir Robert Rich, father of Elizabeth lady Lyttleton. See curious accounts of Mrs. Toft and the Margarita in the 5th vol. of sir John Hawkins's History of Music]. Bought at the sale John duke of Argyll, who bought it at that of Charles Stanhope, esq; by Sebastian Ricci, the landscape in it Marco Ricci.
1842 Sale: day 20, lot 114, bt Hen. Ralph Willett, Esq., 57.15.0; 1999, 9 July, Christie's London Sale, lot 82.

29. Ninon de Lenclos
D 1774, 104 [Great North Bedchamber]: Ninon L'Enclos, the only original picture of her; given by herself to the countess of Sandwich, daughter of Wilmot earl of Rochester, and by her grandson, John earl of Sandwich to Mr. Walpole.
1842 Sale: day 20, lot 98 bt Fuller [for Lord Northwick] £131.5.0.
Note: A pen and ink, and watercolour drawing after this portrait is mounted in Horace Walpole's extra-illustrated copy of *D 1784* (Lewis Walpole Library, Yale University, 49 3582, 161). The drawing is inscribed: 'Ninon de L'Enclos / from an Original Picture / given by herself / to the Countess of Sandwich / and by the present Earl of Sandwich / to Mr. Walpole 1757'.

30. Henry 8ths Family
See Cat. 102, Fig. 149

Gallery

30. Giorgione
D 1774, 70 [Gallery]: A young man's head, æt 18; admirable nature: by Giorgione. [*D 1784*, 51:] This was in the collection of Charles Ist. Vide Topham's Catalogue.
1842 Sale: day 21, lot 92, bt T. B. Brown, Howland-street, £110.5.0 ['A Young Man's Head, dressed in rich black velvet trimmed with fur'].

31. Eagle
See Cat. 138, Fig. 184

32. Vespasian
D 1774, 69 [Gallery]: Vespasian, in bisaltes: a noble bust, bought out of the collection of cardinal Ottoboni. It stands on a Roman sepulchral altar, on which, in bas-relief, is a man sacrificing, with this inscription, TI.CLAUDIUS AUG. L. / DOCILIS / AEDITUS AEDIS / FURTUNAE TULLIANAE.
1842 Sale: day 23, lot 73, bt Hume, Berners-street [for William Beckford], £220.10.0; 1882, June 19, Christie's, Hamilton Palace Collection, His grace the Duke of Hamilton, K.T. First Portion, Lot 190, £336, Agnew; 1893, June 28, Christie's, Collection of Right Hon Revelstoke, Lot 138, to Charles Davis, £157.10.
Note: see pp. 173–4.

33. c/s of Exeter, Vandyck
D 1774, 67 [Gallery]: Chimney side, left hand: … Frances Bridges, daughter of the lord Chandos, and second wife of Thomas Cecil earl of Exeter, on whose left hand she refused to lie on his tomb in Westminster-abbey. This picture, which is an excellent one of Vandyck, belonged to Richardson the painter, who has written a dissertation on eight pages on it in one his books*. it was purchased of Hudson the painter, son-in-law of Richardson [*D 1784*,

49: *This lady was most falsely accused of many crimes, of which she was entirely innocent, and acquitted; of which see an account in Granger's Biographical History of English Portraits, vol. I, p. 548.
1842 Sale: day 21, lot 66, bt Thane, £17.17.0.
Note: see Karen Hearn (ed.), *Van Dyck and Britain*, London: Tate Publishing, 2009, 210–11. Jonathan Richardson the Elder analysed the picture in his *Essay on the Art of Criticism*.

34. Leneve, Corn Jansen
D 1774, 66 [Gallery]: Chimney side, left hand: .... Mr Leneve, master of the company of merchant taylors: a most bright and pure picture, by Cornelius Jansen.
1842 Sale: day 21, lot 59, bt Dommes, £35.14.0; Merchant Taylors' Company, London.

35. Do Sr P Lely
See Cat. 137, Fig. 184

36. D of Bucking, Rubens
D 1774, 65 [Gallery]: East end: ... George Duke of Buckingham, his son [of Sir George Villiers]; a very fine head, by Rubens: the garter is put on the wrong way. *1842 Sale*: day 21, lot 55, bt Farrer, Wardour-street, £23.2.0.

37. Sr Peter Lely's Ld Sandwich
D 1774, 65 [Gallery]: East end: ... Admiral Montagu, earl of Sandwich; by sir Peter Lely: very good head.
1842 Sale: day 21, lot 56, bt Lord Charles Townsend, £33.12.0.
[Holbein Chamber]

38. Holbeins 2 triumphs of riches and poverty
See Cat. 127, Fig. 332

39. ——— Hen 8th terracotta
See Cat. 122, Fig. 328

40. Charlotte de France, by Janet
See Cat. 123, Fig. 63

41. Wolsey's hat
See Cat. 129, Fig. 145

42. Heny 8th bust in box
D 1774, 62 [Holbein Chamber]: On the side opposite to the chimney: ... Head of Henry 8th. with a watch at his neck, carved in box by Holbein.
1842 Sale: day 20, lot 47 bt John Dent, Esq. £39.18.0.

Armoury

43. Armour of Francis 1st
See Cat. 50, Fig. 255

Library

44. Hen 8ths Clock in the library
See Cat. 78, Fig. 56

45. Charter de foresta
See Cat. 80

46. Callot's pocket book
See Cat. 84, Fig. 209

47. 25 medals & coins
i. See Cat. 96, Fig. 319
ii. *D 1774*, 52 [Library]: Catalogue of the 25 most precious coins and medals in the rosewood case: 2 Medal of pope Julius the 3d. in silver, struck on the restoration of the Roman catholic religion in England by queen Mary.
1842 Sale: day 10, lot 44, bt Hen. Ralph Willett, Esq., £8.5.0.
iii. *D 1774*, 52 [Library]: Catalogue of the 25 most precious coins and medals in the rosewood case: 3 A satirical silver medal struck in Holland. On the obverse, the head of Oliver Cromwell laureated in armour. On the reverse he is kneeling in the lap of Britannia, with his breeches down; the French and Spanish ambassadors are contending which shall kiss first; the former says to the latter, *Retire toy, l'honneur appartient au roi mon maitre Louis le Grand*. Vary scarce, from Lord Oxford's collection.
1842 Sale, day 10, lot 53, bt Till, £0.8.0.
iv. *D 1774*, 52 [Library]: Catalogue of the 25 most precious coins and medals in the rosewood case: 4 A silver medal; on one side the head of queen Mary of England, on the other, of Philip II. Both in alto-relievo, and of the most exquisite workmanship. It was a trial-piece, and is certainly the finest modern medal known. It was bought by Mr Walpole in Italy.
1842 Sale: day 10, lot 41, bt Cureton, £0.14.0.
v. *D 1774*, 53 [Library]: Catalogue of the 25 most precious coins and medals in the rosewood case: 5. A large gold medal of Henry 8th. On the reverse, his titles in Hebrew, Greek and Latin. It is the first medal of the English series. From lord Oxford's collection.
1842 Sale: day 10, lot 23, bt Lord Hatherton, £1.16.0.
vi. *D 1774*, 53 [Library]: Catalogue of the 25 most precious coins and medals in the rosewood case: 6. A silver medal of the destruction of the Spanish armada. See an account of this medal, and the preceding [medal of Henry VIII], in Evelyn. From the same [Lord Oxford's] collection.
1842 Sale: day 10, lot 42 bt William Blamire, Esq. £2.16.0
vii. See Cat. 95, Fig. 318
viii. *D 1774* [Library]: Catalogue of the 25 most precious coins and medals in the rosewood case: 8. Fine gilt coin of pope Paul 3d. Reverse, a Ganymede, admirably drawn: this beautiful coin was the work Michael Angelo Buonaroti. From the collection of baron Stosch.
1842 Sale: unidentifiable
ix. *D 1774*, 53 [Library]: Catalogue of the 25 most precious coins and medals in the rosewood case: 9. Silver medal of lord treasurer Southampton; by Abraham Simon.
1842 Sale: unidentifiable
x. See Cat. 97, Fig. 33
xi. *D 1774*, 53 [Library]: Catalogue of the 25 most precious coins and medals in the rosewood case: 11. Gold medal of Nero Claudius Drusus: reverse, trophies, *De Germanis*.
1842 Sale: unidentifiable
xii. *D 1774*, 53 [Library]: Catalogue of the 25 most precious coins and medals in the rosewood case: 12. Gold medal of Trajan; reverse, his forum. These two are very rare.
1842 Sale: unidentifiable
xiii. See Cat. 94, Fig. 317
xiv. *D 1774*, 54 [Library]: Catalogue of the 25 most precious coins and medals in the rosewood case: 14. Gold medal of Othio: very scarce, and finely preserved.
1842 Sale: unidentifiable
xv. *D 1774*, 54 [Library]: Catalogue of the 25 most precious coins and medals in the rosewood case: 15. Ditto of Pertinax: not only very rare, but in the most exquisite preservation.
1842 Sale: unidentifiable
xvi. *D 1774*, 54 [Library]: Catalogue of the 25 most precious coins and medals in the rosewood case: 16. Copper coin of king Ferdinand of Naples; a pun on the reverse; his arms, a *horse*; the motto, *equitas regni*.

1842 Sale: unidentifiable

xvii. *D 1774*, 54 [Library]: Catalogue of the 25 most precious coins and medals in the rosewood case: 17. Silver coin of Eustace, son of King Stephen; very rare: from lord Oxford's collection.

1842 Sale: unidentifiable

xviii. *D 1774*, 54 [Library]: Catalogue of the 25 most precious coins and medals in the rosewood case: 18. A silver half crown of pope Clement 11th. Reverse, the pantheon.

1842 Sale: unidentifiable

xix. *D 1774*, 54 [Library]: Catalogue of the 25 most precious coins and medals in the rosewood case: 19. Copper medal of pope Gregory 13th, on the correction of the calendar: the reverse, which is in beautiful taste, was designed by Parmegiano.

1842 Sale: unidentifiable

xx. *D 1774*, 54 [Library]: Catalogue of the 25 most precious coins and medals in the rosewood case: 20. Silver medal of the same pope, on the massacre of St Barthelemi: on the reverse, the destroying angel murdering the protestants; the legend, *Hugonotorum Strages*. This scandalous medal was called in, and the die broken; which has made it very uncommon.

1842 Sale: unidentifiable

xxi. *D 1774*, 54 [Library]: Catalogue of the 25 most precious coins and medals in the rosewood case: 21. A silver coin struck by the republic of Florence when they declared Jesus Christ their king, to keep off the pope: from baron Stosch's collection: extremely rare.

1842 Sale: unidentifiable

xxii. *D 1774*, 54 [Library]: Catalogue of the 25 most precious coins and medals in the rosewood case: 22. Copper medal of Lorenzo de Medici, who stabbed duke Alexander: the reverse copied from Brutus's medal, with the cap of liberty between the two daggers; the legend, *VIII Id. Jan.* Very rare.

1842 Sale: unidentifiable

xxiii. *D 1774*, 55 [Library]: Catalogue of the 25 most precious coins and medals in the rosewood case: 23. Copper medal of Clement 7th. Reverse, Joseph and his brethren: designed by Raphael.

1842 Sale: unidentifiable

xxiv. *D 1774*, 55 [Library]: Catalogue of the 25 most precious coins and medals in the rosewood case: 24. Coin of Theodore king of Corsica: rare.

1842 Sale: unidentifiable

xxv. *D 1774*, 55 [Library]: Catalogue of the 25 most precious coins and medals in the rosewood case: 25. Brass satirical medal of queen Anne: reverse, the queen and lady Masham embracing; motto, *All for Love.*

1842 Sale: unidentifiable

Breakfast Room

48. Isaac Olivers & Peter Olivers
D 1774, 23 [Breakfast Room]: A young bride, by Isaac Oliver.
1842 Sale: day 11, lot 32, bt Robert Holford, Esq., £105.0.0.
D 1774, 23 [Breakfast Room]: Venetia Stanley lady Digby, aged 19, very beautiful; by Peter Oliver.
1842 Sale: day11, lot 26, bt Miss Burdett Coutts, 25.4.0.
D 1774, 127 [Breakfast Room]: Appendix… Lady Catherine Howard, daughter of H. Fred. earl of Arundel, and first wife of John Digby son of sir Kenelm. On the reverse, in the same enamelled frame, another lady of the family, exquisitely painted by Peter Oliver; probably the second wife of John Digby.
1842 Sale: day 11, lot 55, bt Baroness Anselm de Rothschild, Frankfort, £57.16.0.
See Cats 178, 179, 211, 213–17, 219, Figs 196, 210, 191, 197, 203, 204, 207

49. Cowley in oil
D 1784, 20 [Breakfast Room]: Cowley, by sir Peter Lely; the fine original of Zincke's Cowley in enamel in the cabinet; bought at the sale of Mr Lovibonde in 1776 [with a verse].
1842 Sale: day 11, lot 21, 100gns, to Sir Robert Peel, Bart., £105.0.0. Dulwich Picture Gallery.

50. Petitot's Watch
D 1784, 19 [Breakfast Room]: An exceedingly fine watch, given to general Fairfax by the parliament after the battle of Naseby; by P. Bordier, brother-in-law of Petitot. On one side is Fairfax on horseback, after Vandyck's king Charles; on the other, the house of commons; behind, the battle. It was bought at the sale of Thoresby's museum, who has described it in his Ducatus Leodiensis.
1842 Sale: day 11, lot 41 bt John P. Beavan, Esq., £21.0.0.

51. Charles 2d & Rose the Gardiner
See Cat. 104, Fig. 59

Library

52. Vol of French heads of Court of Francis Ist
See Cat. 81, Fig. 267

Great North Bedchamber

52. Lady Di's 2 flower tubs
See Cat. 253, Fig. 243

53. Ld Clarendon's 12 silver plates
See Cat. 156, Fig. 80

54. Silver Chest of BenvCellini
D 1774, 107 [Great North Bedchamber]: A fine silver trunk to hold perfumes, with bas-reliefs; the top from Raphael's judgment of Paris: the work of Benvenuto Cellini. Bought out of the great duke's wardrobe; a present from sir Horace Mann.
1842 Sale: day 16, lot 48, bt Strong, Bristol, £36.10.0 (a small ebony trunk for perfumes ornamented with bas-reliefs of silver).

55. Lady Di Beauclerc's gipsies
D 1774, 150 [Red Bedchamber]: Additions since the Appendix… Gypsies telling a country-maiden her fortune at the entrance of a beech-wood; a most beautiful drawing in water-colours, designed and executed by lady Diana Beauclerc in 1781; the chef-d'oeuvre of her works.
1842 Sale: day 22, lot101, bt Cain of Richmond, £6.10.0. Probably Victoria and Albert Museum, 9-1883
Note: see *OHG*, 31.

56. ——— masquerade at Vauxhall
D 1784, 89 [Beauclerk Closet]: Appendix … A masquerade at Vauxhall, in bister; by Lady Diana Beauclerc. There is a wonderful expression in the faces, and the attitudes, though some of the figures are quite masked and others have half-masks.
1842 Sale: day 17, lot 35, Hon. Col. D. Damer, M.P. £3.15.0.

57. ———cabinet with drawings
See Cat. 254, Fig. 241

58. Mrs Damer's Dogs
See Cat. 255, Fig. 178

59. Henry 7th
D 1784, 91 [Great North Bedchamber] Appendix ... Henry 7th. A most capital portrait on board, and incomparable for the truth of nature, expression, and chiaro scuro. The character and thought in the countenance, and its exact conformity with the bust by Torreggiani in the Star-chamber, make it unquestionably a portrait for which the king sat; and yet the knowledge of light and shade, not possessed even by Holbein, makes it probable that this picture was retouched by Rubens, of whose colouring it is worthy and resembles.
1842 Sale, day 20, lot 89, bt Viscount Holmesdale, £31.10.0.

60. Heart enamelled, with devices, made for Margaret c/s of Lenox
D 1784, 60 [Tribune]: In the cabinet of enamels and miniatures ... 'A golden heart set with jewels, and ornamented with emblematic figures enamelled, and Scottish mottos; made at the order of the lady Margaret Douglas, mother of Henry lord Darnley, in memory of her husband Matthew Stuart earl of Lennox and regent of Scotland, murdered by the papists.
1842 Sale: day 15, lot 60 bt Farrer, Wardour-street [for Queen Victoria], £136.10.0; Royal Collection.
[About 160 presents in the whole collection]

61. Illuminated Book by Don Julio Clovio
See Cat. 106, Fig. 35

62. Jupiter Serapis
D 1784, 91–2: [Lady Diana Beauclerc's Cabinet]: Appendix...The head of Jupiter Serapis, in basaltes. The divine majesty and beauty of this precious fragment prove the great ideas and consummate taste of the ancient sculptors. This bust was purchased, with the celebrated vase, from the Barberini collection at Rome, by sir William Hamilton; and was sold with the vase to the duchess of Portland, and on her grace's death was bought by Mr. Walpole.
1842 Sale: day 13, lot 82, bt Hume, Berners-street for William Beckford, Esq. £78.15.0; 1882, June 26, Christie's, Hamilton Palace Collection, Second portion, Lot 469 to Castellani for £106.1s.
Note: see p. 176, Fig. 188

63. Pr Arthur& Q Catherine
D 1784, 93 [Beauty Room]: Curiosities added since Book was completed ... Prince Arthur and Catharine of Arragon, on board, the original frame; a present from colonel Myddleton, Esq. Denbighshire, in which county it had remained from death of the prince at Ludlow.
1842 Sale: day 20, lot 79 bt Hor. Rodd, £6.6; 1894, May 11, Christie's, Pryor's Bank, Fulham, Lot 25, £7.5.

64. Mrs Damer's Eagle & her kittens
D 1784, 94 [Library]: Curiosities Added since Book was completed ... The fishing eagle, modelled in terra-cotta, the size of life. This bird was taken in lord Melbourn's park at Brocket-hall, and in taking it one of the wings was almost cut off, and Mrs. Damer saw it in that momentary rage, which she remembered, and has executed exactly. She has written her own name in Greek on the base, and Mr. W. added this line, '*Non me Praxiteles finxit, at Anna Damer*, 1787.'
1842 Sale: day 19, lot 1, bt Sir Alexander Johnston, £7.07.0.
D 1784, 93 [Green Closet]: Curiosities Added since Book was completed ... Two kittens in marble, by Mrs. Damer.
1842 Sale: day 16, lot 21, bt Hon. Col. D. Damer, M.P., £20.9.6
Note: *OHG*, 30.

3. WALPOLE'S ACCOUNT OF THE AESTHETIC EFFECTS AT STRAWBERRY HILL

Ms13-1947 in the Fitzwilliam Museum, Cambridge. It was sold by Sir Wathen Walpole Waller, Christie's, 15 December 1947, lot 50, bought by Maggs, and given by the Friends of the Fitzwilliam Museum, together with other Walpole Mss and a copy of the rules for visitors. It is written by HW, in ink, on four sides of a folded sheet. The layout has been preserved here.

[f.1] Great effects may be produced by the disposition of a House, & by studying lights & shades, and by attending to a harmony of colours. I have practiced all these rules in my House at Strawberrry hill, & have observed the impressions made on Spectators by these arts.

With regard to lights & shades. The first Entrance strikes by the gloom: the Staircase opens upwards to greater light. The blue room relieves the Eye from the conven:tual retirement of the Entrance by discovering a most beautifull landscape from the windows, set off by the overarching trees. The green closet is all light and chearfullness within & without. The Star.chamber and dusky passage again prepare you for solemnity: the Holbein-chamber softens that Idea, yet still maintains a grave tone; for the whole colouring is a kind of Chiaro Scuro. It is hung with purple & has a purple bed. Almost all the pictures are drawings faintly coloured, & the ebony chairs give the darkest shade, while the white fretted cieling & a sprinkling of gold on the frames afford the lights; as the painted glass darkens part of the windows, & heightens the landscapes to which they look. The dusky passage makes the richness & largeness of the gallery appear much more considerable, tho it is much [f.2] ornamented to compensate for its having less prospect than the other rooms. The round room with its great bow-window of painted glass terminates the Gallery to great advantage by the perspective & colours, & has more effect than the same window would have if in the gallery, by leaving some room for expectation. The pic:tures in it are few & in large spaces, but fine, & give an air of repose & grandeur which many pictures destroy. The Gallery is for the pictures, but the pictures in the round room serve as furniture. The Chapel has the true air of a place of Devotion, & that impression makes it please, tho seen after so much larger spaces. The number of curiosities in it takes up the attention, & seem to be the completion of the collection. The sobriety of the Chapel, & the idea of having seen all the House, make the opening of the great bedchamber the more surprising, from its not being expected, & from the striking con:trast between the awe impressed by the Chapel, & the gush of light, gaudiness & grandeur of the bedchamber, in the midst of which Stands the Tapestry bed, glowing with natural flowers in wreaths on a white ground. I have seen a much finer bed of Tapestry at Versailles, the whole effect of which is lost, by the hangings being exactly of the same colours. Here the room is hung with a deep rose colour, which sets off all the others. In the three large [f.3] rooms a harmony is presented, tho there are differences in all according to circumstances. In the gallery, as there is a high surbase of white & gold, the chairs & settees, tho crimson like the hangings, have frames of black & gold, as have the tables. In the round room, crimson likewise, as the damask goes to the skirting board, the chairs are tapestry with green & gold frames that cor:respond with the pillars of the chimney. In the State bedchamber, there are half the chairs of tapestry to suit the bed, with white & gold frames against the damask, while the other half are ebony with deep-rose-:colour'd cushions, to take off from the great gaudiness of the bed & chairs, & to bring back the room to the gothic tone of the House. The tops of the Windows tho adorned with painted glass to suit the rest, have only single shields in each upper pane & a border, while the great size of the rest of the window, which is of plate glass, & the uncommon chearfullness of the Views, make the Outside as beautifull as the Inside.

I do not mention my own House, which is a small one, but by comparison, & as a sample of what might be done on a magificent scale, if perspective, the effects of light & shade, Harmony in the colouring of the furniture & a picturesque taste were observed in the whole. I need not say how much the result of my house is improved by the [f.4] humility of the Entrance, & the simplicity of the first rooms, so little promising the expence of the great Apartment.

Aug. 31.1772

In ~~op~~ hanging pictures, opposition makes harmony. Histo:ries ~~or land~~ should be mixed with Landscapes or heads; & the two latter shd be mixed. Sizes too, thus

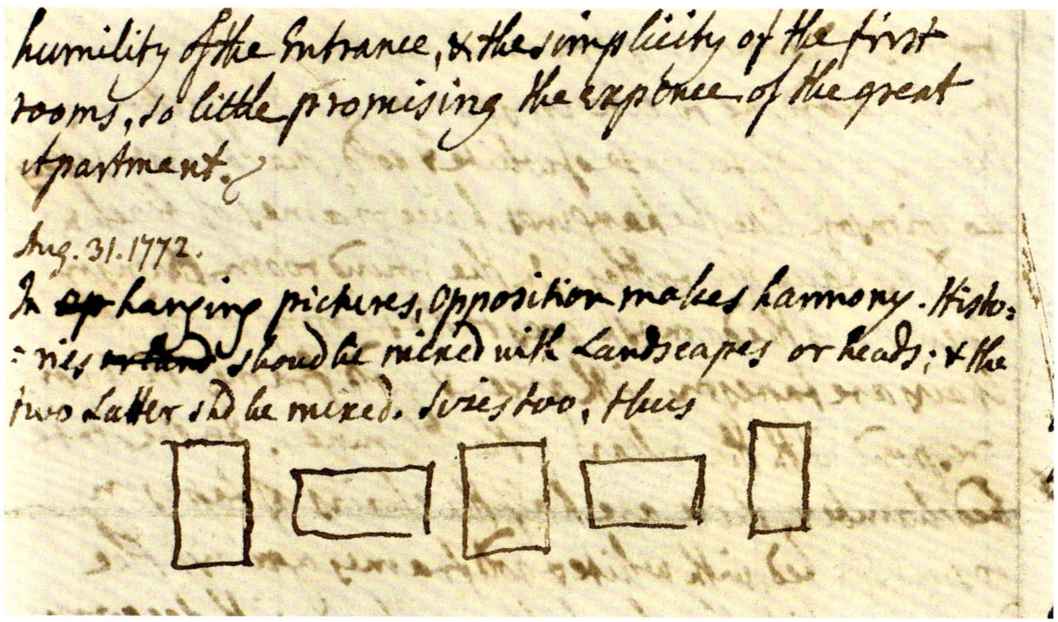

Figure 367. Diagram illustrating Walpole's thoughts on picture hanging, Fitzwilliam Museum, Cambridge. Ms 13-1947

4. HORACE WALPOLE, THE 'STRAWBERRY COMMITTEE' AND THE 'COMMITTEE OF TASTE'

John Riely*

Almost all of the references to the 'committee' or, more fully, the 'Strawberry committee' in Walpole's vast surviving correspondence occur in 1754, the year when the triumvirate of John Chute, Richard Bentley and Walpole himself were busiest consulting among themselves concerning 'Gothic' improvements to Strawberry Hill. While Samuel Johnson defined 'committee' in his *Dictionary* (1755) simply as 'a certain number of persons selected to examine or manage any matter', Walpole may have been thinking of the important public role of investigative committees, and parliamentary committees in particular.

The earliest reference is in a letter from Walpole to Bentley, dated 9 July 1754: 'Sir Charles [Hanbury] Williams brought his eldest daughter [Frances Hanbury Williams] hither [Strawberry Hill] last week: she is one of your real admirers, and…drew a perspective view of the castle from the angle, in a manner to deserve the thanks of the *committee*' (*HW Corres.* 35: 177). The Yale editors, in footnote 7a, quote Mary Berry's identifying note from Walpole's *Works* (1798): 'Mr Walpole in these letters calls the Strawberry committee those of his friends who had assisted in the plans and Gothic ornaments at Strawberry Hill.'

The next two references are in HW to Bentley, 3 November 1754:

> Mr Chute and I have been at Mr Barret's [Thomas Barrett-Lennard, later 17th Baron Dacre] at Belhouse; I never saw a place for which one did not wish, so totally void of faults. What he has done is in Gothic, and very true, though not up to the perfection of the committee… There is a vote of the Strawberry committee for great embellishments to the chapel [at Chute's house, the Vyne], of which it will not be long before you hear something. (*HW Corres.* 35: 183, 185)

This last reference shows that, as is well known, Walpole and Chute sometimes acted independently of Bentley.

The last reference is in HW to Lord Strafford, 30 October 1759: 'I have an additional reason for thanking you now, when you are erecting a building after the design of the Strawberry committee' (*HW Corres.* 35: 296–7). In a footnote the editors point out that this refers to Bentley's design for 'a little gothic building' mentioned elsewhere in his correspondence with Walpole.

George Robins, the auctioneer in Covent Garden who conducted the famous sale of the 'Classic Contents of Strawberry Hill Collected by Horace Walpole' at the behest of Lord Waldegrave in 1842, was apparently the first to confuse matters (in more than one way) in his catalogue description of lot 43 on the 21st day's sale:

> A CONVERSATION, *a highly interesting and valuable picture.* Richard, the second Lord Edgcumbe is seen drawing at a table, in the Library at Strawberry Hill, George James ['Gilly'] Williams is looking over him, and George Augustus Selwyn stands to the other side, with a book in his hand. These gentlemen were the intimate friends of Horace Walpole, and with him formed the well-known Committee of Taste; they were his invariable guests at Christmas and Easter, at Strawberry Hill…[by] SIR JOSHUA REYNOLDS. [Fig. 144]

Walpole in fact regularly referred to these meetings twice a year at SH as his 'out of town party', and its four members certainly did not constitute the Strawberry committee, let alone something called the 'Committee of Taste'. However, this seems to be the earliest use of the phrase 'Committee of Taste' in connection with Walpole and Strawberry Hill. A typically imaginative leap on Robins's part, it was perhaps prompted by Mary Berry's note of 1798 and by Lord Edgcumbe being shown making a drawing. The phrase itself was common enough to have been employed in 1826 by the cookery writer William Kitchener in a dinner invitation. In 1876 it was used by the *New York Times* in aesthetic terms.

W.S. Lewis, in his article 'The Genesis of Strawberry Hill' (*Metropolitan Museum Studies*, vol. 5, no. 1, 1934–6), was the first to call Walpole's 'Strawberry committee' the 'Committee of Taste'. He was perhaps influenced by Austin Dobson's use of the phrase (referring to the Reynolds group) in his book of the 1890s on Horace Walpole, rather than directly by Robins's reference. It would appear that, at this early stage of his Walpolian studentship, Lewis may not have paid close enough attention to Walpole's uses of the phrase 'Strawberry committee' or simply 'the committee' in his letters to Bentley and Lord Strafford. Wyndham Ketton-Cremer, in his biography of Walpole written partly under Lewis's supervision and first published in 1940, also writes of the 'Committee of [or 'on'] Taste', but by 1960, in *Horace Walpole* (his Bollingen Lectures at the National Gallery of Art, Washington), Lewis had come around to indicating that Walpole called it simply 'The Committee' (p. 105) without any mention of 'Taste'. However, in *Selected Letters of Horace Walpole* (Yale University Press, 1973) he included the letter of 3 November 1754 to Bentley and identified 'the committee' in a footnote as the 'Committee of Taste formed by Walpole to remodel Strawberry Hill'. Finally, in the year before he died, Lewis returned, as it were, to the correct formulation 'The Committee' in *Rescuing Horace Walpole* (Yale University Press, 1978, p. 55).

Given this confusion (and most particularly the appearance of the phrase in Ketton-Cremer's standard biography), later writers and commentators, not surprisingly, continued to use the appealing but erroneous 'Committee of Taste' even though there was, quite properly, no entry for it as such in the exhaustive four-volume index of the Yale Correspondence.

* John Riely gratefully acknowledges the assistance of Michael McCarthy in the preparation of this appendix.

SELECT BIBLIOGRAPHY

The literature on Horace Walpole is enormous. This select bibliography lists some of the essential works on Walpole and Strawberry Hill

1. HORACE WALPOLE'S PUBLICATIONS

For a complete list of Walpole's publications, see Hazen's *Bibliography* (1948) cited below

Aedes Walpolianae, or, A Description of the Collection of Pictures at Houghton-Hall in Norfolk, the seat of the Right Honourable Sir Robert Walpole, Earl of Orford, London 1747

Anecdotes of Painting in England and a Catalogue of Engravers, Strawberry Hill Press, 5 vols, 1762–80

The Castle of Otranto, London, 1764

Historic Doubts on the Life and Reign of King Richard the Third, London, 1768

A Description of the Villa of Horace Walpole, Youngest Son of Sir Robert Walpole, Earl of Orford, at Strawberry-Hill, near Twickenham. With an inventory of the furniture, pictures, curiosities &c., Strawberry Hill Press, 1774. (HW added the following appendices to later editions: *c.* 1781 Appendix, with list of books printed at SH; 1784 Additions since the Appendix; 1786 More Additions. All references are to the last edition)

A Description of the Villa of Mr Horace Walpole, Youngest Son of Sir Robert Walpole, Earl of Orford, at Strawberry-Hill, near Twickenham. With an inventory of the furniture, pictures, curiosities &c., Strawberry Hill Press, 1784. (HW added the following appendices to later editions: 1786 Appendix; *c.* 1789 Curiosities Added; *c.* 1791 More Additions. All references are to the last edition)

The Works of Horatio Walpole, Earl of Orford, 5 vols, London, 1798, ed. Mary Berry

2. HORACE WALPOLE AND STRAWBERRY HILL

ADAMS, C.K. and LEWIS, W.S. 'The Portraits of Horace Walpole', *The Walpole Society*, 42, 1970, 1–34

Ædes Strawberrianae. Names of purchasers and process to the sale catalogue of the collection of art and vertû, at Strawberry Hill, formed by Horace Walpole, Earl of Orford, London, 1842; *Names of purchasers and the prices to the detailed sale catalogue of the collection … withdrawn from Strawberry-Hill for sale in London*, London, 1842

BATEY, MAVIS, 'Horace Walpole as Modern Garden Historian', *Garden History: The Journal of the Garden History Society*, 19:1, Spring 1991, 1–11

BROWNELL, MORRIS, *The Prime Minister of Taste*, New Haven and London, 2001

CALLOWAY, STEPHEN, SNODIN, MICHAEL, and WAINWRIGHT, CLIVE, *Horace Walpole and Strawberry Hill*, exh. cat., Orleans House Gallery, Richmond-upon-Thames, 1980

CHALCRAFT, ANNA, and VISCARDI, JUDITH, *Visiting Strawberry Hill, An Analysis of the Eton Copy of 'The Description of the Villa'*, Wimbledon, 2005

—— *Strawberry Hill: Horace Walpole's Gothic Castle*, London 2007

CHASE, ISABEL WAKELIN URBAN, *Horace Walpole: Gardenist, An Edition of Walpole's A History of the Modern Taste in Gardening with an Estimate of Walpole's Contribution to Landscape Architecture*, Princeton 1943

COLE, WILLIAM, *A Journal of my Journey to Paris in the Year 1765*, ed. Francis Griffin Stokes, London 1931

CORNFORTH, JOHN, *Early Georgian Interiors*, New Haven and London 2004

CROOK, J. M., 'Strawberry Hill Revisited', *Country Life*, cliii, 1973, pp. 1598–1602, 1726–30, 1794–97, 1886.

DOBSON, AUSTIN, *Horace Walpole: a Memoir with an Appendix of Books Printed at the Strawberry Hill Press*, 4th edition, ed. Paget Toynbee, Oxford 1927

DUKELSKAYA, LARISSA, AND MOORE, ANDREW, *A Capital Collection: Houghton Hall and the Hermitage*, New Haven and London, 2002

EAVIS, ANNA, AND PEOVER, MICHAEL, 'Horace Walpole's painted glass at Strawberry Hill', *The Journal of Stained Glass*, Vol. 19, no. 3, 1994–5, 280–313

FOTHERGILL, BRIAN, *The Strawberry Hill Set: Horace Walpole and his Circle*, London 1983

GASCOIGNE, BAMBER, and DITCHBURN, JONATHAN, *Images of Twickenham with Hampton and Teddington*, Richmond-upon-Thames, 1981

GUILLERY, PETER, 'Strawberry Hill: Building and Site: Part One: The Building', *Architectural History*, vol. 38, Leeds, 1995, 102–28

HAGGERTY, GEORGE E., 'Queering Horace Walpole', *Studies in English Literature*, 46, 2006, 543–62

HAZEN, A.T., AND KIRBY, J.P., *A Bibliography of the Strawberry Hill Press*, New Haven 1942.

HAZEN, A.T., *A Bibliography of Horace Walpole*, Yale University Press, 1948

—— *A Catalogue of Horace Walpole's Library*, 3 vols, Yale University Press, 1969

JESTIN, LOFTUS, 'Richard Bentley the Younger, 1708–1782: A Critical Biography' (Ph. D. Thesis, Yale University, 1985)

—— *The Answer to the Lyre, Richard Bentley's Illustrations for Thomas Gray's Poems*, Philadelphia 1990

KETTON-CREMER, R.W., *Horace Walpole: A Biography*, London 1940, 3rd edn London and Ithaca, 1964

LEWIS, W.S. *et al*, ed., *The Yale Edition of Horace Walpole's Correspondence*, Yale University Press, 48 vols, 1937–83

—— 'The Genesis of Strawberry Hill', *Metropolitan Museum Studies* 5, part 1, 1934, 57–92

—— *Collector's Progress*, New York, 1951

—— *Horace Walpole's Library*, Cambridge 1958

——*Horace Walpole*, Bollingen Series 35, The A.W. Mellon Lectures in the Fine Arts 9, New York, 1961

—— *A Guide to the Life of Horace Walpole*, New Haven and London, 1973

—— *Rescuing Horace Walpole*, New Haven and London, 1978

MCCARTHY, MICHAEL, *The Origins of the Gothic Revival*, New Haven and London, 1987

MCLEOD, BET, 'The Ceramics at Strawberry Hill', MA Thesis, Cooper-Hewitt/Parsons School of Design, New York, 1993

MERRITT, PERCIVAL, *An Account of Descriptive Catalogues of Strawberry Hill and of Strawberry Hill Sales Catalogues, together with a Bibliography*, Boston, 1915

MILLER, NORBERT, *Strawberry Hill: Horace Walpole und der Ästhetik der schönen Unregelmässigkeit*, Munich, 1986

ROBINS, GEORGE, *A Catalogue of the Classic Contents of Strawberry Hill Collected by Horace Walpole*, April 25th 1842 and 23 following days. (References are from the 6th – penultimate – edition; the first digit refers to the day of the sale, the second to the lot number.)

——*The Collection of Rare Prints ad Illustrated Works, Removed for Sale in London … collected by Horace Walpole*, 13 June 1842 and 9 following days

SABOR, PETER, *Horace Walpole: a Reference Guide*, Boston, 1984

—— *Horace Walpole: The Critical Heritage*, London, 1987

SABOR, PETER, ed., 'Horace Walpole: Beyond *The Castle of Otranto*', *1650–1850: Ideas, Aesthetics, and Inquiries in the Early Modern Era*, vol. 16, forthcoming 2009

SMITH, WARREN HUNTING, ed., *Horace Walpole, Writer, Politician and Connoisseur: Essays on the 250th Anniversary of Walpole's Birth*, New Haven, 1967

SNODIN, MICHAEL, 'Strawberry Hill: Building and Site: Part Two: The Site', *Architectural History*, vol. 38, Leeds, 1995, 102–28

TIPPING, H.A. 'Strawberry Hill, Middlesex', *Country Life*, lvi, 1924, pp. 18–25, 56–64

TOYNBEE, PAGET, *Journal of the Printing-Office at Strawberry Hill*, London and New York, 1923

—— *Strawberry Hill Accounts*, Oxford, 1927

—— *Horace Walpole's Journals of Visits to Country Seats, &c*, The Walpole Society, 16, 1928

WAINWRIGHT, CLIVE, *The Romantic Interior: The British Collector at Home 1750–1850*, New Haven and London, 1989

INDEX

Illustrations are indicated by italicised page numbers. Catalogue entries are referenced by catalogue number. For the catalogue section and the captions only works and lenders are indexed

PHOTOGRAPHIC CREDITS

Note: every effort has been made to credit photographers and sources of all illustrations in this volume; if there are any errors or omissions, please contact Yale University Press so that corrections can be made in any subsequent editions.

Photography © The Art Institute of Chicago: Fig. 286
Reproduced by permission of the Marquess of Bath, Longleat, Warminster, Wiltshire, Great Britain; photo by Blantern & Davis Photography: Fig. 338
Beinecke Rare Book and Manuscript Library, Yale University: Figs. 157, 159, 160, 161, 189, 249
Sarah Campbell Blaffer Foundation, Houston: Fig. 118
© Bristol City Museum and Art Gallery, UK / The Bridgeman Art Library: Fig. 144
By permission of the British Library: Figs. 99, 100, 258
© Trustees of the British Museum: Figs. 33, 54, 60, 87, 125, 126, 140, 146, 164, 165, 166, 167, 168, 182, 183, 186, 223, 224, 228, 230, 317, 318, 319, 330, 332, 352
Photo courtesy of the British Museum: Fig. 328
Trustees of the Ninth Duke of Buccleuch's Chattels Fund, photo by John McKenzie Photography: Figs. 80, 193, 195, 206, 208, 209, 355
Trustees of the Ninth Duke of Buccleuch's Chattels Fund, photo by Antonia Reeve Photography: Fig. 192
Chantilly, musée Condé: Fig. 90
Photo by Martin Charles: Figs. 1, 78, 91, 93, 95, 96, 97, 98, 106
© Governing Body of Christ Church, Oxford: Fig. 145
The Cleveland Museum of Art: Fig. 155
The Corning Museum of Glass: Fig. 9
Licence granted courtesy of The Rt Hon. The Early of Derby 2009: Figs. 30, 43, 85, 124, 178, 198, 267, 310, 331
© Devonshire Collection, Chatsworth. Reproduced by permission of Chatsworth Settlement Trustees: Fig. 122
Wingfield Digby, Sherborne Castle, photo by Peter Booton Photography: Figs. 197, 204, 205, 207
Edinburgh University Library: Fig. 218
© English Heritage Photo Library: Fig. 169
Reproduced by permission of the Provost and Fellows of Eton College: Fig. 190
Fine Arts Museums of San Francisco: Fig. 67
Reproduced by permission of the Syndics of the Fitzwilliam Museum, Cambridge: Fig. 216
Fratelli Alinari Museum of the History of Photography, Florence: Fig. 185
© Culture and Sport Glasgow (Museums): Figs. 83, 151, 256, 320
Courtesy the Knight of Glin: Fig. 300
Gloves Collection Trust, courtesy of the Fashion Museum, Bath and North East Somerset Council: Fig. 117
© Hampshire Record Office: Fig. 94
Marquess of Hertford, Ragley Hall, Warwickshire; photo by John Hammond: half title page, Fig. 3
Houghton Hall, Norfolk, UK: Fig. 59
Courtesy of the Huntington Library, Art Collections, and Botanical Gardens, San Marino, California: Fig. 254
The Lewis Walpole Library, Yale University: endpapers, front cover, back cover, Figs. 12, 14, 17, 20, 21, 22, 24, 25, 26, 28, 29, 32, 36, 37, 38, 39, 40, 44, 45, 46, 48, 52, 53, 64, 66, 72, 77, 89, 92, 101, 104, 108, 113, 114, 115, 120, 128, 131, 132, 134, 135, 136, 137, 138, 139, 141, 142, 143, 156, 162, 163, 170, 171, 172, 175, 176, 179, 187, 188, 213, 214, 220, 232, 233, 234, 235, 236, 237, 245, 250, 251, 252, 253, 260, 261, 262, 264, 265, 266, 268, 270, 271, 272, 273, 274, 275, 276, 280, 281, 282, 283, 284, 285, 287, 288, 289, 290, 291, 292, 293, 294, 295, 296, 297, 298, 304, 312, 315, 316, 325, 326, 333, 342, 350, 359, 363, 365
Image © The Metropolitan Museum of Art: Figs. 31, 50, 215, 306, 308, 335, 344, 345, 356
Photograph © 2009 Museum of Fine Arts, Boston: Fig. 71
© Museum of London: Fig. 358
Image courtesy of the Board of Trustees, National Gallery of Art, Washington: Figs. 75, 269
© National Gallery of Scotland: Figs. 180, 181
© National Maritime Museum, Greenwich, London: Fig. 199
© National Museums Liverpool: Fig. 242
National Museums Scotland: Fig. 219
© Nationalmuseum, Stockholm: Figs. 201, 212
© National Museums Wales / The Bridgeman Art Library: Fig. 149
© National Portrait Gallery, London: Figs. 19, 111, 112, 130, 194, 203, 210, 327, 362
The National Trust for Scotland: Brodick Castle: Fig. 349
Collection of the Duke of Northumberland: Fig. 150
© NTPL/ Derrick E. Witty: Fig. 110
© NTPL/ Nadia Mackenzie: Fig. 107
© NTPL/ John Hammond: Figs. 7, 263
The House of Orange-Nassau Historic Collections Trust: Fig. 347
Philadelphia Museum of Art: Photo by Will Brown: Fig. 217
Private collection: Figs. 62, 70, 279, 303, 307, 321, 353
Private collection / The Bridgeman Art Library: Fig. 10
Private collection, photo by John Hammond: frontispiece, Figs. 42, 57, 243, 339
Private collection, c/o Robert Holden Ltd, London: Fig. 154
Private collection / © Mallett Gallery, London, UK/ The Bridgeman Art Library International: Fig. 364
Private collection, courtesy of the Weiss Gallery: Fig. 63
© Reunion des Musées Nationaux / Art Resource, NY: Fig. 314
Courtesy of Kevin Rogers: Fig. 2
Rosenbach Museum & Library, Philadelphia: Fig. 346
The Royal Collection © 2009 Her Majesty Queen Elizabeth II: Figs. 56, 129, 148, 247
Photo by Natalie Russo: Figs. 6, 13, 18, 23, 47, 49, 55, 58, 61, 76, 81, 88, 102, 103, 119, 133, 173, 174, 231, 238, 239, 241, 244, 301, 302, 305, 311, 322, 336, 337, 361
© The Schroder collection, photo by Ken Adlard: Fig. 340
S. J. Phillips, Limited: Fig. 34
By courtesy of the Trustees of Sir John Soane's Museum: Figs. 73, 74
© The State Hermitage Museum, St Petersburg, 2009: Figs. 8, 82, 121
Stedelijk Museum het Prinsenhof, Delft: Fig. 79
The Friends of Strawberry Hill for the Strawberry Hill Trust: Fig. 277
Courtesy of the Taft Museum of Art, Cincinnati, Ohio: Photo by Tony Walsh, Cincinnati, Ohio: Fig. 299
Photo by Norman Taylor: Fig. 51
© Toledo Museum of Art; all rights reserved: Fig. 147
Lord Tollemache, Helmingham Hall; photo by John Hammond: Fig. 334
© V&A Images/Victoria and Albert Museum, London: front cover, Figs. 5, 27, 41, 65, 84, 86, 105, 116, 123, 127, 152, 191, 225, 226, 227, 229, 240, 278, 309, 329, 341, 343, 348, 351, 357
Courtesy of the Victoria and Albert Museum, London: Fig. 11
The Trustees of the Waldegrave Chattels Trust: Figs. 4, 15, 16, 69, 109, 177, 200, 324
By kind permission of the Trustees of the Wallace Collection, London: Fig. 257
Photo © The Walters Art Museum, Baltimore, Maryland: Figs. 68, 153, 202
Wartburg-Stiftung, Eisenach: Fig. 255
Earl of Wemyss and March, Gosford House, East Lothian: Fig. 184
Photos courtesy of Ellen Page Wilson Photography, 2009: Figs. 221, 222
The Wormsley Library: Figs. 35, 313, 323
Richard Caspole, Yale Center for British Art: Figs. 196, 211, 248, 259, 354, 360
Courtesy of Yale University Library; photo by Photo + Design, Yale University: Figs. 158, 246

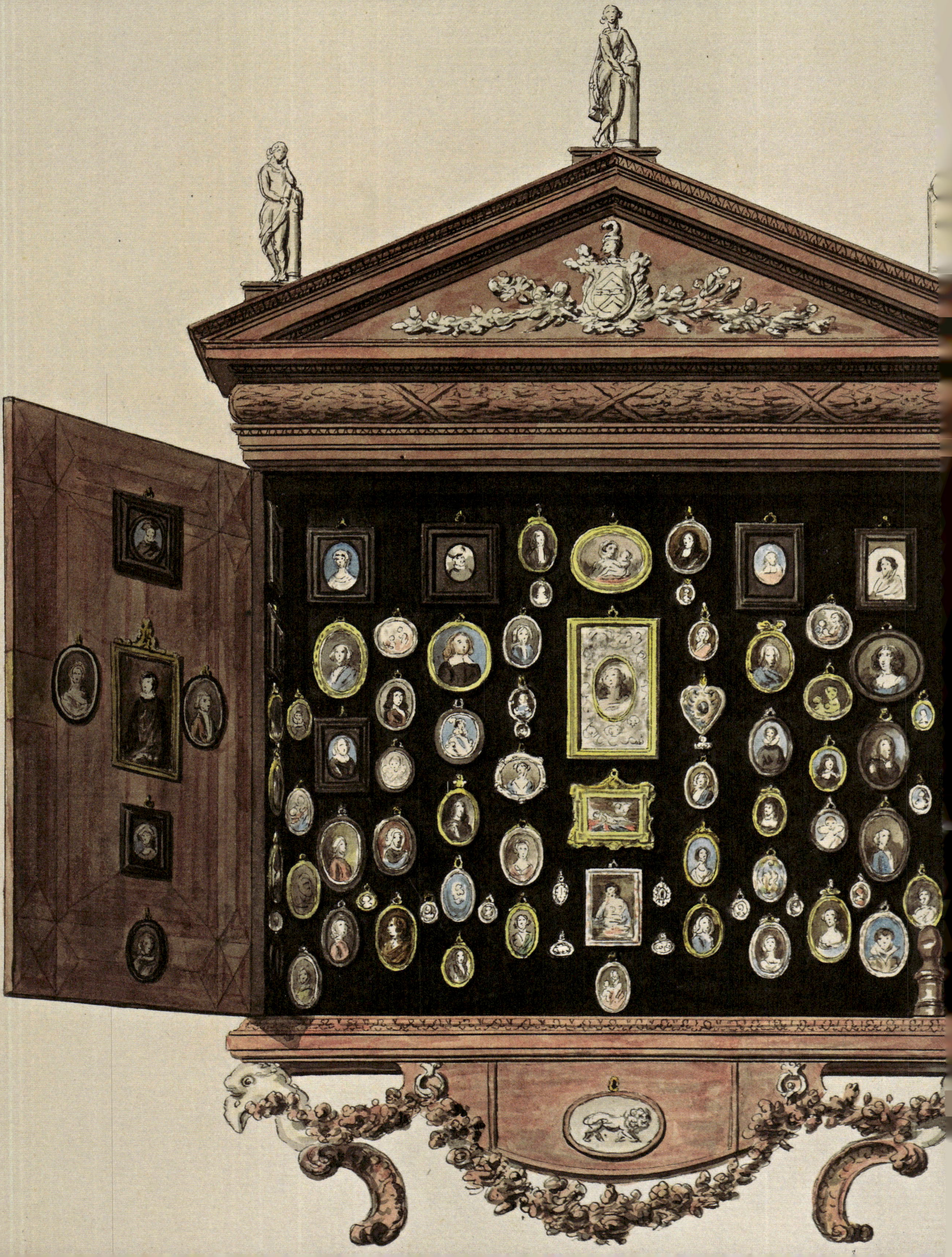